Human Resource Management
Theory and Practice

BRATTON AND GOLD

HRM

 macmillan education · palgrave

© John Bratton and Jeff Gold 1994, 1999, 2003, 2007, 2012, 2017

First edition 1994
Second edition 1999
Third edition 2003
Fourth edition 2007
Fifth edition 2012
Sixth edition published 2017 by
PALGRAVE

Palgrave in the UK is an imprint of Macmillan Publishers Limited, registered in England, company number 785998, of 4 Crinan Street, London, N1 9XW.

Palgrave® and Macmillan® are registered trademarks in the United States, the United Kingdom, Europe and other countries.

ISBN 978–1–137–57259–2 paperback

This book is printed on paper suitable for recycling and made from fully managed and sustained forest sources. Logging, pulping and manufacturing processes are expected to conform to the environmental regulations of the country of origin.

A catalogue record for this book is available from the British Library.

A catalog record for this book is available from the Library of Congress.

Printed in China

There seems to be common ground that university management education has to obsess less on 'employability' and focus on studying the hidden moral assumptions of all the management theory: the efficient distribution of wealth; exploring how management choices affect workers, society and the environment; and alternative governance models and industrial democracy.

John Bratton and Jeff Gold
Work, Employment and Society, 2015, p. 9.

Dear Lecturer

Thank you for adopting Human Resource Management: Theory and Practice. *This sixth edition contains two new chapters: HRM and ethics and Green HRM and environmental sustainability. We reflect also on the effects of economic globalization, the growing body of work advocating for a critical theory approach of HRM and the impact that Britain's vote to leave the European Union or Brexit will have on the HRM function. The effect of economic globalization has had a transformational effect on management processes and caused significant changes in employment relations. Critical HRM education and pedagogy often coalesce around the core themes of de-naturalization, anti-performativity, reflexivity and social justice. In this edition, we introduce the use of the 'sociological imagination' to explain the learning to be gained from teaching HRM that is sensitive to context, power and inequality. In preparing this new edition, we have taken account of comments from the many anonymous users and non-users of the fifth edition from all over the world. The preface provides a complete explanation of our approach to teaching HRM and the structure and content of the text.*

Reflecting the growing interest in analysing the human resources causal chain, particularly the mediating *effects of key variables, this sixth edition contains new material on HRM and line managers and high-performance workplaces. In the shadow of Thomas Piketty's (2014)* Capital, *the rewards chapter contains new material on pay inequality. In the first edition, much was made of the two normative models of HRM: the 'hard' model associated with 'low-road' business strategies that emphasized cost (wage) control, and the 'soft' model, more compatible with 'high-road' business strategies that emphasize competitiveness through strategic learning. The consequences of post-Cold-War economic globalization and neoliberalism have, however, meant that, in the main, the hoped-for 'soft' HRM developmental models exist only as a compelling discourse to mask ever-greater exploitation of employees through precarious 'hard' HR practices. Further evidence of this trend is the recent damning MP's report that criticized Sports Direct CEO Mike Ashley for allegedly adopting a business model that enabled the majority of his staff to be treated 'without dignity or respect' and as 'commodities rather than human beings'. Given this context, features on precarious zero-hour contracts together with international examples, seem highly relevant. For a more detailed description of changes in this edition, see 'New to the sixth edition' in the Preface.*

More than ever, Human Resource Management: Theory and Practice *not only teaches students, but also elicits their responses. Reflective questions and review questions prompt them to consider key concepts and implications. In addition, we are cognizant of the need to offer students greater value for money when they purchase textbooks. Thus, students have free access to an interactive ebook version of the text, and the online resource centre, which offers skill development exercises and other web resources that encourage students to discover more about HRM on their own. Finally, in the context of what has been called a post-crisis critical reflection on management education, we hope this new edition can help management faculty and students to reflect more deeply and critically on the purpose and content of HRM studies.*

This new edition includes a variety of supporting materials to help you improve the student's learning experience and to relate theory to practice. The online resource centre at www.palgravehighered.com/bg-hrm-6e offers downloadable teaching supplements including lecturer notes, teaching tips and lecture enhancement ideas, PowerPoint lecture slides for each chapter and a comprehensive test bank of multiple-choice questions for use in exams, quizzes and tests.

To give your students additional value when using this new edition, we suggest that you make reference to the textbook during your lecture, for instance referring to actual practices as illustrated in the HRM in practice and HRM and globalization features. Ask students to attempt the end-of-chapter case studies in preparation for your seminar or in-class discussion. In addition, do encourage your students to visit the online resource centre and make use of their free access to the interactive ebook version of the book and to watch the HRM as I see it video interviews. The interviews are with practitioners in the field, and feedback suggests that they are highly valued by students.

We would welcome any feedback on these new features or any suggestions on how we can improve the next edition. Please contact us via the email address on the online resource centre.

Best wishes

John Bratton   Jeff Gold

brief contents

contents

III employee performance and development

6 performance management and appraisal
Jeff Gold and Christine Mortimer

7 learning and human resource development
Jeff Gold and Christine Mortimer

IV employment relations   259

list of figures

list of tables

about the authors

John Bratton is a Visiting Professor at Edinburgh Napier University Business School, Edinburgh, UK and Adjunct Professor at Athabasca University, Canada. His research interests and publications have focused on the sociology of work, leadership and workplace learning. He has designed and delivered a wide range of seminars, programmes and executive workshops on strategic learning and labour relations over a career spanning 30 years. John  was the first Director of the Workplace Learning Research Unit at the University of Calgary, Canada, and has been a member of the editorial board of *Leadership*, the *Journal of Workplace Learning* and the *Canadian Journal for the Study of Adult Education*.

In addition to co-authoring the present text, John is author of *Japanization of Work: Managerial Studies in the 1990s* (1992) and *Introduction to Work and Organizational Behaviour* (3rd edn) (2015), and co-author of the following texts: *Workplace Learning: A Critical Introduction* (2003; with J. Helm-Mills, J. Pyrch and P. Sawchuk); *Organizational Leadership* (2004; with K. Grint and D. Nelson) and *Capitalism and Classical Social Theory* (2nd edn; 2014) (with David Denham).

Jeff Gold is Professor of Organization Learning at York Business School, York St John University and Visiting Professor at Portsmouth University, UK. He has designed and delivered a wide range of seminars, programmes and workshops on change, strategic learning, management and leadership, with particular emphasis on participation and distribution. He is a strong advocate of the use of  action modes of research to ensure that rigour is combined with relevance with respect to significant projects to tackle complex business and social issues. He is the co-author of *The Sage Handbook of Professional Doctorates in Business and Management* with Dr Lisa Anderson, Professor Jim Stewart and Professor Richard Thorpe.

about the contributors

Andrew Bratton is a Knowledge Transfer Partnership (KTP) Associate in Business Process Improvement and Knowledge Management at the University of Strathclyde in a high-growth IT consultancy, Glasgow, UK. His teaching and research interests focus on HRM, workplace environmental sustainability and innovation, change management and employee participation in environmental sustainability initiatives. His current research centres on the application of lean practices in small and medium-sized enterprises.

John Burgess is Professor of Human Resource Management, Curtin University, Perth, Australia. His research interests include working time and health, case studies on fragmented working time arrangements and employee health, job readiness in the Asia-Pacific region, country studies of the transition from education to employment, HRM practices of multinational enterprises in Australia, knowledge-sharing mechanisms in the Swan Valley wine tourism cluster and managing the remote workforce in the resources sector.

Kirsteen Grant is a Lecturer in Human Resource Management at Edinburgh Napier University. Her teaching and research interests centre on professional and precarious work, the (changing) nature and expectations of work, talent management, workplace skills utilisation and high-performance working. Her current research is within the UK aviation industry and public services.

Roslyn Larkin is a lecturer in Employment Relations and Human Resource Management at the University of Newcastle, Australia. Roslyn's teaching areas include advanced employee relations/HRM applied through work-integrated learning with partner organizations, international HRM and knowledge management. Her current research interests are ethics in the Australian banking sector, knowledge transfer in small and medium-sized enterprises and regional innovation hubs, and employment for aged care sector personal and direct care workers.

Alan Montague has worked at Royal Melbourne Institute of Technology (RMIT) University, Australia since 1997, initially managing the apprenticeships programme in the VET division. Alan was previously a senior manager within a Federal Government Department, which induced an interest and expertise in labour market complexities and HRM issues. In 2007, Alan moved into higher education and has worked in numerous discipline areas including HRM, human resource development, leadership and ethics. His research and publications include skill shortages, ageing and government education policies.

Christine Mortimer leads international development and business engagement at York St John University Business School, UK. Prior to an academic career, she spent 14 years working in manufacturing across the UK, with particular involvement in cultural change management and the implementation of continuous improvement. Her specialist teaching areas are leadership and management development and practice, operations management, project management, strategy and supporting entrepreneurial businesses and community interest companies. Her current research interests include the interface between business leadership and society, employability and business curriculum design.

Chiara Amati is Lecturer in HRM at Edinburgh Napier University, UK. Chiara is a chartered occupational psychologist who joined Edinburgh Napier University Business School in 2010; she teaches on the MSc in HRM and on related undergraduate courses. Her main area of expertise is the emotional experience of individuals and leaders at work, which includes interest in aspects of job satisfaction, motivation, engagement and workplace stress. Chiara joined the university after a number of years working in a successful commercial psychology consultancy firm, primarily in the area of psychological health and well-being at work.

Feature contributors

Chris Baldry is an Emeritus Professor of the Stirling Management School at the University of Stirling, UK. He has taught several courses, including introductory HRM, international HRM, work and employment, and organizational behaviour. Chris's recent research interests have focused on the changing world of work and employment, including the area of work–life balance. On the basis of his work in the area of occupational health and safety, he was called as an expert witness to the Cullen Inquiry on the Ladbroke Grove rail disaster. His other long-standing interest, in the interface between technological change and work organization, is reflected in his editorship of the journal *New Technology, Work and Employment*.

Bob Barnetson is a Professor of Labour Relations at Athabasca University, Canada. His research interests focus on the political economy of workplace injury with particular attention to farm, migrant and child workers in western Canada. He is the author of *The Political Economy of Workplace Injury in Canada*, co-author of *Health and Safety in Canadian Workplaces*, and co-editor of *Farm Workers in Western Canada*.

David Denham is an Honorary Research Fellow at Wolverhampton University, UK, where he taught a wide variety of sociology courses, including classical social theory, over a career of 35 years. He has published articles on the sociology of law, criminology and the sociology of sport. David is co-author of *Victimology: Victimization and Victims' Rights* (2008) and co-author (with John Bratton) of *Capitalism and Classical Social Theory* (2nd edn) (2014).

Lois Farquharson is Head of the Leadership, Strategy and Organizations Department in the Faculty of Management, Bournemouth University, UK. She is engaged in research around HRM and leadership practice in the public sector, with a particular focus on police forces in England, and has a keen interest in appreciative enquiry as a research method and a tool for leadership development. She teaches in the areas of organizational leadership and change, research methods and HRM practice, and supervises research students in gender, work–life balance, employee engagement and leadership areas.

David MacLennan is an Assistant Professor in the Department of Sociology and Anthropology at Thompson Rivers University, Kamloops, Canada. One of his main research interests is the transition from craft to bureaucratic ways of organizing work and learning. The geographical focus of his work is small cities. His most recent publication is a co-authored paper on how small cities support child development. He is also involved in research on real estate development in the small city.

Martin Reddington runs his own consultancy and is an Associate of the Edinburgh Institute, Edinburgh Napier University, UK.

Lori Rilkoff is Human Resources Director at the City of Kamloops in Canada. She has an MSc in HRM and Training and is a Certified Human Resources Professional. For her work on the City of Kamloops Wellness Works programme, she was selected as part of the City's Innovation Committee in 2008, having 4 years earlier been awarded a Senior Management Award of Excellence for Wellness Works Program Leadership. As a 2010 Innovation Award finalist, she was also recognized by  the British Columbia Human Resources Management Association for the encouragement and promotion of employer-based wellness programmes in the community.

case study grid

Please note that some case studies are fictional, but are based on real situations, and some use pseudonyms to protect the identities of the people and companies.

Chapter	Case study	Geographic focus	Page
1 The nature of contemporary HRM	Knowledge management at Emenee hotels	Australia	33
2 Corporate strategy and strategic HRM	Zuvan Winery	South Africa	67
3 HRM outcomes and line management	Devolement of HR at the City of Kindle	Canada	96
4 Workforce planning and diversity	Showing the impact of adult social care in ABC City Council	UK	137
5 Recruitment, selection and talent management	TNNB Ltd	UK	180
6 Performance management and appraisal	Robertson Engineering	UK	216
7 Learning and human resource development	Volunteers Together	UK	255
8 Reward management and inequality	Cordaval University	Canada	294
9 Labour relations and collective bargaining	Rama Garment factory	India	328
10 Employee relations and voice	Bullying at Fresh Supermarket	USA	362
11 HRM and ethics	Whistleblowing – an Australian context	Australia	387
12 Employee health, safety and wellness	The City of Kamloops	Canada	413
13 HRM and high-performance workplaces	Currency, Inc	International	440
14 Leadership and management development	The City of Sahali	Canada	468
15 Organizational culture and HRM	Big Outdoors	UK	495
16 Green HRM and environmental sustainability	EnergyCo	International	522
17 International HRM and global capitalism	ICAN	Finland, Canada	552

Chapter	Feature type	Feature title	Geographic focus	Page
1	HRM in Practice 1.1	Zero-hours contracts: treating human resources with contempt	🇬🇧 UK	6
1	HRM and Globalization 1.1	Airline service: the demands of emotional labour	🇦🇺 Australia	13
1	HRM in Practice 1.2	New HR practices: the proletarianization of educational work?	🇬🇧 UK	21
1	HRM and Globalization 1.2	The HRM model in advancing economies?	🇨🇳 🇮🇳 China, India	25
1	HRM as I see it	Alison Blayney, Unilever, Part 1	🇬🇧 UK	27
2	HRM in Practice 2.1	Why is self-employment in the UK at a record high?	🇬🇧 UK	42
2	HRM and Globalization 2.1	Business urged to keep on eco-track	🇨🇦 Canada	51
2	HRM in Practice 2.2	More women leaders: the answer to the financial crisis?	🌐 International	53
2	HRM as I see it	Sarah Myers, Sky	🇬🇧 UK	58
2	HRM and Globalization 2.2	The effect of business strategy on workers' psychological health	🇺🇸 USA	61
3	HRM and Globalization 3.1	HRM and performance: evidence from the Middle East	🇹🇷 Turkey	74
3	HRM in Practice 3.1	HR 'can lower NHS death rates'	🇬🇧 UK	78
3	HRM and Globalization 3.2	Evaluating HR practices: the role of qualitative methods	🌐 International	84
3	HRM in Practice 3.2	Can organizations simultaneously be committed to employees and outsource services?	🇬🇧 UK	88
4	HRM and Globalization 4.1	Migrant workers in Qatar: the impact of regulatory failure on workforce planning	🇶🇦 Qatar	111

13	HRM as I see it	Gregor Karolus, Springer Nature, Part 2	Germany, International	435
13	HRM in Practice 13.2	High-performance working in action: public and voluntary sectors	International	437
14	HRM as I see it	Lana Kularajah, Transform Aid International/Baptist World Aid Australia	Australia	461
14	HRM in Practice 14.1	Evaluating the Modern Leaders Programme at Skipton Building Society	UK	465
15	HRM and Globalization 15.1	Is a bullying culture a management strategy? Evidence from Australia	Australia	474
15	HRM and Globalization 15.2	Multiculturalism's magic number	Canada	479
15	HRM as I see it	Keith Stopforth, Bupa Health and Wellbeing	UK	483
15	HRM in Practice 15.1	'Purposeful Darwinism' – Amazon's experiment to motivate staff	USA	489
15	HRM in Practice 15.2	Can we measure changes in organizational culture?	UK	493
16	HRM in Practice 16.1	Carney urges companies to reveal carbon footprint	International	506
16	HRM and Globalization 16.1	US and South African unions form blue–green alliances	USA, South Africa	518
16	HRM as I see it	Markus Hiemann, NHS National Services Scotland	UK	520
17	HRM and Globalization 17.1	Is 'the race to the bottom' an inevitable consequence of globalization?	International	533
17	HRM in Practice 17.1	'We are disposable people …'	UK	535
17	HRM as I see it	Lesley White, Huawei Technologies	UK, China	536
17	HRM and Globalization 17.2	Realizing gender balance in British boardrooms	UK	542
17	HRM in Practice 17.2	Japanese CEO breaks stereotype by firing 14,000 staff	Japan	549

Human Resource Management: Theory and Practice has been written specifically to fulfil the need of undergraduate and graduate courses for an accessible but critical, comprehensive analysis of contemporary HRM.

Overview

It is over 22 years since the first edition of *Human Resource Management: Theory and Practice* was published, yet the management of people continues to present challenges to managers and attract considerable research interest and research funding. As one would expect, the context has profoundly changed: 22 years ago, for example, there was no widespread use of the internet or iPhones, and today it is considered normal behaviour for people to take off their shoes when going through airport security.

Since 1994, HR practices and the HRM academic discourse have responded to ongoing developments, and it is a common cliché to say that we live in 'turbulent' times. In the 1990s, privatization, deregulation and European integration seemed to define the decade. The quintessential 1990s corporate leaders, such as Kenneth Lay of Enron and Bernard Ebbers of WorldCom Inc. in the USA, were portrayed as 'visionaries' and risk-takers. After the dotcom crash, with the global financial crisis and in the wake of corporate scandals, which saw a few of the most egregious fraudsters sent to jail, competence, probity and managerial professionalism were again in high demand. A decade ago, the attacks on New York and Washington led to the ensuing 'global war on terror' and the invasion of Iraq and Afghanistan.

While writing the fifth edition of this book, we witnessed seismic political and economic changes that have reverberated worldwide. In early 2011, it was suggested that the so-called 'Arab Spring' was the equivalent of the 1917 Russian Revolution as pro-democracy revolts stunned North Africa and the Arab world. We experienced the equivalent of the 1929 Great Crash as in 2008 the global financial sector imploded and was put on life support by government bail-outs – to the tune of £737 billion in the case of the UK – and Fred Goodwin of UK's Royal Bank of Scotland was stripped of his knighthood. What started as a banking crisis morphed into a social crisis as the corporate and political elite implemented austerity economics in the form of wage and welfare cuts, spending cuts and tax rises and the privatization of public assets. As others have argued, the object of austerity economics is to impose the cost of the crisis on workers, the poor and pensioners and thereby irreversibly transfer wealth from the poorest to the richest (Chakrabortty, 2016). And as Greek experience has demonstrated, any government that challenges the doctrine of austerity economics will conflict with the European Union (EU) Troika – the European Commission, European Central Bank and the International Monetary Fund – that protects the 1 per cent global elite (Mason, 2016). The latest data show that pay growth has slumped, which means, in the absence of firms investing in plant and machinery, that economic growth depends increasingly on consumers borrowing more on credit cards, overdrafts and loans. The most affluent capitalist economies are therefore at best fragile, with data showing that most are a long way from economic recovery. Over the last decade, widespread bouts of civil disorder have challenged neo-liberalism and austerity economics, and we have witnessed support for radical political parties, both left and right, which speaks to a growing disillusion with precarious free-market capitalism.

And if that were not enough, on 23th June 2016, 17.4 million Britons voted to sever the UK's 43-year membership of the EU. There was market mayhem, with the FTSE 100 falling 8.7 per cent on opening, the pound slumping to a 31-year low and Britain's credit rating being downgraded after this Brexit decision (Parker et al., 2016). The referendum result has left Britain acutely divided, by age, class, education and territory, with prosperous London and Scotland voting by large margins to remain in the EU. Economically depressed post-industrial towns in the north of England, Wales, rural England and seaside towns heavily voted 'Leave'. Although ostensibly about the EU, the Brexit vote can be interpreted as a passionate outcry for help from those who feel they have lost out and been left behind by economic globalization, and who face an increasingly insecure and casualized labour market (Jacques, 2016).

These social fissures are not new but reflect the consequences of post-1990 economic globalization as the old divides of modernity disappear. The causes and effects of Brexit will shape the response of the political class to the unexpected EU referendum vote (Keating, 2016). On 24th June 2016, David Cameron resigned as Prime Minister, and within 19 days Theresa May was appointed in his place. At the time of writing (September 2016), the ramifications of the EU vote and the extraordinary political events following Brexit are highly uncertain.

Three months after the Brexit vote, the UK Government has still not agreed a negotiating position on what Brexit actually means. There is talk of 'soft' Brexit and 'hard' Brexit. Soft Brexit would mean Britain retaining access to the European single market, but continuing to be bound by EU rules and having to pay a membership fee. This arrangement is often called the Norwegian model. Hard Brexit would mean Britain selling goods and services into the EU on the same terms as the USA, China, Canada and so on, but also being able to compel EU countries to export products goods to the UK on the same basis as the rest of the world. In between these two extremes lie a string of compromises (McRae, 2016). David Davis, the UK minister responsible for exiting the EU, said, on behalf of the government, that retaining membership of the European single market was 'very improbable'. However, a senior government official then countered that this statement was only 'his opinion' and not the position of the government. The rest of the EU 27 member states have said that freedom of movement is non-negotiable if the UK is to retain membership of the single market. The UK Government does not yet have an agreed timetable on when Article 50, the mechanism for leaving the EU, will be triggered. With no apparent UK post-Brexit negotiating position, there remains continued uncertainty for businesses, public policy-makers, trade unions and workers across Britain.

The Brexit vote has the potential to be a significant shock for the UK economy (Muscatelli, 2016). Although economic data initially showed a 'dramatic deterioration' in the UK economy (Cadman and Giles, 2016), 3 months later a trio of stronger than expected readings on business activity across manufacturing, construction and service sectors suggests that Britain has escaped a post-Brexit recession (Allen, 2016a). However, it is worth noting that Brexit has, at the time of writing, not yet happened, and these are early days in the post-Brexit economy as far as macro-economic data are concerned (Muscatelli, 2016). It is likely that exiting from the EU has the potential to be a transformational change in how the UK labour market operates across a range of sectors, including the National Health Service, tourism and food-processing, when the employment status of EU nationals remains uncertain (Duffy, 2016). Furthermore, EU member states might seek to lure financial services, banking and digital-based business startups away from London (Oltermann, 2016). Britain is in completely uncharted terrain, and how transformational Brexit is will depend on the outcome of negotiations between the UK and the EU, as well as policy decisions by the UK government.

We focus here on the effects of Brexit on HRM. Arguably, withdrawal from the EU is highly likely to affect the supply of labour and the HR planning and recruitment processes. There is further uncertainty over whether an early casualty of the referendum vote will be the suspension of EU employment law and regulations and the erosion of what remains of British worker and trade union rights and entitlements. Further change is anticipated by Theresa May's promise to ensure that workers are represented on company boards and that shareholders get a binding vote on corporate pay.

These proposed changes in corporate governance will make big business more accountable (Sparrow et al., 2016). Support for Theresa May's proposal has come from Trades Union Congress (TUC) General Secretary Frances O'Grady: 'The TUC has long argued for workers to be given seats on company boards and remuneration committees .... This move would inject a much-needed dose of reality into boardrooms, as well as putting the brakes on the multi-million pay and bonus packages which have done so much to damage the reputation of corporate Britain,' she said (TUC, 2016a). Future research will show whether corporate governance reform ushers in significant change for HR reward practices and employee voice in the workplace. All these developments have to be given consideration, as context matters when studying HRM.

An economic recession is itself a complex phenomenon to analyse. Many theories try to explain it and, depending on our own life experiences and perspectives, we all have our favourite. Some would argue that the challenge ahead is nothing less than replacing the neo-liberal capitalist model. That the so-called 'casino economy' that enabled the City of London to thrive is an unreliable engine of prosperity. That the 2008 financial and economic crisis was a failure of free markets, but also a failure of sovereign government in most developed nations to regulate the financial sector and so protect the public from capitalism's destructive greed. That it represents, as Henry Mintzberg (2009) argues, a monumental failure of management.

Others, however, have argued that the 2008 financial crash is fundamentally a crisis of management education and pedagogy. For years, critics have maintained that North American and European business schools have been teaching an excessively quantitative, socially detached style of management that uncritically accepted the axiomatic notion underpinning neo-liberalism that a sovereign government cannot defy the markets and that, left alone, business can take care of itself.

The thesis that business schools are complicit in the current economic crisis was perhaps best captured by *The Economist*, a venerable bastion of free-market ideology, when in 2009 it asserted that 'This has been a year of sackcloth and ashes for the world's business schools' (Stewart, 2009). The years since 2008 have been a time for some soul-searching among academics responsible for teaching the disgraced bankers and financiers who caused the crisis. In a timely edition of the *British Journal of Management*, Graeme Currie and his colleagues (2010) provided a scathing account of what others have described as 'a fundamental intellectual failure' to subject neo-liberal-inspired business models to critical analysis. Many in academia have begun to acknowledge their (albeit unwitting) complicity in the neo-liberal project to transfer ever-greater wealth to corporate elites (Callahan et al., 2015; Hill, 2014) and, as we have argued elsewhere, that as a field HRM has largely failed to act as an intellectual counterweight to the neo-liberal project against workers and trade unions (Bratton and Gold, 2015).

Approach

So, as we publish this sixth edition of *Human Resource Management: Theory and Practice*, what is the established consensus on HRM in the early twenty-first century? The emerging zeitgeist is critical reflexivity in management education and pedagogy. This approach would take it as given that the practice of management can only be understood in the context of the wider social, economic and political factors that shape or determine organizational life.

The application of C. Wright Mills' *The Sociological Imagination* (1959/2000) – the ability to connect local and personal problems to larger macro and global forces – has obvious and current resonance with HRM education. It would suggest, for example, that an employee's personal troubles caused by job loss resulting from downsizing should be linked to the broader public issue of the contraction of the welfare state, or to how work and capital generally is being relocated offshore in a context of post-Cold-War economic globalization (Gold and Bratton, 2014). It would also suggest linkages when a manager is faced with implementing a strategic reconfiguration of a work system into which she has had no input. For Mills, to make connections of this kind, workplace scholars and students have to develop an ability to change from one perspective to another, and in the process to construct a view of a total market society and its workings. It is the possession of this capacity that differentiates the social scientist from the 'mere technician'. Our aim here is thus to encourage students to ask tough questions about work and employment practices – to educate and not merely train students.

The notion of critical analytical HRM reflects recent contributions to the HRM litera-ture. An approach concerned with the 'what', the 'why' and the 'how' of HRM. A concern with questions of: *What* do managers or HR professionals do? *Why* do they do it, and what affects what they do? *How* are HR practices enacted, and with what effect on employers, employees and society at large? This critical analytical approach to HRM echoes the belief that the contemporary workplace mirrors capitalist society at large, a capitalist society characterized by creativity, innovation and immense material wealth, but also a society that exhibits constant change and adaptability, strategic variation, extreme social inequality and contradiction. Students, in our view, need to develop a complex and context-sensitive understanding of contemporary HRM. This task is made less daunting by the fact that many Millennials, the generation born between around 1977 and 1994, have direct experi-ence of precarious zero-hours employment contracts, insecurity and low wages. The basis for a critical, context-sensitive approach is influenced by recent commentaries from academics such as Peter Boxall, Rick Delbridge, Tom Keenoy and Tony Watson, on 'analytical' and 'critical' HRM, and the ongoing and relevant debate on critical reflexivity in management education and pedagogy.

We do, however, acknowledge that, in an introductory text, there needs to be an oppor-tunity for students to engage in skill development related to HR. This new edition, therefore, still retains a practical element – the 'how to' activities of HRM – and more of this type of material has been placed in the book's online resource centre. Students and lecturers will find there, for example, activities on how to recruit and select, and how to design training programmes.

More broadly, we aim to provide a more critical, nuanced account of the realities of the workplace in market societies, one that encourages a deeper understanding and sensitivity with respect to employment and HR-related issues. We hope that *Human Resource Management: Theory and Practice* captures the range of change evident in today's workplaces and will moreover lead to the kind of sensibilities that encourage the reader to question, to be critical and to seek multicausality when analysing contemporary HRM. This sixth edition of *Human Resource Management: Theory and Practice* has been written for students *looking to be managers in the local or increasingly global arena*, and therefore draws examples of and literature on HRM from Europe, Canada, the USA, China, India, Japan, Australia and other countries. This should help students to compare international developments in HRM and to develop a broader understanding of HRM issues and practices.

New to the sixth edition

Users of previous editions of *Human Resource Management: Theory and Practice* will find that we have retained the overall teaching and learning objectives of the previous versions. However, all the material retained from the fifth edition has been updated and also substantially edited to enhance readability and to allow for a seamless integration of new content.

Despite environmental degradation becoming a major concern for all humankind and there being a continuing interest in sustainability, the texts and discourses of mainstream HRM are largely shaped by entrenched orthodox economic growth models. Indeed, few texts mention, let alone incorporate, HR strategies for creating more sustainable workplaces. In 2017, environmental *sustainability* is an opportunity – a hallmark for organizational change. In this edition, we have therefore included a new chapter on 'green HRM'.

The following is a list of the key changes and additions we have made to this new edition:

Chapter 1 has been updated and revised and sets the theoretical and practical scene for studying HRM, including a consideration of how Brexit will impact on the HRM function.

Chapter 2 incorporates emergent literature on corporate sustainability and outlines the four pillars of sustainability and the links to corporate-level and business-level strategy.

Chapter 3 has been significantly reworked and renamed to reflect the interest in exploring possible causal paths illuminating the HRM–performance relationship and the role of line managers.

Chapter 4 covers developments in workforce planning, along with a discussion of managing diversity in the workplace.

Chapter 5 has been updated and contains new material on recruitment and selection.

Chapter 6 examines new developments in performance appraisal.

Chapter 7 provides an extensive coverage of workplace learning and e-learning, including new material on skills.

Chapter 8 has been significantly reworked and renamed, and includes an expanded discussion on **pay inequality and variable payment schemes**. It also explains some paradoxes and tensions in reward systems in relation to managing the employment relationship.

Chapter 9 has been updated and renamed, and also includes a discussion on trade unions, environmental sustainability, and **union density and inequality**.

Chapter 10 has been rewritten to include new research and developments in **employee voice**.

Chapter 11 is a new chapter on ethics that aims to guide the student through **employment ethics** as it relates to real HR practices, as well as introducing the concept of corporate social responsibility.

Chapter 12 has been rewritten to include new research and developments in **occupational health and safety** illustrated by some examples beyond Europe.

Chapter 13 has been thoroughly restructured and extended to include new research and developments on **high-performance work systems**.

Chapter 14 includes the latest research and practices in organizational **leadership and management development**.

Chapter 15 has been revised and updated, and explains different theoretical perspectives on **organizational culture and climate** and the role of HRM in changing culture.

Chapter 16 is a new chapter that examines the emerging field of **green HRM**.

Finally, **Chapter 17** has been rewritten to introduce new developments in **international HRM**.

This new edition gives consideration to how Britain's vote to leave the **European Union** will impact on the HRM function. It also includes new **HRM in practice** features that illustrate the link between HRM theory and practice in workplaces. The examples take contemporary themes such as zero-hours contracts, sustainability, target culture and workplace violence from a diverse range of organizations.

This edition also includes new **HRM and globalization** features that provide examples of employment practices taken from BRIC countries, as well as Europe, South Africa, North America and the Middle East.

This edition also includes new videos interviews as part of the **HRM as I see it** feature. This consists of video interviews with HR practitioners at companies such as Sky and Unilever (accessible directly through the interactive ebook version of the text), in which they talk about key topics such as recruitment, organizational culture and talent management. These are accompanied by questions in the textbook for students to answer after watching the videos.

Designed specifically to meet the learning needs of international students, this new edition now offers the **Vocab checklists for ESL students** through the new interactive ebook, which helps students to recognize HRM-related terminology and more sophisticated vocabulary used to talk about HRM.

The sixth edition contains many new chapter **case studies**, which are international in scale and accompanied by assignments.

In addition, we have increased the interactive nature of the book, with more opportunities for students to check or reinforce their learning and to expand their knowledge outside the printed text. The reflective questions and HRM web links have all been extended to enhance the learning experience, and there are study tips and practising HRM features online. The interactive ebook offers content more directly for ease of use and navigation.

We believe that this new print and ebook edition of *Human Resource Management: Theory and Practice* and its online resource centre at www.palgravehighered.com/bg-hrm-6e, with three new chapters, an emphasis on dysfunctional aspects of the labour market, ethics, sustainability and 'green' HRM, a greater focus on inequality, gender and diversity, new features focusing on globalization and practitioners' views and, of course, reference to the most recent research and thinking throughout, will help students of HRM to make sense of these exciting developments.

Content

This book is divided into five major parts, which are summarised below. This new structure was suggested by users of the fifth edition. While these parts are, of course, closely interconnected with the external and internal contexts, Parts I, II, III and IV explore the core theories and HR practices that are typically covered in a one-semester HRM module. Part V, on the other hand, retains the updated and reworked chapters from the previous edition, as well as the new chapters, and provides individual lecturers the flexibility and opportunity to examine some contemporary HRM issues in this ever-changing discipline.

Part I introduces the whole arena of contemporary HRM. Chapter 1 discusses the nature and role of HRM and addresses some of the controversial theoretical issues surrounding the debate on HRM. Chapter 2 examines the notion of corporate sustainability and strategic HRM. Chapter 3 critically evaluates the HRM–performance relationship and examines the involvement of line managers in HRM. Chapters 1–3 provide the context of HRM and prepare the groundwork for Parts II, III and IV.

Part II introduces the topic of employee resourcing. Chapter 4 examines key HR practices, including HR planning and talent management. Chapter 5 examines recruitment practices to enable organizations to attract a high-quality pool of job applicants, as well as the use of multiple methods of assessment, all designed to select talented people.

Part III covers employee performance and development. Chapter 6 examines the practice of performance appraisal and provides a critical review of some of the key developments in performance management and appraisal. Chapter 7 explains the link between corporate strategy and human resource development, discusses how human resource development may be implemented and examines the favoured theories of adult learning and HR development practices.

Part IV focuses on employment relations. Chapter 8 presents a model of rewards to help the reader examine the complexities and practices associated with reward management. Research suggests that variable pay systems are increasingly replacing traditional wage schemes, and that these new pay practices go hand in hand with more precarious employment, the decline of union membership and collective bargaining. Chapter 9 highlights the major changes in labour relations, including collective bargaining and partnership strategies. Chapter 10 examines employee 'voice' and considers the context in which employee voice has changed over time.

Part V looks at some of the contemporary HRM issues in the global world. Chapter 11 introduces employment ethics and the concept of social corporate responsibility. Occupational health and safety has long been a neglected area of HRM. We seek to help to shift the balance in Chapter 12, which aims to explore why occupational health and safety is – or ought to be – a central pillar in HRM. Chapter 13 is a thoroughly reworked chapter to cover the major research on high-performance work systems. Chapter 14 examines organizational leadership and explores the favoured theories of leadership and management development practices. Chapter 15 explores the complex notion of organizational culture and climate, and considers the role of HRM in changing culture. Chapter 16 examines the emerging literature on green HRM and includes evidence from the author's own research. Finally, Chapter 17 examines international HRM within the context of post-2008 economic globalization.

Supporting teaching and learning resources

The textual material is complemented by a number of features to help student learning. These include:

Chapter outlines and *chapter objectives* guide students through the material that follows and allow them to check their progress.

HRM in practice examples illustrate current developments or practices in HRM. These are taken from a range of organizations in the EU to reflect the breadth of application of HR theory.

HRM and globalization examples illustrate the practices in HRM in companies outside the EU, which helps students to understand the 'convergence' and 'divergence' debate in the comparative HRM literature.

HRM as I see it video features give some interesting personal views from practitioners and experts in the HRM field in interviews accessible through the interactive ebook, with accompanying questions in the textbook. See pp. xliv–xlv for more details.

Reflective questions challenge the student to think analytically and critically, and to consider the broader relationships and interactions of the topics under discussion.

HRM web links enable students to download statistical information, follow current international developments in HRM practice and even monitor the job market in HRM.

Chapter summaries provide an abbreviated version of the main concepts and theories, which students may find useful for revision and also for checking their understanding of the key points.

Vocab checklists for ESL students accessible in the interactive ebook help international students to recognize the HRM-related terminology and sophisticated vocabulary that they can use to talk about the discipline.

Applying the sociological imagination is a central feature associated with critical HRM education. This concept focuses on the development of a learning culture that focuses less on the 'what' and 'how' of HRM, but shifts the emphasis towards the 'why' of HRM, to the everyday practices and processes and human actions that occur in the workplace and their impact on workers and the local community in which any work organization is situated.

The emphasis is on the idea that, to understand HRM-related 'troubles', both students and educators are required to look beyond them, at the social embeddedness of HRM. Critical HRM education, we contend, adds to a growing body of critical management pedagogy.

Discussion questions test students' understanding of core concepts and can be used to promote classroom or group discussions of different perspectives.

Further reading suggestions provide an elaboration of the key topics discussed in the text.

Chapter case studies demonstrate the application of theoretical material from the text and help students to appreciate the challenges of managing people at work.

Chapter review questions test how much students have learned on completion of the chapter and are useful for revision.

The *reference list* provides students with a comprehensive list of the sources and works cited in the text.

Indexes at the end of the book provide an author index and a subject index to help readers search easily for relevant information or references.

Online resource centre

Lecturers who adopt this textbook for student purchase have access to materials on the password-protected section of the book's online resource centre. Log on to find out more at www.palgravehighered.com/bg-hrm-6e.

The website offers downloadable teaching support and other resources, including:

- Lecture notes for each chapter that expand the content in the book and provide advice for teaching each topic. These include lecture enhancement suggestions providing new ideas for adding further dimensions to lectures, notes to accompany skill development exercises, tips on teaching ESL students and guideline answers to case study questions
- PowerPoint lecture slides for each chapter, including key points and definitions, learning objectives and relevant figures and tables, which you can edit for your own use
- A comprehensive test bank of multiple-choice and essay questions for use in exams, tests and quizzes
- Quick reference grids to readily locate both 'HRM in practice' articles and case studies in terms of context and topic coverage.

Students also have free access to:

- Extensive web links to further resources around the world to help them research topics in more depth
- Summary lecture notes to accompany each chapter topic
- Skill development exercises to improve their professional competencies
- Extra case studies and HRM in practice features
- Study tips and 'practising HRM' features
- Learning tips for ESL students.

Overall, we are confident that the incorporation of new chapters, new material and student-focused features will continue to make *Human Resource Management: Theory and Practice* a valuable learning resource. We are also confident that this book will promote critical reflection so that readers will use multiple perspectives, question, doubt, investigate, be sceptical and seek multiple causes when analysing the problems and challenges of managing people in the workplace. We would welcome any feedback on the text or any suggestions on how we can improve the next edition. Please contact us via the email address listed in the online resource centre.

John Bratton Jeff Gold
September 2016

authors' acknowledgements

No book is ever simply the product of its authors. This book was originally inspired by the teaching and research in which we were involved at Leeds Business School, UK. We continue to be inspired by our students, but we are also indebted to our past and current colleagues for their ideas and encouragement in the writing of six editions of the book.

The sixth edition of *Human Resource Management: Theory and Practice* has been improved by the comments and suggestions of colleagues, anonymous reviewers and students. We have endeavoured to incorporate their insights and criticisms to improve this edition. We are particularly indebted to the following reviewers for their detailed comments: Priyadarshini Baguant, University of Sharjah, United Arab Emirates; Grace Dagher, Lebanese American University, Lebanon; Jason Foster, Athabasca University, Canada; Jo Grady, University of Leicester, UK; Konstantina Kougiannou, Nottingham Trent University, UK; Brigid Milner, Waterford Institute of Technology, Ireland; Rea Prouska, Middlesex University, London, UK; Wilfred Ukpere, University of Johannesburg, South Africa; Andreas Wallo, Linköping University, Sweden; Connie Zheng, Deakin University, Melbourne, Australia; Andrew Zur, University of Melbourne, Australia.

Users familiar with the five previous editions of this book will notice that we have introduced new contributors. In writing this sixth edition, therefore, we are also indebted to Bob Barnetson, Andrew Bratton, John Burgess, David Denham, Kirsteen Grant, Roslyn Larkin, Alan Montague, and Christine Mortimer.

John Bratton: I am indebted to Norma D'Annunzio-Green, Edinburgh Napier University, UK, for her suggestion to include new material on line managers and HRM incorporated in Chapter 3 and for her support. I would like to thank Keith Grint, Les Hamilton, Sue Hughes in the UK; Esa Poikela and Annikki Järvinen in Finland; and Lori and Edward Rilkoff, Bernard Igwe, Bruce Spencer and Albert Mills in Canada for their friendship and support. Special thanks also to Carolyn Forshaw, my wife and partner, who has provided unstinting support with all six manuscripts, and others, over the years. I would like also to dedicate this edition to my children Amy, Andrew and Jennie and my grandchildren Owen (aged 4 years) and Colbie (aged 18 months).

Jeff Gold: I would like to thank colleagues and friends who have provided support in the completion of this book. In particular, I am indebted to Christine Mortimer for her research and contribution to my chapters. A special thanks go to my family, my lovely wife Susan and the families of Katy and Graham, with a special mention to grandson Matthew (aged 5). Thanks also to my ex-colleagues from Leeds Beckett University, my new colleagues at York Business School and those members and friends who are helping me develop a new passion at Ben Rhydding Golf Club.

Finally, we are grateful for the professional advice and support shown by our publisher: Ursula Gavin, Nikini Jayatunga, Isabel Berwick, and on the production side, Georgia Walters and Gogulanathan Bactavatchalane, throughout the project.

tour of the book

Chapter outlines and objectives
Guide you through the material in each chapter and allow your progress to be checked

objectives

After studying this chapter, you should be able to:

1 Define HRM and its relation to organizational management
2 Explain the central features of the contract in the employment relation
3 Summarise the scope of HRM and the key HRM functions
4 Explain the theoretical issues surroun...

Opening vignettes
Show the relevance of each topic and how it links to the chapter content and the real world

Many managers complain that the HR department prevents them from doing what they want, such as hiring someone they 'just know' is a good fit for the job. And HR professionals make them perform tasks they dislike, such as 'playing God', when appraising their employees' performance. These complaints from line managers have a cyclical quality – they are driven largely by the business context. When organizations are experiencing labour problems, whether those are skill shortages, high turnover or low productivity, HR is usually seen as a valued leadership partner. When things are running efficiently, managers tend to think, 'What's HR *doing* for us, anyway?' (Cappelli, 2015, p. 54)

introduction

The contemporary workplace is constantly changing against a backdrop of post-2008 economic austerity that has now reached the proportions of the Great Depression of the 1920s. The changes relate, although not exclusively, to the rise in zero-hour contracts (Brinkley, 2013), the increase of precarious work and insecurity (Standing, 2011), organizational downsizing (Datta et al., 2010), low wages (Flassbeck and Lapavitsas, 2015; Schmitt, 2012), the emasculation of trade union power (Hutton, 2015a) and extreme inequality in income (Stiglitz, 2015a). Analyses of these lab

Reflective questions
Challenge and encourage you to think critically about the broader relationships and interactions between the topics under discussion

reflective question

Based upon your reading or work experience, or that of a family mem organizations manage employees with respect and dignity and in way their full capability and engagement?

HRM web links
Enable you to download statistical information, follow current international developments in HRM practice and even monitor the job market in HRM

HRM web links

Visit the online resource centre at **www.palgravehighered.com/bg-hrm-6e** fo history of the development of HRM over the last 30 years.

We start this introductory chapter by examining the complex debate surr nature and significance of contem

HRM in practice
Illustrate the link between HRM theory and practice in workplaces, covering contemporary themes and a diverse range of organizations

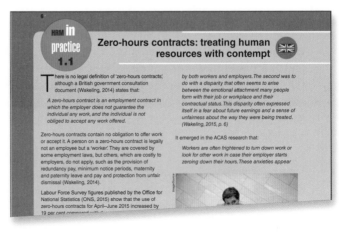

HRM in practice 1.1

Zero-hours contracts: treating human resources with contempt

There is no legal definition of 'zero-hours contracts', although a British government consultation document (Wakeling, 2014) states that:

A zero-hours contract is an employment contract in which the employer does not guarantee the individual any work, and the individual is not obliged to accept any work offered.

Zero-hours contracts contain no obligation to offer work or accept it. A person on a zero-hours contract is legally not an employee but a 'worker'. They are covered by some employment laws, but others, which are costly to employers, do not apply, such as the provision of redundancy pay, minimum notice periods, maternity and paternity leave and pay and protection from unfair dismissal (Wakeling, 2014).

Labour Force Survey figures published by the Office for National Statistics (ONS, 2015) show that the use of zero-hours contracts for April–June 2015 increased by 19 per cent compared with t

by both workers and employers. The second was to do with a disparity that often seems to arise between the emotional attachment many people form with their job or workplace and their contractual status. This disparity often expressed itself in a fear about future earnings and a sense of unfairness about the way they were being treated. (Wakeling, 2015, p. 6)

It emerged in the ACAS research that:

Workers are often frightened to turn down work or look for other work in case their employer starts zeroing down their hours. These anxieties appear

HRM and globalization

Provide examples of employment practices and management in BRIC countries, as well as South Africa and North America, and problematize them

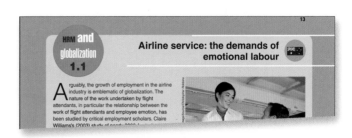

HRM as I see it

Consist of video interviews with HR practitioners in the interactive ebook, accompanied by a summary of the interviewees' qualifications and experience, and questions to think about after watching the videos. See the next page for more detail

Applying the sociological imagination

This concept emphasizes the idea that, to understand HRM-related 'troubles', both students and educators are required to look beyond them, at the social embeddedness of HRM

Chapter summaries

Provide an abbreviated version of the main concepts and theories, useful for your revision and checking understanding of the key points

Vocab checklists for ESL students

Help ESL students to recognize HRM-related terminology and more sophisticated vocabulary used to talk about the discipline

Chapter review questions

Test how much you have learned on completion of the chapter and are useful for revision

Further reading

Offer references that provide an elaboration of the key topics discussed in the text and can be used to help gain a better mark in essays

Case studies

Demonstrate the application of theoretical material from the text and facilitate an understanding and appreciation of the challenges of managing people at work

Interactive ebook

Included free with your copy of the printed book is access to an interactive ebook. Mirroring the pages of the printed book, it allows bookmarking and easy searching. Your unique code (printed on an insert card and placed inside your printed copy) gives you access to the ebook for a whole year, and after the initial download, it can be read offline, giving you the flexibility and convenience to access your ebook anytime and anywhere. Just go to the online resource centre, www.palgravehighered.com/bg-hrm-6e to find details of how to download the ebook.

The ebook contains embedded 'HRM as I see it' videos interviews (see below) and linked vocabulary checklists for ESL students.

HRM as I see it: video and text feature

Video interviews with HR practitioners, linked to chapter content

This exciting feature, expanded for the sixth edition, enables you to learn about how HRM operates *in practice*. In a series of video interviews, HR managers and directors from organizations such as Unilever, Bupa, Sky, Unite the Union and telecommunications company Huawei discuss their activities in the workplace, providing invaluable insights into the 'real world' of HRM. Emphasis is given to HRM's involvement in business strategy, in other words to how it shapes the future direction of organizations, *making a sound knowledge of HRM essential for every future business person.*

Each interview starts with a discussion of why the practitioners decided to work in HR and how they got to where they are now. This is followed by a consideration of selected key topics such as partnership, diversity, organizational culture, trade union relations and recruitment from their point of view, and ends with the HR practitioner giving their advice to those who wish to pursue a career in HR.

HRM as I see it boxes appear in selected chapters of the textbook and provide a description of the organization at which the practitioner is employed and a summary of their qualifications and experience. Simply click on the photo of the interviewee in your interactive ebook to watch the video.

Then try and answer questions on the video that encourage you to think critically about what you have seen, and relate it back to the topics under discussion in the chapter.

There are 14 interviews included in the book. Here is a list of the practitioners and which chapter you can find them in:

Chapter 1: Alison Blayney, HR Business Partner, TIGI Haircare, Unilever, talks in Part 1 of her interview about her role as HR Business Partner.

Chapter 2: Sarah Myers, Director of Talent Management, Sky, discusses how talent management operates in the company, how the recession has impacted on this, and how their approach is firmly tied to the business strategy.

Chapter 4: Karen Jochelson, Director of Policy for Employment and the Economy, The Equality and Human Rights Commission, talks about the work of the Equality and Human Rights Commission on the issue of diversity and what methods can be used to encourage participation of women at board level, provide a better experience for women during pregnancy and maternity cover, and reduce the gender pay gap.

Chapter 5: Alison Blayney, HR Business Partner, TIGI Haircare, Unilever, talks in Part 2 of her interview about the process of recruitment and selection and how these are conducted in the company.

Chapter 7: Helen Tiffany, Managing Director of HR consultancy firm Bec Development, talks about the importance of human resource development and coaching.

Chapter 8: Ruth Altman, an experienced freelance HR practitioner, discusses the challenges faced by HR departments in universities and how higher tuition fees will impact on the reward system at universities.

Chapter 9: Ray Fletcher, Director of Personnel and Development, Unite the Union, considers trade unions in the contemporary workplace, their contribution to workplace learning, and possibilities for union–green coalitions.

Chapter 10: Keith Hanlon-Smith, Employee Relations Director at facilities maintenance company Norland Managed Services, discusses employee relations, the employment relationship and HR as a strategic partner (the Ulrich model).

Chapter 11: Gregor Karolus, Chief HR officer, Springer Nature, talks in the first part of his interview, about the importance of ethics and compliance to a business and how these can be encouraged.

Chapter 13: Gregor Karolus, Chief HR officer, Springer Nature, expands in the second part of his interview, on high-performance workplace systems and how these are implemented in large multi-national companies.

Chapter 14: Lana Kularajah, Senior HR Business Partner, Transform Aid International/ Baptist World Aid Australia, speaks about mentoring programmes in leadership and management initiatives, particularly to encourage female progression to senior management positions.

Chapter 15: Keith Stopforth, Head of Talent and Development, Bupa Health and Wellbeing, talks about the organizational culture at Bupa and how this is implemented, how talent management works in the company and how Bupa views diversity in the workplace.

Chapter 16: Markus Hiemann, Sustainability Manager for NHS National Services Scotland (NSS), discusses the issues surrounding sustainability and green HRM.

Chapter 17: Lesley White, Human Resources Director UK and Ireland, Huawei Technologies, discusses the challenges of working in a UK-based HR department for a company headquartered in China, cultural differences in working and management styles, and the place of HR in Huawei's business strategy.

Online resource centre

Go to www.palgravehighered.com/bg-hrm-6e to access a number of additional resources to aid teaching and learning.

Teaching resources
Instructors who adopt this book on their course gain access to a selection of password protected resources to help plan and deliver their teaching:

- Lecture notes
- Lecture slides
- Testbank of multiple choice and essay questions

Learning resources
Students have free access to:

- HRM web links
- Summary lecture notes
- Skill development exercises
- Extra case studies and HRM features
- Study tips and 'practising HRM' features
- Learning tips for ESL students

key topics grid

Key topic	Relevant chapter(s)	Other relevant material
Ethics, corporate social responsibility and environmental sustainability	Chapter 11: HRM and ethics Chapter 16: Green HRM and environmental sustainability	• Chapter 2, pp. 45–48, 'Strategy, ethics and corporate social responsibility' and 'Corporate sustainability' • Chapter 2, p. 51, 'HRM and globalization 2.1: Business urged to keep on eco-track' • Chapter 2, pp. 67–8, 'Case study: Zuvan Winery' • Chapter 12, pp. 392–5, 'Sustainable health and safety and HRM' • Chapter 13, pp. 440–1, 'Case study: Currency, Inc.' • Chapter 17, p. 535, 'HRM in Practice 17.1: We are disposable people …'
Diversity, gender management and equal opportunities	Chapter 4: Workforce planning and diversity Chapter 5: Recruitment, selection and talent management Chapter 15: Organizational culture and HRM	• Chapter 1, p. 30, content on the feminist paradigm and gender analysis • Chapter 2, p. 53, 'HRM in practice 2.2: More women leaders: the answer to the financial crisis?' • Chapter 7, pp. 230–1, 'Diversity and HRD' • Chapter 8, pp. 279–80 The legal and collective determination of pay • Chapter 9, pp. 328–9, 'Case study: Rama Garment factory' • Chapter 10, pp. 357–8, 'HRM and globalization 10.2: Sexual harassment as gender-based violence in a BRIC economy' • Chapter 14, p. 461, 'HRM as I see it: Lana Kularajah, Transform Aid International/Baptist World Aid Australia' • Chapter 17, pp. 542–3, 'HRM and globalization 17.2: Realizing gender balance in British boardrooms'
Health, safety and wellness	Chapter 12: Employee health, safety and wellness	• Chapter 2, pp. 61–2, 'HRM and globalization 2.2: The effect of business strategy on workers' psychological health' • Chapter 4, p. 111, 'HRM and globalization 4.1: Migrant workers in Qatar: the impact of regulatory failure on workforce planning' • Chapter 9, pp. 302–3, 'Trade unions in action' • Chapter 11, pp. 370–3 'Corporate social responsibility' • Chapter 11, p. 372, 'HRM and globalization 11.1: Toxins and cancer: what price for Canada's oil?' • Chapter 13, pp. 420–1, 'HRM and globalization 13.1: Commuting time in the EU is work time' • Chapter 15, pp. 474–5, 'HRM and globalization 15.1: Is a bullying culture a management strategy? Evidence from Australia' • Chapter 15, pp. 489–90, 'HRM in practice 15.1: 'Purposeful Darwinism' – Amazon's experiment to motivate staff'
Globalization and international HRM	Chapter 17: International HRM and global capitalism	• Chapter 1, p. 25, 'HRM and globalization 1.2: The HRM model in advancing economies?' • Chapter 8, p. 271, 'HRM and globalization 8.1: Building a hybrid at Samsung' • Chapter 13, p. 435, 'HRM as I see it: Gregor Karolus, Part 2, Springer Nature'

Key topic	Relevant chapter(s)	Other relevant material
The global financial crisis	Chapter 1: The nature of Contemporary HRM	• Chapter 2, p. 53, 'HRM in practice 2.2: More women leaders: the answer to the financial crisis?' • Chapter 2, p. 58, 'HRM as I see it: Sarah Myers, Sky' • Chapter 4, pp. 112–13, 'Workforce planning' (content on Northern Rock and workforce planning) • Chapter 7, p. 222, content on global financial crisis and HRD • Chapter 14, p. 445, content on leaders' roles in causing the crisis • Chapter 15, pp. 492–4, 'Paradox in culture management' • Chapter 17, pp. 526–7, introduction
Work–life balance	Chapter 12: Employee health, safety and wellness Chapter 15: Organizational culture and HRM	• Chapter 1, pp. 6–7, 'HRM in practice 1.1: Zero-hours contracts: treating human resources with contempt' • Chapter 4, pp. 121–4, 'Flexibility' • Chapter 13, pp. 420–1, 'HRM and globalization 13.1: Commuting time in the EU is work time' • Chapter 13, p. 422, 'HRM in practice 13.1: The impact of technologies on the practice of HRM'
Organizational culture	Chapter 15: Organizational culture and HRM	• Chapter 1, pp. 15–18, 'Scope and functions of HRM' • Chapter 10, pp. 345–6, 'HRM and globalization 10.1: A warm welcome to the kooky and the wacky' • Chapter 17, p. 536, 'HRM as I see it: Lesley White, Huawei Technologies' • Chapter 17, pp. 547–51, 'The convergence/divergence debate' (covering different organizational cultures in a global working environment)
Leadership management and development	Chapter 14: Leadership management and development	• Chapter 1, pp. 33–4, 'Case study: Knowledge management at Emenee hotels' • Chapter 4, p. 125, 'HRM as I see it: Karen Jochelson, Equality and Human Rights Commission' • Chapter 15, pp. 482–5, 'Managerially oriented perspectives' • Chapter 15, pp. 490–2, 'Leading cultural change'
The voluntary/tertiary sector and HRM in small and medium-sized enterprises		• Chapter 6, pp. 187–8, p. 190, content on performance analysis in small and medium-sized enterprises • Chapter 7, pp. 255–6, 'Case study: Volunteers Together' • Chapter 8, p. 263, material on volunteers and reward management • Chapter 14, p. 447, text on leaders in SMEs and the Third Sector
The public sector		• Chapter 2, p. 39, text on the transformation of the public sector • Chapter 3, p. 78, 'HRM in practice 3.1: HR "can lower NHS death rates"' • Chapter 3, p. 88, 'HRM in practice 3.2: Can organizations simultaneously be committed to employees and outsource services?' • Chapter 4, p. 113, material on workforce planning and the UK NHS • Chapter 4, p. 126, 'HRM in practice 4.2: Planning the headcount on the policy roller-coaster' • Chapter 6, pp. 186–90 and p. 208, material on performance measurement and human resource management in the public and the tertiary sector • Chapter 12, p. 413–14, 'Case study: The City of Kamloops' • Chapter 14, p. 468–9, 'Case study: The City of Sahali' • Chapter 16, p. 520, 'HRM as I see it: Markus Hiemann, NHS National Services Scotland'

publisher's acknowledgements

We would like to thank the many people and organizations who have provided us with artwork or material for the book. In most cases, full references are provided in the source lines; please refer to these for details.

We would also like to thank the people and organizations below for the use of their material:

The Economist Intelligence Unit, for the extracts on page 25. From Economist Intelligence Unit (2006) Foresight 2020: Economic, industry and corporate trends.

http://www.eiu.com/site_info.asp?info_name=eiu_Cisco_Foresight_2020 © Reproduced by permission of The Economist Intelligence Unit.

Emerald Group Publishing Limited, for the extracts on page 176. From Gold, J., Oldroyd, T., Chesters, E., Booth, A. and Waugh, A. (2016) Exploring talenting: talent management as a collective endeavour. *European Journal of Training and Development,* **40**(7): 513–33. Copyright 2016 © Emerald Group Publishing Limited. Reproduced under Emerald Author Rights.

The Globe and Mail, for the extracts on page 479. From Peritz, I. and Friesen, J. (2010) Multiculturalism's magic number. Globe and Mail, October 2, pp. A14–15. Reproduced with permission from The Globe and Mail.

Great Place to Work®, for the extracts on page 493. From Great Place to Work ® (2016) *Baringa Partners: How culture and values drives strategy and success at this top management consultancy, Case Study July 2016.* London: Great Place to Work ® Reproduced with permission.

Harvard Business School Press, for Table 8.5. Reprinted by permission of Harvard Business School Press. From *The Human Equation: Building Profits by Putting People First* by Jeffrey Pfeffer. Boston, MA 1998, p. 116. Copyright © 1998 by the Harvard Business School Publishing Corporation; all rights reserved.

Taylor & Francis Ltd, for the extracts on page 78. From *The link between the management of employees and patient mortality in acute hospitals* by Michael A. West, Carol Borrill, Jeremy Dawson, Judy Scully, Matthew Carter, Stephen Anelay, Malcolm Patterson & Justin Waring (2002). Published in *The International Journal of Human Resource Management* **13**(8): 1299–1310. Reprinted by permission of the publisher (Taylor & Francis Ltd, http://www.tandfonline.com)

ThinkProgress, for the extracts on page 372. From Katie Valentine (2014) Tar Sands Oil Development Is More Toxic Than Previously Thought, Study Finds. February 4. https://

thinkprogress.org/tar-sands-oil-development-is-more-toxic-than-previously-thought-study-finds-aef580e996cd#.ymwjz6ifo. This material was published by ThinkProgress.

John Wiley & Sons, Inc., for the extracts on page 204. From Sullivan, T. A. (2014) Greedy Institutions, Overwork, and Work-Life Balance. *Sociological Inquiry*, **84**(1): 1–15. Copyright © 2013 Alpha Kappa Delta: The International Sociology Honor Society. Reproduced with permission from John Wiley & Sons, Inc.

Sage Publishing, for the extract on page v. From Bratton, J. and Gold, J. (2015) Towards Critical Human Resource Management Education (CHRME): A sociological imagination approach. *Work, Employment and Society*, **29**(3): 496–507. Republished under Sage author rights.

United Nations Development Programme, for the data in Figure 8.4. From Table 3 (Inequality-adjusted Human Development Index), 2015 Human Development Report, United Nations Development Programme (the HDRO calculations are based on data from the World Bank). The HDRO calculations are reproduced here under the Creative Commons 3.0 IGO license (https://creativecommons.org/licenses/by/3.0/igo/). Copyright © 2015 HDRO. To access the data sets go to http://hdr.undp.org/en/composite/IHDI

The entire series of Human Development Index (HDI) values and rankings are recalculated every year using the most recent (revised) data and functional forms. The HDI rankings and values in the 2015 Human Development Report cannot therefore be compared directly to indices published in previous Reports. Please see hdr.undp.org for more information.

The HDI was created to emphasize that people and their capabilities should be the ultimate criteria for assessing the development of a country, not economic growth alone. The HDI can also be used to question national policy choices, asking how two countries with the same level of GNI per capita can end up with different human development outcomes.

Notes on Crown Copyright material

All material credited as Crown Copyright has been licensed under the Open Government Licence v3.0. http://www.nationalarchives.gov.uk/doc/open-government-licence/version/3/ In cases where space wasn't available by the material, these are credited below:

The extracts on page 6 are from Department for Business, Innovation and Skills (2013) *Zero-hours Employment Contracts: Consultation.* London: Department for Business, Innovation and Skills. © Crown copyright 2013; and Wakeling, A. (2014) *Give and Take? Unravelling the True Nature of Zero-hours Contracts.* Acas Policy Discussion Papers. London: Advisory, Conciliation and Arbitration Service. Copyright © Acas, Euston Tower, 286 Euston Road, London NW1 3JJ.

The extracts on page 53 are from HM Treasury Committee (2010) *Treasury Committee Report on Women in The City.* London: TSO. © Crown copyright 2010.

The extracts on page 542 are from Davies, Lord of Abersoch (2011) *Women on Boards.* London: Department of Business, Innovation and Skills. © Crown copyright 2011.

Notes on material from Guardian News & Media Ltd

The following extracts are reproduced with permission from Guardian News & Media Ltd:

The extracts on page 312 are from Dan Milmo (2010) BA told to hit union 'where it hurts' - leaked document. The Guardian, March 27, pp. 1–2. Copyright Guardian News & Media Ltd 2016, www.theguardian.com.

The extracts on page 506 are from Jill Treanor (2015) Mark Carney calls on businesses to disclose carbon footprints. The Guardian, June 26.

https://www.theguardian.com/business/2015/jun/26/mark-carney-calls-on-businesses-to-disclose-carbon-footprints

Copyright Guardian News & Media Ltd 2016, www.theguardian.com.

Short quotations, cited as The Guardian, The Observer, or Courtesy of Guardian News & Media Ltd, are reproduced under The Guardian Open Licence Terms. Please see source lines for details.

Some quotations and extracts are from articles that include links to other sources. Please see below for details:

Page 281: The original extract from the article 'Larry Elliott (2015) Number of UK workers on minimum wage expected to double by 2020. October 1.

https://www.theguardian.com/society/2015/oct/01/number-of-uk-workers-on-minimum-wage-expected-to-double-by-2020' contains the following link:

http://www.resolutionfoundation.org/

Page 339: The original extract from the article 'David Crouch (2015) Ryanair closes Denmark operation to head off union row. July 17.

https://www.theguardian.com/business/2015/jul/17/ryanair-closes-denmark-operation-temporarily-to-sidestep-union-dispute' contains the following link:

http://www.dr.dk/nyheder/penge/ryanairs-kabineansatte-i-billund-vores-arbejde-er-uvaerdigt

Page 474: The original extract from the article 'Alan Yuhas, (2014) Amazon banks on rise of the robots to speed online orders to customers. The Guardian, December 1.

https://www.theguardian.com/technology/2014/dec/01/amazon-robots-online-orders-customers' contains the following links:

https://www.theguardian.com/money/2014/nov/28/being-homeless-is-better-than-working-for-amazon

http://articles.mcall.com/2011-09-18/news/mc-allentown-amazon-complaints-20110917_1_warehouse-workers-heat-stress-brutal-heat

Page 474: The original extract from the article 'Samuel Gibbs (2015) Jeff Bezos defends Amazon after NYT exposé of working practices. The Guardian, August 17.

https://www.theguardian.com/technology/2015/aug/17/jeff-bezos-amazon-working-practices' contains the following link:

http://www.nytimes.com/2015/08/16/technology/inside-amazon-wrestling-big-ideas-in-a-bruising-workplace.html

Page 506: The original extract from the article 'Jill Treanor (2015) Mark Carney calls on businesses to disclose carbon footprints. The Guardian, June 26.

https://www.theguardian.com/business/2015/jun/26/mark-carney-calls-on-businesses-to-disclose-carbon-footprints' contains the following links:

https://www.theguardian.com/environment/2015/mar/03/bank-of-england-warns-of-financial-risk-from-fossil-fuel-investments

https://www.theguardian.com/environment/2014/oct/13/mark-carney-fossil-fuel-reserves-burned-carbon-bubble

Page 542: The original extract from the article 'Jennifer Rankin (2015) Fewer women leading FTSE firms than men called John. The Guardian, March 6.

https://www.theguardian.com/business/2015/mar/06/johns-davids-and-ians-outnumber-female-chief-executives-in-ftse-100' includes the following link:

https://www.theguardian.com/business/2015/feb/04/cable-women-boardroom-mandatory-quotas

Corrections

The article quoted on page 312 'Dan Milmo (2010) BA told to hit union 'where it hurts' - leaked document. The Guardian, March 27, pp. 1–2' includes a correction which can be found here:

https://www.theguardian.com/theguardian/2010/apr/03/corrections-clarifications (please note that the person in question was not referred to in our extract).

Notes on WERS data

We would like to thank the following people for granting us permission to use data from van Wanrooy, B., Bewley, H., Bryson, A. Forth, J., Freeth, S., Stokes, L., and Wood, S. (2013) *Employment Relations in the Shadow of Recession: Findings from the 2011 Workplace Employment Relations Study.* Basingstoke: Palgrave Macmillan; and Kersley, B., Alpin, C., Forth, J., Dix, G., Oxenbridge, S., Bryson, A., and Bewley, H. (2006) *Inside the Workplace: Findings from the 2004 Workplace Employment Relations Survey.* London: Routledge:

John Forth, Alex Bryson, Gill Dix, Lucy Stokes, Stephen Wood, Sarah Oxenbridge, Carmen Alpin, Barbara Kersley, Brigid van Wanrooy, Helen Gray (née Bewley), Stephanie Freeth, ACAS, ESRC, NIESR, WERS, and Policy Studies Institute.

part I

THE CONTEMPORARY HUMAN RESOURCE MANAGEMENT ARENA

Getty Images/Caiaimage

1

part I

THE CONTEMPORARY HUMAN RESOURCE MANAGEMENT ARENA

chapter **1**

the nature of contemporary HRM

Getty

objectives

After studying this chapter, you should be able to:

1 Define HRM and its relation to organizational management
2 Explain the central features of the contract in the employment relationship
3 Summarise the scope of HRM and the key HRM functions
4 Explain the theoretical issues surrounding the HRM debate
5 Appreciate the different approaches to studying HRM

Many managers complain that the HR department prevents them from doing what they want, such as hiring someone they 'just know' is a good fit for the job. And HR professionals make them perform tasks they dislike, such as 'playing God', when appraising their employees' performance. These complaints from line managers have a cyclical quality – they are driven largely by the business context. When organizations are experiencing labour problems, whether those are skill shortages, high turnover or low productivity, HR is usually seen as a valued leadership partner. When things are running efficiently, managers tend to think, 'What's HR *doing* for us, anyway?' (Cappelli, 2015, p. 54)

introduction

The contemporary workplace is constantly changing against a backdrop of post-2008 economic austerity that has now reached the proportions of the Great Depression of the 1920s. The changes relate, although not exclusively, to the rise in zero-hour contracts (Brinkley, 2013), the increase of precarious work and insecurity (Standing, 2011), organizational downsizing (Datta et al., 2010), low wages (Flassbeck and Lapavitsas, 2015), the emasculation of trade union power (Hutton, 2015a) and extreme inequality in income (Stiglitz, 2015). Analyses of these labour market changes driven by neo-liberal economics vary significantly between developed capitalist countries. These changes have been introduced at different times and in different political and economic contexts, and have been accepted or opposed by workers and even managers in different ways and to different degrees (Atzeni, 2014). This diversity makes it even more important to understand the numerous different theories underpinning human resource management (HRM) and to explore the outcome of human resources (HR) practices on organizations, managers and workers and wider society.

As a management function, HRM has been widely documented as playing a fundamental role in designing and bringing about the changes that have given rise to 'labour market flexibility'. Despite the importance and deleterious effects of these transformative changes, mainstream coverage of HRM exhibits a 'dominance of consensus-oriented discourse' that is predominantly managerial in outlook, strategic and prescriptive (Keegan and Boselie, 2006). To put it another way, mainstream accounts tend to focus largely on assumed positive outcomes and the 'how to' of HRM (Watson, 2010). This book tries to take a different perspective: although it is concerned with the way in which organizations manage human capability, both individually and collectively, its coverage of contemporary HRM draws from the conflict and dysfunction-oriented discourse, a discourse being a number of ideas that together form a powerful body of thought that influences how people think and act. Thus, its central aim is to examine HRM theories and practices critically and to expose the tensions inherent in the employment relationship. A further aim is to provide a better understanding of how social relations, leadership, culture and HR policies and practices seek to enlist employee capabilities and engagement – or fail to do so – so that the wider role of HRM within the theory of organizational effectiveness (Boxall et al., 2008) can be examined in ways that will help managers manage workers more equitably and with dignity.

reflective question Based upon your reading or work experience, or that of a family member, do organizations manage employees with respect and dignity and in ways that enlist their full capability and engagement?

HRM itself, as a field of study, has had a controversial recent history. This history helps to explain debates around its precise meaning and significance, and around modes of enquiry, practices and questions related to 'who benefits' from HRM. In the 1980s, the term 'human resource management' or 'HRM' became prevalent and started to replace 'personnel management' (Guest, 1987; Storey, 1989) to describe formally organized activities that specifically dealt with managing workers. For some, the rise of the HRM new orthodoxy is associated with a set of distinctive 'best' practices that aim to recruit, develop, reward and engage employees in ways that create what are called 'high-performing work systems'. For others, HRM is simply a relabelling of 'good' personnel management practices – the 'old wine in new bottles' critique. More profoundly, some detractors argue that HRM grew out of, and is located within, a wider neo-liberal context, and HRM continues to grapple with enduring conflicts and paradoxes associated with managing the employment relationship (Gennard and Kelly, 1997; Legge, 1995). If we understand paradox as two or more positions that sound plausible and well argued yet are contradictory and incompatible with each other, it is argued that successful managers are those who are able to accept the tensions arising from the paradox and are able to handle all its competing positions simultaneously instead of choosing only one of them (Guerci and Carollo, 2016). Further background material on the development of HRM is available on the book's online resource centre.

HRM web links   Visit the online resource centre at **www.palgravehighered.com/bg-hrm-6e** for a short history of the development of HRM over the last 30 years.

We start this introductory chapter by examining the complex debate surrounding the nature and significance of contemporary HRM. After defining HRM, we examine the nature of the employment relationship and HRM functions before exploring some influential theoretical models that attempt to define HRM analytically. At the end of the chapter, we introduce the importance of critical HRM education (CHRME) and the application of the 'sociological imagination'.

Management and HRM

HRM, in theory and in practice, encompasses a multidisciplinary field, bringing together a diverse body of scholarship from various social science disciplines that are concerned with managing work and people. An early definition of HRM by Michael Beer and his colleagues focuses on all managerial activity affecting the employment relationship: 'Human resource management (HRM) involves all management decisions and actions that affect the nature of the relationship between the organization and employees – its human resources' (1984, p. 1). Acknowledging HRM as only one 'recipe' from a range of alternatives, Storey (1995a, 2001) contends that HRM plays a pivotal role in sophisticated organizations, emphasizing the importance of the strategic dimension and employee 'commitment' in generating HR activities. In his view (Storey, 2007, p. 7):

> Human resource management is a distinctive approach to employment management, which seeks to achieve competitive advantage through the strategic deployment of a highly committed and capable workforce using an array of cultural, structural and personnel techniques.

Conceptualizing HRM as a high-commitment management strategy limits the discipline to the study of a relatively small number of distinct organizations, as most firms continue to provide low wages and a minimal number of training opportunities (Bacon and Blyton, 2003). In contrast, Boxall et al. (2008, p. 1) define HRM as 'the management of work and people towards desired ends'. These authors advance the notion of 'analytical HRM' to emphasize that the primary task of HRM scholars is to build theory and gather empirical data in order to identify and explain 'the way management *actually behaves* in organizing work and managing people' (Boxall et al., 2008, p. 4, emphasis added).

This approach to HRM has three interrelated analytical themes. The first is a concern with the '*what*' and '*why*' of HRM – with understanding management and employee behaviour in different contexts and with explaining motives. The second theme is a concern with the '*how*' of HRM, that is, the processes by which it is carried out. In this context, Blau's (1964) influential concept of social exchange theory is often referred to. Social exchange theory draws attention to the psychology of instrumental human behaviour. Its relevance to HRM is defined by an assumption that a resource (human capability and commitment) will continue to flow only if there is a valued return contingent upon it. Social psychologists call this reciprocally contingent flow *reinforcement*, and economists call it *exchange* (Emerson, 1976, p. 359). Therefore employees will feel a sense of obligation to reciprocate when they perceive that they are being treated well by a manager or by their organization (Gilbert et al., 2011a). The third theme is concerned with questions of '*for whom and how well*', that is, with assessing the *outcomes* of HRM. This third characteristic in particular implies a critical purpose and helps us to rediscover one of the prime objectives of the social sciences – that of asking tough questions about power and inequality. It also reminds all of those who are interested in studying the field that HRM is 'embedded in a global economical, political and sociocultural context' (Janssens and Steyaert, 2009, p. 146).

Over 50 years ago, sociologist Peter Berger wrote that the first wisdom of sociological enquiry is that 'things are not what they seem' (1963, p. 23). A deceptively simple statement, Berger's idea suggests that most people live in a social world they do not understand. The goal of sociology is to shed light on social reality using what the late C. Wright Mills called the 'sociological imagination' – the ability to see the relationships between individual life experiences and the larger society, because the two are related (1959/2000). Sociologists argue that the sociological imagination helps people to place seemingly personal troubles, such as losing a job to outsourcing or local environmental degradation, into a larger national or global context. For Watson (2010), a critical approach to studying HRM provides inspiration and an invitation to apply Mills' 'sociological imagination' to matters of HRM 'outcomes' that have 'wider social consequences'. In the context of the post-2008 global recession and the search for the 'new economic philosophy', Delbridge and Keenoy (2010) provide a persuasive argument for critical HRM (CHRM), an intellectual activity, grounded in social science enquiry, that sets HR practices within the context of the prevailing capitalist society, challenges the maxims of what Alfred Schutz has called the 'world-taken-for-granted' and is more inclusive of marginal voices (Bratton and Gold, 2015).

We need a definition of the subject matter that conceptualizes HRM in terms of employment or people management, one that distinguishes it from a set of 'neutral' functional practices, and one that conceives it as being embedded in a capitalist society and its associated ideologies and global structures. The following attempts to capture the essence of what contemporary HRM is about:

> Human resource management (HRM) is a strategic approach to managing employment relations which emphasizes that leveraging people's capabilities and commitment is critical to achieving sustainable competitive advantage or superior public services. This is accomplished through a distinctive set of integrated employment policies, programmes and practices, embedded in an organizational and societal context.

HRM in practice 1.1

Zero-hours contracts: treating human resources with contempt

There is no legal definition of 'zero-hours contracts,' although a British government consultation document (BIS, 2013) states that:

A zero-hours contract is an employment contract in which the employer does not guarantee the individual any work, and the individual is not obliged to accept any work offered.

Zero-hours contracts contain no obligation to offer work or accept it. A person on a zero-hours contract is legally not an employee but a 'worker'. They are covered by some employment laws, but others, which are costly to employers, do not apply, such as the provision of redundancy pay, minimum notice periods, maternity and paternity leave and pay and protection from unfair dismissal (Wakeling, 2014).

Labour Force Survey figures published by the Office for National Statistics (ONS, 2015) show that the use of zero-hours contracts for April–June 2015 increased by 19 per cent compared with the previous year, giving a figure of 744,000 contracts. These contracts account for 2.4 per cent of people in employment. Women, students in full-time education and young or older workers are the groups most likely to be on zero-hours contracts. An ONS survey of businesses covering 2 weeks in January 2015, however, found that there were around 1.5 million contracts that did not guarantee a minimum number of hours. The disparity between the two surveys may be due to people having zero-hours contracts with different employers or having one in addition to their main job. Zero-hours contracts are usually with large employers, especially in the hotel and leisure industries, the National Health Service, the care industry and universities (Inman, 2015). For example, the retailer Sports Direct employs 80 per cent of its staff on zero-hours contracts (The Guardian, 2015).

Wakeling's analysis of zero-hours contracts based upon enquiries to the UK Advisory, Conciliation and Arbitration Service (ACAS) reveals a contradiction between low-commitment contracts and the performance of jobs over a long time that require a high sense of commitment and involvement, such as work as a personal carer with disabled or elderly individuals:

Two broad themes emerged. The first was to do with a lack of clarity over employment status, and a lack of awareness of employment rights, as described

by both workers and employers. The second was to do with a disparity that often seems to arise between the emotional attachment many people form with their job or workplace and their contractual status. This disparity often expressed itself in a fear about future earnings and a sense of unfairness about the way they were being treated. (Wakeling, 2014, p. 6)

It emerged in the ACAS research that:

Workers are often frightened to turn down work or look for other work in case their employer starts zeroing down their hours. These anxieties appear

(continued)

ImageSource

Stop! Zero-hours contracts are seen by their advocates as providing flexibility to industry and additional jobs for employees. Do you think that zero-hours contracts are economically beneficial or do you think they can lead to exploitation, low wages and underemployment for people who really want to work more hours? It was seen in the research quoted above that, in some types of work, people develop an involvement in their work and a commitment to the people who are benefiting from the services they provide. Does this happen because of or despite zero-hours contracts? Do you think that casual employment could fail to nurture and develop workers, and if so, how would you expect employers to engender commitment rather than merely control in employment situations?

Sources and further information: See Department for Business, Innovation and Skills (2013), Inman (2015), Office for National Statistics (2015), The Guardian (2015) and Wakeling (2014) for more information.

Note: This feature was written by David Denham.

Following on from this definition, CHRM underscores the importance of *people* – only the 'human factor' or labour can provide talent to generate value. With this in mind, it goes without saying that any adequate analytical conception of HRM should draw attention to the notion of *indeterminacy*, or uncertainty, which derives from the employment relationship: employees have a *potential* capacity to provide the added value desired by the employer. It also follows from this that human knowledge and skills are a *strategic resource* that needs investment and skilful management. Moreover, the emergent environmental management literature provides a role for HRM in improving an organization's performance in terms of overall *sustainability*. Also implicit within our definition is the need for radical organizational and social change. Another distinguishing feature of HRM relates to the notion of *integration*. A cluster of employment policies, programmes and practices needs to be coherent and integrated with the organization's corporate strategy. Finally, the 2008 collapse of financial services firm Lehman Brothers – the spark that detonated the global financial implosion and recession – the 2011 nuclear crisis in Fukushima, Japan, and the 2015 sovereign-debt financial crisis remind us that the economy and society are part of the same set of processes, and that work and management practices are deeply embedded in the wider sociocultural context in which they operate. The conception of CHRM put forward here resonates with analytical frameworks holding that HR practices can only be understood in the context of economic-societal factors that shape or direct those practices. The approach adopted can be summed up in the succinct phrase 'context matters'.

It is plausible to argue that if the workforce is so critical for sustainability performance, human dignity *in* and *at* work is, or *ought* to be, at the heart of contemporary HRM (Bolton, 2007). The existing literature on dignity *in* and *at* work has revealed conditions that contribute to indignity, the ways in which employees' inherent dignity is undermined and employees' responses to indignity. Framed in positive terms, dignity is affirmed in three ways: 'inherent' dignity as recognized by respectful interaction; 'earned' dignity as recognized by messages of competence; and 'remediated' dignity as recognized by social interactions and organizational practices. Achieving workplace dignity is anything but easy, but research underscores the importance of tackling the phenomenon: 'when dignity is violated, individuals can engage in practices of resistance to reclaim not only a sense of worth but the material resources to affirm their worth' (Lucas, 2015, p. 642). The dignity dimension provides support for a reconceptualized HRM model of empowered, engaged and developed employees – the 'missing "human" in HRM' critique (Bolton and Houlihan, 2007). The demands for dignity in the workplace are a key dimension of CHRM that provides strong support for extending the analysis of HRM outcomes beyond employee performance and commitment to include the 'dignity' aspects of the employment relationship and equality.

To grasp the nature and significance of HRM, it is necessary to understand the management process and the role of HRM within it. But before we do this, we should explain why managing people or the 'human' input is so different from managing other resources.

The meaning of 'human resource'

First and foremost, people are not a commodity so, arguably, referring to employees as a 'human resource' – in which people are seen as another input in the business process – 'dehumanizes workers' (Spencer and Kelly, 2015, p. 78). It is people in organizations who set overall strategies and goals, design work systems and create wealth by producing goods and services. People therefore become human capital by virtue of the roles they assume in the work organization. Schultz (1981, p. 21; quoted in Fitz-enz, 2000, p. xii) defined human capital in this way:

> Consider all human abilities to be either innate or acquired. Every person is born with a particular set of genes, which determines his [or her] innate ability. Attributes of acquired population quality, which are valuable and can be augmented by appropriate investment, will be treated as human capital.

In management terms, 'human capital' refers to the traits that people bring to the workplace – intelligence, aptitude, commitment, tacit knowledge and skills, and an ability to learn. But the contribution of this human resource to the organization is typically variable and unpredictable. This indeterminacy of an employee's contribution to her or his work organization makes the human resource the 'most vexatious of assets to manage' (Fitz-enz, 2000, p. xii) and is helpful in understanding Hyman's (1987) assertion that the *leitmotiv* of HRM is the need to gain both *control over* and *commitment from* workers.

HRM web links

> Visit the online resource centre at **www.palgravehighered.com/bg-hrm-6e** for information on HR professional organizations.

Managing people in a democratic market society extends beyond the issue of control. If the employer's operational goals and the employee's personal goals are to be achieved, there must necessarily be *cooperation* between the two parties. However, different forms of resistance and conflict often accompany this reciprocal cooperation. The nature of employment relations reminds us that people differ from other resources because their commitment and cooperation always has to be won: they have the capacity to resist management's actions and join trade unions to defend or further their interests and rights. At the same time, employment entails an economic relationship and one of control and cooperation. This duality means that the employment relationship is highly *dynamic* in the sense

These chefs provide an example of human capital in the context of a restaurant.

ImageSource/Michael Gross

that it is forged by the coexistence of varying degrees of control, cooperation and conflict (Brown, 1988; Edwards, 1986; Watson, 2004). Thus, HRM is inevitably characterized by structured cooperation and conflict.

The meaning of 'management'

The word *manage* came into English usage directly from the Italian *maneggiare*, meaning 'to handle and train horses' (Williams, 1976). In contemporary workplaces, a manager is an organizational member who is 'institutionally empowered to determine and/or regulate certain aspects of the actions of others' (Willmott, 1984, p. 350). Collectively, managers are traditionally differentiated horizontally by the activities of their function (for example, production manager or HR manager) and vertically by the level at which they are located in their organizational hierarchy (for example, branch manager or line manager). The creation of a formal organizational structure and work configuration is the *raison d'être* for management. Classical management texts present an idealized image of management as a rationally designed system for realizing goals, but there are competing theoretical perspectives, as we will explain below. HRM is often considered to be synonymous with the 'HR department' (Purcell and Kinnie, 2008). Yet, as recent studies suggest, general managers are expected to deliver more effective and cost-efficient solutions (McGuire and Kissack, 2015), and as such occupy a key role in delivering HR interventions, a development we examine in Chapter 3.

The nature of the employment relationship

The nature of the social relationship between employees and their employer is an issue of central analytical importance to HRM. The employment relationship describes an asymmetry of reciprocal relations between employees (non-managers and managers) and their employer. Through the asymmetry of the employment contract, inequalities of power structure both the economic exchange (wage or salary) and the nature and quality of the work performed (whether it is routine or creative). In contemporary capitalism, employment relationships vary: at one end of the scale, they can be short-term, primarily but not exclusively economic exchange for a relatively well-defined set of duties and low commitment; at the other, they can be complex long-term relationships defined by a broad range of economic inducements and relative security of employment, given in return for a broad set of duties and a high commitment from the employee.

The employment relationship can be created in three ways: unilaterally by the employer; bilaterally, by the employer and the trade unions, through a process of collective bargaining; and trilaterally, by employers, trade unions and statutes, through the intervention of the government or state (Kelly, 2005). The (unilateral) *individual* employment relationship between an employer and an individual employee details the terms (wage or salary) and conditions (duties, obligations and other benefits) of the relationship. The (bilateral) *collective* employment relationship is between an employer and a group of employees, the terms and conditions being determined jointly by collective bargaining between the managers, acting on behalf of the employer, and the trade union(s) representing the employees. The terms of the collective agreement between the employer and the trade union are incorporated into the individual employment contracts of all employees (union *and* non-union members) in the bargaining group (Farnham, 2015). What, then, is the essence of the employment relationship? Research into the employment relationship has drawn attention to economic, legal, social and psychological aspects of relations in the workplace.

At its most basic, the employment relationship embraces an *economic relationship*: the 'exchange of pay for work' (Brown, 1988). When people enter the workplace, they enter into a pay–effort bargain, which places an obligation on both the employer and the employee: in exchange for a wage or salary, paid by the employer, the employee is obligated to perform an amount of physical or intellectual labour. The pay–effort bargain is relevant for understanding how far the employment relationship is structurally conflictual or consensual. In the capitalist labour market, people sell their labour and seek to maximize their pay. To the employer, pay is a cost that, all things being equal, reduces profit and therefore needs to be minimized. Thus, as Brown (1988, p. 57) states, 'Conflict is structured into employment relations' as the benefit to one group is a cost to the other.

The 'effort' or 'work' side of the contract also generates tensions and conflict because it is inherently imprecise and indeterminate. The contract permits the employer to buy a potential level of physical or intellectual labour. The function of management is therefore to transform this potential into actual value-added labour. HR practices are designed to narrow the divide between employees' potential and actual performance or, in Townley's (1994, p. 14) words:

> Personnel practices measure both the physical and subjective dimensions of labour, and offer a technology which aims to render individuals and their behaviour predictable and calculable … to bridge the gap between promise and performance, between labour power and labour, and organizes labour into a productive force or power.

The second component of the employment relationship is that it involves a *legal relationship*: a network of contractual and statutory rights and obligations affecting both parties to the contract. Contractual rights are based on case law (judicial precedent), and the basic rules of contract, in so far as they relate to the contract of employment, are fundamental to the legal relationship between the employer and the employee. It is outside the scope of this chapter to provide a discussion of the rules of contract. But, to use Kahn-Freund's famous phrase, the contract of employment, freely negotiated between an individual and her or his employer, can be considered to be the cornerstone of English employment law (Honeyball, 2010).

A complex network of UK and European Union (EU) statutory rights regulates the obligations of employers and employees even though these are not (for the most part) formally inserted into the employment contract itself. Table 1.1 provides an overview of how UK employment legislation has helped to shape the legal regulation of employment relations. In broad terms, the employment laws of the 1979–97 Conservative government sought to regulate the activities of trade unions. Cumulatively, the changes marked 'a radical shift from the consensus underlying "public policy" on industrial relations during most of the past century' (Hyman, 1987, p. 93), which had the effect of tilting the balance of power in industrial disputes towards the employers (Brown et al., 1997). In the late 1990s, under Britain's 'New Labour' government, a plethora of legislative reform in employment extended protection to individual employees. For example, the 2006 Work and Families Act gave additional protections in relation to pregnancy – the right to maternity leave, time off for antenatal care and the right to maternity pay (Lockton, 2010).

Table 1.1 *Selective UK employment statutes and statutory instruments, 1961–2016*

Year	Act
1961	Factories Act (Safety)
1963/72	Contract of Employment Act
1965	Industrial Training Act
1968	Race Relations Act
1970	Equal Pay Act
1971	Industrial Relations Act
1973	Employment and Training Act
1974	Health and Safety at Work etc. Act
1974/76	Trade Union and Labour Relations Act
1975/86	Sex Discrimination Act
1975	Employment Protection Act
1978	Employment Protection (Consolidation) Act
1980	Employment Act
1982	Employment Act
1984	Trade Union Act
1986	Wages Act
1988	Employment Act
1989	Employment Act
1990	Employment Act
1992	Trade Union and Labour Relations (Consolidation) Act
1993	Trade Union Reform and Employment Rights Act

Year	Act
1996	Employment Rights Act
1996	Employment Tribunals Act
1998	Employment Rights (Disputes Resolution) Act
1998	National Minimum Wage Act
1999	Employment Relations Act
2002	Employment Act
2003	National Minimum Wage (Enforcement) Act
2003	Employment Equality (Sexual Orientation) Regulations
2003	Employment Equality (Religion or Belief) Regulations
2004	Gender Recognition Act
2004	Employment Relations Act
2005	Disability Discrimination Act
2006	Employment Equality (Age) Regulations
2006	Work and Families Act
2006	Equality Act
2007	Corporate Manslaughter and Corporate Homicide Act
2010	Equality Act
2016	Trade Union Act

EU employment legislation draws on the Western European tradition, in which the rights of employees are laid down in constitutional texts and legal codes. For example, in 2002, the UK implemented the EU directive mandating that fixed-term employees cannot be treated less favourably than comparable permanent employees in the same firm in terms of wages, benefits and training. New data indicate that the previous wage gap of 4 per cent between male fixed-term and permanent workers closed after 2002, although it is questionable whether this can be ascribed to the new EU law (Salvatori, 2015).

On 24th June 2016, Britain voted to sever the UK's 43-year membership of the EU, triggering turmoil in the global financial markets (Parker et al., 2016). The vote to leave the EU has also prompted questions over what EU employment legislation and directives will be retained, amended or abolished. It remains to be seen what effect this extraordinary political event will have on UK employment laws, but it seems likely that the influence of EU law, which has steadily increased over the four decades of EU membership, will diminish.

HRM web links Visit the online resource centre at **www.palgravehighered.com/bg-hrm-6e** for information on how the UK's decision to withdraw from the European Union might impact on current EU-derived employment rights and the HRM function.

The third distinguishing component of the employment relationship is that it involves a *social relationship*. Employees are not isolated individuals but members of social groups, who observe social norms and mores that influence their actions in the workplace. This observation of human behaviour in the workplace – which has been documented since the 1930s – is highly relevant given the increased prevalence of work teams. Furthermore, unless the employee happens to be an international football celebrity, the employment relationship embodies an uneven balance of power between the parties. The notion in English law of a 'freely' negotiated individual agreement is misleading. In reality, without collective (trade union) or statutory intervention, the most powerful party, the employer, imposes the agreement by 'the brute facts of power' (Wedderburn, 1986, p. 106).

Inequalities of power in turn structure the nature of work. Most employees experience an extreme division of labour with minimal discretion over how they perform their tasks and minimal opportunity to participate in decision-making processes. Thus, the social dimension is concerned with social relations, social structure and power – *people with power over other people* – rather than with the legal technicalities between the parties. As such, employment relations are deeply textured and profoundly sociological (Bratton and Denham, 2014). Looking at the development of the mainstream HRM canon over the last 25 years, it can be seen how little these inherent inequalities figure, despite the fact that they can be readily observed in the contemporary workplace.

In recent years, mainstream HRM scholarship has focused on another component of the employment relationship: the *psychological contract*. This is conceptualized as a dynamic, two-way exchange of perceived promises and obligations between employees and their employer. The concept has become a 'fashionable' framework within which to study aspects of the employment relationship (Guest and Conway, 2002; Rousseau and Ho, 2000). The 'psychological contract' is a metaphor that captures a wide variety of largely unwritten expectations and understandings of the two parties about their mutual obligations. Rousseau (1995, p. 9) defines this as 'individual beliefs, shaped by the organization, regarding terms of an exchange agreement between individuals and their organization'. Guest and Conway (2002, p. 22) define it as 'the perceptions of both parties to the employment relationship – organization and individual – of the reciprocal promises and obligations implied in that relationship'. At the heart of the concept of the psychological contract are levers for individual commitment, motivation and task performance beyond the 'expected outcomes' (Figure 1.1).

Figure 1.1 *The employment and psychological contract between employees and employers*

HRM and globalization 1.1

Airline service: the demands of emotional labour

ImageSource/Christopher Robbins

Arguably, the growth of employment in the airline industry is emblematic of globalization. The nature of the work undertaken by flight attendants, in particular the relationship between the work of flight attendants and employee emotion, has been studied by critical employment scholars. Claire Williams's (2003) study of nearly 3000 Australian flight attendants examined occupational health and safety variables, as well as sexual harassment and passenger abuse, and found a close link between emotional labour and sexual harassment. Research on the link between work and employee emotion goes back to the 1930s. Emotion at work, mainly captured as the 'happy productive worker' hypothesis, has been at the heart of HR since the HR movement of the 1930s. Positive emotion at work offers an apparent win–win situation for organizations and individuals as it suggests that, if a job or work is correctly designed, individuals will feel better and perform better.

However, this framework for interpreting how employees feel at work has tended to eclipse the more critical debates on emotion at work. These highlight that, beyond the more visible efforts aimed at reshaping jobs and job characteristics to achieve the desired emotions in employees, there are more subtle, indirect but still pervasive attempts to manage employees' feelings. As described in the now classic *The Managed Heart* (Hochschild, 1983), there is an exchange between the organization and the individual with regard to employees' feelings at work; feeling at work itself becomes a form of labour (p. 186), referred to as 'emotional labour':

> What was once a private act of emotion management is sold now as labor in the public-contact jobs. What was once a privately negotiated rule of feeling or display is now set by the company's Standard Practices Division … All in all, a private emotional system has been subordinated to commercial logic and it has been changed by it.

Hochschild's publication sparked the start of extensive research in the area of 'emotional labour' and the management of private, individual feelings to achieve the outcome the organization requires. This suggests that each organization, or group within it, has a set of either implicit or explicit rules for displaying emotion, akin at times to job requirements, that regulate when and how certain emotions should or should not be displayed. For example, waiters are expected to smile, to externally display happiness, when taking a customer order, but a surgeon is expected not to display any emotion, even when communicating potentially distressing news to a patient. In this way, the display, or otherwise, of certain emotions becomes part of the job role and is expected, and therefore managed, by the organization. It has also been argued that organizational intervention can change not only what individuals display, but also what they feel at or about work – hence the suggestion that the organization intrudes into the regulation of individuals' private emotions, as in the quote above.

Since the 1980s, our understanding of emotional labour has become more detailed and more sophisticated.

(continued)

Stop! Hochschild's original research was conducted within the airline industry. Consider your own experiences of interacting with flight attendants. What emotions do they typically display in interacting with passengers? To what extent can these be considered authentic, and what display rules might they be following? How might these rules be learnt and managed?

Sources and further information: For further information, see Diefendorff et al. (2006), Fineman (2003), Hochschild (1983) and Williams (2003).

Note: This feature was written by Chiara Amati.

Although it was initially argued that emotional labour applies especially to jobs that involve high levels of direct contact with the public, it is currently considered to be relevant in many other job types and roles, even within leadership and management. Much of the original research into emotional labour argued for an inevitable adverse impact of employees 'faking' certain emotions at work; more recently, however, it has been suggested that this process might manifest itself differently across different situations, with the impact also depending on the individuals concerned and their specific job circumstances. The core importance of understanding aspects of how the organization manages the display of feelings and emotions remains, however, unchallenged, and this is still considered essential for gaining insight into emotion at work.

The psychological contract has a number of important features that employers need to appreciate. First, ineffective practices may communicate different beliefs about the reciprocal promises and obligations that are present (Guest and Conway, 2002). Thus, individuals will have different perceptions of their psychological contract, even when the legal contract is identical. Managers will therefore be faced with a multitude of perceived psychological contracts (PPCs) within the same organization (Bendal et al., 1998). Second, the PPC reaffirms the notion that the employment relationship is thought to be one of exchange – the promissory exchange of offers and the mutual obligation of the employer and employee to fulfil these offers. Third, PPCs are shaped in particular contexts, which includes HR practices. For example, with respect to the training element of the PPC, there is evidence that the perceived investment in employee development relates positively to employees' openness to develop themselves and adapt to organizational change requirements – 'internal employability orientation' – and their active pursuit of new competencies and career trajectories within the organization – 'internal employability activities' (Solberg and Dysvik, 2016). For Rousseau, HR practices, such as investment in HR development (see Chapter 7), 'send strong messages to individuals regarding what the organization expects of them and what they can expect in return' (Rousseau, 1995, pp. 182–3). Again, context and culture is important when evaluating the assumptions underpinning PPCs. A study in the Netherlands, for example, found that the relationship between fulfilment of the psychological contract and work outcomes can be moderated by generational differences (Lub et al., 2016).

HRM web links Visit the online resource centre at **www.palgravehighered.com/bg-hrm-6e** for a bonus HRM in practice feature on employees' experience of 'decent' work.

Changes in the way work is organized have become a ubiquitous part of organizational life (Datta et al., 2010; Mellahi and Wilkinson, 2010; van Wanrooy et al., 2013a). Since 2008, a substantial minority of UK employees has experienced more than one change in their employment conditions, including a wage cut or freeze (32 per cent), an increase in workload (28 per cent) or some reorganization of work (19 per cent) (van Wanrooy et al., 2013a, p. 174). Research suggests that organizations that reorganize the work, such as by increasing workloads or downsizing, can reduce the likelihood of violation of the psychological contract by ensuring that HR practices contribute to employees' perceptions of 'procedural fairness' (Arshad and Sparrow, 2010).

On any reading, the essence of the PPC thesis is the idea that a workforce is a collection of free, independent people, as though individual beliefs are fixed features of an employee's day-to-day behaviour. However, this addresses concerns of individual motivation and commitment within a *unitary* ideological framework. In doing this, in total contrast to critical paradigms, it neglects a well-established body of research grounded in sociology showing that people's beliefs and expectations about employment form *outside* the workplace. For our purposes, we will define paradigms as established frameworks of interrelated values, beliefs and assumptions that social science scholars use to organize their reasoning and research. The work experiences of parents, for instance, shape the attitudes and career aspirations of their teenage children. The idea that family members and peers can influence expectations about work and career opportunities is called 'orientation to work' (Goldthorpe et al., 1968; Hyman and Brough, 1975).

reflective question What do you think of the concept of the psychological contract? How important is it to manage the psychological contract for (1) employees, and (2) managers?

Scope and functions of HRM

HRM is a body of knowledge and an assortment of practices to do with the organization of work and the management of employment relations. The mainstream literature identifies three major subdomains of knowledge: micro, strategic and international (Boxall et al., 2008).

The largest subdomain refers to *micro HRM* (MHRM), which is concerned with managing individual employees and small work groups. It covers areas such as HR planning, job design, recruitment and selection, performance management, training and development, and rewards. These HR subfunctions cover, for instance, numerous evidence-based practices, training techniques and payment systems, many of them informed by psychology-oriented studies of work (see, for example, Warr, 2008). The second domain is *strategic HRM* (SHRM), which concerns itself with the processes of linking HR strategies with business strategies and measures the effects on organizational performance. The third domain is *international HRM* (IHRM), which focuses on the management of people in companies operating in more than one country.

Drawing on the work of Squires (2001), these three major subdomains help us address three basic questions:

- What do HRM professionals do?
- What affects what they do?
- How do they do what they do?

To help us answer the first question – *What do HRM professionals do?* – the work of Harzing (2000), Lewin (2008), Millward et al. (2000) and Ulrich (1997; Ulrich et al., 2007, 2012) identifies the key *MHRM* subfunctions performed by the HR department, including, for example, workforce planning, recruitment and selection, training and development, pay and benefits, employee relations and health and safety. Each function is designed in response to organizational goals and contingencies, and each one contains alternatives from which managers can choose. Some of these functions, such as recruitment, training and pay administration, have been outsourced to specialist companies. Another trend is for key HR functions to be devolved from the HR department to line managers. For some observers, these trends have been characterized as a 'crisis' as HR professionals struggle for relevance and status in post-2008 cost-conscious times (Sparrow et al., 2011).

How the HR function is organized and how much power it has relative to that of other management functions is affected by both external and internal factors unique to the establishment. A regulation-oriented national business system, with strong trade unions, employment laws on equity and affirmative action, and occupational health and safety regulations, elevates the status of the HR professionals and strengthens the corporate HR function. In contrast, a market-oriented corporate culture, minimum investment in employee training and shorter precarious employment contracts is associated with outsourcing and decentralization of the HR function, which weakens the corporate HR function (Jacoby, 2005; Parry, 2011). Perhaps of more concern are studies showing a large gap between what HR professionals see as their role in the organization and how non-HR managers see it (Guest and King, 2001; Hird et al., 2010; Kulik and Perry, 2008). As Lewin (2008) has observed, the main challenge in the twenty-first century is for HR professionals to keep focused on a strategic role in their organization while also performing the essential operational role.

The many functions performed by the HR department and the different roles HR professionals serve in modern organizations depend on the size of the organization. Klass et al.'s (2005) study, for example, found that an increasing number of small and medium-sized organizations – defined typically as those with up to 49 and between 50 and 250 employees, respectively – have turned to external companies for delivering their HR services, a process referred to as 'outsourcing'. Klass et al. argue that the choice is not between an internal HR department and outsourcing the HR services, but is one in which limited resources mean that it is a case of either obtaining HR expertise externally or foregoing such services. In addition, an increasing number of European organizations have redesigned the HR function to enable their HR specialists to 'partner' with line managers to broker HR solutions to workforce issues. This 'devolved' and 'business partnering' model allows the HR function to assume a more strategic role (Andolšek and Štebe, 2005; Chartered Institute of Personnel and Development [CIPD], 2006; Ulrich, 1997; Ulrich et al., 2012).

SHRM underscores the need for the HR strategy to be integrated with other management functions, and highlights the responsibility of line management to foster the high commitment and motivation associated with high-performing work systems. SHRM is also concerned with managing sustainability, including, for example, establishing a low-carbon work system and organization, communicating this vision, setting clear expectations for creating a sustainable workplace, and developing the capability to reorganize people and reallocate other resources to achieve the vision. As part of the integrative process, all managers are expected to better comprehend the strategic nature of 'best' or better HR practices, to execute them more skillfully, and at the same time to intervene to affect the 'mental models', attitudes and behaviours needed to, for instance, build a high-performing sustainable culture (Pfeffer, 2005). Furthermore, national systems of employment regulation shape SHRM: 'the stronger the institutional framework ... the less [sic] options a company may have to impose its own approach to regulating its HRM' (Andolšek and Štebe, 2005, p. 327).

HRM web links Visit the online resource centre at **www.palgravehighered.com/bg-hrm-6e** to read extracts from the 2011 Workplace Employment Relations Survey.

The changing context of work, the peculiarities of national employment systems and national culture shape the employment relationship, and these forces and processes create different tendencies in HR practice operating across national boundaries. As such, they relate to the second question we posed earlier – *What affects what managers and HR professionals do?* The HR activities that managers and HR professionals perform vary from one workplace to another depending upon the contingencies affecting the organization. These contingencies can be divided into three broad categories: external context, strategy and organization.

The external category reinforces the notion that organizations and society are part of the same set of processes – that organizations are *embedded* within a particular capitalist society (see Chapter 15). In the UK, work and employee relations continue to evolve 'in the shadow of the recession' (van Wanrooy, 2013a, p. 1). To meet the challenges posed by global competition, market contraction and government expenditure cuts, organizations have downsized and relentlessly introduced numerous new ways of working and change initiatives (Brown et al., 2009; Farnham, 2015; Van Der Heijden et al., 2015; Wilkinson and Townsend, 2011). Against an ever-changing economic and political backdrop, Brown et al. (2009) have noted the collapse of collective bargaining in the UK (see Chapter 9). The external context impacts on corporate strategies (see Chapter 2), and the internal organizational contingencies, including organizational design and technology (see Chapters 13 and 16, for example), also drive developments in HRM. In addition, pressure on executives to support the firm's short-term share price, which puts the short-term interests of shareholders front- and centre-stage, reduces the incentive to invest long term in employee development and innovation – a phenomenon sometimes called 'quarterly capitalism' (Hutton, 2015b). Together, these global and internal changes and the growing use of migrant labour around the world (Ness, 2014) have created a wide variety of employment relationships and different forms of labour conflicts (Gall, 2014), all of which demands the increasing sophistication of *micro* HRM on the one hand, and increasing diversity on the other (Farnham, 2015). These micro HR functions, when integrated with different *macro* contexts and overall strategy considerations, define the subdomain of *IHRM* (see Chapter 17). It is therefore important to recognize that HR policies and practices are contingent upon external and internal contexts and are fundamentally interrelated.

The third of our three basic questions – *How do managers and HR professionals do what they do?* – requires us to note the skills and key competencies that HR professionals need so that they can accomplish operational functions and strategic functions. Managers use a wide range of technical, cognitive and interpersonal skills and competencies to accomplish their managerial and HR work (Agashae and Bratton, 2001; Ellinger, 2015; Squires, 2001; Ulrich, 1998). Research suggests that personal credibility, the ability to manage change and culture (Ulrich, 1998), communication (Guest and Conway, 2002) and coaching and mentoring (Ellinger, 2015) are the highest key competences managers need to fulfil the HR role.

Managing people is complex, and individual managers vary in terms of their capacity or inclination to use established processes, skills and competencies. Power, for example, is important because it is part of the influence process, as are legal procedures. Overall, these processes and key competencies concern human relationships and go some way to explaining different management styles and the distinction between a manager and a leader (Bratton et al., 2004). The micro, strategic and international domains, the contingencies influencing domestic and international HR practices, and managerial skills are combined and diagrammatically shown in Figure 1.2.

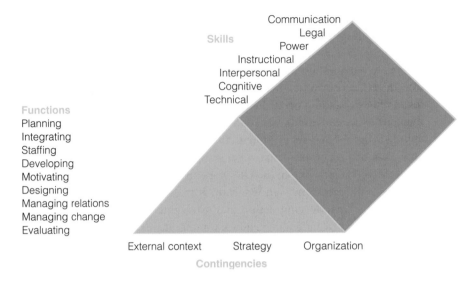

Figure 1.2 *HRM functions, contingencies and skills*
Source: Based on Squires (2001)

The model implies not only that HRM is a multidimensional activity, but also that its analysis has to be multidirectional (Squires, 2001). We might, for that reason, examine the effect of new technology (a contingency) on HR functions, such as training and development, and investigate how HR functions are translated into action, such as learning processes. The model is useful in other ways too: it serves as a pedagogical device that allows its users to discover and connect a specific aspect of HRM within a consistent, general framework. It also helps to develop an 'analytical conception' of HRM by building theory and generating data based on managers' *actual* social actions in managing work and people across workplaces, sectors and different market societies (Boxall et al., 2008) – the classic rhetoric–reality gap notably highlighted by Legge (1995, 2005). It also offers HR specialists a sense of professional 'identity' by detailing professional functions, processes and skills. Finally, it helps HR specialists to look beyond their immediate tasks and to be aware of the 'totality of management' (Squires, 2001, p. 482).

**HRM web
links**   Visit the online resource centre at **www.palgravehighered.com/bg-hrm-6e** to compare the practices that HR professionals are formally accredited to practise with those practices listed in Figure 1.2.

Theoretical perspectives on HRM

Practice without theory is blind. (Hyman, 1989, p. xiv)

So far, we have focused on the meaning of management and on a range of HRM practices used in the contemporary workplace. We have explained that HRM varies across organizations and market societies depending upon a range of external and internal contingencies. In addition, we have identified the skills by which managers accomplish their HRM goals. We now turn to an important part of the mainstream HRM discourse – the search for the defining features and goals of HRM – by exploring the theoretical perspectives in this area.

Over the past 25 years or more, HRM scholars have debated the meaning of the term 'human resource management' and attempted to define its fundamental traits by producing polar or contrasting models with multiple concepts. A number of polar models contrast the fundamental traits of HRM with those of traditional personnel management, while others provide statements on employer goals and HR outcomes. These models help to focus debate around such questions as 'What is the difference between HRM and personnel management?' and 'What outcomes are employers seeking when they implement a HRM approach?' Here, we identify four influential HRM models that seek to demonstrate in analytical terms the distinctiveness and goals of contemporary HRM (Beer et al., 1984; Fombrun et al., 1984; Storey, 1992; Ulrich, 1997). These models fulfil at least four important intellectual functions for those studying HRM:

- They provide an analytical framework for studying HRM (for example, HR practices, situational factors, stakeholders, strategic choice levels and HR and performance outcomes).
- They legitimize HRM. For those advocating 'Invest in People', the models help to demonstrate to sceptics the legitimacy and effectiveness of HRM. A key issue here is the distinctiveness of HRM practices: 'it is not the presence of selection or training but a *distinctive approach* to selection or training that matters. It is the use of high performance or high commitment HRM practices' (Guest, 1997, p. 273, emphasis added).
- They provide a characterization of HRM that establishes the variables and relationships to be researched.
- They serve as a heuristic device – something to help us discover and understand the world of work – that explains the nature and significance of key HR practices and HR outcomes.

The Michigan model of HRM

The Michigan Model developed by Fombrun et al. (1984) is associated with the Michigan Business School. The model's 'cycle' consists of four core HR activities: selection, appraisal, development and rewards. The model emphasizes the fundamental interrelatedness and coherence of HRM activities, which requires HR strategies to have a tight alignment to the overall strategies of the business (see Chapter 2). The Michigan model takes a 'hard' approach to people management, with a focus on performance that is based on human capital theory, in which workers are merely a means to an end or a 'resource' without concern for people's well-being (Lee, 2015, p. 7). The weaknesses of the Michigan model are its prescriptive nature and its focus on just four HR practices. It also ignores different stakeholder interests, situational factors and the notion of management's strategic choice. The strength of the model, however, is that it expresses the coherence of internal HR policies and the importance of 'matching' internal HR policies and practices to the organization's external business strategy (see Chapters 2 and 17). The idea of the 'HRM cycle' is useful as a heuristic framework for explaining the nature and significance of key HR practices that make up the complex field of HRM.

The Harvard model of HRM

As was widely acknowledged in the early HRM literature, the 'Harvard model' offered by Beer et al. (1984) provided one of the first comprehensive statements on the nature of

HRM and the issue of management goals and specific HR outcomes. The Harvard frame-work (Figure 1.3) consists of six basic components:

1 Situational factors
2 Stakeholder interests
3 HRM policy choices
4 HR outcomes
5 Long-term consequences
6 A feedback loop through which the outputs flow directly into the organization and to the stakeholders.

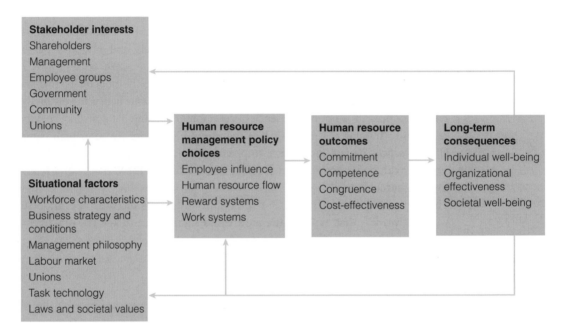

Figure 1.3 *The Harvard model of HRM*

Source: Beer, M., Spector, B., Lawrence, P.R., and Mills, D.Q. (1984), *Managing Human Assets*. New York: Free Press. Reproduced with permission from Michael Beer and Bert Spector.

In the Harvard model of HRM, the *situational factors* influence management's choice of HR strategy. This model incorporates workforce characteristics, management philos-ophy, labour market regulations, societal values and patterns of unionization, and suggests a meshing of 'product market' and 'sociocultural logics' (Evans and Lorange, 1989). Analytically, both HRM scholars and practitioners will be more comfortable if contextual variables are included in the model because this reflects the reality of what they know: 'the employment relationship entails a blending of business and societal expectations' (Boxall, 1992, p. 72).

The *stakeholder interests* recognize the importance of 'trade-offs', either explicit or implicit, between the interests of business owners and the interests of employees and their organizations, the trade unions. Although the model is still vulnerable to the charge of 'unitarism', it is a much more pluralist frame of reference than is found in later models.

HRM policy choices emphasize that management's decisions and actions in HR manage-ment can be fully appreciated only if it is recognized that they result from an interaction

New HR practices: the proletarianization of educational work?

PhotoDisc/Getty Images

The term 'precariat' was introduced by Guy Standing (2011) to reflect the creation of a new class of workers who could be flexible in order to meet the needs of the market as demanded by neo-liberal employment practices. Savage (2015, p. 351) summarizes Standing's identification of the precariat as 'people living and working precariously, usually in a series of short term jobs, without recourse to stable occupational identities or careers, social protection or relevant protective regulation.' As Savage points out, many such workers possess little economic or social capital and have been frequently blamed for their own poverty.

However, not all precarious workers lack social or economic capital. The casualization of teachers and lecturers through the practice of zero-hours contracts helps us to understand that the precariat refers to the structural location of jobs in a globalized market and that people are 'at the mercy of that structure' (Savage, 2015, p. 353). The University and College Union (2015) found that universities and colleges are twice as likely to use zero-hour contracts compared with other employers.

Sixty-one percent of further education colleges in England, Wales and Northern Ireland have teaching staff on zero-hours contracts and 53% of UK universities ... Of the universities that reported they use zero-hour contracts 46% had more than 200 staff on zero-hour contracts ... five institutions had more than 1,000 people on zero-hour contracts.

The University and College Union complained that, without a guaranteed income, workers on zero-hours contracts are unable to make financial or employment plans on a year-to-year or even month-to-month basis.

Casualization and exploitation of supply teachers also occurs in UK schools. In a survey by the teachers' union NASUWT (2014), 71 per cent of supply teachers stated that they were members of the Teachers' Pension Scheme, whilst 39 per cent of those working for agencies were not. When questioned about rates of pay, 56 per cent of supply teachers stated that they

were currently not paid on national pay rates at a level that was in line with their experience. Fifty-seven per cent reported that they had not been made aware that after 12 weeks of working in the same workplace, they would be entitled to the same pay and conditions as permanent members of staff. Sixty-four per cent reported that they had not had any access to continuing professional development.

Stop! Does your university use staff on zero-hours contracts? What impact do you think zero-hours contracts have on the quality of teaching and on staff–student relations? In what ways do the unions argue that lecturers and teachers employed on short-term or zero-hours contracts are exploited?

Sources and further information: See Savage (2015), Standing (2011), NASUWT The Teachers' Union (2014) and University and College Union (2015) for background to this feature.

Note: This feature was written by David Denham.

between constraints and choices. The model shows management as a real actor, capable of making at least some degree of unique contribution within the environmental and organizational parameters that are present, and of influencing those parameters itself over time (Beer et al., 1984).

In terms of understanding the importance of management's goals, the *HR outcomes* of high employee commitment and competence are linked to longer term effects on organizational effectiveness and societal well-being. The underlying assumptions built into the framework are that employees have talents that are rarely fully utilized in the contemporary workplace, and that they show a desire to experience growth through work. Thus, HRM is indivisible from a 'humanistic message' about human growth and dignity at work. In other words, the Harvard framework takes the view that employment relations should be managed on the basis of the assumptions inherent in McGregor's (1960) classic approach to people-related issues, commonly called 'Theory Y', or, to use contemporary parlance, in terms of conditions of human dignity at work.

The *long-term consequences* distinguish between three levels: individual, organizational and societal. At the level of the individual employee, the long-term HR outputs comprise the psychological rewards that workers receive in exchange for their effort. At the organizational level, increased effectiveness ensures the survival of the firm. In turn, at the societal level, as a result of fully utilizing people at work, some of society's goals (for example, employment and growth) are attained. The strength of the Harvard model lies in its classification of inputs and outcomes at both the organizational and the societal level, creating the basis for a critique of comparative HRM (Boxall, 1992). A weakness, however, is the absence of a coherent theoretical basis for measuring the relationship between HR inputs, outcomes and performance (Guest, 1997).

The sixth component of the Harvard model is a *feedback loop*. As we have discussed, situational factors influence HRM policy and choices. Conversely, however, long-term outputs can influence situational factors, stakeholder interests and HR policies, and the feedback loop in Figure 1.3 reflects this two-way relationship.

As Boxall (1992) observed, the Harvard model clearly provides a useful analytical basis for the study of HRM. It also contains elements that are analytical (that is, situational factors, stakeholders and strategic choice levels) and prescriptive (that is, notions of commitment, competence, and so on).

The Storey model of HRM

The Storey (2007) framework attempts to demonstrate the differences between what John Storey terms the 'personnel and industrials' and the HRM paradigm by creating an 'ideal type'. Storey devised the model by reconstructing the 'implicit models' conveyed by some managers during research interviews. We should note that the usage of an 'ideal type' is a popular heuristic tool in the social sciences. It is a 'mental image' and cannot actually be found in any real workplace. Its originator Max Weber wrote, in *The Methodology of the Social Sciences*, that 'In its conceptual purity, this mental construct [*Gedankenbild*] cannot be found empirically anywhere in reality' (Bratton and Denham, 2014, p. 240). An ideal type is not a description of reality; neither is it an average of something, or a normative exemplar to be achieved. It is a *Utopia*. Its purpose is to act as a comparison with empirical reality in order to establish the differences or similarities between the two positions, and to understand and explain causal relationships.

Storey posits that the HRM model emerged in the UK as a 'historically situated phenomenon' and is 'an amalgam of description, prescription, and logical deduction' (Storey, 2001, p. 6). The four main elements in his HRM framework (Table 1.2) are:

- Beliefs and assumptions
- Strategic qualities
- Critical role of managers
- Key levers.

According to the stereotypes depicted in Table 1.2, the HRM 'recipe' of ideas and practices prescribes certain priorities. In this framework, the most fundamental *belief and assumption* is that, ultimately, among all the factors of production, it is labour that really

Table 1.2 *The Storey model of HRM*

Personnel and industrial relations (IR) and human resource management (HRM): the differences		
Dimension	**Personnel and IR**	**HRM**
Beliefs and assumptions		
Contract	Careful delineation of written contracts	Aim to go 'beyond contract'
Rules	Importance of devising clear rules/mutuality	'Can do' outlook; impatience with 'rules'
Guide to management action	Procedures/consistency/control	'Business need'/flexibility/commitment
Behaviour referent	Norms/custom and practice	Values/mission
Managerial task vis-à-vis labour	Monitoring	Nurturing
Nature of relations	Pluralist	Unitarist
Conflict	Institutionalised	De-emphasised
Standardisation	High (for example 'parity' an issue)	Low (for example 'parity' not seen as relevant)
Strategic qualities		
Key relations	Labour–management	Business–customer
Initiatives	Piecemeal	Integrated
Corporate plan	Marginal to	Central to
Speed of decision	Slow	Fast
Critical role of management		
Management role	Transactional	Transformational leadership
Key managers	Personnel/IR specialists	General/business/line managers
Prized management skills	Negotiation	Facilitation
Key levers		
Foci of attention for interventions	Personnel procedures	Wide-ranging cultural, structural and personnel strategies
Selection	Separate, marginal task	Integrated, key task
Pay	Job evaluation; multiple fixed grades	Performance-related; few if any grades
Conditions	Separately negotiated	Harmonisation
Labour–management	Collective bargaining contracts	Towards individual contracts
Thrust of relations with stewards	Regularised through facilities and training	Marginalised (with exception of some bargaining for change models)
Communication	Restricted flow/indirect	Increased flow/direct
Job design	Division of labour	Teamwork
Conflict handling	Reach temporary truces	Manage climate and culture
Training and development	Controlled access to courses	Learning companies

Source: Based on Storey (2007, p. 9)

distinguishes successful firms from mediocre ones. It follows logically from this that employees ought to be nurtured as a valued asset and not simply regarded as a cost. Moreover, another underlying belief is that the employer's goal should not merely be to seek employees' compliance with rules, but to 'strive' for 'commitment and engagement' that goes 'beyond the contract' (Storey, 2001). The *strategic qualities* contained in Storey's framework show that HRM is a matter of critical importance to corporate planning. In Storey's words, 'decisions about human resources policies should … take their cue from an explicit alignment of the competitive environment, business strategy and HRM strategy' (p. 10).

The third component, the *critical role of managers*, argues that line and general managers, and not HR specialists, are vital to the effective delivery of HR practices (Purcell et al., 2009; Storey, 2007). An important reason why line managers are increasingly responsible and accountable for operational HR delivery is that such duties have been dispersed to them (Brewster and Larsen, 2000; Legge, 1995; Storey, 2007). 'If human resources really are so critical for business success, the HRM is too important to be left to operational personnel specialists', writes Storey (2007, p. 10). Research evidence from UK organizations suggests that line managers have emerged in almost all cases as the crucial players in HR issues, and also suggests closer 'relationships' between line managers and the HR department (McGuire and Kissack, 2015; Purcell et al., 2003).

The *key levers* element in the model focuses on the methods used to implement HRM. In researcher–manager interviews on HRM, Storey found considerable unevenness in the adoption of these key levers, such as performance-related pay, harmonization of conditions and investment to produce a work-related learning company. What is persuasive about the HRM narrative is evidence of a shift away from personnel procedures and rules as a basis of good practice, to the management of organizational culture as proof of avant-garde practice. Indeed, Storey notes that this paradigm shift is so significant that 'the twin ideas of "managing culture change" and moving towards HRM [have] often appeared to coincide and become one and the same project' (2007, p. 11).

As HRM has reinvented itself, different models of HR delivery have emerged: HR shared services, centres of expertise, self-service e-HR and HR business partnering. HR shared services are designed to achieve economies of scale, and are tasked with providing cost-effective processes to run transactional HR services such as payroll, monitoring of absence and simple advice for employees. Centres of expertise provide specialist knowledge and development to produce innovations in more complex areas such as leadership and management development. This potential synergy in the centre is designed to achieve economies of skill. Self-service e-HR is part of a wider shift of business operating models towards web-based systems of delivery, note Caldwell and Storey (2007, p. 26). Business partnering involves HR specialists working alongside line managers, perhaps as a member of a project team. The literature suggests that, in large organizations, 'business partnering' that offers a new set of proactive roles for HR specialists has become a dominant model in contemporary redesign of HRM (Ulrich, 1997).

Ulrich's strategic partner model of HRM

To overcome the traditional marginalization of the personnel function and to strengthen the status of the profession, the UK's CIPD has long sought to demonstrate the added value of HR activities in business terms. Such a position requires a transition from the functional HR orientation, with the HR department primarily involved in administering policies,

HRM and globalization 1.2

The HRM model in advancing economies?

Contemporary globalization is the defining political economic paradigm of our time. In terms of HR strategy, HRM policies and practices have to be aligned to the global activities of transnational enterprises, and must be able to attract and retain employees operating internationally but within different national employment structures. The word 'globalization' became ubiquitous in the 1990s. It was, and still is, a thoroughly contested concept depending on whether scholars view it as primarily an economic, a political or a social phenomenon.

In the economic sphere, globalization is understood as a worldwide process of integration of production and consumption resulting from the reduction of transport and communication costs – a global system of economic interdependences. Arguments that build only on these technical conceptions emphasize the positive aspects of globalization, and draw attention to the outsourcing of manufacturing jobs to China and India from high-wage Western economies. The economic argument is captured by these extracts from a Foresight 2020 research report (© reproduced by permission of The Economist Intelligence Unit):

'On a per-capita basis, China and India will remain far poorer than Western markets and the region faces a host of downside risks. Asia will narrow the gap in wealth, power and influence, but will not close it... The pace and extent of globalization will be the single most important determinant of world economic growth. Our baseline scenario is for gradual trade and investment liberalization, but if protectionism were to take greater hold, the consequences for world growth would be substantial and adverse.... Although the industrial base in developed markets will continue to be eroded as jobs transfer to emerging markets, fears of the demise of Western manufacturing are unfounded. Developed manufacturing economies will still hold an advantage in high-value and capital-intensive activities...Despite the expected strong growth in wages in many emerging markets, the differential with average wage levels in the developed world will still be enormous in 2020... In China's case the average wage —at 5% of US and EU15 levels in 2005 — will rise to about 15% of the developed-country average in 2020.'

Writers who conceptualize globalization in terms of politics and power argue that 'big business' has relegated national governments to being the 'gatekeepers' of free unfettered markets. Because there is little competition from alternative ideologies, twenty-first century capitalism 'is more mobile, more ruthless and more certain about what it needs to make it tick' (Giddens and Hutton, 2000, p. 9). Modern capitalism has been called a 'febrile capitalism' that is serving the needs of Wall Street and the financial and stock markets.

© iStockphoto.com/Jessica Liu

Stop! Critics charge that national governments have lost power over their own economies as a handful of large corporations are being permitted to control natural resources and social life. In other words, civil society is perceived principally through the 'prism of economics'. Take a moment to assess critically the various standpoints in the globalization debate. What economic and political forces encourage outsourcing? What are the implications of outsourcing for HRM?

Sources and further information: See Giddens and Hutton (2000), Hoogvelt (2001), Chomsky (1999) and Gereffi and Christian (2009) for more on this. The Foresight 2020 report can be downloaded free of charge; see the link at Economist Intelligence Unit (2006).

Note: This feature was written by John Bratton.

towards a partnership orientation, with the HR professional engaged in strategic decisions that impact on organizational design and organizational performance. In the last decade, the HRM model most favoured to support such a move has been provided by David Ulrich's (1997) business partner model. Ulrich presents a framework showing four key roles that HR professionals must accomplish in order to add the greatest value to the organization. The roles are arranged on two axes that represent focus and activities. HR professionals must focus on both the strategic and the operational, in both the long and the short term. Activities range from managing business processes to managing people, suggesting that there are core competencies that HR professionals must develop to help deliver value to the organization. A core HR competency, according to Ulrich et al. (2012), is that of being both credible (respected, listened to, trusted) and active (taking a position and challenging assumptions).

The two axes delineate four principal roles:

- *Strategic partner* – future/strategic focus combined with business processes
- *Culture and change agent* – future/strategic focus combined with people
- *Administrative expert* – operational focus combined with process
- *Employee champion* – operational focus combined with people.

A later variant of the model integrates the change agent role into the strategic partner role, and gives greater emphasis to HR professionals playing a leadership role (Ulrich and Brockbank, 2005; Ulrich et al., 2009). As such, the first two roles require a strategic orientation; for example, as a strategic partner, HR professionals work with general and line managers to formulate and execute strategy, and as a change agent, they facilitate transformation and significant change. During the 2000s, the Ulrich business partner model was widely espoused in the mainstream HRM literature and gained popularity or what academics call 'rhetorical ascendancy' among HR professionals in the UK and the USA (Caldwell and Storey, 2007). This is explained partly by the perceived increase in status and prestige of HRM, because the strategic partner and change agent roles proved highly attractive to many ambitious HR practitioners, and because of its rhetorical simplicity (Brown et al., 2004). Furthermore, the administrative role provides for processes to 're-engineer' the organization towards great efficiency, while the employee champion relates to listening to employees and providing resources for employees. Research shows, however, that, of the small sample surveyed, few HR practitioners considered their primary roles to be those of the 'less trendy' employee champion and administrative expert (Guest and King, 2004; Hope-Hailey et al., 2005). Despite the popularity of the business partnering model, a survey of managers also revealed that only 47 per cent of those polled believed that Ulrich's model was successful in their organization, and 25 per cent said the model was ineffective (Pitcher, 2008).

Inevitably, perhaps, the role of the strategic business partner attracts most attention, while the employee champion role, which concerns employees' well-being, tends to be devolved to line managers and is therefore likely to be neglected. Inconsistency in HR delivery can be a source of conflict (Caldwell and Storey, 2007; Francis and Keegan, 2006; Marchington et al., 2011). There is another aspect of the business partner model that is problematic. A recurrent theme in SHRM is that organizations need to align or 'match' their HR strategy to their corporate strategy (see Chapter 2). However, the parallel tendency in business partnering to devolve HR activities – what has been called 'centrifugal logic' – may undermine the agenda of 'alignment and integration' in the strategic HRM

HRM as I see it

Alison Blayney Part 1

HR Business Partner, TIGI Haircare, Unilever

www.unilever.co.uk/

Unilever is an Anglo-Dutch global consumer goods company co-headquartered in Rotterdam, the Netherlands, and London, UK. Its products include food, beverages, cleaning agents and personal care products. In 2009, Unilever acquired TIGI , a small B2B business in the professional hair care industry, world leaders in styling and the fastest growing colour brand.

Alison joined Unilever in September 2012 on the Unilever Future Leaders Programme (UFLP), a two to three year programme for graduates who are fast-tracked into management positions. The UFLP prides itself on developing graduates into the business leaders of tomorrow – and quickly. The programme allows real on-the-job responsibility from day one, and all the training and experience needed to become a manager is provided within two to three years.

Over her two-year programme, Alison completed three rotations. First, she worked in the supply chain function in the factory at Unilever's historic home, Port Sunlight, Wirral, where there are three home care and one personal care manufacturing facilities. Moving to Unilever's UK head office, in Leatherhead, Surrey, she worked in the UK and Ireland HR Expertise team, focusing on talent and capability. Next Alison worked in the Global HR Team, based at the London Head Office. In September 2014, Alison moved to TIGI, where she began her first management position as a Global HR Business Partner.

Prior to her Unilever career, Alison worked in a small boutique head-hunting company that specialized in recruiting high-calibre executives and non-executives. This was Alison's first role within HR after graduating from Durham University in 2010.

Click on Alison's photo in your ebook to watch her explaining how she started working in HR and what her role entails. When you have watched her video, try to answer the following questions:

1   What attracted Alison to HRM as a career choice?
2   Thinking of Ulrich's strategic partner model, how does Alison describe her HR role?

dynamic. Post-2008, there has been growing interest in sustainable growth and improved performance through new leadership models, employee engagement and capacity-building (CIPD, 2011). It is suggested, however, that none of these goals can be achieved without an investment in employee learning and development – see Chapter 7 on human resource development, which, at its heart, relates to people learning, growing and flourishing in the context of the workplace (Poell et al., 2015, p. xiii).

HRM web links   Visit the online resource centre at www.palgravehighered.com/bg-hrm-6e for more information on Ulrich's HRM model.

reflective question   Reviewing the four models, what beliefs and assumptions do they imply? How well does each model define the characteristics of HRM? Is there a contradiction between the roles of 'change agent' and 'employee champion' as outlined in Ulrich's model? Is it realistic to expect line managers to be given responsibility for the HRM function?

Studying HRM

It has become commonplace to point out that HRM is not a discipline in its own right, but a field of study drawing on concepts and theories from core social science disciplines including anthropology, economics, psychology, sociology, law and political science. This provides relatively elastic boundaries within which to analyse how the employment relationship is structured and managed. In addition, these elastic boundaries generate multiple ways of making sense of the same organizational phenomenon or the differing standpoints found in the HRM canon. How we understand HRM is very much influenced by key social discourses. Management in the twenty-first century is being influenced by multiple social discourses that include globalization, environmental destruction, social injustice and fundamental neo-liberal economic failure.

Reflexivity is an attitude of attending systematically to the context of knowledge construction, especially to the effect of the researcher, of her or his values, beliefs and interests, at every step of the research process. It is the ability to encounter the familiar as new and to reflect on one's reflection. In understanding the recent debate that management education and pedagogy should be more reflexive and critical (Currie et al., 2010), it is crucial to develop a knowledge base of competing ideological perspectives or paradigms. Each paradigm in the social sciences makes certain bold assertions about the nature of social reality and, in turn, provides legitimacy and justification for people's actions (Babbie and Benaquisto, 2010). When people ask, 'What paradigm are you using?', they might just as well be asking, 'What is your own bias on this aspect of social life?', as each paradigm has a particular bias based on a particular version of knowing about social reality (Hughes, 1990). Paradigms are a 'lens' through which we view the world of work. Thus, when we refer to a particular paradigm to study the HRM phenomenon, we are speaking of an interconnected set of beliefs, values and intentions that legitimize HR theory and practice. For the purpose of developing a critical, analytical conception of HRM, we will in this section compare and contrast three major paradigms – *structural-functionalism*, *conflict* and *feminism* – that have emerged to make sense of work, organizations and HRM.

The intellectual roots of the *structural-functional paradigm* can be traced to the work of the French philosopher Auguste Comte (1798–1857) and French sociologist Emile Durkheim (1858–1917). Comte believed that society could be studied and understood logically and rationally, and he used the term *positivism* to describe this research approach. Durkheim studied social order and argued that the increased division of labour in modern societies created what he called 'organic solidarity', which maintained social harmony: 'The division of labour becomes the chief source of social solidarity, it becomes, at the same time, the foundation of moral order' (Durkheim, 1933/1997, p. 333).

The popularity of the structural-functionalist approach is commonly attributed to the US sociologist Talcott Parsons (Mann, 2011). For Parsons, organizations can function in a stable and orderly manner only on the basis of shared values. In his words: 'The problem of order, and thus the nature of the integration of stable systems of social interaction ... thus focuses on the integration of the motivation of actors with the normative cultural standards which integrate the action system' (1951, p. 36). Although there are variations and tensions, the structural-functional paradigm takes the view that a social entity, such as a whole market society or an organization, can be studied as an organism. Like an organism, a social system is composed of interdependent parts, each of which contributes to the functioning of the whole. A whole society or an organization is held together by a consensus on values – a value system. The view of an organization as a social system thus looks for the 'functions' served by its various departments and members and the common values shared by its members.

It is frequently assumed that managerial functions and processes take place in organizations that are rationally designed to accomplish strategic goals, that organizations are harmonious bodies tending towards a state of equilibrium and order, and that the basic task of managers is to manage resources for formal organizational ends. Thus, the structural-functionalism paradigm, sometimes also known as 'social systems theory', becomes inseparable from the notion of efficiency. The focus of much of the research and literature on management using this 'lens' is about finding the 'winning formula' so that more managers can become 'effective' (Thompson and McHugh, 2009). Common to all variations of structural-functionalism, which is often seen as the dominant or mainstream perspective, is a failure to connect management processes to the 'master' public discourse on market-based societies and globalization.

The intellectual roots of the *conflict paradigm* are most obviously found in the works of the German philosopher Karl Marx (1818–83). In his early manuscripts of 1844, Marx analysed the fundamental contradiction of capitalism that arose from structured tensions between capital (employers) and labour (employees). Specifically, he made the assumption that these two social classes have competing interests. For Marx, the relationship between capitalists and workers was one of contradiction. Each is dependent upon the other, and the two must cooperate to varying degrees. However, there is a fundamental conflict of interest between capital and labour: the capitalist seeks to minimize labour costs; the workers seek the opposite. As a result, economic forces compel employers and employees to cooperate, but also there are forces that simultaneously cause conflict between the two groups. Importantly, workers also experience alienation or 'estrangement' through the act of labour. Marx's alienation theory continues to inform contemporary studies of work and the prerequisites for dignity *in* and *at* work (see, for example, Bolton, 2007).

Similar to Marx, Max Weber's (1864–1920) analyses of advanced capitalist societies centre on work and organizations, especially large bureaucracies. Two themes within Weber's work are especially relevant to understanding contemporary theories of work and management. One is the notion of *paradox* in capitalist societies. In *The Protestant Ethic* (1904–1905/2002), Weber pessimistically warns of creeping rationalization and of the tendency of people to experience a debilitating straight-jacket of rules and control, or what he called the '*iron cage*'. The process of rationalization is, according to Weber, unremittingly paradoxical (Bratton and Denham, 2014). He, and subsequent writers in the Weberian tradition, focused on the notion of '*paradox of consequences*' – two or more positions that each sound reasonable yet conflict or contradict each other. A paradox of consequence results when managers, in pursuit of a specific organizational goal or goals, call for or carry out actions that are in opposition to the very goals the organization is attempting to accomplish. A second theme that lies at the centre of Weber's sociology is his analysis of *power* and domination by social elites (Bratton and Denham, 2014, p. 260). In *Economy and Society* (1922/1968), Weber stresses that power is an aspect of virtually all social relationships. He famously argued that every form of social elite attempts to establish and cultivate belief in its own legitimate authority, which he defined as 'a belief in the legality of enacted rules and the right of those elevated to authority under such rules to issue commands' (Weber, 1922/1968, p. 215).

Critical scholars draw heavily on the works of Marx, and to a lesser extent Weber, to explain management activities in terms of basic 'logics' underlying capitalist production: goods and services are produced for a profit. The motive force of profit is the unifying, quantitative objective of corporate strategies and policies, the touchstone of corporate rationality, the measure of corporate success (Baran and Sweezy, 1968). The agents acting for the capitalists – the managers – decide how and where goods and services are to be produced within the context of the profit imperative that does not allow for substantial differences in management style or approach. Thus, managerial control is a *structural* imperative of capitalist employment relations, causing what Edwards (1986) calls '*structural antagonism*'. Labour process analysis is part of the conflict school of thought. It represents a body of theory and research that examines 'core' themes of technology, skills, control and worker resistance, as well as, more recently, new 'postmodern territories' with a focus on subjectivity, identity and power (Thompson and Smith, 2010). The conflict paradigm, when applied to work organizations, sets out to discover the ways in which power, control, conflict and legitimacy impact on contemporary employment relations. It emphasizes that HRM can only be understood as part of a management process embedded within the wider sociocultural and political economy order of a capitalist society, which determines the nature of work and employment practices (see Delbridge and Keenoy, 2010; Thompson and Harley, 2008; Watson, 2010).

The third social science paradigm examined here, the *feminist paradigm*, traces its intellectual roots to eighteenth-century feminist writings, such as Mary Wollstonecraft's *A Vindication of the Rights of Woman* (1792/2004), and, in the 1960s, to Betty Friedan's *The Feminine Mystique* (1963). Whereas Marx chiefly addressed the exploitation of the working class, the early feminist writers provided a sophisticated understanding of the gender-based, persistent and pervasive injustices that women continue to experience through a variety of 'entrenched social processes, such as patriarchal strategies and sexism' (Bratton and Denham, 2014, p. 10). Researchers looking at the capitalist society from a feminist perspective have drawn attention to aspects of organizational life that have been overlooked by other paradigms. In part, feminist scholarship has focused on gender differences and how they relate to the rest of society. Over the decades, gender has become a concept to be wrestled with, but here we use the word to refer to a set of ideas that focuses on the processes of gender roles, inequalities in society and in the workplace, problems of power, and women's subordination and oppression.

Theoretically, one of the most important consequences of gender analysis is its power to question the research findings and analysis that segregate studies of HRM from those of gender divisions in the labour market (Dex, 1988), patriarchal power (Witz, 1986), issues of workplace inequality (Phillips and Phillips, 1993) and 'dual-role' and work–life issues (Knights and Willmott, 1986; Platt, 1997; Warhurst et al., 2008). More importantly, however, including the dimension of gender in the study of contemporary HRM has the

reflective question It is important to explore your own values and views and therefore your own perspective on HRM. What do you think of these social science paradigms? How do they help us to explain the actions and outcomes of behaviour in organizations? Which perspective seem to you to be more realistic, and why? How do these paradigms help us to understand the uncertainties and conflicts evident in contemporary workplaces?

potential to move the debate forward by examining the people who are deemed to be the 'recipients' of HRM theory and practice (Mabey et al., 1998a). The feminist paradigm takes it as self-evident that gender inequality in the workplace can only be understood by developing a wider gender-sensitive understanding of society and employment practices.

Critique and paradox in HRM

Since Storey's (1989) landmark publication, the HRM canon has been subject to 'external' and 'internal' criticism (Delbridge and Keenoy, 2010). The external critique has come from academics within the broad field of critical management studies and labour process theory. These critics include Alvesson and Willmott (2003), Godard (1991), Thompson and McHugh (2009) and Watson (2004). They expose structured antagonisms and contradictions, and contend that HR practices can only be understood in the context of the wider cultural and political economy factors that shape or direct those practices. Critical management theorists also argue that mainstream HRM researchers have routinely neglected or marginalized those most directly impacted by HR practices – the employees. Generally, there has been an intellectual failure to engage in the process of 'denaturalization' – of questioning 'taken-for-granted' beliefs and assumptions and 'unmasking' the questionable results of HRM research. Finally, critics hold that most HRM researchers have largely failed to subject HR practices to a critical scrutiny of 'unintended consequences' and 'paradox' (Bratton and Gold, 2015) or the 'collateral damage' resulting from their application (Delbridge and Keenoy, 2010, p. 803). The notion of *paradox* has its roots in Weber's classical text *The Protestant Ethic*, as discussed earlier. The process of rationalization is, according to Weber, unrelentingly paradoxical. Predictably, therefore, external critics of HRM consider paradox theory to be a key analytical tool to investigate and critique contemporary organizations (Guerci and Carollo, 2016).

The principal 'internal' critics of HRM provide a sustained critique with respect to the divide between what can be described as the 'rhetoric' and the 'reality' of HRM (Legge, 2005). Townley (1994) offers a sustained analysis and critique based on the writings of the late French philosopher Michel Foucauld (1926–84), and Winstanley and Woodall (2000) present an ethical critique of HRM. More generally, Keenoy and Anthony (1992) have sought to explore the ambiguity associated with the term 'human resource management' itself. This relates to the question of where the emphasis of strategic management policy is placed: is it on the word '*human*' or on '*resource*' in management? This ambiguity has generated the notion of 'soft' and 'hard' HRM and, more recently, provoked a collection titled *Searching for the 'H' in HRM* in the 'moral' market society (Bolton and Houlihan, 2007).

Since the early 1990s, labour market reforms have been high on the political agendas of EU governments. Between 1990 and 2007, the EU countries undertook over 100 deregulatory reforms, of which about a quarter were structural and involved a significant weakening of employment protection for standard workers, while the rest primarily facilitated an extension of more precarious employment (Avdagic and Crouch, 2015). This far-reaching libertarian rebuilding of the employment relationship, especially in the UK, has arguably made British capitalism less inclusive by deterring people from participating fully in the workplace and developing their potential (Hutton, 2015a). The expression of Britain's labour market dysfunctionality is obvious in the growth of precarious employment, which offers less security, less employment protection and fewer rights, entrenched low wages especially for those under 30, the collapse of defined benefit pension schemes, the emasculation of workers' bargaining power, and the rise in excessive pay inequality alongside executive pay that averages 150 times more for mediocre performance.

In this context, studying HRM remains highly relevant. The triple-headed crisis of climate change, global capitalism and Britain's more flexible, which is to say more inhuman, labour market, together with demands for social justice, are the drivers of social change that will cast a long shadow over contemporary organizations and employment activities. Evidence-based analytical HRM is therefore relevant given that its *raison d'être* is to leverage people's knowledge and capabilities and manage employment relationships. In particular, given the growing demands for organizations to develop strategies that are environmentally sustainable and socially just, a reflexive, critical analysis of HRM is increasingly important for understanding organizational life (Bratton and Gold, 2015).

Applying the sociological imagination

The conception of critical HRM put forward in this opening chapter resonates with analytical frameworks holding that HR practices can only be understood in the context of economic-societal factors that shape or direct those practices. With regard to recent concerns about an absence of reflexive critique in business schools, Delbridge and Keenoy's (2010) contribution elaborating what constitutes critical HRM is both important and timely. When scholars call for critical perspectives in HRM practice and research, however, what exactly does 'critical' mean? There are wide-ranging theoretical ideas in critical management studies, but common objectives in all critical studies are to challenge taken-for-granted assumptions and accepted configurations of power and control (Fenwick, 2015).

Using the prism of Mills' sociological imagination, what we have called 'critical human resource management education' or 'CHRME' helps to introduce critical perspectives in HRM and addresses concerns to make the learning culture in business schools more critical. CHRME focuses on the development of a learning culture that focuses less on the 'what' and 'how' of HRM, but shifts the emphasis towards the 'why', with the everyday practices and processes and human actions that occur in the workplace, and their impact on workers and the local community in which any work organization is situated. The emphasis is on the idea that, to understand HRM-related 'troubles', both students and educators are required to look beyond them, at the social embeddedness of HRM. CHRME, we contend, adds to a growing body of critical management pedagogy.

As in previous editions of *Human Resource Management: Theory and Practice*, we are concerned with developing a context-sensitive understanding of work and HR practices. Throughout the book, we emphasize that paradox and antagonism are structured into the employment relationship, that different work regimes and HR strategies and practices can only be understood in the context of the wider cultural-political economy and market factors that direct or influence work and employment. We aim to provide a more critical, nuanced account of the realities of the workplace in capitalist societies, one that encourages a deeper understanding of and sensitivity towards employment and HR-related issues. We hope that *Human Resource Management: Theory and Practice* captures the range of change evident in today's workplaces, and will moreover lead to the kinds of sensibility that encourage the reader to question, be critical and seek multicausality when analysing contemporary HRM.

case study

Knowledge management at Emenee hotels

Getty Images/iStockphoto / Thinkstock \ Nicole S. Young

The setting

Emenee (pseudonym) is an established international hotel chain with over 4500 hotel operations in over 100 countries. It has undertaken two forms of growth: (1) the acquisition of established hotel companies in mature markets, and (2) the development of greenfield sites in emerging markets. When Emenee acquired an existing hotel company in Australia and the South Pacific, it also acquired the vast knowledge base of a mature management and leadership team embedded within that company. Not surprisingly, it was soon recognized that, by leveraging existing systematically arranged knowledge, Emenee could have the advantage of providing mature operational knowledge from the acquired chain at the many greenfield sites it had in the emergent and high-growth Asian market, thus reducing the need for replication of practice and process development.

This realization led to the design and implementation of a vast computerized repository or knowledge library that was accessible to every site manager in every hotel across the Australia/South Pacific/South East Asia region. The system was designed to initiate a long-term knowledge-sharing culture by making it easier to share value-added practices and processes, thus reducing wastage of time and resources through replication.

The problem

The knowledge library operated as a two-way system whereby managers could both add ideas or effective innovative practices and find solutions to some of their own operational problems that demanded new ideas or innovation. To simplify its use, the system was designed to store ideas by hotel function (that is, food and beverage, housekeeping, etc.), with both functional and key word search tools available. Knowledge transfer was considered to have occurred once an idea had been implemented at another site.

Emenee's management realized that they would need to create support systems to motivate sharing between the sites and geographical regions. This opened up an opportunity to embed the desired knowledge-sharing actions and behaviours throughout the performance management system, alongside key performance indicators (KPIs). As a result, for each site manager to pass their annual performance review, they had to retrieve a minimum of two ideas from the system and implement these in their hotel, as well as add two ideas to the system for others to be able to access and use.

On paper, this system worked very well, with site managers seemingly keen to add and implement ideas to pass their annual performance review. This acceptance of the knowledge management system was, however, superficial. In reality, the Australian site managers felt threatened by the pressure and the surveillance nature of the system, saying that it was like having a 'gun pointed at your head'. Further resentment was experienced as managers were forced to share innovation with the managers of the very hotels whose performance was being rated against their on a bi-annual basis. This led to a reluctance to share effective innovations, and resistance against the system by site managers. At a meeting to review the programme, one site manager put the issue like this:

We were mandated through our KPIs, so would that influence me to share? Yes, it would, but it turned into a dog's breakfast, everyone's throwing in ideas just to tick the box.

Two years after the system had been implemented, the link between knowledge-sharing and performance review was severed. Another site manager summed up the outcome this way:

(continued)

34

The link with KPIs might have influenced me to share, but would it be good data going into it? We proved it wouldn't so they had to scrap it and start again [because] they were silly ideas and now it's no longer linked to our KPIs.

The assignment

You are the assistant HR manager of Emenee, based at the head office. You have been asked to prepare a report for the HR manager on why the programme failed and to identify an alternative. In your answer, address the following:

1 Which management systems were at play here, and how did they influence the outcomes?
2 Which other HR practices might help influence a knowledge-sharing culture through the use of the database?
3 How could the main reasons for resistance to the knowledge management sharing system be overcome?

Sources and essential reading

Larkin, R. (2014) Alternative control methods for exploiting subsidiary knowledge within an MNE: quantity versus quality. *Journal of Knowledge Management*, **18**(6): 1184–97.

Larkin, R. and Burgess, J. (2013) The paradox of employee retention for knowledge transfer. *Employment Relations Record*, **13**(2): 32–43.

Note: This case study was written by Roslyn Larkin and is based on the research papers listed above.

 Visit the online resource centre at **www.palgravehighered.com/bg-hrm-6e** for guidelines on writing reports.

summary

➤ In this introductory chapter, we have emphasized the importance of managing people, both individually and collectively, over other 'factor inputs'. We have examined the history of HRM and emphasized that, since its introduction, it has been highly controversial. The HRM phenomenon has been portrayed as the historical outcome of rising neo-liberalism ideology, closely associated with the political era of Margaret Thatcher's Conservative premiership in Britain.

➤ We have conceptualized HRM as a strategic approach, one that seeks to leverage people's capabilities and commitment with the goal of enhancing performance and dignity *in* and *at* work. These HRM goals are accomplished by a set of integrated employment policies, programmes and practices within an organizational and societal context. We suggest that the HRM approach as conceptualized here constitutes critical HRM, extending the analysis of HRM outcomes beyond performance to include equality, dignity and social justice.

➤ To show the multiple meanings of the term 'human resource management', we have examined four theoretical models. We have discussed whether HRM now represents a new orthodoxy; certainly, the language is different.

➤ We have explained that tensions are always present. These include tensions between profitability and cost-effectiveness and employee security; between employer control and employee commitment; and between managerial autonomy and employee dignity. Throughout this book, we illustrate and explain some of these tensions and inevitable paradoxes to encourage a deeper understanding of HR-related issues.

➤ Finally, workplace scholars use a variety of theoretical frames of reference or paradigms – here the focus has been on structural-functionalism, conflict and feminist paradigms – to organize how they understand and conduct research into HRM.

1 What is 'human resource management' and what purpose does it play in work organizations?

2 How, if at all, do the three major paradigms – *structural-functionalism*, *conflict* and *feminism* – help us make sense of work, organizations and HRM?

3 Suppose an entrepreneur is planning to open a chain of high-quality restaurants. What area of HRM would they have to consider and why? If the plan is to open a chain of fast-food outlets, how would the approach to HRM be affected?

4 Based on your own work experience or that of a friend or relative, can you identify three statutory employment rights? Do you think employment rights will be changed as a result of the Brexit vote?

5 How, if at all, do theoretical models of HRM help (1) practitioners and (2) academics?

Visit **www.palgravehighered.com/bg-hrm-6e** to watch John Bratton talking about the sociological imagination, and then answer the following questions:

➤ How can the sociological imagination help you understand why zero-hour contracts have become common practice in the labour market?

➤ Can the personal 'trouble' of an unpaid internee, for example, seeking work experience be explained through the prism the sociological imagination?

Reading these articles and chapters can help you gain a better understanding of the changing role of HRM and potentially a higher grade for your HRM assignment.

➤ Caldwell, R. and Storey, J. (2007) 'The HR function: integration or fragmentation? In J. Storey (ed.) *Human Resource Management: A Critical Text* (3rd edn) (pp. 21–38). London: Thomson Learning.

➤ Cappelli, P. (2015) Why we love to hate HR … and what HR can do about it. *Harvard Business Review*, July/August: 54–61.

➤ Guerci, M. and Carollo, L. (2016) A paradox view on green human resource management: insights from the Italian context. *International Journal of Human Resource Management*, **27**(2): 212–38.

➤ Keegan, A. and Francis, H. (2010) Practitioner talk: the changing textscape of HRM and emergence of HR business partnership. *International Journal of Human Resource Management*, **21**(6): 873–98.

➤ Lub, X.D., Bal, P.M., Blomme, R.J. and Schalk, R. (2016) One job, one deal … or not: do generations respond differently to psychological contract fulfillment? *International Journal of Human Resource Management*, **27**(6): 653–80.

➤ Marchington, M., Rubery, J. and Grimshaw, D. (2011) Alignment, integration and consistency in HRM across multi-employer networks. *Human Resource Management*, **50**(3): 313–39.

➤ Pritchard, K. (2010) Becoming an HR strategic partner: tales of transition. *Human Resource Management Journal*, **20**(2): 175–88.

➤ Solberg, E. and Dysvik, A. (2016) Employees' perceptions of HR investment and their efforts to remain internally employable: testing the exchange-based mechanisms of the 'new psychological contract'. *International Journal of Human Resource Management*, **27**(9): 909–27.

➤ Ulrich, D. and Brockbank, W. (2009) The HR business-partner model: past learnings and future challenges. *People and Strategy*, **32**(2): 5–7.

➤ Ulrich, D., Brockbank, W., Johnson, D. and Younger, J. (2009) Human resource competencies: responding to increased expectations. *Employee Relations Today*, **34**(3): 1–12. Available at: https://deepblue.lib.umich.edu/bitstream/handle/2027.42/57368/20159?sequence=1 (accessed August 8, 2016).

➤ Werner, J. M. (2015) Human resource management and HRD. In R. F. Poell, T.S. Rocco and G.L. Roth (eds.) *The Routledge Companion to Human Resource Development* (pp. 89–98). London: Routledge.

Critical studies are also found among the following:

➤ Blyton, P., Heery, E. and Turnbull, P. (eds) (2011) *Reassessing the Employment Relationship*. London: Palgrave Macmillan.

➤ Delbridge, R. and Keenoy, T. (2010) Beyond managerialism? *International Journal of Human Resource Management*, **21**(6): 799–817.

➤ Dickens, L. (1998) What HRM means for gender equality. *Human Resource Management Journal*, **8**(1): 23–45.

➤ Kochan, T. (2008) Social legitimacy of the HRM profession: a US perspective. In P. Boxall, J. Purcell and P. Wright (eds) *The Oxford Handbook of Human Resource Management* (pp. 599–619). Oxford: OUP.

➤ Legge, K. (2005) *Human Resource Management: Rhetorics and Realities* (anniversary edn). London: Palgrave Macmillan.

➤ McCollum, D. and Findlay, A. (2015). 'Flexible' workers for 'flexible' jobs? The labour market function of A8 migrant labour in the UK. *Work, Employment & Society*, **29**(30):427–43.

➤ Storey J. (ed.) (2007) Human resource management today: an assessment. In J. Storey (ed.) *Human Resource Management: A Critical Text* (pp. 3–20). London: Thompson Learning.

➤ Thompson, P. and Harley, B. (2008) HRM and the worker: labour process perspectives. In P. Boxall, J. Purcell and P. Wright (eds) *The Oxford Handbook of Human Resource Management* (pp. 147–65). Oxford: Oxford University Press.

➤ Watson, T. (2010) Critical social science, pragmatism and the realities of HRM. *International Journal of Human Resource Management Studies*, **21**(6): 915–31.

➤ Williams, C. (2003) Sky service: the demands of emotional labour in the airline industry. *Gender, Work & Organization,* **10**: 513–50.

vocabulary checklist for ESL students

Click here in your interactive ebook for a list of HRM terminology and vocabulary that has appeared in this chapter.

Visit the online resource centre at **www.palgravehighered.com/bg-hrm-6e** for lots of extra resources to help you get to grips with this chapter, including study tips, HRM skills development guides, summary lecture notes, tips for English as a Second Language (ESL) students and more.

THE CONTEMPORARY HUMAN RESOURCE MANAGEMENT ARENA

part 1

chapter **2**

corporate strategy and strategic HRM

Image Source/Innocenti & Lee CM

outline

- ➤ Introduction
- ➤ Strategic management
- ➤ HRM in practice 2.1: Why is self-employment in the UK at a record high?
- ➤ Corporate sustainability
- ➤ Strategic HRM
- ➤ HRM and globalization 2.1: Business urged to keep on eco-track
- ➤ HRM in practice 2.2: More women leaders: the answer to the financial crisis?
- ➤ HRM as I see it: Sarah Myers, Sky
- ➤ HR strategy and organizational dynamics
- ➤ HRM and globalization 2.2: The effects of business strategy on workers' psychological health
- ➤ Critiquing SHRM and models of HR strategy
- ➤ Case study: Zuvan Winery
- ➤ Summary, review questions, further reading and vocabulary checklist for ESL students

objectives

After studying this chapter, you should be able to:

1 Describe the characteristics of strategic decisions and define what is meant by strategy and strategic management

2 Appreciate the meaning of 'quadruple bottom line' as a firm or organization strategy for sustainable work systems

3 Describe how strategic priorities vary by level – corporate, business and operational – and comment on the links between business strategy and HRM

4 Explain three models of HR strategy: control, resource and integrative

5 Comment on the limitations of the literature on strategic HRM and HR strategy

A browse through the business section of any quality newspaper will reveal a ubiquitous use of the word 'strategy'. When supermarket Tesco faced flattened profits to 1 per cent of turnover, newspaper columnist Paul Mason wrote that Tesco's boss Dave Lewis was sticking to the 'strategy' of making Tesco stores the single 'destination' where customers did much or all of their shopping. In search of a new strategy, Mason suggested that Lewis should look to Tesco's most vibrant asset: their employees. 'Everything in the physical architecture of a big supermarket is designed to make the workforce invisible; customer interactions are fleeting; when a person on the till suddenly cracks a pleasantry or reveals some personal detail, it is – in most supermarket groups – as if an unwritten code had been broken. So I would do something that rewarded the workforce for unleashing their wit, knowledge and expertise on the actual customers' (Mason, 2015a, p. S5, courtesy of Guardian News & Media Ltd). If Tesco and other supermarkets followed Mason's advice, they would be looking to change their corporate and HR strategies, which, along with corporate strategy, is the focus of this chapter.

introduction

The idea that employees' 'wit, knowledge and expertise' can play a strategic role in achieving competitive goals is the essence of a field of research labelled 'strategic' human resource management, or SHRM. Just as the term 'human resource management' has been contested, so too has the notion of SHRM. A strategic approach to the management of work and people is concerned with developing and implementing human resources (HR) policies and practices that will enable the organization to achieve its strategic objectives. As a subfield of study, SHRM represents an intersection between the literatures on strategic management and HRM (Allen and Wright, 2008). A stream of empirical research has explored the performance effects associated with SHRM (for example, Guthrie et al., 2009; Martín-Tapia et al., 2009). The SHRM debate focuses on several important questions. First, what determines whether an organization adopts a strategic approach to HRM? Second, can we identify distinct bundles of HR activities with different competitive models? And finally, can SHRM enhance competitive advantage or improve services?

This chapter examines the strategic management process and introduces a new dimension into the debate – the notion of a 'green strategy'. It will then examine different 'models' of HR strategy and the degree to which these types of HR strategy vary systematically between organizations. We then address a number of questions that relate to SHRM and performance, leadership, organizational structure and culture, and trade unions. There is a common theme running through this chapter – that much of the literature reveals structural constraints confirming the complexity of implementing different HRM strategies in the contemporary workplace.

Strategic management

The word 'strategy', deriving from the Greek noun *strategos*, meaning 'commander in chief', was first used in the English language in 1656. The development and usage of the word suggests that it is composed of *stratos* (army) and *agein* (to lead). In a management context, the word 'strategy' has now replaced the more traditional term 'long-term planning' to denote a specific pattern of behaviour undertaken by the senior management of the organization in order to accomplish its performance goals. Hill et al. (2014, p. 3) define a strategy as 'a set of related actions that managers take to increase their company's performance'. Macintosh and MacLean (2015, p. 3) define it more broadly as 'the craft of collectively rising to a significant challenge and accomplishing more than might be reasonably expected as a result of self-knowledge, resolve, foresight, creativity and genuine capabilities cultivated over the medium to long term'. Grant (2010) argues that strategy is simply 'about winning' (p. 4). In for-profit organizations, if a strategy results in superior performance, it is said to have a competitive advantage. Traditionally, an organization's top executives create strategies. In learning organizations, in contrast, the accumulated actions of informed and empowered employees contribute to strategic development (Daft, 2015). In addition, a collaborative strategy can emerge from business partnerships with suppliers and customers, non-profit and environmental agencies and groups. Continuing the focus on supermarkets, Wal-Mart, for example, has enjoyed a competitive advantage over its rivals because it pursues a number of strategies including a lower cost structure, lower prices, a larger market share, lower wages and higher profits than rival supermarkets (Fishman, 2007; Hill et al., 2014). Strategy is therefore the essence of managerial activity.

In the UK, there has been a transformation of public sector organizations through privatization, outsourcing or the application of business-oriented management practices. This development has led some public management authors to advocate that public sector organizations should take generic strategic management models more seriously, even though they may have to be adapted to the still distinctive sectoral culture of public administration (Andrews et al., 2006; Boyne and Walker, 2010; Ferlie and Ongaro, 2015; Vining, 2011). Ferlie and Ongaro (2015), for example, argue that some models of strategic management, typically applied in for-profit organizations, now have enhanced applicability to many contemporary public sector organizations. Although one can see why academics would like to extend models of strategic management into the public sector, this is a contested perspective. Political scientists and sociologists, for instance, might well emphasize the diversity of cultural contexts (for example, England and Scotland) and the continuing distinctively democratic, value-driven nature of public administration. As Ferlie and Ongaro observe, 'The politico-administrative culture and societal contexts shape some of the very basic premises for the management of public service organizations' (2015, p. 221). Clearly, more research is needed in this area.

Whether in private or public sector organizations, a strategy need not necessarily be made explicit or be equated with a formal plan. A strategy is best understood as a pattern of decision-making based on a clear understanding of the 'game' being played and a keen awareness on the part of the players of how to manoeuvre into a position of advantage (Grant, 2010). A successful strategy is consistent with the organization's external environment and with its internal goals, resources, capabilities and shared values. Strategic management is therefore best defined as a continuous process that requires the constant adjustment of three major, interdependent poles: the environment, the resources available and the values of senior management (Figure 2.1).

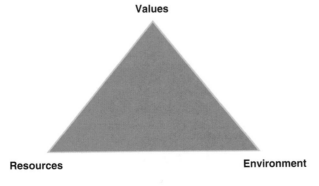

Figure 2.1 *The three traditional poles of a strategic plan or 'game'*
Source: Based on Aktouf (1996)

Model of strategic management

In their overview of the field, Mintzberg et al. (2009) identify no fewer than 10 different schools of strategic management, many of which exhibit different basic assumptions and reflect distinct theoretical perspectives (Ferlie and Ongaro, 2015). What follows, therefore, is an introduction to the field. In the descriptive and prescriptive management texts, strategic management appears as a cycle in which several activities follow and feed on one another. The strategic management process is typically broken down into five steps:

1 Mission and goals
2 Environmental analysis
3 Strategic formulation
4 Strategy implementation
5 Strategy evaluation.

Figure 2.2 illustrates how the five steps interact. At the corporate level, the strategic management process includes activities that range from appraising the organization's current mission and goals, to strategic evaluation.

The first step in the strategic management model begins with top senior managers evaluating their position in relation to the organization's current *mission and goals*. The

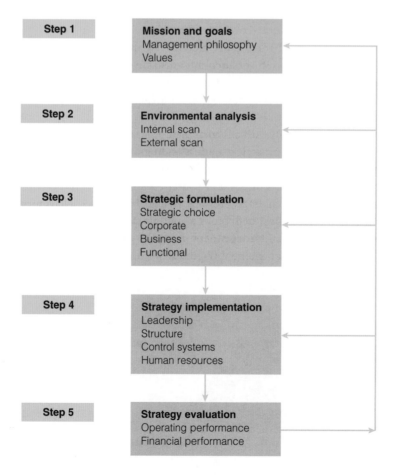

Figure 2.2 *The strategic management model*

mission describes the organization's values and aspirations; it is the organization's *raison d'être* and indicates the direction in which senior management is going. Goals are the formally stated definition of the business scope and outcomes the organization is trying to accomplish (Daft, 2015).

Environmental analysis looks at the organization's internal strengths and weaknesses and at the external environment for opportunities and threats. The factors that are most important to the organization's future are referred to as 'strategic factors' and can be summarized by the acronym SWOT – **S**trengths, **W**eaknesses, **O**pportunities and **T**hreats.

Strategic formulation involves senior managers evaluating the interaction between strategic factors and making strategic choices that enable the organization to meet its business goals. The process, as described here, draws on the 'strategic choice' perspective (Child, 1972). Some strategies are formulated at the corporate, business and specific functional levels. The concept of 'strategic choice' underscores the importance of asking such questions as who makes the decisions and why they are made. It also draws attention to strategic management as a 'political process' whereby decisions and actions on issues are taken by a 'power-dominant' group of managers within the organization. In Child's words (Child, 1972, quoted in McLoughlin and Clark, 1988, p. 41):

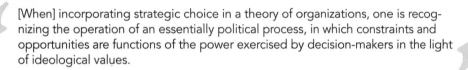

[When] incorporating strategic choice in a theory of organizations, one is recognizing the operation of an essentially political process, in which constraints and opportunities are functions of the power exercised by decision-makers in the light of ideological values.

In a political model of strategic management, it is necessary to consider the distribution of power within the organization: 'where power lies, how it comes to be there, and how the outcome of competing power plays and coalitions within senior management are linked to employee relations' (Purcell and Ahlstrand, 1994, p. 45). The strategic choice perspective on organizational decision-making makes the discourse on strategy 'more concrete' and provides important insights into how the employment relationship is managed.

Strategy implementation is an area of activity that focuses on the techniques used by managers to implement their strategies. In particular, it refers to behaviours that deal with leadership style, the design of the organization, the information and control systems, and the management of HR (see Figure 1.2). Indeed, leadership style is considered to be 'one of the more foundational topics in organizational behaviour' (Judge et al., 2008, p. 334). It is not surprising, then, that a substantial body of research has highlighted the importance of leadership in changing and shaping organizational direction and life (Barling, 2014), in developing HR policies and practices to implement strategic goals (Schuler et al., 2001; Westley and Mintzberg, 2007) and, most recently, in driving pro-environmental behaviours and promoting environmental sustainability (Robertson and Barling, 2015a) (see Table 2.1). Finally, *strategy evaluation* is an activity that determines to what extent the actual change and performance matches the desired change and performance.

The strategic management model depicts the five major activities as forming a rational and linear process. It is, however, important to note that it is a normative model, that is, it shows how strategic management should be done rather than describing what is actually done by senior managers. Mintzberg (2009) believes that the model, uncritically taught to business students, tends to promote an 'excessively analytical, detached style of management' and underestimate the strategic role and contribution of HRM. Strategic management

Why is self-employment in the UK at a record high?

PHOTODISC

The Guardian newspaper, using data from the UK's Office for National Statistics (ONS), revealed that around 15 per cent of those working in the UK are self-employed (Arnett, The Guardian, 2014). This is the highest proportion of the workforce since information on the subject was first collected about 40 years ago. There are 4.6 million people who are self-employed and a further 356,000 people who are self-employed in a second job.

Construction and building is the largest economic sector, with 167,000 people self-employed in 2014, but the ONS states that the largest rise in recent years has been in jobs it describes as 'professional, scientific and technical activities'. Self-employment has also increased among taxi drivers (Monaghan, The Guardian, 2014). At 15 per cent, the rate of self-employment is about average for Europe and only about half of that of Greece, but the UK has had the fastest rate of growth in self-employment. According to the ONS, self-employed people have suffered an average 22 per cent fall in real pay since 2008–09 and receive average earnings of £207 per week – below half that of employees. In addition, they do not receive sick or holiday pay. Self-employment has also been seen to be contributing to the UK's shift to low-paid work (Monaghan, The Guardian, 2014).

The ONS figures show that, before 2009, 32–37 per cent of self-employed individuals transferred to full-time employment, but in the period 2009–14 the rate declined to 23 per cent. The ONS believes this slowdown is due to, first, more people over 65 years of age in both full-time and part-time employment who are continuing to work, and second, the economic downturn since 2008 removing opportunities for people to leave part-time employment (Arnett, The Guardian, 2014).

In August 2015, the UK support organization Citizens Advice published a survey of 491 people who claimed to be self-employed. The report stated:

As many as 460,000 people could be 'bogusly self-employed' meaning workers miss out on holiday pay, government loses tax revenue and responsible businesses could be undercut ... unscrupulous employers can compel staff to be self-employed when they should in fact have employee status.

It was found that one in 10 of the sample of people claiming to be self-employed should have had employment status because of a combination of factors such as having work hours set by an employer, using the business's equipment and having tax deducted from their pay by their employer. On average, self-employed workers lost £1200 per year holiday pay and had to pay an extra £61 in National Insurance contributions compared with those who were employed. Employers could avoid paying the minimum wage, National Insurance, sick pay, holiday pay and pension contributions. The UK government, it was estimated, could as a result lose up to £314 million per year in lost tax and employer's National Insurance contributions.

An optimistic view of self-employment refers to people's desire to work for themselves, innovate and be entrepreneurial. A more pessimistic view is that most self-employed individuals have become so in order to avoid unemployment, may have been forced into self-employment or are just about managing to 'get by', albeit on lower wages.

Stop! What do you think are the benefits and costs of self-employment for (1) the individual, (2) the employer and (3) society?

Sources and further information: See Arnett (2014), Citizens Advice (2015) and Monaghan (2014) for more information on this.

Note: This feature was written by David Denham.

is 'context-sensitive' rather than 'context-free' (Ferlie and Ongaro, 2015, p. 221). It is a practice therefore learned in context. Divorcing the two helps to throw light on the Bank of England's monumental failure of management when 'the collective imagination of many bright people' failed to foresee the timing, extent and severity of the financial crisis occurring in 2008 (Elliott and Treanor, The Guardian, 2015, p. 27; Stewart, 2009). As we have already noted, the idea that strategic decision-making is a political process implies a potential significant gap between the theoretical model and economic and social reality.

Hierarchy of strategy

Another aspect of strategic management in the multidivisional business organization concerns the level to which strategic issues apply. Conventional wisdom identifies different levels of strategy – a hierarchy of strategy (Figure 2.3):

- Corporate
- Business
- Functional.

Corporate-level strategy

Corporate-level strategy describes an organization's overall direction in terms of its general philosophy towards the growth and the management of its various operating units. The term 'corporate' is used in this book because the term 'corporate strategy' denotes the most general level of strategy in an organization and in this sense embraces other levels of strategy in both large and small business enterprises, non-profit organizations and public services. Corporate strategies determine the types of business a corporation wants to be involved in and what business units should be acquired, modified or sold. This strategy addresses the question 'What business are we in?' Devising a strategy for a multidivisional company involves at least four types of initiative:

- Establishing investment priorities and steering corporate resources into the most attractive business units
- Initiating actions to improve the combined performance of those business units with which the corporation first became involved
- Finding ways to improve the synergy between related business units in order to increase performance
- Making decisions dealing with diversification.

Business-level strategy

Business-level strategy deals with decisions and actions pertaining to each business unit, the main objective of a business-level strategy being to make the unit more competitive in its marketplace. This level of strategy addresses the question 'How do we compete?' Although business-level strategy is guided by 'upstream', corporate-level strategy, business unit management must craft a strategy that is appropriate for its own operating situation. In the 1980s, Porter (1980, 1985, 1990, 2004) made a significant contribution to our understanding of business strategy by formulating a framework that described three competitive strategies: cost leadership, differentiation and focus.

The *low-cost leadership* strategy attempts to increase the organization's market share by having the lowest unit cost and price compared with those of competitors. The simple

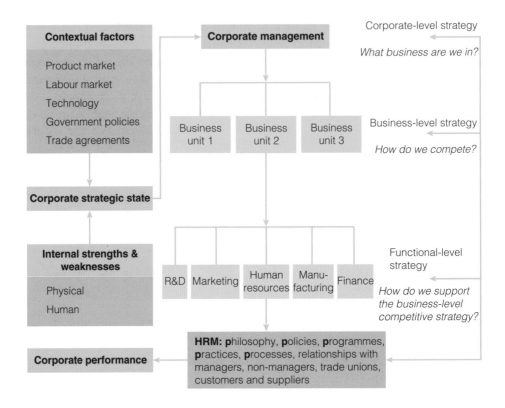

Figure 2.3 *Linking corporate-wide and HRM strategic decision-making*

alternative to cost leadership is the *differentiation strategy*. This assumes that managers distinguish their services and products from those of their competitors in the same industry by providing distinctive levels of service, product or high quality such that the customer is prepared to pay a premium price. With the *focus strategy*, managers focus on a specific buyer group or regional market. A *market strategy* can be narrow or broad, as in the notion of niche markets being very narrow or focused. This all allows the firm to choose from four generic business-level strategies in order to establish and exploit a competitive advantage within a particular competitive scope:

• *Low-cost leadership*, for example Wal-Mart
• *Differentiation*, for example Nudie Jeans
• *Focused differentiation*, for example Mountain Equipment Co-operative
• *Focused low-cost leadership*, for example Rent-A-Wreck Cars.

Miles and Snow (1984) have identified four modes of strategic orientation: defenders, prospectors, analysers and reactors. *Defenders* are companies with a limited product line and a management focus on improving the efficiency of their existing operations. Commitment to this cost orientation makes senior managers unlikely to explore new areas. *Prospectors* are companies with fairly broad product lines that focus on product innovation and market opportunities. This sales orientation makes senior managers emphasize 'creativity over efficiency'. *Analysers* are companies that operate in at least two different product market areas, one stable and one variable. In this situation, senior managers emphasize efficiency in the stable areas and innovation in the variable areas. *Reactors* are companies that lack a consistent strategy–structure–culture relationship.

In this reactive orientation, senior management's responses to environmental changes and pressures thus tend to be piecemeal strategic adjustments. Competing companies within a single industry can choose any one of these four types of strategy and adopt a corresponding combination of structure, culture and processes consistent with that strategy in response to the environment. The different competitive strategies influence the 'downstream' functional strategies.

Functional-level strategy

Functional-level strategy relates to the major functional operations within the business unit, including research and development, marketing, manufacturing, finance and HR. This strategy level is typically primarily concerned with maximizing resource productivity and addresses the question 'How do we support the business-level competitive strategy?' Consistent with this, at the functional level, HRM policies and practices support the business strategy goals.

These three levels of strategy – *corporate, business* and *functional* – form a hierarchy of strategy within large multidivisional corporations. In different corporations, the specific operation of the hierarchy of strategy might vary between 'top-down' and 'bottom-up' strategic planning. The top-down approach resembles a 'cascade' in which the 'downstream' strategic decisions are dependent on higher 'upstream' strategic decisions (Wheelen and Hunger, 2014). The bottom-up approach to strategy-making recognizes that individuals 'deep' within the organization might contribute to strategic planning. Mintzberg (1978) has incorporated this idea into a model of 'emergent strategies', which are unplanned responses to unforeseen circumstances by non-executive employees within the organization. Common to definitions of corporate strategy is the notion that strategy is focused on achieving certain goals and that it 'implies some consistency, integration, or cohesiveness of decisions and actions' (Grant, 2010, p. 16).

Strategy, ethics and corporate social responsibility

The previous sections have discussed decision-making at the three levels of strategy formulation, but have given little consideration to whether strategic decision-making is ethical or unethical. Nor have we considered how society's expectations impact on an organization's strategies. Unethical strategic decisions can have profound long-term implications for a company's profits and brand image. These considerations are the province of business ethics and corporate social responsibility (CSR).

Ethics are a set of moral principles and values that influence the decisions and actions of individuals within the organization. A series of high-profile cases, including those of Bernard Ebbers at WorldCom, Fausta Tonna at Parmalat, Bernard Madoff, former chair of the NASDAQ Stock Market, and Tom Hayes, a former stellar trader at UBS and Citigroup, has drawn public attention to business ethics and *white-collar crime*. In July 2011, the phone-hacking scandal, or 'Hackingate', at News International (UK) brought into sharp focus the unethical behaviour of senior executives in the pursuit of profit. And in September 2015, in another high-profile case of alleged unlawful and unethical behaviour, Volkswagen executives admitted to legal as well as ethical violations of emission laws.

Ethics underscores the notion of *corporate social responsibility*, which is concerned with the ways in which managers' behaviour and actions exceed minimum compliance-based regulations (see, for example, HRM in practice 2.1). CSR concerns the ethical principle that an organization should be accountable for how its corporate strategy might affect suppliers, local communities, society at large and the planet. Unsurprisingly, therefore, public attention has in recent years focused on the need for businesses to define their standards of ethical behaviour, new CSR strategies to be put forward and, moreover, greater government regulation. Business ethics and CSR follow naturally from the discussion of strategic decision-making, and these concepts are examined more thoroughly in Chapter 11, HRM and ethics.

HRM web links   Visit the online resource centre at **www.palgravehighered.com/bg-hrm-6e** for more information on business ethics.

Corporate sustainability

The search for a strategy that provides competitive advantage or superior services is not straightforward. It is typical for these strategic goals to be explainable by identifying resources and human capabilities that competitors find difficult to obtain or imitate (Barney, 1991). Research is beginning to provide an acknowledgement that strategic capability hinges upon issues of environmental sustainability, ethics in strategic decisions and organizational practices and CSR (Ardichvili, 2015; Garavan et al., 2010). A recent recurrent theme in the HRM and human resource development (HRD) literature is that the issues of environmental sustainability, business ethics and CSR are closely interrelated, and that discussions of HRM's and HRD's role should be addressing these three issues as part of the same strategic conversation. To better understand how these three concepts are intertwined, we briefly explore the concept of corporate environmental sustainability. A more thorough account of environmental sustainability can be found in Chapter 16, Green HRM and environmental sustainability.

The term 'sustainability' has its roots in the Latin word *sustinere*, meaning 'to support'. Sumner (2005, p. 81) offers one definition of environmental sustainability:

> a process of change in which the exploitation of resources, the direction of investments, the orientation of technological development, and institutional change are all in harmony and enhance both current and future potential to meet human needs and aspirations.

The concept of sustainability is controversial and elastic, and environmental critics warn that the acceptance and omnipresence of the term 'sustainability' in corporate discourse has come at 'the price of conceptual vagueness, fluidity and co-option' (Sumner, 2005, p. 84). The literature identifies four main approaches to studying sustainability: economic, environmental, social and cultural. The *economic* perspective can be divided into two schools of thinking: neo-classical and ecological. The core premise of neo-classical economics is that firms seek to maximize their profits, reinvesting profits to increase output, in order to sell more and thus further increase profits, ad infinitum. As far as the ecosystem is concerned, it is meant to serve that accumulation and cannot be seen as a value in itself. In contrast, the ecological economic school recognizes that orthodox growth models are responsible for the sustainability crisis. Adherents believe that sustainability involves 'handing down to future generations local and global ecosystems that largely resemble our own' (Goodstein, 1999, p. 109).

reflective
question

Do you believe that society can achieve responsible economic growth, equitable social progress, and effective environmental protection and if so, what, if anything, needs to change?

Speaking about orthodox economic growth models, environmentalists point out that the incessant drive for bigger profits means an accumulation of capital equipment: bigger and bigger plant and machinery, to make more and more cars, and aircraft and so on. It is not only that we are consuming non-renewable mineral resources, such as oil and gas, but that we are destroying the basis of the renewable resources – forests, rivers and oceans – from which we draw our food. This is at the heart of the environmental critique of orthodox economic models. The *environmental* perspective defines sustainability in terms of 'the continued productivity and functioning of the ecosystem' (Brown et al., 1987, p. 716).

The *social* perspective underscores the importance of human society. It involves 'improving the quality of human life while living within the carrying capacity of supporting ecosystems' (Farrell and Hart, 1998, p. 7). The *cultural* perspective, however, sees cultural enrichment as integral to sustainability: the continued satisfaction of basic human needs, as well as 'higher level' cultural necessities (Brown et al., 1987). In terms of values, the environmental, social and cultural perspectives move away from orthodox monetary values towards life values. Thus, in summary, we can identify four interdependent and mutually reinforcing aspects of sustainable development: *sustainable economic growth*, *protection of the environment*, *social equity* and *cultural vitality*. These 'four pillars of sustainability' are expressed visually in Figure 2.4.

The 'four pillars of sustainability' can guide creative thinking and provide a strategic framework for planning corporate-level and business-level strategy. First, corporate strategy should promote sustainable production and consumption, through the appropriate use of environmentally sound technologies and effective demand management. Furthermore, organizational leaders should recognize the intrinsic value of biodiversity and natural ecosystems, and act to protect and restore them. Also, a sustainable corporate strategy recognizes the need for social equity and social change. In addition, the four pillars of sustainability encourage leaders to recognize and build on the

ImageSource/Christopher Robbins

What role do you think HR plays in a sustainable business strategy?

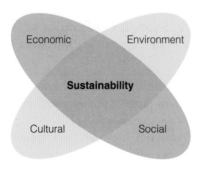

Figure 2.4 *The four pillars of sustainability*

distinctive cultural characteristics, including the shared values, of the cities and communities where their organizations are embedded. These four articulated streams of thinking on environmental sustainability suggest that a successful 'green', low-carbon, sustainable corporate strategy can be expressed as an axiom: the pursuit of *quadruple bottom line* performance – a balance of economic, environmental, social and cultural goals. The issues of a pro-environmental organizational culture and climate and sustainable low-carbon workplace strategy are further examined in Chapters 15 and 16. The literature affirms the need to integrate issues of corporate strategy, sustainability and HRM strategy, and it is to this debate that we now turn.

HRM web links   Visit the online resource centre at **www.palgravehighered.com/bg-hrm-6e** to read a definition of a 'green' economy and for further learning resources on organizational environmental sustainability.

Strategic HRM

SHRM is distinguishable from micro-level HRM in terms of focus and timescale. Whereas micro-level HRM is concerned with day-to-day activities, SHRM is more focused on long-term activities and sustainable organizational outcomes. This also suggests that timescale is another distinguishing factor (Stewart, 2015). The context of SHRM is application within, but not exclusively within, the organization. Recent theoretical frameworks acknowledge, however, that strategic management goals depend very much on 'micro-level' factors: employees' knowledge and ability, employees' self-identity (or identities), employees' attitudes, employees' behaviour and employees' perception of how and why HRM is delivered on the ground, in day-to-day operations (Bowen and Ostroff, 2004; Morris and Snell, 2009; Purcell and Kinnie, 2008). A set or 'cluster' of HR practices is only considered to be strategic if it is integrated with corporate strategy and, because of this, contributes in some sustainable way to the organization's performance.

The SHRM literature is rooted in 'manpower' planning, but it was the influential work of Ouchi (1981) and Peters and Waterman (1982) that encouraged US academics, for example Beer et al. (1984), to develop models of HRM emphasizing its 'strategic' role. Interest in attaching the adjective 'strategic' to the term 'human resource management' can be explained from both the 'rational choice' and the 'constituency-based' perspective. From the 'rational choice' perspective, there is a managerial logic in focusing attention on people's assets to provide a competitive advantage when technological superiority, even once achieved, can soon erode (Barney, 1991). Consistent with Barney's resource-based model (RBM), many mainstream HRM writers go along with the view that 'For a variety of reasons related to changing markets, demands for greater speed and flexibility, and the growing attention to "intangible assets," HR ... has the potential to influence firm performance in a way that was not possible 20 years ago' (Huselid and Becker, 2001, quoted in Guthrie et al., 2009, p. 112). From a 'constituency-based' position, it is argued that HR academics and practitioners have embraced SHRM as a means of securing greater respect for the discipline as a field of study and, in the case of HRM practitioners, of enhancing their status among their peers by appearing more 'strategic' (Bamberger and Meshoulam, 2000).

reflective question 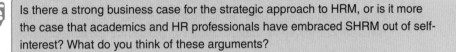 Is there a strong business case for the strategic approach to HRM, or is it more the case that academics and HR professionals have embraced SHRM out of self-interest? What do you think of these arguments?

The precise meaning of 'strategic HRM' and 'HR strategy' remains problematic. It is unclear, for example, which one of these two terms relates to an outcome or a process (Bamberger and Meshoulam, 2000). For Snell et al. (1996, p. 62), 'strategic HRM' is an outcome: 'as organizational systems designed to achieve sustainable competitive advantage through people'. For others, however, SHRM is viewed as a process, 'the process of linking HR practices to business strategy' (Ulrich, 1997, p. 89). Similarly, Bamberger and Meshoulam (2000, p. 6) describe SHRM as 'the process by which organizations seek to link the human, social, and intellectual capital of their members to the strategic needs of the firm'.

According to Ulrich (1997, p. 190), 'HR strategy' is the outcome – 'the mission, vision and priorities of the HR function'. Consistent with this view, Bamberger and Meshoulam (2000, p. 5) conceptualize HR strategy as an outcome: 'the pattern of decisions regarding the policies and practices associated with the HR system'. The authors go on to make a useful distinction between senior management's 'espoused' HR strategy and their 'emergent' strategy. The espoused HR strategy refers to the pattern of HR-related decisions made but not necessarily implemented, whereas the emergent HR strategy refers to the pattern of HR-related decisions that have been applied in the workplace. Thus, 'espoused HR strategy is the road map ... and emergent HR strategy is the road actually travelled' (Bamberger and Meshoulam, 2000, p. 6). Purcell (2001) has also portrayed HR strategy as 'emerging patterns of action' that are likely to be much more 'intuitive' and only 'visible' after the event.

In their in-depth treatment of the field, Boxall and Purcell (2011, p. 65) explain that 'strategic HRM is concerned with the strategic choices associated with the organization of work and the use of labour in firms and with explaining why some firms manage them more effectively than others'. The authors spell out the meaning of their definition by identifying three core questions needed to review a firm's HR strategy: What strengths and weaknesses are apparent in the firm's HR? What threats and opportunities does the firm face in its main employee groups? How effective are the firm's HR planning and reporting processes? A recurrent theme in the literature is the variation in HR strategy, often explained by differences in organizational size, heterogeneous employee groups, the dominant culture in the organization and global location. It is more realistic therefore to think of HR strategy 'as a cluster of HR systems' tailored to different employee groups, rather than as a single set of core HR practices covering the entire workforce (Boxall and Purcell, 2011, p. 67). This diversity in HR strategy is something we explore more fully later in the chapter.

A working definition of SHRM is further complicated when considering HR strategy in multidivisional organizations, operating across a variety of labour and product markets. This raises the question of whether local management should have the autonomy to adapt corporate HR strategy to the local context. Minbaeva and Andersen's (2012) perspective is that HR's strategic role lies in providing support for both centralized and decentralized strategy making by offering aspirations for strategic decisions and by gathering various sources of inspiration for strategy discussions. Globalization has given rise to 'societal analysis' (Maurice and Sorge, 2000), and the national and multinational company has been widely theorized as being embedded in society. Thus, an additional complication in theorizing SHRM is whether the management teams in multinational companies are permitted to adapt the corporate HR strategy to local culture. Chapter 17 examines this issue in more detail. Finally, like strategic management, the extent to which SHRM is 'planned' or 'emergent' depends upon the predictability of, and knowledge about, the external contexts (Boxall and Purcell, 2011; Powell and Wakeley, 2003; Swart et al., 2004).

We begin the discussion of SHRM and HR strategy with a focus on the link between strategy formulation and strategic HR formulation. A range of business–HRM links has been classified in terms of a proactive–reactive continuum (Kydd and Oppenheim, 1990; Purcell and Kinnie, 2008) and in terms of environment–HR-strategy–business-strategy linkages (Bamberger and Phillips, 1991). In the 'proactive' orientation, the HR professional has a seat at the strategic table and is actively engaged in strategy formulation. In Figure 2.3, the two-way arrows on the right-hand side showing both a downward and an upward influence on strategy depict this type of proactive model.

At the other end of the continuum is the 'reactive' orientation, which sees the HR function as being fully subservient to corporate-level and business-level strategy, and organizational-level strategies as ultimately determining HR policies and practices. Once the business strategy has been determined, the emphasis is on the enactment of an HR strategy, as expressed through attitudes (for example, commitment) and behaviour (for example, multitasking), to support the chosen competitive strategy. This type of reactive orientation would be depicted in Figure 2.3 above by a one-way downward arrow from business-level to functional-level strategy. In this sense, an HR strategy is concerned with the challenge of matching the Philosophy, Policies, Programmes, Practices and Processes – the 'five Ps' – in a way that will stimulate and reinforce the different employee role behaviours appropriate for each competitive strategy (Schuler, 1992).

Here we draw on Schuler et al.'s (2001) work to emphasize the strategic 'reactive' role and contribution of HRM. Strategic management plans at corporate and business level provide the context within which HR plans are developed and enacted. HR plans provide a 'map' for managers to follow in order to fulfil the core responsibilities of the HR function, which are to ensure that:

- The organization has the right number of qualified employees
- Employees have the right skills and knowledge to perform efficiently and effectively
- Employees exhibit the appropriate behaviours consistent with the organization's culture and values
- Employees meet the organization's motivational needs.

Business urged to keep on eco-track

BRAND X

When companies make strategic decisions about what they can produce and at what price, they are acting as rational entities, motivated exclusively by profit. The more a company can drive its costs below those of its competitors, the greater the profits it stands to make. Consequently, minimizing any social or environmental problems is not always high on the agenda. Take the example of US corporate giant McDonald's. The greenhouse gas footprint produced from the 550 million Big Mac burgers sold in the USA every year is estimated to be 2.66 billion pounds of carbon dioxide equivalent (Patel, 2009; Rees, 1995). And there are the hidden health costs of treating diet-related illnesses. These social costs are paid for not by McDonald's, but by society. Thinking about food brings together the common valuation of the ecosystem, the need for responsive governments and the need for sustainable corporate strategies.

The Conference Board of Canada proclaims that sustainability should be 'a strategy of choice' on the part of business leaders. As Jayson Myers from Canadian Manufacturers and Exporters (CME) explains:

Going green can help drive sales revenue… With consumers, businesses and governments around the world paying greater attention to reducing their environmental footprint, Canadian manufacturers and exporters are finding significant new business opportunities in providing the necessary solutions that help their customers address environmental concerns (CME and RBC, 2010).

Furthermore, as well as being a marketing opportunity and a point of differentiation, 'going green' can address many other problems that companies face. The CME promotes environmental initiatives as a way of ensuring long-term financial stability. With increasing demand for energy and resources, rising costs, and stricter regulations, investing in more sustainable methods can be a sensible business decision. As the 'Shifting markets, shifting mindsets' report by the CME and the Royal Bank of Canada demonstrates:

Environmental problems are opening the way for innovative solutions in the form of new products, processes and technologies – all aimed at reducing our environmental footprints…There should be no

question about it: making money and enhancing environmental performance go hand-in-hand.

The rationale and business strategy outlined in the Canadian report was also articulated by Chris Huhne, the former British Secretary of State for Energy and Climate Change, at the Trades Union Congress's Climate Change Conference, held in London on 11 October, 2010: 'Our first priority is to build a new kind of economy. One where green growth leads to green jobs. A low-carbon economy that will help us recover at home and compete abroad.'

It is clear that a business strategy which takes environmental and social concerns into account can be competitive. Maximizing profits and reducing harmful practices are not always opposing ideas.

Stop! Using Figure 2.4 as a starting point, what kinds of corporate strategy should organizational leaders be developing? How do local and national attitudes about climate change influence national governments, business strategies and practices? How should 'sustainability' be defined? Who should be responsible for regulating carbon emissions? And, in times of a recession and amidst fears of job losses, should governments relax national emission regulations?

Sources and further information: For more information, see CME and RBC (2010), Huhne, C. (2010), Patel (2009), Rees (1995) and McCarthy (2010).

Note: This feature was written by John Bratton.

These four core activities can be seen as the *leitmotiv* of HRM and, according to Schuler et al. (2001), constitute the four-task model of HRM. The four core HR tasks provide the rationale that guides the strategic choice of HR policies and practices (Table 2.1).

Table 2.1 Strategy implementation and the four-task model of HRM

HR tasks	Major strategic decisions
Employee assignments and opportunities	• How many employees are needed? • What qualifications will the employees need? • What pay and conditions will attract people to the firm?
Employee competencies	• What competencies do employees have now? • What new competencies will be needed in the future? • How can new competencies be purchased or developed?
Employee behaviours	• What behaviours does the firm value? • What behaviours are detrimental to the strategy? • What behaviours need to be modified or eliminated?
Employee motivation	• How much more effort are employees able and willing to give? • What is the optimal length of time for employees to stay with the firm? • Can productivity be improved by reducing absence and tardiness?

Source: Based on information in Schuler et al. (2001)

In the aftermath of the UK voting to exit the EU, the importance of political and economic context as a determinant of HR strategy is self-evident, and context is incorporated into some SHRM models. In the hierarchy of the strategic decision-making model (see Figure 2.3), the HR strategy is influenced by contextual variables: product markets, technology, national government policies, trade unions and European Union policies, for example. Purcell and Ahlstrand argue, however, that those models which incorporate contextual influences as a mediating variable of HR policies and practices tend to lack 'precision and detail' in terms of the precise nature of the environment linkages, and that 'much of the work on the linkages has been developed at an abstract and highly generalized level' (1994, p. 36).

Drawing on the concepts of 'strategic choice' and 'hierarchy of strategy', Purcell (1989) identified what he called 'upstream' and 'downstream' types of strategic decisions. Upstream or 'first-order' strategic decisions are concerned with the long-term direction of the corporation. If a first-order decision is made to take over another enterprise, for example a French company acquiring a water company in southern England, a second set of considerations applies concerning the extent to which the new operation is to be integrated with or separate from existing operations. These processes are classified as downstream, or 'second-order', strategic decisions. Different HR strategies are called 'third-order' strategic decisions because they establish the basic parameters for managing people in the workplace. In Purcell's words, '[in theory] strategy in human resources management is determined in the context of first-order, long-run decisions on the direction and scope of the firm's activities and purpose ... and second-order decisions on the structure of the firm' (1989, p. 71).

The strategic choice perspective defines an organization's strategy as 'sets of strategic choices', which either play a role in underpinning the organization's viability – make-or-break choices – or contribute to creating significant differences in performance outcomes. Boxall and Purcell (2011, pp. 64–5) follow Dyer (1984) in referring to an organization's *'pattern'* of strategic choices in people management, including critical choices about

HRM in practice 2.2

More women leaders: the answer to the financial crisis?

Getty

Governments have spent much time dealing with the recession that resulted from the near-collapse of the financial system in 2008. The role of the financial sector in triggering the economic crisis has brought the key decision-makers into focus and highlighted the lack of women in prominent leadership positions. This has spurred the UK government on to comment on the role of women in the City (HM Treasury Committee, 2010):

Strong and effective corporate governance of the UK financial sector will be an important factor in ensuring the sector's long-term stability, enabling it to help businesses and households in the wider economy … There is a risk of group-think if boards continually recruit individuals who share the same backgrounds and experiences. At the same time, as the economy recovers, it is imperative that businesses are drawing from the widest possible pool of talent, and that means ensuring that women's skills and experiences are utilised to the full … Concern about the under-representation of women on boards can be about business performance as much as fairness. There is a consensus that an effective challenge function within a board is required in financial institutions, and that diversity on boards can promote such challenge. While it is impossible to know whether more female board members would have lessened the impact of the financial crisis, the arguments for fairness, improved corporate governance, a stronger challenge function and not wasting a large proportion of talent seem more than sufficient to conclude that increased gender diversity is desirable.

The European Commission also published a report emphasizing that women in senior positions are the key to economic stability and growth. It suggests that the persistent gender gap has developed from differing perceptions of the roles of men and women in life and work. However, the transformation in attitude and culture necessary to support change seems to be slow in the corporate world, and it can be difficult to change the status quo.

So how do organizations move to change attitudes and perceptions? There are many methods of promoting the advancement of women, such as

training opportunities, flexible working, networks, role models and mentors. However, more quantitative methods can also be used – in Norway, for example, quotas were introduced in law in 2005 for the number of female directors of listed companies because there was a perception that male-oriented boards did not effectively represent companies themselves or the markets they operated in. However, does this quota-based approach result in leadership roles as a 'right' for women rather than being the result of evidenced competence? The case of the public downfall of Lehman Brothers' female chief financial officer is attributed to the company's aggressive HR strategy to improve the representation of women, sexual orientation and ethnic groups; it was found that she did not have the requisite qualifications for the role. On the other hand, the CEO of PepsiCo highlights her hard work and determination in becoming a prominent woman in corporate America without the assistance of quotas.

Stop! What action might HR professionals take to develop a fair and diverse approach to promoting employees to senior leadership roles? What advice would you give organizations about the use of quotas to increase diversity at senior levels?

Sources and further information: See HM Treasury Committee (2010) and Hofman and Hofman (2010) for more on this issue.

Note: This feature was written by Lois Farquharson.

'means and ends'. Case study analysis has highlighted the problematic nature of building models for strategic choice. A study of HRM in multidivisional companies, for example, found that HR strategy is determined by decisions at all three levels and by the ability and leadership style of local managers to follow through goals in the context of specific environmental conditions (Purcell and Ahlstrand, 1994). It is argued, therefore, that the strategic choice perspective might exaggerate the 'choice' in 'strategic choice' – the ability of managers to make strategic decisions independent of the market and the national settings in which they do business. In other words, the extent to which managers have 'choice' is 'variable' in different market society settings (Boxall and Purcell, 2011; Hyman, 1999; Paauwe and Boselie, 2003). On the basis of these definitions and conceptual insights, the next section examines the debate on three SHRM models: 'best fit', 'best practice' and resource-based.

The 'best-fit' model

The best-fit school of SHRM argues that the variety in HR practices observed within and across organizations suggests that managers inevitably adapt HR policy and practices to 'fit' their specific context. This call for the HR function to be 'strategically integrated' is depicted in Beer et al.'s (1984) model of HRM (see Figure 1.3). In this analytical framework, managers are encouraged to develop an internal HR strategy based on a consideration of stakeholder (for example, shareholder) interests and situational factors (for example, workforce characteristics): 'An organization's HRM policies and practices must fit with its strategy in its competitive environment and with the immediate business conditions that it faces' (Beer et al., 1984, p. 25). The Harvard framework focused on the integration of business strategy with a wide range of HR choices. The concept of integration has three aspects:

- Linking of HR policies and practices with the organization's strategic management process
- A need for line managers to internalize the importance of HR
- Integration of the workforce into the organization to foster commitment to or an 'identity of interest' with the strategic goals.

The notion of congruence or 'fit' between an external competitive strategy and an internal HR strategy is a central tenet of Beer et al.'s (1984) HRM model. Beer and his colleagues emphasize the need to analyse the linkages between the two strategies and how each strategy provides goals and constraints for the other. In their words, there must be a 'fit between competitive strategy and internal HRM strategy and a fit among the elements of the HRM strategy' (1984, p. 13). In the case of a subsidiary discount leisure airline (Jang, 2011), for example, consistent with the 'best-fit' model of SHRM, the airline would need to create a low-cost structure of employment relations, which would be quite different from that of the parent airline company. The two distinctive business models would therefore create two systems of employee relations: the 'high road' and the 'low road' (Harvey and Turnbull, 2010).

The relationship between business strategy and HR strategy is said to be 'reactive' in the sense that HR strategy is subservient to 'product market logic' and corporate strategy; the latter is assumed to be the independent variable. As an observer put it, 'HRM cannot be conceptualized as a stand-alone corporate issue ... it must flow from and be dependent upon the organization's (market oriented) corporate strategy' (Miller, 1987, cited in Boxall, 1992, p. 66). There is some theorization of the link between product markets and approaches to people management. Thus, for example, each of Porter's 'generic strategies' described earlier in the chapter involves a unique set of responses from workers and a particular HR strategy designed to develop and reinforce a unique pattern of expected behaviour. HRM is therefore seen to be 'strategic' by virtue of its 'fit' with business strategy and its internal consistency (see, for example, Boxall and Purcell, 2011; Schuler and Jackson, 1987). Research on societal, industrial and organizational fit demonstrates that context matters when examining HR strategy in an organization.

The 'best-practice' model

The best-practice school of SHRM argues that all organizations will see performance improvements if managers identify and enact a universal set of best HR practices. The best-practice school involves senior management identifying the 'leading edge' of best practice, communicating to lower-level managers their commitment to best practices, measuring how well these are being put into practice and rewarding managers for consistently imple-menting them (Boxall and Purcell, 2011). Traditional micro-level HRM research identifies what constitutes 'bad' practice on the one hand, and 'best' practice on the other, in areas such as selection, rewards, performance appraisal and employee voice (see, for example, Johnstone and Ackers, 2015; Schmitt and Kim, 2008; Youndt et al., 1996). Research has also attempted to identify the proportion of highly skilled 'core' employees covered by a partic-ular 'cluster' of best practice (e.g., Osterman, 2000), and whether a set of best practices is associated with a particular organizational culture (for example Pfeffer, 1998) or macro model of best HR practice; this is commonly referred to as high-commitment management or the high-performance workplace (see, for example, Appelbaum et al., 2000; Danford et al., 2008; Den Hartog and Verburg, 2004; Wood, 1996). Whereas US academic Jeffrey Pfeffer (1998) identified seven 'best practices' 'for building profits', European academics Den Hartog and Verburg (2004) isolated eight practices that feature in high-performance workplaces to reinforce desired HR outcomes (Table 2.2).

Table 2.2 *Pfeffer's (1998) and Den Hartog and Verburg's (2004) 'best' practices*

Pfeffer's seven practices	Den Hartog and Verburg's eight practices
1. Employment security	1. Employment skills
2. Selective hiring	2. Autonomy
3. Self-managed teams or teamworking	3. Pay-for-performance
4. High pay contingent on company performance	4. Profit-sharing
5. Extensive training	5. Performance appraisal
6. Reduction in status differences	6. Teamworking
7. Information-sharing	7. Job evaluation
	8. Information-sharing

Research shows that the organizations actually implementing Pfeffer's seven practices are very much in the minority (Kaufman, 2010). Deciding what constitutes 'best' HR practices and isolating the 'core' bundles remains a challenge for academics attempting to measure the HR–performance relationship (Purcell et al., 2009; see Chapter 3). Legge (1978) identified the problem of interest conflicts when she asked the question: For *whom* is 'best practice' best? What if practice is good for shareholders and executives but bad for line managers and workers? This is often the case when the focus is on increasing the share value at the expense of long-term investment in innovation and people (Hutton, 2015b), and when an organization downsizes or relocates part of its operation to a low-wage economy. And what if the practice is good for CEOs but bad for shareholders and/or workers? Arguably, this is the case with CEO remuneration in companies listed on the UK FTSE 100 and US S&P 500 indexes. The UK High Pay Centre reported that, in 2014, the gap between workers' and executive pay widened from 183 to 184 times UK median earnings (O'Grady, 2015). In the USA, the pay of an S&P executive is 373 times that of a regular employee. In contrast, in Germany, which has a stronger employee voice, the equivalent ratio is around 147, and in France and Japan the figures are 104 and 67, respectively. Although it may be unrealistic to see a perfect alignment of interests, Boxall and Purcell's (2011, p. 85) reflective suggestion is that 'a useful test of any best-practice claim is the extent to which it serves employee interests.'

**reflective
question**

Is the growing gap between CEO and regular workers justified? What do these statistics say about HR practices in the UK compared with France, Germany or Japan? Is Boxall and Purcell's 'test' of 'best-practice' realistic?

The 'resource-based' model

The genesis of the resource-based view (RBV) of SHRM can be traced back to Selznick (1957), who suggested that companies possess 'distinctive competence' that enables them to outperform their competitors, and to economist Edith Penrose (1959), who conceptualized the firm as a 'collection of productive resources'. Penrose distinguished between 'physical' and 'human' resources, and drew attention to issues of learning, including the knowledge and experience of the management team. She further emphasized what many organizational theorists take for granted – that human resources are heterogeneous in nature and not perfectly mobile (Penrose, 1959).

Three decades later, Penrose's ideas were rediscovered by, among others, Barney (1991). He argued that '*sustained* competitive advantage' (emphasis added) is achieved not through an analysis of a company's external market position, but through a careful analysis of its skills and capabilities, characteristics that competitors find themselves unable to imitate. Barney identified four characteristics of resources and capabilities – value, rarity, inimitability and non-substitutability – as being important for sustainable advantage. When advanced technology is readily available to competing companies, Cappelli and Singh's (1992) argument is that the sum of people's knowledge and expertise, as well as the social networks that ensure reliable labour, has the potential to provide non-substitutable capabilities that serve as a source of competitive advantage or superior services. Putting RBV in terms of a simple SWOT analysis, this approach highlights the strategic importance of harnessing internal 'strengths' and neutralizing internal 'weaknesses' (Barney, 1991). Relating RBV to the best-fit and best-practice schools of thinking, RBV strategy scholars aim to discover how an organization can build 'an *exclusive* form of fit' (Boxall and Purcell, 2011, p. 97, emphasis in original).

**HRM web
links**

Visit the online resource centre at **www.palgravehighered.com/bg-hrm-6e** for information on how 'corporate' universities help to build 'core' competencies.

The RBV impulse underscores the importance of a learning culture in the workplace (Foley, 2001; Poell et al., 2015; Rebelo and Gomes, 2011). Reflecting on this orientation, 'organic' organizational structures, in terms of utilizing employees' capabilities, flexibility, and communication and shared responsibility, are associated with culture-oriented learning (Rebelo and Gomes, 2011). We should note that employee training and development, the main form of interface between HRM and environmental management – the management of the interaction and impact of human societies on the ecosystem (Jabbour et al., 2010) – is insufficient to promote a learning culture. In fact, Rebelo and Gomes (2011, p. 187) state that 'many training programs did not involve leadership and the promotion of a culture stimulating the transfer and application of newly acquired knowledge in the workplace'. Studies, however, have empirically demonstrated how, all other things being equal, distinctive internal organizational capabilities forming high-performance work systems may potentially account for differences in labour productivity (Guthrie et al., 2009), export performance (Martín-Tapia et al., 2009), product innovation (Wei et al., 2011) and the organization's financial performance (Wei and Lau, 2010).

An important development within the RBV school has been the introduction of the concept of 'dynamic capabilities' (Teece, 2007; Teece et al., 1997). This concept draws attention to the evolution of the organization's competencies and capabilities over time. Such an evolution could enable the firm to respond to discontinuous market conditions or new regulations (for example, a new government policy on renewable energy) and to create new products, services or processes. The concept of dynamic capabilities acknowledges the criticisms that RBV is too static (Ferlie and Ongaro, 2015). Furthermore, the concept of dynamic capabilities emphasizes that the management of knowledge and HRD become fundamental strategic issues (Teece et al., 1997). Indeed, the capacity for organizations to explore and exploit new ideas and technology while simultaneously being able to adapt to changes in the environment may go to the core of effective dynamic capabilities.

The RBV has been part of mainstream strategic management theory for over 20 years, during which time it has been both widely adopted in the SHRM discourse and heavily criticized (Paauwe and Boselie, 2003). The notion of value inherent in the RBV and the fact that the idiosyncratic nature of the resource value is further shaped by any particular organization's specific institutional context has been subject to broad and effective criticism (Kraaijenbrink et al., 2010). Figure 2.5 summarizes the relationship between resources and capabilities, strategies and sustained competitive advantage.

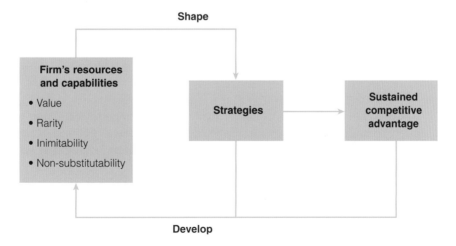

Figure 2.5 *The relationship between resources and capabilities, strategies and sustained competitive advantage*

Source: Based on Barney (1991) and Hill, Jones and Schilling (2014)

HRM as I see it

Sarah Myers
Director of Talent Management, Sky

www.sky.com

Sky entertains and excites more than 10.1 million homes through the most comprehensive multichannel, multiplatform television service in the UK and Ireland. It continues to break new ground with its own portfolio of channels, which includes Sky 1, Sky Living, Sky Arts, Sky Atlantic, Sky Sports, Sky News and Sky Movies. Sky also works with dozens of other broadcasters on the satellite platform, online and on mobile devices. Sky is now leading the UK into the age of high-definition television with Sky+ HD, and has launched Europe's first 3DTV channel, Sky 3D, as well as Sky Anytime+, its internet-delivered video on-demand service. The company is also the UK's fastest-growing broadband and home phone provider.

Sarah Myers joined Sky in 2003. She is a Fellow of the Chartered Institute of Personnel and Development and has an MSc in Human Resources from the London School of Economics. She is also a member of the HR Leadership Alliance for the Heads of Talent Management, an alumna of the School of Coaching and a member of the Editorial Board of *People Management* magazine.

Click on Sarah's picture in your ebook to watch her talking about business strategy and how it related to her work in talent management at Sky. Once you have watched the video try and answer the following questions:

1 What does Sarah mean by looking 'end to end' in talent management?
2 How is development related to talent groups at Sky?
3 In Sarah's view, how is talent linked to succession?

reflective question   Based upon your own work experience, or upon your studies of organizations, is continuous learning in the workplace more or less important for some organizations than others? If so, why?

HR strategy and organizational dynamics

This section examines a point in the SHRM debate raised earlier in this chapter, that HR strategies are not uniform, either between or within organizations, and top management rarely adopt an HR strategy for all their employee groups. Political economists speak of 'varieties of capitalism' (Hall and Soskice, 2009), acknowledging that economic institutions, levels of unionization and legal systems vary across nations. In practice, this means we see a significant variation in the way managers employ and treat people in the modern workplace. The 'variegated' nature of HR strategy is often a reflection of each employee group's power to generate value, the conditions in the labour market and the presence of a countervailing force against management in the form of trade union and legal framework. Thus, the intended HR strategy, designed by senior management to contribute to the accomplishment of the business strategy, should meet tenets of 'social legitimacy' (Boxall and Purcell, 2011, p. 19).

To explore these issues, we introduce the notion of typologies. By using conceptual frameworks, or typologies, academics are able to compare and contrast different configurations or clusters of HR practices and further develop and test theories. This method of analysis is a derivative of Max Weber's (1903–1917/1949) methodological canon called 'ideal type' (see Chapter 1). Weber built his influential theory of bureaucracy, for example, through the use of an abstraction or ideal type. The function of the ideal type is to act as a comparison with complex social realities in order to establish their divergences or similarities, to describe them, and to understand and explain them causally. An ideal type is not a description of reality, nor is it an average of something or a normative exemplar to be achieved: ideal types are logical hypothetical constructs (Bratton and Denham, 2014). The same is true of HR typologies – they are hypothetical constructs that do not necessarily exist in the workplace, but they simplify the multiple complexities of organizational life and help us to understand the nature of HR strategies.

Since the early 1990s, three models for differentiating between 'ideal types' of HR strategy have been proposed: the *control-based model*, the *resource-based model* and the *integrative model*, which combines the first two typologies.

The control-based model

This approach to modelling different types of HR strategy focuses on the complex hierarchy of managers and subordinates and control imperatives, and more specifically on managerial action to direct and monitor subordinates' role performance. According to this perspective, management structures, processes and HR strategy are instruments and techniques to control all aspects of work in order to secure a high level of labour productivity. This focus on monitoring and controlling employee behaviour as a basis for distinguishing different HR strategies has its roots in the labour process theory, a research programme inspired by Harry Braverman's (1974) *Labor and Monopoly Capital*. Adopting a Marxist framework of analysis, Braverman argued that managerial control, primarily through the application of scientific management techniques and controls embodied in machinery, had tightened in the twentieth century.

In the discourses of control strategies, the core premise is that labour's input is indeterminate. This assertion is derived from Marx's analysis of the capitalist labour process and what he referred to as the 'transformation of labour power into labour'. Put simply, when employers hire people, they have only a *potential* or a capacity to work. To ensure that each worker exercises her or his full capacity, the employer or agent (the manager) must organize the tasks, space, movement and time within which workers operate. Workers, however, have divergent interests in terms of pace of work, rewards and job security, and they engage in formal (trade unions) and informal (restrictions of output or sabotage) behaviours to counteract management job controls.

Since the late 1970s, critical workplace scholars have sought to unmask the formal realms of workplace employment relations and conflict to explore the dynamics of managerial control, consent and workers' resistance at the point of production (Thompson and Smith, 2010). They have argued that, as a set of processes and practices that regulates work and people, control strategies bear the imprint of conflicting interests between the employer and employee, a conflict that reflects the nature of the capitalist employment relationship. In an insightful review of managerial control strategies and techniques, Thompson and McHugh state that 'control is not an end in itself, but a means to transform the capacity to work established by the wage relation into profitable production' (2009, p. 105).

What alternative HR strategies have managers used to render employees' behaviour measurable and controllable? Using the core premise of indeterminacy as a framing device to guide their enquiry, researchers have identified several alternative HR strategies. Friedman (1977) articulated the control orientation through the idea of *direct control* and *responsible autonomy*. These contrasting HR strategies reflect differing logics of control depending upon the nature of the product and the labour markets. Edwards (1979) identified dominant modes of control that reflect changing competitive conditions and worker resistance. As a system of individual control, direct supervision was replaced by more complex forms of employer control: bureaucratic and technical. Bureaucratic control includes written rules and procedures covering work. Technical control includes machinery or systems – assembly line, surveillance cameras – that set the pace of work or monitor workers' performance. Edwards also argued that managers use a 'divide and rule' strategy, using gender and race, to foster managerial control. Burawoy (1979), another critical workplace scholar, categorized the development of HR strategies in terms of the transition from despotic to hegemonic regimes. The former were dominated by coercive manager–employee relations; the latter provided an 'industrial citizenship' that regulated the employment relationship through grievance and collective bargaining processes. The growth of employment in new call centres has recently given rise to a renewed focus of interest in the use of technical control systems: the electronic surveillance of the operator's role performance (Callaghan and Thompson, 2001).

The choice of HR strategy is governed by variations in organizational form (for example, size, structure and history), competitive pressures on management and the stability of labour markets. These are in turn mediated by the interplay between superordinate (managerial) and subordinate relations, the transmitter and the recipient of the control strategies involved, and resistance on the part of subordinates (Thompson and McHugh, 2009). Moreover, the variations in HR strategy are not random but reflect two management logics (Bamberger and Meshoulam, 2000). The first is the logic of direct, process-based control, in which the focus is on efficiency and cost containment (within this domain, managers need to monitor and control workers' performance carefully). The second is the logic of indirect outcomes-based control, in which the focus is on actual results (within this domain, managers need to engage workers' intellectual capital, commitment and cooperation). Thus, when managing people, control and cooperation coexist, and the extent to which there is any ebb and flow in intensity and direction between types of control will depend upon the 'multiple constituents' of the management process.

Implicit in this analysis of management control is that the logic underlying an HR strategy will tend to be consistent with an organization's competitive strategy. We are thus unlikely to find organizations adopting a Porterian cost leadership strategy along with an HR strategy grounded in an outcomes-based logic. Managers will tend to adopt process-based controls when the relations between means and ends are certain (as is typically the case among firms adopting a cost leadership strategy), and outcomes-based controls when

reflective question

Thinking about your own experience, how have managers attempted to control you? Was each task closely monitored, or was the focus on the actual outcome? What do you think of the argument that each type of competitive strategy requires a different HR strategy? Again, based on your experience, to what extent were different types of control mechanism related to the organization's product or service?

The effect of business strategy on workers' psychological health

So-called 'breastaurants', such as Hooters, are restaurants that employ scantily clad women to wait on tables in order to attract male customers. This business strategy – with employers sexually objectifying women in order to differentiate their restaurants' products from those of their competitors – has been wildly successful in the USA. Recent efforts to export the Hooters franchise to Australia have been plagued with complaints about unpaid wages, and five restaurants recently fell into voluntary administration (that is, bankruptcy protection) (Bagshaw, 2015).

While Hooters specifically regulates its workers' appearance and wardrobe in order to overtly draw attention to the workers' physical and sexual attributes, many other restaurants encourage their serving staff to wear clothing that encourage men to stare at their bodies. Until recently, there has been no evidence about the emotional and psychological effect on workers of being employed in such sexually objectifying workplaces.

A 2015 US study of workers in breastaurants found that workers experienced unwanted lewd comments, sexual advances and sexual harassment (including stalking) and sexual assault. Not surprisingly, these workers also reported experiencing anxiety, anger and depression as a result of their employment. The way their employers have designed their jobs (so that they intentionally appear as sexually desirable and available) creates situations in which they must routinely cope with customer anger when they fend off unwanted advances (Szymanski and Feltman, 2015a).

While sexual harassment is endemic to the service industry, a comparison of workers in breastaurants to workers in restaurants that did not sexually objectify workers found that breastaurant workers were far more likely to experience negative interactions with customers as well as depression and job dissatisfaction. Indeed, there was a clear inverse relationship between the degree to which workers were forced to put their bodies and sexuality on display and their job satisfaction (Szymanski and Feltman, 2015b).

Given these outcomes, it seems natural to question why women would continue to work at breastaurants if such work is so psychologically damaging. In part, it is about money. Servers at breastaurants make more

BRAND X PICTURES

money then they would in other restaurants. That workers respond to economic incentives is hardly surprising. Whether workers would make the same choice if they had other options is less clear.

(continued)

Stop! Do you agree or disagree with the assertion that employers adopt business strategies with little consideration for the impact of those strategies on workers? If not, what then explains the harmful business strategy adopted by breastaurant operators? Do you think women would continue to work at breastaurants if they could secure equally remunerative employment in non-sexually exploitative restaurants? Why or why not?

Sources and further information: For more information, see Bagshaw (2015) and Szymanski and Feltman (2015a, 2015b).

Note: This feature was written by Bob Barnetson.

From an HR perspective, it is useful to ask why employers would organize work in a manner that is both harmful to their workers and sexually degrading to women. Many worker advocates adopt a Marxist explanation for this behaviour: employer decision-making in capitalist economies is profoundly shaped by the profit imperative. Essentially, employers adopt the most profitable business strategy available to them, with little regard for the costs they place on workers (in this case, psychological injury caused by sexually objectifying work).

While characterizing employers as amoral profit-maximizers may overstate the situation, it is important for HR practitioners to recognize that human costs (which can often be outsourced onto workers) are frequently not central considerations in business strategy decisions. Indeed, employer reluctance to engage HR practitioners as strategic partners in business may (partly) reflect a desire to minimize any consideration of the human costs of business strategies.

the relationship between means and ends is uncertain (for example, with a differentiation strategy). These management logics result in different organizational designs and variations in HR strategy, which provide the source of inevitable structural tensions between management and employees. In the British sociology of work literature, therefore, it is contended that HR strategies contain inherent contradictions.

The resource-based model

As we explained, the RBV model underscores the importance of HRD. Reflecting on this perspective, 'dynamic capabilities' and flexible 'organic' organizational structures and work organization are associated with culture-oriented learning. Jacoby's (2005) engagement in the debate is insightful in that he asserts that investment in competency-building varies between employers depending on whether or not senior management are insulated from shareholder pressure demanding a short-term growth in shareholder value. The more that top managers are insulated from shareholder pressure, the higher the likelihood that they will invest in the resource-based approach to HRM. However, Jacoby's argument would appear to be undermined by Hutton's (2015b) critique of US and UK 'quarterly capitalism' that allegedly puts the short-term interest of shareholders foremost at the expense of long-term investment, including investment in employee training.

An integrative model of HR strategy

Bamberger and Meshoulam (2000) have attempted to synthesize elements of both the control and RBV models, believing that HR strategy must be explained in terms of a framework that encompasses the ebb and flow of the intensity and direction of HR strategy. They have built a model that characterizes the two main dimensions of HR strategy as involving 'acquisition and development' and 'locus of control'.

Acquisition and development is concerned with the extent to which the HR strategy develops internal human capital, as opposed to recruiting human capital from outside the organization. It therefore develops a psychological contract that nurtures social relationships and encourages mutual trust and respect (Rousseau, 1995). Thus, organizations can lean more towards 'making' their workers (by a high investment in training) or more towards 'buying' their workers from the external labour market. They call this the 'make-or-buy' aspect of HR strategy.

Locus of control is concerned with the degree to which the HR strategy focuses on monitoring employees' compliance with process-based standards. The focus here is on controlling the outcomes (the ends) themselves. This strand of thinking in HR strategy can be traced back to the ideas of Walton (1985), who made a distinction between commitment and control strategies (Hutchinson et al., 2000). As Figure 2.6 shows, these two main dimensions of HR strategy yield four different 'ideal types' of dominant HR strategy: *commitment, traditional, collaborative* and *paternalistic.*

Figure 2.6 *Categorizing HRM strategies*
Source: Based on Bamberger and Meshoulam (2000)

The *commitment* HR strategy is characterized as focusing on the internal development of employees' competencies and on outcome-based control. In contrast, the *traditional* HR strategy focuses on the external recruitment of competencies and on behavioural or process-based controls. The *collaborative* HR strategy involves the organization subcontracting work to external independent experts (for example, consultants or contractors); this provides for greater autonomy and performance evaluation primarily by measuring the end results. The *paternalistic* HR strategy offers employees learning opportunities and internal promotion in return for their compliance with process-based control mechanisms. Each HR strategy represents a distinctive HR paradigm, or set of beliefs, values and core assumptions, that guides managers' actions. Lepak and Snell (1999) have developed similar four-cell grids. It is reported that the HR strategies in the diagonal quadrants 'commitment' and 'traditional' are likely to be the most prevalent in contemporary North American workplaces (Bamberger and Meshoulam, 2000).

In summary, research suggests that an organization's HR strategy is typically 'variegated' and is strongly related both to its competitive strategy and the economic-legal institutional framework in which firms are embedded. So, for example, the traditional HR strategy (the bottom right quadrant in Figure 2.6) is most likely to be adopted by management when there is certainty over how inputs are transformed into outcomes and/or when employee performance can be closely monitored or appraised. This dominant HR strategy is more prevalent in firms with a highly routinized transformation process, priority for low cost and stable competitive environment. Under such conditions, managers use technology to control the uncertainty inherent in the labour process and insist only that workers enact the specified core standards of behaviour required to facilitate undisrupted production. Managerial behaviour in such workplaces can be summed up by the managerial edict 'You are here to work, not to think!' Implied by this approach is a focus on process-based control

A teacher is one example of a knowledge worker.

Getty/PhotoDisc

in which 'close monitoring by supervisors and efficiency wages ensures adequate work effort' (MacDuffie, 1995, quoted by Bamberger and Meshoulam, 2000, p. 60). The use of the word 'traditional' to classify this HR strategy and the use of a technological 'fix' to control employees should, however, not be viewed as a strategy only of 'industrial' worksites. Case study research on call centres, workplaces that some organizational theorists label 'post-industrial', reveals systems of technical and bureaucratic control that closely monitor and evaluate their operators (Sewell, 1998; Thompson and McHugh, 2009).

The other dominant HR strategy, the *commitment* HR strategy (the top left quadrant in Figure 2.6), is most likely to be found in organizations in which: (1) management lacks a full knowledge of all aspects of the labour process and/or the ability to monitor closely or evaluate the efficacy of the worker's contribution to the final product or service (as seen, for example, with research and development and healthcare professionals); and/or (2) the predictability of, and knowledge about, the external environment are low (Swart et al., 2004). This typically refers to 'knowledge work'.

In such organizational contexts, managers must rely on subordinates to cope with the uncertainties inherent in the labour process and can thus only monitor and evaluate the final outcomes. This HR strategy is associated with a set of HR practices that aim to develop highly committed and flexible people, internal markets that reward commitment with promotion and a degree of job security, and a 'participative' leadership style that forges a commonality of interest and mobilizes consent to the organization's goals (Hutchinson et al., 2000).

As others have noted, workers experiencing such a work regime and HR strategy do not always need to be overtly controlled because they effectively 'control themselves' (Bratton, 1992; Thompson and McHugh, 2009). To develop cooperation and common interests, an effort–reward exchange based upon investment in learning, internal promotion and internal equity is typically used (Bamberger and Meshoulam, 2000). In addition, such organizations 'mobilize' employee consent through culture strategies, including the popular notion of the 'learning organization'. As one of us has argued elsewhere (Bratton, 2001, p. 341):

> For organizational controllers, workplace learning provides a compelling ideology in the twenty-first century, with an attractive metaphor for mobilizing worker commitment and sustainable competitiveness … [And] the learning organization paradigm can be construed as a more subtle way of shaping workers' beliefs and values and behaviour.

Critiquing SHRM and models of HR strategy

In the last decade, the discourse of SHRM and HR strategy has been 'problematized'. Existing conceptualizations of SHRM are based upon the mainstream rational perspective of managerial decision-making – definable and coherent acts of linear planning, choice and action. Critical workplace scholars have challenged these core assumptions, arguing that strategic decisions are not necessarily the outcome of rational calculation. The assumption that a firm's business-level strategy and HR system have a logical, linear relationship is questionable given the evidence that strategy formulation is informal, politically charged and subject to complex contingency factors, and that key decision-makers often lack information, time and 'cognitive capacity' (Bamberger and Meshoulam, 2000; Mintzberg et al., 1998; Monks and McMackin, 2001; Whittington, 1993). As such, the notion of consciously aligning business strategy and HR strategy applies only to the 'classical' approach to strategy (Legge, 2005). Those who question the classical textbook account of strategic management argue that the image of the corporate manager as a reflective planner and strategist is a myth. Management's strategic actions are more likely to be uncoordinated, frenetic, ad hoc and fragmented' (see, for example, Hales, 1986; Powell and Wakeley, 2003).

Another area of critique is the focus on the connection between external market strategies and the HR function. It is argued that contingency analysis relies exclusively on external marketing strategies (how the firm competes) and disregards the internal operational strategies (how the firm is managed) that influence HR practices and performance (Purcell, 1999). Work motivation and commitment are, as ever, central to managing employment relations, but strategizing 'best fit' or 'best practice' often disregards 'employee interests'. In coping with internal contradictions, the organization not only has to fit HR practices to competitive strategy, but must also integrate business and employee needs (Boxall and Purcell, 2011). In an industry in which a flexible, customized product range and high quality are the key to profitability, a firm can adopt a manufacturing strategy that, via 'high-performance work systems', allows for far fewer employees but within a commitment HR strategy regime. This was the strategy at Flowpak Engineering (Bratton, 1992). In this particular case, the technology and manufacturing strategy became the key intervening variable between the overall business strategy and the HR strategy. Furthermore, a simple SHRM model privileges only one step in the full circuit of industrial capital (Kelly, 1985). To put it another way, conceptions of SHRM look only at the realization of profitability within product markets rather than at the complex contingent variables that constitute the full transformation process.

Within the context of current economic globalization, we also need to view competitive posture as 'multidimensional', with resilient companies being agile at cost leadership and differentiation (Boxall and Purcell, 2011; Purcell, 1999). Furthermore, the sheer size of global markets and the rate of technological obsolescence encourage 'strategic alliances' between rival giants of industry, and between multinational corporations and complementary business partnerships (Hoogvelt, 2001), that can result in an unpredictable variety of control strategies not only between, but also within, organizations (Storey, 1983). In such contexts, managing people is less likely to be based on aligning HR practices to, in Porter's terminology, a 'single strategy' (Boxall and Purcell, 2011).

Social systems are inevitably open and frequently complex and messy (Sayer, 2000). In order to make sense of managerial actions, researchers have to rely on the abstraction and careful conceptualization of multiple practices and forces. But, as Sayer argues, if researchers 'divide what is in practice indivisible, or if they conflate what are different and separable components, then problems are likely to result' (p. 19). Unfortunately, in studies of SHRM, the conceptualization of managerial control can be problematic. The basic premise of the typologies of the HR strategy approach is that a dominant HR strategy is strongly related to a specific competitive strategy. Modelling suggests that the commitment HR strategy is most likely to be adopted when managers use a generic differentiation strategy. This might be true, but the idea that a commitment HR strategy follows from a real or perceived 'added-value' competitive strategy is more difficult in practice. It is misleading to conflate managerial actions and assume that they are not influenced by the indeterminacy of the employment contract and by how to close the 'gap' between an employee's potential and actual performance level. Reflecting on this problem, Colling (1995, p. 29) correctly emphasizes that 'added-value [differentiation] strategies do not preclude or prevent the use of managerial control over employees ... few companies are able to operationalize added-value programmes without cost-constraints and even fewer can do so for very long'. Others have acknowledged that 'It is utopian to think that control can be completely surrendered' in the 'postmodern' work organization (Cloke and Goldsmith, 2002, p. 162).

Consistent with our focus on paradox, management's decisions and actions create potential 'strategic tensions' (Boxall and Purcell, 2011; Thompson and McHugh, 2009; Watson, 1999). Thus, one strategic decision and action might undermine another strategic goal. Complying with the imperatives of a global free market, there is, for example, a tendency in a recession for corporate management to strive for profits by mass redundancies – so-called 'downsizing' – and by applying more intensive performance outcomes to those remaining at unit level. This pattern of action constitutes a strategy even though it manifests a disjunction between organizational design and employment relations. As Purcell (1989, 1995) points out, an organization pursuing a strategy of acquisition and downsizing might 'logically' adopt an HR strategy that includes the compulsory lay-off of non-core employees and, for the identifiable core of employees with rare attributes, a compensation system based on performance results. In practice, the RBV approach predicts a sharp differentiation within organizations 'between those with key competencies, knowledge and valued organizational memory, and those more easily replaced or disposed of' (Purcell, 1999, p. 36). In such a case, the business strategy and HR strategy might 'fit', but, as Legge (2005, p. 128) points out, these HR practices are unlikely to lead to employee commitment and will cause a misfit with employee development or 'soft' HRM values. Thus, achieving the goal of an 'external fit' of business and HR strategy can contradict the goal of employee commitment and cooperation.

The 'best-fit' metaphor for SHRM contends that HR strategy is more effective when it is premeditated to fit specific contingencies in the organization's competitive or political context. It is important to emphasize that, however committed a group of managers might be to a particular HR strategy (for example, the commitment HR strategy), there are external conditions and internal 'structural contradictions' at work that will constrain management action (Boxall and Purcell, 2011; Streeck, 1987). All organizations are embedded in national cultures, and HR strategy will therefore be shaped by economic, technological, political and social factors. Within national boundaries, organizations often have more than one HR system. The kind of analysis explored here is nicely summed up by Hyman's pessimistic pronouncement that 'there is no "one best way" of managing these contradictions, only different routes to partial failure' (1987, quoted in Thompson and McHugh, 2009, p. 110). But reflecting on the SHRM discourse, whatever insights the different perspectives afford into the strategic management process, critical perspectives point out that, as is the case with 'charismatic leadership', 'strategic' is no longer fashionable in management thought and discourse, having gone from 'buzzword to boo-word' (Bratton and Denham, 2014; Thompson and McHugh, 2009, p. 113).

case study

Zuvan Winery

The setting

During the last decade, the wine industry has emerged as an important economic driver for South Africa. According to the South African Wine Industry Information and Systems, the wine industry adds 26.2 billion Rand (US$3.3 billion) to that country's gross domestic product every year. However, the growth of this vital industry has raised concerns as conservationists are worried that some of the region's most vulnerable natural habitats could be targeted in the quest for vineyard expansion.

Located in the Cape Province of South Africa, the Cape Floral Kingdom is one of these areas. As one of the richest plant areas on earth, it has earned international recognition as a global biodiversity hotspot and has been established as South Africa's newest World Heritage Site. It is also where approximately 90 per cent of South Africa's wine production occurs. Following an initial study by the Botanical Society of South Africa and Conservation International, the wine industry and the conservation sector embarked on a pioneering partnership to conserve the rich biodiversity of the Cape Floral Kingdom. The programme they created, called the Biodiversity and Wine Initiative (BWI), aims to:

- Prevent further loss of habitat in critical conservation priority sites
- Increase the total area set aside as a natural habitat in contractually protected areas
- Promote changes in farming practices that enhance the suitability of vineyards as a habitat for biodiversity and reduce farming practices that have negative impacts on biodiversity, both in the vineyards and in the surrounding natural habitat, through the sound management of all the natural resources and the maintenance of functioning ecosystems.

Since 80 per cent of the Cape Floral Kingdom is privately owned, landowner participation in conservation efforts is essential. The BWI lays out specific criteria for wine producers to participate in the programme. The producers must have at least two hectares of natural or restored natural area on the farm that can be conserved, and new vineyards must not be developed in these areas. In addition, they must be registered with the Integrated Production of Wine scheme, which will require compliance with industry-prescribed environmental

© iStockphoto.com/Don Bayley

responsibilities. Although producers might not have implemented all the required management techniques for retaining biodiversity (such as alien clearing, erosion control, rehabilitation of wetlands and rivers, appropriate fire management, etc.), they must have time-based plans and schedules in place to ensure a process of continual improvement.

The problem

South Africa's wine industry employs nearly 276,000 workers, with 58 per cent of employees considered unskilled, 29 per cent semi-skilled and 13 per cent skilled. While most employees receive fair and competitive compensation, training and skills development programmes are lacking, and more than half the wineries in South Africa do not have any dedicated HR resources.

Kamali Masaku heads up the Zuvan Winery, with vineyards that have been owned by his family for several decades. Kamali is one of the landowners in the Cape Floral Kingdom that the BWI has targeted for participation in their programme. Kamali is interested in sustainability and wants to work towards his winery meeting the BWI's criteria. He is, however, concerned that, in order to comply with the BWI's environmental standards and to continue to succeed in the highly competitive wine industry, he will need to have employees with current technical knowledge and skills related to sustainable farming practices. With nearly 65 per cent of his workers considered to be unskilled,

(continued)

Kamali must now make the decision either to invest in the development of their skills or to recruit qualified help from outside his current labour force, although these new employees might demand higher wages. Kamali wants to be sure that his approach to this problem meets with the new business strategy he is about to embark on, with some promise of growth for his winery to cover his expected increased costs.

The assignment

Working either alone or in a study group, prepare a report drawing on this chapter and other recommended material that addresses the following:

1 For employees to be committed to the strategy, they need to understand the business case for sustainable wine production. Why is sustainability important to Zuvan Winery, and what can Kamali do to pursue sustainability for the company's and the community's good?
2 Which HR strategy (commitment, collaborative, paternalistic or traditional) is most likely to be currently used by wine producers in South Africa and other developing countries? Explain your answer.
3 Which HR strategy would be the most effective in helping Kamali with the challenges he will face in pursuing a sustainable approach to wine production? Why?

Essential reading

Browning, V. and Edgar, F. (2004) Reactions to HRM: an employee perspective from South Africa and New Zealand. *Journal of Management and Organization*, 10(2): 1–13.

Budhwar, P. and Yaw, D. (2001) *Human Resource Management in Developing Countries*. London: Routledge.

Grobler, P. and Warnich, S. (2005) Human Resource *Management in South Africa*. Hampshire: Thomson Learning.

Kamoche, K., Debrah, Y. A., Horwitz, F. M. and Muuka, G. N. (2004) *Managing Human Resource Management in Africa*. London: Routledge.

Kidwell, R. and Fish, A. (2007) High-performance human resource practices in Australian family businesses: preliminary evidence from the wine industry. *International Entrepreneurship and Management Journal*, 3(1): 1–14.

For more on the Cape Floral Kingdom and the BWI, go to www.business-biodiversity.eu/default. asp?Menue=155&News=982.

Note: This case study was written by Lori Rilkoff.

 Visit the companion website at **www.palgravehighered.com/bg-hrm-6e** for guidelines on writing reports.

summary

➤ This chapter has examined different levels of strategic management, defining strategic management as a 'pattern of decisions and actions' undertaken by the upper echelon of the company.

➤ Strategic decisions are concerned with change and the achievement of superior performance, and they involve strategic choices. In multidivisional companies, strategy formulation takes place at three levels – corporate, business and functional – to form a hierarchy of strategic decision-making. Corporate and business-level strategies, as well as environmental pressures, dictate the choice of HR policies and practices.

➤ Strategic management plans at corporate level and business level provide the context within which HR plans are developed and implemented. These HR plans provide a map for managers to follow in order to fulfil the core responsibilities of the HR function, which involves managing employee assignments, competencies, behaviours and motivation. These prime responsibilities of the HR function constitute the 'four-task model' of HRM.

➤ When reading the descriptive and prescriptive strategic management texts, there is a great temptation to be smitten by what appears to be the linear and absolute rationality of the strategic management process. We draw attention to the more critical literature that recognizes that HR strategic options are, at any given time, partially constrained by the outcomes of corporate and business decisions, the current distribution of power within the organization and the ideological values of the key decision-makers.

➤ A core assumption underlying much of the SHRM research and literature is that each of the main types of generic competitive strategy used by organizations (for example, the cost leadership or differentiation strategy) is associated with a different approach to managing people, that is, with a different HR strategy.

➤ We critiqued here the 'best-fit' and 'best-practice' models of SHRM on both conceptual and empirical grounds. It was noted that, in the globalized economy with market turbulence, the 'fit' metaphor may not be appropriate when flexibility and a need for organizations to learn more quickly than their competitors seem to be the key to sustainable competitiveness. We also emphasized how the goal of aligning a Porterian low-cost business strategy with an HRM strategy can contradict the core goal of employee commitment. In addition, it was noted that 'best-practice' may serve shareholder or executive interests but may be bad for workers' and society's interests.

➤ The resource-based SHRM model, which places an emphasis on a company's HR endowments as a strategy for sustained competitive advantage, was outlined. In spite of the interest in workplace learning, there seems, however, little empirical evidence to suggest that many firms have adopted this 'soft' HR strategic model.

➤ As part of corporate strategy, we explored the concept of environmental sustainability, which we defined as a process of change in which the exploitation of resources, the direction of investments, the orientation of technological development, and institutional change are all in harmony and enhance both current and future potential to meet human needs and aspirations.

review questions

1 What is meant by 'strategy'? Explain the meaning of 'first-order' and 'second-order' strategies.

2 Explain Purcell's statement that 'trends in corporate strategy have the potential to render the ideals of HRM unobtainable'.

3 What is meant by an 'environmental sustainability' strategy?

4 Why must successful corporate strategies be consistent with the firm's external environment and with its internal environment?

5 'Business-level strategies may be constrained by HR issues but rarely seem to be designed to influence them.' Discuss.

6 What does a 'resource-based' SHRM model of competitive advantage mean? What are the implications for HRM of this business strategy?

further reading

Reading these articles and chapters can help you gain a better understanding and potentially a higher grade for your HRM assignment.

➤ Mainstream notions of strategy are examined in Robert Grant's (2013) *Contemporary Strategic Analysis* (8th edn). Chichester: John Wiley & Sons; T. J. Andersen (2013) *Short Introduction to Strategic Management*, Cambridge: Cambridge University Press; and E. Ferlie and E. Ongaro's (2015) *Strategic Management in Public Service Organizations*, London: Routledge, which examines the case that some models of strategic management have enhanced applicability to many UK contemporary public sector organizations.

The link between SHRM and an organization's survival and sustainable competitive advantage is further explored in:

➤ Allen, M. and Wright, P. (2008) Strategic management and HRM. In P. Boxall, J. Purcell and P. Wright (eds) *The Oxford Handbook of Human Resource Management* (pp. 88–107). Oxford: Oxford University Press.

➤ Barney, J. B. and Clark, D. N. (2007) *Resource-based Theory: Creating and Sustaining Competitive Advantage*. Oxford: Oxford University Press.

➤ Boselie, P. (2010) *Strategic Human Resource Management: A Balanced Approach*. London: McGraw-Hill.

➤ Boxall, P. and Purcell, P. (2011) *Strategy and Human Resource Management* (3rd edn). London: Palgrave Macmillan.

➤ Kamoche, K. (1996) Strategic human resource management within a resource-capability view of the firm. *Journal of Management Studies*, 33(2): 213–33.

➤ Storey, J. (2008) What is strategic HRM? In J. Storey (ed.) *Human Resource Management: A Critical Text* (3rd edn) (pp. 59–78). London: Thompson Learning.

vocabulary checklist for ESL students

 Click here in your interactive ebook for a list of HRM terminology and vocabulary that has appeared in this chapter.

Visit the online resource centre at **www.palgravehighered.com/bg-hrm-6e** for lots of extra resources to help you get to grips with this chapter, including study tips, HRM skills development guides, summary lecture notes, tips for English as a Second Language (ESL) students and more.

chapter 3

HRM outcomes and line management

SuperStock

objectives

After studying this chapter, you should be able to:

1 Explain the importance of measuring the HRM contribution

2 Describe some variables used to measure the value added of HRM

3 Critically evaluate research on the HRM–performance relationship

4 Demonstrate an understanding of the role of line managers in the contemporary workplace

5 Explain the problems and tensions of devolving HRM to line managers

Amazon and Sports Direct are well-known retail giants, with revenues increasing year on year. But the *New York Times* exposé on employment conditions at Amazon claimed that callous managers were guilty of cruel employment practices. In one anecdote, an employee with breast cancer was allegedly put on a 'performance improvement plan' (Elliott, The Guardian, 2015, p. 23). Sports Direct billionaire founder Mike Ashley, when recently cross-examined by MPs about the sexual harassment of female staff, described the accused managers as 'sexual predators … They're repugnant, they're disgusting' (Goodley, The Guardian, 2016, p. 1). This exposé focuses on two themes we cover in this chapter: measuring business performance and the role of line managers in delivering HRM to the workforce.

introduction

Establishing a strong association between strategic human resource management (HRM) and organizational performance (OP) has become a principal area of study over the past two decades. Indeed, this research agenda was once described as the 'holy grail' of HRM. Several explanations have been offered for why this area of research has become so fashionable. Conclusive evidence of the 'bottom-line' contribution of HRM locates the subject, and HRM academics, in business schools on a par with faculty teaching the more quantitatively oriented subjects. By demonstrating measurable outcomes, the position of the human resources (HR) specialist within the organization is also enhanced at a time when the HR function itself is being threatened with marginalization by outsourcing. Research and debate on the strategic HRM (SHRM) and performance causal chain also emphasizes that line managers (LMs) are closely involved in delivering HRM policies (Storey, 1992, 2001); indeed, one persistent mantra is that what constitutes effective HRM policies may well be partly due to the attitude and actions of LMs.

The HRM–performance debate has been intense and often inconclusive among academics. Some contend that the research is too narrowly focused on measures of economic performance at the expense of employee well-being (Delaney and Godard, 2001), making the 'performative intent' of the research an 'ill-fated project' (Delbridge and Keenoy, 2010, p. 804). Others emphasize the importance of contingencies related to context, and the importance of analysing how the 'social relations of productivity' mediates the relationship between specific HR practices and workplace performance in particular contexts (Edwards et al., 2002). Against this backcloth, this chapter begins by examining the rationale of linking the HR function with OP. As a preliminary step towards understanding the effects of HR practices on performance, it discusses a variety of conceptual and methodological concerns. It also examines the role of LMs and reviews the evidence on the rationale and challenges of devolving HRM to LMs; in so doing, it underscores the importance of workplace context when studying the relationships between HR practices, employee flexibility (EF) and performance and OP.

Rationale for evaluating HRM

The current debate on the effects of SHRM on OP has a long academic lineage that predates the modern HRM canon. In the twentieth century, employers and business pundits bemoaned the low productivity of British workers and usually identified various 'restrictive practices' emanating from trade unions as the main culprit behind poor performance (Ahlstrand, 1990; Nichols, 1986). The 'trade unions and productivity' debate, although dominant during the 1960s and 70s, has receded in the twenty-first century as both union membership and union power have significantly declined (van Wanrooy et al., 2013a).

The focus shifted in the 1990s to investigating the impact on business performance of using the HRM paradigm. In Beer et al.'s (1984) canonical model, HR outcomes are seen as having longer term positive effects on individual well-being, organizational effectiveness and societal well-being. The interest in the SHRM–performance nexus also mirrors enthusiasm for the concept of the 'high-performance work system' (HPWS). It is claimed that these new work models can deliver comparative advantage because an integrated 'bundle' of HR practices will have positive, synergistic effects on performance (MacDuffie, 1995). Thus, in terms of improving business performance, designing a bundle or configuration of HR practices becomes *the* issue (Betcherman et al., 1994).

The drive to measure the effects of HRM on performance was given an added boost when management commentators advocated that the HR function should move beyond its administrative role to a strategic 'added-value' role (Boxall and Purcell, 2003; Paauwe, 2004; Ulrich and Beatty, 2001). As Pfeffer (1994, p. 57) argues, 'In a world in which financial results are measured, a failure to measure human resource policy and practice implementation dooms this to second-class status, oversight, neglect, and potential failure.' When HR practitioners are increasingly trying to collaborate with line management, it is ever more apparent that HR specialists need to be able to demonstrate in financial terms the benefits of different HR strategies. This rationale is captured by Fitz-enz's (2000, p. 4) blunt statement that 'if we don't know how to measure our primary value-producing asset, we can't manage it'. However, it is acknowledged that the challenges of measuring the contribution of 'human capital' to the firm's 'bottom line' is 'sometimes subtle, occasionally mysterious, and at times very convincing' (Phillips, 1996a, p. 6). We shall explore later in this chapter whether evidence of the positive effects on performance derived from strategic HR practices is convincing.

reflective question

> According to the late Peter Drucker, 'You can't manage what you can't measure.' At a time when so many people are engaged in so-called knowledge work, how valid is this maxim when strictly applied to managing people?

HRM web links

> Visit the online resource centre at **www.palgravehighered.com/bg-hrm-6e** for information on carrying out research on the relationship between HRM and OP.

Demonstrating the HRM–performance relationship

The research agenda has focused on the search for causal relationships between clusters or bundles of best HR practices and competing performance outcomes (Astakhova and Porter, 2015; Bal and Dorenbosch, 2015; Betcherman et al., 1994; Bou-Llusar et al., 2016; Huselid, 1995; Ichniowski et al., 1996; MacDuffie 1995; Paeleman and Vanacker, 2015; Youndt et al., 1996) (see also HRM in practice 3.1). Establishing the validity of the hypothesized relationships between HR bundles, EF and OP is highly complex (Bou-Llusar et al., 2016; Stavrou et al., 2010). Despite burgeoning research, considerable ambiguity remains over the casual paths of that relationship, ranging from universalistic to contingency

HRM and performance: evidence from the Middle East

© iStockphoto.com/shironosov

One of the challenges of evaluating the impact of HRM on OP is that social and management scientists are often conservative when drawing conclusions. This conservativism is built into the scientific process of formulating, testing and modifying hypotheses. For example, Turkish researchers hypothesized that employee participation in decision-making and problem-solving is associated with a firm's market and financial performance. While the researchers did find a correlation between employee participation and the firm's performance, the correlation was not deemed to be statistically significant (Gurbuz and Mert, 2011).

How do we reconcile the fact that there was a correlation (i.e. increased employee participation was associated with higher OP), but that this finding was not statistically significant? Statistical significance can be a tricky concept to grasp. In everyday conversation, calling something 'significant' means that it is important. In statistical analysis, significance is a measure of how confident researchers are that the result has not been caused by just random chance. That is to say, statistical significance is a measure of the reliability of our conclusions: if we repeated this analysis with data from another workplace, would we get the same result?

So, in saying that these findings about employee participation and OP are not statistically significant, the researchers are not saying the findings are not important. Instead, they are saying they are concerned that the effect might be the result of random chance, and thus the effect they see may not be real. The likelihood that a correlation is the result of a real effect can be estimated statistically. The mathematical probability that an effect is real ranges from 0 (no chance) to 1 (absolute certainty) and is called the 'p-value.' A p-value of 0.1 means there is a 10% chance that the result has been caused by chance alone. Typically, a p-value of less than 0.05 (a 5% chance of random cause) is considered (barely) statistically significant. When $p<0.01$ (a less than 1% chance of random cause), the results are considered to be statistically significant (i.e. there is a real effect) (Institute for Work and Health, 2005).

The reason researchers place such importance on statistical significance is that unreliable results can give rise to false-positive and false-negative findings.

A false-positive result occurs when we conclude that a difference or relationship exists when it does not. Conversely, a false-negative result occurs when we conclude that no difference or relationship exists when it does. False positives and false negatives in research can result in the consumers of research making poor choices in the real world. For example, saying a drug is effective at treating a disease when it actually is not can harm patients by subjecting them to an ineffective course of treatment. These kinds of consequences mean that researchers are often very conservative in drawing conclusions.

This high standard of proof – which may be appropriate in health research due to the potential consequences of false positives and negatives – can act as a barrier to demonstrating the impact of HRM on OP. In short, if a researcher is not 95% confident that results reflect a real effect, the conclusions will be that there is no statistically significant effect. There is no really compelling explanation for using the $p<0.05$ threshold (it is simply accepted practice in statistical analysis), but this cultural practice means that researchers who use a more generous threshold (for example $p<0.1$) are unlikely to have their research published because of this scholarly norm.

Stop! What does this explanation of statistical significance tell you about research findings regarding the relationship between HRM and OP that are statistically significant? Conversely, what questions might you now ask about research findings that are not statistically significant?

Sources and further information: For further information, see Gurbuz and Mert (2011) and Institute for Work and Health (2005).

Note: This feature was written by Bob Barnetson.

(Delery and Doty, 1996). In this section, we summarize selective studies to gain an understanding of the nature of the HRM–performance relationship.

Most of the empirical studies have found a positive association between HR practices and business performance measures. MacDuffie's (1995) landmark publication found strong support for a positive relationship between commitment or high-performance HR practices and intermediate outcomes for individual workers (for example, turnover and sales) and the organization's financial outcomes (market value and profits). In fact, 'A one standard deviation increase in practices is associated with a relative 7.05 per cent decrease in employee turnover (MacDuffie, 1995, p. 667). MacDuffie observed that 'high-performance' HR practices had two major dimensions: workers' skills and work motivation (Table 3.1). The study provided some insight into the 'best-fit' theory, suggesting that although internal fit – the degree to which complementary HR practices are implemented as a cluster – does have a significant and positive effect on financial outcomes, external fit – the degree to which HR strategy is aligned with business strategy – does not (Bamberger and Meshoulam, 2000). Huselid's (1995) findings (Table 3.1) were replicated by Patterson et al.'s (1997) UK study.

Table 3.1 *The two dimensions of high-performance HR practices*

Worker skills and internal processes	Employee motivation
Information-sharing	Performance appraisals to determine pay
Job analysis	Performance to determine promotion
Internal hiring	Qualified applicants per position
Regular attitude surveys	
Quality of work–life programmes	
Participation teams	
Profit-sharing	
Training	
Formal grievance procedures	
Employment tests for hiring	

Source: Republished with permission of Academy of Management, from Huselid, M.A. (1995) The impact of Human Resource Management practices on turnover, productivity and corporate financial performance. Academy of Management Journal, 38(3): 635–72; permission conveyed through Copyright Clearance Center, Inc. Copyright © 1995 Academy of Management.

Pil and MacDuffie (1996) provided further support for the 'internal fit' perspective, suggesting that when team working and complementary HR practices are introduced simultaneously, 'not only does new work practice induce an incremental improvement in performance, but so do the complementary practices' (p. 428). When a new work practice, such as self-managed work teams, is introduced, the greatest positive effect on performance over a period of time – the so-called 'Huselid curve' – will therefore occur when a complementary bundle of HR practices accompanies the new work regime.

Youndt et al.'s (1996) research combined a cluster of HR practices into two indexes – labelled the 'administrative HR system' and the 'human-capital-enhancing HR system' – and found that these impacted positively on OP when the HR practices were aligned with the organization's business strategy. Delaney and Huselid (1996, p. 965) note in another study that 'progressive HRM practices, including selectivity in staffing, training, and incentive compensation, are positively related to perceptual measures of organizational performance'. Betcherman et al. (1994) found a statistically significant association between 'new'

HR practices and lower unit costs. Interestingly, the authors provide support for the idea that context is an important factor. What they call 'innovative' HR practices operate best in certain workplace 'environments'. The more intangible variables, such as 'progressive decision-making' and 'social responsibility', impacted more significantly on performance outcomes than did more tangible incentive-pay plans. Their results suggest (Betcherman et al., 1994, p. 72) that:

Innovative [HRM] practices and programs on their own are not enough to substantially improve performance. What seems more important is that they be introduced into a supportive work environment.

A study by Wright et al. (2003) found evidence that 'progressive' HR practices improve operational performance and profitability at least in part through enhanced employee commitment to the organization. Separate studies by Collings et al. (2010) and Peña and Villasalero (2010) support the contingency 'best-fit' approach. In Peña and Villasalero's (2010) study of the Spanish banking sector, the relationship between HR and OP was found to be moderated by the bank's business strategy: 'There is no one best way to manage human resources without considering the role of business strategy' (p. 2882).

Increasing interest in HPWSs has generated a plethora of research on the relationships between HPWS regimes (see Chapter 13), EF and OP – see, among others, Bou-Llusar et al., 2016; Danford et al., 2008. A key premise of the HPWS is that increased performance stems from employees engaging in informal learning, discretionary decision-making and multitasking. Findlay et al. (2000) found evidence that team working 'increased opportunities for creativity, responsibility and use of worker knowledge' (p. 238). They also found an 'abuse of flexibility' that caused work intensification. The study by Konzelmann et al. (2006) argues that securing full cooperation from employees is required if a cluster of better HR practices is to increase performance. The implications of this observation are profound: 'What secures positive HRM outcomes are, for workers, the quality of consultation and personnel policy [, and in] securing these objectives corporate governance has an important part to play' (Konzelmann et al., 2006, p. 560).

Embedding performance

Reviewing some of the seminal studies on the HRM–performance relationship, Ichniowski et al. (1996) and Coombs and Bierly (2006) concluded that complementary bundles of HR practices gave rise to superior output and quality performances, and that the magnitude of these performance effects was 'large'. Moreover, Ichniowski et al. (1996, p. 32, emphasis added) observed that:

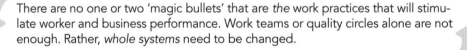

There are no one or two 'magic bullets' that are *the* work practices that will stimulate worker and business performance. Work teams or quality circles alone are not enough. Rather, *whole systems* need to be changed.

As we have already emphasized, organizations and management practices are deeply 'embedded' in the wider society and national institutional environments in which they operate. This is where societal effects are most significant. The point here concerns the ways in which national institutions and culture establish a terrain on which HR strategies may have their effects. The findings from seminal US studies on the HRM–performance relationship may not be generalizable to a polyethnic Europe (Den Hartog and Verburg, 2004; Paauwe and Boselie, 2003). Arguably, in the post-banking crisis era, the effects of which continue to reverberate throughout Europe, drawing attention to the need for government regulation strengthens the need for a change in HR policies and practices.

Looking to European studies, Addison's et al. (2000) findings suggest that, in unionized workplaces, the link between employee involvement (EI) and financial performance is likely to be less clear cut because EI arrangements reflect union power rather than a competitive response to external factors. Addison's et al. study predicts that EI in non-union regimes in Britain will yield positive economic results for the firm, but the union–EI nexus is associated with negative outcomes. Finally, the German evidence indicated that mandatory EI is associated with higher productivity in larger organizations (those employing more than 100 workers) and lower productivity gains in smaller workplaces. Despite these interesting findings, the studies have limited value in demonstrating the relationship between HR strategy and performance because they examined only one HR practice and did not quantify the effect of coherent clusters of HR practices on overall OP. The results therefore need to be read with some caution.

Statistical studies have established causal connections between HR practices and outcome variables. Den Hartog and Verburg's (2004) study of firms in the Netherlands generated data showing a correlation between HR practices associated with HPWSs and culture orientation. Basing their study on a questionnaire completed by senior HR managers and chief executives from 175 Dutch enterprises, the researchers noted increased commitment that resulted in Dutch workers doing more than was typically required in their contract or job description – going beyond contract – which increased economic outcomes. Importantly, work motivation was related to a specific set of HR practices tailored to each specific context: 'The set of practices labelled "Employee skill direction" ... were positively related to workers' willingness to go beyond contract and perceived economic performance of the firm and negatively to absenteeism' (Den Hartog and Verburg, 2004, pp. 74–5). Furthermore, autonomy showed a positive relationship with willingness to go beyond contract, and profit-sharing correlated positively with perceived economic performance, as did pay-for-performance. Den Hartog and Verburg found that the effect of employee skill on innovation was statistically significantly ($p = 0.41$), as was the effect of employee skills on goals ($p = 0.42$). However, employee skill did not significantly affect the firm's performance.

HRM web links → Visit the online resource centre at **www.palgravehighered.com/bg-hrm-6e** for more examples of statistical techniques used to compute the mean differences and measures of association between variables.

Den Hartog and Verburg's (2004) quantitative study emphasized the importance of the context in which companies and HRM systems operated. In the Netherlands, the employment relationship is highly regulated, union density and involvement is more extensive, unlike, for example, the situation in the USA and the UK, and Dutch labour laws ensure employee participation in workplace decision-making. Thus, the idea of a Dutch firm adopting a universal cluster of best HR practices to gain a competitive advantage is more problematic because these firms have less leeway to distinguish themselves from their competitive rivals. Although Dutch laws set the boundaries, the study provides evidence that managers can, within these boundaries, design HR practices to suit the specific needs

HR 'can lower NHS death rates'

The research focus on whether strategic HR practices can demonstrably contribute to the performance of an organization has been described as 'the HRM holy grail' (Purcell and Kinnie, 2008). In the context of changing demographics, the so-called 'grey tsunami' and rising healthcare costs, evidence of an unambiguous causal relationship between HR practices and hospital 'outcomes' would give greater legitimacy to HR professionals. In the UK, West et al. (2002) report a direct link between the quality of HR practices and patient mortality:

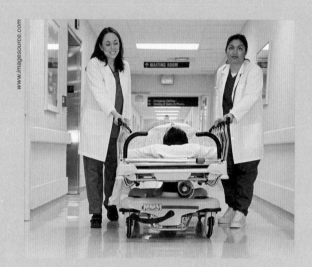

> *Human resource (HR) directors from sixty-one acute hospitals in England (Hospital Trusts) completed questionnaires or interviews exploring HR practices and procedures…The findings revealed strong associations between HR practices and patient mortality generally. The extent and sophistication of appraisal in the hospitals was particularly strongly related, but there were links too with the sophistication of training for staff, and also with the percentages of staff working in teams…*

> *Recent research shows that working in teams in health services is associated with lower levels of stress; that the quality of teamworking processes is linked to ratings of effectiveness and innovation in quality of patient care in primary health care and community mental health care teams; and that multi-disciplinarity in teams is strongly associated with innovation in patient care in primary health care (Borrill et al., 2000)… Accordingly, in the study… patient mortality data were related to these HRM practices.*

Andrew Foster, the HR director for the NHS Executive at the time of the report, highlighted the significance of the findings, as 'With a fixed budget you need an evidence-based case for investment in people issues' (Roberts, 2001).

This study is particularly interesting in that it uses outcomes different from those found in most other studies; however, the method of collecting the observations always needs to be carefully scrutinized. There is, for example, a tendency for some researchers to rely on single indicators of outcomes, to ignore 'multiple' moderating variables, and to use performance indicators across dissimilar workplaces or departments with no regard for how appropriate they are. In this

study, the authors identified certain limitations owing to the sample size and the variability of the sample size between analyses. Although HR Directors from sixty-one hospitals were interviewed, only twenty-one hospitals provided all the required information. Evidently, a hospital respondent may have incomplete knowledge of HR practices. In assessing the links between HRM and death rates, critical scrutiny would also ask whether the researchers were able to control for social variables sufficiently.

Stop! Why is this study considered important? What are the limitations of using a survey to gather data in order to explain the causal links between HR practices and health-related outcomes? Provide an example of variable(s) in a hospital that might cause you to question the research findings. Many non-profit organizations have attempted to measure the effectiveness of HR practices. Why do you think they have done this? In your view, which HR interventions would be most effective in improving healthcare, and why?

Sources and further information: This feature is based on West et al. (2002) and Roberts (2001). For background information to help consider this study, see Gerhart (2008), and Purcell and Kinnie (2008).

Note: This feature was written by John Bratton.

of their organization. The authors, however, acknowledged that future research should focus more on hard economic data rather than on managers' 'perceptions' of performance. The survey study by Astakhova and Porter (2015) focused on the effects of individual factors on firms' performance. The researchers examined the interaction effects between different types of employee's work passion, perceived 'fit' inside the organization and performance. Their results indicated the importance of harmonious work passion related to performance, and concluded that managers responsible for recruitment and selection decisions should take into account not only workers' skills and abilities, but also candidates' passion for the activities involved in doing the job (Astakhova and Porter, 2015).

Buyens and De Vos (2001) conducted a qualitative study to measure the added value of the HR function as perceived by managers in Belgian organizations. The researchers found that, for top managers, the HR function added value through its change programmes following restructuring and downsizing. The findings suggested that LMs had 'a rather traditional view of the HR function' (p. 81) because a majority most frequently mentioned selection and training as the domain in which the HR function added value. The authors acknowledged that the data were 'highly subjective in nature'. Reflecting on the increasing individualization of work, which has seen employees negotiating individual 'idiosyncratic' employment contracts, Bal and Dorenbosch's (2015) large-scale study among establishments in the Netherlands sought to test the effect of individualized agreements on performance. The research found positive relationships between individualized HR practices and OP. Bal and Dorenbosch concluded (p. 54) that:

> [the] availability and use of individualized development HRM positively related to performance growth, and use of work schedule HRM also related positively to performance growth. Moreover, sickness absence is lower in organizations that have individualized work schedules available, while employee turnover is lower in organizations that have individualized pay practices available.

Interestingly, the study provides evidence that employee age moderated the relationships between the use of individualized HR practices and sickness absence and turnover, such that organizations with a high percentage of younger workers benefited from individualized development practices. Bal and Dorenbosch's research demonstrates that, when theorizing about the effects of HR practices on performance behaviours, it is important to take employees' age into account. Furthermore, in line with research on HRM devolved to LMs (Arthur and Boyles, 2007), it is also important to distinguish between the autonomy that LMs have in negotiating and enacting individualized contracts and an organization's HR policy on individualized work agreements.

reflective question What are the strengths and weaknesses of using workplace surveys as a method for collecting data to estimate the causal links between SHRM and performance?

Questioning research on the HRM–performance relationship

Although many studies have found a positive association between HRM and business performance (Coombs and Beirly, 2006), the methodological challenges of demonstrating the causal links between the two measures are formidable (Bou-Llusar et al.,

2016; Gerhart, 2008; Huselid and Becker, 2008). The challenges were summarized by Gerhart (2008), who wrote that 'the 20 per cent effect of HR on firm performance (for an increase in one standard deviation in HR practices) … once corrected … implies that the high firms have … 4.5 times higher performance' (p. 558). The size of the effect is so significant as to perhaps not be credible, comments the author. As some have argued, 15 or more years of extensive research have provided evidence only of a positive association, rather than causation. The research is 'riddled with error both with respect to data on HRM and on outcomes', writes Guest (2011, p. 10). The project to provide an evidence base for the hypothesized connections between SHRM and OP has received extensive criticism. Wright and Gardner (2003, p. 312) provide a bluntly critical assessment:

> Methodologically, there is no consensus regarding which practices constitute a theoretical complete set of HR practices; how to conceptually categorize these practices; the relevance to business strategy; the appropriate level of analysis; or how HR–performance and firm performance are to be measured … Theoretically, no consensus exists regarding the mechanism by which HR practices might impact on firm outcomes.

Ultimately, two kinds of critiques have been made: those dealing with *research design* challenges, and those concerned with *causality*. A variety of research designs is used to study the workplace. In deductive theory construction and hypothesis-testing, designing a study to test the HRM–performance relationship involves specifying precisely *what* HR practices and performance indicators are to be measured, at what *level* (individual, establishment or corporate), and *how*.

Research design issues

Research design issues have been concerned with several aspects: (1) the conceptualization and scope of HR practices that constitute a theoretically coherent set of practices, (2) the appropriate level of analysis, (3) the conceptual construction and measurement of performance, and (4) the mode of data collection.

HR practices: concept, level and measurement

For a positivist, employing survey research methods and analysis, there cannot be a meaningful study of the HRM–performance relationship, let alone an agreement on causality, without precisely specifying the *HR practices* or variables. The researcher, on the basis of theory-derived considerations, has therefore first to specify what HR practices are to be studied and devise measures of these practices, a process referred to as *operationalization*. Conceptualization, then, should produce a specific, agreed-upon meaning for HR practice or a combination of practices for the purpose of the research.

There are a number of challenges in selecting the HR practices used in the analysis. First, there is no agreement on what constitutes core 'HR practices', and ambiguity surrounds which appropriate bundles, clusters or sets of practices have a positive effect on OP. Whereas US academic Jeffrey Pfeffer (1994, 1998) identified seven 'best practices' in successful organizations, European academics Den Hartog and Verburg (2004) isolated eight HR practices to test the HR–performance relationship. Research findings, however, identify only the general presence of HR practices (Purcell et al., 2009), and do not offer insights into the coverage of employees actually *experiencing* those practices. It is noteworthy that Wright et al.'s (2003, p. 32) results were based on data garnered from employees:

using employees as the source of the HR practice measures ensures that the measure represents the *actual* practices rather than the espoused policies of the businesses.

In research into the HRM–performance relationship, there are differences in terms of who or what should be studied, that is, the *unit of analysis*. The most typical units of analysis are individual employees, groups or teams, and organizations. Micro studies focus on the individual or work group, whereas the focal point in macro studies may be a corporation or a public sector establishment (Wright and Boswell, 2002). Although studies into the effects of a singular HR practice have been conducted on an individual's psychological contract (see, for example, Guest, 1998; Rousseau, 1995), many of the empirical studies of the HRM–performance relationship have emphasized the effects of *multiple* or 'bundles' of HR practices at the organizational level. This approach raises various questions concerning the conceptualization of these HR practices as well as the selection of key informants evaluating the causal links between HRM and business performance.

Researchers and informants completing a survey questionnaire might have conceptual disagreements on the definition of an HR practice. Respondents might, for example, define a 'self-directed work team' in different ways, with or without a 'supervisor' or team 'leader' – the proverbial 'apples and oranges'. If informants do not use equivalent definitions in the evaluating process of an HR practice, the veracity of the data estimating the effects on performance will be seriously compromised. Ambiguity over the content of HPWSs plus 'a failure to operationalize HPWS sufficiently' has, for example, been noted (Danford et al., 2008, p. 152), as have the serious difficulties related to specifying the independent variable in HPWSs (Boxall and Macky, 2009).

The second concern relates to the selection of key informants in survey studies. When only a single respondent (typically an HR manager) is selected to evaluate the effects of HR practices, it is assumed that she or he has the competence to provide accurate information about all the variables relevant to the HRM–performance relationship (Gerhart, 2008). This research approach increases the probability that the HRM–performance relationships will be affected by common method variance (CMV), Bou-Llusar et al., (2016, p. 2) argue. CMV may lead to inflated or deflated observed associations between correlations of HR practices and performance variables assessed by the same rater (Craighead et al., 2011). To avoid CMV, it is recommended that researchers collect data from multiple key informants in each establishment to evaluate the effects of HR practices on performance. The use of multiple informants assumes that some managers have more knowledge and information than others in assessing HR practices and performance measures.

However, as Bou-Llusar et al., (2016) point out in their multi-informant study of the relationships between HPWS, EF and OP, drawing conclusions based on pooled data from multiple knowledgeable informants can result in 'ambiguous interpretations' of the relationships because respondents do not use equivalent interpretative frames of reference in the evaluating process. For instance, according to the authors, in the HR manager group the effect of HPWSs on EF is statistically significant ($p = 0.636$), as is the total effect of

HPWSs on OP (p = 0.409). However, EF does not significantly affect OP. In contrast, in the sales manager group, EF has a significant influence on OP (p = 0.405), but the researchers found no statistically significant effect (either direct or indirect) of HPWS on EF or on OP. Although the results are based on a small sample size, the analysis points to 'psychological disagreement' between HR and sales managers (Bou-Llusar et al., 2016, p. 7). This recent study emphasizes that the selection of respondents matters, and in analysing the HRM–performance relationship, pooled data provided by key informants occupying diverse positions in the organization should be examined separately for each manager group to avoid CMV (Bou-Llusar et al., 2016).

Performance: concept and measurement

The focus so far has been on issues concerning the independent variable – HR practices – in the HRM–performance model. We will now examine the problems concerning the *dependent* variable: performance. Performance variables have focused almost exclusively on financial measures (Boselie et al., 2005). Studies rely either on the hard 'objective' performance outcomes reported in published financial statements, or on the subjective assessment of outcomes of a single respondent, usually a senior HR manager. Respondents are asked to estimate the profitability or labour productivity of their organization relative to others in their sector. Both Cully et al. (1999) and Den Hartog and Verburg (2004) measure performance by requesting such information, relative to other firms, using a subjective scale ranging from 'a lot above average' to 'a lot below average'. Guest and his colleagues used both published accounting data and their respondents' evaluations of their companies' performance relative to that of their competitors (Guest et al., 2003). Other workplace scholars have used 'intermediate' or 'proximal' measures of performance (Betcherman et al., 1994; Harter et al., 2002). Typical examples here are the number of occupational accidents/injuries, absenteeism rates, customer satisfaction, the number of formal grievances and complaints, sales per employee, and employee well-being and retention (Bal and Dorenbosch, 2015).

The notion of what constitutes 'superior performance' needs to be disaggregated, and, in order to gain a meaningful insight into what 'performance' means, the researcher and practitioner need to be able to 'compare and contrast performance measures at a variety of individual and organizational levels' (Truss, 2001, p. 1146).

reflective question What do you think of this line of argument? If, indeed, strategic HR practices significantly improve performance, why do a relatively small proportion of workplaces adopt such an HR strategy?

Recent studies evince serious errors in the measurement of performance. As Saks (2000) notes, there is, with the notable exception of Huselid's (1995) study, a tendency for researchers to rely on single indicators of performance, to ignore the relationships between 'multiple measures', and to use performance indicators across dissimilar workplaces with no regard for how appropriate they are, thus rendering comparisons meaningless. A common criticism is the sampling of 'informed' or 'knowledgeable' respondents (Gerhart, 2008). As noted, a single respondent may have incomplete knowledge of HR practices and performance (Bou-Llusar et al., 2016), especially if she or he is located at the corporate office. Further, respondents may be unable or unwilling to disclose commercially sensitive

Poor time-keeping is an example of employee behaviour that can be observed and measured with more reliability than a trait.

© Stockbyte Royalty Free Photos

information on performance indicators to an independent researcher. Survey research designs tend to take no account of the 'lag effect'. It is not credible to argue that HRM drives performance when measurements of the *independent* variable (HR practices) and the *dependent* variable (performance) are conducted in the same time period. Overall, the reliability of the measures is 'frighteningly low' (Gerhart, 2008). Finally, financial performance is only one dimension of organizational effectiveness, which does not acknowledge the goal priorities of different 'varieties of capitalism' (Jacoby, 2005; Paauwe, 2004; Sklair, 2002);.

Critical workplace studies also draw attention to pervasive unfair discrimination on the basis of gender, disability and ethnicity (Carlsson and Rooth, 2008; Dean and Liff, 2010; Riach and Rich, 2002). Decent work is not an intellectual idea; it is a deeply felt aspiration of people in developed and developing societies. The increasing use of non-standard employment contracts engenders 'fear', 'anxiety' and 'demoralization' for those whose choice is limited (Conley, 2008). Studies of cases of sets of HR practices commonly identified with the 'high-performance paradigm' have reported 'work intensification' (see, for example, Findlay et al., 2000) and higher stress levels (Danford et al., 2008).

Mode of data collection: survey or field interview

Having specified what HR practices and performance outcomes to study, and among whom, the researcher has to choose a method of collecting empirical data. In HR–performance research, the choice is often between the use of surveys or field interviews or a multistrategy approach that uses a survey followed by selective case studies and interviews with employees. Each research strategy has its strengths, weaknesses and sets of distinctions. Typically, survey-based research is characterized as being driven by theory-testing, whereas theory emerges from field-based research. A further basic distinction is between quantitative and qualitative data, which is essentially the distinction between numbers and words. Survey research makes observations of social reality more explicit using quantitative data; case study researchers, on the other hand, make observations using qualitative data. A related distinction is sometimes drawn between a quantitative focus on employee behaviour and a qualitative focus on interpretive meanings of employees' behaviour in terms of the values, work norms, culture and occupational community in question.

Evaluating HR practices: the role of qualitative methods

Image Source/Gary Houlder

Variable-based (or quantitative) research is a powerful way of determining whether desirable outcomes in work organizations are the result of HR practices. Individuals engaged in this kind of research typically begin by constructing a variable or performance indicator. They then attempt to determine whether a change in that variable is associated with – perhaps even caused by – a particular HR practice or set of practices.

But while variable-based quantitative research has its strengths, it also has its weaknesses. It forces us to select and preassign meaning to particular features of the social world. In situations where managing across cultures is the challenge, such selective attention, and the preassignment of meaning to behaviours, may lead to superficial or misleading accounts of what is actually going on.

Ideally, HR evaluations would employ mixed methods and bring both quantitative and *qualitative* approaches to bear on the work of evaluation. Qualitative methods start from the assumption that causality in the social world is different from causality in the physical or biological world. The power of a behaviour or verbal statement to bring about a certain outcome depends on the meaning attributed to that behaviour or statement. But the attribution of meaning varies across cultures: different cultures (or subcultures) will attribute different meanings to what, on the surface, appears to be the same behaviour or statement.

In a famous essay on qualitative methods, Clifford Geertz (1973) asks us to reflect on the difference between a blink and a wink. On the surface, both involve a closing and opening of the lid of one eye. However, whether this behaviour is seen as a blink or a wink depends on several factors: the context, the winker's skill at non-verbal communication, and a tacit cultural code that enables someone to distinguish between a blink and a wink. Getting the code wrong could cause a lot of confusion.

This simple example helps us think about how qualitative methods might complement quantitative methods in studying the effects of HR practices. Consider the claim that 'positive affect' boosts morale and motivation in an organizational setting. One could then argue that positive affect is a key leadership quality and refer to studies of US work organizations in which improved worker morale appears to be linked to managers who exhibit an upbeat demeanour.

But smiles and laughter mean different things in different contexts. Picture a young HR graduate assigned to work in an American bank in Moscow. His letters of reference are filled with superlatives: 'This young man has a winning personality: he motivates and inspires those who work alongside him.' Then imagine the surprise when reports from Russia are negative – there are just too many smiles, too much cheerfulness; the American HR graduate is considered superficial, and many find it hard to take him seriously. Others muse, 'Perhaps he is laughing at us?'

Stop! What does this example tell us about the importance of qualitative methods in the evaluation of HR practices? Are there situations, even in the USA and UK, where 'positive affect' becomes a problematic rather than a desirable trait?

Sources and further information: See Geertz (1973) for a discussion of qualitative methods. Connelly and Ruarck (2010) provide an overview of the complex role of emotions in work organizations. For some insights into Russian views of the West, see the commencement speech delivered by Nobel Prize-winning author Alexander Solzhenitsyn at Harvard University in 1978. A pdf transcript of the speech may be found at harvardmagazine.com (July/August 1978; search for 'Solzhenitsyn flays the West') – page 24 of the pdf transcript is especially revealing.

Note: This feature was written by David MacLennan.

reflective
question

> Given the number of variables affecting employment relations, do you think that qualitative, structured interviews can provide a reliable means of measuring the contribution of HR interventions in the workplace?

Theoretical issues: the logic of causality

Apart from the problems with respect to research design, there is theoretical controversy over the nature of the relationship between HRM and performance. Or put another way, *how* exactly does HRM increase performance? A key element of a theory is a causal mechanism, that is, some notion of how the independent and dependent variables are related. The causal mechanism can also be considered as the process, or chain of cause-and-effect linkages, that mediates the causal effect (Remler and Van Ryzin, 2011). The problem of identifying the intermediate variables or processes that would explain how HR practices have their effects on work performance is hardly a new problem. The eighteenth-century Scottish philosopher David Hume, for example, discussed at length the challenges of identifying the 'causal glue' in the cause-and-effect linkage (Hume, 1748/2007). There is no consensus, however, regarding the precise cause-and-effect linkages through which strategic HR practices generate long-term value (Wright and Gardner, 2003). For example, Danford and his colleagues observe that studies may lack robust evidence 'governing direction of causation' (2008, p. 152). The ambiguity surrounding the process is aptly called the 'HR black box': the mediating effects of the core variables and processes that need to be present to produce such a relationship (Boselie et al., 2005).

Explaining the process by which a particular set of HR practices might enhance OP comes down to understanding the logic of causation in social research. Boselie et al. (2005) acknowledge that the 'linking mechanism' between HR practices and performance and the *mediating* effects of other key variables are mostly ignored. The *internal* causal 'mechanism' could, for example, be that employees' work motivation increases performance, or that organizational culture increases employees' long-term commitment and flexibility. Other internal mechanisms could relate to the psychological contract. The logic of causality and the positivist and critical realist view of causation are examined in more detail in the online resource centre for this book. The work of Purcell and Kinnie (2008) lends credence to the view that we need to take account of employees' attitudes and behaviours, culture and LMs' behaviours as 'HRM'.

HRM web
links

> Visit the online resource centre at **www.palgravehighered.com/bg-hrm-6e** for more information on the logic of causality and the positivist and critical realist view of causation.

Line managers as agents of HRM

Studies have established the growth in arrangements allowing HR professionals and LMs to share an organization's HRM responsibility. The focus on the enhanced control by LMs is partly explained by the doctrine that HRM is 'too important' to be left to HR specialists. This thinking goes back three decades to when Guest (1987, p. 51) opined, 'If HRM is to be taken seriously, personnel managers must give it away'. In the 1990s, the delegation of HR responsibilities to LMs, or what some call the 'reinvention' of the HR function, was closely associated with Ulrich's 'business partner' model (Caldwell and Storey, 2007; Larsen and

Brewster, 2003; Storey, 1992, 2001; Ulrich et al., 2007). Those are certainly important developments, but they neglect other significant changes: the parallel disempowerment of trade unionism in private sector workplaces, levels of unemployment and the elimination of almost all restraints on hiring and firing employees, changes which, according to some observers, have empowered management at all levels to 'near-imperial standing' (Hutton 2015a, p. 182). Traditionally, in British labour relations, lay union stewards have been the main conduit for formal representation to employers on a day-to-day basis (van Wanrooy, 2013a). In unionized workplaces, union stewards give employees a voice by negotiating on issues that concern workers and by taking up workers' grievances about rights with management. For example, if an employee is described in an agreement as being entitled to 'reasonable' time off to perform certain duties, a union steward will often be involved in resolving disputes about what the word 'reasonable' means (Burchill, 2014). A union steward is therefore a countervailing influence to LMs' authority and power. However, with statistically significant decreases in this form of representative mechanism, LMs have now gained unrivalled power (see Chapter 9).

The resource-based view of the organization that underpins much of contemporary HRM thinking focuses on internal HR development rather than on the organization's predictable and rationale responses to external labour market forces (Grimshaw and Rubery, 2008). However, there is a plausible argument that the level of unemployment in an occupational labour market will influence the complex realities of the employment relationship between the LM and the other employees she or he manages. The disruption of the dominant model of relatively full employment in the manufacturing sectors has involved complex and interrelated changes in systems of work and supervision, employment security and the employment relationship (Rubery, 2006). There is ample research affirming that work motivation is inherently dynamic and involves changes in both the individual employee and the external environment over time. The effects of post-1990 economic globalization and higher levels of unemployment in post-industrial regions of Europe represent a potent set of influences on employees' motivation (Kanfer et al., 2012) that has yet to be fully taken into account in theories of LM–employee relations. With statistically significant falls in the union steward representative mechanism in UK workplaces and high levels of unemployment, particularly among 18–24-year-olds, this has given LMs unrivalled power.

Often promoted on the basis of their individual performance, LMs have become powerful 'mini-general managers' charged with both operational and HR responsibilities (McGuire and Kissack, 2015, p. 521). Research also identifies important challenges resulting from LM involvement in the HR function. This section examines the role of LM in implementing HR processes, seeking to expose the challenges and tensions facing LMs and the HR function. It offers a theoretical model with which to examine the role of LMs within organizations, as well as the relationship between LMs and the HR function. Theory and research on the relationship between LMs' OP is then detailed, followed by observations highlighting the importance of workplace context when studying the HRM–performance chain.

A model of line managers' responsibilities

The relevant literature differentiates between types of managers occupying various positions in the organization's hierarchy. Studies use the terms 'line managers' (McNeil, 2003), 'first-line managers' (Hales, 2005), 'front-line managers' (Leisink and Knies, 2011) and 'middle managers' (Currie and Proctor, 2001). Nehles et al. (2006, p. 257) define LMs as 'the lowest managers at the operational level, who direct a team of employees on a day-to-day basis and are responsible for performing HR activities'. LMs as defined by the Chartered Institute of Personnel and Development (CIPD, 2015a, p. 1) are those who have 'responsibility for directly managing individual employees or teams [and] report to a higher level of management on the performance and well-being of the employees or teams they manage'. To examine the role of LMs in enacting HRM policies, we need to address two related questions: 'What do LMs do?' and 'How do LMs affect the causal chain linking HR policy inputs to performance outcomes?' Drawing on the work of Mintzberg (1989), Squires (2001) and McGuire and Kissack (2015), a multifaceted model of the roles, skills and behaviours of LMs and the contingencies affecting their behaviours is depicted in Figure 3.1.

reflective question Go back and look at Figure 1.2. As a key element of HRM, what are the three roles of LMs?

In examining the *external context*, we use the concept of STEPLE analysis (Bratton, 2015a) – **S**ocial, **T**echnological, **E**conomic, **P**olitical, **L**egal and **E**cological – to examine the wider global and macro-influences that shape LMs' roles and responsibilities. The external context underscores the need to examine the workplace within its totality, the embedded nature of behaviour and the management processes by which those with most power respond to the forces applied by the external context (see Chapter 1). The *organizational context* describes the regular, patterned nature of work-related activities, technology and processes that is repeated day in and day out. There are (at least) six identifiable variables that impact on the active interplay of people within the structure of the organization: strategy, structure, work, technology, people and control processes. In addition to the physical or material aspects of the organization, there is the less tangible, organizational culture and climate. Working for Amazon, for example, has become synonymous with a corporate culture that monitors its employees' hourly performance. At Amazon, LMs and other employees are allegedly encouraged to contest each other's ideas in the name of 'creative challenge' (Hutton, 2015c). The nature of organizations has undergone seismic changes, and LMs operate in an increasingly 'complex organizational environment' (McGuire and Kissack, 2015, p. 527).

With regard to *LM roles*, Figure 3.1 shows four sets of managerial behaviours: decisional, interpersonal, informational and developmental. Mintzberg usefully distinguishes four *decision-making* roles, those of resource allocator, disturbance handler, negotiator and entrepreneur. He also distinguishes three different *interpersonal* roles – figurehead, leader and liaison – that arise directly from the manager's formal authority. By virtue of these interpersonal encounters with both other managers and other employees, the manager thus acts as a disseminator of information. The manager's three *informational* roles – monitor of information, disseminator of information and spokesperson – flow from the interpersonal roles. McGuire and Kissack (2015) identify six *developmental* roles that should be devolved to LMs: working with HR business partners, workforce planning, coaching and mentoring, fostering a learning climate, career planning and training others. According to McGuire and Kissack, these six activities 'firmly [fix] line managers with responsibility for operational HR delivery as well as giving them a "linking" role, obliging them to work with business partners and the HR function' (2015, p. 525).

As can be seen from Figure 3.1, LMs deliver an array of HR policies: decisions around work level and target setting, communicating with other subordinate employees,

HRM in practice 3.2

Can organizations simultaneously be committed to employees and outsource services?

The outsourcing of the HR function, often associated with neo-liberalism and the business partner model of HRM (see Chapter 1) has resulted in government spending more of taxpayers' money on outsourced public services. In the UK, the amount spent, for example, on justice, welfare and defence increased from £64 billion to £120 billion during the Coalition government years 2010–15. Tens of thousands of staff were transferred to private sector companies as the number of outsourced contracts rose from 526 under the previous Labour government to 1185 under the Coalition government. Companies such as Capita, Serco, G4S, Carillion and BT Group obtained many of the bigger contracts (Plimmer, 2015a). By 2020, the public sector will have decreased by about 1.5 million and:

A new industry of private contractors feeding off contracted-out public work will have been invented, offering even worse pay and conditions than the public sector itself. (Hutton, The Observer, 2015d, courtesy of Guardian News & Media Ltd)

The main driver of the privatization of state public services has been an ideological belief that the public sector is inefficient and that the private sector will be more efficient and introduce innovations that will produce savings and improved quality.

Critics of outsourcing to the private sector argue that 'efficiency' is mainly obtained by lower wages and inferior working conditions for those employees who are transferred from the state sector or those who are later recruited into private providers. They also express concerns about accountability and transparency, especially when companies refuse to disclose information that they claim is commercially sensitive.

Research on pay and conditions in the private-public sector is not extensive, but two surveys bear out Hutton's generalization. A study based on Labour Force Survey data carried out by the New Economics Foundation (Trades Union Congress and New Economics Foundation, 2015) found that workers in the private sector in 2014 were 'less respected.' were 'given more insecure working arrangements' and had 'lower median hourly wages'. In health and social care

occupations, they were less qualified than staff in the public sector. The private sector had a larger proportion of full-time employees who regularly worked in excess of 48 hours, and a higher staff turnover. Newly hired workers were in some cases paid less, providing a potential for a two-tiered workforce. This survey suggested that the unfavourable contrast with the public sector 'would impact indirectly on commitment, motivation and service quality'.

A second source of information involved five case studies of privately contracted services covering supported living in Rochdale, NHS patient transport services in North Staffordshire, support services in West Sussex, the provision of school meals in Newport and support services to the police in Lincolnshire (Smith Institute, 2014). It was found that public sector cuts had had a major impact on outsourcing deals, with low pay, lower staff benefits and work intensification as key features. There was a narrowing of opportunities for progression for low-paid employees. Transferred employees kept their public sector pensions, but new employees had unfavourable pensions. A two-tier workforce was emerging as new starters were being awarded lower rates of pay. None of the case study contracts contained a commitment to pay the living wage. Pay systems had become less transparent, with a danger that equal pay issues might become a problem in the future.

Stop! What do you consider to be the HRM challenges faced by the private companies that now run public services instead of state or local government departments? The trend towards increased outsourcing of services and employment may be considered to be in direct contrast to the 'high-commitment' approach to HRM. If people are the organization's key asset for competitive advantage or superior services, how can organizations simultaneously be committed to employees yet outsource work and use contingent labour?

Sources and further information: For more information, see Hutton (2015d), Lepak and Snell (2008), Plimmer (2015a), Smith Institute (2014) and Trades Union Congress and New Economics Foundation (2015). Information on contracts issued to private firms for construction, cleaning, security, research and training can be viewed at Data.gov.uk Opening up Government; see https://data.gov.uk/

Note: This feature was written by David Denham.

encouraging employee engagement and facilitating employee learning and training. The CIPD (2015a, p. 1) acknowledges that although the policies and practices may be designed by the HR department, 'they cannot be delivered by HR'. The extent to which LMs perform these roles will depend on the organization's hierarchy, the culture, their specific functional responsibilities and the level of education of their co-workers (Sundgren and Styhre, 2006). The CIPD (2015a) observes that the effective delivery of HR policies and practices requires appropriate training and development and a supportive framework to enable LMs to develop self-confidence and to understand their own role in the workplace.

Finally, Figure 3.1, LM skills and behaviours lists various means by which managers communicate ideas, gain acceptance for them, motivate their team of employees to accomplish operational tasks and deliver HR activities. LMs use technical, cognitive and emotional intelligence as well as interpersonal processes and skills to accomplish their work. Power is included in the list because it is part of the influence process. Line management is a blend of social processes, and individuals will vary in terms of their capacity or inclination to use them, but these processes are ultimately about human interaction and relationships. The model is a useful device that helps us to explore the causal chain linking HR policy inputs to performance outcomes, and equally how various contingencies influence the behaviour of LMs.

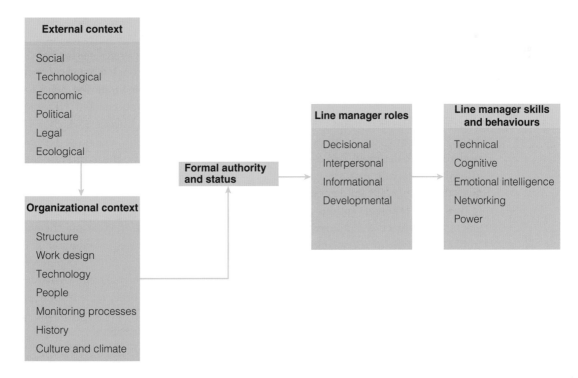

Figure 3.1 *A model of line managers' roles*

reflective question Looking at Figure 3.1, if you were a newly appointed LM, what training and support would you consider for yourself to be essential (1) in the first 4 weeks, and (2) over 12 months? Reflect upon Ulrich's 'business partnering' model (p. 85), and place yourself in the role of an HR specialist. What problems do you foresee from LMs having an HRM role, for example, in training new co-employees?

Line managers and the HRM–performance chain

The second question, 'How do LMs affect the causal chain linking HR policy inputs to performance outcomes?', is concerned with the '*how*' of managing people. In this context, Blau's (1964) influential concept of social exchange theory is often referred to. Social exchange theory draws attention to the psychology of instrumental human behaviour. Its relevance to HRM is defined by an assumption that a resource (human capability and commitment) will continue to flow only if there is a valued return contingent upon it. Social psychologists call this reciprocally contingent flow *reinforcement*, whereas economists call it *exchange* (Emerson, 1976). Therefore employees will feel a sense of obligation to reciprocate when they perceive that they are being treated well by their LM or their organization (Gilbert et al., 2011a). This observation seems to resonate with research suggesting that HR practices experienced or perceived by workers will, to a growing extent, be those delivered by LMs, with many operational HR responsibilities, which means that LMs have to be included in any causal mechanism attempting to measure the HRM–performance relationship.

Research on the HRM–performance relationship (Guest, 2011; Purcell and Kinnie, 2008) has brought into focus the so-called 'HRM black box'. This metaphor captures the complex social interaction found in the workplace, specifically the causal chain linking HR intervention inputs to performance outcomes (Boselie et al., 2005). As discussed earlier, the theory underpinning this 'HRM black box' suggests a casual chain of mediating variables such as employees' attitude, employees' behaviour and employees' performance.

The causal chain or 'HRM black box' can be represented as: Intended practices → Actual practices → Perceptions of practices → Employee attitudes → Employee behaviour → Unit-level performance. This distinguishes between 'intended' and 'enacted' HR practices, and employees' perceptions and experiences of them. Intended practices, which are influenced by organizational values and the tenets of social legitimacy, are those HR policies and practices designed by senior management to help achieve the corporate strategy (Boxall and Purcell, 2011; see Chapter 2). Actual practices are those HR policies and practices that are actually implemented in the workplace.

It is these HR interventions and the way they are implemented by LMs that employees perceive and react to. Employees judge each HR intervention or practice and the way it is applied in terms of its usefulness or satisfaction to them, as well as whether it meets perceived ideas of fairness or equity. Importantly, a bundle of HR practices, as perceived by employees, constitutes an important element in the organizational climate (Ashkanasy et al., 2011; Bowen and Ostroff, 2004). Employee performance has observable responses seen in attitudes, mandatory task behaviour and discretionary behaviour. In turn, the model depicts behaviours influencing unit performance, however this is defined.

Some research reports a positive impact on OP when LMs undertake HR responsibilities. One study, for example, noted that 'line manager behaviour has a significant impact on employee commitment' (Hutchinson and Purcell, 2003, p. 55). Such findings lead some to claim that LMs enable HR strategies to 'come to life' (Hutchinson and Purcell, 2003); they are 'enablers of learning' (Warhurst, 2013) and are 'a critical lynchpin in delivering HRD at the organizational coalface' (McGuire and Kissack 2015, p. 527). The relevant literature draws attention to the importance of high-quality employee–LM dyads, which, it is claimed, strongly influence employees' perceptions of HR practices, and are thus likely to positively or negatively affect OP (Purcell and Kinnie, 2008). Thus, the general consensus is that LMs are seen as pivotal in managing the employment relationship.

On the other hand, some research seems less positive about the involvement of LMs in HRM (Cunningham et. al., 2004; Gibb, 2003; Redman, 2001), and note that the mediating effects of LMs are far from straightforward. Arthur (1994, p. 673) justified his results on the HRM–performance relationship by citing cost savings arising from an empowered workforce with *fewer* LMs. Similarly, other studies on HPWS report a *fall* in the number of LMs following the introduction of self-directed work teams (e.g. Bratton, 1992). Furthermore, research suggests that interpersonal conflicts often plague the relationship between HR professionals and LMs sharing HRM responsibility. As such, a 'perceptual discrepancy' is likely to exist between both parties on the degree of HR devolution, which may eventually lead to bad performance. This discrepancy is rooted in differences in the perception of several factors, including 'red tape', support (personnel) and the age and capability of the LM (Op de Beeck et al., 2015). More generally, studies reveal that some LMs lack commitment, competency and credibility in HRM (Sanders and Frenkel, 2011), that LMs resist taking ownership of additional HR responsibilities (Farnham, 2015), and that they appear to be 'unwilling partners' in HRM (Teo and Rodwell, 2007, p. 278). Such behaviours can therefore cause a disconnection in the theory of the HRM–performance chain (Gratton et al., 1999). Huws and Podro (2012) further observe that outsourcing and global supply chains have deleterious effects on the HR function, including on managing HR practices across organizational boundaries and in relation to 'detachment' from 'key decision-makers'.

Numerous empirical studies have reported on specific HR activities undertaken by LMs. For example, EI in the workplace has attracted the interests of academic and senior managers. For managers, it promises a way of enhancing employee commitment and motivation in the organization (Guest, 2015). However, LMs' capability in, and commitment to, EI processes has produced less positive outcomes for EI (Marchington, 2001). Studies also cast doubt on the ability of LMs to perform their 'disturbance handler' role: Rollinson et al. (1996) found that some LMs were unable to handle grievance and disciplinary cases, and HR specialists had to attend such meetings to 'police' LM behaviour. Studies show a lack of investment in developing LMs' HR knowledge and skills, suggesting that they 'learn by doing' (Townsend et al., 2012). Although 'learning by doing' or informal learning has several advantages, an obvious disadvantage is that 'bad habits and the wrong lessons' can be learned by LMs and passed on to other employees (Dale and Bell, 1999, p. 1). LMs' lack of knowledge and expertise in adult learning principles and practices may undermine the quality of 'on-the-job' training. As McGuire and Kissack observe, outsourcing is omnipresent in modern organizations, and LMs are often asked to interface with external consultants in order to deliver upon devolved training responsibilities; a question thus remains of whether the 'status of HRD does not suffer at the hands of inexperienced line managers' (2015, p. 528). There is also evidence that devolving HR increases role ambiguity and conflict for LMs (Sanders and Frenkel, 2011). The potential for conflict is particularly apparent in the area of performance appraisal. Researchers observe that LMs tend to conduct performance appraisal poorly (Guest and King, 2001; Harris, 2001; Redman, 2001). For example, an employee's age, race, sex and ethnicity can affect an appraisal, and a LM's positive regard for subordinates often results in 'leniency and halo errors, and less inclination to punish poor performance' (Latham et al., 2008, p. 374). The absence of monetary incentives for LMs when delivering HRM is also seen as problematic (Gratton et al., 1999; Hunter and Renwick, 2009; McGuire and Kissack, 2015).

The HR–performance causal chain is based upon high-quality relations between LMs and subordinates, but UK and international studies speak of some LMs exhibiting 'toxic' or 'inappropriate' behaviour. This can include ridiculing subordinate employees in public, promoting divisiveness between individual employees, treating women and ethnic minority employees differently from others, and workplace bullying. Pelletier's (2010) concept of, and empirical support for, 'leader toxicity' draws attention to the limitations of the paradigm of positive, effective LMs delivering HRM. An LM's 'inappropriate behaviour', which is often associated with the presence of a power imbalance (Asch and Salaman, 2002; Keashly and Jagatic, 2011; Saunders et al., 2007), can cause decreased employee commitment, lower job satisfaction and, thus, a disconnection in the causal chain. There are reports, for example, of LMs taking a reactionary position towards 'diversity' issues (Fried et al., 2001), suggestions that some LMs are unable to manage women and black employees (Dominguez, 1992) and 'downwards bullying' behaviours perpetuated by LMs against other subordinate employees (Lewis and Gunn, 2007; Ramsay et al., 2011). Inappropriate behaviour in the workplace, left too long, can become contagious and impact negatively on employee engagement, turnover and, ultimately, the 'bottom line' (Immen, 2011).

Work organizations operate in societies in which there are laws, customs and widely shared social expectations on how people should be treated in the workplace. As the opening vignette on Sports Direct suggests, it is not difficult to see that 'inappropriate' and 'toxic' behaviours by LMs will deplete the moral standing or 'social legitimacy' (Boxall and Purcell, 2011, p. 19) and reputation of the management regime in the organization. This was vividly illustrated recently when Amazon chief executive Jeff Bezos speedily responded to claims of 'shockingly callous' behaviour by managers and advised his employees who experienced such behaviour 'to escalate to HR' (Gibbs, The Guardian, 2015a). The many studies of the LM–HRM nexus suggests that it may not always bring positive outcomes; therefore we have to be cautious of generalizations about the causal chain of LM–HRM–performance.

Finally, research has drawn attention to the unintended consequences of LMs engaging in HRM. First, it is argued that the greater the success of LMs' engagement in HRM, the less need there is for a large costly HR department. Thus, the involvement of LMs in HRM potentially undermines the case that HR professionals should be a 'strategic partner' in the organization. Indeed, the survival of the HR function may be threatened given the reports of 'considerable tension' among LMs in accepting the 'legitimacy of the business partner role' (Higgins and Zhang, 2009), with many LMs viewing the actions of business partners 'as little more than unwarranted imposition and interference with [their] the authority and autonomy' (McGuire and Kissack, 2015, p. 525). Second, it is argued that LMs operate in increasingly complex target-oriented organizational cultures, and, given the pressure for LMs to meet ever-higher targets, this signals a greater priority for immediate operational initiatives over strategic long-term HR initiatives (Heraty and Morley, 1995; McGuire and Kissack, 2015). In essence, the expanded operational/HRM role of LMs captures the classic critique of the HRM model; that is, it attempts to reconcile the 'hard' (resource) and 'soft' (human) elements of the reality of HRM (Bolton and Houlihan, 2007; Legge, 2005).

It is worth emphasizing that the way LMs undertake their HR responsibilities is 'inextricably linked' to the organizational culture and climate (Norton et al., 2015) and leadership behaviours (Robertson and Barling, 2015b). Additionally, situational contingencies and the HR skills and commitment of LMs seem to account for less positive performance outcomes. It is, therefore, unsurprising that we find researchers divided and all see problems arising from LMs acting as agents of HRM. The research suggests that context and the quality of social relations matter.

Context and the social relations of performance

It is often difficult to establish what the context actually is and what different mixes of strategic HR practices are required for each situation; more problematically, quite different sets of HR practices have been effective in distinctly similar situations (Bowen and Ostroff, 2004; Grint, 2001).

As our integrated model of LMs' roles suggests, 'context' involves at least three social structures – meaning relatively stable patterns of social relations and human behaviour – at the global, macro and micro levels. *Global structures* are the patterns of worldwide economic and political relations between countries. *Macrostructures* refer to the pattern of economic and political forces that lie outside the workplace. The ways in which work, technology and people are organized and managed inside the organization make up the *microstructures*. Context can also mean the often intangible aspects of *organizational* life, the patterns of shared assumptions, values and beliefs governing the way in which managers and other employees think about work, and how they act. Collectively, these intangible aspects are referred to as organizational culture and climate (see Chapter 15). Studies of causation in HR have to address complexities and nuances of organizational culture and climate, not least because 'enduring multiple commitments and ties' are 'only partly formed by organizational scripts' (Clegg et al., 1999, p. 9).

The central argument here is that the contemporary workplace is an arena or 'space' in which social relationships shape the beliefs, expectations and behaviour and 'misbehaviour' (Ackroyd and Thompson, 1999) of individual employee–LM dyads that modify and shape how HR policies and practices are enacted. This conceptualization of the contemporary workplace as open, compliant and, importantly, subject to acts of resistance and defiance, means that the positivist generalizations sought by statistical studies of the HR–performance relationship are 'inherently inappropriate' (Edwards and Sengupta, 2010, p. 387). The indeterminacy of an employee's performance makes the 'human' in a theoretical model of HRM and performance the most difficult aspect to test and estimate. Improving our understanding of *how* HR practices increase performance requires us to take account of employees' attitudes, emotions, behaviours and 'misbehaviours', as well as how HR interventions are perceived by employees and their representatives (Bolton, 2005; Edwards and Wright, 2001; Guest, 1997; Purcell and Kinnie, 2008).

We have drawn upon the HR–performance literature to develop an alternative causal HR–performance model, as shown in Figure 3.2. Here causation is *not* understood

Getty

Leading from the front. Managers play a vital role in improving employees' performance. It has been argued that front-line management and a high-quality relationship between the employee and employer lead to positive work attitudes and behaviours, with important consequences for OP.

as regular successions of linear actions (Sayer, 2000). Our development of Purcell and Kinnie's model puts forward an expanded multicausational explanation of how planned HR practices might affect sustainable OP. The model identifies the following key factors: the ability, motivation, expectations, attitudes, emotions, and behaviours of individual employees; the leadership process; work-related learning; and organizational culture. These may nurture creativity, learning and innovation, and a sense of 'shared values', all of which are more likely to persuade employees to go 'the extra mile' and contribute to performance outcomes (Bowen and Ostroff, 2004; Bratton, 2015a; Purcell et al., 2009). These complex human processes, located within the wider context of a sustainable work system and a national and global political economy, suggest *how* HR practices are enacted by general and line managers – a peep inside the metaphorical HR 'black box'. There are limits to what can be reasonably portrayed in a diagram, but Figure 3.2 is meant to convey to the reader the complex, interdependent and mutually reinforcing causal mechanisms that the classical causal model conflates.

In the figure, placing the mediating variables within overlapping circles avoids the tendency to view the HR 'black box' as a series of linear causal steps. Conceptualizing the causal chain as a relational construct has several implications for the way we understand how strategic HR practices influence the attitudes and behaviours of LMs and other employees. First, power is integral to the employer–employee relationship. This means that the causal chain between planned HR practice and performance outcomes is mediated by power between the parties. The balance of power is dynamic, multidimensional and influenced by numerous variables. In particular, labour market conditions, product market competition, employees' skills and organizational bodies such as trade unions, or government intervention such as labour laws, influence it.

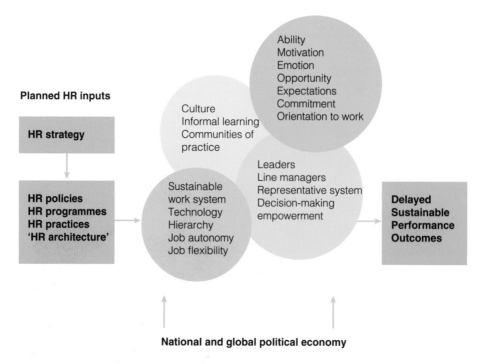

Figure 3.2 *Social relations, HRM and OP*
Source: Inspired by Purcell and Kinnie (2008)

Second, the relation between an LM, a key agent of the organization, and an employee is inherently cooperative and consensual, or defiant and conflictual (Budd, 2004). The indeterminacy of the employment contract focuses attention on the importance of the relational nature of the exchange. Employees' attitudes (for example, commitment), employees' behaviour (for example, effort) and employees' performance (for example, productivity) will be influenced by the socioeconomic context, and will be significantly affected by the quality of the leader/LM–employee relationship. Thus, LMs play an integral role as a purveyor of resources, information and developmental support that extends beyond the formal job description and, importantly, act as a potential champion (or spoiler) of HR policies and practices.

Third, if organizational life is recognized as an arena of complex reciprocal human relations that are socially constructed and embedded in an organizational and national culture, SHRM is more appropriately configured not simply as a 'toolbox' from which a set of practices can deterministically improve performance, but rather as planned practices that *might* be enacted as envisioned. It seems plausible, therefore, that the analytical focus on the causal path between planned HRM and OP has to incorporate issues that are often neglected in the HRM canon, such as conflicts of interest, power, formal and informal employee interactions and employment relations. Thus, the model signals a more inclusive research agenda, which is why, in this edition of the book, we have chosen to focus more on the role of LM and include chapters on HPWSs, leadership and organizational culture.

reflective question Does this causal model predict a particular research design? Can organizational phenomena be understood only by statistical analysis, or is there scope for what Weber called 'verstehen', or interpretive understanding?

Purcell and Kinnie's (2008) causal chain provides both context and nuance for the HR–performance link and the involvement of LM in HRM debates. However, we began this chapter by stating that debate among academics over the connections between bundles of HR practices and OP has been intense and often inconclusive. Indeed, as Guest (2011, p. 3) recently observed, after two decades of research on the HRM–performance relationship we are 'knowledgeable but not much wiser'. Furthermore, debate is still divided over the OP outcomes from involving LMs in the delivery of HRM. The apparent emergence of LMs as key players in delivering HRM policies can be seen as a fundamental shift in attitudes towards individualism leading to 'an upsurge in managerial confidence' (Storey, 2001, p. 10), in, at least in the private sector, a new model work organization that has seen a decline in union membership and influence of shop stewards.

case study

Devolvement of HR at the City of Kindle

The setting

Voluntary turnovers in the Canadian workforce are on the rise, and employers face significant challenges in recruiting and retaining specialized talent. Skill and labour shortages continue to grow, shifting the Canadian labour market from an employers' to an employees' market. This is reflected in the areas of recruiting, hiring, developing and retaining employees. Other external forces are creating an ever-increasing complexity of the HR function in Canadian organizations. New workers' compensation legislation aimed at eliminating bullying and harassment has mandated that annual training be provided to all staff, and that investigations, which can be both time-consuming and costly, be conducted for all claims. In addition, the effective management of the rising number of cases involving mental health issues, including depression and anxiety, in the workplace is requiring substantially more time and resources. Freedom of information legislation, which allows employees to request all personal information held by their employers, has also resulted in more demands being placed on HR professionals, and the number of requests is expected to grow as more employees become aware of this right. Freedom of information requests require HR staff to search through large amounts of historical paper and electronic records, sometimes encompassing an employee's entire employment history.

At the City of Kindle, a medium-sized local government employer located in the interior of British Columbia, Canada, these external impacts add to the internal pressures it already faces. From the 10-year period 2004–14, the City acquired 33 per cent more employees. The result of that growth was an increase of nearly 40 per cent in job postings, and several thousand job applications being reviewed and processed by the HR staff during the year.

The problem

Judy Chow, the HR director at the City of Kindle, had been receiving complaints from several LMs that they were not getting enough time with her staff to help them with their employee issues. Judy had implemented a 'client group' structure for her three HR advisers several years previously (assigning an adviser to one or more departments), and since then they had built very good working relationships with their clients. However, this

PhotoDisc/ Getty Images

had also created more demands on their time as LMs wanted 'their' advisers at every staff meeting, in every interview and at all coaching and disciplinary meetings.

Judy found this somewhat surprising. Recognizing that her staff could not always be available to provide assistance due to their own resource limitations, there had been a very robust leadership development programme in place for many years, providing LMs with the skills and knowledge to carry out basic HR work on their own. Judy was unsure how the department would be able to continue meeting the level of customer service the LMs were demanding while external and other internal pressures were growing. Although there were two clerical staff providing administrative support, she knew that the HR advisers were putting in up to 2 hours of overtime every day and during peak times, and work was being taken home to be completed in the evenings and at weekends. This was not sustainable and would inevitably lead to burnout.

Judy met with the Chief Administrative Officer to get his thoughts. In the past, he had told management that, due to resource limitations, they might have to start doing more HR-related work on their own, but that had not been well received and had basically been ignored. When Judy now suggested that she needed another HR adviser to address the problem, the chief administrative officer was blunt with her. 'Your chances of getting another body in this year's budget are very slim as the

(continued)

city council does not put much priority on internal support functions such as HR,' he said. 'The fact is, you are not seen much in the eyes of the public who vote.' Frustrated, Judy called a meeting with her staff to see if the group could come up with any solutions. 'We are basically victims of our own success as the LMs obviously value your expertise,' she began, 'but at the same time, I sense they are afraid to make a move without your direct involvement.'

Catherine Olmstead, one of the HR advisers, spoke up. 'One of my department client groups has offered to fund another HR position through their budget,' she said. Judy quickly discouraged that idea. 'What they really mean is they want their own HR adviser to be at their beck and call – that's a decentralized system that I strongly oppose,' Judy explained. 'I feel that in an organization of our size, it is realistic and more effective for us to be a centralized function so that we can ensure we are consistent with our approach on issues. As you know, consistency is key in labour relations.'

With no other proposed solutions from her staff, Judy left the room pondering her next steps. She knew a change had to be made, but she sensed it would not be easy regardless of which path she took.

The assignment

Working either alone or in a study group, draw on this chapter, Storey's (1992) model (see p. 22), Ulrich's (1997) business partner model (see p. 24) and other recommended material to answer the following questions:

1 Are there any other options Judy could consider in alleviating the pressures being placed on her department?

2 What do you think might be preventing the LMs from accepting additional HR responsibilities?
3 What would be the advantages and disadvantages of having the LMs act more as 'agents of HRM' at the City of Kindle?

Essential reading

Caldwell, R. (2001) Champions, adapters, consultants and synergists: the new change agents in HRM. *Human Resource Management Journal*, **11**(3): 39–52.
Cunningham, I. and Hyman, J. (1999) Devolving human resource responsibilities to the line: beginning of the end or a new beginning for personnel? *Personnel Review*, **28**(1/2): 9–27.
Hall, I. and Torrington, D. (1998) Decentralisation of the human resources function. In *The Human Resource Function: The Dynamics of Change and Development* (pp. 73–95). London: Financial Times, Pitman Publishing.
Keegan, A. and Francis, H. (2010) Practitioner talk: the changing textscape of HRM and emergence of HR business partnership. *International Journal of Human Resource Management*, **21**(6): 873–98.
Ulrich, D., Brockbank, W., Johnson, D. and Younger, J. (2007) Human resource competencies: responding to increased expectations. *Employee Relations Today*, **34**(3): 1–12.

Note: This case study was written by Lori Rilkoff.

summary

➤ We began this chapter by reviewing some of the literature, arguing that the HRM function is going through a transition in which the evaluation of HRM is being recognized as both fundamental and necessary.

➤ A review of the research undertaken in this chapter shows a substantive body of literature demonstrating that SHRM can and does make a positive and, in some cases, significant impact on organizational outcomes.

➤ We examined the methodological and theoretical concerns relating to HR–performance research. Critics argue that the effectiveness of strategic choices in HR is difficult to measure due to major problems of how to measure the variables and meeting the criteria of causality. We have suggested that the social 'mechanisms' that impact on the causal chain in HR may be better analysed using a multistrategy research design.

➤ We examined the empowerment of LMs. Their enhanced sovereignty is usually related to the 'reinvention' of the HR function. However, the empowerment of LMs was also explained by the parallel disempowerment of workplace trade unionism and the near-elimination of employment rights over hiring and firing.

➤ We introduced a model depicting external and situational forces affecting LMs and four LM roles: decisional, informational, relational and developmental. Reviewing the literature, we identified contrasting findings on LMs delivery of HRM. On the one hand, some studies note that LM behaviour has a significant impact on employee commitment. On the other hand, others reveal that some LMs lack ability and credibility in HRM, which can cause a disconnection in the causal chain of mediating variables, such as attitudes, behaviour and performance.

➤ This chapter has examined the neglected dimension of analysing precisely *how* strategic HR practices improve performance. Our model has a heuristic purpose: it is designed to identify and magnify the influential social processes that shape employees' attitudes, behaviour, social relations and thence performance. Through this lens, social interactions, within definable social structures, play a central role in applying and scaffolding strategic HR policies and practices.

review questions

1   What forces are driving the added-value movement in HRM?

2   To what extent do you agree or disagree with the statement that 'the least important HR practices are measurable, whereas the most important HR practices are not.' Discuss.

3   How can the effect of HR strategy on OP be explained?

4   Why do some academics and practitioners believe that LMs have become the 'lynchpin' through which HR strategy is channelled?

5   What lessons do you think can be learned from the literature in terms of the LMs' responsibilities and involvement in HRM in the environments of small and medium-sized enterprises?

6   What challenges and tensions might organizations encounter when LMs are involved in delivering HR solutions in the workplace?

further reading

Reading these articles and chapters can help you gain a better understanding and potentially a higher grade for your HRM assignment.

➤ Advisory, Conciliation and Arbitration Service (2014) *Front Line Managers*. London: ACAS. Available at: www.acas.org.uk/media/pdf/j/4/Front-line-managers-advisory-booklet.pdf (accessed October 2016).

➤ Astakhova, M. N. and Porter, G. (2015) Understanding the work passion–performance relationship: the mediating role of organizational identification and moderating role of fit at work. *Human Relations*, **68**(8): 1315–46.

➤ Bal, P. M. and Dorenbosch, L. (2015) Age-related differences in the relations between individualized HRM and organizational performance: a large-scale employer survey. *Human Resource Management Journal*, **25**(1): 41–61.

➤ Bou-Llusar, J. C., Beltrán-Martín, I., Roca-Puig, V. and Escrig-Tena, A. B. (2016) Single- and multiple-informant research designs to examine the human resource management–performance relationship. *British Journal of Management*, doi: 10.1111/1467-8551.12177.

➤ Boxall, P. and Macky, K. (2009) Research and theory on high-performance work systems: progressing the high-involvement stream. *Human Resource Management Journal*, **19**(1): 3–23.

➤ Dalziel, S. and Strange, J. (2007) How to engage line managers in people management. *People Management*, **13**(19): 56–7.

➤ Danford, A., Richardson, M., Stewart, P., Tailby, S. and Upchurch, M. (2008) Partnership, high performance work systems and quality of working life. *New Technology, Work and Employment*, **23**(3): 151–66.

➤ Guest, D. (2011) Human resource management and performance: still searching for some answers. *Human Resource Management Journal*, **21**(1): 3–13.

➤ Gurbuz, S. and Mert, I. (2011). Impact of the strategic human resource management on organizational performance: evidence from Turkey. *International Journal of Human Resource Management*, **22**(8): 1803–2.

➤ Hassan, F. (2011) The frontline advantage. *Harvard Business Review*, **89**(5): 106–14.

➤ Huws U. and Podro, S. (2012) *Outsourcing and the Fragmentation of Employment Relations: The Challenges Ahead*. London: Advisory Conciliation and Arbitration Service.

➤ Jacobs, K. (2013) Whose job is it anyway? *Human Resources*, February: 36–9.

➤ Lopez-Cotarelo, J. (2011) HR discretion: understanding line managers' role in human resource management. In: *Academy of Management Annual Meeting, 12th–16th August 2011, San Antonio, Texas*. Available at: http://www2.warwick.ac.uk/fac/soc/wbs/research/irru/publications/recentconf/juan_-_edw_-_lest.pdf (accessed July 30, 2016).

➤ Op de Beeck, S., Wynen, J. and Hondeghem, A. (2015) HRM implementation by line managers: explaining the discrepancy in HR-line perceptions of HR devolution. *International Journal of Human Resource Management*, **27**(17): 1–19.

➤ Purcell, P. and Kinnie, N. (2008) HRM and business performance. In P. Boxall, J. Purcell and P. Wright (eds) *The Oxford Handbook of Human Resource Management* (pp. 533–51). Oxford: Oxford University Press.

vocabulary checklist for ESL students

 Click here in your interactive ebook for a list of HRM terminology and vocabulary that has appeared in this chapter.

Visit the online resource centre at www.palgravehighered.com/bg-hrm-6e for lots of extra resources to help you get to grips with this chapter, including study tips, HRM skills development guides, summary lecture notes, tips for English as a Second Language (ESL) students and more.

part II

EMPLOYEE RESOURCING

STOCK BYTE

BANANASTOCK

part II

EMPLOYEE RESOURCING

chapter 4

workforce planning and diversity

objectives

After studying this chapter, you should be able to:

1 Explain the place of planning in HRM

2 Explain the difference between manpower planning, human resource planning and workforce planning

3 Give details of the use of ICT in workforce planning

4 Understand the requirements for diversity management

5 Explain the various meanings of and approaches to flexible working

6 Outline key ideas in human resource accounting

Meseret Kumulchew was working as a supervisor for Starbucks at Clapham Junction in London. She was responsible for recording the temperature of fridges and water at particular times. However, the company accused her of faking the records when the wrong information was entered. Meseret explained that she was dyslexic and had difficulties with reading, writing and telling the time. In the UK, under the Equality Act 2010, an employer needs to take account of an employee's disability and ensure that 'provisions, criteria or practices' do not put a disabled employee at a disadvantage compared with other employees. A company must take reasonable steps to avoid any disadvantage. The company is responsible for assessing needs and making adjustments. For dyslexia, although it is not automatically seen as a disability, there is still a need to assess and to seek more expert opinion from occupational health professionals on what an employee can and cannot do.

When Meseret described her dyslexia, the company regarded this explanation as unlikely and accused her of making up the data, as a result of which she was disciplined. As a result, her responsibilities were downgraded and she was told to retrain, both of which left her feeling extremely distressed and suicidal. Eventually, Meseret took Starbucks to an employment tribunal, which found in her favour. The tribunal discovered that even though Starbucks had a policy for diversity, which included provisions to remove discrimination, this was not in practice working sufficiently. In Meseret's case, her problems with dyslexia had not been properly assessed and there had not been any reasonable adjustments to her task or alternative ways for her to work, such as working with other staff or delegating tasks.

HRM web links Visit the online resource centre at **www.palgravehighered.com/bg-hrm-6e** to access a recording of an interview with Meseret.

introduction

How certain are you that you can make a plan for the future? As you near the end of your formal education, what kinds of plan can you make so that you will fully utilize your knowledge and skills? Are you more confident of making a plan now the global financial crisis (GFC) of the late 2000s is over? Does the decision made in 2016 for the UK to leave the European Union (EU) affect work opportunities? According to a recent report from the US Economic Policy Institute (Davis et al., 2015), the GFC may have finished in 2009, but its impact is still being felt, and graduates are continuing to face a weak labour market, often competing with others who have gained more experience. Although women are more likely to be employed in sectors such as health and education, considered to be less sensitive to financial downturns, both men and women face a problem of underemployment, something they were probably not planning for when they began their studies. As you might imagine, organizations also seek to plan for the future in order to ensure that the right number of people, with the right kind of talent and skill combinations, get into the right positions at the right time. A plan that achieves this is called a *workforce plan*, and its purpose is to provide some degree of certainty and control over future events. However, as we all know very well, plans do not always work out as intended.

The GFC and uncertainties over the future of the EU have made the process of planning for the recruitment and deployment of a workforce increasingly precarious. The decisions involved in making such plans rely on data that can be used to make choices and forecasts about the future. First, there are forecasts relating to the demand for the workforce, based on the organization's requirements in relation to its environment. Second, there are forecasts for the degree to which the supply of the workforce will match demand for it. In both instances, however, the ability to forecast with any kind of certainty will be reduced, and uncertainty and complexity will be increased. This could mean that plans made through an analysis of past data might become no more than a way of making sense of the past – in other words, they will fail to account for future events, and workforce planners will need to become more creative. The shocks and disturbances of the late 2000s have increased the need for planning to become both an analytical process for predictability and a creative process for working with unpredictability, unknowable shocks and complexity. It also needs to become a continuous process with as much emphasis on doing the planning as having a plan. Furthermore, based on the potential for access to significant amounts of data concerning the workforce, human resources (HR) managers can make use of how the data are analysed – the 'analytics' – to influence key decisions concerning people (Hesketh, 2014).

People and planning

At the start of the twenty-first century, it was claimed that the route to competitive advantage is achieved through people (Gratton, 2000). There was growing evidence that effective HR practices could enhance a company's sustainability and profitability if there was integration with business purpose (Guest et al., 2003), although there was also evidence that many senior managers were failing to recognize this (Caulkin, 2001). Furthermore, according to the resource-based view of the firm, an organization can derive competitive advantage from its resources through the development of human resource management (HRM) systems and routines that are unique to that organization (Barney et al., 2001). Thus, any organization could plan how it would deploy and combine a range of HR practices and achieve high commitment and enhanced performance (Wall and Wood, 2005).

Prior to the GFC and the economic downturn that started in 2008, there was a concern about skills shortages and competition between organizations to attract and develop people who could add most to an organization's performance. This supported the idea of 'HRM as a modernist project' (Legge, 2005, p. 337), pushing to address the traditional weaknesses of personnel managers by constructing a 'hard' version of HRM that is more strategic. Finding a more strategic role has been a long-running feature of HR's story over the last 30 years, requiring a variety of approaches to achieve it (Tamkin et al., 1997). In some cases, this involves supporting business strategy by developing appropriate policies and procedures. In others, it means being proactive and playing a leading role in driving strategy. In recent years, the push for HR to join decision-making at strategic levels has been enabled by the increasing availability and scale of data from many sources, including social media, which can be analysed to reveal key patterns (Hesketh, 2014). HR's position at the strategic table depends on how it makes use of its 'analytics'.

The need for HRM to become more involved in strategic business decision-making is highlighted through the World Employment and Social Outlook 2015 report, which notes that the standard employment model in which workers have a dependent relationship with employers, full-time work and a salary is becoming less dominant. Informal short-term work contracts are becoming the norm, particularly because of the increasingly global nature of supply chains. It is the complication of global supply chains and issues of diversity that has had a great impact on HRM, increasing the need for strategic input (Torres et al., 2015).

The ability to formulate plans has been one of the requirements for joining strategic discussions and, as we will show in this chapter, this ability is connected to priorities for people in organizations and the availability and use of analytics. Thus, in times of relatively full employment, people and their skills have been important because of their scarcity. For example, in the 1960s, the main concerns of manpower planning were an emphasis on the quantities, flows and mathematical modelling of people. During the years of recession in the 1970s and 80s, and then the 1990s, manpower planning was used to reduce or 'downsize' the workforce. A more qualitative view of people underpinned *human resource planning* (HRP), which involved the development and provision of a framework that would allow an organization to integrate key HR practices so that it could meet the needs of its employees, enhance their potential and meet the performance needs of the business strategy.

The uncertainty and complexity of organization and business conditions in the late 2010s is resulting in more varied approaches and methods relating to planning, which we will call *workforce planning*. This will include putting together strategies that aim to develop more people in house and retain key employees (Chartered Institute of Personnel and Development [CIPD], 2009a; Harper et al., 2013), as well as searching for new ways to reduce staffing numbers in the face of fluctuating business conditions and cuts in government funding. Additional challenges facing workforce planners leading up to 2030 focus on issues such as changing demographics, particularly in Western European countries (CIPD, 2012) and disturbances such as the UK's decision to leave the EU. Ageing populations place demand for flexible working and age-diverse working teams, and in service industries and health industries there is a need to ensure that skills are available to address these challenges (Harper et al., 2013). This leads to another vital aspect for the HRM role in workforce planning – ensuring that work is allocated carefully across all areas of an organization to achieve and maintain the well-being and work–life balance of its staff (Hurst and Patterson, 2014; Torres et al., 2015).

reflective question From your experience or reading, how much importance do you think is given to plans for people in organizations? What strategies would enable small organizations to engage in workforce planning?

Manpower planning

What we now call workforce planning was originally referred to as 'manpower planning'. During the twentieth century, this represented a response by personnel and HR managers to ensure that the necessary supply of people was forthcoming to allow targets to be met. In theory at least, a manpower plan could show how the demand for people and their skills within an organization could be balanced by supply. The key stages of this approach are shown in Figure 4.1.

The idea of a balance between demand and supply reflects the influence of the language of classical labour economics, in which movement towards an 'equilibrium' serves as an ideal. Such influences can be found in some of the definitions and explanations of manpower planning put forward over the past 50 years. For example, in 1974, the UK's Department of Employment defined manpower planning as a 'strategy for the acquisition, utilization, improvement and preservation of an organization's human resources'. Four stages of the planning process were outlined:

1 An evaluation or appreciation of the existing manpower resources
2 An estimation of the proportion of currently employed manpower resources that were likely to be within the firm by the forecast date

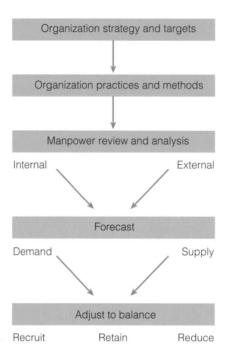

Figure 4.1 *Reconciling demand and supply*

3 An assessment or forecast of labour requirements needed if the organization's overall objectives were to be achieved by the forecast date

4 Measures to ensure that the necessary resources were available as and when required, that is, the manpower plan.

Stages 1 and 2 were linked in the 'supply aspect of manpower', with stage 1 being part of 'normal personnel practice' (Department of Employment, 1974). Stage 3 represents the 'demand aspect of manpower'. There were two main reasons for companies to use manpower planning: first, to develop their business objectives and manning levels; and second, to reduce the 'unknown' factor. Stage 4 requires an interaction between demand and supply so that skills are utilized to the best possible advantage and the aspirations of the individual are taken into account (Smith, 1980).

Because the interaction between these factors was highly complex within a context that included aims of optimization and overall equilibrium, manpower planning became a suitable area of interest for operational research and for the application of statistical techniques (Bartholomew, 1971). In this process, organizations could be envisaged as a series of stocks and flows, and as part of an overall system of resource allocation. Models of behaviour could be formulated in relation to labour turnover, length of service, how quickly promotions occurred and age distribution. These variables could be expressed as mathematical and statistical formulae and equations that would allow solutions to manpower decisions to be calculated. With the growing use of computers, the techniques and models became more ambitious and probably beyond the comprehension of most managers (Parker and Caine, 1996). In large organizations, there was, however, a growth in the number of specialist manpower analysts who were capable of dealing with the complex processes involved.

reflective
question Do you think a manpower system can be adequately represented as a series of
stocks and flows?

Emphasizing statistical models of manpower supply and demand at the expense of the
reality of managing and interacting with people was bound to be met with suspicion,
certainly by employees and their representatives, as well as by managers 'forced' to act on
the results of the calculations. Hence, during the 1970s and 80s, manpower planning
acquired a poor reputation as a system with few benefits and only a few examples of when
'comprehensive and systematic manpower planning [was] fully integrated into strategic
planning' (Cowling and Walters, 1990, p. 6). There were a number of attempts to make
manpower planning techniques more 'user-friendly' to non-specialists. Thus, the fall-out
from theoretical progress in manpower analysis was the application of techniques to help
with 'real' manpower problems (Bell, 1989), for example why one department in an organization seemed to suffer from a dramatically higher employee or labour turnover, or why
graduate trainees were not retained in sufficient number. Personnel managers were able to
build up a 'toolkit' of analytics consisting of key manpower measures relating to, for
example, employee turnover, retention, stability and absenteeism. All of these could be
relatively easily calculated, either monthly or quarterly, and expressed graphically to reveal
trends and future paths.

Through the 1990s, such techniques were incorporated into PC-based computerized
personnel information systems. As the software became more user-friendly, personnel
departments were able to take advantage of this and make themselves more responsive to
business needs. Most large and medium-sized organizations now employ some form of
computerized personnel system, and there are many providers of suitable software; we will
explore such developments later in this chapter.

HRM web
links Visit the online resource centre at **www.palgravehighered.com/bg-hrm-6e** to read a
booklet published in the UK by the Advisory, Conciliation and Arbitration Service, and
for information on many HR software products and suppliers.

Diagnosing manpower problems

The use of manpower planning techniques within computerized personnel information
systems can be seen as part of a continuing search by the personnel function to find areas of
expertise to legitimize its position and prove its value by 'adding to the bottom line'. Thus,
there is an attempt to use manpower information as a way of understanding problems so that
action can be taken as appropriate. In this way, HR managers have been practising what Fyfe
(1986, p. 66) referred to as 'the diagnostic approach to manpower planning'. This approach
built on and broadened the demand and supply approach outlined in Figure 4.1 in order to
identify problem areas and understand why they were occurring. This is shown in Figure 4.2.

The idea of an equilibrium between demand and supply can occur only on paper or on
the digital screen; the more probable situation is one of continuous imbalance as a result of
the dynamic conditions facing any organization, people's behaviour and the imperfections
of manpower models. A diagnostic approach would mean becoming aware of manpower
problems by monitoring statistics such as turnover and stability, as well as by obtaining

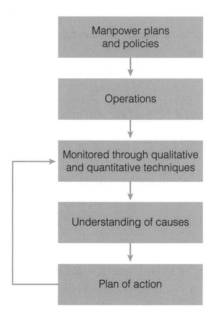

Figure 4.2 *The diagnostic approach to manpower planning*

qualitative data from interviewing staff. Such interviews might reveal concerns with job satisfaction and the career paths open to staff, reflecting the fact that the aspirations they hold are not being met by current practices. Rather than express these aspirations openly for fear of conflict with management, many staff may prefer to seek employment elsewhere. The loss of talented staff has important cost implications, and a diagnostic approach to retention can provide a significant pay-off.

Employee turnover

The reasons for employee turnover are based on complex factors often requiring solutions that are specific to each organization's context. Morrell et al. (2001) have suggested that explanations of voluntary employee turnover fall into two categories:

- *Economic or labour market reasons* – the emphasis being on external factors such as market conditions
- *Psychological reasons* – the emphasis being on feelings and perceptions relating to job satisfaction, involvement and commitment within the psychological contract.

Research on employee turnover has focused on the latter, seeking to explore more closely why voluntary turnover occurs, which is particularly important given the costs of replacing and recruiting new staff, as well as the pressure on the remaining staff to cover the work. For example, employee turnover may rise in times of organizational change; that is, the 'shock' of changes in patterns of work may lead to decisions to quit (Morrell et al., 2004). A better understanding of the psychological features of turnover can allow for more focused interventions and avoid the unnecessary costs involved (see Chapter 1). Morrell et al. (2004) suggested the use of certain measures to minimize the effects of change, including:

- Surveys
- Consultation processes

- Intra- and extra-firm career guidance
- Exit interviews
- Leaver profiling.

In the 2000s, the loss of staff is also seen as the loss of intellectual capital and experience, and the replacement of 'knowledge workers' can be both expensive and time-consuming (Buckingham, 2000; Ton and Huckman, 2008). In addition, Des and Shaw (2001) highlight the importance of social capital – the value of relationships between people, embedded in network links that facilitate the trust and communication that are vital to an organization's overall performance. Social capital is reduced when people leave, with a negative impact on organizational performance (Shaw et al., 2005).

We would usually expect high employee turnover to have a negative impact on performance, but recent research has proved that this is not always the case. Siebert and Zubanov (2009) completed an analysis of employee turnover in a large retail organization in the UK and found differences in commitment among full-time core sales assistants compared with part-timers, differences that affected the turnover–performance relationship. With the full-time staff, there was a negative relationship between turnover and performance, but with the part-timers, the relationship was positive. This suggested a need to consider differences between work systems for different groups in organizations. Thus, full-time or core staff would benefit from high-involvement approaches to their management including less monitoring and control of their performance and more training and career development, whereas part-time or secondary staff would be allocated more routine tasks, more control and less training and career development.

A similar result was found in Budhwar et al.'s (2009) study of high turnover in Indian call centres, where many staff were college graduates with little experience and little intention of staying, meaning that their commitment to working in the organization was limited. Much of the work was considered 'monotonous' and, along with night shifts, affected 'quality of life' and 'work–life balance'. It is hardly surprising that such a work system results in high turnover, but presumably there is a ready supply of staff who can be recruited as substitutes, with only low levels of training needed. Hancock et al. (2013) completed a meta-analysis of 48 studies of employee turnover and organization performance and found a negative relationship. However the strength of the relationship varied, being, for example, stronger in manufacturing and transport, in mid-sized organizations and when performance was mainly focused on customer service.

More recent research into the effects of employee turnover, particularly within a global context, has seen a revival of manpower planning, especially in developing economies such as India and Malaysia (Singh and Jain, 2014). Although many developed Western European economic countries are moving towards workforce planning for reasons discussed below, many of the developing economies are turning to manpower planning as a way to bring their industries and demand for specific labour skills into the organizational business strategy. Singh and Jain (2014), in their quantitative research of manufacturing companies in the Madhya Pradesh area of India, found a significant link between manpower planning and organization growth and development. Likewise, within the growing economy of Bangladesh, a similar link has been reported between entrepreneurial and small business growth, and good manpower planning policies (Amin and Islam, 2013). Dhamija and Gupta (2014) identify a lack of good manpower planning, with employee burnout, a particular issue in India in highly skilled job areas. Within the general manufacturing industry of the Asia-Pacific region, Ali et al. (2015) have identified a 1 per cent increase in employee turnover from 2012 to 2013, which their research suggests is in part a result of poor manpower planning.

HRM web links

Visit the online resource centre at **www.palgravehighered.com/bg-hrm-6e** for UK statistics that measure work-related stress, anxiety and depression.

Human resource planning

There is an acknowledgement that manpower planning does not address some important workforce issues relating to motivation and the link to prospects of promotion. Manpower planning tools do not factor these issues in, which therefore indicates that a more encompassing HR system is required (Guerry et al., 2015). HRM has sought to make an explicit link between strategy, structure and people. During the 1990s, the plan to bring this about was referred to as the HR plan. This also symbolized the intention to link HR practices to superior performance at work. There has been an ongoing debate on the benefits of adopting a 'high-road' HRM strategy (see Chapter 1) of high training, high involvement, high rewards and quality commitment (Cooke, 2000) versus a 'low-road' strategy characterized by low pay, low job security and work intensification. Furthermore, research has suggested the importance of introducing HR practices together in a 'bundle' so that they will enhance and support each other. For example, a plan to introduce performance appraisal on its own will be far less effective without considering training, reward, careers and the attitudes and styles of managers.

It is also important to coordinate implementation (Hoque, 1999), although any plan to do this will be subject to local culture and everyday meanings, which support the 'strength' of the HRM system (Bowen and Ostroff, 2004).

For example, if the organization is pursuing a strategy of increasing its exports, the staff's perception of what they feel the organization is like, based on such factors as policies, rewards and how managers behave towards the staff, will affect how HRM activities such as training and career development affect overall performance. More recent research highlights how different pressures from both within and outside any organization will affect how HRM is implemented (Boon et al., 2009); in the UK, case study research has underlined the need for an integrated system of HRM covering skills, recruitment, absenteeism, reward and encouragement to be innovative in order to achieve superior performance (Department of Trade and Industry, 2005a).

A high-road HRM strategy linked to a high-performing organization requires a belief by management that engagement with people represents the key source of competitive advantage because an organization's route to success is based on having a distinctive product and/or service quality as well as price (MacLeod and Clarke, 2009). Furthermore, the continuing development of those people will be a vital feature of both the formation and the implementation of a business strategy.

Although there is evidence of a correlation between high-road HRM and business performance (Wall and Wood, 2005), such evidence may not always convince managers in their decision-making. A resource-based view of organizations suggests that the distinctive expertise and skills of people are a first-order element of strategy-making and therefore a

HRM and globalization 4.1

Migrant workers in Qatar: the impact of regulatory failure on workforce planning

BRAND X PICTURES

Most states have enacted laws that set out acceptable workplace practices – laws that often reflect global labour standards that are codified in various International Labour Organization conventions. National and subnational laws, in turn, influence workforce planning. For example, limitations on the length of a working day affect the number of workers an employer must hire in order to ensure 24/7 operation of a production line.

Many conservative commentators rail against workplace rules as an unnecessary restraint on the efficient operation of a free market. In this view, the operation of the workplace is a private affair, and working conditions are best left to be negotiated between the employer and the worker. It seems fair, then, to ask what happens when there are no state-enforced rules in the workplace? The case of migrant workers in Qatar offers some alarming answers.

Qatar is hosting the 2022 Fédération Internationale de Football Association (FIFA) World Cup. Approximately 1.4 million migrant workers from across the developing world – including India, Nepal and the Philippines – are building the World Cup venues. These workers arrive in Qatar and are employed under the *kafala* system of indentured servitude. Their passports are routinely seized upon arrival, and they are tied to their employer for a fixed period of time. Workers frequently arrive in debt to recruiters, and the workers' wages are withheld to ensure they do not run away. Work is often for 12 hours per day in heat that frequently exceeds 50°C (Rajouria, 2015).

Not surprisingly, many of these workers die on the job. While workplace injuries claim some, an alarming number of deaths are cases of heart failure (which can be brought on by heat exhaustion) among young men. The exact number of migrant workers killed while building the World Cup stadiums is the subject of intense debate. The government of Qatar says that no migrant workers have died. Organized labour disagrees: a newspaper investigation in 2013 found one Nepalese worker died each day, with Nepalese workers accounting for 40 per cent of the migrant workforce. At this rate, over 4000 migrant workers are expected to die by the end of construction (Pattisson, 2013).

Two aspects of the Qatar example are relevant to HR practitioners. The first is that the regulation clearly has an

effect on the options available to employers when workforce planning. Specifically, the absence of rules allows employers to use their greater labour market power to create highly profitable (albeit rather Dickensian) conditions of work. Historically, such arrangements have often led to significant social instability.

The second aspect is that it is difficult to disentangle employment regulation from other forms of state regulation. For example, the availability of migrant workers to Qatari employers is controlled by state immigration policies. Calls for a deregulation of employment must be viewed with a wider lens to see what sort of knock-on effects deregulation will trigger. The particular constellation of policies operating in Qatar (which allow employers to access migrant workers but deny those workers basic workplace rights) also suggests that the state is not necessarily a neutral actor and is (intentionally or otherwise) colluding with employers in order to achieve some end.

Stop! Can you think of two ways in which state regulation of employment has affected workplace planning in an organization that you are familiar with? Do you think the state should be intervening in the operation of the labour market in these ways? Why or why not? Do you think that knowing there are 4000 dead migrant workers will appreciably affect viewership of the 2022 World Cup? Why or why not?

Sources and further information: For more information, see Pattisson (2013) and Rajouria (2015).

Note: This feature was written by Bob Barnetson.

key element in planning (Liff, 2000). However, HRM is in many cases still not a priority or first-order issue in strategy; indeed, it is often a third-order issue (Coleman and Keep, 2001), so that when difficulties arise, many organizations swiftly move towards a version of HRM in which HR activities are designed to respond to strategy, with people viewed as a resource whose cost must be controlled. We know from experience that, in sectors such as retail banking, when competition and deregulation created conditions of continuous flux, it became easier to adopt a low-road version of HRM resulting in branch closures and the loss of many jobs (Storey et al., 1997).

Another example can be found in the implementation of business process re-engineering (Hammer and Champy, 1993) during the 1990s. This involved a radical change in business processes by applying IT to integrate tasks and produce an output of value to the customer. As the change unfolded, unnecessary processes and layers of bureaucracy were identified and removed, and staff became more empowered to deliver high-quality service and products. Business process re-engineering has, however, almost always been accompanied by unemployment (Grey and Mitev, 1995), a fact that HRP may attempt, with difficulty, to disguise. Downsizing by reducing staff numbers is seen by many organizations as a means of improving their efficiency, productivity and overall competitiveness (Cross and Trava-glione, 2004), but, as we will explore below, redundancy can also have many negative consequences for organizations.

In the UK, specific historical, social, political and institutional contextual features make for a business environment that is largely incompatible with high-road HRM (Cooke, 2000), a situation that is likely to continue given the UK's intended departure from the EU. Thus, with the pressure to sustain or increase profits, employees are more likely to be treated as a 'number' in the quest to reduce costs. This has been a continuing pattern, so that HRP has become a framework to accommodate the 'multifarious practices' of 'pragmatic and oppor-tunistic' organizations (Storey, 1995b). It is perhaps for these reasons that, during the 2000s, the term 'workforce planning' came to be preferred, particularly as organizations began to face growing uncertainty towards the end of the decade (Cappelli, 2009).

reflective question Can an organization claim a high-road approach to HRM while adopting low-road practices? What are the consequences of this?

Workforce planning

In 2008, British bank Northern Rock was nationalized as a consequence of a strategy that failed during the financial crisis. Around 6500 people worked for the bank in 2008, but by June 2010 this figure was close to 4000, with more job losses planned. Like many other organizations, the bank was seeking to plan for the future while facing uncertainty and unpredictability. So the notion of 'right people, right skills, right place and right time' was fraught with difficulty. The trade union suggested that the job cuts were 'short-termist' and likely to worsen unemployment in the UK's North East, where the bank was based. The then-CEO, Gary Hoffman (who resigned in November 2010, intending to join another bank in 2011), said, 'There is still a challenging economic environment and in order to meet our objectives, we must align our staffing level to match the smaller size of the business, increase efficiency and reduce our cost base' (Watchman and Wearden, The Guardian, 2010). But of course it had not been always like this, and pre-2008, Northern Rock, like many other organizations, had faced a different problem: that of finding the right kind of people to support its delivery of services and growth. The search was on to find 'high-potential' individuals in the so-called 'war for talent' (Michaels et al., 2001) as part of a growing interest in talent management (see Chapter 5). Workforce planning is the process of forecasting the supply and demand of skills against the requirements of future production and services delivery in a situation of uncertainty and change. It is a process that must be set in a particular context and can cover many different activities, including analytics such as employee turnover, and the diagnostic and strategic understanding of HRP (Curson et al., 2010); it can also be broader in scope than either of these.

Cappelli (2009) suggests two types of forecast. First, there are internal forecasts to consider the future workforce in terms of numbers and skills or competencies, and how these will be affected by competition for staff and the requirements of the work. Any organization will need to understand the talent of its workforce, how such talent will occupy particular roles, and the relationship between roles. A future perspective will consider the preparation for and movement between roles, including succession-planning and the management of careers. The second type of forecast is the prediction of demand, which has to be considered against the demand for products and services. The latter determines skill requirements for the future and is considered be significant in national efforts to move towards high-value/high-skill production in the UK (UK Commission for Employment and Skills, 2009). However, the most recent global reports on labour and job creation suggest that the organization of workers and employers has become ever more challenging due to global value chains associated with diverse forms of work (Torres et al., 2015).

But it is not just organizations that undertake workforce planning. Governments, for example, are to a greater or lesser extent interested in the supply of skills to match forecasts in demand (Torres et al., 2015). Green et al. (1999) have shown how countries such as South Korea, Singapore and Taiwan – the 'tiger economies' – consider skill requirements against targets for growth, which in turn sets the direction for the supply of skills obtained in schools, colleges and universities. Information for planning is gathered systematically in combination with efforts to persuade employers to demand skills at higher levels.

In sectors such as the UK's National Health Service (NHS), workforce planning faces significant complexities due to the large variety of skill classifications, needs and availability of staff. Curson (2006) sees medical workforce planning as analogous to crystal-ball gazing, and Parsons (2010) views it as both a science and an art because predictions for the future, based on the analysis of trends, can hardly be relied upon when future requirements based on need rather than demand are likely to change so rapidly. Part of the art of workforce planning is the utilization of tools such as simulations and scenarios to create conversations between different stakeholders that then set the direction for action (Micic, 2010). Van Greuningen et al. (2012) have identified weaknesses in the very sophisticated Dutch health workers planning model, in which the importance of interdisciplinary teams is becoming an increasingly vital part of providing holistic healthcare.

The use of ICT in workforce planning

Workforce planning can be supported through the use of information and communication technology (ICT). It is argued that human resource information systems (HRISs) can enhance a more systemic consideration of HR activities and their linkage with the organization's vision and goals (Bhuiyan et al., 2014; Mayfield et al., 2003). Indeed, generating,

Does the UK produce too many graduates?

DIGITAL VISION

A policy report by the CIPD (CIPD, 2015b) starts from a discussion of rising participation rates in higher education in the UK, which have stabilized at around 43 per cent since 2003/04. Following the expansion of higher education in the UK, many graduates have had to find employment in jobs that would previously have been filled by non-graduates. The study shows that the proportion of graduates in professions has increased from 53 per cent to 78 per cent between 1991 and 2014. Almost half of those in managerial and technical professions are now graduates, and graduate employment has increased from negligible proportions to 21 per cent for administrative occupations, 13 per cent for sales and personal service occupations and 8 per cent for low-skilled occupations.

The UK and many European countries have seen:

> graduate supply increase faster than the number of high skilled jobs in which graduates traditionally worked, leading to an occupational filtering down where many graduates find themselves further down the occupational hierarchy. (CIPD, 2015b, p. 4)

The study argues that across Europe, as well as the UK, there has been an increase in graduates entering 'skilled non-manual occupations' such as clerical, service and sales jobs, making it harder for those with medium and low levels of education to find work.

The evidence suggests that a degree 'has become a necessity for getting an ever-larger proportion of jobs'. Higher education can be seen as a 'filtering device' to enable recruiters to identify the most able job applicants. If this is all that is happening, serious questions need to be asked about the role and value of higher education, the quality of graduates and their underutilization. It could, however, be the case that jobs have at the same time been upgraded so that graduates are using their enhanced skills and being more productive. The authors of the CIPD report rejected qualitative research asking graduates about how their skills are utilized because such responses are very subjective and the respondents' perceptions may be inaccurate, creating problems in interpreting the results. The authors of the CIPD study used data concerning influence or discretion over what employees do and their pace of work as a proxy for the skills

requirement of their job. They found that there was upgrading in a number of jobs, but in over half the job groups there was no evidence of this process, and in some cases graduates had less influence and discretion than the non-graduates working alongside them. The data showed extensive graduate underutilization, leading the authors to conclude that alternatives to general degrees such as vocational courses and apprenticeships for preparing young people for entry into the labour market should be considered.

(continued)

Stop! If many graduates do not take any enhanced skills into the labour market, as the CIPD study suggests, should the university participation rate be cut back? Do you think that a university education can be justified on grounds other than to increase productivity, and if so what benefits can you think of for society or the individual?

Sources and further information: For the information quoted here, see CIPD (2015b) and Higher Education Statistics Agency (2015).

Note: This feature was written by David Denham.

A survey of the 2013/14 cohort of UK domicile full-time first-degree graduates, conducted 6 months after graduation, showed an improving job market. Of these graduates, 73 per cent were in work (of whom 69 per cent were in professional occupations), 16 per cent were continuing their studies at postgraduate level or pursuing a professional qualification, and 7 per cent were unemployed (of whom 19 per cent were due to start work in the next month) (Higher Education Statistics Agency, 2015).

capturing, tracking and disseminating organizational knowledge, in all its manifestations in software packages and online, are key features of knowledge management and organizational learning, and both can be facilitated by an HRIS. HRISs have become a form of organizational intelligence, enabling the production of various analytics that enable forecasts and scenarios for future possibilities and unexpected shocks (Hurley-Hanson and Giannantonio, 2008; Nagendra and Deshpande, 2014).

During the 1990s, there was a widespread use of HRISs for transaction applications in operational areas such as employee records, payroll and absence control. This suggests that its primary use was as a means of collecting data for others to use in decision-making, and that it was used much less in expert systems and decision support applications (Kinnie and Arthurs, 1996). Ball (2001, p. 690) concluded at the end of this period that 'HRM still seems to be the laggard in running its own systems' to support decision-making and strategy.

A crucial element in any HRIS is how the information is used, especially in decisions concerning how people are employed at work. It is suggested (Liff, 1997a) that an HRIS can be seen from different viewpoints that in turn affect its use. These viewpoints are that its purpose is:

- To provide an objective view of an organization in which the information used is comprehensive and accurate, allowing the best decisions to be made
- To construct organization realities, including the categories and classifications determining the information that should be collected
- To make sense of what is going on within an organization and what needs to be done, according to how information is interpreted by each person, based on his or her view of life at work.

In three case studies, Liff (1997a) found that each view could be used to explain managers' use of an HRIS. Managers were most attached to an objective view of an HRIS and viewed the information it represented as neutral; that is, skills were defined from a 'rational reassessment of current labels' (Liff, 1997a, p. 27). In addition, there was a belief that the HRIS categories could construct a new approach to managing staff and play a role in 'serving dominant business strategy'. The third view could, however, also be found, especially in the way in which apparent discrepancies in information produced by the system could be understood on the basis of existing knowledge of life at work.

There is increasing research into the use of HRIS systems in countries such as Pakistan and India (Awan and Sarwar, 2014; Jahan, 2014). These studies explore the links between strategic human resource management and the use of HRIS systems, particularly in terms of business process re-engineering. The banking sector is a particular focus for Pakistan in its efforts to secure banking systems for global use. In Bangladesh, HRISs have become an increasingly important tool over the past 5 years, again seen as offering the potential for it to become a more globally recognized economic nation. For countries like Pakistan and Bangladesh, the main limitations to implementation include expense, inconvenience in countries where network connections and electrical supplies are still an issue, and understanding of the type of input information required to constitute quality information for the user (Jahan, 2014).

In the 2000s, there has been an extension of HRISs towards e-HR (Kettley and Reilly, 2003), with many HR departments using the internet and web-enabled technologies to create an organizational network of HR data and information. In addition, there has been a development of new approaches to HR activities such as e-recruitment, e-learning and e-reward. Another approach is to allow staff to access information on HR issues, for example how much holiday they have left for the year, via a business-to-employee (B2E) portal. Advanced B2E solutions include attempts to influence ways of working and relationships, such as enhancing e-working by developments in telephony, shared collaboration spaces, online meeting rooms and shared access to intelligence and knowledge management applications. Furthermore, making such information available on the internet allows it to be accessed by staff from a computer anywhere in the world. As the use of e-HR has become an important part of HR functioning in a globalized world, research has investigated the negative aspects of such systems, which include the vast set-up costs, particularly for developing economies, the inappropriate use of such systems and, most importantly, the loss of the 'human touch' (Francis et al., 2014; Sharma, 2014).

Other ICT developments provide an opportunity for HR departments to work strategically with other functions. Many large and medium-sized organizations have, for example, attempted to integrate all information flows through enterprise resource planning (ERP) software – a typical HR module within ERP might include the items listed in Table 4.1 (see Jackson, 2010). Each heading in the module provides access to a database requiring data to be entered. Once entered, information can then be processed and re-presented for appropriate use. Furthermore, most ERP systems allow for an integration between modules and units within modules, which forms part of an organization's ability to create and manage knowledge (see Chapter 7). Jackson (2010) argues that ERP allows routine HR functions to be consolidated to support business processes, saving cost and securing competitive advantage. However, like all software and technology innovations, it is necessary to consider how change is implemented to secure the benefits and full use of ERP's functionality. This is particularly important when considering the benefits that organizations can gain from cross-disciplinary and diversified teams in terms of responding in an agile way to the rapidly changing external and internal demands (Codreanu and Radut, 2012;

Table 4.1 Headings for a typical HR module within ERP

Application screening	Salary administration
Payroll	Work schedule
Planning	Travel expenses
Recruitment	Benefits administration
Compensation management	Personnel development
Funds and position management	Personnel time management
Time evaluation	Shift planning, training
Event management	

Van Greuningen et al, 2012). The other area that ERP functionality struggles with is the advent of flexible working, particularly in terms of individualized working plans (Kultalahti and Vitala, 2015; Peters et al., 2014).

HRM web links

> Visit the online resource centre at **www.palgravehighered.com/bg-hrm-6e** for information on ERP software.

reflective question

> Do you think that all communications at work can be settled via e-HR and B2E? Is there a 'solution' for all HR issues?

As a consequence of these various technological developments, HR professionals have a significant opportunity to draw upon a large amount of data for use in workforce planning and the production of analytics, which can promote more significant participation in organization decision-making (Hesketh, 2014). However, survey research from the USA suggests that HR managers mostly used spreadsheets and HRIS reports for workforce planning and analytics, although there was generally low satisfaction with either. A significant minority did not conduct workforce planning, and most did not see themselves as 'mature' in the use of workforce analytics (Visier, 2014).

Diversity management

One of the most important trends in recent years has been an interest in the benefits to be achieved by planning for a diverse workforce, known as 'diversity management', and its connection with business and organizational success (Tatli et al., 2007). However, caution needs to be exercised in the development of diversity management as the need for 'fairness' can often lead to the development of 'identity-blind' policies and procedures, which ultimately maintain unequal power relationships between majority and minority groups (Choi and Rainey, 2014). Ashley et al. (2015) highlighted the same issue when investigating the lack of social mobility from university to elite law and accountancy firms in London.

This move towards diversity can be seen as an extension of, but simultaneously a contrast to, the promotion of equal opportunities during the 1970s and 80s. Equal opportunities is the view that people should be treated equally regardless of race, ethnic origin, gender, sexual orientation and other social categorizations, so that 'individuals are enabled freely and equally to compete for social rewards' (Jewson and Mason, 1986, p. 307). Jewson and Mason set equal opportunities within a free-market tradition, and the purpose of legislation and policies was seen as removing obstacles within and distortions to the working of markets. They pointed to a liberal approach based on 'positive action' to ensure fair and meritocratic procedures in organizations, underpinned by antidiscrimination legislation. They contrasted this with a more radical view, highlighting the embedded nature of discrimination, which could not be corrected through fair procedures alone. Instead, disadvantaged groups would need 'positive discrimination' to achieve fairness, although this still remains unlawful in the UK.

There has, however, been a general recognition that equal opportunities based on 'sameness' have not fulfilled their promise, and that while overt discrimination has been largely removed, prejudice and stereotyping remain embedded within organizations and society at large. One of the crucial difficulties is that debates on equality are based on ethical arguments, often framed in terms of either social justice or a business case, which Gagnon and Cornelius (2000) suggest tends to produce sterility when it comes to practice.

Diversity, according to Schneider (2001, p. 27) is 'about creating a working culture that seeks, respects, values and harnesses difference'. The basic contrast with equal opportunities is an acceptance that there are differences between people, that such differences can be valued, and that they are the source of productive potential within an organization. It is suggested that diversity can provide an organization with a valuable resource in competing both globally and locally. Dijk et al. (2012) highlight that there is not only a moral imperative, but also a sound business case with an explicit strategic approach, to valuing individual differences. This will then result in commitment, creativity and competitive advantage for the organization. For example, Barclays Bank in the UK declared the following (Barclays, 2016):

> Barclays ensures that employees of all backgrounds are treated equally and contribute fully to our vision and goals. By deploying a global diversity and inclusion (D&I) strategy which now plays a significant part in our Balanced Scorecard, the diversity of our employees is embedded into our journey to becoming the 'Go-To' bank.

reflective question   How do you think that Barclays can achieve such a vision of diversity and inclusion?

Like Barclays, many organizations are seeking to manage diversity, and this requires organizations to recognize differences. According to Liff (1997b), there are four approaches to managing diversity based on the degree of commitment to social group equality as an organizational objective, and on the perceived relevance of differentiation between social groups for policy-making:

- The first approach might be to *dissolve differences* in order to 'stress individualism' (Liff, 1997b, p. 13), so that everyone's needs and desires for effective working are recognized. This tends to minimize differences, giving little recognition to the value of difference – rather like traditional equal opportunities approaches.
- In contrast, a second approach is to *value differences*. Crucial here is the recognition that past practices have reinforced inequalities and led to under-representation and disadvantage. This may mean that there needs to be a change in practice to create a culture reinforcing the fact that everyone has a valued role in an organization.
- The third approach of *accommodating differences* seeks not to waste talent but to ensure that everyone has an equal chance. This could mean, for example, targeting recruitment for under-represented groups that have the necessary qualifications.
- A fourth approach is to *utilize differences*, recognizing their usefulness and developing policies that value them. Liff uses the example of a career track for 'family' women with career breaks, gradual promotion and part-time work. The crucial feature of the policy would be that this track would be valued in the same way as the traditional track.

It might be argued that the idea of managing diversity is not a great deal more in advance of traditional approaches to equal opportunities. Indeed, many organizations espouse a commitment to equality and diversity that could easily be translated into a focus on 'sameness', rather than tackling the complexity of 'difference'. This is currently being researched in terms of contexts and power relationships, an area that diversity management and HRM have not previously considered (Ahonen et al., 2014). However, in contrast to the preventive stance of equal opportunities, managing diversity takes a more positive line in which an organization seeks to avoid accusations of treating people unequally (Kirton and Greene, 2010). There is also a widening of the coverage beyond traditional concerns with race and gender, and this echoes legislative and regulative support related to age, sexual orientation and disability.

Probably the most important feature is, however, the encouragement from senior management to put diversity at the forefront of its concerns (Celik et al., 2012). Some organizations, for example car manufacturer Ford and telecommunications company BT, have indicated this by the appointment of diversity directors or diversity champions. Thus, there is value to be gained from being diverse, in terms of both orientation towards the external context, by appreciating the diversity of cultures and ethnic backgrounds of staff and customers, and recognition of the variety within an organization.

Diversity needs to be seen strategically (Greene and Kirton, 2011), as part of a cultural change process (Dijk et al., 2012) and one that is good for organizational performance (Pilch, 2006). In the UK, the Confederation of British Industry, the Trades Union Congress and the Equality and Human Rights Commission joined forces to argue that meeting legal and moral requirements on diversity can have clear business benefits (Confederation of British Industry, 2008). Research in Ireland for 132 companies clearly showed a link between high-performance working and organizational outcomes when factors such as diversity were managed in an integrated and cohesive manner (Flood et al., 2008).

There are, however, also doubts. Foster and Harris (2005) and Anand and Winters (2008), for example, have identified that employers and employees are often confused by the simultaneous focus on equality and giving value to difference in the workplace, and question whether diversity is just equality repackaged or genuinely represents something new. In addition, there is a critical engagement with the concept of diversity and its origins (Lorbiecki and Jack, 2000) and a warning against the dangers of an argument that simply serves a business (Western, 2008).

For diversity to be taken seriously, it has to be more than checking possible prejudice in the recruitment literature or expecting line managers to take responsibility for implementing plans (Celik et al., 2012). It needs to be recognized that historical tradition plays a vital role, usually below the surface of consciousness, in maintaining normative value sets that will prevent the agenda of diversity advancing (D'Netto et al., 2014). There needs to be a challenge to and a critique of the attitudes and background assumptions that individuals implicitly hold and that are also embedded in everyday objects and activities that form the commonality of our lives and to which we are bound (Wood et al., 2004). Thus, greater attention to socialization and the development of a culture of tolerance is required if the positive benefits of diversity are to be gained. This implies that implementing a diversity management policy requires cultural change (Wallace et al., 2014) and that it requires tailoring to the specific needs and culture of each organization (Nguyen, 2014). Alcázar et al. (2012) suggest that organizations need to research and analyse their own diversity profile. HRM then needs to consider what patterns of HRM practice can be used, depending on the type of diversity the organization faces and what specific effects it wishes to make. This provides both diversity and HRM with a strategic role in developing diversity management policies within an holistic transformational role (Alcázar et al., 2013).

There is, however, also a potential for greater conflict based on the misunderstandings that are caused when people from different backgrounds and cultures have different points of view and different values; this can, in turn, lead to lower job satisfaction and higher staff turnover (McMillan-Capehart, 2005). Research has also identified that individual interpretations of diversity management affect fundamental understanding. Olsen et al. (2016), in their complex study of gender diversity management, identified that, for example, women in the USA define gender diversity management as meaning the management of the male to female employee ratio and that is standardized to the local demographics – a compliance approach. Conversely, in France, women identified gender diversity management as the need to recognize that different management techniques were required in order to ensure effective management or a business benefit approach.

The CIPD (2010b) found a range of barriers to integrating talent and diversity, such as unsuccessful previous experiences, an exclusive orientation towards talent and a lack of boardroom diversity. However, their research also pointed to some excellent examples of practice in managing diversity in such organizations as BT, The Guardian Media Group and the NHS in the London borough of Tower Hamlets. There is an argument for organizations to appreciate the value that can be provided through the talents of a diverse workforce. However, as Ford et al. (2009) found, such an argument needs to work with the interests of leaders and managers. Nguyen (2014) suggests that diversity management needs tailoring to the specific needs and culture within three levels of an organization – the strategic (culture, vision, mission and business strategy), tactical (staffing and training) and operational (flexible employment and work life balance) – and at each of these levels the line managers need to be involved. Recent research (Agrawal, 2012; Ashikali and Groeneveld, 2015) has identified the role of the line manager or team leader as a factor for the successful implementation of diversity management. Although compliance with the law is expected, many people do not like to be told what to do, and the area of diversity often falls into this category. Payne et al. (2013) have found support for this statement, identifying that worker-directed workplace teams generally facilitate diverse networks through the pursuit of shared organizational goals and objectives. Those workplaces where manager-directed teams operated did not share the same success, leading to a conclusion that perhaps autonomy, co-operative worker action and shared practice can transform the workplace.

In a world where diversity is not simply about race, disability or gender but is now concerned with issues such as transgender individuals (Ozturk and Tatli, 2015), the inclusion of HIV-positive employees in hospitality industries around the world (Yap and Ineson, 2012), the impact of both legal and illegal immigration (Brunow, 2014) and the global supply chain, there is a distinct broadening of the HRM remit. The challenge for HRM is to find ways to enable organizations to maximize the benefits of diversity within a sustainable working environment, by highlighting and engaging with the strategic role of diversity management (Ehrke et al., 2014).

One of the difficulties for HRM is that although diversity management has become an established field of research, there is still a need to develop more conceptual tools to contextualize diversity management processes in socioeconomic and organizational settings (Tatli, 2011). This is primarily due to a gap between how we talk about diversity management – the diversity discourse – and diversity practice. A lack of any agreed definition of diversity impedes how we discuss the issue (Kapoor, 2011). As shown above, the definition of diversity plays an important role in implementing and understanding diversity management, and the definition chosen by an organization will affect how policy is implemented (Olsen and Martins, 2012; Van Ewijk, 2011). The definition adopted affects the understanding of 'what' diversity is for a particular organization, 'why' an organization is implementing diversity management and finally 'how' diversity becomes part of the business strategy (Van Ewijk, 2011). These questions can only be answered through research and analysis conducted by the HRM function (Alcázar et al., 2012, 2013; Nguyen, 2014).

HRM web links Some organizations seek to monitor their progress on diversity issues. Visit the online resource centre at **www.palgravehighered.com/bg-hrm-6e** to learn about one organization's measurement of equality impact.

Flexibility

In planning how to respond to rapid technological and social change, and customer demands, many organizations invoke the idea of 'flexibility'. Furthermore, in recent years, partly as a way of dealing with downturns and upturns in the need for staff, there has been concern about the tendency to offer temporary contracts without the guarantee of work, or what are referred to as 'zero-hours' contracts (Brinkley, 2013). This suggests that the different meanings of the term 'flexibility', and the implications for workforce planning and employment of staff, need to be clarified.

reflective question How many definitions of flexibility can you think of? As you consider these different definitions, examine the implications for skills, the hours and location of work, the type of contract and the overall motivation and satisfaction of people at work.

Stredwick and Ellis (2005) suggest some key advantages of flexible working. For businesses, there is the chance to exploit the 24-hour economy and open new labour markets that avoid traditional working patterns. Employees seem to like flexible working too, achieving 'far more in the flexible mode' with no 'desire to go back to traditional working patterns' (p. 5). Flexibility can also be seen by employees as a means of achieving a more satisfactory work–life balance (Jones et al., 2007), allowing for greater control over their working time, especially for women and those with caring responsibilities (McDonald et al., 2005).

The ambiguity in the definitions of flexibility has allowed a number of interpretations to justify a variety of organizational activities. A key idea has been Atkinson and Meager's (1985) model of a 'flexible firm', which identified four types of flexibility that could be implemented:

- *Functional* – the ability of a firm to match staff skills to tasks as workloads, work methods and technology change
- *Numerical* – a firm's ability to adjust the level of labour inputs to meet fluctuations in output
- *Distancing strategies* – the replacement of internal workers with external subcontractors, that is, putting some work, such as running the firm's canteen, out to contract (now referred to as 'outsourcing')
- *Financial* – support for the achievement of flexibility through the pay and reward structure.

PhotoDisc/Getty Images

Working from home is one definition of flexibility. How many others can you think of?

These flexibilities are achieved through a division of employees into the core workforce and the peripheral workforce. Flexibility here is something done *to* the workforce (Alis et al., 2006). The core group is composed of those employees expected to deliver functional flexibility and includes those with company-specific skills and perhaps high discretionary elements in their work. The peripheral group is composed of a number of different employees, such as those directly employed by a firm as secondary workers to perform work with a low discretionary element, or those employed as required on a variety of contracts, for example part-time, temporary and casual workers. This category of employee might involve highly specialized workers such as consultants as well as low skilled and temporary staff, including those who work with 'zero-hours' contracts. This is therefore not a new kind of employment; the concern is about the growth in such contracts in recent years (Pennycook et al., 2013). Another category comprises trainees and apprentices, some of whom may be being prepared for eventual transfer to the core group.

It is important to remember, when considering the issue of flexibility, that organizations have a choice about the type of flexibility that can be adopted. Moving towards 2020, much research has been completed into the real benefits of 'a flexible firm' (Standing, 2014; Torres et al., 2015; Whyman et al., 2015). It is becoming increasingly obvious that current flexible working practices, despite having benefits, are also creating challenges in terms of social cohesion, wage inequalities, justice, fairness and perceptions of trust (Ryan and Wessel, 2015; Svensson, 2012). They are also affecting expectations and challenges for HRM in engaging in a triangular employee communication system, involving the organization, the worker and various labour market intermediaries such as employment agencies, online job boards and social media sites (Bonet et al., 2013).

The idea of the flexible firm has been recognized for many years, although not without criticism from the start (see Pollert, 1988). It is often accepted as a 'panacea of restructuring' as it combines a variety of changes in the organization of work, such as multi-skilling, job enlargement, teamwork, labour intensification and cost control (Pollert, 1991). More recently, researchers such as Whyman et al. (2015) have begun research into the different aspects of a flexible firm, identifying the importance attached to a firm choosing specific flexible working practices that will enable the corporation to improve performance against a backdrop of the rapidly increasing use of flexible working in the UK. Furthermore, in sectors such as construction, flexibility can take the form of a variety of contract and employment arrangements that HR finds difficult to manage (Raja et al., 2013).

HRM web links

Visit the online resource centre at **www.palgravehighered.com/bg-hrm-6e** to explore different ideas of flexibility.

From 1998 to 2004, the Workplace Employment Relations Survey (Kersley et al., 2006) revealed that a relatively static 30 per cent of workplaces had employees on temporary or fixed-term contracts. The survey showed that 83 per cent of workplaces had part-time employees, a rise from 79 per cent in 1998 (Department of Trade and Industry, 2005b). Part-time employees made up more than half the workforce in 30 per cent of workplaces, with women making up all the part-time staff in 44 per cent of workplaces that employed such staff.

Since 2004, the UK has become widely known for its creative use of flexibility in workforce planning (Brinkley, 2013; Cesyniene, 2015; Whyman et al., 2015). In the UK, full-time standard work opportunities have decreased (CIPD, 2013), with many more flexible and short-term contracts becoming available. It appears that successive generations have adapted to the changing labour market by accepting more non-traditional work arrangements (Lyons et al., 2015) (see Chapter 5 for ideas of career management). In the UK, the idea of groups requiring flexible hours has also been enshrined within the law.

Recent years have seen the acceptance of a range of terms and practices that come under the umbrella of the idea of 'flexibility', with all its definitions and implications. In the UK, partly as a response to EU directives on working time, parental leave and part-time work, and partly as a stimulus to policies on work–life balance, the parents of children under the age of 6 years and of disabled children have the legal right to request more flexible working with respect to hours worked, time, caring duties and possibly location. A key question arises as to whether these will be retained following the UK's intention to withdraw from the EU. The current approach has resulted in a range of possible 'ways of working' such as:

- *Annualized hours* – working time is organized on the basis of the number of hours to be worked over a year rather than a week; it is usually used to fit in with peaks and troughs of work
- *Compressed hours* – which allows individuals to work their total number of agreed hours over a shorter period. For example, employees might work their full weekly hours over 4 rather than 5 days
- *Flexi-time* – employees have a choice about their actual working hours, usually outside certain agreed core times
- *Home-working* – either on a full-time basis or on a part-time basis where employees divide their time between home and office
- *Job-sharing* – which involves two people employed on a part-time basis but working together to cover a full-time post
- *Shift-working* – giving employers the scope to have their business open for longer periods than an 8-hour day
- *Staggered hours* – employees can start and finish their day at different times
- *Term-time working* – employees can take unpaid leave of absence during the school holidays.

Research by Kelliher and Anderson (2008) suggests that such practices are perceived by employees as enhancing job quality, particularly with respect to control, autonomy and work–life balance. There are, however, some downsides to these practices in relation to opportunities for learning and development because remote working means less visibility at work.

Until recently, there had been a shift towards a more employee-friendly approach in the UK and to flexibility that allowed more choice over where and when work could be done.

The onset of the GFC meant a strong association of flexibility with short-term working, which has been shown to have played a key role in preserving jobs, especially among staff with permanent contracts. The effect has been to increase the labour market segmentation between permanent and temporary staff (Hijzen and Venn, 2011). These flexible work practices can also be questioned when considering financial equality on a global scale. The income of the 'super-rich' 1 per cent has risen, but the more alarming statistic relates to the 40 per cent of the global working population at the bottom end who have seen their income fall. It is this group who are most likely to be in informal working arrangements such as zero-hours contracts (Organisation for Economic Co-operation and Development, 2015). It is also felt that the recent recession has accounted for more involuntary part-time work, with the number of homeworkers increasing from 2.3 million in 1997 to 3.5 million in 2012. The past 10 years has also seen an increase – to 22 per cent – in the number of people working in organizations with fewer than four employees, while there has been a drop in those working in organizations of more than 250, from 49 per cent to 40 per cent (CIPD, 2013).

reflective question Considering the next 10 years of your working life, which form of flexible working most appeals to you, and how do you expect employers to respond in terms of pay, conditions and opportunities for learning and development?

Zero-hours contracts

One of the most discussed areas in the non-standard working contracts is that of 'zero-hours' working, in which a person does not have a contract for a fixed number of work hours but is paid only for the hours they actually work (Brinkley, 2013; van Wanrooy et al., 2013b). There is particular concern over the fairness of zero-hours contracts and the abuse with which such systems are used. As with all flexible working arrangements, those who voluntarily choose to work in this way are provided with the flexibility to enable particular lifestyle choices. However, for those who involuntarily find themselves working within these contracts, they can cause hardship and underemployment (Bell and Blanchflower, 2013).

As found by both van Wanrooy et al. (2013b) and Brinkley (2013), there are no reliable statistics, either within the UK or worldwide in Organisation for Economic Co-operation and Development reports, of the number of people working zero-hours contracts, although there is a consensus that the figures are widely under-reported. There is also no knowledge on how many of these people work them voluntarily or involuntarily. Official estimates suggest that, in the UK, less than 1 per cent of the working population – around 250,000 individuals – work under these contracts. However, the CIPD estimates a figure of around 1 million (Brinkley, 2013), with the 2010–15 Conservative Government recognizing the potential for abuse relating to zero-hours contracts (Department for Business, Innovation and Skills, 2015). (See also HRM in practice 1.1 on p. 6.)

Although these contracts can give both employees and employers a great deal of flexibility in planning both work–life balance and workforce planning, the main question currently being raised is whether this develops autonomy and flexibility for the worker or propagates work insecurity (van Wanrooy et al., 2013b). As Brinkley (2013) suggests, zero-hours contracts are based on a specific type of relationship with the worker. Due to reasonably tight working practices legislation in the UK, if the employment is regular and over an

Karen Jochelson

**Director of Policy for Employment and the Economy,
The Equality and Human Rights Commission**

Kent Gavin

The Equality and Human Rights Commission is a statutory body established under the Equality Act 2006. It operates independently to encourage equality and diversity, eliminate unlawful discrimination, and promote and protect human rights. The Commission enforces equality legislation on age, disability, gender reassignment, marriage and civil partnership, pregnancy and maternity, race, religion or belief, sex and sexual orientation. It encourages compliance with the Human Rights Act 1998 and is accredited by the United Nations as an 'A status' National Human Rights Institution.

Karen Jochelson is Director of Policy for Employment and the Economy at the Equality and Human Rights Commission. She provides strategic leadership for the largest delivery programme in the Commission, which uses research, policy development, stakeholder engagement and communications to help employers and employees understand their rights and responsibilities in the workplace, and to ensure everyone has the opportunity to reach their potential. Her team works on projects to reduce pregnancy and maternity discrimination at work, improve business understanding of human rights, and reduce the impact of pay gaps.

Click on Karen's photo in your ebook to watch her speaking about the business case for diversity and methods to encourage diversity at work, and then think about the following questions:

1   Are equality and diversity the same or different?
2   How is diversity linked to innovation at work?
3   What do employers need to do to encourage diversity and what is the part played by line managers? Is espoused policy the same as enacted policy?
4   Can action planning help reduce the gender pay gap?

Visit the online resource centre for more information about the EHRC's work.

---

extended period of time, the worker becomes an employee with specific rights. If, however, there is no regularity of work, the individual is a worker with very few rights, including no paid leave, and faces insecurity and poverty with a growing potential to join others who form part of what is referred to as the 'precariat' (Standing, 2014).

Teleworking

Other significant choices for flexible working are teleworking, telecommuting and/or home-working. According to Duxbury and Higgins (2002, p. 157), such work is 'performed by individuals who are employed by an organization but who work at home or at a tele-center for some portion of their working time during regular business hours'.

Huws (1997) has identified five main types of teleworking:

- *Multisite* – an alternation between working on an employer's premises and working elsewhere, usually at home, but also in a telecottage or telecentre
- *Tele-home-working* – work based at home, usually for a single employer and involving low-skilled work performed by people tied to their homes

HRM in practice 4.2

Planning the headcount on the policy roller-coaster

I n June 2011, the General Teaching Council for Scotland reported that only one in five of the 2009–10 cohort of newly qualified teachers had secured a permanent full-time job. All Scottish probationary teachers are guaranteed a post for 1 year after qualifying, but after that employment in the education sector is not guaranteed. The proportion of new teachers with no job at all had risen from 13.5 per cent to 16.2 per cent, and the number being offered full-time or part-time temporary and supply teaching had also risen (BBC News, 2011).

BANANASTOCK 1996-98 AccuSoft Inc., All right

This is a good example of the difficulties of workforce planning in a large heterogeneous sector such as primary and secondary education, with the additional problem of the time lag between entering a programme of initial professional education and the state of the labour market on completion. The number of teachers required in any year depends on a range of factors such as the number and composition of the school-age population, policy decisions on maximum and minimum class sizes, the rate of teachers leaving the profession and the state of public sector finances. The teaching degree, like most initial degrees in Scotland, is a 4-year course, during which time any of these variables can change. In any part of the public sector, such changes are likely to be a direct result of fluctuations in policy – the 2010 cohort of new teachers had the misfortune to be looking for work at a time of impending cutbacks in public sector financing and of economic conditions that had led many older teachers to postpone early retirement.

Another example of how state policy directly affects workforce planning and composition is given by Stephen Bach's detailed analysis of the use of immigrant nursing staff in the NHS (Bach, 2010). This was driven by the government's perception of a staffing crisis (in relation to policy targets set for the service) and a manipulation of immigration policy to meet the crisis. In the early years of the twenty-first century, the government of the day had pledged to increase the nursing workforce in England by 20,000 additional posts by 2004 and then, in a revised plan, by 35,000 by 2008. Because of the lag in bringing UK-trained nurses into employment, for similar reasons to those we have seen for teachers, the response was actively to step up recruitment from overseas. The government was thus susceptible to criticism that it was poaching trained nursing staff from developing nations.

However, by 2005, staff targets had been exceeded, after which policy priorities changed from staff expansion to curbing expenditure. In the meantime, the number of domestic nurse training places had expanded by a third, so overseas recruitment was drastically reduced. The government changed the immigration points system and removed most nursing grades from the shortage occupation list. This meant that an employer would have to prove it had a vacancy and had been unable to recruit UK or European Economic Area nurses. It also meant that existing work permit-holders were deterred from changing employer in case they lost the right to work in the UK.

Bach's study shows, first, that the supply of immigrant workers has not been the result of an inexorable process of globalization, as is often inferred by populist discussions of immigration. More importantly, it indicates that, in the public sector, workforce planning and the supply and demand of labour are inevitably going to be critically affected as much by state policy as by the normal labour market interplay of supply and demand for suitably qualified people.

Stop! What do you think public sector managers can do to secure a stable and suitably qualified workforce?

Sources and further information: See BBC News (2011) and Bach (2010) for background reading.

Note: This feature was written by Chris Baldry.

- *Freelancing* – work for a variety of different clients
- *Mobile* – work carried out using communication technology such as mobile phones, fax machines and PC connections via the internet, often by professional, commercial, technical and managerial staff who work 'on the road'
- *Relocated back functions (call centres)* – specialist centres carrying out activities such as data entry, airline bookings, telephone banking, telephone sales and helpline services.

The trend towards greater home-working and teleworking is being driven by a variety of factors: technology with the impact of email, the internet and cheaper and faster ICT media; employees demanding and expecting more flexibility and a better work–life balance; and employer initiatives to use home-working to boost productivity, retention and loyalty, and reduce costs (Dwelly and Bennion, 2003).

HRM web links

> Visit the online resource centre at **www.palgravehighered.com/bg-hrm-6e** to explore resources for individuals working (or wanting to work) from home.

A variety of benefits are claimed for teleworking, including a reduction or elimination of travelling to work accompanied by a reduction of stress and negative feelings at work and fewer interruptions, which can in turn increase productivity (Vesala and Tuomivaara, 2015). As technology has moved from basic PC and telephones, home-workers can now teleconference and hold interactive problem-oriented meetings using advanced software such as Windows Meeting Space. One claim is that parents have more time for family responsibilities and so achieve a better work–life balance (Tremblay, 2003), although many mothers would claim that time with children creates its own pressures and stresses (Hilbrecht et al., 2008). In addition, working at home can also mean an imbalance towards work because it is always present (Scott-Dixon, 2004).

Telework is inevitably mainly devoted to information- and knowledge-based services, including professional work. Among such workers, there is the potential for feelings of isolation removed from the constant presence of others to provide social contact, points of comparison and feedback. Golden et al. (2008) completed research on such workers but found that isolation was not related to lower commitment, intention to leave or loyalty to an organization, perhaps because of the benefits of being at home. There was, however, an impact on job performance, especially where workers spent significant time without face-to-face interactions – although some people are likely to benefit from the lack of distractions. Consumer goods company Unilever has moved to a position where all but the production operators can work from home; it calls this move 'agile working'. The main worries employees cite is missing out on social interactions with colleagues (De Leede and Kraijenbrink, 2014; Grossman, 2013). The other important aspect of this type of flexible working is the level of trust required among employees to ensure the system works (Svensson, 2012). Recent research has highlighted that forms of flexible working are not just about technological change, but also require large cultural changes within organizations to ensure that the correct supportive supervision, building of trustful relationships and positive communication develop alongside flexible work systems (Peters et al., 2014); research also suggests, however, that managers are more likely to use task-oriented direction language to motivate teleworkers (Madlock, 2013).

One significant feature of telework has been the growth of call or contact centres, which have been regarded as one of the 'success stories' of the UK economy. Since 2008, however, call centres have also been the focus of significant job losses both in the UK and elsewhere. The operation of call centres is based on the idea that customers can be serviced at a lower cost through the use of telephones and other ICT links, with the possibility of also learning about customers in order to enable cross-selling.

Within this process, there are two key but usually contradictory aims – the needs to be cost-efficient but customer-oriented (Korczynski, 2002). Thus, customers may appreciate staff's time in dealing with their enquiries, but, simultaneously, the length of time taken to respond to customers is being monitored, with pressure to minimize cost. This can place stress on staff and has led to the view of call centres as opportunities for job intensification in which managers can tightly monitor and control staff performance and limit their autonomy (Stredwick and Ellis, 2005). One consequence of this is high rates of absenteeism and turn-over, with terms such as 'sweatshop' and 'slave labour' frequently being applied (Deery and Kinnie, 2004). There is also evidence that long work hours can lead to fatigue and ill-health when balanced against domestic requirements (Bohle et al., 2011; Hyman et al., 2003).

HRM web links   Visit the online resource centre at **www.palgravehighered.com/bg-hrm-6e** to examine the problem of bullying in call centres.

Although there is concern about working conditions in call centres, call centres can alternatively, through attention to the design of jobs, become locations of high-performance work systems, which can positively affect motivation and performance. This allows staff more autonomy as there is less staff monitoring and more focus on team work and leadership (Russell, 2008). The potential here is that, as information and knowledge workers, call-centre staff can significantly enhance the services that call centres provide, although the tension with cost savings can often limit customer interactions with actual employees.

HR practices can play a key role in supporting the creation of high-performance work systems in work cultures, but, as we have already suggested, the 'strength' of an HRM system is demonstrated in the everyday relationships between staff and management. As argued by Wood et al. (2006), there are significant links between the opportunity for relationship-building within call-centre work design and performance, and crucially management's orientation towards these. Interestingly, in comparisons across different countries, it was those countries with coordinated or 'social market' economies, such as Austria, Denmark, Germany, Sweden and the Netherlands, all with more regulated labour markets and institutions, that were associated with better quality jobs and lower turnover in call centres. In countries with liberal market economies, such as the USA and UK, there was a tendency for lower job discretion for workers in call centres (Holman et al., 2007). It is this lack of job discretion and autonomy that recent research has identified in call-centre employee 'burnout, as the balance of emotional work in customer facing activities is incompatible with the focus on efficiency' (Rod and Ashill, 2013).

Offshoring and outsourcing

Although call centres have been an apparent success, many organizations have in recent years sought even more cost savings from flexible working by moving their call centres to countries with low wages but similar or even higher skills. Once the customer is used to the lack of face-to-face contact, why not take the process a step further, removing the now irrelevant geographical boundary? This process is referred to as offshoring.

It is argued that offshoring can create wealth even when workers may lose their jobs in their home country. Farrell (2005, p. 68) argues that the 'price' of an organization's ability to cut costs and create new markets is 'continuous change and higher turnover for workers', which can cause 'pain and dislocation'. To avoid this, it is claimed, labour markets need to become more flexible so that workers can benefit from the gains of globalization as well as suffer the costs. Organizations can include training for re-employment, career guidance and reasonable severance packages in their HR plans. One argument is that although jobs may be lost to low-wage economies, displaced workers can retrain and move to higher valued-added jobs. Offshoring has, therefore, become linked to claims of increasing productivity (Amiti and Wei, 2009).

There is, however, some doubt that highly skilled jobs are safe when economies such as India also aspire to high value-added work (for example, in ICT development). Levy (2005) argues that organizations are developing the ability to integrate geographically dispersed operations, which can mean skilled workers in one location competing with skilled workers in different parts of the world. It is also possible that, where there are shortages of skilled and qualified staff, an organization may prefer to offshore some activities such as innovation to locations where qualified staff are more readily available (Lewin et al., 2009).

In addition to offshoring, an organization can seek to slice up or 'disaggregate' its value chain by outsourcing (Contractor et al., 2010); in this process, an organization seeks to source aspects of its production or service processes by setting up a contractual relationship with an external provider. This allows an organization to focus on its core capability and obtain supporting services such as sales, administration (including HR – see below) and ICT at a lower cost from providers who are in turn able to concentrate on their core capability. According to Harland et al. (2005), in addition to focusing on core activities, the principal drivers for outsourcing are freeing up assets, reducing costs and the potential benefits of working with a supplier or partner who is able to exploit advanced technologies. For example, in the pharmaceutical industry, specialist contract research organizations provide outsourced services in areas such as data management, medical coding and marketing, allowing companies to focus on high-value activities.

As a consequence, it has, in many organizations, become more difficult to speak of a unified entity; instead, in such companies, it is best to consider the working of relationships both internally and externally. Among these relationships will be those characterized by a tight specification of contracts with outsourced service providers, with low trust and pressure to lower costs and compete on price. Colling (2005) refers to these as 'distanced' relationships that can also create difficulties for the contracting organization. An example here is the relationship between British Airways (BA) and its outsourced catering supplier, Gate Gourmet. In 2005, under pressure to reduce costs in the UK, Gate Gourmet sought to make redundancies and change working conditions. This resulted in a dispute with the trade union, which escalated in August 2005 when the company attempted to bring in 130 temporary workers to cope with the peak travel season. This was followed by an unofficial or 'wildcat' strike by workers and the dismissal of 800 staff. There were a number of consequences for BA: first, they could provide no in-flight food; second, some flights were cancelled; and third, around 1000 BA staff, many of them friends and family members of the staff at Gate Gourmet, stopped work in solidarity with them – this led to the delay or cancellation of around 900 flights, at an extra cost of around £45 million.

In contrast, other relationships are more 'engaged', characterized by mutual trust and joint approaches to planning and working via projects and high value-added services in which the outsourced supplier can play a vital role in enhancing decision-making and performance capability through innovation and knowledge production – a typical claim of many consultancies involved in knowledge process outsourcing (Mudambi and Tallman, 2010). Because such relationships are based on a mutual recognition of the contribution of talented staff, it also becomes possible to consider more strategic possibilities for collaboration and cooperation. However, outsourcing can also be associated with uncertainty about the movements of knowledge processes, with the possibility of both positive and negative effects (Edvardsson and Durst, 2014). There are also dangers in disaggregating work, in which parts of skilled work are allocated to less skilled and cheaper workers. Such a process has the potential to continue until the skilled work has been lost (Norlander et al., 2015).

HRM activities are among the services that have been outsourced in recent years. For example, since 2000, BT has outsourced significant HR services to management consultants Accenture. In 2005, this arrangement was extended until 2015, with the formation of a joint venture for a business process outsourcing and transformation contract for the HR administration service (see Saunders and Hunter, 2007). Outsourcing in HR is based on the view that administrative work and operations can be carried out by outside suppliers, leaving HR staff to concentrate on strategic and high value-added work. Sako and Tierney (2005) examined the growth of HR outsourcing, finding that although operations such as payroll administration have been more susceptible to outsourcing, there have been more deals that have bundled processes together, with moves towards a transformational view of HR outsourcing in which an organization seeks consulting and systems integration as part of the bundle. It is argued that because HR suppliers are outside the organization, they are more accountable, can take a more objective view and can gain a more complete understanding of performance. Recent research suggests that, in the face of HR outsourcing based on cost reduction, the role becomes limited, with a loss of strategic influence and less skill development (Glaister, 2014).

Interestingly, research by Woodall et al. (2009) found that, especially in larger organizations, the decision to outsource HR was usually taken because of the success of outsourcing other activities. That is, it was not especially made on the basis of a full understanding of the costs and benefits. It was also found that reductions in core HR staff meant significant challenges in providing a quality service, partly because there was insufficient understanding of the role and activities of HR practitioners.

New workers

For the first time since the beginning of the twentieth century, there are four generations of workers within a majority of organizations: Baby-boomers (born after the Second World War up to around 1965), Generation X (born approximately 1966–76), Generation Y or the Millenials (born around 1977–94) and the new entrants to the workforce, those of Generation Z (born from about 1995) (Lyons et al., 2015). The Baby-boomers are approaching the twilight years of their working life. For many, work has been extended through either choice, necessity or the raising of retirement age. At the other end of the spectrum, the Millenials appear to have some very specific and new demands of employers (Kultalahti and Viitala, 2015). Both groups want some form of individualized work flexibility, the Millenials particularly wanting flexible working conditions, continual feedback from supervisors and the opportunities and flexibility to undertake ongoing learning and training (Hess and Jepsen, 2009). This type of individual flexibility focuses on employees' well-being as opposed to allowing HRM the flexibility to allocate HR in the most effective way. However, recent research suggests that as long as the flexible options are in line with company requirements (Whyman et al., 2015), there is a positive correlation between individualized work arrangements and a reduction of absence in older workers, and between individualized pay and training arrangements and turnover in younger employees (Bal and Dorenbosch, 2015). Generation Z – or the iGen – are, having grown up in a world of technology, increasingly entering the workforce with smartphones in their hands, but this is also a world of uncertainty, recession and labour market flexibility and restructuring (Wachsund and Blind, 2016).

Attitudes to work

With a growing number of temporary, zero-hours, fixed-term and outsourced service contract workers, there has been some interest in the effect of employment status on motivation and commitment to work.

reflective question What do you think would be the effect of being given a fixed-term contract? How would it affect your motivation and satisfaction at work?

Research by Guest et al. (1998) into the views of workers in a variety of different settings found that people on fixed-term contracts generally had a positive psychological contract. Reasons given for this were that they had more focused work to complete and did not have to engage in organizational politics or complete administrative duties. They might also face lower work demands than permanent staff, avoiding stress and taking less work home. Such employees perhaps benefit from a better work–life balance (Hogarth et al., 2001).

McInnis et al. (2009) explored different understandings of contracts and the relation to commitment. They suggested that staff on short-term contracts could be faced with contracts that were organization-centred and set clear terms to define the work to be done – but such contracts had little connection to commitment. Evans et al. (2004), however, examined the work of highly skilled technical contractors in the USA over a period of two and a half years. It was observed that their work was cyclical, involving periods of contract work on projects, and often involved intense activity and pressures from contracting organizations to use their expertise to solve problems, at any time of day. There were also periods between contracts, or 'downtime' – sometimes referred to as 'beach time', 'bench time' or even 'dead time'. They did not consider themselves unemployed at such times – this was normal for contracting. It was found that contractors, even though they were free from normative pressure for permanent employment, did not necessarily enjoy a desirable flexible lifestyle. The contractors often worked longer hours when contracted, and when they were not, they had to continue working to ensure the next contract, using past work to promote their reputations. They had little time to relax.

One of the most persistent findings is the significance of the psychological contract for gaining commitment. How staff perceive their obligations affects their attitudes, motivation and feelings of justice (Battisti et al., 2007). Part of such perceptions relates to the way in which HR practices are employed in combination with an opportunity to innovate within a role. These findings reinforce the view that, in planning to become more flexible, organizations are faced with a choice. Taking an ad hoc approach that is nevertheless driven by cost reduction may produce improved short-term financial results, but is likely to have a negative impact on motivation, innovation and commitment in the longer term. Although the use of outsourcing and temporary and fixed-term contracts may have positive results, a consistent finding in the research is, however, that high-performance HR practices lead to a positive psychological contract and positive organizational outcomes (Kehoe and Wright, 2013). Many organizations have during the twenty-first century been persuaded of the need to focus on their relationship with staff to enhance engagement through developmental HRM that focuses on training and job enrichment (Bal et al., 2013). However, organizations may be tempted by the 'wrong sort of flexibility' (Michie and Sheehan-Quinn, 2001, p. 302), which does not improve productivity or competitiveness (Whyman et al., 2015).

Redundancy

Workforce planning is always a contingent process, and one of the contingent factors is clearly economic conditions. The CIPD (2010a) also identified this factor as a barrier to diversity management, and, in spite of claims that recession provides an opportunity to focus on the talent within organizations, the late 2000s were characterized by job losses in all sectors, the emphasis shifting from the private to the public sector in the UK following the Comprehensive Spending Review in October 2010. However, redundancy, or 'employee downsizing' as it is sometimes referred to, has also been a feature of many economies in the face of global pressures, cost competition and shifts in demand. As Datta et al. (2010, p. 282) argue, it has 'become the norm in many countries'. One assumption is that redundancy stimulates the working of the market and that the availability of highly skilled workers through redundancy will lead to a demand from employers. Research suggests this may not work and that highly skilled workers may become unemployed or underemployed in work not matching their skills (Dobbins et al., 2014). Indeed, a feature of work following the GFC and the following recession is how staff made redundant had to move into lower level work based on lower pay and fewer hours (Warren, 2015).

HRM web links

Visit the online resource centre at **www.palgravehighered.com/bg-hrm-6e** for information on redundancy consultation and notification.

Losing staff has negative consequences for organizations, as well as for those who have been made unemployed. First, and perhaps most obviously, redundancy is a violation of the psychological contract based on a build-up of mutual expectations and obligations between employees and the organization, in which the greater the degree of employees' involvement in their work, the greater their feeling of violation (Stoner and Gallagher, 2010). Second, there is a loss of skill, knowledge, wisdom and social capital – the talent that employees accumulate over years of practice at work. The result of downsizing may thus be a loss of productivity (Yu and Park, 2006).

Third, there is an effect on those employees who remain at work after a period of downsizing. If they respond sympathetically towards those made redundant, they may experience effects such as guilt, lower motivation and commitment, mistrust and insecurity (Thornhill

> *When an employee leaves, they take away more than the contents of their desk. Their skill, wisdom, knowledge and social capital are less easy to replace.*

Photodisc

et al., 1997); this is referred to as 'survivor syndrome'. A further effect, according to Appelbaum and Donna (2000), is that compromising productivity by downsizing is detrimental to the survivors, leading to an increase in absenteeism (Travaglione and Cross, 2006). Managers may suffer, particularly when 'delayering' occurs, through 'burnout' as a consequence of changing workloads and loss of opportunities for progression (Littler et al., 2003); there may also be a decline in loyalty and 'even increases in white collar crime' (p. 226).

Fourth, redundancy is stressful for those made unemployed, possibly due to the process of being made redundant itself and then through the experience of unemployment (Pickard, 2001; see also Richard Sennett's *The Corrosion of Character*, 1998, for an extensive consideration of the debilitating effects of downsizing and job insecurity). Further research has also identified that it is not only those who are directly affected by the downsizing who feel the negative effects. Ashman (2012) conducted a study into those who have to deliver the news, a group he calls 'downsizing envoys'. He found that the attitude and personal conduct of this group are very similar across all sectors, but the emotional stress of fulfilling the role is different depending on the support available and the part played in the decision-making process.

In their wide-ranging review of research, Datta et al. (2010) found that the negative outcomes of redundancy have as much to do with the manner of implementation as with the fact of having been made redundant itself. The way in which change is conducted during downsizing, along with contextual factors such as organizational culture and climate, all affect the outcome (Self et al., 2007). Forde et al. (2008) explored the idea of 'socially responsible restructuring' during a period of mass lay-offs in the UK steel industry. This idea is based on the need to engage with the interests of all stakeholders during the process of restructuring and redundancy as part of an organization's corporate social responsibility agenda, as suggested by the EU (European Commission, 2008). It was found, however, that there were significant gaps between what was said and what was done about the process of restructuring. For example, socially responsible restructuring would suggest allowing time for access to job counsellors and external support agencies, but this was often found to be blocked by managers. In addition, fair and objective criteria for lay-off and redeployment might have been stated, but they were interpreted as inequitable and subjective by employees. It is suggested that HR has a key role to play to ensure 'ethical stewardship' (Forde et al., 2008, p. 22) in situations such as these.

There is also a need for HR to understand the psychological aspects of the 'grief' that often besets individuals. Kübler-Ross (1969) developed an emotional 'grief cycle' while observing the reactions of cancer patients and their families, and this cycle has been adapted and used to track individuals' emotional cycle during downsizing or organizational restructuring (Davey et al., 2013). One of the interesting findings is that individuals often move forwards and then back through the cycle, so HR personnel and managers need to recognize that this happens so they can help employers avoid getting continuously stuck in these mid-cycle stages. Ultimately, however, during periods of recession, the dichotomy particularly between HR accounting and the management of human capital produces conflict, with no easy answer.

Human resource accounting/human capital management

Making people redundant would appear to contradict claims that 'people are our greatest asset' and the fact that people as human capital are a crucial asset in the knowledge economy (Pilch, 2000). As some organizations seek to embrace what is seen as an 'always on' way of working, where employees can become continuously connected to work through mobile technology, staff become amenable to analytics, which can be 'leveraged' when making decisions (Schatsky and Schwartz, 2015) relating to strategy. The ability to derive data for the measurement of HR can also allow people to be valued through use of the language of accounting to represent this value in an organization's financial statement. The process of identifying, quantifying, accounting and forecasting the value of human resources is referred to as *human resource accounting* (HRA) and is based on the view that HRM needs to be measured and expressed in financial terms to gain credibility (Toulson and Dewe, 2004). Failure to do this has been a key factor in reducing the importance of decisions related to HR.

Unlike capital items and materials, people cannot be owned by an organization. They can, however, be said to 'loan' their abilities to perform in return for rewards from the organization (Mayo, 2002). Organizations will seek to obtain the most from such a loan by combining people's knowledge and skills with other resources to add value. Furthermore, such value-adding can increase over time through the knowledge and skills that employees develop from performing their work, and from specific activities such as training and development. An organization might therefore claim that it is important to include such value-adding capability on its balance sheet. There have for many years been attempts to account for the value of people in organizations, with a tendency to treat people in financial terms, 'the dominant image of HRA for many people' (Flamholz, 1985, p. 3) being putting 'people on the balance sheet'. Valid and reliable models of measurement have, however, been lacking, and HRA had 'progressed at something less than a snail's pace' (Turner, 1996, p. 65).

More enthusiasm for HRA was found in Sweden, where many organizations used its key ideas in decision-making, leading to a 'changed way of thinking' about the management of HR (Gröjer and Johanson, 1998, p. 499). Furthermore, HRA statements were included in companies' annual reports. It was found that HRA techniques were useful as management tools, but management were also ambivalent towards HRA since the techniques could also be used to assess the efficiency of the managers themselves (Johanson, 1999).

As a tool that management can use to control costs, HRA can be accused of contributing to a narrow view of people in organizations as being an expense to be minimized and cut when necessary. This view can significantly underrate the value of people in terms of their accumulation of knowledge and understanding as they learn at work, which makes them difficult to replace as well as difficult to copy. People therefore have a value that is greater than simply the cost of their employment. Although that value is difficult to capture in financial terms, knowledge and understanding in an organization form part of its intangible assets or intellectual capital, which includes features such as brand names, as well as knowledge and understanding. Edvinsson and Malone (1997) have suggested that intellectual capital in an organization is composed of two factors. First, there is structural capital, such as hardware and software, trade and brand names, and relationships with customers and suppliers – as Edvinsson and Malone (1997, p. 11) have put it, 'everything left at the office when the employees go home'. Second, there is human capital, which is the knowledge and skills of employees at work as well as their values and culture. In combination, human capital plus structural capital equals intellectual capital.

reflective question | What is the intellectual capital of your course? How is this intellectual capital valued?

Mayo (2002) suggested the use of a 'human capital monitor' to calculate the added value of people in an organization. The key idea is that added value, in the form of both financial and non-financial contributions, can be assessed by considering:

- *People as assets* – composed of employment costs, capability, potential, alignment of values and contributions
  plus

- *People's motivation/commitment* – which is affected by factors in the work environment such as leadership, practical support, reward and recognition, and learning and development.

What is significant about intellectual capital is that, as the knowledge economy advances, the production of new knowledge is a vital differentiator between different organizations (Garvey and Williamson, 2002). However, the difficulty has always been how the accountancy profession should value intangible assets (Cleary, 2010), although there have been moves in recent years to find such an understanding – albeit with limitations. One problem may be that accountants do not believe that human capital valuation should appear on a balance sheet, as indicated by a survey conducted in the US. Reasons given for the belief included difficulty in measurement, too much subjectivity and lack of conformity between organizations. Furthermore, if included, human capital value could be distorted and manipulated (Dean et al., 2012).

In the UK, a central recommendation of the Accounting for People Task Force (2003) was that organizations producing annual operating and financial reviews should include information on 'human capital management' (HCM). There was an acceptance that the lack of agreed measurements and definitions would require an evolutionary approach, and that this could, of course, be used as an excuse to avoid any effort to produce human capital information on management. Toulson and Dewe (2004) called for HR managers to become familiar with a range of measurement practices and tools in order to enhance their understanding of different points of view. Sánchez et al. (2009) developed a model for universities to enable the reporting of intellectual capital.

Recently, and following concerns about corporate governance and financial reporting standards, the Financial Reporting Council (2014) set out changes to company reporting so that it might include an accompanying narrative report covering such issues as human capital. However, it remains left to the discretion of organizations how much information they report on the value of human capital in relation to business performance and development. The argument for HR professionals is therefore to pay more attention to how data can show the link between the value added by people to financial performance and the business or organization's success (CIPD, 2015c). Hesketh (2014) refers to the link between people, their capabilities and the release of sustainable value that is considered in strategy and business models as HCM. He provides a framework for HCM to allow the measurement of capability and how this is contributing to future direction. Crucial to the framework is the generation of good-quality data that need to be analysed so that the outcome, the analytics, can be used in decision-making. HCM could allow more talk about people and value, which is a significant part of an organization's efforts to provide transparent reporting.

HRM web links

Visit the online resource centre at **www.palgravehighered.com/bg-hrm-6e** to access retailer Marks and Spencer's Annual Report.

Showing the impact of adult social care in ABC City Council

The setting

ABC City Council (ABCCC), operating in a large city in the North of England, is facing very difficult decisions with respect to the services it is providing. Over the last 5 years, the budget from central government has been progressively reduced by £130 million and it is forecast to be cut again by a further £45 million. In addition, other sources of funding have also been lost and costs have been rising. The plan is to continue to make savings by finding new ways of delivering internal support services, by managing contracts and purchasing to ensure reduced cost and by selling buildings. There is severe pressure on adult social care, with staff pointing out that any further cuts caused by the continuous pressure to reduce budgets would mean that 'the bone has been reached' and any purpose in providing services would become 'dysfunctional'. Extra powers to raise funds through a council tax would be of minor benefit – only around 2 per cent of the total budget.

PhotoDisc/GettyImages

The problem

The workforce plan includes provision to make 500 staff redundant this year – the council has already seen a 20 per cent reduction in the number of people employed. At the same time, the council recognizes that it needs to become more intelligent about the workforce, especially since it is becoming clear that it is often the most employable staff who 'take redundancy'. There is a clear danger that, in the face of severe budget cuts, the council has responded by working with people numbers at the expense of people qualities and their capabilities. Indeed, as the number employed has fallen, it is evident that the council not only has to do more with fewer staff, but also needs to ensure that quality of service is sustained and even improved.

The expectations of the city's population are rising even though budgets are falling, especially with respect to adult social care as growing numbers of adults are requiring services. Life expectancy for men and women is rising, with predictions for the number of adults over the age of 65 forecast to grow by 65 per cent over the next 20 years.

ABCCC currently employs 2100 staff, around 10 per cent of whom are managers, 12 per cent are professional staff such as social workers, and the rest are a variety of carers and care support staff. An important manifestation of the dilemma being faced is that even senior members of the council and the executive team do not fully appreciate the value of people currently employed in the adult social care

section: they are seen as costs rather than assets. Furthermore, there is little understanding and few data available to investigate factors such as why good people leave employment with the council and how engaged people still working with the council are. The need to demonstrate how value is added by the workforce in adult social care is becoming more obvious in order to: (1) sustain existing resources, and (2) find ways of arguing and competing for more resources.

The assignment

Prepare a short presentation for the adult social care managers on how a link between the staff, their capabilities and sustainable value requires an HCM approach. You should consider how analytics can help to demonstrate the value that is added by adult social care in order to inform future decision-making in the sector.

Essential reading

Hesketh, J. (2014) *Valuing Your Talent*. London: Chartered Institute of Personnel and Development.
Also go to www.valuingyourtalent.com/, a partnership website seeking to help measure the impact and contribution of people to performance.

Note: This case study was written by Jeff Gold.

summary

➤ The shocks and disturbances of the late 2000s have increased the need for workforce planning to become both an analytical process for predictability and a creative process for working with unpredictability, unknowable shocks and complexity.

➤ The standard employment model in which workers have a dependent relationship with employers, full-time work and a salary is becoming less dominant.

➤ Manpower planning in the 1960s and 70s emphasized quantities, flows and mathematical modelling to ensure that the necessary supply of people was forthcoming to allow targets to be met.

➤ Personnel specialists were able to utilize manpower measures of labour turnover, absenteeism and stability to diagnose and solve problems, increasingly aided by PC-based software packages. Manpower planning could play a vital role in the management of the employment relationship.

➤ HRP could be seen to be a continuation and extension of this process, which fully recognizes the potential of people and their needs in the development of strategies and plans. Integrated systems of HR activities are associated with superior performance in high-performing organizations.

➤ Workforce planning is a process of forecasting the supply of and demand for skills against the requirements of future production and services delivery in a situation of uncertainty and change. It is a process supported by the use of ICT, enabling the production of people analytics that can be used to produce various forecasts and scenarios relating to future possibilities and unexpected shocks. Such systems can also be provided over the internet as a feature of e-HR.

➤ There is interest in managing diversity at work. Diversity is a means of creating heterogeneity in the workforce, a variety of experiences, backgrounds and networks enhancing the ability to solve complex problems. Managing diversity needs to be seen as part of cultural change.

➤ In many organizations, the language of flexibility and a range of different practices such as zero-hours contracts have been employed, often without considering their effect on employment relations. There has been a growth in the number of part-time and tele-home-working employees, with government backing for flexible working, as well as in the outsourcing and offshoring of services. There is, however, little evidence of the overall impact on business performance and people's motivation.

➤ Recent years have been characterized by job losses in all sectors. Negative outcomes of redundancy have as much to do with the manner of its implementation, and contextual factors such as the organization's culture and the climate also affect the outcome.

➤ HRA and HCM have been advocated as presenting the value of people as assets, but there has been a lack of agreement on measurements. Using people analytics, HR professionals can pay more attention to how data can show the link between the value added by people to financial performance and the business or organization's success.

review questions

1 'When an organization is mapping out its future needs, it is a serious mistake to think primarily in terms of number, flows and economic models.' Discuss.

2 How is workforce planning linked to strategic planning?

3 What would be your response to the publication of figures showing an above-average turnover of students in a university or college department?

4 How effective are the various approaches to managing diversity in organizations?

5 Are zero-hours contracts acceptable?

applying the sociological imagination

Based on our rationale for what we have called critical human resource management education, presented in Chapter 1, which uses the prism of Mills' sociological imagination to understand HRM-related 'troubles', answer the following question:

➤ How can the sociological imagination help you to understand concerns relating to the lack of women in senior management positions in many organizations?

further reading

Reading these articles and chapters can help you gain a better understanding of the changing role of HRM and potentially a higher grade for your HRM assignment.

➤ Curson, J. A., Dell, M. E., Wilson, R. A., Bosworth, D. L. and Baldauf, B. (2010) Who does workforce planning well?: workforce review team rapid review summary. *International Journal of Health Care Quality Assurance,* **23**(1): 110–19.

➤ Patel, R. (2010) *Working the Night Shift: Women in India's Call Center Industry*. Palo Alto, CA: Stanford University Press.

➤ Schwab, A., Werbel, J. D., Hofmann, H. and Henriques, P. (2016) Managerial gender diversity and firm performance: an integration of different theoretical perspectives. *Group Organization Management,* **41**(1): 5–31.

➤ Skogstad, A., Torsheim, T. and Einarsen, S. (2011) Testing the work environment hypothesis of bullying on a group level of analysis: psychosocial factors as precursors of observed workplace bullying. *Applied Psychology: An International Review,* **60**(3): 475–95.

➤ Standing, G. (2014) Understanding the precariat through labour and work. *Development and Change,* **45(5)**: 963–80.

vocabulary checklist for ESL students

 Click here in your interactive ebook for a list of HRM terminology and vocabulary that has appeared in this chapter.

Visit the online resource centre at **www.palgravehighered.com/bg-hrm-6e** for lots of extra resources to help you get to grips with this chapter, including study tips, HRM skills development guides, summary lecture notes, tips for English as a Second Language (ESL) students and more.

part II

EMPLOYEE RESOURCING

chapter **5**

recruitment, selection and talent management

STOCKBYTE

outline

➤ Introduction
➤ Recruitment and selection policies
➤ HRM and globalization 5.1: Managing discriminatory cultural norms in hiring
➤ Recruitment and attraction
➤ Selection
➤ HRM in practice 5.1: Must you be 'posh' to enter the elite professions?
➤ HRM as I see it: Alison Blayney, Unilever (Part 2)
➤ Talent management and development
➤ HRM in practice 5.2: Talent as a collective endeavour in the West Yorkshire Police
➤ Case study: TNNB Ltd.
➤ Summary, review questions, applying the sociological imagination, further reading and vocabulary checklist for ESL students

objectives

After studying this chapter, you should be able to:

1 Understand the importance of recruitment and selection in the formation of the employment relationship
2 Understand the key features of recruitment and selection policies
3 Explain the nature of attraction in recruitment
4 Explain the effectiveness of various selection methods
5 Understand approaches to identifying and managing talent in organizations

140

The inquiry into the deaths of six people caused by a refuse lorry in Glasgow, Scotland, in December 2014 has heard that the driver had no references on his file and had been suspended from his former job. Harry Clarke, who had been suspended from the First Bus company in December 2010, was at the wheel of the bin lorry when it killed six pedestrians in Glasgow city centre. During a cross-examination at the fatal accident inquiry by Mr Conway, a solicitor acting for one of the families, it emerged that there were no references on Mr Clarke's employment record with Glasgow City Council. This led to the lawyer stating that 'Someone has blundered at Glasgow City Council carrying out a grossly incompetent employment process.' Ms Ham, an HR manager with Glasgow City Council, told the fatal accident inquiry that 'Sometimes documents are misfiled.' Following the inquiry, Glasgow City Council reviewed its recruitment and selection procedures. Much of the mainstream HR literature discusses the recruitment of 'talented' people, but this tragic accident illustrates the importance of effective recruitment and selection processes.

introduction

If you are approaching the end of your studies or are completing further studies to improve your prospects, what is your understanding of the job market? Do you have confidence in finding work that matches your talent? And how do you expect your talent to be managed and developed? All these questions and more require some understanding of what is happening in the job market and organizations. From their side of the market, employers need to seek, recruit, select and then develop people they consider to be talented. What then happens to those considered to be less talented or even untalented (Iles, 2013)? Do they just keep their fingers crossed?

Recruitment and selection have always been critical processes for organizations, and in earlier chapters we discussed ethics in recruitment and selection practices (Chapter 2) and how such practices can change or reinforce a particular culture. As Iles (2013) suggests, how people are recruited and selected on the basis of their contribution, and then their inclusion in or exclusion from a 'talent pool', are ethical issues. Traditional approaches to recruitment and selection attempt to attract a wide choice of candidates for vacancies before screening out those who do not match the criteria set in the job descriptions and personnel specifications. In circumstances where many applicants chase fewer jobs, employers clearly have more power, and therefore many approaches to recruitment and selection emphasize this power.

However, recent surveys (Chartered Institute of Personnel and Development [CIPD] 2015d) from over 500 organizations in the UK suggest that there seem to be recruitment difficulties and shortages of applicants, particularly for roles such as managers and technical specialists, mainly in the private sector. As might be expected at a time of budget cuts, recruitment in the public sector is more restricted. Such difficulties may also be a reflection of some key trends in the structure and nature of jobs in the labour market, where research shows that mid-skilled jobs have been declining, both before and during the global financial crisis – an effect referred to as a 'hollowing out' of labour markets. Furthermore, the expansion of low-skilled and high-skilled jobs has produced a pattern of occupational polarization in what is now called an 'hourglass' structure of the labour market (Gardiner and Corlett, 2015).

reflective question

What are your expectations for employment? What attracts you to employment opportunities in the current economic climate?

ImageSource

Recruitment is a process of attracting the right people to apply for the job.

Recruitment and selection policies

Recruitment and selection is one of the most critical areas within human resource management (HRM). Selecting employees who are able to 'fit' with the organization and perform once they have been employed is risky, and there are no guarantees of future performance (Miles and Sadler-Smith, 2014). Recruitment is strongly connected to workforce planning and the development of accurate job descriptions (Smith, K., 2015). Figure 5.1 shows an overall view of the stages of recruitment and selection, and the connection of these processes to workforce planning.

There are wide variations in recruitment and selection policies and practices, reflecting an organization's strategy and its philosophy towards people management. In large multinational organizations, for example, there is a distinction between policies to attract those destined for

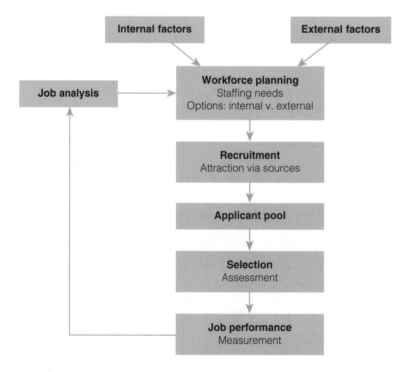

Figure 5.1 *The stages of recruitment and selection*

international careers and policies suited to local conditions (Mahmood, 2015; Phillips et al., 2014). Where indicated by the workforce plan (see Chapter 4), an organization will seek ways of attracting a large pool of applicants and then differentiating between them, in order to avoid the attrition costs of hiring the 'wrong' ones (Nabi et al., 2015; Newell, 2005). There is also a rapidly growing realization of the importance of 'employer branding'. An employer brand brings together the values of the organization and the competencies required of future employees (Das and Ahmed, 2014). This branding plays an important part in, first, attracting the right pool of applicants, and second, ensuring there is a good person–organization (P–O) fit (Jain and Bhatt, 2014; Yu, 2014). Many organizations not only use their websites to promote the brand, but also use social media to engage in transparent relationship-building with potential employees (CIPD, 2015d; Girand et al., 2014).

HRM web links

Visit the online resource centre at **www.palgravehighered.com/bg-hrm-6e** to read an extra HRM in practice feature on how sportswear manufacturer Adidas attracts new staff.

The employer brand will also be reflected in the psychological and behavioural characteristics expected of employees, which are expressed through competency frameworks (Roberts, 1997). Such frameworks have allowed organizations to adopt a range of sophisticated recruitment and selection techniques in order to identify and admit the 'right' people. In this way, as 'organizationally defined critical qualities' (Iles and Salaman, 1995, p. 204), a competency framework augments an organization's power. However, this power is not just with the organization. The values, characteristics and competencies that create the employer brand need to be embedded into the workplace itself; otherwise there is a risk of high attrition created by unfulfilled expectations (Mostafa and Gould-Williams, 2014; Yu, 2014). For example, one tool of assessment we will consider is personality testing. A survey by Piotrowski and Armstrong (2006) found that popular qualities for testing included integrity and potential for violence, and such information can be used to make judgements about who to admit. There are concerns, however, about the validity and reliability of these types of tests (Schmitt, 2014), and the CIPD (2015d) has noticed that, over recent years, the use of these tests has decreased in the UK to around 36 per cent. Crucially, however, such models need to work within the constraints of a legal context and policies for diversity management (Daniels and Macdonald, 2005).

reflective question

How would an employer prove to you that it was seeking to develop its employer brand based on a positive psychological contract? Go to BP Global Careers at http://www.bp.com/en/global/bp-careers.html. How has BP's image and brand been affected by problems such as the 2010 Gulf Oil disaster?

Recruitment and attraction

Recruitment is the process of attracting the interest of a pool of capable people who will apply for jobs within an organization. In this definition, we can highlight three crucial issues. First, there is a need to attract people's interest in applying for employment. This

Managing discriminatory cultural norms in hiring

© Stockbyte Royalty Free Photos

Only 30 per cent of women in Turkey are employed, well below the European Union average of 69 per cent. More troubling is that Turkish women earn 32 per cent less per day than Turkish men, reflecting that they are often limited to precarious, low-wage work (Today's Zaman, 2015). While gender-based wage gaps exist in almost all countries, the relatively few women employed in Turkey reflect a clear cultural belief that women should not work outside the home. Such social norms can find their way into corporate cultures. For example, in August 2015, Turkey's Police Chief Training Center posted a job vacancy that indicated '2,000 deputy police chief candidates will be hired, of which 200 will be women and 1,800 will be male' (*Hurriyet Daily Times*, 2015). This discriminatory advertisement violates both the Turkish constitution and the country's obligations under the United Nations' Convention on the Elimination of All Forms of Discrimination Against Women.

In an increasingly globalizing world, human resource (HR) practitioners may find themselves in the difficult position of having to reconcile their legal obligations not to discriminate with cultural demands to do just that. Although it is easy to condemn discrimination in hiring practices, it is much more difficult for HR practitioners to navigate organizational pressure to act in a discriminatory manner.

Pressure to engage in discriminatory hiring practices is particularly tricky to manage during the recruitment and selection processes. Recruitment and selection are normally very public processes and all actors can watch the process unfolding (unlike, say, performance assessments, which tend to be private affairs). Recruitment and selection also yield definitive outcomes (that is, someone is or is not hired). These characteristics make it harder for HR practitioners to quietly do the right thing (that is, ignore demands to discriminate) because internal stakeholders can see whether or not their demands have been met. And the binary nature of the hiring decision makes it easier for unsuccessful candidates who suspect discrimination to take action because the key facts (that they were not hired) are evident for all to see.

Faced with a demand to discriminate from an organizationally powerful actor, there are three strategies HR practitioners can utilize to 'do the right thing' while minimizing their risk of retribution. The first strategy is to clearly (but tactfully) identify the potential legal, financial and reputational consequences of discrimination for the proponent of this action. Ideally, this should be done in writing and a copy kept. Sometimes simply the act of recording the proposed course of action (and its consequences) in writing can dampen enthusiasm for those actions for fear of the written document being later revealed and triggering sanctions.

The second strategy is to clearly recommend in writing an alternative course of action (one that is not discriminatory) in lieu of the directed course of action. This shifts some measure of responsibility for any negative consequences flowing from any discrimination to the proponent of the discrimination.

If these strategies are not successful, the final option is to bring the matter to the attention of someone with the authority to take action, although this may be a far riskier option, depending upon the circumstances.

Stop! Have you ever seen someone in a position of power in a workplace discriminate against another individual on the basis of their personal characteristics? If you were an HR practitioner who was tasked with resolving this issue, how would you approach that issue? What risks might your approach entail and how would you mitigate them?

Sources and further information: For background information, see Hurriyet Daily Times (2015) and Today's Zaman (2015).

Note: This feature was written by Bob Barnetson.

implies that people have a choice about which organizations they wish to work for, even though during times of recession such choices might be limited. Second, people may be capable of fulfilling a role in employment, but the extent to which this will be realized is not totally predictable. Third, how capability is understood is increasingly determined by an organization's approach to talent management and development (TMD). As we will show, there are some choices to be made, especially in terms of whether there should be an exclusive or an inclusive focus for TMD (Lewis and Heckman, 2006).

Under different labour market conditions, power in the recruitment process will swing between the buyers and sellers of labour – the employers and employees, respectively. It is therefore important to understand that the dimension of power will always be present in recruitment and selection, even in organizations that purport to have a high-commitment HR strategy. Thus, in conditions of recession, employers are likely to reduce recruitment budgets and costs, paying more attention to developing the talent that has already been employed. However, the CIPD has currently noted that recruitment budgets and recruitment itself are on the rise in the private sector, reflecting rising expectations (CIPD, 2015d). Employers both in the UK and globally have noted that there is mounting competition for talented employees (CIPD, 2015d; Gager et al., 2015).

Budgetary factors will also affect how recruitment channels are used, with more use of online recruitment, as we will consider below. Generally, there needs to be an intelligent use of recruitment channels in all circumstances. For example, the ageing profile of the workforce around the world requires an adjustment of recruitment policies (Lyon and Glover, 1998; Connell et al., 2015). Henkens et al. (2005) found that the use of the internet and agencies for recruitment reflected a bias towards younger applicants, whereas older workers were more dependent on formal channels of recruitment such as newspapers and journals. It must, of course, be remembered that many older workers now use IT systems and that not all older workers should be treated the same (Finkelstein, 2015).

In addition, there have been many more graduates leaving university, and graduate employment is becoming very competitive. Many graduates will take longer to find employment that matches their skills and aspirations (Figuerdo et al., 2015). Recent reports have also noted that small businesses now recruit more graduates (70 per cent) than larger companies (64 per cent), and small businesses have the biggest rise in graduate recruitment (Antoun et al., 2015; Gager et al., 2015). This might affect perceptions of the value to be gained from studying for a degree compared with the price of a degree, especially following the introduction of and rise in tuition fees in most parts of the UK. Among today's graduates are those referred to as Generation Y (those born between around 1977 and 1994), as a contrast to Generation X (born around 1965–76). Generation Y are said to be confident and thrive on challenging but flexible work, expecting quick feedback and reward while maintaining a balanced lifestyle (Broadbridge et al., 2009). There is a difference, however, in what recruiters think is important to this generation and what the generation itself thinks. Generation Y value good working relationships, and good relationships with superiors in a company where employee contributions are valued, whereas recruiters consider that strong career paths, strong employee development and flexible working arrangements are what the generation are looking for (Gager et al., 2015; Kultalahti and Viitala, 2015). Also arriving onto the labour market are those born after 1995, referred to as Generation Z or the iGen, who, always having had access in many parts of the world to some form of digital media, are probably even more information-savvy and networked.

HRM web
links

Visit the online resource centre at **www.palgravehighered.com/bg-hrm-6e** to find out
more about Ashridge's Generation Y research project.

reflective
question

Do you consider yourself as part of Generation Y or Z? What are your expectations
for working, and what do you expect in recruitment?

Fitting the person to the environment, organization and job

Effective recruitment depends on the extent to which the overall management philosophy
supports and reinforces an approach to HRM that focuses on the utilization and development of new employees once they have joined an organization (Yu, 2014). Although HR
policies will be designed to achieve particular organizational targets and goals, those policies
will also provide an opportunity for individual needs to emerge and be satisfied, continuing
the development of congruence between the values and competencies required for the job in
question (Jain and Bhatt, 2014). This view assumes that a fit between a person and the environment can be found so that their commitment and performance will be enhanced (Mostafa
and Gould-Williams, 2014). Recent research suggests that this 'fit' is multidimensional, and
that if all areas are addressed, the outcomes in terms of selection and retention will be
improved. Given the cost of recruitment, this is an important consideration. Christensen
and Wright (2011) identified that the focus should be on a person–job (P–J) fit, although
Alniaçik et al. (2013) suggest that the compatibility between the norms and values of the
organization and the values of the employee influences outcomes such as organizational
commitment, job satisfaction and employee turnover. Bringing these thoughts together,
there is an indication that the person–environment fit includes a person–organisation (P–O)
fit, P–J fit, person–group fit and person–supervisor fit (Chuang et al., 2015). If there is a
match between the values within each of these areas expressed by the organization at the
recruitment stage, the organization and the new recruits have a clear understanding of what
is expected of new employees and can therefore manage those expectations.

Taking a strategic view of recruitment requirements starts with the strategic plan.
Research by Tyson (1995) found that although there were many differences between organizations, HRM could help to shape the direction of change, influence culture and 'help
bring about the mindset' that would decide which strategic issues were considered. HR
considerations, including the results of a review of the quantity and quality of people,
should thus be integrated into the plan (see Chapter 4). The goals, objectives and targets
that then emerge set the parameters for performance in an organization and for how work
is organized into roles and jobs.

A key role for HR is to align performance within roles with the organization's strategy,
so recruiting the right people for a role depends on how that role is defined in terms
relating to the performance needed to achieve the strategy (Holbeche, 1999). Once a
recruitment strategy has been formed, an organization might outsource its implementation to reduce costs and take advantage of recruitment expertise, especially where a large
number of staff are to be recruited (Tulip, 2004). Over the last 20 years, recruitment agents
and brokers acting as 'labour market intermediaries' between individual recruits and
recruiting organizations (Bonet et al., 2013) have become significant players in recruitment.

Such intermediaries include recruitment consultancies and temporary employment agencies. The term also includes internet job boards, company websites and social professional networks (Gager et al., 2015). What is important is that such intermediaries can play various roles in recruitment from providing information to matching people to positions, as well as administering the employment relationship. In effect, an agency becomes the employer, but this form of administration of the employment relationship, based on temporary working, is also associated with disadvantage and vulnerability (Cochrane and McKeown, 2015).

Traditionally, creating a specification containing the requirements for a particular role has required the use of *job analysis techniques*; these may include a range of interviews, questionnaires and observation processes that provide information on the work carried out, the environment in which it occurs and, vitally, the knowledge, skills and attitudes needed to perform the job well (Smith, K., 2015). In recent years, information derived from the analysis of work performance has been utilized to create a taxonomy or framework of either criterion-related behaviours or standards of performance referred to as *competencies*. Although most frameworks are developed within organizations and are based on the meanings of behaviour that exist within that organization, there are also frameworks that can be applied more generally or to specific groups in different organizations. Competencies are traditionally linked to the business's objectives and strategies and are critical to gaining the interest and commitment of senior managers. Competency-based HRM provides a strategy to align the organization's strategic direction and the internal skills and behaviours (Chouhan and Srivastava, 2014).

According to the CIPD (2010c, p. 1), competencies are 'the behaviours that employees must have, or must acquire, to input into a situation in order to achieve high levels of performance'. (This definition, focusing on behaviour patterns, differs from the idea of competence used with Vocational Qualifications, which are related to performing activities within an occupation to a prescribed standard.)

HRM web links

Visit the online resource centre at **www.palgravehighered.com/bg-hrm-6e** to learn more about the job assessment software produced by the company SHL, which can be used to develop competencies.

Table 5.1 shows how one large financial services organization in the UK sets out its competencies. Each competency is defined and described by a range of indicators that enables assessment and measurement. The competency of 'creating customer service' is, for example, indicated by:

- Anticipating emerging customer needs and planning accordingly
- Identifying the customers who will be of value to the company
- Recommending changes to current ways of working that will improve customer service
- Arranging the collection of customer satisfaction data and acting on them.

The analysis and definition of competencies should allow the identification and isolation of dimensions of behaviour that are distinct and are associated with competent or effective performance. On this assumption, the assessment of competencies is one means of selecting employees, as will be discussed below. Competencies will enable organizations to

Table 5.1 Competencies in a financial services organization

Personal focus	Self-control Self-development Personal organization Positive approach
Customer focus	Creating customer service Delivering customer service Continuous improvement
Future focus	Delivering the vision Change and creativity
Business focus	Delivering results Providing solutions Systemic thinking Attention to detail
People focus	Developing people Working with others Influencing Leading

form a model of the kinds of employee they wish to attract through recruitment. This also aids in the development of the 'employer brand' which first attracts prospective recruits (Das and Ahmed, 2014; Jain and Bhatt, 2014).

HRM web links

Visit the online resource centre at **www.palgravehighered.com/bg-hrm-6e** to learn more about the competency framework used by the UK Civil Service.

Whatever the model constructed, an organization's commitment to its human resources (HR) processes will form part of its evolving value system and make it even more attractive to those seeking employment. Many organizations seek to express their values by statements of visions and missions. For example, use the internet to find out about the values suggested by terms such as 'The Waitrose Way'. Such statements form part of the image, or 'brand' in TMD terms, that is projected by the company. Projected images, values and information on espoused goals will be made sense of by people in external labour markets, including both those employed and those unemployed. This interaction will determine how attracted potential recruits feel to an organization (Das and Ahmed, 2014).

reflective question

Think about an organization you would like to work for. What images, values and information related to that organization come into your mind? What is the brand of that organization?

The image projected by an organization and the response from potential employees provide the basis for a compatible P–O fit. Schneider (1987), using a theory of interactional psychology, proposed an attraction–selection–attrition framework to explain the workings of this process and the differences between organizations that are caused by the attraction of people to the organization's goals, their interaction with those goals and the fact that 'if they don't fit, they leave' (p. 437). The proposed framework is shown in Figure 5.2. Schneider argued that people are attracted to an organization on the basis of their own interests and personality. Thus, people of a similar type will be attracted to the same place. Furthermore, the attraction of similar types will begin to determine the place. Following selection, people who do not fit, because of either an error or a misunderstanding of the reality of an organization, will leave, resulting in attrition from that organization and weakening its effectiveness. Due to the level of competition between organizations in attracting and recruiting new hires, the attrition rate is something that is high on companies' agendas (Phillips et al., 2014).

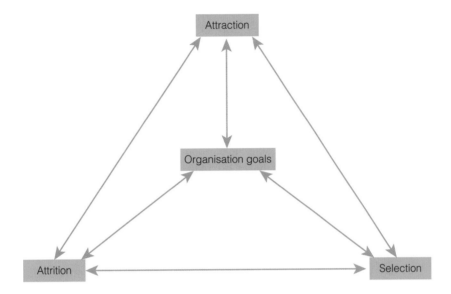

Figure 5.2 *An attraction–selection–attrition framework*

Source: Schneider, B. (1987) The people make the place. Personnel Psychology, 40: 437–53. This material is reproduced with the permission of John Wiley & Sons, Inc. Copyright © 1987 John Wiley & Sons, Inc.

At the heart of the framework lie organizational goals, originally stated by the founder and/or articulated by top managers, and out of these emerge the structures and processes that will form the basis of decisions related to attraction. This framework was supported by research conducted by Judge and Cable (1997), who found that applicants seek P–O fit, attempting to match their values with the reputation surrounding an organization's culture. Understanding the operation of P–O fit can prevent unnecessary and expensive attrition. As we said in Chapter 4, one area that suffers from high staff turnover is call-centre work. McCulloch and Turban (2007) considered P–O fit related to selection in 14 call centres in the USA and Canada among over 200 staff who stayed and those who left, showing that taking P–O fit into account during selection can play a key role in preventing high attrition.

Furthermore, P–O fit can be enhanced by an attention to socialization processes once new employees have been selected (Das and Ahmed, 2014), and in recent years, there has been growing interest in retaining talent through 'onboarding' programmes (Ndunguru, 2012). For example, Google's onboarding programme for software engineers includes face-to-face, online and on-the-job training, mentoring, membership of a support community and practice-based learning, all deemed to be successful in creating a congruence between Google's values and the values of those seeking sustained employment in the company (Johnson and Senges, 2010). Researchers are now investigating best practice in terms of onboarding programmes to understand what works and why (Klein et al., 2015). Research has also identified that positive onboarding experiences among 'millennials' (the newest recruits to the workforce) in particular can aid companies' recruitment as these recruits then share and promote the organization's brand across their social media network (Kaur et al., 2015).

In addition to P–O fit, there is also interest in the extent to which there is a match between an individual's skills, knowledge and abilities and the requirements of a job, referred to as the 'person–job' fit. Research by Carless (2005) found that both P–O and P–J fit were positively linked to attraction – the perception that an organization was a desirable place to work. However, P–J fit becomes more important in relation to a candidate's intention to accept a job offer, suggesting that once applicants move toward job acceptance, they become more concerned with how they will use their abilities than with working in an organization that matches their values (Christensen and Wright, 2011). There is also the issue of person–team fit (De Cooman et al., 2016), which focuses on the issue of team perception and person fit, requiring all team members to perceive both supplementary fit – similar characteristics such as values, abilities and goals – and complementary fit – different characteristics such as abilities and values that enable the development of inclusive teams.

This analysis of attraction, based on images and compatibility of values, and then use of abilities, has been complicated by recent concerns about attracting a more diverse workforce. Recent changes in legislation have also set limits on the expression of values. For example, images used in advertisements for recruits need to take into consideration possible discrimination against older applicants. There are also issues around globalization and the fact that so much recruitment theory is based on developed nations (Ryan and Ployhart, 2013). Views in developed countries tend to adopt an individualist ethos in selection that focus the measurement of individual characteristics such as skills, personality and values (Townley, 2014). Chuang et al. (2015) have researched into the Chinese ideas of person–environment fit and found that, within Chinese organizations, there is a culturally grounded Confucian focus on rationalism, selfhood and appropriateness. This leads to an integrative model with five specific themes: competence at work, harmonious connections at work, balance among life domains, cultivation and realization.

Recruitment channels

The main means of attracting applicants can be summarized as follows:

- Walk-ins
- Employee referrals
- Advertising, particularly online job boards
- Websites
- Labour market intermediaries such as social media, particularly social professional networks, recruitment agencies, professional associations and educational associations.

Advertising and other recruitment literature comprise a common means by which the organization's values, ethos and desired image are made manifest, often in the form of glossy brochures. The utilitarian approach that focused on specifying job details, terms and conditions has been superseded by advertising that attempts to communicate a message about the company image, possibly over a long period of time through 'low-involvement' advertisements. These advertisements seek to create awareness of an organization rather than generate recruits, but aim to raise the degree of attractiveness of the company for potential recruits (Baum et al., 2016). A good example might be the series of adverts for broadband from the UK telephone, mobile, television and internet company BT, which clearly advertises a product but maintains ongoing awareness of BT as a brand and an organization. There has been a marked shift towards recruitment advertisements that are creative and reflect the skills normally used in product marketing. Recruitment advertising is now fully established within mainstream advertising (Baum and Kabst, 2014).

HRM web links

Visit the online resource centre at **www.palgravehighered.com/bg-hrm-6e** to find out about Quality Scouts at the fast-food restaurant McDonald's.

There has been a rapid growth in online recruitment, e-recruitment having become another facet of the rapid progression of e-HRM, particularly on the global stage (Obeidat, 2016). As a result, organizations are advised to consider the design of their websites and the terms that applicants might use to carry out job and vacancy searches (Jansen and Jansen, 2005; Yang et al., 2014). It has also been shown that the usability of a company's website affects an applicant's perception of a job, with a focus on hyperlinks and text rather than graphic images and navigation links (Allen et al., 2013). The number of companies using mobile phone technology has increased by 70 per cent since 2011, and there has been a 90 per cent increase in the number of applicants who have learnt of job opportunities via mobile phone technology (Gager et al., 2015). There are, however, issues with e-recruitment, including the one-way communication system, the fact that it is impersonal and passive, and the fact that it creates an artificial distance between the individual and the company (Stone et al., 2015).

According to the CIPD (2015d, 2015e), 65 per cent of organizations have improved their company website. The survey also noted that use was made of commercial job boards such as Monster (www.monster.co.uk) and StepStone (www.stepstone.com), although evidence suggests that such sites can also attract unsuitable applicants (Parry and Tyson, 2008). Further research also found different attitudes towards commercial job boards in comparison to company websites, including the potential of reaching a wider pool of applicants and the convenience of the method (Parry and Wilson, 2009).

In many cases, especially at a time when there are more applicants than vacancies, online applications via websites can be a way of saving costs in recruitment and also allowing a faster response and turnaround. Although cost-saving is clearly a major benefit, some companies see online recruitment more strategically. For example, when hospitality company Whitbread faced the problem of recruiting managers for its 400-site Brewsters and Brewers Fayre restaurant business, it developed its own recruitment website. The site was searched over 100,000 times in the first 4 months, with 1300 applications. This enabled the company to build a database and maintain contact with potential candidates. Another benefit to the company was its ability to establish consistency in its brand to potential employees (Smethurst, 2004).

As online recruitment has developed, it has been accompanied by the use of tools for filtering applicants and tools for starting the selection process (Parry and Tyson, 2008), probably much valued by employers during a recession when the ratio of applications to positions available is high. Pollitt (2008) reports the approach of the mobile phone company 3, which works with a commercial e-recruitment operator that provides five online 'gateways' for both external and internal recruitment. Applicants can view video clips of employees talking about working for 3, as well as upload their details and create email alerts for jobs that become available. They can also monitor the progress of any application made and receive messages on their mobile technology. Davies (2015) reports the use of a mobile phone game called Firefly Freedom in the recruitment of apprentices for the accountancy firm Deloitte. The game contains a series of tests that provide data on any potential applicant.

HRM web links

> Visit the online resource centre at **www.palgravehighered.com/bg-hrm-6e** to learn about Real Match's Real Time Job Matching process.

reflective question

> Does online recruitment increase the power of employers in the graduate labour market?

In the late 2000s, social networking sites such as Facebook and LinkedIn, and social media such as Twitter, have grown in popularity, and all of these allow information about vacancies in organizations to be shared. While informal 'word of mouth' information about jobs has long been recognized for its accuracy and effectiveness in employee referrals (Van Hoye, 2013), employees can quickly, through social media, refer their friends or contacts towards vacancies – with the company having a mediating effect through its own employer brand management strategy (Uen et al., 2015). It is, of course, also possible for organizations to explore the public pages of network sites to assess the extent and value of a person's links or to find other applicants within a network. Research in Belgium suggests there is some interest among recruiters in the use of social networking sites, especially LinkedIn, but also the possibility that such interest will lead to biased decisions on selection based on profile pictures and personality as indicated by the person's presence on a site (Caers and Castelyns, 2010).

Although social media is becoming a popular recruitment and selection tool for HRM and provides a way of gaining increased information about a potential employer, the legal ramifications are still currently being played out. These include whether decisions made using social media are based on clear job-related behaviours (Curran et al., 2014; Miguel, 2013). Social media does, however, raise the profile of HRM developing a strategic route into employer branding and greater involvement of managers with the recruitment process via social media communities (Girand et al., 2014).

Professional social media sites such as LinkedIn enable recruiters to access a vast number of suitably qualified applicants, so how a potential applicant develops their online persona becomes important (Zide et al., 2014). Facebook, for example, has the added advantage of having sociodemographic filtering, which means that recruitment can be targeted at groups who might normally be hard to reach (King et al., 2014). Downsides to the use of social media are that prospective candidates often do not receive any feedback, and social media provides a platform for negative comments about companies, with a global reach, damaging the employer branding (Iddekige et al., 2013).

Internships or placements

One method of attracting applicants is through internships or placements. These are often used by students for work-based research as part of their programmes (Hynie et al., 2011), but also provide an opportunity for students to gain experience and increase their marketability. If students then take up positions within the organization, the organization gains both through the motivation of students to work and in terms of savings on training and induction. In sectors such as marketing and computing, e-internships are offered allowing interns to work in different geographical locations at reduced cost, mediated by technology (Jeske and Axtell, 2014). Research suggests that experience gained from internships increases employment prospects and starting salaries. Where internees perform well, employers place more value on such programmes (Gault et al., 2010). Because internships and placements offer employers an advanced opportunity to assess potential applicants, a selection process is increasingly used, involving some of the methods we will consider below.

HRM web links Visit the online resource centre at **www.palgravehighered.com/bg-hrm-6e** to explore internship opportunities and the selection process in Yorkshire, UK.

Job descriptions

A further manifestation of the image projected by an organization to which recruits will be attracted is a description of the actual work that potential employees will be required to do. The traditional way of providing such information is in the form of a *job description*, usually derived from a job analysis and a description of the tasks and responsibilities that make up the job. Against each job description, there is normally a specification of the standards of performance. A typical format for a job description is given in Figure 5.3.

JOB DESCRIPTION

Job title

Department

Responsible to …

Relationships

Purpose of job/overall objectives

Specific duties and responsibilities

Physical and economic conditions

Figure 5.3 *Job description format*

In addition to a job description, there is, in the form of a *personnel or person specification*, some attempt to profile the 'ideal' person to fill the job. It is accepted that the ideal person for the job may not actually exist, and that the specification will be used only as a framework within which a number of candidates can be assessed. In the past, a format for a personnel specification has been the seven-point plan, based on the work of Rodger (1970) and shown in Figure 5.4. An alternative to the seven-point plan is Munro-Fraser's (1971) fivefold grading system, as in Figure 5.5. In both forms of personnel specification, it was usual to indicate the importance of different requirements. Thus, certain requirements might be expressed as essential and others as desirable.

PERSONNEL SPECIFICATION

Physical characteristics

Attainment

General intelligence

Specific aptitudes

Interests

Disposition

Circumstances

Figure 5.4 Rodger's seven-point plan

PERSONNEL SPECIFICATION

Impact on other people

Qualification and experience

Innate abilities

Motivation

Adjustment

Figure 5.5 Munro-Fraser's fivefold grading system

Both job descriptions and personnel specifications have been key elements in the traditional repertoire of HR managers. Over the years, various attempts have been made to develop and fine-tune techniques and practices. One such development has been the shift of emphasis in job descriptions away from specifying tasks and responsibilities towards the results or outcomes to be achieved (Plachy, 1987). There has, however, been awareness of the limitations and problems of such approaches. Watson (1994) noted that job analysis, used to produce job descriptions and person specifications, relied too much on the analyst's subjective judgement in identifying the key aspects of a job and deriving the qualities that related to successful performance. In addition, the use of frameworks such as the seven-point plan may provide a 'cloak for improper discrimination' (Watson, 1994, p. 189). Current legislation on discrimination needs to be carefully considered in job descriptions and person specifications. For example, criteria set for physical characteristics might discriminate against applicants with a disability who in fact have the ability to do the job.

HRM web links Visit the online resource centre at **www.palgravehighered.com/bg-hrm-6e** to access examples of job descriptions and personnel specifications from arbitration service ACAS in the UK.

The move towards flexibility and changing work practices (see Chapter 4) has seen the appearance of new forms of work description. It was argued that traditional job descriptions were too narrow and might restrict opportunities for development and growth within jobs (Pennell, 2010). Some organizations have replaced or complemented job descriptions with performance contracts. These contain details of what a job-holder agrees to accomplish over a period of time, summarizing the purpose of a job, how that purpose will be met over the time specified and how the achievement of objectives will be assessed. This approach allows job requirements to be adjusted by agreement between the job-holder and his or her manager. It also allows a clear link to other HR processes such as performance management, appraisal and human resource development. Performance contracts signal to new recruits the expectation that their jobs will change and that they cannot rely on a job description as the definitive account of their work. Adler (2002) referred to this reorientation as performance-based recruitment and selection.

As we have already discussed, competencies are used to create a specification of the characteristics of those sought for particular positions (Industrial Relations Services, 2003a; Roberts, 1997). It has been argued (Feltham, 1992) that the use of competencies allowed organizations to free themselves from traditional stereotypes in order to attract applicants from a variety of sources. Stereotypes of the ideal person may be contained within personnel specifications, and organizations may, despite warnings, be reinforcing the stereotype in their recruitment practices. Competencies appear to be more objective, have a variety of uses in attracting applicants and allow an organization to use more reliable and valid selection techniques.

The test of success of a recruitment process is whether it attracts a sufficient number of applicants of the desired quality within the budget set (Connerley et al., 2003). Traditionally, applications are made by a combination of a covering letter, a completed application form and/or a CV.

Increasingly, such forms can be submitted by email or completed online (Parry and Wilson, 2009). Recruiters might reasonably expect a certain number of applicants per position available, referred to as the recruitment ratio, thus allowing a choice to be made. Too many applicants may reduce the cost per applicant but add further costs in terms of the time taken to screen the applications. Too few applicants may be an indication of a tight labour market. However, it may also be an indication that the values, ethos and image that the organization is projecting onto the market, including information on the work, as provided by job descriptions and specifications, are poor attractors. Recruiters need to monitor the effect of such factors on the recruitment process. If there are insufficient applicants from particular ethnic groups, or too few men or women or disabled applicants, the recruitment process may indirectly discriminate and/or fail to meet legal requirements.

Selection

As we have seen, it is usual for an organization that wishes to recruit new employees to define criteria against which it can measure and assess applicants. Increasingly, such criteria are set in the form of competencies composed of behavioural characteristics and

HRM in practice 5.1

Must you be 'posh' to enter the elite professions?

Despite the expansion in the number of undergraduates since the 1970s, there is evidence that access to elite professions, such as the law, accountancy and medicine, has become more socially exclusive and biased towards the children of middle- and upper middle-class families.

A study by Ashley et al. (2015) examined the non-educational barriers to people from less privileged socioeconomic backgrounds. The main part of the study was based on interviews of personnel involved in recruiting graduates to five elite law firms and five elite accountancy firms in London. Social class was measured according to the taking-up of free school meals, parental attendance at university and the individual's educational background at either a non-selective state school, a selective state school or a fee-paying (private) school. These account for 88 per cent, 4 per cent and 7 per cent of the population respectively.

Ashley et al. report that around 40 per cent of graduate trainees in top law firms were educated at fee-paying schools and that in the accountancy firms in the survey, around 70 per cent of job offers were made to graduates from selective state or fee-paying schools. The primary reason for the lack of diversity in recruitment is explained by the targeting of undergraduates, through campus visits and advertising, at the 24 Russell Group universities (considered the leading universities in the UK), which are research-led and highly selective. Undergraduates from less advantaged social backgrounds constituted 19 per cent of students at Russell Group institutions in 2011/12 compared with 33 per cent for all universities in 2013/14. In addition, in their recruitment activities, elite firms offer students at these privileged universities coaching and advice on the application process and the experience of interviews. Students who apply to these firms from other universities and perhaps less privileged schools and families miss this active assistance and are less likely to be successful. The study suggests that undergraduates from the Russell Group who attended non-selective state schools might feel less welcome and perhaps be deterred from applying.

Applicants to elite professions have to be intelligent, which is assessed by degree results, psychometric tests and A-levels. Privately educated students are

© Stockbyte Royalty Free Photos

more likely to have higher A-level scores, related to small class sizes, which gives them an advantage over less privileged students who have graduated with an equally good first- or upper second-class honours degree.

'Talent' is also measured by the application of non-educational, but desirable, attributes such as strong communication skills, resilience, determination, persuasiveness, drive and a confident manner at the interview, which are sometimes expressed by

(continued)

Stop! Why do you think that private (fee-paying) schools, compared with non-selective state schools, are more successful in instilling in their students those skills and personality traits that are deemed to be desirable by recruiters in the professions?

Sources and further information: See Ashley et al. (2015) for more on this topic.

Note: This feature was written by David Denham.

interviewers as 'polish'. Ashley et al. (2015, p. 11) argue that these:

> *definitions of talent can arguably be closely mapped onto socioeconomic status, including middle class norms and behaviours.*

Members of elite firms have to deal with thousands of applications, so well-tried strategies based on academic achievement and an assessment of 'talent' expedite the process. Consequently, there is little incentive for them to search for talented applicants from a wider range of socioeconomic groups and educational backgrounds. There is a danger, consciously or otherwise, of recruiters selecting candidates who are like themselves, thus disadvantaging applicants from less privileged social backgrounds.

attitudes. Rather than trust to luck, organizations are using more sophisticated selection techniques. Organizations have become increasingly aware of making good selection decisions, as selection involves a number of costs:

- The cost of the selection process itself, including the use of various selection instruments
- The future costs of inducting and training new staff
- The cost of labour turnover if the selected staff are not retained.

The CIPD's research (2015d) on selection methods in the UK has shown an interesting change over the past 5 years. Interviews following a CV/application form is now the most popular form of selection (83 per cent), with the previous most common approach, competency-based interviews, moving into second place (77 per cent). Assessment centres are used by 38 per cent of companies and personal and aptitude tests by 36 per cent.

The configuration of selection techniques chosen will depend on a number of factors. As argued by Wilk and Cappelli (2003, p. 117), it is not simply a case of 'more is better'. Selection methods will depend on the characteristics of the work and the level of pay and training. It is also crucial to remember that decisions are being made by both employers and potential employees, even during a recession, and that the establishment of mutually agreed expectations during selection forms part of the psychological contract (see Chapter 1), which will strongly influence an employee's attitudes and feelings towards the organization (Yang and Yu, 2014). According to Hausknecht et al. (2004), there are good reasons why organizations need to consider the reaction of applicants to selection methods:

- If selection is viewed as invasive, the attraction of the organization may be diminished.
- Candidates who have a negative experience can dissuade others.
- A negative selection experience can impact on job acceptance.
- Selection methods are covered by legislation and regulations relating to discrimination.
- Mistreatment during selection will put off future applications and may also stop applicants from buying the organization's products or using their services.

This still remains the case, although it needs to be remembered that mobile communications and social network sites enable news about a company to travel more quickly and to many more people (Kuhl, 2014).

reflective question How would you react to a negative experience in a selection process?

An important factor is the perception of fair treatment, and this applies to both the methods used and the process as a whole, referred to as procedural justice or fairness (Ababneh et al., 2014; Gilliland, 1993). Bauer et al. (2001) and later Walker et al. (2013) sought to measure the reactions of applications for jobs using a procedural justice scale relating to selection. Walker et al. found that if there was a perception of justice during the selection process, there was a positive relational certainty that improved the attractiveness of the organization. Positive reactions to selection can result in greater efforts to perform, which can in turn help organizations to identify the best candidates (Hausknecht et al., 2004; Walker et al., 2013).

Underlying the process of selection and the choice of techniques are two key principles:

- *Individual differences* – attracting a wide choice of applicants will be of little use unless there is a way of measuring how people differ. People can vary in many ways, for example intelligence, attitudes, social skills, psychological and physical characteristics, experience and so on.
- *Prediction* – recognition of the way in which people differ must be extended to a prediction of performance in the workplace.

Selection techniques will, to a varying degree, reflect these principles of measuring differences and predicting performance. Organizations may increasingly use a variety of techniques, and statistical theory is used to give credibility to those techniques which attempt to measure people's attitudes, attributes, abilities and overall personality. Some commentators would suggest that this credibility is 'pseudoscientific' and that there are still many limitations with selection techniques. Iles and Salaman (1995), for example, claimed that this 'psychometric' model appeared to value:

- *Individualism* – in which individual characteristics are claimed to predict future performance
- *Managerialism* – in which top managers define the criteria for performance
- *Utility* – in which the costs and benefits, in monetary terms, of using different selection techniques are assessed. It must also be remembered that most of the recruitment and selection models previously mentioned are based on experience, theories and knowledge from developed countries (Ryan and Ployhart, 2013).

reflective question What do you think are the implications associated with having individualist, managerialist and utilitarian values in the selection process?

In the context of less developed nations, even where the HR approaches of developed countries are advocated, it is likely that local cultural factors will exert an influence. For example, in China, the notion of *guanxi*, concerned with social networks and social ties through favours, will affect interactions in recruitment and selection (Zhu et al., 2013).

We are once again reminded that power is an important consideration when making decisions about employing people. Selection instruments often seem to be neutral and objective, but the criteria built into such instruments that allow the selection and rejection of applicants make up a knowledge base that provides the organization and its agents with power.

Reliability and validity issues

Two statistical concepts – reliability and validity – are of particular importance in selection. *Reliability* refers to the extent to which a selection technique achieves consistency in what it is measuring over repeated use. If, for example, you were being interviewed by two managers for a job in two separate interviews, you would hope that the interview technique would provide data such that the interviewers agreed with each other about you as an individual. Alternatively, if a number of candidates were given the same selection test, you would want to have some confidence that the test would provide consistent results concerning the individual differences between candidates. The statistical analysis of selection techniques normally provides a *reliability coefficient*, and the higher the coefficient (that is, the closer it is to 1.0), the more dependable the technique.

Validity refers to the extent to which a selection technique actually measures what it sets out to measure. There are different forms of validity, but the most important in selection is criterion validity, which measures the results of a technique against set criteria; this may be the present success of existing employees (concurrent validity) or the future performance of new ones (predictive validity).

Validation is in practice a complex process, and studies involving a large number of candidates would be required in order to allow a correlation coefficient to be calculated – in testing with criteria, this is referred to as a *validity coefficient*. A coefficient of less than 1.0 indicates an imperfect relationship between the test and the criterion. Even if the coefficient indicates such a relationship, a selection technique may, however, still be worth using: that is, you would be better to use the instrument than not use it. In addition, different selection techniques can be assessed in relation to each other according to their validity coefficient results. One difficulty is that it usually takes a long time to conduct validity studies, and by the time such studies were completed, it would be highly likely that the work used to derive some of the criteria would have changed. Validity is also related to the particular environment in which performance is carried out. However, such problems have not stopped many organizations using tests and other selection techniques that have been validated by the test designers in a range of organizations or situations.

CVs and biodata

For many positions, applicants will be asked to provide a CV (a curriculum vitae, also called a résumé), which enables them to set out their experience, skills and achievements. Importantly, it also provides an early chance for the organization to screen the applicants before moving to the next stage of selection. There has been interest in how selectors make decisions on the basis of information contained in CVs, and whether such decisions are informed by the criteria set out in the job descriptions and specifications, or are subject to personal bias. For example, would an applicant who attended a particular university be more likely to be selected on the basis of their CV (see HRM in practice 5.1)? Proença and de Oliveira (2009) examined the assessment of CVs in selection and the reasoning used by selectors. They found some interesting contradictions between the use of objective knowledge and criteria, as set out in the formal documentation, and more implicit knowledge and emotion.

In addition to CVs, there is growing interest in information about a person's past experiences and behaviours in particular situations. This can be gathered by questionnaires including multiple-choice questions and/or scenarios seeking data that can be verified as factual. Such information is referred to as *biodata*. Items can then be scored to predict against aspects of future behaviour such as job performance and absenteeism, results that have been shown to have relatively high validity (see Becton et al., 2009). It can also be scored against the 'Big Five' personality dimensions (which we shall discuss in more detail later in this chapter), adding depth to the personality tests and competency-based recruitment strategies (Cucina et al., 2013). Recent research has found that biodata are a good predictor of voluntary turnover (Breaugh, 2014), which is an important factor when considering attrition and the cost of recruitment. Overall, research is showing that biodata are a strong predictor of future performance and do not have any adverse impacts in terms of gender or ethnicity (Breaugh et al., 2014).

Selection interviewing

Of all the techniques used in selection, the interview is the oldest and most widely used, along with application forms and letters of reference, referred to by Cook (1994, p. 15) as 'the classic trio'. In recent years, with the advent of secure technology, interviews can also take place by video. Various attempts have been made to classify selection interviews, and it may be useful to point out some of the categories that have been developed:

- *Information elicited* – interviews have a specific focus and require information at different levels:
  - An interview may focus on facts. The style of the interview will be direct, based on a question and answer session.
  - An interview may focus on subjective information once the factual information has been obtained.
  - There may also be a focus on underlying attitudes, requiring intensive probing techniques and usually involving qualified psychologists.
- *Structure* – interviews may vary from the completely structured, based on planned questions and responses, to the unstructured, allowing complete spontaneity for the applicant and little control for the interviewer. A compromise between the two extremes is most likely, the interviewer maintaining control by the use of guided questions but allowing free expression on relevant topics.
- *Order and involvement* – the need to obtain different kinds of information may mean the involvement of more than one interviewer. Applicants may be interviewed serially or by a panel.

ImageSource

The selection interview has been the subject of much review and research over the past 60 years. During much of that time, overall results on the validity and reliability of interviews have been disappointing. In 1949, Wagner carried out the first comprehensive review of research associated with the employment interview. Wagner noted that, in the 174 sets of ratings that were reported, the reliability ranged from having a correlation coefficient (r) of 0.23 to one of 0.97, with a median value of $r = 0.57$. In

Have you been through an interview for a job? How reliable do you think selection interviews are?

addition, for the 222 results obtained, the correlation coefficient for validity ranged from $r = 0.09$ to $r = 0.94$, with a median of $r = 0.27$ (Wagner, 1949). Wagner considered such results to be unsatisfactory. This pattern of low-validity results continued in other research for the next four decades. In their review, for example, Ulrich and Trumbo (1965) agreed that the interview seemed to be deficient in terms of reliability and validity, and they were forced to conclude that judgements about overall suitability for employment should be made by other techniques.

There have been two lines of research to examine the reasons behind such poor results for the selection interview. The first focuses on how interviewers process information that leads to a decision on acceptance or rejection. The second focuses on the skills of effective interviewing. Table 5.2 outlines a summary of this research.

Table 5.2 Reasons for poor results from selection interviewing

Processing of information	
Pre-interview	Use of application forms to reject the applicant on grounds of sex, academic standing or physical attractiveness
First impressions	Decisions made quickly lead to a search during the rest of the interview for information to support those decisions. Negative information will be heavily weighted if the decision is rejection, but a positive early decision may lead to warm interviewer behaviour
Stereotypes	Interviewers may hold stereotyped images of a 'good' worker against which applicants are judged. Such images may be personal to each interviewer and are potentially based on prejudice
Contrast	Interviewers are influenced by the order in which applicants are interviewed. An average applicant who follows below-average applicants may be rated as above average. Interviewers may compare applicants against each other rather than against objective criteria
Attraction	Interviewers may be biased towards applicants they 'like'. This attraction may develop where interviewers hold opinions and attitudes similar to those of the applicant
Skills of interviewing	
Structure	Variations in interview structure affect reliability, low scores being gained for unstructured interviews
Questions	Interviewers may use multiple, leading, embarrassing and provocative questions
Listening	Interviewers may talk more than listen, especially if they view the applicant favourably. Interviewers may not be 'trained' to listen effectively
Retention and interpretation	Interviewers may have a poor recall of information unless guides are used and notes made. Interviewers may have difficulty in interpreting the information

By 1982, Arvey and Campion were able to report less pessimism about reliability and validity when interviews were conducted by boards (panels) and based on job analysis and job information. In particular, reference was made to the success of *situational interviews* (Latham et al., 1980). In these, interview questions are derived from systematic job analysis based on a critical incident technique (see Flanagan, 1954). Questions focus on descriptions of what an applicant would do in a series of situations. Responses are judged against benchmark answers that identify poor, average or excellent employees. If interviews could be structured around such questions, they could become more valid (Chapman and

Zweig, 2005), although with well-trained and skilled interviewers, adherence to a less rigid structure can also produce valid interviews (Dipboye et al., 2001).

In addition to situational interviews, Harris (1989) reported on other developments in interview format that relied on job analysis. These included *behaviour description interviews*, which assess past behaviour in various situations, and *comprehensive structured interviews*, which contain different types of question, for example situational, job knowledge, job simulation and work requirements. Such developments have resulted in an enhanced effectiveness of the selection interview and improved scores for reliability and validity. To achieve the benefits of such improvements, organizations need to pay more attention to providing formal training on structured selection interviewing. This is, however, not always easy to achieve since untrained interviewers may believe they are doing a good job in predicting future performance (Chapman and Zweig, 2005).

The use of questions about past behaviour combined with competencies in selection interviews has enhanced effectiveness even further. Pulakos and Schmitt (1995) compared the validity results during the selection process for experience-based (or behavioural) questions and situational questions. The former are past-oriented questions and are based on the view that the best predictor of future performance is past performance in similar situations. Applicants are asked job-relevant questions about what they did in other situations. This contrasts with situational questions, in which applicants are asked what they would do in response to particular events in particular situations. Responses to both types of question can be scored on behaviour scales, but experience-based questions have shown better results with respect to predictions of job performance, that is, predictive validity.

These results can then be used by organizations with competency frameworks. An ICT company has, for example, a competency relating to 'managing meetings'. Interviewers could base their questions around an applicant's past behaviour in managing meetings by asking the applicant to explain what she or he did in managing a specific meeting. Follow-up questions can be used to reveal further features of the applicant's performance, which can then be assessed against the competency indicators. Research by Campion et al. (1997, p. 655) found that these were 'better questions' that enhanced the effectiveness of the interview.

Barclay (1999) found a rapid increase in the use of structured techniques as part of a more comprehensive approach to selection. In particular, it was found that behavioural interviewing was being used systematically, especially in combination with a competency framework. Further research by Barclay (2001) found that behavioural interviewing was referred to in a variety of ways in organizations, for example competency-based interviewing, criterion-based interviewing, skills-based interviewing, life questioning and behavioural event interviewing. It was claimed that, however it was referred to, behavioural interviewing had improved the selection process and decisions made, a finding supported by Huffcutt et al. (2001) in their study of the use of interviews for positions of high complexity.

However, these approaches to interviewing have not been without criticism. First, since behavioural or competency-based questions are based on past behaviour, there is an assumption that behaviour is consistent over time, allowing prediction into the future. This assumption can be challenged on the basis that people do learn from their mistakes and can learn new ways of behaving. Furthermore, it might be suggested that people also tend to behave according to contingent factors such as time, place and especially the presence of others. A second assumption is that the questions allow a fair comparison between different candidates. They might, however, disadvantage those candidates with more limited experience or a poor recall of their experience, even though they might possess attributes or ideas that are not revealed in an interview (Martin and Pope, 2008). Even though a structured approach provides a degree of control over the interview, it might still be possible for applicants to prepare their answers in advance or distort their responses to create a desirable impression (Levashina and Campion, 2006).

More recently, especially in the health and caring professions, there has been an interest in selecting staff on the basis of values, as well as skills, aptitudes and behaviour. The approach, referred to as values-based recruitment, has been particularly prevalent for selection in the UK's National Health Service (NHS), where concerns about the failure of values for safe healthcare were revealed by Francis (2013). In a values-based approach in interview, questions might focus on behaviour in situations but be followed by probing questions to reveal values based on what an applicant considers important and why (Health Education England, 2014).

It is interesting at this point to note that much of the progress in interviews as a selection technique has occurred where organizations have sought to identify behaviour and attitudes that match their models of employees to be selected. This has required an investment in more sophisticated techniques of analysis. It is agreed that traditional job analysis techniques allow the production of job models in terms of tasks and responsibilities; however, organizations faced with change and seeking to employ workers whose potential can be utilized and developed will increasingly turn to techniques of analysis producing inventories of the characteristics and behaviours, such as competencies, that are associated with effective performance in the present and the future.

One consequence of more structured approaches to interviewing, including the training of interviewers, is the impact on applicants' reactions. A review by Posthuma et al. (2002) reported growing research interest in such reactions, generally showing that applicants preferred interviews compared with other selection instruments as the interview had greater *face validity*, which concerns whether applicants judge selection techniques to be related to the job (Smither et al., 1993).

One interesting dilemma, however, emerges for organizations – should the interview focus on establishing a good relationship with an applicant to elicit a positive reaction from the candidate about the selection process, or should the interview be concerned with using a good structure and sophisticated questions that have higher predictive validity? In their research, Chapman and Zweig (2005, p. 697) found that this tension exists, with some interviewers preferring less structure in favour of building a rapport that 'potentially contaminates an otherwise standardized procedure'. Organizations need to recognize that the interview is a source of anxiety for applicants, inevitably affecting their performance. The danger is that an anxiety-affected interview performance may mask an applicant's ability to perform the job (McCarthy and Goffin, 2004). In addition, applicants' self-evaluation can impact on their perception of fairness and reactions to interviews in selection. Applicants who evaluate themselves positively are more likely to view the interview as fair (Nikolaou and Judge, 2007). However, Miles and Sadler-Smith (2014, p. 624) suggest that there is still an 'elephant in the room', and that this is the interviewer(s)' intuition. Selection is a risky proposition for any manager and there is no guarantee that the chosen candidate will perform; many managers therefore still put faith in their own intuition about a candidate.

HRM web links

Selection interviews can be quite daunting for candidates. Visit the online resource centre at **www.palgravehighered.com/bg-hrm-6e** for particular guidance on competency-based interviews.

Psychometric testing

Selection based on competencies, attitudes and/or values has been one result of the increased attention given to identifying psychological factors through testing, and to how such factors predict job performance. Testing, it would seem, offers organizations a cost-effective process in their search for the right people to match the company's personality. For example, during the expansion of the UK coffee house chain Costa, 1800 new 'team' members were sought. The company worked with a testing house to develop a team-member personality questionnaire based on the company's values that measured particular qualities, such as a person's achievement orientation (Dawson, 2005).

We can make the following distinctions between different kinds of test:

- *Ability tests* – these focus on mental abilities such as verbal reasoning and numerical power, but also include physical skills testing such as keyboard speeds. In such tests, there may be right/wrong answers or measurements that allow applicants for a position to be placed in ranked order.
- *Inventories* – these are usually self-report questionnaires about personality, indicating traits, intelligence, values, interests, attitudes and preferences. There are no right/wrong answers but instead a range of choices between possible answers.

Taken together, tests of personality and ability are referred to as *psychometric tests* and have a good record of reliability and validity. Most people have some fears related to any test, and this has caused confusion over the meaning, use and value of psychometric tests. The 1990s saw a rapid growth in the number of organizations using such tests, which was the result of more people, especially HR practitioners, being trained to administer them (McHenry, 1997).

Both forms of test provide a set of norms, developed from the scores of a representative group of people (the 'norm' group) of a larger population, for example UK adult men or women in a sales role. Figures are then expressed in percentiles, which allows for standardization. Thus, a raw score of 120 on a personality test or a section of a test might be placed in the 60th percentile, indicating that the applicant's result is higher than that of 60 per cent of the norm group but less than the score obtained by 40 per cent of the group. If the test had good predictive validity, this would be a valuable indicator allowing a comparison to be made between different applicants. Inventories would also include some allowance for 'distortions' and 'fake' responses (Dalen et al., 2001) as personality tests are generally thought to be less reliable than ability tests. An important issue here is the extent to which a test might discriminate against particular groups of people, which can lead to legal challenges (Jackson, 1996).

reflective question

A personality questionnaire contains the item 'I think I would make a good leader.' This was answered 'true' by twice as many men as women, implying that men are twice as likely to become good leaders. What do you think of such an item and its implication?

Ability tests may be of a general kind, for example those relating to general mental ability or abilities such as verbal fluency and numerical ability. In addition, there are also tests for specific abilities, often referred to as aptitude tests, for example for manual dexterity and spatial ability. Furthermore, there are tests for specific jobs, such as computer aptitude and sales aptitude (Toplis et al., 2005).

For many years, there has been a great deal of interest in the extent to which general mental ability and cognitive abilities can be shown to be valid in terms of predicting performance and can be generalized across a range of occupations (see Schmidt, 2002). For example, Bertua et al. (2005) sought to examine whether general mental ability and cognitive ability tests were valid predictors of job performance and training success in UK organizations. They did this by completing a meta-analysis of 56 papers and books covering 283 samples of testing. The analysis showed that the tests were valid predictors of performance and training success across a range of occupations, including senior managers. This was also the case for changes in the composition of job roles. The authors claimed that the results provided 'unequivocal evidence for the continued and expanded use of general mental ability tests for employee selection in UK organizations' (Bertua et al., 2005, p. 403). The use of skills and general ability tests has not changed over the past 5 years, with around 45–47 per cent of companies still using them (CIPD, 2015d).

HRM web links   Visit the online resource centre at **www.palgravehighered.com/bg-hrm-6e** to learn about the Watson–Glaser test, which measures high-level verbal reasoning abilities and is often used in selecting managers and professionals.

On the personality front, there has, over the past 25 years, been growing interest in what has been referred to as the five-factor model as an explanation of the factors that determine a person's personality (Wiggins, 1996). The Five Factor model – sometimes called the 'Big Five' model of personality – proposes that differences between people can be measured in terms of degrees of:

- *Emotional stability (neuroticism)* – adjustment versus anxiety, level of emotional stability, dependence versus independence
- *Extroversion* – sociable versus misanthropic, outgoing versus introverted, confident versus timid
- *Openness to experience* – reflection of an enquiring intellect, flexibility versus conformity, rebelliousness versus subduedness
- *Agreeableness* – friendliness versus indifference to others, a docile versus a hostile nature, compliance versus hostile non-compliance
- *Conscientiousness* – the most ambiguous factor, seen as educational achievement, or as will or volition.

Salgado (1997) sought to explore the predictive validity of the Five Factor model in relation to job performance through a meta-analysis of 36 studies that related validity measures to personality factors. It was found that conscientiousness and emotional stability showed most validity for job performance, and that openness to experience was valid for training proficiency.

There are, however, doubts about an over-reliance on personality tests with respect to their use in predicting future performance, especially in relation to complex tasks such as management. Within the Five Factor model, for example, conscientiousness has been highlighted as a predictor of overall job performance. However, a study by Robertson et al. (2000) attempted to test the link between conscientiousness and the performance of 453 managers in five different companies. The results showed no overall statistical relationship, although there was a link with particular performance factors such as being organized and being quality-driven. It was also found that there might be an inverse relationship between conscientiousness and promotability. This result supports the view that suitability for complex work cannot be assessed on the basis of a narrow measurement of a psychological profile.

A relatively new slant on testing is using a strengths-based approach (Hossain and Khan, 2015). This uses positive reinforcement of the individual and explores a combination of talent, skills, interest, creativity and culture. Although relatively new in HRM circles, it has been trialled in the UK National Health Service and social services (Ibrahim et al., 2014).

This situation also applies to the assessment of intelligence. Ceci and Williams (2000) suggest that the measurement of intelligence, although used in various ways by HR departments, does have drawbacks if such measurement is based on the assumption that intelligence is a fixed property of individuals. They argue that intelligent behaviour such as complex thinking is strongly connected to the setting, composed of the task, the location and the other people involved.

Limitations on the value of intelligence, as measured by intelligence quotient tests, as a predictor have led to a growing interest in the assessment of another kind of intelligence based on feelings, sensing others' feelings and the ability to perform at one's best in relationship with others. This is referred to as *emotional intelligence* (Dulewicz and Higgs, 2000), and there is mounting evidence that employers are attempting to utilize this view of intelligence in their competency frameworks (Miller et al., 2001). Emotional intelligence has been popularized by the work of Daniel Goleman (2006), who divides emotional intelligence into five emotional competencies:

- The ability to identify and name one's emotional states and to understand the link between emotions, thought and action
- The capacity to manage one's emotional states – to control emotions or to shift undesirable emotional states to more adequate ones
- The ability to enter (at will) into emotional states associated with a drive to achieve and be successful
- The capacity to read, be sensitive to and influence other people's emotions
- The ability to enter and sustain satisfactory interpersonal relationships.

Partly as a consequence of the interest in emotional intelligence, efforts have been made to develop a test with valid and reliable psychometric properties. For example, Akerjordet and Severinsson (2009) describe the design of an Emotional Intelligence Scale and an Emotional Reactions and Thoughts Scale for use in maternity care. Interestingly, they suggested that self-reporting – the fact that respondents evaluate themselves – might pose difficulties.

HRM web
links
Visit the online resource centre at **www.palgravehighered.com/bg-hrm-6e** to find out more about emotional intelligence tests.

Self-reporting in the completion of tests is a key issue considered by Morgeson et al. (2007), who provide a fascinating review of personality testing based on the author's considerable experience and expertise in the field. They conclude that, in view of the self-reporting process that most tests employ, faking should not only be expected, but could also actually be seen as an ability that could be useful in certain situations because it provides evidence of social competence that could help performance. They highlight the generally low-validity figures for such tests, suggesting that measures which are more job-related carry greater face validity because the results can be explained more easily. They also suggest a need for an alternative to self-report measures.

An interesting finding about tests is that academics' debates on validity are not especially significant for practitioners, who tend to choose tests because they are well-known, familiar and easy to use, and therefore tend to be retained over time (Furnham, 2008). This means that the most popular tests are the:

- Myers–Briggs Type Indicator (www.myersbriggs.org/my-mbti-personality-type/mbti-basics)
- 16PF Questionnaire (www.psychometrictest.org.uk/16pf-test/)
- Belbin Team Roles (www.belbin.com/rte.asp?id=8)
- Occupational Personality Questionnaire (www.jobtestprep.co.uk/opq32.aspx).

Online testing

Online testing is also being used for selection and other HR purposes, this being referred to as e-assessment. One feature of testing is to provide a filter for organizations in order to reduce the number of unsuitable candidates (Czerny, 2004), although such a process may also screen out good applicants. The banking organization Lloyds TSB, for example, has an online application form based on its competency framework; this acts as the first stage in filtering applicants. For the second stage, there is a 20-minute numerical reasoning test, also completed online (Pollitt, 2005). The results of this test are then scored electronically, and this feeds into the bank's recruitment management system.

It is claimed that online testing provides organizations with the ability to test at any time and any place in the world, with the added benefit of being able to process the applicants quickly (Lievens and Harris, 2003). Furthermore, as tests are taken, the results can be accumulated and used to improve the validity of the tests. There might even be a correlation between performance in online tests and successful learning at work. One difficulty, however, is that there is a loss of control over the administration of a test; thus, you can take a test at any time and in any place in the world – but also with anyone else to help. Toplis et al. (2005, p. 52) pose the question, 'How do you know who is responding to the test at the end of the line?' There is, however, interest in comparing internet testing with traditional paper and pencil testing. One issue, for example, is whether a person has an understanding of computers, which can affect the perceptions of a test (Weichman and Ryan, 2003) – around the world of course, there are bound to be significant variations in accessing and use of information technology.

Potosky and Bobko (2004) compared the responses of 65 students to internet and paper and pencil versions of untimed and timed tests. They also assessed the students' understanding of computers in advance of the process and their reactions at the end. One interesting finding was the issue of timing; that is, it was reported that time on the internet (virtual time) was different from actual time. This affected the time to find and read the instructions or the time to download a test online. The appearance of a test is also affected online, with fewer items being seen compared with a full paper test. This may also affect the order in which items are responded to since it is easier to move around a paper test compared with its online counterpart. The results showed interesting differences in test performance between the internet and paper and pencil versions of the timed test. For the untimed test, there was little difference.

Another issue is the perception of efficiency and user-friendliness of the website in taking tests online. For example, sites that are difficult to navigate will affect applicants' overall satisfaction, especially in the earlier stages of selection (Sylva and Mol, 2009).

reflective question

> How do you feel about taking a test online?

Whatever developments occur in the use of e-assessment in recruitment, all tests need to conform to the requirements of discrimination laws. In the UK, tests should be endorsed by the British Psychological Society, which will check for any sexual and ethnic bias within them. In addition to this endorsement, the impact of tests needs to be followed up and monitored to ensure that a test does not result in discrimination in practice against one sex or particular ethnic groups. Davies (2015) reports on recent moves by some employers such as the NHS, the BBC and Deloitte to introduce name-blind applications in an effort to avoid discrimination where a person's name might lead to bias against applicants from ethnic minorities.

HRM web links

> Visit the online resource centre at **www.palgravehighered.com/bg-hrm-6e** to try out some emotional intelligence tests for yourself.

Assessment centres

In their examination of organizational selection practices, Wilk and Cappelli (2003) found that as the complexity and demands of work increased, there was a need for a variety of selection methods. Given the weakness of single measures, organizations can combine techniques and apply them together at an event referred to as an assessment centre. Such events may last for 1–3 days, during which a group of applicants for a post will undergo a variety of selection techniques. For example, in the case of Lloyds TSB referred to above (Pollitt, 2005), the last stage of the selection process is attendance at an assessment centre, lasting 24 hours (from 5 pm until 5 pm the following day). Candidates attend in groups of 12 or 24 and are observed by assessors as they complete an interview, a case study presentation, group exercises and a role play. They also complete a numerical reasoning test to verify the online test. The CIPD (2010d) previously found that 42 per cent of organizations used assessment centres during selections, although in the most recent report in 2015 (CIPD, 2015d) , it noted that only 38 per cent of companies were using assessment centres, probably due to the costs involved in providing such centres.

We can make a distinction here between development centres (see Chapter 7), which yield information to help identify development needs, and assessment centres, which are designed to yield information to help make decisions concerning a candidate's suitability for a job. Assessment centres can also be used to select participants for training programmes, especially for leadership and management development (see Chapter 14), and to promote internal applicants to more senior positions (Thornton and Gibbons, 2009).

It is argued that it is the combination of techniques, providing a fuller picture of an applicant's strengths and weaknesses, that makes assessment centres so valuable. Wood-ruffe (2000) outlines four generalizations about assessment centres:

- Participants are observed by assessors who are trained in the use of measurement dimensions such as competencies.
- Assessment is by a combination of methods and includes simulations of the key elements of work.
- Information is brought together from all the methods, usually under competency headings.
- Participants can be assessed in groups.

Although there may be no such thing as a 'typical' assessment centre (Spychalski et al., 1997), the general methods used are group discussions, role plays and simulations, interviews and tests. The following activities were, for example, used in the assessment centre to select customer service assistants for European Passenger Services Ltd (Mannion and Whittaker, 1996, p. 14):

- Structured interview
- Perception exercise
- Communication exercise
- Personality inventory
- Customer service questionnaire
- Tests for clear thinking and numerical estimation.

The objectives for using these methods were to generate information about:

- The ability to work under pressure
- Characteristic behaviour when interacting with others
- Preferred work styles
- The ability to think quickly
- The ability to make quick and accurate numerical estimates
- Experience and aptitude for a customer service role.

The European Passenger Services assessment centre process was judged to be a success, underpinned by the objectives and standardized decision-making of the assessors. Candidates attending an assessment centre would be observed by assessors who should be trained to judge candidates' performance against criteria contained within the dimensions of the competency framework used.

There has been interest in assessment centres that measure dimensions of personality and/or behaviour, based on the judgement of assessors while candidates complete the exercises; these are referred to as dimension-based assessment centres (Lance, 2008). A common problem is that assessors' ratings may be affected if there are too many people to assess at the same time during an exercise (Melchers et al., 2010), and this problem may become more difficult to solve when organizations attempt to save costs by reducing the number of assessors. One possibility is to focus more on interviews with higher validity possibilities that measure dimensions similar to those of an assessment centre, thus screening out applicants who score less well at the interview and reducing the number to measure at the assessment centre (Dayan et al., 2008). Another possibility is using measurement dimensions that are more focused on and specific to particular tasks, in contrast to measurements that are used across all exercises. This approach is a feature of task-based assessment centres, where attention is given to specific dimensions of behaviour for each task, which are observable in the outcomes resulting from participation in that task (Jackson et al., 2010).

reflective
question

> Have any of your colleagues applying for graduate training programmes been put through an assessment centre? What was their reaction to this process?

If your colleagues were to relay to you negative reactions about their experience of selection techniques with one organization, this might affect your image of it. Again, one important issue is the question of face validity – whether applicants feel that the selection techniques are connected to the job. For example, in response to the problem that an assessment centre lacked realism and variety, the accountancy firm Ernst and Young ran its centre in real offices, having candidates answer emails and telephone calls. This apparently made the organization's expectations clearer (Trapp, 2005). Kolk et al. (2003) found no difference to the process in terms of validity when they made an assessment centre more transparent to candidates by revealing, prior to their attendance, the dimensions of assessment that would be observed and used to make judgements. Recent research has also highlighted that the context and composition of the group attending the assessment centre can influence the outcome. Participants' scores may not reflect their skills and abilities (Falk and Fox, 2014), and therefore some standardization of assessment centres may be needed to ensure ongoing validity (Becker et al., 2015). There are also recognized issues concerning the training and size of the assessment team (Wirz et al., 2013).

Pre-employment activities

During recruitment and selection, even in times of recession, both parties in the relationship are making decisions. It is therefore important for an organization to recognize that high-quality applicants, attracted by the organization's image, could be lost at an early stage unless they are supplied with realistic organization and work information. Applicants have expectations about how the organization will treat them, and recruitment and selection represent an opportunity to clarify these.

Realistic job previews (RJPs) have a long history (Baur et al., 2014) and provide a means of achieving this by offering 'accurate, favourable, and unfavourable job-related information to job candidates' (Templer et al., 2006, p. 158). RJPs can take the form of case studies of employees and their work, the chance to 'shadow' someone at work, job sampling and videos, the aim being to enable applicants' expectations to become more realistic. One possibility is therefore that expectations about work and an organization can be lowered, allowing applicants to deselect themselves; however, for those who continue into employment, organizational commitment, job satisfaction, performance and job survival are likely to increase (Baur et al., 2014; Phillips, 1998; Premack and Wanous, 1985).

A key feature of RJPs is their promotion of accurate pre-employment expectations that serve to 'vaccinate' employees for when they are faced with job demands once employed.

Alison Blayney Part 2

HR Business Partner, TIGI Haircare, Unilever

www.unilever.co.uk/

Remind yourself of Alison's background and her experience with Unilever by going back to Chapter 1. Then click on Alison's photo in your ebook to watch the second part of her video, which focuses on recruitment and selection. When you have watched this, try to answer the following questions:

1 How does Alison claim she is proactive in recruiting? What does she mean by 'going beyond normal sourcing strategies' to build talent pools?
2 Is LinkedIn effective for Alison? How does she use the employee referral scheme and who benefits from it?
3 How does Generation Y differ from Generation X? Explain how the employee brand is 'leveraged' to attract Generation Y.

RJPs also serve to communicate an organization's honesty about such demands (Earnest et al., 2011). For example, if the work is located overseas, there is a need for information about living in another country, referred to as a realistic living conditions preview (Templer et al., 2006). Research in Canada by Richardson et al. (2008) highlighted the importance of realistic living conditions previews in revealing non-work factors such as the well-being of the partners and children of those employees who live abroad.

What is clear is that recruitment and selection provide an arena for engagement between organizations and potential employees in which both parties develop an 'image' of each other. If managers fail to understand the mutuality of this process, they endanger the attractiveness of the organization and thereby threaten the organization's ability to recruit good applicants (Hausknecht et al., 2004). In combination with RJPs, organizations such as Siemens and DaimlerChrysler provide applicants with a link to current employees who act as mentors (Spitzmüller et al., 2008), and this can play a role in increasing attraction and improving the quality of socialization of recruits (Baur et al., 2014).

Talent management and development

In recent years, much of the interest in recruitment and selection has been concerned with attracting people with talent. The term 'talent', as part of an employer's branding efforts for future employees (Das and Ahmed, 2014), gained widespread use from the late 1990s and early 2000s when Michaels et al. (2001) declared a 'war for talent'. This was based on the apparent competition between organizations to find and develop 'high-potential' staff. TMD became a significant area of policy activity, accompanied by a growing list of books, conferences and techniques.

There has been and continues to be some confusion and variation in its meaning and use, which, it is argued, is holding back the development of ideas and practices for TMD as a distinct aspect of workplace relations (Gallardo-Gallardo et al., 2013). One concern is that TMD is another repackaging of HR practices as 'old wine in new bottles' (Chuai et al.,

2008). Others argue that talent can be defined and used in any way people want based on their ideas on what they want the term 'talent' to cover (Ulrich, 2011). For example, in organizations composed of knowledge workers where knowledge-sharing and creation are important, Whelan and Carcary (2011) have suggested that organizations need to adopt a 'smart' version of TMD in order to retain staff and their knowledge. This would suggest that TMD should overlap with traditional HRM activities such as recruitment, selection, development, succession-planning and career development. In this sense, TMD, like HRM, is usually considered narrowly with a focus on individuals and how they can benefit organizations. This reinforces the dominance of managerialism and unitarism (Thunnissen et al., 2013), based on the assumption that everyone at work shares mutual goals and interests (Farndale et al., 2010). An important concern shown in evidence on TMD is that it is mainly based on an exclusive categorization of staff, which risks demotivating others who might be seen as less talented or not identified as high potential or a high performer (CIPD, 2015d; Lacey and Groves, 2014).

reflective question | What is your understanding of talent? Do you consider yourself 'high potential'?

Evidence of how TMD is practised in organizations shows that TMD policies need to be set against the context and situation of each organization so that priorities can be achieved (Tansley et al., 2007a). This can lead to a variety of approaches, as shown in Figure 5.6. In this figure, the two dimensions of Exclusive/Inclusive and People/Position provide four possible patterns. First, the 'exclusive people' approach rests on the assumption that key individuals or 'stars' are necessary for the organization's success (Groysberg, 2010). As a consequence, attention is given to those people considered to be 'high potential' and/or 'high performing' (Incomes Data Services, 2010). In contrast, an 'exclusive position' approach starts from the question 'What key positions are needed to meet the strategy?'

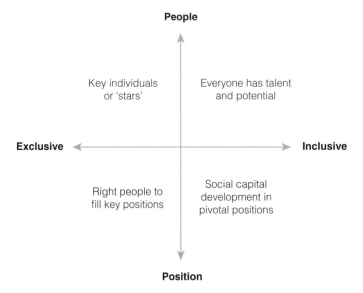

Figure 5.6 Approaches to TMD

People with the right skills and attributes can then be found to fill those positions. Huselid et al. (2005) refer to strategically critical jobs as 'A' positions, filled by 'A' players. Such positions are supported by 'B' positions and 'C' positions – the latter might be seen as jobs that can be outsourced or eliminated. The crucial argument is that improving the performance of 'A' players in 'A' positions will have a more than proportionate impact on the overall performance of the organization. An example might be the performance of customer service staff who have direct interactions with customers.

The 'inclusive people' approach is a recognition that everyone in an organization has talent and the potential for high performance. For example, Cerdin and Brewster (2014) show how, within a global multinational corporation context, TMD is seen as open to all employees as a step in everyone's career development. This approach also gives more attention to the relationships between people and to how work is often organized through teams, for example in legal work and software development. So giving attention to the 'stars' could actually reduce performance overall (Groysberg et al., 2004). The inclusive position approach highlights the importance of developing relationships based on cooperation, trust and goodwill, and accessing networks – referred to as social capital development (McCullum and O'Donnell, 2009). Relationships with others both inside and outside an organization give strategic importance to pivotal positions in providing above-average impact (Collings and Mellahi, 2009).

Succession-planning

Succession-planning has traditionally been concerned with ensuring a smooth replacement for senior managers and leaders, so that there will be less disruption to performance (Giambatista et al., 2005). More recently, succession-planning has been presented as the purpose of TMD, although there may still be some disconnection between TMD and succession processes (Tansley et al., 2007a) if both processes are completed without sharing information. The key link focuses on a plan that considers the organization's future direction and requirements against the capabilities and potential of those selected for a 'talent pool'. Membership of a pool is determined by a selection process including interviews, feedback from a variety of sources or 360-degree feedback, and other assessments. In larger organizations, there can be different pools for different levels. Tansley et al. (2007a) identify four levels:

- Entry level
- Emerging talent
- Rising stars
- Executive talent.

The connections between the levels are referred to as the 'talent pipeline', and this provides an organization with a plan for flexible succession, as well as with a way of motivating internal staff (CIPD, 2009a). There can also be lateral movement between roles, departments and projects. Talent pools and pipelines allow a strategic view of a flow of the right people at the right time, what Ready and Conger (2007) refer to as a 'talent factory'. Part of the planning and selection involves identifying who the right people are for each pool. Succession sometimes has to occur quickly, perhaps in response to an emergency or an absence. At such moments, Rothwell (2011) points to the importance of replacement plans carrying the implication that replacements are not needed on a permanent basis.

A typical approach might be to chart high performers against high potential, as shown in Figure 5.7. Each combination of performance and potential can be used to identify staff for talent pools. The top right corner identifies high performers with high potential, whereas the bottom right corner identifies high performers with low potential. This chart is frequently presented as a 3 × 3 matrix with nine boxes, allowing for more differentiation. Crucially, however, this allows a strategic view of talent from which a plan for succession and development can be made. Decisions relating to development for those considered to be high performers and/or to have high potential to perform include selection for learning and development programmes (see Chapter 7) and making them the focus of attention for coaching and mentoring (Garvey et al., 2014; see Chapter 6). There are also software solutions to help with this process. Pollitt (2007) showed how one organization used software including functions for succession-planning and identifying future blockages to track 300 managers in a global talent pool.

reflective question What approach would you adopt for someone in the top left segment of the chart – that of low performance and high potential?

The value of a grid approach is how it creates debate and discussion concerning TMD, but there could be problems about the adequacy of information to inform decisions about placing people in particular positions on the grid. There might also be a loss of linkage to the organization's strategy (Vaiman et al., 2012).

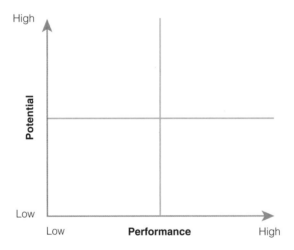

Figure 5.7 *A performance/potential chart*

A further problem is concerned with how even membership of a talent pool might not lead to movement along the pipeline. That is, TMD might result in stagnation for individuals even though they have been identified as talented. This leads to a significant critique of TMD in its focus on employment or HR practices such as attraction, recruitment, selection, appraisal, training and rewarding employees. What is seldom considered is work practices, which concern how work is organized, structured and supported as employees exert effort to achieve particular rewards (Boxall and Macky, 2009). It is quite possible therefore that, even if individuals are considered talented, they will within work practices become dependent on the efforts of others. The critique is deepened further if we consider how work is normally organized. Whereas TMD is mostly concerned with individuals, work often occurs in teams and groups, and is based on relationships within and across networks (Iles et al., 2010). It thus starts to become clearer that TMD is currently more concerned with employment practices and is seldom concerned with work practices, especially those that are not individually based. As Devins and Gold (2014) have argued, workplace performance is often a collective endeavour based on a range of dependent and interdependent relationships to ensure flows and correct responses (Malone et al., 1999). Studies on leadership have shown that work can be seen as conjoint action that requires dependence and mutuality (Spillane, 2006). Therefore even if people are seen as talented, they are required to collaborate with a range of others who may or may not be categorized as talented. However – and this is crucial – without dependencies and mutuality, talent may not be used, so talent work is probably best understood in more collective terms. Gold et al. (2016) show how such work can be understood through a mapping process to find and appreciate collective talent, an example of which is shown in HRM in practice 5.2.

Career management

TMD strategies are increasingly required to focus on the retention of committed staff, who in turn expect their careers to be considered (Scott and Revis, 2008). If an employee is committed to a career, this can complement commitment to an organization provided there is managerial support (Baugh and Roberts, 1994).

In the past, the term 'career' was usually applied to managerial and professional workers, and HR practices provided support for career development along a 'well-made road' via which individual desires for status and fulfilment could be reached (Sennett, 1998, p. 120). Along the way, of course, many employees encountered blocks to their careers, such as a lack of opportunities and support and, for women, cultural and structural prejudices to career progress referred to as the 'glass ceiling' (Davidson and Cooper, 1992). Graduates too might find their aspirations unsatisfied as they experienced a gap between what they expected and what their organizations provided (Pickard, 1997). In addition, those from ethnic minorities could find themselves 'ghettoed' into certain sectors of work (Singh, 2002). For many employees, however, it was indeed possible to embrace the idea of an organizational career that could be planned for the course of a working life, and theoretical models supported a view that careers could be planned and managed (Grzeda, 1999).

Through the 1990s and into the 2000s, there were significant changes in the way in which careers were explained, understood and managed. Various macro- and micro-tensions (Baruch, 2006) – such as competition, recession and short-term financial pressures, a breakdown in functional structures in favour of process structures such as project teams, and even the loss of bureaucratic personnel systems that planned career moves – combined, in some companies, to 'dump the basic idea of the corporate career' (Hirsh and Jackson, 1997, p. 9). Adamson et al. (1998) suggested that there have been three changes in organizational career philosophy:

- An end to the long-term view of the employer–employee relationship
- An end to movement through the hierarchy being seen as career progression
- An end to logical, ordered and sequential careers.

If neither individuals nor organizations can plan for the long term, this suggests that the term 'career', with its implication of predictable progression, may have lost its commonly

HRM in practice 5.2

Talent as a collective endeavour in the West Yorkshire Police

I n order to understand how talent was being used in work practice, HR managers and senior officers in the West Yorkshire Police completed a mapping exercise (shown in Gold et al., 2016) that identified how dependent and interdependent work processes that showed talent in practice were based on people working together rather than focused on particular individuals. One example concerned work on solving street robbery crime and related to how various groups within the police force responded to a spate of street robberies. A key point is how, contrary to reports of 'anecdotal incidents' of teams 'not assisting each other', there was 'a really positive, collaborative response from all teams and departments "doing the right thing"'. Notice how it is collective units that are considered, and not individuals.

Officers from Lates' Response Team 1 attended and took initial details from complainants who were unknown to each other but had both been approached by the same suspects.

The officers identified the scene of the robberies and requested a dog unit (central support) to attend and for further units to make to the area. Officers from Team 1 Rural (a neighbouring geographical area) came in to help with area searches and on identification of the second complainant went to deal with him. (There have been recent anecdotal incidents of neighbouring teams not assisting each other, so this is encouraging!).

Descriptions were obtained and broadcast to officers from Response and Neighbourhood Patrol Teams (NPT) in the area.

A short time later Police Community Support Officers from Team 1 NPT shouted up that they had observed three males and a female who fitted the descriptions given and that they were following them. They gave a commentary and other officers from NPT and Response attended. One of the males ran off but was detained nearby. One of the suspects was found in possession of the complainants' property. The complainants were brought back to the police station and officers from Reactive Criminal Investigation Departments (CID) (statements are usually tasked to uniform by CID, so

ImageSource

their assistance was appreciated) took their statements. Officers from nights (the next shift coming on duty) – Response Team 4 conducted the house searches for the suspects.

Overall a really positive, collaborative response from all teams and departments 'doing the right thing' (Gold et al., 2016).

Sources and further information: For more information on this study, see Gold et al. (2016).

Note: This feature was written by Jeff Gold.

understood meaning. Instead, the career path becomes 'multidirectional' (Baruch, 2004) based on a more dynamic and transactional relationship between people and work (Lee et al. 2011).

An alternative view is that of the 'portfolio career' (Templer and Cawsey, 1999), in which individuals might expect, over the course of their working lives, to work for a variety of different organizations in a variety of positions; as a result, they will need a range of skills, learning new ones as required to enhance their employability. Included in the sequence might be periods of leisure, education and domestic tasks. It is suggested that high-achieving graduates might look to build portfolio careers to seek self-fulfilment by moving from one job to another (Power et al., 2013). A related view is that of the 'boundaryless career' (Arthur and Rousseau, 2000), during which individuals can consider movements between jobs, locations and occupations. Sullivan and Arthur (2006) also refer to psycho-logical mobility, which considers how people perceive their abilities in making career choices in the light of current realities. This reflects an interest in what Khapova et al. (2007, p. 115) see as the 'subjective career' based on an 'individual's interpretation of his or her career situation at any given time'. The boundaryless career, as a concept, has attracted scrutiny, with some suggesting that there are career boundaries, often set by organizations, that continue to enable or constrain, but certainly impact on, careers (Inkson et al., 2012). Nevertheless, around the world there continues to be interest in the notion of the 'boundary career mindset' and how people adapt their expectations of careers in an era of rapid change (Uy et al., 2015).

One way of adapting is for individuals to become proactive in directing their careers, using personal values to evaluate their success, referred to as the 'protean career' (Hall, 2002). This image is part of a general move towards all of us accepting responsibility for our own career development through acquiring employability skills and developing life-long learning (O'Donoghue and Maguire, 2005) rather than assuming employment security (Inkson and King, 2010). Employability is developed through acquiring skills and abilities that are valued by employers, both current and future. Within organizations, this can occur through programmes based on competencies if there is also the support of organizational culture and HR practices (De Vos et al., 2011). These will create positive perceptions for employability and marketability, and Sturges et al. (2010) show the importance of perceptions of the organization's support for career management, espe-cially relationships with managers and others, if staff are to be retained and developed. Furthermore, if such support is absent and job insecurity is perceived, employable staff are more likely to manage their careers in order to take them away from the organization (Kang et al., 2012).

These views of career learning are not, however, universally accepted. For example, Mallon and Walton (2005), in a study of career learning among local government and health workers in the UK and New Zealand, found that few were actively engaging in this. Furthermore, most still saw their careers in terms relating to their employment within their organizations (or previous organizations if workers were now working for themselves). It was still very much the case that definitions of careers were organizationally situated, and that this affected what was deemed relevant to learn. In addition and more generally – as a consequence of the expansion of higher education – there is a growing number of graduates with higher levels of knowledge and skills, but these do not automatically make them employable. Employability, skills and knowledge require a response from employing organizations to say that they are valued (Elias and Purcell, 2003).

reflective
question

> The notion of careers is subject to change and flux. Who do you think should be responsible for the development of people's working lives? How are you making yourself employable, and what are the skills of employability and life-long learning?

HRM web
links

> Visit the online resource centre at **www.palgravehighered.com/bg-hrm-6e** for access to research, models and policies on the importance of employability.

These varying images of what constitutes a career point to a 'pendulum of ownership of career development' by which responsibility swings between the organization and the individual (Hirsh and Jackson, 1997, p. 9). Over the last 20 years, many organizations have engaged in restructuring activities that have led to 'delayering' and the removal of grades. The spread of career development initiatives could thus be seen as a way of empowering and motivating staff who have remained in place as part of a core workforce, and this extends now to TMD strategies. Given the different approaches to TMD we considered above, it is not entirely clear how these will affect patterns of career development. However, we can suggest a segmented pattern encompassing career development for everyone at work, but with different patterns for different work groups:

- Managers and 'high-potential/high-performance' staff – careers managed by the organization, not always for life, but with succession-planning to fill senior positions
- Highly skilled workers – attempts to attract and keep key workers by offering career development paths
- The wider workforce – more limited development opportunities often caused by and resulting in uncertainty over career paths; there is an expectation that these workers should look after themselves.

Lips-Wiersma and Hall (2007) have provided a case study of careers in an organization during change, finding evidence that staff were taking more responsibility for careers but that this was shared with the organization. Thus, where staff were setting their own career goals and aiming to find opportunities such as secondments, HR either helped or initiated projects with secondments, seeking to link the individuals' career aspirations with the culture and direction of the organization. According to Lips-Wiersma and Hall (p. 789):

 career management and development has a significant role to play in achieving mutuality of organizational and individual interests.

For those selected into TMD programmes and pools, it would seem that the benefits include development opportunities that enable career enhancement. Research by the CIPD (2010a) based on surveys and interviews showed, not surprisingly, that selection for such programmes was likely to increase engagement and help employees see a future with their organization, so a career path was clearer. In addition, coaching, mentoring and networking – thus increasing social capital – were more highly valued. The HR function was important in ensuring that the programme was well run and considered effective for the organization.

reflective
question How do you think those not selected for talent pools might respond, and what impact is there on their careers?

Finally, in this section, it is useful to consider Sullivan et al.'s (2007) kaleidoscope career model, which takes a lifespan approach and suggests that each person can seek a best fit of choices based on the parameters of:

- Authenticity – an alignment of internal values with those of the place of work
- Balance – between work and non-work demands, including family, friends and personal interests
- Challenge – of stimulating work and career advancement.

These parameters are interpreted differently over a lifespan and between generations in organizations. For example, those considered to be part of Generation X (born around 1965–76) have a higher preference than Baby-boomers (born approximately 1946–1964) for authenticity and balance (Sullivan et al., 2009). Research suggests that those born after 1976 – Generation Y – as they are very information-savvy and well networked, view trust and relationships with their colleagues more highly but will also form intentions to leave if they become bored, with commitment to an employer viewed less favourably (Solnet et al., 2012).

TNNB Ltd

The setting

TNNB is a family-owned engineering business in the UK that produces electrohydraulic systems for a wide range of customers, mostly for export. It has won two Queens Awards for Export and is regarded as a leader in its sector. Each system is built to order, with a salesperson obtaining the initial details before a design engineer builds a portfolio of images that can be presented to the customer. On approval, which can take anything up to 6 months, a contract is established and the order is handed over to project managers.

The principal tasks of the project managers are to build a relationship with the customer, to draw up a plan with key dates for completion, to ensure safe delivery and check installation, and to make sure that resources are allocated at the right time in the right combination. Project management is complex work, and to ensure delivery against the terms of the contract with the customer, where delays can result in a loss of revenue, it is necessary to establish a strong network of relationships with everyone involved in completing the order. Although a project plan will contain the key details and requirements for completion, it is up to the project manager to track performance, often in parallel streams, so that any disconnections can be prevented or dealt with. As Lewis identifies (Lewis, J. P., 2000), it is always necessary for a project manager to know:

- Where we are
- Where we should be
- How can we get on track again.

The problem

TNNB employs two project managers who can between them be responsible for several projects at a time, usually at different stages of completion. During a period when six projects were in process, it became evident early on that some key stages were not being completed against schedule, the company managers being alerted by the prospect of penalty clauses. Further evidence revealed that one of the project managers had a reputation for being too slow and measured, spending too much time in his office, apparently making a paper plan that seemed to be out of step with events on the ground. He could identify where the project should be, but could seldom identify the current status of the project. The second project manager was more likely to have the opposite problem – good on the live situation of the project but poor at planning, often resulting in reactive scheduling.

TNNB had two managers, cousins within the owning family, and after a brief meeting they decided to take a closer look at what was happening. It soon became clear that there were tensions between the systems engineers and the mechanical design and service engineers. In addition, the project managers were not dealing with this effectively, with the main systems engineer claiming he was 'being let down' and was feeling 'frustrated' through the 'incompetence' of the project managers. He argued that neither project manager seemed to have the necessary skills or talent for the job, and that both were associated with missed deadlines or crisis meetings to get things done at the last minute because no advance information had been provided.

The two project managers were defensive about their work, arguing that management had not prepared them sufficiently for the role. Furthermore, they said that the company's shift to project-based working had, despite its success in the market, not been properly thought through.

The family managers felt threatened by what they found. First, they believed that project-based working with good project managers was the only way they could ensure continued progress in the company. Second, systems engineering added a distinctive feature to the product, and any possibility of losing engineers from this section would cause difficulties. But losing any of their engineers would not be helpful since they were difficult to find, had learnt a lot on the job, which took time, and had mostly been with the company for several years (with some not far from retirement).

The assignment

Working either alone or in a study group, prepare a report drawing on this chapter and other recommended material addressing the following:

1 How would a TMD strategy help this company?
2 What perspective or approach to talent would be appropriate?

3 What policies and practices for TMD are needed now?
4 What policies and practices for TMD are needed in the future?

Essential reading

Lewis, J. P. (2000) *The Project Manager's Desk Reference: A Comprehensive Guide To Project Planning, Scheduling, Evaluation, and System.* New York: McGraw Hill.

Note: This case study was written by Jeff Gold.

summary

➤ This chapter has examined the nature of recruitment, selection and TMD in organizations.

➤ The attraction and subsequent retention of employees is crucial to an employment relationship, which is based on a mutual and reciprocal understanding of expectations. Employers have, however, significant power in terms of recruitment and selection. The overall approach taken will reflect an organization's strategy and its philosophy towards people management.

➤ It is essential that organizations see that, whatever the state of the labour market and their power within it, contact with potential recruits is made through the projection of an 'image' that will impact on and reinforce the expectations of potential recruits.

➤ Competency frameworks have been developed to link HR practices to the key requirements of an organization's strategy. Competencies can be used to form a model or 'image' of the kinds of employee that an organization is seeking to attract and recruit. The response to the image provides the basis for a compatible P–O fit. Images or the 'brand' will feature in recruitment literature and, increasingly, on the internet via e-recruitment.

➤ There has been a growth in online recruitment and the use of social media as a form of e-recruitment. Social networking sites now allow the sharing of information about vacancies and applicants.

➤ Key documents in recruitment and selection are job descriptions and personnel specifications, although there is a growing awareness of the limitations of traditional approaches to their construction. Some organizations have switched to performance contracts, which can be adjusted over time. In addition, personnel specifications may be stated as competencies, which appear more objective.

➤ Selection techniques seek to measure differences between applicants and provide a prediction of future performance at work. Techniques are chosen on the basis of their consistency in measurement over time – reliability – and the extent to which they measure what they are supposed to measure – validity. Applicants' experience of selection methods, especially perceptions of fair treatment, strongly influences their feelings towards the organization.

➤ There are a range of selection techniques, the most common of which is the interview, and this has been the subject of much research. Recent years have indicated that a structured approach and the use of behavioural interviewing based on competencies increase the effectiveness of interviews in selection. The use of competencies in selection is a reflection of the current interest in assessing personality and abilities by the use of psychometric tests. Techniques of selection may be combined in assessment centres to provide a fuller picture of an applicant's strengths and weaknesses.

➤ Online testing allows organizations to process applicants more quickly. This may, however, filter out good applicants as well as unsuitable ones.

➤ TMD has become a significant area of policy activity relating to finding and developing 'high-potential' staff. There are a variety of approaches to TMD based on using dimensions of Exclusive/Inclusive and People/Position.

➤ Succession-planning has been presented as the purpose of TMD, but there are concerns relating to the managerial and unitarist assumptions underpinning TMD.

➤ There are varying images of what constitutes a career with implications for who takes responsibility for management and development of careers.

review questions

1 Who holds the power in recruitment and selection?

2 How does branding and attraction affect people and their image of organizations in recruitment?

3 How can the predictive validity of the employment interview be improved?

4 Should job descriptions be abandoned in recruitment and selection?

5 'Appeal to their guts instead of just their brains.' How far do you agree with this view of graduate recruitment?

6 How can the disconnection between TMD policies and employment practice be reduced?

applying the sociological imagination

Based on our rationale for what we have called critical HRM education, presented in Chapter 1, which uses the prism of Mills' sociological imagination to understand HRM-related 'troubles', answer the following question:

➤ Many TMD schemes focus exclusively on those seen as high performing and/or with high potential, often causing low morale among staff who are excluded. How can the sociological imagination help you understand this problem?

further reading

Reading these articles and chapters can help you gain a better understanding and potentially a higher grade for your HRM assignment.

➤ Anderson, N. and Witvliet, C. (2008) Fairness reactions to personnel selection methods: an international comparison between the Netherlands, the United States, France, Spain, Portugal, and Singapore. *International Journal of Selection and Assessment*, **16**(1): 1–13.

➤ Burton, H., Daugherty, B., Dickins, D. and Schisler, D. (2016) Dominant personality types in public accounting: selection bias or indoctrinated? *Accounting Education*, **25**: 167–84.

➤ Collings, D. G., Scullion, H. and Vaiman, H. (2015). Talent management: progress and prospects. *Human Resource Management Review*, **25**(3): 233–5.

➤ Hollenbeck, J. R., Murphy, K. and Schmitt, N. (2007) Are we getting fooled again? Coming to terms with limitations in the use of personality tests for personnel selection. *Personnel Psychology*, **60**: 1029–49.

➤ Kirves, K., Kinnunen, U., De Cuyper, N. and Mäkikangas, A. (2014) Trajectories of perceived employability and their associations with well-being at work. *Journal of Personnel Psychology*, **13**: 46–57.

➤ Ryan, A.-M. and Ployhart, R. E. (2014) A century of selection. *Annual Review of Psychology*, **65**: 693–717.

vocabulary checklist for ESL students

 Click here in your interactive ebook for a list of HRM terminology and vocabulary that has appeared in this chapter.

➤ Visit the online resource centre at **www.palgravehighered.com/bg-hrm-6e** for lots of extra resources to help you get to grips with this chapter, including study tips, HRM skills development guides, summary lecture notes, tips for English as a Second Language (ESL) students and more.

© Stockbyte Royalty Free Photos

part III

EMPLOYEE PERFORMANCE AND DEVELOPMENT

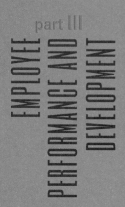

part III

EMPLOYEE PERFORMANCE AND DEVELOPMENT

chapter **6**

performance management and appraisal

BRAND X PICTURES

objectives

After studying this chapter, you should be able to:

1 Explain the purpose and uses of performance management, assessment and appraisal

2 Provide a model of performance management

3 Assess various approaches to understanding performance at work

4 Understand contrasting approaches to assessment and appraisal

5 Explain the use of performance management and appraisal in employee development

6 Understand the use of different performance-rating techniques

Axis Bank is India's third largest private sector lender. Traditionally, its approach to performance management and appraisal has been based on what is called the bell curve system. This is a forced ranking approach to judging performance that rates everyone's performance and ranks them into categories of top performers (possibly the top 10 per cent), medium performers (the next 80 per cent) and then the poor performers (the bottom 10 per cent). The ranking forces managers to make judgements about performance by comparing staff with each other and fitting them into the categories. In some cases, those in the bottom category might be removed or referred elsewhere. In this way, the system provides a warning for those already in or close to the poor performance category. Senior managers at Axis decided that this approach was divisive and over-focused on top performers. Instead, the bank has moved towards a system based on integrated performance management and capability development for all staff. This would also allow Axis to focus more on learning and development as part of performance management, which would help the bank to retain staff who might otherwise be poached by other finance organizations.

introduction

Ever since you arrived at university or college, you knew that there would at some point be an assessment of your work performance. Whether in the form of examinations, assignments, group activities and so on, you have had the chance to demonstrate your capabilities and develop your potential. The results of the assessment are used in an appraisal of what you will do next. So, as in a workplace, your life as a student has to be connected to a performance management system (PMS) in which assessment and appraisal are crucial activities.

Of course, any information you receive about your performance rating as a student will depend on your response to feedback, which in turn will depend on the judgements you make about your own performance, or self-appraisal. Consider for a moment your reactions to the feedback you received on your last assignment. Did you regard the judgement as a valid measurement of your performance? Perhaps you might see more value in receiving feedback from people other than your tutors. You can make use of multisource feedback (MSF) from other students in group work, employers in job placements or even your parents so you get a 360-degree appraisal of your performance. And obviously it is not just students whose performance is assessed. In recent years in the UK, through the National Student Survey, students have been able to provide feedback on the performance of their university or college as a form of upward appraisal.

Because performance management and appraisal are often seen as key features of an organization's drive towards achieving competitive advantage and high performance, such information can be used in goal-setting as part of a performance and development plan (PDP). In this chapter, we will explore the working of PMSs, especially appraisal and assessment, and seek to explain some of the contentious features that have, in the past, failed to find respect among employers and employees alike. The chapter will, however, also explore how performance management has the potential to reverse the negative images of its past so that it can become the source of continuous dialogue between an organization's members.

reflective question How well does the PMS operate in your university or college?

DIGITAL VISION

Every year as exam season rolls around, you are taking part in a performance management system.

Performance measurement and HRM

Performance management refers to the set of interconnected practices designed to ensure that a person's overall capabilities and potential are appraised, so that relevant goals can be set for work and development, and so that, through assessment, data on work behaviour and performance can be collected and reviewed. This has in many organizations resulted in the development of an integrated PMS, often based on a competency framework (Strebler et al., 1997) (see Chapter 5).

At the centre of the PMS is work performance, in which the key ideas are that the principal dimensions of a person's work can be defined precisely in performance terms, allowing measurement over agreed periods of time that also takes account of particular constraints within the performance situation (Furnham, 2004). Measurement yields data that become information, allowing rational, objective and efficient decision-making that can be used in performance appraisals, objective-setting, assessment of development needs, regular feedback to individuals and regular review meetings (Chartered Institute of Personnel and Development [CIPD], 2009b). Through the use of assessment metrics that connect to business objectives, appraisal and performance management provide the possibility of matching human resources (HR) practices with organizational strategy (Rashidi, 2015). Performance management forms the nub of the strategic link between HR inputs and practices and organizational performance (Edgar et al., 2015; Ferguson and Reio, 2010); it is also a vital feature of the development of high-performance work systems (Silvi et al., 2015) and the intent of engaging employees in organization improvement (Brown, D., 2010).

Significant attention has been paid to setting organizational goals and directions so that business performance can be improved, and, importantly, to how such improvements can be measured. Based on the well-known dictum that 'if you can't measure it, you can't manage it', finding ways of measuring performance has become a major preoccupation in many organizations in both the public and private sectors (Moynihan et al., 2012). All organizations have some means of measuring performance, and whichever methods of measurement are chosen, they are considered to play a key role in the efficient and effective management of the organization (Kennerley and Neely, 2002). However, recent research suggests that in public sector organizations there are difficulties in the use of PMSs due to public sector restraints on managers in terms of the variety of organizational actions that can be used, the autonomy of managers in using them and the options available for exploiting the environment (Decramer et al., 2012: Hvidman and Andersen, 2016). Both now and in the future, performance data and indicators that can be quickly produced by information and communication technology are likely to affect decision-making in all sectors (Hatry, 2010), with a direct impact on how performance is managed and goals are set (Kagaari et al., 2010).

It is argued that measurement of performance is an indication of an organization's culture and the strategic thinking of its managers (Pun and White, 2005). Indeed, measurement is a crucial determinant of culture and what managers consider in their thinking. If, for example, turnover and costs are the key measures, these will form the indicators used in setting objectives for others and deciding how achievement is judged. Traditionally, of course, performance measurement has been based on accountancy models, with inbuilt assumptions relating to turnover, costs and especially profit – the bottom line. This provides an underpinning rationale for a 'control approach' to an organization's activities, including performance management and appraisal (Rashidi, 2015). It is argued that the control approach is an outcome of the drive towards rationality and efficiency that is found in our organizations, and in recent years perhaps simply of the drive towards survival, especially in small and medium-sized enterprises (SMEs). Such beliefs may certainly become part of a set of taken-for-granted assumptions that dominate life in organizations and may also be difficult to challenge. This is certainly the case for the HR profession, who have sought to provide a clear link between their activities and organizational outcomes, usually expressed in financial terms (Prowse and Prowse, 2010).

Organizational leaders, managers and employees are often unaware of the ways in which such beliefs are embedded in their actions. For example, much of the language of organizations, and many of the processes developed, can be related back to a mechanical assumption of organizing. Mintzberg (1989, p. 339) argued that the form of structure called 'machine bureaucracy' has dominated thinking on how organizations should be constructed, and that terms such as 'getting organized', 'being rational' and 'achieving efficiency' represent evidence of this domination. As Mintzberg (1990, p. 340) wrote: 'I believe that to most people, what I am calling machine bureaucracy is not just a way to organize, it is the way to organize; it is not one form or structure, it is structure.' This perspective is, however, being challenged by recent research into two very different types of organization. The first comprises public organizations, where the control element of performance management in terms of cost-cutting and efficiency gains is driving organizational objectives (Hvidman and Andersen, 2016; Moynihan et al., 2012). The second type are international organizations and international joint ventures (Larimo et al., 2016), where the head office imposes performance measures on the subsidiaries without due consideration of the local context, including the culture and also relationships with local subsidiaries (Schäffer et al., 2014).

reflective question Does a mechanical assumption of organizing underpin how people talk about work? What effect does such talk have in terms of how judgements and decisions are made?

As we saw in Chapter 4, there have been growing efforts to prove the special value of *people* in organizations by measuring and expressing human resource management (HRM) in financial terms (Toulson and Dewe, 2004). This is a partial acceptance of the control approach that is implied in traditional accountancy models. There has, however, been interest in developing alternatives to financial measures. One example of this is return on investment, which aims to identify value-drivers in organizations (Scott, 1998), such as customer satisfaction and loyalty, and intellectual capital – although the intangibility of these can make some value-drivers difficult to develop. There are, however, measurement models that take a wider view, perhaps more strategic and long term, that encompasses a range of values other than just financial and that can stimulate continuous improvement (Pun and White, 2005). For example, the total quality management (TQM) movement, which emerged in the 1980s and is still prevalent in many organizations, provides tools and measurements to bring about lasting change. The idea of continuous improvement in TQM is referred to as *kaizen*, and there is a close connection to another system of continuous improvement and measure called Six Sigma.

HRM web links   Visit the online resource centre at **www.palgravehighered.com/bg-hrm-6e** to find out about Six Sigma.

The 'excellence model' put forward by the European Foundation for Quality Management (EFQM) provides a way of understanding how the whole organization works based on nine elements of 'excellence', including people. Each element can be judged on a range of criteria, and improvements can then be planned accordingly. For example, one of the criteria for people is that 'people are involved and empowered'. Another holistic measurement framework is Kaplan and Norton's (2000) 'balanced scorecard', in which a variety of perspectives are considered under the headings of customer, financial, internal business, and innovation and learning. Measures can be set for each, and these can then be aligned with strategy. Managers and employees can subsequently develop their own measures in response.

HRM web links   Visit the online resource centre at **www.palgravehighered.com/bg-hrm-6e** for details of EFQM's excellence model and for access to the Balanced Scorecard Institute.

Over the last 15 years, there have been significant efforts to reconfigure the value-drivers in the public sector through greater measurement against targets. In the late 1990s, there was a shift towards a more customer-oriented approach to performance measurement (Mwita, 2000), which was referred to as 'new managerialism'. A Best Value framework was introduced in England in 1997, followed by five dimensions of performance indicator:

- *Strategic objectives* – why the service exists and what it seeks to achieve
- *Cost/efficiency* – the resources committed to a service and the efficiency with which these are turned into outputs
- *Service delivery outcomes* – how well the service is being operated in order to achieve the strategic objectives
- *Quality* – the quality of the services delivered, explicitly reflecting users' experiences of them
- *Fair access* – ease and equality of access to services.

Performance management and the culture of capitalism in Brazil

BANANASTOCK

Although there has been a surge in the number of companies operating outside their home countries, global commerce has a long history. The mercantilist period, for example, which operated in Europe during the sixteenth to eighteenth centuries, was based on the idea that a government could promote a country's economy against competitors through regulation. This saw European companies trade across the world. We tend to think of this trade as being primarily in terms of goods, but mercantilism also entailed the export of culture and technology. In some cases, this diffusion significantly transformed the cultural practices of the mercantilists' trading partners.

An interesting question about present-day multinational enterprises (MNEs) is the degree to which this cultural transfer continues, particularly in relation to emerging markets (EMs), such as Brazil, Russian, India and China. For example, HR practitioners in EM–MNEs must often grapple with the degree to which a company should standardize or localize its performance management practices, such as performance-based bonus systems. The argument for a standardization of performance management practices is that they ensure the subsidiary firms operate in a way that is consistent with the parent company's strategic direction and help the parent company to assess policy and practice compliance. On the flip side, local cultural, legal and political circumstances may augur against imposing foreign performance management practices on local workforces. This tension between localization and standardization – and the two-way flow of HR practices between parent and local operations – has been a core focus of international HRM research.

A recent study of three EM–MNEs that were headquartered in Brazil and had foreign subsidiaries in both developed and developing countries found that the PMSs were Brazilian in design, suggesting that standardization was occurring. Furthermore, each of the Brazilian firms strongly expected subsidiary firms to adopt these standardized practices, reflecting that the performance management targets and objectives were closely linked with corporate strategies (Mellahi et al., 2015).

Resistance to standardized practices among local subsidiaries declined over time. There was no evidence of a reverse diffusion of performance management practices from the subsidiary to the parent company. One possibly important factor in the acceptance of standardized practices was that they were broadly consistent with established global norms, and thus may have been viewed as legitimate practices by subsidiaries regardless of whether local performance management norms were slightly different. Where there were local differences, these tended to be driven by local regulatory and logistical requirements.

This study raises an interesting question about HRM in a global world. The lack of pressure for localization in the companies studied may reflect that the performance management practices imposed by the parent company

(continued)

Stop! Can you think of a widely used performance management practice that you have experienced? When you were subject to this performance management practice, did you think of it as normal? What alternative practices might achieve the same goal in a different way? Why do you think these alternatives are not as widely adopted?

Sources and further information: See Mellahi et al. (2015) for background information.

Note: This feature was written by Bob Barnetson.

were internationally recognized practices (rather than reflecting the Brazilian cultural norms). This suggests that the international standardization of performance management practices may be a form of what is called 'cultural hegemony'. Cultural hegemony is most often defined as the domination of a culturally diverse society by a ruling class, which manipulates the beliefs, perceptions and values of the society such that the worldview of the ruling class becomes widely adopted. Under conditions of global capitalism, it may be that certain practices (for example, performance management schemes) are becoming viewed as the 'natural' or 'normal' way of operating, thereby taking away the legitimacy of local performance management practices.

The overall aim of Best Value was to encourage a reorientation of service delivery towards citizens and customers, and to produce quality-driven organizations (Sheffield and Coleshill, 2001). By 2008, the Best Value performance indicators had been replaced by nearly 200 National Indicators that were used to monitor and measure local government performance, but by 2010 these had been abolished as they were seen by the new UK government to be too much micro-management. Further research has suggested that the assumption of financial control underpinning performance management is a critical feature of performance management within public services (Hvidman and Andersen, 2016; Moynihan et al., 2012). However, local authorities and the public sector as a whole faced large cuts in budgets from 2010 while still being required to meet some standards on front-line services.

Although the public sector is facing significant flux, some attention is being given to community and voluntary groups, of which there are many thousands throughout the UK. Even though such groups are also likely to face funding difficulties, there is interest in how volunteerism as performance can help to meet some of society's needs. One part of what is called the 'third sector' of businesses measures performance against social objectives, in which profits or 'surpluses' are reinvested in projects that help the community or environment. Such social enterprises have been seen as a source of creativity and responsible work that raise the standards of ethical and socially responsible business (Cabinet Office, 2007). There is also an increasing need for Third Sector organizations to embrace performance management as it provides evidence that demonstrates value for money and thereby secures additional funding. It also creates an important vehicle for continuously improving, increasing effectiveness and sustainability (Taylor and Taylor, 2014).

SMEs, usually understood as any business with between 10 and 249 staff, along with businesses with fewer than 10 staff, which are referred to as microenterprises, make up over 95 per cent of all organizations. For many years, there has been concern about their performance and their potential for growth (see Gold and Thorpe, 2010). Research suggests that most SMEs have little time for an analysis of their performance, and that measurement is mostly responsive to problems as they emerge. This, for the most, means a basic profit and loss measurement to ensure survival (Garengo et al., 2005). It has been suggested that, by close attention to helping managers of SMEs deal with their immediate problems and concerns, more complex measures of performance can be introduced (Gold and Thorpe, 2008). However, recent studies into the factors that influence the implementation of PMSs into SMEs have shown that the levers chosen for large firms are not necessarily the most relevant ones for SMEs (Taylor and Taylor, 2014).

HRM web links

Visit the online resource centre at **www.palgravehighered.com/bg-hrm-6e** to access Cranfield University's Centre for Business Performance.

The purpose and processes of performance management

There is considerable pressure on organizations to show that they are organized and systematic in their approach to the management of employee performance, and that there is a clear link between such performance and the organization's goals. The recent interest in talent management policies (see Chapter 5) highlights the importance of ensuring that employees are able to use their talents effectively in the performance of work (Aguinis et al., 2012; Baron, 2009). In addition, effective performance management can result in increased employee engagement (Edgar et al., 2015; Mone et al., 2011).

Activities such as appraisal and assessment have traditionally been completed in isolation and have not always been able to demonstrate their value to organizational performance. Therefore, during the 1990s, there was a growing interest in performance management to ensure that HRM could be seen as being vital to an organization's concerns, leading to improvements in performance and competitive advantage (Armstrong and Baron, 2004). The adoption of a PMS represents an attempt by an organization to show a strategic integration of its HRM processes, which can be linked to the goals and direction of an organization. However, this move relies very much on the role of managers and the quality of their relationships with their employees (Alfes et al., 2012; Sparrow, 2008), and therefore represents something of a conundrum for HR managers. That is, the activities of a PMS, designed and assembled by HR, require the serious attention and commitment of other managers for their effective operation, and this cannot always be assured (Rao, 2007; Rashidi, 2015).

It is a strategic focus on business objectives that gives performance management its distinctive position in HRM (Baron, 2009; Silvi et al., 2015), providing the link between the organization's values, performance and competitiveness (Boudreau and Ramstad, 2009). However, the degree to which strategic aims and a PMS are integrated is open to discussion, creating a gap between the rhetoric and the reality of claims for the contribution of performance management to organizational effectiveness (Brown, D., 2010; Stanton and Nankervis, 2011). There is increasing research into the links between the practice and processes (Guest, 2011) and employees' perspectives of this link (Farndale and Kelliher, 2013) and relationship to performance management, and employee trust and perceptions of justice (Alfes et al., 2012).

reflective question

Why do you think there is so much variation in the impact and benefits of PMSs in organizations?

A key feature of a PMS is its attempt to provide a link between all levels of an organization through goals, critical success factors and performance measures. An organization's goals will thus be derived from business strategy and translated into sector goals, departmental goals, manager goals and employee and/or team goals. As Locke and Latham

(2009, p. 22) have argued, 'Purposeful activity is the essence of living action', and people who commit to goals are likely to exert more effort and sustain it over time. At each stage, there will be an attempt to provide measurable performance indicators of how far the goals have been achieved. Furthermore, in response to the dynamic conditions of globalization and technical change, there is a need to review and reset goals and targets throughout the year (Rose, 2000). A PMS will also provide a means of supporting performance through diagnosing development needs, providing ongoing feedback and review, and coaching where required, and PMSs are becoming an important feature of talent management and development (Aguinis et al., 2012) (see Chapter 5). In a PMS, the attitudes of line managers are crucial because they are the key actors in implementing the various HR processes in the cycle, in particular issues of perceived fairness (Byrne et al., 2012). The integrated nature of a PMS is outlined in the performance management cycle shown in Figure 6.1.

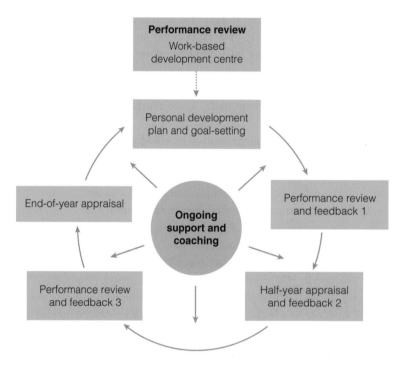

Figure 6.1 *A performance management cycle*

A PMS might, especially for managers, incorporate development centres, which are the same as assessment centres (see Chapter 5) in that assessment tests and exercises are used to provide a report on individual strengths and limitations. Development centres do, however, differ in their emphasis on diagnosing development needs, leading to suggested development activities and a PDP (Ballantyne and Povah, 2004). Although a range of activities may be used, a development centre usually involves psychometrics and feedback from a qualified occupational psychologist, MSF and a self-diagnosis against the organization's competency framework. A PDP also includes an attempt to link the overall business aim with key areas of responsibility, the competencies that are expected to be demonstrated in performing a role, and goal-setting with measurable objectives.

Although development centres are concerned with development needs, their similarity to recruitment assessment centres (see Chapter 5) may make it difficult to escape the tension between judgement and development that is a feature of all processes concerned with assessing and appraising people at work. Carrick and Williams (1999) suggest that development centres may, for some participants, result in the diagnosis of many development needs and have a demotivating influence. Because this may be the expected outcome for some potential participants, this may influence their decision to participate, and their overall performance if they do. As Woodruffe (2000, p. 32) warned, 'Assessment centres masquerading as development centres are wolves in sheep's clothing.'

Research carried out by Halman and Fletcher (2000) highlighted examples of the tensions inherent in development centres and performance management more generally. This related to assessment and performance. In their research, 111 customer service staff attended a development centre. Prior to attending, each person self-assessed his or her performance and was then rated by assessors as part of the development centre. The research revealed a variety of responses to self-ratings depending on whether participants under-rated, over-rated or even accurately rated their performance. For example, those who over-rated their performance tended to make little adjustment in response to any feedback provided, possibly due to their view that they did not need to improve their performance. Another area that is providing some interesting research is the integration of performance appraisals with data gained from recruitment assessment centres (Lopes et al., 2015). This seems to be particularly significant in the first few years of new appointments. We will consider the issues of ratings, judgement and feedback in performance management in more detail below.

reflective question How do you respond to critical feedback when you believe you have performed well?

HRM web links Visit the online resource centre at **www.palgravehighered.com/bg-hrm-6e** to learn more about the British Psychological Society's standards for assessment and development centres.

Once a PDP has been established, then, according to the performance management cycle, work is carried out to meet the objectives set. There should also be ongoing coaching from the immediate manager and support for any training and development needs identified (see Chapter 7). Over the last 10 years, coaching has become a key activity that managers can use to support change and development in organizations. Such is the belief in the value of coaching that many organizations seek to develop a 'coaching culture' (Garvey et al., 2009). There is choice between using coaches from within an organization, especially among line managers, and coaches from outside the organization. Jones et al. (2016) found that coaching was more effective in terms of performance management when conducted by internal rather than external coaches. Internal coaches are able to use workplace coaching, which is effective whether it is face to face or blended with e-coaching (see Chapter 7).

The objectives set in a PDP can be reviewed, perhaps every quarter- or half-year, in order to monitor progress and make any adjustments. During the course of the year,

Twenty-first-century senior HR leaders have a changing role

Early debate on HRM centred on the question 'How does HRM differ from personnel management?' For some, HRM represents a new approach to managing people because, in theory at least, it was envisioned as being integrated into strategic planning. HRM models also make reference to performance outcomes, predicting that a coherent 'bundle' of HR practices will enhance employee commitment and improve performance. To meet the challenges of the twenty-first century, it is argued, organizations therefore need a new senior manager, the 'chief human resources officer' (CHRO).

Deloitte Consulting LLP (2006) considered the role of the CHRO in their report *Strategist & Steward: The Evolving Role of the Chief Human Resources Officer*. The report notes that it is increasingly likely that a CHRO will have to take on these dual roles (strategist and steward), as explained by Jeff Schwartz:

> '*The requirements and perception of HR are changing dramatically as this function's leadership is now expected to play a central role in building and shaping – not just staffing – the enterprise strategy.*'

Schwartz comments that HR leaders have '*longed for*' such a situation, achieving recognition as crucial partners rather than being a '*back-office administrator*.'

In contrast, detractors argue that HRM is more a matter of repackaging 'progressive' personnel management. They emphasize that relatively few

Mat Coleman

organizations have integrated HRM planning into strategic business planning, a central element in the HRM model. They also point to the incontrovertible evidence of a shift towards 'individually oriented' cultures that is symbolized by the growth of contingency pay, as well as the fact that a large proportion of UK firms are still preoccupied with traditional cost-focus strategies. The empirical evidence therefore suggests a lack of fit between knowledge of the normative HRM model and actual management practice.

Stop! Debates on HRM offer an interesting perspective on the issue of state intervention in a market society. Among academics, HRM is highly contentious, and its antecedents, defining characteristics and outcomes are much disputed. What is your view? Is HRM different from personnel management?

Sources and further information: To read Deloitte Consulting LLP's 2006 press release go to http://www.prnewswire.com/news-releases/meet-the-21st-century-chief-human-resources-officer-chro-55779902.html You could also look at Deloitte's Global Human Capital Trends 2016 web page https://www2.deloitte.com/global/en/pages/human-capital/articles/introduction-human-capital-trends.html

For a discussion on employee commitment and HRM, see Guest (1998); for evidence of the growth of 'individualism', see Kersley et al. (2005); and for further insight into the HRM debate, see Legge (2005).

Note: This feature was written by John Bratton.

feedback might be obtained from different sources, this being used to improve perform-ance as well as being fed into the end-of-year review, at which an overall assessment and appraisal might also be carried out. However, it should also be noted that what works well for one organization may fail miserably in another (Hunt, 2015).

Performance, judgements and feedback

A PMS can be used for a variety of purposes, which can be broadly categorized as follows:

- To make administrative decisions concerning pay, promotions and careers, and work responsibilities – the *control purpose*
- To improve performance through discussing development needs, identifying training opportunities and planning action – the *development purpose.*

Both categories require judgements to be made. In the first category, a manager may be required to make a decision about the value of an employee both in the present and in the future, and this may cause some discomfort. For example, several decades ago, McGregor (1957, p. 89) reported that a key reason why appraisal failed was that managers disliked 'playing God', which involved making judgements about the worth of their employees. Levinson (1970) thought that managers experienced the appraisal of others as a hostile and aggressive act against employees that resulted in feelings of guilt over any criticism given. More recent research suggests that there is a correlation between discomfort and being lenient in evaluations, which may also have links to cultural diversity aspects within the workplace (Saffie-Robertson and Brutus, 2014). Such views highlight the tension between appraisal as a process to control employees and appraisal as a supportive development process. It is a tension that has never been resolved and lies at the heart of most debates on the effectiveness of appraisal in particular and, as we will explain below, performance management more generally.

The ability to make judgements about employees' performance that can lead to deci-sions about their contribution, value, worth, capability and potential has to be considered as a vital dimension of a manager's relationship with those employees. Decisions will be interpreted by an employee as feedback, defined as 'actions taken by (an) external agent(s) to provide information regarding some aspect(s) of one's task performance' (Kluger and DeNisi, 1996, p. 254). Gilliland (1993) has pointed to the importance of feedback that is timely as well as informative so that it is perceived as fair. The idea of fairness is something that has attracted a lot of attention in recent years, with researchers such as Qin et al. (2015) looking at how unclear justice decisions in one area of organizational life can result in the employee developing an overall distrust of other areas of organizational justice. What is particularly interesting is the way in which individuals respond to feedback or how people perceive the accuracy of the feedback received, referred to by Anseel and Lievens (2009) as 'feedback acceptance', which is based on the extent to which feedback confirms how people see themselves.

There is no simple formula for how feedback can be used to motivate people, even though managers may be quite convinced, in their own minds, that there is. However, we do know that feedback has a definite influence in terms of demotivation (Coens and Jenkins, 2002). Figure 6.2 shows the range of responses from employees to feedback on their performance at work.

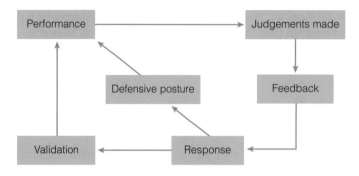

Figure 6.2 *Responses to feedback on performance at work*

reflective
question

> What motivates you to work? Make a list of these factors, and then make another list of what demotivates you. It is likely that the latter will be longer, covering a wide range of factors.

As suggested, the response to feedback can result in two possibilities: validation if there is agreement with the judgement made, or a defensive posture when there is disagreement. The latter is especially likely when feedback is negative or critical, and the impact on subsequent performance can also be negative.

DeNisi and Kluger (2000) conducted a review of research considering the relationship between feedback and performance. They found that, in one-third of cases, feedback had a negative effect on performance. As DeNisi and Kluger highlighted, when feedback has the potential to help someone focus on what is to be done when performing a task or learning details, their performance usually improves. The main danger, however, occurs with feedback that can have a potentially strong impact on an employee's view of 'self', for example their self-belief and self-esteem. The response to feedback, especially critical feedback, is likely to be affective or emotional, which can be detrimental to performance. A further distortion to feedback, especially critical feedback, is based on a desire to see oneself in a positive way, whatever the performance, referred to by Jordan and Audia (2012) as 'the self-enhancement motive'. People like to see themselves as a winner, and this can distort their responses to negative feedback. It is because of such dangers from negative feedback that Kluger and Nir (2009) have suggested a positive approach, especially in appraisal interviews, called *feedforward*. By focusing on positive stories of experience from work that can look forward to provide support so that the employee's performance can improve, a win–win approach will be adopted that avoids them retreating into defensive emotions.

Acceptance of feedback may not, however, be as simple as first thought. Employees themselves seek specific types of feedback depending on the goal that is directing the need for feedback. So, for example, if an employee is wanting feedback related to a learning orientation, they will be more likely to seek feedback that is more self-negative, whereas a performance orientation will prompt seeking for feedback that is more positive. This understanding can help managers when giving the more negative feedback that is sometimes required to improve overall performance. Questions such as 'How do I impede your success?' (Gong et al., 2014, p. 23) from managers will create a safer environment for employees to seek negative feedback.

In addition to unsought feedback being provided to employees on their performance, some employees might prefer to take a more proactive stance, seeking feedback for themselves. Such behaviour may be undertaken in pursuit of a goal, as well as to provide protection for a person's image or ego (Anderson et al., 2003). Contextual factors such as the attitudes of managers and leaders can influence a person's approach to seeking feedback, and given the importance of feedback on each person's sense of self, there is growing interest in creating more open feedback environments (Anseel et al., 2007; Gong et al., 2014).

Particular problems for fostering a diversity agenda can arise from the basis on which many judgements are made in the various processes that form a PMS. PMSs are used for many purposes, including helping in decision-making regarding people's careers, the development they will undertake, the payment they will receive and their future direction in the organization. Well-documented patterns in organizations suggest that some groups suffer disadvantages in these areas (Leyerzapf et al., 2014). For example, fewer women become senior managers or directors of organizations (Sealy et al., 2008) as they hit the so-called 'glass ceiling' for women, suggesting that there are limits on their progress in organizations. There is a similar problem for black, Asian and minority ethnic managers, and there are many reasons for this, largely relating to biased and stereotyped judgements about performance. As in selection decisions (see Chapter 5), distortions occur in how people and their performance are rated (Grote, 1996), such as when managers make judgements based on stereotypes and generalizations, demonstrate similarity bias (rating people who are similar to them more highly) and rely on first impressions or comparisons with others to make judgements (Esfahani et al., 2014).

One explanation for the occurrence of these distortions in judgement with PMS is provided by social role theory (Eagly, 1987). This suggests that social structures influence the roles that people can adopt and the behaviours expected. For example, if it is expected that women will become mothers, this will affect how the different genders are viewed in a PMS. As women leave work to care for children, this reinforces the consistent expectation of the social role of women (Diekma and Eagly, 2000), and even when women return to work, it is expected that there will be conflicts between family and work (Benschop and Doorewaard, 1998). As a consequence, women's performance at work may be less highly rated than men's. However, the recent trend of men taking time away from work for family has also been linked to a poor performance rating; that is, both men and women suffer the family care stereotype (Butler and Skattebo, 2004). A further issue arises from 'gender hierarchy threat' (Inesi and Cable, 2014), which observed when a female subordinate's objective competency and on-the-job performance are approaching those of her male manager.

Evidence shows that taking time off to care for children negatively affects performance ratings for both men and women. Social role theory explains that this is due to the expectations of society around family life.

ImageSource

> Have you ever felt your work performance to be judged unfairly against a social stereotype?

Appraisal interviews

We define 'appraisal' here as a process that provides an analysis of a person's overall capabilities and potential, allowing informed decisions to be made for particular purposes. It is a process that is central to the purpose of stimulating performance (Aguinis, 2009) and an important part of the process is assessment, in which data on an individual's past and current work behaviour and performance are collected and reviewed. The process of appraisal is usually completed from an interview, once or twice a year, between an employee and his or her line manager.

As well as stimulating performance improvement, there are a variety of other declared purposes and desired benefits for appraisal, including:

- Improving motivation and morale
- Clarifying expectations and reducing ambiguity related to performance
- Determining rewards
- Identifying training and development opportunities
- Improving communication
- Selecting people for promotion
- Managing careers
- Counselling
- Discipline
- Planning remedial actions
- Setting goals and targets.

This potential list of purposes for appraisal has led to the view that appraisal is something of a 'panacea' in organizations (Taylor, 1998), although expectations and hopes are more often than not confounded. A recent development has been the link made in many organizations between appraisals as performance reviews and bonus payments.

reflective
question

> Why do you think it is difficult to meet the hopes for and expectations of appraisal systems at work?

When we consider the history of appraisal, it soon becomes apparent that, of all the activities comprising HRM, appraisal is arguably the most contentious and least popular among those who are involved. Managers do not seem to like doing it, and employees see no point in it (Heathfield, 2007). HR managers, as guardians of an organization's appraisal policy and procedures, often have to stand by and watch their work fall into disrepute. Although most organizations seek to complete appraisals in one form or another, often under the heading of Performance Development and Review, with normative guidelines and training available for this, there is evidence of a gap between such goals and what actually happens. For example, guidelines might emphasize a ratio of time to talk that is tilted towards the employee or appraisee, but research suggests that this ratio is in reality rarely achieved. Crucially, negativity is often the main feature of appraisal conversations, which makes the interaction difficult for the participants (Asmuß, 2008; Saffie-Robertson and Brutus, 2014).

Remarkably, despite the poor record of appraisal within organizations, it is an accepted part of management orthodoxy that there should be some means by which performance can be measured, monitored and controlled (Barlow, 1989). Indeed, a failure to show that management is in control would be regarded as highly ineffective by those with an interest in the affairs of an organization. As a result, appraisal systems have for some time served to prove that the performance of employees is under control, or at least to give the appearance of its being so. As Barlow (1989, p. 500) has stated, 'Institutionally elaborated systems of management appraisal and development are significant rhetorics in the apparatus of bureaucratic control.' Research also highlights that the more visible the performance appraisal system is made, the more employees observe the mandatory nature of the system '"forcing" them to pay attention to it', with a focus on ensuring that appraisals are conducted rather than considering the value placed on them (Sumelius et al., 2014). It is not surprising therefore that most appraisal schemes are underpinned by a 'performance control approach' (Randell, 1994, p. 235) with a focus on setting targets or key performance indicators linking individuals to an organization's strategic direction. As one manager in a survey stated (CIPD, 2009b, p. 14):

> Ultimately there is no point doing performance management if it does not deliver the business objectives. It should enable you to take action at the individual level if people are pulling in the right direction ... everyone whatever level they are knows where their personal [key performance indicators] fit.

The idea of control may perhaps lie at the heart of the problem of appraisal in organizations, and this stems from the key points we raised above about judgements and feedback. In any situation when a manager has to provide feedback to employees, there is always a danger that the outcome will be demotivated employees. The seminal study that highlighted this was carried out by Meyer et al. (1965) at the General Electric Company. Although this work was carried out in the mid-1960s, it is remarkable how the lessons have been forgotten and how the mistakes uncovered then have been repeated many times over in many organizations since.

Meyer et al.'s (1965) study looked at the appraisal process at a large plant where appraisal was judged to be good. There were 92 appraisees in the study, who were appraised by their managers on two occasions over 2 weeks. The first interview discussed performance and salary; the second performance focused on improvement. The reactions of the appraisees were gathered by interviews, questionnaires and observation. It was discovered that although the interviews allowed for general praise, criticism was more specific and prompted defensive reactions. Defensiveness on the part of appraisees involved a denial of shortcomings and blaming others. On average, 13 criticisms were recorded per interview, and the more criticism received, the more defensive was the appraisee's reaction. The study revealed that the defensive behaviour was partly caused by most appraisees rating themselves as above average before the interviews – 90 out of 92 appraisees in fact rated themselves as average or above. It was also found that, subsequent to the interviews, criticism had a negative effect on the employees' performance. A summary of some of the conclusions from this study is set out in Figure 6.3.

- Criticism often has a negative effect on motivation and performance
- Praise has little effect – one way or another
- Performance improves with specific goals
- Employees' participation in goal-setting helps to produce favourable results
- Interviews designed primarily to improve performance should not at the same time weigh salary or promotion in the balance
- Coaching by managers should be day to day rather than just once a year

Figure 6.3 *Summary of findings from Meyer et al.'s (1965) study*

Since this study, there has in many respects been a long search to find a way of appraising employees that reduces the negative; however, we should not be surprised to find an attachment by many managers to the idea of control in appraisal (Townley, 1994), and a perception by employees that they are being controlled by appraisal systems. Barlow (1989) took the argument further, pointing out that appraisal serves to make the relationship between managers and employees rational, simple and static whereas it is in fact ambiguous, complex and dynamic. Ambiguity, complexity and dynamism cannot be eliminated in reality, and therein lies the falseness of the appraisal experience. For many employees, appraisal is just not seen as relevant, and this could lie in the fact that performance appraisals are relatively standardized within an organization and do not account for the heterogeneity in both individuals and roles (Sumelius et al., 2014). The following reflects the opinion of one manager on appraisal, gathered during a field study in a sector of the petrochemicals industry (Barlow, 1989, p. 505):

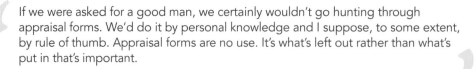

If we were asked for a good man, we certainly wouldn't go hunting through appraisal forms. We'd do it by personal knowledge and I suppose, to some extent, by rule of thumb. Appraisal forms are no use. It's what's left out rather than what's put in that's important.

When an organization seeks to implement strategic changes to improve performance based on principles of learning, communication and employee involvement, there is an apparent contradiction when appraisal is part of performance management, as this is oriented towards control. For example, Soltani et al. (2005) studied a number of organizations that were seeking to utilize the principles of TQM. It was found that although there was a recognition that appraisal should match the requirements of TQM, there was little evidence of this occurring. Indeed, appraisal was often characterized as ineffective, based on high subjectivity that ignored individual objectives, and managers were unqualified in providing feedback. These factors tended to work against the changes sought by using TQM. More recently, appraisals linked to management control and payment rewards have been investigated in banks. There has been clear evidence related to the control element of performance based on long-standing values of a bonus culture in one particular bank that led to long-term commercial problems (Seal and Le, 2014).

Generally, appraisal as an informal and continuous process will make the formal appraisal less isolated and less prone to negativity. It must, however, be acknowledged that, given the importance of appraisal in making judgements and decisions that can have a significant bearing on a person's future, appraisal is bound to be perceived as a political process (Poon, 2004). Employees who believe that their appraisal is based on subjectivity or bias and subjects them to unfair punishments are likely to experience appraisal as being of low quality, resulting in less satisfaction at work, lower commitment and a greater intention to leave (Brown et al., 2010) (although in times of high unemployment, they may remain under sufferance). There are concerns about how bias and prejudice, albeit implicit, might influence ratings during appraisal (Wilson and Jones, 2008). In addition, older employees may miss out on appraisal and on any opportunities arising because their performance might be appraised less often (Grund and Sliwka, 2009). Older employees are also vulnerable to being designated as underperforming and targeted for managed exits from companies through the appraisal system (Scholarios and Taylor, 2014).

It is important that appraisal is perceived to be fair and ethical (Ilgen et al., 1979; Sillup and Klimberg, 2010), particularly with respect to what is called 'procedural justice', which concerns perceptions of *how* appraisal is conducted and completed rather than the outcomes of appraisal (Alfes et al., 2012; Cawley et al., 1998). Research completed in China by Chen et al. (2011), for example, found that perceptions of procedural justice moderated employees' responses to appraisals. They found that if procedural justice was high, this increased employees' acceptance of performance goals, even if the appraisal was negative.

There is still, however, a tendency to associate feedback with criticism, even though most people do their work well most of the time (Swinburne, 2001). One suggestion is that employees may not have realistic expectations about appraisal and perhaps need training on how to use feedback and take action (Cook and Crossman, 2004). Another approach is to work with the feedforward principles referred to above, which can lay the basis for performance improvement that endures, compared with a more traditional approach (Budworth et al., 2015). A connected approach to appraisal focuses on a person's strengths and how these can be expanded in the future (Bouskila-Yam and Kluger, 2011). Weaknesses are not ignored but are minimized, so that a ratio of three positives to one negative is maintained during the interview to ensure positive energy and emotions (Fredrickson and Losada, 2005).

It is also possible to widen the sources of feedback. In recent years, for example, there has been a growth in the popularity of MSF (Smither et al., 2008), during which individuals receive feedback from different people, including peers, subordinate staff, customers and themselves. Feedback received from 'all round' a job is referred to as 360-degree appraisal or feedback, with variations of 180-degree, 270-degree or 540-degree feedback (see below) (McCarthy and Garavan, 2001). The growth in such approaches is based on the view that feedback from different sources allows for more balance and objectivity than can be obtained from the single view of one line manager. We will examine MSF and 360-degree appraisal in more detail later in the chapter.

A further development is the move to online appraisal, probably a feature of integrated HR information system processes or talent management packages (see Chapter 5). The apparent value of such approaches is the way in which information about employees in particular positions is stored against their skills and competencies. HR managers can also monitor the completion of appraisals and consider the pattern of ratings. Payne et al. (2009) compared employee reactions between those who completed online appraisals and those who used a more traditional paper and pencil approach. The results indicated greater participation in the process, in terms of completing self-ratings, by the online appraisees, but there was also a perception that the online process was of lower quality, perhaps because of the limited feedback, which lacked detail. Importantly, for performance appraisal to work and be perceived as fair and effective, there is need to focus less on technology and the structure of procedure, and more on relationships between managers and their staff and the communication between them (Pichler, 2012).

HRM web links   Visit the online resource centre at **www.palgravehighered.com/bg-hrm-6e** for some basic advice on appraisal interviewing and employee performance from the UK's Advisory, Conciliation and Arbitration Service.

Performance and development

It is highly unlikely that the pressure for rationality, efficiency and control in organizations will disappear as it is a powerful force that underlies any organized activity. However, for a PMS to be seen as a driver of organizational performance, it also has to include an alignment with the organization's talent management and development policies based on people first developing skills and then also being challenged to develop themselves (Baron, 2009). This view, of course, provides a contrast to the control orientation of a PMS and questions the underlying principles that are required to develop a culture supporting and reinforcing the ideas and practices of high-performance HRM based on employee engagement, commitment and trust. This can be a painful process. It may, for example, be difficult to resist the requirements of financial controllers seeking to control costs during a recession or at a time of painful budget cuts. It is therefore no surprise that research continues to show ambivalent support for performance management as a helpful process for skill development and careers, with complaints about complexity and too much paperwork/administration (Brown, D., 2010).

In a seminal paper, Walton (1985) wrote about disillusionment with the apparatus of control that assumed low employee commitment and mere obedience, reporting on a number of organizations that had attempted to move towards a workforce strategy based on high employee commitment. Performance management and appraisal can serve as the fulcrum of such a movement, although considerable difficulties can arise (Wilson and Western, 2000). The contrast between control approaches and commitment could not be greater for managers: the former involves a concentration on techniques, the latter a shift towards attitudes, values and beliefs. The skill for HRM practitioners is to acknowledge the importance of the former while arguing for a greater place for the latter.

reflective question   What particular skills are needed by HRM practitioners to argue for two potentially conflicting points of view, such as the need for control and the need for commitment?

A developmental PMS that attempts to harness potential would, for many organizations, mean a more inclusive approach to talent management and development (Iles and Preece, 2010). It has been accepted that discussions of potential and prospects for development have been confined to leaders and managers, thereby sending a strong message to the rest of the organization that only managers are worthy of such attention (Aguinis et al., 2012) – with the implicit assumption that non-managers cannot develop. Changes in employment conditions within organizations have, however, meant that more employees are included in PMS and appraisals. This has also been brought about by changes in organizational structure occurring in the 2000s that have sought to move decision-making to the point of interaction with customers and clients, and see such interactions as the source of creativity. This provides line managers with significant responsibility to ensure that effective communication and feedback are given to employees (Farndale and Kelliher, 2013).

In putting more emphasis on the development of potential, the suspicion that has surrounded control approaches may be reinforced, which should not be surprising as there has been pressure to shift the orientation for some time. As long ago as 1983, Harper suggested dropping the word 'appraisal' because it put employees on the defensive. He recommended instead a shift towards future-oriented review and development that actively involved employees in continuously developing ways of improving their performance in line with their needs, similar to Kluger and Nir's (2009) feedforward interview process referred to earlier. Moving in such a direction requires a more flexible approach on the part of line managers. It also results in inevitable tensions because such objectives might be concerned with immediate performance set against current tasks and standards, whereas employees and even their managers might also be concerned with a variety of work and personal changes such as a change of standards, task, job role or even career, which can be considered as an on-the-job experiential learning approach (Pulakos et al., 2015).

Once employees have been encouraged to pay attention to their progress at work, the organization must be able to respond to their medium- and long-term aspirations. The manager's role will be to resolve the inevitable tension that will result between individual goals and the manager's interpretation of organizational goals. But how can data about employees be gathered for such purposes? Of necessity, there has to be a shift in attention towards the performance of work. This will provide a link to the value of a PMS as a means of recognizing employees via feedback on what they have done and how they have done it, that is, their work performance so as to engage them in a dialogue about improving their performance (Armstrong and Baron, 2004; Farndale and Murrer, 2015) that considers the importance of trust and perceptions of justice, particularly when considering required job resources within an organization (Farndale et al., 2015). In such a context, it becomes possible to identify how learning and development can help employees to meet their needs and aspirations.

The performance of a work task can be presented as a relationship between means and outcomes (Ouchi, 1979). The means take the form of the attributes, skills, knowledge and attitudes (competencies) of individual employees that are applied to a task in a specific context. The outcomes take the form of results achieved, which may be measurable either quantitatively or qualitatively against an explicit or implicit standard or target. Between means and outcomes lies the behaviour of the individual in a transformation process, as shown in Figure 6.4.

Although all phases of this process can form the focus of performance management, particular attention to behaviour in the transformation process will reveal how an individual has applied knowledge, skills and attitudes to practice when carrying out a task; this will include taking account of all aspects of the context, including time and place, machinery and equipment, other employees and other circumstances. For example, the presence of a manager might have an impact on an employee's performance. There is significant interest

HRM in practice 6.2

Schools as 'greedy institutions' and the loss of teachers from the profession

UK government figures show that four out of 10 newly qualified teachers leave the profession within 5 years (Harris, The Guardian, 2014). Record numbers of teachers are also leaving in mid-career. According to a union leader, the profession has become 'incompatible with normal life' (Weale, The Guardian, 2015). Government-commissioned research based upon the workload diaries of 1004 teachers showed that:

> On average, all school teachers report working over 50 hours per week, with primary and secondary school headteachers reporting more than 60 hours … Teachers of all types work around 12 hours a week outside what might be regarded as their normal working week. (Department for Education, 2014, p. 5)

In addition to planning, preparation and assessment, teachers also referred to the need to perform unnecessary and bureaucratic tasks for inspections by the Office for Standards in Education, Children's Services and Skills (Ofsted), the completion of forms and paperwork, marking and recording pupil progress, which many thought involved unnecessary duplication.

The idea of the 'greedy institution' developed by the American sociologist Lewis Coser (Sullivan, 2014) helps us to understand the crisis in work–life balance, which appears to be a crucial driver in the exodus of teachers from their profession. In Sullivan's words (2014, pp. 2–3):

> [Coser] describes how different kinds of organized groups compete with each other for the limited energies and time commitments of individuals. These competing groups include our families, employers, churches, clubs, and so on. Today we might also include time for getting exercise, informal time with friends, and time for running errands as competing commitments.
>
> The competing claims on our time and energy remain manageable as long as these organizations make only limited, reasonable demands on us. But some organizations overstep their bounds and begin to make absolute unlimited claims on their members, taking up more and more of their life space, until no room is left in the workers' lives for anything else. These are greedy institutions.

ImageSource

Educational policies over the past 20 years have put pressure on schools to become greedier and demand more of teachers' time. Schools have been put in a quasi-market situation where they compete to attract applications from parents armed with a growing amount of information derived from league table rankings that are based on mandatory teacher assessments and tests taken by children at age 7 and 11 years, which are

(continued)

Stop! What do you understand by the term 'greedy institution'? What do you understand by the idea of work–life balance, and would you be prepared to sacrifice some of your non-work activities to devote more time to work? How could performance assessment and review help teachers cope with pressures faced?

Sources and further information: For background information, see Department for Education (2014), Harris (2014) Sullivan (2014) and Weale (2015). For further reading on work–life balance, see Noon et al. (2013).

Note: This feature was written by David Denham.

known as SATs. According to Harris (The Guardian, 2014), these are reasons why teachers have to spend so much time recording data and filling in spreadsheets, 'leaving no room for the kind of human values that were once at the centre of what teachers did'.

Harris also cites the role of the inspection agency Ofsted, which can descend on a school at short notice and judge whether a school is 'outstanding' or 'good',

'requires improvement' or is 'inadequate'. In order to be ready for an inspection, teachers have to spend hours compiling data on their activities 'just in case the inspectors turn up', as one teacher interviewed by Harris (The Guardian, 2014) put it. Changes to the national curriculum and sometimes a school's transformation into an academy also involve extra form-filling for teachers.

Figure 6.4 *Performance as a transformation process*

in this part of the transformation process, because it is in practice that new knowledge can be created (Newell et al., 2002). Research has partly focused on the importance of knowledge that people learn informally in practice, which is acquired intuitively and implicitly, often without intention (Sternberg and Horvath, 1999). Such knowledge is often referred to as 'tacit knowledge', a rather ambiguous term but one that is seen as key in knowledge creation as it emerges from practice (Nonaka et al., 2000a), and as a key feature of strategic human resource development and workplace learning (see Chapter 7).

We must also remember that practice occurs in a context, that contextual factors can have a significant bearing on overall performance, and that these need to be considered in the various PMS processes of managing, measuring, assessing and rewarding performance. Thus, paying attention to how an employee performs will provide rich data on that employee's current effectiveness and potential for further development. If, for example, we assume that an employee has been trained to complete a basic task, attention to practice in the transformation process will provide data on a number of issues. The first time she completes the task, an assessment of her behaviour will reveal nervousness until completion, when the results achieved can be compared against a standard. This nervousness can be corrected by adjustments to the employee's skills and practice until she has gained confidence. Further study reveals that, once confidence has been gained, the employee will perform with some sense of rhythm and flow that achieves a perfect result.

Given static conditions and standards, this is as far as the employee can go in this task. She can continue to perform with confidence, but after some time this becomes too easy. This feeling prompts her to ask for some adjustment, possibly at first to the work targets and then to an extension of tasks within the job. The important point is that ease within the transformation process, as assessed by the employee and others, leads to developmental adjustments. Continued attention to the process may eventually result in a further range of adjustments, such as increased responsibility through job enlargement and job enrichment, and a reconsideration of the employee's future direction within the organization. On the way, the organization may benefit from her rising efficiency and effectiveness, including better standards.

Through paying attention to the behaviour of an employee during the transformation process, data can thus be provided for a whole gamut of developmental decisions over time, starting with adjustments to reach minimum standards and then addressing career changes and progression. Through appraisal, individual employees are able to set targets, objectives and goals for each stage.

The focus on practice as the starting point for PMS processes is brought into greater prominence when we consider that many people now perform tasks that are knowledge-intensive within what is recognized as a knowledge economy and a knowledge society (Bednall et al., 2014; Rohrbach, 2007). Highly skilled jobs require significant and ongoing learning, or life-long learning. Furthermore, such work often requires a response to unusual or changing situations, where on-the-spot decisions are needed with little time for considered deliberation. This is not atypical of professional work or work requiring high levels of expertise (Beckett, 2000).

A number of techniques have been developed that allow for a consideration of practice against the various stages of the transformation process. The ability to employ various techniques in performance management will depend on a number of contingencies. Ouchi (1979) has provided a framework specifying these and allowing for a choice to be made; Figure 6.5 has been adapted from his work. This framework can be used to reconcile the dilemma that organizations may face in performance management and appraisal, that is, the dilemma between the desire to maintain control, and the desire to foster a developmental emphasis. Forms of control depend on the feasibility of measuring the desired performance – 'the ability to measure either output or behaviour which is relevant to the desired performance is critical to the "rational" application of … bureaucratic forms of control' (Ouchi, 1979, p. 843).

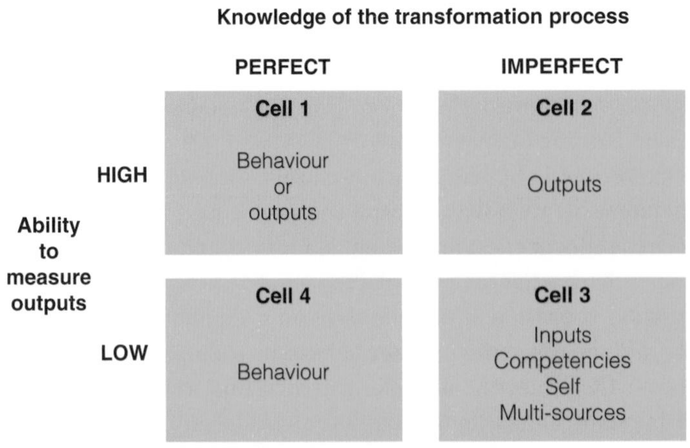

Figure 6.5 *Contingencies in performance management*

Source: Adapted with permission from Ouchi, W. G. A conceptual framework for the design of organizational control mechanisms. Management Science, 25(9): 833–48, (September 1979). Copyright © 1979, the Institute for Operations Research and the Management Sciences, 5521 Research Park Drive, Catonsville, Maryland 21228. http://www. informs.org.

In Ouchi's framework, if an organization either has a high ability to measure outputs or behaviour, or has perfect knowledge of the transformation process involved in production, it could opt for a bureaucratic control approach and base appraisal on behaviour, output measurements or both. Thus, in cell 1, typical of traditional manufacturing and service organizations where work process steps can be clearly stated, both behaviour and output techniques can be used. Appraisal interviews or online measures can include ratings against dimensions drawn from a competency framework, with a focus on behaviour or outputs that can be assessed.

In cell 2, only outputs can be successfully measured, perhaps because work processes cannot be directly observed; this may occur with field sales workers, for example. The key issue here seems to be how such outputs are judged and the criteria utilized. Research by Pettijohn et al. (2001), for example, which sought to understand salespersons' perspectives of appraisal, found that although appraisal was a common practice within sales management, there was some dissatisfaction with the criteria used. In particular, salespersons preferred to be appraised with respect to customer satisfaction and the product knowledge that lay within their control. The failure to include such criteria had implications for morale, turnover and overall performance. Even if outputs provide more objective measurement criteria, it is still possible for subjective criteria to affect how sales staff are evaluated. Factors such as physical attractiveness and being in favour with a supervisor can affect the judgement of a salesperson's performance (Vilela et al., 2007).

Approaches are now moving from cell 1 to cell 2 in areas such as police work (Shane, 2010), where performance appraisal has traditionally been based on a model of compliance and control that fits a bureaucratic framework. Instead, it is argued that there could be a stronger focus on what the police achieve, as indicated by empirical measures.

In cell 4, employees' behaviour can be observed, but outputs are more difficult to discern; this may be the result of groups of employees producing group outputs or measurable outputs over a long period of time, for example in research work. Particular difficulties occur when appraisal, which is inherently an individual process, is applied to a group or team – you may already have had experience of group work and the problems that occur when a group mark is given for assessed work. In the workplace, there may be variations of effort and variations in the skill required. There is also variability in the life of teams, some teams coming together for a single project, others working together over several tasks. In addition, a team may increasingly have to operate over different locations.

All this suggests that the performance management of teams requires a consideration of relevant circumstances rather than a 'one-size-fits-all' prescription (Scott and Einstein, 2001), including considering the situations faced and the beliefs and motives of team members (Chang et al., 2008). Van Vijfeijken et al. (2002) suggest that the effective management of group performance requires a combination of goal-setting and rewards based on the group's performance. This needs to consider the degree of interdependence between tasks completed by group members, the complexity of tasks and the interdependence of goals, which considers how one person's goal is affected by or affects the attainment of goals by others.

In all the above cases, the logic of control may be extended to some form of performance- or merit-related pay system. In cell 3, however, there is an imperfect knowledge of transformation and a low ability to measure outputs directly, making bureaucratic control more difficult. Ouchi refers to this cell as a 'clan' based on a ritualized, ceremonial or 'cultural' form of control arising from shared attitudes, values and beliefs. Cell 3 would include the work of professionals and knowledge workers, as well as most managers and, increasingly, forms of work organization in which higher levels of discretion and autonomy are granted to individual employees. It also includes teams within a network, where expertise must be used selectively and leadership shared between team members (Friedrich et al., 2009) and recent approaches to crowdsourcing for the development of new products and services (Simula and Ahola, 2014). In such situations, behaviour, although difficult to observe formally, can be observed by those present at the point of production.

A university can, for example, try to bureaucratically control who becomes a member of the academic staff through its selection processes; hence it is possible to assess 'inputs' through qualifications, publications and other attributes. Once in place, however, performance is much more difficult to assess and appraise. Some universities have used competency frameworks. For example, one institution is seeking to base performance management on an 'assessment of the outcomes and competence requirements established during the Performance and Development Review'. The difficulty here is the attempt to measure outcomes when the work is non-standardized.

Consider further the work of professionals in the public sector, in which performance management and appraisal have been seen as a shift towards managerialist language and techniques (Hvidman and Andersen, 2016). In response to deregulation and competition, often sponsored by central government as part of the trend referred to as new managerialism or new public management (Pollitt, 2000), there have been various attempts to curtail the power of professionals within the public sector and remove or usurp their monopoly (Exworthy and Halford, 1999). Research so far suggests the emergence of new relationships and a reordering of professions and management: head teachers, for example, require leadership skills that include the assessment of their staff.

In the UK's National Health Service (NHS), with over 1 million employees, many of whom are professionally qualified, appraisal was developed in the 1980s and has been seen as one of the tools necessary to bring about a change in culture. Research by Redman et al. (2000) found that, after several years of experience, appraisal was generally valued, particular strengths being the setting of objectives, personal development planning and, where they occurred, quarterly 'mini' reviews. There was, however, also evidence of 'patchy application' (p. 59). Although there remains little systematic evidence of PMS in the NHS, the evidence that does exist points to the importance of feedback and participation in setting goals (Patterson et al., 2007). Recent research on the talent management process in the NHS has suggested lack of clarity and measurement difficulty in areas where there was a poor infrastructure for data collection and sustainability (Powell et al., 2013).

HRM web links Visit the online resource centre at **www.palgravehighered.com/bg-hrm-6e** to access a website for NHS employers with advice and links for the appraisal process.

Generally, the performance management of people whose work is knowledge-based is difficult to observe and requires a longer timeframe for measurement. Reilly (2005) suggests that performance management cannot be imposed in such circumstances. Furthermore, such workers tend not to want hierarchical career progression, and many will resist moves into managerial posts. Career-planning tools can help them to determine their own career paths.

Approaches to rating performance

We can see that there are a number of opportunities for performance-rating to occur. The different approaches to rating can be classified as inputs, results and outcomes, and behaviour.

Rating *inputs* is a broad and potentially vague category that has traditionally been concerned with listing traits or personality attributes. Typical attributes are dependability, loyalty, decisiveness, resourcefulness and stability. Because such attributes may be difficult to define, there will be little agreement on their presence in employees between the different groups using lists of measures. The use of personality attributes in performance management and appraisal can lack reliability, giving rise to charges of bias, subjectivity and unfairness. This is usually the case when managers attempt to measure their employees in appraisal interviews. As indicated above, many organizations now prefer to use reliable and valid psychometric instruments as a way of helping employees to diagnose strengths and weaknesses for a development plan.

Ratings based on the *results and outcomes* of work performance provide the most objective technique for collecting data for appraisal. When available, measurements can be taken at different points in time and comparisons made with objectives. Typical measurements might relate to production, sales, the number of satisfied customers or customer complaints combined with the use of objective-setting and review as part of the PMS. Ratings might utilize the language of standards as set out in vocational qualifications (see Chapter 7). Such standards attempt to describe what competent people in a particular occupation are expected to be able to do. The outcomes achieved can be assessed against performance criteria for each standard. It is not surprising that most measurements are quantifiable, although many organizations will attempt to modify quantification with qualitative measurements or comments.

The attractiveness of results and outcomes as objective sources of data makes them a feature of many PMSs, allowing decisions to be made on a person's ranking against others that appear neutral and rational. In turn, the results can feed decisions on issues such as pay based on a 'forced distribution', for example the top 10 per cent, next 20 per cent and so on (Bevan, 2014), sometimes referred to as the bell curve system. This can also lead to a certain degree of manipulation and inflated ratings among managers. A key question is whether such approaches reflect performance control or development approaches. Factors for consideration will relate to how objectives, targets and goals are set, how managers and employees interact in work towards achieving them, and whether the employees use the measurements as feedback in order to develop further. As Pettijohn et al. (2001) found, it is important that the criteria used to judge performance are controllable by those being judged: a failure here affects morale and overall performance.

During the 1960s, for example, there was a growth in schemes of management by objectives, which were designed to control the performance of managers and stimulate them in terms of their development. If this could be achieved, it was believed, the needs of managers and of the organization could be integrated. Such schemes, however, soon came under attack, and many fell into disrepute. Levinson (1970, p. 134) attacked the practice of management by objectives as self-defeating because it was based on 'reward–punishment psychology', which put pressure on individuals without there being any real choice of objectives. Modern approaches to objective-setting will face similar charges unless managers pay as much attention to the process by which objectives are set as to the content and quantification of objectives, and the environment in which employees work towards achieving them.

Attention to the *behaviour* of employees as practised in the transformation process will reveal how an individual has applied aptitudes, attitudes and competencies to the performance of work and will provide rich data on current effectiveness and the potential for further development. This attention can occur continuously, taking into account both subjective and objective data. Such an approach forms the foundation of a PMS concerned with the direction of performance and support for employees' continuing development. Once these processes have been established, employees may be more willing to accept more codified approaches to rating their behaviour. Frameworks of competencies associated with effective performance can, for example, provide the integrating link within a PMS between identifying key performance factors and setting objectives that can then be reviewed and rated; there is, however, evidence that the competencies identified are not always included in the appraisal process (Abraham et al., 2001).

Two kinds of ratings scale can be developed:

- *Behaviour-anchored rating scales* (BARSs) provide descriptions of important job behaviour 'anchored' alongside a rating scale. The scales are developed by generating descriptions of effective and ineffective performance from people who know the job; these are then used to develop clusters of performance and scales (Rarick and Baxter, 1986). Each scale describes a dimension of performance that can be used in appraisal. For example, in a scale developed for the behaviour of 'planning', the performance scale could vary from 'Excellent' to 'Unacceptable', and in between would lie a range of possible behaviours with varying degrees of effectiveness (Khanna and Sharma, 2014).
- *Behavioural observation scales* (BOSs) involve the people doing the rating assessing the frequency of specific job-related behaviours that are observable. Figure 6.6, for example, shows BOSs that have been derived from a financial services company.

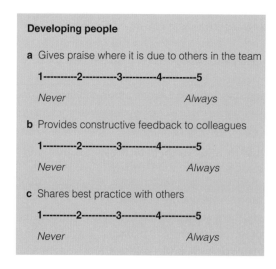

Figure 6.6 *BOSs in a financial services company*

Both BARSs and BOSs are based on specific performance and on the descriptions of employees involved in a particular job. Research by Tziner et al. (2000) provided a comparison between BARSs and BOSs with respect to how satisfied those being rated were with their appraisal, and to the setting of goals to improve performance. It was found that goals developed using BOSs were more specific than those set using a BARS since they were based on what a 'rater' actually observed rather than on evaluation. Furthermore, since BOSs require a rating of several behaviours rather than the identification of a single 'anchor', as in BARSs, this reduces bias and allows more specific feedback, allowing clearer goals to be formed. What is particularly interesting is the potential for such instruments to enhance self-appraisal and allow a dialogue between employees and others based on more objective criteria.

Self-appraisal

Referring back to our earlier analysis, we saw that there have been significant problems associated with performance appraisal. These stemmed mainly from the way in which systems were put in place as a way of superiors evaluating employees for a variety of purposes, for example improving performance, pay and promotion. What cannot be escaped, however, is that all employees have an opinion on how well they are performing, the rewards they desire and deserve, and the training they require. That is, whatever techniques of appraisal are employed, self-appraisal and self-rating will always be there too. When the emphasis of PMS is on evaluation and control, it is only to be expected that differences will exist between an individual's self-appraisal and the appraisal of his or her superior. Campbell and Lee (1988) put forward a number of discrepancies between self-appraisal and supervisory appraisal:

- *Informational* – there is disagreement over the work to be done, how it is done and the standards to be used in judging the results.
- *Cognitive* – behaviour and performance are complex, and appraisers attempt to simplify this complexity. Different perceptions result in disagreement between appraisers and appraisees.
- *Affective* – the evaluative nature of performance control appraisal is threatening to appraisees and triggers defence mechanisms, leading to bias and distortions in interpreting information. Appraisers also may find appraisal threatening.

All this suggests that self-appraisal in an environment of evaluation and control is not effective, which is not surprising. Campbell and Lee (1988, p. 307), however, suggested that 'such pessimistic conclusions did not rule out the possibility that self- appraisals can be used as important developmental and motivational tools for individuals'. We have already shown that employees are able to observe their own performance and obtain data for appraising strengths and weaknesses, and for identifying future goals, from the processes of working. Self-appraisal as a minimum condition allows the emergence of data for use in a discussion about performance, especially where the work is complex or knowledge-intensive (Ryan and Tipu, 2009). The extent to which employees are able to appraise themselves objectively becomes a question of how willing they are to seek and accept feedback from their work behaviour and the environment they are in. Employees can learn to appraise themselves and will treat this as part of their own development if they can see its value for themselves rather than viewing it as a manipulative management tool.

HRM web links Visit the online resource centre at www.palgravehighered.com/bg-hrm-6e to access examples of appraisal forms, including self-appraisal from ACAS, UK.

Multisource feedback

Self-appraisal for development will not occur unless it is set in an environment that facilitates and encourages such a process. If a positive experience is gained from self-appraisal, employees may then be willing to share their thoughts on the process with others. Many organizations have sought to increase the amount of feedback received and the number of sources of feedback. Kettley (1997) claimed that the popularity of MSF had arisen from a number of factors:

- It is a way of empowering employees and promoting teamwork by allowing employees to appraise their managers.
- It increases the reliability of appraisals and balance in 'flatter' (that is, less hierarchical) organizations.
- It reinforces good management behaviour by allowing people to see themselves as others see them.

The various sources of feedback might include:

- The immediate manager
- Staff (upward appraisal)
- Peers (peer appraisal)
- The manager and/or other staff (180-degree appraisal)
- The manager, staff and peers (360-degree appraisal)
- The manager, staff, peers, customer, suppliers and others (540-degree or 720-degree feedback).

As the number and range of MSF schemes have grown, so too has interest in their impact. This has been particularly so in the rating of innovation competencies (Potočnik and Anderson, 2012). The crucial factor is the extent to which self-rating is supported by the ratings of others. What do you think the outcome would be if a manager had a positive perception of his or her performance but was rated less well by others, for example staff and internal customers? Yammarino and Atwater (1997) have provided an examination of possible HRM outcomes based on the range of agreements between 'self' and 'other' ratings. For example, where self-ratings are higher than the ratings of others, this is likely to lead to negative outcomes, whereas self-ratings that are lower than the ratings of others will result in a mixture of positive and negative outcomes.

MSF is growing in popularity, but there is evidence of both benefits and difficulties with it. For example, *upward appraisal* for managers, where managers start from a low or moderate rating and the feedback process is sustained over time, leads to performance improvement; there is less impact, however, on managers who already have a high performance rating (Reilly et al., 1995). Managers prefer feedback from people they can specify, although staff, understandably perhaps, prefer anonymity (Antonioni, 1994). Most importantly, upward appraisal provides a powerful message to managers that performance will be assessed and improvement is expected. Managers can prepare themselves by becoming aware of the behaviours being assessed.

However, managers can also treat ratings with ambivalence or worse. For example, Atwater et al. (2000) found that managers who faced feedback from staff during a period of organizational change demonstrated a low impact from the feedback where the change had been cynically introduced. Research by Van Dierendonck et al. (2007) in the NHS suggested that upward appraisal had only a small positive effect but, more importantly, that there was a gap between the self-ratings of managers and those of their staff. This led to some reduction of ratings by managers but no change of behaviour. Perhaps one of the most valued features of upward appraisal is the opportunity for staff to express their views in a constructive manner, which adds to their sense of being included (Howe et al., 2011; MacKie, 2015).

Peer appraisal appears to be especially suitable for professional and knowledge-based workers such as doctors, teachers and researchers. The responses can be unpredictable, but research suggests that some will undertake further learning as a consequence (Colthart et al., 2008), and that peer-led discussions about learning and development are more acceptable than other alternatives (Main et al., 2009). There are, however, some possible tensions, since peers in managerial roles are usually connected with each other through their work or more informal relationships, and may be unwilling to offer formal feedback or make comparisons between their peers. Within teams, peer feedback can lead to resistance and avoidance of blame if the team is not performing well (Peiperl, 2001).

reflective question Do you review the performance of your group after any work completed? Do you provide feedback to each other?

Moving round from upward and peer appraisal, *360-degree appraisal* completes the circle of MSF. The purpose of 360-degree feedback is to facilitate behavioural change (Harrington, 2012) through assessment and development, and this change should be achievable, positive and measurable in order to be effective (Leslie, 2011). Such a move does, however, require confidence and trust in the way it works because the outcome can become demoralizing and negative for the target group of appraisees, usually managers and leaders. 360-degree appraisal usually requires ratings from a sample of relationships, probably no fewer than eight. The feedback is collected by questionnaire, increasingly completed online, which can speed up the process (Mason et al., 2009) and can be seen as a more objective approach.

As with all approaches to appraisal, there can be both positive and negative reactions. Where appraisees are open-minded and willing to use the views of others to assess their self-perceptions, the process can be positive (Taylor and Bright, 2011). Individuals can, however, be hurt by too much negative feedback, and there may be confusion over whether the process is for development or for judgement relating to pay or promotion (Handy et al., 1996). Research into leadership development in a university in Australia (Drew, 2009) suggests that responses range from 'no surprising feedback' (that is, just reinforcement and affirmation) to 'new insights' that lead to plans for change. These types of mechanism have perhaps been put to better use within coaching and mentoring for improved performance, where opportunities to discuss the various feedbacks is provided (Nieminen et al., 2013: Nowack and Mashihi, 2012).

The value of the 360-degree appraisal will also depend on how the process is positioned in an organization, on how a climate of support is established and facilitated for its implementation, and on how the negative effects are ameliorated. In particular, organizations need to consider employees' willingness to give and receive feedback and to use the various rating techniques (Vukotich, 2014). Training programmes are crucial before implementing MSF schemes. It would also seem that such schemes have more value as processes for development and performance improvement rather than as mechanisms of judgement related to pay and promotion (McCarthy and Garavan, 2001).

Smither et al. (2005) sought to explore the impact of MSF on performance over time by examining 24 studies. However, they found only small improvements in performance, suggesting that other factors were also important. Their research suggested that the following factors were important in determining how much improvement in performance might result from MSF:

- The characteristics of the feedback
- Initial reactions to the feedback
- Personality
- The feedback orientation of those receiving feedback
- The perceived need for change
- Beliefs about change
- Goal-setting
- Taking action.

Each of these factors could have an impact ranging from the nature of the feedback, for example positive or negative, to beliefs about the ability to take action. There are no clear paths to performance improvement from MSF feedback. Instead, the process will benefit some employees and not others. In particular, an organization needs to assess the impact of any MSF feedback scheme and provide support by developing a coaching culture (DeNisi and Kluger, 2000), especially as a common problem reported by managers is a lack of interest on the part of others (including the employees' immediate line managers) (Garavan and McCarthy, 2007). In addition, as we indicated earlier, perceptions of procedural justice are important in appraisal, and this is significant for the acceptance of MSF, as is the decline in managers' cynical attitudes towards MSF (McCarthy and Garavan, 2007). Smither et al. (2008) showed how wider features of context can affect the impact of MSF over time. They found that, 9 months after completing MSF, 145 managers tended to recall strengths rather than weaknesses, and there was little evidence of performance improvement. MSF needs to be supported by reviews, coaching and perhaps learning projects, especially since the process is often used with development programmes for leaders and managers (see Chapter 14).

HRM web links   Visit the online resource centre at **www.palgravehighered.com/bg-hrm-6e** to check the approach to a 360-degree review.

Given the potential for tension between performance management and appraisal that is oriented towards judgements, in contrast to being oriented towards development, there needs to be some way of providing reconciliation. The development of competency frameworks, along with other measurement devices, has improved the reliability and validity of feedback on employees' attitudes, aptitudes and performance. This still does not, however, remove the underlying emphasis on control. Indeed, some would claim that the use of the various techniques within a PMS serves to enhance the 'manageability' of employees (Townley, 1994). PMSs also place a great deal of faith in the support of the management team as the assessors and facilitators of other people's development. There is no guarantee of either, and our understanding of what really happens in performance management and in organizations generally is still limited.

Importantly, so much of the literature concerning performance management and appraisal works from the neo-human relations assumption that all employees have an interest in achieving the objectives set or in responding to measurements when they have participated in the process (Newton and Findlay, 1996). Employees do, of course, have an interest in what they do at work, but they also have many other interests with only a tangential connection to workplace performance, possibly including many activities that work against management requirements for performance, such as gossiping and having fun, as well as more serious forms of behaviour such as theft of the organization's property (Ackroyd and Thompson, 1999). Additionally, a PMS can also play a key role in uncritically informing the behaviours of managers and staff that shape the fate of the wider economy and national welfare (Bakir, 2013).

Robertson Engineering

The setting

Robertson Engineering is a family-owned business that designs and manufactures equipment for mining. Based in the North-East of England, the company grew by serving local coal mines, but since the 1980s it has sought new customers. Having survived the demise of the UK market, the business has been successful in securing contracts for Chinese and Australian mining companies. There are currently 45 staff, but this is likely to grow over the next few years.

The company's MD is Bill Robertson. He is a third-generation owner of the business and recognizes that more attention needs to be given to performance management. In particular, there needs to be a more systematic process so that talent can be identified to enable growth. Although he believes that things are happening informally, the MD is aware that he needs to demonstrate, using objective data, that he has control of the business. This means that people's performance has been agreed against targets that are tied to business objectives.

Image Source/Gary Houlder

The problem

Until recently, any assessment of performance had been undertaken rather informally. This is traditional in small businesses, and most of the staff were used to a 'friendly chat' with their line manager. There are four line managers, and they had all been appointed from within the business and therefore had close relationships with the people they managed. Owing to the size of the business, Bill ran 'a tight ship', with only the line managers between him and the rest of the staff, so performance management was very much left to the managers.

When action or changes, such as promotions or replacements of staff, were needed, Bill relied on information from the managers to make a quick decision. It had always been the case that people were promoted from within, and that training needs could be identified 'as and when' needed. This did not please everyone, and Bill knew that some of the staff were not always happy with the way managers made judgements about work performance, or with their support (or lack of support) for training. Most of the time, however, any clear differences and variations in performance could be 'smoothed over', and the annual company profit share tended to satisfy the bulk of the workforce.

There had been little attention given to setting goals, and hardly any attempt had been made to record and monitor targets. Because production tended towards fairly lengthy timescales, it was felt that as long as people knew when delivery was required, and that everyone had a 'rough' idea when their input was needed, goals could be 'loose'. As long as delivery was achieved on schedule, profit would be secured.

But some changes were needed, and Bill saw an increasing connection between the performance management of staff and the expansion of the business, although he did not want to lose the informality that had come from being a smaller business. He certainly did not want to create a bureaucratic process of unnecessary form-filling. He was also aware that many staff were very sensitive to feedback, and this could become difficult if judgements about performance were written down formally.

But there was an attraction in understanding more about staff performance, albeit through the eyes of line managers, and he wanted individuals to have their own development plans. Being an engineer, he could also see the logic of a talent pipeline and, as most staff were likely to stay with the company, some connection to career development. Indeed, he could see how performance management might provide him with the perfect process to move the business forward.

The assignment

Working as a group or on your own, prepare a report for Bill that outlines the way forward. You will need to consider:

(continued)

1 An appropriate approach to performance management in this organization

2 The purpose of the exercise, and what skills would be needed by the managers

3 The issue of staff sensitivity to feedback

4 Whether training would be needed, and what methods would be used.

Note: This case study was written by Jeff Gold.

summary

➤ The key idea of a PMS is that the principal dimensions of a person's work can be precisely defined in performance terms, allowing measurement over agreed periods of time, and that it also takes account of particular constraints within the performance situation. Performance management forms the nub of the strategic link between HR inputs and practices, and organizational performance.

➤ Through its link to measurement, performance management provides evidence that management is rationally, efficiently and effectively controlling an organization. There are, however, measurement models that take a wider view, perhaps more strategic and long term, and that encompass a range of values (not just financial) and can stimulate continuous improvement.

➤ Research evidence shows the importance of performance management, with a wide range of activities featured. Different criteria are used to judge performance and to help diagnose development needs, providing a link to the organization's goals. A performance management cycle integrates various HR processes, including development centres, objective-setting and personal development planning, feedback and reviews. There is, however, often a gap between the rhetoric and the reality of claims for its contribution to organizational effectiveness.

➤ Performance management has a 'control' purpose to aid decisions about pay, promotion and work responsibility, and a 'development' purpose in improving performance, identifying training opportunities and planning action.

➤ A PMS might incorporate development centres, which are the same as assessment centres in that assessment tests and exercises are used to provide a report on individual strengths and limitations. However, they differ in their emphasis on diagnosing development needs, leading to suggested development activities and a PDP.

➤ Managers have a vital role to play in providing feedback, both formally as part of a PMS and informally as part of everyday work. The acceptance of feedback as valid will depend on its frequency as part of an ongoing relationship and on how well managers understand the perceptions of their staff.

➤ The performance control approach to appraisal is still seen as evidence of rationality and efficiency at work. Such beliefs often become taken-for-granted assumptions and difficult to challenge. Employees who believe that their appraisal is based on subjectivity or bias and subjects them to unfair punishments are likely to experience appraisal as being of low quality.

➤ A more developmental approach to performance management and appraisal has to include an alignment with talent management policies based on people developing their skills and being challenged to develop themselves.

➤ Performance can be rated in different ways. Inputs, in the form of personality attributes or traits, may lack reliability and may be seen as subjective and unfair. Results and work outcomes allow quantifiable measurement and are therefore seen as being more objective. Rating behaviour within performance allows the use of such techniques as BARSs and BOSs.

➤ Performance might be reviewed and appraised using a variety of MSF processes, including self-appraisal and feedback from managers, peers, subordinates and others as part of a 360-degree appraisal process.

1   What should be the purpose of performance management and appraisal?

2   What is the role of 'objectives' in performance management? Can performance be 'managed by objectives'?

3   Does a PMS enhance strategic integration within HRM?

4   Can knowledge workers and/or professionals be performance-managed?

5   Do you think that students should have more say in appraising and assessing themselves and each other?

6   Do you think that appraisal and assessment techniques enhance the 'manageability' of employees?

Reading these articles and chapters can help you gain a better understanding of the changing role of HRM and potentially a higher grade for your HRM assignment.

➤ Bednall, T. C., Sanders, K. and Runhaar, P. (2014) Stimulating informal learning activities through perceptions of performance appraisal quality and human resource management system strength: a two-wave study. *Academy of Management Learning and Education*, **13**(1): 45–61.

➤ DeNisi, A. and Smith, C. E. (2014) Performance appraisal, performance management, and firm-level performance: a review, a proposed model, and new directions for future research. *Academy of Management Annals*, **8**(1): 127–79.

➤ O'Toole, L. J. and Meier, K. J. (2014) Public management, context, and performance: in quest of a more general theory. *Journal of Public Administration and Theory*, **25**(1): 237–56.

➤ Shaout, A. and Yousif, M. K. (2014) Employee performance appraisal system using fuzzy logic. *International Journal of Computer Science and Information Technology*, **6**(4): 1–19.

➤ Viera, R., O'Dwyer, B. and Schneider, R. (2016) Aligning strategy and performance management systems: the case of the wind farms industry. *Organization and Environment*, doi: 10.1177/1086026615623058.

 Click here in your interactive ebook for a list of HRM terminology and vocabulary that has appeared in this chapter.

Visit the online resource centre at **www.palgravehighered.com/bg-hrm-6e** for lots of extra resources to help you get to grips with this chapter, including study tips, HRM skills development guides, summary lecture notes, tips for English as a Second Language (ESL) students and more.

chapter 7

learning and human resource development

Image Source/John Rowley_ Peter

Sofaworks was a UK-based retail business for all kinds of sofa – leather, fabric, corner and recliners. Previously operating as a family-owned business that sold its own products, from 2002 it switched to sourcing products from all over the world at lower cost. From February 2016, the company rebranded to become Sofology, seeking to differentiate itself from the competition by moving towards a 'coaching style' to sales that focused on customer requirements. This contrasted with a commissioned-based approach. This new approach included the use of an iPad for taking orders. The rebranding also involved the use of a mascot, Neal the sloth.

The change of strategy followed a review based on customer feedback that suggested a lack of differentiation from other furniture retailers. In response to the change of business strategy, the learning and development strategy had to change too. This involved retraining around 500 retail staff to develop coaching behaviours with the customer, based on how interactions with customers reduced the pressure for a sale but allowed them to 'enjoy' the experience of making a choice about a sofa. The coaching approach to selling is more open and empowering for the customer. As customers leave the store, they score the service, and this affects the level of team bonus in the store. The results suggest improved sales, higher staff engagement and the employment of more female staff.

introduction

Imagine you have finished your degree and have accepted a position as a graduate trainee in marketing at a leading pharmaceutical company. On the first day, you discover that the company sees human resource development (HRD) as an investment in the learning of its people, and not just as training as a short-term cost. The company claims to embrace key aspects of the country's concern for increasing skills with a well-established apprenticeship system in which trainees work towards vocational qualifications. This sets your expectation that HRD is considered to be a strategic consideration in the organization. Soon afterwards, you meet with the marketing director, who outlines how you will access the company's learning resources, many of which are now available online as e-learning. He also tells you that your line manager has responsibility to help you complete a training needs analysis, so that measurable objectives can be set for any training undertaken, against which outcomes can be evaluated.

Soon after starting with the company, you meet with other graduates on a 3-day training programme. You learn a lot, but on your return to work, you find that no one is prepared to follow up and help you transfer your learning into work practice. In particular, your line manager takes little interest, whereas you soon find out that other graduates have benefited from their managers acting as coaches and helping trainees to integrate work and learning. However, your own experience suggests little support and, even more problematically, the work you are given does not provide sufficient challenge. Both these features provide barriers to further learning and development.

The meaning of HRD

There has been significant interest in the link between a nation's skills base and the ability of that country to compete in the global economy. Further links are made between skills and ideas such as social mobility, engagement and sustainability (Department for Business, Innovation and Skills, 2010). In organizations, it is often argued that learning and development provides a strong indication of benevolent intentions and commitment to staff

(Gold et al., 2013). For an individual, acquiring skills and knowledge to work and live is considered a requirement for employability and lifelong learning (Beckett and Hager, 2015). There is also evidence that high skill levels that are combined with high discretion in work performance and decision-making can be linked to a measurable improvement in an organization's performance (Camps and Luna-Arocas, 2012). However, this link is likely to be affected by how learning and development are perceived by staff, as well as the support provided by others such as leaders and managers (Sung and Choi, 2014) and the role played by those who deliver programmes and events.

Delivering learning and development programmes is often the task of experts in human resource development, or HRD. After many years of low organizational awareness of their expertise (Gold et al., 2003), HRD practitioners now form a significant section of the Chartered Institute of Personnel and Development (CIPD) in the UK, where they are able to present themselves as the experts in the development of knowledge, skills and learning, and as proactive in their approach to change (Mankin, 2001). Accompanying this growth, there has been more focus on the theoretical basis of HRD (Woodall, 2001), with new journals and conferences being devoted to HRD as a separate discipline rather than as a subdiscipline of human resource management (HRM). Despite this interest, there are, however, differing views about the meaning of HRD and its purpose. For example, 'human resource development' as a term is seldom used by professionals in practice (Sambrook and Stewart, 2005) – they prefer terms such as 'training', 'development' or 'learning and development'. This tends to mean that HRD is seen as an academic subject, although there are some interesting efforts by academics in HRD to make connections to practice (see Gold and Stewart, 2011).

It is suggested in discussions that there are two purposes of HRD:

- To improve people's performance
- To help people learn, develop and/or grow.

Over many years, these purposes have become the focus of some key debates and, more recently, of some of the challenges facing those in HRD. In the 1970s and 80s, the dual purpose of HRD could be presented as an either/or choice, such as in Nadler's definition (quoted in Nadler and Nadler, 1989, p. 4) that:

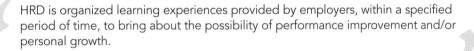

> HRD is organized learning experiences provided by employers, within a specified period of time, to bring about the possibility of performance improvement and/or personal growth.

The 'and/or' proviso in this definition has been subject to a more critical treatment in which the 'performative' focus is seen to dominate over a more empowering 'learning' focus (see Rigg et al., 2007). This critique might also point to the way in which definitions such as Nadler's explicitly suggest that it is employers who make the provision and do something to employees, so that employers might then expect outcomes serving the interests of the organization. Other writers, such as Stewart (2007), have attempted to neutralize this connection by seeing HRD as 'constituted by planned interventions in organizational and individual learning processes' (p. 66). The value of this definition is the way in which learning processes can work at different levels, a theme we will explore more carefully later in the chapter; it also highlights that interventions are not owned by any particular group or person. For example, employees could provide their own interventions or access activities from outside the organization, perhaps via a social networking link, that are shared with others at work.

We might also suggest that some learning processes might not be planned at all but might emerge more informally through everyday work, problems and interactions, increasingly enabled by mobile technology and media in online communities (Ziegler et al., 2014). Crucially, it may be recognized that informal learning needs to be shared and utilized (Marsick and Watkins, 2001), but, as we will explore later, this is not a particularly straightforward process. However, given such possibilities, we will suggest our own definition of HRD to be:

any intervention or activity that enables and results in learning at work.

 reflective question   How much of your learning is achieved informally? Who influences such learning?

While the purpose and meaning of HRD have been debated, those involved in its practice have not enjoyed a particularly favourable status. Short et al. (2009, p. 421) refer to HRD as a 'weakened profession' in relation to other professions in an organization. Considering events linked to the global financial crisis (GFC) that began in 2008, HRD practitioners may have allowed decisions to be made without critique or challenge because of their lack of influence; they became bystanders (MacKenzie et al., 2012). An analysis of documentation relating to the GFC in the UK, the USA and Ireland (MacKenzie et al. 2014) revealed that some organizations were obsessed with results that could not be criticized by others in those organizations. HRD professionals, for example, had to operate in such contexts and fall into a line that sought the pursuit of results. On the basis of this apparent weakness, MacKenzie et al. put out a 'call to action for the HRD profession' to pursue 'legitimacy' anew (p. 49), and Gold and Bratton (2014) have argued for critical HRD education to be introduced as a key feature of professional HRD programmes based on the use of what we have outlined throughout this book as the sociological imagination.

Strategy, HRD and workplace learning

Strategic work at whatever level of consideration – for a nation, an organization, groups of sizes within and between organizations or individuals – is concerned with considering the long term and the future, with survival and sustainability as the key purposes. As a result of strategic understanding, strategies, polices and plans can be made, which can then be assessed and reviewed. Increasingly, it is becoming recognized that what is significant is the quality of the practice of strategy-making and doing.

At a national level, there have been ongoing concerns about the UK's strategy for competing in knowledge-based economies based on high-level skills and talent (Leitch, 2006). The intent is that, in order to sustain the economy, we need a transformation based on economically valuable skills and employment practices that will utilize those skills (UK Commission for Employment and Skills [UKCES], 2011). To achieve this, employers need, however, to have ambitious plans for the development of their products and services so that high-level skills are demanded. As argued by Keep et al. (2006), any strategy for skill use has to be seen in combination with innovative product and investment activities. An interesting finding from a survey of UK skills was that half of employers reported an underuse of skills, and 4.3 million workers were reported as being over-skilled and over-qualified for the work they were doing (UKCES, 2014).

HRD is a key feature of a 'high-road' HRM strategy (Cooke, 2000) based on high involvement, high rewards and high-quality commitment. HRD has a pivotal role in the integration of practices with links to high-performance working (Tamkin, 2014), in which high-level skills and high discretion in the performance of work allow decision-making to be decentralized to those people closest to the customers. Two important implications arise from this view. First, employees are recruited for a skilled working role that will require learning and change, rather than for a job that might soon become obsolete. Employees are expected to retrain, and indeed many employees undertake courses of self-study in order to continue their learning and remain 'employable'. Employees are therefore carefully selected as much for their ability to learn as for their current repertoire of skills. Once recruited, employees become worth investing in, although the form of this investment may be subtler than simply possessing a large training budget. That is, learning becomes embedded into workplace practice as an ongoing process.

Second, line managers are fully involved in their subordinates' development, to such an extent that the differentiation between learning and working becomes virtually impossible to discern (and include in a budget). There is an emphasis on informal learning and an appreciation of its value, where line managers adopt a coaching role as facilitators of learning (Ellinger, 2013).

reflective question Do you recognize the image of line managers portrayed here? What factors might prevent its realization?

In earlier chapters, we briefly examined HRD and workplace learning. The emergent literature on low-carbon sustainable work systems, for example, emphasized the pivotal role of HRD (Chapter 2) and how both mainstream and critical scholars stress that both HRD and workplace learning can create a 'strong' corporate culture. McGoldrick and Stewart (1996) have argued that HRD has a strategic function; they identified leadership as a key variable in linking strategy, culture, the commitment of employees, and approaches and responses to changed and changing internal and external conditions. The findings of Camps and Luna-Arocas (2012) show that the link between high-performance working and organizational performance is mediated by what they call organization learning (OL) capabilities, which includes such factors as the value of learning, involvement in decision-making, communication and the use of errors for improvement rather than blame.

Over the years, managers in organizations and writers have viewed the process of planning strategy as deliberate and purposeful. Mintzberg (1990) labels this the 'design school' model of strategic work. The key features of this approach are a prescription to assess external and internal situations, uncovering threats and opportunities, strengths and weaknesses, and the declaration of an intent incorporating the values and visions of the strategy-makers. This is followed by an attempt to formulate strategies that simply and clearly reconcile the gap between perceptions of current reality and desires for the future.

It would thus seem that the extent to which HRD becomes a feature of strategy depends on the ability of senior managers to sense important environmental trends and signals in HRD terms, that is, in terms of learning for employees. In the same way, it is argued that HRD professionals can make their work strategic by integrating it into the organization's long-term planning, resulting in HRD plans and policies that seek to improve performance (Garavan, 2007). This view of strategic HRD (SHRD) is almost entirely responsive to organizational strategy. It is for others to define the needs relating to the work to be carried out and the skills and knowledge necessary for implementation. Mayo (2004) argues that SHRD must be business-led in order to create value. This requires a recognition of the drivers in terms of:

- The medium- to long-term goals of the business, covering its mission, vision and values, principles and beliefs about people and their development, while maintaining core competencies
- Current goals and objectives relating to the strategies of various business units, manpower plans and change programmes
- Problems and issues that require an HRD response, such as waste, ineffectiveness, compliance with regulations and the needs of individuals and teams.

Many organizations have, for example, sought to use continuous improvement of their processes and procedures in order to create value for customers, a focus referred to as a strategy for 'lean' production. Such a strategy involves a consideration of technology and measurement, and also the creation of a learning culture with support from HRD. Alagaraja and Egan (2013) provide a case study of the implementation of a lean strategy, in which the HRD personnel were able to integrate their systems, practices and policies in line with phases of the strategy. They were responsible for key activities such as management development, skill assessment and training, and the development of problem-solving groups. HRD specialists were thus responsive by providing solutions, although they did not lead the implementation process.

HRM web links   Visit the online resource centre at **www.palgravehighered.com/bg-hrm-6e** to learn more about Henry Mintzberg.

Workplace learning and knowledge creation

A contrast to this responsive view of SHRD is derived from Mintzberg (1987), who suggested that strategies can emerge from the actions of employees, such as a salesperson's work with customers. Through employees' interaction with production processes, customers, suppliers and clients, both internal and external to their organization, employees can monitor, respond to and learn from evolving situations. As a result of such interactions, employees develop what Yanow (2004) refers to as 'local knowledge', and if senior managers can value this more carefully, it can flow to create knowledge that will inform the organization's strategy.

This view of SHRD gives attention to how learning in the workplace can contribute to dealing with change, coping with uncertainty and complexity in the environment, and creating opportunities for sustainable competitive advantage (Antonacopoulou et al., 2005;

Bratton et al., 2004). As argued by Billett (2006), the workplace provides the space for learning where most people gain skills and knowledge every day of their working lives. What is termed workplace learning has therefore become a key idea in recent years (Poell, 2013).

An important feature of workplace learning is the way it casts a whole organization as a unit of learning, allowing leaders and managers to take a strategic view and others to think in terms of how their learning impacts on the wider context. It is an idea that unifies a diverse set of influences and disciplines within HRD (McCormack, 2000), such as training and organizational development, and knowledge and information systems. For example, learning within organizations is increasingly related to the use of mobile technologies and applications, or 'apps', that allow knowledge to be articulated in a digital form, which is then shared via social media (Gu et al., 2014). There has been a growth in efforts to capture knowledge that is generated by workplace learning, and the creation and management of knowledge are now considered as a source of competitive advantage. The economy has become knowledge-based (Organisation for Economic Co-operation and Development, 1996), the basic idea being that knowledge becomes the key ingredient of products and services. Differences between organizations and nations will therefore depend on the extent to which information can be obtained, turned into knowledge and applied to production.

The emphasis on knowledge has resulted in a plethora of new concepts, such as knowledge workers, knowledge-intensive organizations, knowledge networks and knowledge societies. There is also an emphasis on the skills of employees who are recast as knowledge workers. They are the owners of intellectual capital since it is people who are able to construct, manipulate and apply new knowledge, adding value to what is produced. Accumulation of human capital has therefore become one of the reasons for an investment in HRD (Garavan et al., 2001). Knowledge that is created through learning provides a crucial link to the release of sustainable value, which can be used strategically if a framework for human capital management (CIPD, 2015e) is used (see Chapter 4). For example, in e-commerce, learning can begin from the moment a potential customer comes online and points a 'mouse' or 'finger-pad' at a company's web page. Thereafter, depending on which choices have been made and whether or not a decision has been made to purchase, data are generated through the electronic systems in place and, importantly, are collected over time for analysis (Yen, 2014). It is humans who eventually make use of this information to create knowledge, and this highlights a key point – while more attention is increasingly being paid to the systems and technologies of knowledge management than to learning within the workplace, Scarbrough and Swan (2001, p. 8) argue that there is a 'glossing over the complex and intangible aspects of human behaviour'. So much of what counts for knowledge is created and used in practice that it becomes difficult to separate knowledge from what Tsoukas (2000) calls a 'knowing subject', who always exists in a place of action, in a social context.

In considering knowledge creation, it is common to distinguish between 'knowing-that' and 'knowing-how'. The former is concerned with knowledge about facts and explanations for facts that are explicit and communicable, whereas the latter refers to the ability to do something in a particular situation. Knowing-that is based on knowledge that has been *codified*, for example written into books, journals or papers on the internet, and therefore becomes communicable. It is this knowledge that lies at the heart of the digital revolution. Knowing-how is, however, particularly important in the performance of skilled work. Whereas performance may require knowing-that, dealing with the particulars of a

HRM in practice 7.1

Managing knowledge

© Stockbyte Royalty Free Photos

In June 2011, a Work Foundation (Levy et al., 2011) report concluded that Britain could not pin its hopes for the future on finance or manufacturing, but had to concentrate on developing a 'knowledge economy' for lasting growth. The report defined a knowledge economy as one in which value is created from exploiting knowledge and technology rather than from physical assets and manual labour (Levy et al., 2011).

This theme has for over a decade underpinned the rise of the concept of knowledge management, on the grounds that, for a company to develop internal processes of constant innovation, the knowledge and ideas of its employees must be seen as an asset to be developed and diffused to everyone in the organization. This has been criticised as an attempt to capture workers' 'tacit knowledge' – the unwritten knowledge that they carry in their heads that is based on their cumulative experience of doing the job.

McKinlay (2002) examined attempts to create knowledge management systems in an international pharmaceutical company. Pharmaceuticals is seen as one of the key knowledge-based sectors, and more than two-thirds of McKinlay's survey respondents explicitly regarded themselves as 'knowledge workers'. The aim of the project was to diffuse small-scale and local innovations rapidly across the entire organization.

However, the approach taken by management was to use IT to create centralized databases of good ideas and lessons learned. McKinlay concluded that this had been fairly ineffective in developing innovative knowledge management processes. One reason was that workers actually developed their tacit knowledge through face-to-face interaction with other team members. 'In this sense, tacit knowledge was context-specific, generated and bounded by interpersonal relationships' (McKinlay, 2002, p. 79) – the complete opposite of searching a central database for ideas or solutions. In practice, constructing the database simply became another item on project managers' checklists in the drug development process. The database was validated by the number of hits registered by particular sites, and there was no qualitative measure of its impact on organizational performance.

The second reason why this approach was ineffective was the challenge to ownership of the expertise. On the one hand, knowledge management expected individuals voluntarily to hand over the very experience

that defined them as experts, while, on the other, searching the database could be seen as a sign that the individual's experience was inadequate.

However, one section of the technical workforce had developed their own knowledge management system, which operated more like a social network site. Members were encouraged to engage in dialogue and self-reflection, follow links to related sites and above all take time – no short-term deadlines were involved. The objective was to deepen expertise within existing project teams and create and capture knowledge through a more organic process. But although this seemed to be both popular and successful, it remained limited to a minority of employees. In the main knowledge management programme, there remained a tension between the functional hierarchy in the organization, with its preference for centralized data, and the creation of genuine information networks that, by their very nature of open access, challenged the hierarchical structures.

Stop! Do you think that knowledge management is just another management technique, or does it require a whole new approach to management and organizational structure?

Sources and further information: See Levy et al. (2011) and McKinlay (2002) for more on this topic.

Note: This feature was written by Chris Baldry.

situation, especially a new or unexpected situation, 'cannot be accomplished by procedural knowledge alone or by following a manual' (Eraut, 2000a, p. 128). Such knowledge is personal, based on the requirements of the situation and the understanding of the person carrying out the performance. This is referred to as *tacit knowledge*; it is the ability to deal with different situations, known and unknown, often responding spontaneously to surprise through improvisation and without thought (Schön, 1983).

reflective question To work out the difference between codified and tacit knowledge, think about riding a bike. Could you codify the explanation into a manual for riding bikes?

It is likely that it will be very difficult to explain the skill of riding a bike because the understanding is tacit and difficult to put into words (Polanyi, 1967); however, there are different views on whether this is possible (Beckett and Hager, 2002). Collins (2001) suggests a range of possibilities for tacit knowledge ranging from 'concealed knowledge' or 'the tricks of the trade', which is deliberately concealed and not passed on to others, to 'uncognized/uncognizable' knowledge, in which humans do things such as speak acceptably formed phrases in their native language without knowing how they do it. Gourlay (2006), however, argues that the term 'tacit knowledge' is used where people cannot 'give an account' (p. 67) of an action or behaviour for which there is evidence. This could relate to situations in which there are uncertainties, failures or surprises that Spender (2008, p. 166) calls 'knowledge-as-practice'; these can be a source of creativity but can also be constrained by situational factors. Encouraging the sharing of tacit knowledge is now recognized as beneficial for innovation and effectiveness (Arnett and Wittman, 2014).

Interestingly, tacit knowing by individuals is a starting point for a range of ideas concerning how learning by individuals can become shared by teams and organizations as a whole. Such ideas are concerned with OL. For example, Crossan et al. (1999, p. 525) present four processes in a '4I' model:

- *Intuiting* – individuals see patterns in their experience that provide new insights, which they translate into metaphors for possible communication to others.
- *Interpreting* – individuals explain their insights to themselves and then others through talk, and these then become possible ideas for application.
- *Integrating* – the group shares in the understanding and takes action as a consequence.
- *Institutionalizing* – the learning at individual and group levels becomes organizational through 'systems, structures, procedures and strategy'.

Crossan et al. suggest that these processes are unlikely to flow without difficulty. For example, power and politics are likely to play a role (Lawrence et al., 2005) in the way in which ideas are accepted, rewarded or rejected. Another model, presented by Nonaka et al. (2000b), considers how tacit knowledge is transferred through face-to-face experiences in a socialization phase that creates a shared space for knowledge creation, referred to as 'Ba'. This can enable or inhibit knowledge conversion between people and consists of a physical space such as an office, a virtual one such as an email, wiki and social media, or a mental one such as shared experiences. These models acknowledge the importance of context in learning and knowledge creation. It is within a context that individuals encounter everyday possibilities for learning such as solving a problem or facing a challenge or surprise. Events act as a trigger that requires their further interpretation, and this usually occurs informally and incidentally (Marsick and Watkins, 2001); however, there is a desire to utilize informal learning to underpin improvements in organizational performance (Fuller et al., 2003). An example of this is the study of lawyers completed by Gold et al. (2007), which focused on the situations in practice when lawyers had to perform under pressure, for example in court, or with clients. Individual professionals were able to present their views of the events and derive learning, which they validated with others.

HRM web links

> Visit the online resource centre at **www.palgravehighered.com/bg-hrm-6e** for more on Nonaka's 'Ba' concept.

It is a key feature of workplace learning that it is an everyday process where people become enmeshed in a 'web of relations' composed of actions that they complete with others, based on a set of values that are socially formed. Workplace learning can be helped or hindered by such values (Fenwick, 2008). This links to another view of OL based on what groups practise and on the values, beliefs and norms that are shared between group members by talk, rituals, myths and stories. This is a cultural view of OL developed by Yanow (2000) and highlights how, in any place we refer to as an organization, there will be a variety of groups, all practising or 'organizing' according to the meanings they have made within the group. OL is therefore concerned with what people do in their local situation. This also means that OL is not concerned only with change, innovation or finding new ways to compete. Because OL is based on the meanings made within groups, it can also be concerned with sustaining the group and its practices – which those outside the group, such as managers, may call 'resistance' to change and learning. However, this view of OL is important for SHRD, especially where work is structured around projects and the development and sharing of knowledge between project teams (Mueller, 2015).

The cultural view supports a key idea of how learning, mostly informal and improvisational, is 'situated' in a particular context and is a function of the activity that occurs at a local level within a community of practice (CoP) (Lave and Wenger, 1991). As originally developed, learning within a CoP is likely to be at variance with what is supposed to happen, at least in the eyes of managers, who will have formed and espoused abstract versions of what should be learnt but will miss vital details in the process. Learning is strongly related to becoming a practitioner within a CoP, with its own norms, stories and views about what is effective. This makes the task of achieving the benefits of OL even more complex. Brown and Duguid (1991, p. 53) have argued that an organization needs to be conceived as a 'community-of-communities'. During the 1990s and 2000s, some managers sought to work with the idea of CoPs to provide an infrastructure of support so that they could be made 'a central part of their companies' success' (Wenger and Snyder, 2000, p. 145). However, there has been criticism of how far managers can form and manipulate CoPs (Roberts, 2006); we would suggest that the ongoing and everyday processes that make up life within CoPs are not amenable to easy control by managers, nor are they easy to study, with the result that a wide variety of meanings and uses is attached to CoPs (Li et al., 2009). Nevertheless, CoPs provide a powerful image for the creation of knowledge that can be used for strategic advantage (Saint-Onge and Wallace, 2012).

reflective
question   How far are students members of a CoP? Do they practise according to their own norms, stories and views about what is effective? What difficulties does this cause?

The learning organization

The learning organization is seen as a strategy for performance improvement and competitive advantage (Weldy, 2009), using ideas from CoPs and OL models. In the UK, the idea was first developed by Pedler et al.'s (1988) learning company project report, which provided the following definition of a learning organization: an organization that facilitates the learning of all its members and continuously transforms itself. Pedler et al. (1991) went on to provide a list of dimensions of a learning company that could be used to differentiate it from a non-learning company. Among these were a learning approach to strategy, participative policy-making, 'informating' (that is, the use of information technology to inform and empower people), reward flexibility and self-development opportunities for all.

Another source of encouragement for the learning organization was Senge's (1990) idea of five disciplines that were required as a foundation:

- Personal mastery
- A shared vision
- Team learning
- Mental models
- Systems thinking.

HRM web
links Visit the online resource centre at **www.palgravehighered.com/bg-hrm-6e** to learn more about Peter Senge's view of learning organizations.

Still another view was presented by Watkins and Marsick (1996), who developed a model and a survey instrument, the Dimensions of the Learning Organization Questionnaire (DLOQ), which examined seven dimensions of the learning organization: continuous learning, dialogue and enquiry, team learning, embedded systems, empowerment, system connections, and leadership. The DLOQ continues to be used around the world as the basis for strategic work in HRD to create a learning organization culture (Kim et al., 2015).

However, this is not an easy process as the idea of the learning organization is difficult to implement (Garavan, 1997) and is best compared with a journey, possibly one that is never completed. For Örtenblad (2004), the vagueness of the idea of the learning organization can also be a source of creativity, although he argued that there is a need for some clarity to avoid the concept becoming a mere fashion. He suggested that overly bureaucratic organizational structures might pose particular difficulties; as a result, some have suggested that smaller organizations might be more suited to the idea because their structures are relatively organic and flexible, with less bureaucracy (Birdthistle and Fleming, 2005), or that digital organizations may be appropriate because of their knowledge-based work and workforce (Cabanero-Johnson and Berge, 2009).

Part of the journey towards the image of a learning organization is to use instruments such as the DLOQ as a form of organizational needs assessment to begin the journey. For example, Jamali et al. (2009) show its use in the IT and banking sectors in Lebanon. The

DLOQ can highlight the different perceptions at different levels of leaders and teams, as well as weaknesses such as lack of communication, involvement, engagement or participation, which are seen as necessary for enacting the learning organization (Song et al., 2014; Weldy and Gillis, 2010).

Integrating workplace learning and strategic HRD

Giving attention to workplace learning and the potential for knowledge creation allows for a more reciprocal and proactive influence on organizational strategy. Slocum et al. (2014) refer to the 'essential investment' in people that feeds the development of ideas for products and services and finding markets and customers. In this process, HRD specialists can play an important role by developing new ideas that both match strategy and take it forward. They can also develop facilitating and change management skills (McCracken and Wallace, 2000), which they are able to do because managers themselves appreciate the emergent features of strategy-making and provide support for learning activities. This is accompanied by managers acting as key advocates of HRD, recognizing that people are more likely to be productive when they feel that their work is personally meaningful and not simply a means to another end (Boud and Garrick, 1999). One important effect is that leaders and managers become more accepting of ideas that can feed strategy from others within the organization, thereby creating a culture that supports learning through an understanding of how workplace learning links to SHRD. For example, Watson and Harmel-Law (2010) show how workplace learning in a Scottish law firm could benefit the organization, although there was a need for support from others, and contextual factors such as structure and pressure to meet income targets could provide obstacles to learning.

A particular problem, however, even within organizations where strategic management is taken seriously, is that the focus in most cases remains on profit maximization, cost minimization and marketing, which makes HRD and skills a fourth-order consideration (Coleman and Keep, 2001). Choosing a path other than skills and learning lies at the core of a UK problem of low-priced, low-quality production and a low demand for skills. Thus, if an organization chooses a production process that implies a low product specification in terms of skills, this has a corresponding impact on the demand for skill (as products with a high specification tend to be more complex and need frequent updating and/or alteration of the specification) (Green et al., 2003). This maintains what Keep (2004, p. 16) refers to as an organization's 'low skills trajectory'. It is a continuing problem with which successive governments, especially in the UK, have been concerned, but without finding a solution. Keep and James (2012) point to the existence of 'bad jobs', which are low paid and which provide little incentive for learning at work.

Diversity and HRD

The issue of diversity is prompting many organizations to find a training response, and this needs to be considered strategically (Home Office, 2003). As we identified in Chapter 4, a number of changes in the legal context are widening the coverage of antidiscrimination legislation, and this is coinciding with a broadening of philosophies that seek to shift the idea of equal opportunities at work towards diversity and inclusion, often emphasizing the business benefits. A CIPD (2012) survey in the UK found that many organizations had policies to support an inclusive culture and practices such as HRD. However, there was less evidence of measuring change and using Key Performance Indicators to monitor impact.

Diversity is usually considered in terms of a need to conform with the law and therefore as a cost, but there are signs that a more inclusive culture is being given prominence.

Developing an inclusive culture is inevitably a difficult issue, but a common view is that HRD and training activities have an important part to play, even though such activities frequently 'hope' to raise awareness leading to a change of behaviour that will eliminate discrimination (Tamkin et al., 2002). Awareness programmes are a common form of diversity training, seeking to enable participants to become aware of their prejudices and/or disseminating information on issues such as changes in the law. Such programmes can, however, also be criticized for being too generalized and not focusing on the skills needed for changing behaviour. Kulik and Roberson (2008) suggest that awareness training has not been as effective as skills-based training that considered behaviour, with particular attention to interactions between people that enable the promotion of diversity at work. Skills-based learning for improving interactions is often based on Bandura's (1986) social learning theory, in which behaviour change can occur by role modelling new behaviours. Participating in role play can sensitize participants to diversity issues within interactions, allowing practice in a relatively supportive and safe environment, with feedback from an experienced coach. In general, research suggests that, in diversity programmes, skill-based or knowledge-based outcomes tend to be stronger than changes in attitudes (Kalinoski et al., 2013).

It needs to be recognized that the shift towards diversity and inclusion requires the adoption of a long-term view of cultural change – it is not a 'one-size-fits-all' or a 'one-off' effort but has to be continuous. The strategy needs to be problem-oriented by identifying the issues that need to be confronted so that it is clear what is being tackled; in this way, any learning can be matched to need and designed to provide a more integrated approach rather than just stand-alone events (Bezrukova et al., 2012).

Crucially, for such learning to have any chance of being effective, it requires a supportive learning climate (see below) and support from senior managers and leaders who are basing their support on a clear business case for diversity, with this communicated throughout the organization. Metcalfe (2010), for example, shows how the computer company HP made diversity central to its leadership development, with a focus on how diversity issues were communicated and represented, including questions of cultural values, beliefs and norms. Such processes can provide a space for a critical confrontation of deeply embedded prejudices, which Wood et al. (2004) argue is required if the aspirations of the diversity agenda are to be seriously considered. It is also apparent that HRD academics need to embrace diversity more seriously since it remains the case that the focus on performance is likely to squeeze out the complexity and critique needed to increase the amount of attention being given to diversity (Bierma, 2010). However, diversity training, sometimes called sensitivity training, needs to be considered carefully. In one university, students were asked to write down their stereotypes of ethnic and religious groups and give views on issues such as gay marriage. It was a process that created discomfort with what appeared, leading to national media attention and legal claims (Johnson, B., 2015).

National HRD

While organizations wrestle with the ideas and practices for SHRD, at a national level there is interest in how a country views the contribution of skills towards its economic and social life. The interest in skills finds expression in the policies and practices of the state, its agents and its influence on organizations. Through such moves, a national HRD (NHRD) agenda has been established. McLean (2004) suggested that interest in NHRD arises from such issues as the need to alleviate poverty, improving the quality of people's lives, technological advances and globalization, and labour shortages, so that more attention is paid to upskilling employees. Alagaraja and Wang (2012) point out the need to consider the societal context and the differences between developed and emerging economies when considering NHRD strategy.

In the UK, decisions about HRD are taken principally by those in organizations in what is referred to as a voluntarist approach. The government's role in this approach is to encourage organizations to take responsibility for their own training and development and for financing it. This can be contrasted with a more interventionist approach in which the government or its agents seek to influence decision-making in organizations and make decisions in the interests of the economy as a whole. These two approaches are often combined, albeit usually with a preference for one against the other, as shown in Figure 7.1. In countries such as France, Belgium, Denmark, Spain, France, Italy, Cyprus and the Netherlands, there are systems of training levies, often backed by government, to provide the main revenue for training. In the UK, in sectors such as construction and engineering construction, there are statutory levies on organizations for training. This levy is an annual sum of money as a proportion of payroll, which is then used as a grant to organizations to fund training. If an organization does not provide training, it pays the levy but does not receive any grant (UKCES, 2012). Mostly in the UK, the voluntarist approach relies heavily on market forces for skills, in particular on the views of decision-makers in organizations. However, in 2015, the UK government announced the introduction of an 'apprenticeship levy' from April 2017 for companies with turnovers of more than £3 million, which was to be equal to 0.5 per cent of the wage bill. The purpose of this was to raise around £3 billion for apprenticeship training. All companies were to receive £15,000 to offset the charge, but there have been concerns about bureaucracy, and some employers have seen the idea as an extra 'payroll tax' (Johnson, C., 2015).

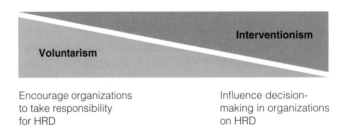

Figure 7.1 *Voluntarism versus interventionism in HRD*

reflective question Do you think a levy system is a fair approach to encouraging organizations to devote resources to HRD?

Decisions on funding people's skills are underpinned by assumptions about the worth of investing in skills as a form of capital. People's performance and the results achieved can then be considered as a return on investment (ROI) and assessed in terms of costs and benefits (see Chapter 4). This view is referred to as *human capital theory* (Garrick, 1999). Although this theory may be dominant, it may also obscure key processes such as how management can ensure successful performance, and how costs and benefits can be measured. Furthermore, it can present HRD in fairly narrow terms based on tangible and measurable benefits (Heyes, 2000), which may place a restriction on activities that have an uncertain pay-off over a longer time period. Investment can therefore become reduced to a cost. Furthermore, as argued by McLean and Kuo (2014), human capital theory is basically concerned with the supply of skills and does not sufficiently consider the actions of firms or government in creating demand for products and services that have an impact on earnings and employment. Thus, Taylorist–Fordist approaches to control (see Chapter 13) can, through job design and the deskilling of jobs in order to reduce training costs, hold sway in many organizations. In such conditions, HRD becomes subservient to accounting procedures that measure the cause-and-effect relationships between programmes and output and profit in the short term. If a relationship cannot be shown, there will be pressure to provide the proof or cut the cost of the training, providing a powerful barrier to OL. For example, many HRD professionals come under pressure to prove the 'bottom-line value' of their work and show an ROI in evaluation (Burkett, 2005).

reflective question To what extent do the above features of human capital theory influence the learning programmes in which you are involved?

Human capital theory may be dominant in HRD but can be contrasted with a softer and more *humanist* view of people and their potential. A *developmental humanistic approach* based on the personal empowerment of the workforce through learning highlights how individuals are most productive when they feel that their work is personally meaningful rather than simply a means to an end. Learning provides a way of coping with change and fulfilling ambitions. HRD can therefore move beyond the technical limitations of training and embrace the key ideas of learning and development implied in such concepts as the learning organization and life-long learning. The tensions between human capital theory and the developmental humanist view still, however, require those involved in HRD to present their arguments in appropriate terms. It is for such reasons that the case for a more critical approach to HRD is presented (Bierema and Callahan, 2014).

These views provide a background against which the case for HRD is made at the different levels of individuals, the organization and the economy/society. Of particular concern in the UK has been what has been called the 'low-skills equilibrium', in which the economy becomes trapped in a cycle of low value added, low skills and wages, and high unemployment (Wilson and Hogarth, 2003). The main idea, first suggested by Finegold and Soskice (1988), is that products are specified in low skill terms because of the need to keep costs down. As Wilson and Hogarth (2003, p. viii) argue, 'Other things being equal, the lower the specification, the lower the skill intensity of the production process ... [and therefore] the lower the demand for skill.' This problem has dogged many efforts to raise skills levels in the UK and is now recognized as a crucial factor to tackle (UKCES, 2011); however, it remains to be seen how this will happen.

Clearly, understanding skills and how skills are defined is central in NHRD. Felstead et al. (2002) suggest that 'skill' can mean:

- Competence to carry out a task
- A hierarchy of skill levels that are dependent on the complexities and discretions involved
- A variety of types, including generic skills applied in diverse situations, and specific skills suitable for particular contexts.

Most decisions on the definition of skills take place in organizations, exposed to factors such as the structure of domestic markets, short-term financial pressure, models of competitive advantage based on economies of scale, central control, cost containment and standardization (Wilson and Hogarth, 2003). These all combine to design tasks to a low specification, requiring low skills and providing low value added (Bloom et al., 2004). Even if an organization reports a deficiency in skills, these can easily be defined in low skills terms, in what Bloom et al. (2004, p. 12) call a 'latent skills gap', where organizations can accept and adjust to low skill requirements, losing awareness of the restriction that this imposes.

It has become a crucial feature of the case for HRD that there needs to be an association between skills and organizational performance (Tamkin et al., 2004). A key area is the perceptions of leaders and managers with respect to product and service specification and the level of skills and capabilities required as technology changes (Green et al. 2003). Studies of high-performing organizations suggest that skill development is focused on performance and is continuous. In addition, it is not just a matter of technical skills but of 'creating a work environment in which employees can learn all the time as part of their normal work and where they can take advantage of the system for performance and innovation' (Sung and Ashton, 2005, p. 26). Sung and Choi's (2014) 5-year study of over 200 manufacturers shows that HRD improves employee commitment and competence to improve performance if there is support from managers who perceive the benefits of HRD. How far employers, especially those in smaller and medium-sized enterprises, become oriented towards HRD, particularly the offer of high-skilled and higher pay work, has been a concern of successive governments in the UK.

The GFC may have reinforced a trend for technological changes that hollow out internal labour markets, which sees medium-skilled jobs disappear at a faster rate than low-paid unskilled ones (Autor, 2010). Gallie (2007) points to another trend of dual labour markets, one part for high-skill, better paid and more secure jobs that provide opportunities for progression, learning and development, and another for low-paid jobs that often lack opportunities for learning and development. The latter category can involve those who have been identified as the 'precariat', a new social class that have little job security, often working in low-paid jobs on zero-hours contracts (Atkinson 2010; Holmes and Mayhew, 2010). Such trends can only accelerate through disruptive technologies such as advanced robotics, cloud technologies and 3D printing, which are likely to lower costs of production and replace people in many sectors (Ifenthaler, 2015). This is bound to raise difficult questions for governments, organizations and individuals in terms of training, skill development and continuous learning.

HRM web links | Visit the online resource centre at **www.palgravehighered.com/bg-hrm-6e** for more information on how NHRD is developed by different bodies in the UK.

Implementing HRD

Although there are many recommendations to adopt a more strategic approach to HRD and make it more business-driven, there remains the crucial factor of how HRD is implemented. A number of uncertainties and tensions arise here. Who, for example, should take responsibility for HRD? Should it be HRD specialists, with their sophisticated repertoire of interventions and techniques? Or should it be line managers, who are close to work performance and are able to influence the way in which people learn and develop, as well as the environment in which this occurs? How should needs be identified, and whose interests should they serve?: those of employees seeking opportunity and reward for the sacrifice of their effort, or those of the organization in the pursuit of goals and targets? What activities should be used, and will these activities add value? How does HRD relate to business goals? A crucial feature of HRD, given the claims made for its connection with high-performance working and knowledge creation, is the measurement and assessment of learning. In any organization, a range of factors influence learning, and HRD practitioners may not be the best people to make judgements about its impact (Clarke, 2004). Furthermore, budgets for HRD activities have come under significant pressure in recent years, especially in the public sector, where most practitioners expect a decline in budgets (CIPD, 2015e).

Overall, there may be still insufficient evidence about what is happening inside organizations when HRD is considered, which is compounded when we consider both formal and informal approaches to learning at work. For example, line managers seem to offer low support for formal training but play a crucial role as coaches in what is learnt informally on an everyday basis (Beattie et al., 2014). So although it is becoming clearer that the formal aspects of HRD, such as plans, policies and activities, can have a crucial impact, informal features may be of even greater importance.

reflective question How do your peers, colleagues and/or managers influence everyday learning where you are?

Formal models of implementation have shown a remarkable tendency to match the conventional wisdom of how organizations should be run. Depending on the resources committed to their activities, trainers have had to justify this commitment by adhering to prescriptive approaches. Employees traditionally learnt their jobs by exposure to experienced workers who would show them what to do ('sitting by Nellie'). Much learning undoubtedly did occur in this way, but as a learning system it was haphazard and lengthy, and bad habits as well as good could be passed on. In some cases, reinforced by employers' tendencies to deskill work, employees were unwilling to give away their 'secrets' for fear of losing their jobs. Most importantly, line managers did not see it as their responsibility to become involved in training, thus adding to the forces that served to prohibit any consideration of valuing employee potential.

Theories of learning

How we understand and explain learning in organizations is, of course, crucial to any attempt to implement HRD. Throughout the twentieth century, there were many ideas concerning learning, and a traditional distinction was usually made between *associative learning* (or behavourism) and *cognitive learning*; the main differences between the two traditions are summarized in Table 7.1.

Table 7.1 *Traditions of learning*

Associative learning or behaviourism	Cognitive learning
Learning in terms of responses to stimuli: 'automatic' learning	Insightful learning
Classical conditioning (Pavlov's dogs)	Thinking, discovering, understanding, seeing relationships and meaning
Operant or instrumental conditioning	New arrangements of previously learned concepts and principles

We can see how the nature of the work that employees are required to perform will lead to the acceptance of a particular view of learning. It will also underpin much of a manager's understanding of human behaviour and motivation. The reduction of work into low-skilled and repetitive tasks will therefore favour associative and behaviourist views of learning even where, in the initial phases of learning, knowledge and understanding are required. The main thrust of the learning is to produce behaviour that can be repeated time after time in relatively unchanging conditions. More complex work favours a need for knowledge, understanding and higher order cognitive skills, underpinned by cognitive learning theories. The work of writers such as Anderson (1981), for example, considered learning from an information-processing perspective in which learners seek to solve problems by seeking relevant information, and then matching and processing the information into a solution to provide knowledge and understanding before execution through action.

Behaviourist and cognitive theories of learning are viewed by Beckett and Hager (2002, p. 98) as representing a 'standard paradigm of learning'. The basic assumption here is that the 'human mind' is viewed as a 'stock room' that is at first empty but gradually becomes filled with knowledge. Both theories have value in HRD. For example, behaviourist theories underpin the importance of reinforcement and feedback in learning, including the opportunity to practise new skills. Coaching by managers has a part to play in this process. Cognitive theories focus on how learners process information through thinking and memory, organized into patterns or schema to attend to what is happening (Sadler-Smith, 2006). Tests such as the Cognitive Styles Index (Allinson and Hayes, 1996) suggest that people process information somewhere between two preferences:

- *Analytical* – a preference for step-by-step models and structured decision-making
- *Intuitive* – a preference for less structure and more openness and creativity.

reflective question What is your preference for decision-making? Do you recognize different preferences among others when you work in a group?

Research also suggests that it is possible to consider both analytical and intuitive processing together. For example, a high preference for both would indicate versatility and openness but also structured thinking (Hodgkinson and Clarke, 2007). There has been a growing interest in the use of cognitive styles in organizations, and a recent review by Armstrong et al. (2012) recommends a need to extend research into the use of and impact of measuring cognitive styles in such areas as team leadership, group problem-solving and conflict, particularly in the context of social interactions, for example collaboration in teams.

Recent years have seen an interest in the connection of cognitive theories, the working of the brain and central nervous system and the philosophy of human reasoning, referred to as *neurocognitive theory* (Brandon and Anderson, 2009). Studies of the brain, referred to as neuroscience, have uncovered many functions of each part of the brain. Based on such knowledge, which is continuously emerging, cognition can be viewed as an integration of networks from different areas of the brain (Meehan and Bressler, 2012). These discoveries are affecting some key issues in learning. For example, neuroscience is helping us to understand how people might link reinforcement to reward-associated behaviour in the midbrain and the use of video games in developing skills, referred to as the 'gamefication' of learning (Howard-Jones, 2014).

HRM web links Visit the online resource centre at **www.palgravehighered.com/bg-hrm-6e** for more information on the Society for Neuroscience.

Although research on behaviourist and cognitivist learning, along with neurocognitive theory, is continuing, it is important to remember that learning always occurs in a context. The interaction of learners with their context is often referred to as *experiential learning*. Kolb (1984), for example, has provided an integrated theory of experiential learning in which learning is prompted through the interaction between a learner and her or his environment. The theory stresses the central role of individual needs and goals in determining the type of experience sought and the extent to which all stages of learning are completed. For learning to occur, all the stages of a learning cycle should be completed. Individual learners will, however, have an established pattern of assumptions, attitudes and aptitudes that will determine their effectiveness in learning.

According to Kolb, learning occurs through grasping an experience and transforming it. Transformation of the impact of experience on the senses (concrete experience) allows, through internal reflection (reflective observation) the emergence of ideas (abstract conceptualization), and this can be extended into the external world through new actions – active experimentation. Unless the process can be completed in full, learning does not occur, and individuals may not begin the journey to qualitatively finer and higher forms of awareness, which may be called development.

Kolb's model has been very influential for many HRD practitioners and has also heightened awareness of the factors that contribute to learning or prevent learning at work. Learning activities at work could thus be designed on the basis of individual and group learning preferences. Learners might also attempt to overcome their blocks to learning. Individuals might, for example, lack the belief that they can take action in certain situations, or they might have negative feelings about certain activities. The important point about such blocks is that they are based on personal meanings, feelings and emotions towards learning, and this connects with other models of learning, for example *neurolinguistic programming*, which examines the way in which learners represent the world in their brains and order their thoughts by language to produce largely automatic actions (Tosey, 2010). Learners can examine how such processes occur and how they can model themselves on the processes of others whom they see as more effective. Harri-Augstein and Webb (1995) presented an approach to learning based on uncovering personal meanings and myths that produce 'robot-like' performance and appear very difficult to change. It is suggested that, through critical awareness, learners can begin to experiment and change. Such views of learning link to a growing interest in adult learning and development, and the importance of reflection to examine behaviour and assumptions and premises about learning (Mezirow, 1991).

Kolb's experiential learning model is one of a number that have led to the popularity of assessing the approach to learning through learning style questionnaires. However, research by Coffield et al. (2004), examining 69 learning style instruments, found that many had psychometric drawbacks and were not recommended for use in education or training. One criticism is that experiential learning models are overly focused on individuals at the expense of their interaction and involvement with others (Holman et al., 1997). Others point to the importance of critical reflection allowing more attention to be paid to questioning assumptions relating to context, as well as to considering more collaborative ways of learning (Bergsteiner et al., 2010; Reynolds, 2009). In addition, there has been growing interest in how people learn on an everyday basis, mostly with others in an informal manner, through their participation in practice.

There has been an increasing influence of the work of Russian psychologist Lev Vygotsky and his sociocultural theory of human development (Wells, 1999). Vygotsky (1978) suggested that learning occurs through participation in actions and interaction with others. The result of what happens socially is an internalization of understanding within the individual. This process from the outside to the inside is principally mediated through the use of 'tools' such as language and other social symbols. Using the work of Vygotsky, Gold and Yeo (2013) combined it with Bakhtin's (1981) philosophy of language to set up an integrated experiential learning approach that brings together social context, cognition and action.

A systematic training model

Whatever theory of learning is selected, it needs to inform how HRD is implemented. The preferred routine is to adopt a systematic training model, an approach that emerged during the 1960s under encouragement from the industrial training boards. The approach was based on a four-stage process, shown in Figure 7.2, and was widely adopted, becoming ingrained in the thinking of most training practitioners. Buckley and Caple (2007, p. 24) suggest it emphasizes 'logical and sequential planning and action'.

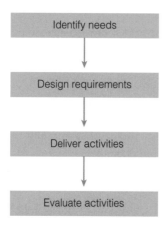

Figure 7.2 A four-stage model of training

What do you think is the best way to deliver training in an organization?

Stockbyte/ Punchstock

This model neatly matches the conception of what most organizations would regard as rationality and efficiency, a consistent theme in many HRM processes. There is an emphasis on cost-effectiveness throughout: training needs are identified so that wasteful expenditure can be avoided, objectives involving standards are set, programmes are designed and implemented based on the objectives, and outcomes are evaluated or, more precisely, validated to ensure that the programme meets the objectives originally specified and the organizational criteria. There is a preference for off-the-job learning, partly because of the weaknesses identified in the 'sitting by Nellie' approach, and partly to formalize training so that it is standardized, measurable and undertaken by specialist trainers. The trainers can focus on the provision of separate training activities that avoid the complexity of day-to-day work activities and make evaluation all the easier.

In this systematic model, the assessment and analysis of training needs is concerned with identifying gaps between work performance and standards of work or performance criteria that have a training solution. Once these have been identified, clear and specific objectives can be established that can be used to design learning events and evaluate the outcomes. Training needs can exist and be identified throughout an organization. Boydell (1976) identified three possible levels for this: organization, job or occupation, and individual. Needs are in theory identified at the corporate or organizational level and fed through to the individual level. The approach reflects a mechanistic view of organizations and the people within them. In particular, there is an emphasis on the flow of information down the hierarchy to individuals, whose training needs are assessed against standards defined by others. Each person has a responsibility to perform against the standard and to receive appropriate training if they are unable to meet the standard. Table 7.2 provides a list of possible approaches to assessment and analysis of training needs.

Table 7.2 *Assessment and analysis of training needs*

Organizational	Job/occupation	Individual
• Culture audit and diagnosis • Skills audit • Development of competency framework • HR plan • Analysis of performance management data • Critical incidents • External research • Benchmarking • External assessment, e.g. the Investors in People awards in the UK and worldwide	• Job analysis • Job documents – descriptions, specifications • Problem-centred analysis • Key task analysis • Competency analysis • Job or occupation standards (defined within vocational qualifications)	• Performance management and appraisal data including multisource feedback • Direct observation • Performance standards measurement • Assessment/development centre results • Completion of psychological tests • Self-appraisal

A consideration of needs will then allow plans for development activities to be drawn up. These may take the form of on-the-job or work-based opportunities supported by line managers and others, off-the-job courses run by specialists and, increasingly, open and distance learning or e-learning activities (see below). A key feature in completing a plan is to consider what is called learner readiness, which is concerned with how people might retain knowledge and skill from the opportunities they take and how motivated they are to apply learning (Bhatti et al., 2013).

The last stage of the model is evaluation. Although a number of writers have pointed out the value of evaluation at each stage (Donnelly, 1987), the image of evaluation held by many trainers is that of a final stage added on at the end of a training course. In such cases, evaluation serves to provide feedback to the trainers, so that small adjustments and improvements may be made to activities. Evaluation can also provide data to prove that the training meets the objectives set, so that expenditure on training may be justified.

reflective question

> The four-stage model (Figure 7.2) may be rational and efficient, but is it a model of HRD?

HRM web links

> Visit the online resource centre at **www.palgravehighered.com/bg-hrm-6e** to access resources and ideas for HRD activities.

The basic elements of the four-stage training model have remained in place, and most organizations that claim to have a systematic and planned approach to training will have some representation of it. A number of refinements have also been made by advocates of a more realistic and more sophisticated model. Donnelly (1987) argued that senior management may, in reality, abdicate responsibility for the training policy to the training department, with a consequent potential for widening the gap between training and organizational requirements. Essential prerequisites for any effort to implement a training model are a consideration of budgets, attitudes, abilities and culture or climate. A key requirement of training activity is that it should be relevant and 'reflect the real world'.

We can, however, easily see how training could become either isolated from organizational strategy or reactive to it. Bramley (1989) argued that the training subsystem may become independent of the organizational context. He advocated turning the four stages into a cycle that was open to the context by involving managers in analysing work situations to identify desirable changes, and then designing and delivering the training to bring the changes about. Evaluation occurs throughout the process, with an emphasis on managers taking responsibility for encouraging the transfer of learning that occurs during training into workplace performance. In this way, the model is made effective rather than mechanistically efficient. Garavan et al. (1999a, p. 171) suggest that a 'jug and mug' metaphor could be suited to the trainer role here, with a very passive involvement of learners at any stage.

Refinements to the basic form of the systematic model imply that a more sophisticated view of training needs to be taken. This essentially involves taking account of reality and organizational context. Implicit in such a view are the inherent limitations of the reality found in the organization, which may prevent the basic model operating or may maintain training activity at a low level. The reality may thus be little consideration for training in

HRM and globalization 7.1

Access to informal workplace learning opportunities

I t is self-evident that many jobs require workers to continually learn new skills and information. Yet employer support for formal training appears to be distributed unevenly among workers, with older workers and women frequently reporting fewer opportunities for training. Indeed, formal workplace training tends to be concentrated among the best educated workers who already hold prestigious jobs. Yet workplace learning is not confined to formal training opportunities: workers have always learned on the job. The opportunities for such informal learning are, however, shaped by the degree of flexibility built into jobs by employers, including the opportunity for workers to participate in decision-making and problem-solving.

A recent German study examined whether the same pattern of bias – against female, older and less educated workers – that is often found in formal training also exists in the availability of informal training opportunities. The researchers reported (Harteis et al., 2015, p. 77) that the:

> kind of occupation individuals are participating in crucially shapes their opportunities for workplace learning. Again, this finding is consistent with studies conducted with older employees in both Australia and Singapore that found employees in higher status occupations (professional, para-professional, administrative) reported little in the way of age-related discrimination or constraints on opportunities for maintaining their employability.

This analysis suggests that neither age nor gender is a significant predictor of workers' opportunities to apply their knowledge in the workplace and thereby to participate in informal learning. This greater availability of informal learning opportunities to workers in higher status occupations mirrors the research on the availability of formal learning opportunities.

Yet examining which workers can best access workplace learning opportunities presents only part of the picture. It is also important to look at the overall level of workplace training. While the annual training participation rate in the UK consistently hovered around 65 per cent between 2006 and 2012, the duration of training (as measured by the number of days during which some training occurred) fell by 32

© Stockbyte Royalty Free Photos

per cent, from 51.2 to 34.9 annual days per worker (Green et al., 2016).

Examining 4-week training estimates bolstered this finding. The percentage of UK workers engaged in training during the previous 4 weeks has long held steady at approximately 13 per cent. Yet, over time, the proportion of training lasting less than a week has risen from a third in the mid-1990s to over half in 2012. What this examination of training volume tells us is that not only is formal and informal workplace learning allocated unevenly, but the overall volume of training also appears to be significantly declining. And this decline has occurred regardless of gender, age or occupation.

(continued)

Stop! What do you make of the idea that workplace training is allocated in ways that disadvantage female and older workers? Does this ring true to you? Which explanation for the overall decline in training volume do you prefer? And why?

Sources and further information: For background information, see Green et al. (2016) and Harteis et al. (2015).

Note: This feature was written by Bob Barnetson.

This leaves us with the question of how we can reconcile these data with the idea that workplace learning is critical to organizational success and the mantra of the so-called knowledge economy. It may be that managers have become sceptical about the value of training or that the overall increase in education levels has made job-specific training less necessary. It may also be that training methods have become more efficient or that non-formal learning opportunities are displacing formal training. At present, there is no compelling reason to prefer any of these explanations.

relation to organizational strategy, but instead a culture that emphasizes short-term results measured against set standards. Organizational politics may interfere with decisions on training needs (Clarke, 2003), or managers may simply refuse to accept responsibility for supporting the transfer of learning where training is undertaken. These are all features of an organization's learning climate, a consideration of which is essential for implementing HRD.

Taylor (1991) argued that it is possible to present two views of why systematic training models may not match organizational reality. In the first, referred to as the *rehabilitative critique*, it is proposed that the concepts of the systematic model are sound and can be used as an approximation of reality, serving to highlight the problems to be overcome at each stage by refining techniques. In identifying training needs, for example, trainers may not have access to the 'real' learning needs of the organization because of a lack of access to information and low credibility with senior managers. The refinement would be for trainers to raise the profile of training. However, the second view – the *radical critique* – argues that the systematic model is based on flawed assumptions and is merely a 'legitimizing myth' (Taylor, 1991, p. 270) to establish the role of the trainer and allow management's right to define skill within the employment relationship. It is often assumed, for example, that training is in everyone's best interest. In times of change, however, the definition of skill and the redesign of work, which determine and are determined by employee learning, may lead to a divergence of interest between employees and management, and may unbalance the employment relationship between them.

Taylor (1991) concluded that although systematic models might have helped to profes-sionalize the training activity and provide a simple and easily understood explanation of training procedures, such models were incomplete and really only suitable for organiza-tions operating in stable environments where goals could be clearly set, outcomes measured and mere compliance obtained from employees. According to Taylor (1991, p. 273), however:

> Continued adherence towards what is still essentially a mechanistic procedure may well prevent trainers tapping into the more nebulous but powerful organizational forces such as mission, creativity, culture and values.

Thus, in recent years, there has been greater interest in considering some of the key contextual issues that make training, and learning generally, more effective. This may include factors such as the motivation and interests of learners, the support from managers and leaders, and the overall learning culture. Instead of being systematic, trainers need to become systemic in their thinking about the learning process at work (Chiaburu and Tekleab, 2005); that is, they need to understand the various factors that have an impact on HRD, the interdependence and tensions between the factors and how they combine to produce (or not) training, learning and development in all parts of the organization.

An integrated and systemic approach

In contrast to the mechanistic view of training implied by the systematic approach described above, many organizations, especially those facing uncertain environments and the expectation of rapid and continuous change, have sought a more integrated and systemic approach in recent years. It is an approach that highlights key interdependencies within organizations, such as the link to strategy, the role of line managers, the link to team-based learning and knowledge transfer (Hirsh and Tamkin, 2005). It is therefore an approach to which the label 'human resource development' seems more suited.

Sloman (2005) suggested a shift from training, which is principally instructor-led and involves content-based interventions, to learning based on the self-direction of staff and learning from work, with managers taking responsibility to support this process. For HRD professionals, there is a need to engage with the reality of the organization at both the strategic and the operational level in order to provide value and enhance their credibility. The image is closer to that of what is called a 'business partner', in which HRD works alongside business units as an agent or facilitator of change. The notion of partnership is drawn from Ulrich's (1997) views on how human resources (HR) can add value and deliver results, and from more recent work on HR transformation (Ulrich et al., 2009). Gubbins and Garavan (2009) suggest a variety of HRD roles ranging from traditional trainer roles to those of a strategic business partner, as shown as Figure 7.3.

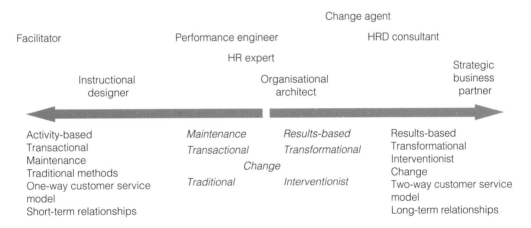

Figure 7.3 *Changing HRD roles*

Source: Gubbins, C. and Garavan, T. N. (2009) Understanding the HRD Role in MNCs: The Imperatives of Social Capital and Networking. Human Resource Development Review, 8(2): 245–75. Copyright © 2009 by SAGE Publications, Inc. Reprinted by Permission.

Following Ulrich (1997), HRD professionals have three possibilities:

- To provide routine transactional services such as traditional training programmes, as part of a *shared service* provision with other HRM professionals
- To become more specialist by providing leading and complex HRD processes that are valued by others within a *centre of excellence*, perhaps by using the latest research in collaboration with universities
- To become a strategic *business partner*, working with business leaders on the organization's agenda for the future.

In most cases, but especially as strategic business partners, HRD professionals have issues and possibilities similar to those of others in HRM. There is a need to develop a knowledge and understanding of how to add value that meets the needs of key stakeholders. For some, this means HRD becoming what the CIPD (2010f) calls an insight- and business-driven discipline, possibly in contrast to a people-driven discipline. Others, however, would argue against such prioritization and the potential for this to drive out concerns for people and their development and well-being (Keegan and Francis, 2010).

The context of enacting an HRD role has a vital impact on its value. Any HRD policy has to be translated into the structures, systems and processes that might be called a learning climate or environment. The learning climate in an organization is composed of subjectively perceived physical and psychosocial variables that will fashion an employee's effectiveness in realizing his or her learning potential (Temporal, 1978). Such variables may also act as a block to learning. Physical variables cover the jobs and tasks that an employee is asked to undertake, the structure within which these are set, and factors such as noise and the amount of working space. Of particular significance is the extent to which the work carried out can be adjusted in line with employee learning, for example following the completion of an HRD activity.

Psychosocial variables may be more powerful; these include the norms, attitudes, processes, systems and procedures operating in the workplace. They appear within the relationships in which an employee is involved, for example with managers, work colleagues, customers and suppliers. Fuller and Unwin (2003), drawing on their research of apprenticeship learning, have suggested that an organization's learning environment can be considered as expansive or restrictive – as two ends of a continuum. At the more expansive end, an organization is characterized by such factors as access to learning and a range of qualifications, a vision of workplace learning and career progression, the valuation of skills and knowledge, and managers as facilitators of development. In contrast, a restricted environment is characterized as having little or no access to qualifications, a lack of vision, recognition and support for learning, and the presence of managers as controllers of development.

reflective question Consider any organization you have worked in. Which end of the expansive–restrictive continuum most accurately describes its stand on learning?

At the heart of the learning climate or learning environment lies the line manager–employee relationship. HRD requires the integration of various activities such as identifying needs, choosing learning activities and supporting the application of new skills to work, and the key to achieving this lies in the thoughts, feelings and actions of line managers. Some organizations have recognized this and have included 'developing others' within their competency frameworks for managers (Industrial Relations Services, 2001). Gibb (2003) provides a number of advantages arising from the greater involvement by line managers in HRD:

- Development will become possible for a wider range of staff and encourage a proactive approach to life-long learning.
- There is likely to be a better link between organizational and individual needs because line managers are more likely to understand the requirements of work as well as the organizational goals.
- Helping others to learn is a learning process for line managers too.

- The involvement of line managers can lead to better relations and more help to support change in organizations.

Of course, as identified by Gibb, there might also be some difficulties. For example, pressures of work may reduce the opportunities for HRD, and managers may not have the skills or positive attitudes for developing others. In addition, by giving responsibility to line managers, the role of specialist HRD practitioners may be reduced and the provision of resources outsourced. Nevertheless, there has been growing interest in how a line manager can support HRD, especially through coaching (see later in the chapter).

Evaluation and transfer of training

For HRD to be effective, it is important to provide evidence of impact and added value. This requires attention to evaluation and the transfer of learning. Figure 7.4 shows a model of learning transfer within HRD adapted from the work of Baldwin and Ford (1988, p. 65). The framework specifies six crucial linkages, indicated by the arrows in Figure 7.4. We can, for example, see that new skills can be learnt and retained, but support and opportunity to use the learning must be provided in the work environment. The influence of the framework can be seen in the work of Holton et al. (2007), who have developed a Learning Transfer System Inventory that allows an organization to diagnose the factors affecting or preventing the transfer of learning. The items in the inventory relate to:

- Motivational factors relating to the expectations that people have about applying new skills
- Secondary influences concerning the degree of preparedness of learners, and their belief or conviction in their ability to use their skills
- Environmental elements such as supervisor support or sanctions, and peer support
- Ability elements relating to the opportunity to apply new skills, the energy and workload of learners and the way in which training is designed to link to work performance.

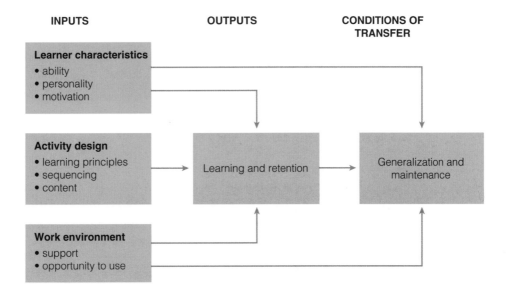

Figure 7.4 *A framework for the transfer of training*

Source: Adapted from Baldwin, T.T. and Ford, J. K. (1988) Transfer of training: A review and directions for future research. Personnel Psychology, 41(1): 63–105. Reproduced with the permission of John Wiley & Sons, Inc. Copyright © 1988 John Wiley & Sons, Inc.

Managers' support activities can include goal-setting, reinforcement activities, encouragement to attend and modelling of behaviours, all part of their role as coaches to motivate their staff to transfer learning to work (Gegenfurtner et al., 2009). In addition, HRD activities need to be designed to enable transfer. This can begin before employees attend events by providing information about the events and how the learning can be applied (Culpin et al., 2014). A key feature of any design is to allow for practice that includes features of the work context (Grossman and Salas, 2011), so the design of HRD events that take place away from the work setting needs to be sensitive to events as they happen within work. This will enhance employees' perceptions of the value of and potential to use what is being learnt (van der Locht et al., 2013). In addition, event providers need to employ a style of delivery that stimulates participants and helps them to relate the learning to their experience and increase their intentions to transfer it to their work situations (Rangel et al., 2015).

On returning to work, a culture of learning and support from managers has a direct effect on staff's motivation for training and learning (Chiaburu and Tekleab, 2005), and is therefore central to learning transfer and the overall learning climate. Also important is the support of peers and other staff, especially in the short term (Homklin et al., 2014). After HRD input, Billett (2001) suggests that the successful development of workplace knowledge is particularly underpinned by the degree to which 'affordances' are provided within the workplace: that is, opportunities are given for learners to engage with learning at work and be supported by managers as coaches and by others.

Activities to support learning transfer within HRD are also a key feature of the evaluation of HRD. As we indicated above, within the mechanistic view of training, evaluation often appears as the final stage. The key purpose of evaluation is to show how training input leads to particular outputs and outcomes. In a well-known model of evaluation (Kirkpatrick, 1998), for example, measurements can be taken at four stages to show a chain of causality in order to prove a result (Figure 7.5).

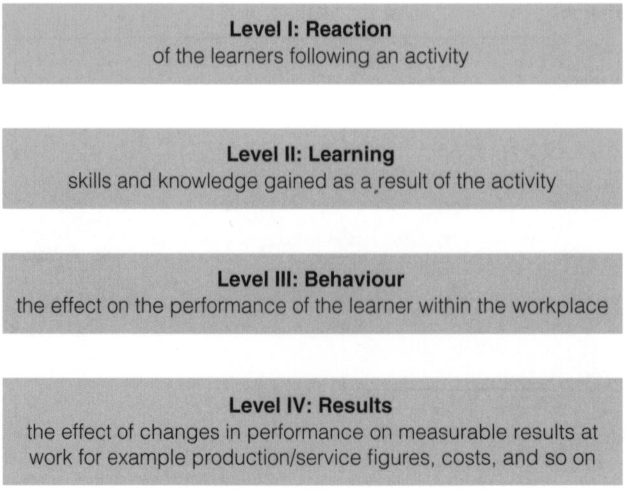

Level I: Reaction
of the learners following an activity

Level II: Learning
skills and knowledge gained as a result of the activity

Level III: Behaviour
the effect on the performance of the learner within the workplace

Level IV: Results
the effect of changes in performance on measurable results at work for example production/service figures, costs, and so on

Figure 7.5 *Levels of evaluation for training*
Source: Based on Kirkpatrick (1998)

This view of evaluation matched the mechanistic view of training and became the orthodoxy for many years, with a number of adaptations to improve its working. For example, Phillips (1996b) added another stage beyond 'Results'. This stage required an effort to assess the costs and benefits so that the programme's net benefits, or what is usually called the 'return on investment', could be measured, calculated by the ratio of programme benefits to programme costs, and expressed as a percentage (Phillips, 2005). Phillips gives an example of a programme with a cost of £35,000 that produces benefits of £105,000. Here, the net benefit is £70,000, so the ROI is (£70,000/£35,000) × 100 per cent = 200 per cent. Phillips points to the use of such calculations as evidence to prove the value of HRD and as a key part of the process of communicating value-add by training to different audiences. Although HRD staff may not have the time to devote to data collection, it is increasingly possible to complete the process leading to the calculation of ROI by using specialized software (Burkett, 2005).

Proving the worth of HRD by producing an acceptable ROI is certainly becoming more important. However, there have been persistent doubts about the efficacy and value of this when applied to many training and development activities (Guba and Lincoln, 1989), especially in terms of the idea that training outcomes can be quantified and measured as if in a chain of causality. As we have indicated above, there are key factors in the organizational context, such as the support of others and opportunities for application, that affect employees' ability to use new skills and knowledge, and in turn affect overall their work performance. Thus, whereas the mechanistic view of training will seek to use evaluation to prove the worth of training, ultimately to the organization, in terms of cost savings and profit improvement, an integrated approach will seek to use evaluation to improve the quality of HRD activities and enhance participants' learning in the activities. It achieves this by providing data for feedback and review discussions, especially between participants and their managers or peers, so that opportunities for application and continued learning can be identified.

Anderson (2007), for example, points to the need for any approach to evaluation to include the values of those receiving the learning and training. The task initially becomes one of developing the metrics that will reflect the needs of decision-makers so that they can assess whether investment in learning is contributing to organizational performance. As the metrics are formed, it becomes possible to employ a range of methods for evaluation, as well as to involve others in the process. Managers, for example, can indicate the value of HRD and how they are playing a role in evaluation and data generation to support action, but they can also show why action is not occurring, for example after a training event. Torres et al. (2005) suggest that evaluation can link HRD to ongoing learning through:

- Feedback from evaluation to make changes
- Integrating change with work activities and the organization's systems, culture, leadership and communication infrastructure
- An attempt to align meanings, values and feelings through questions, surfacing assumptions and allowing dialogue.

Linking HRD to its impact on work activities and beyond represents a shift from the linear reasoning of mechanistic models, because it becomes possible to raise important issues about what may be, or importantly may not be, occurring to allow HRD to have an impact on performance. Establishing the metrics strategically allows them to become part of the meanings made that will be evaluated by managers and those participating in HRD. It can identify any barriers to the use of learning and show how these can be tackled with the support of managers and others (Mooney and Brinkerhoff, 2008). In this way, an organization engages in what Preskill (2008) calls 'evaluation capacity-building', so evaluation becomes purposeful and useful in improving the impact of HRD and enhancing the learning climate and workplace learning.

Coaching

Coaching has become a significant activity in the implementation of HRD, with recent survey evidence indicating its use in three-quarters of organizations overall and 86 per cent of public sector organizations. Talent management and development (see Chapter 5) is also most effectively developed through organized coaching opportunities (CIPD, 2015e).

Originally a development within the sporting field aimed at improving performance (Evered and Selman, 1989), coaching was adapted during the 1970s and 80s as a management activity to enhance employees' development, with particular emphasis on how the transfer of learning from formal training courses into workplace activity could be enabled. There has been a growing interest in coaching, with conferences, books, journals and training materials devoted to coaching now more readily available. Coaching is mainly concerned with current performance and development issues, based on a relationship between a line manager and an employee, and structured around specific issues and goals (Gray, D. E., 2010; Sikora and Ferris., 2014). The role of line managers as coaches has therefore become a key focus of interest (Ellinger, 2013). It can be contrasted with mentoring, which tends to focus on long-term issues such as careers and personal development (see Chapter 14). There are also other variations in coaching, such as peer and team coaching (Godfrey et al., 2014; Parker et al., 2008), as well as executive coaching and business coaching for managers in small and medium-sized enterprises (see Chapter 14).

The particular focus of attention in coaching is on combining performance improvement with HRD (Megginson and Pedler, 1992), increasingly as part of a talent management and development agenda (see Chapter 6). The performance focus is not, however, without tension, and the quandary of being accountable for performance and HRD could lead to a regression into stereotyped management behaviour that focuses narrowly on performance (Phillips, 1995). However, recent research has revealed an alternative challenge for HR departments, which is that front-line managers may not be interested in or capable of coaching (Beattie et al., 2014), or may lack confidence in using coaching skills to improve performance (Turner and McCarthy, 2015).

Gold et al. (2010) have suggested that coaching provides two benefits for an organization: first, managers who are coached are more likely to improve their own performance, and second, managers who coach are more likely to learn about their staff and improve their performance. Other benefits include the relief of stress, and by experiencing how to show compassion to others, there is increased leadership sustainability through restoration of the body's natural healing and growth processes (Boyatzis et al., 2006). However, a longitudinal study of 714 managers and their teams identified specific tensions that revolved around whether the coaching was facilitative, leading to a positive effect on team performance, or pressure-based, which tended to highlight tensions within the team negatively impacting on team performance (Weer et al., 2015). As was found in Chapter 6 when discussing appraisals, there is also a view that coaching success is mediated by the perception of the manager's trustworthiness and ability to have honest conversations (Godfrey et al., 2014; Kim et al., 2015).

**reflective
question** Can coaching be both performance-focused and development-focused?

Although evidence on the value of coaching is still emerging, this has not prevented interest in the development of a coaching culture or coaching organization (Garvey et al., 2014). Based on their study of major organizations, Clutterbuck and Megginson (2005a, 2005b) have provided a framework for developing a coaching culture based on a consideration of:

- Coaching linked to business drivers
- Encouraging and supporting coaches
- The provision of training for coaches
- Reward and recognition for coaching
- A systemic perspective
- Management of the move to coaching.

Godfrey et al. (2014) have added to this list, suggesting that it is also important to take into account the context, of both the organization and the experience of the team. This coincides with evidence from recent research by Jones et al. (2016) that internal coaches are more effective than those who are external to the organization. The other area identified was that of culture.

Any attempt to bring about a change in culture is difficult, but coaching can itself support such changes (Stober and Grant, 2008). Research suggests that organizations are taking a variety of routes in embedding coaching. For example, Knights and Poppleton (2008) found three approaches in a study of 20 organizations:

- Centralized and structured – senior managers provide high support and formal structures to ensure consistency, as, for example, found in London's Metropolitan Police.
- Organic and emergent – based on informality and networks, coaching evolves slowly according to the context of practice, as in, for example, the international emergency assistance organization the Cega Group.
- Tailored middle ground – this involves a blend of the previous two approaches, with some degree of direction for consistency but also a response to the particulars of the context. This can be seen in, for example, the BBC, where coaching started with a small group of committed coaches but grew, requiring structure and direction.

For a coaching culture to emerge, there needs, at some stage in all cases, to be momentum based on good practice, training for coaches and support from senior managers who see the value of coaching. As more coaches become involved, there is a need for guidance from 'master-coaches' (Garvey et al., 2009) and coaching supervisors, who provide an opportunity for coaches to share learning and problems. This also, however, requires care since coaching often involves revealing thoughts and feelings (Butwell, 2006).

A growing number of models and skills for coaches have been presented. The best known is probably Whitmore's (2002) GROW model, which provides a direction for a conversation between the:

- *Goal* – establish a clear objective to be achieved
- *Reality* – establish the current performance and situation
- *Options* – find ideas and alternatives
- *Will or Way Forward* – commitment to action.

Whitmore's model is particularly useful for introducing coaching into organizations, although it can be criticized for its lack of theoretical underpinning. Barner and Higgins (2007), for example, suggest that all coaching practice is implicitly based on a theoretical model and that these models need to be more clearly understood and articulated.

HRM web links

> Visit the online resource centre at **www.palgravehighered.com/bg-hrm-6e** for information on 14 models of coaching. What theories, if any, underpin the models?

Increasing efforts are being made to specify the behaviours or competencies needed for coaching. Anderson et al. (2009) have identified the following coaching behaviours for managers:

- Shared decision-making
- Listening
- Making action plans
- Questioning
- Giving feedback
- Developing staff personally and professionally.

Building trustful relationships based on honest communication is also important (Godfrey et al., 2014). In addition, it has been identified, as we have seen elsewhere, that any behaviour is performed in a context that can help or hinder its enactment; for example, priority for coaching has to be provided by senior managers. It has been found that multi-source feedback (see Chapter 6) is also detrimental to a positive coaching outcome (Jones et al., 2016), and this is thought to be created by a concentration on the feedback rather than the coaching opportunity.

Although models and skills provide some degree of clarity for training programmes and qualifications, allowing a degree of prespecification of what is to be learned, there are also reasons to believe that coaches are in many cases faced by complex and ambiguous interactions with those they are coaching. Coaching is a process that is inevitably dynamic and not easily captured by models or specified skills. Thus coaches are often required to respond spontaneously to the words of the person they are coaching, with little time for deliberating or specifying a model (Gold et al., 2010). At such moments, coaches have to respond with what they have available – their experience and wisdom derived from such experience – a process referred to as *bricolage*, a term developed by the French anthropologist Claude Levi Strauss.

HRM web links

> Visit the online resource centre at **www.palgravehighered.com/bg-hrm-6e** for information about the European Mentoring and Coaching Council and the *International Journal of Evidence Based Coaching and Mentoring*.

HRM in practice 7.2

Ensuring the transfer of learning for managers at BUPA Care Homes

As a major provider of care provision for the elderly, BUPA Care Homes has over 300 homes in the UK. Each is managed by a Home Manager (HM), with a First Line Manager (FLM) reporting to them. James, the company's learning and development manager, had developed an FLM programme. Although there had been support for the programme from FLMs, HMs were struggling to see 'what is in it for us'. They were very much concerned with compliance and a 'what gets measured, get's done' mentality. There was little incentive for HMs to take a longer term view and invest in a programme that might reap rewards further down the line. There was also little clarity over the role of the HMs in this training, and a possibility that HMs might also feel threatened by newly empowered FLMs. James saw the need to build an appropriate performance measure in to the FLM programme so that HMs could link their accountability for performance to it.

James sought to increase the HMs' accountability for the FLMs' performance after they had attended the programme. First, he ensured that a robust learning review (which considered learning and more importantly their actions as a result of their learning)

Getty Images/iStockphoto / Thinkstock Catherine Yeulet

was built into the programme design by introducing the concept of 'action challenges' – a method of transferring learning into real workplace actions. Second, he supported this by introducing a new performance management process that provided HMs with the tools to make their FLMs' development seem more 'core' and hence more sustainable. Finally, James realigned the HMs' objectives and expectations with those of senior leaders in order to reinforce the importance being placed on FLM development.

Stop! How can we ensure that learners can gain value from attending HRD events? As we have made clear, it is important to provide evidence of impact and added value for HRD to be effective. Who must take responsibility for ensuring that learning is transferred from HRD events such as training to the workplace?

Sources and further information: See Gegenfurtner et al., 2009, Culpin et al., 2014 and Rangel et al., 2015. Improving learning transfer is a key issue for those involved in the practice of HRD with ideas and methods discussed in practitioner journals, such as https://trainingmag.com/improving-learning-transfer.

Note: This feature was written by Jeff Gold.

HRM as I see it

Helen Tiffany

Managing Director, Bec Development

www.becdevelopment.co.uk

Bec Development is a people development consultancy firm, working with clients to implement growth in their organizations. It specializes in learning and development, and offers:

- Training, delivered via workshops, seminars and courses
- Management development, to embed new behaviours and bring about change
- Leadership development through 360-degree feedback, psychological profiling, assessment centres and strategy days
- Coaching, including team, one-to-one and executive coaching
- Facilitation, by brainstorming and strategizing with clients
- Organizational development, including staff surveys, training needs analysis, talent development and competency frameworks.

Helen and her team work closely with each of their clients and their board of directors to help implement change through staff development, in line with the strategic aims of their clients' organizations. She is a Fellow of the CIPD, sits on the Council for the Association for Coaching and is a member of the executive board for Mentoring Digital Minds.

Click on Helen's picture in your ebook to watch her talking specifically about coaching, and then think about the following questions:

1 What is 'unique' about the sector in which Helen works? Does this affect the approach to HRD?
2 How does Helen's view of HR relate to business strategy? How can this be achieved?
3 According to Helen, why has coaching become so important? Why is it having such a large impact?

Learning technologies (e-learning)

One area in which the technology revolution is having a massive impact in HRD is the provision of learning technologies, or e-learning. Until very recently, the term 'e-learning' covered a range of different activities involving the delivery of HRD activities, including computer-based training, web-based training and online learning. Preceding these terms were those of 'distance learning' and 'flexible learning'. Through the rapid investment in web facilities, all these terms have now been incorporated under the heading 'e-learning'. Indeed, on 18th November 2015, a search for 'e-learning' on Google returned 315,000,000 hits – the corresponding number in 2011 was 139,000,000 hits, and in 2006 this had been only 63,000,000.

It is difficult to define e-learning precisely, and any attempt to pin it down is likely to be superseded by events. However, by 2015, the CIPD (2015e, p. 15) had replaced it with the term 'learning technologies', which has been defined as:

> The broad range of communication and information technologies that can be used to support learning (such as online or mobile learning).

Research has suggested a number of benefits of e-learning, including the ability to learn 'just in time' at the learner's pace and convenience, the provision of updateable materials, a reduction in delivery costs and, particularly relevant for modern global institutions, the ability to standardize training processes (Pollard and Hillage, 2001; Bharti, 2015). However, as Zainab et al. (2015) have identified, managers and policy-makers in developing countries need to be aware of several specific requirements when making decisions to invest in e-learning. These include perceived cost, computer self-efficacy, technological infrastructure, internet facilities, power supplies and organizational, technical and government support. There is also the possibility of collaborative working, sometimes with learners spread over large distances, with tutor support, flexibility of access from anywhere at any time and monitoring of learners' progress. Most computer-mediated conferencing systems enable a moderator to track participation and adjust provision as required, and according to the CIPD survey (CIPD, 2015e), this has created a 29 per cent increase in the use of virtual workshops and webinars. The survey found that e-learning was being used in 75 per cent of organizations, rising to 88 per cent in the public sector. On top of this, there has been a 17 per cent increase in the use of mobile devices for learning, making it much more difficult for firms to control and monitor learning time (Stewart, 2010). Such figures are, however, very likely to underplay the unplanned and informal use of the technology and networks both at work and beyond.

On the downside, a learner clearly needs access to ICT with an internet or network connection. This can be expensive to set up and requires collaboration between IT and HRD/learning specialists. The CIPD survey suggested that there is a lack of confidence in using learning technology within HR departments, which creates tension when there is a predicted growth in areas such as e-learning, virtual classrooms and social learning. As a result, learning technologies are more commonly used in larger organizations. However, even in larger organizations, research has found that a blended approach of online/mobile learning and face-to-face sessions is more popular (Alghafri, 2015).

One way to address the lack of technical expertise within HR departments is to create corporate universities (CUs). Cunningham et al. (2000) have suggested that most CUs are simply rebadged training departments, but it also argued that a CU reflects an organization's strategic priority for learning, especially where staff are dispersed globally (Paton et al., 2007). Gibb (2008, p. 143) suggests that a CU reflects an aspiration to 'create a strategic learning organization that functions as the umbrella for a company's total education requirements.' The key features that make a CU distinctive are, according to Paton et al. (2007):

- *Corporate-level initiatives* in large, highly complex and differentiated settings – CUs will have a presence on the board. They may be distinct from the HRD function within large business units. They aim to deliver a specific corporate contribution, avoiding the replication or duplication of what is being managed or delivered at a local level.
- *The pursuit of continuing corporate alignment* – the CU is seen as a vehicle by which the control of HRD activities, broadly interpreted, can most effectively be aligned with strategic priorities, such as post-merger integration, customer loyalty and developing leadership.
- *Raising standards, expectations and impact* – the CU reflects the strategic priority afforded to learning. Issues might be ensuring the highest quality of provision, including harnessing the best available technology to create a virtual learning platform across global sites.

Further features of a CU include an influence on training and development for the entire value chain, including customers and suppliers, and, of course, the use of the label 'university', with its implications of high standards and rigour. There are, however, bound to be doubts about how far these can be compared with more traditional universities (Walton, 2005).

HRM web links

> Visit the online resource centre at www.palgravehighered.com/bg-hrm-6e to access Peugeot-Citroen's Corporate University and for more information on Salmon's five-stage model.

It is clear that everyone can join online groups, build networks and communities through social networking sites, add to and use wikis and even create new identities. Martin et al. (2009) have expressed a concern regarding control of learning; however, more recent research has recognized that the lack of control is actually a valuable asset.

A key concept in the twenty-first century is that of knowledge management, which enables the development of different applications of knowledge to known scenarios (Salerno et al., 2015). Semantic web vision uses both formal and informal learning systems, specifically using informal learning as a mechanism to generate unpredictable links to resources. This new learning technology makes use of ontological modelling – a term used in information and computer science that relates to naming and defining various types that can be found in any particular domain being considered, such as data models or attributes of people and the relationships between them. It is suggested that competencies for ontological modelling are required in any role (Sumithra, 2015). Both semantic web vision and the use of subject matter or domain experts defining competencies within ontological modelling allow training courses to be tailored and targeted to specific people in specific roles, enabling the generation of new competencies that are required (Bajenaru et al., 2015; Salerno et al., 2015).

The role of HRD specialists will inescapably be affected as learners move from being present in training rooms to being members of virtual communities. A key issue will be how learning theories can be used in different aspects of e-learning environments. For example, behaviourist theories might be incorporated into staged learning and social learning theories to develop support processes and communities online (Gillani, 2003). There will be many opportunities for knowledge-sharing through a variety of modes of contact and timings of interaction. Much will, however, depend, as we indicated earlier, on the nature of the demand for skills within organizations, which will have a knock-on effect on the supply of e-learning materials and activities. It will also depend on where the development of learning technologies sits within an organization.

case study

Volunteers Together

The setting

The Third Sector consists of many thousands of community and voluntary sector groups that seek to serve a public or community purpose. These can range from well-known charities such as Oxfam and Barnardo's to smaller voluntary groups operating in local areas. A growing feature of the Third Sector includes businesses with social objectives, where profits or 'surpluses' are reinvested into community or environmental projects. Such social enterprises are seen as sources of socially and environmental responsible work that can raise the standards of ethical business.

Volunteers Together (VT) is a coordinating body for the Third Sector in a large city in the north of England. Located in a converted primary school close to the city centre, its status is guaranteed by a trust, although its day-to-day operations are in the hands of a Chief Officer (CO), two managers and five staff who all work on full-time contracts. In addition, there are around 30 volunteers. The overall task is to provide leadership and support for a wide range of Third Sector groups in the city, which before the 2008 recession numbered close to 5000. Since the recession, however, the number of groups has fallen to around 4000. The main reason for this has been a lack of funds and support, especially from the city council, which provides statutory funding. In addition, donations from private sources have suffered considerably.

The problem

At a recent strategic 'away day', all the staff worked on a new vision for VT – to ensure the development and sustainability of harmonious, thriving communities and neighbourhoods. This is to be achieved by:

- Ensuring that the value of the sector is recognized by strategic partners (both statutory and private) as being key to the development of a healthy, harmonious, sustainable city
- Striving to provide services that impact on the lives of the citizens by supporting and developing:
  - Community development, empowerment and engagement
  - Cooperative activity in neighbourhoods and communities
  - Environmental sustainability and respect for the local environment

Image Source Image Source/Bill Miles

  - Community-led organizations aimed at meeting local needs
  - Community ownership (of decisions and the allocation of resources)
  - Volunteers and volunteering opportunities
- Supporting the development and sustainability of community anchors in all neighbourhoods as the 'hubs' for the local delivery of support services.

One of the main outcomes to be achieved relates to how value and impact can be shown. In the discussions that followed between the CO and his full-time staff, they realized that much of this had to be done through the volunteers, who tended to be 'clueless' on issues relating to proving the value of money spent, or on responding to any formal mechanisms to share the ideas and knowledge that they had gained from working with the groups.

Volunteers tended to have their own way of working, based on lots of energy and goodwill towards the groups they favoured. In many cases, this meant spending more time with some groups and less time with others. It also meant avoiding any attempt to meet what they saw as

(continued)

'time targets'; after all, they were volunteers and unpaid, so it should be left to them to decide how time should be allocated to the groups and which groups should benefit from their attention.

They also established deep affection and friendships within certain groups. They would see such relationships as vital to their work, but also were unwilling to reveal too much about a group beyond the confines of the relationship. While the full-time VT staff were entitled to know some basic information, because such information could also be used to decide which groups should and should not receive support for their activities, the volunteers recognized they had to take care how much was revealed. However, the CO knew that VT's survival would rely on creating a flow of knowledge between those who worked with Third Sector groups and VT's full-time staff.

The assignment

Working in a group or on your own, help the CO consider how he can enhance OL in VT and beyond. You might consider the following questions:

1 To what extent can OL ideas help this organization?
2 How can knowledge gained by volunteers from their interactions become organizational knowledge?
3 How can learning and development activities help this organization to show the value and impact of its work?

Further reading

A useful source of reading for social enterprises is provided by Ridley-Duff, R. and Bull, M. (2016) *Understanding Social Enterprise*. London: Sage.

Note: This case study was written by Jeff Gold.

summary

➤ Most attempts to define HRD suggest that it has two purposes – first, to improve the performance of people, and second, to help people learn, develop and/or grow.

➤ There have been ongoing concerns about the UK's strategy for competing in knowledge-based economies based on high-level skills and talent.

➤ For HRD to become a feature of organizational strategy, senior managers must incorporate the need for learning into their consideration of trends and signals in the environment, such as changes in markets and technology. A strategy for HRD can often respond to organizational strategy by using competencies to set performance expectations and targets.

➤ Workplace learning casts a whole organization as a unit of learning and unifies the diverse set of influences and disciplines within HRD, such as training and organization development, knowledge and information systems.

➤ The creation of knowledge and its management are now considered as a source of competitive advantage. The economy has become knowledge-based, the basic idea being that knowledge becomes the key ingredient of products and services.

➤ HRD and training activities have an important part to play in implementing diversity policy through awareness programmes and skills-based development.

➤ NHRD concerns how a country views the contribution of skills towards its economic and social life; this finds expression in the policies and practices of the state, its agents and organizations.

➤ Decision-makers in organizations determine the demand for skills, taking a broadly human capital view that may lead to a restricted approach to HRD. In contrast, some organizations adopt a developmental humanist approach, which can lead to a greater focus on the potential of people for learning.

➤ The understanding of skills and how skills are defined is central to NHRD. Low skill levels among many workers remain a problem in the UK.

➤ A systematic approach to training is still preferred in many organizations; this emphasizes the need for cost-effective provision. Recent years have seen attempts to develop a more integrated approach that recognizes interdependencies with organizations, the importance of line managers and HRD professionals as business partners.

➤ The learning climate or learning environment in an organization greatly influences the effectiveness of its HRD policies, especially the relationships between managers and employees.

➤ To support HRD, managers have been encouraged to become coaches with a growing interest in developing the idea of a coaching culture or coaching organization. Coaching can provide a link between HRD activities, transfer to work and evaluation.

➤ Learning technologies materials and approaches may need to be blended with more traditional approaches for effectiveness. Mobile learning, or m-learning, is difficult for organizations to control.

review questions

1   What is meant by SHRD and how is it connected with organizational strategy?

2   What should be the role of government in HRD?

3   What are the requirements for effective learning at work?

4   Learning is a 'good thing' for everyone. Discuss.

5   What should be the role of managers in HRD?

6   How can organizations and individuals benefit from learning technologies?

applying the sociological imagination

Based on our rationale for what we have called Critical Human Resource Management Education, or 'CHRME', presented in Chapter 1, which uses the prism of Mills' sociological imagination to understand HRM-related 'troubles', answer the following question:

➤ Far too many jobs are low skilled and low paid, so require only basic training. How can the sociological imagination help you understand this problem?

further reading

Reading these articles and chapters can help you gain a better understanding and potentially a higher grade for your HRM assignment.

➤ Gedro, J., Collins, J. C. and Rocco T. S. (2014) The 'critical' turn: an important imperative for human resource development. *Advances in Developing Human Resources*, **16**(4): 529–35.

➤ Haynes, R. and Alagaraja, M. (2016) On the discourse of affirmative action and reservation in the United States and India: clarifying HRD's role in fostering global diversity. *Advances in Developing Human Resources*, **18**: 69–87.

➤ Keep, E. and Mayhew, K. (2010) Moving beyond skills as a social and economic panacea. *Work Employment & Society*, **24**(3): 565–77.

➤ McGuire, D. (2011) Foundations of human resource development. In McGuire, D. and Jorgenson, K. (eds) *Human Resource Development* (pp. 1–11). London: Sage.

➤ Shuck, M. B., Rocco, T. S. and Albornox, C. A. (2011) Exploring employee engagement from the employee perspective: implications for HRD. *Journal of European Industrial Training*, **35**(4): 300–25.

vocabulary checklist for ESL students

 Click here in your interactive ebook for a list of HRM terminology and vocabulary that has appeared in this chapter.

Visit the online resource centre at **www.palgravehighered.com/bg-hrm-6e** for lots of extra resources to help you get to grips with this chapter, including study tips, HRM skills development guides, summary lecture notes, tips for English as a Second Language (ESL) students and more.

EMPLOYMENT RELATIONS

259

part IV

EMPLOYMENT RELATIONS

chapter **8**

reward management and inequality

IMAGE SOURCE

objectives

After studying this chapter, you should be able to:

1 Explain the key objectives of reward management

2 Evaluate different approaches to reward that seek to align pay systems with an organization's business strategy

3 Explain the manner and extent to which pay influences employees' attitudes and behaviour

4 Define and evaluate different reward systems and structures related to the job, person and performance

5 Describe and evaluate job evaluation as a method for developing a pay system

6 Explain how governments and trade unions intervene in the pay determination process

7 Explain the importance of inequality in understanding reward management

8 Describe some paradoxes and tensions in pay systems in relation to managing the employment

When Britain's then-Chancellor George Osborne announced the new compulsory Living Wage during his 2015 budget speech, many political pundits applauded him. Eighteen years after passing the UK's National Minimum Wage Act 1998, tens of thousands of care workers are still being paid below the national minimum wage despite new regulations designed to ensure they are paid fairly (Merrill, 2016). In a damning government report, the billionaire owner of Sports Direct Mike Ashley was found to have broken the law by failing to pay staff the minimum wage (Goodley, 2016). Indeed, 70 per cent of households in Britain saw their incomes fall or remain stagnant in the decade after the financial and economic crisis that began in 2008 (Elliott, 2016). Yet CEOs' pay has been steadily rising, being, in 2016, 183 times the average UK employee, up from 160 times just six years before. This has prompted widespread reaction, including the Institute of Directors urging BP shareholders to think twice before supporting a decision to award £14 million to CEO Bob Dudley in a year when the oil company suffered its worst ever losses (Macalister, 2016). The debates around low pay and income inequality alongside exorbitant CEO executive pay are a reminder that HRM operates in an arena of continuous tension that is inherent in the generation of added value, and of society's moral values related to employment and disquiet about growing inequality.

introduction

Pay is the centerpiece of the employment relationship as it underscores the fact that the relationship constitutes an economic exchange (Arrowsmith et al., 2010), that is, the payment employees receive in exchange for their physical and/or mental effort. The more prescriptive approaches emphasize that employee reward (monetary and non-monetary), if managed correctly, can be an effective human resources (HR) tool to improve employee performance, motivation and satisfaction. Contemporary strategic human resource management (HRM) theory focuses on the challenges of integrating employee rewards into either 'best practice' or 'best fit' models. The concept of the psychological contract suggests that any 'incongruence' of expectation concerning the rewards employees receive when they join the organization can lead to a perceived violation of the contract (Rousseau and Ho, 2000). Critics of British pay systems point out that despite its centrality to employee well-being, the incidence of low-wage work is 'stubbornly high', and 'gender discrimination is strongly entrenched in pay practices in the UK' (Grimshaw and Rubery, 2010, p. 357).

This chapter provides a conceptual model for reviewing and understanding key developments in reward management. It considers the nature of rewards before examining pay levels and the legal and collective determination of pay. We conclude with a critical look at income inequality and the position of pay in the prescriptive HRM model, which reveals tensions and contradictions.

The nature of reward management

In the literature, the term 'compensation' is used as an alternative to 'reward' (Martocchio, 2015). Although both terms are problematic, we consider that the new vocabulary of 'reward management' best captures the 'new pay' paradigm in Britain, which focuses on the employee's market worth, flexibility and performance (Corby et al., 2009). Managers typically define reward as the package of monetary rewards (wages, salaries and benefits) that an employee receives, but employees generally define it even more narrowly as just the wage or salary received from the employer for their work. The reward function does not operate in isolation and has major knock-on effects on other HR policies and practices (Martocchio, 2015). To understand the crucial role that reward plays in managing the employment relationship, it is necessary to conceptualize it in its broadest sense.

An organization can provide two broad types of reward: *extrinsic* and *intrinsic*. Extrinsic rewards satisfy an employee's basic needs for survival, security and recognition, and derive from factors associated with the job context. This includes financial payments, working conditions and managerial behaviour. Intrinsic rewards refer to psychological 'enjoyment' and the satisfaction of 'challenge' (Bratton, 2015), sometimes called 'psychic income', that a worker derives from her or his paid work. These rewards derive from factors inherent in the way in which the work is designed, that is, the job content. Therefore, for our purposes, we will define reward in the following terms:

> Reward refers to a package of monetary, non-monetary and psychological payments that an organization provides for its employees in exchange for a bundle of valued work-related behaviours.

This definition draws attention to the multifaceted nature of the employment relationship, which involves complex, multiple exchanges. Reward is primarily but not exclusively the exchange of pay and other tangible monetary benefits, and possibly other intangible benefits such as a positive emotion (Kessler, 2007). The mix of extrinsic and intrinsic rewards provided by the employer is termed its *reward system*. The monetary element can be divided into pay, consisting of the employee's wages or salary, and non-pay benefits, including, for example, medical insurance and a pension. Combined pay and non-pay benefits constitute the *payment system*, but it is pay that has traditionally been the centrepiece of the reward system. The management of rewards must meet numerous economic and behavioural objectives (Figure 8.1).

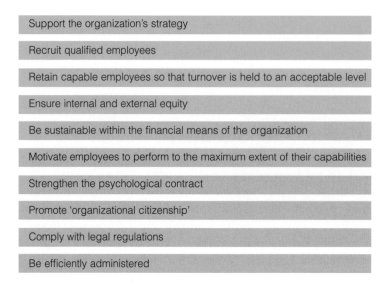

Support the organization's strategy

Recruit qualified employees

Retain capable employees so that turnover is held to an acceptable level

Ensure internal and external equity

Be sustainable within the financial means of the organization

Motivate employees to perform to the maximum extent of their capabilities

Strengthen the psychological contract

Promote 'organizational citizenship'

Comply with legal regulations

Be efficiently administered

Figure 8.1 *Objectives of the reward system*

The reward system consists of the integrated policies, processes, practices and administrative procedures for implementing the system within the framework of the HR strategy. A reward strategy comprises an organization's plan and actions pertaining to the mix and total amount of direct pay (for example, salary) and indirect monetary payments (benefits, shares) paid to various categories of employee. Two key questions pertain to any pay strategy: 'How should monetary payments be paid?' and 'How much should be paid?' The optimal choice ultimately depends on the objectives of the reward system. Reward may include at one extreme, direct pay only, and at the other extreme no pay whatsoever. In terms of the latter, it is easy to think, 'Who works for nothing?', but an increasing number of companies are using unpaid internships (Boffey, 2012) and many voluntary organizations, such as Oxfam, Médicins Sans Frontières and food banks, rely upon unpaid volunteers. The point here is that the amount of pay (extrinsic) reward needed to hire people will vary depending upon the availability of other (intrinsic) rewards that the organization offers (Long, 2010).

To fully understand the conceptual analysis of the place of rewards within an HR strategy, it is first necessary to recall the nature of the employment relationship, discussed in Chapter 1. We noted there that the wage–effort exchange is central to the employment relationship. All pay systems contain two elements that are in contradiction with each other:

- *Cooperation* between employee and employer or manager is an essential ingredient of the employment relationship if anything is to be produced. Cooperation is fostered through the logic of financial gain for the worker.
- *Conflict* is engendered through the logic that makes the 'buying' of labour the reward for one group and the cost for the other.

These two features of the employment contract mean that employees and those responsible for reward management have different objectives when it comes to monetary rewards. For employees, the pay cheque is typically the major source of personal income and hence a critical determinant of an individual's standard of living and social well-being. Employees constantly seek to maximize their pay because of inflation and rising expectations. The employer, on the other hand, is interested in the absolute cost of the rewards because of its bearing on profitability or cost-effectiveness. The importance of this varies with the type of organization. The relative labour costs in a petroleum refinery, for example, are minimal, whereas in healthcare they are substantial.

This fundamental tension underpinning the exchange makes the employment relationship unstable, and this

What are the rewards of voluntary service? Is monetary payment always necessary as a reward system?

IMAGE SOURCE / BILLMILES

employment relationship, in the context of global capitalism, is constantly being adjusted. Furthermore, the employees' contribution, or 'effort' itself, is 'a highly unstable phenomenon', and a payment system forms part of an array of managerial strategies to control the contribution or 'effort' of people (Baldamus, 1961; Watson, 2008). Unsurprisingly therefore, it has been conceded that the satisfactory management of pay is an essential, although not sufficient, condition of the satisfactory management of people (Brown, 1989).

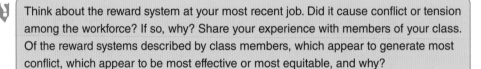

reflective question Think about the reward system at your most recent job. Did it cause conflict or tension among the workforce? If so, why? Share your experience with members of your class. Of the reward systems described by class members, which appear to generate most conflict, which appear to be most effective or most equitable, and why?

A model of reward management

To help us examine the complexities and principles underpinning the 'new pay agenda', we have developed a pay model that serves as both a framework for analysing reward management and a guide for the chapter (Figure 8.2). The model contains five basic building blocks:

- Strategy
- Reward objectives
- Reward options
- Reward techniques
- Reward competitiveness.

Our model shows first that reward management is linked to an organization's overarching strategic goals. *Strategy* focuses on those reward choices that support the organization's strategic goals. Going back to our discussion on corporate strategy (see Chapter 2), this means that each business strategy – and in this example we used Porter's (1980) typology of cost leadership and differentiation – should be supported by a different HR strategy, including a package of rewards – the principle of *strategic pay*.

Reward objectives

The *reward objectives* emphasize the linkage between a reward system and employees' attitudes and behaviours. There are three principal objectives that are desired by management – membership behaviour, commitment behaviour and performance behaviour – and seminal motivation theories suggest that the reward system can play an essential role in eliciting all three (Long, 2010). Financial rewards can stimulate desirable employee behaviours (for example, performance) and discourage unfavourable ones, such as absenteeism. Research suggests that rewards can have positive connotations for potential applicants and influence membership behaviour or recruitment (Kuhn, 2009, p. 1646). Commitment behaviour is an elusive construct and, depending on the writer's perspective, is discussed in terms of 'organizational citizenship behaviour' (Long, 2010) or 'compliance' and 'control of meaning', that is, psychosocial factors subject to manipulation by management (Thompson and McHugh, 2009).

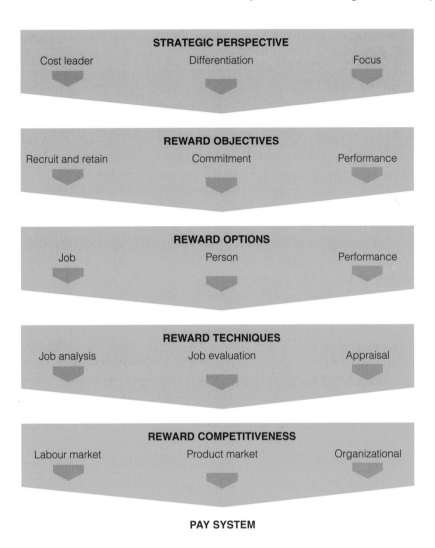

Figure 8.2 *A model for reward management*

Research on reward outcomes has two major shortcomings. First, the focus has traditionally been on financial rewards, whereas scholars have recently highlighted the added value of focusing on non-financial rewards (Hofmans et al., 2013). Second, reward theorists have traditionally attempted to unravel the reward–satisfaction relationship for the 'average' employee, thereby neglecting potential individual employee differences in this relationship (De Gieter and Hofmans, 2015).

Pay and employee behaviours lie at the heart of the employment relationship. People seek employment to earn money to live. In this context, pay theorists Gomez-Mejia et al. assert that 'money is the quintessence of all business language' (2010, p. 5). Although the incentivizing effect of money should never be underestimated (Boxall and Purcell, 2011, p. 207), especially for the 5.2 million workers in Britain earning less than a living wage (TUC, 2015), much organizational behaviour research has focused on the question 'Can money motivate employees?'

For managers, discovering what motivates different categories of employees is of the same magnitude as finding the Holy Grail (Bratton, 2015, p. 157). The different answers reflect a fundamental tension between economic and psychological theories of motivation. On the one hand, labour economists argue that pay incentives can achieve performance targets by paying more to spur extra effort ('tournament theory'). On the other hand, the primacy of money is challenged by social psychologists who have drawn attention to employees' 'hierarchy of needs' (Maslow, 1954), cognitive choices (Adams, 1965; Locke, 1968; Vroom, 1964) and importance of 'self-concept' (Fairholm, 1996; Leonard et al., 1999) as inner sources of energy that motivate 'non-calculative-based' workplace behaviour.

Sisodia et al. (2014) go as far as to assert that employees crave 'psychic income' as well as financial income: 'people want work that engages them wholly, that fulfills their emotional and social needs, that is meaningful – in short, work that is psychologically rewarding' (p. 62). Thus, the message for practitioners is that it is inappropriate to assume that all rewards have the same influence on the attitudes and behaviours of every individual employee. Studies demonstrate that financial rewards stimulate extrinsic but not intrinsic motivation (Deci and Ryan, 2000). De Gieter and Hofmans's (2015) study is individual-sensitive, finding support for the presence of individual differences in the relationship between satisfaction with different reward types and turnover intentions, but, importantly, not with task performance. Given the different schools of thought, it is not surprising that reward theorists disagree over the strength of the pay–performance link. Caruth and Handlogten (2001, p. 4) express the received wisdom of the reward–performance relationship thus:

> A compensation system that rewards employees fairly according to efforts expended and results produced creates a motivating work environment.

The research on performance behaviour highlights the importance of relationships between line managers and employees: what LMs do and how well they do it. Blinder's (1990, quoted by Kessler, 1995, p. 261) insightful conclusion is particularly helpful: 'Changing the way workers are treated may boost productivity more than changing the way they are paid.' Put another way, creating dignity *at* work (Bolton, 2007) may improve performance behaviour more than money does.

HRM web links

Visit the online resource centre at **www.palgravehighered.com/bg-hrm-6e** for a bonus HRM in practice feature on bargaining performance related-pay at Severn Trent Water.

Reward options

The third box of Figure 8.2 shows three *reward options*: job, person and performance. *Job-based* pay is a system whereby the level of pay, expressed in either hourly (waged) or fixed (salary), is assigned to the jobs that employees perform. Jobs of similar value to the organization are assigned to the same pay grades: the higher the value of the job, the higher the pay grade. In establishing the internal value of its jobs, an organization has to consider both external and internal labour market equity (Kessler, 2007). Job-based pay systems are considered to reinforce bureaucratic hierarchical structures, encourage a 'command and control' style of management, and be less compatible with team-based work systems (Guthrie, 2008).

HRM in practice 8.1

'Duvet days' or 'presenteeism'?

Getty Images/iStockphoto / Thinkstock Jason Stitt

The annual absence and workplace health survey for 2010 from the Confederation of British Industry (CBI) claimed that employee absence cost the UK an estimated £17 billion in 2009, with an average rate of absence of 6.4 days per employee. However, only a third of employers believed that all sickness absence was genuine. Such data underpin the regular accusations in the media about 'sicknote Britain', that British workers are inclined to use sickness absence as an excuse to enjoy a 'duvet day' off work.

Much of this popular discourse fails to distinguish between absence and 'absenteeism': it is the latter term that indicates *voluntary* absence – a deliberate decision to stay away. Absence on its own can be seen as an unlooked-for response to illness or family emergency. In industrial sociology, voluntary absence was traditionally seen as one manifestation of industrial conflict – one of the ways in which an individual worker, with no means of collectively remedying an unfavourable work situation, could balance the wage–effort equation by temporarily absenting him- or herself.

However, as Taylor et al. (2010) have demonstrated, this interpretation may no longer be valid, as government and management policies have become more stringent. Since the Statutory Sick Pay Act of 1994, management has been increasingly concerned with minimizing the cost of sickness absence, including sick pay, lost productivity and the cost of staff cover. The CBI literature emphasizes employee well-being policies and rehabilitation for those on long-term sick leave; case study research, however, indicates that company policies frequently use the 'Bradford factor' calculation, which penalizes multiple short-term sickness absences, and commonly feature return to work interviews following an illness. The result, argue Taylor et al., is that employees are now under pressure to attend work even if they are still ill, for fear of triggering disciplinary action.

In their detailed analysis of absence statistics, Taylor et al. demonstrate a series of fallacies behind the popular view of sickness absence. What the CBI terms 'non-genuine' absence accounts for only 12 per cent of the total days lost due to absence, and there is no evidence that 'sickies' are linked to long weekends or major sporting events. Indeed, rates of sickness absence have decreased over the past decade. International comparisons are tricky because of different bases for measurement, but UK sickness absence does not seem to rank particularly highly; where it is seen to be higher, this may have more to do with the British culture of long working hours rather than any predisposition to take time off.

Both government and employer data sets indicate that absence is more likely to occur in larger organizations and among female workers (especially single mothers), the young (short-term absences), older workers (long-term absences) and manual compared with professional grades. When absence figures are adjusted for age, gender and size of the organization, the discrepancy between rates for the public and private sectors virtually disappears. In addition, public sector workers seem more likely to display 'presenteeism' – continuing to work when ill – because of factors such as job insecurity, the lack of cover when absent and a sense of responsibility to service users.

Although managerial desire to reduce voluntary absence is understandable, the question raised by research is whether draconian sickness absence policies can prove counterproductive. Return to work interviews, while ostensibly about helping the employee, may, if conducted in a disciplinary fashion, contribute to a low-trust culture, the opposite of the stated goals of HRM. In addition, workers who continue to work while ill have been shown to contribute to productivity losses greater than those produced by absenteeism.

Stop! Should sickness absence policies give priority to employee well-being or to cost minimization?

Sources and further information: For further information, see Taylor et al. (2010).

Note: This feature was written by Chris Baldry.

Person-based pay is a system whereby pay is assigned to the breadth and/or depth of knowledge, formal qualifications, skills or competencies possessed by an individual employee. Under this type of pay regime, pay enhancements are awarded when employees are certified as having acquired additional knowledge, qualifications or skills that are of value to the organization. Research suggests that person-based pay systems are a 'better fit' with high-involvement work systems (Guthrie, 2008; Lawler, 2000).

Performance-based pay is a system tied to employees' 'effort' or performance. The performance might derive from the contributions of the individual or a team (Table 8.1). *Individual* pay is directly related to the individual's commitment of time, performance or a combination of both. *Team* pay systems have become more prevalent in Europe and North America with the popularity of high-performance work systems. *Organizational* pay, such as profit-sharing, is seen by managers as a way of increasing organizational performance through employee involvement in decision-making (Pendleton, 1997) and by encouraging stronger employee identification with the business (Long, 2010).

Table 8.1 Types of employee pay

Type of reward	Examples	Type of behaviour
Individual rewards	Basic wage overtime payments by results Commission merit pay or performance-related pay Benefits	*Time*: maintaining work attendance *Energy*: performing tasks *Competence and performance*: completing tasks without errors
Team rewards	Team or group bonus gain-sharing	*Cooperation*: with co-workers
Organizational rewards	Profit-sharing profit-related employee share incentive plan	*Commitment*: to strategic goals

reflective question If you are an employer, paying employees only when the desired performance takes place sounds like 'common sense'. Can you think of any circumstances in which individual-based performance pay would be advantageous or disadvantageous for a particular organization?

HRM web links Go to the online resource centre at **www.palgravehighered.com/bg-hrm-6e** for more information on team and profit-related pay systems.

There is considerable disagreement over the effects of pay on the performance of the individual or group. The argument involves fundamental issues of causality and the HR 'black box' problem (see Chapter 3). That said, different pay systems appear to encourage or reinforce different modes of behaviour. Payment-by-results (PBR) schemes, for example, encourage volume output, while profit-related pay schemes (for example, bonuses) may foster employees' loyalty and commitment (Kessler, 2007), and a team-based pay system may facilitate the sharing and creation of tacit knowledge and informal learning among team members (Kim and Gong, 2009). These alternative pay systems, which are explained later in the chapter, offer managers a choice of pay contingencies that best fits their organization.

Reward techniques

The fourth component is *reward techniques*. Job analysis and job evaluation highlight the importance attached to internal labour market equity, that is, the pay relationships between jobs within a single organization. *Job analysis* refers to the systematic process of collecting and evaluating information about the tasks, responsibilities and context of a specific job. The basic premise underlying job analysis is that jobs are more likely to be described, differentiated and equitably evaluated if accurate information is available to decision-makers (Milkovich et al., 2013). *Job evaluation* involves systematically comparing jobs in terms of their relative contributions to the organization's goals. We will examine job evaluation in more detail below. *Appraisal* is an HR practice used to evaluate a person's overall capabilities and potential, enabling informed decisions to be made for the purpose of performance. From differing perspectives, the practice has come under much critical scrutiny in recent years. Research shows that a reliance on 'subjective global ratings' for measuring employees' performance is 'notoriously subject to individual supervisory biases and political decisions' (Kepes et al., 2009, p. 525). Performance appraisal is examined in more detail in Chapter 6.

Reward competitiveness

The fifth component of the model is *reward competitiveness*. This draws attention to the importance of external equity and, by implication, why the organization needs to pay 'competitive' labour market rates for a given occupation. The organization has three options: to be a pay leader, to match the market rate or to lag behind what competitive organizations are paying. Kessler (2007, p. 167) argues that external equity is an 'imperative' if it is going to 'win the talent war' of attracting and retaining talented people. Research suggests that pay sends 'signals' to prospective applicants regarding the organization's values and culture (Barber and Bretz, 2000; Guthrie, 2008). Reward competitiveness has typically been analysed in terms of three contingencies: labour market, product market and organizational.

Labour market

The study of pay requires a context. Managers may typically be heard saying, 'Our pay levels are based upon the market.' In neo-classical economic theory, pay is the outcome of the forces of the demand for and supply of labour. Most markets, including labour, are not, however, perfect but have what economists call 'imperfections' on both the demand (for example, discrimination) and the supply (for example, membership of a professional body) side. Government actions affect both the demand and the supply of labour, and consequently pay. Legislation can, for example, restrict the supply of labour – a law setting minimum age limits would restrict the supply of young people. Government action can also affect the demand for labour. It is a major employer and therefore a dominant force in determining pay in and beyond the public sector, and government expenditure can affect consumer demand for goods and services and hence indirectly the labour market.

Product market

The degree of competition between producers and the level of the demand for products or services are two key product market factors affecting the ability of the firm to change the prices of its products and services. If prices cannot be changed without negative effects on revenue, the ability of the organization to pay higher rates is constrained. The product market factors thus set the limits within which the pay level can be established.

Organizational

Doeringer and Piore's (1971) classic study of internal labour markets explained that job evaluation and organizational culture and practice took precedence over external labour market information in shaping internal pay systems. In other words, they considered the implications of internal HR strategies for the overall functioning of the labour market (Grimshaw and Rubery, 2008, p. 79). One important critique of Doeringer and Piore's general theory is that they neglected to consider 'societal effects' on pay systems. Kessler (2007, p. 175) argues that 'real societal pressures … have propelled external and internal equity to the centre of the pay agenda'. In the UK, legislation on equal pay, the radically changed nature of labour markets, the 'collapse of collective bargaining' (Brown et al., 2009, p. 354), and the organization's own culture and HR practices shape pay structures (Corby et al., 2009). In many developed countries, the legal and collective determination of pay is a major element of the reward competitiveness part of the model and is examined below.

Job evaluation and internal equity

Pay equity requires that equal pay be paid for jobs of equal 'worth' or value to the organization, which academics argue is central in reward management (Gomez-Mejia et al. 2010, p. 5). Thus, traditional pay models emphasize the importance of internal equity, and the method most often used to establish and maintain internal constancies is job evaluation. Formal job evaluation is a generic label for a variety of processes used to establish pay structures by systematically comparing jobs in terms of their relative contributions to the organization's overarching goals (Egan, 2004; Milkovich et al., 2013). It can be defined as:

A systematic process designed to determine the relative worth of jobs within a single work organization.

The goal of job evaluation is to achieve internal equity by determining a hierarchy of jobs that is based on the relative contribution of each job to the organization. This hierarchy is then used to allocate rates of pay to jobs regardless of the employee working in that role. The importance to managers of job evaluation has increased because of equal pay legislation, which requires, either implicitly or explicitly, that gender-neutral job evaluation schemes be adopted and used to determine and compare the value of jobs within the organization.

Job evaluation is often misunderstood, so the following three characteristics of all formal job evaluation methods need to be emphasized:

- The technique is systematic rather than scientific: it depends on a series of subjective judgements.
- The premise that job evaluation is based on the worth of the job rather than on the worth of the employee in that particular job is fundamental (Risher, 1978; Welbourne and Trevor, 2000).
- The validity of the job evaluation process, or how accurately the method assesses job worth, is suspect (Collins and Muchinsky, 1993).

Building a hybrid at Samsung

Image Source

Globalization is often portrayed as a kind of hydraulic system: ideas and practices from developed countries somehow 'flow' to other parts of the world. According to this model, those on the receiving end of this 'flow' welcome the new practices from the West, assuming that their lives and their workplaces will improve as a consequence of new, and improved, ways of doing things.

Of course, the reality is exceptionally more complex than this, and to learn more about the challenges of exporting and importing HR practices, it is helpful to look closely at Samsung's approach to reward management. Widely recognized as a paradigm of success in the global economy, senior executives at Samsung knew that, to stay on top, they would have to think critically about the approaches to HR that had enabled them to succeed in the past. Company chairman Lee Kun-Hee anticipated that Koreans would not necessarily wholeheartedly welcome new management practices from the West. Strongly influenced by Japanese cultural values, Samsung placed considerable emphasis on Confucian respect for one's elders. However, given the choice between Western and Eastern approaches to reward management, Lee Kun-Hee refused to choose one over the other and instead opted for a hybrid approach blending the best of the West and the East.

But endorsing a hybrid ideal is one thing; implementing it is another. What makes it particularly difficult to introduce new management practices is that the practices already in existence tend to be embedded. For example, promotion on the basis of seniority is part of a cluster of related social practices, and it is difficult to call into question one element of the cluster without calling into question the whole cluster. Obviously, this kind of fundamental cultural challenge would be unacceptable to most Koreans. One of the keys to Kun-Hee's success was his flexible 'trial and error' approach. In some instances, Kun-Hee was willing to backtrack, to revert to the traditional Korean way when there was significant resistance to the Western way.

Stop! As a young HR graduate, you have an opportunity to spend a year in Korea interning at a company that produces various electronic devices. You are invited to participate in a group discussion in which the 'pros and cons' of seniority-based versus merit-based approaches to reward and promotion will be debated. How can you state your pro-merit position without offending the seminar's Korean participants? Can respect for competence and respect for one's elders be reconciled? Are national cultures homogenous? Is it possible that Korea has an indigenous cultural tradition that challenges patriarchal authority and values merit as much as seniority?

Sources and further information: For further information, see Khanna et al. (2011). Sociologist Talcott Parsons offered a classic statement of the notion of clusters of traits in his discussion of pattern variables. To learn more about pattern variables, go to Wikipedia's entry for Parsons and check out the web links at the end of the entry.

Note: This feature was written by David MacLennan.

Studies have suggested that formal job evaluation offers an opportunity for discretionary decision-making, with 'departmental power' thus affecting the outcome (Welbourne and Trevor, 2000). A critical perspective also emphasizes the fact that job evaluation ratings are often gender-biased by, for example, giving a higher weighting to physical demands and continuous service, which tend to favour men, and by the gender linkage of job titles. In one study, for example, evaluators assigned significantly lower ratings to jobs with a female-stereotyped title, such as 'secretary', than to the same job with a more gender-neutral title, for example 'assistant' (McShane, 1990).

Job evaluation is not scientific, but it can bring a degree of objectivity to the decision-making process. Most organizations use 'analytical' job evaluation – in which jobs are broken down into individual elements (Egan, 2004) – involving four steps:

1 Gathering the data
2 Selecting compensable factors
3 Evaluating the job
4 Assigning pay to the job.

Let us look at each of these in turn.

Gathering the job analysis data

Information must be collected via a method of job analysis, and validity should be a guiding principle in this first step. The job analyser must accurately capture all the job's content because ambiguous, incomplete or inaccurate job descriptions can result in jobs being incorrectly evaluated.

Selecting compensable factors

Compensable factors are the factors the organization chooses to reward through differential pay. The most typical compensable factors are skill, effort, knowledge, responsibility and working conditions.

Evaluating the job

There are four fundamental methods of job evaluation:

- Ranking
- Job-grading
- Factor comparison
- The point method.

The latter is the most commonly used evaluation technique. For comparison purposes, we will provide brief descriptions of the other methods but will focus here on the point method.

In *ranking*, jobs are ordered from the least to the most valued in the organization, this rank order or hierarchy of jobs being based on a subjective evaluation of relative value. In a typical factory, we might finish up with the rank order shown in Table 8.2; in this example, the evaluators have agreed that the job of inspector is the most valued of the six jobs listed. Rates of pay will then reflect this simple hierarchy. This method has a number of advantages: it is simple, fast and inexpensive. The ranking method will be attractive for small organizations and for those with a limited number of jobs. Obvious disadvantages are that it is crude and entirely subjective; the results are therefore difficult to defend, and legal challenges might make the approach costly.

Table 8.2 *Typical job-ranking*

Job title	Rank
	Most valued
1. Forklift driver	1. Inspector
2. Machinist	2. Machinist
3. Inspector	3. Secretary
4. Secretary	4. Forklift driver
5. File clerk	5. Labourer
6. Labourer	6. File clerk
	Least valued

Job-grading, or job classification, works by placing jobs in a hierarchy or series of job grades. It is decided in advance how many grades of pay will be created, the jobs falling into each grade being based on the degree to which the jobs possess a set of compensable factors. The lowest grade will be defined as containing those jobs that require little skill and are closely supervised. With each successive grade, skills, knowledge and responsibilities increase. Grade A will, for example, include jobs that require no previous experience, are under immediate supervision and need no independent judgement. Grade F, however, will contain jobs that require apprenticeship training under general supervision with some independent judgement. In our example in Table 8.2, the file clerk and the machinist might be slotted into grades A and F, respectively. The advantage of this method is that it is relatively simple, quick and inexpensive. A disadvantage is that complex jobs are difficult to fit into the system, as a job may seem to have the characteristics of two or more grades.

Factor comparison evaluates jobs on the basis of a set of compensable factors. Internal jobs are compared with each other across several factors, such as skill, mental effort, responsibility, physical effort and working conditions. For each job, the compensable factors are ranked according to their relative importance in each job. Once each bench-mark job has been ranked on each factor, the decision-maker allocates a monetary value to each factor. This is typically done by deciding how much of the pay rate is associated with skill requirement, how much with mental effort and so on across all the compensable factors.

In a typical job ranking system like the one in Table 8.2, this forklift driver is neither the most valued nor the least valued employee. How fair do you think this ranking method is?

The main disadvantage of this approach is that it is complex, and translating a factor comparison into actual pay rates is a cumbersome exercise. Because of its complexity, it is used less frequently than the other methods.

The *point method* is the most frequently used of the four techniques. Like the factor comparison method, it develops separate scales for each compensable factor in order to establish a hierarchy of jobs. But instead of using monetary values, points are assigned. Each job's relative value, and hence its location in the pay structure, is determined by adding up the points assigned to each compensable factor.

The exercise starts with the allocation of a range of points to each compensable factor. Any number between 1 and 100 points might be assigned to each factor. Next, each of the factors is given a weighting, which is an assessment of how important one factor is in relation to another. In the case of the machinist, for example, if skill is felt to be twice as important as working conditions, it is assigned twice as many points (20 versus 10). The results of the evaluation might look like those displayed in Table 8.3. The point values allocated to each compensable factor are then added up across factors, allowing jobs to be placed in a hierarchy according to their total point value. In our example in Table 8.3, this would mean that the machinist's wage rate would be twice that of the labourer. Such a differential might be unacceptable, but this difficulty can be overcome by tailoring the job evaluation scheme to the organization's pay policy and practical objectives.

The advantage of the point system is that it is relatively stable over time and, because of its comprehensiveness, is more acceptable to the parties involved. Its shortcomings include a high administrative cost, which might be too high to justify its use in a small workplace. A variation of the point system is the widely used 'Hay plan', which employs a standard point matrix applicable across organizational and national boundaries. Decision-makers should, however, be aware that, as far as job evaluation is concerned, there is no perfect system because the process involves subjective judgement.

Table 8.3 Point system matrices

Job title	Factor					
	Skill	Mental effort	Responsibility	Physical effort	Working conditions	Total
Forklift driver	10	10	10	10	5	45
Machinist	20	15	17	8	10	70
Inspector	20	20	40	5	5	90
Secretary	20	20	35	5	5	85
File clerk	10	5	5	5	5	30
Labourer	5	2	2	17	9	35

Assigning pay to the job

The final outcome of the evaluation exercise is a hierarchy of jobs in terms of their relative value to the organization. Assigning pay to this hierarchy of jobs is referred to as 'pricing the pay structure' and requiring a policy decision on the pay structure in the organization. Despite its reported demise, job evaluation is 'alive and kicking in the public sector, driven in large part by concern about pay for work of equal value' (Corby et al., 2009, p. 8).

 HRM web links   Go to the online resource centre at **www.palgravehighered.com/bg-hrm-6e** for published pay surveys.

Establishing pay structure and levels

This section examines two aspects of pay structure: *pay dispersion* and the *basis of the pay level*. Pay structures can range from a relatively flat or 'egalitarian' pay distribution, with limited differences across levels and jobs or positions, to pay distributions that are 'hierarchical', displaying wide differences across levels and positions. Pay survey data appear to show a trend towards pay structures that are hierarchical and 'tournament-like' – high pay for a few at the top of the pay structure and low pay for the vast majority at the bottom (Guthrie, 2008; Hutton, 2015a; Piketty, 2014; Stiglitz, 2015). UK earnings statistics show that, in 2014, the median annual UK wage for full-time employees was £27,271 (£25,635 for women). The chief executives of FTSE 100 companies, on the other hand, have seen their remuneration more than quadruple between 2000 and 2014. Average CEO pay was £4.9 million in 2014 up from £4.129 million in 2013. We look at the 'tournament-like' pay phenomenon in more detail when we examine income inequality below.

With respect to the basis of the pay level, any job reflects its relative and absolute worth. A job's relative worth to the organization is determined by its ranking through the job evaluation process, whereas its absolute worth is influenced by what the labour market pays for similar jobs. In Britain, since the 2008 global recession, the issue of pay and the value we assign to it has become particularly divisive.

reflective question Thinking about the average UK wage in relation to the pay for selected occupations, what do the various pay scales suggest about the value we assign to jobs? What is a job worth? Is gender important in valuing jobs?

Table 8.4 shows the value we assign to a range of occupations. To answer the question 'How do organizations assign a pay rate?', most organizations rely on pay surveys of 'benchmark' jobs. The data from these are used to anchor the organization's pay scale, other jobs then being slotted in on the basis of their relative worth to the organization.

Table 8.4 UK salaries for selective occupations and CEOs, 2014

Über-salary earners	Frank Chapman, British Gas	£28.00 million
	Bob Diamond, Barclays	£27.00 million
	Mick Davies, Xstrata	£27.00 million
	Bob Dudley, BP	£14.00 million
	Willie Walsh, BA	£6.40 million
Over £40,000	IT director	£80,215
	Air traffic controller	£75,416
	Medical practitioner	£69,463
	Police inspector	£58,533
	HE teaching professional	£40,054
£30,000–£40,000	Social services director	£39,698
	Paramedic	£36,771
	Crane driver	£35,458
	Coalminer	£33,102
	Probation officer	£30,026

£20,000–£30,000	Primary teacher	£29,908
	Web designer	£29,856
	Midwife	£29,529
	Nurse	£26,252
	Forklift truck driver	£21,345
Under £20,000	Refuse collector	£19,945
	Bank clerk	£19,557
	Van driver	£18,322
	Chef	£17,513
	Teaching assistant	£11,916

Sources: Office for National Statistics (2015), © Crown copyright; Macalister (2016) and Topham (2015), courtesy of Guardian News & Media Ltd.

In determining the pay level, an organization will have to combine the results of the job evaluation process (internal equity criteria) and labour market data (external competitiveness criteria) on a graph, as depicted in Figure 8.3. The horizontal axis depicts an internally consistent job structure based on job evaluation, each grade being made up of a number of jobs (A–O) within the organization. The jobs in each category are considered equal for pay purposes – they have about the same number of points. Each grade has its own pay range defining the lower and upper limits of pay for jobs in that grade, and all the jobs within the grade have the same range. Jobs in grade 1 (that is, jobs A, B and C), for example, have lower points and pay range than jobs in grade 2 (D, E and F). The actual minimum and maximum pay rates paid by the organization's competitors are established by survey data. Individual levels of pay within the range may reflect differences in performance or seniority. As depicted, organizations can structure their rate ranges to overlap a little with adjacent ranges so that an employee with experience or seniority might earn more than an entry-level person in the pay grade above.

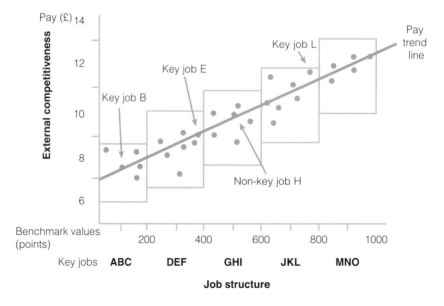

Figure 8.3 *The construction of a pay level*

Each dot on the graph in Figure 8.3 represents the intersection of the going pay rate (the vertical axis), as determined by the pay survey, and the point value (horizontal axis) for a particular benchmark job. Key jobs B, E and L are, for example, worth 100, 375 and 750 points respectively and are paid £7.50, £9.00, and £11.80 an hour. A pay trend line is drawn through the dots, as close to as many points as possible, using a statistical technique called the least squares method. The pay trend line serves as a reference line around which pay structures and rates are established for non-benchmark jobs in the organization.

There are two steps in this process. The first step is to locate the point value for the non-benchmark job on the horizontal axis; the second is to trace the line vertically to the pay trend line and then horizontally to the pay scale. The amount on the vertical axis is then the appropriate pay rate for the non-benchmark job. Non-benchmark job H is, for example, worth 500 points. By tracing a vertical line up to the pay trend line and then horizontally to the vertical pay scale in Figure 8.3, it can be seen that the appropriate pay rate for job H is £10.00 per hour. Thus, both market survey information and job evaluation translate the concepts of external competitiveness and internal equity into pay practices.

Once a pay trend line has been established, management has three choices: to *lead* the competition, to *match* what other organizations are paying or to *lag* behind what competitors are paying their employees – establishing a lag or lead policy by shifting the pay trend line down or up. The least-risk approach is to set the pay level to match that of the competition, although some organizations may set different pay policies for different categories of employee with different skill sets. An organization could, for example, adopt a 'lead' policy for jobs critical skills, such as computer design engineers, a 'match' policy for less critical skill sets and a 'lag' policy for jobs that could be easily filled in the local labour market.

The construction of a pay structure, as depicted in Figure 8.3, using both equity (job evaluation) and labour market data (pay surveys) presents a largely deterministic view of reward management (Gomez-Mejia et al. 2010, p. 13). This prescriptive approach has been questioned in a number of related ways. First, research confirms considerable divergent pay practices between and within organizations. In 2010, 40 per cent of UK organizations (729 respondents) used labour market rates (rather than a job evaluation database) to determine pay levels (Chartered Institute of Personnel and Development [CIPD], 2010e). Gomez-Mejia et al. (2010) report that it is not unusual to find 3 to 1 differences in pay level for identical job titles in the same labour market. Second, external and internal equity considerations are 'largely inappropriate' in terms of upper management pay and scientific professionals (Gomez-Mejia et al. 2010, p. 14). Third, the pay issues and challenges found in each organization are typically unique and less structured than traditional models suggest. As Gomez-Mejia et al. observe, 'considerable creativity is required to synthesize large amounts of external and internal information and to develop a pay policy (p. 13). Thus, while guided by external and internal equity considerations, the organization's pay policy will be determined by many factors, including HR strategy, work design and organizational values and norms. Finally, prescriptive pay models neglect 'societal effects' and wider socioeconomic, political and cultural factors, which shape – if not determine – pay practices.

Internships in Australia: valuable experience or exploitation?

While there are many reasons for working, the need to earn money is certainly a common one. Historically, many young workers have volunteered their time with community groups or taken paid internships with companies to gain the experience and skills necessary to land a job. Recently, there has been an international trend towards unpaid internships. Essentially, students and recent graduates perform work (that normally would earn them a pay cheque) for free in the hope of getting a leg up.

In early 2015, Australia's Federal Circuit Court fined employer Crocmedia $24,000 for breaching minimum wage conditions. Crocmedia had already made restitution for paying the two interns at the heart of the case in the sums of AU$19,341 and AU$5767. Prior to the case, the interns had received wages of AU$2940 and nothing respectively. Another intern reported discovering that she would be forced to sign away her occupational health and safety rights if she accepted an internship (Ma, 2015).

The growth in unpaid internships has multiple explanations. The root cause is that employers in capitalist economies face profound pressure to maximize profitability. Unpaid workers can dramatically reduce labour costs and contribute to that goal. At the same time, youth unemployment rates are high (approximately 13 per cent in Australia), leading many young people to take any advantage or opportunity available to them in a poor job market. One Australian law firm went so far as to charge unpaid interns AU$22,000 for the privilege of working for nothing!

In a case of 'being a day late', Australia's productivity commission warned, in August of 2015, that it was concerned that some employers might be tempted to use unpaid interns to complete the work that would normally be done by paid workers. Against the need to regulate such arrangements, it said, was the fact that unpaid interns had little incentive to stay with an employer if the employer was not providing the interns with something of value (Han, 2015).

The notion that internships are a choice is a tricky one. Workers are certainly choosing to take unpaid internships. But employers may be constraining the range of choices available to those workers via hiring practices that select candidates with such work experience on their résumé. Furthermore, the 'choice' rationale ignores the potential for exploitation – in the form of long hours and dangerous working conditions – that comes with unregulated work.

The analysis of unpaid internships in Canada suggests that they have a negative impact on the overall economy, contributing to youth unemployment. Unpaid internships also appear to be shifting from traditional occupations – medicine and skilled trades – into traditionally female-dominated occupations. That is, these internships may be further disadvantaging young women, who already face a significant wage gap should they become employed. There is also some suggestion that the educational aspect of these internships is giving way to employers simply using interns as a source of free labour (Langille, 2013).

From a social justice perspective, internships raise many troubling questions. Yet HR practitioners may face significant organizational pressure to incorporate unpaid interns because they can significantly lower labour costs. An important question to ask is whether the apparent costs of using unpaid labour are offset by the additional supervisory workload as well as the heightened risk of error by untrained staff and possible harm to the company's reputation should their unpaid internships attract bad press.

Stop! In what circumstances might you accept an unpaid internship? And, if you were an HR practitioner, in what circumstances might you offer one? What would your primary motivation be for doing so? What would be the risks of such a decision?

Sources and further information: For background information, see Han (2015), Langille (2013) and Ma (2015).

Note: This feature was written by Bob Barnetson.

The legal and collective determination of pay

In European Union member states and North America, employment legislation directly affects employees' pay (see Table 1.1 for an outline of the key legislation related to pay). In addition, pay and conditions of employment are determined through collective bargaining.

Equal Pay and National Minimum Wage legislation are two examples of the legal determination of rewards. *Equal pay* legislation has existed in the UK for over three decades, but its origins can be traced back to 1919 when the International Labour Organization (ILO) made the concept of equal pay for work of equal value one of its founding principles. Then, in 1951, the ILO passed Convention 100: 'Each member shall ... ensure the application to all workers of the principle of equal remuneration for men and women workers for work of equal value.' In 1972, the UK became bound to Article 19 of the EU's Treaty of Rome, which stated that 'Each member state shall ... maintain the application of the principle that men and women should receive equal pay for equal work.' The Equal Pay Act 1970 inserts into contracts of employment an implied term, the 'equality clause'. This enforces equal terms in the contract of employment for women in the same employment, requiring the elimination of less favourable terms where men and women are employed on similar work and where a job evaluation assessor has rated the work as equivalent in the same employment. In the case of the UK however, it remains to be seen whether equal pay legislation will change as a result of Brexit.

HRM web links   Go to the online resource centre at www.palgravehighered.com/bg-hrm-6e to find details of a film on the campaign for equal pay for women.

Despite the existence of equal pay legislation in the UK since 1975, the income disparity between men and women is still widely acknowledged (Grimshaw and Rubery, 2010). In 2014, the gender gap was 9.4 per cent, although this is the lowest since records began in 1997. The gender–pay dynamics that produce the pay gap are complex and are, as indicated, rooted in societal values and norms as well as in management practices and the organization's culture. In all developed countries, for example, women, especially mothers, work fewer paid hours than their spouses. The magnitude of the gender gap varies significantly by country, ranging from 2 to 20 hours per week (Landivar, 2015). In the workplace, there is gender bias in job evaluation and a 'masculine logic' (Fletcher, 1999) of effectiveness operating that leads to the undervaluing of many jobs, both full time and part time, that are associated with female labour. Pay inequality is also shaped by the degree of occupational sex segregation, that is, the gap between the types of job performed by men and those performed by women, which is acknowledged to be an important source of gender discrimination in pay practices (see, for example, Grimshaw and Rubery, 2010). Research by the UK's CIPD in 2015 (CIPD, 2015f) found that only 25 per cent of employers had performed any analysis of whether they were paying women as much as men, ahead of new rules (Equality Act 2010 (Gender Pay Gap Information) Regulations 2016) that will compel organizations to publish data on their gender pay gap (Davies, 2016). With such a tardy response by companies to act on the gender pay gap, it is perhaps unsurprising that the ILO recently forecast that, globally, this will not close until 2085 (Topping, 2015, p. 1).

HRM web links   Go to the online resource centre at **www.palgravehighered.com/bg-hrm-6e** to compare men's and women's pay levels.

In the UK, the Labour government introduced a statutory national minimum wage of £3.60 an hour in April 1999, which, for adults, had reached over 80 per cent higher in October 2014. In 2015, then-Chancellor George Osborne introduced plans for a new compulsory minimum wage for over-25s – the 'National Living Wage' – which will increase hourly pay for about 6 million of the UK's 31 million workers. The new national living wage was set at £7.20 an hour in April 2016, due to rise to 60 per cent of median hourly earnings by 2020 (O'Connor, 2015). Since 1999, however, there have been reports of enforcement and of non-compliance among employers of migrant workers (Colling, 2010), apprentices, social care, unpaid interns and seafarers (Low Pay Commission, 2015), and research suggests that employment equity laws in the private sector have failed to deal with low pay resulting from discrimination against visible minorities (Friesen, 2011). Over the last two decades, the national minimum wage has extended legal regulation into payment systems, and it is now possible to argue that the protection of low-wage employees increasingly relies on legal rights rather than collective bargaining (Dickens and Hall, 2010).

reflective question   It has been pointed out by some that minimum wage regulations increase the cost of doing business and cause unemployment. What do you think of this argument? Go to www.fraserinstitute.ca and www.clc-ctc.ca for contrasting views on this issue.

HRM web links   Go to the online resource centre at **www.palgravehighered.com/bg-hrm-6e** to find more information on employment legislation in different countries and evidence of discrimination in recruitment practices.

The collective determination of pay and conditions of employment takes place in most developed economies through collective bargaining. The framework within which negotiations over pay take place can be either at the level of the workplace, at corporate level or at industry level. Although collective bargaining is a very complex phenomenon depending on underlying cost structures, strategy and power (see Chapter 9), much of the focus is on bilateral negotiations between the employer and union(s) over pay and conditions of employment. In the UK, between 1945 and the 1980s, the collective determination of pay was dominant. Since the 1990s, unlike other member states in the European Union albeit not unique to the UK, collective bargaining over pay has collapsed for employees in the private sector (see Chapter 9). This means that pay arrangements for a vast majority of workers in the private sector are determined unilaterally by management, an important factor, it is argued, in explaining the UK's high incidence of low-paid work (Grimshaw and Rubery, 2010).

HRM in practice 8.2

Is the statutory national living wage a departure from a deregulated labour market?

Conservative governments of the 1980s and 90s pursued policies designed to deregulate the labour market. Neo-liberal theories assume that economies are more successful if employers can take decisions free from the constraints of government intervention such as employment protection legislation and the power of trade unions to negotiate wages and working conditions. The New Labour government elected in 1997 halted the momentum of deregulation through the minimum wage, the strengthening of some trade union rights and the adoption of European directives that limited the length of the working week. The Coalition government of 2010–15 continued to attack regulations on the free market such as restricting the scope of employment protection laws (Noon et al., 2013).

Collective bargaining declined from 60 per cent of UK workplaces in the 1980s to 29 per cent in 2012 (European Trade Union Institute, 2015). The reasons for this change are partly the product of anti-union laws but also the decline of manufacturing, which reduced the membership and influence of trade unions. Globalization, increased competition and the privatization of many state-controlled industries further contributed to the decline in the influence of trade unions.

In April 2013, 5.2 million, or 22 per cent, of employees were low paid (up to £7.69 an hour) – when measured in terms of hourly wages, this was below two-thirds of the gross median hourly pay of all employees (Corlett and Whittaker, 2014). Alongside a national minimum wage, a strategy to improve employees' living standards was to supplement low wages with tax credits. However, as the number in low-paid jobs increased, welfare payments became burdensome and the payment of a supplementary income to the low paid was seen as a subsidy to employers who paid low wages. Large numbers of low-paid workers provide a problem for capitalism as they depress both tax revenue and the demand for goods.

In a surprise announcement in the summer budget of 2015, the Conservative government announced that the minimum wage (then £6.50 per hour) would be replaced by a national living wage starting at £7.20 in April 2016 and rising to at least £9 by 2020. One in 50 employees were entitled to the minimum wage when it was set at a low level in 1999, and by 2015 the number earning the minimum wage had increased to one in 20. According to

Image Source/Image Source/Bjarte Rettedal

research by the Resolution Foundation (quoted in Elliott, 2015, courtesy of Guardian News & Media Ltd), the new national living wage would greatly increase the proportion of workers whose wages were set by the state to more than 10 per cent of the UK workforce by 2020:

> It will mean that around one in seven private sector workers will have their pay directly set by the government by 2020 ....The Resolution Foundation report found that in some regions – the north-east, East Midlands and Wales – one in seven workers would be on the minimum wage by 2020. In the hospitality sector, 40% of employees will be earning the wage, while women and older workers are also particularly likely to be affected.

The role of the government in setting a statutory pay floor seems to be a major departure from a deregulated labour market.

Stop! HRM has been seen as bypassing collective bargaining, and remuneration policy has been part of the HRM function to secure employee commitment. Do you think the government has taken over pay policy?

Sources and further information: See Corlett and Whittaker (2014), Elliott (2015), European Trade Union Institute (2015) and Noon et al. (2013) for background information. You can read more about the work of the Resolution Foundation online, at http://www.resolutionfoundation.org/.

Note: This feature was written by David Denham.

The strategic pay paradigm

The 'new pay agenda', with its focus on aligning reward with corporate strategy, caught the zeitgeist (Corby et al., 2009): the espoused theory of strategic pay starts with corporate strategy and work design. It is predicated on the notion of 'strategic choice', which involves managers choosing a pay system that is judged through rational deliberation to be the most fitting (Trevor, 2009). Key to this argument is the assumption that the closer the alignment or 'fit' between the pay system and corporate strategy, the more effective the organization (see, for example, Gomez-Mejia et al., 2010; Mintzberg et al., 1998; Pfeffer, 1998). Pfeffer (1998, p. 99) explained the notion of alignment like this:

> The diagnostic framework is premised on the idea of alignment, that is, that an organization does specific things to manage the employment relationship and these practices need to be first, internally consistent or aligned with one another, and second, externally consistent, in the sense that the organization's procedures produce behaviours and competencies required for it to compete successfully given its chosen marketplace and way of differentiating itself in that marketplace.

Let us illustrate the 'strategic' approach to reward with an example involving two organizations with two different corporate strategies and completely different payment systems. Precision Engineering produces high-quality, customized machine tools for the aerospace industry. The manufacturing process is organized around self-managed work teams. Rather than pay an hourly wage rate to the skilled machine operators, which is the industry norm, the company pays a base salary, additional pay being awarded if the workers learn new skills. All employees receive an excellent benefits package and profit-sharing bonuses based on company profits. Labour costs at Precision Engineering are above the industry average. The culture at Precision Engineering encourages informal workplace learning, and, not surprisingly, labour turnover is extremely low.

Seafresh Foods, in contrast, operates a plant that produces fish fingers. The work is organized around a conveyor belt, with workers stationed along the assembly line performing each step in the process, from gutting the fish to packaging. The work requires little training and is monotonous. The process workers at Seafresh Foods are paid an hourly wage rate that is 10 per cent above the minimum wage, and there are no additional payments or benefits. Labour turnover exceeds 100 per cent a year.

reflective question Think about the business strategy and reward systems at these two companies. How can Precision Engineering compete when it pays above the industry average? And how can Seafresh Foods survive with such a high turnover? Go back to Chapter 2 and look again at the 'integrative model'.

The strategic approach would suggest that, despite the two completely different payment systems at Precision Engineering and Seafresh Foods, both are effective (Long, 2010) – each payment system is aligned with the firm's business strategy. Again, using Porter's (1980) typology – differentiation and cost leadership – Precision Engineering is following a differentiation competitive strategy, with a focus on high-quality machine tools. Owing to the complexity of the production process, high-skilled workers are given a considerable amount of autonomy. The pay system (base pay, benefits and pay-for-knowledge) therefore supports the 'high-commitment' HR strategy (see, for example, Guest, 1997). Is this altruism or good business? Precision Engineering's pay system is good business for the following reasons:

- There is higher productivity resulting from increased functional flexibility.
- A highly skilled and flexible workforce reduces machine downtime and scrap rates.
- The use of self-managed work teams eliminates the amount paid to supervisors and quality control inspectors as team members undertake these tasks for themselves.
- Low turnover means that recruitment and training costs are reduced.

In contrast, Seafresh Foods depends for its survival on following a cost leadership strategy (in which low-cost production is essential). This competitive strategy requires low-skilled employees and little employee commitment because managers exert control using technology (the speed of the assembly line). Labour turnover is high, but unskilled workers are easy to recruit and training costs are low. At Seafresh Foods, the reward system (only a near-minimum wage) supports a 'traditional low-commitment' HR strategy. The business cases for paying a wage rate higher than the market rate, for egalitarian pay structures and for superior benefits to employees is illustrated by a study comparing Costco Wholesale Corporation to its fierce rival Sam's Club, a division of Wal-Mart Stores. For Costco, a wage rate 42 per cent higher than the rate at Sam's Club 'translates into more efficiency' (Guthrie, 2008, p. 344).

The strategic approach has been used as an analytical tool for explaining developments in and factors influencing the choice of pay systems over the last two decades. The multiple competitive demands, for example deregulation, global cost pressures and flexible work methods, explain why managers may choose a PBR pay scheme based on individual performance. In contrast, where the product market requires a high-quality manufacturing strategy, they may choose a pay-for-knowledge and profit-sharing scheme. As Corby and her colleagues (2009, p. 7) note, one major objective of the 'new pay' paradigm is the 'individualization of reward packages, an objective that fits with a wider social decline in collectivism'. The current literature on the 'new pay agenda' has emphasized the need for organizations to adopt 'good' reward practices that encourage a constellation of attitudes and behaviours meeting the perceived needs of the contemporary workplace, as illustrated in Table 8.5.

Table 8.5 *Alignment of business strategy, work design and reward practices*

Bureaucratic 'old' job-based pay model	Post-bureaucratic 'strategic' pay model
Base wage or salary	Variable pay
Based on cost of living and labour market	Based on organizational performance
Evenly distributed between employees	Differentiated
Correlated with seniority	Based on individual performance
Based on individual performance	Based on team (unit) and organizational performance
Viewed as a result of behaviour values	Used as a means of communicating

Source: Reprinted by permission of Harvard Business School Press. From The Human Equation: Building Profits by Putting People First by Jeffrey Pfeffer. Boston, MA 1998 p. 116. Copyright © 1998 by the Harvard Business School Publishing Corporation; all rights reserved.

In the 1990s, the basic premise of the strategic approach to pay argued that the pay system should be aligned to the organization's business strategy. Pay can therefore be a strategic 'lever' to improve organizational performance. As two American reward theorists, Gomez-Mejia and Balkin, explain (1992, p. 4):

> The emerging paradigm of the (pay) field is based on a strategic orientation where issues of internal equity and external equity are viewed as secondary to the firm's need to use pay as an essential integrating and signalling mechanism to achieve overarching business objectives.

A reward management survey by the CIPD (cited by Kessler, 2007, p. 162) reported that, among organizations with a reward strategy, almost 80 per cent indicated that 'supporting business goals' was their principal reward objective. In 2010, it was reported that 35 per cent of UK organizations (729 respondents) responding to a CIPD survey had a written reward strategy (CIPD, 2010e). These findings appear to give support to Gomez-Mejia and Balkin's statement.

Variable pay schemes in UK workplaces

Despite the simplicity of the title 'variable pay scheme' (VPS), this pay practice has been defined in different ways and comes in many guises. Lazear (2000, p. 410) defines variable pay as 'pay that is tied to some measure of worker output'. Historically, the most typical form of variable pay was merit pay or *performance-related pay* (PRP). The principle of PRP can be characterized by the linking of an individual employee's pay increase to an appraisal process. As part of the new pay agenda, PRP has moved away from subjective assessments based on individual behavioural traits (individual inputs) towards those assessed against an objective criterion (that is, individual outputs). PRP has also been extended from managerial and professional occupations downwards to other job categories in general. The contemporary PRP scheme, it is claimed, is based solely on performance and tied more closely to the overall objectives of the organization.

Kessler and Purcell (1992) characterize PRP as a means of translating and signalling market-based organizational goals into personalized performance criteria. PRP is not to be confused with PBR pay schemes. Van Wanrooy et al. (2013a) explain the difference between these two similar pay schemes. Whereas PRP is determined through a *subjective* assessment of individual performance by a manager, PBR is measured according to *objective* criteria – the amount done or its value, rather than the hours worked (2013a, p. 95). Another pay incentive scheme is profit-related pay, which links part or whole of employees' pay to the profit levels of all or part of the organization.

VPSs can therefore take several forms: PRP or merit pay, PBR and profit-related pay. The Workplace Employment Relations Survey (WERS) found that 55 per cent of all UK workplaces used at least one form of VPS in 2011, compared with 54 per cent in 2004 (Table 8.6). However, there was substantial variation across sectors, with private sector workplaces almost three times as likely as public sector workplaces to use at least one VPS, at 59 per cent and 21 per cent respectively. In the private sector, 28 per cent of employees received PRP compared with only 7 per cent of public sector employees. In the financial services, 65 per cent of employees were in receipt of PRP compared with just 4 per cent in education (van Wanrooy et al., 2013a). In the most recent CIPD reward management survey, 74 per cent of employer respondents reported using individual performance as a criterion to move an employee through their pay band. A use of PRP, for either individual or groups of employees, was reported by 49 per cent of respondents (CIPD, 2015f, p. 3), down on the 65 per cent reported in 2012. The decrease, however, obscures a number of developments, such as a move away from individual PRP towards a combination of individual, group and/or profit-related VPSs. Parallel with the general growth in the primacy of VPSs is the significant fall in the number of UK workplaces where pay is determined jointly by union–management collective bargaining (Arrowsmith and Marginson, 2011; van Wanrooy et al., 2013a).

Table 8.6 *VPSs in all UK workplaces, 2004 and 2011*

Type of reward scheme	2004 (%)	2011 (%)
Any payments by results or merit pay	40	41
Merit or performance-related pay (PRP)	15	21
Any payments by results (PBR)	31	29
Any profit-related pay	30	29
Any employee share plans	16	9
At least one VPS	54	55

Source: van Wanrooy, B., Bewley, H., Bryson, A. Forth, J., Freeth, S., Stokes, L., and Wood, S.(2013a, pp.96) Employment Relations in the Shadow of Recession: Findings from the 2011 Workplace Employment Relations Study. Basingstoke: Palgrave Macmillan. Reproduced with the permission of the authors and sponsors.

Comparative studies have found a growing use of incentive pay systems that link pay to performance, at both the individual and collective levels, in Britain and European Union member states (Arrowsmith et al., 2010; Marsden and Belfield, 2010). In British retail banking, various forms of performance-related bonus are now 'strongly embedded' as tools to motivate and control employees through pay (Arrowsmith and Marginson, 2011). There have also been attempts to re-engineer the architecture of pay determination in the UK public sector, with a movement from seniority-based progression to pay more explicitly linked to performance results (Perkins and White, 2009). Under the 'new pay' paradigm, the reality for the vast majority of employees in UK workplaces, especially in the private sector, is that management sets pay unilaterally.

HRM web links Visit the online resource centre at www.palgravehighered.com/bg-hrm-6e to read a bonus HRM in practice feature on performance-related pay.

The interest in variable or contingency pay arrangements can best be understood in terms of psychological theory and political ideology. Unitary theoretical explanations suggest that profit-related pay schemes indirectly affect organizational performance through a casual chain of mediating variables such as individual behaviour, for example attracting talented people with a preference for share ownership (Lazear, 2000) and employee retention (Sengupta et al., 2007), and employees' attitudes, such as fostering 'psychological ownership' (Pierce et al., 2009). As Heery (2015, p. 27) observes, psychological reasoning is used to penetrate the 'black box' of HRM and thereby explain the link between financial participation and performance.

The interest in VPSs can also be explained by neo-liberal ideology. In North America and Britain, there has since the 1980s been a concerted ideological campaign against automatic annual pay increases and 'artificially inflated' public sector pay. This dominant thinking has encouraged a movement towards linking pay to individual performance and local labour markets (Curnow, 1986; Grimshaw and Rubery, 2010; Pendleton, 1997; Sisson and Storey, 2000). The growth of VPSs raises concerns for both equity and organizational performance. In the absence of a joint regulation of pay, many individual employees will be unlikely to address problems of inequality and indignity at work. In addition, it is plausible that organizations will be disadvantaged because of the lack of engagement of unions' and employees' 'voice', which can potentially contribute to innovation in the workplace and higher productivity (Scottish Government, 2014).

Criticism of the 'new pay agenda' in the UK has revolved around not only its ideological significance, but also the fact that the so-called 'strategic' paradigm has not been universally applied across UK workplaces (Corby et al., 2009; Kessler, 2007). Indeed, the WERS data set suggests that almost 60 per cent of workplaces had *not* adopted PRP schemes by 2013. Despite the hype surrounding the 'strategic' approach to pay, various studies show that there is in practice evidence of 'rowing back', with workplaces establishing broadbanded pay structures to represent graded pay structures or 'even *de facto* traditional salary structures' (Corby et al., 2009, p. 7). Kessler (2007) suggests that internal and external equity, rather than corporate strategy, has come to dominate the pay agenda. Research shows that, despite the contemporary prescriptive – 'How to' – rhetoric on rewards, there is extreme pay inequality, and that millions of young people across Europe 'occupy their hours with "bullshit jobs" that pay little' (Mason, The Guardian, 2015b). A further critique relates to gender pay inequality. The pay gap in the UK is still obstinately wide nearly 50 years after the passing of the 1970 Equal Pay Act, which is not surprising given Grimshaw and Rubery's (2010, p. 357) observation that 'gender discrimination is strongly entrenched' in UK pay structures.

With regard to the specific notion of strategic pay, the principle of 'fit' commonly cited in the strategic HRM literature is fraught with theoretical and practical difficulties. First, at the theoretical level, rational decision-making, which underpins the pay–strategy link, assumes that managers have perfect knowledge and the cognitive ability to organize and process all the relevant information. In practice, however, decision-makers may not know whether a pay–strategy decision is 'optimal' because they have only imperfect knowledge and limited calculative ability (Trevor, 2009). Second, the casual mechanistic relationship between pay and organizational performance is a hypothesis based on the assumption that pay practices change employees' attitudes and employees' behaviour in ways that advance organizational goals. This is somewhat at odds with the expanded multicausational approach, which privileges social relations between line managers and other employees and 'bundles' of HR practices as the key levers (see Chapter 3).

At the practical level, empirical support for strategic pay theory is limited. Kessler (2007) notes how survey data show that only a small proportion – 6 per cent – of organizations responding reported that their pay strategy was 'fully aligned' with their business strategy. Furthermore, using PBR schemes to achieve corporate goals is not as straightforward as prescriptive pay theorists suggest. This is plagued by operational constraints and difficulties (Arrowsmith and Marginson, 2010), especially in relation to objective-setting, performance measurement and pay determination. In practice, a pay system, as a social construct, is invariably subject to social and power pressures, and as such is inevitably customized and subverted to meet context-specific demands. Recent pay literature suggests that 'theory is out of step with reality and may represent a largely unattainable ideal in practice' (Gomez-Mejia et al., 2010, p. 13 ; see also Marsden and Belfield, 2010; Trevor, 2009). This echoes other studies suggesting that new work systems have explained management's decision to favour 'simplified, aggregate forms of bonus over individual payment-by-results as part of a wider change agenda' (Arrowsmith and Marginson, 2010, p. 309). Finally, the 'new pay' paradigm is widely presumed to entail negative consequences for the regulation of pay by trade unions and for economic inequality.

Inequality, paradox and reward management

Income inequalities are extremely high globally, and have been rapidly increasing over the last three decades (Savage, 2015). In 2016, it was reported that half a billion people in 25 of the west's richest countries suffered from flat or falling pay between 2005 and 2014 (Elliott, 2016, p. 11). Yet the world's 20 richest men and women had a combined wealth that was £595 billion more than the poorest 80 per cent of the world's population in 2016 (Ruddick, 2016). If equality is judged in terms of equality of income, equality of opportunity or education equality, then inequality is a persistent feature of the human condition, or, to use Owen Jones's metaphor, inequality runs through Britain 'like it is a stick of rock' (Jones, The Guardian, 2016, p. 33). Inequalities exist in all aspects of life – access to education, healthcare, the legal system – and not just in income (Wilkinson and Pickett, 2010). There is compelling evidence too that extreme inequality damages economies (Hutton, 2015a; Piketty, 2014; Stiglitz, 2013). Here the aim is to understand how inequality affects employees' commitment, trust and behaviours.

reflective question Take a moment to ask yourself how you understand the term 'equality'? Thinking about the values underpinning HRM, how does extreme inequality impact on the employment relationship?

Equality can be defined as the state of being equal, especially in status, rights or opportunities. The principle of and our belief in social equality are rooted in a body of intellectual thought that we associate with the Enlightenment and social unrest in Europe and North America in the eighteenth century. The ideology of the French Revolution, found in the famous Declaration of the Rights of Man and the Citizen (1789), proclaims that 'men are born free and remain free and equal in rights' and goes on to state that 'social distinctions can be based only on common utility' (Piketty, 2014, p. 479). Although the first statement asserts the principle of absolute equality, the second sentence alludes to the existence of very real inequalities.

Since 1945, in Western Europe at least, political discourse on the redistribution of wealth within society has been based around a logic of human rights and a principle of equal access to certain resources that are deemed to be fundamental: education, health and retirement (Piketty, 2014). For our purposes, perhaps the most important point to be taken from the debate surrounding the concept is that equality is socially constructed. It concerns practices, policies and the organizational structures that shape them and is typically understood to be subjective (Colquitt et al., 2001). The concept of 'social equality' will serve as the starting point for discussing the connection between capital and inequality in the context of the post-2008 work organization. Employment and pay equity legislation is defined as those laws that are intended to eliminate established inequalities in pay received by women and (often specifically identified) members of minority groups working for a given employer (Godard, 2005).

Income inequality is "the extent to which income is distributed unevenly in a group of people" (see https://www.equalitytrust.org.uk/how-economic-inequality-defined for a more detailed discussion). It has been a universal feature of capitalist societies, even if the degree of inequality has varied enormously. Wilkinson and Pickett's work The Spirit Level (2010) identifies a number of ways of measuring income inequality. For example, you might analyse the proportion of all incomes which the richer and poorer halves of the population receive. Wilkinson and Pickett note that typically the richest half of the population receive approximately 75 or 80 per cent of all income, and the poorest half only 25 or 20 per cent. Another way to measure income inequality is to compare the average income of the richest 20% of the population to the average income of the poorest 20%. Figure 8.4 shows the size of income inequalities across selective

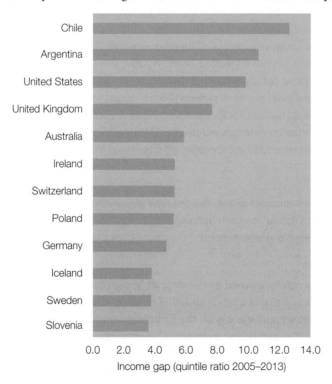

Figure 8.4 *Income inequality in selective countries*

Source: Table 3 (Inequality-adjusted Human Development Index), 2015 Human Development Report, United Nations Development Programme (the HDRO calculations are based on data from the World Bank). The HDRO calculations are reproduced here under the Creative Commons 3.0 IGO license (https://creativecommons.org/licenses/by/3.0/igo/). Copyright © 2015 HDRO. To access the data sets go to http://hdr.undp.org/en/composite/IHDI. Please also refer to the Publisher's Acknowledgements on page xlix for further information.

capitalist countries. At the top are the most unequal countries, and at the bottom are the most equal. For the most equal countries in this graph, Slovenia, Sweden and Iceland, the richest 20 per cent are less than four times as rich as the poorest 20 per cent. However, at the top of the chart, in Chile the richest 20 per cent get almost thirteen times as much as the poorest. Argentina, the United States and the United Kingdom are also very unequal.

An alternative method for measuring income inequality is the Gini Coefficient. This measures income inequality across a whole society instead of just comparing its "extremes" (Wilkinson and Pickett, 2010). The Gini Coefficient would be equal to 100 if one person received all the income and everyone else received nothing (maximum inequality). The Gini Coefficient would equal 0 if everyone received exactly the same amount of income (perfect equality). Figure 8.5 shows the rate of income inequality in selective European Union countries in 2014.

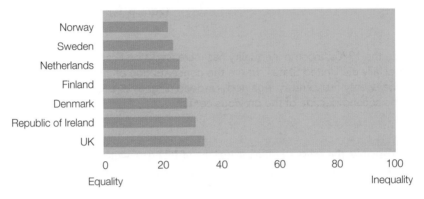

Figure 8.5 *Rate of income inequality in selective EU countries in 2014*

Source: Eurostat http://ec.europa.eu/eurostat/statistics-explained/index.php/Income_distribution_statistics (accessed August 2016). Copyright © European Union, 1995–2016.

HRM web links

Visit the online resource centre at www.palgravehighered.com/bg-hrm-6e to find more information and data examining equality across different countries.

As well as measuring income inequality, we can also look at pay inequality (which unlike income inequality discounts money received from other sources). One way to do this is to compare the pay rates of the top 1 per cent with the other 99 per cent of society, typically the pay of corporate CEOs and average workers in the same organization. CEO's pay is notoriously complex, with separate components paying off on different timescales. In 2016, a London School of Economics report showed that the average pay package of the CEOs of Britain's FTSE 100 companies was £4.6 million (US$6.4 million) a year (Boffey, 2016a). The median pay for CEOs was slightly lower, at £3.873 million. In 2014, the ratio between the average pay of FTSE 100 CEOs and the average wage of UK employees was 184:1 (Caulkin, 2004), whereas in 1998, the corresponding ratio was 47:1. In the 1980s, using a different methodology but nonetheless still indicating a trend, the ratio was around 20:1. A similar trend of average CEO pay has been recorded in the USA. In 2016, the ratio of America's top CEOs' pay to the average wage of US employees was 340:1 (Kasperkevic, 2016). According to the detailed Office for National Statistics annual salaries survey of 2014, British workers who were employed full time earned an average of £27,271. But by around 10 am on 2nd January 2014, the top FTSE 100 CEOs had already been paid that amount.

PhotoDisc/Getty Images

It has been argued that CEOs' performance bears little relation to the high salaries they command.

The statistics suggest that the rate of income inequality is greater in those countries that most closely embrace the neo-liberal troika of deregulation, privatization and flexible labour markets (Bratton and Denham, 2014). French economist Thomas Piketty's economic tome *Capital* offers detailed evidence on the structured pattern of income inequality with a focus on the USA, the UK and France. He observes (2014, p. 15):

 Since the 1970s, income inequality has increased significantly in the rich countries, especially the United States, where the concentration of income in the first decade of the twenty-first century regained – indeed, slightly exceeded – the level attained in the second decade of the previous century.

Arguably, the most significant insight of Piketty's work is that it shows that, if unregulated, capitalism can be expected to produce rates of return on investment that are so much higher than overall rates of economic growth that the only possible outcome is an even greater inequality in income (Graeber, 2014).

Following the cataclysm that befell many EU economies, especially Britain, in 2008, income inequality has featured prominently in public debate. There are many reasons for the dramatic rise of income inequality, and space only permits a mention of a few. These include the decline in union membership (see for example, Figure 9.1), the growth in precarious employment and zero-hour contracts, the erosion of workers' protections, the process used to set CEOs' pay and the ideology of 'meritocratic extremism' (Piketty, 2014). The widening pay gap between CEOs and workers can be partly explained by peer group analysis involving a comparison of what other company CEOs have received. Although this process appears to be based on market forces, it is in reality a 'rigged game' because peers 'cherry-pick' higher paid CEOs, but they do not reflect the company's performance (Hutton, 2015a; Piketty, 2014). The 'stratospheric' pay of CEOs has also been explained by Piketty as a form of 'meritocratic extremism', by which he means the apparent social norm in some modern societies, especially those of the USA and UK, 'to designate certain individuals as "winners" and to reward them all the more generously if they seem to have been selected on the basis of their intrinsic merits' (Piketty, 2014, p. 334). The justification for the growth in CEO pay has, however, little to do with real company performance. Piketty observes (p. 335):

 If executive pay were determined by marginal productivity, one would expect its variance to have little to do with external variances [for example, variations in the exchange rate] and to depend solely or primarily on nonexternal variances [for example, leadership]. In fact, we observe just the opposite: it is when sales and profits increase for external reasons that executive pay rises most rapidly.

Will Hutton, in his book *How Good We Can Be* (Hutton, 2015a), draws similar conclusions and observes that British CEO pay, once adjusted for the size of the corporation under management, is the 'highest in the world' and much higher than in EU member states and Japan (p. 95). The 'absurdly high' pay of British 'super-managers', as Piketty calls them, has little to do with their personal performance. Moreover, many CEOs of FTSE 100 companies are unexceptional, and, 'for every appointment of a CEO, another 100 people could have filled the role just as ably, and ... many chosen for the top jobs were "mediocre"' (Boffey, 2016a, p. 1).

reflective question

> How much more than the average worker *should* CEOs make? Hint: in the 1970s, management guru Peter Drucker suggested a cap on the ratio of CEO to average worker salary of 25 to 1. In 2013, the Swiss electorate voted in a referendum against a ratio between CEOs' and employees' pay of 12:1. What criteria should be used to justify CEO pay?

But what is the relevance of inequality, in all its dimensions, to HRM? Evidence suggests that employees' motivation is influenced by relative, rather than absolute, rewards. Employees compare their pay with that of comparable co-workers or 'referent others' (Corby et al., 2009, p. 12). These are typically their own co-workers (internal equity), but this may extend to those doing comparable jobs in other organizations (external equity). Although the evidence is mixed, some studies suggest that a more 'egalitarian' pay structure enhances employees' cooperation and satisfaction (Guthrie, 2008, p. 355). The extravagant CEO pay phenomenon can have a malign organizational effect, inviting scepticism and resentment on the part of low-paid workers, which can deplete commitment. Collectively, if the perception of negative inequity is strong and is shared by a sufficient number of workers, unionization and conflict can occur.

HRM web links

> Visit the online resource centre at **www.palgravehighered.com/bg-hrm-6e** to find more information on social equality.

Let us finish our discussion of reward management by examining some of the tensions and contradictions inherent in pay systems. At both practical and theoretical levels, reward management has an interlocking set of tensions and paradoxes. For employers, reward is a cost, but for employees, it is typically their only source of income. Each party attempts to secure a pay outcome that, from their position, is more satisfactory. Thus, conflict is structured into the management of pay. Furthermore, pay is subject to contradiction or 'strategic tension', shaped and negotiated through social and power relations rather than straightforward 'rational' processes (Boxall et al., 2008).

In addition to this, reward exhibits the 'overarching tension' between neo-classical economic theories and social psychological theories with regard to the management conundrum of employee motivation (Corby et al., 2009). Economists argue that pay incentives can motivate workers; work psychologists and sociologists argue that workers' needs and social norms have a major influence on work motivation. This tension is documented

Ruth Altman
Freelance HR practitioner

R uth has worked across a variety of sectors and industries throughout her career, including several positions as HR Director. She was previously Director of HR and Development for Cranfield University, which she left in summer 2011 to move back into consultancy and interim work.

Her route through HR has been first as an HR generalist working with the business, gaining experience in more specialist areas such as reward, industrial and employee relations, organization development, change management and delivering management development programmes. She then took up more overarching strategic HR roles. More recently, Ruth was a member of the Universities Human Resources Executive and the Higher Education Sector's HR professional body, for which she chaired the annual national conference committee. She has also been a judge for the sector's marketing and communications initiatives, the Heist Awards.

Click on Ruth's picture in your ebook to watch her talking about the challenges of working in a HR department at a university, and how higher university fees will impact on the reward system in universities. Then think about the following questions:

1 How does Ruth explain the development of the psychological contract at work?
2 How are changes in universities affecting HR?
3 How can a HR department really 'add value'?

in workplace research reporting that individually based pay-for-performance schemes can undermine work team effectiveness, and that team-based pay schemes are also imbued with the 'free-rider' problem (Guthrie, 2008).

The 'new pay agenda' seeks to increase employees' commitment, motivation and flexibility. At the lower end of the pay scale, managers' attempts to change workers' commitment through PRP arrangements might, however, be undermined if pay to superior performers could not be fulfilled because of the company's poor financial performance. Disappointment might also lead to a breach of the psychological contract rather than increased commitment. We should also note Pfeffer's (1998) argument that PRP creates tensions that can undermine workers' 'intrinsic motivation'. Furthermore, PRP is prone to the 'twin vices of subjectivity and inconsistency' (Kessler, 1994) and might become discredited in the eyes of subordinates because of perceived 'procedural injustices' caused by subjective and inconsistent appraisals by line managers (see Chapter 3). The Chartered Institute of Personnel and Development (CIPD) reported that the growing disparity between pay at the low and higher ends of the pay scale created a 'real sense of unfairness' that impacted negatively on employees' motivation at work' (Treanor, The Guardian, 2015a, p. 35). PRP arrangements can have other unintended consequences, such as employees falsifying data to improve their perceived performance. Five G4S Lincolnshire police control-room staff were suspended in 2016 after allegedly making more than a thousand bogus 999 'test calls' in order to meet their target of answering 92 per cent of calls within 10 seconds (Travis,

The Guardian, 2016, p. 11). At the top end of the pay scale, the worst fears about PRP systems materialized in the 2008/09 global financial crisis when the perversions of the bonus culture encouraged high-risk behaviour (Martin, 2014).

Finally, we should appreciate the relationship between 'reward options' and power. The choice of a pay system does not operate in a vacuum but is dictated by perceptions of power on the part of management and labour. This suggests we can predict that pay systems will change according to their effectiveness in terms of the relationship of effort to pay and shifts in power. The balance of power is therefore a strategic factor that helps to explain the choice of pay arrangements within any HR strategy. In addition, the 'new pay' paradigm has some 'ethical deficiencies', but these are examined in Chapter 11.

case study

Cordaval University

The setting

The Canadian university sector has recently experienced major changes and increasingly faces new challenges of rising tuition fees for students, changing political agendas, squeezed public funding and an unpredictable demand from international students. The increase in student fees has sharpened students' focus on the value they receive from their universities. Running parallel is the entry into the sector of new universities created by rebranding well-established 2-year colleges into 'applied' universities. Globalization has created a booming market in higher education, and, aided by the dissolution of national market borders, international partnerships have developed to create 'superuniversities' with overwhelming competitive advantages over locally or regionally focused institutions.

Located in eastern Canada, Cordaval University, created from an applied university-college, gained university title in 2004. The university employs 400 full-time and 150 part-time teaching staff. The university's student numbers have grown steadily in the past few years, with a current headcount of 25,000 full-time and part-time students. The university's core activity is helping students to succeed. The vast majority of students attend the university to improve their career prospects or to change career. Cordaval offers programmes across a comprehensive range of disciplines. The university's strategic plan is to deliver high-quality innovative, flexible programmes both on and off the campus. In setting a course to achieve its new strategic vision, the university has established five strategic goals:

- Helping every career-motivated student to achieve his or her career aspirations
- Consistently delivering academic excellence
- Building the university's track record in applied research
- Developing the capacity to generate income
- Contributing to the cultural and economic prosperity of the region
- Establishing a school of law.

The problem

The Ad Hoc Joint Committee established by the University's Board of Governors, which consisted of representatives from the teaching staff, deans, students' union and HR, chaired by the President, Dr Sara

Ferguson, was mandated to develop an action plan to create a school of law (goal 6). This was to consist of a Dean of Law, executive assistant and four teaching faculty, paid a salary scale between $106,360 and $136,905.

At the first meeting, Malcolm O'Reilly, the Human Resource Adviser for Cordaval University, presented data on salary structures from other Canadian universities that were offering law degrees. In closing his presentation, he remarked that while Cordaval's teaching staff were on average paid at levels below those of comparable universities (see the table for Cordaval's salaries), there was insufficient funding to raise academic salaries across the board. This would not change any time soon because:

We can recruit in most disciplines; it's only in law that we anticipate a problem. We have little choice but to create a new higher salary structure for law lecturers that is competitive with the labour market. Funding will not provide sufficient money to maintain equitable pay differences between new law lecturers and current teaching staff.

Bill Warren from the Department of Philosophy, History and Politics forcefully countered:

Arts and social science teaching staff are underpaid relative to other universities, and we are struggling to recruit good people because of this. Paying higher salaries just to law professors will demotivate staff and undermine efforts to develop interdisciplinary degrees.

Dr Michael Peters, from the department of anthropology, geography and sociology, then spoke up:

> What is vexing is inequity within the social science school. I have colleagues who routinely, year after year, teach far fewer students than the contract limit. Yet we're all equally responsible for the same standards of teaching, research and service, not to mention pay. It's not hard to think that good teachers and vibrant disciplines are being 'rewarded' with more work. Poor teachers in moribund disciplines are, in a sense, rewarded with more pay.

Dr John Rickman, a professor of English, remarked:

> What does annoy me is that I periodically hear justifications of administrative salaries being what they are – exorbitant when compared with teaching salaries – in terms of some wider 'market'. We have to pay this dean this much because that's the 'going rate' at Calgary, but we never hear the same argument when it comes to teaching faculty. What about the rest of us?

Another member of the Ad Hoc Committee, Dr Chris Woodstock, an executive member of the University Teaching Union (UTU) said, 'Michael's and John's views illustrate the position of UTU. A new pay structure only for law professors is very divisive and in the long-term will prove disastrous for employee relations at the university'.

Dr Ferguson then summed up the contributions from around the table. Finally, following extended discussion, it was agreed that John Rickman, Chris Woodstock and Malcolm O'Reilly would draft a discussion paper for the next meeting on what could be done to address the salary problem that existed at Cordaval university.

The assignment

Working in a small group, and role-playing the members of the subcommittee, prepare a report for the Ad Hoc Joint Committee drawing on the material from this chapter, addressing the following:

1 Based on the data collected by the HR department, what reward problems exist at Cordaval University?
2 Is the proposal from the HR adviser for a differential salary structure favouring law lecturers justifiable?
3 Does the proposal to pay higher salaries to one particular group of teaching staff impact positively or negatively on the strategic plan? Explain your answer.
4 What reward policy would you suggest to the university?
5 How should the university address the problem of disgruntled lecturers who feel underpaid?

Salary schedules at Cordaval University

Step	Current pay ($)	Academic rank
21	**106,905**	Full professor ceiling
20	104,723	
19	102,541	
18	100,359	
17	**98,178**	Associate professor ceiling
16	95,451	
15	92,723	
14	89,996	
13	87,269	
12	**84,542**	Assistant professor ceiling
11	81,269	
10	78,542	
9	**76,360**	Full professor floor
8	73,176	
7	70,496	
6	67,816	
5	**65,136**	Associate professor floor
4	62,456	
3	59,776	
2	57,095	
1	**54,415**	Assistant professor floor

Essential reading

Long, R. (2010) Evaluating the market. In *Strategic Compensation* (4th edn) (pp. 333–58). Toronto: Nelson.

Pfeffer, J. and Langton, N. (1993) The effect of wage dispersion on satisfaction, productivity, and working collaboratively: evidence from college and university faculty. *Administrative Science Quarterly*, **38**: 382–407.

Shaw, J. D., Delery, J. E., Jenkins, G. and Gupta, N. (1998) An organizational-level analysis of voluntary and involuntary turnover. *Academy of Management Journal*, **41**: 511–25.

Tien, F. F. and Blackburn, R. (1996) Faculty rank system, research motivation, and faculty research productivity: measure refinement and theory testing. *Journal of Higher Education*, **67**(1): 2–22.

Note: This case study was written by John Bratton.

 Visit the online resource centre at **www.palgravehighered.com/bg-hrm-6e** for guidelines on writing reports.

summary

➤ This chapter has emphasized that reward management is central to the effective management of the employment relationship. The pay model we have developed shows that reward is multidimensional and emphasizes two fundamental policy issues: *internal* and *external equity*.

➤ A reward system is a key mechanism that can influence each step of the strategy process. Although this view has been contested, we explained that the current new pay literature stresses that an 'effective' pay system is one that is aligned with the organization's business strategy.

➤ We discussed why no single best pay system exists. A pay system that may seem highly appropriate in one period, with a particular organization and work design supporting a management strategy, or with a particular group or individual employees, can be highly inappropriate in the next, when the business strategy and organizational design or individual employees change.

➤ We explained that changes in reward systems reflect shifts in management thinking. The adoption of more variable pay systems is ideologically driven to encourage labour flexibility, although there is an apparent lack of consensus on the type of pay system that might encourage behavioural change.

➤ We have also examined how government intervenes *directly* in the pay determination process. We examined equal pay, national minimum pay legislation and how they impact on pay determination.

➤ We have explored the issue of wage inequality and some of the strategic tension in reward systems. Under the logic of political economy, pay systems cannot remove the contradictory tensions that bedevil employment relations. We also focused on some 'ethical deficiencies' with respect to contingency pay increasing employee risk.

review questions

1 Explain the statement 'The design of reward systems is contingent upon the organizational context in which they must operate.'

2 Is money the prime driver of employee performance?

3 Do financial rewards have the same effect on the turnover intentions and task performance behaviour of all employees?

4 'New payment systems generate greater employee risk and diminish democratic rights in the workplace.' Discuss.

5 Do incentive-pay schemes have a motivational or a demotivational effect on employees?

6 'Equal pay for women will be secure only when its justice is adequately understood and practised by men' (Wedderburn, 1986). Do you agree or disagree? Discuss.

further reading

Reading these articles and chapters can help you gain a better understanding and potentially a higher grade for your HRM assignment.

➤ Alvaredo, F., Atkinson, A., Piketty, T. and Saez, E. (2013) Top 1 per cent in international and historical perspective. *Journal of Economic Perspectives*, **27**(1): 3–20.

➤ Arrowsmith, J. and Marginson, J. (2011) Variable pay and collective bargaining in British retail banking. *British Journal of Industrial Relations*, **49**(1): 54–79.

➤ Chartered Institute of Personnel and Development (2015) *Reward Management: Annual Survey Report, 2014–15*. London: CIPD.

➤ Corby, S., Palmer, S. and Lindop, E. (eds) (2009) *Rethinking Reward*. Basingstoke: Palgrave Macmillan. Read pp. 102–19.

➤ De Gieter, S. and Hofmans, J. (2015) How reward satisfaction affects employees' turnover intentions and performance: an individual differences approach. *Human Resource Management Journal,* **25**(2): 200–16.

➤ Heery, E. (2000) The new pay: risk and representation at work. In D. Winstanley and J. Woodall (eds) *Ethical Issues in Contemporary Human Resource Management* (pp. 172–88). Basingstoke: Palgrave.

➤ Kessler, I. (2007) Reward choices: strategy and equity. In J. Storey (ed.) *Human Resource Management: A Critical Text* (3rd edn) (pp. 159–76). London: Thomson Learning.

➤ Kessler, I. and Purcell, J. (1992). Performance related pay: objectives and application. *Human Resource Management Journal,* **2**(3): 16–33.

➤ Landivar, L.C. (2015) The gender gap in employment hours: do work-hour regulations matter? *Work, Employment & Society,* **29**(4): 550–70.

➤ Martocchio, J. J. (2015) *Strategic Compensation: A Human Resource Management Approach* (8th edn). New York: Pearson Prentice-Hall.

➤ van Wanrooy, B., Bewley, H., Bryson, A. et al. (2013) Pay and rewards. In *Employment Relations in the Shadow of Recession: Findings from the 2011 Workplace Employment Relations Study* (pp. 77–100). London: Palgrave Macmillan.

vocabulary checklist for ESL students

Click here in your interactive ebook for a list of HRM terminology and vocabulary that has appeared in this chapter.

Visit the online resource centre at **www.palgravehighered.com/bg-hrm-6e** for lots of extra resources to help you get to grips with this chapter, including study tips, HRM skills development guides, summary lecture notes, tips for English as a Second Language (ESL) students and more.

part IV

EMPLOYMENT RELATIONS

chapter 9

labour relations and collective bargaining

Getty

objectives

After studying this chapter, you should be able to:

1 Define and describe contemporary trends in labour relations

2 Describe the core legal principles relating to union–management relations

3 Explain and critically evaluate different types of union–management strategy

4 Explain the pattern of trade union membership and union structure

5 Understand the nature of collective bargaining over pay and its links to the rise of income inequality

6 Critically evaluate the importance of 'partnership' for labour relations

Junior doctors in NHS England in 2016 gave public notice that they would walk out on strike as part of the long-running contract dispute (Cooper, 2016). In August 2015, members of four rail unions took part in strike action causing the entire London underground to close. London's then-Major, Boris Johnson, urged the unions to put the latest 'incredibly generous' offer from management to their members. The train drivers' leader, Mick Whelan, said, 'Our members have ejected the latest offer from the company because they are forcing through new rosters without agreement and offer no firm commitments on work–life balance for trainers' (Press Association, The Guardian, 2015). Despite the fact that the number of days lost to strikes is currently running at its lowest since records began in 1893, there has, unsurprisingly, been much public criticism of the strikes. Context, however, is paramount. As one senior trade union official acutely put it: 'no strike in our country could inflict the sort of economic damage which the banks and finance houses have' (Kenny, The Guardian, 2011, p. 30). In terms of the general public's perception of unions, less well-known perhaps, is the joint statement by then Prime Minister David Cameron and Brendan Barber former general secretary of the TUC urging workers to vote to remain in the European Union referendum (Cameron and Barber, 2016) or the presence of union 'Disability Champions' and 'Green Reps' in workplaces.

introduction

The central significance of the union actions described here is to remind us that the employment relationship, that human resource management (HRM) seeks to shape and manage is dynamic in the sense that it involves both collective conflict and cooperation. There is an underlying conflict of interest between employers and workers that emerges during periods of change or crisis. On the other hand, the overwhelming need to develop a sustainable, low-carbon economy acts on all parties to induce high levels of cooperation. Since the 1980s, underpinning neo-liberalism are the ideas that unfettered markets 'know best' and that trade unions are a matter of irrelevance – dinosaurs from the past. We, however, disagree. Social inequality, human dignity *in* and *at* work, worker physical and mental well-being, and the development of sustainable strategies emphasize the importance of a union voice in the contemporary workplace.

As explained in Chapter 1, there can be an individual employment relationship or a collective employment relationship, with the former determined unilaterally by the employer, and the latter bilaterally or jointly by the employer and a trade union(s). The focus of this chapter is the collective employment relationship, that is, the relationship between management and organized labour, including the balance of power between the parties, and the process of collective bargaining.

We will begin the chapter by defining labour relations and the scope of this interdisciplinary field of study. Next we will examine a number of strategic decisions that management must take with regard to trade unions. After providing an overview of the legal context of industrial relations, the chapter will examine trends in UK trade union membership and collective bargaining. Finally, the chapter will turn to the issue of social partnership, 'worker commitment' and an assessment of the unions' response to post-2008 wage austerity and other developments in the workplace.

reflective question It is important to examine your own values and life experiences, and therefore your own perspective on trade unions. Do you think that unions have a role to play in the new knowledge-based economy or are they 'dinosaurs' from a past era?

The nature of labour relations

As a field of study, the academic community has used different terms to describe the collective employment relationship, including 'industrial relations', 'labour relations' and 'union–management relations' (see Burchill, 2014; Colling and Terry, 2010; Farnham, 2015; Gunderson et al., 2005; Kelly, 2005). Traditionally, the preferred term was 'industrial relations' to describe the study and practice of management and trade union relations, together with collective bargaining between the two parties. It is argued that the term 'industrial relations' and its traditional subject boundaries have now become outdated (Wood, 2000). In this edition of the book, we will use the term 'labour relations' because it is less synonymous with heavy manufacturing and mining, which has been in decline for at least three decades in the UK. In post-industrial economies, the term 'labour relations' provides a better descriptor of the collective employment relationship in both private and public sector organizations, although we acknowledge that we use the terms interchangeably. The relevance of the term '*trade*' unions is also open to debate. For some, the term is an anachronism and it would be better to adopt the North American term 'labour' unions. However, we justify the use of the term 'trade unions', in part, in recognition of the terminology used in UK employment law (Burchill, 2014).

Over the past three decades, labour relations in Britain has been so radically transformed by a combination of economic, political and social factors that it is argued that the 2016 workplace would be 'incomprehensible' to the average employee in work in 1980 (Brown et al., 2009, p. 1). The Workplace Employment Relations Study (WERS) surveys have demonstrated with clarity the transformation 'in the shadow' of the post-Lehman Brothers crisis (van Wanrooy et al., 2013a). Running parallel with (and not unrelated to) these changes has, of course, been the ascendancy of the HRM paradigm. Some critics argue that particular patterns of HRM are inconsistent with the traditional British system of labour relations, albeit for very different reasons (Godard, 2005; Guest, 1995; Wells, 1993). Others, however, maintain that analytical HRM is not a union-avoidance strategy (Boxall, 2008).

The radical transformation of the British system of labour relations has not been limited to the UK. In the European Union (EU), the traditional pattern of labour relations has also undergone profound modifications in the intervening period. European trade unions have been weakened both numerically and politically. The response to intensified global competition has not, however, been the same in every EU member state. Thus, in some respects, the pattern of European labour relations systems has always sharply diversified, 'a contradictory mix of market liberalization and social regulation', representing a complex interaction between 'Europeanization' and 'Anglicization' forms of employment relations (Hyman, 2010).

In light of these profound contextual and institutional changes, it has become widely accepted that labour relations must be reconceptualized and extend its focus beyond traditional issues to a broader concern with all the forces and processes that shape the employment relationship (Colling and Terry, 2010; Gunderson et al., 2005). Moreover, it is acknowledged that any reconceptualization of labour relations must focus analysis on the three defining features of the employment relationship (Colling and Terry, 2010, pp. 7–8):

- It is *indeterminate*, which derives from the fact that the labour contract involves an exchange for money for a *potential* level of performance;

- *Power* is unequally distributed between the parties; and
- The employment relationship is *dynamic*.

A contemporary labour relations perspective also acknowledges that the category of 'worker' is itself contested, and that it is necessary to consider the influence of patriarchy, allowing for interests grounded in gender, ethnicity and other identities (Heery, 2009). The principal institutions and processes that encompass the field of study are, moreover, not gender-neutral but reflect 'masculine priorities and privilege' in work organizations (Wajcman, 2000, p. 183).

Understanding why employees join trade unions

Trade unions in the UK have approximately 6.4 million members, which amounts to about one-quarter of the labour force. In 2015 the proportion of male employees who were in a trade union was 22.3 per cent, lower than the number of female trade union members, at 27.7 per cent (Department for Business, Innovation and Skills, 2015). In the EU, about one in four employees is a member of a trade union. Significant variations exist, however, between EU members states: in 2013, the EU's four most populated states had different rates of unionization, with Italy at 36 per cent, the UK at 25 per cent, Germany at 18 per cent and France at 7.9 per cent. The Nordic countries have some of the highest rates of union membership: Denmark at 68.5 per cent, Sweden at 68.9 per cent, Finland at 69 per cent and Norway at 54.6 per cent. In Canada, 27.2 per cent of the workforce are members of a trade union, and in the USA, the figure in 2013 was 10.8 per cent. World-wide, trade unions have approximately 320 million members (Visser, 2013). It is therefore important to understand the decision to join a trade union from an individual employee's perspective.

Workers join unions for a wide variety of reasons (Schnabel, 2003). First, they may be motivated to join a union for *economic* reasons. In a classic study, Sidney and Beatrice Webb (1911) suggested that workers' pursuit of improved pay and conditions expressed a basic motive to reduce domination by their employers. Workers may also join a union because of perceived and actual extreme income equality (Checchi et al., 2010). Equity theory proposes that workers will engage in social action to the extent that they perceive the situation to be equitable (Bratton, 2015).

In addition to economic and equity rationales, employees also join unions because they want to gain a *voice* in decision-making in their workplace. Joining a union may bring workers the benefit of an indirect voice mechanism, which can potentially allow them to improve conditions, resolve irritating problems or address unreasonable workplace behaviour. In a democratic society, workers may make a decision to unionize in order to lobby politicians for political action on work-related or societal improvements. The participation of unions in civil society can also help to bring about the demise of authoritarian regimes. The democratization of Poland, for example, was led by the trade union Solidarity (Frost and Taris, 2005, p. 40).

In a survey of UK workplaces, workers disclosed that they had decided to join a union to improve their pay and conditions and for collective protection against management's actions (Waddington and Whitston, 1997). The findings from workplace surveys in the UK and North America suggest that workers' perceptions of the imbalance of power between 'them' (the management) and 'us' (the workers) necessitate some form of collective voice or representation in the form of a union.

What factors make unions relevant today? What factors make them irrelevant? And what do employees want from unions?

Trade unions in action

In a non-unionized workplace, managers have flexibility in designing work, selecting, promoting and training people, and determining rewards and other human resources (HR) practices, but much of this can change when workers join a union. After recognizing the union, representatives from union and management negotiate a collective agreement that spells out the details of the employment relationship that will be jointly determined. This can typically include establishing some control over core HR policies and practices, including rewards, recruitment and selection, training and employee development and health and safety:

- First and foremost, unions seek to counter downward pressures on wages caused by fluctuations in the labour market, and to control *rewards* and attempt to maximize the pay side of the wage–effort contract.
- In the area of *recruitment and selection*, unions, in some industries at least (for example, construction, film and theatre), have had some control over external recruiting.
- Unions also take an active interest in work-related *learning* and *employee development*, trying to ensure that training opportunities are distributed equitably and that employers adhere to the principle of maintained earnings during training.
- Perhaps most controversially, the whole practice of *employee performance appraisal* poses challenges to the unions. The central tenet of traditional unionism has been the collectivist culture, namely the insistence on rewards according to the same definite standard and its application in the workplace. Such collectivist goals have resulted in unions strongly resisting all forms of performance appraisal based on individual performance.

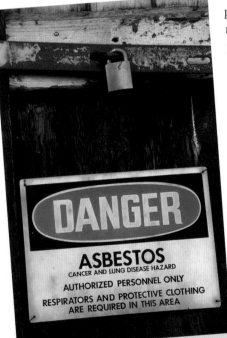

- Occupational *health hazards* and environmental pollution disproportionately affect those in the lower social class strata, the working class. Unions have a long history of campaigning and negotiating for the removal of toxic substances and for healthier and safer workplaces.

These examples illustrate that the importance of 'economic forces in determining behaviour' (Burchill, 2014, p. 1) and the 'control over work relations' (Hyman, 1975, p. 31) is a central feature of labour relations, which here we define as:

> The *relations* between organized employees (represented by a union) and management, the *processes* that regulate the employment contract, the *context* within which a union and an employer interact.

Occupational health hazards are just one of the issues that unions campaign against.

Photodisc

Let us briefly expand on the components of this definition. The '*relations*' between the workforce and management are both economic and social: they are an economic relation because employers buy employees' potential physical and mental abilities, and they are a social relation because, when employees enter into a contract, they agree to comply with the employer's standards and rules. These relationships between the workforce and management may be played out in different arenas – at workplace level, at industry level and at national level – where union, employer and government representatives participate in a social dialogue on economic and employment-related issues.

The word '*processes*' refers to collective bargaining, by which unions represent their members' interests through formal negotiations with management representatives. Through collective bargaining, a hierarchy of rules and regulations affecting employment and workplace behaviour is generated, and this is the process that may provide the focal point for studying the *mediating* effects of key variables in the HRM–performance casual chain, often referred to as the 'HR black box' (see Chapter 3).

The third key feature of the definition, '*context*', refers to the economic, legal and political conditions and constraints within which management and union relations take place. Our definition of labour relations recognizes the fluidity of contexts and the processes of control over the employment relationship. This dynamic mix means that, in a unionized environment, managing the interactions between union and management representatives can be a significant area of HRM activity.

HRM web links

Visit the online resource centre at **www.palgravehighered.com/bg-hrm-6e** for information on economic, political and collective bargaining developments in the EU and industrial relations in North America, Australia and South Africa.

The legal context of labour relations

Trade unions and collective bargaining processes and outcomes are strongly influenced by *legislation* and through *third-party intervention* (as, for example, in the UK, by the Advisory, Conciliation and Arbitration Service – ACAS). Labour law is an aspect of labour relations that interacts with the institutions, processes and behaviour of the key actors in the system. As a body of statutes and cases, labour law regulates union organization and governance, the main concerns being relations between different unions, union recognition by employers, collective bargaining and manifestations of collective workplace conflict, such as strikes. Whereas individual labour law governs the relations between individual employees and their employer, collective labour law therefore governs the collective aspects of the employment relationship.

When trade unions organized in eighteenth-century Britain, they faced illegality under both criminal and civil law. The Combination Acts of 1799 and 1800 were only part of a battery of more than 40 statutes that criminalized trade union activities. The Conservative governments of the 1980s and 90s significantly remodelled the legal framework for labour relations that had been established between 1870 and 1906 (McIlroy, 1988).

The Employment Relations Act 1999 provides a more supportive statutory framework for union organization and governance and collective bargaining, including provision for statutory union recognition, changed balloting procedures and increased protection for union members when participating in official industrial action (see Emir, 2014). Reviewing trade union rights under the New Labour government, from 1997, Smith and Morton (2006, p. 414) argue that partnership agreements 'entrench employers' power'. They also contend that, to strengthen workers' power, legislation is needed to establish 'a statutory right of trade unions to have access to, and assembly at, the workplace'.

The Conservative Government's Trade Union Act 2016 aims to reform various aspects of the law on trade union activities and industrial action. Key features of the Act include the following: a new 'opt-in' process for union political funds; a new minimum voter turnout – at least 50 per cent of eligible members must have voted in favour of strike action – a requirement made in no other part of British democracy; additional minimum thresholds for workers in 'important public services', for example health services, education, fire services and transport services; and a new definition of and restrictions on picketing at or near a place of work in contemplation or furtherance of a trade dispute for the purpose of obtaining or communicating information. Labour relations scholars and a United Nations (UN) body have expressed concerns about the Act, suggesting that the 'draconian' provisions amount to 'the most sustained attack on trade union and workers' rights since the Combination laws of the early 19th century' (Stuart et al., 2015, p. 30). The International Labour Organization, a UN agency dealing with employment and union issues, expressed concern that the Trade Union Act 2016 contravenes international labour law (Perraudin, 2016). Some of the key UK legislative provisions related to industrial relations are shown in Table 9.1.

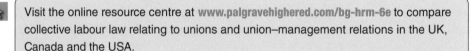

HRM web links

Visit the online resource centre at **www.palgravehighered.com/bg-hrm-6e** to compare collective labour law relating to unions and union–management relations in the UK, Canada and the USA.

reflective question

What is your view – should trade unions have more or fewer rights?

Pre-Brexit – Britain's decision to leave the EU – EU law and regulations have also influenced British labour relations. In 2007, for example, the landmark judgements of the European Court of Justice in the Viking and Laval cases adopted the legal concept of proportionality. The general principle of proportionality is complex, but briefly it entails a three-part test: first, is the measure suitable to achieve a legitimate objective?; second, is the measure necessary to achieve that objective or are less restrictive means available?; and third, does the measure have an excessive effect on the applicant's interests? The application of proportionality in labour relations meant that, irrespective of national law, work stoppages that interfered with freedom of movement were lawful only if they satisfied a 'proportionality' test. That is, they had to be both appropriate and necessary (Hyman, 2010).

A direct consequence in the UK of ever-complex legal rules regulating strike action was the injunction preventing the airline cabin crew's union Unite calling a strike against British Airways in 2010. The landmark decision by Mr Justice McCombe granted the injunction against the strike, overturning an 81 per cent vote by BA's cabin crew in favour of industrial action. The judge ruled that Unite had not complied with a particularly esoteric point of the

Table 9.1 Main UK legislative provisions related to industrial relations, 1980–2016

Act	Date	Coverage
Employment Act	1980	Public funds for union ballots (since repealed) Provision for codes on picketing and closed shops
Employment Act	1982	New definition of a 'trade dispute'
Trade Union Act	1984	Compulsory secret ballots for union positions and before industrial action; otherwise no immunity
Employment Act	1988	Greater control to members of union governance
Employment Act	1990	Abolition of the closed shop and immunity in respect of secondary industrial action
Trade Union and Labour (Consolidation) Act	1992	Consolidation of all relevant law on unions and labour relations together with ACAS. Code provides for disclosure of information to unions for collective bargaining purposes
Trade Union Reform and Employment Rights Act	1993	Independent scrutineers of union elections given more powers. Voting fully postal
Employment Relations Act	1999	New statutory framework for collective bargaining, including provision of statutory union recognition, changed balloting procedures and increased protection for union members when participating in official industrial action
Employment Relations Act	2004	Union recognition rights for the purpose of conducting collective bargaining. Outlines additional responsibilities of the Central Arbitration Committee to facilitate collective bargaining
Trade Union Act	2016	Introduced 'opt-in' process for union political funds. A 50% turnout threshold for ballots on industrial action; 40% of those eligible to vote must back action for strikes in core public services. Notice of industrial action to the employer increased from 7 to 14 days (unless the employer agrees to 7 days' notice).

1992 Trade Union and Labour Relations (Consolidation) Act that orders unions to notify not just the result of any secret ballot to all eligible voters, but also the exact breakdown of votes, including spoiled ballot papers, of which there were 11 (Milmo and Pidd, 2010). Reacting to the verdict, the joint general secretaries of Unite, Tony Woodley and Derek Simpson (quoted by Milmo and Pidd, 2010, p. 1, courtesy of Guardian News & Media Ltd), said:

> This judgement is an absolute disgrace and will rank as a landmark attack on free trade unionism and the right to take industrial action. Its implication is that it is now all but impossible to take legally protected strike action against an employer who wishes to seek an injunction on even the most trivial grounds.

The traditional attitude of the UK courts is that there is no 'right to strike' in the UK: Parliament has granted unions immunities not rights (as set out in the case *Express Newspapers* v. *McShane*, 1979). The judge in this case, Lord Denning, held that unions had no right 'to break the law or do wrong by inducing people to break contracts … only immunity if they did'. Pre-Brexit, that view was open to question once UK law incorporated the European Convention on Human Rights through the Human Rights Act 1998. Article 11 of the Convention recognizes a right to freedom of association, which has been interpreted as incorporating a right to strike. In *British Airways Plc* v. *Unite Union* (2010), Judge McCombe seemed to resurrect Lord Denning's view.

Wikum Jayatunga

Although the traditional attitude of the UK courts is that there is no 'right to strike', there is a consensus that some form of a right to strike must be respected if that is really the democratic will of union members.

However, at the Court of Appeal it was held that Unite had complied with the Trade Union and Labour Relations (Consolidation) Act 1992. The Lord Chief Justice described the ballot as having been 'impeccably conducted'. The Court of Appeal did not clarify the argument of whether the right to strike is recognized in the UK as a fundamental human right: 'The judgments of the majority do, however, seem to assume that some form of a right to strike must be respected if that is really the democratic will of union members' (Eady and Motraghi, 2010, p. 1). Despite promoting 'social partnerships' and, most recently, 'employee representation' on company boards, the effects of the legal strategies pursued by governments has thus considerably restricted lawful industrial action (Dickens and Hall, 2010). The ramifications of the UK withdrawal from the EU for labour law will take years to emerge and will not become clear until we know what elements of EU law/regulations are passed into UK law (Hillage, 2016).

HRM web links

Visit the online resource centre at **www.palgravehighered.com/bg-hrm-6e** for information on what Brexit means for employment law and on the role of ACAS.

Management strategies

Management plays a predominant role in constructing collective relations in the workplace, with managers shaping the options and largely determining the outcomes (Hyman, 1997b). Unilateral regulation is that part of the employment relationship managed by managers alone, and it is the preferred method of managing labour around the globe (Farnham, 2015). Numerous studies have investigated how British managers, responding to changes in forms of contemporary work and organizational design, public policy and employment law and the global economy, have reorganized the conduct of workplace collective employment relations (Cully et al., 1999; Kersley et al., 2006; van Wanrooy et al., 2013a).

A labour relations strategy refers to the plans and policies chosen by management to deal with trade unions (Gospel and Littler, 1983). The idea of choice among alternative labour relations strategies is closely linked to the concept of 'HR strategy'. The choice of a strategy towards unions is substantially constrained by a number of complex factors, including historical legacies, path dependency, union power, existing bargaining structures and global competition (Hyman, 1999; Jacoby, 2005; Thompson and Ponak, 2005). The 'varieties of capitalism' literature has also highlighted the importance of culture and national institutions that substantially constrain – as well as explain – the choice of a

HRM and globalization 9.1

Wal-Mart resists unions across North America

Wal-Mart Stores is the world's largest company in terms of revenue and employee numbers. It operates over 11,000 discount department and warehouse stores in 28 countries, including Asda in the UK and Best Price in India. In North America, Wal-Mart has faced significant criticism of its employment practices, including gender discrimination in its pay and promotion practices, refusing to accommodate other medical restrictions of pregnant women, and condoning the harassment of older employees (American Association of Retired Persons, 2014).

Wal-Mart is also known to fiercely oppose unionization. In 2004, 190 Canadian workers in Jonquière, Quebec voted to unionize with the United Food and Commercial Workers Union. The Jonquière store was the first successful unionization of an entire Wal-Mart store in North America. Shortly thereafter, Wal-Mart closed the store. After years of litigation, the Supreme Court of Canada ruled that the shutdown was an illegal effect to avoid the union. Despite Wal-Mart's claim that the store was closed due to poor performance, the Supreme Court upheld the original arbitrator's decision, which read (Marin, Huffington Post/The Canadian Press, 2014):

> It was in fact reasonable to find that a reasonable employer would not close an establishment that 'was performing very well' and whose 'objectives were being met' to such an extent that bonuses were being promised.

Wal-Mart's response to the Jonquière campaign was not unusual. In 2000, the meat department in a Texas Wal-Mart had voted to unionize. Two weeks later, Wal-Mart announced that it was moving to use pre-packaged meat and eliminated meat-cutters at 180 stores across the US (Greenhouse, 2015). Wal-Mart has also disciplined and terminated workers for protests demanding higher wages.

Wal-Mart's union-avoidance practices are hardly unique, and unionization rates in Canada (30 per cent) and the USA (11 per cent) have dropped to post-war lows. Unionization also tends to be concentrated in the public sector, with unionization rates in the private sector just above half of the national average.

The decline in North American unionization can be attributed to many things. Changing worker preferences for unionization, changes in the law that make unionization and collective bargaining more difficult, and decreasing employer acceptance of unions are often mooted as explanations.

In response to declining memberships, some union activists have suggested fundamental changes in North American unionism. For example, unionization in Canada and the USA is based upon majoritarian exclusivity. If a majority of workers decide (often through a vote) to be represented by a union, every worker (whether they like it or not) is exclusively represented by that union. The unionization of large companies often occurs on a site-by-site basis. If the majority votes against unionizing, then no workers are represented.

A controversial alternative to majoritarian exclusivity – called minority unionism – operates in New Zealand. Minority unionism grants workers the right to be represented by a union even if the majority of their co-workers do not want it. In this way, it better matches demand for with access to union representation. It also means that workers within a single workplace can select different unions to represent them.

Some Wal-Mart workers in the USA have adopted this approach, striking for better wages and working conditions. The logic of minority unionism is to improve working conditions immediately and thereby build support for the union. This may eventually lead to the union winning a representation vote among a majority of workers.

Stop! What motivates employers to resist unionization? What does this say about the differing interests of workers and employers in the workplace? What does the limited success that workers have enjoyed at unionizing Wal-Mart Stores suggest about the legal framework governing unionization and collective bargaining?

Sources and further information: For background information, see American Association of Retired Persons (2014), Greenhouse (2015) and Marin (2014).

Note: This feature was written by Bob Barnetson.

labour relations strategy. Although it is simplifying a complex phenomenon, the various strategic alternatives can, for analytical purposes, be classified into four broad labour relations strategies (Thompson and Ponak, 2005): union acceptance, union resistance, union replacement and union avoidance.

The *union-acceptance* strategy is defined here as a decision by top managers to accept the legitimacy of the union role and, in turn, of collective bargaining as a process for regulating the employment relationship to support their corporate strategy. The most fundamental employment policy decision made by senior management is whether to manage its workforce bilaterally with trade unions or unilaterally (Farnham, 2015). Survey evidence indicates that, even in the inimical environment of the 1980s, a number of important Japanese companies chose a union-acceptance strategy, albeit in a modified form, to achieve their employment objectives (Bassett, 1987; Wickens, 1987). In the UK in 2011, survey data indicated that the number of senior managers opting for a bilateral arrangement had significantly declined. In the private sector, for example, the proportion of workplaces adopting a union-acceptance/recognition strategy was only 16 per cent, compared with 44 per cent in the public sector (Kersley et al., 2006; van Wanrooy et al., 2013a).

Management's choice of a union-acceptance strategy will be influenced by their assessment of whether bilateral arrangements will benefit or damage the organization. The extant literature on the direct relationship between unions and organizational performance, however, shows inconsistent results and emphasizes the difficulty of generalizing across different industries, countries, years and workplace HR and labour relations practices (Verma, 2005). The collective voice/institutional response model (Freeman and Medoff, 1984), proposes that unions have two faces: a voice and a monopoly face with positive and negative effects for organizational performance, respectively. Thus, it is argued that although unions have the capacity to formally represent employee voice and to mitigate conflict through dispute resolution procedures in the workplace, to generate productivity-enhancing ideas and reduce costs associated with turnover, they have also the ability to raise wages above competitive levels, negatively impact employment growth, and increase the likelihood of costly and dysfunctional forms of workplace conflict.

Pohler and Luchak (2015) argue that determining whether unions are a benefit or a detriment to an organization will depend on whether a cooperative or competitive union–management relationship exists between the parties. Their research found that where management's intentions towards cooperation were clear and where they espoused a 'high employee-focused' strategy, the union was more likely to reciprocate with cooperative behaviours that would create the potential for win–win outcomes. In contrast, the presence of a 'low employee-focused' strategy tends to send a mixed signal to the union about whether or not its interests are aligned with those of management. In this situation, the union is more likely to respond by seeking to regulate work effort and to resist the potential threat to itself and its membership, with negative implications for organizational performance (Pohler and Luchak, 2015). The existing literature reports that non-union strategy is the most common form of employment relationship globally (Farnham, 2015), and three strategies can create a non-union environment.

First, the *union-resistance* strategy describes a decision by senior managers to limit the spread of unionization to other sections of the company's workforce, although they accept the legitimacy of their existing unions. For example, the spread of unionization among knowledge workers is discouraged by communicating to this group of employees that improvements in pay and conditions are due to management initiative, not union pressure.

ImageSource

Some organizations go to great lengths to prevent union action, monitoring who and what staff are talking about.

The study by Heery and Simms (2010, p. 9) gives two graphic illustrations of outright anti-union action by employers:

> Example 1: There are surveillance cameras at the only entrance of the building. Staff were afraid to even stop and speak to us at the gate. Management had previously sacked the last employee who spoke about getting a union.
>
> Example 2: When we first started the [union] campaign factory-gating, the factory manager, who is Asian, called all the Asian workers together on the shopfloor and told them that he would sack anyone who joined the union. That week, he phoned them all at home and told them again that they would be sacked.

Second, the *union-replacement* strategy means that top management have decided to achieve their strategic goals without any consultation or agreement with trade unions. De-recognition refers to a decision by management to withdraw from collective bargaining in favour of unilateral arrangements for the governance of employment relations. Several studies provide convincing evidence of de-recognition or substitution practices in Britain (see, for example, Claydon, 1989; Heery and Simms, 2010; Smith and Morton, 1993). The union-replacement scenario describes a case in which a relatively weak union is de-recognized and management install a non-union employee representation arrangement as 'a deliberate attempt to pre-empt the return of a union voice' (Butler, 2009, p. 207).

HRM web links

> Visit the online resource centre at **www.palgravehighered.com/bg-hrm-6e** for information on how industrial relations strategies in Britain have changed over the past two decades.

Throughout the 1990s, a union-replacement strategy was evident in UK workplaces. Survey results showed that 6 per cent of all established workplaces de-recognized unions between 1990 and 1998 (Millward et al., 2000). Bacon and Storey's (2000) analysis reveals a 'disjuncture between unions and "new" corporate thinking'. One manager (quoted in Bacon and Storey, 2000, p. 412) expressed the new management thinking towards unions like this:

> Collectivism via trade unions is something we want to remove … We are not anti-union; it is just that they are incompatible with our current direction. I think we can win by edict in the current climate and drive through changes against any opposition and hope that in the end people will see there is no choice.

One interesting aspect of Bacon and Storey's study is the evidence suggesting that British management did not take full advantage of its power. Two reasons are given for this. First, the 'heavy threats' to the unions contributed to higher levels of mistrust of management. This observation can be linked to the importance of the psychological contract. With this in mind, Bacon and Storey's (2000, p. 423) note that managers were 'reluctant to sacrifice employee trust' is important. The second reason managers did not use their power to de-recognize the unions was because the very threat of such action alone 'allowed managers to introduce many of the changes they had wanted to drive through' in the workplace (Bacon and Storey, 2000, pp. 413–14). Overall, then, although most managers have an enduring preference for non-union relations (what is referred to as 'unitarism'), pragmatic considerations in these cases deterred the adoption of a union-replacement strategy.

The third strategy, *union avoidance*, is defined here as a decision to maintain the status quo of a non-union workforce by barring union members from employment, often referred to as 'blacklisting'. In 2016, for example, major UK construction companies, including Robert McAlpine and Balfour Beatty, issued an "unreserved and sincere" apology in the high court to hundreds of building workers for putting them on an illegal blacklist and denying them work for two decades (Boffey, 2016b, p. 10). Legal strategies to avoid unions include HR policies that give employees a 'voice', such as non-union grievance procedures (see Chapter 10). The retail giant Marks & Spencer exemplifies the union-avoidance strategy, which was explained like this by the company's CEO, Lord Sieff, in 1981 (quoted by Purcell and Sisson, 1983, p. 114):

> Human relations in an industry should cover the problems of the individual at work … the contribution people can make, given encouragement – these are the foundations of an effective policy and a major contribution to a successful operation.

HRM web links Visit the online resource centre at www.palgravehighered.com/bg-hrm-6e for information on how many work organizations in the UK have negotiated partnership agreements.

In Britain, Heery and Simms (2010) concluded that, between 1998 and 2004, a period that was relatively favourable to trade unions under a Labour government, there was no single dominant labour relations strategy – 'support, suppression and substitution' were all evident. The significance of this debate for labour relations strategies is this: the HRM model is not restricted to a 'union-exclusion' environment. Guest (1995) analyses the strategic options in terms of labour relations that are available to management, the 'new realism' option appearing to illustrate the case of HRM and labour relations operating in tandem. Within the EU legislative framework, British labour relations have been 'Europeanized' (Hyman, 2010), and prior to 2008/09 managers were beginning to take a more proactive approach towards union involvement in workplace decision-making. However, Hyman (2015, p. 269) argues that globalized financial capitalism 'is one of the grave diggers of social democracy'. He suggests that the decline of union organization over the past 30 years is 'in part ideological in causation' (p. 273). As an important constituent of social democracy, the travails of trade unions will fluctuate as management labour strategies change depending on the ideological and economic climate. In addition, different labour strategies can be applied to different firms within the same industrial sector and to different groups of employee within the same organization. With this caveat in mind, the economic down-turn from Brexit (Fletcher, 2016) and the growing globalization of corporate structures will compel senior management to make strategic choices about their business processes and how they will arrange related aspects of HR practices, including labour relations.

Trade unions

Most students using this textbook will probably be surprised to learn that, four decades ago, British trade unions were considered to be powerful social institutions that merited close study. Indeed, an eminent labour relations scholar referred to trade unions as 'one of the most powerful forces shaping our society' (Clegg, 1976, p. 1). Between 1968 and 1979, trade union membership increased by 3.2 million to 13.2 million, and trade union density – the proportion of employees who are in a union – exceeded 50 per cent. The sheer scale of union organization represented a 'decade of exceptional union growth' (Bain and Price, 1983, p. 6). In contrast, union membership in Britain has collapsed since 1979: whereas in 1979, 53 per cent of workers were union members, this had fallen to 25 per cent by 2015. This section examines recent trends in union membership before examining union structure, in the belief that a knowledge of these developments is important for understanding the debate on HRM, unions and income inequality.

Union membership

The decline in aggregate membership of British trade unions is well documented and is shown in Table 9.2. In 1979, when the late Margaret Thatcher was first elected Prime Minister of Britain, union membership stood at over 12 million. Since then, membership has fallen by over 6 million, or 49.9 per cent. Union density is higher among women than men – 27.7. per cent compared with 22.3 per cent in 2015.

Table 9.2 *Union membership in the UK, 1971–2015*

5-year annual average	Members (000s)	% of employed
1971–75	11,548 (+1.5)	50.0
1976–80	12,916 (+1.5)	55.9
1981–85	11,350 (–3.5)	49.1
1986–90	10,299 (–1.7)	44.6
1991–95	8,740 (–4.0)	37.8
1996–2000	7,910 (–9.5)	34.2
2003–05	7,772 (–1.7)	33.6
2006–11	7,436 (–4.3)	28.0
2011–15	6,463 (–13.1)	25.0

Source: Data from Sneade, A. (2001) Trade union membership 1999–2000: an analysis of data from the Certification Officer and the Labour Force Survey. Labour Market Trends, September: 433–41. © Crown copyright 2001; gov.uk; and EurWORK, Eurofound: http://www.eurofound.europa.eu/observatories/eurwork. Used with permission.

Table 9.3 describes the pattern of union membership across major sectors of the British economy from 1980 to 2016. Union presence at workplace level remained stable in the early 1980s at 73 per cent, but then fell sharply to 64 per cent in 1990, then 54 per cent in 1998,

HRM in practice 9.1

BA told to hit union 'where it hurts'

The HRM–trade union debate poses some interesting questions for academics and practitioners alike. For example, can a worker be simultaneously committed to the goals of both the organization and the trade union? How does the HRM concept of 'high employee commitment' present a threat to unions? And can the HRM model function alongside traditional collective bargaining? Depending upon the answers to these, and other, questions, management may choose to deal with trade unions in different ways. Consider this recent industrial relations case (Milmo, 2010, copyright Guardian News & Media Ltd 2016):

DIGITALVISION

> British Airways commissioned an adviser who told it to 'force the issue' with the cabin crew union that is leading the strike action against the company by 'hitting the leadership … where it hurts' … Union insiders said it amounted to a blueprint for the company's hardline approach to industrial relations. 'It confirms everything that we have argued all along – that this company has a secret union-busting agenda which in the final analysis is the reason why so many passengers are suffering the inconvenience of this dispute …' The advice includes recommendations to the airline on:
>
> - Taking an 'anti-Bassa' [the union] approach
> - Recognizing 'there is no prospect of … partnership' under the union's current leadership
> - Seeking help from Bassa's parent union, then the Transport and General Workers' Union, in a 'divide and rule' approach. The document states: 'The

> management team should agree and express a determination to force the issue with Bassa. Some consideration should be given to hitting the leadership of Bassa where it hurts. Ground rules for paid time off for trade union duties is an area which needs to be very closely examined.'

This chapter identifies four broad industrial relations strategies: union acceptance, union resistance, union replacement and union avoidance. It also examines the concept of 'social partnerships'. For some, social partnerships provide a philosophy based on the employer and union working together to achieve common goals such as fairness and competitiveness (Verma, 1995). Critics, however, argue that partnership can potentially weaken the growth of workplace unionism (Kelly, 1996).

Stop! Having outlined above the broad strategies pursued by organizations, what type of industrial relations strategy is BA following? What are the constraints on management if they introduce non-union worker representation at BA?

Sources and further information: The extract is taken from Dan Milmo's (2010) Guardian article 'BA told to hit union where it hurts'. For more information, see Verma (1995), Kelly (1996), Godard (1997) and Williams et al. (2011).

Note: This feature was written by John Bratton.

continuing downwards to 25 per cent in 2016. Union presence differed significantly across the broad sectors of the economy. The decline in union presence was most marked in private manufacturing – down from 77 per cent in 1980 to just 42 per cent of workplaces in 1998. Union density in both private manufacturing and services was around 2.7 million or just 14 per cent in 2016. The trade union presence in public sector workplaces over the three decades fell from 99 per cent in 1980 to around 3.7 million or 54.3 per cent in 2015. Furthermore, in both private manufacturing and services, the decline was 'more substantial in small workplaces' and among traditionally 'male-dominated' workplaces (Millward et al., 2000, p. 86).

Table 9.3 *Union presence by broad sector, 1980–2015*

	Percentages						
	1980	**1984**	**1990**	**1998**	**2004**	**2011**	**2015**
All establishments	73	73	64	54	34	28	25
Sector of ownership							
Private manufacturing	77	67	58	42	n/a	14	14
Private services	50	53	46	35	22[1]	15[1]	13[1]
Public sector	99	100	99	97	64	56	54

[1]*This figure only refers to the 'private' sector – both manufacturing and services. Figures are rounded n/a, not applicable*

Source: British Employment Relations 1980–1998, as portrayed by the Workplace Industrial Relations Survey Series, 1st edition, p. 85, by Alex Bryson, John Forth and Neil Millward. Copyright © 2000 Routledge. Reproduced with permission of Taylor & Francis Books UK. Other sources: Kersley et al. (2006, p.12) and van Wanrooy et al. (2013a), both reproduced with permission of the authors and sponsors; https:// www.gov.uk/government/statistics/trade-union-statistics-2014 and the Certification Officer website, both © Crown copyright; and the Trades Union Congress website, © Trades Union Congress, reproduced with permission.

A closer look at the 2015 data reveals some interesting long-term trends in UK trade union membership. Female employees are more likely to be a trade union member. The proportion of female employees who were in a union was 27.7 per cent, compared with 22.3 per cent for male employees. Thus, the relative declines in the proportion of unionized employees who are in a union over the last decade has been much weaker for women. A higher proportion of UK born employees are in a trade union compared with non-UK born employees. About 26 per cent of UK-born employees were in a union, compared with 18 per cent for non-UK-born employees. The proportion of employees who were union members was greater for employees with a higher qualification, such as a degree, compared with those with no qualifications: about 31 per cent of employees with a degree or equivalent were in a trade union, compared with less than 20 per cent of employees without formal qualifications. Employees who worked in larger workplaces (with 50 or more employees) were more likely to be in a union and were more likely to have their pay affected by a collective agreement. The proportion of employees who belonged to a trade union in larger workplaces was 33 per cent, compared with 16 per cent in the workplaces with fewer less than 50 employees. Permanent employees were more likely than those in temporary jobs to be union members in all occupations. In 2014–15, the proportion of permanent employees who were union members was 26 per cent, compared with 15 per cent for temporary employees (Department for Business, Innovation and Skills, 2015).

reflective question Can you think of any environmental factors (for example, new legislation) that might lead workers to join unions? What internal factors (for example, perceived violation of the employment contract) can affect unionization?

HRM web
links

Visit the online resource centre at **www.palgravehighered.com/bg-hrm-6e** for further
information on union presence in the workplace in different countries.

Interpreting union decline

Although the general pattern clearly indicates that union membership and union density
in the UK have fallen sharply and continually since 1979, there is a debate over the precise
scale of the trend, its cause and its likely duration. Part of the problem is measurement.
The key statistic of union density can be measured in nine different ways depending on
which of three different data series for potential membership and trade union membership
is used (see Kelly and Bailey, 1989).

Bain and Price (1983) developed an influential explanation of variations in the rate of
unionization. The central argument here is that variations in union density over time were
explained by the business cycle, public policy, the restructuring of work and industry, and,
moreover, employer policy. Employer resistance to unions also has a decisive influence on
trade union recruitment. Others argue that although employer policy towards unions is a
significant influence, effective campaigning by unions can neutralize employer resistance
(Bronfenbrenner, 1997).

Although Bain and Price's approach is comprehensive, it is difficult to disentangle the
relative importance of each of the determinants in interpreting aggregate union decline in
the UK. Within the business cycle framework, it is contended that high levels of unemployment have eroded the constituencies of manual workers, from which unions have
traditionally recruited (Disney, 1990; Waddington, 1992). Following the election of a
Conservative government in 1979, public policy towards trade unions was overtly hostile.
Freeman and Pelletier (1990) estimate that the labour relations laws of the Thatcher
government reduced union density by 1–1.7 percentage points per year from 1980 to 1986.
This type of analysis is, however, fraught with problems: it is difficult to disentangle cause
and effect when dealing with trade union law (Disney, 1990).

The continual restructuring within the UK economy from manufacturing to service and
the growth of precarious employment also affects union membership (Doherty, 2009).
Another significant development is the collapse of compulsory unionism – the 'closed
shop' – among non-manual workers (Wright, 1996). Employers' policies will significantly
influence workers' support for unionization. As noted, the strategic de-recognition of
unions has been associated with the growing adoption of the 'Americanized' HRM model
(Brown et al., 1997). Hyman (2015) argues that part of the neo-liberal agenda is an 'ideological revolution' against unions.

With the Labour Government's 1999 Employment Relations Act, the climate for union
recognition became more favourable (Wood et al., 2002). The whole rhetoric of the New
Labour government towards the trade unions encouraged employers and workers to
reassess the benefits of unionization. At the time of writing, it is too early to assess whether
the new Conservative Government's Trade Union Act 2016, will place unions on the
defensive and cause the climate for union recognition to be less favourable. However,
recent analysis of union decline over the past three decades emphasizes the interplay
between the effects of globalization, particularly imports of manufactured goods from
developing countries and financialization, that is, the increasing role of finance and financial actors in developed economies rather than manufacturing activities and actors

(Vachon et al., 2016). The increasing number of workers on precarious contracts, the adverse political and legal environments and the growing number of firms adopting a union-exclusion strategy will also negatively affect union development and density.

HRM web links

Visit the online resource centre at www.palgravehighered.com/bg-hrm-6e for further information on the union-renaissance report and the latest figures for union recognition agreements.

Union structure

The word 'structure' in relation to trade unions denotes the 'external shape' of trade unions (Hyman, 1975) or job territories – the areas of the labour market from which the union aims to recruit. There are many variants of union structure within countries, traditionally expressed in terms of the four classic ideal types: craft, industrial, general and white-collar unions. In practice, however, these classical union structures have never existed in their true forms (Ebbinghaus and Waddington, 2000). In the British contemporary trade union movement, the wave of union mergers over the past three decades reflects the 'deep crisis' in unionization and has resulted in the formation of 'super-unions' (Ebbinghaus and Waddington, 2000).

UK trade unions recorded a total membership of 6,449,000 in 2015. The major unions, with a membership of over 100,000, accounted for 4,940,000 members, or 77 per cent of the total. Table 9.4 illustrates the wave of mergers and amalgamations of Trades Union Congress (TUC)-affiliated trade unions since 1979. It shows that the number of trade unions affiliated to the TUC has fallen from 109 to 52, almost entirely as a result of mergers. The three largest unions, with a membership of over, 3,193,000 (Table 9.4), accounted for 49.5 per cent of TUC union membership in 2015. This illustrates a philosophy of 'big is best' to encourage 'natural growth', and an 'industrial logic' (Waddington, 1988) in order to avoid the duplication of administrative costs. In 2007, for example, the union Unite was formed by the merger of Amicus and the TGWU, amid expectations that the new enlarged union would give employees the largest resources in industrial disputes. In explaining merger activity, formal union links to the British Labour Party, what is called a 'political logic', are also influential (Waddington and Whitston, 1994).

The structure of British trade unions is recognized to be complex, diverse and 'chaotic' – as observed by Hyman (1997a) – and the competitive scramble to seek membership anywhere has created trade union structures that can seem bewildering and incomprehensible. The membership distribution between individual trade unions is skewed. At one extreme, there are a relatively small number of trade unions with a disproportionate share of the total union membership, whereas at the other there are a large number of unions with very small memberships. As the data in Table 9.4 show, the 10 largest TUC-affiliated unions have a membership of 4.9 million, 76.5 per cent of total TUC membership – close to 80 per cent of all TUC membership. The major structural characteristic of British trade unions in 2015 was the predominance of horizontal or 'conglomerate' unions, that is, large individual unions whose members were distributed over a wide range of different industries. In the past decade, parallel trends of restructuring have become evident among trade unions in other developed capitalist economies (see, for example, Ebbinghaus and Waddington, 2000; Streeck and Visser, 1997; Visser and Waddington, 1996).

Table 9.4 *Largest TUC-affiliated unions, 1979–2015*

Ranking union (size)	Affiliated membership			Website (www)
	Membership (000s)		% change	
	1979	2015	1979–2015	
1. UNITE[1]	5,058	1,310	(–) 74.1	unitetheunion.org.uk
2. UNISON[2]	1,697	1,266	(–) 25.4	unison.org.uk
3. GMB	967	617	(–) 36.2	gmb.org.uk
4. USDAW	470	433	(–) 7.9	usdaw.org.uk
5. NUT	n.d.	330		teachers.org.uk
6. NASUWT	197	293	(+) 48.7	nasuwt.org.uk
7. PCS	291	247	(–) 15.1	pcs.org.uk
8. CWU[3]	124	201	(+) 62.1	cwu.org
9. ATL[4]	n.d.	127		atl.org.uk
10. PROSPECT[5]	n.d	116		prospect.org.uk
Total TUC membership	**12,175**	**6,449**	**(–) 47.0**	tuc.org.uk
Number of TUC unions	**109**	**52**	**(–) 52.3**	

[1]*Formed by the merger in 2007 of TGWU and Amicus (Amicus having been created by the 2002 merger of the AEEU and MSF)*

[2]*Formed by the merger in 1992 of NALGO, NUPE and COHSE*

[3]*Growth has been caused by merger activity within the communications industry.*

[4]*New union entering top 10 through merger activity – ATL represents education professionals across the UK*

[5]*New union entering top 10 through merger activity – PROSPECT represents scientists, engineers, managers and other specialists across the private and public sector n.d., no data*

Source: TUC (2015) TUC Directory 2015. London: TUC. Available at: www.tuc.org.uk/sites/default/files/TUC_Directory_2015_Digital_Version.pdf
© Trades Union Congress, reproduced with permission.

HRM web
links

For further information on union membership, governance, services and policies, go to any of the websites listed in Table 9.4.

Collective bargaining

The previous sections have examined the principal 'actors' in labour relations: management and the unions. We will now focus our attention on a central activity that regulates the collective employment relationship for over 9 million UK workers – collective bargaining. In any democratic society, the freedom for workers to bargain collectively is a core human right (Adams, 2006). In Canada, for example, the Charter of Rights protects the right to collective bargaining in the workplace. In a landmark judgement in Canada in 2007, Chief Justice Beverley McLachlin and Mr Justice Louis LeBel (quoted by Makin, 2007, p. A4) wrote:

> The right to bargain collectively with an employer enhances the human dignity, liberty and autonomy of workers by giving them the opportunity to influence the establishment of workplace rules and thereby gain some control over a major aspect of their lives, namely their work.

HRM as I see it

Ray Fletcher OBE
Director of Personnel and Development, Unite the Union

www.unitetheunion.org

Unite is a large trade union that was formed by a merger between two of Britain's leading unions, the TGWU and Amicus. It is a democratic and campaigning union that strives to achieve equality in the workplace for its members, as well as advancing its members' interests politically. Unite is active on a global scale and represents over 1.3 million members in the UK, Republic of Ireland, North America and the Caribbean.

Ray Fletcher worked in personnel in the automobile and building materials industries before moving over to the not-for-profit sector, where he became Executive Director of HR and External Affairs at Remploy. Remploy seeks to provide sustainable employment opportunities for disabled people, and Ray was awarded an OBE in 2004 for his work there. Ray currently works at Unite. He is a Fellow of the Chartered Institute of Personnel and Development and the Chartered Institute of Marketing, and has 40 years' experience in personnel.

Click on Ray's picture in your ebook to watch him talking about trade unions in the contemporary workplace, their contribution to workplace learning and possibilities for union–green coalitions, and then think about the following questions:

1 According to Ray, in the context of change and restructuring, does the role of HR change?
2 What does Unite do to promote learning at work?
3 Can a balance be found between green policies and the interests of union members?

We define collective bargaining here as:

> An institutional system of formal negotiation in which the making, interpretation and administration of rules, as well as the application of statutory controls affecting the employment relationship, are decided within union–management negotiating committees.

Several important points arise from this definition. First, formal collective bargaining is a process through which representatives of the union and management *jointly* determine some of the rules and regulations relating to the employment contract. As such, it is a form of workplace democracy, which has been well articulated by Chamberlain and Kuhn (1965; quoted in Adams, 2006). The ethical principle underlying the concept of collective bargaining as a process of industrial governance is that those who are integral to the conduct of the enterprise should have a voice in decisions of concern to them. Collective bargaining is therefore a correlation of political democracy.

The second important point is that there are two types of rule: *substantive* and *procedural*. Substantive rules establish terms and conditions of employment, such as pay, working hours and holidays, whereas procedural rules regulate the way in which substantive rules are made and interpreted, and indicate how workplace conflicts are to be resolved.

Building employers blacklisted thousands of workers

Getty Images/moodboard RF Thinkstock Images moodboard

For many years, workers and trade unionists had suspected that large British construction companies were operating a secret blacklist of trade union activists. Some skilled workers suspected blacklisting because they had not been able to secure work for years even when the construction industry was booming. David Clancy, the chief investigator at the regulatory agency the Information Commissioner's Office, after a leak about the conspiracy and months of searching, raided the hub of the operation in a small anonymous office in Droitwich, in the West Midlands. In February 2009, Clancy and his officers found a database managed by a secretive and unregistered organization called the Consulting Association, which was run by its Director Ian Kerr with the assistance of a couple of part-time staff including his wife (Smith and Chamberlain, The Guardian, 2015). Files were found bearing the names, addresses and National Insurance numbers of 3213 workers, with comments by managers and newspaper clippings about individuals and their involvement in various trade union and political activities. Files included phrases such as 'will cause trouble, strong TU [trade union]' and 'ex-shop steward, definite problems' (quoted in Smith and Chamberlain, The Guardian, 2015). Many individuals were included because they had voiced concerns about health and safety procedures.

In oral evidence to MPs (House of Commons, 2012), Kerr described how, in return for an annual subscription and a fixed fee per enquiry, he would check applicants for work against his database, which contained information on individuals supplied by managers and from his own monitoring of left-wing organizations. The HR departments of construction firms submitted lists of job applicants, and Kerr contacted the head managers of HR departments if he possessed information on any of the individuals. Kerr admitted that no more than 30 per cent of his files had been seized, and that after the raid he had smashed his computer hard drive and memory sticks and burned all his files. It was later discovered that he had intelligence on environment campaigners, journalists, politicians, academics and teachers, firefighters and postal staff (Syal, The Guardian, 2015; Evans, The Guardian, 2015). Blacklisting ruined people's chances to earn a living and created stress and illness.

In October 2015, eight major construction firms admitted their role in the collection of defamatory information on workers and 'submitted an "unprecedented" apology to the High Court for anxiety and distress' caused to over 600 workers (Syal, The Guardian, 2015). The defendants in the case were

(continued)

Stop! The activities of the Consultancy Association were illegal – what laws do you think were broken? Have you worked in HR and been asked to submit details to an organization that collects data on applicants including their trade union or political activities? If so what was your reaction? If, in the future, you were employed in HR, how do you think you would react if asked to submit details of job applicants to a vetting organization? The Consultancy Association was closed down after its discovery, but do you think there might be other organizations still doing the same kind of scrutiny of job applicants?

Sources and further information: For more information, see Evans (2015), House of Commons (2012), Smith and Chamberlain (2015) and Syal (2015).

Note: This feature was written by David Denham.

Balfour Beatty, Carillion, Costain, Kier, Laing O'Rourke, Sir Robert McAlpine, Skanska UK and Vinci. Payments for settlement could cost up to £250,000 in some cases, but the companies are still contesting the effects of their actions on individual workers. The union Unite has called for full compensation and a reinstatement of workers in their jobs.

Unions have called for a public enquiry into the blacklisting and safeguards to ensure that it cannot occur again. A further cause for concern is the allegation by a former undercover police officer that information gathered by the secret services and the police about legitimate political activities of workers was shared with the blacklisters (Evans, The Guardian, 2015).

Third, the parties negotiating the collective agreement also *enforce* the agreement. Unlike, for example, Canada and the USA, the British system of collective bargaining is perhaps most noted for its lack of legal regulation. Collective agreements are, with a few exceptions, not regarded as contracts of legal enforcement between the parties (see Davies and Freedland, 1994).

The fourth significant point to note is that informal relations help to shape and lubricate the formal collective employment relationship. The influential Donovan Commission reported that Britain had both a 'formal system' of labour relations consisting of trade unions and employers' associations, and an 'informal system' created 'by the actual behaviour of managers, shop stewards and workers' (Donovan, 1968, p. 12). This classic study observed that informality informed workplace negotiations because of the predominance of unwritten understandings and of custom and practice. Recent research has shed further light on the role and importance of informal social relations and the complexity of the interdependencies, levels of trust and reciprocal obligations that define and lubricate the formal negotiating process itself (Findlay et al., 2009; Sennett, 2012). As Sennett (2012) observes, workers forge informal bonds and friendships with co-workers including managers, and although these do not eliminate conflict, they help to create civility in the organization.

Collective bargaining structure

The structure of collective bargaining is the framework within which negotiations take place and defines the scope of the employers and employees covered by the collective agreement. In Britain, for much of the post-1945 period, there was no single uniform structure of collective bargaining, the major structural characteristic of the system being wide variety. Collective bargaining was conducted at several levels – workplace, corporate or industry-wide. In practice, survey evidence showed that collective bargaining structures were closely linked with business structures and 'profit centres'. Union recognition and collective bargaining coverage – the percentage of employees whose pay and working conditions are negotiated between a union and their employer – are mutually dependent. Industry-wide collective agreements covering core pay, hours and holidays items were, however, never strong in Britain (Hutton, 2015a, p. 184), and responsibility for pay bargaining migrated to individual enterprises even before Prime Minister Thatcher's assault on trade union bargaining power. In the early 1980s, around 70 per cent of employees had their pay determined by collective bargaining between employers and trade unions. But from 1980–84 onwards, collective bargaining coverage started to decline and this continued into the twenty-first century, albeit at a slower rate than in the 1980s and 90s. The demise of pay bargaining is a significant feature of the 'transformation' in UK workplace employment relations (Millward et al., 2000, p. 234).

Table 9.5 *Coverage and scope of collective bargaining and union presence in Britain, 2004–11 (percentages)*

	Private sector		Public sector		All workplaces	
	2004	2011	2004	2011	2004	2011
Employees covered by collective bargaining	16	16	68	44	28	23
Unions recognized	29	31	94	96	45	47
Pay bargaining	61	56	56	52	58	54
Hours	50	37	55	45	52	42
Holidays	52	41	51	44	51	43

Source: Data from van Wanrooy, B., Bewley, H., Bryson, A. Forth, J., Freeth, S., Stokes, L., and Wood, S. (2013a, pp.79-81) *Employment Relations in the Shadow of Recession: Findings from the 2011 Workplace Employment Relations Study.* Basingstoke: Palgrave Macmillan. Reproduced with the permission of the authors and sponsors.

Data from the 2013 WERS record the decline of collective bargaining in Britain. In 2011, collective bargaining over pay was no longer the norm in Britain (Table 9.5). Although 31 per cent of private sector workplaces had a recognized trade union, only 16 per cent of employees had their terms and conditions determined by collective bargaining. Indeed, WERS reported that in 2011 the employer had negotiated over pay in only 56 per cent of private sector workplaces where trade unions were formally recognized for negotiation. The proportion of workers covered by collective agreements broadly reflects the pattern of union density, and the latest findings on the scope of collective bargaining in the private sector are strongly reminiscent of those published in earlier WERS studies (Brown, W., 2010; Cully et al., 1999; Kersley et al., 2006; van Wanrooy et al., 2013a).

By the early twenty-first century, collective bargaining coverage in the private sector had thus diminished to 'a patchy and highly localised protection to a small and shrinking minority of workers' (Brown and Nash, 2008, p. 102). The WERS survey demonstrates that the low incidence of pay bargaining in most of the unionized sector, even when the unions are recognized by the employer for this purpose, is a defining feature of labour relations in Britain (van Wanrooy et al., 2013a). As Brown (Brown, W., 2010, p. 258) observes, the demise in collective bargaining coverage has meant that, for the vast majority of private sector workers, 'the only cushion against the vagaries of an open labour market has been provided by the state' through the statutory national minimum wage. The steep decline in collective bargaining coverage appears to be largely confined to the UK. The coverage rate is as high as 70 per cent or more in western EU member states, such as Belgium, Denmark, Finland, France, Italy, the Netherlands and Sweden.

HRM web links Visit the online resource centre at **www.palgravehighered.com/bg-hrm-6e** for further information on union membership in the EU.

Collective bargaining over pay, effort level and the control of work is the *raison d'être* of trade unionism, but the data underscore how little involved unions are in pay bargaining and other aspects of the employment contract in twenty-first-century Britain. There has been considerable debate over the causes of the sustained collapse in collective bargaining. The contraction of employment in the manufacturing sector, anti-union legislation and

Conservative governments' overt hostility to collective bargaining during the 1980s and early 1990s are commonly assumed to have undermined union strength and collective bargaining. Arguably, the 'golden age' of collective bargaining was relatively short-lived – from 1950 to 1960 – since when it has been going downhill. However, by focusing on collective bargaining and formal 'rule-making', this perspective arguably downplays the daily interaction between workers and line managers, as the informal 'rules of the game' are negotiated on a day-to-day basis (Krahn et al., 2011).

Brown (Brown, W., 2010, p. 262) suggests that the collapse of collective bargaining has been caused by the destabilizing forces of globalization and privatization: 'Legislative restraints on trade unions may have accelerated the process, but it was tougher competitive environments that reduced the share of profits that [the unions] could win for their members'. Globalization may have had a profound effect, but this does not fully explain why collective bargaining, as a system of workplace governance, remains relatively stable in EU member states. The focus on the precipitous decline in union density may be obscuring other factors underlying the collapse of collective bargaining, for example the shift in power towards management. As Hyman (1975, p. 26) explains, employment is a power relationship in which conflict is always a likelihood:

> In every workplace there exists an invisible frontier of control, reducing some of the formal powers of the employer: a frontier which is defined and redefined in a continuous process of pressure and counter-pressure, conflict and accommodation, overt and tacit struggle.

In the UK, post-2008 austerity, the absence of support from the state for unions and a decline in labour's bargaining power has contributed to the diminishing significance of collective bargaining as a means of regulating the employment relationship (Sullivan, 2010). UK survey data illustrate this shift in the balance of power between employers and unions. In private sector employment, the proportion of workplaces in which managers *did not* negotiate over pay and conditions of employment, even though unions were recognized in their workplace, increased from 28 per cent to 37 per cent between 2004 and 2011 (van Wanrooy, et al., 2013a).

HRM web links Visit the online resource centre at **www.palgravehighered.com/bg-hrm-6e** for more information on the WERS 2011 survey first findings, and EU data.

The collective agreement: an overview

The outcome of collective bargaining is a collective agreement that provides for the terms and conditions of employment of those employees covered by the agreement, also specifying the procedure that will govern the relationship between the signatories. In Britain, the terms of the collective agreement are binding in law on the parties if they are incorporated into the individual contract of employment (see Emir, 2014, for a legal discussion on incorporation). For management, the formal negotiation of a collective agreement is an instrument for rewriting the 'rules' governing the workplace. For trade unions, the process of negotiating a collective agreement offers an opportunity for union representatives to become 'embedded' in workplace governance (Findlay et al., 2009). A key determinant of the contents of the agreement is the balance of power between the parties (Brown, W., 2010).

HRM web
links

Visit the online resource centre at www.palgravehighered.com/bg-hrm-6e for suggestions on how to write a collective agreement.

Union density, collective bargaining and rising income inequality

Wage austerity has been a feature in both the UK and the EU's largest economy, Germany, in the post-2008 period (see Flassbeck and Lapavitsas, 2015). In the USA and France, similar trends have been documented (Piketty, 2014; Stiglitz, 2015). Alongside wage austerity, there has also been a rise in pay inequality, which we detailed in Chapter 8. Over the past three decades, we have witnessed 'stratospheric levels' of inequality, with top UK executives now earning 184 times more than the average full-time worker.

The more orthodox explanations of growing income inequality underscore changes in the labour market, a contraction of manufacturing, low productivity and a squeeze on wages from growing competition from China as part of the globalization phenomenon. Important as those economic forces are, this narrative neglects, in Britain's case, a 'home-grown' explanation: the emasculation of British trade unions and the collapse of collective bargaining. Economists Kumhof et al. (2012) pinpointed the rise of inequality to the decline of collective bargaining and its effect on real wages. They hypothesized that a cumulative decline in collective bargaining power of 10 per cent would result in a 7 per cent decline in real wages. This, Hutton (2015a, p. 180) observes, 'is what happened: the fall in union density … was associated with an accumulative decline in real wages 7 per cent below what they would otherwise have been.'

The available data show a correlation between reduced levels of union density and income inequality (Ewing and Hendy, 2013) and, concomitantly, low levels of private sector collective bargaining over workers' pay in the UK (Figure 9.1). The 'transformation' in the system of collective bargaining has been well documented (Millward et al., 2000), showing that the percentage of private sector employees covered by pay bargaining fell from around 48 per cent in the mid-1980s to 16 per cent in 2011 (Kersley et al., 2006; van Wanrooy et al., 2013a). Figure 9.1 shows, between 1979 and 2011, a correlation between falling levels of union density and pay bargaining and a widening gap between the incomes of rich and poor in the UK (Wilkinson and Pickett, 2010). Since 1979, income inequality, as shown by the Gini Coefficient, has increased significantly, levelling in the 1990s and, after a slight fall, reaching a new peak of 0.36 in 2011. As Wilkinson and Pickett (2010, p. 239) observe, 'Few other developed countries have shown quite such dramatic increases over this period.'

The cumulative decline in collective bargaining power and real wages partly explains why the UK, along with the USA, Portugal and Singapore, is one of the lowest ranked economies for equality (see Figure 8.4). The concept of distributive justice – the outcomes and allocations emerging from organizational processes – is useful to help us understand the possible reaction to extreme income inequality (Bratton, 2015). Interested readers can look at the primary sources, but, for our purposes, we can say that organizational justice (or at least perceptions of it) correlates highly with positive workplace outcomes including more positive evaluations of managers (Ball et al., 1993), enhanced organizational citizenship behaviour (Organ, 1990), lower turnover and absenteeism (Masterson et al., 2000), and higher levels of trust between managements and their workforces (Folger and

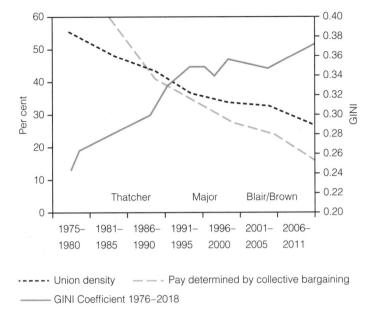

------ Union density   — — - Pay determined by collective bargaining

——— GINI Coefficient 1976–2018

Figure 9.1 UK trade union density, private sector collective bargaining and rising income inequality

Sources: data from All Change At Work?: British Employment Relations 1980–1998, as portrayed by the Workplace Industrial Relations Survey Series, 1st edition, by Alex Bryson, John Forth and Neil Millward. Copyright © 2000 Routledge. Reproduced with permission of Taylor & Francis Books UK. Other data: Kersley et al. (2006) and van Wanrooy et al. (2013a), both reproduced with permission of the authors and sponsors; the TUC (2011) © Trades Union Congress, reproduced with permission; and the Family Resources Survey and Family Expenditure Survey (via the Institute for Fiscal Studies and the Equality Trust (see https://www.equalitytrust.org.uk/how-has-inequality-changed), © Crown copyright.

Cropanzano, 1998). Those positive outcomes may explain an emerging accord that Britain's flexible labour market has become 'too flexible', entrenching low pay and low productivity, and discouraging investment (Hutton, 2015a).

reflective question

> What do you think of the hypothesis that the decline in union density and the collective bargaining power of unions is the principal cause of income inequality and low productivity?

Union strategies and paradox

The precipitous decline in union density and collective bargaining coverage provides the backcloth for examining very divergent union renewal strategies. At its core, a union renewal strategy seeks to deliver sustainable increases in workplace power for both unions and their members (Simms and Holgate, 2010). In his study of British trade unions, Heery (2005, p. 103) argues that union strategy is not simply a pragmatic adjustment to a changing national business system: 'It is also an expression of internal politics, dialogue and power … [thus] union politics matter.' Efforts by unions to reverse the steep decline in union density and bargaining coverage have prompted a body of scholarship on union renewal (see, for example Hickey et al., 2010). It would be misleading to develop a typology of union strategies – one with mutually exclusive categories – but, for our purposes, we have identified two dominant strategic approaches for the renewal of British trade unions: organizing strategy and partnership strategy.

HRM and globalization 9.2

The role of unions in South Africa

© iStockphoto.com/RapidEye

For decades, the apartheid policies of South Africa were condemned by nations around the world. Studies of South Africa during this period reveal persistent patterns of inequality, which appeared to have changed little since the early days of colonialism. The reasons for this were obvious. Laws and policies supported by the South African state provided a foundation on which the exploitation of the black African majority could be pursued without sanction. South Africa embodied what Charles Tilly (2008) calls 'categorical inequality', an asymmetrical situation in which the advantages enjoyed by one category of persons are directly related to the disadvantages experienced by another.

All this began to change in the late 1970s and early 1980s. Crucial to the change were penalties imposed on South Africa by the international community. Also important were various forms of social protest, protests that often united groups with different ethnic and racial backgrounds. During this period, unions acted as agents of change. According to Barchiesi (2008, p. 121), the success of unions as change agents may be attributed to three factors: 'their capacity to forge broad social alliances with unwaged sectors …, their ability to put pressure on ruling parties … [and] their internal democratic practices.'

In the postapartheid period, the ability of unions to act as agents of progressive change has diminished. As elsewhere, integration with the global economic system has gone hand in hand with changing belief systems. There is a trend among some South African politicians to endorse versions of neo-liberalism – the belief that the state's role in society, including in protecting workers and the environment, should be cut back.

When neo-liberalism emerges as the dominant political belief system, corporations and employers are empowered. This is due in part to the so-called 'race to the bottom' (see Chapter 17). When one country fails to enforce rules protecting workers, other countries feel compelled to do the same. Unions find themselves in a vulnerable position, as governments move to privatize public services, and corporations threaten to send work 'off shore' if union demands are too high. In one case discussed by Barchiesi (2008), a third union-weakening strategy is identified: the company supplements its workforce by local outsourcing, hiring workers from a labour brokering agency. These workers are on fixed-term contracts and do not receive medical insurance. Barchiesi concludes that, due in part to this general climate of neo-liberalism and its associated HR practices, union traditions of collective action and democratic practice in South Africa are being eroded.

It is important to note that the vulnerable situation unions find themselves in is not limited to places such as South Africa where restrictions against unions have only recently been lifted. Even in the USA, where unions have been considered to be a legitimate and valuable part of civil society, their very right to exist has been challenged: in Madison, Wisconsin, the governor sought to enact legislation that would all but eliminate unions and collective agreements in the public sector.

Stop! Are you familiar with other situations in which unions have been agents of progressive social change? In the USA, there has been a decline in the percentage of workers enrolled in unions but events in Madison suggest that unions can still play a role in articulating a vision of the just society. Explain.

Sources and further information: See Barchiesi (2008) and Tilly (2008) for more information on this topic.

Note: This feature was written by David MacLennan.

The *organizing strategy* is internally focused and places a renewed emphasis on 'organizing the unorganized'. The insider–outsider literature generally proposes that only the 'insiders' – full-time permanent workers – enjoy trade union representation and protection against dismissal (Pulignano et al., 2015). Thus, a sustained attempt is made to recruit 'outsiders' – zero-hour, part-time workers – who are outside the traditional white male norm of full-time employment. The organizing strategy includes a change in union priorities, such that they accommodate a more diverse workforce, 'issue-based' recruiting, for example focusing on 'justice, dignity and respect' issues (Heery, 2002, 2004, 2005), and the use of social media to mobilize members and non-members around campaigns, especially in the UK and countries of the Eurozone (Panagiotopoulos and Barnett, 2015). The aim is to establish an effective workplace union organization that can be self-sustaining in terms of recruitment and service to its members. In this, Bacon and Hoque (2015) provide thought-provoking research on the role and influence of 'disability champions'. Similar to union health and safety representatives, workplace union representatives can conduct disability audits and help to improve employers' equal opportunities practices with regard to disability. Hickey et al. (2010) note an interesting paradox: when statutory procedures, rather than 'pure bargaining power', provide for workplace union organization, the disassociation between the two may have a detrimental effect on employees' commitment to the union. An analysis of successful union renewal campaigns shows support for a strategy that combines both 'bottom-up' grassroots activism and 'top-down' leadership-driven strategies tailored to the specific context (Hickey et al., 2010).

The second dominant approach for the renewal of unions is the *social partnership strategy*. This strategy is externally focused, with its emphasis on labour relations embedded in 'union-friendly' employment law. Central to the argument is the belief that renewal requires trade unions to take advantage of the facilitating effect of employment law and EU social policy in order to develop a new form of workplace governance in increasingly complex competitive environments (see, for example, Terry, 2003). As noted elsewhere, post-Brexit, what elements of EU directives are passed into UK law remains uncertain. The theoretical basis of the approach can be traced back to North American literature on 'strategic partnerships', 'mutual gains' and 'win–win' principles: reciprocal employer–trade union commitments to deliver mutual gains and establish the basis for trust and cooperation to develop high-performance work systems (Betcherman et al., 1994; Kochan et al., 1986; Verma, 1995).

Following the election of the 'New Labour' government in the UK in 1997, a partnership approach, part of the government's broader 'Third Way' philosophy, to labour relations became increasingly popular and was adopted by some employers. The TUC published *Partners for Progress: New Unionism in the Workplace* (TUC, 1999), which advocated 'pragmatic partnership' agreements between local union representatives and managers. In the context of falling membership, the unions presented themselves to potential members and employers alike as 'facilitators of cooperative collective relationships' that would have mutual economic benefits (Brown, 2000, p. 303).

The term 'partnership' is used in a variety of ways. With this caveat in mind, it can be applied to quasi employment relations government bodies; for example, unions play an important and constructive role with the UK Equal and Human Rights Commission, the Low Pay Commission, the Health and Safety Executive, the UL Commission for Employment and Skills and ACAS. Partnership can also apply to tripartite discussions and involvement between employers and union representatives and the government. For example, addressing the 2010 TUC Green Growth Conference, Frances O'Grady, TUC Deputy General Secretary, outlined a partnership approach: 'We want a mature debate about how we can accelerate progress towards a low-carbon, ecofriendly economy ... And we want to work with ministers and with industry to achieve a *just transition* to a greener economy' (O'Grady, 2010).

At *societal level*, there is scope for trade unions to take responsibility for the two major social needs – lowering inequality and re-enfranchising workers. Hutton (2015a), in *How Good We Can Be*, argues for a new union and management partnerships in which unions pioneer profit-sharing and employee share ownership schemes and provide skilled pension fund trustees and remuneration directors to determine executive pay. He advocates that trade unions should be reinvented around the Nordic model with new forms of workplace organization that replace collective bargaining with 'collective creativity' and union engagement in life-long learning (Cassell and Lee, 2009). This approach envisions unions to be like premodern town guilds, guardians of skills and fair wages, pioneers in the rein-vention of the public sector and of the new digital economy, rather than confrontational representatives of a shrinking manual working class: 'In this conception the unions do not fight capitalism; they continually reshape and reconfigure it' (Hutton, 2015a, p.188).

HRM web links

Visit the online resource centre at **www.palgravehighered.com/bg-hrm-6e** for further information on trade union strategies for a 'green' economy.

At *workplace level*, 'partnership' agreements promote innovation and organizational change in exchange for a union 'voice' in work-related issues. According to Roche (2009), partnership-related practices give rise to 'win–win' or 'mutual gains' for each of the main stakeholders: employers, employees and unions. Employers appear to gain with respect to organizational commitment, the climate of employment relations and the quality of managerial supervisory relations. Partnership-related practices improve the intrinsic aspects of work, such as work autonomy, job satisfaction and fairness, for employees. In addition, the trade unions gain with respect to union commitment, influence, the likelihood of increased membership and social legitimacy.

An analysis of the partnership agreements signed in Britain between 1990 and 2007 shows that most have only modest objectives and are 'substantially hollow', although they do offer unions increased involvement in management's decisions (Samuel and Bacon, 2010). Partnership agreements can potentially give unions a place at the 'strategy table' by portraying themselves as authoritative partners in economic management (Martin, 2010; Munro and Rainbird, 2000).

reflective question

What do you think of workplace partnerships? How does the partnership strategy reframe employment relations? What are the advantages and disadvantages of partnership?

Partnership agreements also have their detractors (see, for example, Bacon and Storey, 2000; Clayton, 1998; Kelly, 1996; O'Dowd and Roche, 2009; Watson et al., 2009). Clayton (1998), for example, remains sceptical about the likelihood of workplace partnership devel-oping as a vehicle for reconstituting trade union power in response to long-term decline. To paraphrase Guest (2001), UK management is currently driving the bus, and although the unions may be invited along for the ride, they will remain in the passenger seats to offer guidance only; they will not be trusted to do any driving. Kelly (1996, p. 101) argues that, rather than strengthening the unionization process, partnership can potentially 'weaken or inhibit the growth of workplace union organization', and partnership agreements may form part of 'a longer term *non-union* strategy' (Bacon and Storey, 2000, p. 410).

At a more theoretical level, Watson and his colleagues (2009) note that the partnership model is a problematic concept because of its variety of meanings and potential denial of the 'dual nature' of the employment relationship that involves both cooperation *and* conflict (2009). An analysis of the characteristics of British corporate governance – a preference for short-term financial performance and the maintenance of shareholder values (Purcell, 1995) – suggests that British business is an infertile environment for social partnership (Heery, 2002).

Table 9.6 *The benefits and costs of a partnership strategy*

	Benefits	**Costs**
For organizations	• Efficiency gains • Lower absenteeism/turnover • Better union–management relations • Potential for improved performance	• Greater investment in work-related learning and other HR programmes • Having to share information • Having to share decision-making
For workers	• Access to work-related learning • Potentially increased skills • Discretion over the work process	• A need for greater commitment to the firm • Job loss and lower income growth • Greater work intensification and job-related stress
For unions	• Participation in decision-making • Affirmation of an independent voice for workers • Access to information • Improved status	• A move away from job control unionism • Isolation from union members • Leaders challenge

Source: Based on Betcherman et al. (1994)

In the long run, partnership is likely to be sustained if it holds the promise of real benefits for the employer, employees and unions. The interests of employers and labour are not identical, so an effective approach to partnership must involve acceptable trade-offs – the trade-offs associated with the partnership model shown in Table 9.6. It is hard to disentangle the effects of partnership. With this in mind, the challenge for trade unions is to transcend the polarized positions of outright opposition to partnership and cooperation, and focus on a strategy to extract the potential from partnership without avoiding traditional union-building activities.

The outcome is indeterminate and will depend upon the ongoing interaction between union and management, and, as Heery (2002) concludes, upon whether the 'qualitative' gains (for example, 'voice' and dignity) are not heavily outweighed by 'quantitative' losses (for example, job loss and inequality). The debate on 'union renewal' and 'social partnerships' occurred, of course, before the financial crisis that erupted in 2008 and has continued to reverberate around the globe (Nolan, 2011). A key focus of contemporary debate is the destructive contradiction between unsustainable short-term 'quarterly focused' business strategies that destroy the ecosystem and those which partner with trade union and environmental movements in the quest to achieve a *just*, low-carbon, ecofriendly economy (see, for example, Klein, 2015).

HRM web links

For further information on trade union 'partnership arrangements', visit the online resource centre at **www.palgravehighered.com/bg-hrm-6e** and read the additional HRM in practice feature.

Rama Garment factory

The setting

In the early twentieth century, the rapid expansion of industry and the growth of the working class in India led to an increase of skilled and literate workers who set the stage for unions to flourish in the workplace. The country's first trade union was formed in 1918, followed by the creation of the regulatory India Trades Union Act in 1926.

In 2012, only 6 per cent of the 487 million workforce in India were unionized, and of these most were employed by government, state-owned enterprises and large private sector companies. India has among the lowest trade union densities in the Asia-Pacific region, and the rate continues to decline.

Men overwhelmingly represent the majority of trade union membership in the country. The active participation of women in the trade union movement has historically been low, with social, historical, biological and religious constraints creating barriers to the higher paying opportunities that unionized workplaces can offer. Although the trade unions were successful in helping to establish the Maternity Benefit Act in 1961, Indian women are still under-represented at all levels of union leadership and decision-making, and their issues have not taken centre stage in union struggles.

One striking exception to trade union membership for women is in the garment industry, a major source of exports for India. More than 80 per cent of the 3 million people who work in the industry are women, and women can make up as many as 70 per cent of total union members. However, despite the presence of unions in the industry, the work is still characterized by long hours, low wages and minimal regulation.

The problem

Twenty-year-old Asha recently arrived in Baddi, an industrial town in northern India, to find work in the garment factory industry. She had followed her cousin Devi, who had fled their rural village several months earlier after failing to find local work that would pay enough to help support her family. Although both women knew the wages in Baddi's garment industry were low, a job in a factory would still pay more than they could earn performing the traditional agricultural or domestic work available to women in their village. Asha's father was severely ill, and her mother was depending on Asha to provide additional money for his medication. The women

also wanted to continue their education, a goal that would be highly unlikely if they remained at home.

Devi, who had had some experience as a seamstress, quickly found work in the tailoring section at one of the newer Baddi factories called Rama. She told Asha that the factory management preferred to hire young women, saying that women were more efficient and disciplined than men. Devi managed to get Asha an interview with the supervisor of the factory she worked for.

At the interview, the supervisor talked to Asha about job responsibilities and salary, and then ended the meeting by saying that she should not get involved in any kind of unionism. 'It's unproductive,' he said. 'You must pay attention only to your work.' Asha nodded and was happy to learn that she was hired for the job, although the money she would earn would still not be enough to pay for all of her father's medical bills.

On her first day on the job, Asha noticed that although there were a few men on the factory floor, the vast majority of her co-workers were women. The work was routine and the hours were long, but Asha was appreciative of the opportunity the factory management had given her. Within her first few weeks, she was able to send home money to help support her parents and buy her father's medicine.

Shortly after Asha had completed her first year at the factory, her father's condition worsened and he required more medication, putting a further strain on the family's finances. Kapil, who had been hired at the same time as

Asha, approached her when they began their shift. He told her that he had contacted a trade union leader to start the process of unionizing the workers and asked for her support. 'The union can help improve our working conditions and get us an increment in pay.' Kapil stressed that he needed the women in the factory to get involved as there were far more of them than men. 'We will never become unionized unless the women come forward,' he said. 'It's for their benefit too.' He asked Asha to meet him the next day to work out a strategy to get the other women to support the idea.

When Asha told Devi what Kapil had said, Devi warned Asha about talking to Kapil any further about unions. 'We cannot take this risk as it is the best work option we have. The men are always trying to bring in the union because it is easier for them to find work elsewhere if the factory lets us go. The other women will not cooperate with the men in trying to unionize our workplace.' Later that day, Asha read a notice that management had posted on the factory floor bulletin board warning that other factories in Baddi had been shut down because of unions protesting against work conditions. It also mentioned that management was reviewing possible pay increments, but only if the factory remained non-unionized.

Asha spent that night worrying about how she was going to continue to support her family and wondered if helping Kapil bring in the union was the right thing to do.

The assignment

Working either alone or in a study group, prepare a report drawing on this chapter and other recommended material addressing the following:

1 How does India's patriarchal society play a role in Asha's situation and for Indian women in general?
2 What type of industrial relations strategy is Rama's management applying? What national features of India's society and economy might be contributing to their choice of strategy?
3 If you were Asha, would you help Kapil bring in the union? Why or why not?

Essential reading

Chakravarty, D. (2007) 'Docile oriental women' and organised labour: a case study of the Indian garment manufacturing industry. *Indian Journal of Gender Studies*, **14**(3): 439–60.
Gani, A. (1996) Who joins the unions and why? Evidence from India. *International Journal of Manpower*, **17**(6–7): 54.
Mathias, P. and Davis, J. (eds) (1996) *International Trade and British Economic Growth: From the Eighteenth Century to the Present Day*. Oxford: Blackwell.
Mohanty, M. (ed.) (2004) *Class, Caste, Gender: Readings in Indian Government and Politics*. New Dehli: Sage.
Ramaswamy, E. and Schiporst, F. (2000) Human resource management, trade unions and empowerment: two cases from India. *International Journal of Human Resource Management*, **11**(4): 664–80.
Ratnam, V. (2006) *Industrial Relations*. New Dehli: Oxford University Press.
Saraswati, R. and Bagchi, D. (eds) (1993) *Women and Work in South Asia: Regional Patterns and Perspectives*. New York: Routledge.

Note: This fictional case study was written by Lori Rilkoff, and is based on research by Chakravarty, 2007.

 Visit the online resource centre at **www.palgravehighered.com/bg-hrm-6e** for guidelines on writing reports.

summary

➤ This chapter recognizes that managing work and people in the workplace includes a collective dimension. Research indicates that a union-avoidance strategy is the one most frequently adopted by UK and US companies. We have emphasized that the selection of a labour relations strategy involves managers considering a number of complex economic, political, legal and historical factors. Given the different conditions, each labour relations strategy is likely to be unique and display contradictory practices.

➤ We have also examined union membership, union structure and collective bargaining, and union strategies. In a nutshell, the dramatic reduction in union membership and collective bargaining coverage has led to a shift in power towards management. The argument here is that this shift in power makes it more likely that employers will be tempted to take the short-term 'low road' to profitability that can potentially violate the psychological contract.

➤ When analysing four fundamental factors influencing labour relations – the state of the labour market, management's strategic capacity, labour's strategic capacity and the legal and political context of labour relations – in the fifth edition of this book, we said that we thought the jury was still out on whether the present economic crisis would accelerate labour relations trends, and the 2013 WERS data suggest the demise of the unions has at least been stabilized.

➤ We have presented data showing, between 1979 and 2011, reduced levels of union density pay bargaining alongside a widening gap between the incomes of rich and poor in the UK. Since 1979, income inequality, as shown by the Gini Coefficient, has increased significantly, reaching a new peak in 2011.

➤ This chapter examined two dominant union strategies: organizing strategy and partnership strategy. We noted that the long-term success of the partnership strategy will depend upon ongoing union–management relations and on whether or not the qualitative gains are heavily outweighed by quantitative losses. We also emphasized the apparent contradiction in the two union strategy alternatives.

review questions

1 What is meant by the term 'labour relations', and why are labour relations strategies said to be the result of strategic choices?

2 Are trade unions good or bad for work organizations?

3 Why do employees join trade unions? How can contextual factors explain the development of British trade unions?

4 To what extent is collective bargaining in Britain too fragmented to function effectively in a global market?

5 What contradictions might be found in the twin goals of union renewal and social partnership?

6 Given the present economic crisis, what are the benefits, if any, of a 'social partnership' involving the union movement, environmental movements, employers and government to develop a sustainable green economy?

further reading

Reading these books, articles and chapters can help you gain a better understanding and potentially a higher grade for your HRM assignment.

➤ Bacon, N. and Hoque, K. (2015). The influence of trade union Disability Champions on employer disability policy and practice. *Human Resource Management Journal*, **25**(2): 233–49.

➤ Bacon, N. and Samuel, P. (2010) The contents of partnership agreements in Britain 1990–2007. *Work, Employment & Society*, **24**(3): 430–48.

➤ Brown, W. and Nash, D. (2008) What has happening to collective bargaining under New Labour? Interpreting WERS 2004. *Industrial Relations Journal*, **39**(2): 91–103.

➤ Burchill, F. (2014). *Labour relations*. London: Palgrave Macmillan. This is an accessible and engaging introduction to labour relations.

➤ Butler, P. (2009) Non-union employee representation: exploring the riddle of managerial strategy. *Industrial Relations Journal*, **40**(3): 198–214.

➤ Charlwood, A. (2002) Why do non-union employees want to unionize? Evidence from Britain. *British Journal of Industrial Relations*, **40**(3): 463–91.

➤ Findlay, P., McKinlay, A., Marks, A. and Thompson, P. (2009). Collective bargaining and new work regimes: 'too important to be left to bosses'. *Industrial Relations Journal*, **40**(3), 235–51. This provides an insight into the formal negotiation process.

➤ Heery, E. and Simms, M. (2010) Employer responses to union organizing: patterns and effects. *Human Resource Management Journal*, **20**(1): 3–22.

➤ Hutton, W. (2015) 'Reinventing unions to save them'. In *How Good We Can Be* (pp. 185–9), London: Abacus.

➤ Pohler, D. and Luchak, A. (2015) Are unions good or bad for organizations? The moderating role of management's response. *British Journal of Industrial Relations*, **53**(3): 423–59.

➤ Vachon, T.E., Wallace, M. and Hyde, A. (2016) Union Decline in a Neoliberal Age: Globalization, Financialization, European Integration, and Union Density in 18 Affluent Democracies, *Socius: Sociological Research for a Dynamic World* Volume 2: 1–22. DOI: 10.1177/2378023116656847

 Click here in your interactive ebook for a list of HRM terminology and vocabulary that has appeared in this chapter.

vocabulary checklist for ESL students

Visit the online resource centre at **www.palgravehighered.com/bg-hrm-6e** for lots of extra resources to help you get to grips with this chapter, including study tips, HRM skills development guides, summary lecture notes, tips for English as a Second Language (ESL) students and more.

part IV

EMPLOYMENT RELATIONS

chapter **10**

employee relations and voice

© Royalty-Free/Corbis

objectives

After studying this chapter, you should be able to:

1 Appreciate the importance of workplace communication in managing people

2 Define employee voice and explain the context in which employee voice has changed over time

3 Explain the types of employee voice mechanism used in practice, why managers might want to increase their use and the potential impact on organizational performance

4 Identify some ethical issues and their relevance to employee relations

5 Describe the major issues relating to sexual harassment and bullying in the workplace and the implications for managing employee relations

6 Explain the concepts, values and legal framework that underpin workplace grievance

DMW, an IT consulting company, was awarded first position in the 2015 Best Workplaces Programme in the small business category. Chris Dean, DMW's managing director, attributed the success to the company's 'people-centred ethos and commitment to effective communication' and 'high workplace engagement'. 'When we treat our staff with respect and give them an equal voice in helping to set the direction of DMW I have been continuously surprised at the innovation that they show,' he said (Great Place to Work Institute, 2015, p. 14). Less positive, reports in 2016 exposed the 'workhouse or gulag' conditions at Mike Ashley's Sports Direct, which included a 'six strikes and you're out' policy that sees workers dismissed for six infringements within 6 months (Goodley, The Guardian, 2016, p. 1) and highlighted the problems of working mothers – 20 per cent of working mothers said they experienced harassment or negative comments related to their pregnancy or flexible working from their employer or colleagues (Gallagher, 2016). These reports highlight the importance of three themes we examine in this chapter: communications, employee voice and individual legal rights that protect employees against inequitable treatment in the workplace.

introduction

As explained in the introductory chapter, the employment relationship can be created in three ways: unilaterally, bilaterally and trilaterally (the employer, unions and statutes). Whereas the field of 'labour relations' addresses the bilateral (collective) dimension of the employment relationship, 'employee relations' primarily focuses on the unilateral (individual) dimension of the employment relationship between an employer and individual employee. The individual employment relationship is based on managerial prerogative, the ideological assumption that managers, as agents of capital, have 'the right to manage', and is based on managerial power (Farnham, 2015). In the post-1980 period, and with the emergence of neo-liberal thinking, interest in the individual employment relationship surged and the term 'employee relations' became fashionable among some British academics (Leat, 2007). Here, we use the label 'employee relations' to encompass an assortment of human resources (HR) practices that seek to shape and regulate the employment relationship through communications, employee voice, individual grievance-handling and managerial disciplinary action. Although management-oriented, these HR practices provide an opportunity to create and maintain dignity *at* work (Bolton, 2007).

In this chapter, we will explain the nature of employee relations before exploring key issues related to workplace communication. We will then go on to explain the terms and the various forms of employee voice before examining the process governing individual employees' grievances and discipline.

The nature of employee relations

Exactly what constitutes employee relations is not explicable. The term is used in different ways and tends to encompass both collective and individual dimensions, union and non-union relationships. As we noted in Chapter 9, some authors use the terms 'industrial relations' and 'employee relations' interchangeably, while other scholars argue that there identifiable differences in the subject matter that justify the use of each term. Blyton and Turnbull (2004) adopted the term 'employee relations' partly because 'industrial relations' was too closely associated with trade unions, collective bargaining and industrial action, although they acknowledge that 'the management of employees, both individual and collective, remain a central feature of organizational life' (p. 3). Marchington and Wilkinson

(1996) justify the use of the term 'employee relations' principally because it is increasingly used by practitioners to describe workplace employment relations, both collective and individual, and it epitomizes the shift in focus to management issues; however, they acknowledge that they use the terms interchangeably. Other scholars define employee relations to include both non-union and union dimensions of the employment relationship. Leat (2007, p. 7), for example, uses the term 'employee relations' to:

> Encompass both individual and collective dimensions, union and non-union relationships, the changing nature of work and the employment relationship, and the wider contexts within which the employment relationship occurs. I do not take a managerial perspective or standpoint.

From a managerial perspective, the Chartered Institute of Personnel and Development (CIPD) justifies the use of the term 'employee relations' because 'the term 'industrial relations' is no longer widely used by employers and does not describe today's employment relationships, except in specific sectors, and even there in modified form'. The CIPD (2016, p. 1) views employee relations primarily as:

> A skill-set or a philosophy, rather than as a management function or well-defined area of activity … the emphasis of employee relations continues to shift from 'collective' institutions … to the relationship with individual employees, the ideas of 'employee voice' and the 'psychological contract' have been accepted by employers and reflected in their employee relations policies and employee relations skills and competencies are seen as critical to achieving performance benefits.

The literature presents a number of different definitions and perspectives, which arguably views employee relations as a wider concept than the traditional term 'industrial relations'. Here, the term 'employee relations' is used to encompass both individual and collective dimensions of the employment relationship, but the focus is given to the individual employee relations processes, skills and competencies as opposed to the collective relationship. As such, we examine an assortment of HR policies and practices that shape and influence the individual employment relationship with the objective of improving organizational performance – workplace communication, employee voice, employee rights and grievance-handling, and employee discipline – as shown in Figure 10.1.

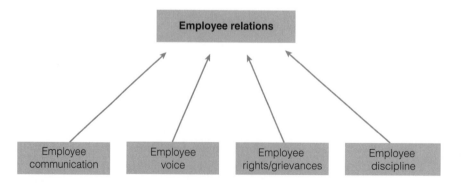

Figure 10.1 *Four important dimensions of employee relations*

The focus here on the individual employment relationship should not be interpreted to mean that 'union voice' is unimportant in the workplace – far from it. Edwards and Sengupta's (2010) evidence highlighting the 'social relations of performance' as a contested arena indicates that both employee voice and union voice are important for the achievement of both worker influence and sustainable organizational performance.

To emphasize Edwards and Sengupta's (2010) point, the four dimensions of employee relations can be operationalized both informally or formally and without or with a union voice. The concepts of *formal* and *informal* employee relations relate to the nature of relationships and the processes in the workplace. A formal communication process mirrors the literal structure of the organization with its organizational chart and hierarchical reporting relationships. Informal communication, often called the grapevine, is the unstructured and informal communication network based around social relationships rather than organizational charts. A formal employee voice scheme can include managers, individual employees and/or their union representatives participating in decision-making on committees or a governing body, such as a works council. On the other hand, employee voice may be informal, for example a line manager listening to suggestions from their subordinates. Furthermore, if an employee's conduct or performance does not meet organizational standards or targets, a line manager can seek to improve the employee's behaviour through informal conversations. However, if the employee's poor conduct or performance continues, a formal disciplinary procedure can be activated. The formal disciplinary procedure should – at the very least – comply with the statutory dismissal and disciplinary procedures and might include union participation in the proceedings. Thus, there can be a significant interaction between individual and collective forms of employee voice, grievance-handling, and disciplinary procedures.

reflective question

Looking at the four key dimensions of employee relations, how can HR practices in each area impact positively and negatively on individual employee relationships? Try to think about your own work experience of 'good' and 'poor' employee relations.

The antecedents of managerial leadership behaviours and the focus on 'leader–member exchange' as it applies to the HRM–performance debate underscore the importance of interpersonal *communications* in the workplace. Communication scholars emphasize the different ways in which managers communicate the content of a message to their subordinates, and how those ways of communicating affect the quality of the individual employment relationship. Witherspoon (1997, p. x), a specialist in leadership and communication, argues that 'leadership is to a great extent a communication process'. In our three-dimensional model of management (see Figure 1.2), communication is part of the process of influence by which line managers 'personalize' and enact HR practices, which is an element of the HR 'black box'. (See Chapter 3 for an extended discussion on the so-called HR 'black box'.)

Over the past decade, interest in the various aspects of *employee voice* has grown considerably in Europe and North America (Dundon et al., 2004; Gollan, 2006; Johnstone and Ackers, 2015; Marchington, 2008; Mayrhofer et al., 2000). The concept of 'employee voice' is ambiguous, with a variety of meanings, but despite this, 'voice can perhaps best be seen as the Holy Grail of employee relations; it is the promise of a harmonious and effective employment relationship built on trust, fairness, and respect' (Emmott, 2015, p. vii). For Marchington (2008), employee voice appears to be a vogue term used to describe HR practices designed to permit workers some 'say' in workplace decision-making. Some writers define employee voice in terms of two-way communication between management and employees (Bryson, 2004), whereas others suggest that it is best understood as a complex set of HR practices that are dialectically fashioned by internal management choice on the one hand, and external regulation on the other (Dundon et al., 2004). Processes that provide for employee voice include direct employee involvement and participation in workplace decision-making, whether via upward quality control techniques or indirect participative arrangements such as a works council.

It is suggested that allowing employees a bigger voice plays a critical role in constructing a high-involvement workplace and improving 'bottom-line' results for the organization. Taras and Kaufman (2006) observe that employee voice mechanisms aim to encourage cooperative and productive modes of employment interaction. According to Dundon et al. (2004), employee voice can be viewed as:

- A form of contribution to decision-making
- An articulation of individual dissatisfaction (or satisfaction)
- A demonstration of collective organization.

At the heart of HR strategy is the extent to which employees have a voice in workplace decision-making. The search for causal links between strategic HRM and organizational performance has elevated the importance of understanding the relationship between employee voice and performance. Employee voice practices can thus be seen as a management-designed means to transform the climate of employee relations by long-term changes in workers' attitudes and commitment that shape 'organizational citizenship' (Guest, 2008). However, Boxall and Purcell (2011) remind us that managers' choices in employee voice arrangements are not solely about the economic 'bottom line'. The beliefs and values of managers, employees and society at large, the notion of social legitimacy, provide a crucial non-economic dimension.

The third dimension of employee relations is *employee rights and redress of grievances*. A set of individual employment *rights* affects the nature of employee relations. The right to be treated fairly and equitably is embedded in UK and European Union (EU) legislation, which attempts to regulate the behaviour of employers and employees in the workplace. An important aspect of fairness and dignity at work is to allow individual employees to express their dissatisfaction about issues that impact on their work experience, and to receive redress for alleged unfair or unreasonable treatment through a formal grievance process, which might involve a union representative.

Employee discipline, the fourth key dimension in employee relations (Figure 10.1), is the regulation of employee behaviour to produce predictable and effective performance (Torrington, 1998). When other employee relations practices fail to create, or reinforce, desirable employee attitudes and behaviours, managers may resort to disciplinary action to encourage compliance with organizational rules, values and standards. This ranges from the threat of being dismissed to the subtle persuasions of mentoring. Maintaining discipline is one of managers' central activities. A framework of legal rules and procedures surrounds the disciplinary process to provide a fair and consistent method of dealing with alleged inappropriate or unacceptable behaviour. In a union workplace, the employee normally has the right to be accompanied by a union representative at the disciplinary meeting.

As in other areas of human resource management (HRM), the ethical dimension of employee relations policy and practice has tended to be downplayed in most HRM texts, where the focus of debate has been on 'best fit' versus 'best HR practices' (Winstanley and Woodall, 2000). Ethical considerations inevitably require managers to reflect on what constitutes ethical employee relations practice in an increasingly diversified workplace (see Chapter 11). Research continues to reveal in detail problems of work-related discrimination, harassment and inequitable managerial behaviour. Indeed, since the start of the economic recession in 2008, analysis of large-scale survey data has suggested that non-nationals in some EU states experience higher rates of work-based discrimination, and that there is substantial variation in discrimination across national-ethnic groups (Kingston et al., 2015). Since the 2016 EU referendum, the UK has seen a major increase in reports of racist and xenophobic incidents, with the National Police Chiefs' Council reporting a 57 per cent increase in hate crime in the days following the vote. The surge in racist incidents since Brexit prompted the Trades Union Congress to publish a guide that government, employers and unions can follow to challenge and defeat racist behaviour, including zero-tolerance policies in the workplace (Trades Union Congress, 2016). We will now examine in more detail each of the key dimensions of employee relations.

 HRM web links Visit the online resource centre at **www.palgravehighered.com/bg-hrm-6e** for more information on combatting racist behaviour after the EU referendum.

Employee communication

We need to begin with a notion of what is meant by employee communication. One simple definition focuses on information disclosure: '*Employee communications* means the provision and exchange of information and instructions which enable an organization to function efficiently and employees to be properly informed about developments. It covers the information to be provided, the channels along which it passes, and the way it is communicated' (Advisory, Conciliation and Arbitration Service, 2014, p. 1). Employee communication involves exchanging information and sharing ideas, feeling and opinions. Meaning is a core concept in communication, and researchers in this field of study define their discipline in complex behavioural and contextual terms. Byers (1997), for example, incorporates three ideas associated with communication – behaviour, meaning and context – and defines communication in the workplace as (p. 4):

> Both behaviours and symbols, generated either intentionally or unintentionally, occurring between and among people who assign meaning to them, within an organizational setting.

HRM web links For more information on management employee relations practices, visit the online resource centre at **www.palgravehighered.com/bg-hrm-6e** and read the bonus HRM in practice feature on creating union-free workplaces.

Keith Hanlon-Smith

Employee Relations Director, Norland Managed Services

www.norlandmanagedservices.co.uk

Norland Managed Services is a provider of hard services-led facilities maintenance and support services in the built environment. It works for national and global organizations to fulfil their building management requirements, its aim being to maintain and enhance its clients' buildings so that those clients can focus on their core business. It has counted among its customers Bloomberg, the O_2 Arena, Scottish Power, Southampton University, Experian and Manchester and Stockport Primary Care Trusts.

Keith Hanlon-Smith joined Norland in 2006, having previously worked as an HR Manager at Sony DADC and Quantum Business Media, and been Employee Relations Manager at Earls Court Olympia Ltd. He is a member of the HR Professionals Network.

Click on Keith's picture in your ebook to watch him talking about employee relations, the employment relationship, and how Norland's HR practices fit with its business strategy, and then think about the following questions:

1 How is HR embedded in the business at Norland Managed Services?
2 What is Keith's view on changes in employee relations?
3 How does Keith think that 'agendas' affect priorities?

Communication is symbolic, which means that the words managers and workers speak and the gestures they make have no inherent meaning. Symbolic meanings conveyed both verbally and non-verbally only 'gain their significance from an agreed-upon meaning' (Martin and Nakayama, 2000, p. 61).

Downward communication patterns from managers to non-managers need to be explored within the wider context of organizational culture and management practices. Information exchange and the transmission of meaning are the very essence of organizational life. Information about the organization – its production, its products and services, its external environment and its people – is a prerequisite for effective employee involvement in decision-making. A strong advocate of high-involvement work systems, Pfeffer (1998, p. 93), not surprisingly, argues that 'the sharing of information on such things as financial performance, strategy, and operational measures conveys to the organization's people that they are trusted'. Employee communications can be simply viewed as the process by which information is exchanged between a sender and a receiver, but the communication process is complicated by organizational characteristics such as hierarchy and power relations, and by the fact that managers and non-managers all have idiosyncrasies, abilities and biases.

The role of employee communication can be seen in studies of managers and their work. Mintzberg's (1973) ground-breaking study found that managers spend a vast proportion of their working time on interpersonal communications; indeed, he argues that the business

HRM **in practice** 10.1

Ryanair accused of 'management by fear'

A bitter dispute between Danish unions and Ryanair led to the airline withdrawing from Billund airport, which is used by many visitors to access the Legoland theme park. The Guardian newspaper reported that, after introducing flights to Copenhagen in spring 2015, the airline came under attack from Danish unions who accused it of violating workers' rights. The unions and Ryanair cabin staff claimed that, in some months, wages were as low as €500 (£348) and that they were less than half the salaries paid by other comparable low-cost airlines. The Flight Personnel Union, which organizes pilots and cabin crew in Denmark, expressed its shock that pay and conditions were being undermined, and the union campaigned to persuade the airline to negotiate. An ex-Ryanair pilot who was involved in the campaign accused Ryanair of 'management by fear' and of failing to trust and respect employees. Staff, he claimed (Crouch, 2015, courtesy of Guardian News & Media Ltd):

Getty Images/Fuse Thinkstock Images Fuse

> are ordered where to work and when to take holidays, and are under pressure to meet targets to sell merchandise. Pilots compete to save fuel, with their performance disclosed in the crewroom for all their colleagues to see.

These practices, he thought, were features of the worst type of competition. The union wanted the airline to make modest increases in its prices in order to pay for decent pay and conditions, and to sign a collective agreement that subscribed to Danish labour customs and practices. Armed with a tribunal ruling that allowed unions to pursue sympathy action against the airline anywhere in the country, even though they had no members among Ryanair staff, the unions planned to launch a boycott of the airline because of its refusal to align itself with Denmark's generous working conditions. In response, the airline pulled out of its operation in Denmark, making the industrial action illegal, but it continued to fly passengers to and from Danish airports using planes and staff based in Britain, Lithuania and Ireland.

Ryanair said that it 'does not negotiate with unions because for 30 years its people have preferred to negotiate directly with the company' (quoted in Crouch, The Guardian, 2015). The company refused to comment on the criticisms from the unions, but it did not expect the negative publicity from unions and some Social Democratic politicians. Even before this incident Ryanair had acquired a low reputation in Denmark. Ryanair claims to be Europe's largest airline, and its budget prices attract huge numbers of customers. Crouch portrays the dispute as one between 'hard headed corporate culture and the Scandinavian ideal of consensus and equity'. The union's aim was to have a signed collective agreement as a basis of 'fair competition with other airlines' (quoted in Crouch, The Guardian, 2015). What this incident exemplifies is a conflict between a view that governments must regulate markets and business to achieve social goals of equality, fair rewards for work and social welfare, and a neo-liberal view that people are better off when entrepreneurs and workers exercise their property rights within free markets without restrictions from governments or trade unions.

Stop! What do you think about Ryanair's ability to evade Denmark's employment relations policies? Since the 1970s, neo-liberal economic principles have become the norm in many countries, but are they good for workers and or consumers?

Sources and further information: For more on this, see Crouch (2015), Harvey (2005) and Hall (2011).

Note: This feature was written by David Denham.

of managers is communications. In our discussion of management, communication is an important skill for 'getting things done' (see Figure 1.2). Communication strategies will be determined by the way work is designed; for example, the more the organization relies on knowledge workers and innovation to competitively survive, the more important communications become.

All managers engage in *downward* communication in one form or another, but communication scholars emphasize that, to be effective, employee communication must be a two-way process to give employees the opportunity to participate on a regular basis. Researchers, academics and practitioners have also stressed some key issues related to communications in the workplace (Figure 10.2).

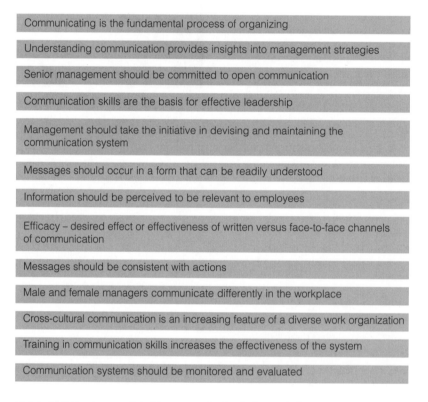

Communicating is the fundamental process of organizing

Understanding communication provides insights into management strategies

Senior management should be committed to open communication

Communication skills are the basis for effective leadership

Management should take the initiative in devising and maintaining the communication system

Messages should occur in a form that can be readily understood

Information should be perceived to be relevant to employees

Efficacy – desired effect or effectiveness of written versus face-to-face channels of communication

Messages should be consistent with actions

Male and female managers communicate differently in the workplace

Cross-cultural communication is an increasing feature of a diverse work organization

Training in communication skills increases the effectiveness of the system

Communication systems should be monitored and evaluated

Figure 10.2 *Key issues related to communication in the workplace*

Employee communications in the workplace is a process by which information is exchanged between a sender and a receiver. Employees have three basic methods of transmitting information:

- Verbal
- Non-verbal
- Written.

Verbal communication ranges from a casual conversation between two employees to a formal speech by the managing director. In face-to-face meetings, the meaning of the information being conveyed by the sender can be expressed through gesture or facial expressions, which are referred to as *non-verbal* communication. *Written* communication ranges from a casual email note to a co-worker to an annual report. Social media platforms, including Facebook, Twitter, blogs, LinkedIn, podcasts, YouTube and wikis, are an increasingly popular form of communication within and across organizations and are revolutionizing business communications (although not without some cost in terms of employee stress; see Chapter 12). The content of any message consists of what is being communicated, and the way in which content is communicated, through the various channels, describes the sender's communication style. In turn, different communication styles will also, importantly, affect the perception of a message or set of messages.

reflective question Thinking about social media systems, what are (1) the positives and (2) the negatives for managing the employment relationship? Thinking globally, how does this new communications technology impact on international HRM?

The orthodox managerial approach to viewing employee communications has its limitations in that it characterizes communication as a linear process and ignores different cultures and subcultures, organizational hierarchies and power relationships (Coates and Pichler, 2011; Rees, 1998; Tan, 1998). People communicate differently depending on their class, gender, organizational setting and national culture. Language is particularly associated with class in the UK. Research suggests that there is sometimes implicit prejudice against certain accents or regional dialects (Plimmer, 2015b, p. S1). An accent is nothing more or less than a speech pattern and everyone has one, 'but it can be a huge barrier at work, affecting productivity, engagement and morale' (Judy Ravin, president and cofounder of Accents International and quoted by Plimmer, 2015b, p. S1).

Language is also associated with gender relations and power. In this context, it is argued that written communication is an ideological act in the process of gender redefinition. The interplay of language and power comes through clearly in how individuals in developed countries use masculine words to signify greater force, significance or value. For instance, the positive word 'seminal', meaning ground-breaking, is derived from the word 'semen' or 'male seed'. The positive adjective 'virtuous', meaning morally worthy, is derived from the Latin word *vir*, meaning man. In contrast, the disparaging adjective 'hysterical' comes from the Greek word *hustera*, meaning uterus or womb (Bratton, J., 2015).

Ethnographic research shows that most workplaces are predominantly masculine domains with masculine norms of behaviour, which of course includes ways of communicating (see, for example, Coates and Pichler, 2011). Language scholars posit that language and gender intersect, and this contributes to different interpretations of meaning in workplace communications. Effective communicators, both female and male, typically draw on a diverse discursive repertoire of social and linguistic practices, ranging from normatively 'feminine' to normatively 'masculine' ways of talking (Holmes, 2006). Studies suggest, for example, that male managers tend to be loud, direct, dominant and aggressive. Women, on the other hand, tend to be more open, self-revealing and polite when they speak, and are superior at decoding non-verbal communication (Aries, 1996). Effective communicators also adroitly select their linguistic practices in response to the interactional context in which communication occurs. Each message may have multiple layers of meaning. Culture, because it shapes our perception of reality, influences communication processes: 'All communities in all places at all times manifest their own view of reality in what they do: The entire culture

You don't need to know what this man is saying to realize that he has an aggressive communication style.

Photoalto

reflects the contemporary model of reality' (Burke, 1985, quoted in Martin and Nakayama, 2000, p. 62).

These limitations of the traditional approaches to employee communication, in particular simply viewing communication as a linear process, are particularly significant to international HRM, in which managers have to be aware of, and sensitive to, the cultural situation in which the organization is embedded (see Chapter 17). Arguably, the traditional approach is a contextually impoverished model of employee communication that needs to be improved upon by sensitivity to cross-cultural norms, as well as to the organizational context that gives rise to the shared meanings through which interpersonal communication occurs.

reflective question

Thinking about your own work experience or the experience of a friend, relative or family member, can you think of a situation in which you have perceived differences in communication style between men and women? How important is it to recognize that communication is 'culture-bound'?

HRM web links

Visit the online resource centre at **www.palgravehighered.com/bg-hrm-6e** for more information on electronic business communication.

Direct communication methods

Survey evidence indicates that managers use a variety of structured arrangements for communicating directly with their subordinates, including regular meetings between senior managers and the entire workforce, team briefings, problem-solving, employee surveys, suggestion schemes and regular use of email (see, for example, van Wanrooy et al., 2013a). Table 10.1 lists the most frequently discussed direct communication or 'voice' mechanisms in the UK, and shows the proportion of workplaces operating such schemes.

Table 10.1 Use of direct two-way communication methods, 2004–11, by sector ownership

	% of all workplaces					
	2004			2011		
	Private	Public	All	Private	Public	All
Meetings between senior managers and workforce	45	54	46	45	50	46
Team briefings + question time	34	57	37	37	59	40
Problem-solving groups	16	28	18	13	25	14
Employee surveys	31	61	35	33	75	38
Suggestion schemes	24	31	25	23	40	25
Regular use of email to workforce	33	52	35	46	73	49

Source: Data from van Wanrooy, B., Bewley, H., Bryson, A. Forth, J., Freeth, S., Stokes, L., and Wood, S. (2013a, p. 65) Employment Relations in the Shadow of Recession: Findings from the 2011 Workplace Employment Relations Study. Basingstoke: Palgrave Macmillan. Reproduced with the permission of the authors and sponsors.

The data show that although the prevalence of general face-to-face meetings was stable between 2004 and 2011, the prevalance of problem-solving groups declined. Around 18 per cent of all workplaces had such groups in 2004, but by 2011 the figure had fallen to 14 per cent. The incidence was lower in the private sector (13 per cent) than in the public sector (25 per cent). The issues commonly discussed at these two types of meeting included production issues, planning, training, and health and safety. When there is time for employees to raise questions or make comments, team briefings are considered to be an effective way of increasing the two-way communication flow. Mechanisms designed specifically to elicit information from employees about workplace issues include suggestion schemes and employee surveys. While the prevalence of employee suggestion schemes between 2004 and 2011 was stable (25 per cent of all workplaces), the incidence of respondents reporting having conducted an employee attitude survey within the previous 2 years increased from 35 to 38 per cent.

HRM web links

Visit the online resource centre at **www.palgravehighered.com/bg-hrm-6e** for further details on the research methods used and outcome of the surveys, including information on how managers communicate with their subordinates.

Employee voice

The second key dimension of employee relations is employee voice. Historically, in European economies, trade unions provided workers with a 'voice' for dealing with workplace issues. As already noted above, since 1980 an increasing number of UK employers have relied less upon the union voice, and turned more to direct employee voice arrangements (Benson and Brown, 2010; Burchill, 2014; Farnham, 2015; Johnstone and Ackers, 2015; Marchington, 2008; van Wanrooy et al., 2013a).

'Employee voice' is the current fashionable term to use to describe a whole variety of HR practices and structures that give employees access to and involvement, both directly and indirectly, in management decision-making in the workplace (Boxall and Purcell, 2011). Previous variants to describe these activities have included 'industrial democracy', 'employee participation' and 'employee involvement' (Marchington, 2008). The terms 'employee participation' and 'employee involvement' have, however, different meanings. In essence, employee participation involves workers exerting a countervailing and upward pressure on management control, which need not imply unity of purpose between managers and non-managers. Employee involvement is, in contrast, perceived to be a softer form of participation, implying a commonality of interest between employees and management, and stressing that involvement should be directed at the workforce as a whole rather than being restricted to trade union channels. As Guest (1986, p. 687) states: 'involvement is considered to be more flexible and better geared to the goal of securing commitment and shared interest'.

In recent years, the concept of '*employee engagement*' has attracted much attention from academics and practitioners (Guest, 2015). It is a contested phenomenon (Farnham, 2015), and global interest has produced a multitude of definitions. In the UK, MacLeod and Clarke (2009, p. 9) define employee engagement as 'a workplace approach designed to ensure that employees are committed to their organization's goals and values, motivated to contribute to organizational success, and able at the same time to enhance their own sense of well-being'. The definition suggests that, to be engaged, employees must have a cognitive understanding of the organization's goals and values, an emotional or effective attachment to these goals and values and a motivation to exert discretionary effort beyond the requirements of the formal contract. Bridger (2015) identifies three dimensions to employee engagement: *intellectual* engagement – employees thinking about the job and how to do it better; *affective* engagement – employees feeling positively about doing a good job; and *social* engagement – employees activity taking opportunities to discuss work-related improvement. It can thus be seen as a management tool 'to leverage the employment relationship to the benefit of the organization' (Guest, 2015, p. 61). Engagement can also be seen as a two-way process: managers must try to engage their subordinates, who in turn have a choice about the level of engagement they offer their employer. Defined this way, employee engagement is a psychological state characterized by vigour, dedication and absorption into their work role the antithesis of Marx's notion of alienation (Bratton, 2015). Contemporary usage of the term echoes Blau's (1964) theory of a 'norm of reciprocity'. HR practices can strengthen employee engagement, but it is also acknowledged that the 'enablers' or antecedents for employees to engage their attitudes and behaviours include leadership, engaging line managers, integrity, trust and voice (Guest, 2015).

When people talk about participation or involvement or engagement, they are reflecting their own attitudes and work experiences, as well as their own hopes for the future. Managers tend to talk about participation when in fact they mean consultation. In this context, consultation, which is explored more fully later in the chapter, usually means a structure for improving communications, either top-down, or upwards in the form of problem-solving. When offered consultation, employees, and in unionized workplaces union representatives, tend to believe, however, that they are about to be given participation. Differing expectations among employees will affect their attitude, their propensity to participate and ultimately the success of participation techniques in the organization. A vital first step, if there is to be any meeting of minds, is therefore to create a common language and conceptual model.

Definitions of employee voice do not always reflect the range of possibilities available – from having some say over how work is designed and executed, to exerting a significant influence over strategic decisions. George Strauss maintains that meaningful employee participation in decision-making demands that workers are able to exert influence over their working environment. He defines participation as 'a process which allows employees to exert some influence over their work and the conditions under which they work' (Strauss, 1998, p. 15). Strauss (2006, p. 803) observes that employee voice 'is meaningless if the message is ignored'. He adds, 'that for me, it is actual influence, not a *feeling of influence* that is important' (Strauss, 2006, p. 778, emphasis added). The process of employee voice should provide workers or their representatives with the opportunity to take part in and influence decisions that affect their working lives. As such, an employee voice environment creates an alternative network to traditional hierarchical patterns (Stohl and Cheney, 2001).

There are two types of participation, or what we call here employee voice: direct and indirect. The first, *direct*, refers to those forms of voice in which individual employees, albeit often in a very limited way, are given input or 'say' in decision-making processes that affect their everyday work routines. Examples of direct employee voice include task-based quality problem-solving participation, and high-performance work systems (HPWS).

HRM and globalization 10.1

A warm welcome to the kooky and the wacky

One of the biases of traditional HR practice is the tendency to see employees as somehow subsumed by their work role rather than being people with a broad range of passions, interests and abilities. This narrow view of the employee goes hand in hand with a narrow view of employee voice. 'He never asks me about myself, my family or my life outside work' is a complaint that captures an employee's dismay at not being recognized as a person.

At the other end of the continuum is a workplace where workers are recognized as people who have lives and interests outside work, and sometimes this recognition goes even further. Rather than maintaining the traditional sharp boundary between work and life outside the workplace, some employers will celebrate a culture that spans both work *and* leisure. Such an approach has the potential to enhance employee voice and secure high levels of employee identification with the work organization.

Take the case of the Dogfish Head Brewery in Delaware, USA. The company is not shy about its workplace culture, which is in fact very much a part of its 'brand'. A quick glance at the company website illustrates this:

> *Dogfish Head? An unconventional company? No way …*
>
> *Okay, so maybe we are a little nuts! We brew strange concoctions of beer, sell silly accessories with our name on it and have our own music group, The Pain Relievaz!*
>
> *We like to keep it a little kooky and wacky around the Dogfish joint!*

It would be tempting to see this as a simple marketing strategy: the company brands itself a certain way to sell a product (beer) to a niche market. But it seems that the company culture is more than this here. The website also lists a range of activities, mainly related to keeping fit and protecting the environment, that suggest commitment to a 'triple bottom line': people, community and environmental responsibility. Most importantly, many of these activities appear to involve both workers *and* managers. Indeed, Dogfish Head Brewery seems like a great place to work if you are particularly green or have a penchant for mountain biking!

Getty

Stop! What if you do not like mountain biking? Might the Dogfish Head approach to employee voice produce problematic divisions between a group of 'insiders' and a group of 'outsiders'?

What about the global perspective? Is the potential of the Dogfish Head approach limited to countries, like the USA, where egalitarian values are celebrated as part of the national culture? Would the idea of working together and playing together be palatable in countries where traditional hierarchies influence a broad range of everyday interactions?

Sources and further information: For a classic statement on the failure of traditional models of organization to recognize the whole person, see Beetham (1978). For a glimpse of the Dogfish Head Brewery culture, check out their website at www.dogfish.com.

Note: This feature was written by David MacLennan.

(continued)

Indirect voice refers to those forms of participation in which representatives of the main body of employees participate in the decision-making process. Examples of indirect voice include joint consultative committees and 'worker directors', both models that are associated with the broader notion of 'industrial democracy' (Bullock, 1977). A current example of indirect voice is UK Prime Minister Theresa May's proposal to add employee representatives to company boards. May's proposal would likely not match Germany's system, which requires half the seats on the company board that makes strategic decisions, but would, if implemented, go some way to make big business more accountable (Sparrow et al., 2016). As a consequence of the precipitous decline in union membership density, recent research has tended to focus on non-union models of employee representation (Butler, 2009; Kim et al., 2010; Marchington, 2008).

The plurality of ways in which employee voice works gives rise to differing degrees of scope, significance and influence in the workplace. Figure 10.3 provides a framework within which different forms of employee voice can be examined and shows the relationship between thee constituent elements:

- The *forms* of voice – direct and indirect
- The *level* of voice in the organizational hierarchy
- The *degree* of voice
- The *influence* of voice.

Figure 10.3 shows a continuum of employee voice from a situation in which employees have no autonomy (for example, downward communication), through problem-solving and team-based arrangements to enable a voice on operational decisions, to works councils with full involvement and a potentially high influence on strategic decision-making. Current methods of employee voice fall along this continuum. Marchington and Wilkinson (2000) call this continuum an 'escalator' of participation.

Research on employee voice arrangements in multinational corporations (MNCs) reveals a complex picture. Studies have found that UK-owned MNCs are more likely to have a hybrid arrangement of union and non-union employee representation, consistent with a shift away from union-based employee representation. US-based MNCs have a preference for direct forms of employee voice. Nordic-based and Japanese-based MNCs are, however, no more likely to have employee representative structures than their US counterparts. In the main Anglophone countries, there is a trajectory towards non-union employee representation (Marginson et al., 2010). Indirect employee voice through the process of collective bargaining was examined in Chapter 9. Before examining forms of employee voice in detail, however, let us address the question, 'Why the enthusiasm for employee voice?'

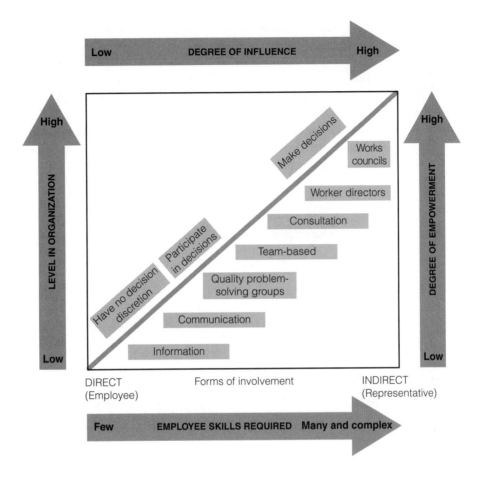

Figure 10.3 Framework for analysing employee voice

HRM web links

Visit the online resource centre at www.palgravehighered.com/bg-hrm-6e for general information on employee voice schemes in Britain and Canada.

reflective question

These different forms of employee voice need to be understood as part of an HR strategy. Before reading on, review Figure 2.6 and its accompanying text. What is the connection between business strategy, HR strategy and employee voice? Thinking about the post-2008 debate on bankers' bonuses, which forms of employee voice would improve transparency and curb excessive executive bonuses?

A general theory of employee voice

Management has to continually address two interlinked problems – those of control and commitment – with regard to managing the employment relationship. Fox (1985) argues that, faced with the management problem of securing employees' compliance, identification and commitment, management has adopted a range of employment strategies including employee voice. The current enthusiasm for improved employee voice needs to be viewed within the context of changing business and corresponding HR strategies in which its purpose is to secure employee support, engagement and commitment to new work designs in order to improve performance (Marchington, 2008). The engagement–performance link is based on a number of assumptions, the first being that giving workers more autonomy over work tasks will strengthen the emotional and intellectual connection the workers have with their job, co-workers or organization, which will in turn result in enhanced individual and organizational performance. The engagement–commitment cycle is depicted in Figure 10.4. Lubricating the whole engagement performance process is a communication style that attempts to build a strong internal culture encouraging initiative, learning, creativity and greater employee identification with the organization.

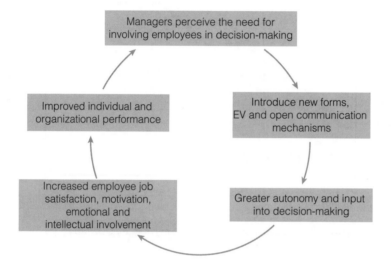

Figure 10.4 *The engagement–commitment cycle. (EV, employee voice)*

reflective question   What do you think of the assumptions underpinning the engagement–commitment cycle? Can the growth of employee voice be explained by employers' 'needs', or are there other reasons driving this HR practice?

Management scholars have put forward three main reasons – *ethical, economic* and *behavioural* – for why senior management introduce employee voice arrangements (Verma, 1995). The ethical reason has roots in the argument that, in a democratic society, workers should have a say in how their workplaces are run when the outcomes of any decisions impact on their lives. Employee voice therefore presents a socially acceptable management style. Employee voice reflects well on the company's image or 'brand' and their desire to project 'a socially responsible stance on such issues' (Marchington and Wilding, 1983, p. 32).

The economic reason for employee voice is championed by the 'model of excellence' school in North America, and is derived from the utilitarian principle that employee voice improves the quality of decision-making and performance. Research demonstrates that employee voice potentially improves productivity and energizes workers (Verma and Taras, 2001), increases employees' job satisfaction (Sisodia at al., 2014), heightens trust in management (Mabey et al., 1998a) and reduces work-related stress (Mackie et al., 2001). Thus, research appears to support the theory that giving employees a voice on a range of workplace decisions benefits both the organization and the workforce (Heller et al., 1998).

The behavioural justification for employee voice derives from the perennial managerial problems associated with perceived dysfunctional behaviour, in particular resistance to change, absenteeism and conflict (Beer et al., 1984). Employee voice is seen as a solution to these dysfunctional human behaviours. According to Beer et al. (1984, p. 53), by introducing employee voice schemes:

> Employers hope that participative mechanisms will create a greater coincidence of interests between employers and employees, thereby increasing trust, reducing the potential for conflict, and increasing the potential for an effective mutual influence process.

Surveys of managers have shown that employee voice is typically initiated and operated by management, with the objective of enhancing employees' commitment to organizational goals (Butler, 2009; Marchington, 2008) and improved employee perceptions of the employment relations climate (Pyman et al., 2010). In an interesting study arguing that work remains a significant locus of personal identity, Doherty (2009, p. 97) notes that what provoked most discontent among workers was the belief that they had insufficient 'say or voice' about issues affecting their working lives.

In addition, workplace scholars have noted that interest in non-union employee voice arrangements coincided with the rise of HRM (Benson and Brown, 2010) and the global decline in union density, while also prompting renewed debates over the need for union voice in the contemporary workplace (Budd et al., 2010). Three decades ago, Beer et al. (1984, p. 153) noted that 'Some companies introduce participative methods at the shop floor in the hope that a greater congruence of interest will make it less likely that workers will organize.' Employee voice practices might go hand in hand with changes in an organization's culture away from a collective trade union focus and towards an individual-oriented focus (Batstone and Gourlay, 1986). As part of a union-avoidance strategy, direct employee voice can 'emulate a unionized workplace' and thus make it 'difficult for a union to sell something that is already being provided by management' (Knight, 2011, p. 22). Other scholars, sceptical of employee voice practices, see the processes being used to 'educate' and 'reconstitute the individual', thereby making workers' behaviour and performance more manageable (Townley, 1994).

HRM web links Visit the online resource centre at **www.palgravehighered.com/bg-hrm-6e** for more examples of companies introducing employee voice practices.

Indirect employee voice

Joint consultation is a key type of employee voice (Cregan and Brown, 2010). In its simplest form, joint consultation may take the form of an informal exchange of views between a group of workers and their manager on an incoming piece of technology or a reorganization of the office. When, however, the size of the organization makes it difficult for workers to access management, a more formal and indirect employee voice network needs to be established. The committee usually includes representatives of management and workers. The intent is to provide a meeting forum that acts as a channel for employee voice on matters affecting the workplace.

Joint consultation is different from collective bargaining, examined in the last chapter. The difference rests on the idea that both conflict and a common interest are inherent elements of the employment relationship that need to be handled in different ways. Joint consultation is viewed as a means of promoting action when there are no obvious conflicts of interest, whereas collective bargaining is a means of reconciling divergent interests, although we should stress that every aspect of the employment relationship has the potential for conflict. The balance between joint consultation and collective bargaining will depend upon the power of trade unions (Daniel and Millward, 1983).

Joint consultative committees

Joint consultative committees (JCCs) are workplace-based committees of managers and other employees that are concerned with consulting, rather than negotiating, about workplace change. In some organizations, they are known as works councils, and union representatives often sit on JCCs but, equally, many function without union involvement (van Wanrooy et al., 2013a). Survey evidence of private sector workplaces in the UK found that the overall proportion of the workplaces with JCCs fell between 1984 and 1998 from 34 per cent to 28 per cent (Cully et al., 1998). The 2011 Workplace Employment Relations Study data reveal the latest figures on the extent of JCCs (Table 10.2). In 2004, 9 per cent of all workplaces had a JCC on site, compared with 8 per cent in 2011, a difference that was not statistically significant. By size, there has been a statistically significant increase in JCCs on site in organizations with 100–249 employees, from18 per cent in 2011 compared with 9 per cent in 2004 (van Wanrooy et al., 2013a).

Table 10.2 *Incidence of JCCs: 2004 and 2011*

	2004	**2011**
All workplaces	9	8
Organization size, by employees		
5–49	3	3
50–99	10	12
100–249	9	18
250–999	14	13
1000–9999	13	11
10,000 or more employees	17	14

Source: Data from van Wanrooy, B., Bewley, H., Bryson, A. Forth, J., Freeth, S., Stokes, L., and Wood, S. (2013a, p.62) Employment Relations in the Shadow of Recession: Findings from the 2011 Workplace Employment Relations Study. Basingstoke: Palgrave Macmillan. Reproduced with the permission of the authors and sponsors.

Studies show that union membership status has a significant impact on workers' willingness to participate in joint consultation arrangements (Cregan and Brown, 2010). Union members were more willing to participate 'the more likely they expected the JCC to result in instrumental gains' (p. 344). Importantly, union members were willing to participate in JCC arrangements in order to 'build on union-based instrumental gains and to fill the gaps left by collective bargaining' (p. 344). A contrasting early study by MacInnes (1985) reminds us that the separation of joint consultation from collective negotiations is often attempted by simply excluding from the negotiating agenda any item that is normally the subject of collective bargaining. The result can be the creation of the 'canteen, car park, toilet paper syndrome' and has prompted some observers to characterize the subject matter of JCCs as a 'diet of anodyne trivia and old hat' (Cregan and Brown, 2010, pp. 103–4).

Although we always have to be careful when making international comparisons – because, for example, researchers often define HR practices differently – survey studies show that, across Western Europe between 1997 and 2000, employee voice practices and downward and upward communication increased by an average of 52 per cent (Mayrhofer et al., 2000). In Canada, 43 per cent of workplaces reported some form of employee voice in decision-making (Verma and Taras, 2001). These findings need to be contrasted with more critical studies suggesting that employee voice in decision-making has not shown any sign of substantive improvement (Thompson and McHugh, 2009).

The structure and operation of joint consultative committees

The structure of a JCC is guided by the organization's goals, philosophy and strategy. JCCs of necessity require a high-trust relationship and regular disclosure of information to all participating parties. Managers have to decide how much information will be disclosed, by whom and how. Management's role in a consultative structure is generally to communicate information and be fully involved in the process; anything less than this will result in decisions being made or agreed upon without their knowledge or support. Managers may adopt either of two broad approaches: they can integrate the two processes of consultation and negotiation within the collective bargaining machinery, or they can agree to maintain a separate machinery of joint consultation and regulation:

Three main reasons have been identified for integrating consultative and negotiating machinery:

- Communicating, consulting and negotiating are integrally linked together in the handling of employee relations.
- Union representatives need to be fully involved in the consultative process, if only as a prelude to negotiations.
- As the scope of collective bargaining expands, the issues left are otherwise allocated to what may be viewed as an irrelevant process.

On the other hand, substantive reasons have been cited for establishing separate consultative and collective bargaining structures:

- Separation may help to overcome organizational complexity.
- The fact that collective bargaining deals with substantive or procedural issues, whereas consultation addresses other issues of common interest, forces the two structures apart.
- Regular JCC meetings and the publication of minutes ensure that joint consultation is accorded a proper place in the organizational system and confirms management's commitment and responsibility to consulting with its employees.

An example of a joint consultation and collective bargaining structure in the public sector is shown in Figure 10.5.

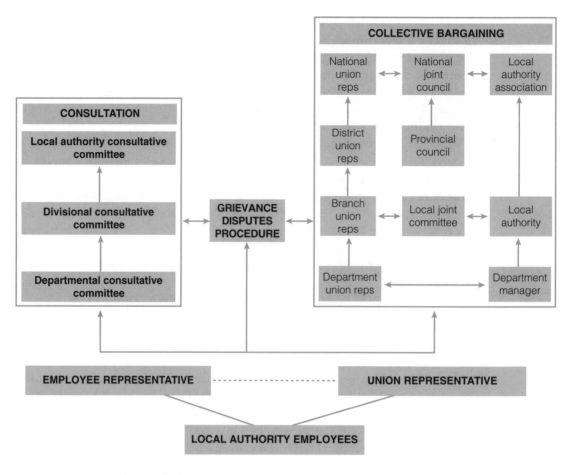

Figure 10.5 *Example of joint consultation and collective bargaining in municipal government*

When there are two sets of arrangements, the JCC's terms of reference need to be specified by defining both its subject matter and the nature of its authority. The subject matter may be defined in terms of:

- Excluding from its deliberation anything that is subject to joint regulation, that is, substantive (for example, pay and vacation time) and procedural (for example, discipline and grievance processes) matters
- Enumerating the items that are to be regarded as matters for joint consultation (for example, a corporate plan, HR trends and education and training)
- Items chosen on an ad hoc basis, deciding whether or not an issue should be dealt with in the joint regulation process.

HRM web links

Visit the online resource centre at www.palgravehighered.com/bg-hrm-6e for more information on JCCs in the UK, South Africa and Australia.

European Works Councils

In the post-Brexit economy, it is worth comparing employee voice mechanism in the EU. European Works Councils (EWCs) are not the same as JCCs: whereas JCCs are voluntary committees, and as such can be withdrawn by management, the term 'European Works Council' is used to describe only mandatory consultative committees. Since 1945, Germany has made works councils part of its employment relations landscape, and much of the early research focused on German 'co-determination' (*Mitbestimmung*) and workers' voice manifested in the Works Constitution Act. Frege (2002, p. 223) defines works councils as:

> Institutionalized bodies of collective worker participation at the workplace level, with specific informatory, consultative and codetermination rights in personnel, social and economic affairs.

Works Councils are legally independent of trade unions, and their members are elected in a ballot of *all* employees rather than just union members. The key functions of EWCs are:

- Establishing two-way communication between employees and management, and union and management
- Maintaining peaceful and cooperative employment relations (as EWCs are not allowed to initiate a stoppage of work)
- Providing training for representatives.

In the UK, managers, trade unions and academics have become increasingly interested in the EWC model. There are three principal reasons for this heightened interest. First, EU legislation has focused attention on EWCs. The 1994 EWC Directive required organizations employing more than 1000 employees in EU member states (excluding the UK) and with at least two establishments in different member states, comprising at least 150 employees (again excluding the UK), to set up works councils. The principal objective of the EWC Directive is to induce organizations to set up an EWC voice system for the purpose of informing and consulting employees. In December 1999, the 1994 EWC Directive became law in the UK. Since 1994, over 600 European companies have negotiated agreements with unions to establish EWCs (Gilman and Marginson, 2002).

Second, the decline of union membership in Britain and bargaining power over the past three decades has induced union leaders to explore the extension of unions' and workers' rights outside the traditional collective bargaining arena, under the umbrella of EU employee governance law – EU employment rights was an important reason why British unions opposed Brexit in the 2016 referendum on Britain's continued membership of the EU. Third, in the 'transitional economies' of Central Europe, the EWC model has evoked debate on the conditions for the successful implementation of EWCs (Frege, 2002). Although still in its infancy, at least in the UK, EWCs are 'the most prominent, widespread and powerful form of industrial democracy in contemporary capitalist societies' (Frege, 2002, p. 221).

EWCs have differing degrees of power (Mayrhofer et al., 2000). In Germany, for example, employee representatives can resort to the courts to prevent or delay managerial decisions in areas such as changing working practices and dismissals. The range of issues discussed and the degree of legislative support for EWCs would, note Mayrhofer et al. (2000, p. 226), 'shock US managers brought up on the theories of "manager's right to manage"'. Evaluating the existing literature, Frege (2002, p. 241) concludes that 'we know much about the ontology of works councils (what is a works council, what does it do) but much less about the determinants, outcomes and underlying causal relations'.

In terms of links between EWCs and organizational performance, Addison et al. (2000) have made a contribution to the debate. Using economic data from Germany and Britain, they argue that mandatory indirect participation in decision-making would appear to be associated with higher productivity in workplaces with more than 100 workers and in economies with centralized pay bargaining (for example, Germany). In a recent study, it was found that Germany's employee voice rights provided a 'crucial source of counter-vailing power in negotiations over work reorganization' (Doellgast, 2010, p. 395).

Employee voice and paradox

The types of employee voice arrangements initiated by management performance contain contradictions and paradoxes. Stohl and Cheney (2001) analyse four main types of employee voice paradox: structure, agency, identity, and power. They propose that paradox is inherent in employee voice processes and that these paradoxes set limits that constrain the effectiveness of employee voice networks.

Organizational *structures* are created to govern employee voice, but most employee voice arrangements eliminate workers from the most influential network – the executive. Strauss (1998) explains this potential paradox. Direct employee voice mechanisms provide opportunities to make changes only at the margins of managerial decision-making. Senior management make the 'really important decisions', for example investment in sustainable energy. Put another way, 'Learn, innovate and voice your opinions as I have planned!'

The idea of *agency* relates to an individual's sense of being and a feeling that she or he can or does make a difference (Giddens, 1984). One paradox of agency references the tensions and contradictions present in HPWSs, in which teams may rely on the active subordination of team members to the will of the team. Thus, 'Do things our way but in a way that is still distinctively your own!'

The paradox of *identity* addresses issues of boundaries, space and the divide between the in-group and the out-group (Stohl and Cheney, 2001). This paradox is linked to the notion of employee commitment. At one level, employee voice implies commitment to the processes of learning and dialogue. At another level, however, 'commitment is expected to equal agreement' (Stohl and Cheney, 2001, p. 380). In a so-called 'learning organization', the paradox of identity may be expressed as 'Be a self-directed learner to meet organizational priorities.'

The fourth paradox is that of *power*, which centres on issues of access to resources, opportunities for independent voice and the shaping of employee behaviour. Stohl and Cheney (2001, p. 388) provide persuasive evidence of employee voice regimes 'getting workers to make decisions that management would have made themselves'. In other words, 'Be an independent thinker, just as I have commanded you!'

Furthermore, contemporary arrangements of employee voice also raise ethical concerns (see Chapter 11). The growing interest in the ethics of employee voice might reflect a degree of unease over the shift in power towards employers and management resulting from the decline in union influence, the growth of precarious employment and exorbitant salary increases for corporate executives (see Chapter 8). That paradoxes and contradictions are found within the existing employee voice literature should be no surprise. These mirror the inherent contradiction contained within the employment relationship, that is, management's need to be able to manage workers as an objectified commodity, but at the same time to call upon employees' cooperation (Clayton, 2000). As stated elsewhere, it is also a mistake to assume that employee voice and engagement can serve as an effective alternative to other more robust forms of employee voice such as collective bargaining (Heery, 2000). These ethical and structured contradictions partly account for the continued scepticism towards employee voice on the part of critical workplace researchers (see Thompson and McHugh, 2009). The challenge for both managers and workers is whether creativity and innovation can emerge from these paradoxes.

Employee rights and grievances

The third key dimension of employee relations is the set of individual employment rights and a process to handle individual complaints made to management.

Employee rights

Individual legal rights that protect employees against inequitable behaviour on the part of managers or other co-workers shape the equality of employee relations. A fundamental tenet underpinning effective employee relations is that employees must have confidence in management's intention to be fair and equitable. The right to be treated fairly and equitably, with its links to concepts of rights, obligations and 'social justice', has, of course, an ethical dimension (Winstanley and Woodall, 2000) and a 'dignity *at* work' dimension (Bolton, 2007). Employee rights and dignity at work are closely connected, and indeed 'Employment rights are human rights' (Barber, 2007, p. vii) that form an integral part of a workplace where employees can expect respect, and dignity both *in* and *at* work.

As we have explained elsewhere (see, for example, Chapter 1), individual employment rights, embodied in UK and EU legislation, regulate the behaviour of employers and employees. The Sex Discrimination Acts of 1975 and 1986, the Race Relations Act 1976, the Disability Discrimination Act 2005 and the Equality Act 2006, for example, address issues of discrimination and harassment with regard to an employee's gender, disability, ethnicity, race or sexual orientation. To comply with the legislation, HR professionals have developed codes of practice as a guide to better HR practices.

Employee grievances

A key indicator of fairness and dignity in the workplace is the ability of an employee to raise concerns or express dissatisfaction about workplace issues, and receive redress for unfair treatment. A grievance is simply a complaint by an employee that the behaviour of another employee or management has been unfair or damaging to her or him. The formal grievance procedure plays an important role in introducing democracy into the workplace (Craig and Solomon, 1996) and is also a form of *direct* employee voice (Marchington, 2008). From management's perspective, the formal grievance procedure allows an employee to express dissatisfaction that, if not resolved, can result in unsatisfactory (mis) behaviour (Ackroyd and Thompson, 1999) and performance.

The non-union models of grievance-handling vary widely from one workplace to another and may have fewer than or as many procedural steps as are found in union models; in all instances, the grievance-handling process mirrors the management hierarchy. At a minimum, prescriptive HRM advisers recommend that a grievance workplace policy should:

- Investigate the complaint
- Take appropriate action to resolve the complaint to the mutual satisfaction of the complainant and the management
- Resolve the grievance in a timely manner (see Gennard and Judge, 2005, p. 300).

Employee complaints that require formal grievance management cover a myriad of workplace issues, including undignified or demeaning treatment by front-line managers or other co-workers, workplace bullying and harassment.

Sexual harassment as an employee relations issue

Recent analysis has shown that the negative consequences of sexual harassment and a misogynistic workplace extend beyond individual targets to include co-workers, work groups and whole organizations (Miner-Rubino and Cortina, 2004). As Keith (2000, p. 287) points out, sexual harassment 'poisons the atmosphere in the workplace'. It is an important issue for management, centring as it does on issues of social justice and efficiency. Sexual harassment in the workplace is unlawful, and the courts have increasingly viewed its prevention as the employer's responsibility. The legal concept of 'detriment' is important here. Sexual harassment is a 'detriment' per se; it can lead to an employment-related detriment to the female employee and, as such, has serious implications for management. In 1986, the European Parliament passed a resolution on violence against women, commissioning a report on the dignity of women at work, which led to the adoption of the EU code of practice (Figure 10.6).

The allegations of sexual impropriety against US President Bill Clinton in 1998 and, in 2011, the case of former International Monetary Fund chief Dominique Strauss-Kahn highlighted some of the difficulties seen in cases of sexual harassment in the workplace.

The EU code of practice defines sexual harassment as 'unwanted conduct of a sexual nature' affecting 'the dignity of women and men at work'. It defines harassment as largely subjective, in that it is for the individual to decide whether the conduct is acceptable or offensive.

The code says that member states should take action in the public sector and that employers should be encouraged to:

- issue a policy statement
- communicate it effectively to all employees
- designate someone to provide advice to employees subjected to harassment
- adopt a formal complaints procedure
- treat sexual harassment as a disciplinary offence.

Figure 10.6 *The European code on sexual harassment*

Source: Adapted from http://eur-lex.europa.eu/legal-content/EN/TXT/?uri=uriserv%3Ac10917b © European Union, 1998–2016

HRM and globalization 10.2

Sexual harassment as gender-based violence in a BRIC economy

BANANASTOCK

Pavitra Bhardwaj, 35, set herself on fire in front of the Dehli Secretariat in 2013 to protest sexual harassment by her employer. Bhardwaj had been dismissed from her position as a laboratory attendant at BR Ambedka College in 2012 after unsuccessfully complaining about sexual harassment by the school's principal. Bhardwaj later succumbed to her injuries and the principal was cleared of all charges (Gohain, 2013).

The Bhardwaj case draws our attention to an important issue in employee relations: workplace sexual harassment remains endemic throughout the world. For example, in Singapore, 54 per cent of workers report experiencing some form of workplace sexual harassment – from clients, co-workers and supervisors. Of those workers reporting sexual harassment, 79 per cent were women (AWARE, 2015). Studies of workplaces in the EU typically find that 40–50 per cent of women experience sexual harassment in the workplace (European Commission, 1998).

Sexual harassment is one of the thorniest issues that HR practitioners generally have to deal with. Victims are often reluctant to come forward and are sometimes traumatized by their experiences. The evidence of the harassment can be incomplete and ambiguous. In addition, complaints can divide a workplace along both friendship and gender lines. In the end, the complainant and the alleged harasser are often both dissatisfied with the outcome of any investigation, and privacy considerations often make it impossible to bring closure to the issue for other workers who are indirectly affected by the complaint.

These characteristics of sexual harassment can often make line managers reluctant to deal with instances of alleged harassment or raise the issue in workplace training sessions. That said, there are strong legal and moral reasons why HR practitioners need to promptly act on complaints and seek to prevent harassment from occurring wherever possible.

In most jurisdictions, sexual harassment is deemed to be a form of gender discrimination in that workers are treated differently on the basis of their gender. This places a legal onus on employers to prevent and respond to sexual harassment. While cases of sexual harassment tend to be dealt with individually, it is helpful for HR practitioners to recognize that the

pervasive nature of sexual harassment suggests it is not just an instance of individual misconduct, but is also indicative of systemic inequality between men and women, and a form of gender-based violence.

(continued)

Stop! Have you ever witnessed, experienced or taken part in sexual harassment in the workplace? How did this conduct affect the victim? Do you agree with the assertion that pervasive sexual harassment is indicative of systemic inequality and a form of gender-based violence? Why or why not?

Sources and further information: For background reading, see AWARE (2015), European Commission (1998) and Gohain (2013).

Note: This feature was written by Bob Barnetson.

Seeing sexual harassment as systemic inequality helps us understand why a significant number of (typically) men believe that making inappropriate comments or sexual advances, staring at women's bodies or sexually assaulting women is acceptable workplace conduct. Men's greater power in the workplace and society both creates 'space' for this conduct to occur and blunts social and legal sanction when it does.

Sexual harassment is also an example of gender-based violence in that it inflicts physical, emotional or sexual harm or suffering on (mostly) women. This harm impairs the ability of women to enjoy their lives and exercise their fundamental rights and freedoms. And, sometimes, it is so harmful and so difficult to remediate that women – like Pavitra Bhardwaj – take desperate action to bring it to a stop.

The first issue is credibility because there is seldom a witness to support whether the conduct being complained about actually happened. There were, for example, no witnesses to the alleged conduct of Mr Clinton and the White House employee Monica Lewinsky or to the sexual encounter between Mr Strauss-Kahn and the hotel maid, Nafissatou Diallo, a 32-year-old immigrant from Guinea. Credibility and circumstantial evidence are under scrutiny here. Who has more credibility? Is there indirect evidence that might support or dismiss the allegations?

The Clinton case raises another issue that often applies to workplace investigations: the question of containment. In the presidential investigation, the public prosecutor apparently had no interest in limiting the scope of the investigation, but for many HR professionals, containment, in addition to what is legitimate and necessary in terms of conducting the investigation into a complaint of sexual harassment, is also an issue. The aim will be to contain the allegation and limit knowledge about the complaint to those who need to know.

Workplace sexual harassment is 'the most intimate manifestation of employment discrimination faced by women' (Keith, 2000, p. 277), and legal protection against it is complex and sensitive. There is concern expressed by some authors about how women are treated in law, contending that women are disadvantaged because of a patriarchal or sexist jurisprudence. Debono (2001), for example, found that there are sexist elements to the jurisprudence related to workplace sexual harassment decisions in the UK, the USA and New Zealand. Although the legislation is progressive, it is argued that 'sexist attitudes still remain with those who have the power to use the legislation to compensate the victims' (Debono, 2001, p. 338). The intervention of co-workers witnessing sexual harassment is another response to the problem. McDonald's et al. (2016) study of sexual harassment in Australian workplaces reveals that, despite the hidden nature of sexual harassment, the intervention of bystanders who are not direct targets can potentially be an effective response to the persistent and damaging problem of workplace sexual harassment.

One of the most significant developments in the workplace in the last decade has been the use of social networking. Although there are obvious benefits, organizations also recognize these developments present risks to employees and employers alike. The use of Facebook, for instance, in the workplace presents a danger to employees from the posting of inappropriate material that can be discriminatory, derogatory or threatening. Two employment tribunal cases demonstrate this point. In *Otomewo* v. *Carphone Warehouse Ltd* (ET/2330554/2011), cyberbullying occurred when an employee posted comments about a colleague's sexual orientation using social media. In *Taggart* v. *TeleTech UK Ltd*

(NIIT/704/11), damage was caused by disparaging comments on Facebook about a colleague's alleged sexual promiscuity. Both cases illustrate that employers can be held vicariously liable for the actions of employees on social networking sites if they occur 'in the course of employment', but employers should not disregard employee conduct which 'takes place outside the workplace'. Studies tend to emphasize that exposure to workplace bullying impacts negatively on the quality of employee relations and is, moreover, associated with impaired employee well-being and individual and organizational performance (see HRM in practice 10.2 and the section on workplace bullying in Chapter 12).

Employee discipline

So far, we have looked at communication practices, management-initiated employee voice and employee rights and grievances. To complete the discussion on employee relations, we must examine a fourth set of HR policies and practices that affect the quality of employee relations: that of *employee discipline*.

When employee voice mechanisms fail to create or reinforce desirable employee attitudes and behaviours, managers may resort to disciplinary action. Indeed, there is evidence that there has been an increased use of formal disciplinary processes since employee voice arrangements were introduced. Mabey et al. (1998a) found a disjuncture between the rhetoric of empowerment and the practical reality of total quality management. Their study found that workers had 'negative perceptions' of total quality management because of a culture incorporating the 'excessive use of disciplinary actions against individuals' (Mabey et al., 1998a, p. 66). In recent years, rates of disciplinary sanctions and dismissals have increased, providing further evidence of the general movement from collective relations towards the individualization of the employment relationship in the UK (Knight and Latreille, 2000).

The modern workplace is pervaded by rules established by management to regulate workers' behaviour. Indeed, it is argued that obedience underscores the relationship between employer and employee: 'There is certainly nothing more essential to the contractual relation between master and servant than the duty of obedience' (Cairns, 1974, quoted in Wedderburn, 1986, p. 187). Disciplinary practices, ranging from oral warnings to termination of the employment relationship, aim to make workers' behaviour predictable. The employment relationship involves a legal relationship, and for those employers and managers who share a less-than-sophisticated management style known as 'my way or the highway', there is a framework of legal rights regulating the disciplinary process.

The purpose of this section, with supporting material in the online resource centre, is modest: to provide an overview of the disciplinary concepts, practices, procedures and statutory rights found in the workplace. UK students and practitioners requiring a detailed knowledge of employment law relating to discipline and dismissal are advised to refer to Selwyn's *Law of Employment* (Emir, 2014) or a similar text.

HRM web links

Visit the online resource centre at **www.palgravehighered.com/bg-hrm-6e** to compare employment standards legislation relating to discipline at work in the UK and Canada.

Bullying at work: 'My life became a living hell ...'

PhotoDisc/Getty Images

I n 2009, Swansea County Court found Carmarthenshire NHS Trust liable for substantial compensation to Mrs Nanette Bowen, who had been signed off work indefinitely with stress and panic attacks following a 3-year campaign of bullying by her boss. Nanette, an information manager who had worked for the trust for more than 28 years, was not allowed to provide information without her new boss's written consent, had been made to complete a daily form so he could see what she was doing, had her responsibility for hiring staff removed, had been subject to sexual innuendo and aggression, and been banned from attending important meetings (Trades Union Congress, 2009).

Research shows that such a case is anything but unusual. The first national survey of workplace bullying at the end of the 1990s by Hoel and Cooper (2000) surveyed over 5000 employees and managers in 70 different organizations spanning all major sectors of employment. They found that one in 10 respondents reported being bullied within the previous 6 months, and that when the reporting period was extended to the previous 5 years, the incidence rose to a quarter of all respondents.

It is important to note that bullying is a long-term situation – a one-off argument does not count as bullying – and that a power imbalance usually makes it difficult for the bullied person to defend themselves. Subsequent surveys typically show that two-thirds of reported cases of bullying involve managers or supervisors as the perpetrators, while a third allege bullying by colleagues or peers (often, however, connected to the presence of a bullying manager). Some researchers have made a further distinction between 'victimization', in which the target of the abusive behaviour is an individual, and 'oppressive work regimes', where everyone is subject to the experience (Hoel and Beale, 2006).

The negative consequences for the organization of a persistent culture of bullying include increases in the rate of sickness absence, lowered productivity arising from lowered morale and commitment, and an increase in labour turnover. This suggests that the effects of bullying extend further than the victim to create a negative organizational atmosphere that includes those who have been bullied in the past and those who persistently witness bullying behaviour.

Leaving the organization may, however, only be possible when jobs are relatively plentiful: in times of job shortage, workers may feel they have no option but to continue to endure abusive treatment. This suggests that the concept of power imbalance extends to the wider socioeconomic context to include, in the last couple of decades, the unitary nature of HRM; this has seen a subsequent decline in trade union and collective representation in the workplace, and an intensification of managerial control resulting from recent economic crises and the increased market pressures felt by the private and public sectors alike.

Hoel and Cooper (2000) suggest that management styles need to be analysed in order to achieve the key HRM goals of enhanced employee commitment and engagement. Managers should move away from the 'confrontational' and 'macho' attitudes typical of a US style of management, and instead develop a cooperative style based on personal and professional qualities such as integrity and a regard for the needs of the individual and the group.

Stop! Have you experienced bullying in any job you have had? What did you see as the cause at the time? Why do you think that the incidence of workplace bullying seems to be on the increase?

Sources and further information: See Hoel and Beale (2006), Hoel and Cooper (2000) and Trades Union Congress (2009) for background to this case. Further information can be found in Trades Union Congress (2007).

Note: This feature was written by Chris Baldry.

Disciplinary concepts

Discipline can be defined as the process that maintains compliance with employment rules in order to produce a controlled and effective performance. The purpose of discipline in the workplace is threefold:

- *Improvement* – the disciplinary process is seen as one of counselling the disobedient employee back to acceptable behaviour.
- *Punishment* – the disciplinary process is seen as being about imposing penalties.
- *Deterrent* – the process is seen as educational to deter others.

Corrective discipline refers to management action that follows the infraction of a rule. In North America, the 'hot-stove rule' is used to guide correct discipline. This states that disciplinary action (for example, warnings or suspension from work) should have the same characteristics as the penalty an individual receives from touching a hot stove. These characteristics are that discipline should be, with warning, immediate, consistent and impersonal. Most organizations apply a policy of *progressive discipline*, which means that the employer notifies employees of unacceptable conduct and provides them with an adequate opportunity to correct it. However, UK research on corrective discipline has found that managers have different handling styles when dealing with disciplinary situations. The less serious disciplinary cases tend to attract a prescriptive autocratic style, whereas cases that are potentially more serious to the organization tend to be handled with less prescriptive approaches and involve the employee to a greater extent, which, in theory, is more likely to bring about the desired change in the behaviour of the employee (Rollinson et al., 1996).

Disciplinary rules and procedures are designed for promoting orderly employee relations as well as fairness and consistency in the treatment of individuals (Klass, 2009). *Rules* set standards of conduct and performance in the workplace, whereas *procedures* help to ensure that the standards are adhered to and also provide a fair method of dealing with alleged failures to observe them. A disciplinary process typically incorporates the requirements of *natural justice*, which means that employees should be informed in advance of any disciplinary hearing of the alleged misconduct, be given the right to challenge the alleged evidence, have the right to representation and to have witnesses, and be given the right to appeal against any decisions taken by management (Emir, 2014).

HRM web links Visit the online resource centre at **www.palgravehighered.com/bg-hrm-6e** and look at the text entitled 'Managing employee discipline' for information and guidance on how to manage employee discipline, including the recommended disciplinary procedures of the UK's Advisory, Conciliation and Arbitration Service.

reflective question   How important is it for an organization's disciplinary process to be seen to be 'equitable'?

case study

Bullying at Fresh Supermarket

The setting

Recent studies have underscored the severe harm that workplace bullying can cause to employees, producing damaging mental and physical symptoms in its victims. For employers, the negative effects of bullying include higher costs associated with high turnover rates, absenteeism, reduced productivity, legal costs and damage to the company's reputation. In the UK, legal cases have demonstrated that employers can be held vicariously liable for the actions of their employees if they occur 'in the course of employment', but that employers should not disregard employee conduct that 'takes place outside the workplace' (see, for example, *Otomewo* v. *Carphone Warehouse Ltd* [ET/2330554/2011] and *Taggart* v. *TeleTech UK Ltd* [NIIT/704/11]).

Fresh Supermarket is one of the world's largest retailers, with stores throughout North America and Western Europe. It brands itself as a business that regards its employees highly. This multinational company has a number of HR policies designed to reflect its concern for its employees. First, Fresh Supermarket has developed an open door communication policy. This encourages its employees to report on a confidential basis concerns about how its employees are treated or how stores are operated. It also has a policy on prevention of violence in the workplace, undertaking to take all employee reports of incidents seriously and to protect employees making a complaint from acts of retaliation. In addition, the giant retailer has a harassment and discrimination policy, developed to protect employees from unwelcome conduct that offends a person's feelings. During orientation sessions, Fresh Supermarket emphasizes to all new hires that its employees must treat each other with dignity and respect. This case arises out of events that took place at its Lancaster store located in South Central Pennsylvania, a town of over 59,000 people, which is one of the oldest inland towns in the USA.

The problem

Carol Bryman began working for Fresh Supermarket in 2001. She was well regarded by her co-workers and immediate supervisor. In 2006, Ruth Douglas, the Store Manager, chose Carol over four other candidates as her assistant line manager responsible for the fresh produce. She told her that she was the 'most promotable' of everyone in the store. She was happy to have her on her

STOCKBYTE

management team because she was a real 'go-getter'. Carol was to report directly to the line manager Tomaz Polski. Initially, her relationship with Polski was cordial and positive, and her performance appraisals were excellent.

In 2013, when the meat adulteration scandal was reported in Europe, Polski asked Bryman to falsify a log recording temperatures in the meat and dairy coolers. Bryman refused. Polski, worried that the incomplete logs would negatively affect the store's ratings in an upcoming inspection, threatened to discipline Bryman. Concerned about her future employment, Bryman approached the store manager to express her concerns. When Polski heard of the complaint, he called her into his office and subjected her to a stream of abuse and profane language. Later that day in the staff canteen, Polski demeaned her in front of other employees. Bryman complained of Polski's escalating harassment to the store manager. She told Ruth Douglas, 'I'm totally stressed out. I'm unable to eat or sleep, I have abdominal pain, and I've lost weight.' After hearing Bryman's account, Douglas called the area HR manager responsible for the six stores in South Central Pennsylvania.

The assignment

Assume that you are the area HR manager. Working either alone or in a study group, prepare a report drawing on this chapter and other recommended material, which considers the following points:

1 Discuss the issue from the company's point of view. What comments would you make to the store manager?
2 What follow-up action should the store manager, and the HR department take? For example, do you recommend disciplinary action against Polski? Would you reconsider the company's open door, prevention of violence and harassment polices?

Essential reading

Advisory, Conciliation and Arbitration Service (2014) *Bullying and Harassment at Work: Guidance for Employees*. Advice leaflet. London: ACAS. Available at: www.acas.org.uk/index.aspx?articleid=797 (accessed August 2016).

Chartered Institute of Personnel and Development (2016) *Harassment and Bullying at Work*. Factsheet. London: CIPD.

Crush, P. (2015) Inexperienced managers 'reluctant' to confront bullies at work, research reveals. *PM Daily*, November 16.

Lewis, G. (2015) Bullying remains rife and unchecked in UK workplaces, research finds. *PM Daily*, August 25.

Note: This case study was written by John Bratton with research help from Bob Barneston.

 Visit the online resource centre at **www.palgravehighered.com/bg-hrm-6e** for a bonus case study on evidence-based management and direct employee voice, and for guidelines on writing reports.

---

summary

➤ This chapter has conceptualized employee relations as an assortment of rules, regulations and HR policies. The focus of study is, however, the individual employment relationship as opposed to the collective employment relationship. Employee relations is driven by management's concern with how to gain employees' commitment to the organization's goals and operational objectives.

➤ We have examined four dimensions of employee relations: workplace communications, employee voice, employee rights and grievances, and discipline.

➤ Communicating is the fundamental process of managing people in the workplace. It includes written, verbal and non-verbal communication, which flows downwards, upwards and horizontally in organizations.

➤ Employee voice provides an opportunity for workers to take an active role in the decision-making process within their organization. Employee voice may be direct or indirect, formal or informal, voluntary or legislated; it may range from a manager simply exchanging information with employees, to their complete participation in a major investment decision.

➤ Employee voice can be seen to be a logical development in employee relations to enlist employees' skills and cooperation. Data provide evidence that British managers are adopting employee voice arrangements. Critics, as discussed, argue, that employee voice schemes might be used to marginalize the role of the unions.

➤ Employee relations are buttressed by a framework of individual legal rights protecting employees against inequitable or inappropriate behaviour by managers or other co-workers. Formal non-union grievance procedures are a form of employee voice, designed to allow employees to articulate dissatisfaction about an issue directly to management. For managers, a grievance process can be seen as a useful mechanism to identify and resolve inappropriate behaviour, such as bullying or harassment.

➤ Employee discipline is the fourth dimension of employee relations examined in this chapter. Discipline practices vary between national legal systems, but to command support among the workforce, to avoid litigation and to avoid violations of the psychological contract, managers should design and apply practices with due regard to the requirements of *natural justice.*

review questions

1 What are the links between HR strategies and employee voice and communication practices?

2 Discuss some of the issues that should be considered when communicating effectively with employees in the organization.

3 Explain the difference between participation and involvement in the workplace.

4 'Collective voice achieves what the lone voice could never do: it humanizes and civilizes the workplace.' Do you agree or disagree? Why?

5 Explain the difference between grievance and discipline in the organization. What are the various steps when handling an employee grievance effectively? What is the purpose of discipline in the organization?

6 What is meant by 'sexual discrimination'? Explain why an effective response to incidents of sexual harassment in the workplace is important for the employer and manager.

further reading

Reading these articles and chapters can help you gain a better understanding and potentially a higher grade for your HRM assignment.

➤ Aylott, E. (2014) *Employee Relations*, London: Kogan Page.

➤ Bridger, E. (2015) *Employee Engagement*. London: Kogan Page.

➤ Budd, J., Gollan, P. and Wilinson, A. (2010) New approaches to employee voice and participation in organizations. *Human Relations*, **63**(3): 303–10.

➤ Doellgast, V. (2010) Collective voice under decentralized bargaining: a comparative study of work reorganization in US and German call centres. *British Journal of Industrial Relations*, **48**(2): 375–99.

➤ Gollan, P. J. (2006) Editorial: Consultation and non-union employee representation. *Industrial Relations Journal*, **37**(5): 428–37.

➤ Guirdham, M. (2015) *Work Communication: Mediated and Face-to-Face Practices*. London: Palgrave Macmillan.

➤ Hall, M. and Marginson, P. (2005) Trojan horse or paper tigers? Assessing the significance of European Works Councils. In B. Harley, J. Hyman, and P. Thompson (eds) *Participation and Democracy at Work* (pp. 204–21). Basingstoke: Palgrave Macmillan.

➤ Johnstone, S. and Ackers, P. (2015) *Finding a Voice at Work?* Oxford: Oxford University Press.

➤ Kamenou, N. and Fearfull, A. (2006) Ethnic minority women: a lost voice in HRM. *Human Resource Management Journal*, **16**(2): 154–72.

➤ Kingston, G., McGinnity, F. and O'Connell, P. (2015) Discrimination in the labour market: nationality, ethnicity and the recession, *Work, Employment & Society*, **29**(2): 213–32.

➤ Lucas, K. (2015) Workplace dignity: communicating inherent, earned, and remediated dignity. *Journal of Management Studies*, **52**(5): 621–42.

➤ Marchington, M. (2008) Employee voice systems. In P. Boxall, J. Purcell and P. Wright (eds) *The Oxford Handbook of Human Resource Management* (pp. 231–50). Oxford: Oxford University Press.

➤ Marchington, M. and Cox, A. (2007) Employee involvement and participation: structures, processes and outcomes. In J. Storey (ed.) *Human Resource Management: A Critical Text* (pp. 177–94). London: Routledge.

➤ McDonald, P. Charlesworth, S. and Graham, T. (2016) Action or inaction: bystander intervention in workplace sexual harassment. *International Journal of Human Resource Management*, **27**(5): 548–66.

➤ Rollinson, D., Hook, C., Foot, M. and Handley, J. (1996). Supervisor and manager styles in handling discipline and grievance: Part 2: Approaches to handling discipline and grievance. *Personnel Review*, **25**(4), 38–55.

➤ Simpson, S. (2015) Age equality: five examples of discrimination against young workers. *Personnel Today*, October 26 (accessed November 9, 2015).

vocabulary checklist for ESL students

Click here in your interactive ebook for a list of HRM terminology and vocabulary that has appeared in this chapter.

 Visit the online resource centre at www.palgravehighered.com/bg-hrm-6e for lots of extra resources to help you get to grips with this chapter, including study tips, HRM skills development guides, summary lecture notes, tips for English as a Second Language (ESL) students and more.

part V

CONTEMPORARY ISSUES: HRM IN A GLOBAL WORLD

Getty Images/iStockphoto / Thinkstock \ Jacob Wackerhausen

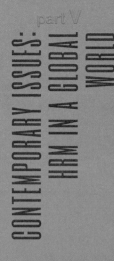

chapter **11**

HRM and
ethics

ImageSource

objectives

After studying this chapter, you should be able to:

1 Understand the role of ethics and corporate social responsibility in an organization

2 Assess the alternative dimensions of ethical theory and apply them to HRM issues

3 Explain the competing roles of the HRM function in business ethics

4 Debate the context of ethics in a corporatist environment

More than four decades after the Equal Pay Act 1970 was introduced, the gender pay gap in Britain is still £5732, or 24 per cent (Allen, 2016b). Is this right? Is the payment of at least a minimum wage a human right? Although there is nothing illegal about outsourcing labour, should managers or society be concerned if that outsourced work takes place in an unhealthy and unsafe worksite or is undertaken by workers paid a fraction of the wage rate paid to workers in developed countries? What should we do if we see one of our co-workers harassing another employee, mentally, sexually or physically? Do we 'turn the other cheek' because we may worry that we'll be labelled a troublemaker? It is easy to see how the 'unwritten' rules we have been taught affect the decisions we make as individuals. For example, social mores compel us to tell the truth rather than lie to our friends. But what guides decision-making by managers? Organizations are compelled to make decisions within the framework of a business model, but consumers, governments and civil society are now increasingly placing corporate decision-making in the moral spotlight. This chapter focuses on the belief that managers' behaviour is not above being the subject of standards of right and wrong.

introduction

Shareholders, business owners, managers, employees and consumers of products and services are affected by the ethical conduct of businesses on a daily basis. For example, as an employee, we expect to be treated fairly within the principles of equity in terms of recruitment and pay, and to be provided a safe workplace free from both physical and psychological harm. We expect organizations to uphold strict hygiene principles when producing or distributing food-based products, as well as the highest safety standards when designing motor vehicles, aeroplanes and other forms of transport. When we invest in business, we expect decisions about our investment to be transparent and non-harmful to our environment rather than based on shortcuts and greed that favour the few at the cost of the many and the planet. Thus, whether it is the gender pay gap, outsourcing, inappropriate behaviour in the workplace or investment decisions, ethical questions are central to managing both work and people.

Although business ethics can be quite complex, this chapter provides a starting point for the key areas of interest from a business and human resource management (HRM) perspective. In doing so, it introduces you to some of the principles and developing themes of ethics in a business environment. It introduces ethical theories and considers the competing interests and tensions for human resources (HR) practitioners as the 'ethical guardians' of organizations.

Business ethics

Ethics are a set of moral principles and values that influence the decisions and actions of individuals within the organization. Carroll and Buchholtz (2008, p. 242) define business ethics as 'the discipline that deals with what is good and bad and with moral duty and obligation [and can] be regarded as a set of moral principles or values'. In a globalized economy, Morrison (2015a) provides a compelling case for seeking and establishing ethical guideposts in strategic management decisions, across national boundaries: 'ethical questions are central to how the business sees its role in the world. They concern who we are and what we should be doing' (p. 4). Therefore business ethics deals with 'what is perceived as good and bad behaviour in a business organization's interaction with its multiple stakeholders and what the business' obligations are to its stakeholders, the society, and, ultimately, to the world and the environment' (Ardichvili, 2015, p. 299).

Any set of ethical principles does not emerge in a vacuum, but instead reflects the cultural values and norms of society (see Chapter 15). For example, bribing officials for contracts is regarded as bad in most cultures but an acceptable business practice in others. *Ethical dilemmas* arise when two or more values conflict, for example when a pharmaceutical company has to meet profit targets but this involves testing a new drug on animals. The degradation of the environment is another classical illustration of an ethical dilemma. Petroleum companies extracting 'dirty oil' from the oil sands in Alberta, Canada, or drilling in the Gulf of Mexico, satisfy shareholders' interests in preference to reducing pollution.

The regulatory context determines the minimum obligations that an organization has towards its various stakeholders, and ethical decision-making is mainly legally driven. That is, compliance-based codes guide managers' actions in terms of the improper use of the organization's resources or conflicts of interest. The *ethical stance* is the extent to which an organization will exceed its minimum obligations to stakeholders and society at large (Johnson et al., 2005). In an ever-more globalized economy, Carroll (2004, p. 35) argues that there is evidence of more organizations undergoing 'a program of moral reform' that involves writing value-based ethical policies that are compatible with cross-global operations. The aim is to help managers make informed decisions when faced with new ethical situations.

Ethics permeates the employment relationship. The debate on whether HR practitioners can be a source of moral authority speaks to the growing interest in 'ethical stewardship' in decision-making and the role of the HR professional as 'a guardian of ethics'. However, with much of the research focusing on strategy and efficacy, ethics has been largely left out of the HRM discourse (Ashman and Winstanley, 2006). The centrality of ethics in the employment relationship is evident in the core HR processes. Ethics impacts on the recruitment and selection of employees (for example, in avoidance of discrimination), on rewards (for example, through notions of fairness), on training and development (for example, in terms of equal opportunities), on health and safety (for example, by the full disclosure of harmful chemicals, including any harmful long-term effects) and on the protection of whistleblowers (Winstanley and Woodall, 2000).

Corporate social responsibility

Ethics underscores the notion of *corporate social responsibility* (CSR), which is concerned with the ways in which managers' behaviour and actions exceed minimum compliance-based regulations. McWilliams and Siegel (2001, p. 117) argued that CSR could be defined in terms of 'actions that appear to further some social good, beyond the interests of the firms and that which is required by law'. CSR concerns the ethical principle that an organization should be accountable for how its corporate strategy might affect suppliers, local communities, society at large and the planet. Twenty-seven years after the disastrous oil spillage from the *Exxon Valdez* on 24th March 1989, there is evidence that the concept of CSR is increasingly gaining popularity in advanced market societies (Koleva et al., 2010). In 2001, the European Commission defined CSR as 'a concept whereby companies integrate social and environmental concerns in their business operations and in their interactions with their stakeholders on a voluntary basis' (quoted by Koleva et al., 2010, p. 274). It is a concept whose time has come (Yakabuski, 2008).

HRM web
links

Visit the online resource centre at **www.palgravehighered.com/bg-hrm-6e** for more information on CSR.

The intellectual roots of CSR can be found in the *stakeholder theory* of the firm, which contends that firms should be managed not purely in the interests of maximizing shareholder return, but also in the interests of a range of stakeholders that have a legitimate interest in the organization, including employees, customers, the local community, suppliers, the environment and society in general (Donaldson and Preston, 1995).

The concept of CSR is problematic because it is people rather than organizations that engage in unethical behaviour. And, of course, only people and not inanimate objects, such as organizations, can be responsible for unethical actions. Examples of corporate social irresponsibility abound. In Bhopal, India, for example, a chemical plant owned by the US global company Union Carbide operated under conditions considered illegal in the USA. On 3rd December 1984, the plant experienced a major leak. Within hours, 3000 people were dead, with 15,000 more dying in the aftermath; 200,000 were seriously injured, and 500,000 still carry special health cards. Eventually, Union Carbide paid out just $470 million in compensation (Saul, 2005). See also HRM in practice 2.1 for another example of corporate irresponsibility.

The Corporate Manslaughter and Corporate Homicide Act 2007 came into force in the UK as a result of concerns over the difficulties of obtaining prosecutions of individual executives when serious mismanagement had led to the death of either an employee or a member of the public. In response to this, the Act created organizational liability for when the actions of an organization fell far below what could reasonably be expected (Lockton, 2010).

reflective
question

Is it socially responsible when corporations encourage host countries to overlook health and safety or deregulate employment standards as a price for relocating?

Ethical behaviour and CSR are a function of the individual's values, the organizational culture in which the decision-making process is occurring and power resources. Managers who lack a strong moral commitment are much less likely to make unethical decisions if they are constrained by a societal and organizational culture that disapproves of such actions. Conversely, a manager with integrity can be corrupted by an organizational culture that 'turns a blind eye' or permits or encourages unethical action. In the UK, the act of whistleblowing, as a practice that exposes unethical or illegal processes and practices, has been given some protection by the 1998 Public Interest Disclosure Act. Early evidence suggests that the Act has helped to improve ethical standards in the workplace and reduce the number of cases of injustice to whistleblowers (Weale, 2000). The balance of power between employees and employers increases the tendency towards whistleblowing. Skivenes and Trygstad (2010, p. 1091) note that the more equitable power balance found in the Norwegian model of labour relations illustrates this because 'Norwegian employees, to a great extent, perceive their whistle-blowing activity as positive and effective'.

Toxins and cancer: what price for Canada's oil?

Getty

Sustainable economic development has primarily been focused on economic growth. However, Janet Morrison (2015a) reminds us that, from an ethical perspective, sustainability is about sustaining the means by which each individual can attain a good life, and ensuring social justice and observing human rights. In Canada, these two aspects of development have come into conflict over the expansion of tar sands pipelines in Alberta.

Tar sands, also known as oil sands, are a mixture of sand, clay, water and bitumen, a tar-like substance which can be turned into oil. Extracting and refining the tar sands is challenging, energy intensive and poses risks to human health, as reported by ThinkProgress (2014):

> The Canadian government has likely underestimated the health risks of Alberta's tar sands development, according to a new study. The study, published Monday in the Proceedings of the National Academy of Sciences, focused on polycyclic aromatic hydrocarbons (PAH), persistent chemicals that are released during tar sands mining and processing and that have been associated with cancer in humans. Researchers compared the official records of PAH levels from the Athabasca Tar Sands Region to measurements from other scientific studies, and found that actual PAH emissions may be two to three times higher than recorded in environmental reviews.

Canada's tar sands development covers a huge area, about 140,000 square kilometres, larger than most EU member states. Greenpeace notes that First Nations communities (aboriginal groups) in the area show 'unusually high levels of rare cancers and autoimmune diseases' and that their way of life is under threat. At the same time, the extraction and refining processes produce more carbon dioxide than for conventional oil and use more water, much of which is contaminated by toxic substances (Union of Concerned Scientists, no date). However, exploiting the tar sands, the 'third-largest proven crude oil reserve in the world' brings economic growth (Alberta Energy). Both the Canadian and local governments support an increase in production, but can Canada realize the economic benefits while also protecting the natural environment and the people living there?

Stop! What are the ethical issues involved in extraction of fossil fuels in (1) rich developed countries and (2) developing countries?

Sources and further information: The extract by Valentine (2014) is from material published by ThinkProgress https://thinkprogress.org/. See Alberta Energy, Union of Concerned Scientists, Greenpeace, Dower (2004), Vidal (2013) and Morrison (2015a) for more information.

Note: This feature was written by John Bratton.

The existence of a website that encourages whistleblowing – WikiLeaks – may cause corporations to act accountably. In newly released cables, for example, US diplomats around the world are found to have lobbied for genetically modified crops as 'a strategic government and commercial imperative' in response to moves by France to ban a genetically modified Monsanto corn variety in 2007 (Vidal, 2011). The release of confidential and embarrassing US diplomatic and corporate documents by WikiLeaks has carried with it some uncomfortable lessons, not least for open government and corporate accountability and transparency (Gilmore, 2010; Saunders, 2010). The full implications of WikiLeaks for corporate whistleblowing are beginning to be realized. This twenty-first-century Jeremy Bentham-style 'Panopticon' may do what legislation has only partially succeeded in doing – actually provoking universal transparency and corporate citizenship.

CSR, however, has its critics. For some, corporate 'greening' strategy initiatives, for instance, represent a form of 'green-washing' – the marketing or rebranding of goods to capitalize on a new zeitgeist – or may be seen as a public relations ploy to deflect public criticism away from environmentally irresponsible corporate practices. CSR activities can placate politicians and discourage regulatory controls, or can be characterized as a marketing strategy that misleads consumers into believing that they are helping the planet by buying 'green products'. In an era of largely unfettered global capitalism, the idea of good corporate citizenship is a self-regulatory response to public concerns that it is still too marginal to make a real difference to irresponsible unethical corporate behaviour. A more effective response to flagrantly dishonest action will occur through greater scrutiny, transparency and regulation. For example, a reformed global financial system undertaken by the G20 group of countries would have profound consequences for corporate- and business-level strategies. The literature affirms the need to integrate issues of corporate strategy, sustainability and HRM strategy, and it is to this debate that we now turn.

Ethical theories and cultural context

Ethics and morals enter into day-to-day transactions – should you buy 'free-range' eggs? Organic foods? Recycled products? Furniture that uses rainforest timbers? Products with extensive 'throw-away' packaging? A petrol-fuelled car? Ethical decisions confront us as consumers. As such, these issues also confront firms that produce products since consumers consider more variables than just the price, quality and appearance of the product.

But are not markets amoral, as they are only operative for transacting business and are removed from ethics? All markets involve ethical and moral issues. What is produced for the market is determined by 'effective' demand – that

You encounter ethics in your everyday life without even realizing it. A decision to buy a product has ethical implications.

Getty

is, by those consumers who can afford to purchase products. As such, the functioning of markets is not independent of the distribution of income and wealth. The greater your income, the greater the opportunity to participate in the market and determine what is going to be produced. Aside from the distributional dimension of markets, there are legal and moral constraints over markets. There are restrictions on certain products (for example, ice, cocaine and heroin); other products are controlled by prohibitions and restrictions over sales of, for instance, tobacco and alcohol to minors and controls over poisons and pesticides; and there are prohibitions over buying and selling people (slavery). Markets are thus not unfettered by moral dimensions. The government influences markets (for example, through taxes), which involves judgements about what products are desirable and undesirable. Finally, markets may not produce commodities that the community desires as they may be too expensive to provide as a private product or it may be difficult to establish a price and charge users. How can a price be applied to defence, street lighting, law and order or public health? The community in these cases makes a collective judgement about providing (public) goods across the community.

In this section, we examine the main ethical frameworks that govern economic activity and the operations of business. Under what conditions should organizations and businesses be regulated in order to meet the established ethical standards of the community? The three main schools of ethics are consequentialism (utilitarianism), deontological ethics (duty) and virtue ethics (behaving as a virtuous person).

Utilitarianism

Utilitarianism is a branch of ethics that is most commonly associated with Jeremy Bentham (1748–1832) and John Stuart Mill 1806–1873). It is forward-looking and as such is often discussed under the name 'consequentialism'. For consequentialists, actions and behaviours are evaluated as right or wrong, or good or bad according to their consequences. The guiding principle of consequentialism is the greatest good for the greatest number (or utility), or, ethically right thing to do is that which maximizes pleasure and minimizes pain (Grace and Cohen, 2000; Mallin and Ow-Yong, 2010). Those actions that make the individual and the community better off can be justified. Organizations thus need to evaluate the consequences of their actions. Within this approach, a major division is that of 'action' versus 'rules'. As Nathanson (2015, pp. 3, 5) writes:

> Act utilitarians believe that whenever we are deciding what to do, we should perform the action that will create the greatest net utility. In their view, the principle of utility, that is do whatever will produce the best overall results should be applied on a case by case basis. The right action in any situation is the one that yields more utility (i.e. creates more well-being) than other available actions. ... [For rule utilitarians,] a) a specific action is morally justified if it conforms to a justified moral rule; and b) a moral rule is justified if its inclusion into our moral code would create more utility than other possible rules (or no rule at all). According to this perspective, we should judge the morality of individual actions by reference to general moral rules, and we should judge particular moral rules by seeing whether their acceptance into our moral code would produce more well-being than other possible rules.

In other words, every action is evaluated for its effects, or a set of rules are developed that are used to guide individuals towards taking the right decision. An example is road rules, where it can be assumed that most individuals would consider the consequences of their action. Road rules (for example, traffic lights, give way signs and one-way roads) guide them towards making decisions that improve happiness. Utilitarianism guides public policy and public debate – What are the consequences? Who benefits? Who loses? How big are the losses and gains? The problem is that benefits and costs may not be immediately obvious (see the impact of climate change and smoking), they are not the same for everyone and maximization of utility may mean very big gains or sacrifices for a few people. For example, there may be rules that limit the number of taxis, the number of hotel licenses or the number of doctors who are registered – an orderly and controlled market generates public gains, but those who hold licenses have a vested interest in a system that limits and controls entry to their industry.

Deontology

Rather than focusing on consequences, deontology is either backward- or present-looking. It is rules-based and requires people simply to do the right thing. Of all deontologists, Immanuel Kant (1724–1804) is arguably the most widely known. Kantian ethics is based on the premise that the motive for an action is more important than the consequences of the action. An act is either morally justified or it is not. Pleasure and happiness in themselves are not morally justified; it is the motives behind actions that are morally justified. Instances of companies misinforming regulators, misleading creditors and concealing fraudulent behaviour (consider the case of the energy and commodities company Enron) demonstrate that the motives (lying and misinforming) could not justify the actions that in the short term protected shareholders. What, then, are the principles for guiding decisions?

Kant (2012) proposed three key guiding decisions, which he referred to as 'categorical imperatives'. The first imperative is 'act only in accordance with that maxim through which you can at the same time will that it become a universal law' (p. 12). A second imperative is 'So act that you use humanity, whether in your own person or in the person of any other, always at the same time as an end, never merely as a means' (p. 16). The third formulation by Kant focuses on a consensus of universal laws. This takes some explaining. Kant envisaged 'a systematic union of various rational beings through common laws' (2012, p. 58). The categorical imperative was to:

> determine ends in terms of their universal validity, if we abstract from the personal differences of rational beings as well as from all the content of their private ends we shall be able to think of a whole of all ends in systematic connection (a whole both of rational beings as ends in themselves and of the ends of his own that each may set himself), that is, a kingdom of ends, which is possible [as] the principle, namely the idea of the will of every rational being as a *will giving universal law* (p. 58). Put simply, Kant considered that it was possible for rational beings to establish guiding ethical rules for humanity.

Again the problems are that individual and collective moral standards may differ, and that decisions often involve more than one moral issue. Do firms source supply from the cheapest provider? Should medicines that effectively treat a condition be supplied if they also have adverse consequences? Should a merger proceed if it results in job losses?

Virtue ethics

Virtue does not require actions but is embodied in a person's character. Virtue ethics is associated with Plato and Aristotle. Individuals should aspire to lead a virtuous life, but what are these virtues, and how are they justified? Aristotle suggested that there are moral and intellectual virtues. The most important intellectual virtue is wisdom, while the moral virtues include courage, justice and prudence. For each virtue, there is a vice – generosity versus selfishness, for example. For virtue ethics, there are a number of challenges – What are the core virtues? Do they rank equally? Who decides what is virtuous? Do the virtues change through time and across countries and communities? Virtue ethics does not evaluate decisions but the system of beliefs. We can see manifestations of virtue ethics from corporate websites and from the discussion of politicians and political parties in terms of 'what they stand for'.

The context of behaviour and decisions

You are either morally motivated or you are not. You lead a virtuous life by a set of tenets that ensure that you do the right thing, but many moral decisions are judged by the context in which they are made. First-century Rome had few rights for slaves and non-Roman citizens, limited franchise and an established class system that determined rank and rights. Values and what is considered as virtue are culturally dependent and can change through time and across countries. We can observe that attitudes to women, disabled individuals, members of minority cultures and indigenous communities have changed through time. Similarly, what is regarded as being acceptable and responsible business behaviour has also changed over time. Behind the local and corporate values lie systems of belief that are often encoded in religion and legislation. As values change, there is often conflict and confusion – consider, for example, community division over online gambling, retail businesses trading on a Sunday, same-sex marriage and no-fault divorce laws.

The idea of institutional embeddedness governing decisions and behaviour is one that is found in international business studies. Should multinational corporations be allowed to avoid local taxes? Can international hotels operate with bars and gambling facilities in countries that prohibit alcohol and gaming? Should international publishers censor press coverage in countries where the media are controlled? The rules of the game, the acceptable systems of behaviour and values, do differ across the globe. On the one hand, it is suggested that globalization is a force for homogeneity and we should see a convergence of business systems and the institutions supporting them. However, local conditions, customs and beliefs remain important. Can an international hamburger chain offer beefburgers in a country that regards the cow as sacred? Can international beverage chains sell liquor in countries where alcohol is illegal? Should an international mining company pay bribes to local officials in return for mining rights in a country where bribery is an acceptable business practice? Local laws, customs and ethical beliefs mean that decisions and behaviour will differ internationally. However, if corporations practised virtue ethics, would the decisions and behaviours be identical everywhere?

Organizations are inanimate and it is difficult to reconcile organizations with ethical positions. However, organizations do add legitimacy to the context in which they operate by accepting and conforming to local laws even if they are discriminatory, oppress minorities, punish dissent and impinge on human dignity. We can observe numerous examples of companies that operated in support of harsh and extreme regimes in, for example, Nazi Germany, apartheid South Africa and Fascist Italy. More recent examples are of companies and countries that have broken United Nations trade sanctions that applied to the military regime in Myanmar. For example, the mining company Rio Tinto is under investigation by the UK Government for sanction-breaking operations in Myanmar

(Amnesty International, 2015a). In 2006, the Australian Wheat Board was found to be engaging in bribery and in sanction-breaking deals with Iran (Anonymous, 2006).

HRM web links

Visit the online resource centre at **www.palgravehighered.com/bg-hrm-6e** to access a podcast on the Australian Wheat Board scandal.

Rights-based ethics: human rights and core labour standards

The rights approach to ethical behaviour suggests that there are inviolable rights or standards that should be the standard by which to judge behaviour. These rights include free speech, freedom from slavery and equal opportunity (non-discrimination). They are represented by the United Nations Universal Declaration of Human Rights (1948) and form the foundation for the development of laws across many nations.

These rights are supported by the majority of countries across the globe and are encoded in national laws. In turn, they form the basis for the standards by which business and governments can be judged in their interactions with the community. Breaches of human rights are reported and publicized by such organizations as Amnesty International and Human Rights Watch. Examples of ongoing campaigns include Amnesty's campaign against Shell and the Nigerian Government to systematically address oil spills in the Niger Delta. In its report, Amnesty claims that the rights of local communities to a livelihood and quality of life have been infringed (Amnesty International, 2015b). Human Rights Watch has a number of campaigns against mining practices in Uganda and Tanzania that are dangerous, displace traditional communities and employ child labour (Human Rights Watch, 2013, 2014).

Labour rights build on human rights and develop codes of labour practice that are monitored by the International Labour Organization (ILO). The ILO was established in 1919 and was the first specialist agency developed by the United Nations in 1946. The ILO is a tripartite organization that represents employers, employees and governments: 'The main aims of the ILO are to promote rights at work, encourage decent employment opportunities, enhance social protection and strengthen dialogue on work-related issues' (International Labour Organisation, 2015). The ILO is responsible for the development and implementation of standards linked to employment:

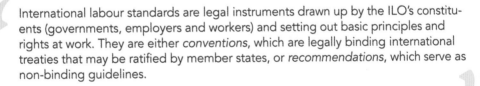

International labour standards are legal instruments drawn up by the ILO's constituents (governments, employers and workers) and setting out basic principles and rights at work. They are either *conventions*, which are legally binding international treaties that may be ratified by member states, or *recommendations*, which serve as non-binding guidelines.

The ILO assists member countries in applying standards and conventions, and monitors the application of those standards. The core labour standards or fundamental conventions include freedom of association, the right to collectively organize, an absence of discrimination in employment and an absence of forced labour (slavery).

There are also many technical conventions that are linked to specific industries (for example, shipping and mining) and specific conditions (such as occupational health and safety). The ILO publishes regular country reports on the ratification and implementation of conventions. For example, not all countries have ratified the core labour standards. The USA has not ratified any of the core standards, and the freedom of association and collective bargaining has not been ratified by Saudi Arabia, New Zealand and Singapore. Similarly, the discrimination in employment convention has not been ratified by Japan, Kuwait or Singapore. Signing up to the conventions means that governments will attempt to enforce the principles through national legislation, and this in turn provides a contextual system of behaviour for organizations. However, since the core labour standards are based on human rights, there is a moral basis for organizations to do the 'right thing' irrespective of whether they are required to do so by national governments.

HRM: how do ethical principles apply?

As we have read, ethics is all about what we should do, and how we should behave. Within an organization, our behaviour is often a reflection of the formal and informal systems that manage and control our work from day to day. As HR managers are responsible for building capabilities and shaping culture through their employees (Tharp, 2015), some of the formal systems lie within the HR domain. As such, the HR manager has an opportunity to create and reinforce ethical organizational cultures.

Ethics in recruitment and selection

The recruitment and selection process has a significant role when it comes to establishing an ethical organizational culture. Creating job descriptions, writing advertisements, forming a selection committee and finally selecting the right person for the job must on the one hand be undertaken ethically and fairly, while simultaneously sending signals about the organization's ethical values to the potential candidate.

A source of help for HR managers to incorporate an ethical culture is protectionist legislation. Such legislation in Australia, and many other developed nations, includes equal employment opportunity, occupational or workplace health and safety, and antidiscrimination legislation, legislation covering harassment and bullying among many others. Within the recruitment and selection process, opportunity and outcomes must be consistent with the basic tenets of procedural fairness, which focuses on equitable processes.

The transparent and accurate setting of minimum qualifications for a position is one way in which the HR manager can ensure that fairness of substance and procedure are captured. Writing minimum qualification statements that genuinely reflect the needs of the position according to the necessary skills, qualifications and attitudes reduces the chance of a line manager inadvertently or otherwise (see, for example, Scott, 2005) proposing a work model that is modelled around an identified candidate rather than the requirements of the job. In this capacity, the HR manager can work as the ethical business partner of the line or section manager to ensure that legal, ethical and strategic considerations are met.

Through the interview and verification or checking process, HR managers can similarly assume a dual role to support an ethical culture. First, they can ensure that all candidates are treated in accordance with the principles of fairness and equity of process and selection. Second, they can ensure that the right people are recruited. For the HR manager, this role extends beyond ensuring that the candidate's skills and qualifications are right for the job to ensuring that the person has the right attitude and values for the organization. Tools such as psychometric testing to evaluate integrity, providing situational examples designed to assess the candidate's values and conducting reference checks are all useful resources to evaluate a candidate's fit into the ethical organization (see Chapter 5). Trevino and Nelson (2011) suggested an even higher imperative to get the decision right when recruiting for a leadership role, as HR managers must withstand the pressures of the market or culture of the industry, where high levels of integrity are vital. This will be discussed critically in a following section.

reflective
question

If the violation of employment laws results in unethical practice, does the application of employment laws result in ethical outcomes?

Ethics in human resource development

Scott (2005) referred to the various forms of training that an organization may provide to employees. General training may include the principles of equal employment opportunity and procedural and distributive justice. Safety training is crucially important and can be invoked through legislation provisions such as occupational/workplace health and safety regulations or through the organization's own commitment to ensuring a safe work environment for all employees by minimizing risk and ensuring that an employee's actions and behaviour do not put others at risk. Values training that is consistent with the organization's ethical culture can also be important here (see, for example, Trevino and Nelson, 2011).

The start of a new employee's ethical acculturation is through induction or orientation training. After recruitment and selection, this is the first point, beyond the statements that are usually outlined on company websites, to formally communicate to the employee the organization's values and ethical culture. This is typically achieved through an introduction to the company's mission and values statements and codes of conduct (discussed in more detail below). Furthermore, specific ethics training can be incorporated into both induction training for new employees and ongoing regular refresher training for existing staff. Trevino and Nelson (2011) introduce the term 'cascading' to refer to ethics initiatives that flow down through the organizational levels from senior management, thus identifying the role of senior management in ethics training initiatives. The concept of cascading therefore also includes each level of management as the initiatives flow through the whole organization.

Ethics in performance management and rewards

Rewards systems may be used to promote and reinforce ethical behaviour. Some of the many appropriate behaviours include acting with integrity, respecting others, reliability, and openness to and acceptance of diversity. Although rewards (or discipline) can be distributed in many ways, an alignment between rewards and a well-designed performance management system can translate and reinforce an ethical culture.

Ethical behaviour can be measured within the performance management system through performance, conduct or both, and should be evaluated in much the same way as physical performance and general workplace conduct. The baseline for appropriate ethical conduct may be provided within the organization's policies, mission or value statements or code of conduct. This is discussed in more detail below.

Ethics and employee well-being: values and codes of practice

An organization has numerous ways in which to communicate and instil an ethical culture into its members. Values are often found within mission statements, each contributing to a code of conduct similar in essence to the often cited Johnson and Johnson credo.

HRM web links

> Visit the online resource centre at **www.palgravehighered.com/bg-hrm-6e** to access the Johnson and Johnson credo.

Codes of conduct are, however, not limited to organizations but often extend to industries developed to guide their members toward ethical behaviour. One of the oldest ethical codes comes from the medical industry and is known as the Hippocratic Oath, named after the ancient Greek physician Hippocrates. Although modernized over time to reflect changes in medical practice, the oath binds physicians all over the world to uphold ethical standards in their treatment of patients. At a national level, industries are represented by peak bodies. In Australia, for example, the code of ethics of the Australian Medical Association represents guiding principles with respect to patient care, research, teaching and conduct for more than 27,000 doctor members. Similar bodies exist in many countries – in the UK, the British Medical Association has a similar role. In other industries such as law, rules of professional conduct are communicated through industry societies and councils.

Although possibly different in constitution, the HR profession also has peak industry bodies that develop and deliver codes of conduct and expected ethical behaviours to their members. For example, the Chartered Institute of Personnel and Development (CIPD) is a professional body for HR with 140,000 members (see www.cipd.co.uk). A code of professional conduct including ethical standards and integrity is expected to be upheld by each member, and a breach may result in expulsion from membership. The Australian peak body, the Australian Human Resources Institute (AHRI), although it has its own 'model of excellence' to communicate its members' expected ethical behaviours, has a mutual recognition arrangement with the CIPD, allowing for cross-body benefits and accountabilities to members.

HRM web links

> Visit the online resource centre at **www.palgravehighered.com/bg-hrm-6e** to compare the ethical statements in the codes of conduct of the UK's CIPD and Australia's AHRI.

Whistleblowers

Whistleblowing relates to reporting unethical behaviour. Reporting may occur through websites such as WikiLeaks (see above) or can occur internally, employees reporting a particular matter through the chain of command (Grace and Cohen, 2000). Where an

Organizations with an unethical culture that frown upon whistleblowing tend to ostracize those who have been brave enough to speak out.

Image Source/David Ryle

organization has an ethical culture (Trevino and Nelson, 2011), employees will be encouraged through both formal and informal systems to speak up about ethical concerns.

Some organizations have whistleblowing hotlines or internal processes to encourage the reporting of ethical misbehaviour, but in too many cases unpleasant side effects have meant that many people who could report ethical misconduct think twice about doing so. For example, Grace and Cohen (2000), reporting on the fate of a group of American whistleblowers, identified lawsuits, divorce, alcohol abuse and attempted suicide as just some of the fallout that the whistleblowers encountered. One example among many is the suspected suicide of the Newscorp hacking scandal whistleblower, Sean Hoare (The Guardian, 2011). So why may whistleblowers suffer retaliation or punishment? One reason is that they are often viewed negatively as tell-tales (Trevino and Nelson 2011) or trouble-makers (Lewis, D., 2000), especially where the complaint has been made publicly. Contrary to this is the view that whistleblowing represents loyalty that leads management to address areas of concern before they become public (Lafer, 2002). In this sense, it is the role of the HR department to have not only a designated process for reporting, but one that is effective and safe.

The gaps in human rights

In 2004, Joel Bakan released an exposé of 'The Corporation'. Declaring the for-profit contemporary corporation as a pathological institution and a dangerous possessor of power, Bakan's key premise is 'that the corporation is an institution, whose legally defined mandate is to pursue relentlessly and without exception, its own self-interest' (Bakan, 2004, p. 1).

This case raises issues surrounding the 'problem of dirty hands'. While typically associated with politicians and governments, the quote below from Machiavelli, cited by Cohen and Grace (1998, p. 37), personifies industries as needing to behave unethically in order to be competitive.

> there is such a gap between how one lives and how one ought to live that anyone who abandons what is done for what ought to be done learns his ruin rather than his preservation; for a man who wishes to make a vocation of being good at all times will come to ruin among so many who are not good. Hence it is necessary for a prince who wishes to maintain his position to learn how not to be good, and to use this knowledge or not to use it according to necessity

HRM as I see it

Gregor Karolus Part 1
Chief HR Officer, Springer Nature

www.springernature.com

Springer Nature is one of the world's leading global research, educational and professional publishers, home to an array of respected and trusted brands providing quality content through a range of innovative products and services. These include academic monographs and textbooks, influential journals, language learning resources and schools books among many others. The company numbers almost 13,000 staff in over 50 countries and has a turnover of approximately €1.5 billion. Springer Nature was formed in 2015 through the merger of Nature Publishing Group, Palgrave Macmillan, Macmillan Education and Springer Science+Business Media.

Over his long career, Gregor has risen up the ranks of HR positions in large international organizations operating from his native Germany. His experience began at Helmholtz Zentrum München, a research institute, as Assistant to the Board of Directors and then Deputy Director of HR, before moving to the media company Bertelsmann, where he held several roles including functions in Personal Development, and was Divisional Director of HR. Now, as Chief HR Officer for Springer Nature, he heads up the centralized HR organization, with an international staff of 150 people.

Click on Gregor's photo in your ebook to watch him speaking on the important of ethics and compliance, and then think about the following questions:

1   What does business ethics mean to Gregor Karolus?
2   Why does Gregor believe that whistleblowers can have a positive impact on the organization?
3   What example does he give to illustrate his point?

Is it therefore this underlying premise of the contemporary business that produces unethical behaviours in executives? Table 11.1 illustrates examples of fines and outcomes in response to executive misconduct (Shumaker, Loop and Kendrick, 2013).

From a stakeholder perspective, injury from high-risk behaviours and misbehaviours on the part of executives is caused to employees, commercial partners, shareholders, the families of those affected and the community at large. So where is the role for HR? An examination of the websites of Australia's big banks identifies only a token presence of HR on the governance boards and executive teams, but would an increased presence be enough to provide ethical guardianship within such major institutions? Peck Kem (2015) calls for the HR function to build more muscle if it is to have an impact on the future. In this sense, the muscles are agility, resilience and 'the courage to call out the gorilla in the room when nobody else dares to, simply because it is the right thing to do' (Peck Kem, 2015, p. 387). Finally, Peterson (2015, p. 55) states that 'As growing numbers of organizations become global enterprises, entering markets with vastly differing ethical codes, the human resources profession must take leadership in ensuring those norms are upheld.'

HRM in practice 11.1

Banks: who do they serve?

A recurring theme in the ethics of banking relates to where risk and responsibility lie (Morrison, 2015b). Many bank executives, especially in the USA and UK, have been criticized for excessive risk-taking and a culture of greed in the years leading up to the catastrophic banking crisis that began in 2008. The events in the finance sector, among many others, bring into question the place of ethics in large corporations. Ethical scandal is consistent across the globe in the industry, and the following insight into the Australian banking industry provides just one example:

On 21 April 2015, four of Australia's most prominent corporate executives in the banking sector apologised before an Australian Senate Inquiry for the unprincipled practices of financial advisers within their organisations. The inquiry focussed on a cultural environment where many financial advisers within these organisations adopted dubious practices. Convincing evidence presented within this Senate Inquiry, as well as Australia's media, showed Australia's largest banks had allowed a culture in which financial advisers lacking ethical principles were able peddle high risk investments to their clients and for many, numbering in the thousands, resulted in major financial loss.

One bank is on record as having received a warning of the practices of rogue financial advisers in 2008, seven years earlier, by an internal whistle-blower but the bank ignored the warning. This particular bank was among others offering dubious financial advice to the peril of thousands of vulnerable clients. The banks' clients were linked to high risk investments at odds with the safe investments they sought. Reports alleged that documents were forged and shredding had occurred to conceal the scandalous behaviour. Circumstances suggest that these criminal activities were fraudulent as forgery, deceptive and unprincipled conduct prevailed within a distorted business model within Australia's leading banks. This calls into question some fundamental issues pertaining to the role of human resource management (HRM) in these organisations. Simply stated, what had happened was that the practices and behaviour of financial advisers and their managers had become distorted from honest and decent business practices.

The evidence indicated that thousands of clients of these four big Australian banks were innocent victims of bad advice and many lost their life savings. The reports raised terms such as white collar criminality and questioned why such criminals working in this industry sector had escaped the justice system.

Greed in the form of kickbacks from companies where the clients' money was invested, combined with internal financial bonuses, were reported to be a contributing factor in poor advice provided by the financial advisers.

The plot worsens. It was reported that one bank had paid compensation but only on the condition that hundreds of victims signed confidentiality agreements, referred to as 'gag' clauses by one Senator during the inquiry hearing. When questioned the bank had admitted that some compensation payments were insufficient – or other terms could be unfair or unethical – but this bank was shielded from subsequent indemnity it would seem. Clients of the bank who signed these agreements may be fearful of speaking freely due to the possibility of legal reprisals. It is arguable that this issue pulls ethical issues undertaken by staff in the bank to an even deeper abyss.

(continued)

Stop! What are the ethical factors associated with a 'light-touch' regulation of the banking system?

Source and further information: See Martin (2013) and Morrison (2015b) for more information.

Note: This feature was written by Alan Montague.

It has been reported that more than 40 advisers have been dismissed from big Australian banks since the media began to focus on this scandal. It has also been reported that many have obtained employment in other organisations in the financial planning sector. This raises two key issues. The first is if the banks chose to retrench financial advisers why does it appear that the banks did not call on the judiciary to examine potential white-collar crime and possibly prevent these undisciplined individuals plying their dubious practices elsewhere on unsuspecting clients? The second issue relates to those who managed the financial advisers who lost their jobs. What penalties did they face? Both questions remain unanswered but are issues of concern from a HRM-ethical perspective.

Table 11.1 *Fines and outcomes in response to executive misconduct*

Year	Fine	Company and outcome
2005	$84 million	DuPont Dow Elastomers LLC
2005	$185 million	Hynix Semiconductor Inc
2011	$31 million	Hitachi – 4 executives jailed
2011	$148 million	Singapore Airlines – 17 executives jailed
2011	$214 million	Nippon Cargo Airlines
2011	$300 million	Samsung Electronics
2011	$375 million	British Airways
2011	$890 million	TFT-LCD – 22 executives jailed
2011	$1 billion	MasterCard and Visa – 7 executives jailed
2011	$1.4 billion	Pilkington Glass (UK) and Asahi Glass (Japan) price fixing auto glass.
2012	$450 million	Hoffmann – LaRoche (vitamins)
2012	$500 million	Au Optronix (LCD panels)

Tension and paradox: is ethical action possible?

Writers on business ethics have been slow to incorporate national culture and politics into their thinking. The social codes of guilt, embarrassment and shame are deeply rooted within society's unwritten rules. They are tied intimately to moral conduct (Fineman, 1999). Ethics in HRM is predicated on the assumption that moral behaviour is important, but problematic for the HR manager. An ethical organization has been characterized as one that has an ethical culture which should be thought of as a slice of the larger organization culture (Trevino and Nelson, 2011).

To create an ethical culture, it is argued that both the formal and informal systems must be aligned. That is, the message from each must be consistent through actions, behaviours and values. For example where recruitment and selection processes should be based on principles of distributive and substantive fairness. Similarly, performance management systems should evaluate not only performance, but also values and honesty. Where alignment occurs, the informal systems will openly reward those who exhibit such characteristics, reinforcing the formal ethical system with the informal. Problems, however, ensue where there is a misalignment or tension between the formal and informal systems. Where the formal and informal ethical cultures are out of alignment, 'employees' perceptions of informal cultural systems influence their ethics-related behaviour more than the formal systems', warn Trevino and Nelson (2011, p. 180). Ethical leadership is a way in which organizations can align their formal and informal ethical culture through the message that the CEO is sending to the employees and the community at large.

Of course, the ability to establish an ethical framework through which employees interact will be challenged if the employees' perception of the organization is at odds with the ethical message. From an HR perspective, we can see this where values of ethical behaviour are frequently touted but only behaviours (even unethical) that impact on the bottom line are rewarded, and misconduct fails to be disciplined (Trevino and Nelson, 2011). Organizations in which self-interest is high on the agenda, or those organizations which operate in industries that place a high emphasis on financial outcomes, will often experience unethical behaviour (Trevino and Nelson, 2011). Staff see that self-interested behaviour is rewarded by the company culture rather than being punished. Such behaviour is demonstrated where white-collar crimes appear as part of the overall industry culture.

The global business landscape presents new moral parameters of increasing complexity for the HR role, with Kryscynski and Ulrich (2015, p. 377) declaring HR as a 'cultivator of organizational paradoxes' and competing demands, many of which raise both ethical and strategic dilemmas for the HR manager. Indeed some writers, for example, Peterson (2015), claim that with the growth of global enterprises, HR professionals should take up the ethical leadership role, viewing it as imperative that HR should become the ethical champion.

The possibility to do this, however, becomes a dilemma when testing the legitimacy of the HR profession (Kochan, 2004) and arises from the dual role that the HR professional must assume in the organization. The HR professional must act on the one hand as the strategic partner of management (Sheehan et al., 2013), but on the other as an advocate and supporter of employee interests (Kochan, 2004). Furthermore, Scott's (2005) argument regarding the ability of the HR manager to be an ethical champion is distinguished through its emphasis on the title rather than the organization's stakeholders. Here Scott argues that the HR title belies an ethical approach as it is more about managing humans as a resource rather than as 'autonomous individuals with legitimate rights and interests' (Scott, 2005, p. 173).

These dilemmas and tensions surface in some of the more critical HRM literature. Moreover, for critical management scholars, there is a debate on whether the ethical treatment of workers within organizations is possible and, at a more abstract level, whether mainstream business ethicists have failed to make a connection between ethical action and politics.

There appear to be at least six main barriers to ethical behaviour:

First, the fundamental contradiction between capital and labour renders any attempt to make employment conditions more ethical a 'problematic' endeavour (Clayton, 2000).

Second, constraints are placed on managers' ethical behaviour by global capitalism. Beyond legal constraints and the notion of CSR, customer power in the form of boycotts can compel multinational corporations to act ethically. However, as evidenced by Starbucks, Amazon and Facebook's behaviour over paying their corporation tax in 2016, if public shaming and threats of consumer boycotts are needed to persuade multinational corporations to act ethically, "their 'morality' is not truly ethical, at least from a Kantian viewpoint, as it is motivated by self-interest" (Legge, 2000, p. 38).

Third, the growth of precarious employment has demonstrated the unethical basis of much contemporary HR practice as it shifts the burden of risk from employers to employees or recent graduates. Heery's (2000) criticism of the 'new pay' paradigm (see Chapter 8) is based on its 'ethical deficiencies'. Heery argues that increased employee risk and diminished collective representation are present in reward systems. Variable pay represents a dramatic growth in 'pay-at-risk' as a larger proportion of pay is contingent on individual or organizational performance (see Chapter 8). Furthermore, the absence of a strong trade union voice in the pay-setting process arguably means that the 'new' pay is potentially 'unjust' and that 'it affords little scope for the exercise of democratic rights by citizens' in the workplace (Heery, 2000, pp. 182–3).

Fourth, organizations pursuing profit maximization first and foremost tend normatively to pursue a 'minimalist' ethical position (Winstanley and Stoney, 1999).

Fifth, the focus on the HRM–performance link (see Chapter 3), where superior performance is achieved through 'strategic fit', limits the use of costly ethical employment standards (Woodall and Winstanley, 2000).

Finally, business ethics writings have been critiqued for failing to differentiate enough from individualistic discourse on 'good' corporate citizenship and politics – a discourse on political power. At an abstract level, Wray-Bliss (2005), using Foucauldian-inspired writing (see Chapter 1), has (re)introduced an appreciation of the political nature of nominally individual ethical acts. He also draws out the importance of power relations in capitalist society and emphasizes the point that, to effectively challenge unethical corporate behaviour, people need to engage in a political process (Willmott, 1993). This suggests that although organizations have in many cases embraced the rhetoric of CSR, their actions have lagged behind this, and it takes political action to persuade organizations to act ethically.

case study

Whistleblowing – an Australian context

The setting

Compensating whistleblowers in the UK and Australia for exposing corporate misconduct to benefit the public has permeated the discourse on ethics with added rigour in 2014 and 2015, respectively. Many academic commentators currently consider that the protection of insiders who blow the whistle, at great risk to their health, well-being and career, is totally inadequate.

The problem

The issue of rewarding whistleblowers was a question posed by the Chairman of the Australian Securities and Investment Commission (ASIC). ASIC is Australia's corporate, markets and financial services regulator – also known metaphorically as the 'corporate watchdog'. ASIC's role is to ensure that Australia's financial markets are underpinned by transparent integrity, so that investors and consumers have the capacity to make informed decisions. The Chairman's view was that whistleblowers should be compensated, potentially, for their lifetime. The exposure of corporate misconduct is common in Australia, as it is on a global basis. Therefore, an Australian Senate Economics Committee aims to lead a discussion paper that highlights this issue to raise awareness. This may result in the formulation of legislation that provides protection and fair compensatory rewards for whistleblowers.

In the corporate world, unethical behaviour is strewn with cases where greed has superseded the ethical foundations of human perpetrators. Whistleblowers have an enormous impact on corporations, legal regulations and regulators, laws and innocent victims to induce measures of redress. Wage fraud by prominent retailers and financial advice by leading banks are two main issues that have been prominent in Australia's media in 2014 and 2015. Whistleblowers in these areas have forced ethical changes in organizations. For example, banks have compensated innocent people who were the victims of unethical and substandard financial advice but have now collectively received tens of millions of dollars, and more is to follow – much more. Individuals employed by a prominent retail franchise are being paid fairly and compensated for many hours where they were short-changed on their salaries. This retail franchise is destined to face the judiciary, with a class action having been initiated by franchisees and disgruntled staff in separate actions.

Image Source/TODD WARNOCK

Some whistleblowers anonymously supply information about covert or illegal behaviour in the organizations where they work – known as a 'Deep Throat' approach – due to fear of retaliation and career suicide. Many employees are aware of corporate scandals but choose to do nothing and stay silent. Many possibly live in fear that they are a part of the fraudulent behaviour and may themselves face penalties in time, but consider that the risks of whistleblowing outweigh the responsibility for undertaking it.

The USA provides a superior safeguard and reward for whistleblowers, Bradley Birkenfeld being an outstanding example. Birkenfeld was a banker who was paid a record $104 million by the Internal Revenue Service in 2012 for exposing former banking executive superiors who coached US clients to conceal large sums of money in Swiss bank accounts. In the USA, successful whistleblowers can and have received considerable monetary settlements, sometimes to the tune of multiple millions of dollars. The amount generally depends on the type of fraud exposed and may take account of the level of work undertaken to ensure that the fraud allegation results in prosecution under the US False Claims Act. The USA represents a comprehensive contrast to Australia, where whistleblowers are reported to suffer stressful situations, retaliation, possible threats, anxiety and financial hardship if they are dismissed by an employer for their honesty.

As many corporations have experienced, whistleblowers aim to protect against greed-fuelled unethical behaviour by staff that tarnishes the image of

(continued)

an organization. It is a pity that a whistleblower did not expose a prominent car manufacturing company before it was revealed to be developing a component that would conceal the emission of impurities that were deemed illegal in many countries. The cost to the company of a whistleblower not speaking out may escalate to billions of dollars.

The assignment

Working individually, or in a group, prepare a brief report to respond to the following questions:

1 What role should HRM perform to shield whistleblowers from inappropriate threats or unethical retribution in cases where they are acting honestly to thwart fraudulent behaviour or damage to the environment?
2 For most Australian whistleblowers, publicly disclosing damaging information about a company, despite this being motivated by well-justified ethics, poses great risks and often carries a steep price in terms of a person's career. Given this information what level of compensation in your group's view should be paid to whistleblowers?
3 What penalties for corporate misconduct should occur?
4 What range of penalties should HRM departments impose on the perpetrators of fraudulent behaviour or work practices that are damaging to the broader society?
5 From an HRM perspective, what action should be considered for the managers and executives who have managed the work of financial or environmental fraudsters?
6 Undertaking your own research in your group or individually, identify some famous whistleblowers and prepare a brief outline of some interesting and notable examples.

Note: This case study was written by Alan Montague, Roslyn Larkin and John Burgess.

summary

➤ Business ethics are moral principles and values that influence the decision-making of individuals within the organization. Business ethics considers the organization's interaction with its stakeholders and environment.

➤ Ethical decision-making within the organizational environment may be legally driven. For example, within the regulatory environment, legislation including equal employment opportunity, occupational or workplace health and safety, antidiscrimination legislation and many others exist to determine the minimum obligations of the organization toward its many stakeholders.

➤ CSR is concerned with ways in which managers' behaviours exceed minimum compliance-based regulation. CSR is intellectually grounded within the stakeholder theory of the firm, supporting the legitimate interest of many stakeholders (employees, customers, suppliers, the environment, shareholders and society at large) in the organization.

➤ Key ethical frameworks include the following: utilitarianism or consequentialism, whereby actions and behaviours are evaluated as right or wrong, or good or bad, according to their consequences; deontology, or Kantian ethics, which is based on the premise that the motive for an action is more important than its consequences; virtue ethics, which does not require action but is embodied through the aspiration that individuals should lead a virtuous life; and rights-based ethics, as represented by the United Nations, which includes free speech, freedom from slavery and equal opportunity.

➤ Labour rights are built on human rights with labour practice monitored by the ILO, a tripartite organization representing employers, employees and governments. The ILO promotes rights at work through its labour conventions or recommendations to member countries.

➤ Within an organization, the HR department has an opportunity to create and/or reinforce an ethical organizational culture through its activities of recruitment and selection, human resource development, performance management and reward, as well as through support mechanisms such as codes of conduct and whistleblower programmes. Codes may be developed internally from the organization or externally through industry bodies.

➤ One of the primary challenges for HR as an 'ethical guardian' is the dual role that the HR professional must assume. On the one hand, HR is management's strategic partner, whereas on the other it is an advocate of employee interests. This duality of role is recognized as a significant tension for the future impact of HR's ethical leadership.

review questions

1 What are the links between business ethics and CSR?

2 Utilitarianism is the most universal of the ethical frameworks. Do you agree?

3 Virtue ethics apply universally. Do you agree? Why or why not?

4 In what ways can the HR manager work as an ethical business partner of the organization?

5 Why are whistleblowers often viewed negatively? Why are they viewed positively?

6 In ethics, why do we consider the HR professional as performing a dual role?

further reading

Reading these articles and chapters can help you gain a better understanding and potentially a higher grade for your HRM assignment.

➤ Commonwealth of Australia (2015) Scrutiny of financial advice. Proof Committee Hansard Senate Economics References Committee (Public) Friday, 6 March 2015 Melbourne.

➤ De Roeck, K., Marique, G., Stinglhamber, F., and Swaen, V. (2014) Understanding employees' responses to corporate social responsibility: mediating roles of overall justice and organisational identification. *International Journal of Human Resource Management*, **25**(1): 91–112.

➤ Kohn, S. (2011). *Whistleblower's Handbook: A Step-by-Step Guide to Doing What's Right and Protecting Yourself*. Lanham, MD: Rowman & Littlefield.

➤ Mintz, S. L. (2015). Issue: Ethics and financial services. Available at: http://businessresearcher. sagepub.com/sbr-1645-95217-2661757/20150316/ethics-and-financial-services (accessed August 1, 2016).

➤ Morrison, J. (2015) *Business Ethics: New Challenges in a Globalized World*. London: Palgrave.

➤ Muchlinski, P. (2012) Implementing the new UN corporate human rights framework: implications of corporate law, governance and regulation. *Business Ethics Quarterly*, **22**(1): 145–77.

➤ Sheedy, E. A. and Griffin, B. (2014) Empirical analysis of risk culture in financial institutions: interim report. Available at: www.lse.ac.uk/accounting/CARR/events/Sheedy-Risk-Culture-Paper-Nov-14.pdf. (accessed August 1, 2016).

➤ UN Human Rights Council (2011) Guiding principles on business and human rights. Available at: www.ohchr.org/EN/Issues/Business/Pages/BusinessIndex.aspx (accessed August 1, 2016).

➤ Winstanley, D. and J. Woodall (eds) (2000) *Ethical Issues in Contemporary Human Resource Management*. Basingstoke: Palgrave Macmillan.

vocabulary checklist for ESL students

 Click here in your interactive ebook for a list of HRM terminology and vocabulary that has appeared in this chapter.

Visit the online resource centre at www.palgravehighered.com/bg-hrm-6e for lots of extra resources to help you get to grips with this chapter, including study tips, HRM skills development guides, summary lecture notes, tips for English as a Second Language (ESL) students and more.

HRM web links

Visit the online resource centre at www.palgravehighered.com/bg-hrm-6e for a group assignment on ethics in HRM.

part V

CONTEMPORARY ISSUES: HRM IN A GLOBAL WORLD

chapter **12**

employee health, safety and wellness

PhotoDisc/Getty Images

outline

➤ Introduction
➤ Sustainable health and safety and HRM
➤ HRM in practice 12.1: Employees going to work even if they are ill
➤ The importance of health, safety and wellness
➤ HRM and globalization 12.1: The social construction of workplace injury in North America
➤ Workplace health and safety issues
➤ HRM in practice 12.2: Work-related stress
➤ HRM in practice 12.3: Juggling work and life and – the work–life boundary
➤ Workplace wellness
➤ Paradox in workplace health and safety
➤ Case study: The City of Kamloops
➤ Summary, review questions, further reading and vocabulary checklist for ESL students

objectives

After studying this chapter, you should be able to:

1 Explain the benefits of a health, safety and wellness strategy
2 Describe some common hazards in the contemporary workplace
3 Describe the components of a workplace wellness programme
4 Critique management strategies for health and safety in the workplace

When TV audiences around the world watched the dramatic rescue of 33 trapped Chilean miners in October 2010, they may have found the news uplifting, but for occupational health and safety activists, it was a reminder that work can be a life and death experience. Most mornings, we turn the door handle and set off to work in offices, banks, schools, hospitals, universities, construction sites and other workplaces. Most of us assume that we will return home safely at the end of the working day, but many workers unfortunately will not. In 2014–15, 142 British workers lost their lives through a workplace fatality, and a further 629,000 employees suffered a reportable work-related injury (Health and Safety Executive, 2015). At a different level, unsocial working hours can impact negatively on workers' health. For example, the Rail, Maritime and Transport union said the Eurostar dispute, which began on 12th August 2016, had been caused by the company's failure to honour a 2008 agreement to ensure that train managers could expect a good work–life balance in terms of unsocial hours and duty rosters (Topham, 2016).

introduction

These data and the Eurostar reported dispute underscore two important realities about work: first, it can be an unhealthy, even deadly, experience; and, second, health and safety in the workplace is all too often mismanaged. Work systems and practices that offer safe and healthy working conditions reduce accidents and help to create dignity *at* work (Bolton, 2007). The World Health Organization (WHO, 2016) defines 'health' as 'a state of complete physical, mental and social well-being and not merely the absence of disease or infirmity'. According to this definition, managers and, in workplaces where they are organized, trade union representatives are immersed in one of society's greatest challenges – the design and maintenance of sustainable work systems that both support the organization's objectives and provide an environment that is safe and healthy for its workers. Thus, the links with the design and quality of jobs examined in Chapter 13 are a primary focus. Most recently, the industrial pollution of global and local ecosystems has brought into full relief the need for work systems to operate without compromising the health of the local community or destroying the ecosystem.

We will begin this chapter by considering the importance of health and wellness in the management of work and people. After giving an overview of some health hazards in the modern workplace, we look at the importance of health and wellness before examining the paradoxes surrounding the issue of health and wellness so that there can be a better understanding of the complexities of the employment relationship.

HRM web links

Visit the online resource centre at **www.palgravehighered.com/bg-hrm-6e** for details on a short film on the rescue of the Chilean miners.

reflective question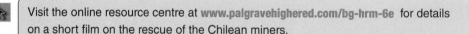

Who are the stakeholders in health and safety? What are the responsibilities of employers to ensure that work is conducted in a safe and healthy environment?

Sustainable health and safety and HRM

Traditionally, occupational health and safety (OHS) encapsulated quite distinct yet intrinsically related concepts concerned with the identification and control of work-induced ill-health and accidents. Whereas accidents are visible or measurable, not without cause and largely preventable, work-induced ill-health is largely invisible and can develop over a long period of time, as in the case of asbestosis (Cullen, 2002). Although workplace health and safety have long been legitimate areas for regulation, as evidenced by health and safety legislation, greater visibility has in recent years been given to employees' well-being (Black and Frost, 2011; van Wanrooy et al., 2013a).

The concept of workplace wellness goes beyond the regulation and management of work-related health and safety, to focus on shaping employees' entire lifestyle and well-being. Employee well-being has two dimensions: the 'emotional affect' that is pleasure or displeasure gained from paid work, and the degree of mental arousal experienced by the employee (van Wanrooy et al., 2013a). The emerging literature on sustainable business strategies, the 'quadruple bottom line performance' (see Chapter 2), and the links between inequality and health and well-being (Wilkinson and Pickett, 2010) is widening the scope and coverage of 'green' health and safety management. Recent research published in *The Lancet* medical journal shows massive regional variations in life expectancy and ill-health caused by wide income inequality (Boseley, 2015). What is important to recognize is that concerns about ill-health are no longer limited to areas of industrial work. Front-line office workers, managers and professionals are demanding to work in a 'healthy organization', and employers and policy-makers are increasingly acknowledging the adverse economic consequences of employee ill-health.

People living in the locale of industrial polluters – mines, agriculture, chemicals and forestry – and environmental movements are beginning to hold organizations accountable for widespread damage to ecosystems. The instances here are numerous, but well-known examples include the massive oil spill in the Gulf of Mexico in 2010 when BP's wellhead burst, and toxic pollution by the US corporation Union Carbide in Bhopal, India in the 1980s (see Chapters 2 and 11). Another case is the industrial poisoning of an entire community's water supply, and the subsequent corporate cover-up, by the US Pacific Gas and Electric Company (PG&E) in Hinkley, USA – the legal fight against PG&E was dramatized in the 2000 film *Erin Brockovich*. A more recent example can be found in Western Canada in 2012, where research has shown that oil sand production is responsible for high levels of toxins in the Athabasca watershed. The pollution has been held responsible for rare human cancers diagnosed in residents of Fort Chipewyan (Weber, 2011). In Europe, environmental activists are proposing to the United Nations that 'ecocide' – the extensive destruction, damage to or loss of ecosystems in a given territory, whether by human agency or by other causes – be declared an international crime against peace (Jowit, 2010).

Such experiences and campaigns have brought into the modern discourse on low-carbon economies a recognition that OHS and the protection of ecosystems form an important subgroup of organizational contingencies affecting corporate strategy. Moreover, they underscore the need to develop a proactive human resource management (HRM) strategy that can contribute to the management of health, wellness and environmental-related risks.

Although there has been a deluge of research on HRM problems and issues, it is unfortunately true, apart from a few notable cases (Nichols, 1997; Taylor and Connelly, 2009), that workplace health and safety is under-researched by workplace scholars, partly because it has entered the HRM discourse in only a marginal way. Rising costs associated with work-induced injuries and ill-health, issues relating to the psychological contract, new laws and growing concerns about protecting ecosystems are important reasons why workplace health, safety and wellness should be part of any introduction to the field of HRM.

HRM in practice 12.1

Employees going to work even if they are ill

A survey by the CIPD (Chartered Institute of Personnel and Development/Simplyhealth, 2012) found that the average level of employee absence had fallen by about 1 day compared with the previous year, and that almost a third of employers had reported an increase in the number of people going into work ill. Absenteeism, whether caused by illness or an employee taking a day off, is an easily observable phenomenon, but attendance at work when ill is not such an obvious problem. The term 'sickness presenteeism' refers to people going in to work even if they are suffering from an illness that they think would justify sickness absence. Reasons for employees going to work despite suffering from illness include maintaining a good relationship with colleagues, not wanting to lose time for doing work, avoidance of job stress on return to work, high workload and job insecurity, especially the fear that absenteeism could be used in selection for redundancy.

Commenting on the CIPD report, Dr Jill Miller, Research Adviser at the CIPD stated that presenteeism can damage a company's productivity:

Not only can illnesses be passed on to other colleagues, but ill employees are likely to work less effectively than usual, may be more prone to making costly mistakes and take longer to recover from their illnesses (CIPD/Simplyhealth, 2012).

It has been calculated that, 'presenteeism accounts for 1.5 times more working time lost than absenteeism' (Ashby and Mahdon, 2010). Organizations have taken steps to reduce absenteeism due to ill-health, including well-being strategies whereby managers are trained to manage people effectively to reduce stress and use methods to direct people to occupational health services and provide support to help them stay in or return to work. Little is known about the long-term health implications for individuals who frequently go in to work despite feeling ill.

A study of 11,793 Swedish police officers aimed to identify factors in the work environment that were associated with sickness presenteeism (Leineweber et al., 2011). Officers were asked the simple question, 'How many times during the past 12 months did you go to work even though you should have been off sick due to

the state of your health?' Respondents were deemed to have been sickness-present if they stated they had been to work at least twice on occasions when they judged that they could have taken sick leave. Sickness presence was common, as 46.5 per cent of respondents had gone to work despite feeling sufficiently ill to justify a sickness absence. Differences were found according to sex, age, seniority and self-rated health. Male respondents aged over 54 years and supervisors stated

(continued)

Stop! HR departments have done much to reduce absenteeism by, for example, the introduction of well-being strategies, recording of absenteeism with official targets, and interviews with employees on their return to work, which may be helpful but could be interpreted as a form of coercion. What can be done to reduce sickness presenteeism, which may be more harmful than absenteeism to the organization and the employee?

Sources and further information: For more on this issue, see Ashby and Mahdon (2010), CIPD/Simplyhealth (2012) and Leineweber et al. (2011).

Note: This feature was written by David Denham.

more often that they had not been ill at all. Women and subordinates were the most likely to report extreme sickness presenteeism (10 times or more).

The study concluded that work environment factors such as support from colleagues and supervisors, poor leadership, low control and high stress are associated with sickness presenteeism. Support from colleagues and control over work tasks also interacted with age, showing that poor support from colleagues and low control contributed to presenteeism among older employees.

But there is another important reason why HRM scholars and practitioners need to pay more attention to health and wellness: if strategic HRM means anything, it must encompass the development and promotion of a set of health and wellness policies to protect the organization's most valued asset – its people.

The employer has a legal duty to maintain a healthy and safe workplace. When considering the question of how important OHS may be, although economic cost and human resources (HR) considerations will always be predominant for the organization, the costs of ill-health and work-related accidents are not only borne by the victims, the families and their employers: they are also clearly borne by the tax-payer and public sector services. The healthcare sector, for example, bears the costs of workplace ill-health and accidents. Reliable estimates of the total cost of occupational ill-health and accidents are incomplete, which is perhaps symptomatic of the low priority given to this area of work. In 2015, the Health and Safety Executive (HSE) estimated the cost of workplace injuries and ill-health to be £14.2 billion (HSE, 2015), but Georgiou et al. (2009) put the figure higher.

HRM web links Visit the online resource centre at **www.palgravehighered.com/bg-hrm-6e** for further information on the cost of workplace injuries and ill-health.

HRM web links Visit the online resource centre at **www.palgravehighered.com/bg-hrm-6e** for a brief history of the changing approaching to workplace health and safety.

The importance of health, safety and wellness

There are strong economic, legal, psychological and ethical reasons why managers should take health and safety seriously, and these will be discussed in turn below.

Economic considerations

In the UK, the Health and Safety Commission (HSC) and the Department of the Environment, Transport and the Regions (2000) document made the 'business case' for health and safety in the workplace. In considering the economics of an unhealthy and unsafe workplace, it is necessary to distinguish between costs falling upon the organization and costs falling upon government-funded bodies such as hospitals. It is not difficult for an organization to calculate the economic costs of a work-related accident. In addition to direct costs related to lost production due to accidents and illness, there are also indirect costs. These include the overtime payments necessary to make up for lost production, the cost of retaining a replacement employee and the legal cost associated with court hearings in contested cases. The indirect costs of workplace accidents and illnesses also fall on society through the extra need for healthcare provision. The economic costs of work-related accidents, and the techniques for assessing them, require further research (Georgiou et al., 2009). A safe and healthy work environment, built on sustainable principles, can reduce operating costs and improve organizational effectiveness (Dyck, 2002; Mearns and Hope, 2005).

Legal considerations

With respect to workplace health and safety, the legal rights of employees can be categorized into two broad categories: *individual* and *collective*. The first source of individual rights evolves from common law. Every employer has a vicarious common law duty to provide a safe working environment for her or his employees. But the primary source of individual rights arises from statute law. In Britain, an example is the Health and Safety at Work Act 1974. Within the European Union (EU), individual rights stemming from directives under Article 189 of the Treaty of Rome are, pre-Brexit, a second important source of legislated protection standards promoting safe working environments.

The main source of collective health and safety rights arises from the negotiated collective agreements between union and management. In current labour law, Canadian, American and New Zealand workers have legal rights to refuse to perform unsafe or unhealthy work (Pye et al., 2001). In the EU and the USA, failure to provide a safe working environment may result in the employer being prosecuted for *corporate manslaughter*. Health and safety legislation is discussed more fully in the next section.

HRM web links Visit the online resource centre at **www.palgravehighered.com/bg-hrm-6e** for further information on the development of health and safety legislation and details of relevant websites.

Psychological considerations

Apart from economic and legal considerations, a healthy and safe work environment helps to facilitate employee commitment and improve industrial relations. In Beer et al's (1984) model of HRM, it is recognized that, going beyond the legal requirement of 'due diligence', a healthy organization can have a strong positive effect on the psychological contract by strengthening employees' commitment, motivation and loyalty (p. 153):

> There is some evidence to indicate that work system design may have effects on physical health, mental health, and longevity of life itself.

A survey of UK workplaces found a strong association between worker reports of a 'healthier workplace' and greater experience of HR practices. With respect to work-related stress, a 'healthier workplace' and a more positive state of the psychological contract were associated with lower reported levels of stress (Guest, 2008).

Ethical considerations

Sustainable business practices and health are inextricably linked, and health issues have implications for corporate responsibility and managerial ethics. Gewirth (1991) argues that

HRM and globalization 12.1

The social construction of workplace injury in North America

PhotoDisc/ Getty Images

Canadian newspapers routinely report on injuries that occur in workplaces. But is their coverage accurate? The evidence definitively says no. Canadian newspapers dramatically over-report occupational fatalities. Although fatalities comprise only 0.4 per cent of serious workplace injuries each year, they are the subject of 61.2 per cent of newspaper stories. In addition, reporters also almost entirely ignore injuries to women, so although men experience 62.9 per cent of all serious workplace injuries in Canada, injuries to men comprise 95.6 per cent of the newspaper coverage.

Injuries caused by contact with objects or equipment, and by fires and explosions, comprise 24.0 per cent of all workplace injuries in Canada but are the subject of 58.9 per cent of all newspaper reports. By contrast, bodily reactions and exertions cause 42.1 per cent of all injuries but, over a 5-year period, were never mentioned in newspapers. Finally, newspaper stories over-report injuries in blue-collar occupations: injuries in the construction, mining and petroleum industries comprise 12.3 per cent of all injuries but account for 44.6 per cent of newspaper stories (Barnetson and Foster, 2015).

This bias in newspaper accounts is important because injuries have a dual nature. On the one hand, workplace injuries are specific harms experienced by workers. On the other hand, workplace injuries are social constructions. That is to say, what we consider to be a workplace injury (and what we do not) reflects a shared understanding that emerges from our personal experiences and from knowledge we have gleaned from other sources, including the media.

If media reports tells us that workplace injuries are primarily an issue affecting men in blue-collar occupations who are often killed due to contact with objects or in explosions, this bias cannot but help shape what we recognize as hazards in our workplaces. Is speeding up the work of a cashier so much so that her wrists ache really a problem? If so, it certainly isn't important enough to make the papers. Is a steam burn from the cappuccino machine worth bothering about? Maybe, but it isn't like you lost your life in a mineshaft collapse.

Constructing workplace injuries as traumatic, physical injuries that only happen to workers in certain industries reduces the pressure on employers to take action on the most common kinds of injuries (muscle strains and sprains) in the industries where most injuries happen (manufacturing and healthcare). Ignoring sprains and strains in healthcare, for example, means that employers do not have to redesign work in potentially expensive ways, such as by buying expensive lifts. Instead, this cost of production is transferred from the employer to nurses and healthcare aides (mostly women) in the form of workplace injuries.

Emphasizing acute physical injuries also delegitimizes injuries that have a long latency period or are otherwise difficult to see, such as the psychological damage caused by workplace bullying. Human resource practitioners must be mindful of how media misrepresentations of workplace injuries can blind managers and workers to hazardous working conditions and obscure the presence of serious occupational injuries.

Stop! Do newspapers in your country misrepresent workplace injuries? Why do newspaper reports so profoundly misrepresent the nature of occupational injuries? How do these misrepresentations affect workplace health and safety? And what, specifically, might explain the near absence of women from media reports of workplace injury?

Sources and further information: See Barnetson and Foster (2015) for the study discussed in this feature.

Note: This feature was written by Bob Barnetson.

those individuals who contribute to the causation of work-related diseases (for example, asbestosis, lung cancer and exposure to second-hand smoke) and who do so knowingly can be held to be both causally and morally responsible for their action. Doherty and Tyson (2000) argue persuasively that managers are not innocent bystanders with regard to employee health and well-being: their actions – such as the choice of production processes and substances, or speeding up work – have adverse effects on employees' work–life balance, as well as their physical and mental well-being.

A major challenge to managers is clearly to provide a safe and healthy work environment for their employees, but, in addition to a pervasive portfolio of OHS legislation, economic and moral reasons dictate such a policy, and the HR practitioner has an important role advising line managers on the content and legal obligations of this.

reflective question

> What are your views? Do employers have a moral responsibility to provide a safe and healthy workplace?

Workplace health and safety issues

This section examines several health issues of special concern to today's managers – sick building syndrome (SBS), workplace stress, workplace violence, bullying, alcohol abuse, smoking, and acquired immune deficiency syndrome (AIDS) – and explains the meaning of workplace wellness.

Sick building syndrome

Interest in the physical aspects of the work building, as a factor affecting employee performance, goes back to at least the 1930s with Mayo's Hawthorne experiments in the USA (see Chapter 13). Most recently, the construction of 'closed' office buildings with air-conditioning systems has focused research attention on the working conditions of knowledge workers.

In 1982, SBS was recognized by the WHO as occurring where a cluster of work-related symptoms of unknown cause were significantly more prevalent among the occupants of certain buildings in comparison with others. Researchers have identified numerous symptoms of SBS, including eye, nose and throat irritation, a sensation of dry mucous membranes and skin, skin rashes, mental fatigue, headaches, a high frequency of airway infection and cough, nausea, dizziness, hoarseness and wheezing (Bain and Baldry, 1995). The HSC calculated in the 1990s that the staff of 30–50 per cent of newly 'remodelled' buildings in Britain suffered a high incidence of SBS-related illnesses. In Canada, it has been estimated that there are 1800 'sick' buildings affecting 250,000 office workers. Based on such data, the problem of SBS seems to have been 'severely underestimated' (Bain and Baldry, 1995, p. 21), and from the worker well-being perspective, it is a significant problem (Redman et al., 2011, p. 23).

The causes of SBS have been linked to inadequate ventilation, unsuitable lighting and airborne pollutants. Others have focused less on technical explanations and emphasized managerial contingencies. Bain and Baldry (1995) and Bain et al. (1999), for example, propose that, in a context of high energy costs, SBS is related to cost reductions and the intensification of knowledge work. They conclude that 'Changes in the balance of power in the office environment have undoubtedly made it easier for management to gain employee acceptance of much more demanding practices and patterns of work' (Bain and Baldry, 1995, p. 30).

SBS is negatively associated with job satisfaction and is associated with 'increased management-employment conflict' (Redman et al., 2011, p. 23). SBS is also a 'stressor' and positively associated with emotional exhaustion, which can increase labour costs via lower performance and absenteeism. This may in turn undermine the empowerment approach associated with high-commitment work models as managers resort to disciplinary measures to reduce absenteeism.

Workplace stress

The word 'stress' is now part of the regular vocabulary of managers and other employees. Although a certain degree of stress is normal in life, if stress is repeated or prolonged, individuals experience physical and psychological discomfort. There is widespread recognition that tension and stress have increased in UK workplaces (Green, 2004; Kelliher and Anderson, 2010), and this is supported by evidence of work intensification. The capacity of 'smart' mobile phones, such as the iPhone, to create a 24/7, on-demand lifestyle, and to result in the intrusion of work into private life, has been identified by some academics as a potential stressor (Bittman et al., 2009). There is a general consensus that stress and stress-related ill-health can impact negatively on job performance. Figure 12.1 illustrates some common symptoms of stress.

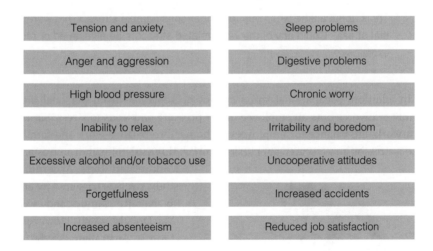

Tension and anxiety	Sleep problems
Anger and aggression	Digestive problems
High blood pressure	Chronic worry
Inability to relax	Irritability and boredom
Excessive alcohol and/or tobacco use	Uncooperative attitudes
Forgetfulness	Increased accidents
Increased absenteeism	Reduced job satisfaction

Figure 12.1 *Typical symptoms of workplace stress*

HRM web links   Visit the online resource centre at www.palgravehighered.com/bg-hrm-6e for further information on workplace stress.

Much research into job-related stress has tended to focus on 'executive burnout' and individuals in the higher echelons of the organizational hierarchy, but stress affects employees at lower levels too. Early US studies have found that the two most stressful jobs are a manual labourer and a secretary (Craig, 1981). In the UK, the 2011 Workplace Employment Relations

Survey found that 55 per cent of employees felt 'tense' because of their job some of the time (van Wanrooy et al., 2013a). The survey also found that 'higher job demands, or greater work intensity, were associated with lower levels of contentment' (van Wanrooy et al., 2013a, p. 131). A 2004 UK survey found a strong association between employee reports of lower levels of work-related stress and a more positive state of the psychological contract and a 'healthier workplace' (Guest, 2008). In addition to the physical and psychological disabilities that stress causes, occupational stress costs individuals and business considerable sums of money (Coutts, 1998). The HSE has, for example, estimated that workplace stress, depression and anxiety cost the British economy £530 million annually (HSE, 2007).

Researchers have explored the antecedents of workplace stress. Research has investigated *work-related* factors, such as role ambiguity and job design, and *individual* factors, such as debt worries and workplace bullying (Hadikin and O'Driscoll, 2000). Changes in the labour market, such as non-standard hours and employment insecurity, can be a cause of work-related stress. Zeytinoglu's et al. (2015) research, for example, examines associations between home care workers' health and non-standard hours and insecurity. The authors found that part-time and casual hours and job insecurity were positively and significantly associated with symptoms of stress, and these results have implications for employers, HR managers, trade unionists and policy-makers. Workplace stress that is associated with work overload and unrealistic time deadlines, for example, will put an employee under pressure. Workplace sexual harassment is another source of stress.

reflective question Think about a time when you felt under considerable stress. What were the causes of that stress? Could any of the work-related stressors be eliminated or reduced? If not, explain why.

In addition, occupational stress cannot be separated from personal life: illness in the family or divorce puts an employee under pressure and leads to stress. Similarly, the notion of a work–life balance for employees – the need to balance work and family activities – is also a stressor, and research appears to support this dual-role syndrome as an explanation of work-related stress. According to a Canadian study, stress is triggered by employees trying to balance family and work (Ross and MacDonald, 1997). However, Zheng's et al. (2016) Australian study of employees' perception of work–life balance found that individual employees with positive attitudes and life coping strategies were more capable of achieving overall well-being. Thus work-related stress can be seen to be a multifaceted workplace phenomenon caused by multiple social factors.

Getty Images/Hemera / Thinkstock / Cathy Yeulet

Stress caused by the 'dual-role' syndrome.

In the HRM canon, work-related stress is underanalysed, the prevailing view being that occupational stress is a personal problem. It is now recognized, however, that work-related stress is a major health problem and that it is a management's responsibility to provide the initiative to eliminate or reduce the causes of work-related stress.

Workplace violence

For many employees at the front end of service delivery, violence is a critical safety issue. According to the British Crime Statistics, there were during 2013/14 an estimated 583,000 incidents of violence at work, comprising 269,000 physical assaults and 314,000 threats (HSE, 2015). The HSE describes workplace violence as 'Any incident in which a person is abused, threatened, or assaulted in circumstances relating to their work' (HSE, 2011). Surveys have found that between 40 and 90 per cent of women suffer some forms of violence and harassment during the course of their working lives. There are three major types of workplace violence:

- *Type 1* – the perpetrator of the violence has no legitimate relationship with the targeted employee and enters the workplace to commit a criminal act (for example, robbery). Retail and service industry employees and taxi drivers are those most exposed to this type of workplace violence.
- *Type 2* – the perpetrator is an employee or former employee of the organization, typically a 'disgruntled employee' who commits a violent act against a co-worker or supervisor for what is perceived to be unfair treatment.
- *Type 3* – the perpetrator is a recipient of a service provided by the targeted employee. Bus drivers, social workers, healthcare providers and teachers are particularly vulnerable to this type of workplace violence.

Montgomery and Kelloway (2002) identify three groups of employee at particular risk of experiencing workplace violence: those who interact with the public; those making decisions that influence other people's lives; and those denying the public a request or a service. Given the growth of the call-centre model for customer service, chronic exposure to 'phone rage' is also a growing problem in some workplaces. Capita UK estimates that the top three triggers of phone rage are:

- The phone not being answered in reasonable time
- The customer feeling processed, or a victim of a faceless corporation
- Standard greetings and pleasantries that do not sound sincere.

Research shows that much of workplace violence goes unrecorded. However, the consequences of workplace violence go beyond immediate physical injury or death. The trauma caused by the violence has negative results for both the individual employee's well-being (that is, in terms of impaired mental and physical health) and the organization (that is, decreased commitment, retention and performance; Montgomery and Kelloway, 2002).

HRM web links ▶ Visit the online resource centre at www.palgravehighered.com/bg-hrm-6e for more material on violence in the workplace.

HRM in practice 12.2

Work-related stress

© Stockbyte Royalty Free Photos

The incidence of work-related stress appeared to increase rapidly at the end of the twentieth century, bringing into the spotlight the importance of the health and well-being of employees at work. An extensive research drive followed, attempting to better understand the consequences for individuals (for example, psychological and physical ill-health), for teams (such as conflict between team members) and for organizations (for example, short- and long-term absence). Significant effort was also invested in understanding the work-related causes of stress and the effectiveness of different interventions for preventing, managing and treating it. As a result, plentiful amounts of information and resources are now available for organizations to better manage this aspect of their employees' experience, and the advice given to HR and organizations is fairly consistent. Most advocate a series of linked interventions to manage stress, prioritizing an employee risk assessment of specific work characteristics identified as potentially stressful. Employees are typically asked to rate features of their jobs, such as the amount of control and discretion allowed in their role, usually via questionnaires.

Many of these approaches can genuinely describe themselves as evidence-based, in that they directly link to recent research. Examples are the HSE's Management Standards for Work-related Stress and the toolkits and training courses specifically available for HR practitioners. But, for all this, are these approaches missing something? There are those who think so, as Kevin Daniels, who has researched and written about work-related stress for over a decade describes (2011, p. 33):

> *The dominant approach to policy and practice in the areas of work stress and well-being has focused on jobs and job redesign, but has evolved to ignore how workers interpret their work and how they act to shape their work.*

Recent, and not so recent, research reveals a much more active role for individual employees in shaping how they think, feel and behave at work. It portrays a more complex and dynamic interaction between individuals, for example their personality, coping styles, expectations and motivations, and their work. Individuals make decisions about their choice of jobs and therefore about their exposure to potential stressors; once in the job,

they differently interpret its remit, and their coping abilities can influence how they respond to potentially stressful situations. These differences of interpretation can be the result of their personality, abilities and previous experience, and also of the group, organization or national culture they work in.

This brings into question approaches to work-related stress that assume relatively universal relationships between stable, 'bad' work characteristics and related emotional and physical distress, as seen in popular measurements of stress at work. More flexible and employee-centred methods might therefore be needed to generate meaningful insight into employees' experience at work.

Stop! What do you think of the idea of standardized measures of stress at work? What are the advantages of this approach, but what might its limitations be, in light of the discussion above? How might greater sensitivity to the more dynamic interaction between individual, job and organization be achieved?

Sources and further information: For more on Kevin Daniels' research, see Daniels (2006, 2011). For background information, see also Cox et al. (2000), Hagger (2009), Longua et al. (2009) and Rick and Briner (2000).

Note: This feature was written by Chiara Amati.

Workplace bullying

Described as the 'silent epidemic' (McAvoy and Murtagh, 2003), workplace bullying is becoming a troublesome and ubiquitous reality of institutional life (Soylu and Sheehy-Skeffington, 2015). Understanding the phenomenon and its complexity is especially important given the increased involvement of line managers in HRM. Research has highlighted the severe harm that bullying can cause to individuals, yielding damaging mental and physical symptoms in its victims, including post-traumatic stress disorder and depression; identity crises; damaged self-esteem; emotional damage, such as humiliation, doubt and stress; violation of the psychological contract; vicious cycles of counterproductive work behaviour; and violation (Field, 1996; Fox and Stallworth, 2005; Hoel et al., 2011; O'Moore et al., 1998; Parzefall and Salin, 2010). Targeted employees may experience a range of negative effects, including feelings of frustration and/or helplessness, loss of confidence, insomnia and stress-related symptoms. It is a significant issue for employee well-being and dignity *at* work (Bolton, 2007). Researchers have observed the negative effects of bullying on the organization, including higher costs associated with high turnover rates, absenteeism, reduced productivity and organizational performance, legal costs, damage to the company's reputation, and decreased loyalty and commitment to the company (Branch et al., 2009; Fox and Stallworth, 2005; Glambek et al., 2014; Hoel et al., 2011).

Recent research into workplace bullying supports the notion that it is an elusive, complex social phenomenon, which, according to some, has its origins outside the organization (Soylu and Sheehy-Skeffington, 2015). An important variation to the concept of workplace bullying, and possibly a societal – gender or/and religious – dimension, is that bullying is deployed 'strategically' to achieve goals beyond those of the perpetrators themselves. Thus, according to Soylu and Sheehy-Skeffington's (2015) study, bullying is used either as a calculated means of getting rid of unwanted employees, or as a subtle, but no less pernicious, means of achieving the dominance of one sociocultural worldview over another, and in turn a mechanism through which inequality is maintained and reproduced.

Although there has been increased research on workplace bullying, an agreed definition of the phenomenon remains elusive (Saunders et al., 2007). Workplace bullying is often defined as an extreme case of 'dysfunctional organizational behaviour' (Soylu and Sheehy-Skeffington, 2015) or multiple 'negative behaviours'. Definitions of bullying emphasize that the victim regularly faces repeated exposure to unwanted negative acts, be they personal or work-related, over a long period of time, that it is predominantly psychological in nature, and that there exists a power imbalance between the protagonists (Hoel and Einarsen, 1999). Workplace bullying (Einarsen et al., 2011, p. 4) is:

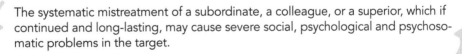

The systematic mistreatment of a subordinate, a colleague, or a superior, which if continued and long-lasting, may cause severe social, psychological and psychosomatic problems in the target.

Examples of such behaviours include persistent abusive verbal comments, threats, ridicule, unjustified criticism, the spreading of malicious rumours, knowingly assigning inappropriate tasks, planned social isolation, and denigration of personal habits or beliefs (Einarsen et al., 2011). Thus, although it is a form of aggression, some bullying behaviour can be observable, but other instances can be subtle and difficult to observe.

The definitions of workplace bullying incorporate several inappropriate and dysfunctional behaviours. First, workplace bullying is about a personalized attack on one employee by another employee, persistently over a period of time, using behaviours that are emotionally and psychologically punishing. Second, workplace bullying introduces a dynamic into the employment relationship that involves a purposed attempt by one employee to injure another employee's self-esteem, self-confidence and/or reputation, or to undermine their competence to carry out their work duties effectively (Oade, 2009). Third, definitions of workplace bullying emphasize the existence of an imbalance of power between the bully and the recipient (Keashly and Jagatic, 2011). Research has identified a link between economic conditions and bullying, with studies predicting that the threat of job loss is likely to cause an increase in workplace bullying, as is the decline of trade unions and of collective representation (Hirch, 2010). In summary, the most salient characteristics of bullying in the workplace are the use of persistent extreme dysfunctional behaviours coupled with the inability of the target to defend themself because of a power imbalance between the target and the perpetrator.

Although there is little OHS legislation that specifically deals with workplace bullying, bullying is often addressed in unionized workplaces through collective agreement clauses dealing with harassment. Many organizations choose to address the issue of workplace bullying because it has a detrimental effect on individual and, through increased absenteeism, increased turnover, decreased productivity and work motivation, also on organizational performance. The negative consequences of workplace bullying extend beyond the perpetrator–victim relationship, possibly into 'injustice and psychological contract breach perceptions' (Parzefall and Salin, 2010, p. 774), thereby supporting the notion of a connection between attitudinal change in victims and witnesses, and the effective management of the issue.

Fox and Cowan (2015) contend that because HR professionals have the prime responsibility for dealing with the victim and perpetrator of bullying, they should have a voice in assessing and dealing with cases of bullying. However, they also report that HR professionals experience difficulties in effectively responding to employees' complaints of bullying due to a number of factors, including conflicts among multiple HR roles in the organization, a paucity of specific organizational policies and guidelines for dealing with bullying, and ambiguous definitions and criteria for behaviour to be considered bullying. A policy on bullying should protect the rights and dignity of the targeted individual. The most important component of any workplace bullying prevention programme is commitment on the part of senior management. As noted, the causes of workplace bullying are complex and, as such, a 'one-size-fits-all' approach is unlikely to effectively address the multiple aspects of the phenomenon. Any effective policy needs to incorporate 'prevention, resolution, and support' (McCarthy et al., 2002, p. 528). The Canadian Centre for Occupational Health and Safety (2001) recommends that a preventive policy on workplace bullying must:

- Be developed by management and employee representatives
- Define workplace bullying in precise, concrete language
- Provide clear examples of inappropriate or unreasonable behaviour
- Precisely state the consequences of making threats or committing acts
- Outline the process by which preventive measures will be developed
- Encourage the reporting of all incidents of workplace bullying
- Make a commitment to provide support services to victims.

In conclusion, Aryanne Oade writes, 'Being subject to workplace bullying is among the most horrible workplace experiences you might have' (2009, p. 159). Although workplace bullying is underanalysed, research shows a detrimental effect on individual and organizational performance, which consequently necessitates a response from management and employee representatives, including an effective preventive policy and processes. HR practices designed at helping employee victims of bullying, violence or harassment might include counselling, discipline and assignment to other supervisors (Biron, 2010).

HRM web links

Visit the online resource centre at www.palgravehighered.com/bg-hrm-6e for further information on workplace bullying.

HRM web links

Visit the online resource centre www.palgravehighered.com/bg-hrm-6e for a bonus HRM in practice feature on workplace bullying.

Alcohol abuse

Recent UK research on 'binge-drinking' shows that this social phenomenon has significantly increased in Britain over the last two decades, particularly among women, and is estimated to cost the country £20 billion a year. There is no international agreed definition of binge-drinking, but the Institute of Alcohol Studies (IAS) defines it as the consumption of more than the recommended number of alcoholic drinks in a single drinking session. In 2010, one in four adults in Britain were reported to be binge-drinkers, and the UK was ranked number one in Europe for alcohol consumption. Data show a narrowing of an alcohol gender gap that has persisted for decades (IAS, 2013). The reported proportion of women binge-drinking increased from 8 per cent to 15 per cent between 1998 and 2006. Over the same period, binge-drinking among men increased only slightly, from 22 to 23 per cent.

According to the IAS, binge-drinking is now so routine that young adults find it difficult to explain why they do it. In a 'culture of intoxication', it is unsurprising that alcohol misuse in the UK accounts for more than 20,000 premature deaths per year. There were 8697 alcohol-related deaths in 2014, more than double the 4144 recorded in 1991. Of these, 5687 deaths were among males (65 per cent of the deaths) and 3010 among females (35 per cent of the deaths), with rates of 19.4 deaths per 100,000 males and 9.6 per 100,000 females (Office for National Statistics, 2014).

In the context of the workplace, the excessive consumption of alcohol is both a health problem and a job performance problem in every occupational category, be it manual, white collar or managerial. In alcohol abuse, behavioural problems range from tardiness in the early stages to prolonged absenteeism in later ones. The direct and indirect costs of alcohol abuse to employers include the costs of accidents, lower productivity, poor-quality work, bad decisions, absenteeism and managers' lost time in dealing with employees with an alcohol problem.

Employers have been advised to have a written statement of policy regarding alcohol abuse, which can be discussed and agreed with employees and, where applicable, union representatives. The policy should recognize that alcohol abuse is an illness, and it should be supportive rather than punitive or employees will hide their drink problem for as long as possible. The HSE advocates that a policy should encourage any employee who believes that she or he has a drink problem to seek help voluntarily, and should, subject to certain provisions, give the same protection of employment and pension rights as those granted to an employee with problems that are related to other forms of ill-health. Research in Scotland estimated that 20 per cent of employers had a policy to deal with problem drinkers. In addition to preparing a policy, management can devise a procedure for dealing with alcohol abuse; to encourage employees to seek advice, it is suggested that this procedure should be separate from the disciplinary procedure. Finally, the HRM department is advised to establish links with an external voluntary organization to obtain help and develop an employee assistance programme (EAP).

HRM web links   Visit the online resource centre at **www.palgravehighered.com/bg-hrm-6e** for fact sheets on alcohol consumption and binge-drinking.

Smoking

The tragic death of non-smoker Dana Reeve, the 44-year-old widow of Superman actor Christopher Reeve, in March 2006, highlighted the dangers of both active and passive smoking. In 2014, smoking accounted for approximately 100,000 deaths a year in the UK (Action on Smoking and Health, 2015). Smoking is unlawful in the workplace in the USA, Canada, the UK and some EU member states, and the only place where a smoker can jeopardize the health of a non-smoker is at home. In the past, managers in Britain agreed that successful non-smoking policies required consultation with employees and, in a unionized workplace, a joint approach by management and the trade union. While North American and UK legislation banning smoking in public spaces has significantly addressed the problem of passive smoking, smoking in the workplace is in many other countries a major problem because active smoking may be a fire hazard or hygiene risk. In addition, the estimated cost attributable to absenteeism and lost productivity associated with active smoking is said to be approximately US$825 per employee per year (Montgomery and Kelloway, 2002). Figure 12.2 shows employers' costs associated with workplace smoking (money that 'goes up in smoke') and why it is important for employers to introduce effective non-smoking policies.

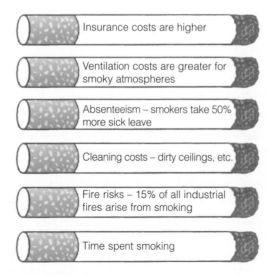

Insurance costs are higher

Ventilation costs are greater for smoky atmospheres

Absenteeism – smokers take 50% more sick leave

Cleaning costs – dirty ceilings, etc.

Fire risks – 15% of all industrial fires arise from smoking

Time spent smoking

Figure 12.2 *Smoking-related costs*

Juggling work and life and the work–life boundary

When a long-hours culture is combined with an increase in the proportion of women in the labour force and changes to the pattern of the working day, with many services now being offered on a 24-hour basis, we have a phenomenon that has for two decades been the subject of ongoing academic and policy debates – the so-called work–life balance or work–life boundary.

In 2004, an editorial in The Guardian newspaper commented:

> As you hunt for the Easter eggs or visit the garden centre this weekend, spare a thought for the nearly 3 million British workers for whom the Easter break represents a pay cut …. It is a reminder of the peculiarity of the British work culture: compared to the rest of Europe, Britain has fewer bank holidays, takes less holiday and its men work the longest hours (courtesy of Guardian News & Media Ltd).

In the UK, working long hours has traditionally been a way in which workers on a low basic wage could bump up their take-home pay. More recently, there has in addition been a widespread diffusion of *unpaid* overtime. Here, long hours are worked because of more subjective pressures such as not wishing to let the customer or team colleagues down, or wanting to meet management expectations about employee commitment. The result has been that, despite finally signing up to the EU Working Time Directive in 1997, a high proportion of employees in the UK continue to work more than the Directive's maximum of 48 hours a week.

The first policy response to these tensions between work and domestic responsibilities was the promotion of so-called 'family-friendly' employment policies in which employers were encouraged to consider flexible patterns of working to fit in with employees' domestic responsibilities. Since 2003, employees have had the right to request flexible working but, even where this has been practised, it has been only a limited response to perceived imbalance: it focuses only on working parents, it has often been defined in ways that suit the employer's workflow rather than the employees' non-work responsibilities, and it looks only at patterns of working time.

In their examination of call centres and software production, Jeff Hyman and his colleagues (Hyman et al., 2003) made a useful distinction between tangible and intangible work-related incursions into domestic life. The tangible, or quantitative, factors include expectations to work overtime, perhaps at short notice and often unpaid, unpredictable shift patterns, and an explicit or implicit expectation to take work home to get the job done. The intangible or qualitative aspect includes exhaustion, feelings of stress and disturbed sleep patterns, and tendencies to worry about work after hours.

Hyman et al. found that, for both groups of 'new' workers, organizational pressures resulted in work intruding into non-work areas of employees' lives but, because of the different nature of the labour processes, this was manifested in different ways. For call-centre work, directly reliant on a particular technological system, only managers were likely to take work home with them. For the others, spillover was experienced through juggling complex patterns of working hours with domestic responsibilities and

(continued)

Stop! Has any job you have had ever made your non-work life difficult to manage (for example, part-time work alongside your studies as a student)? Can there even be a satisfactory balance between work and non-work life? What would be the conditions for this to occur?

Sources and further information: For the information quoted in this feature, see The Guardian (2004) and Hyman et al. (2003). To find out more on work–life balance, see Hogarth et al. (2000), Houston (2005) and Zheng et al. (2016).

Note: This feature was written by Chris Baldry.

aspects of occupationally induced ill-health such as fatigue and stress. For the more autonomous software workers, much of the work was conceptual and less bounded by the actual workplace. Many software workers took work home and thought about work-related problems after hours. Although simple adjustments to starting and finishing times would not in themselves provide an adequate framework for work–life balance, there were fewer intangible extensions of work demands on home life where employees perceived the organization to have a supportive family-friendly culture.

HRM web links

Visit the online resource centre at **www.palgravehighered.com/bg-hrm-6e** for fact sheets on smoking statistics.

Acquired immune deficiency syndrome

Three decades ago, AIDS became a workplace health and safety issue. It is the most serious disease caused by HIV (the human immunodeficiency virus, or the 'AIDS virus'). HIV impairs the body's defence or immune system and leaves it vulnerable to life-threatening illnesses. One manager with experience of managing the HIV/AIDS problem captured the complexity surrounding the issue: 'I was not trained to manage fear, discrimination, and dying in the workplace' (Smith, 1993, p.48). A modern textbook on HRM in the twenty-first century would be incomplete if it contained no reference to HIV/AIDS. In 2016, the WHO has reported that 42 million people are infected with HIV/AIDS, 75 per cent of whom are in sub-Saharan Africa.

Human rights legislation impacts on HR policies and practices. In Canada, for example, mandatory testing for HIV/AIDS is regarded as a serious intrusion on individual rights, and employers are prohibited from subjecting job applicants to any type of medical testing for the presence of the HIV/AIDS virus. Furthermore, the employer is obligated to accommodate the needs of an employee with a disability such as HIV/AIDS by, for example, redefining work assignments. The fear of catching HIV can, however, create problems for managers because employees might refuse to work with a person with HIV/AIDS (Gopalan and Summers, 1994).

A workplace policy for HIV/AIDS should protect the human rights and dignity of those infected with HIV and

Smoking can be both a health problem and a job performance problem.

BRANDX

those who have AIDS, and should not allow discriminatory action in the provision of services and employment. HIV/AIDS policies and procedures need to be developed through a team approach that includes workers and, if present, trade unions. As with any HRM policy, any policy or programme for HIV/AIDS requires a clear endorsement from top management down if it is going to be successful. The Global Business Coalition (2011) recommends that HIV/AIDS workplace policy should:

• Make an explicit promise to undertake corporate action
• Commit to confidentiality and non-discrimination for all employees
• Ensure consistency with the appropriate national laws
• Encourage all employees (regardless of their HIV status) to support an inclusive and non-stigmatizing workplace
• Provide guidance to supervisors and managers
• Explain to employees living with HIV/AIDS the type of support and care they will receive, so that they are more likely to come forward for counselling and testing
• Help stop the spread of the virus through prevention programmes
• Make the policy available to all employees, in a format that is easily understood
• Manage the impact of HIV/AIDS with the ultimate aim of cutting business costs.

HRM web links

Visit the online resource centre at **www.palgravehighered.com/bg-hrm-6e** for further information on HIV/AIDS in the workplace in the UK, Canada, South Africa and Australia.

It was reported that few North American companies surveyed had a workplace policy for HIV/AIDS and, unsurprisingly, smaller organizations were less likely to have such a policy (Green, 1998). More worrying perhaps is the finding that there is, among employers, a 'declining interest' in HIV/AIDS education in the workplace. In 1997, 18 per cent of US companies surveyed provided HIV/AIDS education for their employees, compared with 28 per cent in 1992 (Green, 1998). Companies that have encountered the problem of managing HIV/AIDS in the workplace have found that it is better to expect a problem and be proactive in educating employees on the issues raised by HIV/AIDS. The chairman of Levi Strauss, Robert Hass, confirms the need for senior management support: '[HIV/AIDS] is frequently viewed as something that the personnel department should take care of, but there has to be support from the top. You can't do it with one flyer' (Smith, 1993, p. 48). As attitudes and legal considerations change, HIV/AIDS has important implications for HRM policy, programmes and practices.

Workplace wellness

News reports in 2015 that NHS staff in England were to be offered a programme of fitness activities and healthy options for meals highlights the growing recognition of the value of workplace wellness programmes (Merrifield, 2015). Workplace wellness models typically focus on individual behaviour and offer programmes and activities promoting individual behavioural change. Smoking, binge-drinking patterns, poor diet and lack of physical exercise have all been identified as lifestyle problems impacting on the health of the workforce. Here, consistent with the literature, workplace wellness will refer to any voluntary health-improving programme and activity instigated by the employer to effect changes in non-occupational health behaviours. Smoking cessation, personal fitness programmes and EAPs are early examples of workplace health-improvement initiatives. A wide variety of initiatives that fall under the wellness promotion strategy have been instigated in establishments with 500 or more employees, including part or all the following:

- A smoke-free workplace
- Employer-sponsored sports
- Discounted gym facilities
- Health examinations offered to employees
- 'Health fairs' hosted on the premises
- Wellness newsletters
- Smoking cessation incentives
- Weight loss incentives
- Blood pressure and cholesterol testing
- Energy-based therapy seminars
- EAPs.

An EAP provides confidential professional assistance to employees and their families to help resolve problems affecting their personal lives and, in some cases, their job performance. Typically, an EAP provides services in such areas as alcohol and drug abuse, legal, financial, marriage and crisis counselling. These various workplace wellness initiatives tend to operate independently and focus on individual employee goals; few organizations integrate wellness programmes and initiatives into an overall HR strategy with concrete measures and expected targets (Dyck, 2002). See Chapter 3 for evaluating HR programmes.

reflective question

> Haunschild (2003) posits that characterizing wellness management as merely a 'healthy' philanthropic act is naive and neglects intended control strategies. Can you think how wellness programmes can act against the interests of the employee?

HRM web links

> Visit the online resource centre at www.palgravehighered.com/bg-hrm-6e for more information on workplace wellness programmes and policies.

Paradox in workplace health and safety

The notion of paradox and ethics that we have discussed in other areas of HRM is also apparent in OHS and wellness. Citing global competition and the need for level playing fields, most employers since the Industrial Revolution have opposed environmental and OHS regulation. The complaints of the corporate elite about agreements on climate change emission targets, such as the Kyoto (1997) and Paris (2015) Accords are a notable recent example of employer resistance. Arguably, HRM (at least the rhetoric) has raised the ethical stakes over OHS. Yet, despite this claim, the driving force for the majority of employers to provide a safe and healthy working environment has all too often been framed through a 'business case' lens, for example in terms of the reduction in sick leave and time lost from accidents. This is especially true for mental well-being, as evidenced by the *Walker* v. *Northumberland* [1994] case (Doherty and Tyson, 2000, p. 103).

Paradox stems from the multiple consequences of a single management action that seem to conflict with those of another. The work-related symptoms of stress presented in Figure 12.1 can be illuminated using a concrete health and wellness case. Portable computers, mobile phones, email and social media have enabled us all to be connected to the organization 24 hours a day, 7 days a week. These high-tech instruments have, however, produced adverse results, for example, inability to relax, causing some observers to describe them as 'electronic versions of a ball and chain, keeping us in work mode around the clock' (Drohan, 2000, p. B15). The intended consequence of these high-tech instruments is improved productivity, but the unanticipated consequence of high-tech communications has yielded a major problem of stress and burnout caused by the inability of individuals to maintain a boundary between work and home. This unintended consequence of the high-tech revolution can counteract the positive consequences.

OHS and wellness form an important part of the HRM context, but it is not simply a technical issue of, for example, supplying hard hats and goggles. Above all, OHS underscores the fact that employment relations involve an economic and power relationship. In terms of economics, 'pure market' ideology panders to the shareholder, and 'profitability over safety' is favoured (Glasbeek, 1991, p. 196). With regard to power, it is argued (Sass, 1982, p. 52; quoted in Giles and Iain, 1989) that:

> In all technical questions pertaining to workplace health and safety there is the social element. That is … the power relations in production: who tells whom to do what and how fast.

Wellness management also contains a social element. It is arguably about organizations attempting to appropriate the employee's whole body as a matter of surveillance and control (Haunschild, 2003), and wellness management represents a process of discipline since activities such as medical screening and lifestyle counselling are connected to selection and promotion (Townley, 1994). It is interesting to note that interest in wellness management increased rapidly in the USA at a time when the regulatory power of the official health and safety agency, the Occupational Safety and Health Administration, had allegedly been curtailed under the Clinton and Bush junior administrations (Cullen, 2002).

The economic cost of OHS and wellness is a double-edged sword for the organization. On the one hand, OHS measures that protect employee well-being from physical or chemical hazards can conflict with management's objective of containing production costs. On the other, as we have explained, effective health and wellness interventions can improve the performance of both employees and the organization by reducing the cost associated with accidents, disabilities, absenteeism and illness.

To manage the employment relationship effectively, it also needs to be recognized that the employer's perspective on OHS and wellness issues can affect an individual's beliefs, levels of trust and psychological contract (Guest, 2008). Talk of a reciprocal commitment and a psychological contract has a hollow ring for many manual workers: more pressing may be malodorous processes and dangerous work systems. Critical, too, is the ability of global companies to relocate to other parts of the world to avoid stringent health and safety laws and regulations. Global trading agreements, such as the North American Free Trade Agreement and the Transatlantic Trade and Investment Partnership, put growth and protectionist polemics ahead of concern for the environment and community health (Klein, 2015, p. 84). Following the catastrophic events in Japan in 2011, when damage to the Fukushima nuclear power plant after an earthquake and tsunami led to a radiation leak, there is growing public awareness about the links between work systems, OHS and environmental protection. An appreciation of OHS provides a better understanding of managing the employment relationship. Indeed, the discussion on paradox goes back to basics in reminding us of some of the complexities and tensions inherent in the employment relationship. The key point is that OHS and wellness policies and practices must, as with other aspects of the HR strategy, be properly integrated in the sense that they are both complementary to and compatible with corporate strategy.

case study

The City of Kamloops

The setting

In Canada, cities typically provide a range of municipal services, including the police, fire protection, road management, public transit, utility services, land use planning and development, taxation and local economic development (Governance Network, 2002). Local governments provide more jobs than any other level of government in Canada, employing over 350,000 people in 2016. In that year, local governments in British Columbia employed approximately 10 per cent of that total.

There are a number of the challenges facing local governments. These have included remaining competitive in terms of attracting people and investment in a global economy, considering citizens' demands for approaches to economic development that were environmentally sustainable, and responding to increasingly sophisticated tax-payer expectations relating to accountability and performance. In addition, the transfer of service responsibility from other levels of government and fiscal realities puts immense pressure on local governments to review their corporate management. The consideration of innovative and alternative service delivery has also created a requirement for organizational change and staff development to meet the needs of local governments in this new environment.

Kamloops is one of the largest cities in the central interior of British Columbia, Canada, with a city population base of 85,000. The local government, or what is known as the City of Kamloops, has over 500 full-time equivalent employees. Approximately 60 per cent of the staff are represented by the Canadian Union of Public Employees, the rest being divided between firefighters represented by the International Association of Fire Fighters, and management, who are non-unionized. In the previous 2 years, the organization had experienced a major change in its senior management staffing, with a new City Mayor, new Chief Administrative Officer and new Human Resources Director taking over the helm from long-standing incumbents. With its new leadership, the City of Kamloops embarked on a quality improvement initiative labelled Quest for Quality, with the goal of becoming an employer of choice in Canada and improving its capability to face both external and internal challenges. One of the main objectives of Quest for Quality was to provide employees with the most

enjoyable and fulfilling working environment possible and help them to balance this with their home and personal lives.

Shortly after these changes, a disability management programme was also introduced. The programme provided managers with consistent attendance data through bi-weekly payroll reports, showing details on when staff were absent and the status of their leave banks. In addition, training on attendance management and a coaching process were offered to managers to help them deal with staff who had consistently high absenteeism rates. Canadian Union of Public Employees outside workers, such as labourers and equipment operators, historically had higher rates of absenteeism compared with the other employee groups at the City of Kamloops, and emphasis was made, particularly by the Occupational Health and Safety Division, on decreasing the number of days on which these employees missed work.

As a proactive measure within the disability management programme and in line with the Quest for Quality undertaking, the City also implemented a wellness initiative. The HR department approached wellness as one piece of a healthy workplace approach,

(continued)

which also included developing a safer physical environment and a positive organizational culture. The wellness initiative itself focused on increasing and recognizing staff involvement in both mental and physical health activities, and supporting healthy lifestyles, behaviours and coping skills for employees. As a result, the organization provided two company gyms at the worksite, as well as educational workshops on such topics as nicotine cessation, diabetes and osteoporosis. An EAP providing short-term counselling and health testing for blood sugar level, cholesterol level and bone density were also offered to staff on a regular basis. A walking programme, which supplied staff with pedometers and incentives for individual participation, was used to encourage employees' involvement in physical activity.

The problem

At the monthly meeting of the HR department, the wellness initiative was item 3 on the agenda. When the issue was reached, the HR Coordinator, Lori Brown, explained how it was expected that, over time, the wellness initiative would contribute to general staff morale. George Brotherton, who had been sceptical about the wellness efforts, said, 'I'm not sure whether the City can continue with this initiative; there are more pressing matters that we must address.' Lori responded that the employees had continually expressed a high level of satisfaction with the wellness events and offerings, and senior management was pleased with the positive feedback they had received about the initiative. The HR Director, who was chairing the meeting, asked Lori whether she could prepare a report for the next meeting to justify the portion of the HR department's budget that was being spent on the wellness initiative.

The assignment

Working either alone or in a small group, prepare a report drawing on the material from this case study and addressing the following:

1 What challenges does the HR department face in identifying the contribution that the wellness initiative has provided towards the City's goals?
2 What benefits could the organization see as a result of this wellness initiative?
3 What recommendations would you make with regard to a process for evaluation?

Essential reading

Governance Network (2002) *At the Crossroads of Change: Human Resources and the Municipal Sector*. Ottawa: Federation of Canadian Municipalities.

Health Canada (1998) *Influencing Employee Health. Workplace Health System*. Ottawa: Canadian Fitness and Lifestyle Research Institute.

Go to the City of Kamloops website at www.kamloops.ca.

Visit the Canadian Healthy Workplace Week website at www.healthyworkplacemonth.ca.

To find out about how to implement a healthy workplace, go to wellnessproposals.com/wellness-articles/workplace-wellness-programs-2/.

Note: This case study was written by Lori Rilkoff.

 Visit the online resource centre at **www.palgravehighered.com/bg-hrm-6e** for guidelines on writing reports.

---

summary

➤ Employee OHS and wellness should be an important aspect of managing the employment relationship. This chapter has established the importance of workplace health and wellness from an economic, legal, psychological and moral perspective.

➤ In this chapter, we have examined some contemporary health issues, such as SBS, workplace stress, alcoholism, smoking, workplace violence, bullying and HIV/AIDS, as well as key elements of a workplace wellness programme.

➤ Critical analysis of OHS and wellness management draws attention to the fact that employment relations involve an economic and power relationship. Shareholder interests and return on investment may come before workers' health and safety. Wellness management is arguably a distraction because it manages the consequences rather than causes of ill-health.

➤ In this chapter, we have examined how the economic cost of workplace health and wellness is a double-edged sword for the organization. On the one hand, it protects employees' well-being from physical or chemical hazards, but it can also be at odds with management's objective of containing costs. Effective health and wellness interventions can, however, improve the performance of employees and the organization by reducing the cost associated with accidents, disabilities, absenteeism and illness.

review questions

1 'Spending money on a health and wellness programmes is a luxury most small organizations cannot afford.' Build an argument to support this statement, and an argument to negate it.

2 Explain the role of an HRM specialist in providing a safe and healthy environment for employees.

3 Explain the symptoms and causes of job stress and what an organization can do to alleviate them.

4 Explain how an HR professional can justify a workplace wellness programme.

5 What is workplace bullying and why is it important for managers to understand its antecedents and its effects on targets?

6 What role can line managers play in the development of a sustainable and healthy workplace?

further reading

Reading these articles and chapters can help you gain a better understanding and potentially a higher grade for your HRM assignment.

➤ Bain, P. (1997) Human resource malpractice: the deregulation of health and safety at work in the USA and Britain. *Industrial Relations Journal*, **28**(3): 176–91.

➤ Chamberlain, L. J., Crowley, M., Tope, D. and Hodson, R. (2008) Sexual harassment in organizational context. *Work and Occupations*, **35**(3): 262–95.

➤ Fox, S. and Cowan, R. L. (2015) Revision of the workplace bullying checklist: the importance of human resource management's role in defining and addressing workplace bullying. *Human Resource Management Journal,* **25**(1): 116–30.

➤ Hoel, H. and Einarsen, S. (1999) *Workplace Bullying*. London: John Wiley.

➤ Loudoun, R. and Johnstone, R. (2009) Occupational health and safety in the modern world of work. In A. Wilkinson, N. Bacon, T. Redman and S. Snell (eds) *The Sage Handbook of Human Resource Management* (pp. 286–307). London: Sage.

➤ Mayer, B. (2009) *Blue-Green Coalitions: Fighting for Safe Workplaces and Healthy Communities*. Ithaca, NY: Cornell University Press.

➤ Oade, A. (2009) *Managing Workplace Bullying*. Basingstoke: Palgrave Macmillan.

➤ Parzefall, M.-R. and Salin, D. (2010) Perceptions of and reactions to workplace bullying: a social exchange perspective. *Human Relations*, **63**(6): 761–80.

➤ Soylu, S. and Sheehy-Skeffington, J. (2015) Asymmetric intergroup bullying: the enactment and maintenance of societal inequality at work. *Human Relations*, 1–31.

➤ Storey, R. (2004) From the environment to the workplace … and back again? Occupational health and safety activism in Ontario, 1970s–2000+. *Canadian Review of Sociology and Anthropology*, **41**(4): 419–47.

➤ Walters, D. (2004) Worker representation and health and safety in small enterprises in Europe. *Industrial Relations Journal*, **35**(2): 169–86.

➤ Zeytinoglu, I. U., Denton, M., Plenderleith, J. and Chowhan, J. (2015) Associations between workers' health, and non-standard hours and insecurity: the case of home care workers in Ontario, Canada. *International Journal of Human Resource Management*, **26**(19): 2503–22.

➤ Zheng, C., Kashi, K., Fan, D., Molineux, J. and Shan E. M. (2016) Impact of individual coping strategies and organisational work–life balance programmes on Australian employee well-being. *International Journal of Human Resource Management*, **27**(5): 501–26.

Click here in your interactive ebook for a list of HRM terminology and vocabulary that has appeared in this chapter.

vocabulary checklist for ESL students

Visit the online resource centre at **www.palgravehighered.com/bg-hrm-6e** for lots of extra resources to help you get to grips with this chapter, including study tips, HRM skills development guides, summary lecture notes, tips for English as a Second Language (ESL) students and more.

part V

CONTEMPORARY ISSUES: HRM IN A GLOBAL WORLD

chapter **13**

HRM and high-performance workplaces

© Royalty-Free/Corbis

outline

➤ Introduction

➤ The nature of work and job design

➤ HRM and globalization 13.1: Commuting time in the EU is work time

➤ HRM in practice 13.1: The impact of technologies on the practice of HRM

➤ The development of work systems

➤ HRM and globalization 13.2: Bureaucracy, work and HRM

➤ High-performance workplaces

➤ HRM as I see it: Gregor Karolus, Springer Nature, Part 2

➤ Tension and paradox

➤ HRM in practice 13.2: High-performance working in action: public and voluntary sectors

➤ Case study: Currency, Inc.

➤ Summary, review questions, further reading and vocabulary checklist for ESL students

objectives

After studying this chapter, you should be able to:

1 Explain the nature of work and the core dimensions of job design

2 Understand how management decisions concerning job and work design affect employee commitment, well-being and performance, employment relations and organizational and societal outcomes

3 Define job design and describe specific work organization strategies

4 Understand the theoretical arguments underpinning high-performance work systems

5 Explain the main principles of high-performance work systems

6 Understand the relationship between different job and work designs and human resources strategies

417

Workplaces that are perceived to have a change-quality, technology-driven culture and are characterized by support for creativity, open communications, effective knowledge management and the core values of respect and integrity have strong effects on talent attraction and retention and are also highly conducive to the development of high-commitment and motivating work systems (Kontoghiorghes, 2015). These characteristics are often associated with a trend in workplace design called high-performance work systems. The focus on contemporary work designs in debt-choked post-2008 economies can, however, easily distract us from more persistent trends and features of the workplace: work intensification, heightened managerial control and consequential work-related stress. The way work is organized in the workplace is, therefore, inseparable from the study of the management of the people doing the work.

introduction

The way work is organized is a critical internal contingency affecting both micro and strategic human resource management (HRM). Management is the architect of job and work design, and different strategies have created a myriad of contrasting types of jobs and work systems. For example, there are jobs that provide employees with no variation in the tasks performed, their work activities being closely supervised. In contrast, other jobs may require employees to perform a wider range of tasks within a self-managing team. There is a well-established body of research traversing organizational behaviour, labour relations and HRM that explores how different work design systems have important consequences for employee outcomes such as job satisfaction, skills and work-related stress, for organizational outcomes such as performance, as well as for societal outcomes such as social stability and sustainability. There is also another body of academic work, known as labour process theory that focuses on the dynamics of managerial control, employee consent and resistance at the point of service or production, and emphasizes the continuity and limited effects of new work systems.

In this chapter, we define work and explain how different work design strategies have different effects on employee commitment and performance. We then examine the implications of different work design configurations for managing the employment relationship. We conclude by examining evidence of tension and paradox in work redesign that questions the widespread claims that various forms of high-performance work systems (HPWSs), for example, can truly reconcile the 'needs' of both the employees and the organization.

reflective question What is your own experience of work? Have you or your friends had jobs in which you were expected to 'check your brains at the door'? Have you experienced work in a team? How do you feel about working at home? What are the implications of new ways of working (1) for young people, women and ethnic minorities, and (2) for HRM?

The nature of work and job design

Filling in the forms to apply for a student loan is not seen as work, but filling in forms may be part of a clerical worker's job. Similarly, when a mature student looks after her or his own child, this is not seen as work, but if she or he employs a child-minder, it is, for the minder, paid work. We can see from these examples that work cannot be defined simply by the content of the activity. So when we refer to the term 'work', what do we mean? Work is not just an activity, something one *does*, but something a person *has* (Gorz, 1982). We can begin to understand the complexity of work and its social ramifications by exploring the following definition:

> Work refers to physical and mental activity that is carried out to produce or achieve something of value at a particular place and time; it involves a degree of obligation and explicit or implicit instructions, in return for a wage or salary. (Bratton, 2015, p. 41)

This definition draws attention to some central features of work. First, the most obvious observation is that work involves 'physical and mental' activity for the purpose of adding 'value', which suggests that the activities of both a construction worker and a computer systems analyst can be considered to be work. 'Mental activity' also includes the commercialization of human feeling, or what is called 'emotional work' (Bolton, 2005; Brook, 2009; Hochschild, 1983). The fact that the service sector provides the most employment in Britain (Nixon, 2009) emphasizes how important it is to analyse the full array of emotional work that takes place in the workplace, as well as the processes by which emotional labour is extracted and exploited (Bolton, 2009).

Second, work is structured spatially – geographically – and, by time and people's spatial embedding, shapes work and management practices (Herod et al., 2007). Throughout most of the twentieth century, work was typically carried out away from home and at set periods of the day or night. Thus, 'place and time' locates work within a social context. With the iPhone symbolizing the 'work anywhere' culture of our times (Donkin, 2010), the mass timetable of the '8 to 5' factory world, and the '9 to 5' office world, has given way to a complex flexi-place, flexi-time world.

HRM web links

> Visit the online resource centre at **www.palgravehighered.com/bg-hrm-6e** to read a bonus HRM in practice feature on home working.

Third, work always involves social relations between people: between employer and employee, between first-line manager and other employees, between co-workers and, in some workplaces, between manager and trade union representatives. Social relations in the workplace can be cooperative or conflictual, hierarchical or egalitarian. Thus, to be 'in work' is to have a definite relationship with some other who has control of the time, place and activity.

The fourth element of work is a payment. Pay is typically of two types: *extrinsic* and *intrinsic*. The employee provides physical effort and/or mental application, and accepts fatigue and the loss of control over her or his time. In return, the extrinsic work rewards that he or she usually receives consist of (primarily) a wage or salary and possibly bonuses. The intrinsic rewards the worker might get from the job include status and peer recognition.

We should note that not all work, either physical or mental, is remunerated. Some of it is household-based work – cooking, child-rearing, cleaning and so on – and some of it is done voluntarily, for the good of society, for instance working for a Food Bank. These

Commuting time in the EU is work time

Working from one's home or one's car is an increasingly common arrangement in developed countries. Employer choices around the design of work often bring to the surface conflicting interests and raise questions about the application of employment law – much of which is still premised on notions of traditional jobs and workplaces – to these new arrangements.

The Court of Justice of the European Union recently ruled that the time spent commuting by workers without a fixed place of work – such as repair workers and salespeople – should be counted as working time. This includes time workers spend travelling from home to their first appointment of the day and the time spent travelling from their last appointment to their homes (Court of Justice of the European Union, 2015).

This ruling arose from a Spanish case. Tyco, a company that installs anti-theft devices, closed down its provincial offices in 2011 owing to a restructuring, and reassigned all roving staff to its main office in Madrid. In reality, these workers were now based out of their vehicles and often faced up to 3-hour commutes each way to various worksites from their homes. In this new arrangement, Tyco did not count commuting time at the beginning and end of the working day as working time, although previously it had included time spent travelling between a provincial office (where the vehicles were located) and a worksite as working time. This change in Tyco's work system significantly reduced its cost of wages by externalizing the costs of the workers' travel time onto the workers themselves. More concerning for the Court of Justice was the impact that the change had on the health and safety of the workers, as protected by the Working Time Directive of the European Union (EU):

> Requiring [the workers] to bear the burden of their employer's choice would be contrary to the objective of protecting the safety and health of workers pursued by the directive, which includes the necessity of guaranteeing workers a minimum rest period. (Court of Justice of the European Union, 2015, p. 2)

The Working Time Directive contains a number of restrictions that affect employers' decisions about job design. In this case, the employer's decision to move workers to home offices and not compensate travel time put the employer in violation of the Working Time Directive's requirement that workers work no more than 48 hours (on average) in a working week. Other provisions in the directive fix daily and weekly rest periods, daily breaks and annual vacations, all of which constrain employers' discretion in relation to the organization of work (European Commission, 2003).

(continued)

Stop! Why do you think Tyco restructured its operation? If you were a Tyco worker who found yourself based from home, what concerns would you have about this decision? If you were an HR professional employed by Tyco, what advice would you give the employer about this decision?

Sources and further information: For background information, see Centers for Disease Control (2004), Court of Justice of the European Union (2015) and European Commission (2003).

Note: This feature was written by Bob Barnetson.

The evidence that long daily and weekly working hours are harmful to workers is fairly compelling. Workers' performance on psycho-physiological tests declines when workers work long hours, particularly when 12-hour shifts are combined with working weeks of more than 40 hours. From a safety perspective, long working hours entail a reduction in cognitive functioning and vigilance as well as an increased number of injuries. Workers are also less productive as working time increases, working both more slowly and with higher error rates.

This case is an example of how the interests of employers and workers are not always in alignment around the design of work. Although both Tyco and its employees benefit from a profitable company, this reorganization did not necessarily distribute the cost of production evenly between Tyco's managers and workers. The (rather predictable) result of the redesign of work was conflict and reputational harm for Tyco. A thorny question for human resources (HR) practitioners is whether these costs outweigh the benefits for the reorganization.

activities are unpaid yet are identical to those in some paid jobs, such as working in a nursery or a warehouse. This book concentrates on paid work, and as a consequence we largely omit the critically important area of unpaid work, although that is not to suggest that we see it as unimportant.

reflective question How is the growth of the 'service economy' transforming the nature of work and the skills required?

Job design is at the core of any *work system*, but what are the core dimensions of job design for individual employees, and how does job design influence employee and line management behaviour? A job comprises one or more tasks that an employee performs in the workplace, and job design and redesign has been one of the most regularly researched topics in the field of work motivation and organizational behaviour (Fried et al., 1998). The design of jobs for individual employees or work teams has emphasized improved performance outcomes for the organization and a reversal of the negative effects of the division of labour (Linstead et al., 2009). The critical literature on job design has questioned the view that job redesign is primarily motivated by a management ideology of improving the quality of work (Thompson and McHugh, 2009). Job design focuses directly on work-related tasks or activities that employees undertake to design, produce and deliver a good or service for the organization. In the literature, *job design* refers to the actual 'content and method of jobs' that employees perform in their jobs (Wall and Clegg, 1998, p. 337). Job design itself is at the core of a *work system*, defined here as a particular configuration of job tasks and the overarching relationships between these job tasks and the operational exigencies, leadership style and management policies and practices found in the organization (Beer et al., 1984; Cordery and Parker, 2008).

A multitude of different approaches can be taken in designing jobs. At its most basic level, job design decisions produce low or high levels of horizontal and vertical job-related tasks or activities. The core dimensions of job design are shown in Figure 13.1.

The horizontal axis in Figure 13.1 represents the functional or technical tasks that are required to produce a product or service. Job design choices can entail only one simple task or a series of tasks combined in one job, depicted as a movement along the horizontal

The impact of technologies on the practice of HRM

Different forms of technology and technological change have been at the heart of many of the issues concerning the management of people and the work of HR professionals for a good number of years. In more recent times, however, these issues have emanated from the role of newer technologies in transforming societies, economic progress and how we work.

These more macro and intellectual concerns have been accompanied by the actual influence of technologies on the *practice* of HRM. For example, Sparrow et al. (2004) singled out technology as a transforming force, especially in the e-enablement of HRM and its impact on the creation and transfer of knowledge. With the new knowledge-based technologies advancing at a rapid pace, people management becomes an important mechanism for enabling organizations to translate investments more rapidly into better performance. This HRM–performance perspective has a focus on high-performance work practices, leading to 'smarter working' and 'best practice' (Boxall and Macky, 2009).

However, this focus assumes a universalist bundle of practices that somehow result in mutual gains for both employer and employee. Analysts from a critical HRM perspective have called for practitioners and researchers to reflect more carefully upon the shrinking 'human face' of HR from its customer base, and the implications for HR professionals themselves in terms of career opportunities and the development of new capabilities. Practitioners and researchers are also being encouraged to focus on identifying the *processes or pathways* that lead to sustainable individual, team and organizational performance. The emergence of social media technologies provides an opportunity to do this; these represent a move away from technology mostly operating on prescriptive, organization-centred systems to collaborative, web-based applications.

There are, of course, concerns on the part of organizations for their reputation in relation to employee 'misbehaviour' on blogs and social networking sites, and critical HRM analysts draw attention to the 'tyrannical dimension' of new technology, such as its role in enabling people to work

longer hours and intensify their work. There is, however, growing evidence that these media have enormous potential to change the way in which people collaborate, communicate, organize their work and give voice to their opinions and expectations, especially when they are physically dispersed across time and space (Martin et al., 2009). Used in this way, they can help to unlock the nature of people management tensions associated with the need to maintain control *and* seek commitment from workers, and there is also a need for more skilled and pragmatic approaches to managing these at the workplace.

Examples of this approach can be found that help us to understand the tensions associated with the economic and social exchange processes underpinning the employer and the corporate brand (Francis and Reddington, 2012) – an area of increasing interest to HR professionals.

Stop! There are many opportunities for academics and practitioners to collaborate in finding out how different organizations innovate and effectively exploit new HR technology. What is your view on how this might be done?

Sources and further information: For further information, see Boxall and Macky (2009), Francis and Reddington (2012), Martin et al. (2009) and Sparrow et al. (2004).

Note: This feature was written by Martin Reddington.

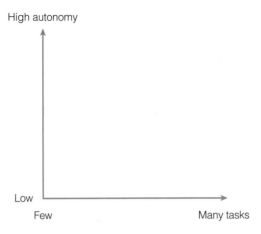

Figure 13.1 *The core dimensions of job design for individual employees*

axis. Horizontal job enlargement has the effect of increasing cycle times and creating more complete and, hopefully, more meaningful jobs. The technical dimension, then, is concerned with the range of tasks undertaken by employees and raises issues of multi-skilling and functional flexibility. The vertical axis, on the other hand, represents the decision-making aspects of work activities, and shows the extent of employees' autonomy in the job. The extent to which the job allows employees to exercise choice and discretion in their work runs from low to high.

The two core dimensions enable us to contrast two jobs, shown as A and B in Figure 13.2. The characteristics of job design A limit the content or scope of the job, giving minimal, if any, discretion over how work-related tasks are performed. The focus is on a rapid completion of tasks and close supervision.

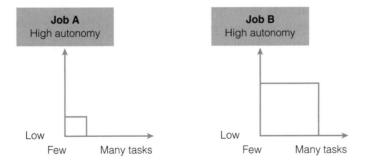

Figure 13.2 *Alternative job designs for an employee*

In contrast, job B is designed with more tasks and offers the employee more autonomy over how those tasks are performed. The focus is on improving job satisfaction by allowing the worker to complete several tasks with some self-supervision. During the last millennium, these core job design concepts have been central to the work redesign process in North America and Western Europe. Next, we trace the innovations in job and work systems since the beginning of modernity.

The development of work systems

The HPWS is neither new nor radical. The assumptions underpinning the high-performance work model originate in the limits of classical bureaucratic work designs and in the post-bureaucratic systems (see HRM and globalization 13.2) that heralded the self-management movement in the 1980s. This section gives an overview of these developments to give context and a deeper understanding of the contemporary notion of high-performance work.

Classical work systems

We begin by studying what others call 'classical' approaches to designing work systems. These are considered classical partly because they are the earliest contributions to management theory, but partly because they identify ideas and issues that keep occurring in contemporary literature, albeit using a different vocabulary (Grey, 2005).

Innovations in how work is designed interested Adam Smith (1723–90). In Smith's book *The Wealth of Nations*, he observed that the division of labour leads to productivity (output per worker) increases because of enhanced dexterity, and specialization stimulates the invention of new machinery. Smith's early example of job design was taken from the production of nails. He wrote (1776/1982, p. 109):

> Man draws out the wire; another straightens it; a third cuts it; a fourth points it; a fifth grinds it at the top for receiving the head … the important business of making a pin is, in this manner, divided into eighteen distinct operations.

In the nineteenth century, Charles Babbage pointed out that the division of labour gave the employer a further advantage: by simplifying tasks and allocating fragmented tasks to unskilled workers, the employer could pay a lower wage, and thus 'dividing the craft cheapens its individual parts' (Braverman, 1974, p. 80).

Marx gave a more critical interpretation of the division of labour. While not disagreeing with Smith that it increased labour productivity, he argued that division of labour also stultified human creativity and that, as such, it 'alienated labour' (Bratton and Denham, 2014, p. 104). The influence of Smith's and Babbage's theories on the design and management of work can be found in Frederick W. Taylor's book *The Principles of Scientific Management*, published in 1911. Frederick W. Taylor (1856–1915) pioneered the scientific management movement often referred to as *Taylorism*. This form of job design, it is argued, is 'both a system of ideological assertions and a set of management practices' Littler (1982, p. 51). Taylor was appalled by what he regarded as inefficient working practices, what he called 'natural soldiering', and set out to analyse 'scientifically' all the tasks to be undertaken and then to design jobs to eliminate time and motion waste. Taylor's approach to job design was based on five main principles:

- Maximum job fragmentation
- The divorce of planning and doing
- The divorce of 'direct' and 'indirect' labour
- The minimization of skill requirements and time for learning the job
- The reduction of material-handling to a minimum.

Thus, the centrepiece of scientific management was the separation of tasks into their simplest constituent elements, and as such Taylorism was 'a dynamic of skilling' (Littler, 1982, p. 52). Some writers argue that Taylorism was a relatively short-lived phenomenon that died in the economic depression of the 1930s, while others have argued that, in the late twentieth century, the direct and indirect influence of Taylorism on job design factory was extensive (Littler and Salaman, 1984, p. 73).

reflective question

> Can you think of jobs in the retail and service sector that support the charge that work systems in the modern workplace continue to be imbued with neo-Taylorism?

The American car-maker Henry Ford applied the major principles of Taylorism, but also installed specialized machines and perfected the flow-line principle of assembly work; this kind of job design has, not surprisingly, come to be called Fordism. This classical work system is characterized by two essential features: first, a system of conveyor lines that feed components to different work stations to be worked on; and second, the standardization of parts to gain economies of scale and lower unit costs. Management's control over the work system was enhanced by detailed time and motion studies that attempted to discover the shortest possible task-cycle time. Ford's concept of people management was simple: 'The idea is that man [sic]... must have every second necessary but not a single unnecessary second' (Ford, 1922, quoted in Beynon, 1984, p. 33). Recording job times meant that line managers could closely monitor their subordinates' performance.

Ford's production system was, however, not without its problems. Workers found the repetitive work boring and unchallenging, job dissatisfaction being expressed in high rates of absenteeism and turnover. Taylor-style job design techniques also carried control and coordination costs. Specialization needed extensive planning and supervision, so Ford had to employ an increasing number of production planners, controllers, supervisors and inspectors to meet quality standards. The economies of the extended division of labour thus tended to be offset by the dis-economies caused by management control structures. Despite these limits, Taylorism and Fordism became the predominant approach to job design in vehicle production in the USA and Europe.

In the 1920s, Harvard Business School professor Elton Mayo (1880–1949) applied the insights of social psychology to the design of work and to management practice. He criticized F. W. Taylor for focusing solely on

Many factories operate on classic Fordist principles to allow economies of scale and efficient production. But how highly would they rank on staff satisfaction and motivation?

Getty

Bureaucracy, work and HRM

Bureaucracy is something everyone loves to hate. And with good reason. Everyday life presents us with a never-ending sequence of bureaucratic encounters that tax our patience and leave us speechless. The state of frustration many people feel when reflecting on their encounters with bureaucracy is a good starting point for thinking about work and work systems. But if we are seeking to understand the challenges of work design in a globalizing world, we have to proceed cautiously. Whatever the faults of the thing itself, the idea of bureaucracy has served as a useful conceptual reference point for thinking about organizations and the work processes situated within them. As we enter the pre-bureaucratic and post-bureaucratic worlds associated with globalization, this conceptual reference point will serve as a valuable navigational tool.

What is the meaning of pre- and post-bureaucratic in this context? With regard to pre-bureaucratic worlds, we can recall the work of Max Weber, who wrote the classic analysis of bureaucracy. For Weber, bureaucracy was to be understood in contrast to patrimony, the organization of social activities based on one's personal relationships to powerful people (usually men). In societies where patrimony is the dominant organizing principle, it is not what you know, but who you know, that determines your position in various organizations. In many traditional societies, patrimonial values continue to exert a strong influence on people's thinking, and HR professionals may find themselves working in these pre-bureaucratic societies.

With regard to post-bureaucratic worlds, Andrew Abbott has recently argued that what we have traditionally designated as organizations are being altered in fundamental ways. As a result in part of the changes we associate with globalization, 'organizations are responding not so much by changing organizational policies as by dismantling and reassembling what in mid-twentieth-century-terms we would have called the organization itself' (Abbott, 2009, p. 419). Abbott's analysis suggests we may be entering a post-bureaucratic era, and some people consider that this is a good thing. But we must be careful not to lose sight of certain desirable features of bureaucracy, features (like

Image Source/Image Source/EMMERICHWEBB CM

the obligation to hire the most qualified person for the job) that classical bureaucratic theory helped to identify.

The point is that we must recognize that bureaucracy is not just a thing: it is also a conceptual model or 'thinking tool' that for many decades served as a basic reference point in discussions about organizations. The idea of bureaucracy helped people to think about the organizational settings of work processes and about optimal ways of linking the setting and the work process. In a period of globalization and rapid social change, when HR practitioners are likely to encounter both pre- and post-bureaucratic environments, it will be helpful to have a clear understanding of what bureaucracy was.

Stop! Consider the phrase 'use your discretion'. How would the meaning of this phrase vary depending on whether one was working in a bureaucratic or a non-bureaucratic setting? As an HR professional, you typically urge your co-workers to 'use your discretion' when dealing with unforeseen circumstances on the job. How might your co-workers misinterpret your advice if they were not familiar with the organizational norms of bureaucratic settings?

Sources and further information: For more information, see Abbott (2009) and also Swedberg (2005).

Note: This feature was written by David MacLennan.

the engineering aspects of work and for believing that employees were solely motivated by extrinsic (money) rewards.

In 1928, Mayo's research at the Hawthorne Works of the Western Electric Company in the USA found that not only economic incentives, but also the working environment and social relations motivated workers. The message for management was quite clear: rather than depending on management controls and extrinsic rewards, management needed to influence the work group by cultivating an organizational climate that met the social needs of workers. This ushered in what became known as the *human relations movement*, which advocated worker participation and non-authoritarian first-line managers to promote a climate of good human relations, in which both the quantity and quality of the service or the goods demanded by the organization could be met. During the 1960s and early 1970s, job design was further influenced by the *neo-human relations* and the 'quality of working life' movement. The neo-human relations approach to job design emphasized the fulfilment of social needs by recomposing fragmented work tasks, which challenged the core principles of Taylorism. Advocates of neo-human relations emphasized five core principles:

- The principle of closure, whereby the scope of the job is such that it includes all the tasks to complete a product or process, thus satisfying the social need for achievement
- A good design incorporating control and monitoring tasks, by which the individual or group assumes responsibility for quality control
- Task variety, whereby the worker acquires a range of different skills so that job flexibility is possible
- Self-regulation of the speed of work
- That the design should encompass a job structure allowing some social interaction and a degree of cooperation between workers (Littler and Salaman, 1984).

Competitive pressures in the 1970s compelled an increasing number of Western companies to reassess Taylorism and consider ways to redesign jobs. The earliest suggested antidote to Taylorism was the use of *job rotation*, which simply involves the periodic shifting of a worker from one work-simplified task to another (Figure 13.3). The advantage of job rotation is, it was argued, that it reduces the boredom and monotony of doing one simplified task by diversifying a worker's activities. An alternative approach involved the horizontal expansion of tasks, referred to as *job enlargement* (Figure 13.4). Instead of only grilling hamburgers, for example, a griller's job could be enlarged to include mixing the meat for the burger or preparing a side salad to accompany the order. With a larger number of tasks per worker, the time-cycle of work increases, thus reducing repetition and monotony.

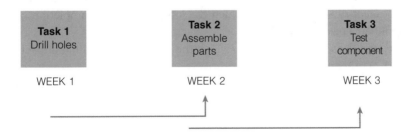

Figure 13.3 An example of job rotation

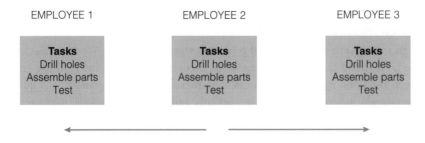

Figure 13.4 *An example of job enlargement*

A later and more sophisticated effort to overcome some of the major shortcomings of Taylorism was the vertical expansion of jobs, often referred to as *job enrichment*. This approach takes some authority from the immediate supervisors and adds it to the job (Figure 13.5). Increased vertical scope gives the worker additional responsibilities, including planning and quality control. For example, the fast-food worker from our previous example might be expected not only to grill the burgers and prepare the salad, but also to order the produce from the wholesaler and inspect the food on delivery for its quality.

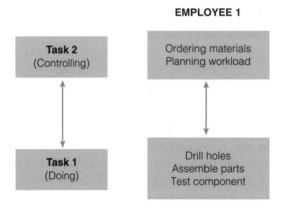

Figure 13.5 *An example of job enrichment*

Hackman and Oldham's (1980) seminal model of job enrichment – the *job characteristic model* – is an influential approach to job design. This model proposed five core job characteristics:

- *Skill variety* – the degree to which the job requires a variety of different activities in carrying out the work, requiring the use of a number of the worker's skills and talents
- *Task identity* – the degree to which the job requires the completion of a 'whole' and identifiable piece of work
- *Task significance* – the degree to which the job has a substantial impact on the lives or work of other people
- *Autonomy* – the degree to which the job provides the worker with substantial freedom, independence and discretion in terms of scheduling the work and determining the procedures to be used when carrying it out
- *Feedback* – the degree to which the worker possesses information related to the actual results of his or her performance.

The chef/manager of a small restaurant would, for example, have a job high on skill variety (requiring all the skills of cooking plus the business skills of keeping accounts, and so on), high on task identity (starting with raw ingredients and ending with appetizing meals), high on task significance (feeling that the meals have brought pleasure to the customers), high on autonomy (deciding the suppliers and the menus) and high on feedback (visiting the customers after they have finished their meals). In contrast, a person working for a fast-food chain grilling hamburgers would probably have a job low on skill variety (doing nothing but grilling hamburgers throughout the shift), low on task identity (simply grilling burgers and seldom preparing other food), low on task significance (not feeling that the cooking makes much of a difference when the burger is to be covered in tomato ketchup anyway), low on autonomy (grilling the burgers according to a routine, highly specified procedure) and low on feedback (receiving few comments from either co-workers or customers).

Critical workplace scholars offered a more critical and ideological evaluation of job enrichment (Thompson and van den Broek, 2010). Friedman's (1977) influential study argues that although job enrichment techniques may increase job satisfaction and commitment, the key focus remains on managerial control. Thompson (1989) offers one of the most penetrating early critiques of job redesign. He argues that many job enrichment schemes 'offer little or nothing that is new, and are often disguised forms of intensified [managerial] control' (1989, p. 141). Ritzer's (2004) 'McDonaldization of society' is best known for applying elements of job design to control workers in the fast-food industry:

> Bureaucracies emphasize control over people through the replacement of human judgment with the dictates of rules, regulations, and structures. Employees are controlled by the division of labor, which allocates to each office a limited number of well-defined tasks. Incumbents must do the tasks, and no others, in a manner prescribed by the organization. They may not, in most cases, devise idiosyncratic ways of doing those tasks. Furthermore, by making few, if any, judgments, people begin to resemble human robots or computers. Having reduced people to this status, leaders of bureaucracies can think about actually replacing human beings with machines. (Ritzer, 2000, p. 24)

Interactive service fast-food work is characterized as low-paid, low-skilled, low-autonomy and poor career prospects. The term 'McJob' (Etzioni, 1988) embodies the worst elements of service sector employment. In spite of the research indicating that 'McJobs' are boring, unchallenging and controlling, some scholars have suggested that fast-food work and HR practices are a more nuanced phenomenon that allows for unambiguously negative outcomes, but also offer positive outcomes as a potential 'stepping-stone' to a rewarding career (Daniels, 2004) and 'job security' to younger and older employees (Gould, 2010, p. 799).

In the past two decades, the 'call-centre discourse' has been part of the dominant rhetoric of the new economy. Critical researchers have drawn attention to contemporary Taylorist-type surveillance in call centres. Various metaphors have been used to capture call-centre work: 'electronic sweatshops' or the 'electronic panopticon', the 'assembly-line in the head' and the often-quoted 'electronic Taylorism' (for example, Callaghan and Thompson, 2001; Sewell, 1998; Taylor, 2010; Taylor and Bain, 1998; Thompson and McHugh, 2009). Such arguments echo earlier debates on deskilling in manual and routine clerical work.

© Royalty-Free/Corbis

In the past two decades, the call-centre model has emerged as a dominant work design form.

Contemporary, post-bureaucratic approaches to job design have grown out of, draw upon and have sometimes reacted against classical approaches to work practices (Grey, 2005). For many scholars, the paradigm shift in work redesign that has occurred over the past two decades revolves around variants of team-based working, including 'flexible specialization', 'Japanese work systems', 'business process re-engineering' (BPR) and HPWS.

reflective question You have probably experienced group working as part of your business programme. Have you enjoyed the experience? What are the advantages and disadvantages of group projects? Why have 'team' projects become common practice in many business schools?

If corporate giants, such as the Ford Motor Company, had once been the model of mass production, Toyota became the model for redesigning assembly lines. According to US academics Piore and Sabel (1984), the Fordist model is incapable of responding quickly in highly competitive consumer industries. The alternative was *'flexible specialization'*, which presented a revival of the 'craft paradigm', which Piore and Sabel (p. 17) described as:

A strategy of permanent innovation: accommodation to ceaseless change, rather than an effort to control it [based] on flexible – multiuse – equipment; skilled workers; and the creation, through politics, of an industrial community that restricts the forms of competition to those favoring innovation.

The flexible specialization model was the antithesis of Taylorism; it had the following features:

- The small-scale production of a large variety of products for differentiated markets
- The utilization of highly skilled workers exercising considerable control and autonomy over the labour process
- The use of process and information technology
- Strong networks of small producers that achieved flexibility and efficiency through collaboration (Appelbaum and Batt, 1994).

In Europe, Atkinson's (1984) flexible firm model provoked extensive attention from policy-makers, management theorists and practitioners. Atkinson's analysis became *de facto* British government policy in the late 1980s and 90s (Sisson and Storey, 2000). The flexible firm model is important in the new economy discourse because it gave theoretical legitimacy to flexible employment arrangements and thereby contributed to the growth of non-standard labour and 'looser organizational boundaries' that tolerate 'outsiders' coming into the organization (Felstead and Jewson, 1999). Classical work design systems were further modified by the influence of Japanese and American work practices.

Japanese and American work design practices

Three decades ago influential management consultants proclaimed the need for Western companies to embrace the 'art of Japanese management' (Grey, 2005). The *'Japanese way of work'* set off a process of job and work redesign, and concomitant changes in managing the employment relationship (Bratton, 1992; Thompson and McHugh, 2009).

The stereotypical Japanese job and work systems involved both horizontal and vertical job enlargement. Machines are arranged in a group or 'cell' – cellular technology – and multiskilled workers have flexible job boundaries including self-inspection, which means that the team completes a whole component from start to finish. The Japanese management work system was also based on total-quality control and the practice of zero or low inventory known as just-in-time. In the USA, these practices were studied and implemented as part of the *'lean production'* movement (Womack et al., 1990). The work team makes production and quality-improvement decisions. In other words, the form of job design resembles job B shown in Figure 13.2 above.

Academics differ over whether or not the Japanese model constitutes a significant departure from traditional job design principles. While some argue that 'Japanization of work' is distinctive because it creates a complex web of *dependency relationships* that calls for adroit management (Oliver and Wilkinson, 1988), others emphasize that the Japanese model constitutes a sophisticated control system designed to influence expectations and encourage peer-group pressure or 'clan' control that create a culture reproducing the conditions of their own subordination (Bratton, 1992; Burawoy, 1979; Grey, 2005; Wells, 1993).

HRM web links

> Visit the online resource centre at **www.palgravehighered.com/bg-hrm-6e** for insights into how different companies and unions (in the UK, USA and Australia) view the introduction of work teams.

The Japanese model is no longer avant-garde, but numerous US and European studies show that team-based work systems have become the dominant reality (see, for example, Fröbel and Marchington, 2005). Recent contributors to the 'team debate' use a multitude of new acronyms such as BPR and HPWS to describe self-managed work teams designed to enhance organizational performance as well as employee voice. A 'repackaged' version of the Japanese model, BPR falls within the post-bureaucratic genre (Albizu and Olazaran, 2006; Champy, 1996; Hammer, 1997). The BPR job redesign movement declares that work systems have to be 'radically' changed so that the re-engineered organizations can become adaptable and oriented towards continuous change and renewal. According to the re-engineering guru James Champy (1996, p. 3), BPR is 'about changing our managerial work, the way we think about, organize, inspire, deploy, enable, measure, and reward the value-adding operational work. It is about changing management itself.'

Central to re-engineered work systems, argues Willmott (1995), is the 'reconceptualization of core employees' from being considered a variable cost to being represented as a valuable asset capable of serving the customer without the need for a command and control style of leadership. With the ascendancy of 'customer democracy', employees are encouraged to exercise initiative in creating value for customers and thereby profits for the company. According to Hammer (1997, pp. 158–9):

> Obedience and diligence are now irrelevant. Following orders is no guarantee of success. Working hard at the wrong thing is no virtue. When customers are kings, mere hard work – work without understanding, flexibility, and enthusiasm – leads nowhere. Work must be smart, appropriately targeted, and adapted to the particular circumstances of the process and the customer … Loyalty and hard work are by themselves quaint relics … organizations must now urge employees to put loyalty to the customer over loyalty to the company – because that is the only way the company will survive.

This passage is most revealing. It presents the debate on employee commitment, shared commitment and reciprocity in a different light. Furthermore, in the re-engineered organization, responsibility for the fate of employees shifts from managers to customers. In Hammer's (1997, p. 157) opinion, 'The company does not close plants or lay off workers – customers do, by their actions or inactions.'

Unlike earlier movements in work system redesign, re-engineering is market-driven. In essence, it views the management of people through an economic prism focusing on the relationship between the buyer and the seller of services or goods rather than between the employer and employee. In contrast to Beer's et al. (1984, p. 153) 'four Cs', consisting of commitment, competence, cost-effectiveness and congruence, Hammer and Champy (1993) emphasize only 'three Cs' – customers, competition and change. Moreover, reflecting the rhetoric of 'free markets', they emphasize that a government policy of 'tough love' towards business has created the need for BPR. For Champy (1996, p. 19), using a mixture of language discarded by the political 'old Left' and terminology of the 'new Right', 'a dictatorship of the customariat or … a market democracy … is the cause of a total revolution within the traditional, machine-like corporation.'

Some workplace scholars have, however, been highly critical of re-engineering. Grint and Willcocks (1995), for example, offer a scathing review of BPR, arguing that it is not new and pointing out that it is essentially political in its rhetorical and practical manifestations. Willmott is similarly scornful of BPR, emphasizing that re-engineering is 'heavily top-down' and pointing out that the re-engineered organization, using information technology, while creating fewer hierarchical structures, also produces 'a fist-full of dynamic processes … notably, the primacy of hierarchical control and the continuing treatment of employees as cogs in the machine' (Willmott, 1995, p. 91). Moreover, BPR does not obviate the inherent conflict of interest between employers and employees. When examined in the context of employee relations, BPR can be interpreted 'as the latest wave in a series of initiatives … to increase the cooperation/productivity/adaptability of staff' (Willmott, 1995, p. 96). The antecedents of HPWS can be found in the neo-human relations and team-based movements developed over the last four decades.

HRM web links   Visit the online resource centre at **www.palgravehighered.com/bg-hrm-6e** for an introductory guide to BPR.

High-performance workplaces

High-performance working is a concept that currently dominates the HRM literature. However, in the absence of any widely accepted blueprint definition of high-performance working, one way of understanding the concept is to consider it as a strategic and holistic approach to managing people and work through the successful implementation of high-performance work practices. These are HR interventions and actions that contribute, at an operational level, to the totality of high-performance working at an organizational level.

As our review of post-bureaucratic work regimes suggests, the fundamental assumptions behind high-performance work configurations are neither new nor radical (Sung and Ashton, 2005); instead, this approach is the means through which synergies may be derived from successfully combining a number (or 'bundles') of high-performance work practices that can lead to superior performance (Boxall, 2012). The inference is that the achievement of high-performance working requires a deliberate and sustained focus on not only ensuring effectiveness in how people are managed and developed strategically in their workplace, but, importantly, in how work and jobs are organized and designed operationally to enable higher levels of workplace skills utilization (Grant et al., 2014). Indeed, Belt and Giles (2009, p. 3) suggest that high-performance working is 'a general approach to managing organizations that aims to stimulate more effective employee involvement and commitment in order to achieve high levels of performance'. The existence and 'strength' (Bowen and Ostroff, 2004, p. 204) of a sustainable high-performance work climate can therefore underpin increased levels of job autonomy and commitment, which can in turn give rise to higher levels of skills utilization and organizational performance (Boxall et al., 2015).

Characteristics of high-performance working

Perhaps the most important defining characteristic of an HPWS is that it 'possesses autonomy in the performance of its daily work activities' (Nijholt and Benders, 2010, p. 381). As noted earlier, this proposition shifts the historical emphasis on work from core employees being considered as a variable cost, to their being regarded as a valuable asset capable of serving the customer without the need for a command and control style of leadership (Willmott, 1995). By comparing the key characteristics of the contemporary high-performance work paradigm with the traditional bureaucratic model of work organization, we can see in Table 13.1 that the high-performance working focus places much greater emphasis on employee value and on fostering a work environment in which workers can fully participate.

High-performance working is generally enacted through mutual employer–employee reciprocation: employers develop high-commitment and trust-building work practices, and, in return, employees experience higher levels of job autonomy and involvement (Thompson, 2003). The approaches most commonly attributed to high-performance working are high-involvement and high-commitment management (Boxall and Macky, 2009) and high-engagement management (Bridger, 2015), three management positions that arguably infer a more than a semantic difference (see Chapter 10). Indeed, it can be argued that where intrinsically motivating high-involvement (for example, employee suggestion, empowerment and decision-making) practices are used, mutually reinforcing extrinsic high-commitment (for example, benefit and reward) practices are also required. Therefore, through for example effective job design, team working, leadership and

Table 13.1 *The traditional and high-performance work models*

Work characteristic	Traditional focus	High-performance work focus
Competitive advantage	Cost	Quality
Resources	Capital	People and information
Quality	What is affordable	No compromise
Focal point	Profit	Customer
Structural design	Hierarchical	Flattened and organic
Control	Centralized	Decentralized
Leadership	Autocratic	Distributive and participative
Labour	Homogeneous	Culturally diverse
Work organization	Specialized and individual	Flexible and teams
Communications	Vertical	Horizontal and upward

continuous development practices, workers experience (or perceive) higher levels of participation and involvement and may subsequently be more inclined to experience higher levels of job commitment and/or organizational engagement.

Enacting high-performance working

Sustainable high-performance working is not generally achievable solely by upskilling workers; instead, 'high performance is some kind of function of an employee's skills, motivation, and the opportunity to deploy skills' (Bloom et al., 2004, p. 40). Often referred to as the AMO (**A**bility, **M**otivation and **O**pportunity) framework (see, for example, Macky and Boxall, 2007), this proposition adds weight to our earlier definition of high-performance working as a 'strategic and holistic' approach to the management of people and work. For example, it would be disadvantageous for organizations to have highly skilled but demotivated and underutilized workers, and, equally, to have highly motivated but incompetent workers (Guest, 2006). Macky and Boxall (2007) explain that improved organizational performance is realized via three causal routes: (1) employee ability setting the upper limit of performance; (2) motivation influencing the extent to which that ability is applied; and (3) opportunity concerning the removal of barriers for able and motivated employees to participate and apply their skills effectively. The challenge for organizations therefore centres on simultaneously focusing on and balancing all three aspects (ability, motivation and opportunity). In addition, the development of a strong and sustainable organizational climate for high performance tends to evolve over a considerable period of time, and employee reactions to high-performance work practices are likely to be shaped by workers' past experiences of HR interventions, actions and work practices (Kinnie et al., 2005).

HPWS are most often presented as being positive for workers in that they provide for more skills and autonomy and thereby contribute to increased job satisfaction and commitment (Boxall et al., 2015). It has been argued to the contrary, however, that rather than being about working 'smarter', HPWSs have in instances been associated with increased work intensification (Ramsay et al., 2000) and other forms of 'controlled participation' (Edwards et al., 2002). Danford et al. (2008) and Godard (2004) also provide critical accounts of HPWSs, and Bratton's (1992) study of teams further reminds us of the need to develop a context-sensitive understanding of self-managed teams. These critical accounts

HRM as I see it

Gregor Karolus Part 2

Chief HR Officer, Springer Nature

www.springernature.com

Remind yourself of Gregor's background and experience from Chapter 11. Click on Gregor's photo in your ebook to watch the second part of his video as he speaks about implementing HPWSs, and then think about the following questions:

1 Why did Gregor move to HR?
2 How can HR play a positive role in creating a high-performance workplace?
3 Why does Gregor believe that trust is important in an HPWS?

suggest that HPWSs and high-performance work practices may not necessarily have universally 'positive' or 'negative' outcomes for workers (Heffernan and Dundon, 2016). Rather, outcomes can vary depending on contingencies such as hierarchy and social relations within the workplace, and the presence and power of trade unions (see, for example, Edwards et al., 2002).

Figure 13.6 depicts the well-documented HR causal chain (see, for example, Purcell and Hutchinson, 2007), and illustrates the potential impact of perceptions in influencing the effectiveness of high-performance work practices. Acknowledging the complexity inherent in predicting causal order (Wright et al., 2005), Figure 13.6 illustrates that between the actual implemented work practices and the subsequent behavioural change lies the 'black box' (Messersmith et al., 2011), that is, the elusiveness of how employees might react to, perceive and experience new work practices (Khilji and Wang, 2006) in the quest for improved organizational performance.

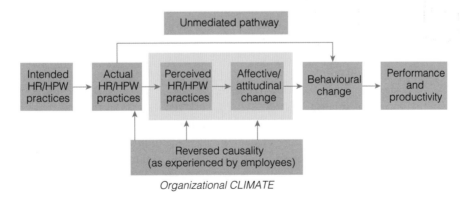

Figure 13.6 *Causal chain of HR/high-performance work practices*

Identifying high-performance work practices

Fuelling the degree of conceptual complexity enveloping the concept of high-performance working itself is the lack of an agreed list(s) of concomitant high-performance work practices. Of course, as mentioned earlier, the success of high-performance work practices largely depends on the effectiveness of their implementation within a conducive organizational climate. There is, however, some debate in the HRM–performance literature concerning the extent to which high-performance work practices can be universally applicable to all organizational contexts (best practice), or whether they are more effective when contingently aligned to particular business needs (best fit) (see Chapter 3). Boselie et al. (2005, p. 73) also observe that 'no accepted theory exists that might classify different practices into "obligatory", and '"optional", "hygiene" factors and motivators"'. Other commentators, however, have distinguished between 'hygiene' and 'core' (Tamkin et al., 2010) and 'enabling' and 'performance' (Stevens, 2005) practices. The former within both interpretations are the work practices that encompass the day-to-day HR basics and must be present, but are not sufficient in their own right, to facilitate sustainable high performance. From an organizational climate perspective, a realization of high-performance working also seems to require the presence of the latter of each pair, which are those work practices needed to drive and support behavioural and organizational change. Therefore, increased organizational performance is not necessarily derived from the number of high-performance work practices implemented (it is not a case of 'more is better'), or even necessarily by the particular work practices selected. Instead, it is the ways in which the work practices are strategically selected and contingently aligned to each other and to a particular organizational context that can increase performance through employee behaviours (Guest and Conway, 2011). The difficulty for employers is that many are unlikely to know at the outset which particular work practices are best suited to their organization and, importantly, how these should be configured, aligned and measured (Hughes, 2008). It is in part for this reason that, while many organizations appear to utilize a number of potential high-performance work practices, Warhurst and Findlay (2012, p. 9, emphasis in original) suggest that 'few firms in the UK have anything that might be loosely accepted as an HPW *system*'.

Tension and paradox

We started this chapter by examining the meaning of work in contemporary Western society and then went on to evaluate three contrasting and significant work system designs: the classical Taylorism and Fordism, the neo-human relations and US/Japanese self-management models. Bolton's (2007) work reminds us of the centrality of work system design to human dignity *in* and *at* work. The ways in which work is organized and managed can all operate to promote or deny dignity. According to Bolton, the notion of dignified work is about much more than escaping routine and mundane work or attaining a state of 'self-actualization'. But neither is it an individual thing. Instead, it is a multifaceted phenomenon that embodies both objective factors (for example, job security) and subjective factors (for example, respect). As such, job and work designs that offer a degree of responsible autonomy and social esteem and respect provide 'dignity *in* work'; work configurations that offer, among other things, 'voice' and safe and healthy working conditions, afford 'dignity *at* work' (Bolton, 2007).

We complete this chapter by examining identifiable tension and paradox in job redesign. Paradox is evident in work system design, and there are a number of ways in which to think

High-performance working in action: public and voluntary sectors

HRM in practice 13.2

This 'insight' is based on a snapshot of a larger comparative analysis of two different organizational contexts. The first is a large public sector healthcare organization, while the second is a small charity operating in the voluntary sector. Five overarching and interrelated groupings of high-performance work interventions and practices, as shown in Table 13.2, inform the conceptual underpinning and were explored through a series of interviews with line managers and focus groups with employees.

Table 13.2 High-performance work groupings and implementation

High-performance work grouping	Workplace implementation
Autonomy and empowerment	Employees are able and trusted to participate fully in the workplace through applying discretionary behaviour and contributing to the decision-making processes that affect their job
Work organization and job design	Work and jobs are organized and designed in ways that maximize employees' contributions
Leadership and management	Leaders and managers empower and support employees to recognize and apply their skills effectively in the workplace
Teamwork and collaboration	Teamwork practices contribute positively to organizational performance through enabling collaborative working and shared decision-making
Learning environment	Training and learning opportunities exist, and employees' are able and empowered to apply their learning in the workplace

There are both similarities and differences in the extent of the high-performance work climate and the perceived effectiveness of high-performance work practices within the two diverse organizational contexts. A notable finding replicated across both organizations is the importance of a shared organizational purpose in driving job satisfaction and commitment, for example, *'when the service user is at the heart of everything that is going on people deliver, and people do it because what motivates them is care, and values around care'.*

However, while heavily regulated and prescriptive roles are necessary within the risk-critical nature of the public sector organization, the hierarchical structure and demarcated roles and grades are viewed as potential inhibitors of job autonomy. Interestingly, the notion of responsible autonomy is complex. Within both organizations, people reflected on having 'nominal responsibility' for tasks, but not necessarily true autonomy (or ownership) of them. Line managers also commented that lack of employee autonomy and involvement could in turn lead to *'a lack of willingness to change and learn new skills'* and, highlighting the importance of job design, voiced that in such circumstances *'employees can become complacent … or they are not proactive in maintaining their skill set if their job does not allow [this]'.* Both organizations believed that job descriptions could be restrictive in the sense that they could offer greater flexibility through becoming more 'outcome-focused' as opposed to 'task-driven', with emphasis placed on the holistic nature of combining a number of jobs within a team context.

Within the constraints of time and role barriers, line managers in both organizations talked about

(continued)

'*continuously seeking out development opportunities for employees*' and of using participative and coaching styles of leadership to encourage more employee ownership of tasks and involvement in decisions. Financial constraints in the voluntary sector have led to line managers seeking innovative ways to harness and utilize people's skill sets. A manager highlighted that while opportunities are not always work-related, '*what they do is bring people together as a team and strengthen our team-based culture*'. In addition, making reference to high-commitment-building practices within the voluntary sector, it was recognized that '*although we can't pay good wages here, we have got good terms and conditions … it shows that we really care for our people*'.

Managers from both organizations signalled a need (and opportunity) to consider people's interests more broadly in terms of their job commitment to and motivation for applying discretionary effort at work. For instance, there was a need to '*look at people more holistically to tap into their motivation in terms of strengths and what excites them*', and a view that '*if you can tap into things that people love doing and are passionate about, then they are so much more motivated to perform*'.

Stop! What does the analysis tell us about the importance of organizational climate for sustainable high performance?

Sources and further information: For further information, see Grant and Maxwell (2015).

Note: This feature was written by Kirsteen Grant and the quotations are from her own work, referenced above.

about and conceptualize this paradox. Here we use a simple model presented by Jaffee (2001) and illustrated in Figure 13.7. The model shows that paradox stems from what is called 'differentiation–integration tension'. This refers to the inherent tension between management strategies for achieving a rational division of economic activities and, simultaneously, for ensuring that these activities are coordinated and integrated. Differentiation and the division of labour are fundamental management principles that underscore organizational goals to control costs and the quality of their products or services. As organizations increase in size and complexity, integration becomes an issue. How do different workers, departments and managers coordinate and integrate their interdependent activities?

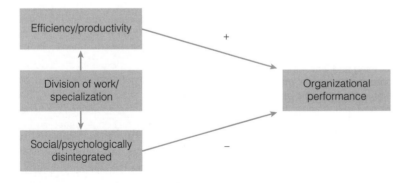

Figure 13.7 *The work design–human factor paradox*

Source: Adapted from Jaffee, D. (2001) Organization Theory: Tension and Change. Boston: McGraw-Hill. Copyright © 2001 Professor David Jaffee. Reproduced with permission.

The tension between differentiation and integration within the organization can be illustrated by a familiar manufacturing strategy: that management initially redesigns work involving a rigid division of labour and highly specialized tasks (for example, Fordism). The intended consequence is to rationalize the business and make the workers more efficient and productive. The unintended consequence, however, is a work experience that produces low levels of job satisfaction, motivation and commitment. This, as we discussed earlier, can limit the positive contribution made by the specialization of labour. Delbridge and Turnbull (1992) have detailed the limitation and potentially negative outcomes for workers in fast paced work regimes, which 'creates *extraordinary pressures* on employees and work organization' (Scarbrough, 2000, p. 16, emphasis added). Topcic et al.'s (2016) recent study suggests that some HPWSs are more strongly associated with negative pressures on employees than others. Drawing on two different job design configurations, Topcic et al.'s research differentiates between a 'challenge demand' HPWS model – focusing on performance evaluation and ongoing learning – and a 'job resource' model centred around flexible working hours and participation in decision-making. The research found a positive relationship between the challenge demand model and enhanced individual stress among employees. These kind of pressures may 'drive out HR support activities ... needed to sustain employee motivation and morale' (Scarbrough, 2000, p. 16).

The crux of this problem is the managerial 'control' of labour's input. Management, as Geary and Dobbins (2001, p. 5) remind us, is not simply about controlling the labour process; it is also about enlisting workers' knowledge, creativity and discretionary efforts:

Management remains caught between two opposing imperatives: attempts at regulating employees too tightly run the risk of endangering the employees' creativity and commitment to management goals, while empowering employees runs the risk of reducing management control.

This fundamental paradox at the heart of the employment relationship becomes even more acute when managers redesign organizational structures and introduce flexible non-standard work patterns – sometimes called 'precarious employment' – that create a disad-vantaged and marginalized workforce, the 'precariat'. The notion of tension and paradox in work system design is apparent in the debate on team-based designs. While many scholars (see, for example, Piore and Sabel, 1984) consider that self-managed teams reverse Taylorism, others note that new post-bureaucratic designs have, paradoxically, revitalized Weber's typology of bureaucracy. New performance-related incentives, for example, have generated behavioural rules that reinforce bureaucratic control: 'Thus, intriguingly, the use of bureaucratic control emerges as the main element of labour control in this type of work-place' (Pulignano and Stewart, 2006, p. 104).

Legge's (2007) analysis of the networked organizational configuration identifies the tension that occurs when employers strive for both control *and* commitment. Organizational fragmentation resulting from global supply chains and interorganizational business arrangements are, she deftly observes, likely to 'inhibit the development of commitment to a common organizational culture and often involve the disruption of the psychological contract' (Legge, 2007, p. 53). Work team 'empowerment' does not eliminate worker resistance, and managerial control continues to be contested (McKinlay and Taylor, 1998).

case study

Currency, Inc.

The setting

In today's modern office, employees generate over half a kilogram of waste paper per employee per day, and this is increasing by 20 per cent each year. Although it was originally believed that the use of computers would decrease the reliance on paper, the networked access to the internet and company intranet typically results in more documents being printed. It is estimated that digital documents are being copied onto paper an average of 11 times. The introduction of an email system alone can cause a 40 per cent increase in paper use. Nearly half of the paper being used is considered to be high grade, which can easily be recycled.

The environmental impacts caused by a paper-hungry society are astounding. Over 40 per cent of the solid mass in landfills is created by paper and paperboard waste, and the paper industry ranks fourth in contribution to greenhouse gas emissions, with more than 100 million trees destroyed each year to produce junk mail. If the USA could cut office paper use by just 10 per cent, it would prevent the emission of 1.6 million tons of greenhouse gases, which is the equivalent of taking 280,000 cars off the road. Eliminating paper waste in landfills would almost double the lives of current landfill sites.

In their book *The Myth of the Paperless Office*, authors Abigail Sellen and Richard Harper say that organizations have increasingly striven to become 'paperless' in the hope of not only reducing the costs directly associated with paper, but also achieving greater efficiency, to 'move forward' and motivate change. However, Sellen and Harper caution that concentrating on a goal to eliminate paper can prevent organizations from identifying organizational work practices and value systems that really should be the focus of change.

The problem

Currency Inc., a medium-sized financial firm located in the City of Johannesburg, South Africa, had gone through tremendous changes in the past year: a merger with another company, a new CEO and lay-offs caused by a decline in the country's economy. Many of those affected by the lay-offs had been with Currency for most of their careers, and their abrupt departures caused fear and distrust among the employees who had remained. Absenteeism due to stress suddenly became commonplace.

Image Source

At the first stakeholder meeting of the year, the company's new CEO, Kagiso Maree, introduced herself to the audience as an 'environmental champion'. Her inaugural presentation focused on the 'green' strategies she intended to implement in the company, proclaiming that 'financial firms are the "watchdog" of the business world and we need to set an example in South Africa by demonstrating environmentally friendly practices.' She laid out a corporate programme targeted at saving energy and conserving resources, with an initial focus on eliminating paper use. Currency, she said, would be a paperless organization within two years.

Once she had identified the areas of the business involving the most paper use, Kagiso assigned to several managers the task of implementing the new policies and processes targeted at eliminating paper use. Foremost on the agenda was the implementation of an electronic records retention system to reduce paper usage and the installation of scanners to discourage the printing of documents. This was followed by the roll-out of a new corporate policy allowing only double-sided printing for any company documents that had to be produced in hard copy. Photocopiers and printers were adjusted to default to this setting.

Such policies and attempts to implement the new 'green' initiatives were quickly met with uncertainty, cynicism and scepticism on the part of the workers. The new systems were left untouched or were underused because employees found either the hardware or the applications too confusing and even difficult to use. Employees quickly figured out ways around using the new technology and returned to their previous use, and waste, of paper.

Jokes about the next policy mandating 'paperless toilets' began to circulate throughout the offices. Returning to work after a holiday weekend, several managers found their office floors covered in hundreds of documents, with single-sided printing, produced by photocopiers that had been left to run continuously until depleted of paper. Kagiso, shocked at the workplace response, quickly assembled her management team for an urgent meeting to review why the new corporate programme had failed to gain acceptance by the employees.

The assignment

Working either alone or in a study group, prepare a report drawing on this chapter and other recommended material addressing the following:

1 How might the rise in staff absenteeism have been an indication of how workers would react to the new 'green' strategies?

2 Although minimum waste is also a component of Japanese management techniques, which aspect of the Japanese approach is obviously lacking at Currency Inc. and might have increased the likelihood of the employees accepting the company's new 'green' initiatives?

Essential reading

Ackroyd, S. and Thompson, P. (1999) *Organizational Misbehaviour*. Thousand Oaks, CA: Sage.

Alvesson, M. (1996) *Communication, Power and Organization*. Berlin: Walter De Gruyter.

Maclagan, P. (2008) Organizations and responsibility: a critical overview. *Systems Research and Behavioral Science*, **25**(3): 371–81.

Sellen, A. and Harper, R. (2002) *The Myth of the Paperless Office*. Cambridge, MA: Massachusetts Institute of Technology.

Thompson, P. and McHugh, D. (2009) Power, conflict and resistance. Chapter 9 in *Work Organisations: A Critical Approach* (4th edn). Basingstoke: Palgrave Macmillan.

Note: This case study was written by Lori Rilkoff.

Visit the online resource centre at **www.palgravehighered.com/bg-hrm-6e** for guidelines on writing reports.

summary

➤ We started this chapter by defining work as a physical and mental activity performed to produce or achieve something of value at a particular place and time, under explicit or implicit instructions, in return for a reward.

➤ Research testifies that management's mantra is 'flexibility'. The current literature is couched in the language of 'high-involvement', but it appears that, in most cases, the 'quality' of work requiring extensive training does not match the rhetoric, and 'non-educative work is systemic' (Bratton, 1999, p. 491).

➤ Critical workplace scholars argue that 'new' work regimes embody neo-Taylorist principles and a technical mode of managerial control. The research on non-standard employment and the 'McDonaldization of work' suggests both change and continuation in work design.

➤ We have cautioned against conceptualizing new work systems as a smooth transition from one ideal-type model to another. The tendency to compress the specific into categories of general trends not only compresses variations in work design, but also attaches a false coherence to emerging work forms. Change is sporadic and subject to constant renegotiation.

> HPWSs are a complex 'interlocking' arrangement of technical, behavioural and cultural dimensions. In the context of capitalist employment relationships, tension and unintended consequences will arise with each new work system, making it imperative to understand how new forms of work can change employees' perceptions of the content of the psychological contract.

review questions

1 Why define 'work' by its social context rather than by the content of the activity itself?

2 Explain the limits of Taylorism as a job design strategy.

3 'Job rotation, job enlargement and job enrichment are simply attempts by managers to control individuals at work.' Do you agree or disagree? Discuss.

4 Students often complain about doing group projects. Why? Relate your answer to autonomous work teams. Would you want to be a member of such a work group? Discuss your reasons.

5 'McJobs' is a term often used by critics of the 'new economy' to capture the realities of workplace life confronting young people today. What kinds of job does the term 'McJobs' refer to? How do the job design concepts discussed in this chapter help you to understand the term 'McJobs'? Is it an accurate description of employment today? Why does capitalism always seem to produce new work systems, and what are some of its features today?

6 What might be some of the positive and negative impacts of HPWS on employees?

further reading

Reading these articles and chapters can help you gain a better understanding and potentially a higher grade for your HRM assignment.

> Appelbaum, E. (2002) The impact of new forms of work organization on workers. In G. Murray, J. Belanger, A. Giles and P. A. Lapointe (eds) *Work and Employment Relations in the High Performance Workplace* (pp. 120–49). London: Continuum.

> Baldry, C., Bain, P., Taylor, P. and Hyman, J. (2007) *The Meaning of Work in the New Economy*. Basingstoke: Palgrave Macmillan.

> Belt, V. and Giles, L. (2009) *High Performance Working: A Synthesis of Key Literature. Evidence Report no. 4*. Wath-upon-Dearne: UK Commission for Employment and Skills.

> Bolton, S. C. (ed.) (2007) (ed.) *Dimensions of Dignity at Work*. Amsterdam: Elsevier.

> De Menezes, L. and Wood, S. (2006) The reality of flexible work systems in Britain. *International Journal of Human Resource Management*, **17**(1): 106–38.

> Docherty, P., Kira, M. and Shani, A. (2009) *Creating Sustainable Work Systems* (2nd edn). London: Routledge.

> Edgell, S. (2012) *The Sociology of Work* (2nd edn). London: Sage.

> Flecker, J. and Meil, P. (2010) Organizational restructuring and emerging service value chains: implications for work and employment. *Work, Employment & Society*, **24**(4): 680–98.

> Godard, J. (2004) A critical assessment of the high-performance paradigm. *British Journal of Industrial Relations*, **42**(2): 349–78.

> Grant, K. and Maxwell, G. (2015) High performance work practices: exploring manager and employee perceptions in Scotland. Paper presented at the 33rd International Labour Process Conference, April13–15, Athens.

> Ritzer, G. (2004) *The McDonaldization of Society* (Revised New Century edn). Thousand Oaks, CA: Pine Forge Press.

> Sung, J. and Ashton, D. (2005) *High Performance Work Practices: Linking Strategy and Skills to Performance Outcomes*. London: Department of Trade and Industry/Chartered Institute of Personnel and Development.

> Topcic, M., Baum M. and Kabst, R. (2016) Are high-performance work practices related to individually perceived stress? A job demands-resources perspective. *International Journal of Human Resource Management*, **27**(1): 45–66.

Click here in your interactive ebook for a list of HRM terminology and vocabulary that has appeared in this chapter.

Visit the online resource centre at **www.palgravehighered.com/bg-hrm-6e** for lots of extra resources to help you get to grips with this chapter, including study tips, HRM skills development guides, summary lecture notes, tips for English as a second language (ESL) students and more.

vocabulary checklist for ESL students

chapter 14

leadership and management development

© Royalty-Free/Corbis

outline

➤ Introduction

➤ Meanings of leadership, management, and leadership and management development

➤ Defining leadership and management development

➤ Strategic leadership and management development

➤ Implementing leadership and management development

➤ HRM as I see it: Lana Kularajah, Transform Aid International/Baptist World Aid Australia

➤ HRM in practice 14.1: Evaluating the Modern Leaders Programme at Skipton Building Society

➤ Case study: The City of Sahali

➤ Summary, review questions, further reading and vocabulary checklist for ESL students

objectives

After studying this chapter, you should be able to:

1 Understand the meanings of leadership, management and leadership and management development (LMD)

2 Assess the requirements for strategic leadership and management development

3 Explain various models of leadership and management for development purposes

4 Explain key approaches to implementing and evaluating leadership and management development

5 Understand how leadership and management development can be used with leaders and managers in small and medium-sized enterprises

How much do you trust people with the title 'leader'? Certainly, in the popular media there has been scathing criticism of some corporate leaders. In 2016 alone, Sir Philip Green, ex-owner of the retail giant British Home Stores, was severely criticized by MPs for putting 11,000 jobs at risk and leaving BHS with a £571m pension deficit (Butler and Ruddick, The Guardian, 2016). So too was Mike Ashley, the boss of Sports Direct. His behaviours were described as 'unacceptable', and contributed to employment conditions at the company's warehouse in Shirebrook, Derbyshire described as 'more like those in a workhouse or gulag' (Goodley, The Guardian, 2016).

introduction

I n academic journals, leaders have been considered blameworthy for various failings. Board (2010), for example, suggested that leaders helped to cause the global financial crisis of 2008 and will probably contribute to the next one too. Collinson (2012) argued that leaders in particular have been too 'positive', which leaves them unprepared for unexpected events or to listen to others who can see the problems. He employs the metaphor of 'Prozac' to consider this – referring to the medication Prozac that is used to treat depression, anxiety and, in this case, obsessive compulsive symptoms. Those involved in leadership and management development (LMD), such as trainers and consultants, have also been criticized because they did not do enough to stop leaders and managers taking their organizations in the wrong direction (MacKenzie et al., 2014).

Nevertheless, there is still a concern, as there has been for many years, that we need high-quality leaders and managers. The Chartered Management Institute (2014) reported that the weakness in management and leadership was holding back the UK's economic performance. But questions remain over what we mean by high-quality managers and leaders, and how they can be developed. There are also debates about terms such as 'leadership', which can be open to so many different meanings in organizations. Kelly (2014, p. 913), for example, asks us to pose the question for any organization, 'Where is the leadership?' Of course, everyone has their own model of leadership and management, often based on prejudiced experience. In addition, most people who manage or lead learn from experience, especially in organizations such as small and medium-sized enterprises (SMEs), where few resources are available for formal development events or a strategic approach. If you talk to anyone who works as a leader or manager about their learning, you will often find that most learning occurs at work, and that they are made aware of this learning process through reflection on practice. Learning and development also often rely on the support of others through coaching and mentoring, or by working in an action learning group with other leaders and managers on problems that they face. However, this can also make LMD less formal and more difficult to evaluate. This chapter will consider such issues. One issue is whether leaders are different from managers. This question has been debated for many years without conclusion. Suffice it to say that the terms are often used interchangeably, and we will do the same, although there may be times when one term is more preferred.

Meanings of leadership, management and LMD

If we consider what leaders and managers actually do, one starting point might be to refer to various studies of the work of those who lead and manage. For example, the work of F. W. Taylor (1911), recognized as the founder of scientific management, in the early part of the twentieth century, and of Henri Fayol (1949), who identified the basic functions of planning, organizing, coordinating, commanding and controlling, are often invoked as the foundations of what leaders and managers are supposed to do. Taylor sought to define the role of managers by analysing work tasks so that those managers could find the 'one best way' to control work and reduce waste (see Chapter 13). Such studies, albeit influential, have not always been useful for leaders and managers in helping them to decide what to do and how to learn what to do in the particular circumstances they face. These challenges, which continue to the present day, have not, however, prevented the formation of a continuous stream of ideas and models that seek to overcome them. It is not our intention to cover such developments, but suffice it to say that many theories about management and leadership exist (see Dinh et al., 2014 for a review of leadership theories) and form the basis of leadership and management qualifications such as the Master's in Business Administration (MBA) or other training programmes.

reflective question What do you understand by human relations theories? What has been the influence of such theories on how leaders and managers motivate others or on what styles of behaviour they need to learn?

The reality of leadership and management at work

Although much effort is expended in forming *theories* about leaders and managers, other studies have focused more carefully on what leaders and managers *actually do* at work. For example, Rosemary Stewart (1975) studied the work of hundreds of managers in the UK and found that most:

- Worked at a brisk pace with little free time
- Spent a lot of time interacting with people
- Based a lot of their work on personal choice
- Did not work according to neat, well-organized models.

In the USA, John Kotter (1982) studied those in general management positions and found that they spent a lot of time dealing with issues through conversations. Managers seldom had a formal plan but worked with an informal 'agenda' to build a network so that they could achieve their objectives.

Another study by Henry Mintzberg (1973), of senior managers, also found fragmentation and variety in the way they worked, with an emphasis on verbal rather than written communication and a high use of networks (see Chapter 3, pp. 86–9 and Figure 3.1). Mintzberg suggested a range of roles for managers:

- *Interpersonal* – such as figurehead, leader or liaison
- *Informational* – such as monitor, disseminator or spokesperson
- *Decisional* – such as entrepreneur, disturbance-handler, resource allocator or negotiator.

Mintzberg's view was that 'leader' was just one role within management and so raised the crucial question of whether leadership is in fact different from management. Certainly, since the 1970s when Mintzberg completed his work, there has been growing attention to this matter, with much discussion on how leaders deal with flux, fast change and transformation, while managers deal with day-to-day operations and transactions (Bennis and Nanus, 1985). Questionnaires have even been developed which allow the assessment of leaders and managers as transformational and transactional (see Bass and Avolio, 1990). However, the model of transformational/transactional leadership has been criticized in recent years with respect to its measurement and providing a link between transformational leadership and organization performance (Van Knippenberg and Sitkin, 2013).

Rather than there being a separation between leadership and management, especially in terms of roles, we would suggest that, in practice, aspects of the two are found together. There is a tendency, however, in uncertain and difficult times for leaders to be given prominence, with the expectation that they will provide direction and maintain engagement (Holbeche, 2008). But even this tendency can be misleading as it can result in particular individuals being identified as 'leaders' – as Alimo-Metcalfe and Alban-Metcalfe (2005) showed, leadership can instead be found at all levels of an organization. In fact, there is now significant interest in plural forms of leadership (Denis et al., 2012) and how leadership, as a process of influence and mutual working, becomes distributed across teams and groups, as well as whole organizations (Thorpe et al., 2011).

This factor has implications for developing leaders and managers, as does the variety of work contexts in which leading and managing occur. For example, although most attention is given to work in larger organizations, where roles can be clearly defined, most work units throughout the world are SMEs or microbusinesses, and many of these are family owned. In such organizations, the term 'leadership' seems to have little meaning or value (Kempster and Cope, 2010). We need to remember that there are also differences between leading and managing in the public sector, the professions and voluntary organizations and social enterprises – known as the Third Sector, and across boundaries between organizations, both physically and virtually. In addition, given the variety of purposes in organizations, there are sure to be different values at work, along with different perspectives on the ethical and moral considerations of decision-making (Robinson, 2010) and the impact of decisions on the environment (Western, 2008).

Defining leadership and management development

Burgoyne et al. (2004) suggested that it is difficult to generalize about developing leaders and managers because of the variations in the contexts and the situations faced. As we have suggested, there are debates about the meanings of leadership and management, as well as about the meanings of such terms in different work contexts. Nevertheless, some generalization is possible, even if some accuracy is lost in application. For example, Gold et al. (2010) suggest two possible definitions of LMD. The first of these is applicable where it is believed possible to specify a 'correct' or 'best way' to lead or manage:

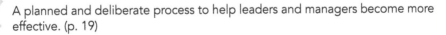

A planned and deliberate process to help leaders and managers become more effective. (p. 19)

Planning and deliberation is based on the existence of specified ideas, models and theories that leaders and managers need to learn in order to practise. Such a definition underpins many of the LMD courses and programmes available, including those that provide accreditation.

In contrast, a second definition gives more prominence to how leaders and managers really work and how learning can occur within their work:

A process of learning for leaders and managers through recognised opportunities. (p. 19)

This definition provides a recognition of how LMD might occur more informally without planning and deliberation. A key issue, however, is how leaders and managers might come to recognize learning opportunities as part of their work. Writers such as Vince and Reynolds (2010) point to the importance of reflection in capturing learning from work and events, allowing sense to be made and changes in practice to be considered. Such a process can also become more public, allowing learning to be shared with others. It is probably best to see these two definitions as contrasting poles of a dimension, as shown in Figure 14. 1.

LMD is planned
and deliberate

LMD is recognized
from work and
events

◄─────────────────────────────────────►

Figure 14.1 *Planned versus recognized LMD*

As a contrasting dimension, it is possible to see how, even in planned LMD programmes, such as a strategy workshop for senior managers, there is also the possibility for informal learning to occur as participants share ideas and catch up with the latest gossip and stories about the business. Equally, some events can be planned to allow learning to emerge. For example, outdoor management development programmes have to be to some extent planned, but much of the learning will need to be recognized through reviews and discussion. Within these definitions, there is a wide range of LMD processes, which we will consider in more detail below.

reflective question   How much of your learning is planned and how much is based on informal recognition?

Strategic leadership and management development

There is a general view that LMD is part of a 'formula for success' for a national economy. However, there are also many detractors from this view (Holmes, 1995), based on the difficulty of demonstrating how LMD affects the performance of leaders and managers, as well as the overall performance of organizations and nations (Tamkin and Denvir, 2006). Nevertheless, for over 30 years, there have been calls for the nation and organizations to take a more strategic approach to LMD. For example, in 2002, the Council for Excellence in Management and Leadership (CEML, 2002) called for a strategic body to oversee LMD based on dissatisfaction with the quality of leadership and management, and on a mismatch between the demand and supply of LMD opportunities. Efforts have been made to show the link between good management practice and performance (Advanced Institute of

Management, 2009) for example the model developed by Tamkin and Denvir (2006), shown as Figure 14.2.

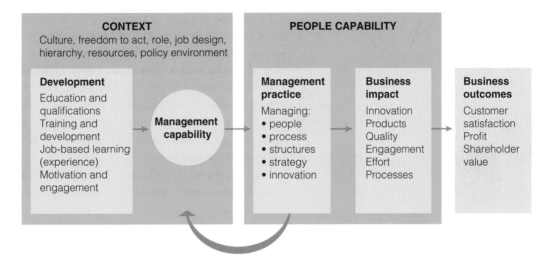

Figure 14.2 *A model of impacts on organizational performance*

Source: Tamkin, P. and Denvir, A. (2006, p.13) Strengthening the UK Evidence Base on Management and Leadership Capability. Brighton: IES. Copyright © 2006 Institute for Employment Studies. Reproduced with permission.

Strategy and LMD in organizations

In the face of change and turbulence, such as increasing globalization, greater customer demand, technological advances and economic instability, LMD could be seen as a deliberate attempt to implement a strategic response (Brown, 2007). There seem to be two possible purposes for LMD strategies (Chartered Institute of Personnel and Development, 2002):

- To sustain the business by developing leaders and managers with the skills to carry out determined roles
- To advance the business by developing new models in fast-moving sectors and turbulent environments.

The first might be considered to be the orthodox view, reflecting what Garavan et al. (1999b, p. 193) call 'the functional performance rationale' for LMD, implying a causal link between strategy, LMD and performance. This approach involves:

1   Setting the organization's strategy in response to an assessment of changes in the environment
2   Agreeing the response with the various stakeholders and interested parties
3   Using the strategy to provide guidance on the requirements for leaders and managers in terms of numbers, skills and performance
4   Using the LMD policy to translate the requirements in order to provide LMD activities
5   Assessing the outcomes to provide feedback to the organizational strategy.

Included in any policy for LMD are responses to identified weaknesses and improvements for performance, succession planning, values to be promoted (for example, diversity and ecology), new services or products to be pursued and requirements for new leader-managers.

Stockbyte

> Identifying high potential staff and developing them as leaders and managers can be an important way of making strategy, instead of simply responding to it.

The second purpose of advancing the business by developing new models suggests that LMD can also play a role in *making* strategy as well as *responding* to strategy. This also connects to a recent interest in talent management (see Chapter 5). For example, Tansley et al. (2007b) showed how a number of organizations were developing a 'talent pipeline' for senior positions by strategically identifying staff of high potential and performance for development as leaders and managers.

Allowing LMD to influence strategy formation creates a link between what leaders and managers learn and the organization's future activities. This might require a change in understanding how strategy is made. According to Mintzberg et al. (1998), most approaches to strategy are based on a *prescription* of how strategy should be carried out – this could include what leaders and managers must learn and do. This can be contrasted with a learning approach that considers the value of using ongoing actions and decisions as the source of change. In this way, strategy is said to *emerge*, often in an unplanned way. An LMD strategy would need to include how this can be achieved and also how, as Mintzberg et al. (p. 195) suggested, 'Real learning takes place at the interface of thought and action, as actors reflect on what they have done'. It should include a recognition of how learning is part of leaders' and managers' everyday practice.

reflective question   How could 'real learning' by you and your friends be achieved and influence strategy in your current work organization or college?

According to Brown (2005), a strategic approach to LMD can stimulate change-enhancing capability in management. In addition, if consistency at different levels of leadership and management can be maintained during a strategic initiative, a significant improvement in performance can occur (O'Reilly et al., 2010). There is still, however, little evidence that a strategic approach to LMD is being taken. Part of the reason seems to be a failure to distinguish between future-oriented or strategic skills and general business skills, mainly based on a conservative approach taken by LMD providers who tend to focus on short-term issues (Clarke et al., 2004), and a lack of influence of human resource development (HRD) and LMD at board level (Mackenzie et al., 2014). This is in the face of some evidence demonstrating a good relationship between manager effectiveness and higher performing organizations (McBain et al., 2012)

reflective question   Is there a strategic case for LMD?

**HRM web
links**

Visit the online resource centre at www.palgravehighered.com/bg-hrm-6e for access to
the Leadership Academy for the NHS.

Implementing leadership and management development

Evidence shows that an investment in LMD can have an impact on an organization's
performance and productivity, although this is unlikely to occur in a straightforward
manner. In implementing LMD, there are some key issues to consider, such as:

- What is understood as leadership and management?
- How can leaders and managers be assessed in terms of their development?
- How do leaders and managers learn?
- What activities can be provided for LMD?
- How can LMD activities add value?

As we seek to answer these questions in what follows, keep in mind the dual aspects of the
definitions considered earlier, in which the two perspectives of planned processes and recognized opportunities were presented. In particular, in current times, leaders and managers
can share views about work and learning via social media (Ravenscroft et al., 2012).

Models of leaders and managers

As we have already indicated, there has been an ongoing search to find particular meanings for what leaders and managers are supposed to do and the behaviours they are
required to perform. The search continues to the present day, with new models of an
'excellent' leader or an 'effective' manager readily available. Some models are even presented
in terms of being 'scientifically' valid and can be used to measure 'true' aspects of a person's
personality or behaviour.

**reflective
question**

Write down the six most important behaviours that you would expect a good manager
to demonstrate. Compare your response with those of three other people. How far do
you agree and disagree with each other?

Suffice it to say that many models of leaders and managers have been presented. One
distinction can, however, be made between models that are meant to apply to all leaders
and managers in all situations – referred to as *generic models* – and models that are
developed for application in a specific organization – referred to as *organization-specific*
models. For example, as part of their work for the CEML, Perren and Burgoyne (2002)
presented a model of abilities for generic leaders and managers, shown in Figure 14.3.

Such frameworks are useful for assessing the needs of leaders and managers, and LMD
activities can be stimulated by both the frameworks themselves and managers' needs. The
precise meanings of each cluster of abilities, such as 'Manage resources', still need to be determined, but the terms can be employed in all organizations. In contrast, organization-specific
models use the meanings that are understood within an organization and are more specific to
a particular context. In many organizations, models of leadership and management are

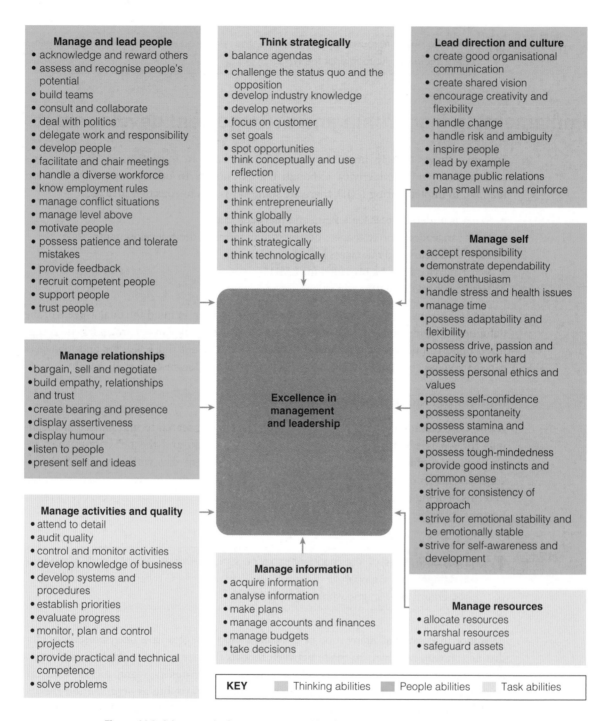

Figure 14.3 *A framework of management and leadership abilities*

Source: Perren, L. and Burgoyne, J. (2002) Management and Leadership Abilities: An Analysis of Texts, Testimony and Practice. Report from the SME working group. London: Council for Excellence in Management and Leadership. © Crown copyright 2002.

expressed as competencies, which, as we considered in Chapter 6, are descriptions of the behaviours, attributes and skills that people need to perform work effectively, or the outputs to be achieved from such work that can be assessed against performance criteria.

For many years, there has been an interest in the behaviours of leaders and managers in relation to high performance. One of the first models dealing with this was presented in the USA by Boyatzis (1982); this consisted of five clusters of competencies which emerged from his research, shown as Figure 14.4. Boyatzis made it clear that competencies alone would not explain performance: it was also necessary to consider the environment and context in which performance was taking place, as well as the particular requirements of the work. Such limitations have not, however, prevented the development of a large number of competence frameworks for both generic and organization-specific purposes. Another example of a generic leadership framework of competencies is presented by Bass and Avolio (2004), whose Multifactor Leadership Questionnaire allows a leader's style to be assessed against four leadership dimensions –

a transformational leadership – concerned with the stimulation and inspiration of followers

b transactional leadership – concerned with getting followers to comply with instructions

c laissez-faire leadership – a passive contrast to transformational and transactional leadership

d outcomes of leadership – concerned with the followers' extra effort, the effectiveness of a leader's behavior and the followers' satisfaction.

Goal and action cluster	Leadership cluster	Human resource cluster	Directing subordinates cluster	Focus on others cluster
• efficiency orientation • proactivity • diagnostic use of concepts	• self-confidence • use of oral presentations • logical thought • conceptualization	• use of socialized power • positive regard • managing group process • accurate self-assessment	• developing others • use of unilateral power • spontaneity	• self-control • perceptual objectivity • stamina and responsibility • concern with close relationships

Figure 14.4 *Boyatzis' competency clusters*
Source: Based on from Boyatzis (1982)

Another generic model is concerned with defining a set of standards for leaders and managers. In the UK, such a model was developed in 1991 to fit into the Vocational Qualifications framework in an effort to provide qualifications for leaders and managers. Since that time, the model has been revised several times, with the most recent revision in 2008. The model, known as the Management Standards, are based on a mapping exercise to identify the functions of managers at work. Six functional areas can be identified, as shown in Figure 14.5.

Whereas generic models can be used by all leaders and managers in any context or to cover a group of professionals who might work in different contexts, organization-specific models are expressed in terms of what is understood to be meaningful in one particular context. They provide clarity for leaders and managers, aligned with business requirements. For example, within one organization in the UK there was a need for more focus on the future, with competencies including 'Delivering the vision' and 'Change and creativity'.

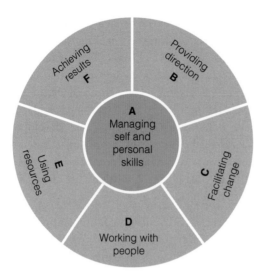

Figure 14.5 *Functional areas of management and leadership standards*

Source: © *The Management Standards Centre (available via www.management-standards.org). Reproduced with permission.*

HRM web links

> Visit the online resource centre at **www.palgravehighered.com/bg-hrm-6e** for more information on the functional areas of management and leadership defined by the Management Standards Centre and how they might be used, as well as a range of qualifications for leaders and managers provided by the Institute for Leadership and Management and the Chartered Management Institute.

Both generic and organization-specific models of competencies are popular and represent well-supported views of what leaders and managers need to learn. They are therefore the most common approach to assessing and developing leaders and managers, now becoming almost 'ubiquitous' (Bolden and Gosling, 2006, p. 147). The danger here is that the presentation of a framework of competencies can easily become confused with the reality of leading and managing. This warning has not, however, prevented the spread of the idea of competencies to include emotional intelligence (Goleman, 2006) and social and cultural competence (Boyatzis, 2008), despite the difficulties of putting these into practice.

Ever since competencies for leaders and managers appeared, they have met with critical comments. Some of the criticism relates to the vague terms and the use of language that people find difficult to understand, along with a proliferation of paperwork that can shift attention away from the purpose of LMD (Gold et al., 2010). Perhaps of more concern is the way in which competencies can falsely bring order to what is complex activity. As Lawler (2005) suggests, competencies can minimize the fluid and objective experience of leaders and managers. However, those who control the competence frameworks gain a degree of power over such experience, which can also result in pressure to control performance. Other criticisms of competencies claim that they do not relate sufficiently to business needs (Canals, 2014) and can lead to discrimination against women (Javidan et al., 2016).

Assessing the need for LMD

The various models and frameworks of leadership and management can be used to help leaders and managers determine their needs for LMD. This is not, however, an especially straightforward process since it requires an assessment of behaviour and/or performance, which, as we saw in Chapter 6, requires judgements to be made. Assessment of needs is usually incorporated into a performance management system that allows discussions of performance in the context of the organization's objectives. For example, when the phone company O_2 was preparing for its launch in 2002, all senior managers were assessed against a competence framework, resulting in a personal report containing skills gaps against which LMD, supported by coaching, could be provided.

As we also indicated in Chapter 6, judgement in assessment involves feedback. Leaders and managers, like everyone else, will vary in their response to feedback on their performance. Research by Judge et al. (1997) pointed to the importance of key psychological factors such as self-esteem, self-efficacy, locus of control and neuroticism, which affect responses. Some leaders and managers thrive on feedback, and actively seek it, which can play a role in improving their performance. VandeWalle et al. (2000) showed the importance of a manager's learning-goal orientation in seeking feedback that was then used to develop new skills, although contextual factors such as leadership, the frequency of positive feedback and the quality of relationships also play a role (Anseel et al., 2015).

reflective question Are you a feedback-seeker? Do you seek feedback to develop new skills, or do you use feedback to avoid negative judgements?

As we have shown in previous chapters (Chapters 5 and 6), assessment/development centres, appraisal and multisource feedback can be used to assess performance and determine HRD needs. For leaders and managers, multisource feedback can involve:

- Appraisal by staff – *upward appraisal*
- Appraisal by fellow managers – *peer appraisal*
- Appraisal by the higher level senior manager – *top-down appraisal*
- Appraisal by the manager and/or staff/peers – *180-degree appraisal*
- Appraisal by the manager, staff and peers – *360-degree appraisal*
- Appraisal by the manager, staff, peers, customers, suppliers and others who are in an interdependent relationship with the manager – *540-degree appraisal*.

Multisource feedback is a demanding approach to LMD, and since it involves feedback from different angles, it needs to be supported (Brutus and Derayeh, 2002), with the results used to set goals for action that are in turn complemented by coaching (Luthans and Peterson, 2003). However, all assessments of leaders and managers involve self-appraisal, which inevitably carries face validity but is likely to be distorted by bias and disagreements with the views of others, as we showed in Chapter 6. Upward appraisal can complement self-appraisal and can be viewed positively if it is anonymous and provides constructive feedback (Antonioni, 1994). Yet where leaders and managers rate themselves more highly than staff rate them, this is unlikely to lead to changes in their behaviour, although some might reduce their own ratings in response to lower staff ratings (Dierendonck et al., 2007). They might also distort negative feedback by attributing the cause to factors other than their own behaviour, such as others, the situation and so on (Jordan and Audia, 2012).

Peer appraisal is more likely to lead to LMD if negative evaluation can be avoided. Leaders and managers are probably anxious to avoid disturbing relationships with each other, so will be less inclined to give formal feedback on performance; they may, however, do so informally (Peiperl, 2001). Peer appraisal is also likely to be accepted in professional environments such as schools and hospitals (Dupee et al., 2011).

Moving from upward and peer appraisal to 360-degree appraisal provides a more rounded view of performance but requires confidence and trust on the part of leaders and managers since the barrage of feedback received could potentially make the process deeply negative and demoralizing (Gold et al., 2010). For such reasons, 360-degree appraisal schemes can become unworkable (Fletcher, 1998). The balance of such schemes has to be tilted toward development, and this needs to be made clear to leaders and managers in both words and actions in order to avoid confusion and possible cynicism. More research on how self-awareness is measured and affected by assessment methods is needed (Day et al., 2014).

Whatever emerges from the process, goals need to be set, motivation for applying learning discussed, LMD undertaken and support provided if improvements in performance are to be achieved (Smither et al., 2008; Bhatti et al., 2013). As with any approach to LMD, personal development plans that are meaningful to leaders and managers can be motivating and effective in creating a virtuous process of performance, review and learning (see McCall, 2010).

Approaches to learning in LMD

As in all HRD activities, learning is central, and in LMD the topic of learning has received significant attention from researchers. One of the reasons for this is that LMD often requires an investment of resources that can easily be wasted if the way in which leaders and managers learn is not considered in the delivery of LMD activities. Gold et al. (2010) highlight the learning processes that work well for leaders and managers as one of three aspects that need to be considered for effectiveness in LMD. In addition to this, the meaning of effective behaviour for leaders and managers needs to be identified, and processes developed that will help leaders and managers achieve this behaviour.

These aspects of effectiveness in LMD can create difficulties where, for example, people other than the leaders or managers decide what leaders and managers need to learn. Generic or generalized skills or knowledge, for example, can result in problems of transfer of learning (Gilpin-Jackson and Bushe, 2007), or even worse, if leaders and managers see little value in undertaking LMD, referred to by

Image Source

For LMD to be effective it is important to think of leaders and managers as adult learners, and consider not only their drivers and motivators, but also the considerable resource-rich experience they bring to learning.

Gold et al. (2010, p. 115) as 'vicious learning'. To avoid such an effect, it is important to pay attention to what leaders and managers see as relevant in their roles, working with principles set by Malcolm Knowles (1998), as follows:

- The learner is largely self-directed but has a conditioned expectation to want to be dependent and to be taught.
- The learner arrives with experience, which in effect means that, with many kinds of learning, adults are themselves a very rich resource for each other, and that there is a wide range of experience in any group.
- Adults are ready to learn when they have a need to perform better in some aspect of their lives.
- For the most part, adults do not learn for the sake of learning – they learn in order to be able to perform a task, solve a problem or live in a more satisfying way.
- Although adults will respond to some external motivators (for example, a better job or a salary increase), the more potent motivators are internal – self-esteem, recognition, greater self-confidence and self-actualization.

reflective question 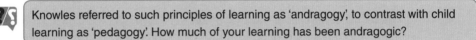 Knowles referred to such principles of learning as 'andragogy', to contrast with child learning as 'pedagogy'. How much of your learning has been andragogic?

Both andragogy and pedagogy are found in approaches to LMD. Holman (2000) has provided a framework that shows how the approach of the learner is considered in LMD:

- *Academic liberalism* – the pursuit of objective knowledge as principles and theories, through access to expertise via books, seminars and so on.
- *Experiential liberalism* – experience is the source of learning that provides ideas for practice, through reflection on practice.
- *Experiential vocationalism* – profiles of skills and competencies, defined by organizations or an occupational area, which need to be learned for practice as considered earlier in the models and frameworks of competencies.
- *Experiential critical* – leaders and managers, through a questioning of assumptions that underpin their practice, find a degree of 'emancipation' from particular aspects of their lives at work that reflect dominant or powerful forces.

Within the framework, you might be able to identify some of the theories of learning that we considered in Chapter 7. For example, cognitive theories might be more prominent in situations where leaders and managers are required to learn ideas and knowledge presented to them, and behaviour theories when particular skills have to be put into practice and then reinforced through feedback. Experiential learning, especially the learning styles models presented by Kolb (1984) and Honey and Mumford (1996) in the UK, have been very influential in LMD. This relates partly to their value in enabling leaders and managers to assess their learning preferences and styles through questionnaires, and to the value of the learning cycle in helping with the design of LMD events.

As we indicated in Chapter 7, there has been some critique of 'learning style questionnaires'. Reynolds' (1997) main argument against the models of learning styles is the decontextualization of learning and the prominence given to individuals; this reduces the complexity of a leader or manager's interaction within their context. Nevertheless, it is still possible to make use of experiential learning in LMD, especially if the social and political features of organizational life can be incorporated (Reynolds, 2009). One approach is to learn in and from practice, and this is connected to Lave and Wenger's (1991) situated learning theory. The key idea is that learning occurs through practice at work, often informally and incidentally. There is a link here to the idea of 'natural learning', identified by Davies and Easterby-Smith (1984) as a crucial source of LMD, especially by dealing with problems and finding new ways of handling difficult situations. Situated learning provides a theory to explain these processes by showing how learning occurs within a 'community of practice' where newcomers or 'novices' learn to participate in the community by assisting and learning from more experienced members. Such newcomers remain on the 'periphery' of the community but learn to move from this position by observing others and copying them (Fox, 1997). Informal or natural learning is particularly important for leaders and managers of SMEs (Fuller-Love, 2006), where most learning happens by solving problems, making mistakes, copying others and so on (Beaver et al., 1998; Gibb, 1997). Furthermore, such working is seldom recognized by the managers *as learning*.

Providing activities for LMD

There has never been a shortage of ideas for LMD. As the CEML (2002) report suggested, there is a large supply of opportunities, but the supply is 'mixed on quality' and 'confusing' (p. 4). Much of the provision is generic so is less likely to accommodate the specific circumstances of leaders, managers and their organizations. Furthermore, as Bolden (2005) points out, there tends to be an overemphasis on individual development rather than the development of leadership and management capacity. Following Day (2001), especially with reference to leadership development, there can be a choice between a focus on individuals or on LMD activities that instead build networks and relationships and allow ideas to be shared throughout an organization. This view allows more recognition of what Gronn (2008) refers to as hybrid configurations of leadership, ranging from the individual as a solo leader to a collective and distributed understanding of leadership. This variation is shown as a dimension in Figure 14.6. This dimension of possible targets for LMD also presents a problem for those appointed as individual leaders because it suggests that influence and power can be exerted throughout an organization (Harris, 2008).

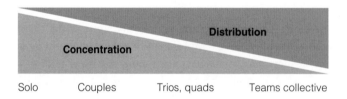

Figure 14.6 *Concentration and distribution in LMD*

Source: Ross, L., Rix, M. and Gold, J. (2005) Learning distributed leadership, Part 1. Industrial and Commercial Training, 37(3): 130–7. Copyright © Emerald Group Publishing Limited 2005.

Although the focus of LMD can vary, so too can the approach to LMD, as we have already indicated in Figure 14.1. Based on the two definitions of LMD presented, we can also see how this is supported by different theories of learning, with informal and unplanned learning often occurring. Working with a typology based on that suggested by Rodgers et al. (2003a, 2003b), which combines Figures 14.1 and 14.6, we propose considering some of the main types of LMD provision. The typology is shown as Figure 14.7. This can be used to consider LMD activities, which can also be combined to form programmes, sometimes lasting several months. A quick search on Google will reveal the vast range of activities available for LMD, from the obvious training courses in leadership skills or strategy to the use of drama, poetry, film and Shakespeare for learning (see Edwards et al., 2015). Here, we can only provide brief coverage of some of the key activities indicated by Figure 14.7.

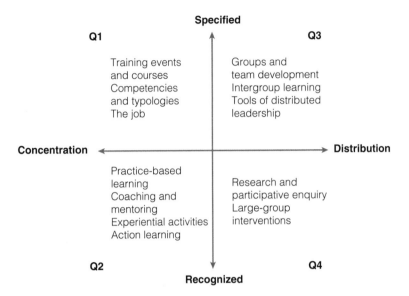

Figure 14.7 *A typology of LMD activities*

Source: Adapted from Rodgers, H., Gold, J., Frearson, M., Holden, R. (2003) The rush to leadership: explaining leadership development in the public sector. Paper presented at the Leadership Conference, Lancaster, UK.

Q1

Training events and courses

These are usually focused on individuals or small groups and teams. Training forms the basis of what most people understand as LMD (Suutari and Viitala, 2008). Events are often based on theories, models and ideas that are presented as 'best practice'. They are often delivered 'off-site', and therefore away from the location of practice. We can also include in this section formally organized courses, which may lead to accreditation in the form of a qualification, such as an MBA. Research suggests that leaders and managers value qualifications that impact on abilities (McBain et al., 2012). In either case, there is usually a clear understanding of the objectives or outcomes to be achieved or assessed. Of course, such a specification can create a gap between what individual leaders and managers *need* and what is *provided* (Antonacopoulou, 1999). Formal qualifications such as MBAs are considered to be too focused on skills of analysis at the expense of implementation (Mintzberg, 2004).

Competencies and typologies

LMD events and activities are often based on models of behaviours, skills and so on. There are many such models, such as Belbin's team role inventory (Belbin, 1981) for developing management teams, which are often based on a questionnaire to allow diagnosis or even feedback from others.

> How do you feel about completing questionnaires to assess your management, leadership, group or team role preferences?

The job

Plans can be made for leaders and managers to learn about the roles they undertake. For example, any change in job or job content can provide an opportunity for LMD, although this is not always grasped by leaders and managers. For example, new customers provide a chance for leaders and managers to develop new relationships, which can lead to increased orders for products or services. Other planned approaches can include a secondment as part of a succession plan (Kur and Bunning, 2002).

Q2

Practice-based learning

While formal moves into and between jobs can provide sources for LMD, it is also clear that many leaders and managers learn informally, perhaps by accident or incidentally through experience and practice (Marsick and Watkins, 1990). Crucially, many opportunities go unnoticed, so leaders and managers need to make such learning more deliberate by reviewing and reflecting on the actions taken (Eraut, 2000b). Learning from work is now considered to be a crucial source of LMD, and recognizing the possibilities for this is seen as a way of questioning assumptions that underpin actions, allowing new thoughts and ideas to emerge (Raelin, 2011). Projects relating to specific tasks or problems are a way of making learning explicit, benefiting both participants and the organization; if accreditation can be gained, they also allow rigour and theoretical contribution to be considered (Rounce et al., 2007).

One of the difficulties of practice-based learning relates to the requirement for recognition, as many leaders and managers learn without being aware that they have learned (Kempster, 2009). For this reason, as suggested above, review and reflection are advocated as ways in which leaders and managers 'can engage more directly and effectively with their worlds' (Sadler-Smith, 2006, p. 185). Review and reflection allow a consideration of what has happened in key events, but also act to bring to the surface attitudes and perspectives on meaning, revealing the assumptions that are being made. Reflection and a subsequent analysis of events that uncovers underlying assumptions can be threatening, but is also a way by which leaders and managers can become more critical of their practice and find new ways of taking action (Mezirow, 1990). There are links between practice-based learning and leaders and managers taking responsibility for their own development, usually referred to as self-development (Pedler et al., 2013), and action learning (see below). In addition, given the critique of leaders and managers in recent years (Kelly, 2014), if leaders and managers can learn to reflect critically on their practice, they might avoid some of the negative impressions that are formed about their behaviour.

> How much time have you taken over the reflective questions in this book, and how beneficial have you found it to reflect on such questions?

HRM as I see it

Lana Kularajah

Senior HR Business Partner, Transform Aid International/Baptist World Aid Australia

www.bwaa.org.au

Transform Aid International/Baptist World Aid Australia is an Australian international aid and development agency, which works together with churches, denominations and agencies to end poverty through community development, child centred community development and disaster management with Christian partner organisations in 18 countries across Asia, Africa and the Pacific. They also educate and empower supporters in Australia via advocacy programs and marketing resources. Transform Aid International is based in Sydney, Australia.

Lana Kularajah is an HR professional with more than 10 years' experience, having started as an HR Assistant. Her career has been focused in the not-for-profit sector, in community services and now in an international aid agency. Her early role as a generalist HR professional in a large community services organisation involved working within the complex Australian industrial relations environment, implementing industrial relations reforms. Her current role in a small not-for-profit agency involves all aspects of HR management, and some of the key priorities have been devising and implementing a leadership development program and establishing the HR function.

Click on Lana's photo in your ebook to watch her talking about mentoring programmes in leadership and management initiatives, then think about the following questions:

1   How does Lana distinguish between hard and soft skills in leadership? What are the individual and organisational challenges for LMD?
2   How does Lana view the dangers of leadership development as a 'tick-box' exercise?
3   What did Lana's organisation do to ensure more 'voices of influence' were heard? How did this benefit women or minority groups?
4   Why was mentoring introduced and who did it help?

Coaching and mentoring

Leaders and managers learn better when they receive support from others in helping to identify opportunities for learning and reviewing what happened. Much of this is unplanned, and the main learning experience of many leaders and managers seems to be 'being thrown in at the deep end', along with watching others as role models (Watson and Harris, 1999, p. 107). To make learning more explicit, coaching and mentoring are identified as important. As we have already indicated in Chapter 7, coaching has seen significant growth in the UK (Institute of Leadership and Management, 2011), and many organizations are seeking to develop coaching cultures. In addition to coaching by line managers, there has for senior managers been the development of *executive coaching*, in which someone outside the organization provides the service. Research suggests that this leads to the formation of more specific goals, more effort to make improvements and better ratings from staff (Smither et al., 2003). Gender does not seem to make a difference here – male managers can be coached by women and vice versa, with the same effect (Gray and Gore-gaokar, 2010). Beattie et al. (2014) show that coaching can take a number of forms, including peer coaching and team coaching.

Whereas coaching and executive coaching can help leaders and managers learn from everyday issues and their work, *mentoring* is seen as a process for the longer term and, in contrast to coaching, is usually undertaken by a more experienced manager as mentor in relation to a more junior manager as mentee or protégé. It is often informal and is concerned with careers, personal growth and all-round development (Mumford, 1993). Research has shown the success of mentoring for personal development and careers in such contexts as medicine (Sambunjak et al., 2006). However, mentoring does not always work, and it can even lead to negative experiences such as the mentor taking undue credit for the mentee's accomplishments (see Simon and Eby, 2003, for more problems). It is therefore important for both parties in a mentoring relationship to understand what they want. Both parties must also be willing to learn (Garvey et al., 2014).

Experiential activities

Drawing on experiential learning theories, activities can be provided to stimulate the involvement of leaders and managers so they can reflect on aspects of their roles, including key features of organizational life that are often left unconsidered such as unfair selection practices or the pride staff have in working with members of the public (Reynolds and Vince, 2007). Activities can be challenging, which also allows emotions to be revealed, in particular where problems that do not have clear outcomes are set. Such problems provide points of analogy for leaders and managers, who can then, through review and reflection, consider possibilities for work application. Experiential learning is often associated with management development undertaken outdoors, focusing on personal and team development, although there is danger of a poor transfer of learning into practice (Lau and McLean, 2013). Outdoor management development requires a balance between task completion and the chance to discuss learning and application at work, making use of models such as Adair's (2005) action-centred leadership model, which considers task needs, individual needs and team needs.

Experiential activities can be extended beyond outdoor management development to include the use of drama (Olivier and Verity, 2008), music, comedy and the arts in general. In addition, sports such as golf, rugby and even falconry have been used as sources of experience for learning about leadership and management. Garavan et al. (2015) show that what they refer to as 'arts-based' LMD can have a positive impact in terms of emotional intelligence and the feedback orientations of leaders and managers.

reflective question Is there a link between learning to play golf and leading at work?

Action learning

Leaders and managers form a small group or 'set' of between five and eight participants to work on difficult problems, agreeing to take action and then at subsequent meetings reviewing the learning from the actions taken. Pedler (2008) suggests that the process of action learning can help individuals, teams and organizations to deal with change and innovation.

Reg Revans (1982) was the originator of action learning, developing the process in the UK during the 1950s. This was based on the assumption that leaders and managers learn best by working on real problems that are important to them by meeting with a group or set of other leaders and managers as 'comrades in adversity' (Revans, 1982, p. 636). Participants agree to help each other through questions and discussion that enable possible actions to emerge. The attention to questions in action learning is given prominence in Revan's well-known learning equation of $L = P + Q$, where P is the programmed knowledge or answers already available to deal with problems in the form of books or theories found in articles or even the views of experts, and Q is the questioning insight that arises from thinking about and reflecting on problems when no one has an answer, using questions about possibilities that lead to actions. By then taking action and reporting on the learning, leaders and managers can advance their understanding of how to live and act in their roles (Anderson and Gold, 2009). Action has to be taken beyond the set, requiring interaction between the participant and the situation he or she is trying to influence, referred to by Revans as system gamma. More recently, others have developed a more critical approach to action learning that makes the tensions and power dynamics arising from such interactions more explicit (Ram, 2013).

HRM web links

> Visit the online resource centre at **www.palgravehighered.com/bg-hrm-6e** for more about action learning.

Q3

Groups, teams and community development

Research on distributed leadership shows the importance of working with groups and teams in order to create alignment between them (Leithwood et al., 2008). There are well-known models of group and team development, and leaders and managers can become more involved as team coaches, a role that helps teams to improve their performance through reflection and dialogue (Clutterbuck, 2007).

Intergroup learning

Groups and teams increasingly need to find ways of collaborating across boundaries, both within and between organizations and across cultures (Bochner, 2013). Since each group or team can be seen as a figuration of shared leadership, working across boundaries becomes an example of 'co-configuration' (Victor and Boynton, 1998, p. 195). This requires joint training in skills of debate and dialogue to bring to the surface differing values, cultures and disciplines (Tomlinson, 2003).

Tools of distributed leadership

As research into distributed leadership has continued, it has also become more possible to specify how to implement this approach in practice. It is important for distributed leadership to be recognized in contexts where staff have greater discretion for making decisions with implications for joint working, such as projects within and between organizations (Bolden, 2011). It becomes essential to align work practices for change and performance improvement (Heck and Hallinger, 2010).

Q4

Research and participative enquiry

Specified approaches to distributed leadership will only go so far since much of the influence that is exercised as leadership occurs in daily practice that is not easily seen or understood; the effects are likely to be emergent (Spillane et al., 2008). Action-oriented approaches to research and enquiry, to make improvements by involving many others, allow leaders and managers to learn about how influence can be exerted as leadership while seeking to align activities and intervene where necessary. One approach to participation is found in appreciative enquiry (Reed, 2007), a process that reveals how good practice occurs and identifies the values that inform practice. Gold (2014) shows how appreciative inquiry can be combined with action learning to attempt a shift of culture in one organization during a time of significant change.

HRM web links   Visit the online resource centre at **www.palgravehighered.com/bg-hrm-6e** to learn more about appreciative enquiry.

Large-group interventions

It is possible for leaders and managers to use large-group interventions to create a momentum for 'whole-systems change'. The outcomes are emergent, and the processes require the engagement and commitment of participants to generate ideas and take action. One approach, for example, is to use open space technology (Owen, 2008) – conferences in which the agenda is set by participants who respond to a key question that is important. The events at the conference emerge from the participants, as do the actions that are agreed.

Across all quadrants, it is likely that leaders and managers will complete some of the activities using digital media to access online and virtual provision. LMD has to include approaches to blended learning, in which at least part of the learning is delivered via online media, and the creation of learning communities. Fleck (2012) argues that blended learning and the development of a learning community allows more scope for integrating a diverse range of perspectives from different locations, cultures and political contexts. As many existing leaders and managers, as

Stockbyte/Punchstock

Open space technology encourages participants to take control of their learning and can be a powerful source of momentum for change.

HRM in practice 14.1

Evaluating the Modern Leaders Programme at Skipton Building Society

Skipton Building Society's Modern Leaders Programme (MLP) aims to develop leadership capability and align leaders with the organization's strategy. A key aspect has been to develop culture in line with the declared values of One Team, Ownership and Trust. The backdrop was years of underinvestment in people while the organization was focusing on surviving the economic recession. Delivering The MLP has involved significant internal resources, and the process by which evaluation assesses the impact on both individuals and the organization has been woven into the programme's design from the outset.

Crucially, senior managers from the Executive team, or 'Exco', have been involved throughout. A Steering Group was set up before the programme started, with a remit to both receive and provide challenge related to the changes (both expected and unexpected) that were noticed as the programme developed. The learning and development team recognized that both quantitative and qualitative measures would be needed. The Steering Group comprised the Chief HR Officer, Chief Operating Officer and Distribution Director, Head of Organisational Development and Leadership and Learning Manager. The group met on a 6-weekly basis and reviewed the impact of learning on performance across the Skipton. Data reviewed includes shifts in 360° ratings for leaders before and after the programme, trends identified by the review and assessment process and performance results. Early decisions for the Steering Group were largely related to programme design and the pace of the roll-out. This allowed decisions to be made regarding the content and mix of groups, for example in terms of a cohort's blend of head office and branch distribution, to ensure the maximum cultural impact.

Three-way contracting between a peer coach, line manager and leader allowed clear learning objectives to be agreed at the outset of the programme. A 360° view based on a behavioural framework, current development plan and performance objectives has contributed to shaping the clearly defined learning objectives. This process was repeated at month 10, and the change in performance and effectiveness in role was evaluated. It was noticed that some 360° scores have gone down as more honest, and challenging feedback is both asked for and provided by leaders, as they become more skilled and recognize the value that feedback can have on changing performance.

Peer coaching groups have provided leaders with the space to develop trusting relationships with colleagues from across the Skipton. Over the five peer coaching sessions required, leaders have been able to develop from a directive style of offering solutions and advice to colleagues, to a more collaborative and then non-directive style of support. The value of the experience is shown by the fact that some groups have continued to meet long after completing the required number of sessions. There are also 'Alumni' events based on open space working, enabling those who have completed the programme to meet to create learning sessions together.

The review and assessment process provides a clear statement of intent that learning and shifting performance is not optional. At month 13, the review and assessment is separate from the learning experience, and the Head of Organisational Development and Leadership, and the Learning Manager are not involved in assessing the impact that learning has had on individuals. This ensures that leaders do not see time spent learning as purely about 'passing a test' at the end of the programme. Two Exco members are involved in the review and assessment days, and the highly supportive nature of the day and the time taken to provide high-quality feedback has meant that leaders continue to learn through this experience as well.

Stop! Leadership development is an important activity undertaken by many organizations. But is the investment in leadership development programmes worth it? How can an organization justify the investment in leadership programmes and do such programmes impact on organisation performance?

Sources and further information: Easterby-Smith (1994) provides a good consideration of the purpose of evaluation in leadership development. Thorpe et al. (2009) present a view of evaluation that takes account of wider system impacts on leadership development, and methods to ensure data is collected to show added value.

Note: This feature was written by Jeff Gold.

well as future leaders and managers, adopt technologies that connect them to sources of knowledge, Siemens (2014) argues, the technology in turn affects how leaders and managers think. This would suggest even more need for leaders and managers to become critical of how they learn.

Can LMD activities add value?

Given that significant resources can be devoted to LMD through the activities referred to above, it becomes crucial to show that value has been added. This is especially true in times when there is competition for resources, such as during a recession, and politics is bound to play a role (Kim and Cervero, 2007). Thorpe et al. (2009) argue that evaluation of LMD is straightforward to consider – find what works and what does not, learn the lessons, and then apply the lessons. However, as we have already shown in Chapter 7, evaluation is not an easy process, especially where there is a desire to show a return on investment – something of a holy grail in HRD (Russ-Eft and Preskill, 2005) – and, we would suggest, also when the value added can often be something of an 'act of faith'.

reflective question Why do you think that it might be difficult to evaluate LMD, and why might the value added by LMD activities be an 'act of faith'?

In Chapter 7, we presented mechanistic ideas of evaluation, usually connected to levels or stages of results, such as the Kirkpatrick (1998) model. This also has strong appeal in LMD, but, as Gold et al. (2010) suggest, there are also difficulties with such models based on the fact that:

- LMD is more than just attending training courses and needs to include less formal activities
- Leaders and managers often complete and participate in a range of LMD activities, formally and informally, which occur in relation to each other
- Leaders and managers learn in different ways and differ in how they seek activities
- Leadership and management work takes place in different contexts, and this affects how far leaders and managers can use ideas they learn as part of LMD and change their behaviour.

Issues such as these affect decisions relating to why LMD is being evaluated and how techniques of evaluation can be used. Easterby-Smith (1994) suggested that there are four reasons to evaluate LMD – proving, improving, learning and controlling – and that the choice of purpose is decided on grounds of expediency such as stakeholders' interests. Anderson's (2007) consideration of evaluation, for example, gives prominence to the needs of decision-makers so that they can assess whether investment in learning is contributing to organizational performance. Thorpe et al. (2009) argue that evaluation of LMD has to be holistic to take account of wider system impacts, but also has to acknowledge the need for data to show evidence of value added. Figure 14.8 shows the key features of this view.

As leaders and managers participate in a range of LMD events, whether formal or informal, the intentions of the participants, perhaps as goals and plans, are both used as data and monitored as learning proceeds, perhaps through reviews with a coach or a group of peers. The effects of the system become apparent in terms of how leaders and managers

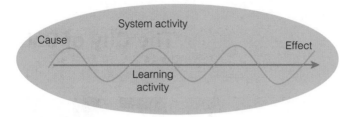

Figure 14.8 *Holistic evaluation*

Source: Thorpe, R., Gold, J., Anderson, L., Burgoyne, J., Wilkinson, D. and Malby, B. (2008) Towards 'Leaderful' Communities in the North of England (2nd edn). Cork: Oak Tree Press. Copyright © Oak Tree Press. Reproduced with permission.

can apply learning, and also in how the effects might be prevented from being applied due to the factors we identified in Chapter 7 as the learning climate or environment. Holistic evaluation was the approach employed at Skipton Building Society for its Modern Leaders Programme (see HRM in practice 14.1). The approach allowed evaluation to support a transfer of learning as well as improve the programme and provide evidence to show a return on investment. An impact assessment completed 5 months after the programme had finished showed a consistent strong impact and transfer (Hall et al., 2014). The programme at Skipton ran over 3 years and involved more than 20 cohorts of 15 leaders and managers. Using an evolutionary evaluation (Urban et al., 2014), it was apparent that there were different phases of the programme with variation between cohorts. The programme evolved from initiation, where evaluation was concerned with ensuring satisfaction and with the participants' reactions, to improving the programme through to stability, where evaluation was concerned with measureable impact and then cost-effectiveness.

reflective question What can be done to improve a return on investment in LMD programmes?

case study

The City of Sahali

The setting

The city of Sahali is located in the central interior of British Columbia, Canada. Like the rest of the Canadian public sector, the City Council is facing a wave of retirements as the working population ages and the first group of 'Baby-boomers' begin to leave the workplace. This year, the largest group of employees in the known history of the City gave notice to retire, with increasing numbers of retirements from the higher levels of management being predicted. Even more problematic, there have been, as a result of recent retirements, major changes in the senior management team, including a new City Mayor, Chief Administrative Officer and Human Resources Director.

Getty Images/iStockphoto Thinkstock Images monkeybusinessimag

The problem

There has been a clear need to develop these new leaders, and their future successors, in order to cope with ongoing internal and external demands and tax-payers' expectations. As a result, the City recently made the decision to hire a private consulting firm to develop and provide a customized leadership development training programme called Leading for Excellence. Although the City's unions were in support of the initiative, this was to require a large amount of staff time and financial resources. Based on the needs identified by the City's Human Resources Department, the training programme's curriculum focused on three main areas:

- Module I: Self-management – management roles, values, skills, and time and stress management (2 days)
- Module II: Management of the team – interpersonal communication, coaching and performance management (2 days)
- Module III: Management of the organization – understanding the organization and how to create more interdepartmental collaboration (2 days).

The fourth module, which lasted 1 day, focused on the integration of learning, motivation, learning from peers and creating successful daily habits.

Module participants were divided into departmental groups of either management or union supervisory staff. Their inclusion in the training programme was prompted by a recognition of the important role that union supervisors play in implementing HR policies and providing leadership to staff on a daily basis, and by a desire to promote unionized staff into management posts as vacancies became available. Managers or union supervisors attended the first three modules with their group, and joined their counterparts from the same department in the fourth module. The intent was to keep a department's managers and union supervisors apart for the first three modules in order to encourage open and honest discussion.

Shortly after the training programme had been completed, Jennifer Chang, the City's new Human Resources Director, scheduled a meeting with her staff. The first item on the agenda was to discuss how to justify the expenditure for training that was earmarked in the department's budget. At the meeting, Jennifer expressed a concern that evaluating the effectiveness of the training had not been considered when the programme had been designed or developed. Janna McCormick, a junior HR Adviser, was adamant that it was too late. She remarked, 'We don't have a baseline measure prior to the training to compare with changes after the programme was completed.'

Senior HR Adviser, Nathan Cole, disagreed, saying it was still possible. He suggested, 'We can determine whether desired behaviour has been brought back into the workplace by surveying those who work with the participants and who may observe changes in their behaviour. We can also see if there are any organizational changes resulting from this changed behaviour.' Jennifer asked Nathan to submit a proposal on how such an evaluation could be undertaken so that it could be given to senior management staff at their next meeting.

The assignment

Working either alone or in a group, prepare a report drawing on this chapter and other researched material, addressing the following:

1 What challenges does the Human Resources Department face in identifying any changes resulting from the training?
2 What sources could the Human Resources Department draw upon to gather data to evaluate the training's organizational impact?
3 What recommendations would you make in regard to evaluating future leadership training programmes?

Note: This case study was written by Lori Rilkoff and Jeff Gold.

summary

➤ Leaders and managers and those involved in their development have been considered to be partly to blame for the global financial crisis that began in 2008.

➤ There are differing meanings of leadership and management, both in theory and in practice. It is suggested that both leadership and management occur in practice, but in uncertain and difficult times, leaders tend to be given prominence.

➤ LMD can be defined as a planned and deliberate process, and also as a process of learning that emerges and has to be recognized.

➤ There are different purposes for LMD strategies, including sustaining the business by developing leaders and managers with the right skills, or advancing business by developing new models based on what leaders and managers learn.

➤ There are both generic and organization-specific models of leadership and management, expressed as skills, attributes or competencies. Models of leadership and management, especially competencies, have been subjected to critical comment.

➤ Models and frameworks of leadership and management can be used to help leaders and managers determine their needs for learning and development, but this is not a straightforward process as it requires an assessment of behaviour and/or performance. Many leaders and managers face multisource feedback.

➤ There are many LMD activities that focus on individuals and more collective units. Activities can also be specified and pre-set, or recognized and emergent, requiring reflection and review. Generic or generalized skills or knowledge can result in problems with the transfer of learning.

➤ Evaluation needs to consider wider system impacts as well as the collection of data to show evidence of value added. Evaluation can also help leaders and managers prepare to cope with difficulties in applying learning.

review questions

1 How would LMD in an architect's firm differ from that in a financial services organization?
2 What strategy for LMD is needed to avoid unethical and dangerous decisions for organizations and the wider society?
3 Do competency frameworks provide the best way of assessing and developing leaders and managers?
4 360-degree feedback is 'scary' but 'powerful' for leaders and managers. Discuss.
5 How can evaluation of LMD become more than an 'act of faith'?

further reading

Reading these articles and chapters can help you gain a better understanding and potentially a higher grade for your HRM assignment.

➤ Antonacopoulou, E. P. (2006) *Introducing Reflexive Critique into the Business Curriculum: Reflections on the Lessons Learned*. London: Advanced Institute of Management.

➤ Hezlett, S. (2016) Enhancing experience-driven leadership development. *Advances in Developing Human Resources*, **18**(3): 369–89.

➤ Mabey, C. (2013) Leadership development in organizations: multiple discourses and diverse practice. *International Journal of Management Reviews*, **15**(4): 359–80.

➤ Mavin, S. (2006) Venus envy: problematizing solidarity behaviour and queen bees. *Women in Management Review*, **21**(4): 264–76.

➤ Moen, F. and Skaalvik, E. (2009) The effect from executive coaching on performance psychology. *International Journal of Evidence Based Coaching and Mentoring*, **7**(2): 31–41.

➤ Raelin, J. A. (2014) The ethical essence of leaderful practice. *Journal of Leadership, Accountability and Ethics*, **11**(1): 64–72.

vocabulary checklist for ESL students

 Click here in your interactive ebook for a list of HRM terminology and vocabulary that has appeared in this chapter.

Visit the online resource centre at **www.palgravehighered.com/bg-hrm-6e** for lots of extra resources to help you get to grips with this chapter, including study tips, HRM skills development guides, summary lecture notes, tips for English as a Second Language (ESL) students and more.

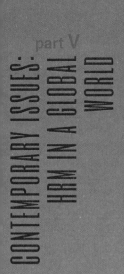

chapter 15

organizational culture and HRM

Getty

objectives

After studying this chapter, you should be able to:

1 Explain the relationship between national culture and organizational culture

2 Define organizational culture and be aware of notions of dominant culture, cultural diversity, subcultures and countercultures

3 Explain different theoretical perspectives on organizational culture

4 Understand how senior managers strive to change the culture of their organization and the role of human resource management in the change process

In 2015, credit card company Capital One scooped the award for 'Best Workplaces – Large Category' – for the third consecutive year. 'Capital One is a unique place to work that is fun, values-based and every bit committed to customer care. It is a place where employees feel empowered to make a difference. Where communication forms one of a set of values that underpin the company's vision, which is designed to transform and develop a culture built around responsible lending, customer care and support', explains Karen Bowes, VP International HR and Sustainability (Great Place to Work Institute, 2015, p. 21). An organization's 'culture' refers to an amorphous collection of interrelated values, understandings and behaviours that is shared by its workforce. For some, it 'smacks of a lack of communication, or at least trust' (Ambasna-Jones, The Guardian, 2016, p. 25). Academic research, however, reports on workplace cultures that are far less stimulating than Capital One's. Workplaces with a 'binge-working culture' (Campbell, 2010), a 'long-hours culture' in which employees regard long working days as 'a badge of honour' (Chatzitheochari and Arber, 2009), work that is not fun but centrally driven by a 'tick-box culture' (Travis, The Guardian, 2011) and an absence of diversity perpetuating 'pinstripes and braces' and the 'laddish' culture (Dunkley, 2015, p. 4).

introduction

Workplace norms of work and leisure activities can be seen as an expression of organizational culture and power. The work–life balance discourse can illustrate that the different ways in which we *experience* work are shaped by a form of hegemony, and by what we believe, what we value and what we see as legitimate (Kärreman and Alvesson, 2009; Schneider, 2000). These intangible informal structures or 'ways of doing' work can be thought of as 'organizational culture' (Ashkanasy et al., 2011). Understanding organizational culture is an important consideration for managers as well as for the recruitment of talented employees. Norton at al. (2015, p. 325), for example, observed that, 'Without a cultural framework to provide meaning, [management] interventions may only be short-lived', and ethical high performance organizational cultures have strong effects on attracting and retaining talent (Kontoghiorghes, 2015). In the human resource management (HRM) canon, organizational culture has been described as a 'key lever' and the 'holy grail' to release consensus, flexibility and commitment (Beer et al., 1984; Storey, 2007). Critical management scholars, however, are highly sceptical about claims of managing cultures, regarding such claims as naive and as doing little to remove the 'structured antagonism' found in the employment relationship (Edwards, 1986, 1995).

This chapter begins by introducing the concept of national culture and discusses its relevance to the contemporary workplace. We will then explore the complex concept of organizational culture – what it is, and how it manifests itself within the modern workplace. We examine different theoretical perspectives on organizational culture, and finally we will take a critical look at the clusters of HRM practices that are used to change and manage culture.

reflective question

Based upon your own experience of work or of being a customer of an organization, is it possible to recognize a different tone or 'feel' within organizations? How do the intangible 'ways of doing' things at your university compare, for instance, with your employment experience?

Culture and modernity

The word 'culture' is one of the most complicated words in the English language (Williams, 1983). In everyday language, the word 'culture' is loaded with evaluative connotations related to social class, power and status (Parker et al., 2003). The complexity of its modern usage can be appreciated when, in everyday speech, we refer to rock music as 'popular culture' and opera as 'high culture'. In the latter case, culture is associated with the arts, refinement and a privileged education. When anthropologists and sociologists use the term 'culture', it includes such social activities, but it also emphasizes that a national culture has a 'collectivizing effect' and creates differences between populations.

A 'culture' refers to an imperfect collection of interrelated understandings and behaviours shared by a people, which are shaped by ways of thinking and acting, by identities and by the material artefacts that together shape a people's way of life. As such, culture includes all the things people learn while growing up among a particular group: attitudes, beliefs about how people should act in particular situations, how females and males should interact, perceptions of reality and so forth. By definition, culture is collective, it is shared by a group of people, and it is socially learned and transmitted from one generation to the next (Giddens, 2009; Macionis and Gerber, 2011). You might think of culture as a societal tapestry of woven threads that makes each society unique or, on a larger scale, as a national characteristic such as 'Englishness'. The central implication for human resources (HR) practice is that culture constrains and enables social action, conditioning social structure or relatively stable patterns of individual behaviour and motivations (Figure 15.1).

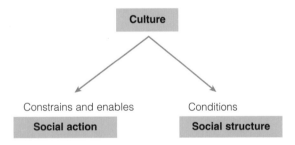

Figure 15.1 *The dynamics of culture*

Source: *Parker, J., Stanworth, H., Mars, L. and Ransome, P. (2015) Explaining Social Life: A Guide To Using Social Theory. Basingstoke: Palgrave Macmillan. Reproduced with permission from John Parker, Hilary Stanworth, Leonard Mars and Harriet Ransome.*

HRM web links Visit the online resource centre at **www.palgravehighered.com/bg-hrm-6e** for more on organizational culture and an article on culture and leadership.

Cultural scholars contend that the culture of a human society is a manifestation of a complex interplay of symbols, laws, values, beliefs and practices that are learned and exhibited by its members (Adler and Gundersen, 2008). Importantly, and prescient in the light of the Brexit vote, it is argued that when institutions, organizations or management functions, such as HRM, are viewed through the lens of national culture, then like a prism, culture 'bends and shapes the image' that we see and raises questions about continuity, change and resilience and new meanings of 'Europeanness' (Dickmann et al., 2016, p. 424).

Is a bullying culture a management strategy? Evidence from Australia

Is a bullying workplace culture a management strategy? Ben Farrell, an Australian employed by Apple, quit his job in early 2015, alleging a culture of harassment and intimidation. Among Farrell's claims are that Apple placed a performance note on his HR file after he missed a business trip because his pregnant wife was hospitalized after falling down some stairs, and that Apple demanded Farrell do work when he himself was hospitalized with a viral infection (Francis, 2015).

Almost 7 per cent of Australian workers reported bullying in the second half of 2012. In this study, bullying was defined as offensive behaviour occurring repeatedly over time, and the victim experienced difficulties defending him- or herself. This was much higher than international comparators, which run between 1 and 4 per cent (Occupational Health News, 2013). Bullying can result in a number of negative outcomes, including elevated rates of illness and staff turnover.

The issue of bullying in the workplace is, however, not just an Australian problem. Global firms such as Amazon have been accused of having a high-pressure workplace climate with a bullying management style. For example, the company reportedly culls the so-called worst performers in its workforce each year. This creates an organizational incentive for employees to work very hard as well as to identify and target other workers for complaints in order to survive the cuts. Coupled with high-pressure management, Amazon is able to extract the maximum productivity from its workforce at the least cost. Consider this example, courtesy of Guardian News & Media Ltd (Yuhas, 2014):

> *Some [Amazon] fulfillment center employees have complained of a brutal pace…In 2011, for instance, workers at a Pennsylvania warehouse described debilitating heat and distances, saying the company kept ambulances outside for employees who suffered heat stroke, exhaustion or collapse. (Amazon has since installed air conditioning.)*

Other workers report being pushed out of the organization after suffering from health issues such as cancer and miscarriage, rather than being given time to recover. The toll of these management practices is profound:

ImageSource

Bo Olson, a former employee from the company's book marketing department, described Amazon as a place where … "nearly every person I worked with, I saw cry at their desk"… One woman interviewed

(continued)

Stop! Have you ever experienced bullying in the workplace? What strategies did you use (or wished you had used) to respond to the bullying? Do you agree or disagree with the notion that bullying may be used as a management strategy? Why or why not?

Sources and further information: For background information, see Francis (2015), Gibbs (2015b), Gracely (2014), Kantor and Streitfeld (2015), Occupational Health News (2013) Soper (2011) and Yuhas (2014).

Note: This feature was written by Bob Barnetson.

said she had paid a freelancer in India to enter data out of her own pocket to get more done (Gibbs, 2015b, courtesy of Guardian News & Media Ltd).

Not surprisingly, the average work tenure at Amazon is roughly 1 year. The idea that an employer would intentionally subject workers to bullying treatment sits at odds with the widely held belief that bullying represents individual cases of misconduct. It also suggests that relying upon employers to manage bullying in the workplace is not necessarily a good idea. Yet these conclusions should hardly be surprising; employers in capitalist economies must respond to the profit imperative and, given the ongoing success of Amazon, bullying employees appears to be a successful way to do so.

Symbols, for example in languages, intellectual life and religion, are ideas that convey meaning between individuals and groups, and one important aspect of culture is language. Words and utterances can have different meanings depending on the context. In Japan, for example, some utterances may be lost in translation. When government officials or business people say that they will take something 'into serious consideration', they mean 'no' (Buruma, 2011), but expatriate managers do not always understand this. Take also the symbol of the cross, which has a powerful meaning for Christians but little meaning for Buddhists. The Confederate flag, however, has a powerful meaning for Christians and non-Christians alike, as a searing symbol of the nineteenth-century American slave-holding states (Manji, 2010).

Symbols also influence the essential *values* that people hold about society and the world around them. Values have profound, although partly unconscious, effects on people's behaviour in different situations. A *norm* is a shared ideal (or rule) about how people ought to act in certain situations, or about how particular people should act toward particular other people. The different ways in which people act and interact with others, and the tendency for people to view their own way of life as 'natural', can cause personal disorientation or 'culture shock' for tourists and immigrants experiencing a new country (Macionis and Gerber, 2011). Shared symbols, values and behaviour, however, change over generations. An interesting example of this is the controversy at Oriel College, Oxford University, over statues of Cecil Rhodes. In 2015, students organized an online petition calling on the University to take down the statue of Cecil Rhodes because the statue was, in their view, 'open glorification of the racist and bloody project of British colonialism'. The process by which each generation or other new members of society learn the values and way of life of their society is called *socialization*.

A mixture of factors distinguishes 'capitalist modernity'. This term has come to define the vast and largely unregulated expansion of the production and consumption of commodities, their related national markets, individualism and secularization over the last 200 years (Sayer, 1991). Late modernity is associated with the production of information, conspicuous consumption, especially in the area of leisure, global markets and social networks. The dynamics of late modernity, it is argued, have brought an 'extensification of contemporary culture' (Lash, 2010, p. 2). Take, for example, the iconic coffee chain Starbucks: there are many stores not just in every European capital, but in seemingly every district of Beijing, Delhi, Johannesburg and Buenos Aires too. Multinational corporations and global intergovernmental organizations, such as the International Monetary Fund, the

United Nations and the World Bank, as well as non-governmental organizations such as Oxfam, are driving this growing extensification of contemporary urban life. Moreover, 'time' and 'space' have taken on a new meaning in contemporary culture with today's global capitalism. City-dwellers increasingly face the choices and uncertainties of a globalized market society, with experiences that cut across all spatial boundaries of social class and nationality or ethnicity, and of religion and ideology, and whose reference point is both global and local (Giddens, 1990; Harvey, 1994).

In this context of seismic shifts in how contemporary societies are organized and are an increasing extension of social structures – the patterns of social relations that bind people together and give shape to their lives – people acquire new values, beliefs and practices from the groups to which they belong. A national culture has a number of essential features: it is *collective, socially learned, transmitted, shared* and a product of human socialization and social interaction. These defining aspects of national culture are important in understanding the complexity of culture and how people seek to assert their social uniqueness over time and place; moreover, they help us to see how a society's beliefs and values can guide and shape the employment relationship.

Europe, North and South America, South Africa and Asia and the Middle East are culturally diverse. Within their borders lie many cultures and subcultures formed by divisions such as social class, ethnicity and gender, this tapestry of multiple subcultures being in turn locally differentiated. A stream of studies describes the cultural traits found in Eastern and Western societies, perhaps the best known being Hofstede et al.'s (2010) study, which measured national culture in 64 countries. Hofstede's data, based on one global corporation, IBM, initially identified four independent dimensions of national cultural differences:

- *Power distance* – the extent to which those who are less powerful accept that power is distributed unequally
- *Individualism* versus *collectivism* – the degree to which members of society are integrated into communities
- *Masculinity* versus *femininity* – the general acceptance of sex-biased values and the sexual division of labour
- *Uncertainty avoidance* – society's tolerance for ambiguity and uncertainty, which ultimately deals with the search for truth.

HRM web links Visit the online resource centre at **www.palgravehighered.com/bg-hrm-6e** for access to more information on the works of Geert Hofstede.

Since early modernity, the moral values of societies on both sides of the Atlantic have had a strong influence on the management of people. The value-loaded notion of 'fairness', for example, underwrites the structure of rewards and work obligations. This is illuminated by the maxim 'A fair day's wage for a fair day's work' (Hyman and Brough, 1975). Changing 'life' values have also altered rates of participation in the labour market and challenged traditional gender roles in the workplace. In addition, different national cultures have influenced the thinking of Western scholars on the best way to motivate employees and on how to close the 'commitment gap' (see Chapters 1 and 3). In Maslow's theory of work motivation, for instance, higher order self-actualization is seen as the supreme human need. But this assumption presupposes an *individualist* culture in which the ties between individuals are loose and everyone is expected to look after themselves and their immediate families.

Renewed interest in the culture–performance link has generated studies comparing North American and East Asian cultural values. Faced with reports of superior Japanese management practices, researchers examined whether the 'commitment gap' between North American and Japanese workers can be attributed to differences in cultural values and national character (Lincoln and Kalleberg, 1992). In some national cultures, the values of *collectivism* and sharing are cited as a defence against an ideology seeking to lower taxes and privatize public services:

> It's the difference between being human beings and animals. With animals, when one of them gets old, they let it die, they eat it. We want to take care of our people, our youths, our students, our elderly. We are the most egalitarian society [Quebec] in North America and we want to keep it that way. (Séguin, 2010, p. A16)

Hofstede's argument for cultural homogeneity has attracted considerable criticism. The empirical basis for his proposal is a statistical averaging of his quantitative data – survey responses from IBM's employees. But an average of personal values claiming to measure the values of a national culture is about as meaningful as an average of personal income. As has been well established elsewhere, in the same way as there is a wide variance in personal income in any population, so there is a wide dispersion in the personal values of that population (McSweeney, 2002).

Among the developed countries in the global economy, few are likely to exhibit a singular culture, being more likely to be plural, with hyphenated identities such as African-American, Chinese-Canadian, French-Canadian, Anglo-Indian and so on. In support of the cultural diversity argument, experts document almost 7000 languages worldwide, suggesting the existence of that many distinct cultures (Macionis and Gerber, 2011). In the countries located in the Asian region, there are at least seven major official languages, and people believe in widely different religions and philosophies, ranging from Buddhism and Hinduism to Islam and Christianity. Within the European Union, there are 23 official and working languages. And within the UK, the question of whether or not Scotland, Wales, Northern Ireland or England has its own distinct culture evokes strong responses. Scotland, for example, as a land of lochs, mountains and tartan, forms a compelling image that transmits 'potent resonances for culture' (McCrone, 2001, p. 37).

The empirical evidence at the centre of Hofstede's argument for a 'national culture' contains contradictions and paradoxes. In reality, people live and work in multiple cultures. The quest for a 'unified' culture is therefore doomed to ignore the fragmentation and complexities of contemporary society. To argue that research on the relationship between national values and organizational cultures is 'loose' (Hofstede et al., 2010) is not to imply that cultural undercurrents do not structure human behaviour in subtle but highly regular ways, or that, as citizens and as employees, we do not carry our cultural heritage and social identities into the workplace. We talk and act in a particular way that reflects both our collective unconsciousness and our ethical standards (Saul, 2008). In other words, cultural plurality does not entirely remove national or regional norms from Western societies. Amidst the plurality, national culture translates into organizations by influencing the core values and beliefs that constitute their organizational cultures (see, for example, Zhang and Begley, 2011).

reflective question

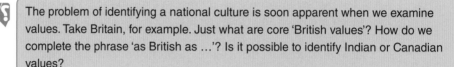

The problem of identifying a national culture is soon apparent when we examine values. Take Britain, for example. Just what are core 'British values'? How do we complete the phrase 'as British as …'? Is it possible to identify Indian or Canadian values?

Organizational culture

In the current organizational literature, the word 'culture' is used to capture various 'ways of doing' and employees' interactions, as in 'bonus culture', 'binge-working culture' or 'masculine culture'. When academics and executives debate the merits of transforming or managing 'organizational culture', what exactly is it that they are trying to change or manage? The notion of organizational culture is equally as complex as that of national culture, and equally it lends itself to very different uses. In the literature, the terms 'corporate culture' and 'organizational culture' are common. The distinction between the two is that the former is devised and transmitted downwards to subordinates by senior management as part of a strategy of mobilizing employee commitment and portrays the workforce as 'culture-takers'. Organizational culture, on the other hand, is a product of employees' creativity and portrays the participants as 'culture-makers' (Linstead and Grafton Small, 1992) and, as such, is 'always capable of being rewritten or reimagined' (Dickmann et al., p. 424).

Some cultural researchers use the terms *culture* and *climate* interchangeably (Schneider, 2000). These are complementary constructs, but they reveal overlapping nuances in the social and psychological life of complex organizations. Organizational culture refers to the intangible or 'hidden' elements of the social context of organizations, such as assumptions, beliefs and values (Ashkanasy et al., 2011). In contrast, organizational climate relates to employees' perceptions and evaluations of tangible workplace attributes, such as their shared perceptions of low-carbon policies, procedures and practices that senior managers support and reward (Norton et al., 2015). Culture scholars tend to use qualitative methodology derived from anthropology to examine symbolic and cultural forms of organizations. Climate researchers, however, attempt to measure individuals' perceptions of workplace conduct and the meaning they assign to it using quantitative methods, such as regression analysis. The distinction between culture research and climate research therefore lies in the different methodology traditions, what they consider to be significantly meaningful and the agenda underlying each approach. More critical interpretations contend that the psychological treatment of culture largely reflects 'a neo-human relations agenda' (Parker, 2000).

The different approaches generate different definitions of organizational culture. An early definition by Smircich focuses on values that guide employees' conduct at work and shape their interactions. Organizational culture (Smircich, 1983, p. 344) is the:

> Social or normative glue that holds an organization together … The values or social ideals and the beliefs that organization members come to share. These values or patterns of beliefs are manifested by symbolic devices, such as myths, stories, legends and specialized language.

HRM and globalization 15.2

Multiculturalism's magic number

Getty Images / Thinkstock Valueline

In the first decade of the new millennium, questions have been raised about the so-called multiculturalism experiment. In Europe, Chancellor Angela Merkel has claimed that German multiculturalism has 'utterly failed', and the Netherlands, the UK and France have all, to differing degrees, blamed multiculturalism for weakening their national social cohesion. Even in Canada, one of the world's most multicultural societies, 'its reality remains complex and at times volatile' (Peritz and Friesen, 2010, p. A14).

High levels of immigration in the last three decades have transformed Canada from a bilingual – English and French – two-culture society to a cultural mosaic. Immigration statistics reveal just how much Canada has changed. Before 1961, about 91 per cent of immigrants to Canada came from Western Europe, especially the UK, and less than 5 per cent came from Asian and Middle Eastern countries. Canadians celebrated their European cultural inheritance but gave 'scarcely a nod, let alone a meaningful nod, in the direction of the First Nations, the Métis, the Inuit' (Saul, 2008, p. 4).

Between 1991 and 2001, however, European immigrants constituted 20 per cent of total immigration, while immigrants from Asia and the Middle East made up 58 per cent. Between 2011 and 2016, Asia (including the Middle East) provided Canada's largest source of immigrants. These changes in the pattern of immigration were the result of a deliberate change in public policy. Canadian society is now officially multicultural in that this aim is embodied in government social policy designed to encourage ethnic or cultural heterogeneity. Quebec has become the crucible for a Canadian debate over identity, values and how far newcomers should be accommodated at work and in other areas of life. In 2008, Quebec established a telephone 'hotline' to tackle matters of linguistic, ethnic and religious accommodation. The following three cases from The Globe and Mail (Peritz and Friesen, 2010) provide a window into managing the multicultural workplace:

- *Case 1 – A Sikh employee in a food warehouse wants to wear a kara – a bangle-type metal bracelet that represents an expression of the Sikh faith. The warehouse has a ban on jewellery for employees who handle food, for hygiene purposes. The company wants to know if it should accommodate the employee's request.*

- *Case 2 – A college student wears a Muslim face veil, or niqab, that covers her entire body except for a slit for the eyes. She has agreed to pose for her student ID bare-faced, but doesn't want the image to be entered into a college-wide computer database. The college seeks a policy that balances its security needs with the student's wishes.*

- *Case 3 – A Muslim schoolteacher requests each Friday afternoon off to attend prayers at his mosque. The school board wants to know how to accommodate him.*

Multiculturalism has generated controversy because people need to rethink their core values and norms. The issue of reasonable accommodation in multicultural workplaces has become a microcosm of the diversity dilemma: it affects the psychological contract, it is linked to the topic of dignity at work (Bolton, 2007), and it has repercussions for HRM.

Stop! If you were the HRM manager employed at these three workplaces, what advice would you give to each? What types of cultural knowledge might be common in a workplace in your home country? How would you react if you were asked by an employer to remove an article of faith, for example a cross or a kara?

Sources and further information: See Peritz and Friesen (2010), Saul (2008), Bolton (2007) and Taylor and Bain (2005) for more information. Watch the film Slumdog Millionaire (2009) for an insight into culture training at Indian call centres. And go to this book's online resource centre for more information about multiculturalism in Canada.

Note: This feature was written by John Bratton.

In contrast, a definition focusing on shared meanings and symbolism is articulated by Alvesson (2002, pp. 3–4):

> For me values are less central and less useful than meanings and symbolism in cultural analysis … Culture is not primarily 'inside' people's heads, but somewhere 'between' the heads of a group of people where symbols and meanings are publicly expressed, for example, in work group interactions, in board meetings but also in material objects. Organizational culture then is central in governing the understanding of workplace interactions, events and processes. It is the context in which these phenomena become comprehensible and meaningful.

A synthesis of the definitions captures the essential elements of organizational culture. It concerns the importance of shared values, beliefs and language that shape and perpetuate organizational reality, so that employees' work conduct is more predictable and governable.

reflective question Reading the two definitions of organizational culture, does your university have a culture? How does this differ within and between the different faculties, schools or departments of the university?

To understand organizational culture, we must examine its parts, even though any organizational culture is greater than the sum of its parts. Drawing on the work of Edgar Schein (2010), Figure 15.2 shows three fundamental levels of organizational culture:

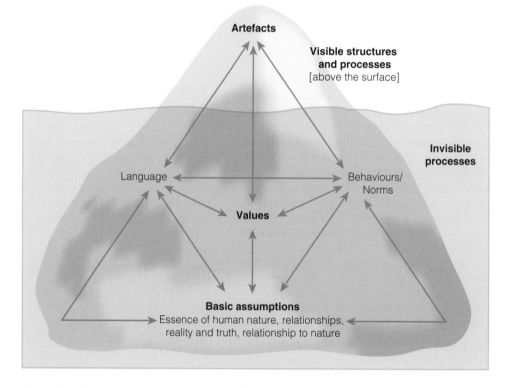

Figure 15.2 *The three levels of organizational culture*

Source: Adapted from Schein, E.H. Organizational culture and leadership, 4th ed. John Wiley & Sons, Inc., 2010. Copyright © 2010 John Wiley & Sons, Inc. Republished with permission of Professor Edgar H Schein and John Wiley & Sons, Inc.; permission conveyed through Copyright Clearance Center, Inc.

Leather, tattoos and long hair could be considered an expression of this motorcycle club's visual culture.

artefacts, values and *basic assumptions*. These can be imagined as an iceberg. The uppermost subtriangle might be viewed as the 'tip of the iceberg', representing the observable parts of organizational culture, which are embedded in shared values, basic assumptions and beliefs that are invisible to the human eye. Each level of culture influences another level.

The first level comprises the visible, the *artefacts* and material objects such as buildings, technology, art and uniforms that the organization 'uses' to express its culture. For example, when a company uses only email for internal communication, the cultural message is that IT is a highly valued resource. Displaying art on office walls signals to members and visitors that creating a stimulating cultural context in which employees can explore ideas and aesthetics is highly valued (Harding, 2003). Other examples are the wearing of professorial apparel, the doctor's white coat in the National Health Service (NHS) and the black gown worn by academics at official university ceremonies. The visible culture also includes *language*.

How managers describe other employees is an example of using symbols to convey meaning to each other. For example, Wal-mart refers to its employees as 'associates', and at Disneyland they are known as 'cast members'. Social *behaviour* is another aspect of observable organizational culture, including rituals and ceremonies. *Rituals* are collective routines that 'dramatize' the organization's culture. For example, the office party can be viewed as a ritual for *integrating* new members into the organization. *Ceremonies* are planned and represent more formal social artefacts than rituals, as in, for example, the 'call to the bar' ceremony for graduating lawyers.

The second level of organizational culture comprises perceived shared work-related *values*, which are invisible. Previous studies suggest that perceived organizational ethical values refer to workers' beliefs concerning what practices are acceptable or appropriate in their organization (Biron, 2010). Perceived organizational values are therefore the standards of desirability by which employees evaluate aspects of their work or profession and make choices between options (Warr, 2008). For example, in healthcare, standard medical practice is influenced by a belief in evidence for practice or by a commitment to patient-centred care. In many universities, practice is influenced by the espoused value 'We are a teaching-centred institution'. Employment-related espoused values possess six characteristics (Warr, 2008):

- They involve a moral or ethical statement of 'rightness'.
- They pertain to desirable modes of behaviour at a given point in time.
- They directly influence employees' behaviour and experiences, and act as significant moderators.
- They are typically associated with strategic goals and address questions such as 'What are we doing?' and 'Why are we doing this?'
- They guide the selection and evaluation of the organization's members.
- They may vary with respect to male/female, demographic and cultural differences.

The term 'shared' in cultural analysis implies that organizational members are a whole. Each member has been exposed to a set of dominant values, although not every member may internalize and endorse these. Despite the substantial evidence that perceived organizational values influence the behaviour of workers, the practical application of the insights generated by this research has been limited (Biron, 2010).

The third level of organizational culture relates to *basic assumptions*, which are invisible, unconscious, taken for granted, difficult to access and highly resistant to change. These are the implicit and unspoken assumptions that underpin everyday choices and shape how members perceive, think and emotionally react to social events. For example, in the NHS, assumptions about the relative roles of doctors and nurses, about patients' rights or about the sources of ill-health underpin everyday decisions and actions (Davies, 2002). The basic assumptions or beliefs about human nature, human relationships, relationships to nature and how the world works form the base from which employees, who enter the workplace as social beings with life histories and experiences, build their values of how the world *should* be. Assumptions and values then guide employees' workplace conduct and shape their interactions, as do the artefacts with which members surround themselves. Organizational culture manifests itself most clearly through the organization's policies and practices (Zhang and Begley, 2011).

HRM web links

Visit the online resource centre at **www.palgravehighered.com/bg-hrm-6e** for more information about the work of Schein.

reflective question

Thinking about your own university or college, does the culture manifest itself through policies or practices? For instance, do you expect *and* experience a student-centred focus? Do teaching staff primarily focus on their teaching or their research interests? Is there a 'publish or perish' culture? Try to assess your answer at three levels: observable artefacts, shared values and basic assumptions of the culture.

Perspectives on organizational culture

The family tree of the different perspectives on organizational culture is rooted in classical sociological theory. The work of the German sociologist Max Weber is representative of the canonical literature on understanding employees' work conduct as a cultural phenomenon: individuals behave 'not out of obedience, but either because the environment approves of the conduct and disapproves of its opposite, or merely as a result of unreflective habituation to a regularity of life that has *engraved itself as a custom*' (Weber, 1922/1968, p. 312, emphasis added). Much contemporary writing in culture analysis can be divided into two schools of thought: managerialist and critical.

Managerially oriented perspectives

This body of writing examines culture from the premise that it can play a role in building organizational consensus and harmony, and can improve performance. From this

HRM as I see it

Keith Stopforth
Head of Talent and Development, Bupa Health and Wellbeing

www.bupa.co.uk

Bupa is an international private healthcare company with bases on three continents and over 10 million customers in over 200 countries. Bupa provides health insurance, care homes, health assessments, occupational health services and child care, and runs its own hospital, Bupa Cromwell Hospital, in London. The company also owns several healthcare companies overseas, including Sanitas in Spain and IHI Danmark in Denmark.

Keith Stopforth has been with Bupa since 2001, most recently with Bupa Health and Wellbeing in the UK, having previously worked as a sales manager and then branch training manager at Prudential. Keith is currently developing his skills in executive coaching and mentoring. He is a member of the Talent Forum 2011.

Click on Keith's picture to watch him talking about talent management, organizational culture and diversity at Bupa, and then think about the following questions:

1 What is Keith's view of organizational culture and the role of the HR department in 'shaping' culture?
2 What is the role of competencies in this process?
3 How does Bupa embrace diversity? What opportunities are provided to encourage prospective employees, and how do you think these could be applied in other companies?

viewpoint, organizational culture is a *variable* – an attribute that an organization possesses or '*has*' and, as such, can be created by corporate managers.

This standpoint is associated with the *structural-functionalist* approach to cultural analysis. Its theoretical roots date back to Auguste Comte (1798–1857) and Emile Durkheim (1858–1917) and, in the twentieth century, to the US sociologist Talcott Parsons (1902–79) (see Chapter 1). The central premise of the structural-functionist approach is that cultural processes can create organizational stability and consensus. The task of senior management is therefore to focus on how culture can be managed and disseminated downwards to organizational members.

Within this genre, Peters and Waterman's influential book *In Search of Excellence* is probably the best known example of the 'has' school. These gurus view culture as an elixir that binds together the specific human qualities that lead to a maximizing of employees' commitment to providing a high-quality service or product – what is sometimes called a 'commitment-excellence organization'. Thus, mainstream theorists are said, in Martin's (1992) words, to follow an '*integration*' perspective. In this sense, management-inspired cultural processes and interventions attempt to alleviate the many forms of the ever-present conflict that arises from managing the labour process. This approach focuses on building a culture that binds members together around the same core values, beliefs and norms, which are considered to be prerequisites for achieving the organization's strategic goals. For integration or functionalism theorists, culture is conceptualized as 'organization-wide agreement with values espoused by top management' (Martin and Frost, 1996, p. 600). The notion of 'cultural engineering' – creating the 'right' kind of culture to align with strategic goals – is seen as a 'lever' for fostering commitment and loyalty in the workforce.

What constitutes the 'right culture' for excellence is, however, a matter of debate. A popular approach is the contingency theory, which is based on the belief that senior managers need to consider both external and internal variables when deciding what kind of culture best fits their organization. Deal and Kennedy (1982), for example, identify important contingencies such as the level of risk, the size and design of the organization, ownership and governance, technology and the need for innovation. In the leadership literature, a connection between leadership, culture and employees' commitment to the organization has often been theoretically proposed. Employee organizational commitment is the degree to which employees identify with the organization's goals and values, their willingness to exceed a minimum level of effort on behalf of the organization, and their intention to remain with the organization.

Specifically, recent studies have found that 'transformational' leadership behaviour is an antecedent variable in regard to employee commitment. For example, Simosi and Xenikou (2010, p. 1611) conclude that both transformational leadership behaviour and contingent reward were found to be 'significantly and positively related to affective and normative commitment' as well as to employees' feeling of obligation to remain in the organization. Champy contends that 'values are our moral navigational devices' and that, for real change to occur, leaders need 'cultural warriors' at every level of the organization to communicate new values to their peers (1996, p. 79). Whereas management gurus such as Peters and Waterman, Deal and Kennedy, and Champy focus on values that foster 'strong' corporate cultures, researchers have in recent years argued that cultural diversity and the changing nature of the employment relationship have heightened how important it is to understand the dynamics of employee commitment as a potential determinant of motivation (see, for example, Becton and Field, 2009; Mathew and Ogbonna, 2009; Su et al., 2009).

Contingency studies do draw attention to cultural heterogeneity, and Martin (1992) refers to these as the *differentiated* perspective. An organization such as the UK's NHS might have one dominant culture expressing its core values, but it also has sets of *subcultures* defined by professions, function and space. An image of professional groups with strong norms and values potentially challenging aspects of the organization's core values is associated with Ouchi's (1980) concept of the 'clan', itself drawn from Durkheim's theory of mechanical solidarity. A study of healthcare providers revealed that 'complex multiple cultural values are often hierarchical and are commonly interpreted in ways that ascribe differentiated, fragmented and collective meaning' (Morgan and Ogbonna, 2008, p. 61). Healthcare professionals may collectively interpret the espoused value of providing the 'best possible care' for patients, but that 'care' will be delivered differently by the various professional groups. For doctors, this may mean eradicating the cause of illness, whereas for occupational therapists it may mean helping patients achieve greater mobility (Fitzgerald and Teal, 2004). In contrast, a macho and aggressive subculture might exist among male workers doing mundane or unpleasant work (Ackroyd and Crowdy, 1990).

Subcultures help to bind workers together, to cope with shared frustrations and to preserve a distinctive identity (Bolton, 2005). The analyses of subcultures reveal a wide variation in values, work conduct and assumptions – these are, however, a normal part of organizational life.

reflective question Do you think a complex organization like the UK's NHS has subcultures? What are the implications for HRM practices if core subcultures exist?

A sociologically informed analysis of culture also acknowledges the existence of *countercultures* in work organizations. These create their own form of organizational reality through a subculture that actively opposes the dominant values and norms (Martin and Siehl, 1983). For example, a policy change focusing on 'putting customers first' may produce countercultures as some staff may be reluctant to abandon professional or trade norms and may strongly reject service-oriented values. Mergers and acquisitions may also produce countercultures. There may be a 'clash of corporate cultures' when the values, beliefs and norms held by members of an acquired organization are inconsistent with those of the acquiring organization. The debate on the existence of subcultures and countercultures emphasizes the complexities and interwoven character of organizational culture and avoids an overly static and monolithic picture of everyday organizational life.

Critically oriented perspectives

Critical cultural scholars share a similar view that values and norms are deeply embedded in society. In contrast to the structural-functionalist perspective that understands culture as something an organization '*has*', critical workplace theorists proceed from the idea that the organization '*is*' a culture. The central premise is that, at its roots, the work organization is a manifestation of human consciousness, a source of power, a socializing and controlling force. Moreover, adherents of the 'is' view of culture are likely to play down any outcomes in terms of efficiency that result from changes in the culture (Alvesson, 2002). Here, three critically oriented perspectives – symbolic-interactionist, conflict and feminist – will serve as alternative lenses through which to understand organizational culture.

The *symbolic-interactionist* approach understands organizational culture as the sum of all the employees' interactions. In this school of thought, culture plays the role of a 'carrier' for shared meaning (hence 'symbolic') and is produced by workers and managers in face-to-face encounters (hence 'interactionist') as they go about their everyday workplace activities. The culture of the organization is created

The office water cooler is a well-known location for sharing workplace stories.

PhotoDisc/ Getty Images

by its members and reproduced by the networks of symbols and meanings that employees share and that make shared work conduct possible. The analysis of organizational culture can therefore occur through studying observable artefacts, language, action and the beliefs and values of organizational members.

In the realm of shared *artefacts*, displayed mission statements, framed photographs of individuals and ceremonies, technology and displayed art are all manifestations of culture. *Language* is explored to see how it is used to communicate effectively in order to make work conduct possible. Story-telling touches all of us, reaching across cultures and generations (Fulford, 1999). In workplaces, shared *stories*, *myths* and *legends* serve to construct a common ground for understanding work behaviour. For example, an account of a dramatic event in the past history of the company serves to create a shared meaning of how workers are expected to handle problems in the present.

Also scrutinized is shared work *action*. Rites commonly found in the workplace are those of recognition (for example, an employee of the month award) and of conflict (for example, a disciplinary hearing). Shared *beliefs* and *values* are examined too. In workplace talk, the espousal of 'values' or perceived 'ethical values' is omnipresent; this can concern either legislative provisions that are not always heeded (for example, antidiscrimination laws) or values that are not adequately supported or funded by the organization. Employee groups will wrap their proposals around a 'values' rhetoric to elevate these demands over more pedestrian ones. By highlighting day-to-day social interaction, this analysis explains why organizational cultures are enduring. However, research suggests that a lack of organizational support and mistreatment and indignity at work can undermine the normative influence of perceived ethical values (Biron, 2010). Furthermore, a common critique of this approach relates to its underemphasis of how larger social structures cause disagreement on meanings.

Unlike the integration perspective, the *critical perspective* explores how values, beliefs and norms develop to sustain inequalities and the power of employers. It sets out to develop an understanding of organizational culture by situating it in the context of capitalist relations of domination and control. The intellectual roots of this analysis are found in the canonical text written by Karl Marx and Friedrich Engels. In the 1859 preface to *The Critique of Political Economy*, Marx wrote: 'The mode of production of material life conditions the social, political and intellectual life process in general. It is not the consciousness of men that determines their being, but, on the contrary, their social being that determines their consciousness' (Tucker, 1978, p. 4). For Marx, cultural knowledge is socially produced on the basis of particular structures of economic relationships. Furthermore, in *The German Ideology*, Marx and Engels (1998) reiterate the point that ideas about how the world works: perceptions of reality and so forth are cultural constructs that reflect constellations of class interests – typically those of society's most powerful social elite. Moreover, dominant ideas in society are directly interwoven with the economy and with work-related activities. Many conflict theorists agree with Marx's assertion that social elites use *ideology*, a non-material element of culture, to shape the thoughts and actions of other social classes, as, for example, in the popular idea that markets can best decide society's economic priorities because 'governments cannot pick winners'. Public discourse often supports these views, since no alternatives are debated or offered.

Conflict perspectives call attention to the perpetual tension, conflict and resistance that exists between different employee groups. The structured antagonism between capital and labour, and, in tandem with this, managerial control, focuses on the '*who*' of power over other people and the '*how*' of employee commitment. Here, the focus is on 'strong' corporate cultures as an employment strategy to develop a sense of 'community' and to activate employee emotion, which might lead to enhanced loyalty and commitment to the company (Ray, 1986; Thompson and McHugh, 2009). Around this thesis, a body of literature has developed which argues that cultural control overlaps and exists alongside, rather than replaces, more traditional forms of management control strategies, such as bureaucracy, technology and the more traditional HRM policies and practices, for example completing forms or 'punching in' at the start of a working day. In this sense, systems of cultural hegemony do not replace but instead *complement* other employment strategies adopted over time that aim to increase the loyalty and control of employees, and ultimately their efficiency.

reflective question What national (macro) and global forces drive the development of employment strategies? To what extent have the reverberations of the economic crises since 2008 caused managers to change the mix of employment strategies, including cultural control, with which they experiment?

The picture represented by critical workplace scholars is one that represents contradictory and unstable organizational cultures. Drawing on the postmodernist discourse, this approach has been referred to as the *fragmentary* perspective (Martin, 2002). As such, organizational culture is characterized by ephemerality, ambiguity and change, and exposes claims of unified corporate cultures. Culture is 'a loosely structured and incompletely shared system that emerges dynamically as cultural members experience each other, events, and the organization's contextual features' (Martin, 1992, p. 152). The value of this fragmentary approach lies in its exposure of the naivety of using a culture metaphor to describe the organization – it is naive to think that there is no ambiguity in what cultural members believe and do. For example, it might expose claims of truth such as 'We are an equal opportunity employer' while masking the gender or race inequality arising from a male-dominant or white-dominant workplace (Martin, 2002).

The *feminist perspective* argues that gender is a central aspect of work and organizations. Why, 40 years after the

If you were asked to picture a firefighter, would you imagine a man or a woman? Feminist perspectives would argue that gender ideology would expect this woman to be at home rather than putting out fires.

Getty Images/VStock RF Thinkstock Images Vstock LLC

passing of the UK Sex Discrimination Act, and in an age of alleged equality of opportunity (in developed economies at least), is the gender gap so enduring in the workplace? Understanding the gender problem in organizational culture analysis is important for at least four reasons:

- First, virtually every human culture known to exist has been dominated by its men, and *external* societal values associated with notions of masculinity and femininity are often reflected in work-related processes. For example, it is common to find processes that privilege the rationality and 'objectivity' associated with masculine attributes while suppressing emotion, which is associated with family and other feminine attributes.
- Second, gender inequality is supported by ideology that seeks to 'naturalize' gender roles. As Eagleton (1983, p. 135) remarks, 'Ideology seeks to convert culture into Nature'. The idea that a woman's place is in the home, or a woman is incapable of performing the duties of a firefighter, illustrates the existence of this ideology.
- Third, *inside* the workplace, practices involved in recruitment, selection and appraisal often conform to and extend the sex-biased societal values that reinforce job segregation – the tendency for men and women to work in different occupations – as well as systemic discrimination against women.
- Finally, some organizations (for example, schools and the media) play a direct part in the socializing processes by which people acquire gender identities (Aaltio-Marjosola and Mills, 2002). For example, the social association between masculinity and physical hazards contributes to the gendered nature of 'the way things are done' in an organization, justifying 'masculine occupations'.

Feminist perspectives have brought about a major shift in our ways of thinking about culture and knowledge, and also about the way in which the political impinges upon and permeates all of our ways of thinking and acting, both public and private. The argument is that, with notable exceptions, mainstream analysis has generally reflected dominant social beliefs about gender roles that men inhabit the 'public' domain of action, decision-making, power and authority, while women inhabit the 'private' domestic world. Thus, critical feminist scholars have contended that the standard treatment of organizational culture neglects how gender, a patriarchal system, subtle stereotyping, social networks that unintentionally exclude women, systemic discrimination, female-hostile banter and sexuality, that is, sexual characteristics and sexual conduct in the workplace, profoundly shape work cultures. Although sexuality serves to affirm men's sense of shared masculinity, it can serve to make women feel uncomfortable, and leaving the organization is often seen as the only alternative (Brewis and Linstead, 2000). Organizational culture is often a crucial determinant of sexual harassment (Chamberlain et al., 2008) that can be an entrenched feature of workplaces through pornographic pin-ups, taunting and innuendo, and predatory conduct.

National culture, with its societal value system and norms, is deeply intertwined with organizational culture in a dialectical relationship, each being fashioned and refashioned by the other. Including the gender-sexuality paradigm in the study of organizational culture has pushed the boundaries of the differentiation approach by addressing concerns of inequality and discriminatory workplace practices. As sociologist Judy Wajcman observes, the contemporary workplace is not gender neutral; indeed, 'gender is woven into the very fabric of bureaucratic hierarchy and authority relations' (Wajcman, 1998, p. 47). In broad terms, work cultures can be studied from three perspectives, those of *integration, differentiation* and *fragmentation*. Joanne Martin (1992) argues that all three are necessary to fully understand how culture operates in the workplace. Each of the major perspectives we have

HRM in practice 15.1

'Purposeful Darwinism' – Amazon's experiment to motivate staff

In a 5000-word report, the New York Times published a survey based on interviews with more than 100 current and former Amazon executives and engineers who described how they experienced both its punishing work discipline and what 'many called its thrilling power to create'. Amazon is the most valuable retailer in the US (worth $250 billion) partly because it has extracted so much effort from its employees. The study delves into the secret life in the corporation's offices where tens of thousands of white-collar workers have been recruited to expand its retail empire. The survey states:

it is conducting a little-known experiment in how far it can push white-collar workers, redrawing the boundaries of what is acceptable. (Kantor and Streitfield, New York Times, 2015).

The company collects a huge amount of data on the performance of every employee, and each month they have to explain their performance based upon these data. Employees are ranked annually, and the lowest ranked are fired. Those with the highest ranking are well compensated, but constant performance monitoring and a system whereby individuals can be secretly reported to management, along with a culture that encourages self-monitoring, leads to a breakdown between work and private life. Workers documented having to answer emails or keep in touch with work late at night and during vacations. If they failed to do so, they could be criticized by their supervisors. Employees frequently worked 80 hours per week. A former HR director has called the annual culling of staff 'purposeful Darwinism'. This struggle for survival among staff is supposed to increase their performance, but respondents believe it encourages people to sabotage the reputations of others to protect their jobs and to erect a barrier against cooperation between workers.

The survey found examples of a lack of empathy towards anyone who needed a respite from the oppressive work regime. People were encouraged to leave if they were ill or needed to care for sick or dying relatives. These circumstances particularly affect women, and several women in the survey stated that when they suffered ill-health and could not commit to an 80-hour week, they were given a low performance rating. A woman who had miscarried twins was

BRANDX

pressured by her boss to go on a business trip the day after she had had surgery.

Many employees cannot endure the pressure of this tough environment, resulting in a huge turnover of staff: the median tenure of employees is a year. The company aims to give good compensation to the best employees,

(continued)

Stop! Do you think that the trade-off between increased efficiency and high-pressure working conditions with its reduction of a balance between work and private life is reasonable? Read the article by Spicer listed below and then consider whether or not you think that the 'rank and yank' system is really able to motivate employees or is counterproductive.

Sources and further information: For background to this feature, see Kantor and Streitfeld (2015) and Spicer (2015).

Note: This feature was written by David Denham.

whom it drives hard. Workers in their twenties fear that they will be replaced by younger ones who will work even harder.

Amazon's intense use of staff whose response is to move on is only sustainable if there are large numbers of well-qualified people who wish to work for the company. Critics argue that Amazon's managerial style destroys the lives of individuals and undermines organizational performance (Spicer, 2015).

examined can be used as a theoretical compass for navigating through the myriad and competing views found in the organizational culture and HRM literature.

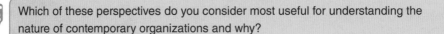

reflective question Which of these perspectives do you consider most useful for understanding the nature of contemporary organizations and why?

Managing culture through HRM

Organizational cultures are amazingly stable and enduring. From an integrationist perspective, a strong culture can produce a common value system that is consistent with organizational goals such as higher productivity. From this point of view, corporate culture functions as the ultimate form of management control – a self-controlled, committed workforce dedicated to management's expectations and goals. Thus, developing a 'strong' culture in which members of the organization develop a fierce loyalty to the organization offers the possibility to close the 'commitment gap' in the employment relationship, thereby releasing the workers' creative and productive capacity.

As was noted in Chapter 1, an important goal of HRM is to manage the psychological contract, to change the employment relationship from a binary *low-trust* and *low-commitment* relationship to a participatory *high-trust* and *high-commitment* relationship, as well as to capture, manage and control emotion in the organization (Bolton, 2005; Legge, 2005). Contemporary workplace scholars, drawing heavily on Erving Goffman's (1967) work comparing human interactions with drama, argue that a robust corporate culture provides normative and behavioural 'scripts' for employees to follow. The 'scripts' are written by management and reflect the big issues of productivity, organizational flexibility, social legitimacy and 'strategic tensions'. The scripts may also provide clear expectations of work behaviour for new initiatives such as high-performance work systems, or may be used to capture and manage employees' emotional labour (du Gay, 1996).

The role of HRM in translating and crafting an organization's culture has received substantial attention in both the popular and the academic HRM literature. It has been argued, for example, that 'the HR professional must recognize, articulate, and shape a company's culture' (Brewster et al., 2008, p. 312). Several researchers have examined the phenomenon of organizational culture in multinational corporations. The issue they have focused on is whether the subsidiaries of multinational corporations generate 'third cultures', that is hybrid versions of their home and host country cultures (Hui and Graen, 1997; Zhang and Begley, 2011). Amid culturally diverse environments, although an organizational culture may be partly crafted by senior managers, it is not effortlessly manipulated by them. Indeed, as HRM is one of the main transmitters of company policies and practices, changes in HR policies and practices that run counter to, or do not blend with, perceived organizational values will usually meet with resistance from managers and other employees, and may fail (Biron, 2010; Gahan and Abeysekera, 2009; Zhang and Albrecht, 2010). In this context, leadership theorists (see, for example, Bass and Riggio, 2006) and HRM scholars have tried to identify effective ways to change manifestations of organizational culture: visible *artefacts*, including language and shared behaviour; work *values*, which are invisible, but can be espoused; and various sets of HR practices that reinforce the culture.

Figure 15.3 draws from Norton's et al., (2015, p. 337) work, which itself extends the work of Hatch (1993) and Schein (1990). The conceptual framework shows the antecedents – societal values, beliefs and laws, organizational design and leader behaviours – and the influence of HR practices that can create and shape an organization's culture. Climate is shown as an artefact of culture (Schein, 1990). Organizational culture influences employee behaviour through employee perceptions of climate (for example, policies, procedures and practices), which translate organizational beliefs and values into behavioural norms (Norton et al., 2015). The model implies that an organization's social context is not a matter of *being*, but continually of *becoming*. In other words, it is a dynamic process through which organizational life and behavioural norms respond to external and internal pressures including HR practices. For the organization and individual employees, the social context impacts on performance and employees' well-being – the outcomes.

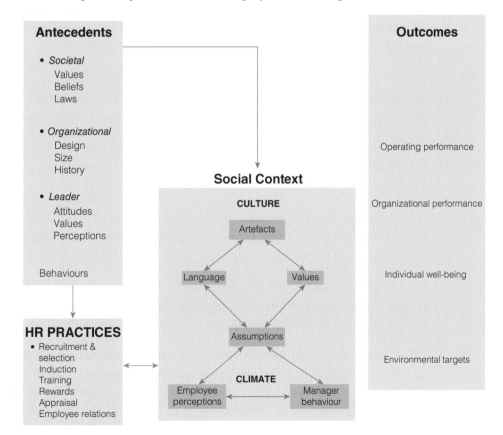

Figure 15.3 *Changing organizational culture through HR practices*
Source: Inspired by Norton et al. (2015, p. 337)

Evidence suggests that a galaxy of HR practices can create a strong culture. People are key carriers of values into the workplace. Thus, one way to change or reinforce a particular culture is through the 'individual–organizational fit' (Purcell et al., 2009), and in this regard, HR *selection* practices are an important means of 'knowing' and managing a culture change (Townley, 1994). Personality- and competency-based tests represent the psychological calculation of an applicant's suitability and enable managers to find talented individuals who seem to 'fit' the new culture. Changing and managing culture involves formal and informal work-related learning, a process sociologists call *socialization*. By means of socialization, employees learn the symbols and meanings and shared practices of an organization.

In addition, the performance appraisal system is a systematic HR practice used to classify and rank employees hierarchically according to how well they integrate the newly defined set of beliefs, values and actions into their normal ways of doing things. The newly espoused values are incorporated into the appraisal system to enable employees to be compared with each other, to render them 'known' and to reinforce the desired cultural change. HR *reward* practices can have a reinforcing or 'refreezing' effect when the appraisal system connects desired work behaviours with rewards. For example, given the general commodification of education, new contracts in universities reinforce a 'research culture' in which promotion and pay are tied to research productivity rather than teaching excellence. Administrators or managers can furthermore reinvigorate the culture change process and increase discretionary behaviour with new formal *training* and, importantly, the informal learning of organizational values and routines. The cluster of HR practices mentioned above is a conduit through which dominant shared values can be both carried into the organization and enacted (Purcell et al., 2009). The most sceptical detractors claim that HR practices can help to sustain 'cultural doping' so that individual employees exhibit shared values and routines – how work is performed – congruent with those of their organization (Alvesson and Willmott, 1996). In strong cultures, a metaphorical 'glue' therefore bonds employees and encourages each to internalize the organization's culture because it fulfils their need for social affiliation and identity.

Paradox in culture management

Assuming that top managers are able to change to a strong one-culture organization, is this necessarily desirable? If the central premise of the 'has' theory is that ideas within a social work group are homogeneous, unified and uncontested, a strong one-culture organization can have unintentional consequences. It can give members an organizational identity, reinforce complex friendship networks and employee engagement, and strongly influence designated behaviour without the need for costly bureaucratic controls. However, if fundamental changes are needed, a strong corporate culture can be an impediment to a management mantra of creative thinking, informal learning and innovation. Although the prescriptive literature presents organizational culture as a variable that can be easily manipulated to produce ideal types of coherence and integration to 'fit' new organizational goals, careful consideration should be given to the unintended or paradoxes of such a strategy.

These tensions surface in the relevant literature. Management scholars, who primarily understand the one-culture phenomenon as a unifying force, focus on the counterforces that challenge strong corporate cultures. The lay-off of workers in response to periods of recession and deep cuts in government expenditure are, however, a compelling

HRM in practice 15.2

Can we measure changes in organizational culture?

Much cultural analysis is framed within a workforce commitment–performance relationship in which a configuration of a 'strong' culture produces a loyal workforce and superior performance. The new recognition that in order to provide superior services, especially in service-oriented, team-based workplaces, managers need to enlist the know-how of all their employees places a premium on interpersonal communication (Guirdham, 2011). A culture that emphasizes communication, trust and transparency has helped Baringa Partners, a management consultancy firm, to become a Master Best Workplace: over the last decade it has won its category of the Best Workplaces awards three times and has been ranked in the top ten workplaces (by size) nine times, as shown by these extracts from the Great Place to Work® case study (2016):

"I couldn't recommend working at Baringa more. Even as we grow in numbers, the leadership team are doing everything in their power to ensure we maintain the culture that is so unique."

Baringa credits its success to a strong focus on an open, respectful, non-hierarchical, entrepreneurial and flexible culture which prioritizes caring for, and development of, the individual. […] There are groups and committees across different practice areas of the organization where employees can address challenges, and regular 'Big Ideas' evening and breakfast sessions which offer any employee, who wishes, the chance to help develop ideas for the company's future.

"We try to be very non-hierarchical in the way that we interact," says Dan Look, Senior Partner. "Of course there is a structure in the company, but the conversation is really fluid."

Baringa typically promotes from within, running promotion rounds every quarter… The vast majority of recruitment comes from either employee referrals

(33 per cent) or directly from the website (41 per cent). Baringa also makes sure it's a genuinely fun place to work with annual weekends away for employees and their families, gala dinners, Christmas parties for grown-ups and children…

Despite these impressive accounts of culture management, demonstrating a relationship between a 'strong' culture and superior performance is not without its problems. Ideally, the methodology would permit a calculation of how different cultures – 'weak' versus 'strong' – affect performance, while controlling the other factors influencing performance. The data must demonstrate the extent to which the staff internalize new core values, using a particular set of performance variables over a period of time.

Stop! What HR practices did Baringa use to create a successful culture? How can we be confident about the culture–performance link? What credible evidence do we need to explain the impact of culture on performance?

Sources and further information: See Great Place to Work® (2016) and Guirdham (2011) for more on this topic. Also review Chapter 3, 'HRM and Performance', and look at Ashkanasy et al. (2000).

Note: This feature was written by John Bratton.

reinforcement of the two-culture, or 'us and them', organization. The rationales for investing in training and enlisting employees' tacit knowledge have a similar unintended consequence for managers. The learning-creativity paradigm as a source of competitive advantage and high-quality services is based on critical open dialogue activities that might be considered to be deviant behaviour (Coopey, 1996). Furthermore, initiatives are often the result of workers challenging conventional ideas and solutions and effectively 'rule-breaking'. In other words, a creative culture requires a nurturing and celebration of the creative potential of deviant thinking and action (Bratton and Garrett-Petts, 2008) and can, as such, be viewed as a counterforce to cultural homogeneity.

Organizational culture is embedded in powerful informally shared social interactions and norms. For this reason, the most sceptical detractors argue that culture *as a whole* cannot be 'created, discovered or destroyed by the whims of management' (Meek, 1992, p. 209). Willmott (1993) notes a potentially manipulative intent of corporate agendas for culture change, and details the resistance to strong cultures, or what he calls 'corporate culturalism', that is found among powerful professional groups. For example, in the public sector domain, it is suggested that professionals, may 'evade commercial feeling rules' (Bolton, 2005, p. 108). Sociological studies describe all kinds of unusual and idiosyncratic employee conduct that creates small spaces of 'uncolonized terrain, a terrain which is not and cannot be managed' (Gabriel, 1995, p. 478). The scope for employees to offer 'empty performances' and to be indifferent to officially sponsored values is nicely captured by Goffman's classic study (1961, p. 267; also quoted in Bolton, 2005, p. 138):

> Whenever we look at a social establishment … we find that participants decline in some way to accept the official view of what they should be putting into and getting out of the organization … Where enthusiasm is expected, there will be apathy, where loyalty, there will be disaffection; where attendance, absenteeism; where robustness, some kind of illness; where deeds are to be done, varieties of inactivity … Wherever worlds are laid on, underlives develop.

Furthermore, Ackroyd and Thompson's (1999) concept of 'misbehaviour' emphasizes not only the messy reality of conflict in the workplace, but also the fact that employee resistance to new 'Big Ideas' can be less overt, less familiar, less observable and barely manageable.

Not surprisingly, therefore, critical workplace scholars tend to be highly sceptical about claims of managing cultures, regarding such claims as naive. In particular, the preoccupation with culture obscures enduring structural inequalities, antagonism and conflict (Edwards, 1995). As demonstrated during the global financial crisis that began in 2008, culture does nothing to remove the need for top management to try to reduce labour costs, intensify the pressure of work and render employees redundant. The binary conflict of interest between capital and labour that exists within a 'negotiated order' of mutual cooperation suggests that the significance of organizational culture cannot be grasped unless it is related to structures of power – *power over other people* – within a context of market exigencies. These arguments stress that culture can never be wholly managed because it emerges from complex processes involving how employees construct their sense of identity in ways that are beyond management's control. At the very best, culture-change interventions are only successful at the observable behavioural level rather than the subconscious level (Ogbonna, 1993).

Big Outdoors

The setting

Despite being one of the largest and most developed markets in the world, the retail industry for sports and camping goods in the UK has faced several challenges in recent years. This has come as a result of rising consumer debt, unemployment and demographic shifts causing a movement away from traditional competitive sports. However, the consumer's continued focus on recreational activities, as well as the development of 'extreme' sports such as rock-climbing, ice-climbing and caving, has helped to maintain growth levels. The rising participation of retirees in hill-walking has also helped to protect the market from more serious reversals. Many retail outlets are now offering specialized services and specific brands to attract this new demographic and lure back their cautious loyal customers.

The problem

Established in 1984, Big Outdoors is an outdoor and sporting goods retail firm specializing in hiking and camping equipment. It currently employs 13 full-time workers with an additional 18 part-time workers to assist with increased sales on weekends. As the firm sells to the low end of the market, most of the employees are students supplementing their income to pay for their education who have very little training or experience in the activities the store sells supplies for. The majority of the staff are between the ages of 18 and 23 years old. The hourly pay rate is only slightly more than the minimal wage, and staff turnover is high.

Recently, Big Outdoors was sold to a new owner, Jonathan Tempest, an avid rock-climber, who plans to introduce better quality merchandise with a focus on the high end of the market. His personal business philosophy is 'Focus on high-quality merchandise and excellent customer service, and profit will take care of itself.' With his strong background in the recreational retail industry, Jonathan recognizes that this will require a new business plan as well as a shift in the organization's culture. As the firm is too small to have an in-house HR department to help make these changes, Jonathan decides to hire a local HR consulting firm. He also creates a team of the most experienced employees to provide input into any changes that will be made.

At the first meeting with the consultant Kelly Maynard, Jonathan introduces the team members and lays out his plan to change the firm's merchandise and market focus. However, he admits he is struggling over how to

BANANASTOCK

approach changing the overall culture to fit the new direction of the company. Jonathan stresses he wants the team to take a lead role in this aspect. Kelly asks to have some time to study the firm's current HR practices, including its recruitment, training and reward processes, before she makes any recommendations to Jonathan.

The assignment

Acting as the consultant, prepare a report drawing on the material from this chapter addressing the following:

1 What change interventions can Jonathan introduce in order to create a culture at Big Outdoors that is more aligned with the new strategic vision?
2 What do you think of Jonathan's decision to create an employee team? What role, if any, should members of that team play in implementing a cultural change in the organization?

Essential reading

Burke, W. (2011) *Organizational Change: Theory and Practice*. Los Angeles: Sage.

Schein, E. (2010) *Organizational Culture and Leadership*, 4th edn. San Francisco, CA: Jossey-Bass.

Tushman, M. and O'Reilly, C. (1996) Ambidextrous organizations: managing evolutionary and revolutionary change. *California Management Review*, **38**(4): 8–30.

Note: This case study was written by Lori Rilkoff.

 Visit the online resource centre at **www.palgravehighered.com/bg-hrm-6e** for guidelines on writing reports.

summary

➤ In this chapter, we have explored the nature of organizational culture – a unique configuration of shared artefacts, common language and meanings and shared values that influences ways of doing things in the workplace. The culture of an organization influences what employees should think, believe or value.

➤ We have discussed how national culture and organizational culture are deeply intertwined – each influencing the other, with the latter embedded in society. Yet we have noted that standard accounts of organizational culture have tended to neglect how gender, patriarchy and sexuality in society and in the workplace profoundly influence the dynamics of organizational culture.

➤ We explained that culture analysis can be divided into different schools of thought. The functionalist perspective stresses that culture can play a role in building consensus and harmony, and emphasizes how this can improve performance. It views organizational culture as a variable – it is something that an organization 'has' and can, as such, be produced and managed.

➤ The prescriptive literature tends to present too uniform a view of organizational culture. Alternative approaches point out the existence of subcultures and counterculture. These concepts are important if we believe that organizations consist of individuals and work groups with multiple sets of values and beliefs.

➤ The critical perspective focuses on a sociological concern to describe and critically explain cultural processes, how culture emerges through social interaction, power relations, communities of practice and norms. It also focuses on connections between social inequalities and patriarchal systems *outside* the workplace, and socialization processes and conduct *inside* it. Viewed through a sociologist's lens, culture is something that a work organization '*is*'.

➤ We have emphasized that a set of integrated HR practices is both a carrier through which dominant values are expressed and enacted, and also, by their outcomes, an expression of deep-rooted values. Well-established HR practices have been used to manage culture. However, we have emphasized that managers must be aware of the messy realities that shape complex organizations.

review questions

1 How does national culture relate to organizational culture?

2 Review the functionalist and critical perspectives on organizational culture described in this chapter. Which perspective do you find most appealing and plausible? Why?

3 What impact do expectations about gender have upon workplace activities and HR practices? To what extent, if at all, do notions of masculinity and femininity reinforce or challenge traditional notions of organizational culture?

4 What role can HRM play in creating a more customer-oriented culture?

further reading

Reading these articles and chapters can help you gain a better understanding and potentially a higher grade for your HRM assignment.

➤ To understand the importance of avoiding 'quick fixes' when it comes to organizational culture, see Alvesson, M. (2002) *Understanding Organizational Culture*. London: Sage.

➤ For understanding the difference between organizational culture and organizational climate, see Norton, T. A., Zacher, H. and Ashkanasy, N. M. (2014) Organizational sustainability policies and employee green behaviour: the mediating role of work climate perceptions, *Journal of Environmental Psychology*, **5**: 444–66.

➤ For a comparative study of the importance of organizational culture for recruiting and retaining talented employees, see Kontoghiorghes, C. (2016) Linking high performance organizational culture and talent management: satisfaction/motivation and organizational commitment as mediators. *International Journal of Human Resource Management*, **27**(16): 1833–53.

➤ The links between work values in countries with a different cultural heritage are explored in Warr, P. (2008) Work values: some demographic and cultural correlates. *Journal of Occupational and Organizational Psychology*, **81**: 751–75. See also de Cieri, H. (2008) Transnational firms and cultural diversity. In P. Boxall, J. Purcell and P. Wright (eds) *The Oxford Handbook of Human Resource Management* (pp. 509–29). Oxford: Oxford University Press.

➤ For insight into 'green' workplaces, see Docherty, P.,. Kira, M. and Shan, A. B. (2009) *Creating Sustainable Work Systems* (2nd edn). London: Routledge; Jabbour, C. J. C. (2011) How green are HRM practices, organizational culture, learning and teamwork? A Brazilian study. *Industrial and Commercial Training*, **43**(2): 98–105; and Wehrmeyer, W. (1996) *Greening People: Human Resources and Environmental Management*. Sheffield: Greenleaf Publishing.

➤ More critical accounts of culture management can be found in: Legge, K. (2005) HRM: from compliance to commitment, In *Human Resource Management: Rhetorics and Realities* (pp. 209–40). Basingstoke: Palgrave Macmillan; McSweeney, B. (2002) Hofstede's model of national cultural differences and their consequences: a triumph of faith – a failure of analysis. *Human Relations*, **55**(1): 89–118; Morgan, P. I. and Ogbonna, E. (2008) Subcultural dynamics in transformation: a multi-perspective study of health care professionals. *Human Relations*, **61**(1): 39–65; and Parker, M. (2000) *Organizational Culture and Identity*. London: Sage.

vocabulary checklist for ESL students

Click here in your interactive ebook for a list of HRM terminology and vocabulary that has appeared in this chapter.

Visit the online resource centre at **www.palgravehighered.com/bg-hrm-6e** for lots of extra resources to help you get to grips with this chapter, including study tips, HRM skills development guides, summary lecture notes, tips for English as a Second Language (ESL) students and more.

chapter 16

green HRM and environmental sustainability

© iStockphoto.com

objectives

After studying this chapter, you should be able to:

1 Explain the nature of environmental sustainability

2 Identify the main drivers of sustainable workplace practices and behaviours

3 Explain the benefits expected from implementing sustainability initiatives

4 Explain the role of HRM in creating a low-carbon workplace

The Paris accord on climate change was hailed as historic, with nearly 200 nations agreeing to limit warming to 1.5°C, measured in relation to pre-industrial temperatures. However, 8 months after the target was set, leading climate scientists have warned that the Earth is perilously close to breaking through the 1.5°C limit (McKie, 2016). The environmentalist George Monbiot argues that, on current trends, with 15 of the 16 warmest years occurring in the twenty-first century, humanity already faces an 'existential crisis' (Monbiot, The Guardian, 2016, p. 29). The world's fight against unmanaged climate change demands real commitments from individual governments, multi-national corporations, communities and consumers to wean themselves off fossil fuels. Work organizations are significant contributors to climate change, and they have the potential to positively affect it through the actions of their managers and employees.

introduction

The scientific evidence is clear: human action has already exceeded Earth's regenerative capacity, and economic activity is responsible for the degradation of the environment (Ones and Dilchert, 2012). The world's leading climate scientists report that more than half of the global carbon dioxide allowance has been used up, and, unless checked, the accumulation of carbon in the atmosphere will warm the planet by more than 2°C by 2045. The 2013 Intergovernmental Panel of Climate Change Working Group report (Working Group Contribution to the IPCC Fifth Assessment Report Climate Change, 2013 , p. 4) states that:

> Warming of the climate system is unequivocal, and since the 1950s, many of the observed changes are unprecedented over decades to millennia. The atmosphere and ocean have warmed, the amounts of snow and ice have diminished, sea level has risen, and the concentrations of greenhouse gases have increased.

The report is significant because some have argued that this would result not so much in climate change but, ever more catastrophically, 'climate chaos'. The scientific evidence from 209 leading climate scientists is clear: the planet is past halfway to triggering dangerous climate change, and they are 'unequivocal' that global warming is a result of human actions (Harvey, The Guardian, 2013). Canadian environmentalist Naomi Klein (2015, p. 11), in her book *This Changes Everything*, reminds us of the challenges facing governments and organizations when she observes that preliminary data show that, in 2013, global carbon dioxide emissions were 61 per cent higher than they were in 1990, *'when negotiations toward a climate treaty began in earnest'* (p. 11, emphasis added).

It is within this context that there has been more incentive for organizations to report on their environmental sustainability activities, and in parallel with this, there has been the development of 'sustainable' or 'green' human resource management (HRM) (Ehnert et al., 2016). Here, environmental sustainability incorporates ecological or environmental considerations (for example, carbon emissions) with organizational needs (for example, profitability) in such a way as to reduce destruction and promote benefits for the environment (Norton et al., 2015). That organizations are both part of the problem as well as part of the solution to carbon accumulation is not in doubt. The question examined in this chapter, however, is to what extent do people-oriented management practices contribute to changing behaviours that can create more environmentally sustainable workplaces? As mentioned in Chapter 2, that researchers and organizational leaders are giving greater attention to organizational environmental sustainability can be explained as part of a wider consideration of corporate social responsibility (CSR) and should come as no surprise given that climate change and environmental destruction have become a major concern for humanity (Klein, 2015).

This chapter therefore begins by introducing the concept of organizational environmental sustainability and discusses its importance to contemporary management. The chapter then identifies the main drivers of sustainable workplace practices and behaviours before going on to explain the role of HRM in creating low-carbon workplaces (LCWs) – what they are, and how effective they are at encouraging low-carbon behaviours.

reflective question 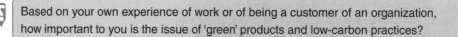 Based on your own experience of work or of being a customer of an organization, how important to you is the issue of 'green' products and low-carbon practices?

The meaning of environmental sustainability

The meaning of sustainability has developed over several decades and is multidimensional. The term 'sustainability' has its roots in the Latin word *sustinere*, meaning 'to hold up'. Throughout much of the late twentieth century, where sustainability did enter management parlance, it was largely viewed from a narrow liberal-economic perspective, with sustainability understood simply as a management practice, with little consideration of conflicting employee and managerial interests. 'A popular term, *sustainability* has become one of those motherhood concepts that is hard to oppose, but difficult to pin down' (Sumner, 2005, p. 76, emphasis in original).

The broader discourse of sustainability evolved in the 1970s and 80s with publications of critical academic work on the ecological limits of liberal economic growth (for example, Carson, 1962; Meadows et al., 1972; Schumacher, 1973). The issue of sustainability was initially debated at the 1972 United Nations Conference on the Human Environment in Stockholm (Buttel, 1998; Mebratu, 1998; cited in Sumner 2005, p. 79). A significant development came with the formation of the United Nations' World Commission for Environment and Development (WCED), which subsequently provided the now classical definition of sustainable development: 'development that meets the needs of the present without compromising the ability of future generations to meet their own needs (1987, p. 43).

Conceptually, the meaning of sustainability, as cited in the Brundtland Commission, 'can be understood as an overarching worldview recognizing the interconnectedness of ecological, social, and economic factors in human activity' (Docherty et al., 2009, p. 6). The Commission's report also introduced 'the concept of justice (within and between generations, global justice and justice through participation and democratic arrangements) as a central issue in relation to efforts to enhance sustainability' (Lund, 2004, p. 43).

'Sustainability science' is an interdisciplinary field that seeks to enhance sustainability by integrating knowledge from a range of disciplines including natural sciences, engineering, social sciences and the humanities (Kates et al., 2001). The challenge for sustainability science is to ensure that knowledge production is a communal effort that links academic research with industry and government, and benefits individuals and society (Wiek et al., 2012). Sustainability science is embedded within broader social processes of understanding, and thus contributes to organizational decision-making processes through the creation of knowledge (particularly analyses of risks and consequences) derived from emergent interdisciplinary enquiry (Kasemir, 2003). Although it is recognized that there is a multiplicity of viewpoints, sustainability is for an increasing number of organizational and environmental writers the ultimate goal – that is, 'living within the regenerative capacity of the biosphere' (Wackernagel et al., 2002, p. 9266). Importantly, in terms of managing work and people, scholars of sustainability science advocate participatory and collaborative approaches to the co-generation of knowledge and environmental decision-making (Blackstock et al., 2007).

This chapter focuses on environmental sustainability. Environmental management is an attempt to control the human impact on and interaction with the natural environment in order to preserve natural resources. At the organizational level, corporate environmental performance refers to 'organizational performance in managing natural resources and the natural environment in the process of conducting business' (Ones and Dilchert, 2012, p. 450). Corporate environmental performance includes both environmental outcomes and the pro-environmental initiatives that organizations implement. The former represent the ecological impact or 'footprint' of organizational activities; the latter focus on what organizations do for environmental sustainability. In the workplace, this includes encouraging energy efficiency, waste reduction and recycling, water conservation, and employees' use of alternative low-carbon forms of transportation (for example, a bus, train or bicycle). At the individual level, workplace pro-environmental behaviour can be defined as 'a systematic set of actions from a collective network of organizational actors spread across a company, team, and/or value chain' (Kennedy et al., 2015, p. 370). For employees, this entails changes to their existing job duties, additional requirements of their position and, in some cases, the creation of entirely new occupational opportunities, such as 'environmental manager' (Ones and Dilchert, 2012).

Although environmental sustainability has been debated for decades, it is an emerging concept in the business world, and the existing literature provides numerous and varied interpretations of it. In contemporary management parlance, sustainability has been used to refer to values and ethics, as well as goals such as CSR.

Some organizations offer incentives to those who choose low-carbon methods of travelling to work. For example, 'Cycle to Work' schemes provide financial assistance to purchase a bicycle.

ImageSource

In 1997, expert John Elkington, for example, coined the term 'triple bottom line' or 'P3' – People, Planet and Profit – which emphasizes that, in sustainable workplaces, human and social resources along with ecological and economic resources should be able to grow and develop. From a work systems perspective, sustainability has been described as an ongoing process of efficiency *and* improved environmental and social performance (Docherty et al., 2009). For Norton and his colleagues (2015), organizational efficiency and improvements to the planet are combined in the concept of 'environmental sustainability'. In the organizational context, this means that environmental sustainability incorporates business needs (for example, profitability) with environmental consideration (for example, lower carbon emissions) in such a way as to be ecologically beneficial to the planet.

Thus, pro-environmental low-carbon behaviours are necessary but not sufficient for environmental (corporate) sustainability. Popular corporate strategy authors have been optimistic, arguing that although the concept is understood to mean different things to different people, it has nevertheless made a positive social and environmental impact. For example, management strategy expert Michael Porter, championing the concept of creating shared value, has argued that the ongoing efforts of certain corporations are helping to transform sustainability from a 'cliché term' to an innovative and enduring business strategy (Porter and Kramer 2006, 2011).

The burgeoning literature demonstrates that sustainability is no longer a fringe issue. Corporate titans, for example retailer Wal-Mart (Wal-Mart, 2015), Google (Google, 2015) and British Petroleum plc. (BP, 2015) have embraced elements of sustainability. In the twentieth century, occupational health and safety was always an issue for trade unions, but in the twenty-first century, institutions such as the International Labour Organization, the European Trade Union Confederation and the British Trades Union Congress (TUC) in the UK have also embraced the wider concept of sustainability. Sustainability is particularly relevant to 'mission-driven organizations such as governments, charities, and universities, because they are not evaluated in traditional financial terms, and have missions that go beyond the bottom line' (Boudreau and Ramstad, 2005, p. 130). This trend towards sustainability, no doubt influenced by the environmental movement of the 1980s and the CSR movement of the 1990s, has influenced organizational leaders to become increasingly aware of the need to build positive relations with stakeholders, both internal and external to the organization (Harrison and Freeman, 1998).

The concept of sustainability has evolved since its first usage over 30 years ago. There is a general consensus in the literature that the concept of sustainability is linked to nature, the notion of resource conservation, and as outlined by Dyllick and Hockerts (2002), present-day interpretations of the term have been influenced primarily by three different stakeholder groups: ecologists, business strategy scholars, and the United Nations (WCED, 1987). While its origin begins with the natural environment, the concept often embodies a human emphasis, 'reflecting not only a concern for our future, but also an unease with our current situation and an emphasis on human agency' (Sumner, 2005, p. 78). Instead of helping to improve our understanding of sustainability, these contradictory interpretations and their tensions indicate the kind of problem that sustainability can pose, both in evaluating the literature and in terms of employers and employees working in partnership towards more sustainable outcomes in the workplace. Following the perspective throughout this textbook, sustainability is examined here through a prism that recognizes that the employment relationship is, by necessity, cooperative but also entails unavoidable structural conflict between the managers and workers.

The workplace, behaviours and environmental management systems

The extant literature on sustainable workplaces raises the possibility that work organizations, through appropriate processes, policies and practices, can make strategic choices that can enhance natural resource efficiency and reduce the amount of greenhouse gases emitted into the atmosphere. It is in the workplace therefore where human resources (HR) policies and practices have their effects on the issue of work itself and, by extension, on employee behaviour, labour productivity and environmental sustainability (Bratton and Bratton, 2015). It is to the workplace that one must look to examine how managers' and workers' behaviours and own goals combine to create an LCW regime that governs how work is actually performed (Kersley et al., 2006; van Wanrooy et al., 2013b). The workplace is a site where social relationships shape interests, motives and the actions of managers and workers, and where cooperation and resistance around management objectives takes place in a 'contested terrain' (Edwards, 1979). Workplace sustainability is therefore more than a technical challenge – it goes to the very heart of managing people.

Ultimately, the solution to reducing carbon emissions in the workplace lies with the social sciences that are tasked with changing employee behaviour. In this regard, Renwick et al. (2016) observe, the embedded nature of green HRM (GHRM) workplace-level practices, and therefore the role of HRM, is to identify the challenges in terms of employee behaviour. The object is to develop policies and practices to bring about specified pro-environmental behaviours in alignment with the organization's strategic goals. Ones and Dilchert (2012) define pro-environmental behaviours as 'individual behaviours contributing to environmental sustainability' (for example, purchasing an ecofriendly vehicle or recycling). These behaviours are rooted in individuals' own lifestyle and initiative. In contrast, employee pro-environmental behaviours entail a certain degree of managerial oversight or control. They are defined as 'scalable actions and behaviours that employees engage in that are linked with and contribute to or detract from environmental sustainability' (2012, p. 452). This definition therefore focuses on what employees do and excludes those behaviours under the control of the employee. Employee pro-environmental behaviours mostly comprise task performance or organizational citizenship (commitment and engagement) behaviours. Empirical research in this area has

The decision to buy an electric car would be an example of an individual behaviour.

Photoalto

demonstrated that effective environmental management depends, to a large extent, on various behaviours intended to reduce pollution, minimize waste, contribute to eco-innovations and participate in recycling programmes (Boiral et al., 2015; Cox et al., 2012).

Within the emergent sustainable workplace literature, it has been argued that in order to work towards the goal of environmental risk management, organizational managers must develop an environmental management system (EMS). An EMS is the most widely recognized tool for managing the impacts of an organization's activities on the environment. It refers to the management of an organization's environmental impact in a comprehensive, systematic, planned and documented manner. It incorporates people, procedures and working practices into a formal structure, involves all members of an organization as appropriate, promotes continual improvement including periodically evaluating environmental performance, and actively engages senior management in support of the EMS (see, for example, Zutshi and Sohal 2004). EMS enables organizations to achieve more environmentally sustainable processes, practices and outcomes (see, for example, Jabbour et al., 2010). Thus, the focus is on improving environmental performance and maintaining compliance with environmental regulations. As EMS and risk management are analogous activities, EMS supports an organization's overall approach to environmental risk management.

reflective question What internal and external factors drive organizations to introduce low-carbon practices?

Drivers of workplace sustainability

Managers attempting to create sustainable workplaces are often less effective than they might be because they do not understand the 'drivers' of change (Jørgensen et al., 2008). Here, drawing on data from the author's own research, we give a brief overview of the internal and external drivers towards sustainable LCWs. In order to create a LCW, change agents need to know and reflect upon a number of mediating variables in cause and effect, including employees' attitudes (for example, commitment to the workplace), employees' behaviours (for example, conforming to a 'green' policy), external regulatory bodies and the management of organizational risk. Change agents also need to understand that their own leadership behaviour and the organization's culture and climate directly and indirectly affect managers' and other employees' behaviours and the overall success of a low-carbon strategy (see Chapters 14 and 15).

Despite the research on organizations' sustainability strategies, it remains unclear why some organizations adopt sustainability initiatives beyond regulatory compliance (Delmas and Toffel, 2004; Gabzdylova et al., 2009). The drivers of sustainability initiatives can be grouped into internal and external drivers. Internal drivers include the personal or ethical values of managers, employee environmental champions, a desire to reduce operational costs, employee engagement, the organizational culture, investor pressure and, since the 1990s, CSR (Gabzdylova et al., 2009; Hanna et al., 2000; Walker et al., 2008). External drivers of change, on the other hand, are associated with legislative and regulatory compliance. For example, the Scottish government's new procurement policy is designed to encourage companies to develop a sustainable and socially just corporate strategy. According to Infrastructure Secretary Keith Brown:

> Our model of procurement, putting the social, economic and environmental aspects of sustainability at the heart of all we do, remains the foundation of our approach. Employers must now recognize, as many already do, that if you want to do business with the public sector in Scotland, you have to be a responsible employer and value your workers. … Companies will also be required to commit to giving workers an 'active voice' in the workplace. (Brown, 2015, p. 1)

Other external drivers of change include increased energy costs, gaining competitive advantage, access to government funds, stakeholder and customer pressures for sustainable business models, products and services, as well as pressures from suppliers, environmental groups, trade unions and public opinion that impinge on the organization (see, for example, Haigh and Jones, 2006). Guerci et al's (2016) study of HR managers and supply chain managers operating in Italy examined how low-carbon HR practices can be implemented in response to stakeholder pressures. The authors found that 'green' HR practices mediated the relationship between pressures on environmental issues from external stakeholders (customers and regulatory stakeholders) and environmentally sustainable performance.

Change management 'trigger-response' theories, proposing that the stimulus of external change prompts management action, have been critiqued on the grounds of 'environmental determinism' (Duncan, 1972), and for considering that the external 'context' and 'organization' are discrete spheres, which tends to downplay the importance of strategic choice (Child, 1972). Changes in these various internal and external drivers might cause managers to consider the need for sustainability initiatives, but every organization has its own peculiar history and context. The context and character of the sector in which the organization is located shapes some of these drivers of change. The top six internal and external drivers encountered in Bratton's (2016, p. 103, unpublished) study of six work-places in Scotland are shown in Table 16.1.

Table 16.1 *Rank order of environmental managers' perceptions of drivers of sustainability initiatives*

Internal	External
1. Reducing organizational risk exposure	1. Regulatory compliance
2. New product/service opportunities	2. Reducing the impact on the local environment
3. Promoting social responsibility	3. Providing assurance to stakeholders and regulators
4. Ethical reasons	4. Customer demand
5. Reducing costs/efficiency savings	5. Maintaining rapport with government agencies and non-governmental organizations
6. Health and safety	6. Maintaining a 'licence to operate'

Source: Bratton, A. (2016) 'Creating Sustainable Workplaces Together: Employee Relations Practice & Environmental Management', unpublished PhD thesis.

With regard to internal factors, reducing organizational risk exposure was considered to be 'very important' in four out of the six cases. Risk has been defined as 'an uncertain (generally adverse) consequence of an event or activity with respect to something that humans value' (International Risk Governance Council 2005, p. 4). Correspondingly, risk governance is concerned with the identification, assessment, management and communication of risks in a broad context (IRGC, 2005). Concern with reputational risk was highlighted in the author's research in six case studies. In this research, several interviewees reported that because their organization was well known and in the public eye, they were

Carney urges companies to reveal carbon footprint

Organizations introduce sustainability strategies for both internal and external reasons. The internal reasons include the personal pro-environmental values of leaders, environmental champions, among the managers, the need to reduce operational costs and pressure from investors. The external drivers of change, on the other hand, are associated with legislative and regulatory compliance and pressure from consumers. Customer boycotts can be effective. If an organization adopts an environmentally sustainable business model because of customer boycotts, its action is driven by self-interest, especially if the customer happens to be a pension fund looking for 'green' investment. Greater transparency on the organization's carbon emissions may act to drive change, as the following report (copyright Guardian News & Media Ltd 2016) suggests:

Getty

> *Mark Carney [the governor of the Bank of England] has called for companies to disclose their carbon footprints to help investors to make clearer decisions about whether or not to back them. 'One of the best things that can be done is disclosure of carbon footprint.'*
>
> *It is not the first time Bank officials have intervened on the subject of climate change and its impact on businesses. Paul Fisher, the deputy head of its regulatory arm, said in March [2015] that insurance companies could be hit if their investments in fossil fuels ended up being worthless. He described such assets as potentially 'stranded' if policy changes limited the use of fossil fuels. At a World Bank meeting a year ago [in 2014], Carney said the vast majority of fossil fuel reserves may be unburnable if the world was to limit temperature rises to 2°C. Such restrictions could send shockwaves through the financial markets. Carney, speaking at a conference on inclusive capitalism, said investors needed information on carbon footprints to make judgements about companies.* (Treanor, The Guardian, 2015b, p. 42)

The potential for fossil fuel assets to be 'stranded' perhaps helps to explain the cool response from the oil and energy companies to the 2015 Paris accord on climate change. Coal and oil executives shrugged off any suggestion that the agreement would have any impact on their businesses, and the 1.5°C goal was described as merely 'aspirational' (Clark and

Sevastopulo, 2015, p. 1). There are multiple external and internal drivers that cause organizations to create LCW. The STEPLE framework – **S**ocial, **T**echnological, **E**conomic, **P**olitical, **L**egal and **E**cological – provides a wide-ranging audit of the organization's external context with the purpose of using the information to guide strategic decisions around issues such as environmental sustainability (see Bratton, 2015).

Stop! Mark Carney warned that the 'age of irresponsibility' was coming to an end. What is the most effect way to make multinational corporations act responsibly towards the natural environment: is it through legislation, market forces or consumer boycotts? In the light of the Paris accord, what role do organizational leaders have in promoting workplace pro-environmental behaviours? And, in times of recession in the oil industry, and amidst downsizing, what role, if any, has the HR professional?

Sources and further information: For background information, see Treanor (2015b), Clark and Sevastopulo (2015) and Bratton (2015). More discussion can be found in Mackey and Sisodia (2014), Guerci et al. (2016) Carrington (2015), Shankleman (2014), and Llanwarne (2016).

Note: This feature was written by John Bratton.

under considerable pressure and scrutiny from different stakeholders to address environmental issues that arose from their operations. For example, commenting on the potential reputational risk associated with poor recycling performance on trains, a graduate environmental manager argued that, 'It is very visual that we don't do it. All it takes is a couple of concerned people on the train to say, "you are not recycling, I'll Tweet that or Facebook that"' (Bratton, 2016, p. 105, unpublished).

Research has also demonstrated that the reduction of operating costs is a key driver of change. In Bratton's (2016, unpublished) study, the majority of respondents indicated that reducing costs was either a 'very important' or 'important' driver. In all six cases, sustainability initiatives involving electricity use were seen as an effective strategy to reduce overall energy costs. In the public sector cases, energy reduction programmes were seen as a strategy to reduce costs and maintain service levels. Unsurprisingly, in the transport industry, a significant motivator behind the implementation of low-carbon technology was the desire to reduce fuel costs. For example, transport companies recognized that pollution reflects hidden costs and that, by implementing eco-driving training and driver assistance technology management aimed at preventing unnecessary pollution, they could improve fuel efficiency and decrease the overall cost of fuel. In the public sector cases, government budget cuts and increased energy prices provided the financial context to certain sustainability initiatives. This was most evident in one case where the recent 'agile' working and office rationalization programme was predominantly marketed as first a cost-saving measure and second a carbon reduction initiative. The driver was explained like this:

> The services are now recognizing that reducing energy costs is one of the measures that they can take to reduce their overall costs. There is a lot of talk in the council about revenue generation and ideas for that, but gradually people are coming around to the idea that resource efficiency and reducing consumption can also come from the bottom-up to support that. (Bratton, 2016, p. 108, unpublished).

The evidence suggests that, in the context of UK and Scottish government budget cuts, sustainability activities were seen as a strategy to control and reduce operating costs and maintain service levels. These findings are consistent with research by Cox et al. (2012) and Zibarras and Ballinger (2011) that reports initiatives to reduce energy as one of the most common sustainability initiatives.

Table 16.1 shows that the promotion of social responsibility and ethical considerations ranked third and fourth, respectively, of the internal drivers. In three cases, health and safety was a 'very important' consideration. The mantra of CSR is based on the belief that organizations are expected to provide 'green' measures that reduce carbon emissions or waste (Docherty et al., 2009). Again, in Bratton's (2016, unpublished) research of Scottish private and public sector organizations, a number of interviewees expressed a 'moral' imperative for their sustainability initiatives, articulating a belief that encouraging low-carbon behaviour is the 'right' thing to do. For example, in both the public and private sector, ethical considerations motivated senior managers to increase engagement in sustainability at a workplace level. The notion of ethical environmental behaviour was expressed in such terms: 'To start with (economics) was not a driver it was mostly it is the right thing to do' (Bratton, 2016, p. 106, unpublished).

With regard to external factors, research found that regulatory compliance seems to underpin the different sustainability initiatives, and is the context for other observed drivers (Bratton, 2016, unpublished). The study found that, in four out of six case studies, environmental managers considered that meeting regulatory compliance requirements was 'very important'. In all of the cases, sustainability initiatives involving waste and recycling were driven by the Waste (Scotland) Regulations 2012. In terms of energy initiatives, at one company in the study government legislation drove investment in sustainability initiatives through a combination of higher costs associated with increased taxes and reputational risk. Environmental legislation underpinned many of the sustainability initiatives, and provided the context for other observed drivers.

The Climate Change (Scotland) Act 2009 is the centerpiece of the Scottish Government's climate change policy framework. The Act includes an emissions target, set for the year 2050, for a reduction of at least 80 per cent from the baseline year, 1990. The Act requires public sector bodies to engage in climate change mitigation and adaptation activities, integrate greenhouse gases into decision-making, and act in way that it considers most sustainable. For example, the Act requires public bodies to set annual greenhouse emissions targets and demonstrate compliance with duties through transparent and open reporting.

In Bratton's (2016, unpublished) study, interviewees from both public and private sector organizations noted the Act and highlighted their responsibility to reduce greenhouse gas emissions and to help with decarbonizing the economy. For example, the Programme Manager at one public sector organization described the role of government legislation in shaping organizational activities like this: 'We are a public body so we are required to carry out a number of duties laid down in the Climate Change legislation of 2009 that the Scottish Government passed and we have an obligation to work toward the low-carbon Scotland' (Bratton, 2016, p. 111, unpublished). The Climate Change Act (Scotland) 2009 was often noted as a key driver for sustainability initiatives. Other common external drivers were reducing the overall impact on the local environment and providing assurance to stakeholders and regulators, which were ranked second and third, respectively.

reflective question What benefits can organizations, employees and society expect from investment in sustainable low-carbon practices?

Benefits expected of implementing sustainability initiatives

From a management and cost-savings perspective, a range of benefits is associated with implementing low-carbon initiatives (Zutshi and Sohal, 2004). Organizational decision-makers expect both quantifiable and non-quantifiable benefits from investment in sustainable practices. For example, Mike Barry, Head of Sustainable Business at retailer Marks and Spencer (M&S), argues that energy efficiency in 2011/12 saved the company £22 million; using fewer raw materials and reducing packaging saved £16.3 million; using less vehicle fuel saved £2.1 million; and waste reduction and recycling more saved £6.3 million (M&S, 2012). The perceived benefits of pro-environmental behaviours and initiatives are typically classified as 'internal' and 'external' (Hillary, 2004; Zutshi and Sohal, 2004). Internal benefits are those deemed to have positive outcomes resulting directly from low-carbon sustainability practices and relate to the internal operation of the organization. The internal benefits can be grouped into three categories: (1) organizational benefits; (2) financial benefits; and (3) people benefits (Hillary, 2004). The expected internal benefits identified are presented in Table 16.2.

Table 16.2 *Expected internal benefits of sustainability initiatives categories and examples*

Organizational benefits	Financial benefits	People benefits
Encouraging innovation	Cost savings from material, energy and waste reductions and efficiencies	Improved employee motivation, awareness and qualifications
Investment in training	Access to government funds and assistance	Enhanced skills and improved knowledge
Improved working conditions and safety		Providing a forum for dialogue between employees and management
Reduced costs or efficiency savings		Financial or non-monetary rewards linked to environmental performance
Demonstrating environmental responsibility		Providing a socially responsible workplace
		Long-term job security

Source: Bratton, A. (2016, p. 119) 'Creating Sustainable Workplaces Together: Employee Relations Practice & Environmental Management', unpublished PhD thesis.

Focusing on the social construction of change through training and learning can have far-reaching effects. The process influences not only how job tasks are undertaken, but also how employees relate to, and learn from, others, including change agents. Learning in the workplace can promote 'action learning' (Gold et al., 2013) and provide opportunities for 'reflexive practice' (Cunliffe, 2004), all of which can help managers and other employees to learn about and facilitate sustainable practices. In Bratton's (2016, unpublished) research, the importance of investing in workplace training and learning was explained by an Energy Efficiency Manager like this:

> We do have an e-learning course on sustainability which line-managers can go through to help their understanding ... There are two separate modules. There is one that is a global module and then there is another one that is a (company) module that explains what we do in terms of sustainability. (Bratton, 2016, p. 120, unpublished).

The evidence suggests that investment in learning may potentially help managers and workers to make sense of the need to change to low-carbon behaviours, which can facilitate innovation, make savings from energy and waste reductions, and increase employees' motivation and environmental awareness (Brio et al., 2007; Dyllick and Hockerts, 2002; Carmona-Moreno et al., 2012). External benefits are positive outcomes from the implementation of sustainability practices that relate to the external interaction of the organization. External benefits can be grouped into three categories (1) commercial benefits; (2) environmental benefits; and (3) communication benefits (Hillary, 2004). The expected external benefits identified are presented in Table 16.3.

Table 16.3 Expected external benefits of sustainability initiatives categories and examples

Commercial benefits	Environmental benefits	Communication benefits
Gaining new customers/business and satisfying existing customers	Improved environmental performance	Creating a positive public image
Gaining a competitive/marketing advantage	Increased energy and material efficiencies	Developing better customer relationships
Developing more environmentally friendly products and services	Increased recycling	Developing better cooperation and relationships with regulators and administrative bodies
Continuing to operate/stay in business	Reduced pollution	Developing better cooperation and relationships with suppliers
	Improved biodiversity	Improving communication with stakeholders
		Setting an example for other organizations in the sector

Source: Bratton, A. (2016, p. 120) 'Creating Sustainable Workplaces Together: Employee Relations Practice & Environmental Management', unpublished PhD thesis.

The evidence suggests that external benefits are linked to gaining new customers and achieving a competitive advantage, reducing waste and energy consumption, improving environmental performance, and improving the organization's public image and stakeholder relations (for example, Morrow and Rondinelli, 2002; Zutshi and Sohal, 2004). These expected and achieved benefits are, it seems, driving organizations to adopt sustainability practices as a part of their operations. The top three internal and external benefits are shown in Table 16.4.

Table 16.4 Rank order of managers' perceptions of internal and external benefits of sustainability initiatives

Internal	External
1. Improved employee engagement	1. Better product/service offerings
2. Providing a socially responsible workplace	2. Improved brand
3. Lower operating costs for products and services	3. Increased competitive advantage

Source: Bratton, A. (2016, p. 103) 'Creating Sustainable Workplaces Together: Employee Relations Practice & Environmental Management', unpublished PhD thesis.

In the author's study, environmental managers ranked 'Improved employee engagement' as the top internal benefit. In three cases, managers considered this benefit 'significant' and in two cases 'very significant'. One manager explained how the corporate-led sustainability initiatives contributed to employee engagement like this:

> When you look at a part of the university as a community that is working together on something and you try to implement programmes which get them to spend more time together not competing from research money, but actually working together on things that has a huge benefit improving the whole institution, improving people's quality of life, improving people's quality of work ... Now whether or not you are doing it for the purposes of sustainability actually doesn't matter so much, but sustainability has given us an opportunity to implement that type of programme because actually getting people to work together like that is more effective than trying to control everything from the centre (Bratton, 2016, p. 122, unpublished).

This evidence suggests that employee engagement processes 'builds' a sense of shared goals and culture that potentially improves social relations by fostering a 'community' and creates opportunities for shared learning and innovation. This observation supports Hanna et al. (2000) and Russo and Fouts's (1997) findings on the 'human' dimension of corporate sustainability.

Ranked third in the list of external benefits is 'increased competitive advantage'. In two cases, this variable was considered a 'significant' benefit, and in two other cases it was deemed 'very significant'. One manager at one transport company explained how the organization's environmental performance contributed to their overall competitive advantage like this: 'We are very much seen as an industry exemplar when it comes just to public transport in general and there is an expectation upon us that almost without asking people expect us to operate at a high degree of sustainability anyway' (Bratton, 2016, p. 123, unpublished).

This finding is consistent with other studies that examine the commercial benefits of implementing sustainability practices (for example, Hillary, 2004; Zutshi and Sohal, 2004), and with Cox et al.'s (2012, p. 3) observation that: 'Pragmatic motivations for cost reduction can sit comfortably alongside pro-environmental objectives'.

Creating a low-carbon workplace through leadership and culture change

Can HR practices contribute to workplace environmental sustainability? A growing body of research has highlighted the importance of leadership (Robertson and Barling, 2015a) and organizational culture and climate (Norton et al., 2015) to both organizational and employee-level pro-environmental performance. Within the strategic management context, the goal of environmental leadership is to motivate followers to achieve high levels of environmentally related performance. Egri and Herman (2000, p. 572) defined environmental leadership as 'the ability to influence individuals and mobilize organizations to realize a vision of long-term ecological sustainability'. This definition is based on the notion that guided by eco-centric values and assumptions, environmental leaders seek to change economic and social systems that they perceive as currently and potentially threatening to the health of the biophysical environment. Robertson and Barling's (2015a) framework for environmental leadership underscores the importance of leaders, inspired by their own personal values, striving 'to influence others at all levels of the organization in an effort to benefit the natural environment' (p. 166). Environmental leaders typically demonstrate transformational patterns of behaviour including charisma, two-way communication, values of collaboration, and orientation towards changing work systems that reduce the environmental impact of an organization. It has been argued that 'leaders' supportive behaviours have been shown to be a crucial component of environmental leadership' (Robertson and Barling, 2015a, p. 170).

A 'sustainability leader' can extend beyond senior managers (Ferdig, 2007; Schein, 2010). Robertson and Barling (2015a, p. 169) found that pro-environmental leaders are more likely to (1) possess personal values that go beyond self-interest, (2) have favourable attitudes toward the natural environment, (3) perceive social pressure to support environmental and sustainability initiatives, and (4) view environmental issues as commercial opportunities for their organization. Other studies have identified different types of behaviours enacted by sustainability leaders, including line management supportive behaviours (Ramus, 2001). These behaviours include encouraging innovation among employees, competence-building, communicating ideas on sustainability, dissemination of information, rewards and recognition, and management of goals and responsibilities by disseminating environmental targets and responsibilities. Kotter (2012) points to the importance of leadership behaviours that encourage employee involvement and participation in organizational change. Participation at all levels of management is essential to the introduction of environmental sustainability change (Davis and Coan, 2015). However, internal workplace stakeholders – specifically front-line managers – are seen to be critical to the overall success of an organization's low-carbon strategy (Bratton and Bratton, 2015).

Supporting the change process, findings across several studies consistently show that, when implementing sustainability initiatives, managers and leaders need to consider organizational culture and climate (Norton et al., 2015; Russell and McIntosh, 2011) (see Chapter 15). Norton and his colleagues (2015) argue that, in creating a pro-environmental workplace, it is imperative that the organization's culture emphasizes values toward the natural environment in such a way that employees have shared perceptions of those values – what Norton et al. call organizational 'climate' (p. 322). A pro-environmental organizational culture is defined as:

> A pattern of shared basic assumptions learned by a group as it adapts to the challenges posed by human activity's impact on the natural environment in a way that permits day-to-day functioning, which has worked well enough to be considered valid and, therefore, to be taught to new members as the correct way to perceive, think, and feel in relation to environmental sustainability. (Norton et al., 2015, p. 329–30).

A pro-environmental climate at the individual level – defined as 'employees' shared perceptions of pro-environmental policies, procedures, and practices that an organization rewards and supports' (Norton et al., 2015, p. 335) – acts as a mediator between the perception of, for instance, pro-environmental HR policies and the pro-environmental behaviour of employees. Research strongly suggests leaders and organizational culture and climate influence employees' and their organizations' environmental performance. There is debate regarding whether organizations need to have an underlying 'moral commitment to sustainability' (Davis and Coan, 2015, p. 247), which suggests that there is a need for the principles, assumptions and values that underpin the organization's norms and rules to be changed if sustainability is to be achieved (see, for example, Hayes, 2014). This introduces the concept of 'cultural congruence', that is, in order for an organization to become environmentally sustainable, its underlying values and assumptions must be aligned with sustainability interventions in such a way that employees' attitudes and behaviours scaffold the organization's overall low-carbon strategic objectives (Davis and Coan, 2015; Russell and McIntosh, 2011). A sustainable LCW is therefore associated with specific pro-environmental attitudes, values and behaviours. Taken together, the available research findings identify two key antecedents or enablers of pro-environmental behaviours and initiatives, which are pro-environmental leadership and a pro-environmental culture and climate.

Creating a low-carbon workplace through HR practices

What role do HRM variables or practices play in developing employees' pro-environmental behaviours? Fernandez et al. (2003, p. 641) highlight the important role of HRM in environmental sustainability:

> The impact on performance will take place when the human resource management system is inserted into the organization's architecture and environmental awareness becomes part of a company's culture.

The established use of HR processes in occupational health and safety, minimum waste production as part of a 'lean' manufacturing system (see Chapter 13) and cultural management make HRM well positioned to coordinate the goal of a low-carbon sustainable organization (Jabbour et al., 2010; Oliveira and Pinheiro, 2009).

Scholarship investigating the connections between HRM and environmental management has been called GHRM (Renwick et al., 2013; Jackson and Seo, 2010). An early contribution to the field of study was Wehrmeyer's (1996) book *Greening People: Human Resources and Environmental Management*. As discussed in Chapters 1 and 2 of this text, HRM is associated with a distinctive managerial philosophy and style, and organizational culture, and there has been wide debate around 'best-fit' and 'best-practice' as a way to link HRM to corporate strategy in order to enhance organizational performance (Boxall and Purcell, 2011). Extending the concept of the high-performance workplace to include environmental sustainability, an LCW has been defined (Bratton and Bratton, 2015, p. 277) as:

> A planned approach to organization design, culture, and HR practices to deliver low-carbon outcomes in the workplace as well as to align the organization and its processes to achieve innovation and sustainable high-quality results for the organization, workforce, and customers.

An LCW requires new roles and low-carbon behavioural activities for managers and other employees. Low-carbon behaviours occur at three levels: individual, social, and material (Cox et al., 2012):

- Individual-level influences act on individual motivations (for example, personal rewards)
- Social-level influences act on employees when operating in teams or groups (for example, social norms, shared understandings and communities of practice)
- Material level influences act on organizational structure and processes (for example, products, technology and environment).

The research by Cox et al. (2012) suggests that behavioural interventions tend to be most successful when they consider these three contexts – individual, group and material – holistically, and not simply focus on trying to change individual employee attitudes or just installing new technology. In other words, when establishing an LCW, the goal should be to take an integrated approach that raises awareness and improves understanding with individuals employees and groups, builds social meaning and norms around pro-environmental low-carbon or 'sustainable' working practices, and supports employees with the technology they need, backed up with consistent policies.

What HR practices do you think could encourage pro-environmental behaviours and why? Can you think of any unintended consequences arising from green HR practices?

HRM scholars have tried to identify effective ways to change manifestations of a low-carbon organizational culture through modified HR practices. The emergent literature on GHRM emphasizes that a set of integrated HR practices covering recruitment, selection, performance management, training and development, rewards and employment relations can promote pro-environmental behaviours at work and build a more environmentally sustainable organizational culture (Figure 16.1).

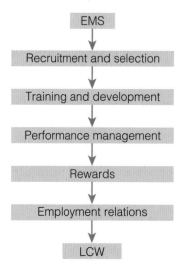

Figure 16.1 *Creating an LCW through HR practices*

Existing GHRM studies highlight the opportunity for improved environmental performance when the goals, policies and procedures of EMSs are more closely aligned or 'embedded' (Purcell and Kinnie, 2008) with HR practices and wider activities of the organization (see, for example, Brio et al., 2008; Chen, 2011; Jørgensen, 2000). However, this convergence, between HR practices and organizational culture is considered secondary in classic studies of organizational sustainability (see, for example, Shrivastava, 1995; Wehrmeyer, 1996).

A central question that arises from the literature is whether effective environmental sustainability initiatives can develop from top-down management driven exercises, or whether they are more likely to be successful if they are part of a more grass-roots, employee-led initiative for environmental sustainability in the workplace. To date, much of the GHRM research has focused on HR practices: recruitment and selection, performance management and appraisal, rewards, and training and workplace learning.

Recruitment and selection

Environmental sustainability has become an important dimension shaping the recruitment and selection process. Research suggests that attracting top candidates is easier for organizations known for their superior environmental stewardship (Guerci et al., 2016; Gully et al., 2013; Rupp et al., 2013). An Italian study found, for example, that 'green recruiting practices' could have a distinct and direct effect on attracting applicants (Guerci et al., 2016). One obvious way to build a sustainable workplace is through self-selection of prospective employees. For example, German companies such as chemical and pharmaceutical company Bayer and engineering company Siemens use their environmental reputation to attract competent employees who are committed to the environment (Jabbour and Santos, 2008). The published research suggests that given a choice, people are attracted to green employers that are keenly attuned to climate change issues and have a strong ecological approach (Philips, 2007). Environmentally sensitive job previews combined with accurate portrayal of the organization's culture can attract talented people with values that match and promote sustainability (Jabbour, 2011; Wehrmeyer, 1996).

Another way to embed ecological values in the workplace is by selecting people with green-related skills and values. As Townley (1994) points out, selection practices are an important means of 'knowing' and managing a culture change. The selection process may be designed to ensure that 'employees committed to the environmental issue have a potential to be hired more than those who do not show an ability to lead the environmental management in a company' (Jabbour and Santos, 2008, p. 53). Studies also suggest that it may be expedient to start hiring managers who have a proven track record of environmental performance and value environmental protection (see, for example, Ramus, 2002). Personality- and competency-based tests provide the tools that enable managers to find talented individuals who seem to fit the new culture. Selection tests based on attitudinal and behavioural profiling can also be used to screen applicants for green values. However, as discussed in Chapter 5, the validity and predictive power of these assessment techniques have both been subject to challenge.

Training and workplace learning

Consensus is growing among academics that the issues of sustainability, organizational change and training and learning are closely interrelated. Training and workplace learning are a primary intervention for developing pro-environmental behaviours (Garavan and McGuire, 2010). Much of company training appears to be related to improving employees' health and safety, energy-saving and waste management. For example, the US company 3M has encouraged employees to find creative ways to reduce pollution through their Pollution Prevention Pays (3P) programme, which has saved the company close to $300 million (Renwick et al., 2008). Training and learning is a necessary component of advanced environmental management systems. The literature suggests that a major factor in a successful EMS is a comprehensive training programme that provides all employees, at all levels of the organization, with the tools and understanding necessary to conduct themselves in an environmentally aware manner, foster innovation, make environmentally responsible decisions and contribute to continued environmental improvements (Daily and Huang, 2001; Ulhoi and Madsen, 1996).

Research suggests that the level of employee environmental awareness is one of the most important predictors of the level of adoption and success of an organization's environmental initiatives. Perron et al. (2006, p. 553) report, for example, that the intent of clause 4.4.2 of ISO 14001 is to 'ensure that employees at all levels of the organization understand the goals of the EMS and the ways their job activities impact the environment and the achievement of EMS goals'. This understanding allows employees to participate in environmental management efforts, and could lead to improved environmental performance of an organization. Zilahy's (2003) study of the factors restricting the implementation of energy efficiency improvement indicates that perhaps the most salient restrictive factor was the level of employee environmental awareness. Research findings support the importance of employees being well versed in environmental issues, environmental processes and the overall functioning of environmental management systems to ensure that an organization's environmental targets and objectives were achieved (see, for example, Sammalisto and Brorson, 2008).

Performance management and appraisal

Emergent studies in environmental management (Cox et al., 2012; Garavan and McGuire, 2010; Govindarajulu and Daily, 2004) suggest that, in those organizations with proactive environmental sustainability programmes, environmental criteria are systematically integrated into employee performance appraisal systems (PASs). These PASs are designed to improve the effectiveness of environmental management over time by guiding employees' actions toward the environmental performance outcomes desired by the organization. Milliman and Clair (1996) advocate for PASs that encourage environmental activities at work. Jabbour et al. (2010) report that Brazilian manufacturing companies are establishing environmental objectives for their employees, whose performance is evaluated as one of the criteria of the performance appraisal. For example, the business services Xerox Company has a reward system that recognizes employees who meet certain levels of innovation in terms of how they deal with waste reduction, reuse and recycling (Milliman and Clair, 1996). Without performance appraisal, pro-environmental behaviours may come to a standstill. Chinander (2001) highlights how many environmental management programmes fail to emphasize the importance of feedback on environmental issues. Continual feedback ensures that employees are aware of their responsibilities and communicates the link between their environmental performance outcomes and rewards (Govindarajulu and Daily, 2004).

Reward management

Conventional wisdom suggests that a well-designed reward system can help to motivate employees to achieve satisfactory performance levels, including in environmental performance (see Chapter 8). The organization's reward system provides a good indication of the seriousness of its commitment to environmental sustainability management. It has been argued that the existence of rewards systems that take environmental performance into account is an indirect reflection of the level of management commitment to environmental management (Berrone and Gomez-Mejia, 2009; Jabbour and Santos, 2008; Patton and Daley, 1998). The rewards can be monetary or non-monetary, and could be tied to individual, group or organizational actions (Milliman and Clair, 1996; Ramus and Steger, 2000).

Monetary rewards may be one of the strongest motivators for encouraging employees to participate in environmental improvement activity. For example, aligning compensation practices with environmental strategy has been implemented in North American companies such as Huntsman Chemical, Browning-Ferris Industries and Coors Brewing Company (Milliman and Clair, 1996), where financial rewards are tied to employees' environmental performance. In this regard, managers will need to determine whether environmental responsibilities and initiatives should be incorporated into managers' and employees' performance appraisal. Denton (1999) observes that, even in some of the best-known

An award is one method of showing public recognition for the environmental activities of staff members.

companies for encouraging environmental initiatives, financial rewards are rarely tied to environmental performance.

Studies suggest that many workplaces are encouraging environmental activities using non-monetary rewards such as employee recognition schemes, time off from work, gift certificates and paid vacations (Govindarajulu and Daily, 2004). For example, Dow Chemical, a leading American multinational corporation, motivates its employees by awarding plaques to employees who develop innovative waste reduction ideas (Denton, 1999). Some employees may be more motivated by formal or informal recognition rather than financial incentives. Empirical findings from six environmentally proactive European firms have shown that two of the most important factors for engaging employees and encouraging creative ideas are management support and company environmental awards (Ramus, 2002). This suggests that front-line managers should seek environmental ideas from all employees, and seek opportunities to provide feedback to encourage employees' engagement in environmental sustainability. Whether rewards are monetary or non-monetary in nature, the reward system has to be supported by an effective communication plan (Parker and Wright, 2001), rewards must be tied to the achievement of environmental objectives (Starik and Rands, 1995), and they must be consistent with other aspects of the rewards system (May and Flannery, 1995).

Employment relations

Whereas 'informal social relations' addresses the 'individualist' dimensions of the employment relationship, 'employment relations' primarily focuses on the collectivist aspects of the employer–employee relationship. The nature and role of informal social relations provide an essential dimension of workplace relations that must be encompassed within the broader domain of employment relations (Morgan, 1993), and an HR strategy aiming to support and facilitate corporate environmental sustainability. Recognizing this complexity in human relations in the workplace is necessary given the change component of environmental management and those workplace relations that are seen as a product of a historical process, ultimately shaping productive performance (Edwards et al., 2002). Underlying these arguments is the important assumption that HRM and employment relations are 'embedded' within a socioeconomic, institutional and societal context (see, for example, Renwick et al., 2013). Adopting this context-sensitive perspective, it is argued, helps to explain why environmental management initiatives are successful in one context and not another. The notion that context matters and that workplace employment relations have undergone a transformation over the last three decades – the rise of employee voice (see Chapter 9) and the decline in trade union membership and collective bargaining coverage – informs the analysis of GHRM in this chapter.

US and South African unions form blue–green alliances

Getty

Reducing carbon emissions impacts differently on employers and trade unions, and while trade unions globally are beginning to support environmental issues, in some instances forming links with environmental groups – a blue–green alliance – unions and their members are affected in different ways. For example, curbing the use of fossil fuels, nuclear energy and air travel will have a negative effect on employment and union membership in those sectors. Increasing the supply of renewable energy through the use of onshore and offshore wind, wave power or tidal power will create new employment opportunities. There is little hope, writes Canadian environmental activist, Naomi Klein, of bringing the fossil fuel companies onside to renewable energy – the profits they stand to lose are too great. However, that is not the case for workers whose jobs are tied to fossil extraction and combustion. She writes (2015, pp. 126–7):

> *What is known is this: trade unions can be counted on to fiercely protect jobs, however dirty, if these are the only jobs on offer. On the other hand, when workers in dirty sectors are offered good jobs in clean sectors (like the former autoworkers at the Silfab factory in Toronto, Canada), and are enlisted as active participants in a green transition, then progress can happen at lightening speed.*

Given the will, there is a great opportunity to create decent, fairly paid, green jobs. In the USA, this path is advocated by the BlueGreen Alliance, a coalition of America's major labour unions and environmental organizations. They believe that the creation of good jobs goes 'hand-in-hand' with the protection of the environment (BlueGreen Alliance). For example, one of the many enterprises that they support is energy efficient housing products. As governments look to reduce carbon emissions and people become more aware of energy cost savings, the markets for these products are predicted to grow from $300 billion dollars globally in 2014 to $620 billion dollars in 2023 (Navigant Research quoted in BlueGreen Alliance Foundation, 2016).

In South Africa, a country with a heavy economic reliance on fossil fuels and high unemployment and inequality, the need for good, green jobs is equally pressing. Here the *One Million Climate Jobs Campaign*, an alliance of 'labour, social movements, community organizations and environmental NGOs' argues for the transition to a 'just' low-carbon economy, which prioritizes workers and the poor. Their research shows that there is the potential for 'at least a million climate jobs to be created' in renewable energy, energy efficient products and building new, zero carbon emitting housing (van Neikerk, 2015).

There is a debate on whether the market will create climate jobs on a large scale or whether this can only be done by government involvement and thoughtful policy and planning. The body representing British trade unions, the TUC, in its document *One Million Climate Jobs*, estimated that 1 million workers could be employed for a decade for less than the government gave to the banks in 1 year (TUC, 2010). The climate case for rethinking government intervention, long-term planning and alternative business models is particularly strong when it comes to energy and transport. Since economy and ecology have the same root, perhaps it is not so remarkable that trade unions around the world are beginning to cooperate and form alliances with the environmental movement.

Stop! What do you think of Klein's argument? To what extent can it be argued that the contradictory position of capital and labour renders any cooperation between work organizations, unions and environmental groups to curb carbon emission a problematic endeavour?

Sources and further information: Klein (2015), BlueGreen Alliance Foundation (2016), van Neikerk (2015), International Labour Organization (2012), Neale (2011) and TUC (2010). You can read about the BlueGreen Alliance at https://www.bluegreenalliance.org.

Note: This feature was written by John Bratton.

Employee voice can operate both informally or formally and with or without a trade union voice. As explained in Chapter 10, employee voice may be informal, for example a line manager listening to suggestions from an individual or team members. On the other hand, a formal employee voice scheme can include managers, individual employees and/or their union representatives participating in decision-making in a work group. The important point about employement relations is that both informal and formal modes potentially involves dialogue – employees 'think[ing] together in relationship' (Isaacs, 1999, p. 19, cited by Jabri, 2012, p. 172) – and this process can play a key role in facilitating organizational change and, specifically, in getting organizational actors to think about and engage in sustainability initiatives. Markey et al.'s (2016) study of almost 700 Australian workplaces, for instance, found strong associations between worksite activities for the reduction of carbon emissions and employees' participation in motivating, developing and/or implementing these decarbonizing measures.

Although trade union membership and influence has significantly declined over the last four decades (see Chapter 9), unions in the developed economies have responded to climate change issues. For example, in Britain in 2010, the TUC published its One Million Climate Jobs campaign, which aimed to initiate a debate on 'just transition'. This aims to create a sustainable and just economy while protecting jobs. The TUC (2010, p. 6) focuses on what it calls 'climate jobs':

> We mean climate jobs, not 'green jobs'. Climate jobs are jobs that cut down the amount of greenhouse gases we put into the air and thus slow down climate change. 'Green jobs' can mean anything – jobs in the water industry, national parks, landscaping, bird sanctuaries, pollution control … All these jobs are necessary. But they do not affect global warming. We mean jobs that tackle the main sources of emissions.

The TUC's programme examines a range of climate change jobs and suggests ways to pay for these. Although trade unions globally are beginning to support environmental issues, for example, the anti-fracking movement in the USA and the UK, the labour movement is divided. The union that organizes many workers in the UK gas industry, the GMB, argues the case for fracking like this:

> Gas is absolutely integral to life in Scotland and the UK … Is it kinder to the environment for gas to be transported thousands of miles across continents and oceans before we use it in Britain? … GMB's position on fracking must therefore be consistent with the need to organize the shale gas industry if it does develop, as well our duty to protect the future of the UK gas industry and the thousands of GMB members it currently employs (Smith, G., 2015, p. 20)

Trade union and employee participation and engagement or 'voice' can be seen as the Holy Grail of employment relations (Emmott, 2015, vii). Moreover, voice is seen as central to creating a sustainable workplace (Brio et al., 2007; Lund, 2004). Mechanisms to allow trade unions and workers to have a 'voice' in workplace decision-making are both the oldest and the most recent topic of debate in contemporary employee relations. While recent GHRM studies have tended to focus on non-union processes, most only go so far as to suggest that, in order for sustainability initiatives to be effective, managers should utilize various employee representation arrangements to encourage employees' 'voice' or engagement (Chen, 2011; Hanna et al., 2000).

HRM as I see it

Markus Hiemann
Sustainability Manager for NHS National Services Scotland

NHS National Services Scotland (NSS) provides national strategic support services and expert advice to NHS Scotland, including national screening and specialist services, procurement, legal services and public health intelligence.

Markus Hiemann is the Sustainability Manager for NSS and is responsible for the Health Board's sustainability strategy and delivery of Good Corporate Citizenship programmes across areas such as workforce, procurement, facilities, transport, community engagement and climate change adaptation.

Before joining NSS, Markus worked as a project manager in contract research, providing drug development and commercial outsourcing services to the pharmaceutical industry. In 2002, he transitioned to the public sector in a customer relations and communications role for the Public Health & Intelligence Business Unit. Originally from Barcelona, Spain, Markus has lived in the USA and Belgium, and now calls Edinburgh home.

Click on Markus's photo in your ebook to watch him speaking about ways to encourage sustainability and how it relates to HR practice, and then think about the following questions:

1 How has the idea of sustainability evolved over time?
2 Should sustainability be driven from the top down or from the bottom up?
3 How can sustainability goals be combined with performance management?

HRM web links

Visit the online resource centre at **www.palgravehighered.com/bg-hrm-6e** for more information on the trade union response to the climate change crisis.

Critique and paradox in environmental management

The prescriptive literature presents organizational culture and HR practices as variables that can be easily manipulated to produce ideal types of integration to 'fit' new corporate goals. But as we have explained in previous chapters, consideration should be given to the paradoxes of such a strategy. Despite attempts by the trade union movement to build alliances to produce sustainable, low-carbon growth, there is evidence that many employers consider union involvement as a challenge to management prerogative. Furthermore, the 'green bargaining agenda', based on ecofriendly principles and insights, is not without contradictions. The trade union movement can potentially act as the pivotal agency of environmental and social change (Mayer, 2009; Hampton, 2015), but as in the case of nuclear energy and fracking, unions face barriers to playing this role because they can find themselves representing workers on opposite sides of conflicts related to environmental protection and job security. For environmental movements, the generation of nuclear energy and fracking is unsustainable, yet job security is a major issue for the unions representing workers at nuclear power plants (Oates, 1996; Smith, G., 2015).

Mainstream environmental studies tend to fail to engage sufficiently with conflicts of interest in the capitalist employment relationship. Critical authors three decades ago argued that the term 'sustainability' had become a purposeful distraction, 'deliberately vague ... so that endless streams of academics and diplomats could spend comfortable hours trying to define it without success' (O'Riordan, 1985, p. 37). Later, others added to this critique, arguing that the sustainability debate had become too 'technocratic, mere rhetoric, inegalitarian, and ... a *smokescreen for perpetuation of the status quo, vacuous, politically correct sloganeering*' (Buttel, 1998, p. 262, emphasis added). Informed by a social justice perspective, a number of critical social scientists (see, for example, Agyeman and Evans, 2004) and environmental advocacy associations (for example, Friends of the Earth Scotland) are attempting to reorient the term 'sustainability' around concepts of equity, social justice, participatory democracy and ecological limits. This more inclusive view of sustainability is captured by Agyeman et al. (2002, p. 78), who argue that:

> Sustainability ... cannot be simply a "green", or "environmental" concern, important though "environmental" aspects of sustainability are. A truly sustainable society is one where wider questions of social needs and welfare, and economic opportunity are integrally related to environmental limits imposed by supporting ecosystems.

There is a requirement to define environmental sustainability that recognizes the need to ensure a better quality of life for *all*, in the present and into the future, in an equitable manner, while preserving supporting ecosystems (Agyeman et al., 2003; Dobson, 1998), that is, an economy that meets emission targets and is environmentally sustainable and socially just. This more inclusive approach to environmental sustainability focuses on four core areas: quality of life, present and future generations, equity and justice in resource allocation, and living within ecological limits. While orthodox notions of corporate sustainability have little to say about contemporary human conditions, the definition suggested here includes ideas of both intra- and intergenerational equity (equality within and between different generation groups). This new, more egalitarian perspective of sustainability draws the connection between environmentalism, equity and fairness.

reflective question   Does the primacy of the profit motive prevent organizations adopting a strategy that is environmentally sustainable and socially?

HRM web links   Visit the online resource centre at **www.palgravehighered.com/bg-hrm-6e** for more information on a 'green' economy.

Emerging definitions of environmental sustainability are shifting towards 'Just sustainability' (the nexus between social justice and environmentalism), a broader approach that prioritizes social justice but does not downplay notions of ecological limits. The 'environmental justice' definition has more explicit emphasis on the social conditions of citizens and workers, both locally and internationally, and also acknowledges that multiple stakeholder decision-making starts to address environmental and social inequality (see, for example, Benn et al., 2009; Bullard, 1990; Carlsson and Berkes, 2005; Robbins, 2004; Razzaque and Richardson, 2006; Schlosberg, 1999).

case study

EnergyCo

The setting

EnergyCo is a large energy company which upholds its competitive position in the market thanks to a diverse energy mix. It prides itself on its investment in renewable energy and is one of the major players in this area. The company produces and supplies both electricity and gas, and also offers contracting services. EnergyCo has expanded its workforce significantly over the last few years and now has a large workforce based across multiple sites, a significant percentage of which is unionized. At a strategic level, sustainability is considered a priority and its importance is communicated to all employees. Internal communications, such as newsletters and electronic notifications, and training workshops all highlight the company's sustainability principles. These principles are also demonstrated through EnergyCo's employee and community projects, and of course through its investment in renewable energy and energy efficiency at its sites.

The problem

Performance measurement and appraisal are often seen as key features of an organization's strategic drive to achieving an LCW. In terms of environmental management, performance appraisal aims to guide employees' actions toward desired environmental performance outcomes. Mainstream GHRM scholars suggest that, without performance appraisal, employee environmental improvement efforts may falter.

However, integrating performance appraisal with sustainability objectives presents many challenges, particularly the *measurement* of environmental performance across the organization. At EnergyCo, environmental performance is an aspect of work that is formally evaluated for the majority of employees. The formal link between employee environmental performance and pay is established in the company's PAS, first introduced in 2013. At least in theory, the PAS has the potential to influence EnergyCo's employees' performance rating and annual incremental pay.

In practice, however, managers and workers have expressed concern that the introduction of the PAS had led to an increase in their workload. At a meeting held to discuss some of the issues, one EnergyCo manager

Image Source/Christopher Robbins

said: 'the PAS system has intensified our work by "squeezing complex jobs into standardised measures" and she questioned the assumption that there was "a link between individual effort and reward".' Another manager at the meeting expressed concern that the PAS could 'potentially have a negative impact on line-manager and employees relations'. The manager explained:

> [The PAS] is a distraction. You are obviously the guys' managers, but at the same time because you are spending so much time with them you need to get along with them as well.

Mhairi White, the HR director, who was chairing the meeting, summarised the main concerns of the managers and added that their experiences mirrored published evidence drawing attention to the added pressure on line mangers when pay is linked to performance. She promised to take a second look at the present PAS system to see whether it could be improved. Mhairi White prides herself on her use of evidence-based HR management to design policies.

The assignment

Working as a group or on your own, prepare a report for Mhairi White, drawing on the material from this chapter and addressing the following:

1 How can performance appraisal activities help this organization meet its sustainability objectives? What role, if any, should line managers play in implementing sustainability initiatives?
2 What are the challenges associated with integrating performance appraisal with sustainability objectives?
3 What changes would you suggest to EnergyCo's PAS system?

Essential reading

Brio, J. A., Fernandez, E. and Junquera, B. (2007). Management and employee involvement in achieving an environmental action-based competitive advantage: an empirical study. *International Journal of Human Resource Management*, **18**(4): 491–522.

Daily, B. F. and Huang S. (2001). Achieving sustainability through attention to human resource factors in environmental management. *International Journal of Operations and Production Management*, **21**: 1539–52.

Jabbour, C. J. C. (2011) How green are HRM practices, organizational culture, learning and teamwork? A Brazilian study. *Industrial and Commercial Training*, **43**(2): 98–105.

Note: This case study was written by John Bratton and Andrew Bratton.

summary

➤ This chapter has critically evaluated an eclectic body of literature covering environmental sustainability. In addition, we have identified the importance of the workplace as a site for sustainability.

➤ We explained that an EMS is the most widely recognized tool for managing the impacts of an organization's activities on the environment. An EMS refers to the management of an organization's environmental impact in a comprehensive, systematic, planned and documented manner. EMSs incorporate people, procedures and working practices.

➤ With regards to drivers of change, all the evidence points to a variety of internal and external drivers, including organizational values, regulation, demand from customers, society and competition, for implementing sustainability initiatives. A common feature that all organizations share is that meeting regulatory compliance requirements seems to underpin the different sustainability initiatives and is the context for other observable drivers.

➤ GHRM studies highlight the opportunity for improved environmental performance when the goals, policies and procedures of EMSs are more closely aligned or 'embedded' with HR practices and wider activities of the organization.

➤ Finally, the chapter focused attention on the limitations of GHRM studies, including insufficient attention to the importance of context, insufficient recognition of alternative voices, particularly those of employees and unions, and the 'fatally flawed' assumption that line managers enact sustainable HR policies and practices.

review questions

1 What is meant by a sustainable workplace?
2 What are the internal and external drivers of change towards more sustainable workplace practices?
3 What impact do low-carbon behaviours have on organizational performance?

4   Explain the role of leadership and organizational culture in the creation of a low-carbon organization?

5   What role can HRM play in creating an LCW? What are the challenges?

further reading

Reading these articles and chapters can help you gain a better understanding and potentially a higher grade for your HRM assignment.

➤   Agyeman, J. and Evans, B. (2004) 'Just sustainability': the emerging discourse of environmental justice in Britain? *Geographical Journal*, **170**(2): 155–64.

➤   Beard, C. and Rees, S. (2000) Green teams and the management of environmental change in a UK county council. *Environmental Management and Health*, **11**(1): 27–38.

➤   Berrone, P. and Gomez-Mejia, L. (2009) The pros and cons of rewarding social responsibility at the top. *Human Resource Management*, **48**(6): 957–69.

➤   Bratton, A. and Bratton, J. (2015) Human resource management approaches. In J. Robertson and J. Barling (eds) *The Psychology of Green Organizations* (pp. 275–95), New York: Oxford University Press

➤   Cox, A., Higgins, T., Gloster, R. and Foley, B. (2012) The impact of workplace initiatives on low carbon behaviours – CASE study report. Scottish Government. Available at http://www.scotland. gov.uk/Publications/2012/03/2237 (accessed August 13, 2016).

➤   Jabbour, C. J. C., Santos, F. C. A. and Nagano, S. M. (2010) Contributions of HRM throughout the stages of environmental management: methodological triangulation applied to companies in Brazil. *International Journal of Human Resource Management*, **21**(7): 1049–89.

vocabulary checklist for ESL students

 Click here in your interactive ebook for a list of HRM terminology and vocabulary that has appeared in this chapter.

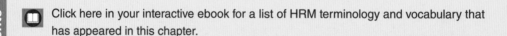 Visit the online resource centre at **www.palgravehighered.com/bg-hrm-6e** for lots of extra resources to help you get to grips with this chapter, including study tips, HRM skills development guides, summary lecture notes, tips for English as a Second Language (ESL) students and more.

chapter 17

international HRM and global capitalism

Getty Images/iStockphoto / Thinkstock Catherine Yeulet

outline

objectives

After studying this chapter, you should be able to:

1 Explain how developments in global capitalism affect corporate strategies and patterns of employment relations

2 Describe the difference between strategic international HRM and international HRM

3 Explain how strategic international HRM is linked to different global business strategies

4 Outline some key aspects and contemporary issues in international HRM

5 Comment on whether globalization is driving processes of convergence or divergence in HRM policies and practices

European Union member states and most economies have enacted laws setting out acceptable workplace practices that often reflect International Labour Organization (ILO) standards. News of fatal accidents and the appalling living conditions of migrants construction workers in Qatar building football stadiums (Rajouria, 2015), and alleged abuses, including erratic or reduced payment of wages, passport confiscation, intimidation and debt bondage. Pattisson (2016, p. 14), offers an alarming insight into what happens when there are no state-enforced employment rules presenting what can be called a 'dark' side of international HR management. The reality of managing people in a global environment is also concerned with the challenges connected with regional wars and terrorism (Bader and Berg, 2014). This contemporary issue is illustrated, for example, with the mass evacuation of European workers in Libya in 2011. As antigovernment protests spread to Tripoli, oil companies, such as Royal Dutch Shell PLC and BP, organized flights to evacuate their expat workers or their families from the country (Winfield, 2011).

introduction

The success of global business strategies, observes Lasserre (2012, p. 335, emphasis in original) relies on the *'quality of the people'* who are in charge of its implementation. The field of *international* human resource management (IHRM) refers to all human resources (HR) practices used to manage people in companies operating in more than one country. It can be distinguished from domestic HRM by the fact that core HR activities have to be culturally sensitive and effective in a cross-cultural, multinational context (French 2010; Scullion and Linehan, 2005). As such, it is different from a related, but separate, field called *comparative* HRM, which identifies and analyses the role of institutions, culture and other societal conditions in understanding differences and similarities in HRM across countries (Bryson and Frege, 2010; Szamosi et al., 2010).

The proliferation of interest in IHRM springs directly from the globalization of markets, international commodity chain configurations (Morris et al., 2009), new 'boundaryless' work organizations and the impact of these changes on national patterns of labour markets and employment relations. Practitioner interest stems from the acknowledgement that international managers need a global 'mindset' supported by appropriate knowledge and competencies. A global mindset is the ability to develop and interpret criteria for business and HRM performance that are independent of the beliefs, values and assumptions of a single country, and to implement those criteria appropriately across cultures (Kedia and Mukherji, 1999, cited by Kramar and Syed, 2012, p. 61). Practitioner interest also stems from the recognition that female global managers face many challenges combining careers that entail international business travel and integrating family across cultures (Fischlmayr and Puchmüller, 2016).

Academic interest stems from neo-liberal capitalism – deregulation, privatization and the shrinking of the state. The dominance of neo-liberalism ideology and the global financial crisis (GFC) that started in 2008 has significantly reshaped employment systems in the European Union. First, there has been a decisive weakening of the social contract between trade unions, corporate capital and the state. A key part of this social contract has been the building of a robust system of European social dialogue, including collective bargaining. Second, and concomitantly, the GFC has weakened trade unions and collective bargaining across member states. Moreover, across the EU trade unions have been unable to mount an effective challenge to austerity economics, all of which it is argued has stalled the social dimension to European integration (Dickman et al., 2016, pp. 42–3). Thus, the phenomenon of internationalization of HR practices has immense potential to foster a global approach to managing human capital following the paradigmatic Anglo-American model (Farazmand, 2002; Sparrow et al., 2004). The so-called 'gig economy' captures the potential of internationalizing HR practices. Workers can drive their own car and earn instantly as a taxi driver for Uber. Or workers can use their bike or scooter to deliver fast-food for Deliveroo. In both cases the workers are supported by iPhone technology. The reality of this new employment model, however, is precarious employment, which offers zero-hour contracts, insecurity and fewer employment rights (Mason, 2016).

This chapter begins with an overview of three alternative theories relating to the impact of global processes on domestic patterns of employment relations. This is followed by an examination of the international aspects of key HR practices in companies operating outside their parent country. We will conclude by examining a pivotal argument in IHRM on whether global capitalism is causing a convergence or a divergence in employment management.

HRM web links

> Visit the online resource centre at **www.palgravehighered.com/bg-hrm-6e** for information on how the UK's decision to withdraw from the European Union might impact on UK HRM and IHRM.

Typologies of global business strategy

The domain of IHRM connects to issues of significance in the field of global business and the process of internationalization (Boxall et al., 2008; Morris et al., 2009). Global business strategies are connected to the generic business-level strategies of cost leadership and differentiation that were examined in Chapter 2. A global business strategy means effectively and efficiently matching the internal strengths of a multinational corporation (MNC) (relative to its competitors) with the opportunities and challenges found in geographically dispersed markets that cross international borders. Such matching is said to be a precondition for creating value and satisfying stakeholder goals, both domestically and internationally (Verbeke, 2013). A useful starting point for understanding global business theories is the model developed by Bartlett and Ghoshal (1989). These two international business theorists suggest that global corporations typically face tension from two types of business pressure. MNCs face, on the one hand, demands for global cost reductions and integration, and, on the other hand, demands for differentiation and local responsiveness. The demand to control costs and integrate has its roots in the classical management theory that there is 'one best way' to manage.

Global companies strive for global efficiency by rationalizing their product lines, standardizing their parts design and integrating their global manufacturing and control systems. The pressures for integration can be high in technologically intensive enterprises or where the product is universal and requires minimal modification to local needs. This typically occurs with goods such as petroleum, steel and chemicals, and is also typical for consumer electronics, for instance mobile phones and personal computers. Demands for integration are also high in industries in which there is excess capacity or in which consumers face low switching costs. For example, the demand for integration has been globally intense in the steel industry, in which differentiation is difficult and price is the main competitive variable (Hill et al., 2014).

Differences in the national infrastructure can be a barrier for MNCs.

Countering global strategies and organizational efficiency imperatives are local realities and a need for local responsiveness. Companies have to satisfy consumers' tastes and preferences in diverse locations, so competitive advantage may be derived from producing a product or service that is more sensitive to national cultures and local tastes in the host countries where the MNC operates. Culture differentiates one locale from another, and the duality of culture – its pervasiveness yet its uniqueness – impacts on global business strategy (Mintzberg et al., 2008). Pressures to be locally responsive arise from consumer tastes and preferences, differences in the host country's infrastructure and the regulations of the national business environment imposed by the host government. For example, when the Swedish home furnishing company IKEA entered the US market in the 1990s, it offered cut-price standardized products, which had sold well across Europe, based on huge economies of scale. However, IKEA soon found that it had to be responsive to North American tastes and physiques: IKEA's glasses were too small for North American consumers, who tend to add ice to their drinks, and Swedish beds were too narrow for American body sizes (Hill et al., 2014).

A second set of demands for local responsiveness arises from differences in the host country's infrastructure. For example, some EU member states use 240-volt consumer electric systems, whereas in North America 110-volt systems tend to be standard. Thus, differences in the national infrastructure require MNCs to customize domestic electrical appliances. This diversity in infrastructure has been identified as a barrier to European competitiveness and was behind the Single Europe Act of 1986. The Act aimed to stimulate pan-European trade by harmonizing technical standards governing the production and distribution of goods (Hendry, 1994).

A third set of demands for local responsiveness emanates from nationally based regulatory regimes constructed and maintained by host governments. The regulation of employment relations, consumer products (for example, automobile exhaust emissions), ecological controls and local testing (for example, clinical trials of pharmaceutical products according to domestic standards) may dictate that MNCs be responsive to local conditions. Global corporations can be enticed to relocate by national governments deregulating safety, environmental or employment standards.

The major chemical accident that occurred in Bhopal, India, for example, illustrates the dangers implicit in reducing standards to attract investment from developed countries. A chemical plant owned by the US MNC Union Carbide engaged in chemical production under conditions that would have been illegal in the USA. On 3rd December 1984, the plant experienced a major leak. Within hours, 3000 people were dead, 15,000 more dying in the aftermath. A further 200,000 were seriously injured, and half a million still carry special health cards. Eventually, the MNC paid out just $470 million in compensation (Saul, 2005). More recently, the Indian government gave tax exemptions and deregulated the telecommunications industry in order to increase foreign investment in call centres (Maitra and Sangha, 2005).

Thus, through a wide variety of national or regional policy mechanisms, national governments can effectively shape national business systems and therefore the competitive dynamics within a market (Whitley, 1999). Prahalad and Doz (1987, p. 251) suggest that, because governments influence competitive outcomes, 'MNCs can approach strategy as a process of "negotiation" with host governments'; they call this process 'negotiated strategies'. Overall, MNCs are crucial agents in the transformation of national employment management systems (Marginson and Meardi, 2010). They are widely held to have differing preferences over arrangements for managing the employment relationship: union representation, non-union representation or none at all, direct or indirect forms of employee voice (Marginson et al., 2010). The point we wish to make here is, therefore, that the cost efficiency–responsiveness strategic mix may well depend on the MNC's calculation to exploit cross-national differences, including the model of capitalism that prevails in the host country and that country's political will to protect the planet and safeguard the health and safety of its people.

The integration–responsiveness grid

Local realities are the classic barrier to universal theories of global efficiency. Two pressures – cost efficiencies and rationalization, and differentiation and local responsiveness – form the two dimensions of what Barlett and Ghoshal (1989) describe as the integration–responsiveness grid. Imagine a box with 'Demand for global integration' on the left side going from low to high, and along the base are 'demands for local responsiveness', going from low to high. Next superimpose into the box Prahalad and Doz's (1987) four typologies – global, multidomestic, international and transnational. At the bottom left corner, there would be an example of an international strategy (e.g., Procter and Gamble) with low demands for global integration and low demands for local responsiveness. Moving up, a global strategy is found at the top left, high global integration and low local responsiveness (e.g., Texas Instruments). Shifting across is a transnational strategy at the top right corner of the box, high global integration and high local responsiveness (e.g., Unilever). Finally, a multi-domestic strategy will be at the bottom right corner of the box, with low global integration and high local responsiveness (e.g., ITT). These four typologies are offered as solutions to the dual pressure for cost efficiency and responsiveness.

Global strategy

Global corporations that pursue a global strategy focus on increasing profit margins through cost-efficiencies arising from economies of scale and economies of location. These MNCs are pursuing a low-cost leadership strategy. The operations of the MNCs will be concentrated in a few favourable host economies and will tend not to customize their goods to local situations. A global strategy is typically associated with high demands for integration and low demands for local responsiveness. Texas Instruments, a company that once dominated the market in pocket calculators and digital watches by focusing persistently on cost reductions and price at the expense of understanding consumers' needs, is an example of an MNC that, until 1982, followed a global strategy (Hill et al., 2014).

Multidomestic strategy

Companies pursuing a multidomestic strategy design their operations to maximize local responsiveness. These MNCs tend to customize both their product offering and their marketing strategy to different local customer tastes and preferences. A multidomestic company such as the technology company ITT developed a 'strategic posture and organizational ability that enables it to be very sensitive and responsive to differences in national environments' (Bartlett and Ghoshal, 1989, p. 14). A multidomestic strategy is typically associated with low demands for integration and high demands for local responsiveness.

International strategy

Global corporations pursuing an international strategy create competitive advantage through a global diffusion of the company's distinctive competencies where its local competitors lack these resources and the capability to integrate and effectively rationalize their value-added activities abroad. An international strategy is typically associated with low demands for integration and low demands for local responsiveness. MNCs pursuing an international strategy tend to centralize their research and development activities in the parent country, but also tend to establish operations in each major national economy in which they do business. The US-based company Procter & Gamble is an example of an MNC that has pursued an international strategy: 'it set up miniature replicas of the domestic organization to adapt P&G products without deviating from the "Procter way"' (Bartlett and Ghoshal, 1989, p. 15).

Transnational strategy

Companies following a transnational strategy strive for competitive advantage worldwide by rationalizing and integrating resources to achieve superior cost efficiencies from economies of scale and economies of location, by being sensitive to and capable of responding to local needs, and by sharing knowledge throughout their global operations. In a transnational company, knowledge and distinctive competencies flow to and from each of the company's operations as part of a larger process of 'global learning' that encompasses 'every member of the company' (Bartlett and Ghoshal, 1989, p. 59).

In essence, a transnational company simultaneously achieves low-cost leadership and a competitive advantage in terms of differentiation. The effect is 'a complex configuration of assets and capabilities that are distributed, yet specialized [and] the company integrates the dispersed resources through strong interdependencies ... Such interdependencies may be reciprocal rather than sequential' (Bartlett and Ghoshal, 1989, p. 60). Thus, a world-scale production plant in Mexico may depend on world-scale component plants in Australia, France and South Korea; major sales subsidiaries worldwide may in turn depend on Mexico for their finished products. The transnational company's resources and capabilities are represented as an integrated network, a term emphasizing the significant flows of components, products, resources, information and people. Unilever is an example of an MNC that has pursued a transnational strategy, with 17 different and largely decentralized detergent plants in Europe alone.

HRM web links Visit the online resource centre at **www.palgravehighered.com/bg-hrm-6e** to explore the structures of some large MNCs.

The integration–responsiveness grid is a simple and impressive model for explaining the strategic choices shaping the strategies and organizational networks of MNCs. Case study research confirms Bartlett and Ghoshal's typology of MNCs that is explained here (see Harzing, 2000; Morris et al., 2009), but we should end this introduction to international business strategies by noting the shift in economic thinking on globalization since the GFC and by providing a word of caution related to Bartlett and Ghoshal's model.

We should note that, since the financial meltdown in 2008, the theory of 'efficient markets' and the supposedly unmitigated virtues of self-regulation have, unsurprisingly, been severely discredited (see, for example, Nolan, 2011; Rodrik, 2011). Mainstream economists, in questioning the wisdom of the globalization narrative, have joined long-standing critics of unfettered global capitalism. Rodrik argues (2011, p. xv) that there has been an extraordinary shift in the intellectual debate. Among dominant mainstream economists, we have, for example, Paul Krugman, the 2008 recipient of the Nobel Prize in Economic Sciences, arguing that trade with low-income economies is no longer too small to have an effect on inequality in rich developed economies, and Larry Summers, former economic adviser to Barack Obama, US President from 2009 to 2016, deliberating about the negative impact of a 'race to the bottom' in national regulations and labour standards.

With regard to the integration–responsiveness model, we should note that the typologies proposed by Bartlett and Ghoshal depict a theoretical or 'ideal type' of global strategy that global corporations should strive for if they wish to attain superior performance outcomes. But the evidence suggests that few global companies truly pursue a transnational strategy. Rather, it is far more likely that managing the conflicting pressures for global rationalization and integration (low-cost leadership) and local responsiveness (differentiation) sets the context for IHRM.

reflective question Can you think of three globalizing and three localizing forces in business today?

International human resource management

As companies increasingly seek to leverage human capital to compete in global markets, academics and practitioners alike have increasingly begun to explore the international potential of strategic HRM. In so doing, they have generally addressed the complexities of organizing work and managing employees with heterogeneous beliefs and values, and cognitive and emotional orientations. Thus, MNCs, on the one hand, need to have a set of explicit or implicit corporate shared values and beliefs that help integration and interpersonal collaboration across different units of the organization (Barlett and Ghoshal, 1989, 2002). Yet, on the other hand, HR practices must be sensitive to, and adapted to fit, domestic legal requirements and local cultural expectations and norms (Kramar and Syed, 2012). HR policies and practices relating to global and local recruitment and selection, international training and learning, international reward management, performance appraisal and the management of expatriate personnel (people living and working outside their native country) define IHRM.

In this section, we will seek to understand the explicit connection between global competition and HRM in MNCs. We will identify three alternative theories relating to the impact of global processes on domestic patterns of employment relations. We will then explain the concepts of strategic IHRM (SIHRM) and critically examine the links between global strategic management and SIHRM and IHRM. Finally, we will look at a model of SIHRM first developed by Schuler et al. (1993).

Global capitalism and employment relations

The social networking platform Facebook, with roughly 1 billion account-users globally, exemplifies the globalization of capitalism and the converging lifestyles worldwide (Cavusgil et al., 2014). The developments in international capitalism have generated a debate on how globalization impacts on domestic patterns of employment relations. The existing literature identifies three alternative approaches to this: economic, institutionalist and integrated (Bamber et al., 2004).

The *economic* approach follows the classical neo-liberal premise that global business activity has become so interconnected, and that competitive imperatives are so dominant, that they offer little scope for domestic differences in patterns of employment relations. This influential economic approach predicts that international markets operate in accordance with universal principles and will result in a 'convergence' of national employment relations. Economic imperatives will, for example, create 'efficiencies' by driving wages down and eroding employment standards.

The *institutionalist* approach to the impact of globalization contends that global forces are more fluid in their dynamics and more contradictory in their outcome. Moreover, nationally based regulatory institutions form an independent dynamic that structures, controls and legitimates business activities and outcomes. Global trends are mediated by national or local institutional regimes and changed into 'divergent' power struggles over particular national employment practices (Hyman, 1999). By highlighting national differences in how societies shape economic and social outcomes, the institutionalist approach emphasizes the variability of market economies and highlights why 'varieties of capitalism' are likely to persist in the future (see, for example, Hall and Soskice, 2009). Furthermore, nationally embedded institutions, for example universities, can confer a comparative competitive advantage, especially in the sphere of innovation.

Bamber et al. (2004) have put forward an *integrated* approach to globalization and national patterns of employment relations. They suggest that both global economic trends and nationally based institutions are important in structuring national patterns of employment relations. However, because different kinds of market economy are integrated into the global economy in different ways, global economic pressures are likely to be divergent. The integrated approach thus focuses on the effects of global economic developments on the 'interests of different groups of employers, workers and policy-makers within different institutional settings' (Bamber et al., 2004, p. 1483).

IHRM and SIHRM

Before we consider models of SIHRM that have been developed to explain how the HRM function is configured in global companies, it is important to distinguish between IHRM and SIHRM. There are competing definitions of IHRM, although most scholarship in the field has focused on issues associated with the cross-national transfer of expatriates (that is, how to recruit and manage individual managers in international job assignments; see, for example Dowling et al., 2008; Kochan et al., 1992; Shenkar, 1995; Tung, 1988).

Taylor et al. (1996, p. 960) define IHRM as:

HRM and globalization 17.1

Is 'the race to the bottom' an inevitable consequence of globalization?

The effects of globalization can be seen everywhere: few people would question this basic proposition. But when pressed to provide an account of how globalization produces these effects, even the most astute observer may pause. Too often, the particular causal mechanisms of globalization are not specified, and we are left imagining a mysterious force impacting on the world in ways that mere mortals can do little to influence.

To move beyond this kind of abstraction, it helps to reflect critically on general claims about globalization. We often encounter the argument that globalization is responsible for the 'race to the bottom', a phrase referring to the fact that, in order to compete with companies in the developing world – or in some cases, with local rivals – managers believe they must reduce costs and opt for traditional low-trust, authoritarian HR practices.

This seems to offer a rather narrow range of options for managers working in more developed economies: they can send work to the developing world, they can import models of compensation and work organization characteristic of the developing world, or they can blend the two low-cost options together. Regardless of which low-cost option is selected, worker compensation and the quality of work are compromised. In this vision of globalization, managers are portrayed as passive agents responding predictably to global forces beyond their control. It implies that if management do not adapt by joining their competitors in this 'race to the bottom', they will be responsible for the failure of their companies. This view, however, is fundamentally flawed.

The reality is in fact more complex. Compare the HR practices of retailers Wal-mart and Costco. Wal-mart is the champion of low costs, and this is reflected in its workplace environment (low pay, limited benefits, significant work intensification). However, Wal-mart's competitor Costco uses a different management model, offering its employees better compensation and a better quality work environment. Judging from the value of Costco stocks, the choice not to participate in 'the race to the bottom' has paid off.

A recent study of the airline industry provides a more in-depth analysis. The authors identify a trend towards differentiation in the airline industry in which established airlines have created subsidiaries to compete in the low-cost market. One might expect this to lead to a 'race to the bottom', but while there is some evidence of this, there is a notable exception. 'Go' (part of the airline British Airways) was able to reduce its costs without overly harsh reductions in worker compensation and without sacrificing the quality of the work environment. Go maintained a quality of customer service that made it the preferred choice in this sector of the industry. The authors (Harvey and Turnbull, 2010, pp. 239–40) concluded that:

> *the scope for managerial choice in the civil aviation industry should not be underestimated ..., nor should the competitive advantage that can be secured from high road employee relations, even when the airline's business strategy might appear to position the company in the 'low end' of the market.*

Stop! Managers may choose not to participate in the 'race to the bottom'. But how much freedom do they have?

Sources and further information: See Harvey and Turnbull (2010) for more information. Type the phrase 'race to the bottom' into the search engine Google Scholar to find out what other researchers have said about this important global process.

Note: This feature was written by David MacLennan.

> The set of distinct activities, functions and processes that are directed at attracting, developing and maintaining a MNC's human resources. It is thus the aggregate of the various HRM systems used to manage people in the MNC, both at home and overseas.

Scullion (2001, p. 288) defines IHRM as the 'HRM issues and problems arising from the internationalization of business, and the HRM strategies, policies and practices which firms pursue in response to the internationalization process'. More recent definitions have extended the term to cover the need to adapt to local contexts, the global coordination of overseas subsidiaries, global knowledge management and global leadership (Scullion and Linehan, 2005).

IHRM tends to celebrate a developed nation hegemonic culture, one that emphasizes the subordination of domestic culture and domestic employment practices to corporate culture and corporate HRM practices (Boxall, 1995). As such, many contemporary studies of IHRM tend to be seen as a managerial strategic instrument unashamedly connected to the neo-liberalism agenda (Farazmand, 2002). It is the principal discourse of neo-liberalism that provides insights into related debates around labour market rigidities, flexibility, outsourcing, privatization, European integration, shifting macro-economic policy paradigms and international HR practices. IHRM is thus the sum of the various HRM policies and practices used to manage people in companies operating in more than one country.

As we showed in Chapter 2, strategic HRM is the process of explicitly linking the HRM function with the strategic management goals of the organization. Thus, SIHRM is the process of explicitly linking IHRM with the strategy of the global company. In defining SIHRM, we draw on the work of Scullion and Linehan (2005) and Björkman and Stahl (2006). Schuler et al. (1993, p. 720) define SIHRM as the 'HRM issues, functions and policies and practices that result from the strategic activities of multinational enterprises and that impact the international concerns and goals of those enterprises'. Emphasizing that the study of IHRM is a relatively new area of research, Björkman and Stahl (2006, p. 1) define the field as 'all issues related to the management of people in an international context'. Here, SIHRM is defined as:

> An array of HR practices and issues related to the management of people that arises from the global competitive activities of MNCs and that explicitly link international HR practices and processes with the worldwide strategic goals of those companies.

SIHRM builds on strategic HRM that aims to connect HRM explicitly with strategic management processes. In so doing, SIHRM recognizes the need to address the tension between the global and the local. This tension is related to balancing the strategies of global competitiveness (rationalization and integration) and local responsiveness (flexibility) that are pursued by MNCs while simultaneously leveraging global learning within and across the MNC. As such, SIHRM links 'IHRM explicitly with the strategy and with the MNC' (Scullion and Linehan, 2005, p. 23). This highly dynamic and complex context is the arena of SIHRM.

A model of SIHRM

We have focused so far on some global business strategies and the meaning of IHRM and SIHRM. We will now identify some conceptual models of SIHRM developed to explain the

HRM in practice 17.1

'We are disposable people …'

In April 2011, the union Unite held a demonstration outside the giant 220-acre Thanet Earth greenhouse complex in Kent, UK, claiming that agency workers were being treated like 'sweatshop labour', denied holiday pay and employed as permanent casual labour with no proper contracts. A migrant worker was reported as saying: 'The agencies have done whatever they want, and Thanet Earth and the supermarkets have let them. When we have asked for our rights we have been told: "You can find another job." We are disposable people to Tesco, Sainsbury's, M&S and the rest.' Thanet Earth, which supplies the major supermarkets with salad produce, refuted the claims, saying that all the agencies supplying its labour had been fully vetted by the Gangmasters Licensing Authority (Quinn, The Guardian, 2011).

MACMILLAN AUSTRALIA

This was the latest episode to add to the growing concern over the employment conditions faced by the large number of migrant workers in the UK, particularly in agriculture. The Gangmasters Licensing Authority itself was set up in the aftermath of the death of Chinese shellfish collectors in Morecombe Bay in 2004 with the aim of regulating casual labour agencies and gangmasters. There is, however, evidence that parts of the agriculture sector are still ignoring or undermining minimum labour standards; in October 2010, for example, a group of Romanian children were found picking onions in Worcestershire.

Agriculture has always been characterized by a seasonal use of temporary labour as the agricultural cycle makes it uneconomical to retain a permanent labour force: the use of labour contractors makes achieving numerical flexibility easier for the grower. Rogaly (2008) looked at the increasing use of migrant workers in this sector and concluded that the shift of power away from producers to a small number of powerful retailers had pressured growers to intensify production to compensate for the smaller margins dictated by the supermarkets. This was done through a combination of innovations in growing techniques, manipulation of piecework regimes and innovations in labour control.

Migrants have a strong monetary incentive, and the cutting of piecework rates ensures a higher daily output before the minimum wage equivalent is reached. Growers have preferred non-UK nationals because of

their 'work ethic', but these workers form a vulnerable group in the labour market due to factors such as immigration status, a general lack of information and language barriers. Rogaly argues that this vulnerability is used to ensure a compliant labour force. The agencies can exercise power over the workers through being the source of information about jobs, offering transport to the work location and providing credit and, importantly, accommodation. Such workers are more amenable to working irregular hours and may be easier to dispose of when harvesting is over: 'they can easily be turned on and they can easily be turned off', said one grower.

Stop! Should we be prepared to pay more for our food if it guarantees better working conditions for food production workers?

Sources and further information: See Quinn (2011). For background information, see Rogaly (2008) and McKay and Markova (2010).

Note: This feature was written by Chris Baldry.

HRM as I see it

Lesley White
Human Resources Director UK and Ireland, Huawei Technologies

www.huawei.com

Huawei is a multinational networking and telecommunications company that provides information and communications technology solutions and products to its customers. These solutions and products, including telecom networks, devices and cloud computing, are used in over 140 countries and serve more than a third of the world's population, making the company the largest of its kind in China and the second largest in the world. Huawei is headquartered in Shenzhen in China.

Lesley White is an HR professional with more than 20 years' experience, having started as an HR Assistant. She specialized for 9 years in European compensation and benefits, designing reward strategies and associated policies to attract, retain and motivate employees. Her current role covers all areas of HRM, with a key focus on strategy planning and implementation.

Click on Lesley's photo in your ebook to watch her talking about the challenges of working in a UK-based HR department for a company headquartered in China, cultural differences in working and management styles, and the place of HR in Huawei's business strategy, and then think about the following questions:

1   What does Lesley feel are the key features of working in HR in a global organization?
2   In Lesley's view, how do Chinese managers respond to directives compared with Europeans, and why?
3   How is information-sharing affected by culture?

processes and roles of IHRM, and how external and internal factors impact on HRM in MNCs. Models of SIHRM have been developed by De Cieri and Dowling (1999), Schuler et al. (1993) and Taylor et al. (1996). In Figure 17.1, we present an integrative model that draws primarily from Schuler et al. (1993) and is informed by the work of Bartlett and Ghoshal (1989) and Taylor et al. (1996).

Schuler et al.'s original integrative framework consisted of four core components:

- Exogenous factors
- Endogenous factors
- SIHRM
- The pressures and goals of the MNC.

To this, we have added a fifth component – the corporate SIHRM orientation. The lines and arrows in Figure 17.1 denote the reciprocal relationships between exogenous factors, SIHRM and the pressures and goals of the MNC.

Briefly, *exogenous factors* relate to issues external to the MNC. They include, for example, industry characteristics, the technology available and domestic characteristics such as domestic employment relations. De Cieri and Dowling (1999) argue that exogenous factors exert a direct influence on endogenous factors, SIHRM and the pressures and goals

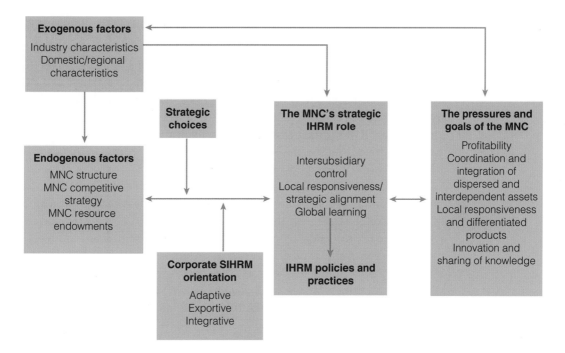

Figure 17.1 *An integrated framework of SIHRM*

Source: Based on Schuler et al. (1993, p. 722), Scullion and Linehan (2005, p. 31), Taylor et al. (1996, p. 965) and Bartlett and Ghoshal (1989, p. 67)

of the MNC. *Endogenous factors* relate to internal organizational issues, such as work design, intraorganizational networks and coordination and control systems.

SIHRM relates to issues of coordination and control, local responsiveness and worldwide learning. It is concerned with 'Developing a fit between exogenous and endogenous factors and balancing the competing demands of global versus local requirements as well as the needs of coordination, control and autonomy' (Schuler et al., 1993, p. 451). *Pressures and goals of the MNC* relate to profitability, the dual demands for cost reductions and local responsiveness, and the global transfer of innovation. The model suggests that there are reciprocal relationships between exogenous factors, SIHRM and the pressures and goals of the MNC (Scullion and Linehan, 2005). SIHRM is expected to buttress the MNC's global goals. Finally, the corporate *SIHRM orientation* refers to the general philosophy or approach taken by the MNC's top management in designing its total IHRM system.

One of the numerous HRM issues facing MNCs is the extent to which HR practices should be transferred across borders (Stahl and Björkman, 2006, p. 3). Taylor et al. (1996) help to explain why MNCs choose different HRM orientations in different countries by drawing upon the resource-based theory of the firm and resource dependence. Resource-based theory proposes that, in order to provide added value to the organization, the SIHRM system of global affiliates should be built around the company's critical HRM competencies. The resource dependence framework helps to identify those situations in which MNCs will exercise control over their subsidiaries' SIHRM systems. In Figure 17.1, we show the corporate SIHRM orientation impacting on the SIHRM role of MNCs. Taylor et al. propose that the HR strategy of MNCs follows three generic SIHRM orientations: *adaptive*, *exportive* and *integrative*:

- An *adaptive* SIHRM orientation constructs HRM systems for subsidiaries that reflect the local context. This approach gives more emphasis to differentiation and less to integration. Top managers at corporate head office adopt local HR practices by hiring knowledgeable and competent indigenous HR practitioners.
- An *exportive* SIHRM orientation focuses on replicating in an MNC's overseas affiliates the HR practices used by the corporation in its parent country. This approach gives more emphasis to integration and less to differentiation.
- An *integrative* SIHRM orientation focuses on transferring the 'best' HR policies and practices from any of the company's affiliates worldwide to construct a global HRM system. Taylor et al. contend that the SIHRM orientation of the MNC determines its overall approach to managing the tension between integration and control pressures, and local responsiveness and differentiation pressures. The central theoretical argument of the integrative model is, therefore, that IHRM should be explicitly related to the MNC's global business strategy, and that its changing forms must be understood in relation to the strategic evolution of the MNC (Scullion and Linehan, 2005; Scullion and Starkey, 2000; Taylor et al., 1996).

reflective question What type of SIHRM orientation would you expect to find at Texas Instruments, ITT and Unilever? Why?

The integrated model is useful for understanding the link between international business strategy and IHRM in the global corporation, and for identifying a comprehensive range of factors that influence SIHRM in MNCs. However, models are just that: they are a conceptual construct and have been criticized because the alleged direction of the causal relationships within them is uncertain. For example, the argument that exogenous factors exert a direct impact on endogenous factors may privilege external factors as the actor when MNCs have actually become global giants that wield titanic political power. Arguably, corporations in fact determine the rules of the game, and governments enforce the rules laid down by others (Hertz, 2002). The MNC is the actor.

Although the framework in Fig 17.1 covers a wide range of relevant issues, the issue of transplanting HRM practices and values from developed countries into culturally diverse domestic environments needs to be researched through a critical lens. Global companies share with their domestic counterparts the intractable problem of managing the employment relationship to reduce the indeterminacy that results from the unspecified nature of the employment contract (see Chapter 1). If we adopt Townley's (1994) perspective on IHRM, the role of knowledge to render people in the workplace 'governable' is made highly problematic by the intertwining of highly complex local, regional, national and global cultures (Crane, 1994). It is the *complexity* of operating in different socioculturally diverse environments and employing different national categories of workers, rather than the HR practices as such, that differentiates national and international HRM (Dowling et al., 2008).

HRM web links Visit the online resource centre at **www.palgravehighered.com/bg-hrm-6e** for further information on cultural diversity.

reflective
question

How has globalization changed the nature of intercultural HRM competencies?

The internationalization of HRM practices

The global strategies examined above, in particular the supposed ascendancy of the transnational corporation with global communication networks, has far-reaching implications for the function and practices of IHRM. When leveraging their core HR activities, MNCs must achieve a dynamic balance between the pressures for central control and the pressures for local responsiveness across diverse national locations, intercultural business contexts (Adler, N. J., 2002) and business cultures (Brewster and Bennett, 2010). One important aspect of the internationalization of HRM relates to the 'best practice' versus 'best fit' debate. The former argues for the universal application of certain HR practices, while the latter recognizes the importance of context and societal embeddedness in HRM. It is argued that MNCs in general engage in the straightforward transfer of their own, 'nationally idiosyncratic' HRM policies and practices across borders (Sayim, 2010).

As an independent variable, however, sociocultural embeddedness can have an important influence on the development of IHRM policies and practices and their subsequent effect on global performance (Paauwe and Boselie, 2008, p. 167). Expatriate managers, for example, are required to fit in and be 'legitimated' by the host country nationals (HCNs) but local legitimacy is also dependent on compliance with local norms and mores (Brewster and Bennett, 2010).

In shaping international HR policies and practices, an MNC will need to consider a number of objectives. First, each area of HR activity, like structure and systems, should be consistent with its business strategy, and hence contribute to the MNC's international performance. In sectors such as consumer electronics and clothing – both labour-intensive and prone to intense global competition – HR practices are found to be associated with cost-reduction strategies, narrowly designed jobs, low levels of spending on recruitment, selection and induction, and minimal investment in training. In contrast, MNCs producing sophisticated technical/high value-added products in the same host country are found to employ HR practices associated with Schuler's (1989) 'quality enhancement and innovation' strategies with, for example, high levels of training and employee participation. Although it is not the sole factor, business strategy, which directs work configuration in commodity chains, is an important determinant of HR practices (Morris et al., 2009, p. 368).

Second, the array of HR practices needs to recruit, retain, motivate and facilitate the transfer of talented employees internationally. Third, the MNC will want to ensure that the HR practices are equitable and comply with the host-country's cultural values (Zhang and Albrecht, 2010) and employment standards. As a whole, the above considerations inevitably raise the potential for countless complexities (Dowling et al., 2008; Varma et al., 2011).

To provide insight into the potential complexities, here we add the dimension of cultural diversity and extend Fombrun et al.'s HRM model (see Chapter 1) to briefly examine the international aspects of recruitment and selection, rewards, training and development, and performance appraisal, as well as the issue of repatriation. Others have noted that cultural diversity represents a variable that poses significant challenges for managing people in an international context. MNCs typically have multicultural workforces made up of employees with a variety of ethnic, racial, religious and cultural values and mores.

Indeed, it has been suggested that the central *modus operandi* of the global company is the creation and effective management of multicultural work teams that represent diversity in competencies, levels of experience, and cultural and language backgrounds (Dickmann et al., 2016; Dowling et al., 2008). A deep sensitivity for cultural diversity implies that researchers and practitioners should attempt to understand the goals and outcomes of HR practices within the wider sociocultural context of societal values and mores.

reflective question

> As we have discussed, the global company is characterized by geographical dispersion, demands for rationalization and differentiation, and cultural diversity. When an MNC adopts a global business strategy, what new challenges does it present for managing Fombrun et al.'s four dimensions of recruitment and selection, rewards, training and development, and performance appraisal?

HRM web links

> Visit the online resource centre at **www.palgravehighered.com/bg-hrm-6e** for information on IHRM issues, policies and practices from the Society for Human Resources Management.

International recruitment and selection

MNCs do not simply transmit capital: they invariably transmit management 'know-how'. Expatriate managers play a critical role in the transfer of both explicit knowledge and the tacit knowledge of the MNC's practices and management style to the overseas affiliates (Gamble, 2003). As such, international staffing is a crucial aspect of the management of people in the MNC, and is increasingly seen as one of the core HR practices used by global enterprises to control and coordinate their spatially dispersed global operations (Collings and Scullion, 2007).

The use of expatriates to staff vacant positions in subsidiaries in host countries is a widespread practice. In the case of European MNCs, 54 per cent of the managers of their overseas subsidiaries have been reported to be expatriates, and in North American and Japanese MNCs the pattern has been similar, with figures of 51 per cent and 75 per cent, respectively (Bonache and Fernández, 2005, p. 115). It is not surprising, therefore, that, in most IHRM publications, recruitment and selection is seen primarily as an issue of expatriate selection. Selection is, however, important beyond simply staffing key technical or managerial positions. Intercultural phenomena suggest that mastering cultural differences may be crucial for successful organizational performance. As such, it is argued that recruitment and selection is at the heart of the dilemma of centralization (cost efficiencies) versus decentralization (local responsiveness). The handling of this balance invokes issues of 'ethnocentricity', the belief in the inherent superiority of one's own culture or race, as well as 'managerial empathy' towards the local peoples (Torbiörn, 2005).

Much of the IHRM literature on staffing has focused on two alternative categories of recruitment and selection: parent country nationals and HCNs (Tung, 1998). Drawing from these two pools of potential employees seems logical in global recruiting as they mirror the wider dilemma of central versus de-central or local, in that the choice is whether to transfer the dominant norms of the MNC's national culture or make use of those of the local culture. In theory, a varied sociocultural context requires a selective use of parent country nationals and HCNs across staffing decisions. In practice, however, expatriate selection appears to be more a matter of 'good luck than good management' (Anderson, 2005, p. 580). In addition, because the locus of decision-making is embedded in the local culture and norms where the MNC's corporate office is located, expatriate staff at the company's head office may have little idea what culturally derived expectations are needed to 'fit' the local context (Gamble, 2003). Moreover, informal ad hoc selection practices may be frequent, and decisions of intercultural reach may frequently be affected by illogical or irrational elements such as ethnocentrism, ignorance and stereotyping (Torbiörn, 2005).

Furthermore, local culture and norms where the MNC's corporate office is located can exhibit discriminatory staffing practices. Senior managers might presume that skill-accredited immigrant professionals can access positions in the corporation to match their skills and qualifications. However, Almeida's et al. (2015) research examines the influence of similarity effect in recruitment decision-making involving immigrant information technology professionals in Australia. In particular, the authors investigated how the level of exposure to diversity, the decision-maker's origin and the diversity of clientele can moderate the assessment of the candidate's fit to the organization. The study assessed how apparel, name, accent and any overtly expressed religious affiliations influence employers' and recruitment managers' perceptions. The findings indicate that decision-makers with lower levels of exposure to diversity or working in organizations with mostly Anglo-American clients are more likely to be negatively influenced by non-Anglo personal attributes, and are more concerned about how Chinese Indian and South-East Asian candidates would 'fit' into the organization.

The discriminatory effect can also extend to gender. In 1911, feminist activist Clara Zetkin founded International Women's Day. A century later, research shows that, despite women's increased presence in organizational hierarchies in developed countries, the number of female expatriates remains only a fraction of those in senior management positions, and 'only in rare circumstances' are female managers offered global assignments (Linehan, 2005, p. 197). The low number of women chosen for global assignments provides evidence that staffing decisions in MNCs may often be irrational and sometimes discriminatory. In all capitalist countries, it is argued, men control economic and political power – management is consequently androcentric.

Numerous studies (see, for example, Adler, 1994; Caligiuri and Tung, 1999; Linehan, 2005; Punnett et al., 1992; Taylor and Napier, 1996) point to stereotypical perceptions of women's managerial abilities and business acumen, traditional attitudes towards women's family roles, the need to accommodate dual-career couples, and general discrimination against women as major social barriers to women expanding their career horizons via access to global management positions. Countering one myth, studies by Adler (1987) and Taylor and Napier (1996) found that there were no significant differences between male and female expatriates in their business performance, even in male-dominated cultures such as South Korea and Japan. As in all HR practices, an MNC will, in developing a recruitment and selection policy, need to understand the role of cultural values as a contributor to its strategic development (Zhang and Albrecht, 2010).

reflective question The term 'glass border' describes the irrational assumptions held by parent-country senior management about the suitability of female managers for overseas appointments. To what extent is gender still relevant as a criterion for selecting female expatriates? If gender is still relevant, what can be done to promote equal opportunity for female managers to undertake international assignments?

Realizing gender balance in British boardrooms

It has long been recognized that there is a 'glass ceiling' preventing women from achieving top positions in management. In 2010, only 12.5 per cent of board members of FTSE 100 companies were women, which represented a slow increase compared with 9.4 per cent in 2004 (Davies, 2011). At that rate, it would take 70 years for gender-balanced boardrooms to be realized. The report carried out by Lord Davies, then UK Minister for Trade, set a target of 25 per cent, for 2015. The report made a strong business case for raising female participation on the boards of Britain's largest companies and argued (Davies, 2011, p. 7) that:

> *The issues debated here are as much about improving business performance as about promoting equal opportunities for women. There is a strong business case for balanced boards. Inclusive and diverse boards are more likely to be effective boards, better able to understand their customers and stakeholders and to benefit from fresh perspectives, new ideas, vigorous challenge and broad experience. This in turn leads to better decision-making.*

The report quotes a wide range of research by academics and business consultants that compares firms and countries with greater female business leadership experience. The report claimed that research shows that company performance is increased when women are appointed. Women, it is thought, improve decision-making because they bring broader experiences and backgrounds to the task; they prepare more conscientiously for meetings and ask awkward questions. All male boards often have members with similar education, backgrounds and networks, which makes them more vulnerable to 'groupthink', whereas women can bring different perspectives to the decision-making process. Studies of the dynamics of group opinion formation suggest that the existence of three women is enough to change a boardroom's dynamics. Davies, as well as other studies suggest that:

> *a 'critical mass' of 30% or more women at board level or in senior management produces the best financial results.* (Davies, 2011, p. 8)

and that:

> *a gender-balanced board is more likely to pay attention to managing and controlling risk.* (Davies, 2011, p. 9)

Getty

Davies resisted calls for the establishment of quotas and instead recommended a voluntary approach involving a series of targets and monitoring at various levels of organizations. The UK target of 25 per cent female representation set for 2015 was almost met, with a figure of 23.5 per cent being reported. A BBC report (Hope, 2015) shows that there is still much to be achieved, as only 18 per cent of directors of the FTSE 250 firms are currently women. In addition, it is predicted that the representation of women is likely to

(continued)

Stop! Can you think of additional factors that prevent women from occupying top managerial posts? For example, do different national cultures promote or hinder female representation on governing bodies? Do you think that a combination of target-setting and company monitoring will eventually produce gender-balanced company boards?

Sources and further information: For more information, see Davies (2011), Hope (2015), Goodley (2015) and Rankin (2015).

Note: This feature was written by David Denham.

stagnate because there are not enough women in suitable, lower positions to gain the necessary experience to progress to the board. Other barriers to executive progression need to be addressed because:

most are non-executive, part-time directors. Smashing the glass ceiling for chief executive and chair jobs is proving harder: only 3.5% of these roles are occupied by women. (Rankin, 2015, courtesy of Guardian News & Media Ltd).

International rewards

Reward management (salary, allowances and incentive bonuses) generally needs to support overall business strategy in order to attract, retain and motivate needed employees (see Chapter 8). Managing international rewards requires that managers responsible for implementing HR policies and practices are familiar with a range of other issues, including the HCNs, the host country's employment law, national labour relations, the availability of particular allowances or benefits, and currency fluctuations in particular host countries. Even within the 'scant' international reward literature, much of the focus has been on reward management for expatriates and far less on other categories of workers, such as host country and third-country nationals (Mahajan, 2011).

Although the issue of generous remuneration packages for globally mobile corporate elites has become part of the public discourse on what constitutes 'responsible capitalism', most of the reward literature deals with technical rather than strategic or ethical issues of rewards, that is, with how to design effective remuneration packages for expatriates (Bonache and Fernández, 2005). Part of that technical discussion includes deciding which currency it is beneficial to pay rewards in so that, in terms of tax efficiency, the outcome motivates the expatriate. Bonache and Fernández (2005) present a theory-based approach to expatriate rewards based on the costs and benefits. They suggest that when salary and non-salary costs (for example, training) are taken into account, and in certain circumstances (for example, the need to exploit company-specific knowledge), expatriates can be a cost-effective solution. Other studies provide evidence that effective performance management requires expatriates to know whether and how their performance in their overseas assignment is linked to pay and the next step in their career (Tahvanainen and Suutari, 2005).

In terms of strategic issues, there is limited evidence to suggest that international rewards systems misaligned with the values and beliefs of the local host country cause negative outcomes for the MNC. Negative effects in terms of the organization arise, when, without reasonable justification, expatriates' rewards significantly exceed those rewards paid to their local colleagues. This internal inequity can cause HCNs to withhold technical and social support from expatriates. Research also suggests that pay systems that are aligned with the host country's values and beliefs, and are perceived to be fair and socially responsive to HCNs, are likely to render positive outcomes such as 'extra-role behaviour' and support for expatriates (Mahajan, 2011).

Cross-cultural research draws attention to the salience of national culture as an enduring set of beliefs that shapes employees' behaviour. These beliefs shape the attitudes of HCNs, including whether a pay system is perceived as fair and locally responsive. Recent research has highlighted the universality of concepts of the 'work-life' balance and the psychological contract from developed nations. Global work–life initiatives present unique challenges for HR departments in MNCs because of the complexity of implementing policies that require sensitivity to local issues such as cultural traditions and legislation. For global managers, this suggests that it is important to guard against biases related to developed countries' notions of progress when constructing global work–life initiatives (Bardoel, 2016).

Other studies have highlighted the universality of the psychological contract framework in explaining negative effects in terms of employees' reactions to a reduction in rewards. Chambel and Fortuna's (2015) study provides an empirical test of the psychological contract violation (PCV) that was caused by the pay reduction of Portuguese civil servants. The evidence confirms that the PCV of the employing organization mediates the relationships between the PCV of the public institution and the commitment and turnover intentions of civil servants. In developing an international reward policy, an MNC will need to include the HCNs' perspective. According to Mahajan, a 'cultural alignment' pay system will be more acceptable than ethnocentric reward policies to HNCs 'as it increases perceived status similarity and reduces intergroup conflict between expatriates and HCNs [and] will facilitate adjustment of expatriates and favourably impact overall effectiveness of [MNCs]' (2011, p. 131). While there is evidence of 'strong "pull" factors' for the transfer of contemporary reward practices to HCNs (Sayim, 2010), the need to elicit HCN's voluntary cooperation and knowledge-sharing with expatriates makes international reward management inevitably complex.

International training and development

The transnational strategy focuses attention on the issue of 'best fit' between an MNC's global business strategy and training interventions. Within the global integration versus host country responsiveness framework, the notion of strategic alignment suggests that international training and development will vary and take one of three forms: centralized, synergistic or local (Caligiuri et al., 2005). Evidence suggests that MNCs pursuing a global strategy will tend to place greater emphasis on training rather than development. The general objective of the training interventions will be to provide managers and key technical personnel with the competencies needed to transfer the distinctive competencies and organizational culture successfully from the parent headquarters to the subsidiaries. MNCs pursuing a multidomestic strategy tend to transfer almost all their HR practices to the host country subsidiaries. Local managers at the affiliate make decisions on the types of training intervention required. MNCs pursuing a transnational strategy clearly require the most complex training and development strategy. The transnational strategy requires that managers be recruited from a worldwide pool of employees, regardless of nationality.

Prescriptive HRM advisers tend to view training intervention as a strategic instrument to nurture a 'strong' culture, or what Bartlett and Ghoshal (1989, p. 175) call the 'global glue' that counterbalances the centrifugal forces of decentralized operations and processes. A particular focus in this area has been the pre-departure training of expatriates to be 'interculturally competent', which refers to the ability of the effective manager to have both 'communicative competence' – that is, the ability to communicate both verbally and non-verbally with HCNs – and 'cognitive competence', which avoids the use of crude stereotypes to judge people (see, for example, Mabey et al., 1998b). According to Caligiuri et al. (2005, p. 76), training interventions in the transnational MNC aim to help managers 'to work, think and behave synergistically across borders with people from diverse cultural backgrounds'. However, international research suggests also a positive correlation between training interventions and organizational outcomes that go beyond the construction or reconstruction of organizational culture. Gathering data from 277 establishments in South Korea, Choi and Yoon (2015) investigated how and when investment in employee training leads to improved organizational outcomes. Their findings showed that employees' commitment and competence mediated the relationship between the training investment and organizational outcomes. The study also found that this mediated relationship via employee commitment and competence was stronger when the HR function within an organization was 'highly strategically oriented' (p. 2632). Irrespective of global business strategy and training and performance linkages, training and development interventions in MNCs typically include cross-cultural training and competencies associated with global leadership. Table 17.1 summarizes these interventions and their respective goals. (See Chapter 7 for a further discussion on learning and development.)

Table 17.1 Examples of training and development interventions in MNCs

Training and development initiatives	Goals
Cross-cultural orientation (predeparture)	Comfortably live and work in host country
Cross-cultural training (in-country)	Increase cross-cultural adjustment
Diversity training	Increase ability to understand and appreciate multiple cultural perspectives
Language training	Fluency in another language
Traditional education in international management	Increase international business acumen and knowledge
Individualized coaching or mentoring on cultural experiences	Build cultural awareness; work on cultural 'blind spots'; develop competencies for becoming an effective global leader
Immersion cultural experiences	Build extensive understanding of the local culture and increase ability to understand and appreciate multiple cultural perspectives
Cross-border global teams with debriefing	Learn skills to be a better leader (or team member) with multiple cultures involved in the team
Global meetings with debriefing or coaching	Learn skills to conduct a better meeting when multiple cultures are involved in the meeting
International assignment rotations with debriefing or coaching	Develop a deep appreciation for the challenges of working in another culture; increase global leadership competence

Source: Caligiuri, P. M., Lazarova, M. and Tarique, I. (2005, p. 77) Training, learning and development in multinational organizations. In H. Scullion and M. Linehan (eds) International Human Resource Management (pp. 71–90). Basingstoke: Palgrave Macmillan. Reprinted with permission from Hugh Scullion and Margaret Linehan.

International performance appraisal

As we discussed in Chapter 6, performance appraisal has become a key feature of the employment relationship. The desire to control and predict an employee's current and potential performance has resulted in both national and global firms developing integrated performance appraisal systems. In keeping with the critical perspective of HRM, some have argued that the diffusion of performance appraisal systems is associated with low trade union density (Brown and Heywood, 2005), and is indicative of increasing attempts on the part of employers to individualize the employment relationship; this will cause greater risk by, first and foremost, increasing the proportion of pay that is contingent on assessments of individual, group or organizational performance (Heery, 2000). Appraisal systems have also been critiqued on the grounds that they weaken trade union influence over pay determination (see, for example, Gunnigle et al., 1998). Here, we will consider questions of 'why' and 'how' related to international performance appraisal.

Sparrow et al. (2004) argue that five interrelated organizational 'drivers' – core business cost efficiencies, information exchange, building a global presence, global learning and localized decision-making – are together creating an obvious logic of being as effective as possible across the organization's whole international operations, as well as creating a need for the cross-national transfer of better HR practices such as performance appraisal. Notably, performance appraisal is the favoured way to ensure that strategic employee competencies, employee behaviour and motivation are enacted effectively in the host country.

In Eastern Europe, following the collapse of the Soviet Union in 1991, the 'Washington Consensus' dominated the ideology of most newly elected governments. This was the ideology of wide-scale privatization, deregulation and free markets, all promoted by the International Monetary Fund and the World Bank. The new dominant ideology and the orientation towards the European Union (EU) urged Eastern European managers into new roles requiring increased autonomy and performance appraisal (Koubek and Brewster, 1995; Prokopenko, 1994). According to Shibata (2002), in Asia, when the Japanese 'bubble economy' collapsed in the 1990s, Japanese companies began to be attracted to the performance appraisal systems that had long been found in North American business organizations. Chou's (2005) study examines the implementation of performance appraisal in the civil service in China in the 1990s. It is suggested that changes occurred to improve personnel practices and government capacity in both central and local government.

How far does performance appraisal in an international context resemble the Anglo-American model and practice? Performance appraisal is a political activity. It is about gathering relevant information on an employee's competencies and behaviour; about making judgements of a subordinate's work effort, the level of reward and career paths; about motivation (being inspired by positive appraisal) – and in some cases it involves termination of employment. To perform successfully in a host country, a manager requires technical skills, interpersonal skills, adaptability and cultural sensitivity. Expatriate performance in an international context is, however, affected by volatility in the international environment (for example, fluctuating currency exchange rates), which is outside the expatriate's scope of control, and by cultural and political factors inside the host country (for example, acts of terrorism).

The complexity of the task is compounded by differences in societal values. For example, Chou (2005) found that Anglo-Saxon-style performance appraisal was undermined in China because of the collectivist, relationship-oriented or 'Communist neo-traditionalism' sociopolitical culture. The study found that many managers 'manipulated appraisal results' and refrained from rating subordinates' performance as 'unsatisfactory' because of the importance placed on a 'reciprocal relationship and organizational harmony' (Chou, 2005, p. 54). Evidence suggests that the internationalization of performance appraisal demands sensitivity to different cultural and sociopolitical experiences. This section also illustrates that the cross-national transfer of Anglo-Saxon HR practices for selection, rewards, training and appraisal will require some degree of cultural sensitivity, as well as consultation with HCNs about local suitability (Mabey et al., 1998b).

HRM web links Visit the online resource centre at **www.palgravehighered.com/bg-hrm-6e** for more information on Geert Hofstede's extensive work on organizational culture.

reflective question If you were an expatriate, how would you feel about returning to your old position in the company after 5 years working at one of the company's overseas subsidiaries? Can you think of any problems you would encounter on your return to your parent country and company?

Repatriation

Much of the early research on IHRM focuses on expatriates returning to the parent company – repatriation. The main reason for a premature return or an ineffective international assignment is a failure of the expatriate and his or her family to adapt to the new setting (Fischlmayr and Kollinger, 2010). In the context of SIHRM discussed in this chapter, managing expatriates or 'flex-patriates' (Mayerhofer et al., 2004) returning to the parent company may be the least of the challenges facing a global manager, as our opening chapter statement on events in the Middle East testifies. Nonetheless, for many MNCs, the failure to repatriate managers successfully has caused many expatriates to resign from the company owing to what has been termed re-entry shock.

The complexity of the repatriation problem varies from individual to individual. Linehan and Mayrhofer (2005) point out that a violation of the psychological contract may lead to a negative psychological reaction to repatriation. Anecdotal and empirical evidence of re-entry shock indicates that loss of autonomy, loss of status and loss of career opportunities, together with problems of family members readjusting to the parent culture, are often relevant (for example, Brewster and Scullion, 1997; Fischlmayr and Kollinger, 2010; Linehan and Mayrhofer, 2005). Nga Thi Thuy Ho et al.'s (2016) study, for example, found three pull–push factors associated with home and host countries that have a significant impact on expatriates' self-initiated intention to re-expatriate: dissatisfaction with their career and life in their home country, culture shock, and the family and quality-of-life outcomes of re-expatriation. Recent expatriate research has shown that HR managers need to develop a formal and informal mentorship system to help expatriates cope with social isolation abroad and assist in balancing expatriate work–life relationships. This is especially the case for female expatriates, given the fact that they in general invest more time in family activities (Fischlmayr and Kollinger, 2010). Even before the attacks on the World Trade Center in New York in 2001 and the revolts in North Africa in 2011, MNCs had begun to experience difficulty attracting managers to accept overseas assignments. The security issue will be an additional contributing factor in this reluctance to go abroad.

The convergence/divergence debate

Critical IHRM scholars support conceptualizations of organizational culture (see Chapter 15) as being continuously constructed and reconstructed through human interactions between specific social contexts (Frenkel, 2008). From this perspective, critical scholars view the corporate culture of MNCs as a powerful strategic tool not just to facilitate integration and cooperation, but rather to exert control over the domestic workforce (Peltonen, 2006, cited by Kramar and Syed, 2012, p. 62; Said, 1993).

The contentious nature of employment relations and HR practices in MNCs highlights that a common theme in the comparative HRM literature has been 'convergence' and 'divergence' in HR practices, resulting from globalization, in different regions of the world. Historically, orthodox economists have held the belief that unfettered flows of international trade would allow rich and poor economies eventually to converge to similar levels of per capita income, as capital investment would migrate from developed economies, where it would be abundant and returns limited, to developing economies, where capital would be scarce and returns higher. This convergence process should also, according to prevailing management wisdom, result in a convergence of national business environments, including HR practices, towards homogeneity. The power of capital from the parent country and the weakness and 'receptiveness' of the subordinate host country both underscore ideas of how globalization creates uniformity in national business patterns (Rowley and Bae, 2002).

The major challenge to a universal vision of order, equilibrium and convergence arises from local rationalities, local realities, local ideologies and local culture (Clegg et al., 1999). An example of divergence theory applied to IHRM is the freedom of lesbian, gay, bisexual and transgender (LGBT) expatriates to disclose their identity when on international assignments. Although LGBT+ people are becoming acknowledged in diversity management practices, they are under-researched in IHRM. In Paisley and Yayar's (2016) study, the concept of convergent and divergent intersectionality – interconnected social categorizations such as race, class, gender, and sexual orientation as they apply to a given individual or group, which is regarded as creating interdependent systems of disadvantage or discrimination – is introduced to explain how the multiple identities of LGBT+ expatriates are redefined during an international work assignment.

Evidence of continued diversity in local or national patterns of economic activity and employment relations has contributed to the notion of 'varieties of capitalism' (see Hall and Soskice, 2001; Hancke, 2009). Within the 'varieties of capitalism' literature, academics have highlighted the importance of national culture, national economic and political conditions, institutions and historical legacies that substantially shape employment relations (Bryson and Frege, 2010). For Whitley (1999, p. 3), although the global economy continues to be more interconnected, 'societies with different institutional arrangements will continue to develop and reproduce varied systems of economic organization with different economic and social capabilities in particular industries and sectors'. Echoing this perspective, Sheldon and Sanders (2016) underscore the importance for HRM researchers to understand the existence of distinct national contexts. When it comes to studying China, for example, the authors posit that researchers have, in practice, been unwilling to contextualize HRM beyond the organization or, perhaps the industry. Adopting a different research perspective, the authors highlight two important contextual conceptions of 'differences': diversity within China, especially where related to space and place; and rising evidence of expressed differences of interests within China's labour markets. Such context-sensitive studies suggest that, with the existence of distinct national contexts and cross-cultural differences, the idea of the 'universalist' assumption that Anglo-American HRM techniques are directly transferable is wrong (Elenkov, 1998), and that strikingly resilient differences in cultural and institutional contexts produce divergent employment relationships and HR practices (Clark and Pugh, 2000; Paik et al., 1996).

Japanese CEO breaks stereotype by firing 14,000 staff

Japan's business system is the most advanced of those in the Asia-Pacific countries reviewed here. Research into traditional HR practices has usually emphasized six characteristics of Japanese employment relations: recruitment and selection, training, the lifetime employment contract, seniority-based rewards, the consensus decision-making process and enterprise trade unionism. The traditional Japanese approach to HR so eulogized by managers in developed countries is, of course, a simplistic and sanitized version of reality, as this discussion of Sanyo Electric Co. illustrates:

In 2005 the struggling electronics firm broke with tradition and appointed a former TV anchorwoman, Tomoyo Nonaka, as chief executive, in what was deemed one of the 'most off-the-wall CEO choices in Japanese corporate history' (Pitts, 2005). Yet despite having no management experience, Nonaka quickly initiated a major restructuring programme. The first stage, euphemistically named 'Streamlining', involved approximately 14,000 job losses, equivalent to 15% of the workforce, and the closure of several 'underperforming sites' (Sanyo Electric Co., Ltd., Annual Report 2006). Nonaka tried to mask these cuts by focusing attention on the company's new vision, Think GAIA, alluding to the Greek 'Mother Earth' mythological figure, with the motto 'We Seek to be a Company That Delights the Earth' (Sanyo Electric Co., Ltd., Sustainability Report 2006). However, things didn't quite work out. Nonaka resigned in 2007 as Sanyo's difficulties escalated. Nonaka's unusual appointment was, nonetheless, an example of Japan's desire for 'fresh faces' to breathe life into suffering companies, instead of selecting the typical 'middle-aged' man (Pitts, 2005).

Critical workplace scholars have challenged different aspects of the Japanese HRM model, particularly in the context of globalized capitalism. Relevant here is Whittaker's (1990) study, which notes that one of the 'pillars' of Japanese employment – 'lifetime employment' – is highly selective and, where it does exist, excludes part-time, short-term or peripheral workers. Others have noted that, since the 1997 financial crisis, Japanese companies have found it difficult to maintain lifetime employment security and the *nenko* automatic pay increase system (see, for

example, Benson, 1996). HRM is universal in the sense that every employer has to manage, in some way, people. However, the practice of HRM varies within and across borders.

Stop! Is this case an example of the destructive 'strategic tension' between global corporations that promote the 'low road' to profitability? Does it provide evidence of the persistence of capitalist employment relations or of a 'convergence' HRM practices? Is there evidence of HRM models converging and, if so, towards which model?

Sources and further information: The quotes and statistics are taken from Pitts (2005), Sanyo Electric Co., Ltd., Sustainability Report 2006 and Sanyo Electric Co., Ltd., Annual Report 2006. To read about Nonaka's resignation, go to http://news.bbc.co.uk/1/hi/business/6467677.stm For an analysis of the 2007–08 financial meltdown and its impact on employment relations, see the article 'Money, markets, meltdown' (Nolan, 2011).

Note: This feature was written by John Bratton.

Does globalization bring into being a convergence of HR practices? To address this conundrum, we have drawn on Rowley and Bae's (2002) model (Figure 17.2). The two dimensions in Rowley and Bae's framework are the unit of analysis – *country* versus *organization* – and the foci – *practices* versus *people*. Changes in HR practices within the organization are mediated by environmental changes and universal 'best practices'. However, the framework draws attention to 'gaps' between universalism versus national culture, and HR practices newly adopted versus the organizational culture or the 'shared mindset' of people in the workplace. For example, the change from a regulated to a more market-driven form of capitalism in China, India and Singapore, with its greater flexibility and unemployment, would provide a cultural shock for the nationals of these countries.

Different national institutional systems, which comprise laws, frames of reference and core values and norms, can explain the 'divergence' between the parent and host local establishments. Brewster (2001) makes a strong case for only a remote likelihood of a common HRM model emerging in the foreseeable future because the idiosyncratic national institutional settings are so variable in host country nationals (HCNs). Jacoby's (2005) study of Japan and the USA also argues the case for a persistence of varieties of employment management practices. Consequently, institutional change to facilitate movements towards US-inspired market-oriented HR practices and employment management has been slow in Japan.

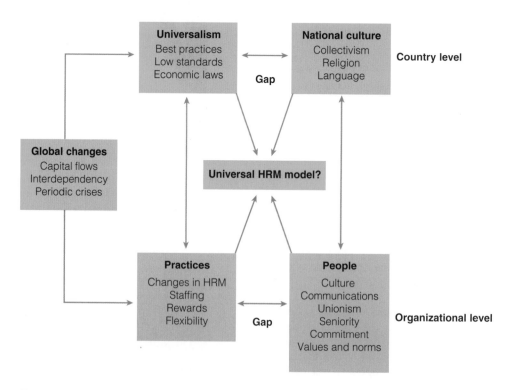

Figure 17.2 *Globalization and HRM models*
Source: Based on Rowley and Bae (2002), p. 543

Similarly, Rowley and Bae (2002) engage in the convergence/divergence debate by pointing out the gap between changes in HR practices and what they call the 'shared mindset' of managers and workers. Successful transfer, it is argued, depends upon two processes:

- The *'implementation'* of the HR practices, whereby workers in the recipient organization change their observable behaviours in respect of the transferred practice
- The *'internalization'* of the HR practices, whereby people fully accept and approve the practices.

The gaps therefore reflect a failure to instil HR practices with embedded core 'values'. Thus, 'even if there are "best practices", they would not bring positive effects until people fully accepted and approved them', assert Rowley and Bae (2002, p. 544). The gaps problematize any grand narrative on the conversion to either European or Asian models of HRM and on their efficacy. Brewster captured the inconclusiveness of the convergence/divergence debate when he concluded (2007, p. 212):

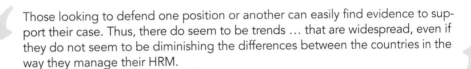

Those looking to defend one position or another can easily find evidence to support their case. Thus, there do seem to be trends … that are widespread, even if they do not seem to be diminishing the differences between the countries in the way they manage their HRM.

Understanding the disjuncture between universal theory and idiosyncratic national institutions and cultures becomes a key competency of the global manager. Although the debate remains equivocal, we can be more confident in affirming that the study of IHRM is no longer a marginal area of interest. Increasingly, as the globalization of world markets continues apace, global managers will be expected to undertake overseas assignments, and IHRM and comparative HRM research will be an important resource for training expatriate managers (Budhwar and Boyne, 2004).

case study

ICAN

The setting

ICAN, established in 1972 in Finland by Vesa Stroh, has experienced considerable growth since Finland joined the EU in the 1990s, to become one of the EU's largest manufacturers of home furnishings. The parent company is located in Tampere and employs 1750 employees made up of skilled and semi-skilled workers. Two hundred and thirty employees work in design and development and other highly skilled areas. All the employees belong to one trade union. The company has a profit-sharing scheme and an excellent pension scheme.

Since 1972, ICAN has sold a basic range of typically 'Scandinavian' home furnishings in six stores, only one of which – in Helsinki – is inside Finland. The company remains primarily production-oriented, its Finnish management and design group deciding what it is going to manufacture in the most cost-effective way and then how it will sell it to the European homeowner, often with very little market research outside Finland. The company has emphasized its Finnish roots in its European advertising, including the adoption of the colours blue and white, from the Finnish national flag, for its retail outlets and advertising material.

The foundation of ICAN's success has been to offer consumers good value for money, distinctive branding and a good network of suppliers. A supplier for ICAN gains long-term contracts and leased equipment from the company. In return, ICAN demands an exclusive contract and low prices. ICAN's expatriate managers seconded to the subsidiary standardize products and integrate production to gain maximum savings on the final products at a low cost. ICAN sells its avant-garde furniture to customers as self-assembly kits. In this way, the company reaps economies of scale from the large production runs. In 2012, only 13 per cent of its sales were generated in Finland, the balance coming from Germany (33 per cent), Sweden (22 per cent), The Netherlands (11 per cent) and the UK (21 per cent). This strategy allows ICAN to match its competitors on quality but undercut them by up to 30 per cent on price, while maintaining an after-tax return on sales of around 7 per cent.

The problem

In 2013, ICAN decided to establish a factory in Montreal and two retail stores in Canada, followed by six in the USA. The Canadian subsidiary was built on a green-field site on the east side of Montreal and employed 320

Fancy

employees by the end of 2014. Informed that trade union density in Canada was well below that of Finland, expatriate managers were told that unionization was a 'non-issue' and that the company's profit-sharing scheme, similar to the Finnish scheme, would ensure employee loyalty and commitment. The production side of the business was meeting output targets. Preliminary reports, however, indicated that the new North American retail stores were not meeting sales and profit targets as planned. Finnish home furnishings, which sold well in Western Europe, clashed with Canadian and US tastes and sometimes physiques. In addition, the new Canadian factory was experiencing quality control problems and some challenges in managing the workforce.

Vesa Engeström, the factory manager, called a meeting of the Canadian management team. Yrjö

Alvesson, an experienced Finnish marketing manager, gave the first presentation to the assembled ICAN managers. He explained that sales had not reached expected targets because the standard furniture did not meet North American tastes and preferences. He said, for example, 'Our Finnish kitchen cupboards are too narrow to take large dinner plates needed for pizza. And our beds are too narrow for American preferences.'

Christian Poikela, the HR manager at the Canadian subsidiary, explained that some of the Canadian managers resented the degree of control exerted over how they managed their units. In addition, he had heard through various managers and supervisors that some employees had been overheard talking about 'bringing in a union' to achieve higher wages. Jonathan Pyrch, one of three Canadian-born and Canadian-educated managers present at the meeting, interjected at this point and said, 'The union isn't the problem; it's poor communications. Many staff can't understand the expatriate managers! I've heard that shop-floor supervisors leave their encounters with Finnish managers feeling frustrated by their inability to understand and relate to them.' Poikela also said that shop-floor staff were reluctant to work at weekends. 'The fact that Quebec, like the other provinces in Canada, has its own labour relations statutes makes dealing with Canadian unions more difficult and frustrating, especially if we open a factory in Calgary,' he added. What legal rights do unions have in this province, asked Engeström? 'I'm unsure, but I'll investigate,' replied Poikela.

The assignment

Given the pressures facing ICAN in the marketplace, prepare a written report to Christian Poikela:

1. Explaining how ICAN can be both competitive and locally responsive, and detailing why ICAN's SIHRM orientation should be linked to its international business strategy and what this would mean for the role of the HRM department at ICAN's Canadian subsidiary
2. Explaining the types of competency you feel the managers at the Canadian subsidiary need, and whether expatriate or local managers can supply these competencies.

Note: This case study was written by John Bratton.

Visit the online resource centre at **www.palgravehighered.com/bg-hrm-6e** for guidelines on writing reports.

summary

➤ In this chapter, we explored how global corporations typically face tension from two types of business pressure: on the one hand, pressures for global cost reductions and rationalization, and on the other hand, demands for differentiation and local responsiveness.

➤ We also discussed how IHRM is closely tied to international business strategies and briefly explained four fashionable business strategies – global, multidomestic, international and transnational – as solutions to the dual pressure for cost-efficiencies and responsiveness.

➤ The chapter explained that the driving force behind the growth of interest in SIHRM and IHRM is the resurgence of neo-liberalism and the growth in global markets. Critics argue that globalization has created the new international division of labour, causing the transfer from old industrialized regions of high-wage manufacturing jobs to low-wage developing economies.

➤ An integrative model explored how IHRM should be explicitly linked to the global business strategy of the MNC and how its changing forms must be understood in relation to the strategic evolution of the MNC.

➤ We discussed how the cross-national transfer of Anglo-Saxon HR practices will require some degree of cultural sensitivity, as well as consultation with HCNs about local suitability.

➤ We discussed how variations in national regulatory systems, the labour markets and cultural and polyethnic contexts are likely to constrain or shape any tendency towards 'convergence' or a 'universal' model of 'better' HR practice. The sheer variation of capitalist economies and cultures makes claims for convergence both simplistic and problematic.

➤ Finally, in this chapter, it has been easier to formulate questions than answers, and we have taken the easier rather than the more difficult route. Yet there is value in asking questions. Questions can stimulate reflection and increase our understanding of IHRM. Our object here has been to do both.

review questions

1 What is meant by SIHRM and IHRM?

2 Explain how MNCs address the tension between the dual imperatives of global integration and local responsiveness.

3 Discuss how differences in national institutional systems influence a corporation's decision to locate its profit-making operations.

4 Explain how a need for rationalization and standardization over foreign operations varies with the business strategy and distinctive competencies of an MNC.

further reading

Reading these articles and chapters can help you gain a better understanding and potentially a higher grade for your HRM assignment.

➤ For an introduction to the issues of globalization, see Hancke B. (ed.) (2009) *Debating Varieties of Capitalism: A Reader*. Oxford: Oxford University Press; Mason, P. (2016) *Post-capitalism: A Guide to Our Future*. London: Penguin.

➤ For more specialized texts on IHRM, refer to Dickmann, M., Brewster, C. and Sparrow, P. (eds.) (2016) *International Human Resource Management: Contemporary HR Issues in Europe* (3rd edn). Abingdon: Routledge.

➤ For an accessible introduction to some of the issues discussed in this chapter, refer to Cappellen, T., Zanoni, P. and Janssens, M. (2012) Human resource management in contemporary transnational companies. In R. Kramar and J. Syed (eds.) *Human Resource Management in a Global Context* (pp. 55–76). Basingstoke: Palgrave.

➤ This article examines the multiple roles of HR managers and shows that these HR roles have different impacts depending on the aspect of organizational performance: Galang, M. C. and Osman, I. (2015) HR managers in five countries: what do they do and why does it matter? *International Journal of Human Resource Management*, **27**(13): 1341–72.

➤ Global pay systems are examined in Mahajan, A. (2011) Host country national's reactions to expatriate pay policies: making a case for a cultural alignment pay model. *International Journal of Human Resource Management*, **22**(1): 121–37.

➤ The following article argues that HR practices in MNCs can best be understood in the context of worldwide commodity chains. Arguably, much of the case for cultural alignment can be made for other HR practices. Morris, J., Wilkinson, B. and Gamble, J. (2009) Strategic international human resource management or the 'bottom line'? The case of electronics and garments commodity chains in China. *International Journal of Human Resource Management*, **20**(2): 348–71.

➤ Paisley, V. and Yayar, M. (2016) Lesbian, gay, bisexual and transgender (LGBT) expatriates: an intersectionality perspective. *International Journal of Human Resource Management*, **27**(7): 766–80.

➤ Sheldon, P. and Sanders, K. (2016) Contextualizing HRM in China: differences within the country. *International Journal of Human Resource Management*, **27**(18): 2017–33.

➤ Almeida et al. provide insight into how recruiters can be negatively influenced by the non-Anglo personal attributes of candidates: Almeida, S., Fernando, M., Hannif, Z. and Dharmage, S. C. (2015) Fitting the mould: the role of employer perceptions in immigrant recruitment decision-making. *International Journal of Human Resource Management*, **26**(22): 2811–32.

➤ For information on testing the concept of the psychological contract in an international context, see Chambel M. J. and Fortuna, R. (2015) Wage reduction of Portuguese civil servants and their attitudes: the psychological contract perspective. *International Journal of Human Resource Management*, **26**(22): 2853–71.

➤ The mediating role of training investment on South Korean organizations is examined in Choi, M. and Yoon, H. J. (2015) Training investment and organizational outcomes: a moderated mediation model of employee outcomes and strategic orientation of the HR function. *International Journal of Human Resource Management*, **26**(20): 2632–51.

➤ Bardoel, E. A. (2016). Work–life management tensions in multinational enterprises (MNEs). *International Journal of Human Resource Management*, **27**(15): 1681–709.

➤ Nga Thi Thuy Ho, Pi-Shen Seet and Jones, J. (2015) Understanding re-expatriation intentions among overseas returnees – an emerging economy perspective. *International Journal of Human Resource Management*, **27**(17): 1938–66.

➤ Stahl, G. K. and Björkman, I. (eds) (2006) *Handbook of Research in International Human Resource Management*. Cheltenham: Edward Elgar.

vocabulary checklist for ESL students

Click here in your interactive ebook for a list of HRM terminology and vocabulary that has appeared in this chapter.

Visit the online resource centre at **www.palgravehighered.com/bg-hrm-6e** for lots of extra resources to help you get to grips with this chapter, including study tips, HRM skills development guides, summary lecture notes, tips for English as a Second Language (ESL) students and more.

references

Aaltio-Marjosola, I. and Mills, A. J. (eds) (2002) *Gender, Identity and the Culture of Organizations*. London: Routledge.

Ababneh, K. I., Hackett, R. D. and Schat, A. C. (2014) The role of attributions and fairness in understanding job applicant reactions to selection procedures and decisions. *Journal of Business and Psychology*, **29**(1): 111–29.

Abbott, A. (2009) Organizations and the Chicago School. In P. Adler (ed.) *Oxford Handbook of Sociology and Organization Studies: Classical Foundations* (pp. 399–420). Oxford: Oxford University Press.

Abraham, S. E., Karns, L. A., Shaw, K. and Mena, M. A. (2001) Managerial competencies and the managerial appraisal process. *Journal of Management Development*, **20**(10): 842–52.

Accounting for People Task Force (2003) *Report of the Accounting for People Task Force*. London: Department for Trade and Industry.

Ackroyd, S. and Crowdy, P. A. (1990) Can culture be managed? Working with 'raw' material: the case of the English slaughtermen. *Personnel Review*, **19**(5): 3–13.

Ackroyd, S. and Thompson, P. (1999) *Organizational Misbehaviour*. Thousand Oaks, CA: Sage.

Action on Smoking and Health (2015) Fact sheet. Smoking statistics: illness and death. November. ash.org.uk/files/documents/ASH_107.pdf (accessed August 15, 2016).

Adair, J. (2005) *Effective Leadership Development*. London: Chartered Institute of Personnel and Development.

Adams, J. S. (1965) Inequality in social exchange. In L. Berkowitz (ed.) *Advances in Experimental Social Psychology* (pp. 267–99). New York: Academic Press.

Adams, R. J. (2006) *Labour Left Out*. Ottawa: Canadian Centre for Policy Alternatives.

Adamson, S. J., Doherty, N. and Viney, C. (1998) The meanings of career revisited: implications for theory and practice. *British Journal of Management*, **9**(4): 251–9.

Addison, J., Siebert, W., Wagner, J. and Wei, X. (2000) Worker participation and firm performance. *British Journal of Industrial Relations*, **38**(1): 7–48.

Adler, L. (2002) *Hire With Your Head*. Chichester: John Wiley & Sons.

Adler, N. J. (1987) Pacific basin managers: a gaijin, not a woman. *Human Resource Management*, **26**(2): 169–92.

Adler, N. J. (1994) Competitive frontiers: women managing across borders. In N. J. Adler and D. N. Izraeli (eds) *Competitive Frontiers: Women Managers in a Global Economy* (pp. 22–40). Oxford: Blackwell.

Adler, N. J. (2002) Global managers: no longer men alone. *International Journal of Human Resource Management*, **13**(5): 743–60.

Adler, N. J. and Gundersen, A. (2008) *International Dimensions of Organizational Behavior* (5th edn). Mason, OH: Thomson/South-Western.

Advanced Institute of Management (2009) *Closing the UK's Productivity Gap: The Latest Research Evidence*. London: AIM.

Advisory, Conciliation and Arbitration Service (2014) *Employee Communications and Consultation*. London: ACAS.

Agashae, Z. and Bratton, J. (2001) Leader–follower dynamics: developing a learning organization. *Journal of Workplace Learning*, **13**(3): 89–102.

Agrawal, V. (2012) Managing the diversified team: challenges and strategies for improving performance. *Team Performance Management*, **18**(7/8): 384–400

Aguinis, H. (2009) *Performance Management* (2nd edn). Upper Saddle River, NJ: Pearson Prentice-Hall.

Aguinis, H., Gottfredson, R. K. and Joo, H. (2012) Using performance management to win the talent war. *Business Horizons*, **55**: 609–16.

Agyeman, J. and Evans, B. (2004) 'Just sustainability': the emerging discourse of environmental justice in Britain. *Geographical Journal*, **170**(2): 155–64.

Agyeman, J., Bullard, R. D. and Evans, B. (2002) Exploring the nexus: bringing together sustainability, environmental justice and equity. *Space and Polity*, **6**(1): 77–90.

Agyeman, J., Bullard, R. and Evans, B. (2003) *Just Sustainabilities: Development in an Unequal World*. New York: MIT Press.

Ahlstrand, B. W. (1990) *The Quest for Productivity*. Cambridge: Cambridge University Press.

Ahonen, P., Tienari, J., Merilanlnen, S. and A. Pullen (2014) Hidden contexts and invisible power relations: a Foucauldian reading of diversity research. *Human Relations*, **67**: 263–86.

Akerjordet, K. and Severinsson, E. (2009) Emotional intelligence, Part 1: The development of scales and psychometric testing. *Nursing and Health Sciences*, **11**: 58–63.

Aktouf, O. (1996) *Traditional Management and Beyond*. Montreal: Morin.

Alagaraja, M. and Egan, T. (2013) The strategic value of HRD in lean strategy implementation. *Human Resource Development Quarterly*, **24**(1): 1–27.

Alagaraja, M. and Wang, G. (2012) Development of a national HRD strategy model. *Human Resource Development Review*, **11**(4): 407–29.

Alberta Energy. Oil Sands. Online, available at http://www.energy.alberta.ca/oilsands/oilsands.asp (Accessed December 2016).

Albizu, E. and Olazaran, M. (2006) BPR implementation in Europe: the adaptation of a management concept. *New Technology, Work and Employment*, **21**(1): 43–58.

Alcázar, F. M., Fernandex, P. M. R. and Gardey, G. S. (2012) Transforming human resource management systems to cope with diversity. *Journal Business Ethics*, **107**: 511–31.

Alcázar, F. M., Fernández, P. M. R. and Gardey, G. S. (2013) Workforce diversity in strategic human resource management models. *Cross Cultural Management*, **20**(1): 39–49.

Alfes, K., Shantz, A. and Truss, C. (2012) The link between perceived HRM practices, performance and well-being: the moderating effect of trust in the employer. *Human Resource Management Journal*, **22**(4): 409–27.

Alghafri, A. A. (2015) Literature review on: 'The Advantages and Disadvantages of Implementing E-HRM for an Organisation, E-Learning as an Example'. *American Journal of Economics*, **5**(2): 51–5.

Ali, N. N. K., Wilson, P. and Yazmin, I. (2015) Symptoms versus problems (SVP) analysis on job dissatisfaction and managing employee turnover: a case study in Malaysia. *International Journal of Economics, Commerce and Management*, **3**(4). Open access at ijecm.co.uk.

Alimo-Metcalfe, B. and Alban-Metcalfe, J. (2005) Leadership: time for a new direction. *Leadership*, **1**(1): 51–71.

Alis, D., Karsten, L. and Leopold, J. (2006) From gods to goddesses. *Time and Society*, **15**(1): 81–104.

Allen, K. (2016a) Record jump for services sector after July's slump. The Guardian, September 6, p. 18.

Allen, K. (2016b) Gender pay gap: women earn £300,000 less than men over working life. The Guardian, March 7, p. 1.

Allen, D., Biggane, J. E., Pittis, M., Otondo, R. and Van Scotter, J. (2013) Reactions to recruitment web sites: visual and verbal attention, attraction, and intentions to pursue employment. *Journal of Business Psychology*, **28**(3): 263–85.

Allen, M. R. and Wright, P (2008) Strategic management and HRM. In P. Boxall, J. Purcell and P. Wright (eds) *The Oxford Handbook of Human Resource Management* (pp. 88–107). Oxford: Oxford University Press.

Allinson, C. W. and Hayes, J. (1996) The Cognitive Style Index: a measure of intuition-analysis for organizational research. *Journal of Management Studies*, **33**(1): 119–35.

Almeida, S., Fernando, M., Hannif, Z. and Dharmage, S. C. (2015) Fitting the mould: the role of employer perceptions in immigrant recruitment decision-making. *International Journal of Human Resource Management*, **26**(22): 2811–32.

Alniaçik, E., Alniaçik, U., Erat, S. and Akcin, K. (2013) Does person-organization fit moderate the effects of affective commitment and job satisfaction on turnover intentions? *Procedia – Social and Behavioral Sciences*, **99**: 274–281.

Alvesson, M. (2002) *Understanding Organizational Culture*. London: Sage.

Alvesson, M. and Willmott, H. (1996) *Making Sense of Management: A Critical Analysis*. London: Sage.

Alvesson, M. and Willmott, H. (eds) (2003) *Studying Management Critically*. London: Sage.

Ambasna-Jones, M. (2016) It's time for CEOs to trust their tech teams. The Guardian, June 1, p. 25.

American Association of Retired Persons (2014) Wal-Mart charged with age discrimination. blog.aarp.org/2014/03/28/wal-mart-charged-with-age-discrimination/ (accessed July 18, 2016).

Amin, M. R. and Islam, M. J. (2013) Organizational effectiveness and efficiency through manpower planning and development: a study on selected service and manufacturing organizations of Bangladesh. *World Journal of Social Sciences*, **3**(5): 49–66.

Amiti, M. and Wei, S.-J. (2009) Service offshoring and productivity: evidence from the US. *World Economy*, **32**(2): 203–23.

Amnesty International (2015a) UK: Investigate Rio Tinto's role in potential Burma sanctions busting. Press Release. Amnesty International UK.

Amnesty International (2015b) Nigeria: Executive summary – Niger Delta evolution: Amnesty International's work in oil pollution and corporate accountability in the Niger Delta. https://www.amnesty.org/en/documents/afr44/2626/2015/en/ (accessed August 26, 2016).

Anand, R. and Winters, M.-F. (2008) A retrospective view of corporate diversity training from 1964 to the present. *Academy of Management, Learning and Education*, **7**(3): 356–72.

Anderson, B. A. (2005) Expatriate selection: good management or good luck? *International Journal of Human Resource Management*, **16**(4): 567–83.

Anderson, C., Keltner, D. and John, O. P. (2003) Emotional convergence between people over time. *Journal of Personality and Social Psychology*, **84**: 1054–68.

Anderson, J. (ed.) (1981) *Cognitive Skills and their Acquisition*. Hillsdale, NJ: Laurence Erlbaum.

Anderson, L. and Gold, J. (2009) Conversations outside the comfort zone: identity formation in SME manager action learning. *Action Learning: Research and Practice*, **6**(3): 229–42.

Anderson, V. (2007) *The Value of Learning: A New Model of Value and Evaluation*. London: Chartered Institute of Personnel and Development.

Anderson, V., Rayner, C. and Schyns, B. (2009) *Coaching at the Sharp End: The Role of Line Managers in Coaching at Work*. London: Chartered Institute of Personnel and Development.

Andolšek, D. M. and Štebe, J. (2005) Devolution or (de) centralization of HRM function in European organizations. *International Journal of Human Resource Management*, **16**(3): 311–29.

Andrews, R., Boyne, G. A. and Walker, R. M. (2006) Strategy content and organizational performance: an empirical analysis. *Public Administration Review*, **66**(1): 52–63.

Anonymous (2006) Wheat scandal. *The Economist*. January 26. www.economist.com/node/5452325 (accessed August 26, 2016).

Anseel, F. and Lievens, F. (2009) The mediating role of feedback acceptance in the relationship between feedback and attitudinal and performance outcomes. *International Journal of Selection and Assessment*, **17**(4): 362–75.

Anseel, F., Lievens, F. and Levy, P. (2007) A self-motives perspective on feedback-seeking behavior: linking organizational behavior and social psychology research. *International Journal of Management Reviews*, **9**(3): 211–36.

Anseel, F., Beatty, A. S., Shen, W., Lievens, F. and Sackett, P. R. (2015) How are we doing after 30 years? A meta-analytic review of the antecedents and outcomes of feedback-seeking behaviour. *Journal of Management*, **41**(1): 318–48.

Antonacopoulou, E. P. (1999) Training does not imply learning: the individual perspective. *International Journal of Training and Development*, **3**(1): 14–23.

Antonacopoulou, E., Ferdinand, J., Graca, M. and Easterby-Smith, M. (2005) *Dynamic Capabilities and Organizational Learning: Socio-political Tensions in Organizational Renewal*. AIM Working Paper Series. London: Advanced Institute of Management.

Antonioni, D. (1994) The effects of feedback accountability on upward appraisal ratings. *Personnel Psychology*, **47**(2): 349–56.

Antoun, C., Zhang, C., Conrad, F. G. and Schober, M. F. (2015) Comparisons of online recruitment strategies for convenience samples Craiglist, Google AdWords, Facebook and Amazon Mechanical Turk. *Field Methods*, **28**(3): 231–46.

Appelbaum, E. and Batt, R. (1994) *The New America Workplace: Transforming Systems in the United States*. Ithaca, NY: ICR/Cornell University Press.

Appelbaum, E., Bailey, T., Berg, P. and Kalleberg, A. (2000) *Manufacturing Advantage: Why High-Performance Systems Pay Off*. Ithaca, NY: ILR Press.

Appelbaum, S. H. and Donna, M. (2000) The realistic downsizing preview: a management intervention in the prevention of survivor syndrome, Part I. *Career Development International*, **5**(7): 333–50.

Ardichvili, A. (2015) Organizational sustainability, corporate social responsibility and business ethics. In R. F. Poell, T. S. Rocco and G. L. Roth (eds) *The Routledge Companion to Human Resource Development* (pp. 298–306). London: Routledge

Aries, E. (1996) *Men and Women in Interaction: Reconsidering the Differences*. New York: Oxford University Press.

Armstrong, M. and Baron, A. (2004) *Managing Performance* (2nd edn). London: Chartered Institute of Personnel and Development.

Armstrong, S. J., Cools, E. and Sadler-Smith, E. (2012) Role of cognitive styles in business and management: reviewing 40 years of research. *International Journal of Management Reviews*, **14**: 238–62.

Arnett, D. and Wittman, M. (2014) Improving marketing success: the role of tacit knowledge exchange between sales and marketing. *Journal of Business Research*, **67**: 324–31.

Arnett, G. (2014) Why is UK self-employment at a record high? The Guardian, August 20.

Arrowsmith, J. and Marginson, P. (2010) The decline of incentive pay in British manufacturing. *Industrial Relations Journal*, **41**(4): 289–311.

Arrowsmith, J. and Marginson, P. (2011) Variable pay and collective bargaining in British retail banking. *British Journal of Industrial Relations*, **49**(1): 54–79.

Arrowsmith, J., Nicholaisen, H., Bechter, B. and Nonell, R. (2010) The management of variable pay in European banks. *International Journal of Human Resource Management*, **21**(15): 2716–40.

Arshad, R. and Sparrow, P. (2010) Downsizing and survivor reactions in Malaysia: modelling antecedents and outcomes of psychological contract violations. *International Journal of Human Resource Management*, **21**(11): 1793–815.

Arthur, J. (1994) Effects of human resources systems on manufacturing performance and turnover. *Academy of Management Journal*, **37**: 670–87.

Arthur, J. B. and Boyles, T. (2007) Validating the human resource system structure: a levels-based strategic HRM approach. *Human Resource Management Review*, **17**(1): 77–92.

Arthur, M. B. and Rousseau, D. M. (eds) (2000) *The Boundaryless Career*. Oxford: Oxford University Press.

Arvey, R. D. and Campion, J. E. (1982) The employment interview: a summary and review of recent research. *Personnel Psychology*, **35**: 281–322.

Asch, D. and Salaman, G. (2002) 'The challenge of change', *European Business Journal*, **14**(3): 133–43.

Ashby, K. and Mahdon, M. (2010) *Why do Employees Come to Work when Ill?* London: Work Foundation.

Ashikali, T. and Groeneveld, S. (2015) Diversity management in public organizations and its effect on employees' affective commitment: the role of transformational leadership and the inclusiveness of the organizational culture. *Review of Public Personnel Administration*, **35**(2): 146–68.

Ashkanasy, N. M., Broadfoot, L. E. and Falkus, S. (2000) Questionnaire measures of organizational culture. In N. M. Ashkanasy, C. P. M. Wilderom and M. F. Peterson (eds) *Handbook of Organizational Culture and Climate* (pp. 131–45).Thousand Oaks, CA: Sage.

Ashkanasy, N. M., Wilderom, C. P. and Peterson, M. F. (2011) Introduction to the handbook of organizational culture and climate. In N. M. Ashkanasy, C. P. Wilderom and M. F. Peterson (eds) *Handbook of Organizational Culture and Climate* (2nd edn) (pp. 3–10). Thousand Oaks, CA: Sage.

Ashley, L., Duberley, J., Sommerlad, H. and Scholarios, D. (2015) *A Qualitative Evaluation of Non-educational Barriers to the Elite Professions*. London: Social Mobility and Child Poverty Commission.

Ashman, I. (2012) *Downsizing Envoys: A Public/Private Sector Comparison*. London: Advisory, Conciliation and Arbitration Service.

Ashman, I. and Winstanley, D. (2006) The ethics of organizational commitment. *Business Ethics: A European Review*, **15**(2): 142–53.

Asmuß, B. (2008) Performance appraisal interviews. *Journal of Business Communication*, **45**(4): 408–29.

Astakhova, M. N. and Porter, G. (2015) Understanding the work passion–performance relationship: the mediating role of organizational identification and moderating role of fit at work. *Human Relations*, **68**(8): 1315–46.

Atkinson, J. S. (1984) Manpower strategies for flexible organizations. *Personnel Management*, August: 28–31.

Atkinson, J. S. and Meager, N. (1985) Introduction and summary of main findings. In *Changing Work Patterns* (pp. 2–11). London: National Economic Development Office.

Atkinson, W. (2010) *Class, Individualization and Late Modernity: In Search of the Reflexive Worker*. Basingstoke: Palgrave Macmillan.

Atwater, L. E., Waldman, D. A., Atwater, D. and Cartier, P. (2000) An upward feedback field experiment: supervisors' cynicism, reactions and commitment to subordinates. *Personnel Psychology*, **53**(2): 275–97.

Atzeni, M. (ed.) (2014) *Workers and Labour in a Globalised Capitalism*. Basingstoke: Palgrave.

Australian Human Resources Institute. AHRI model of excellence. https://www.ahri.com.au/about-us/model-of-excellence (accessed October 2016).

Autor, D. (2010) *The Polarization of Job Opportunities in the US Job Market*. Washington, DC: Center for American Progress.

Avdagic, S. and Crouch, C. (2015) Symposium introduction: Labour market reforms, employment performance, employment quality, and changing social risks. *British Journal of Industrial Relations*, **53**(1): 1–5.

Awan, A. G. and Sarwar, G. H. (2014) Integrated role of HRIS and SHRM (SHRIS) in banking sector of Pakistan. *Global Journal of Human Resource Management*, **3**(1): 45–61.

AWARE (2015) Workplace sexual harassment: Statistics. Singapore: Association of Women for Action and Research. www.aware.org.sg/ati/wsh-site/14-statistics/ (accessed August 24, 2016).

Babbie, E. and Benaquisto, L. (2010) *Fundamentals of Social Research* (2nd edn). Toronto, Ontario: Nelson.

Bach, S. (2010) Managed migration? Nurse recruitment and the consequences of state policy. *Industrial Relations Journal*, **41**(3): 249–66.

Bacon, N. and Blyton, P. (2003) The impact of teamwork on skills: employee perceptions of who gains and who loses. *Human Resource Management Journal*, **13**(2): 13–29.

Bacon, N. and Hoque, K. (2015) The influence of trade union disability champions on employer disability policy and practice. *Human Resource Management Journal*, **25**(2): 233–49.

Bacon, N. and Storey, J. (2000) New employee relations strategies in Britain: towards individualism or partnership? *British Journal of Industrial Relations*, **38**(3): 407–27.

Bader, B. and Berg, N. (2014) The influence of terrorism on expatriate performance: a conceptual approach. *International Journal of Human Resource Management*, **25**(4): 539–57.

Bagshaw, E. (2015) Three Sydney Hooters restaurants go into administration after superannuation claims. *Sydney Morning Herald*, July 16. www.smh.com.au/business/three-sydney-hooters-restaurants-go-into-administration-after-superannuation-claims-20150716-gidm2q.html (accessed May 26, 2016).

Bain, G. S. and Price, R. (1983) Union growth: determinants, and density. In G. S. Bain (ed.) *Industrial Relations in Britain* (pp. 3–33). Oxford: Blackwell.

Bain, P. and Baldry, C. (1995) Sickness and control in the office – the sick building syndrome. *New Technology, Work and Employment*, **10**(1): 19–31.

Bain, P., Taylor, P. and Baldry, C. (1999) Sick building syndrome and the industrial relations of occupational health. *International Journal of Employment Studies*, **7**(1): 125–48.

Bajenaru, L., Borozan, A. M. and Smeureanu, I. (2015) Using ontologies for the e-learning system in healthcare human resources management. *Informatica Economica*, **19**(2).

Bakan, J. (2004) *The Corporation: The Pathological Pursuit of Power and Profit*. New York: Free Press.

Bakhtin, M. M. (1981) *The Dialogic Imagination: Four Essays by M.M.Bakhtin* (ed. M. Holquist). Austin, TX: University of Texas Press.

Bakir, C. (2013) *Bank Behaviour and Resilience: The Effect of Structures, Institutions and Agents*. Basingstoke: Palgrave Macmillan.

Bal, P. M. and Dorenbosch, L. (2015) Age-related differences in the relations between individualized HRM and organisational performance: a large-scale employer survey. *Human Resource Management Journal*, **25**(1): 41–61.

Bal, P. M., Kooij, D. T. A. M. and De Jong, S. B. (2013) How do developmental and accommodative HRM enhance employee engagement and commitment? The role of psychological contract and SOC strategies. *Journal of Management Studies*, **50**(4): 545–72.

Baldamus, W. (1961) *Efficiency and Effort: An Analysis of Industrial Administration*. London: Tavistock.

Baldwin, T. T. and Ford, J. K. (1988) Transfer of training: a review and directions for future research. *Personnel Psychology*, **41**: 63–105.

Ball, G., Trevino, L. and Sims, H. (1993) Justice and organizational punishment: attitudinal outcomes of disciplinary events. *Social Justice Research*, **6**: pp. 39–67.

Ball, K. (2001) The use of human resource information systems: a survey. *Personnel Review*, **30**(6): 677–93.

Ballantyne, I. and Povah, N. (2004) *Assessment and Development Centres*. Gower: Aldershot.

Bamber, G., Ryan, S. and Wailes, N. (2004) Globalization, employment relations and human indicators in ten developed market economies: international data sets. *International Journal of Human Resource Management*, **15**(8): 1481–516.

Bamberger, P. and Meshoulam, I. (2000) *Human Resource Management Strategy*. Thousand Oaks, CA: Sage.

Bamberger, P. and Phillips, B. (1991) Organizational environment and business strategy: parallel versus conflicting influences on human resource strategy in the pharmaceutical industry. *Human Resource Management*, **30**, 153–82.

Bandura, A. (1986) *Social Foundations of Thought and Action*. Englewood Cliffs, NJ: Prentice Hall.

Baran, P. A. and Sweezy, P. A. (1968) *Monopoly Capital*. London: Penguin.

Barber, A. E. and Bretz, R. (2000) Compensation, attraction and retention. In S. Rynes and B. Gerhart (eds) *Compensation in Organizations: Current Research and Practice* (pp. 32–60). San Francisco, CA: Jossey-Bass.

Barber, B. (2007) Foreword. In S. Bolton (ed.) *Dimensions of Dignity at Work* (pp. viii–x). Amsterdam: Elsevier.

Barchiesi, F. (2008) Wage labour, precarious employment, and social inclusion in the making of South Africa's postapartheid transition. *African Studies Review*, **51**(2): 119–42.

Barclay, J. (1999) Employee selection: a question of structure. *Personnel Review*, **28**(1/2): 134–51.

Barclay, J. (2001) Improving selection interviews with structure: organisations' use of 'behavioural' interviews. *Personnel Review*, **30**(1): 81–101.

Barclays Bank (2016) Diversity and inclusion. https://www.home.barclays/citizenship/our-approach/diversity-and-inclusion.html (accessed August 30, 2016).

Bardoel, E. A. (2016) Work–life management tensions in multinational enterprises (MNEs). *International Journal of Human Resource Management*, **27**(15): 1681–709.

Barling, J. (2014) *The Science of Leadership: Lessons from Research for Organizational Leaders*. New York: Oxford University Press.

Barlow, G. (1989) Deficiencies and the perpetuation of power: latent functions in management appraisal. *Journal of Management Studies*, **26**(5): 499–517.

Barner, R. and Higgens, J. (2007) Understanding implicit models that guide the coaching process. *Journal of Management Development*, **26**(2): 148–58.

Barnetson, B. and Foster, J. (2015) If it bleeds, it leads: the construction of workplace injury in Canadian newspapers, 2009–2014. *International Journal of Occupational and Environment Health*, **21**(3): 258–65.

Barney, J., Wright, M. and Ketchen, D. J. (2001) The resource-based view of the firm: ten years after 1991. *Journal of Management*, **27**: 625–41.

Barney, J. B. (1991) Firm resources and sustained competitive advantage. *Journal of Management*, **17**(1): 99–120.

Baron, A. (2009) *Performance Management: A Discussion Paper*. London: Chartered Institute of Personnel and Development.

Bartholomew, D. J. (1971) The statistical approach to manpower planning. *Statistician*, **20**: 3–26.

Bartlett, C. A. and Ghoshal, S. (1989) *Managing across Borders: The Transnational Solution*. Boston, MA: Harvard Business School Press.

Bartlett, C. A. and Ghoshal, S. (2002) *Managing across Borders: The Transnational Solution* (3rd edn). Boston, MA: Harvard Business School Press.

Baruch, Y. (2004) Transforming careers: from linear to multidirectional career paths. *Career Development International*, **9**(1): 58–73.

Baruch, Y. (2006) Career development in organizations and beyond: balancing traditional and contemporary viewpoints. *Human Resource Management Review*, **16**(2): 125–38.

Bass, B. M. and Avolio, B. J. (1990) *Multifactor Leadership Questionnaire*. Palo Alto, CA: Consulting Psychologists Press.

Bass, B. M. and Avolio, B. J. (2004) *The Multifactor Leadership Questionnaire (Form 5X)*. Palo Alto, CA: Mind Garden.

Bass, B. M. and Riggio, R. (2006) *Transformational Leadership* (2nd edn). Mahwah, NJ: Lawrence Erlbaum.

Bassett, P. (1987) *Strike Free: New Industrial Relations in Britain*. London: Papermac.

Batstone, E. and Gourlay, S. (1986) *Unions, Unemployment and Innovation*. Oxford: Blackwell.

Battisti, M., Fraccaroli, F., Fasol, R. and Depolo, M. (2007) Psychological contract and quality of organizational life: an empirical study on workers at a rest home. *Industrial Relations*, **62**: 664–88.

Bauer, T. N., Truxillo, D. M., Sanchez, R. J., Craig, J. M., Ferrera, P. and Campion, M. A. (2001) Applicant reactions to selection: development of the selection procedural justice scale (SPJS). *Personnel Psychology*, **54**(2): 387–421.

Baugh, S. G. and Roberts, R. M. (1994) Professional and organizational commitment among engineers: conflicting or complementing? *IEEE Transactions on Engineering Management*, **41**: 108–14.

Baum, M. and Kabst, R. (2014) The effectiveness of recruitment advertisements and recruitment

websites: indirect and interactive effects on applicant attraction. *Human Resource Management*, **53**(3): 353–76.

Baum, M., Schafer, M. and Kabst, R. (2016) Modeling the impact of advertisement-image congruity on applicant attraction. *Human Resource Management*, **55**(1): 7–24.

Baur, J. E., Buckley, M. R., Bagdasarov, Z. and Dharmasiri, A. S. (2014) A historical approach to realistic job previews: an exploration into their origins, evolution, and recommendations for the future. *Journal of Management History*, **20**(2): 200–23.

BBC News (2007) Female boss exits Sanyo hotseat. March 19. http://news.bbc.co.uk/1/hi/business/6467677.stm (accessed December 2016).

BBC News (2011) Fewer new Scottish teachers find permanent jobs. June 15, 2011. http://www.bbc.co.uk/news/uk-scotland-13773708 (accessed October 2016).

Beattie, R. S., Kim, S., Hagen, M. S., Egan, T. M., Ellinger, A. D. and Hamlin, R. G. (2014) Managerial coaching: a review of the empirical literature and development of a model to guide future practice. *Advances in Developing Human Resources*, **16**(2): 184–201.

Beaver, G., Lashley, C. and Stewart, J. (1998) Management development. In R. Thomas (ed.) *The Management of Small Tourism and Hospitality Firms* (pp. 156–73). London: Cassell.

Becker, B. and Huselid, M. (2006) Strategic human resource management: where do we go from here? *Journal of Management*, **32**(6): 898–925.

Becker, N., Höft, S., Holzenkamp, M. and Spinath, F. M. (2015) The predictive validity of assessment centers in German-speaking regions. Boston, MA: Hogrefe Publishing.

Beckett, D. (2000) Making workplace learning explicit: an epistemology of practice for the whole person. *Westminster Studies in Education*, **23**: 41–53.

Beckett, D. and Hager, P. (2002) *Life, Work and Learning: Practice in Postmodernity*. London: Routledge.

Beckett, D. and Hager, P. (2013) *Life, Work and Learning*. London: Routledge.

Becton, J. B. and Field, H. S. (2009) Cultural differences in organizational citizenship behaviour: a comparison between Chinese and American employees. *International Journal of Human Resource Management*, **20**(8): 1651–69.

Becton, J. B., Matthews, M. C., Hartley, D. L. and Whitaker, D. H. (2009) Using biodata to predict turnover, organizational commitment and job performance in healthcare. *International Journal of Selection and Assessment*, **17**(2):190–202.

Bednall, T. C., Sanders, K. and Runhaar, P. (2014) Stimulating informal learning activities through perceptions of performance appraisal quality and human resource management system strength: a two-wave study. *Academy of Management Learning and Education*, **13**(1): 45–61.

Beer, M., Spector, B., Lawrence, P. R., Quin Mills, D. and Walton, R. E. (1984) *Managing Human Assets*. New York: Free Press.

Beetham, D. (1978) *Bureaucracy*. Minneapolis, MN: University of Minnesota Press.

Belbin, M. (1981) *Management Teams*. London: Heinemann.

Bell, D. (1989) Why manpower planning is back in vogue. *Personnel Management*, July: 40–3.

Bell, D. N. F. and Blanchflower, D. G. (2013) Underemployment in the UK revisited. *National Institute Economic Review*, **224**(1). F8–22.

Belt, V. and Giles, L. (2009) *High Performance Working: A Synthesis of Key Literature*. Evidence Report No. 4. Wath-upon-Dearne: UK Commission for Employment and Skills.

Bendal, S. E., Bottomley, C. R. and Cleverly, P. M. (1998) Building a new proposition for staff at NatWest UK. In P. Sparrow and M. Marchington (eds) *Human Resource Management: The New Agenda* (pp. 90–105). London: Financial Times/Pitman.

Benn, S., Dunphy, D. and Martin, A. (2009) Governance of environmental risk: new approaches to managing stakeholder involvement. *Journal of Environmental Management*, **90**(4):1567–75.

Bennis, W. and Nanus, B. (1985) *Leaders*. New York: Harper & Row.

Benschop, Y. and Doorewaard, H. (1998) Covered by equality. The gender subtext of organizations. *Organization Studies*, **19**(5): 787–805.

Benson, J. (1996) Management strategy and labour flexibility in Japanese manufacturing enterprises. *Human Resource Management Journal*, **6**(2): 44–57.

Benson, J. and Brown, M. (2010) Employee voice: does union membership matter? *Human Resource Management Journal*, **20**(1): 80–99.

Berger, P. L. (1963) *Invitation to Sociology*. New York: Anchor Books.

Bergsteiner, H., Avery, G. C. and Neumann, R. (2010) Kolb's experiential learning model: critique from a modeling perspective. *Studies in Continuing Education*, **32**(1): 29–46.

Berrone, P. and Gomez-Mejia, L. (2009) The pros and cons of rewarding social responsibility at the top. *Human Resource Management*, **48**(6): 957–69.

Bertua, C., Anderson, N. and Salgado, J. (2005) The predictive validity of cognitive ability tests: a UK meta-analysis. *Journal of Occupational and Organizational Psychology*, **78**: 387–409.

Betcherman, G., McMullen, K., Leckie, N. and Caron, C. (1994) *The Canadian Workplace in Transition*. Queen's University, Kingston, Ontario: IRC Press.

Bevan, S. (2014) *Performance Management: HR Thoroughbred or Beast of Burden?* London: Work Foundation.

Beynon, H. (1984) *Working for Ford*. Harmondsworth: Penguin.

Bezrukova, K., Jehn, K. and Spell, C. (2012) Reviewing diversity training: where have we been and where are we going. *Academy of Management Learning*, **11**(2): 207–17.

Bharti, P. (2015) Impact of e-HRM system on organizational performance: a case study on banking sector. Paper presented at the International Conference of Advance Research and Innovation .

Bhatti, M. A., Battour, M. B., Sundram, V. P. K. and Othman, A. A. (2013) Transfer of training: does it truly happen? *European Journal of Training and Development*, **37**(3): 273–97.

Bhuiyan, F., Chowdhury, M. M. and Ferdous, F. (2014) Historical evolution of human resource information system (HRIS): An interface between HR and computer technology. *Human Resources Management Research*, **4**(4): 75–80.

Bierema, L. L. (2010) Resisting HRD's resistance to diversity. *Journal of European Industrial Training*, **34**(6): 565–76.

Bierema, L. and Callahan, J. (2014) Transforming HRD: a framework for critical HRD practice. *Advances in Developing Human Resources*, **16**(4): 429–44.

Billett, S. (2001) Learning through work: workplace learning affordances and individual engagement. *Journal of Workplace Learning*, **13**(5): 209–15.

Billett, S. (2006) Constituting the workplace curriculum. *Journal of Curriculum Studies*, **38**(1): 31–48.

Birdthistle, N. and Fleming, P. (2005) Creating a learning organization within the family business: an Irish perspective. *Journal of European Industrial Training*, **29**(9): 730–50.

Biron, M. (2010) Negative reciprocity and the association between perceived organizational ethical values and organizational deviance. *Human Relations*, **63**(6): 875–97.

Bittman, M., Brown, J. and Wajcman, J. (2009) The mobile phone, perpetual contact and time pressure. *Work, Employment and Society*, **23**(4): 673–91.

Björkman, I. and Stahl, G. K. (2006) International human resource management research: an introduction to the field. In G. K. Stahl and I. Björkman (eds) *Handbook of Research in International Human Resource Management* (pp. 1–14). Cheltenham: Edward Elgar.

Black, C. and Frost, D. (2011) *Health at Work: An Independent Review of Sickness Absence*, http://www.dwp.gov.uk/policy/welfare-reform/sicknessabsence-review/ (accessed November 2016).

Blackstock, K. L., Kelly, G. J. and Horsey, B. L. (2007) Developing and applying a framework to evaluate participatory research for sustainability. *Ecological Economics*, 60(4): 726–42.

Blau, P. (1964) *Exchange and Power in Social Life*. New York: Wiley.

Blinder, A. (ed.) (1990) *Paying for Productivity*. Washington, DC: Brooking Institute.

Bloom, N., Conway, N., Mole, K., Moslein, K., Neely, A. and Frost, C. (2004) *Solving the Skills Gap*. Summary Report from the AIM/CIHE Management Research Forum. London: Advanced Institute of Management Research.

BlueGreen Alliance (no date) *About us*, https://www.bluegreenalliance.org (accessed December 2016).

BlueGreen Alliance Foundation (2016) Energy Efficient Housing Products for Multifamily Buildings, https://www.bgafoundation.org/news/energy-efficient-housing-products-for-multifamily-buildings (accessed December 2016).

Blyton, P. and Turnbull, P. (2004) *The Dynamic of Employee Relations* (3rd edn). Basingstoke: Palgrave Macmillan.

Board, D. (2010) Leadership: the ghost at the trillion dollar crash? *European Management Journal*, 28(4): 269–77.

Bochner, S. (2013) *Cultures in Contact: Studies in Cross-Cultural Interaction*. Oxford: Elsevier.

Boffey, D. (2012) Revealed: class divide at the heart of unpaid internships. *The Observer*, December 2, p. 16.

Boffey, D. (2016a) Top headhunters admit: UK bosses' pay 'absurdly high'. *The Observer*, March 6, p. 1.

Boffey, D. (2016b) Bosses "tried to destroy evidence of blacklist", say building workers. *The Observer*, May 15, p. 10.

Bohle, P., Willaby, H., Quinlan, M. and McNamara, M. (2011) Flexible work in call centres: working hours, work-life conflict and health. *Applied Ergonomics*, 42(2): 219–24.

Boiral, O., Paillé, P. and Raineri, N. (2015) The nature of employees' pro-environmental behaviors. In J. L. Robertson and J. Barling (eds) *The Psychology of Green Organizations* (pp. 12–33). New York: Oxford University Press.

Bolden, R. (2005) *What Is Leadership Development?* Exeter: Leadership South West.

Bolden, R. (2011) Distributed leadership in organizations: a review of theory and research. *International Journal of Management Reviews*, 13(3): 251–69.

Bolden, R. and Gosling, J. (2006) Leadership competencies: time to change the tune? *Leadership*, 2(2): 147–63.

Bolton, S. C. (2005) *Emotion Management in the Workplace*. Basingstoke: Palgrave Macmillan.

Bolton, S. C. (ed.) (2007) *Dimensions of Dignity at Work*. Amsterdam: Elsevier.

Bolton, S. C. (2009) Getting to the heart of the emotional labour process: a reply to Brook. *Work, Employment and Society* 23(3): 549–60.

Bolton, S. C. and Houlihan, M. (eds) (2007) *Searching for the Human in Human Resource Management: Theory, Practice and Contexts*. Basingstoke: Palgrave Macmillan.

Bonache, J. and Fernández, Z. V. (2005) International compensation: costs and benefits of international assignments. In H. Scullion and M. Linehan (eds) *International Human Resource Management* (pp. 114–30). Basingstoke: Palgrave Macmillan.

Bonet, R., Cappelli, P. and Hamori, M. (2013) Labor market intermediaries and the new paradigm for human resources. *Academy of Management Annals*, 7(1): 339–90.

Boon, C., Paauwe, J., Boselie, P. and Den Hartog, D. (2009) Institutional pressures and HRM: developing institutional fit. *Personnel Review*, 38(5): 492–508.

Borrill, C., West, M.A., Shapiro, D. and Rees, A. (2000). Team Working and Effectiveness in Health Care. *British Journal of Health Care*, 6: 364–71.

Boseley, S. (2015) Life expectancy soars – for the wealthy. The Guardian, September 15, p. 2.

Boselie, P., Dietz, G. and Boon, C. (2005) Commonalities and contradictions in HRM and performance research. *Human Resource Management Journal*, 15(3): 67–94.

Boud, D. and Garrick, J. (eds) (1999) *Understanding Learning at Work*. London: Routledge.

Boudreau, J. W. and Ramstad, P. M. (2005) Talentship, talent segmentation, and sustainability: a new HR decision science paradigm for a new strategy definition. *Human Resource Management*, 44(2): 129–36.

Boudreau, J. and Ramstad, P. (2009) *Beyond HR: The New Science of Human Capital*. Boston, MA: HBR Press.

Bou-Llusar, J. C., Beltrán-Martín, I., Roca-Puig, V. and Escrig-Tena, A. B. (2016) Single- and multiple-informant research designs to examine the human resource management–performance relationship. *British Journal of Management*, 27(3): 646–68.

Bouskila-Yam, O. and Kluger, A. (2011) Strength-based performance appraisal and goal setting. *Human Resource Management Review*, 21: 137–42.

Bowen, D. E. and Ostroff, C. (2004) Understanding HRM–firm performance linkages: the role of the 'strength' of the HRM system. *Academy of Management Review*, 29(2): 203–21.

Boxall, P. F. (1992) Strategic human resource management: beginnings of a new theoretical sophistication? *Human Resource Management Journal*, 2(3): 60–79.

Boxall, P. F. (1995) Building the theory of comparative HRM. *Human Resource Management Journal*, **5**(5): 5–17.

Boxall, P. (2008) The goals of HRM. In P. Boxall, J. Purcell and P. Wright (eds) *The Oxford Handbook of Human Resource Management* (pp. 48–67). Oxford: Oxford University Press.

Boxall, P., Hutchison, A., and Brigitta Wassenaar, B. (2015) How do high-involvement work processes influence employee outcomes? An examination of the mediating roles of skill utilisation and intrinsic motivation. *The International Journal of Human Resource Management* 26.13: 1737–1752.

Boxall, P. and Macky, K. (2009) Research and theory on high-performance work systems: progressing the high-involvement stream. *Human Resource Management Journal*, **19**(1): 3–23.

Boxall, P. F. and Purcell, J. (2003) *Strategy and Human Resource Management*. Basingstoke: Palgrave Macmillan.

Boxall, P. and Purcell, P. (2011) *Strategy and Human Resource Management* (3rd edn). London: Palgrave Macmillan.

Boxall, P., Purcell, J. and Wright, P. (2008) Human resource management: scope, analysis and significance. In Boxall, J. Purcell, and P. Wright (eds) *The Oxford Handbook of Human Resource Management* (pp. 1–16). Oxford: Oxford University Press.

Boxall, P., Hutchison, A. and Wassenaar, B. (2015) How do high-involvement work processes influence employee outcomes? An examination of the mediating roles of skill utilisation and intrinsic motivation. *International Journal of Human Resource Management*, **26**(13): 1737–52.

Boyatzis, R. (1982) *The Competent Manager: A Model for Effective Performance*. New York: John Wiley & Sons.

Boyatzis, R. (2008) Competencies in the 21st century. *Journal of Management Development*, **27**(1): 5–12.

Boyatzis, R. E., Smith, M. L. and Blaize, N. (2006) Developing sustainable leaders through coaching and compassion. *Academy of Management Learning and Education*, **5**(1): 8–24.

Boydell, T. H. (1976) *Guide to the Identification of Training Needs* (2nd edn). London: BACIE.

Boyne, G. A. and Walker, R. M. (2010) Strategic management and public service performance: the way ahead. *Public Administration Review*, **70**(1): 185–92.

BP (2015) Sustainability Report 2015. www.bp.com/content/dam/bp/pdf/sustainability/group-reports/bp-sustainability-report-2015.pdf (accessed September 12, 2016).

Bramley, P. (1989) Effective training. *Journal of European Industrial Training*, **13**(7): 2–33.

Branch, S., Ramsey, S. and Barker, M. (2009) Workplace bullying. In T. Redman and A. Wilkinson (eds) *Contemporary Human Resource Management* (3rd edn) (pp. 517–41). London: Prentice Hall.

Brandon, R. and Anderson, O. R. (2009) A new neurocognitive model for assessing divergent thinking: applicability, evidence of reliability, and implications for educational theory and practice. *Creativity Research Journal*, **21**(4): 326–37.

Bratton, A. (2016) 'Creating Sustainable Workplaces Together: Employee Relations Practice & Environmental Management', unpublished PhD thesis, University of Strathclyde, Glasgow, Scotland.

Bratton, A. and Bratton, J. (2015) Human resource management approaches. In J. Robertson and J. Barling (eds) *The Psychology of Green Organizations* (pp. 275–95): New York: Oxford University Press.

Bratton, J. (1992) *Japanization at Work: Managerial Studies for the 1990s*. Basingstoke: Palgrave Macmillan.

Bratton, J. (1999) Gaps in the workplace learning paradigm: labour flexibility and job design. Paper presented at the 1st International Conference on Researching Work and Learning, University of Leeds, UK.

Bratton, J. (2001) Why workers are reluctant learners: the case of the Canadian pulp and paper industry. *Journal of Workplace Learning*, **13**(7/8): 333–43.

Bratton, J. (2015) *Work and Organizational Behaviour*, London: Palgrave.

Bratton, J. and Denham, D. (2014) *Capitalism and Classical Sociological Theory* (2nd edn). Toronto, Ontario: University of Toronto Press.

Bratton, J. and Garrett-Petts, W. (2008) Art and workplace learning: innovation, and the economic development of Canadian small cities. In D. Livingstone, K. Mirchandani and P. Sawchuk (eds) *The Future of Lifelong Learning and Work: Critical Perspectives* (pp. 85–98). Rotterdam: Sense Publishers.

Bratton, J. and Gold, J. (2015) Towards critical human resource management education (CHRME): A sociological imagination approach. *Work, Employment and Society*, **29**(3): 496–507.

Bratton, J., Grint, K. and Nelson, D. (2004) *Organizational Leadership*. Mason, OH: Thomson/South-Western.

Braverman, H. (1974) *Labor and Monopoly Capital*. New York: Monthly Review Press.

Breaugh, J. A. (2014) Predicting voluntary turnover from job applicant biodata and other applicant information. *International Journal of Selection and Assessment*, **22**(3): 321–32.

Breaugh, J., Labrador, J., Frye, K., Lee, D., Lammers, V. and Cox, J. (2014) The value of biodata for selecting employees: comparable results for job incumbent and job applicant samples? *Journal of Organizational Psychology*, **14**(1): 41–51.

Brewis, J. and Linstead, S. (2000) *Sex, Work and Sex Work: Eroticizing Organization*. London: Routledge.

Brewster, C. (2001) HRM: 'the comparative dimension'. In J. Storey (ed.) *Human Resource Management: A Critical Text* (pp. 255–71). London: Thompson Learning.

Brewster, C. (2007) HRM: the comparative dimension. In J. Storey (ed.) *Human Resource Management: A Critical Text* (3rd edn) (pp. 197–214). London: Thompson Learning.

Brewster, C. and Bennett, C. V. (2010) Perceptions of business cultures in eastern Europe and their implications for international HRM. *International Journal of Human Resource Management*, **21**(14): 2568–88.

Brewster, C. and Larsen, H. H. (eds) (2000) *Human Resource Management in Northern Europe: Trends, Dilemmas and Strategy*. Oxford: Blackwell.

Brewster, C. and Scullion H. (1997) A review and an agenda for expatriate HRM. *Human Resource Management Journal*, **7**(3): 32–41.

Brewster, C., Carey, L., Grobler, P., Holland, P. and Warnich, S. (2008) *Contemporary Issues in Human Resource Management*. Cape Town: Oxford University Press.

Bridger, E. (2015) *Employee Engagement*. London: Kogan Page.

Briley, M. (2014) Antitrust Compliance Programs: Their Need and Operation, Schumaker, Loop and Kendrick, LLP, Insights, Fall 2014, online: available at http://www.slk-law.com/portalresource/lookup/poid/Z1tOl9NPIuKPtDNIqLMRVPMQiLsSw4JCv03D/document.name=/Antitrust%20Compliance.pdf (accessed 24th November 2016).

Brinkley, I. (2013) *Flexibility or Insecurity? Exploring the Rise in Zero Hours Contracts*. London: Work Foundation.

Brio, J. A., Fernandez, E. and Junquera, B. (2007) Management and employee involvement in achieving an environmental action-based competitive advantage: an empirical study. *International Journal of Human Resource Management*, **18**(4): 491–522.

Brio, J. A., Junquera, B. and Ordiz, M. (2008) Human resources in advanced environmental approaches: a case analysis. *International Journal of Production Research*, **46**: 6029–53.

Broadbridge, A., Maxwell, G. A. and Ogden, S. M. (2009) Selling retailing to Generation Y graduates: recruitment challenges and opportunities. *International Review of Retail, Distribution and Consumer Research*, **19**(4): 405–20.

Bronfenbrenner, K. (1997) The role of union strategies in NLRB certification elections. *Industrial and Labor Relations Review*, **50**(2): 195–212.

Brook, P. (2009) In critical defence of 'emotional labour': refuting Bolton's critique of Hochschild's concept. *Work, Employment and Society*, **23**(3): 531–48.

Brown, A. (2005) Implementing performance management in England's primary schools. *International Journal of Productivity and Performance Management*, **54**(5/6): 468–81.

Brown, B., Hanson, M., Liverman, D. and Merideth, R. (1987) Global sustainability: towards a definition. *Environmental Management*, **11**(6): 713–19.

Brown, D. (2010) *Performance Management: Can the Practice Ever Deliver the Policy*. Brighton: Institute of Employment Studies.

Brown, D., Caldwell, R., White, K., et al. (2004) *Business Partnering: A New Direction for HR*. London: Chartered Institute of Personnel and Development.

Brown, J. S. and Duguid, P. (1991) Organizational learning and communities-of-practice: toward a unified view of working, learning and innovation. *Organization Science*, **2**(1): 40–7.

Brown, K. (2015) Scottish National Procurement Conference 2015: Keynote speech. www.gov.scot/Topics/Government/Procurement/Procurement-News/NatConf08/CabSecSpeech (accessed August 26, 2016).

Brown, M. and Heywood, J. (2005) Performance appraisal systems: determinants and change. *British Journal of Industrial Relations*, **43**(4): 659–79.

Brown, M., Hyatt, D. and Benson, J. (2010) Consequences of the performance appraisal experience. *Personnel Review*, **39**(3): 375–96.

Brown, P. (2007) Strategic management development. In R. Hill and J. Stewart (eds) *Management Development, Perspectives from Research and Practice* (pp. 40–59). London: Routledge.

Brown, W. (1988) The employment relationship in sociological theory. In D. Gallie (ed.) *Employment in Britain* (pp. 33–66). Oxford: Blackwell.

Brown, W. (1989) Managing remuneration. In K. Sisson (ed.) *Personnel Management in Britain* (pp. 249–70). Oxford: Blackwell.

Brown, W. (2000) Putting partnership into practice in Britain. *British Journal of Industrial Relations*, **38**(2): 299–316.

Brown, W. (2010) Negotiation and collective bargaining. In T. Colling and M. Terry (eds) *Industrial Relations: Theory and Practice* (3rd edn) (pp. 253–74). Chichester: John Wiley & Sons.

Brown, W. and Nash, D. (2008) What has happening to collective bargaining under New Labour? Interpreting WERS 2004. *Industrial Relations Journal*, **39**(2): 91–103.

Brown, W., Deakin, S. and Ryan, P. (1997) The effects of British industrial relations legislation. *National Institute Economic Review*, **161**: 69–83.

Brown, W., Bryson, J. and Whitfield, K. (2009) *The Evolution of the Modern Workplace*. Cambridge: Cambridge University Press.

Brunow, S. B. U (2014) Effects of cultural diversity on individual establishments. *International Journal of Manpower*, **35**(1/2): 166–86.

Brutus, S. and Derayeh, M. (2002) Multi-source assessment programs in organizations: an insider's perspective, *Human Resource Development Quarterly*, **13**: 187–201.

Bryson, A. (2004) Management responsiveness to union and nonunion worker voice in Britain. *Industrial Relations*, **43**(1): 213–41.

Bryson, A. and Frege, C. (2010) The importance of comparative workplace employment relations studies. *British Journal of Industrial Relations*, **48**(2): 231–4.

Buckingham, G. (2000) Same indifference. *People Management*, **6**(4): 44–6.

Buckley, R. and Caple, J. (2007) *The Theory and Practice of Training* (5th edn). London: Kogan Page.

Budd, J., Gollan, P. and Wilinson, A. (2010) New approaches to employee voice and participation in organizations. *Human Relations*, **63**(3): 303–10.

Budd, J. W. (2004) *Employment with a Human Face: Balancing Efficiency, Equity, and Voice*. New York: Cornell University Press.

Budhwar, P. S. and Boyne, G. (2004) Human resource management in the Indian public and private sectors: an empirical comparison. *International Journal of Human Resource Management*, **15**(2): 346–70.

Budhwar, P., Verma, A., Malhotra, N. and Mukherjee, A. (2009) Insights into the Indian call centre industry: can internal marketing help tackle high employee turnover. *Journal of Services Marketing*, **23**(5): 351–62.

Budworth, M.-H., Latham, G. and Manroop, L. (2015) Looking forward to performance improvement: a field test of the feedforward interview for performance management. *Human Resource Management*, **54**(1): 45–54.

Bullard, R. D. (1990) *Dumping in Dixie: Race, Class, and Environmental Quality*. Boulder, CO: Westview Press.

Bullock, Lord (1977) *Report of the Committee of Inquiry on Industrial Democracy*. Cmnd 6706. London: HMSO.

Burawoy, M. (1979) *Manufacturing Consent: Changes in the Labour Process Under Monopoly Capitalism*. Chicago, IL: Chicago University Press.

Burchill, F. (2014) *Labour Relations* (4th edn). Basingstoke: Palgrave Macmillan.

Burgoyne, J., Hirsh, W. and Williams, S. (2004) *The Development of Leadership and Management Capability and its Contribution to Performance: The Evidence, the Prospects and the Research Need*. Report No. 560. London: Department for Education and Skills.

Burke, J. (1985) *The Day the Universe Changed*. Boston, MA: Little, Brown.

Burkett, H. (2005) ROI on a shoestring: evaluation strategies for resource-constrained environments or ROI on a shoestring. *Industrial and Commercial Training*, **37**(2): 97–105.

Buruma, I. (2011) Political aftershock: public trust breakdown. *Globe and Mail*, April 8, p. A15.

Butler, A. B. and Skattebo, A. L. (2004) What is acceptable for women may not be for men: the effect of family conflicts with work on job performance ratings. *Journal of Occupational and Organizational Psychology*, **77**: 553–64.

Butler, P. (2009) Non-union employee representation: exploring the riddle of management strategy. *Industrial Relations Journal*, **40**(3): 198–214.

Butler, S. and Ruddick, G. (2016) Sir Philip Green's reputation ripped apart in damning report on BHS demise. The Guardian, 27 July. Available at https://www.theguardian.com/business/2016/jul/25/bhs-demise-sir-philip-green-reputation-torn-apart-in-damning-report (accessed October 2016).

Buttel, F. H. (1998) Some observations on states, world orders, and the politics of sustainability. *Organization and Environment*, **11**(3):261–86.

Butwell, J. (2006) Group supervision for coaches: is it worthwhile? A study of the process in a major professional organization. *International Journal of Evidence Based Coaching and Mentoring*, **4**(2): 43–53.

Buyens, D. and De Vos, A. (2001) Perceptions of the value of HR function. *Human Resource Management Journal*, **11**(3): 70–89.

Byers, P. Y. (ed.) (1997) *Organizational Communication: Theory and Behavior*. Boston: Allyn & Bacon.

Byrne, Z. S., Pitts, V. E., Wilson, C. M. and Steiner, Z. J. (2012) Trusting the fair supervisor: the role of supervisory support in performance appraisals. *Human Resource Management Journal*, **22**(2): 129–47.

Cabanero-Johnson, P. and Berge, Z. (2009) Digital natives: back to the future of microworlds in a corporate learning organization. *Learning Organization*, **16**(4): 290–7.

Cabinet Office (2007) *Social Enterprise Action Plan: Scaling New Heights*. London: Cabinet Office.

Cadman, E. and Giles, C. (2016) Business activity at post-crisis low. *Financial Times*, July 23, p. 1.

Caers, R. and Castelyns, V. (2010) LinkedIn and Facebook in Belgium: the influences and biases of social network sites in recruitment and selection procedures. *Social Science Computer Review*, **29**(4): 437–48.

Caldwell, R. and Storey, J. (2007) The HR function: integration or fragmentation? In J. Storey (ed.) *Human Resource Management: A Critical Text* (3rd edn) (pp. 21–38). London: Thomson Learning.

Caligiuri, P. M. and Tung, R. (1999) Comparing the success of male and female expatriates from a U.S. based company. *International Journal of Human Resource Management*, **10**(5): 763–82.

Caligiuri, P. M., Lazarova, M. and Tarique, I. (2005) Training, learning and development in multinational organizations. In H. Scullion and M. Linehan (eds) *International Human Resource Management* (pp. 71–90). Basingstoke: Palgrave Macmillan.

Callaghan, G. and Thompson, P. (2001) Edwards revisited: technical control and worker agency in call centres. *Economic and Industrial Democracy*, **22**: 13–37.

Callahan, J., Stewart, J., Rigg, C., Sally Sambrook, S. and Kiran Trehan, K. (eds) (2015) *Realising Critical Human Resource Development: Stories of Reflecting, Voicing, and Enacting Critical Practice*. Newcastle upon Tyne: Cambridge Scholars.

Cameron, D. and Barber, B. (2016) On Europe even we can agree: it's better in. The Guardian, April 28, p. 30.

Campbell, D. (2010) The binge working culture is taking its toll. *The Observer*, May 16, p.37.

Campbell, D. J. and Lee, C. (1988) Self-appraisal in performance evaluation. *Academy of Management Review*, **13**(2): 3–8.

Campion, M. A., Palmer, D. K. and Campion, J. E. (1997) A review of structure in the selection interview. *Personnel Psychology*, **50**: 655–702.

Camps, J. and Luna-Arocas, R. (2012). A matter of learning: how human resources affect organizational performance. *British Journal of Management*, **23**:1–21.

Canadian Centre for Occupational Health and Safety (2001) *Violence in the Workplace Prevention Guide*. https://www.ccohs.ca/products/publications/violence.html (accessed October 2016).

Canals, J. (2014) Global leadership development, strategic alignment and CEOs commitment. *Journal of Management Development*, **33**(5): 487–502.

Cappelli, P. (2009) A supply chain approach to workforce planning. *Organizational Dynamics*, **38**(1): 8–15.

Cappelli, P. (2015) Why we love to hate HR … and what HR can do about it. *Harvard Business Review*, July–August: pp. 54–61.

Cappelli, P. and Singh, H. (1992) Integrating strategic human resources and strategic management. In D. Lewin, O. S. Mitchell and P. Sherer (eds) *Research Frontiers in Industrial Relations and Human Resources* (pp. 165–92). Madison, WI: Industrial Relations Research Association.

Carless, S. A. (2005) Person–job fit versus person–organization fit as predictors of organizational attraction and job acceptance intentions: a longitudinal study. *Journal of Occupational and Organizational Psychology*, **78**: 411–29.

Carlsson, L. and Berkes, F. (2005) Co-management: concepts and methodological implications. *Journal of environmental management*, **75**(1): 65–76.

Carlsson, M. and Rooth, D. (2008) *Is it Your Foreign Name or Foreign Qualifications? An Experimental Study of Ethnic Discrimination in Hiring*. IZA Discussion Paper No. 3810. Bonn: Institute for the Study of Labor.

Carmona-Moreno, E., Céspedes-Lorente, J. and Martinez-del-Rio, J. (2012) Environmental human resource management and competitive advantage. *Management Research: Journal of the Iberoamerican Academy of Management*, **10**(2): 125–42.

Carrick, P. and Williams, R. (1999) Development centres – a review of assumptions. *Human Resource Management Journal*, **9**(2): 77–92.

Carrington, D. (2015) Bank of England warns of huge financial risk from fossil fuel investments. The Guardian, March 3. https://www.theguardian.com/environment/2015/mar/03/bank-of-england-warns-of-financial-risk-from-fossil-fuel-investments (Accessed December 2016).

Carroll, A. B. and Buchholtz, A. K. (2008) *Business and Society: Ethics and Stakeholder Management* (7th edn). Mason, OH: South-Western Cengage Learning.

Carroll, W. K. (2004) *Corporate Power in a Globalizing World: A Study of Elite Social Organization*. Don Mills, Ontario: Oxford University Press.

Carson, R. (1962) *Silent Spring*. New York: Houghton Mifflin Harcourt.

Caruth, D. and Handlogten, G. (2001) *Managing Compensation: A Handbook for the Perplexed*. Westport, CT: Quorum.

Cassell, C. and Lee, B. (2009) Trade union representatives: progressing partnerships? *Work, Employment and Society*, **23**(2): 213–30.

Caulkin, S. (2001) The time is now. *People Management*, **7**(17): 32–4.

Caulkin, S. (2015) Money for less than nothing. simoncaulkin.com/article/227/ (accessed September 10, 2016).

Cavusgil, S. T., Knight, G., Riesenberger, J. R., Rammal, H. G. and Rose, E. L. (2014) *International Business*. Sydney: Pearson Australia.

Cawley, B. D., Keeping, L. M. and Levy, P. E. (1998) Participation in the performance appraisal process and employee reactions: a meta-analytic review of field investigations. *Journal of Applied Psychology*, **83**(4): 615–33.

Ceci, S. and Williams, W. (2000) Smart bomb. *People Management*, **6**(17): 32–6.

Celik, H., Abma, T., Klinge, I. and Widder, G. (2012) Process evaluation of a diversity training program: the method strategy. *Evaluation and Programme Planning*, **35**: 54–65.

Centers for Disease Control (2004) Overtime and extended work shifts: recent findings on illness, injuries and health behaviours. Washington: CDC.

Cerdin, J.-L. and Brewster. C. (2014) Talent management and expatriation: bridging two streams of research and practice. *Journal of World Business*, **49**(2): 245–52.

Cesyniene, R. (2015) The most recent trends and emerging values in HRM: comparative analysis. *Engineering Economics*, **44**(4): 50–5.

Chakrabortty, A. (2016) Austerity is far more than just cuts. It's about privatizing everything we own. The Guardian, May 24, p. 29.

Chakravarty, D. (2007) 'Docile oriental women' and organised labour: a case study of the Indian garment manufacturing industry. *Indian Journal of Gender Studies*, **14**: 439–60.

Chambel M. J. and Fortuna, R. (2015) Wage reduction of Portuguese civil servants and their attitudes: the psychological contract perspective. *International Journal of Human Resource Management*, **26**(22): 2853–71.

Chamberlain, L. J., Crowley, M., Tope, D. and Hodson, R. (2008) Sexual harassment in organizational context. *Work and Occupations*, **35**(3): 262–95.

Chamberlain, N. and Kuhn, J. (1965) *Collective Bargaining* (2nd edn). New York: McGraw-Hill.

Champy, J. (1996) *Reengineering Management: The Mandate for New Leadership*. New York: HarperCollins.

Chandler, A. (1962) *Strategy and Structure*. Cambridge, MA: MIT Press.

Chang, T., Liao, J. and Xinyan, W. (2008) The effect of team-based performance appraisal on knowledge sharing: constructing and verifying an influencing model. *International Journal of Data Analysis Techniques and Strategies*, **1**(2): 153–72.

Chapman, D. S. and Zweig, D. I. (2005) Developing a nomological network for interview structure: antecedents and consequences of the structured selection interview. *Personnel Psychology*, **58**: 673–702.

Chartered Institute of Personnel and Development (2002) *Developing Managers for Business Performance*. London: CIPD.

Chartered Institute of Personnel and Development (2006) *Offshoring and the Role of HR*. London: CIPD.

Chartered Institute of Personnel and Development (2009a) *Fighting Back Through Talent Innovation*. London: CIPD.

Chartered Institute of Personnel and Development (2009b) *Performance Management in Action*. London: CIPD.

Chartered Institute of Personnel and Development (2010a) *The Talent Perspective. What Does It Feel Like To Be Talent-Managed?* London: CIPD.

Chartered Institute of Personnel and Development (2010b) *Opening Up Talent For Business Success*. London: CIPD.

Chartered Institute of Personnel and Development (2010c) Competency and competency frameworks. www.cipd.co.uk/subjects/perfmangmt/competnces/comptfrmwk.htm (accessed January 12, 2011).

Chartered Institute of Personnel and Development (2010d) *Resourcing and Talent Planning*. London: CIPD.

Chartered Institute of Personnel and Development (2010e) *Reward Management: Annual Survey Report 2010*. London: CIPD.

Chartered Institute of Personnel and Development (2010f) *Next Generation HR*. London: CIPD.

Chartered Institute of Personnel and Development (2011) *Sustainable Organisation Performance*. London: CIPD.

Chartered Institute of Personnel and Development (2012) *Diversity and Inclusion – Fringe or Fundamental*. London: CIPD.

Chartered Institute of Personnel and Development (2013) *Megatrends: The trends shaping work and working lives*. London: CIPD.

Chartered Institute of Personnel and Development (2015a) *The Role of Line Managers*. London: CIPD.

Chartered Institute of Personnel and Development (2015b) *Over-qualification and skills mismatch in the graduate labour market*. London: CIPD.

Chartered Institute of Personnel and Development (2015c) *Human Capital Reporting: Investing for Sustainable Growth*. London: CIPD

Chartered Institute of Personnel and Development (2015d) *Resourcing and Talent Planning*. London: CIPD.

Chartered Institute of Personnel and Development (2015e) *Learning and Development Survey*. London: CIPD.

Chartered Institute of Personnel and Development (2015f) *Reward Management: Annual Survey Report, 2014–15*. London: CIPD.

Chartered Institute of Personnel and Development (2016) Factsheet. Employee relations: an overview. London: CIPD. www.cipd.co.uk/hr-resources/factsheets/employee-relations-overview.aspx (accessed August 3, 2016).

Chartered Institute of Personnel and Development/Simplyhealth (2012) *Absence Management Survey*. London: CIPD/Simplyhealth.

Chartered Management Institute (2014) *Management 2020. The Commission on the Future of Management and Leadership*. London: CMI.

Chatzitheochari, S. and Arber, S. (2009) Lack of sleep, work and long hours culture: evidence from the UK Time Use Survey. *Work, Employment and Society*, **23**(1): 30–48.

Checchi, D., Visser, J. and van de Werfhorst, H. (2010) Inequality and union membership: the influence of relative earnings and inequality attitudes. *British Journal of Industrial Relations*, **48**(1): 84–108.

Chen, T., Wu, P. and Leung, K. (2011) Individual performance appraisal and appraisee reactions to workgroups. *Personnel Review*, **40**(1): 87–105.

Chen, Y.-S. (2011) Green organizational identity: sources and consequence. *Management Decision*, **49**(3): 384–404.

Chiaburu, D. and Tekleab, A. (2005) Individual and contextual influences on multiple dimensions of training effectiveness. *Journal of European Industrial Training*, **29**(8): 604–26.

Child, J. (1972) Organizational structure, environment and performance: the role of strategic choice. *Sociology*, **6**(1): 1–22.

Chinander, K. R. (2001) Aligning accountability and awareness for environmental performance in operations. *Production and Operations Management*, **10**(3): 276–91.

Choi, M. and Yoon, H. J. (2015) Training investment and organizational outcomes: a moderated mediation model of employee outcomes and strategic orientation of the HR function. *International Journal of Human Resource Management*, **26**(20): 2632–51.

Choi, S. and Rainey, H. G. (2014) Organizational fairness and diversity management in public organizations: does fairness matter in managing diversity. *Review of Public Personnel Administration*, **34**(4): 307–31.

Chomsky, N. (1999) *Profit over People*. New York: Seven Stories Press.

Chou, B. K. (2005) Implementing the reform of performance appraisal in China's civil service. *China Information*, **19**(1): 39–65.

Chouhan, V. S. and Srivastava, S. (2014) Understanding competencies and competency modeling — a literature survey. *IOSR Journal of Business and Management*, **6**(1): 14–23.

Christensen, R. K. and Wright, B. E. (2011) The effects of public service motivation on job choice decisions: disentangling the contributions of person-organization fit and person-job fit. *Journal of Public Administration Research and Theory Advance Access*, **21**(4): 723–43.

Chuai, X., Preece, D. and Iles, P. (2008) Is talent management just 'old wine in new bottles'? *Management Research News*, **31**(12): 901–11.

Chuang, A., Hsu, R. S., Wang, A-C. and Judge, T. A. (2015) Does West "fit" with East? In search of a Chinese model of person-environment fit. *Academy of Management Journal*, **58**(2): 480–510.

Citizens Advice (2015) Bogus self-employment costing millions to workers and Government. www.citizensadvice.org.uk/about-us/how-citizens-advice-works/media/press-releases/bogus-self-employment-costing-millions-to-workers-and-government/ (accessed October 2016).

Clark, P. and Sevastopulo, D. (2015) Climate agreement obstacles rise as oil and coal groups play down impact. *Financial Times*, December 14, p. 1.

Clark, T. and Pugh, D. (2000) Similarities and differences in European conceptions of human resource management. *International Studies of Management and Organizations*, **29**(4): 84–100.

Clarke, M., Butcher, D. and Bailey, C. (2004) Strategically aligned leadership development. In J. Storey (ed.) *Leadership in Organizations* (pp. 271–92). London: Routledge.

Clarke, N. (2003) The politics of training needs analysis. *Journal of Workplace Learning*, **15**(4): 141–53.

Clarke, N. (2004) HRD and the challenges of assessing learning in the workplace. *International Journal of Training and Development*, **8**(2): 140–56.

Claydon, T. (1989) Union de-recognition in Britain in the 1980s. *British Journal of Industrial Relations*, **27**(2): 214–24.

Clayton, T. (1998) Problematizing partnerships: the prospects for a cooperative bargaining agenda. In P. Sparrow and M. Marchington (eds) *Human Resource Management: The New Agenda* (pp. 180–92). London: Financial Times Management.

Clayton, T. (2000) Employee participation and involvement. In D. Winstanley and J. Woodall (eds) *Ethical Issues in Contemporary Human Resource Management* (pp. 208–23). Basingstoke: Palgrave Macmillan.

Cleary, P. (2010) Human resource accounting. In D. McGuire and K. M. Jorgensen (eds) *Human Resource Development* (pp. 44–54). London, Sage.

Clegg, H. (1976) *Trade Unionism Under Collective Bargaining*. Oxford: Blackwell.

Clegg, S., Hardy, C. and Nord, W. (eds) (1999) *Managing Organizations: Current Issues*. Thousand Oaks, CA: Sage.

Cloke, K. and Goldsmith, J. (2002) *The End of Management and the Rise of Organizational Democracy*. San Francisco, CA: Jossey-Bass.

Clutterbuck, D. (2007) *Coaching the Team at Work*. London: Nicholas Brealey.

Clutterbuck, D. and Megginson, D. (2005a) *Making Coaching Work: Creating a Coaching Culture*. London: Chartered Institute of Personnel and Development.

Clutterbuck, D. and Megginson, D. (2005b) How to create a coaching culture. *People Management*, April 21: 44–5.

CME and RBC (2010) 'Report on Business & the Environment: Manufacturing 2011. Shifting markets, shifting mindsets: Creating value through cleaner & greener manufacturing.' Online: available at http://www.enviro-stewards.com/wp-content/uploads/2010/12/RBC-CME_Report-on-Business-and-The-Environment-Manufacturing_FINAL.pdf (accessed December 2016).

Coates, J. and Pichler, P. (eds) (2011) *Language and Gender: A Reader* (2nd edn). Chichester: Wiley-Blackwell.

Cochrane , R. and McKeown, T. (2015) Vulnerability and agency work: from the workers' perspectives. *International Journal of Manpower*, **36**(6): 947–65.

Codreanu, D. E. and Radut, C. (2012) Development and market of ERP systems. *Anale. Seria Stiinte Economice*, **18**(2); 378–83.

Coens, T. and Jenkins, M. (2002) *Abolishing Performance Appraisals*. San Francisco, CA: Berrett-Koehler.

Coffield, F., Moseley, D., Hall, E. and Ecclestone, K. (2004) *Learning Styles and Pedagogy in Post-16 Learning: A Systematic and Critical Review*. Wiltshire: Learning and Skills Research Centre.

Cohen, S. and Grace, D. (1998) *Business ethics*. Oxford: Oxford University Press.

Coleman, S. and Keep, E. (2001) Background literature review for PIU project on workforce development. www.cabinet-office.gov.uk/innovation/2001/workforce/literaturereview.pdf (accessed 2002).

Colling, T. (1995) Experiencing turbulence: competition, strategic choice and the management of human resources in British Airways. *Human Resource Management*, **5**(5): 18–32.

Colling, T. (2005) Managing human resources in the networked organization. In S. Bach (ed.) *Managing Human Resources* (pp. 90–112). Oxford: Blackwell.

Colling, T. (2010) Legal institutions and the regulation of workplaces. In T. Colling and M. Terry (eds) *Industrial Relations: Theory and Practice* (3rd edn) (pp. 323–46). Chichester, John Wiley & Sons.

Colling, T. and Terry, M. (eds) (2010) Work, the employment relationship and the field of industrial relations. In T. Colling and M. Terry (eds) *Industrial Relations: Theory and Practice* (3rd edn) (pp. 3–25). Chichester: John Wiley & Sons.

Collings, D. and Mellahi, K. (2009) Strategic talent management: a review and research agenda. *Human Resource Management Review*, **19**(4): 304–13.

Collings, D. G. and Scullion, H. (2007) Global staffing and multinational enterprise. In J. Storey (ed.) *Human Resource management: A Critical Text* (3rd edn) (pp. 215–31). London: Thomson Learning.

Collings, D. G., Demirbag, M., Mellahi, K. and Tatoglu, E. (2010) Strategic orientation, human resource management practices and organizational outcomes: evidence from Turkey. *International Journal of Human Resource Management*, **21**(14): 2589–613.

Collins, H. M. (2001) Tacit knowledge, trust, and the Q of sapphire. *Social Studies of Science*, **31**(1): 71–85.

Collins, J. M. and Muchinsky, P. M. (1993) An assessment of the construct validity of three job evaluation methods: a field experiment. *Academy of Management Journal*, **36**: 895–904.

Collinson, D. (2012) Prozac leadership and the limits of positive thinking. *Leadership*, **8**(2): 87–107.

Colquitt, J. A., Conlon, D. E., Wesson, M. J., Porter, C. O. and Ng, K. Y. (2001) Justice at the millennium: a meta-analytic review of 25 years of organizational justice research. *Journal of Applied Psychology*, **86**(3): 425–45.

Colthart, I., Cameron, N., McKinstry, B. and Blaney, D. (2008) What do doctors really think about the relevance and impact of GP appraisal 3 years on? A survey of Scottish GPs. *British Journal of General Practice*, **58**: 82–7.

Confederation of British Industry (2008) *Talent Not Tokenism: The Business Benefits of Workforce Diversity*. London: CBI/TUC/EHRC.

Conley, H. (2008) The nightmare of temporary work: a comment on Fevre. *Work, Employment and Society*, **22**(4): 731–36.

Connell, J., Nankervis, A. and Burgess, J. (2015) The challenges of an ageing workforce: an introduction to the workforce management issues. *Labour and Industry*, **25**(4): 257–64.

Connelly, S. and Ruarck, G. (2010) Leadership style and activating potential moderators of the relationships among leader emotional displays and outcomes. *Leadership Quarterly*, **21**: 745–64.

Connerley, M. L., Carlson, K. D. and Mecham, R. L. (2003) Evidence of differences in applicant pool quality. *Personnel Review*, **32**(1): 22–39.

Contractor, F. J., Kumar, V., Kundu, S. K. and Pedersen, T. (2010) Reconceptualizing the firm in a world of outsourcing and offshoring: the organizational and geographical relocation of high-value company functions. *Journal of Management Studies*, **47**(8): 1417–33.

Cook, J. and Crossman, A. (2004) Satisfaction with performance appraisal systems. *Journal of Managerial Psychology*, **19**(5): 526–41.

Cook, M. (1994) *Personnel Selection and Productivity*. Chichester: John Wiley & Sons.

Cooke, F. L. (2000) *Human Resource Strategy to Improve Organisational Performance: A Route for*

British Firms? Working Paper No. 9. Economic and Social Research Council Future of Work Programme. Swindon: ESRC.

Coombs, J. E. and Bierly, P. E. (2006) Measuring technological capability and performance. *R&D Management*, **36**(4): 421–38.

Cooper, C. (2016) Junior doctors to stage first full NHS walkout. *The Independent*, March 24, p. 14.

Coopey, J. (1996) Crucial gaps in the 'learning organization'. In K. Starkey (ed.) *How Organizations Learn* (pp. 348–67). London: International Thomson Business.

Corby, S., Palmer, S. and Lindop, E. (eds) (2009) *Rethinking Reward*. Basingstoke: Palgrave Macmillan.

Cordery, J. and Parker, S. K. (2008) Work Organization. In P. Boxall, J. Purcell and Wright, P. (eds) *The Oxford Handbook of Human Resource Management* (pp. 187–209). Oxford: Oxford University Press.

Corlett, A. and Whittaker , M. (2014) *Low Pay Britain 2014*. The Resolution Foundation.

Council for Excellence in Management and Leadership (2002) *Managers and Leaders: Raising Our Game*. London: CEML.

Court of Justice of the European Union (2015) The journeys made by workers without fixed or habitual place of work between their homes and the first and last customer of the day constitute working time. Press release. September 10. curia.europa.eu/jcms/upload/docs/application/pdf/2015-09/cp150099en.pdf (accessed September 11, 2016).

Coutts, J. (1998) Workplace stress more prevalent than illness, injury. *Globe and Mail*, April 8, p. A2.

Cowling, A. and Walters, M. (1990) Manpower planning – where are we today? *Personnel Review*, **19**(3): 3–8.

Cox, A., Higgins, T., Gloster, R. and Foley, B. (2012) The impact of workplace initiatives on low carbon behaviours: case study report. www.scotland.gov.uk/Publications/2012/03/2237 (accessed August 13, 2016).

Cox, T., Griffiths, A., Barlowe, C., Randall, R., Thomson, L. and Rial-Gonzalez, E. (2000) Organizational interventions for work stress: a risk management approach. HSE Contract Research Report. London: HSE.

Craig, A. W. J. and Solomon, N. (1996) *The System of Industrial Relations in Canada* (5th edn). Scarborough, Ontario: Prentice-Hall.

Craig, M. (1981) *Office Worker's Survival Handbook*. London: BSSR.

Craighead, C. W., Ketchen, D. J., Dunn, K. S. and Hult, G. T. M. (2011) Addressing common method variance: guidelines for survey research on information technology, operations, and supply chain management. *IEEE Transactions on Engineering Management*, **58**(3): 578–88.

Crane, D. (ed.) (1994) *The Sociology of Culture*. Cambridge, MA: Blackwell.

Cregan, C. and Brown, M. (2010) The influence of union membership status on workers' willingness to participate in joint consultation. *Human Relations*, **63**(3): 331–48.

Cross, B. and Travaglione, A. (2004) The times they are a-changing: who will stay and who will go in a downsizing organization? *Personnel Review*, **33**(3): 275–90.

Crossan, M., Lane, H. and White, R. (1999) An organizational learning framework: from intuition to institution. *Academy of Management Review*, **24**: 522–37.

Crouch, D (2015) Ryanair closes Denmark operation to head off union row. 17 July. The Guardian, https://www.theguardian.com/business/2015/jul/17/ryanair-closes-denmark-operation-temporarily-to-sidestep-union-dispute (accessed October 2016).

Cucina, J. M., Caputo, P. M., Thibodeaux, H. F., MacLane, C. N. and Bayless, J. M. (2013) Scoring biodata: is it rational to be quasi-rational? *International Journal of Selection and Assessment*, **21**(2): 226–32.

Cullen, L. (2002) *A Job To Die for: Why so Many Americans Are Killed, Injured or Made Ill at Work and What To Do About It*. Monroe, ME: Common Courage Press.

Cully, M., O'Reilly, A., Woodland, S. and Dix, G. (1998) The 1998 Workplace Employee Relations Survey, first findings. www.dti.gov.uk/emar (accessed 2011).

Cully, M., Woodland, S., O'Reilly, A. and Dix, G. (1999) *Britain at Work*. London: Routledge.

Culpin, V., Eichenberg, T., Hayward, I. and Abraham, P. (2014) Learning, intention to transfer and transfer in executive education. *International Journal of Training and Development*, **18**(2): 132–42.

Cunliffe, A. L. (2004) On becoming a critically reflexive practitioner. *Journal of Management Education*, **28**(4): 407–26.

Cunningham, I., James, P. and Dibben, P. (2004) Bridging the gap between rhetoric and reality: line managers and the protection of job security for ill workers in the modern workplace. *British Journal of Management*, **15**(3): 273–90.

Cunningham, S., Ryan, Y., Stedman, L., Bagdon, K., Flew, T. and Coaldrake, P. (2000) *The Business of Borderless Education*. Canberra: Department of Education, Training and Youth Affairs.

Curnow, B. (1986) The creative approach to pay. *Personnel Management*, October: 32–6.

Curran, M. J., Draus, P., Schrager, M. and Zappala, S. (2014) College students and HR professionals: conflicting views on information available on Facebook. *Human Resource Management Journal*, **24**(4): 442–58.

Currie, G. and Procter, S. (2001) Exploring the relationship between HR and middle managers. *Human Resource Management Journal*, **11**(3): 53–69.

Currie, G., Knights, D. and Sgtarkey, K. (2010) Introduction: a post-crisis critical reflection on business schools. *British Journal of Management*, **21**: 1–5.

Currie, L. (2015) What if an entire company bullies employees? Alaska Dispatch News. September 15. www.adn.com/article/20150901/lynne-curry-what-if-entire-company-bullies-employees (accessed September 12, 2016).

Curson, J. (2006) Crystal-ball gazing: planning the medical workforce. *British Journal of Hospital Medicine*, **67**(8): 1141–7.

Curson, J. A., Dell, M. E., Wilson, R. A., Bosworth, D. L. and Baldauf, B. (2010) Who does workforce planning well? : workforce review team rapid review summary. *International Journal of Health Care Quality Assurance*, **23**(1): 110–19.

Czerny, A. (2004) Not so quick and easy. *People Management*, February 26: 14–15.

Daft, R. (2015) *Organizational Theory and Design* (12th edn). Boston, MA: Cengage Learning.

Daily, B. F. and Huang S. (2001) Achieving sustainability through attention to human resource factors in environmental management. *International Journal of Operations and Production Management*, **21**: 1539–52.

Dale, M. and Bell, J. (1999) *Informal Learning in the Workplace*. London: Department for Education and Employment.

Dalen, L. H., Stanton, N. A. and Roberts, A. D. (2001) Faking personality questionnaires in personnel selection. *Journal of Management Development*, **20**(8): 729–41.

Danford, A., Richardson, M., Stewart, P., Tailby, S. and Upchurch, M. (2008) Partnership, high performance work systems and quality of working life. *New Technology, Work and Employment*, **23**(3): 151–66.

Daniel, W. W. and Millward, N. (1983) *Workplace Industrial Relations in Britain*. London: Heinemann.

Daniels, C. (2004) 50 best companies for minorities. *Fortune*, **149**(13): 136–42.

Daniels, K. (2006) Rethinking job characteristics in work stress research. *Human Relations*, **59**(3): 267–90.

Daniels, K. (2011) Stress and well-being are still issues and something still needs to be done: or why agency and interpretation are important for policy and practice. In G.P. Hodgkinson and J. K. Ford (eds) *International Review of Industrial and Organizational Psychology*, (26): 1–46.

Daniels, K. and Macdonald, L. (2005) *Equality, Diversity and Discrimination*. London: Chartered Institute of Personnel and Development.

Das, S. C. and Ahmed, I. Z. (2014) The perception of employer branding to enhance recruitment and selection processes. *European Journal of Business and Management*, **6**(6): 138–44.

Datta, D., Guthrie, J., Basuil, D. and Pandey, A. (2010) Causes and effects of employee downsizing: a review and synthesis. *Journal of Management*, **36**(1): 281–348.

Davey, R., Fearon, C. and McLaughlin, H. (2013) Organizational grief: an emotional perspective on understanding employee reactions to job redundancy. *Development and Learning in Organizations: An International Journal*, **27**(2): 5–8.

Davidson, M. J. and Cooper, C. L. (1992) *Shattering the Glass Ceiling*. London: Paul Chapman.

Davies, H. (2002) Understanding organizational culture in reforming the National Health Service. *Royal Society of Medicine Journal*, **95**(3): 140–2.

Davies, J. and Easterby-Smith, M. (1984) Learning and developing from managerial work experiences. *Journal of Management Studies*, **21**(2): 168–83.

Davies, P. and Freedland, M. (1994) *Labour Law: Text and Materials*. London: Weidenfeld & Nicolson.

Davies, R. (2015) It's all to play for as employers turn to recruitment apps. *The Observer*, November 29, p. 44.

Davies, R. (2016) Companies slow to act on gender pay gap. The Guardian, March 11, p. 15.

Davies, Lord (2011) *Women on Boards*. London: Department of Business, Innovation and Skills.

Davis, A., Kimball, W. and Gould, E. (2015) *The Class of 2015*. Economic Policy Institute Briefing Paper No. 401. Washington, DC: EPI.

Davis, M. C. and Coan, P. (2015) Organizational change. In Robertson, J. L. and Barling, J. (eds) *The Psychology of Green Organizations* (pp. 244–74). New York: Oxford University Press.

Dawson, M. (2005) Costa's 'filter' gets the right employees. *Human Resource Management International Digest*, **13**(4): 21–2.

Day, D. (2001) Leadership development: a review in context. *Leadership Quarterly*, **11**(4): 581–613.

Day, D. V., Fleenor, J. W., Atwater, L. E., Sturm, R. E. and Mckee, R. A. (2014) Advances in leader and leadership development: a review of 25 years of research and theory. *Leadership Quarterly*, **25**(1): 63–82.

Dayan, K., Fox, S. and Kasten, R. (2008) The preliminary employment interview as a predictor of assessment center outcomes. *International Journal of Selection and Assessment*, **16**(2): 102–11.

Deal, T. E. and Kennedy, A. A. (1982) *Organization Cultures: The Rites and Rituals of Organization Life*. New York: Addison-Wesley.

Dean, D. and Liff, S. (2010) Equality and diversity: the ultimate industrial relations concern. In T. Colling and M. Terry (eds) *Industrial Relations Theory and Practice* (3rd edn) (pp. 422–46). Chichester: John Wiley & Sons.

Dean, P. C., McKenna, K. and Krishnan, V. (2012) Accounting for human capital: is the balance sheet missing something? *International Journal of Business and Social Science*, 3(12): 61–4.

Debono, J. (2001) Sexual harassment in employment: an examination of decisions looking for evidence of a sexist jurisprudence. *New Zealand Journal of Industrial Relations*, 26(3): 329–40.

Deci, E. L. and Ryan, R. M. (2000) The "what" and "why" of goal pursuits: human needs and the self-determination of behavior. *Psychological Inquiry*, 11(4): 227–68.

De Cieri, H. and Dowling, P. (1999) Strategic human resource management in multinational enterprises: theoretical and empirical developments. In P. Wright, L. Dyer, J. Boudreau and G. Milkovich (eds) *Research in Personnel and Human Resource Management* (pp. 305–27). Stanford, CT: JA Press.

De Cooman, R., Vantilborgh, T., Bal, M. and Lub, X. (2016) Creating inclusive teams through perceptions of supplementary and complementary person–team fit. *Group Organization Management* 41(3): 310–34.

Decramer, A., Smolders, C., Vanderstraeten, A. and Christiaens, J. (2012) The impact of institutional pressures on employee performance management systems in higher education in the low countries. *British Journal of Management*, 23(S1): S88–103.

Deery, S. and Kinnie, N. (2004) *Call Centres and Human Resource Management: A Cross-national Perspective*. Basingstoke: Palgrave Macmillan.

De Gieter, S. and Hofmans, J. (2015) How reward satisfaction affects employees' turnover intentions and performance: an individual differences approach. *Human Resource Management Journal*, 25(2): 200–16.

Delaney, J. T. and Goddard, J. (2001) An industrial relations perspective on the high-performance paradigm. *Human Resource Management Review*, 11: 395–429.

Delaney, J. T. and Huselid, M. A. (1996) The impact of HRM practices on perceptions of organizational performance. *Academy of Management Journal*, 39(4): 949–69.

Delbridge, R. and Keenoy, T. (2010) Beyond managerialism? *International Journal of Human Resource Management*, 21(6): 799–817.

Delbridge, R. and Turnbull, T. (1992) Human resource maximization: the management of labour under JIT system. In P. Blyton and P. Turnbull (eds) *Reassessing Human Resource Management* (pp. 56–73). London: Sage.

De Leede, J. and Kraijenbrink, J. (2014) The mediating role of trust and social cohesion in the effects of new ways of working: a Dutch case study. In T. Bondarouk and M. R. Olvias-Lujan (eds) *Human Resource Management Social Innovation and Technology*. Advanced Series in Management No. 14 (pp. 2–20). Bingley: Emerald Publishing Group.

Delery, J. and Doty, H. (1996) Modes of theorizing in strategic human resource management: tests of universalistic, contingency and configurational performance predictions. *Academy of Management Journal*, 39: 802–35.

Delmas, M. and Toffel, M. W. (2004). Stakeholders and environmental management practices: an institutional framework. *Business strategy and the Environment*, 13(4), 209–222.

Deloitte Consulting (2006) Meet The 21st Century Chief Human Resources Officer (CHRO). http://www.prnewswire.com/news-releases/meet-the-21st-century-chief-human-resources-officer-chro-55779902.html (accessed July 14, 2016).

Den Hartog, D. N. and Verburg, R. M. (2004) High performance work systems, organizational culture and firm effectiveness. *Human Resource Management Journal*, 14(1): 55–78.

Denis, J.-L., Langley, A. and Sergib, V. (2012) Leadership in the plural. *Academy of Management Annals*, 6(1): 211–83.

DeNisi, A. and Kluger, A. (2000) Feedback effectiveness: can 360-degree appraisal be improved? *Academy of Management Executive*, 14(1): 129–39.

Denton, D. K. (1999) Employee involvement, pollution control, and pieces to the puzzle. *Environmental Management and Health*, 10: 105–11.

Department for Business, Innovation and Skills (2010) *Skills for Sustainable Growth*. London: Department for Business, Innovation and Skills.

Department for Business, Innovation and Skills (2013) *Zero-hours Employment Contracts: Consultation*. London: Department for Business, Innovation and Skills.

Department for Business, Innovation and Skills (2015a) *Trade Union Membership 2014: Statistical Bulletin*. London: Department for Business Innovation and Skills.

Department for Business, Innovation and Skills (2015b) *Evaluation of the Employer Ownership of Skills Pilot*. London: Department for Business Innovation and Skills.

Department for Education (2014) *Teachers' Workload Diary Survey 2013*. London: Department for Education Research Report.

Department of Employment (1974) *Company Manpower Planning*. Manpower Papers No. 1. London: HMSO.

Department of Trade and Industry (2005a) *People, Strategy and Performance: Results from the Second Work and Enterprise Business Survey*. London: DTI.

Department of Trade and Industry (2005b) *Inside the Workplace: First Findings from the 2004 Workplace Employment Relations Survey* (WERS 2004). London: DTI.

Des, G. G. and Shaw, J. D. (2001) Voluntary turnover, social capital and organizational performance. *Academy of Management Review*, **26**: 446–56.

Devins, D. and Gold, J. (2014) Re-conceptualising talent management and development within the context of the low paid. *Human Resource Development International*, **17**(5): 514–28.

Devlin, K. (2015) Osborne's policy is not a living wage, says think tank which inspired it. *The Herald*, July 11, p. 6.

De Vos, A., De Hauw, S. and Van der Heijden, B. (2011) Competency development and career success: the mediating role of employability. *Journal of Vocational Behavior*, **79**: 438–47.

Dex, S. (1988) Gender and the labour market. In D. Gallie (ed.) *Employment in Britain* (pp. 281–309). Oxford: Blackwell.

Dhamija, A. and Gupta, R. K. (2014) Impact of inefficient manpower planning on burnout. *Global Journal of Multidisciplinary Studies*, **3**(6). Open access available at www.gjms.co.in.

Dickens, L. and Hall, M. (2010) The changing legal framework of employment relations. In T. Colling and M. Terry (eds) *Industrial Relations: Theory and Practice* (3rd edn) (pp. 298–322). Chichester: John Wiley & Sons.

Dickmann, M., Brewster, C. and Sparrow, P. (eds) (2016) *International Human Resource Management: Contemporary HR Issues in Europe* (3rd edn): Abingdon: Routledge.

Diefendorff, J., Richard, E., Erin, R. M. and Croyle, M. H. (2006) Are emotional display rules formal job requirements? Examination of employee and supervisor perceptions. *Journal of Occupational and Organisational Psychology*, **79**(2): 273–98.

Diekma, A. B. and Eagly, A. H. (2000) Stereotypes as dynamic constructs: women and men of the past, present, and future. *Personality and Social Psychology Bulletin*, **26**: 1171–88.

Dierendonck, D., Haynes, C., Borrill, C. and Stride, C. (2007) Effects of upward feedback on leadership behaviour toward subordinates. *Journal of Management Development*, **26**(3): 228–38.

Dijk, H., Engen, M. and Paauwe, J. (2012) Reframing the business case: a values and virtues perspective. *Journal of Business Ethics*, **111**: 73–84.

Dinh, J., Lord, R. G., Gardner, W., Meuser, J., Liden, R. C. and Hu, J. (2014) Leadership theory and research in the new millennium: current theoretical trends and changing perspectives. *Leadership Quarterly*, **25**(1): 36–62.

Dipboye, R. L., Gaugler, B. B., Hayes, T. L. and Parker, D. (2001) The validity of unstructured panel interviews: more than meets the eye? *Journal of Business and Psychology*, **16**: 35–49.

Disney, R. (1990) Explanations of the decline in trade union density in Britain: an appraisal. *British Journal of Industrial Relations*, **28**(2): 165–77.

D'Netto, B., Shen, J., Chelliah, J. and Monga, M. (2014) Human resource diversity management practices in the Australian manufacturing sector. *International Journal of Human Resource Management*, **25**(9): 1243–66.

Dobbins, T., Plows, A. and Lloyd-Williams, H. (2014) *Work, Employment and Society*, **28**(4): 515–32.

Dobson, A. (1998) *Justice and the Environment: Conceptions of Environmental Sustainability and Dimensions of Social Justice*. Oxford: Oxford University Press.

Docherty, P., Kira, M. and Shani, A. B. (2009) *Creating Sustainable Work Systems* (2nd edn). London: Routledge.

Doellgast, V. (2010) Collective voice under decentralized bargaining: a comparative study of work reorganization in US and German call centres. *British Journal of Industrial Relations*, **48**(2): 375–99.

Doeringer, P. and Piore, M. J. (1971) Internal labor markets and manpower adjustment. New York: D. C. Heath.

Doherty, M. (2009) When the working day is through: the end of work as identity? *Work, Employment and Society*, **23**(1): 84–101.

Doherty, N. and Tyson, S. (2000) HRM and employee well-being: raising the ethical stakes. In D. Winstanley and J. Woodall (eds) *Ethical Issues in Contemporary Human Resource Management* (pp. 102–15). Basingstoke: Palgrave.

Dominguez, C. M. (1992) Executive forum – the glass ceiling: paradox and promises. *Human Resource Management*, **31**: 385–92.

Donaldson, T. and Preston, L. E. (1995) The stakeholder theory of the corporation: concepts, evidence and implications. *Academy of Management Review*, **20**(1): 15–19.

Donkin, R. (2010) *The Future of Work*. Basingstoke: Palgrave Macmillan.

Donnelly, E. (1987) The training model: time for a change. *Industrial and Commercial Training*, May/June: 3–6.

Donovan, L. (1968) Report of the Royal Commission on Trade Unions and Employers Associations. Cmnd 3623. London: HMSO.

Dower, N. (2004) Global economy, justice and sustainability. *Ethical Theory and Moral Practice*, **7**(4): 399–415.

Dowling, P. J., Festing, M. and Engle Allen, D. (2008) *International Human Resource Management* (5th edn). London: Thomson Learning.

Drew, G. (2009) A '360' degree view for individual leadership development. *Journal of Management Development*, **28**(7): 581–92.

Drohan, M. (2000) Technology comes with a price: stress and depression. *Globe and Mail*, October 11, p. B15.

du Gay, P. (1996) *Consumption and Identity at Work*. London: Sage.

Duffy, J. (2016) 'My whole world has collapsed' … fear and uncertainty for EU nationals after Brexit. *Sunday Herald*, July 10, p. 12.

Dulewicz, V. and Higgs, M. (2000) Emotional intelligence: a review and evaluation. *Journal of Managerial Psychology*, **15**(4): 341–72.

Duncan, R. B. (1972) Characteristics of organizational environments and perceived environmental uncertainty. *Administrative Science Quarterly*, **17**(3): 313–27.

Dundon, T., Wilkinson, A., Marchington, M. and Ackers, P. (2004) The meaning and purpose of employee voice. *International Journal of Human Resource Management*, **15**(6): 1149–70.

Dunkley E. (2015) Banks tackled for not ending culture of 'pinstripes and braces'. *Financial Times*, 19 November, p. 4.

Dupee, J. M., Ernst, N. P. and Caslin, K. E. (2011) Does multisource feedback influence performance appraisal satisfaction? *Nursing Management*, **42**(3): 12–16.

Durkheim, E. (1933/1997) *The Division of Labor in Society*. New York: Free Press.

Duxbury, L. and Higgins, C. (2002) Telework: a primer for the millennium introduction. In Cooper, C. L. and Burke, R. J. (eds) *The New World of Work: Challenges and Opportunities* (pp. 157–200). Oxford: Blackwell.

Dwelly, T. and Bennion, Y. (2003) *Time To Go Home: Embracing the Home-working Revolution*. London: Work Foundation.

Dyck, D. E. (2002) *Disability Management: Theory, Strategy and Industrial Practice* (2nd edn). Markham, Ontario: Butterworths.

Dyer, L. (1984) Studying human resource strategy: an approach and an agenda. *Industrial Relations*, **23**(2): 156–69.

Dyllick, T. and Hockerts, K. (2002) Beyond the business case for corporate sustainability. *Business Strategy and the Environment*, **11**(2): 130–41.

Eady, J. and Motraghi, N. (2010) United action. *New Law Journal*, 160 (7423).

Eagleton, T. (1983) *Literary Theory: An Introduction*. Minneapolis, MN: University of Minnesota Press.

Eagly, A. (1987) Sex differences in social behavior: a social-role interpretation. Hillsdale, NJ: Lawrence Erlbaum.

Earnest, D. R., Allen, D. G. and Landis, R. S. (2011) Mechanisms linking realistic job previews with turnover: a meta-analytic path analysis. *Personnel Psychology*, **64**(4): 865–97.

Easterby-Smith, M. (1994) *Evaluating Management Development, Training and Education* (2nd edn). Aldershot: Gower.

Ebbinghaus, B. and Waddington, J. (2000) United Kingdom/Great Britain. In B. Ebbinghaus and J. Visser (eds) *The Societies of Europe: Trade Unions in Western Europe Since 1945* (pp. 705–56). Basingstoke: Palgrave Macmillan.

Economist Intelligence Unit (2006) Foresight 2020: Economic, industry and corporate trends. Available at www.eiu.com/site_info.asp?info_name=eiu_Cisco_Foresight_2020 (accessed August 26, 2016).

Edgar, F., Geare, A., Halhjem, M., Reese, K. and Thoresen, C. (2015) Well-being and performance: measurement issues for HRM research. *International Journal of Human Resource Management*, **26**(15): 1983–44.

Edvardsson, I. R. and Durst, S. (2014) Outsourcing of knowledge processes: a literature review. *Journal of Knowledge Management*, **18**(4): 795–811.

Edvinsson, L. and Malone, M. S. (1997) *Intellectual Capital*. London: Piatkus.

Edwards, G., Elliott, C., Iszatt-White, M. and Schedlitzki, D. (2013) Critical and alternative approaches to leadership learning and development. *Management Learning*, **44**(1): 3–10.

Edwards, G., Schedlitzki, D., Ward, J. and Wood, M. (2015) Exploring critical perspectives of toxic and bad leadership through film. *Advances in Developing Human Resources*, **17**(3): 363–75.

Edwards, P. K. (1986) *Conflict at Work: A Materialist Analysis of Workplace Relations*. Oxford: Blackwell.

Edwards, P. K. (1995) The employment relationship. In P. K. Edwards (ed.) *Industrial Relations: Theory and Practice in Britain*. Oxford: Blackwell.

Edwards, P. and Sengupta, S. (2010) Industrial relations and economic performance. In T. Colling and M. Terry (eds) *Industrial Relations: Theory and Practice* (3rd edn) (pp. 378–97). Chichester: John Wiley & Sons.

Edwards, P. and Wright, M. (2001) High involvement work systems and performance outcomes: the strength of variable, contingent and context bound relationships. *International Journal of Human Resource Management*, **124**: 568–85.

Edwards, P., Belanger, J. and Wright, M. (2002) The social relations of productivity. *Relations Industrielles/Industrial Relations*, **57**(2): 309–28.

Edwards, R. (1979) *Contested Terrain: The Transformation of the Workplace in the Twentieth Century*. London: Heinemann.

Egan, J. (2004) Putting job evaluation to work: tips from the front line. *IRS Employment Review*, (792): 8–15.

Egri, C. P. and Herman, S. (2000) Leadership in the North American environmental sector: values, leadership styles, and contexts of environmental leaders and their organizations. *Academy of Management Journal*, **34**(4): 571–604.

Ehnert, I., Parsa, S., Roper, I., Wagner, M and Muller-Camen (2016) Reporting on sustainability and HRM: a comparative study of sustainability reporting practices by the world's largest companies. *International Journal of Human Resource Management*, **27**(1): 88–108.

Ehrke, F., Berthold, A. and Steffens, M. C. (2014) How diversity training can change attitudes: increasing perceived complexity of superordinate groups to improve intergroup relations. *Journal of Experimental Social Psychology*, **53**: 193–206.

Einarsen, S., Hoel, H., Zapf, D. and Cooper, C. L. (2011) The concept of bullying and harassment at work: the European tradition. In S. Einarsen, H. Hoel, D. Zapf and C. L. Cooper (eds) *Bullying and Harassment in the Workplace* (2nd edn) (pp. 3–41). Boca Raton, FL: Taylor & Francis.

Elenkov, D. (1998) Can American management concepts work in Russia?: a cross-cultural comparative study. *California Management Review*, **40**(4): 133–56.

Elias, P. and Purcell, K. (2003) *Measuring Change in the Graduate Labour Market*. Research Paper No. 1. Bristol: Employment Studies Research Institute.

Ellinger, A. (2013) Supportive supervisors and managerial coaching: exploring their intersections. *Journal of Occupational and Organizational Psychology*, **86**(3): 310–16.

Ellinger, A. D. (2015) Coaching and mentoring. In R.F. Poell, T. S. Rocco and G. L. Roth (eds) (2015) *The Routledge Companion to Human Resource Development* (pp. 258–71). London: Routledge.

Elliott, L. (2015) Amazon delivers a speedy response. The Guardian, August 18, p. 23.

Elliott, L. and Treanor, J. (2015) Bank of England's disarray in the face of financial crisis revealed. The Guardian, January 7, p. 27.

Elliott, L. (2015) Number of UK workers on minimum wage expected to double by 2020. The Guardian, October 1. https://www.theguardian.com/society/2015/oct/01/number-of-uk-workers-on-minimum-wage-expected-to-double-by-2020 (accessed August 28, 2016).

Elliott, L. (2016) Banking crisis blamed for pay freeze decade. The Guardian, July 14, p. 11.

Emerson, R. M. (1976) Social exchange theory. *Annual Review of Sociology*, **2**: 335–62.

Emir, A. (2014) *Selwyn's Law of Employment* (18th edn). Oxford: Oxford University Press.

Emmott, M. (2015) Foreword. In S. Johnstone and P. Ackers, *Finding a Voice at Work?* (pp. vii–xii) Oxford: Oxford University Press.

Equality Trust (2015) How has inequality changed? https://www.equalitytrust.org.uk/how-has-inequality-changed (accessed August 15, 2016).

Eraut, M. (2000a) Non-formal learning and tacit knowledge in professional work. *British Journal of Educational Psychology*, **70**: 113–36.

Eraut, M. (2000b) Non-formal learning, implicit learning and tacit knowledge in professional work. In F. Coffield (ed.) *The Necessity of Informal Learning* (pp. 12–31). Bristol: Policy Press.

Esfahani, A. N., Abzari, M. and Dezianian, S. (2014) Analyzing the effect of performance appraisal errors on perceived organizational justice. *International Journal of Academic Research in Accounting, Finance and Management Sciences*, **4**(1): 36–40.

Etzioni, A. (1988) *The Moral Dimension*. New York: Free Press.

European Commission (1998) Sexual harassment at the workplace in the European Union. Directorate-General for Employment, Industrial Relations and Social Affairs. www.un.org/womenwatch/osagi/pdf/shworkpl.pdf (accessed July 16, 2016).

European Commission (2003) Working conditions – Working Time Directive. ec.europa.eu/social/main.jsp?catId=706&langId=en&intPageId=205 (accessed July 16, 2016).

European Commission (2008) *Restructuring in Europe*. Brussels: European Commission.

European Trade Union Institute (2015) Collective Bargaining in the United Kingdom. http://www.worker-participation.eu/National-Industrial-Relations/Countries/United-Kingdom/Collective-Bargaining (accessed November 2016).

Evans, A. L. and Lorange, P. (1989) The two logics behind human resource management. In P. Evans, Y. Doz and A. Laurent (eds) *Human Resource Management in International Firms: Change, Globalization, Innovation* (pp. 144–62). Basingstoke: Palgrave Macmillan.

Evans, J. A., Kunda, G. and Barley, S. A. (2004) Beach time, bridge time, and billable hours: the temporal structure of technical contracting. *Administrative Science Quarterly*, **49**: 1–38.

Evans, R. (2015) Blacklisted: the secret war between big business and union activists – a book review. The

Guardian, July 9. https://www.theguardian.com/uk-news/undercover-with-paul-lewis-and-rob-evans/2015/jul/09/blacklisted-the-secret-war-between-big-business-and-union-activists-a-book-review (accessed July 15, 2016).

Evered, R. D. and Selman, J. C. (1989) Coaching and the art of management. *Organizational Dynamics*, Autumn: 16–32.

Ewing, K. D. E. and Hendy, J. (2013) *Reconstruction after the Crisis: A Manifesto for Collective Bargaining*. Liverpool: Institute of Employment Rights.

Exworthy, M. and Halford, S. (eds) (1999) *Professionals and the New Managerialism in the Public Sector*. Buckingham: Open University Press.

Fairholm, G. W. (1996) Spiritual leadership: fulfilling whole-self needs at work. *Leadership and Organizational Development*, **17**(5): 11–17.

Falk, A. and Fox, S. (2015) Gender and ethnic composition of assessment centers and its relationship to participants' success. *Journal of Personnel Psychology*, **13**: 11–20.

Farazmand, A. (2002) Privatization and globalization: a critical analysis with implications for public management education and training. *International Review of Administrative Sciences*, **68**: 355–71.

Farndale, E. and Kelliher, C. (2013) Implementing performance appraisal: exploring the employee experience. *Human Resource Management*, **52**(6): 879–97.

Farndale, E. and Murrer, I. (2015) Job resources and employee engagement: a cross-national study. *Journal of Managerial Psychology*, **30**(5): 610–26.

Farndale, E., Scullion, H. and Sparrow. P. (2010) The role of the corporate HR function in global talent management. *Journal of World Business*, **45**(2): 161–8.

Farndale, E., Biron, M., Briscoe, D. R. and Raghuram, S. (2015) A global perspective on diversity and inclusion in work organisations. *International Journal of Human Resource Management*, **26**(6): 677–87.

Farnham, D. (2015) *The Changing Faces of Employment Relations*. London: Palgrave.

Farrell, A. and Hart, M. (1998) What does sustainability really mean? The search for useful indicators. *Environment*, **40**(9): 4–31.

Farrell, D. (2005) Offshoring: value creation through economic change. *Journal of Management Studies*, **42**(3): 675–83.

Fayol, H. (1949) *General and Industrial Management*. London: Pitman.

Felstead, A. and Jewson, N. (1999) Flexible labour and non-standard employment: an agenda of issues. In A. Felstead and N. Jewson (eds) *Global Trends in Flexible Labour* (pp. 1–20). Basingstoke: Palgrave Macmillan.

Felstead, A., Jewson, N., Phizacklea, A. and Walters, S. (2002) Opportunities to work at home in the context of work–life balance. *Human Resource Management Journal*, **12**(1): 54–76.

Feltham, R. (1992) Using competencies in selection and recruitment. In S. Boam and P. Sparrow (eds) *Designing and Achieving Competency* (pp. 89–103). Maidenhead: McGraw-Hill.

Fenwick, T. (2008) Understanding relations of individual and collective learning in work. *Management Learning*, **39**(3): 227–43.

Fenwick, T. (2015) Conceptualizing critical HRD (CHRD). In R. F. Poell, T. S. Rocco and G. L. Roth (eds) (2015) *The Routledge Companion to Human Resource Development* (pp. 113–23). London: Routledge.

Ferdig, M. A. (2007) Sustainability leadership: co-creating a sustainable future. *Journal of Change Management*, **7**(1): 25–35.

Ferguson, K. L. and Reio, T. G. (2010) Human resource management systems and firm performance. *Journal of Management Development*, **29**(5): 471–94.

Ferlie, E. and Ongaro, E. (2015) *Strategic Management in Public Service Organizations*. London: Routledge.

Fernandez, E., Junquera, B. and Ordiz, M. (2003) Organizational culture and human resources in the environmental issue. *International Journal of Human Resource Management*, **14**(4): 634–56.

Field, T. (1996) *Bullying in Sight*. Didcot: Success Unlimited.

Figuerdo, R., Rocha, V. and Teixeira, P. (2015) Should we start worrying? Mass higher education, skill demand and the increasingly complex landscape of young graduates' employment. *Studies in Higher Education*. http://dx.doi.org/10.1080/03075079.2015.1101754.

Financial Reporting Council (2014) *Guidance on the Strategic Report*. London: Financial Reporting Council.

Findlay, P., McKinlay, A., Marks, A. and Thompson, P. (2000) Flexible when it suits them: the use and abuse of teamwork skills. In S. Procter and F. Mueller (eds) *Teamworking* (pp. 222–43). Basingstoke: Palgrave Macmillan.

Findlay, P., McKinlay, A., Marks, A. and Thompson, P. (2009) Collective bargaining and new work regimes: 'too important to be left to bosses'. *Industrial Relations Journal*, **40**(3): 235–51.

Finegold, D. and Soskice, D. (1988) The failure of training in Britain: analysis and prescription. *Oxford Review of Economic Policy*, **4**(3): 21–53.

Fineman, S. (1999) Emotion and organizing. In S. R. Clegg and C. Hardy (eds) *Studying Organization: Theory and Method* (pp. 289–310). London: Sage.

Fineman, S. (2003) *Understanding Emotion at Work*. London: Sage.

Finkelstein, L. M. (2015) Older workers, stereotypes, and discrimination in the context of the employment relationship. In P. M. Bal., D. T. A. M. Kooij and D. M. Rousseau (eds) *Aging Workers and the Employee-Employer Relationship* (pp. 13–32). Heidelberg: Springer.

Fischlmayr, I. and Kollinger, I. (2010) Work-life balance – a neglected issue among Austrian female expatriates. *International Journal of Human Resource Management*, **21**(4): 455–87.

Fischlmayr, I. C. and Puchmüller, K. M. (2016) Married, mom and manager – how can this be combined with an international career? *International Journal of Human Resource Management*, **27**(7): 744–65.

Fishman, C. (2007) *The Wal-Mart Effect: How an Out-of-town Superstore Became a Superpower*. London: Penguin.

Fitz-enz, J. (2000) *The ROI of Human Capital*. New York: AMACOM.

Fitzgerald, A. and Teal, G. (2004) Health reforms, professional identity and occupational sub-cultures: the changing interprofessional relations between doctors and nurses. *Contemporary Nurse*, **16**: 9–19.

Flamholz, E. (1985) *Human Resource Accounting*. Los Angeles, CA: Jossey-Bass.

Flanagan, J. C. (1954) The critical incident technique. *Psychological Bulletin*, **51**(4): 327–59.

Flassbeck, H. and Lapavitsas, C. (2015) *Against the Troika: Crisis and Austerity in the Eurozone*. London: Veso.

Fleck, J. (2012) Blended learning and learning communities: opportunities and challenges. *Journal of Management Development*, **31**(4): 398–411.

Fletcher, C. (1998) Circular argument. *People Management*, October 1: 46–9.

Fletcher, J. K. (1999) *Disappearing Acts: Gender, Power and Relational Practices at Work*. Cambridge, MA: MIT Press.

Fletcher, N. (2016) One month after the referendum, are predictions of Brexit blight coming true? *The Observer*, 24 July, p. 42.

Flood, P., Mkamwa, T., O'Regan, C. et al. (2008) *New Models of High Performance Work Systems: The Business Case for Strategic HRM, Partnership and Diversity and Equality Systems*. Dublin: NCPP and Equality Authority.

Foley, G. (2001) *Strategic Learning: Understanding and Facilitating Organizational Change*. Sydney: Centre for Popular Education.

Folger, R. and Cropanzano, R. (1998) *Organizational Justice and Human Resource Management*. Thousand Oaks, CA: Sage.

Fombrun, C. J., Tichy, N. M. and Devanna, M. A. (eds) (1984) *Strategic Human Resource Management*. New York: John Wiley & Sons.

Ford, J., Tomlinson, J., Sommerlad, H. and Gold, J. (2009) 'Just don't call it diversity': developing a programme for the business case for diversity in West Yorkshire. Paper presented at the HRD conference, Newcastle-upon-Tyne.

Forde, C., Stuart, M., Gardiner, J., Greenwood, I., MacKenzie, R. and Perett, R. (2008) *Socially Responsible Restructuring in an Era of Mass Layoffs*. CERIC Working Paper No. 5. Leeds: Leeds University.

Foster, C. and Harris, L. (2005) Easy to say, difficult to do: diversity management in retail. *Human Resource Management Journal*, **15**(3): 4–17.

Fox, A. (1985) *Man Mismanagement* (2nd edn). London: Hutchinson.

Fox, S. (1997) From management education and development to the study of management learning. In J. Burgoyne and M. Reynolds (eds) *Management Learning* (pp. 21–37). London: Sage.

Fox, S. and Cowan, R. L. (2015) Revision of the workplace bullying checklist: the importance of human resource management's role in defining and addressing workplace bullying. *Human Resource Management Journal*, **25**(1): 116–30.

Fox, S. and Stallworth, L. E. (2005) Racial/ethnic bullying: exploring links between bullying and racism in the US workplace. *Journal of Vocational Behavior*, **66**(3): 438–56.

Francis, A. (2015) 'Toxic': Australian ex-Apple employee accuses tech giant of workplace bullying. *Sydney Morning Herald*. April 10. http://www.smh.com.au/digital-life/digital-life-news/toxic-australian-exapple-employee-accuses-tech-giant-of-workplace-bullying-20150410-1mi5sc.html (accessed October 2016).

Francis, H. and Keegan, A. (2006) The changing face of HRM: in search of balance. *Human Resource Management Journal*, **16**(3): 231–49.

Francis, H. and Reddington, R. (2012) Employer branding and organisational effectiveness. In Francis, H., Holbeche, L. and Reddington, R. (eds) *People and Organisational Development: A New Agenda for Organisational Effectiveness* (pp. 260–85). London: Chartered Institute of Personnel and Development.

Francis, H., Parkes, C. and Reddington, M. (2014) E-HR and international HRM: a critical perspective on the discursive framing of e-HR. *International Journal of Human Resource Management*, **25**(10): 1327–50.

Francis, R. (2013) *Report of the Mid Staffordshire NHS Foundation Trust Public Inquiry*. London: HMSO.

Fredrickson, B. L. and Losada, M. F. (2005) Positive affect and the complex dynamics of human flourishing. *American Psychologist*, **60**(7): 678–86.

Freeman, R. and Medoff, J. (1984) *What Do Unions Do?* New York: Basic Books.

Freeman, R. B. and Pelletier, J. (1990) The impact of industrial relations legislation on British union density. *British Journal of Industrial Relations*, **28**(2): 141–64.

Frege, C. M. (2002) A critical assessment of the theoretical and empirical research on works councils. *British Journal of Industrial Relations*, **40**(2): 221–48.

French, R. (2010) *Cross-Cultural Management in Work Organizations* (2nd edn). London: Chartered Institute of Personnel and Development.

Frenkel, M. (2008) The multicultural corporation as a third space: rethinking international management discourse on knowledge transfer through Homi Bhabba. *Academy of Management Review*, **33**(4): 924–42.

Fried, Y., Cummings, A. and Oldham, G. R. (1998) Job design. In M. Poole and M. Warner (eds) *The IEBM Handbook of Human Resource Management* (pp. 532–43). London: International Thomson Business Press.

Fried, Y., Levi, A. S., Billings, S. W. and Browne, K. R. (2001) The relation between political ideology and attitudes toward affirmative action among African-Americans: the moderating effect of racial discrimination in the workplace. *Human Relations*, **54**(5): 561–84.

Friedan, B. (1963) *The Feminine Mystique*. New York: DeU.

Friedman, A. (1977) *Industry and Labour: Class Struggle at Work and Monopoly Capitalism*. London: Macmillan.

Friedrich, T. L., Vessey, W. B., Schuelke, M. J., Ruark, G. A. and Mumford, M. D. (2009) A framework for understanding collective leadership: the selective utilization of leader and team expertise within networks. *Leadership Quarterly*, **20**: 933–58.

Friesen, J. (2011) Wage gap wider for children of immigrants. *Globe and Mail*, February 26, p. A15.

Fröbel, P. and Marchington, M. (2005) Teamworking structures and worker perceptions: a cross-national study in pharmaceuticals. *International Journal of Human Resource Management*, **16**(2): 256–76.

Frost, A. and Taris, D. (2005) Understanding the unionization decision. In M. Gunderson, A. Ponak and D. Taras (eds) *Union-Management Relations in Canada* (5th edn) (pp. 23–57). Toronto: Pearson.

Fulford, R. (1999) *The Triumph of Narrative*. Toronto, Ontario: Anansi.

Fuller, A. and Unwin, L. (2003) Fostering workplace learning: looking through the lens of apprenticeship. *European Educational Research Journal*, **2**(1): 41–55.

Fuller, A., Ashton, D., Felstead, A., Unwin, L., Walters, S. and Quinn, M. (2003) *The Impact of Informal Learning at Work on Business Productivity*. London: Department of Trade and Industry.

Fuller-Love, N. (2006) Management development in small firms. *International Journal of Management Reviews*, **8**(3):175–90.

Furnham, A. (2004) Performance management systems. *European Business Journal*, **16**(2): 83–94.

Furnham, A. (2008) HR professionals' beliefs about, and knowledge of, assessment techniques and psychometric tests. *International Journal of Selection and Assessment*, **16**(3): 300–5.

Fyfe, J. (1986) Putting people back into the manpower planning equation. *Personnel Management*, October: 64–9.

Gabriel, Y. (1995) The unmanaged organization: stories, fantasies and subjectivity. *Organizational Studies*, **16**(3): 477–501.

Gabzdylova, B., Raffensperger, J. F. and Castka, P. (2009) Sustainability in the New Zealand wine industry: drivers, stakeholders and practices. *Journal of Cleaner Production*, **17**(11): 992–8.

Gager, S., Bowley, R., Cruz, E. and Batty, R. (2015) Global recruiting trends. LinkedIn.

Gagnon, S. and Cornelius, N. (2000) Re-examining workplace equality: the capabilities approach. *Human Resource Management Journal*, **10**(4): 68–87.

Gahan, P. and Abeysekera, L. (2009) What shapes an individual's work values? An integrated model of the relationship between work values, national culture and self-construal. *International Journal of Human Resource Management*, **20**(1): 126–47.

Gall, G. (2014) New forms of labour conflict: a transnational overview. In M. Atzenti (ed.) *Workers and labour in Globalised Capitalism* (pp. 210–29). London: Palgrave.

Gallagher, P. (2016) Working mothers struggle with discrimination. *The Independent*, March 23, p. 22.

Gallardo-Gallardo, E., Dries, N. and González-Cruz, T. F. (2013) What is the meaning of 'talent' in the world of work? *Human Resource Management Review*, **23**(4): 290–300.

Gallie, D. (2007) Production regimes, employment regimes and the quality of work. In D. Gallie (ed.) *Employment Regimes and the Quality of Work* (pp. 1–34). Oxford: Oxford University Press.

Gamble, J. (2003) Transferring human resource practices from the United Kingdom to China: the limits and potential for convergence. *International Journal of Human Resource Management*, **14**(3): 369–87.

Garavan, T. N. (1997) The learning organization: a review and an evaluation. *Learning Organization*, **4**(1): 18–29.

Garavan, T. (2007) A strategic perspective on human resource development. *Advances in Developing Human Resources*, **9**(1): 11–30.

Garavan, T. and McCarthy, A. (2007) Multi-source feedback and management. In R. Hill and J. Stewart (eds) *Management Development Perspectives from Research and Practice* (pp. 231–50). London: Routledge.

Garavan, T. and McGuire, D. (2010) Human resource development and society: human resource development's role in embedding corporate social responsibility, sustainability, and ethics in organizations. *Advances in Developing Human Resources*, **12**(5): 487–507.

Garavan, T. N., Heraty, N. and Barnicle, B. (1999a) Human resource development: current issues, priorities and dilemmas. *Journal of European Industrial Training*, **23**(4/5): 169–79.

Garavan, T., Barnicle, B. and O'Suulleabhain, F. (1999b) Management development: contemporary trends, issues and strategies. *Journal of European Industrial Training*, **23**(4/5):191–207.

Garavan, T. N., Morley, M., Gunnigle, P. and Collins, E. (2001) Human capital accumulation: the role of human resource development. *Journal of European Industrial Training*, **25**(2–4): 48–68.

Garavan, T., Heraty, N., Rock, A. and Dalton, E. (2010) Conceptualizing the behavioral barriers to CRS and CS in organizations: a typology of HRD interventions. *Advances in Developing Human Resources*, **12**(5): 587–613.

Garavan, T. N., McGarry, A., Watson, S., D'Annunzi-Green, N. and O'Brien, F. (2015) The impact of arts-based leadership development on leader mind-set: a field experiment. *Advances in Developing Human Resources*, **17**(3): 391–407.

Gardiner, L. and Corlett, A. (2015) *Looking Through The Hourglass*. London: Resolution Foundation.

Garengo, P., Biazzo, S. and Bititci, U. (2005) Performance measurement systems in SMEs: a review for a research agenda. *International Journal of Management Reviews*, **7**(1): 25–47.

Garrick, J. (1999) The dominant discourses of learning at work. In D. Boud and J. Garrick (eds) *Understanding Learning at Work* (pp. 216–29). London: Routledge.

Garvey, B. and Williamson, B. (2002) *Beyond Knowledge Management*. Harlow: Pearson Education.

Garvey, R., Stokes, P. and Megginson, D. (2009) *Coaching and Mentoring: Theory and Practice*. London: Sage.

Garvey, R., Megginson, D. and Stokes, P. (2014) *Coaching and Mentoring* (2nd edn). London: Sage.

Gault, J., Leach, E. and Duey, M. (2010) Effects of business internships on job marketability: the employers' perspective. *Education and Training*, **52**(1): 76–88.

Geary, J. F. and Dobbins, A. (2001) Teamworking: a new dynamic in pursuit of management control. *Human Resource Management Journal*, **11**(1): 3–23.

Geertz, C. (1973) Thick description: toward an interpretive view of culture. In *The Interpretation of Cultures* (pp. 3–32). New York: Basic Books.

Gegenfurtner, A., Veermans, K., Festner, D. and Gruber, H. (2009) Motivation to transfer training: an integrative literature review. *Human Resource Development Review*, **8**(3): 403–423.

Gennard, J. and Judge, G. (2005) *Employee Relations* (4th edn). London: Chartered Institute of Personnel and Development.

Gennard, J. and Kelly, J. (1997) The unimportance of labels: the diffusion of the personnel/HRM function. *Industrial Relations Journal*, **28**(1): 27–42.

Georgiou, S., Thomson, M., Richardson-Owen, A. and Edwards, H. (2009) The costs of workplace injuries and work-related ill health in the UK. *Ege Academic Review*. eab.ege.edu.tr/pdf/9_3/C9–53-M13 pdf (accessed 2010).

Gereffi, G. and Christian, M. (2009) The impacts of Wal-Mart: the rise and consequences of the world's dominant retailer. *Annual Review of Sociology*, **35**: 573–91.

Gerhart, B. (2008) Modelling HRM and performance linkages. In P. Boxall, J. Purcell and P. Wright (eds) *The Oxford Handbook of Human Resource Management* (pp. 552–80). Oxford: Oxford University Press.

Gewirth, A. (1991) Human rights and the prevention of cancer. In D. Poff and W. Waluchow (eds) *Business Ethics in Canada* (2nd edn) (pp. 205–15). Scarborough, Ontario: Prentice Hall.

Giambatista, R. C., Rowe, W. G. and Riaz, S. (2005) Nothing succeeds like succession: a critical review of leader succession literature since 1994. *Leadership Quarterly*, **16**: 963–91.

Gibb, A. A. (1997) Small firms training and competitiveness: building on the small business as a learning organisation. *International Small Business Journal*, **15**(3): 13–29.

Gibb, S. (2003) Line manager involvement in learning and development: small beer or big deal? *Employee Relations*, **25**(3): 281–93.

Gibb, S. (2008) *Human Resource Development: Process, Practices and Perspectives* (2nd edn). Basingstoke: Palgrave Macmillan.

Gibbs, S. (2015a) Amazon chief urges staff to report callous managers directly to him. The Guardian, August 18, p. 2.

Gibbs, S. (2015b) Jeff Bezos defends Amazon after NYT exposé of working practices. The Guardian, August 17. https://www.theguardian.com/technology/2015/aug/17/jeff-bezos-amazon-working-practices (Accessed December 2016).

Giddens, A. (1984) *The Constitution of Society*. Berkeley, CA: University of California Press.

Giddens, A. (1990) *The Consequences of Modernity*. Cambridge: Polity Press.

Giddens, A. (2009) *Sociology* (6th edn). Cambridge: Polity Press.

Giddens, A. and Hutton, W. (2000) In conversation. In W. Hutton and A. Giddens (eds) *On the Edge: Living with Global Capitalism* (pp. 1–51). London: Jonathan Cape.

Gilbert, C., De Winne, S. and Sels, L. (2011a) The influence of line managers and HR departments on employees' affective commitment. *International Journal of Human Resource Management*, **22**(8): 1618–37.

Gilbert, C., De Winne, S. and Sels, L. (2011b) Antecedents of front-line managers' perceptions of HR role stressor. *Personnel Review*, **40**(5): 549–69.

Giles, A. and Iain, H. (1989) The collective agreement. In J. Anderson, M. Gunderson and A. Ponak (eds) *Union–Management Relations in Canada* (2nd edn). Don Mills, Ontario: Addison-Wesley.

Gillani, B. B. (2003) *Learning Theories and the Design of E-Learning Environments*. Lanham, MD: University Press of America.

Gilliland, S. W. (1993) The perceived fairness of selection systems: an organizational justice perspective. *Academy of Management Review*, **18**: 694–734.

Gilman, M. and Marginson, P. (2002) Negotiating European Works Councils: contours of constrained choice. *Industrial Relations Journal*, **33**(1): 36–51.

Gilmore, S. (2010) WikiLeaks just made the world more repressive. *Globe and Mail*, November 30, p. A19.

Gilpin-Jackson, Y. and Bushe, G. R. (2007) Leadership development training transfer: a case study of post-training determinants. *Journal of Management Development*, **26**(10): 980–1004.

Girand, A., Fallery, B. and Rodhain, F. (2014) Integration of social media in recruitment: a delphi study. *Social Media in Human Resources Management, Advanced Series in Management*, **12**: 97–120

Glaister, A. (2014) HR outsourcing: the impact on HR role, competency development and relationships. *Human Resource Management Journal*, **24**(2): 211–22.

Glambek, M., Matthiesen, S. B., Hetland, J. and Einarsen, S. (2014) Workplace bullying as an antecedent to job insecurity and intention to leave: a 6-month prospective study. *Human Resource Management Journal*, **24**(3): 255–68.

Glasbeek, H. (1991) The worker as a victim. In D. Poff and W. Waluchow (eds) *Business Ethics in Canada* (2nd edn) (pp. 199–204). Scarborough, Ontario: Prentice Hall.

Global Business Coalition (2011) Fighting HIV/AIDS in the workplace: a company management guide. Available at http://archive.gbchealth.org/system/documents/category_13/91/Fighting-HIVAIDS-in-Workplace.pdf?1315342567 (accessed October 2016).

Godard, J. (1991) The progressive HRM paradigm: a theoretical and empirical re-examination. *Relations Industrielles/Industrial Relations*, **46**(2): 378–99.

Godard, J. (1997) Managerial strategies, labour and employment relations and the state: the Canadian case and beyond. *British Journal of Industrial Relations*, **35**(3): 399–426.

Godard, J. (2004) A critical assessment of the high-performance paradigm. *British Journal of Industrial Relations*, **42**(2): 349–78.

Godard, J. (2005) *Industrial Relations: The Economy and Society* (3rd edn). Concord, Ontario: Captus Press.

Godfrey, M. M., Andersson-Gare, B., Nelson, E. C., Nilsson, M. and Ahlstrom, G. (2014) Coaching interprofessional health care improvement teams: the coachee, the coach and the leader perspectives. *Journal of Nursing Management*, **22**(4): 452–64.

Goffman, E. (1961) *Asylums: Essays on the Social Situation of Mental Patients and Other Inmates*. New York: Doubleday Anchor.

Goffman, E. (1967) *Interaction Ritual: Essays on Face-to-Face Behavior*. New York: Doubleday Anchor.

Gohain, M. P. (2013) Ex-DU employee, who set herself on fire alleging sexual harassment, dies in hospital. October 7. timesofindia.indiatimes.com/city/delhi/Ex-DU-employee-who-set-herself-on-fire-alleging-sexual-harassment-dies-in-hospital/articleshow/23632995.cms (accessed August 16, 2016).

Gold, J. (2014) Revans reversed: focusing on the positive for a change. *Action Learning: Research and Practice*, **11**(3): 264–77.

Gold, J. and Bratton, J. (2014) Towards critical human resource development education (CHRDE): using the sociological imagination to make the HRD profession more critical in the post-crisis era. *Human Resource Development International*, **17**(4): 400–15.

Gold, J. and Stewart, J. (2011) Theorising in HRD. *Journal of European Industrial Training*, **35**(3): 196–8.

Gold, J. and Thorpe, R. (2008) 'Training, it's a load of crap!': the story of the hairdresser and his 'suit'. *Human Resource Development International*, **11**(4): 385–99.

Gold, J. and Thorpe, R. (2010) Leadership and management development in SMEs. In J. Gold, R.

Thorpe and A. Mumford (eds) *The Gower Handbook of Leadership and Management Development* (pp. 133–50). Aldershot: Gower.

Gold, J. and Yeo, R. (2013) Experiential learning and learning cycles – towards an integrative perspective. In C. Valentin and J. Walton (eds) *Human Resource Development: Practices and Orthodoxies* (pp. 33–57). Basingstoke: Palgrave Macmillan.

Gold, J., Rodgers, H. and Smith, V. (2003) What is the future for the human resource development professional? A UK perspective. *Human Resource Development International*, **6**(4): 437–55.

Gold, J., Thorpe, R., Woodall, J. and Sadler-Smith, E. (2007) Continuing professional development in the legal profession: a practice-based learning. *Management Learning*, **38**(2): 235–50.

Gold, J., Thorpe, R. and Mumford, A. (2010) *Leadership and Management Development*. London: Chartered Institute of Personnel and Development.

Gold, J., Holden, R., Iles, P., Stewart, J. and Beardwell, J. (eds) (2013) *Human Resource Development: Theory and Practice* (2nd edn). Basingstoke: Palgrave Macmillan.

Gold, J., Oldroyd, T., Chesters, E., Booth, A. and Waugh, A. (2016) Exploring talenting: talent management as a collective endeavour. *European Journal of Training and Development*, **40**(7): 513–33.

Golden, T., Veiga, J. and Dino, R. (2008) The impact of professional isolation on teleworker job performance and turnover intentions: does time spent teleworking, interacting face-to-face, or having access to communication-enhancing technology matter? *Journal of Applied Psychology*, **93**(6): 1412–21.

Goldthorpe, J. H., Lockwood, D., Bechhofer, F. and Platt, J. (1968) *The Affluent Worker: Industrial Attitudes and Behaviour*. Cambridge: Cambridge University Press.

Goleman, D. (2006) *Emotional Intelligence* (10th anniversary edition). London: Bantam.

Gollan, P. J. (2006) Editorial: Consultation and non-union employee representation. *Industrial Relations Journal*, **37**(5): 428–37.

Gomez-Meija, L. and Balkin, D. (1992) *Compensation, Organizational Strategy, and Firm Performance*. Cincinnati, OH: South-Western.

Gomez-Mejia, L. R., Berrone, P. and Franco-Santos, M. (2010) *Compensation and Organizational Performance: Theory, Research, and Practice*. London: Routledge.

Gong, Y., Wang, M., Huang, J. C. and Cheung, S. Y. (2014) Toward a goal orientation-based feedback-seeking typology implications for employee performance outcomes. *Journal of Management*, **20**(10): 1–27.

Goodley, S. (2015) Cable hints at mandatory EU quotas for female executives. The Guardian, February 4. https://www.theguardian.com/business/2015/feb/04/cable-women-boardroom-mandatory-quotas (Accessed December 2016).

Goodley, S. (2016) Ashley admits 'I broke law': the scandal of Sports Direct. The Guardian, June 8, p. 1.

Goodstein, E. S. (1999) *Economics of the Environment*. Englewood Cliffs, NJ: Prentice Hall.

Google (2015) *Google Green*. https://www.google.com/green/bigpicture/ (accessed April 14, 2016).

Gopalan, S. and Summers, D. (1994) AIDS and the American manager: an assessment of management's response. *SAM Advanced Management Journal*, **59**(4): 15–26.

Gorz, A. (1982) *Farewell to the Working Class*. London: Pluto.

Gospel, H. F. and Littler, C. R. (eds) (1983) *Managerial Strategies and Industrial Relations*. London: Heinemann.

Gould, A. (2010) Working at McDonalds: some redeeming features of McJobs. *Work, Employment and Society*, **24**(4): 780–802.

Gourlay, S. (2006) Towards conceptual clarity for 'tacit knowledge': a review of empirical studies. *Knowledge Management Research and Practice*, **4**(1):60–9.

Governance Network (2002) *At the Crossroads of Change: Human Resources and the Municipal Sector*. Ottawa: Federation of Canadian Municipalities.

Govindarajulu, N. and Daily, B. F. (2004) Motivating employees for environmental improvement. *Industrial Management and Data System*, **104**: 364–72.

Grace, D. and Cohen, S. (2000) *Business Ethics: Australian Problems and Cases* (2nd edn). Oxford: Oxford University Press.

Gracely, N. (2014) 'Being homeless is better than working for Amazon.' The Guardian, November 28. https://www.theguardian.com/money/2014/nov/28/being-homeless-is-better-than-working-for-amazon (Accessed December 2016).

Graeber, D. (2014) Savage capitalism is back – and it will not tame itself. The Guardian, May 30. https://www.theguardian.com/commentisfree/2014/may/30/savage-capitalism-back-radical-challenge (accessed August 30, 2016).

Grant, K. and Maxwell G. (2015) High performance work practices: exploring manager and employee perceptions in Scotland. Paper presented at the 33rd International Labour Process Conference, Athens, April 13–15.

Grant, K., Maxwell, G. and Ogden, S. (2014) Skills utilisation in Scotland: exploring the views of managers and employees. *Employee Relations*, **36**(5): 458–79.

Grant, R. (2010) *Contemporary Strategic Analysis* (7th edn). Chichester: John Wiley & Sons.

Gratton, L. (2000) A real step change. *People Management*, **6**(6): 26–30.

Gratton, L., Hope-Hailey, V., Stiles, P. and Truss, C. (1999) Linking individual performance to business strategy: the people process model. In R. Schuler and S. Jackson (eds) *Strategic Human Resource Management* (pp. 142–58): Oxford: Blackwell.

Gray, D. E. (2010) *Business Coaching for Managers and Organizations – Working with Coaches that Make the Difference*. Amherst, MA: HRD Press.

Gray, D. E. and Goregaokar, H. (2010) Choosing an executive coach: the influence of gender on the coach-coachee matching process. *Management Learning*, **41**(5): 525–44.

Gray, J. (2010) Very good one for the party's bigoted tendency. The Guardian, May 8, p. 39.

Great Place to Work® (2016) *Baringa Partners: How culture and values drives strategy and success at this top management consultancy, Case Study July 2016*. London: Great Place to Work®.

Green, F. (2004) Why has work effort become more intense? *Industrial Relations* 43: 709–41.

Green, F., Ashton, D. N., James, D. and Sung, J. (1999) The role of the state in skill formation: evidence from the Republic of Korea, Singapore and Taiwan. *Oxford Review of Economic Policy*, **15**(1): 82–96.

Green, F., Mayhew, K. and Molloy, E. (2003) *Employer Perspectives Survey*. Warwick University: Centre for Skills, Knowledge and Organisational Performance.

Green, F., Felstead, A., Gallie, D., Inanc, H. and Jewson, N. (2016) The declining volume of workers' training in Britain. *British Journal of Industrial Relations*, **45**(2): 422–48.

Green, J. (1998) Employers learn to live with AIDS. *HR Magazine*, **43**(2): 62–7.

Greene, A. and Kirton, G. (2011) Diversity management meets downsizing: the case of a government department. *Employee Relations*, **33**: 22–39.

Greenhouse, S. (2015) How Walmart persuades its workers not to unionize. *The Atlantic*. June 8. www.theatlantic.com/business/archive/2015/06/how-walmart-convinces-its-employees-not-to-unionize/395051/ (accessed July 18, 2016).

Greenpeace Canada. Tar sands. Online, available at http://www.greenpeace.org/canada/en/campaigns/Energy/tarsands/ (Accessed December 2016).

Grey, C. (2005) *Studying Organizations*. London: Sage.

Grey, C. and Mitev, N. (1995) Reengineering organizations: a critical appraisal. *Personnel Review*, **24**(1): 6–18.

Grimshaw, D. and Rubery, J. (2008) Economics and HRM. In P. Boxall, J. Purcell and P. M. Wright (eds) *The Oxford Handbook of Human Resource Management* (pp. 68–87).Oxford: Oxford University Press.

Grimshaw, D. and Rubery, J. (2010) Pay and working time: shifting contours of the employment relationship. In T. Colling and M. Terry (eds) *Industrial Relations Theory and Practice* (3rd edn) (pp. 347–77). Chichester: John Wiley & Sons.

Grint, K. (2001) *The Arts of Leadership*. Oxford: Oxford University Press.

Grint, K. and Willcocks, L. (1995) Business process re-engineering in theory and practice: business paradise regained? *New Technology, Work and Employment*, **10**(2): 99–108.

Gröjer, J.-E. and Johanson, U. (1998) Current development in human resource accounting and costing. *Accounting, Auditing and Accountability*, **11**(4): 495–505.

Gronn, P. (2008) The future of distributed leadership. *Journal of Educational Administration*, **46**(2): 141–58.

Grossman, R. and Salas, E. (2011) The transfer of training: what really matters. *International Journal of Training and Development*, **15**(2): 103–20.

Grossman, R. J. (2013) Phasing out face time: flexibility rules at Unilever – as long as the work gets done. *HR magazine*, **58**(4): 32–8.

Grote, R. (1996) *The Complete Guide to Performance Appraisal*. New York: American Management Association.

Groysberg, B. (2010) *Chasing Stars: The Myth of Talent and the Portability of Performance*. Princeton, NJ: Princeton University Press.

Groysberg, B., Nanda, A. and Nohria, N. (2004) The risky business of hiring stars. *Harvard Business Review*, **82**(5): 93–100.

Grund, C. and Sliwka, D. (2009) The anatomy of performance appraisals in Germany. *International Journal of Human Resource Management*, **20**(10): 2049–65.

Grzeda, M. M. (1999) Re-conceptualizing career change: a career development perspective. *Career Development International*, **4**(6): 305–11.

Gu, J., Churchill, D. and Lu, J. (2014) Mobile Web 2.0 in the workplace: a case study of employees' informal learning. *British Journal of Educational Technology*, **45**(6): 1049–59.

Guardian (2004) Women come off worse. April 10. www.guardian.co.uk/news/2004/apr/10/leadersandreply.mainsection (accessed September 2, 2016).

Guardian (2011) News of the World phone-hacking whistleblower found dead. www.theguardian.com/media/2011/jul/18/news-of-the-world-sean-hoare (accessed September 14, 2016).

Guardian (2015) Sports Direct: a mega-success, but also big British capitalism at its grubbiest. The Guardian, September 9, p. 34.

Guba, E. G. and Lincoln, Y. S. (1989) *Fourth Generation Evaluation*. London: Sage.

Gubbins, C. and Garavan, T. (2009) Understanding the HRD Role in MNCs: the imperatives of social capital and networking. *Human Resource Development Review*, **8**: 245–75.

Guerci, M. and Carollo, L. (2016) A paradox view on green human resource management: insights from the Italian context. *International Journal of Human Resource Management*, **27**(2): 212–38.

Guerci, M., Longoni, A. and Luzzini, D. (2016) Translating stakeholder pressures into environmental performance – the mediating role of green HRM practices. *International Journal of Human Resource Management*, **27**(2): 262–89.

Guerry, M. A., Berghe, G. V. and Feyter, T. (2015) Balancing attainability, desirability and promotion steadiness in manpower planning systems. *Journal of the Operational Research Society*, **66**(12): 2004–14.

Guest, D. E. (1986) Worker participation and personnel policy in the UK: some case studies. *International Labour Review*, **125**(6): 406–27.

Guest, D. E. (1987) Human resource management and industrial relations. *Journal of Management Studies*, **24**(5): 503–21.

Guest, D. E. (1995) Human resource management, trade unions and industrial relations. In J. Storey (ed.) *Human Resource Management: A Critical Text* (pp. 110–41). London: Routledge.

Guest, D. E. (1997) Human resource management and performance: a review and research agenda. *International Journal of Human Resource Management*, **8**(3): 263–76.

Guest, D. E. (1998) Beyond HRM: commitment and the contract culture. In P. Sparrow and M. Marchington (eds) *Human Resource Management: The New Agenda* (pp. 37–51). London: Financial Times/ Pitman.

Guest, D. E. (2001) Industrial relations and human resource management. In J. Storey (ed.) *Human Resource Management: A Critical Text* (2nd edn) (pp. 96–113). London: Thomson Learning.

Guest, D. (2006) High-performance working: HRM and performance. In S. Porter and M. Campbell (eds) *Skills and Economic Performance* (pp. 173–195). London: Caspian Publishing for the Sector Skills Development Agency.

Guest, D. (2008) HRM and the worker: towards a new psychological contract? In P. Boxall, J. Purcell and P. Wright (eds) *The Oxford Handbook of Human Resource Management* (pp. 128–46). Oxford: Oxford University Press.

Guest, D. (2011) Human resource management and performance: still searching for some answers. *Human Resource Management Journal*, **21**(1): 3–13.

Guest, D. (2015) Voice and employee engagement. In S. Johnstone and P. Ackers (eds) *Finding a Voice at Work?* (pp. 44–66). Oxford: Oxford University Press.

Guest, D. E. and Conway, N. (2002) Communicating the psychological contract: an employer perspective. *Human Resource Management Journal*, **12**(2): 22–38.

Guest, D. and Conway, N. (2011) The impact of HR practices, HR effectiveness and a 'strong HR system' on organisational outcomes: a stakeholder perspective. *International Journal of Human Resource Management*, **22**(8): 1686–02.

Guest, D. and King, Z. (2001) Voices from the boardroom report: state of the profession survey. *Personnel Today*, pp. 10–11.

Guest, D. and King, Z. (2004) Power, innovation and problem solving: the personnel managers' three steps to heaven? *Journal of Management Studies*, **41**(3): 401–23.

Guest, D. E., Davey, K. and Patch, A. (1998) *The Impact of New Forms of Employment Contract on Motivation and Innovation*. London: Economic and Social Research Council.

Guest, D. E., Michie, J., Conway, N. and Meehan, M. (2003) Human resource management and corporate performance in the UK. *British Journal of Industrial Relations*, **41**(2) 291–314.

Guirdham, M. (2011) *Communicating Across Cultures at Work* (3rd edn). Basingstoke: Palgrave Macmillan.

Gully, S. M., Phillips, J. M., Castellano, W. G., Han, K. and Kim, A. (2013) A mediated moderation model of recruiting socially and environmentally responsible job applicants. *Personnel Psychology*, **66**: 935–73.

Gunderson, M., Ponak, A. and Taras, D. (eds) (2005) *Union–Management Relations in Canada* (5th edn). Toronto, Ontario: Pearson.

Gunnigle, P., Turner, T. and D'Art, D. (1998) Counterpoising collectivism: performance-related pay and industrial relations in greenfield sites. *British Journal of Industrial Relations*, **36**(4): 565–79.

Gurbuz, S. and Mert, I. (2011) Impact of the strategic human resource management on organizational performance: evidence from Turkey. *International Journal of Human Resource Management*, **22**(8): 1803–22.

Guthrie, J. P. (2008) Remuneration: pay effects on work. In P. Boxall, J. Purcell and P. Wright (eds) *The Oxford Handbook of Human Resource Management* (pp. 344–63). Oxford: Oxford University Press.

Guthrie, J. P., Flood, P., Liu, W. and MacCurtain, S. (2009) High performance work systems in Ireland: human resource and organizational outcomes. *International Journal of Human Resource Management*, **20**(1): 112–25.

Hackman, J. R. and Oldham, G. R. (1980) *Work Redesign*. New York: Addison-Wesley.

Hadikin, R. and O'Driscoll, M. (2000) *The Bullying Culture: Causes, Effect, Harm Reduction*. Melbourne: Books for Midwives.

Hagger, M. (2009) Personality, individual differences, stress and health. *Stress and Health: Journal of the International Society for the Investigation of Stress*, **25**(5): 381–6.

Haigh, M. and Jones, M. T. (2006) The drivers of corporate social responsibility: a critical review. In *GBER 2006: Proceedings of the 2006 Global Business and Economics Research Conference* (pp. 1–8).

Hales, C. (2005) Rooted in supervision, branching into management: continuity and change in the role of first-line manager. *Journal of Management Studies*, **42**(3): 471–506.

Hales, C. P. (1986) What do managers do? A critical review of the evidence. *Journal of Management Studies*, **23**(1): 88–115.

Hall, D. T. (2002) *Careers In and Out of Organizations*. Thousand Oaks, CA: Sage.

Hall, F., Petrossian, B., Spackman, T. and Gold, J. (2014) 'I would recommend it to anyone!' Transferring leadership development and evaluating for impact at Skipton Building Society. Paper presented at the HRD Conference, Edinburgh, June.

Hall, P. and Soskice, D. (2001) *Varieties of Capitalism*. Oxford: Oxford University Press.

Hall, P. A. and Soskice, D. (2009) An introduction to varieties of capitalism. In B. Hancke (ed.) *Debating Varieties of Capitalism: A Reader* (pp. 21–74). Oxford: Oxford University Press.

Hall, S. (2011) The march of the neoliberals. The Guardian. September 12. www.theguardian.com/politics/2011/sep/12/march-of-the-neoliberals (accessed August 14, 2016).

Halman, F. and Fletcher, C. (2000) The impact of development centre participation and the role of individual differences in changing self-assessments. *Journal of Occupational and Organizational Psychology*, **73**: 423–42.

Hammer, M. (1997) *Beyond Reengineering*. New York: HarperCollins.

Hammer, M. and Champy, J. (1993) *Reengineering the Corporation*. London: Nicholas Brealey.

Hampton, P. (2015) *Workers and trade unions for climate solidarity: Tackling climate change in a neoliberal world*. London: Routledge.

Han, M. (2015) Commission warns against using unpaid interns instead of paid employees. *Financial Review*. August 6. www.afr.com/news/economy/employment/productivity-commission-warns-companies-over-using-unpaid-interns-instead-of-paid-employees-20150804-girqy8 (accessed July 2016).

Hancke, B. (2009) (ed.) *Debating Varieties of Capitalism: A Reader*. Oxford: Oxford University Press.

Hancock, J., Allen, D. G., Bosco, F., McDaniel, K. R. and Pierce, C. A. (2013) Meta-analytic review of employee turnover as a predictor of firm performance. *Journal of Management*, **39**(3): 573–603.

Handy, L., Devine, M. and Heath, L. (1996) *360° Feedback: Unguided Missile or Powerful Weapon?* Berkhamsted: Ashridge Management Research Group.

Hanna, M. D., Newman, W. R. and Johnson, P. (2000) Linking operational and environmental improvement through employee involvement. *International Journal of Operations and Production Management*, **20**: 148–65.

Harding, K. (2003) A leap of faith. *Globe and Mail*, January 8, p. C1.

Harland, C., Knight, L., Lamming, R. and Walker, H. (2005) Outsourcing: assessing the risks and benefits for organisations, sectors and nations. *International Journal of Operations and Production Management*, **25**(9): 831–50.

Harper, P., Kleinman, E., Gallagher, J. and Knight, V. (2013) Cost effective workforce planning: optimising the dental team skill-mix for England. *Journal of Enterprise Information Management*, **26**(1/2): 91–108.

Harper, S. C. (1983) A developmental approach to performance appraisal. *Business Horizons*, September/October: 68–74.

Harri-Augstein, S. and Webb, I. M. (1995) *Learning To Change*. Maidenhead: McGraw-Hill.

Harrington, A. (2012) Numbers, Words and Anonymity in 360-degree Feedback: A Qualitative Study. Loughborough University, PhD thesis.

Harris, A. (2008) Distributed leadership: according to the evidence. *Journal of Educational Administration*, **46**(2): 172–88.

Harris, J. (2014) Teachers: life inside the exam factory. The Guardian. March 14. https://www.theguardian.com/education/2014/mar/14/teachers-life-inside-the-exam-factory (accessed September 12, 2016).

Harris, L. (2001) Rewarding employee performance: line manager's values, beliefs and perspectives. *International Journal of Resource Management*, **12**(7): 1182–95.

Harris, M. M. (1989) Reconsidering the employment interview: a review of recent literature and suggestions for future research. *Personnel Psychology*, **42**: 691–726.

Harrison, J. S. and Freeman, R. E. (1999) Stakeholders, social responsibility, and performance: empirical evidence and theoretical perspectives. *Academy of Management Journal*, **42**(5): 479–85.

Harteis, C., Billett, S., Goller, M., Rausch, A. and Seifried, J. (2015) Effects of age, gender and occupation on perceived workplace learning support. *International Journal of Training Research*, **13**(1): 64–81.

Harter, J., Schmidt, F. and Haynes, T. (2002) Business unit level relationships between employee satisfaction, employee engagement and business outcomes: a meta analysis. *Journal of Applied Psychology*, **87**(2): 268–79.

Harvey, D. (1994) *The Conditions of Postmodernity: An Enquiry into the Origins of Cultural Change*. Oxford: Blackwell.

Harvey, D. (2005) *A Brief History of Neoliberalism*. Oxford: Oxford University Press.

Harvey, F. (2013) IPCC: 30 years to climate calamity if we carry on blowing the carbon budget. The Guardian, September 27, p. 17.

Harvey, G. and Turnbull, P. (2010) On the go: walking the high road at a low cost airline. *International Journal of Human Resource Management*, **21**(2): 230–41.

Harzing, A. W. (2000) An empirical analysis and extension of the Bartlett and Ghoshal typology of multinational companies. *Journal of International Business Studies*, **31**(1): 101–20.

Hatch, M. J. (1993) The dynamics of organizational culture. *Academy of Management Review*, **18**(4): 657–93.

Hatry, H. P. (2010) Looking into the crystal ball: performance management over the next decade. *Public Administration Review*, **70**(Suppl. 1): s208–11.

Haunschild, A. (2003) Humanization through discipline? Foucault and the goodness of employee programmes. *Journal of Critical Postmodern Organization Science*, **2**(3): 46–59.

Hausknecht, J., Day, D. and Thomas, S. (2004) Applicant reactions to selection procedures: an updated model and meta-analysis. *Personnel Psychology*, **57**: 639–83.

Hayes, J. (2014) *The theory and practice of change management*. London: Palgrave Macmillan.

Health Education England (2014) *Values-Based Framework*. London: HEE.

Health and Safety Commission and Department of the Environment, Transport and the Regions (2000) *Revitalizing Health and Safety*. Strategy Statement. London: DETR.

Health and Safety Executive (2007) Workplace stress costs Great Britain in excess of 530 million. http://news.hse.gov.uk/2007/11/12/workplace-stress-costs-great-britain-in-excess-of-530-million/ (accessed September 14, 2016).

Health and Safety Executive (2011) Statistics on violence at work. www.hse.gov.uk/violence (accessed 2012).

Health and Safety Executive (2015) Health and Safety Executive Annual Report. www.hse.gov.uk/statistics/fatals.htm (accessed September 9, 2015).

Heathfield, S. (2007) Performance appraisals don't work – what does? *Journal for Quality and Participation*, Spring: 6–9.

Heck, R. and Hallinger, P. (2010) Testing a longitudinal model of distributed leadership effects on school improvement. *Leadership Quarterly*, **21**(5): 867–85.

Heery, E. (2000) The new pay: risk and representation at work. In D. Winstanley and J. Woodall (eds) *Ethical Issues in Contemporary Human Resource Management* (pp. 172–88). Basingstoke: Palgrave.

Heery, E. (2002) Partnership versus organizing: alternative futures for British trade unionism. *Industrial Relations Journal*, **33**(1): 20–35.

Heery, E. (2004) The trade union response to agency labour in Britain. *Industrial Relations Journal*, **35**(5): 434–50.

Heery, E. (2005) Sources of change in trade unions. *Work, Employment and Society*, **19**(1): 91–106.

Heery, E. (2009) The representation gap and the future of worker representation. *Industrial Relations Journal*, **40**(4): 324–36.

Heery, E. (2015) Frames of reference and worker participation. In S. Johnstone and P. Ackers (eds) *Finding a Voice at Work?* (pp. 21–43) Oxford: Oxford University Press.

Heery, E. and Simms, M. (2010) Employer responses to union organizing: patterns and effects. *Human Resource Management Journal*, **20**(1): 3–22.

Heffernan, M., and Dundon, T. (2012) Researching Employee Reactions to High Performance Work Systems in the Service Sector: The Role of Organisational Justice Theory. 16th ILERA (IIRA) World Congress.

Heller, F., Pusic, E., Strauss, G. and Wilpert, B. (1998) *Organizational Participation: Myth and Reality*. Oxford: Oxford University Press.

Hendry, C. (1994) The single European market and the HRM response. In P. Kirkbride (ed.) *Human Resource Management in Europe* (pp. 93–113). London: Routledge.

Henkens, K., Remery, C. and Schippers, J. (2005) Recruiting personnel in a tight labour market: an analysis of employers' behaviour. *International Journal of Manpower*, **26**(5): 421–33.

Heraty, N. and Morley, M. (1995) Line managers and human resource development. *Journal of European Industrial Training*, **19**(10): 31–7.

Herod, A., Rainnie, A. and McGrath-Champ, S. (2007) Working space: why incorporating the geographical is central to theorizing work and employment practices. *Work, Employment and Society*, **21**(2): 247–64.

Hertz, N. (2002) *The Silent Takeover: Global Capitalism and the Death of Democracy*. London: Arrow.

Hesketh, A. (2014) *Managing the Value of Your Talent*. London: Chartered Institute of Personnel and Development.

Heyes, J. (2000) Workplace industrial relations and training. In H. Rainbird (ed.) *Training in the Workplace* (pp. 148–68). Basingstoke: Palgrave Macmillan.

Hickey, R., Kuruvilla, S. and Lakhani, T. (2010) No panacea for success: member activism, organizing and union renewal. *British Journal of Industrial Relations*, **48**(1): 53–83.

Higgins, P. and Zhang, L. F. (2009) The thinking styles of human resource practitioners. *Learning Organization*, **16**(4): 276–89.

Higher Education Statistics Agency (2015) Destinations of UK domicile full-time first degree graduates. www.hesa.ac.uk/pr/3646-press-release-219 (accessed August 24, 2015).

Hijzen, A. and Venn, D. (2011) *The Role of Short-time Work Schemes During the 2008–09 Recession*. OECD Social, Employment and Migration Working Paper No. 115. Brussels: OECD Publishing.

Hilbrecht, M., Shaw, S., Johnson, L. C. and Andrey, J. (2008) 'I'm home for the kids': contradictory implications for work–life balance of teleworking mothers. *Gender, Work and Organization*, **15**(5): 454–76.

Hill, B. (2014) Critical HRD – a Mithrider? *Advances in Developing Human Resources*, **16**(14): 407–16.

Hill, C. W., Jones, G. and Schilling, M. (2014) *Strategic Management Theory: An Integrated Approach* (11th edn). Stamford, CT: Cengage Learning.

Hillage, J. (2016) What does Brexit mean for employment? June. www.employment-studies.co.uk/news/what-does-brexit-mean-employment (accessed August 1, 2016).

Hillary, R. (2004) Environmental management systems and the smaller enterprise. *Journal of Cleaner Production*, **12**(6): 561–9.

Hirch, A. (2010) Bullying in the workplace on the rise. The Guardian. January 4. https://www.theguardian.com/money/2010/jan/04/bullying-workplace-recession (accessed October 2016).

Hird, M., Sparrow, P. and Marsh, C. (2010) HR structures: are they working? In P. Sparrow, M. Hird, A. Hesketh and C. Cooper (eds) *Leading HR*. London: Palgrave Macmillan.

Hirsh, W. and Jackson, C. (1997) *Strategies for Career Development: Promise, Practice and Pretence*. Report No. 305. Brighton: Institute for Employment Studies.

Hirsh, W. and Tamkin, P. (2005) *Planning Training for your Business*. Report No. 422. Brighton: Institute of Employment Studies.

HM Treasury Committee (2010) *Treasury Committee Report on Women in The City*. London: TSO.

Hochschild, A. R. (1983) *The Managed Heart: Commercialization of Human Feeling*. Berkeley, CA: University of California Press.

Hodgkinson, G. P. and Clarke, I. (2007) Exploring the cognitive significance of organizational strategizing: a dual-process framework and research agenda. *Human Relations*, **60**: 243–55.

Hoel, H. and Beale, D. (2006) Workplace bullying, psychological perspectives and industrial relations: towards a contextualised and interdisciplinary approach. *British Journal of Industrial Relations*, **44**(2): 239–62.

Hoel, H. and Cooper, C. (2000) *Destructive Conflict and Bullying at Work*. Manchester: Manchester School of Management, UMIST.

Hoel, H. and Einarsen, S. (1999) *Workplace Bullying*. London: John Wiley & Sons.

Hoel, H., Sheehan, M. J., Cooper, C. L. and Einarsen, S. (2011) Organisational effects of workplace bullying. In Einarsen, S., Hoel, H., Zapf, D. and Cooper, C. (eds) *Bullying and Harassment in the Workplace: Developments in Theory, Research, and Practice* (2nd edn) (pp. 129–48). London: Taylor & Francis.

Hofman, A. and Hofman, T. (2010) Why are senior woman so rare in finance? *Financial Times*. May 20. https://www.ft.com/content/69ca3d46-6444-11df-8618-00144feab49a (accessed October 2016).

Hofmans, J., De Gieter, S. and Pepermans, R. (2013) Individual differences in the relationship between satisfaction with job rewards and job satisfaction. *Journal of Vocational Behavior*, **82**(1): 1–9.

Hofstede, G. Hofstede, Gert Jan and Minkov, M. (2010) *Cultures and Organizations: Soft-ware of the Mind* (3rd edn). London: McGraw-Hill.

Hogarth, T., Hasluck, C. and Pierre, G. (2000) *Work–Life Balance 2000: Baseline Study of Work–Life Balance Practices in Great Britain*. Summary Report. London: DfEE.

Hogarth, T., Hasluck, C., Pierre, G., Winterbotham, M. and Vivien, D. (2001) *Work–Life Balance 2000: Results from the Baseline Study*. Department for Education and Employment Research Report No. 249. London: DfEE.

Holbeche, L. (1999) *Aligning Human Resources and Business Strategy*. Oxford: Butterworth Heinemann.

Holbeche, L. (2008) Developing leaders for uncertain times. *Impact*, (23): 6–9.

Holman, D. (2000) Contemporary models of management education in the UK. *Management Learning*, **31**(2): 197–217.

Holman, D., Pavlica, K. and Thorpe, R. (1997) Rethinking Kolb's theory of experiential learning in management education: the contribution of social constructionism and activity theory. *Management Learning*, **28**(2): 135–48.

Holman, D., Batt. R. and Holtgrewe, U. (2007) The Global Call Centre Report: international perspectives on management and employment. www.ilr.cornell.edu/globalcallcenter (accessed July 7, 2016).

Holmes, C. and Mayhew, K. (2010) *Are UK Labour Markets Polarising?* SKOPE Research Paper No. 97. Warwick: Warwick University, Centre for Skills, Knowledge and Organisational Performance.

Holmes, J. (2006) *Gender Talk at Work*. Oxford: Blackwell.

Holmes, L. (1995) HRM and the irresistible rise of the discourse of competence. *Personnel Review*, **24**(4): 34–49.

Holton, E. F., Bates, R. A., Bookter, A. I. and Yamkovenko, V. B. (2007) Convergent and divergent validity of the learning transfer system inventory. *Human Resource Development Quarterly*, **18**(3): 385–419.

Home Office (2003) *Diversity Matters*. London: Home Office.

Homklin, T., Takahashi, Y. and Techakanont, K. (2014) The influence of social and organizational support on transfer of training: evidence from Thailand. *International Journal of Training and Development*, **18**(2): 116–31.

Honey, P. and Mumford, A. (1996) *Manual of Learning Styles* (3rd edn). Maidenhead: Honey Publications.

Honeyball, S. (2010) *Honeyball and Bower's Textbook on Employment Law* (11th edn). Oxford: Oxford University Press.

Hoogvelt, A. (2001) *Globalization and the Postcolonian World* (2nd edn). Basingstoke: Palgrave Macmillan.

Hope, K. (2015) FTSE 100 firms appoint more women to their boards. www.bbc.co.uk/news/business-32038561 (accessed July 15, 2016).

Hope-Hailey, V., Farndale, E. and Truss, C. (2005) The HR department's role in organizational performance. *Human Resource Management Journal*, **15**(3): 49–66.

Hoque, K. (1999) Human resource management and performance in the UK hotel industry. *British Journal of Industrial Relations*, **37**(3): 419–43.

Hossain, M. S. and Khan, S. (2015) Strength based approach (SBA) and its various relationships: a literature review. *Platinum Global Journal of Social Science and Humanities*, **1**(1): 1–9.

House of Commons (2012) Blacklisting in employment: oral evidence taken before the Scottish Affairs Committee. November 27, 2012.

Houston, D. M. (ed.) (2005) *Work–Life Balance in the 21st Century*. Basingstoke: Palgrave Macmillan.

Howard-Jones, P. (2014) *Neuroscience in Learning*. London: Chartered Institute of Personnel and Development.

Howe, C. L., Auflick, P. and Freiberger, G. (2011) Upward evaluation at the Arizona Health Sciences Library. *Journal of the Medical Library Association*, **99**(1): 91–4.

Huffcutt, A. I., Weekly, J. A., Wiesner, W. H., DeGrout, T. G. and Jones, C. (2001) Comparison of situational and behavior description interview questions for higher-level positions. *Personnel Psychology*, **54**(3): 619–44.

Hughes, J. (1990) *The Philosophy of Social Research* (2nd edn). Harlow: Longman.

Hughes, J. (2008) *The High Performance Work Paradigm: A Review and Evaluation*. Learning as Work Research Paper No. 16. Cardiff: Cardiff School of Social Sciences, Cardiff University.

Huhne, C. (2010) The Rt Hon Chris Huhne MP's speech to the TUC annual Climate Change Conference. Online, available at https://www.gov.uk/government/speeches/the-rt-hon-chris-huhne-mps-speech-to-the-tuc-annual-climate-change-conference (Accessed December 2016).

Hui, C. and Graen, G. (1997) Guanxi and professional leadership in contemporary Sino-American joint ventures in mainland China. *Leadership Quarterly*, **8**(4): 451–65.

Human Rights Watch (2013), Child Labor and Mercury Exposure in Tanzania's Small-Scale Gold Mines. Online, available at https://www.hrw.org/publications?topic[0]=9682 (Accessed November 2015).

Human Rights Watch (2014), The Impact of Mining on Human Rights in Karamoja, Uganda. Online, available at https://www.hrw.org/report/2014/02/03/how-can-we-survive-here/impact-mining-human-rights-karamoja-uganda (Accessed October 2015).

Hume, D. (1748/2007) *An Enquiry Concerning Human Understanding* (ed. P. Millican). Oxford: Oxford University Press.

Hunt, S. T. (2015) There is no single way to fix performance management: what works well for one company can fail miserably in another. *Industrial and Organizational Psychology*, **8**(1): 130–9.

Hunter, W. and Renwick, D. (2009) Involving British line managers in HRM in a small non-profit work organization. *Employee Relations*, **31**(4): 398–411.

Hurley-Hanson, A. and Giannantonio, C. (2008) Human resource information systems in crises. Paper presented at the Academy of Strategic Management Conference, Tunica.

Hurriyet Daily Times (2015) Outrage over gender discrimination in Police Chief Training Centre job posting. August 17. www.hurriyetdailynews.com/outrage-over-gender-discrimination-in-police-chief-training-center-job-posting.aspx?pageID=238&nID=87094&NewsCatID=339 (accessed July 14, 2016).

Hurst, K. and Patterson, D. K. (2014) Health and social care workforce planning and development – an overview. *International Journal of Health Care Quality Assurance*, **27**(7): 562–72.

Huselid, M. A. (1995) The impact of HRM practices on turnover, productivity, and corporate financial performance. *Academy of Management Journal*, **38**(3): 635–72.

Huselid, M. A., Beatty, R. W. and Becker, B. E. (2005) A players or A positions? The strategic logic of workforce management. *Harvard Business Review*, **83**(12): 110–17.

Hutchinson, S. and Purcell, J. (2003) *Bringing Policies to Life*. London: Chartered Institute of Personnel and Development.

Hutchinson, S., Purcell, J. and Kinnie, N. (2000) Evolving high commitment management and the experience of the RAC call centre. *Human Resource Management Journal*, **10**(1): 63–78.

Hutton, W. (2015a) *How Good We Can Be*. London: Abacus.

Hutton, W. (2015b) Quarterly capitalism is short-term, myopic, greedy and dysfunctional. *The Observer*, July 26, p. 32.

Hutton, W. (2015c) Once, firms cherished their workers. Now they are seen as disposable. *The Observer*, August 23, p. 34.

Hutton, W. (2015d) Doctors, teachers, the police-public servants are demoralised. *The Observer*. October 18. https://www.theguardian.com/commentisfree/2015/oct/18/doctors-teachers-police-public-servants-demoralised (accessed October 2016).

Huws, U. (1997) Teleworking: *Guidelines for Good Practice*. Report No. 329. Brighton: Institute for Employment Studies.

Huws, U. and Podro, S. (2012) *Outsourcing and the Fragmentation of Employment Relations: The Challenges Ahead*. London: Advisory Conciliation and Arbitration Service.

Hvidman, U. and Andersen, S. C. (2016) Perceptions of public and private performance: evidence from a survey experiment. *Public Administration Review*, **76**(1): 111–20.

Hyman, J., Baldry, C., Scholarios, D. and Bunzel, D. (2003) Work–life imbalance in call centres and software development. *British Journal of Industrial Relations*, **41**(2): 215–39.

Hyman, R. (1975) *Industrial Relations: A Marxist Introduction*. Basingstoke: Palgrave Macmillan.

Hyman, R. (1987) Trade unions and the law: papering over the cracks? *Capital and Class*, (31): 43–63.

Hyman, R. (1989) *The Political Economy of Industrial Relations*. Basingstoke: Palgrave Macmillan.

Hyman, R. (1997a) The future of employee representation. *British Journal of Industrial Relations*, **35**(3): 309–36.

Hyman, R. (1997b) Editorial. *European Journal of Industrial Relations*, **3**(1): 5–6.

Hyman, R. (1999) National industrial relations systems and transnational challenges: an essay review. *European Journal of Industrial Relations*, **5**(1): 89–110.

Hyman, R. (2010) British industrial relations: the European dimension. In T. Colling and M. Terry (eds) *Industrial Relations: Theory and Practice* (3rd edn) (pp. 54–79). Chichester: John Wiley & Sons.

Hyman, R. (2015) Making voice effective: imagining trade union responses to an era of post-industrial democracy. In S. Johnstone and P. Ackers, *Finding a Voice at Work?* (pp. 265–77) Oxford: Oxford University Press

Hyman, R. and Brough, I. (1975) *Social Values and Industrial Relations*. Oxford: Blackwell.

Hynie, M., Jensen, K., Johnny, M., Wedlock, J. and Phipps, D. (2011) Student internships bridge research to real world problems. *Education and Training*, **53**(1): 45–56.

Ibrahim, N., Michail, M. and Callaghan, P. (2014) The strengths based approach as a service delivery model for severe mental illness: a meta-analysis of clinical trials. *BMC psychiatry*, **14**(1): 243.

Ichniowski, C., Kochan, T., Levine, D., Olson, C. and Strauss, G. (1996) What works at work: overview and assessment. *Industrial Relations*, **35**(3): 299–333.

Iddekinge, C. H. van., Lanivich, S. E., Roth, P. L. and Junco, E. (2013) Social media for selection? Validity and adverse impact potential of a Facebook-based assessment. *Journal of Management*, doi:10.1177/0149206313515524.

Ifenthaler, D. (2015) Disruptive technologies affecting academia and professional practice. *Technology, Knowledge and Learning*, **20**(1): 1–3.

Iles, P. (2013) Commentary on "The meaning of 'talent' in the world of work". *Human Resource Management Review*, **23**: 301–4.

Iles, P. and Preece, D. (2010) Talent management and career development. In Gold, J., Thorpe, R. and Mumford, A. (eds) *Gower Handbook of Leadership and Management Development* (pp. 243–60). Aldershot: Gower Press.

Iles, P. and Salaman, G. (1995) Recruitment, selection and assessment. In Storey, J. (ed.) *Human Resource Management* (pp. 203–33). London: Routledge.

Iles, P., Preece, D. and Chuai. X. (2010) Talent management as a management fashion in HRD: towards a research agenda. *Human Resource Development International*, **13**(2): 125–45.

Ilgen, D. R., Fisher, C. D. and Taylor, M. S. (1979) Consequences of individual feedback on behavior in organizations. *Journal of Applied Psychology*, **64**(4): 349–71.

Immen, W. (2011) Duking it out with bad managers. *Globe and Mail*, January 21, p. B14.

Incomes Data Services (2010) *Talent management. HR studies*. No. 918. London: IDS.

Industrial Relations Services (2001) *Competency Frameworks in UK Organisations*. London: IRS.

Industrial Relations Services (2003) Sharpening up recruitment and selection with competencies. *IRS Employment Review*, **782**: 42–9.

Inesi, M. E. and Cable, D. M. (2014) When accomplishments come back to haunt you: the negative effect of competence signals on women's performance evaluations. *Personnel Psychology*, **68**(3) : 615–57.

Inkson, K. and King, Z. (2010) Contested terrain in careers: a psychological contract model. *Human Relations*, **64**(1): 37–57.

Inkson K., Gunz, H. and Roper, J. (2012) Boundaryless careers: bringing back boundaries. *Organization Studies*, **33**(3): 323–40.

Inman, P. (2015) Zero-hours contracts up by almost 20% since last year. The Guardian, March 9, p. 4.

Institute of Alcohol Studies (2013) Binge drinking: nature, prevalence and causes. www.ias.org.uk/What-we-do/Publication-archive/The-Globe/Issue-3–2013/Binge-drinking-is-an-underrecognized-problem-among-US-women-and-girls.aspx (accessed September 14, 2016).

Institute of Leadership and Management (2011) *Creating a Coaching Culture*. London: ILM.

Institute for Work and Health (2005) What researchers mean by … statistical significance. www.iwh.on.ca/wrmb/statistical-significance (accessed September 14, 2016).

International Labour Organization (2012) *Working Towards Sustainable Development Opportunities for Decent Work and Social Inclusion in a Green Economy*. Geneva: ILO.

International Labour Organisation (ILO) (2015) http://www.ilo.org/global/about-the-ilo/lang--en/index.htm (accessed October 2015).

International Risk Governance Council (2005) *Risk Governance: Towards an Integrative Approach*. White paper. Geneva: IRGC.

Isaacs, W. (1999) *Dialogue and the Art of Thinking Together*. New York: Doubleday.

Jabbour, C. J. C. (2011) How green are HRM practices, organizational culture, learning and teamwork? A Brazilian study. *Industrial and Commercial Training*, **43**(2): 98–105.

Jabbour, C. J. C. and Santos, F. C. A. (2008) The central role of human resource management in the search for sustainable organizations. *International Journal of Human Resource Management*, **19**: 2133–54.

Jabbour, C. J. C., Santos, F. C. A. and Nagano, S. M. (2010) Contributions of HRM throughout the stages of environmental management: methodological triangulation applied to companies in Brazil. *International Journal of Human Resource Management*, **21**(7): 1049–89.

Jabri, M. (2012) *Managing Organizational Change*. Basingstoke: Palgrave.

Jackson, C. (1996) *Understanding Psychological Testing*. Leicester: BPS Books.

Jackson, D. J. R., Stillman, J. A. and Englert, P. (2010) Task-based assessment centers: empirical support for a systems model. *International Journal of Selection and Assessment*, **18**(2): 141–54.

Jackson, L. (2010) Enterprise resource planning systems: revolutionizing lodging human resources management. *Worldwide Hospitality and Tourism Themes*, **2**(1): 20–9.

Jackson, S. E. and Seo, J. (2010) The greening of strategic HRM scholarship. *Organization Management Journal*, **7**: 278–90.

Jacoby, S. M. (2005) *The Embedded Corporation: Corporate Governance and Employment Relations in Japan and the United States*. Princeton, NJ: Princeton University Press.

Jacques, M. (2016) The death of neoliberalism. *The Observer*, August 21, pp. 31–3.

Jaffee, D. (2001) *Organization Theory: Tension and Change*. Boston: McGraw-Hill.

Jahan, S. (2014) Human resources information system (HRIS): a theoretical perspective. *Journal of Human Resource and Sustainability Studies*, **2**(2): 33–9.

Jain, N. and Bhatt, P. (2014) Employment preferences of job applicants: unfolding employer branding determinants. *Journal of Management Development*, **34**(6): 634–52.

Jamali, D., Sidani, Y. and Zouein, C. (2009) The learning organization: tracking progress in a developing country. *Learning Organization*, **16**(2): 103–21.

Jameson, F. (1991) *Postmodernism, or The Cultural Logic of Late Capitalism*. London: Verso.

Jang, B. (2011) Air Canada to launch cut-rate carrier. *Globe and Mail*, April 12, pp. B1, B4.

Jansen, B. and Jansen, K. (2005) Using the web to look for work. *Internet Research*, **15**(1): 49–66.

Janssens, M. and Steyaert, C. (2009) HRM and performance: a plea for reflexivity in HRM studies. *Journal of Management Studies*, **46**(1): 143–55.

Javidan, M., Bullough, A. and Dibble, R. (2016) Mind the gap: gender differences in global leadership self-efficacies. *Academy of Management Perspectives*, **30**(1): 59–73.

Jepsen, D. and Hess, D. M. (2009) Career stage and generational differences in psychological contracts. *Career Development International*, **14**(3): 261–83.

Jeske, D. and Axtell, C. (2014) e-Internships: prevalence, characteristics and role of student perspectives. *Internet Research*, **24**(4): 457–73.

Jewson, N. and Mason, D. (1986) The theory and practice of equal opportunities policies: liberal and radical approaches. *Sociological Review*, **34**(2): 307–34.

Johanson, U. (1999) Why the concept of human resource costing and accounting does not work. *Personnel Review*, **28**(1/2): 91–107.

Johnson, B. (2015) When diversity training goes wrong: a case study analysis of the University of Delaware residential education program. *Performance Improvement*, **54**(6): 13–19.

Johnson, C. (2015) Autumn statement: Apprenticeships levy to raise £3bn. www.bbc.co.uk/news/business-34923235 (accessed September 14, 2016).

Johnson, M. and Senges, M. (2010) Learning to be a programmer in a complex organization. *Journal of Workplace Learning*, **22**(3): 180–94.

Johnson, G., Scholes, K. and Whittington, R. (2005) *Exploring Corporate Strategy: Text and Cases* (8th Edition). Harlow: Pearson Education.

Johnstone, S. and Ackers, P. (2015) *Finding a Voice at Work?* Oxford: Oxford University Press.

Jones, A., Visser, F., Coats, D., Bevan, S. and McVerry, A. (2007) *Transforming Work*. London: Work Foundation.

Jones, O. (2016) Our private school elite's dominance is not just unfair – it damages us all. The Guardian, February 25, p. 33.

Jones, R. J., Woods, S. A. and Guillaume, Y. R. (2016) The effectiveness of workplace coaching: a meta-analysis of learning and performance outcomes from coaching. *Journal of Occupational and Organizational Psychology*, **89**(2): 249–77.

Jordan, A. and Audia, P. (2012) Self-enhancement and learning from performance feedback. *Academy of Management Review*, **37**(2): 211–31.

Jørgensen, T. H. (2000) Environmental management systems and organizational change. *Eco-Management and Auditing*, **7**(2): 60–6.

Jørgensen, H. H., Owen, L. and Neus, A. (2008) *Making change work*. www-07.ibm.com/au/pdf/making_change_work.pdf (accessed July 4, 2015).

Jowit, J. (2010) British lawyer wants UN to declare 'ecocide' a crime. The Guardian, April 10, p. 21.

Judge, T. A. and Cable, D. M. (1997) Applicant personality, organizational culture and organization attraction. *Personnel Psychology*, **50**: 359–94.

Judge, T. A., Locke, E. A. and Durham, C. C. (1997) The dispositional causes of job satisfaction: a core evaluation approach. *Research in Organizational Behaviour*, **19**: 151–88.

Judge, T.A., Fluegge-Woolf, E., Hurst, C. and Livingston, B. (2008) Leadership. In J. Barling and C. L. Cooper (eds) *The SAGE Handbook of Organizational Behaviors*, Volume 1: *Micro approach* (pp. 334–52). London: Sage.

Kagaari, J. R. K., Munene, J. C. and Ntayi, J. M. (2010) Performance management practices, information and communication technology (ICT) adoption and managed performance. *Quality Assurance in Education*, **18**(2): 106–25.

Kalinoski, Z. T., Steele-Johnson, D., Peyton, E. J., Leas, K. A., Steinke, J. and Bowling, N. A. (2013) A meta-analytic evaluation of diversity training outcomes. *Journal of Organizational Behavior*, **34**: 1076–4.

Kanfer, R., Chen, G. and Pritchard, R. D. (eds) (2012) *Work motivation: Past, Present and Future*. New York: Routledge.

Kang, D.-S., Gold, J. and Kim, D. (2012) Responses to job insecurity. *Career Development International*, **17**(4): 314–32.

Kant, I. (2012) *Groundwork of the Metaphysics of Morals* (eds M. J. Gregor and J. Timmermann). Cambridge: Cambridge University Press.

Kantor, J. and Streitfeld, D. (2015) Inside Amazon: wrestling big ideas in a bruising workplace. *New York Times*. August 15. http://www.nytimes.com/2015/08/16/technology/inside-amazon-wrestling-big-ideas-in-a-bruising-workplace.html (accessed October 2016).

Kaplan, R. and Norton, D. (2000) *The Strategy-focused Organization: How Balanced Scorecard Companies Thrive in the New Business Environment*. Boston, MA: Harvard Business School Press.

Kapoor, C. (2011) Defining diversity: the evolution of diversity. *Worldwide Hospitality and Tourism Themes*, **3**(4): 284–93.

Kärreman, D. and Alvesson, M. (2009) Resisting resistance: counter-resistance, consent and compliance in a consulting firm. *Human Relations*, **62**(8): 1115–44.

Kasemir, B. (2003). Public participation in sustainability science: A handbook. Cambridge: Cambridge University Press.

Kasperkevic, J. (2016) America's top CEOs pocket 340 times more than average workers. The Guardian. May 17. https://www.theguardian.com/us-news/2016/may/17/ceo-pay-ratio-average-worker-afl-cio (accessed July 25, 2016).

Kates, R. W., Clark, W. C., Corell, R. et al. (2001) Sustainability science. *Science*, **292**(5517): 641–2.

Kaufman, B. (2010) SHRM theory in the post-Huselid era: why its fundamentally misspecified. *Industrial Relations*, **49**(2): 286–313.

Kaur, P., Sharma, S., Kaur, J and Kumar, S. (2015) Using social media for employer branding and talent management: an experiential study. *IUP Journal of Brand Management*, **12**(2): 7–20.

Keashly, L. and Jagatic, K. (2011) North American perspectives on hostile behaviors and bullying at work. In S. Einarsen, H. Hoel, D. Zapf and C. Cooper (eds) *Bullying and Harassment in the Workplace: Developments in Theory, Research, and Practice* (2nd edn) (pp. 41–71). London: Taylor & Francis.

Keating, M. (2016) Where next for a divided kingdom? *Scottish Left Review*, Issue 94 (July/August): 5–6.

Kedia, B. L. and Mukherji, A. (1999) Global managers: developing a mindset for global competitiveness. *Journal of World Business*, **34**(3): 230–51.

Keegan, A. and Boselie, P. (2006) The lack of impact of dissensus inspired analysis on developments in the field of human resource management. *Journal of Management Studies*, **43**(7): 1491–1511.

Keegan, A. and Francis, H. (2010) Practitioner talk: the changing textscape of HRM and emergence of HR business partnership. *International Journal of Human Resource Management*, **21**(6): 873–98.

Keenoy, T. and Anthony, P. (1992) HRM: metaphor, meaning and morality. In P. Blyton and P. Turnbull (eds) *Reassessing Human Resource Management* (pp. 233–55). London: Sage.

Keep, E. (2004) Trapped on the low road? *Adults Learning*, February: 16–17.

Keep, E. and James, S. (2012) A Bermuda triangle of policy? 'Bad jobs', skills policy and incentives to learn at the bottom end of the labour market. *Journal of Education Policy*, **27**(2): 211–30.

Keep, E., Mayhew, K. and Payne, J. (2006) From skills revolution to productivity miracle: not as easy as it sounds? *Oxford Review of Economic Policy*, **22**(4): 539–59.

Kehoe, R. R. and Wright, P. M. (2013) The impact of high performance HR practices on employees' attitudes and behaviour. *Journal of Management*, **39**: 366–91.

Keith, M. (2000) Sexual harassment case law under the Employment Contracts Act 1991. *New Zealand Journal of Industrial Relations*, **25**(3): 277–89.

Kelliher, C. and Anderson, D. (2008) For better or for worse? An analysis of how flexible working practices influence employees' perceptions of job quality. *International Journal of Human Resource Management*, **19**(3): 421–33.

Kelliher, C. and Anderson, D. (2010) Doing more with less? Flexible working practices and the intensification of work. *Human Relations*, **63**(1): 83–106.

Kelly, J. E. (1985) Management's redesign of work: labour process, labour markets and product markets. In D. Knights, H. Willmott and D. Collinson (eds) *Job Design: Critical Perspectives on the Labour Process* (pp. 30–51). Aldershot: Gower.

Kelly, J. E. (1996) Union militancy and social partnership. In P. Ackers, C. Smith and P. Smith (eds) *The New Workplace and Trade Unionism* (pp. 77–91). London: Routledge.

Kelly, J. E. (2005) Industrial relations approaches to the employment relationship. In J. A.-M. Coyle-Shapiro, L. Shore, S. Taylor and L. Tetrick (eds) *The Employment Relationship: Examining Psychological and Contextual Perspectives* (pp. 48–64). Oxford: Oxford University Press.

Kelly, J. E. and Bailey, R. (1989) Research note: British trade union membership, density and decline in the 1980s. *Industrial Relations Journal*, **20**(1): 54–61.

Kelly, S. (2014) Towards a negative ontology of leadership. *Human Relations*, **67**(8): 905–22.

Kempster, S. (2009) *How Managers Have Learnt To Lead*. Basingstoke: Palgrave Macmillan.

Kempster, S. and Cope, J. (2010) Learning to lead in the entrepreneurial context. *International Journal of Entrepreneurial Behaviour and Research*, **16**(1): 5–34.

Kennedy, S., Whiteman, G. and Williams, A. (2015) Workplace pro-environmental behavior as a collective driver for continuous improvement. In J. L. Robertson and J. Barling (eds) *The Psychology of Green Organizations* (pp. 351–77). New York: Oxford University Press.

Kennerley, M. and Neely, A. (2002) A framework of the factors affecting the evolution of performance measurement systems. *International Journal of*

Operations and Production Management, **22**: 1222–45.

Kenny, P. (2011) Quoted in the Editorial. The Guardian, June 7, p. 30.

Kepes, S., Delery, J. and Gupta, N. (2009) Contingencies in the effects of pay range on organizational effectiveness. *Personnel Psychology*, **62**, 497–531.

Kersley, B., Alpin, C., Forth, J. et al. (2005) *Inside the Workplace: First Findings from the 2004 Workplace Employment Relations Survey (WERS 2004)*. London: DTI/ESRC/ACAS/PSI.

Kersley, B., Alpin, C., Forth, J. et al. (2006) *Inside the Workplace: Findings from the 2004 Workplace Employment Relations Survey*. London: Routledge.

Kessler, I. (1994) Performance pay. In K. Sisson (ed.) *Personnel Management* (2nd edn). Oxford: Blackwell.

Kessler, I. (1995) Reward systems. In J. Storey (ed.) *Human Resource Management: A Critical Text* (pp. 254–79). London: Routledge.

Kessler, I. (2007) Reward choices: strategy and equity. In J. Storey (ed.) *Human Resource Management: A Critical Text* (3rd edn) (pp. 159–76) London: Thomson Learning.

Kessler, I. and Purcell, J. (1992) Performance related pay: objectives and application. *Human Resource Management Journal*, **2**(3): 16–33.

Kettley, P. (1997) *Personal Feedback: Cases in Point*. Report No. 326. Brighton: Institute for Employment Studies.

Kettley, P. and Reilly, P. (2003) *e-HR: An Introduction*. Report No. 398. Brighton: Institute of Employment Studies.

Khanna, M. and Sharma, R. K. (2014) Employees performance appraisal and its techniques: a review. *Asian Journal of Advanced Basic Science*, **2**(2): 51–8.

Khanna, T., Song, J. and Lee, K. (2011) The paradox of Samsung's rise. *Harvard Business Review*, **89**(7/8): 142–7.

Khapova, S. N., Arthur, M. B. and Wilderom, C. P. M. (2007) The subjective career in the knowledge economy. In H. Gunz and M. Peiperl (eds) *Handbook of Career Studies* (pp. 114–30). Thousand Oaks, CA: Sage.

Khilji, S.E. and Wang, X. (2006) 'Intended' and 'implemented' HR: the missing linchpin in strategic human resource management research. *International Journal of Human Resource Management*, **17**(7): 1171–89.

Kim, H. and Cervero, R. M. (2007) How power relations structure the evaluation process for HRD programmes. *Human Resource Development International*, **10**(1): 5–20.

Kim, H. and Gong, Y. (2009) The roles of tacit knowledge and OCB in the relationship between group-based pay and firm performance. *Human Resource Management Journal*, **19**(2): 120–39.

Kim, J., MacDuffie, J. P. and Pil, F. (2010) Employee voice and organizational performance: team versus representative influence. *Human Relations*, **63**(3): 371–94.

Kim, J., Egan, T. and Tolson, H. (2015) Examining the Dimensions of the Learning Organization Questionnaire: a review and critique of research utilizing the DLOQ. *Human Resource Development Review*, **14**(1): 91–112.

King, D., O'Rourke, N. and DeLongis, A. (2014) Social media recruitment and online data collection: a beginner's guide and best practices for accessing low-prevalence and hard-to-reach populations. *Canadian Psychology*, **55**(4): 240–9.

Kingston, G., McGinnity, F. and O'Connell, P. (2015) Discrimination in the labour market: nationality, ethnicity and the recession. *Work, Employment and Society*, **29**(2): 213–32.

Kinnie, N. J. and Arthurs, A. J. (1996) Personnel specialists' advanced use of information technology. *Personnel Review*, **25**(3): 3–19.

Kinnie, N., Hutchinson, S., Purcell, J., Rayton, B. and Swart, J. (2005) Satisfaction with HR practices and commitment to the organization: why one size does not fit all. *Human Resource Management Journal*, **15**(4): 9–29.

Kirkpatrick, D. L. (1998) *Evaluating Training Programs* (2nd edn). San Francisco, CA: Berrett-Koehler.

Kirton, G. and Greene, A. (2010) *The Dynamics of Managing Diversity: A Critical Approach*. London: Elsevier.

Klass, B. S. (2009) Discipline and grievances. In A. Wilkinson, N. Bacon, T. Redman and S. Snell (eds) *The Sage Handbook of Human Resource Management* (pp. 322–35). London: Sage.

Klass, B., Gainey, T., McClendon, J. and Yang, H. (2005) Professional employer organizations and their impact on client satisfaction with human resource outcomes: a field study of human resource outsourcing in small and medium enterprises. *Journal of Management*, **31**(2): 234–54.

Klein, N. (2015) *This Changes Everything*, London: Penguin.

Klein, H. J., Polin, B. and Sutton, K. L. S. (2015) Specific onboarding practices for the socialization of new employees. *International Journal of Selection and Assessment*, **23**(3): 263–83.

Kluger, A. N. and DeNisi, A. S. (1996) The effects of feedback interventions on performance: a historical review, a metaanalysis, and a preliminary feedback intervention theory. *Psychological Bulletin*, **119**: 254–84.

Kluger, A. N. and Nir, D. (2009) The feedforward interview. *Human Resource Management Review*, **20**: 235–46.

Knight, J. (2011) Union-free shops strong in HR. *Canadian HR Reporter*, February 28: 20–2.

Knight, K. and Latreille, P. (2000) Discipline, dismissals and complaints to employment tribunals. *British Journal of Industrial Relations*, **38**(4): 533–55.

Knights, A. and Poppleton, A. (2008) *Developing Coaching Capability in Organisations*. London: Chartered Institute of Personnel and Development.

Knights, D. and Willmott, H. (eds) (1986) *Gender and the Labour Process*. Aldershot: Gower.

Knowles, M. (1998) *The Adult Learner* (5th edn). Houston, TX: Gulf Publishing.

Kochan, T. (2004) Restoring trust in the human resource management profession. *Asia Pacific Journal of Human Resources*, **42**(2): 132–46.

Kochan, T. E., Katz, H. and McKersie, R. (1986) *The Transformation of American Industrial Relations*. New York: Basic Books.

Kochan, T. E., Batt, R. and Dyer, L. (1992) International human resource studies: a framework for future research. In D. Lewlin, O. Mitchell and P. Sterer (eds) *Research Frontiers – Industrial Relations and Human Resources* (pp. 309–37). Madison, WI: Industrial Relations Association, University of Wisconsin.

Kolb, D. A. (1984) *Experiential Learning*. Englewood Cliffs, NJ: Prentice Hall.

Koleva, P., Rodet-Kroichvili, N., David, P. and Marasova, J. (2010) Is corporate social responsibility the privilege of developed market economies? Some evidence from Central and Eastern Europe. *International Journal of Human Resource Management*, **21**(2): 274–93.

Kolk, N., Born, M. and van den Flier, H. (2003) The transparent assessment centre: the effects of revealing dimensions to candidates. *Applied Psychology: An International Review*, **52**(4): 648–68.

Kontoghiorghes C. (2015) Linking high performance organizational culture and talent management: satisfaction/motivation and organizational commitment as mediators. *International Journal of Human Resource Management*, **27**(16): 1833–53.

Konzelmann, S., Conway, N., Trenberth, L. and Wilkinson, F. (2006) Corporate governance and human resource management. *British Journal of Industrial Relations*, **44**(3): 541–67.

Korczynski, M. (2002) *Human Resource Management in Service Work*. Basingstoke: Palgrave Macmillan.

Kotter, J. P. (1982) *The General Managers*. New York: Free Press.

Kotter, J. (2012) How the most innovative companies capitalise on today's rapid-fire strategic challenges– and still make their numbers. *Harvard Business Review*, **90**(11): 43–58.

Koubek, J. and Brewster, C. (1995) Human resource management in turbulent times: HRM in the Czech Republic. *International Journal of Human Resource Management*, **6**(2): 223–47.

Kraaijenbrink, J., Spender, J-C. and Groen, A. (2010) The resource-based view: a review and assessment of its critiques. *Journal of Management*, **36**(1): 349–72.

Krahn, H., Lowe, G. and Hughes, K. (2011) *Work, Industry, and Canadian Society* (6th edn). Toronto, Ontario: Nelson Education.

Kramar, R. and Syed, J. (2012) *Human Resource Management in a Global Context*. Basingstoke: Palgrave.

Kryscynski, D. and Ulrich, M. (2015) HR as the cultivator of organizational paradoxes. In D. Ulrich, W. Schiemann and L. Sartain (eds) *The Rise of HR: Wisdom from 73 Thought Leaders*. Alexandria, VA: HR Certification Institute.

Kübler-Ross, E. (1969) *On Death and Dying*. New York: Macmillan.

Kuhl, J.S. (2014) Investing in Millennials for the future of your organization. *Leader to Leader* 71: 25–30.

Kuhn, K. M. (2009) Compensation as a signal of organizational culture: the effects of advertising individual or collective incentives. *International Journal of Human Resource Management*, **20**(7): 1634–48.

Kulik, C. and Perry, E. (2008) When less is more: the devolution of HR's strategic role and construed image. *Human Resource Management*, **47**(3): 541–58.

Kulik, C. T. and Roberson, L. (2008) Common goals and golden opportunities: evaluations of diversity education in academic and organizational settings. *Academy of Management Learning and Education*, **7**(3): 309–31.

Kultalahti, S. and Viitala, R. (2015) Generation Y – challenging clients for HRM? *Journal of Managerial Psychology*, **30**(1): 101–14.

Kumhof, M., Lebarz, C., Rancière, R., Richter, D. A. and Throckmorton, N. (2012) *Income Inequality and Current Account Imbalances*. IMF Working Paper 12/08. Washington, DC: International Monetary Fund.

Kur, E. and Bunning, R. (2002) Assuring corporate leadership for the future. *Journal of Management Development*, **21**(9/10): 761–79.

Kydd, B. and Oppenheim, L. (1990) Using human resource management to enhance competitiveness: lessons from four excellent companies. *Human Resource Management Journal*, **29**(2): 145–66.

Lacey, M. Y. and Groves, K. (2014) Talent management collides with corporate social responsibility: creation of inadvertent hypocrisy. *Journal of Management Development*, **33**(4): 399–409.

Lafer, G. (2002) The critical failure of workplace ethics. In J. Budd and J. Scoville (eds) *The Ethics of Human Resources and Industrial Relations* (pp. 273–97). Labour and Employment Relations Series. Ithaca, NY: ILR Press.

Lance, C. E. (2008) Why assessment centers do not work the way they are supposed to. *Industrial and Organizational Psychology: Perspectives on Science and Practice*, **1**: 84–97.

Landivar L. C. (2015) The gender gap in employment hours: do work-hour regulations matter? *Work, Employment and Society*, **29**(4): 550–70.

Langille, A. (2013) Lost in transition: the impact of unpaid internships on Ontario's youth. www.youthandwork.ca/2013/08/lost-in-transition-impact-of-unpaid.html (accessed July 19, 16).

Larimo, J., Le Nguyen, H. and Ali, T. (2016) Performance measurement choices in international joint ventures: what factors drive them? *Journal of Business Research*, **69**(2): 877–87.

Larsen, H. and Brewster, C. (2003) Line management responsibility for HRM: what's happening in Europe? *Employee Relations*, **25**(3): 228–44.

Lash, M. L. (2010) *Intensive Culture: Social Theory, Religion and Contemporary Capitalism*. London: Sage.

Lasserre, P. (2012) *Global Strategic Management* (3rd edn). London: Palgrave.

Latham, G. P., Saari, L. M., Pursell, E. D. and Campion, M. A. (1980) The situational interview. *Journal of Applied Psychology*, **65**: 422–7.

Latham, G., Sulsky, L. M. and MacDonald, H. (2008) Performance management. In P. Boxall, J. Purcell and P. Wright (eds) *The Oxford Handbook of Human Resource Management* (pp. 364–81). Oxford: Oxford University Press.

Lau, P. Y. Y. and Mclean, G. (2013) Factors influencing perceived learning transfer of an outdoor management development programme in Malaysia. *Human Resource Development International*, **16**(2): 186–204.

Lave, J. and Wenger, E. (1991) *Situated Learning. Legitimate Peripheral Participation*. Cambridge: Cambridge University Press.

Lawler, E. (2000) *Rewarding Excellence*. San Francisco, CA: Jossey-Bass.

Lawler, J. (2005) The essence of leadership? Existentialism and leadership. *Leadership*, **1**(2): 215–31.

Lawrence, T. B., Mauws, M. K., Dyck, B. and Kleysen, R. F. (2005) The politics of organizational learning: integrating power into the 4I framework. *Academy of Management Review*, **30**(1): 180–91.

Lazear, E. P. (2000) The power of incentives. *American Economic Review*, pp. 410–14.

Leat, M. (2007) *Exploring Employee Relations* (2nd edn). Oxford: Butterworth-Heinemann.

Lee, C., Liu, J., Rousseau, D. M., Hui, C. and Chen, Z. X. (2011) Inducements, contributions, and fulfillment in new employment psychological contracts. *Human Resource Management*, **50**: 201–22.

Lee, M. (2015) The history, status and future of HRD. In R. F. Poell, T. S. Rocco and G. L. Roth (eds) (2015) *The Routledge Companion to Human Resource Development* (pp. 3–12). London: Routledge.

Legge, K. (1978) *Power, Innovation, and Problem-solving in Personnel Management*. London: McGraw-Hill.

Legge, K. (1995) *Human Resource Management: Rhetorics and Realities*. Basingstoke: Macmillan.

Legge, K. (2000) The ethical context of HRM: the ethical organisation in the boundaryless world. In D. Winstanley and J. Woodall (eds) *Management, Work and Organizations: Ethical Issues in Contemporary Human Resource Management* (pp. 23–40). Basingstoke: Macmillan Business.

Legge, K. (2005) *Human Resource Management: Rhetorics and Realities* (anniversary edn). Basingstoke: Palgrave Macmillan.

Legge, K. (2007) Networked organizations and the negation of HRM? In J. Storey (ed.) *Human Resource Management: A Critical Text* (3rd edn) (pp. 39–56). London: Thomson Learning.

Leineweber, C., Westerlund, H., Hagberg, J., Svedberg, P., Luokkala, M. and Alexanderson, K. (2011) Sickness presenteeism among Swedish police officers. *Journal of Occupational Rehabilitation*, **21**: 17–22.

Leisink, P. L. and Knies, E. (2011) Line managers' support for older workers. *International Journal of Human Resource Management*, **22**(9): 1902–17.

Leitch, S. (2006) *Prosperity For All in the Global Economy – World Class Skills*. London: HM Treasury.

Leithwood, K., Mascall, B. and Strauss, T. (eds) (2008) *Distributed Leadership According to the Evidence*. London: Routledge.

Leonard, N. H., Beauvais, L. L. and Scholl, R. W. (1999) Work motivation: the incorporation of self-concept-based processes. *Human Relations*, **52**(8): 969–98.

Lepak, D. P. and Snell, S. A. (1999) The strategic management of human capital: determinants and implications of different relationships. *Academy of Management Review*, **24**(1): 1–18.

Lepak, D. and Snell, S. (2008) Employment subsystems and the 'HR architecture'. In P. Boxall, J. Purcell and P. Wright (eds) *The Oxford Handbook of Human Resource Management* (pp. 210–30). Oxford: Oxford University Press.

Leslie, J. (2011) *360 Degree Feedback: Best Practice to Ensure Impact*. Greensboro, NC : Center for Creative Leadership.

Levashina, J. and Campion, M. A. (2006) A model of faking likelihood in the employment interview. *International Journal of Selection and Assessment*, **14**: 299–316.

Levinson, H. (1970) Management by whose objectives? *Harvard Business Review*, July/August: 125–34.

Levy, C., Sissons, A. and Holloway, C. (2011) *A Plan for Growth in the Knowledge Economy*. London: Work Foundation.

Levy, D. L. (2005) Offshoring in the new global political economy. *Journal of Management Studies*, **42**(3): 685–93.

Lewin, A., Massini, S. and Peeters, C. (2009) Why are companies offshoring innovation? The emerging global race for talent. *Journal of International Business Studies*, **40**: 901–25.

Lewin D. (2008) HRM in the 21st century. In C. Wankel (ed.) *Handbook of 21st Century Management*. London: Sage.

Lewis, D. (2000) Whistleblowing. In D. Winstanley and J. Woodall (eds) *Ethical Issues in Contemporary Human Resource Management* (pp. 267–77). New York: Palgrave Macmillan.

Lewis, D. and Gunn, R. (2007) Workplace bullying in the public sector: understanding the racial dimension. *Public Administration*, **83**(3): 641–65.

Lewis, J. P. (2000) *The Project Manager's Desk Reference: A Comprehensive Guide To Project Planning, Scheduling, Evaluation, and System*. New York: McGraw Hill.

Lewis, R. E. and Heckman, R. J. (2006) Talent management: a critical review. *Human Resource Management Review*, **16**(2): 139–54.

Leyerzapf, H., Abma, T. A., Steenwijk, R. R., Croiset, G. and Verdonk, P. (2014) Standing out and moving up: performance appraisal of cultural minority physicians. *Advances in Health Sciences Education*, **20**(4): 995–1010.

Li, L. C., Grimshaw, J. C., Nielsen, C., Judd, M., Coyte, P. C. and Graham, I. (2009) Use of communities of practice in business and health care sectors: a systematic review. *Implementation Science*. https://implementationscience.biomedcentral.com/articles/10.1186/1748-5908-4-27 (accessed October 2016).

Lievens, F. and Harris, M. M. (2003) Research on internet recruiting and testing: current status and future directions. In C. L. Cooper and I. T. Robertson (eds) *International Review of Industrial and Organizational Psychology*, **16**: 131–65.

Liff, S. (1997a) Constructing HR information systems. *Human Resource Management Journal*, **7**(2): 18–31. (4)

Liff, S. (1997b) Two routes to managing diversity: individual differences or social group characteristics. *Employee Relations*, **19**(1): 11–26.

Liff, S. (2000) Manpower or human resource planning – what's in a name? In S. Bach and K. Sisson (eds) *Personnel Management* (3rd edn) (pp. 93–110). Blackwell: Oxford.

Lincoln, J. and Kalleberg, A. (1992) *Culture Control and Commitment*. Cambridge: Cambridge University Press.

Linehan, M. (2005) Women in international management. In H. Scullion and M. Linehan (eds) *International Human Resource Management* (pp. 181–201). Basingstoke: Palgrave Macmillan.

Linehan, M. and Mayrhofer, W. (2005) International careers and repatriation. In H. Scullion and M. Linehan (eds) *International Human Resource Management* (pp. 131–55). Basingstoke: Palgrave Macmillan.

Linstead, S. and Grafton Small, R. (1992) Corporate strategy and corporate culture: the view from the checkout. *Personnel Review*, **19**(4): 9–15.

Linstead, S., Fulop, L. and Lilley, S. (2009) *Management and Organization: A Critical Text* (2nd edn). Basingstoke: Palgrave Macmillan.

Lips-Wiersma, M. and Hall, D. T. (2007) Organizational career development is not dead: a case study on managing the new career during organizational change. *Journal of Organizational Behavior*, **28**: 771–92.

Littler, C. R. (1982) *The Development of the Labour Process in Capitalist Societies*. London: Heinemann.

Littler, C. R. and Salaman, G. (1984) *Class at Work: The Design, Allocation and Control of Jobs*. London: Batsford.

Littler, C. R., Wiesner, R. and Dunford, R. (2003) The dynamics of de-layering: changing management structures in three countries. *Journal of Management Studies*, **40**(2): 225–56.

Llanwarne, A. (2016) The circular economy: implications for the environmental movement: report for Scottish Environment LINK. www.scotlink.org/wp/files/Circular-economy-report_External-draft-19-February.pdf (accessed July 10, 2016).

Locke, E. A. (1968) Towards a theory of task motivation and incentives. *Organizational Behavior and Human Performance*, **3**: 152–89.

Locke, G. and Latham, E. (2009) Has goal setting gone wild, or have its attackers abandoned good scholarship? *Academy of Management*, February: 17–23.

Lockton, D. J. (2010) *Employment Law* (7th edn). Basingstoke: Palgrave Macmillan.

Long, R. (2010) Evaluating the market. In *Strategic Compensation* (4th edn) (pp. 333–58). Toronto: Nelson.

Longua, J., DeHart, T., Tennen, H. and Armeli, S. (2009) Personality moderates the interaction between positive and negative daily events predicting negative affect and stress. *Journal of Research in Personality*, **43**(4): 547–55.

Lopes, S. A., Sarraguça, J. M. G., Lopes, J. A. and Duarte, M. E. (2015) A new approach to talent management in law firms: integrating performance appraisal and assessment center data. *International Journal of Productivity and Performance Management*, **64**(4): 523–43.

Lorbiecki, A. and Jack, G. (2000) Critical turns in the evolution of diversity management. *British Journal of Management*, **11**: S17–31.

Low Pay Commission (2015) *National Minimum Wage*. Cm 9017. London: HMSO.

Lub, X. D., Bal, P. M., Blomme, R. J. and Schalk, R. (2016) One job, one deal … or not: do generations respond differently to psychological contract fulfillment? *International Journal of Human Resource Management*, **27**(6): 653–80.

Lucas, K. (2015) Workplace dignity: communicating inherent, earned, and remediated dignity. *Journal of Management Studies*, **52**(5): 621–42.

Lund, H. L. (2004) Strategies for sustainable business and the handling of workers' interests: integrated management systems and worker participation. *Economic and Industrial Democracy*, **25**(1): 41–74.

Luthans, F. and Peterson, S. J. (2003) 360-degree feedback with systematic coaching: empirical analysis suggests a winning combination. *Human Resource Management*, **42**: 243–56.

Lyon, P. and Glover, I. (1998) Divestment or investment? The contradictions of HRM in relation to older employees. *Human Resource Management Journal*, **8**(1): 56–68.

Lyons, S. T., Schweitzer, L. and Ng, E. S. W. (2015) How have careers changed? An investigation of changing career patterns across four generations. *Journal of Managerial Psychology*, **30**(1): 8–21.

M&S (2012) *How We Do Business Report*. www.corporate.marksandspencer.com/howwedobusiness (accessed October 20, 2013).

Ma, W. (2015) Unpaid internships could be a thing of the past. February 3. www.news.com.au/finance/work/unpaid-internships-could-be-a-thing-of-the-past/story-fnkgbb6w-1227205291252 (accessed July 11, 2016).

Mabey, C., Skinner, D. and Clark, D. (eds) (1998a) *Experiencing Human Resource Management*. London: Sage.

Mabey, C., Salaman, G. and Storey, J. (eds) (1998b) *Human Resource Management: A Strategic Introduction*. Oxford: Blackwell.

Macalister, T. (2016) BP boss's pay deal attacked by Institute of Directors. The Guardian, 14 April, p. 22.

McAvoy, B. R. and Murtagh J. (2003) Workplace bullying: the silent epidemic. *British Medical Journal* **326**(7393): 776–7.

McBain, R., Ghobadian, A., Switzer, J., Wilton, P., Woodman, P. and Pearson, G. (2012) *The Business Benefits of Management and Leadership Development*. London: Chartered Management Institute.

McCall, M. (2010) Recasting leadership development. *Industrial and Organizational Psychology*, **3**(1): 3–19.

McCarthy, A. M. and Garavan, T. N. (2001) 360° feedback processes: performance improvement and employee career development. *Journal of European Industrial Training*, **25**(1): 5–32.

McCarthy, A. and Garavan, T. (2007) Understanding acceptance of multisource feedback for management development. *Personnel Review*, **36**(6): 903–17.

McCarthy, J. and Goffin, R. (2004) Measuring job interview anxiety: beyond weak knees and sweaty palms. *Personnel Psychology*, **57**: 607–37.

McCarthy, P., Henderson, M., Sheehan, M. and Barker, M. (2002) Workplace bullying: its management and prevention. In *Australian Master OHS and Environmental Guide 2003* (pp. 519–49). Sydney: CCH Australia.

McCarthy, S. (2010) Business urged to keep on eco-track. *Globe and Mail*, November 24, p. B4.

McCormack, B. (2000) Workplace learning: a unifying concept. *Human Resource Development International*, **3**(3): 397–404.

McCracken, M. and Wallace, M. (2000) Towards a redefinition of strategic HRD. *Journal of European Industrial Training*, **24**(5): 281–90.

McCrone, D. (2001) *Understanding Scotland*. London: Routledge.

McCulloch, M. and Turban, D. (2007) Using person–organization fit to select employees for high-turnover jobs. *International Journal of Selection and Assessment*, **15**(1): 63–71.

McCullum, S. and O'Donnell, D. (2009) Social capital and leadership development. *Leadership and Organization Development Journal*, **30**(2): 152–66.

McDonald, P., Brown, K. and Bradley, L. (2005) Explanations for the provision utilisation gap in work–life policy. *Women in Management Review*, **20**(1): 37–55.

McDonald, P., Charlesworth, S. and Graham, T. (2016) Action or inaction: bystander intervention in workplace sexual harassment. *International Journal of Human Resource Management*, **27**(5): 548–66.

MacDuffie, J. P. (1995) Human resource bundles and manufacturing performance: organizational logic and flexible production systems in the world of auto industry. *Industrial and Labor Relations Review*, **48**: 197–221.

McGoldrick, J. and Stewart, J. (1996) The HRM–HRD nexus. In J. McGoldrick and J. Stewart (eds) *Human Resource Development* (pp. 9–27). London: Pitman Publishing.

McGregor, D. (1957) An uneasy look at performance appraisal. *Harvard Business Review*, **35**(3): 89–94.

McGregor, D. (1960) *The Human Side of Enterprise*. New York: McGraw-Hill.

McGuire, D. and Kissack, H. (2015) Line managers and HRD. In R. F. Poell, T. S. Rocco and G. L. Roth (eds) (2015) *The Routledge Companion to Human Resource Development* (pp. 521–30). London: Routledge.

McHenry, R. (1997) Tried and tested. *People Management*, January 23: 32–7.

McIlroy, J. (1988) *Trade Unions in Britain Today*. Manchester: Manchester University Press.

MacInnes, J. (1985) Conjuring up consultation. *British Journal of Industrial Relations*, **23**(1): 93–113.

McInnis, K. J., Meyer, J. P. and Feldman, S. (2009) Psychological contracts and their implications for commitment: a feature-based approach. *Journal of Vocational Behavior*, **74**: 165–80.

Macintosh, R. and McLean, D. (2015) *Strategic Management*. London: Palgrave.

Macionis, J. and Gerber, L. M. (2011) *Sociology* (7th Canadian edn). Toronto, Ontario: Pearson.

McKay, S. and Markova, E. (2010) The operation and management of agency workers in conditions of vulnerability. *Industrial Relations Journal*, **41**(5): 446–60.

MacKenzie, C., Garavan, T. and Carberry, R. (2012) Through the looking glass: challenges for human resource development (HRD) post the global financial crisis—business as usual? *Human Resource Development International*, **15**: 353–64.

MacKenzie, C., Garavan, T. and Carberry, R. (2014) The global financial and economic crisis. Did HRD play a Role? *Advances in Developing Human Resources*, **16**: 34–53.

Mackey, J. and Raj Sisodia (2014) A healthy, vibrant environment. In *Conscious Capitalism* (pp. 139–152): Boston, MA: Harvard Business Review Press.

MacKie, D. (2015) Who sees change after leadership coaching? An analysis of impact by rater level and self-other alignment on multi-source feedback. *International Coaching Psychology Review* **10**(2): 118–30.

Mackie, K. S., Holahan C. and Gottlieb, N. (2001) Employee involvement management practices, work stress, and depression in employees of a human services residential care facility. *Human Relations*, **54**(8): 1065–92.

McKie, R. (2016) Scientists warn world will miss key climate target. *The Observer*, August 7, p. 1.

McKinlay, A. (2002) The limits of knowledge management. *New Technology Work and Employment*, **17**(2): 76–88.

McKinlay, A. and Taylor, P. (1998) Through the looking glass: Foucault and the politics of production. In A. McKinlay and K. Starkey (eds) *Foucault, Management and Organizational Theory* (pp. 173–90). London: Sage.

Macky, K. and Boxall, P. (2007) The relationship between 'high-performance work practices' and employee attitudes: an investigation of additive and interaction effects. *International Journal of Human Resource Management*, **18**(4): 537–67.

McLean, G. N. (2004) National human resource development: what in the world is it? *Advances in Developing Human Resources*, **6**(3): 269–75.

McLean, G. and Kuo, C. (2014) A critique of human capital theory from an HRD perspective. *HRD Journal*, **5**(1): 11–21.

MacLeod, D. and Clarke, N. (2009) *Engaging for Success: Enhancing Performance through Employee Engagement*. London: Department for Business, Innovation and Skills.

McLoughlin, I. and Clark, J. (1988) *Technological Change at Work*. Milton Keynes: Open University Press.

McMillan-Capehart, A. (2005) A configurational framework for diversity: socialization and culture. *Personnel Review*, **34**(4): 488–503.

McNeil, C. M. (2003) Line managers: Facilitators of knowledge sharing in teams. *Employee Relations*, **25**(3): 294–307.

McRae, H. (2016) It might sound scary, but in the long-term a 'hard Brexit' without access to the single market could work out for the best. July 20. www.independent.co.uk/voices/it-might-sound-scary-but-in-the-long-term-a-hard-brexit-without-access-to-the-single-market-could-a7146681.html (accessed September 12, 2016).

McShane, S. L. (1990) Two tests of direct gender bias in job evaluation ratings. *Journal of Occupational Psychology*, **63**: 129–40.

McSweeney, B. (2002) Hofstede's model of national cultural differences and their consequences: a triumph of faith – a failure of analysis. *Human Relations*, **55**(1): 89–118.

McWilliams, A. and Siegel, D. (2001) Corporate social responsibility: a theory of the firm perspective. *Academy of Management Review*, **26**(1): 117–27.

Madlock, P. (2013) The influence of motivational language in the technologically mediated realm of telecommuters. *Human Resource Management Journal*, **23**(2): 196–210.

Mahajan, A. (2011) Host country national's reactions to expatriate pay policies: making a case for a cultural alignment model. *International Journal of Human Resource Management*, **22**(1): 121–37.

Mahmood, M. (2015). Strategy, structure, and HRM policy orientation: Employee recruitment and selection practices in multinational subsidiaries. *Asia Pacific Journal of Human Resources*, 53(3): 331–350.

Main, P., Curtis, A., Pitts, J. and Irish, B. (2009) A 'mutually agreed statement of learning' in general practice trainer appraisal: the place of peer appraisal by experienced course members. *Education for Primary Care*, **20**(2): 104–10.

Maitra, S. and Sangha, J. (2005) Intersecting realities: young women and call centre work in India and Canada. *Women and Environments*, Spring/Summer: 40–2.

Makin, K. (2007) Collective bargaining is a right, top court rules. *Globe and Mail*, June 9, p. A4.

Mallin, C. and Ow-Yong, K. (2010) The UK alternative investment market–ethical dimensions. *Journal of Business Ethics*, **95**(2): 223–39.

Mallon, M. and Walton, S. (2005) Career and learning: the ins and the outs of it. *Personnel Review*, **34**(4): 468–87.

Malone, T. W., Crowston, K. G., Lee, J. et al. (1999) Tools for inventing organizations: toward a handbook of organizational processes. *Management Science*, **45**(3): 425–43.

Manji, I. (2010) How complex the culture of fear. *Globe and Mail*, November 26, p. A21.

Mankin, D. P. (2001) A model for human resource development. *Human Resource Development International*, **4**(1): 65–85.

Mann, D. (2011) *Understanding Society* (2nd edn). Don Mills, Ontario: Oxford University Press.

Mannion, E. and Whittaker, P. (1996) European Passenger Services Ltd – assessment centres for recruitment and development. *Career Development International*, **1**(6): 12–16.

Marchington, M. (2001) Employee involvement. In J. Storey (ed.) *Human Resource Management: A Critical Text* (pp. 232–52). London: Thomson Learning.

Marchington, M. (2008) Employee voice systems. In P. Boxall, J. Purcell and P. Wright (eds) *The Oxford Handbook of Human Resource Management* (pp. 231–50). Oxford: Oxford University Press.

Marchington, M. and Wilding, P. (1983) Employee involvement inaction? *Personnel Management*, December: 73–82.

Marchington, M. and Wilkinson, A. J. (1996) *Core Personnel and Development*. London: Institute of Personnel and Development.

Marchington, M. and Wilkinson, A. (2000) Direct participation. In S. Bach and K. Sisson (eds) *Personnel Management: A Comprehensive Guide to Theory and Practice* (Chapter 14). Oxford: Blackwell.

Marchington, M., Rubery, J. and Grimshaw, D. (2011) Alignment, integration and consistency in HRM across multi-employer networks. *Human Resource Management*, **50**(3): 313–39.

Marginson, P. and Meardi, G. (2010) Multinational companies: transforming national industrial relations? In T. Colling and M. Terry (eds) *Industrial Relations: Theory and Practice* (3rd edn) (pp. 207–30). Chichester: John Wiley & Sons.

Marginson, P., Edwards, P., Edwards, T., Ferner, A. and Tregaskis, O. (2010) Employee representation and consultative voice in multinational companies operating in Britain. *British Journal of Industrial Relations*, **48** (1): 151–80.

Marin, S. (2014) Supreme Court of Canada: Wal-Mart must pay for closing unionized store. Huffington Post/ The Canadian Press. June 27. www.huffingtonpost. ca/2014/06/27/walmart-canada-supreme-court_n_ 5537051.html (accessed September 14, 2016).

Markey, R., McIvor, J. and Wright, C. F. (2016) Employee participation and carbon emissions reduction in Australian workplaces. *International Journal of Human Resource Management*, **27**(2): 173–91.

Marsden, D. and Belfield, R. (2010) Institutions and the management of human resources: incentive pay systems in France and Great Britain. *British Journal of Industrial Relations*, **48**(2): 235–83.

Marsick, V. and Watkins, K. (1990) *Informal and Incidental Learning in the Workplace*. London: Routledge.

Marsick, V. J. and Watkins, K. (2001) Informal and incidental learning. *New Directions for Adult and Continuing Education*, **89**: 25–34.

Martin I. (2013) *Making It Happen: Fred Goodwin, RBS and the Men Who Blew up the British Economy*. London: Simon & Schuster.

Martin, D. (2010) The removal of workplace partnership in the UK Civil service: a trade union perspective. *Industrial Relations Journal*, **41**(3): 218–32.

Martin, G., Reddington, M. and Kneafsey, M. B. (2009) *Web 2.0 and Human Resource Management: Groundswell or Hype?* Research into Practice Report. London: Chartered Institute of Personnel and Development.

Martin, I. (2014) *Making It Happen*. London: Simon & Schuster.

Martin, J. (1992) *Cultures in Organizations: Three Perspectives*. New York: Oxford University Press.

Martin, J. (2002) *Organizational Culture: Mapping the Terrain*. Thousand Oaks, CA: Sage.

Martin, J. and Frost, P. (1996) The organizational culture war games: a struggle for intellectual dominance. In S. R. Clegg, C. Hardy and W. R. Nord (eds) *Handbook of Organizational Studies* (pp. 599–621). London: Sage.

Martin, J. and Siehl, C. (1983) Organizational culture and counterculture: an uneasy symbiosis. *Organizational Dynamics*, **122**: 52–65.

Martin, J. N. and Nakayama, T. K. (2000) *Intercultural Communications in Context* (2nd edn). Mountain View, CA: Mayfield.

Martin, P. and Pope, J. (2008) Competency-based interviewing – has it gone too far? *Industrial and Commercial Training*, **40**(2): 81–6.

Martín-Tapia, I., Aragón-Correa, J. A. and Guthrie, J. (2009) High performance work systems and export performance. *International Journal of Human Resource Management*, **20**(3): 633–53.

Martocchio, J. J. (2015) *Strategic Compensation: A Human Resource Management Approach* (8th edn). New York: Pearson Prentice-Hall.

Marx, K. and Engels, F. (1998) *The German Ideology*. New York: Prometheus Books.

Maslow, A. (1954) *Motivation and Personality*. New York: Harper & Row.

Mason, P. (2015a) My radical plan to reinvent Tesco. The Guardian, April 27, p. S5.

Mason, P. (2015b) Paying everyone a basic income would kill off low-paid menial jobs. The Guardian, February 1.

Mason, P. (2016) *PostCapitalism: A Guide to our Future*. London: Penguin.

Mason, R., Power, S., Parker-Swift, J. and Baker, E. (2009) 360-degree appraisal: a simple pragmatic solution. *Clinical Governance*, **14**(4): 295–300.

Masterson, S., Lewis, K., Goldman, B. and Taylor, M. (2000) Integrating justice and social exchange: the differing effects of fair procedures and treatment on work relationships. *Academy of Management Journal*, **43**: 738–48.

Mathew, J. and Ogbonna, E. (2009) Organizational culture and commitment: a study of an Indian software organization. *International Journal of Human Resource Management*, **20**(3): 654–75.

Maurice, M. and Sorge, A. (eds) (2000) *Embedding Organizations*. Amsterdam: John Benjamins Publishing.

May, D. R. and Flannery, B. L. (1995) Cutting waste with employee involvement teams. *Business Horizons*, **38**: 28–38.

Mayer, B. (2009) *Blue-Green Coalitions: Fighting for Safe Workplaces and Healthy Communities*. Ithaca, NY: Cornell University Press.

Mayerhofer, H., Hartmann, L., Michelitsch-Riedl, G. and Kollinger, I. (2004) Flexpatriate assignments: a neglected issue in global staffing. *International Journal of Human Resource Management*, **15**(8): 1371–89.

Mayfield, M., Mayfield, J. and Lunce, S. (2003) Human resource information systems: a review and model development. *Advances in Competitiveness Research*, **11**(1): 139–51.

Mayo, A. (2002) A thorough evaluation. *People Management*, **8**(7): 36–9.

Mayo, A. (2004) *Creating a Learning and Development Strategy*. London: Chartered Institute of Personnel and Development.

Mayrhofer, W., Brewster, C., Morley, M. and Gunnigle, P. (2000) Communication, consultation and the HRM debate. In C. Brewster, W. Mayrhofer and M. Morley (eds) *New Challenges for European Human Resource Management* (pp. 222–44). Basingstoke: Palgrave Macmillan.

Meadows, D. H., Meadows, D. L., Randers, J. and Behrens, W. W. (1972) *The Limits to Growth*. Universe Books: New York.

Mearns, K. and Hope, L. (2005) *Health and Well-being in the Offshore Environment: The Management of Personal Health*. Research Report No. 305, London: Health and Safety Executive.

Mebratu, D. (1998) Sustainability and sustainable development: historical and conceptual review. *Environmental Impact Assessment Review*, **18**(6): 493–520.

Meehan, T. and Bressler, S. (2012) Neurocognitive networks: findings, models, and theory. *Euroscience and Biobehavioral Reviews*, **36**(10): 2232–47.

Meek, L. (1992) Organizational culture: origins and weaknesses. In G. Salaman (ed.) *Human Resources Strategies* (pp. 198–229). London: Sage.

Megginson, D. and Pedler, M. (1992) *Self Development*. Maidenhead: McGraw-Hill.

Melchers, K. G., Kleinmann, M. and Prinz, M. A. (2010) Do assessors have too much on their plates? The effects of simultaneously rating multiple assessment center candidates on rating quality. *International Journal of Selection and Assessment*, **18**(3): 329–41.

Mellahi, K. and Wilkinson, A. (2010) Slash and burn or nip and tuck? Downsizing, innovation and human resources. *International Journal of Human Resource Management*, **21**(13): 2291–305.

Mellahi, K., Frynas, J. and Collings, D. (2015) Performance management practices within emerging market multinational enterprises: the case of Brazilian multinationals. *International Journal of Human Resource Management*, **27**(8): 876–905.

Merrifield, N. (2015) NHS to launch major staff fitness and healthy food programme. *Nursing Times*. September 2. www.nursingtimes.net/clinical-archive/public-health/nhs-to-launch-major-staff-fitness-and-healthy-food-programme/5090020.fullarticle (accessed July 15, 2016).

Merrill, J. (2016) Care workers 'are not being paid the minimum wage'. *The Independent*, March 23, p. 20.

Messersmith, J. G., Patel, P. C. and Lepak, D. P. (2011) Unlocking the black box: exploring the link between high-performance work systems and performance. *Journal of Applied Psychology*, **96**(6): 1105–18.

Metcalfe, B. D. (2010) Leadership and diversity development. In Gold, J., Thorpe, R. and Mumford, A. (eds) *Gower Handbook of Leadership and Management Development* (pp. 151–73). Aldershot: Gower Publishing.

Meyer, H. H., Kay, E. and French, J. R. P. (1965) Split roles in performance appraisal. *Harvard Business Review*, **43**: 123–29.

Mezirow, J. (1990) *Fostering Critical Reflection in Adulthood*. San Francisco, CA: Jossey-Bass.

Mezirow, J. (1991) *Transformative Dimensions of Adult Learning*. San Francisco, CA: Jossey-Bass.

Michaels, E., Handfiled-Jones, H. and Axelrod, B. (2001) *The War for Talent*. Boston, MA: Harvard Business School Press.

Michie, J. and Sheehan-Quinn, M. (2001) Labour market flexibility: human resource management and corporate performance. *British Journal of Management*, **12**(4): 287–305.

Micic, P. (2010) *The Five Futures Glasses*. Berlin: Springer.

Miguel, R. F. (2013) LinkedIn for hiring decisions: a content validity framework. In R. F. Miguel (Chair): The promise and perils of social media data for selection. Symposium presented at the Society for Industrial and Organizational Psychology, Houston, TX, USA.

Miles, A. and Sadler-Smith, E. (2014) "With recruitment I always feel I need to listen to my gut": the role of intuition in employee selection. *Personal Review*, **43**(4): 606–27.

Miles, R. and Snow, C. (1984) Designing strategic human resources systems. *Organizational Dynamics*, Summer: 36–52.

Milkovich, G., Newman, J. and Cole, N. (2013) *Compensation* (11th edn). New York: McGraw-Hill.

Miller, L., Rankin, N. and Neathey, F. (2001) *Competency Frameworks in UK Organizations*. London: Chartered Institute of Personnel and Development.

Miller, P. (1987) Strategic industrial relations and human resource management – distinction, definition and recognition. *Journal of Management Studies*, **24**(4): 347–61.

Milliman, J. and Clair, J. (1996) Best environmental HRM practices in the U.S. In W. Wehrmeyer (ed.) *Greening People: Human Resources and Environmental Management* (Chapter 2). Sheffield: Greenleaf.

Mills, C. Wright (1959/2000) *The Sociological Imagination*. Oxford: Oxford University Press.

Millward, N., Bryson, A. and Forth, J. (2000) *All Change at Work: British Employee Relations 1980–1998*. London: Routledge.

Milmo, D. (2010) BA told to hit union 'where it hurts'. The Guardian, March 27, pp. 1–2.

Milmo, D. and Pidd, H. (2010) Union cries foul after court blocks BA cabin crew strike. The Guardian, May 18, p. 1.

Minbaeva, D and Andersen, T. J. (2012) *The Role of Human Resource Management in Strategy Making*. Working Paper. Copenhagen: Copenhagen Business School.

Miner-Rubino, K. and Cortina, L. M. (2004) Working in a context of hostility towards women: implications for employees' well-being. *Journal of Occupational Health Psychology*, **9**(2): 107–22.

Mintzberg, H. (1973) *The Nature of Managerial Work*. London: Harper & Row.

Mintzberg, H. (1978) Patterns in strategy formation. *Management Science*, **24**(9): 934–48.

Mintzberg, H. (1987) Crafting strategy. *Harvard Business Review*, July/August: 66–75.

Mintzberg, H. (1989) *Mintzberg on Management*. New York: Collier/Hamilton.

Mintzberg, H. (1990) The design school: reconsidering the basic premises of strategic management. *Strategic Management Journal*, **11**: 171–95.

Mintzberg, H. (2004) *Managers Not MBA's: A Hard Look at the Soft Practices of Managing and Management Development*. San Francisco, CA: Berrett-Koehler.

Mintzberg, H. (2009) America's monumental failure of management. *Globe and Mail*, March 16, p. A11.

Mintzberg, H., Ahlstrand, B., Lampel, J. (1998) *Strategic Safari: The Complete Guide Through the Wilds of Strategic Management*. New York: Free Press.

Mintzberg, H., Ahlstrand, B., Lampel, J.B. (2008) *Strategy Safari: The Complete Guide Through the*

Wilds of Strategic Management (2nd edition), London: FT Prentice Hall.

Mintzberg, H., Ahlstrand, B., Lampel, J. (2009) *Strategic Safari: The Complete Guide Through the Wilds of Strategic Management* (2nd edn). Harlow: Pearson Education.

Monaghan, A. (2014) Self-employment in UK at highest level since records began. August 20. www.theguardian.com/uk-news/2014/aug/20/self-employment-uk-highest-level (accessed September 9, 2016).

Monbiot, G. (2016) The climate crisis is already here – but no one's telling us. The Guardian, August 3, p. 29.

Mone, E., Eisinger, C., Guggenheim, K., Price, B. and Stine, C. (2011) Performance management at the wheel: driving employee engagement in organizations. *Journal of Business and Psychology*, **26**(2): 205–12.

Monks, K. and McMackin, J. (2001) Designing and aligning an HR system. *Human Resource Management Journal*, **11**(2): 57–72.

Montgomery, J. and Kelloway, K. (2002) *Management of Occupational Health and Safety* (2nd edn). Scarborough, Ontario: Nelson Thomson Learning.

Mooney, T. and Brinkerhoff, R. (2008) *Courageous Training: Bold Actions for Business Results*. San Francisco, CA: Berett-Koehler.

Morgan, D. E. (1993) The nature of workplace relations: a typology of social relations and analysis of industrial relations systems. *Economic and Labour Relations Review*, **4**(1): 140–66.

Morgan, P. I. and Ogbonna, E. (2008) Subcultural dynamics in transformation: a multi-perspective study of healthcare professionals. *Human Relations*, **61**(1): 39–65.

Morgeson, F. P., Campion, M. A., Dipboye, R. L., Hollenbeck, J. R., Murphy, K. and Schmitt, N. (2007) Reconsidering the use of personality tests in personnel selection contexts. *Personnel Psychology*, **60**: 683–729.

Morrell, K. M., Loan-Clarke, J. and Wilkinson, A. J. (2001) Unweaving leaving: the use of models in the management of employee turnover. *International Journal of Management Reviews*, **3**(1): 219–44.

Morrell, K. M., Loan-Clarke, J. and Wilkinson, A. J. (2004) Organisational change and employee turnover. *Personnel Review*, **33**(2): 161–73.

Morris, J., Wilkinson, B. and Gamble, J. (2009) Strategic international human resource management or the 'bottom line'? The case of electronics and garments commodity chains in China. *International Journal of Human Resource Management*, **20**(2): 348–71.

Morris, S. and Snell, S. (2009) The evolution of HR strategy: adaptations to increasing global complexity.

In A. Wilkinson, N. Bacon, T. Redman, and S. Snell (eds) *The SAGE Handbook of Human Resource Management* (pp. 84–99). London: Sage.

Morrison, J. (2015a) *Business Ethics: New Challenges in a Globalized World*, London: Palgrave.

Morrison J. (2015b) Financial markets: what role for ethics? In *Business Ethics* (pp. 150–80). London: Palgrave.

Morrow, D. and Rondinelli, D. (2002) Adopting corporate environmental management systems: motivations and results of ISO 1401 and EMAS certification. *European Management Journal*, **20**(2): 159–71.

Mostafa, A. M. and Gould-Williams, J. S. (2014) Testing the mediation effect of person-organization fit on the relationship between high performance HR practices and employee outcomes in the Egyptian public sector. *International Journal of Human Resource Management*, **25**(2): 276–92.

Moynihan, D. P., Pandey, S. K. and Wright, B. E. (2012) Prosocial values and performance management theory: Linking perceived social impact and performance information use. *Governance*, **25**(3): 463–83.

Mudambi, S. M. and Tallman, S. (2010) Make, buy or ally? Theoretical perspectives on knowledge process outsourcing through alliances. *Journal of Management Studies*, **47**(8): 1434–56.

Mueller, J. (2015) Formal and informal practices of knowledge sharing between project teams and enacted cultural characteristics. *Project Management Journal*, **46**(1): 53–68.

Mumford, A. (1993) *How Managers Can Develop Managers*. Aldershot: Gower.

Munro, A. and Rainbird, H. (2000) The new unionism and the new bargaining agenda: UNISON–employer partnerships on workplace learning in Britain. *British Journal of Industrial Relations*, **38**(2): 223–40.

Munro-Fraser, J. (1971) *Psychology: General, Industrial, Social*. London: Pitman.

Muscatelli, A. (2016) Brexit … if you think the worst is over, think again. *Sunday Herald*, August 28, p. 35.

Mwita, J. I. (2000) Performance management model. *International Journal of Public Sector Management*, **13**(1): 19–37.

Nabi, G, Wei, S., Rja, M., Zhao, S. and Ahmed, B. (2015). So Far Where Se Stand in the Recruitment and Selection Studies? A Review Study Based on Earlier Studies. *International Journal of Human Resource Studies*, 5(2): 135–151.

Nadler, L. and Nadler, Z. (1989) *Developing Human Resources*. San Francisco, CA: Jossey-Bass.

Nagendra, A. and Deshpande, M. (2014) Human resource information systems (HRIS) in HR planning and development in mid to large sized organizations. *Social and Behavioral Sciences* **133**: 61–7.

NASUWT The Teachers' Union (2014) *Supply Teachers: A Survey of their Experiences*. Birmingham: NASUWT.

Nathanson, S. (2015) Act and rule utilitarianism. Internet Encyclopaedia of Philosophy. Available at http://www.iep.utm.edu/util-a-r/ (accessed October 2016).

Navigant Research (2015) Energy Efficient Buildings: Global Outlook. Online, available at https://www.navigantresearch.com/research/energy-efficient-buildings-global-outlook (Accessed December 2016).

Ndunguru, C.A. (2012) Executive onboarding: how to hit the ground running. *Public Manager*, **41**(3): 6–9.

Neale J. (2011) *Our Jobs, Our Planet: Transport Workers and Climate Change*. Brussels: European Transport Workers Federation.

Nehles, A. C., Van Riemsdijk, M., Kok, I. and Looise, J. C. (2006) Implementing human resource management successfully: a first-line management challenge. *Management Revue*, **17**(3): 256–73.

Ness, I. (2014) Labour migration and emergent class conflict: corporate neo-liberalism, worker mobility and labour resistance in the US. In M. Atzenti (ed.) *Workers and Labour in Globalised Capitalism* (pp. 230–50): London: Palgrave.

Newell, S. (2005) Recruitment and selection. In S. Bach (ed.) *Managing Human Resources* (pp. 115–47). Oxford: Blackwell.

Newell, S., Robertson, M., Scarbrough, H. and Swan, J. (2002) *Managing Knowledge Work*. Basingstoke: Palgrave Macmillan.

Newton, T. and Findlay, P. (1996) Playing God? The performance of appraisal. *Human Resource Management Journal*, **6**(3): 42–58.

Nga Thi Thuy Ho, Pi-Shen Seet and Jones, J. (2016) Understanding re-expatriation intentions among overseas returnees – an emerging economy perspective. *International Journal of Human Resource Management*, **27**(17): 1938–66.

Nguyen, S. (2014) The critical role of research in diversity training: how research contributes to an evidence-based approach to diversity training. *Development and Learning in Organizations: An International Journal*, **28**(4): 15–17.

Nichols, T. (1986) *The British Worker Question: A New Look at Workers and Productivity in Manufacturing*. London: Routledge & Kegan Paul.

Nichols, T. (1997) *The Sociology of Industrial Injury*. London: Mansell Publishing.

Nieminen, L. R., Smerek, R., Kotrba, L. and Denison, D. (2013) What does an executive coaching intervention add beyond facilitated multisource feedback? Effects on leader self-ratings and perceived effectiveness. *Human Resource Development Quarterly*, **24**(2): 145–76.

Nijholt, J. J. and Benders, J. (2010) Measuring the prevalence of self-managing teams: taking account of defining characteristics. *Work, Employment and Society*, **24**(2): 375–85.

Nikolaou, I. and Judge, T. (2007) Fairness reactions to personnel selection techniques in Greece: the role of core self-evaluations. *International Journal of Selection and Assessment*, **15**(2): 206–19.

Nixon, D. (2009) 'I can't put a smiley face on': working-class masculinity, emotional labour and service work in the 'new economy'. *Gender, Work and Organization*, **16**(3): 300–22.

Nolan, P. (2011) Money, markets, meltdown: the 21st-century crisis of labour. *Industrial Relations Journal*, **42**(1): 2–17.

Nonaka, I., Toyama, R. and Nagata, A. (2000a) A firm as a knowledge creating entity: a new perspective on the theory of the firm. *Industrial and Corporate Change*, **9**(1): 1–20.

Nonaka, I., Toyama, R. and Konno, N. (2000b) SECI, Ba and leadership: a unified model of dynamic knowledge creation. *Long Range Planning*, **33**: 5–34.

Noon, M., Blyton, P. and Morrell, K. (2013) *The Realities of Work* (4th edn). London: Palgrave Macmillan.

Norlander, P., Erickson, C., Kuruvilla, S. and Kannan-Narasimhan, R. (2015) India's outsourcing industry and the offshoring of skilled services work: a review essay. *E-Journal of International and Comparative Labours Studies*, **4**(1): 1–24.

Norton, T. A., Zacher, H. and Ashkanasy, N. M. (2015) Pro-environmental organizational culture and climate. In J. Robertson and J. Barling (eds) *The Psychology of Green Organizations* (pp. 322–48). Oxford: Oxford University Press.

Nowack, K. M. and Mashihi, S. (2012) Evidence-based answers to 15 questions about leveraging 360-degree feedback. *Consulting Psychology Journal: Practice and Research*, **64**(3): 157.

Oade, A. (2009) *Managing Workplace Bullying*. Basingstoke: Palgrave Macmillan.

Oates, A. (1996) Industrial relations and the environment in the UK. In W. Wehrmeyer (ed.) *Greening People: Human Resources and Environmental Management* (pp. 117–40). Sheffield: Greenleaf.

Obeidat, S. (2016) The link between e-HRM use and HRM effectiveness: an empirical study. *Personnel Review*, **45**(6): 1281–301.

Occupational Health News (2013) Australian has worst bullying rates. February 28. sites.thomsonreuters.com.au/workplace/2013/02/28/australia-has-worst-bullying-rates/ (accessed August 10, 2016).

O'Connor, S. (2015) Minimum wage gamble shocks business lobby. *Financial Times*, November 30, p. 9.

O'Donoghue, J. and Maguire, T. (2005) The individual learner, employability and the workplace. *Journal of European Industrial Training*, 29(6): 436–46.

O'Dowd, J. and Roche, W. K. (2009) Partnership structures and agendas and managers' assessments of stakeholder outcomes. *Industrial Relations Journal*, 40(1): 17–39.

Office for National Statistics (2014) Alcohol related deaths in the United Kingdom: registered in 2014. www.ons.gov.uk/peoplepopulationandcommunity/healthandsocialcare/causesofdeath/bulletins/alcoholrelateddeathsintheunitedkingdom/registeredin2014#summary (accessed August 17, 2016).

Office for National Statistics (2015) Employee contracts that do not guarantee a minimum number of hours: 2015 update. https://www.ons.gov.uk/employmentandlabourmarket/peopleinwork/earningsandworkinghours/articles/contractswithnoguaranteedhours/2015-09-02 (accessed October 2016).

Ogbonna, E. (1993) Managing organizational culture: fantasy or reality. *Human Resource Management Journal*, 3(2): 211–36.

O'Grady, F. (2010) Keynote address to TUC green Growth Conference. October 13. www.tuc.org.uk/social/tuc-18662-f0.cfm (accessed October 15, 2010).

O'Grady, F. (2015) Rising executive pay is a disgrace, says TUC. Bulletin, August 17. London: Trades Union Congress.

Oliveira, O. J. and Pinheiro, C. R. (2009) Best practices of the implantation of ISO 14001 norms: a study of change management in two industrial companies in the Midwest region of the state of Sao Paulo, Brazil. *Journal of Cleaner Production*, 17: 883–5.

Oliver, N. and Wilkinson, B. (1988) *The Japanization of British Industry*. Oxford: Blackwell.

Olivier, R. and Verity, J. (2008) Rehearsing tomorrow's leaders: the potential of mythodrama. *Business Strategy Series*, 9(3): 138–43.

Olsen, J. E. and Martins, L. L. (2012) Understanding organizational diversity management programs: a theoretical framework and directions for future research. *Journal of Organizational Behavior*, 33: 1168–87.

Olsen, J. E., Parsons, C .K., Martins, L. L. and Ivanaj, V. (2016) Gender diversity programs, perceived potential for advancement and organizational attractiveness: an empirical examination of women in the United States and France. *Group and Organization Management*, 41(3): 271–309.

Oltermann, P. (2016) Berlin is beckoning to Britain's startups. But will they leave? *The Observer*, July 10, p. 42.

O'Moore M., Seigne E., McGuire, L. and Smith M. (1998) Victims of workplace bullying in Ireland. *Irish Journal of Psychology*, 19(2–3): 345–57.

Ones, D. S. and Dilchert, S. (2012) Environmental sustainability at work: a call to action. *Industrial and Organizational Psychology*, 5: 444–66.

Op de Beeck, S., Wynen, J. and Hondeghem, A. (2015) HRM implementation by line managers: explaining the discrepancy in HR-line perceptions of HR devolution. *International Journal of Human Resource Management*, 27(17): 1–19.

O'Reilly, C., Caldwell, D. F., Chatman, J. A., Lapiz, M. and Self, W. (2010) How leadership matters: the effects of leaders' alignment on strategy implementation. *Leadership Quarterly*, 21(1): 104–13.

Organ, D. (1990) The motivational basis of organizational citizenship behavior. In L. Cummings and B. Staw (eds) *Research in Organizational Behavior*, Volume 12 (pp. 43–72). Greenwich, CT: JAI Press.

Organisation for Economic Co-operation and Development (1996) *The Knowledge-based Economy*. Paris: OECD.

Organisation for Economic Co-operation and Development (2015) *In It Together: Why Less Inequality Benefits All*. Paris: OECD Publishing

O'Riordan, T. (1985) Research policy and review 6. Future directions for environmental policy. *Environment and Planning A*, 17(11): 1431–46.

Örtenblad, A. (2004) The learning organization: towards an integrated model. *Learning Organization*, 11(2): 129–44.

Osterman, P. (2000) Work reorganization in an era of restructuring: trends in diffusion and effects on employee welfare. *Industrial and Labor Relations Review*, 53(2): 179–96.

Ouchi, W. (1979) A conceptual framework for the design of organizational control mechanisms. *Management Science*, 25(9): 833–48.

Ouchi, W. G. (1980) Markets, bureaucracies, and clans. *Administrative Science Quarterly*, 25(1): 129–41.

Ouchi, W. (1981) *Theory Z: How American Companies Can Meet the Japanese Challenge*. Reading, MA: Addison-Wesley.

Owen, H. (2008) *Open Space Technology: A User's Guide* (3rd edn). San Francisco, CA: Berrett-Koehler.

Ozturk, M. B. and Tatli, A. (2015) Gender identity inclusion in the workplace: broadening diversity management research and practice through the case of transgender employees in the UK. *International Journal of Human Resource Management*, doi.org/10.1080/09585192.2015.1042902

Paauwe, J. (2004) *HRM and Performance: Achieving Long-term Viability*. New York: Oxford University Press.

Paauwe, J. and Boselie, P. (2003) Challenging 'strategic HRM' and the relevance of the institutional setting. *Human Resource Management Journal*, **13**(3): 56–70.

Paauwe, J. and Boselie, P. (2008) HRM and social embeddedness. In P. Boxall, J. Purcell and P. Wright (eds) *The Oxford Handbook of Human Resource Management* (pp. 166–84). Oxford: Oxford University Press.

Paeleman, I. and Vanacker, T. (2015) Less is more, or not? On the interplay between bundles of slack resources, firm performance and firm survival. *Journal of Management Studies*, **52**: 819–48.

Paik, Y., Vance, C. and Stage, H. (1996) The extent of divergence in human resource practice across three Chinese national cultures: Hong Kong, Taiwan and Singapore. *Human Resource Management Journal*, **6**(2): 20–31.

Paisley, V. and Yayar, M. (2016) Lesbian, gay, bisexual and transgender (LGBT) expatriates: an intersectionality perspective. *International Journal of Human Resource Management*, **27**(7): 766–80.

Panagiotopoulos, P. and Barnett, J. (2015) Social media in union communications: an international study with UNI global union affiliates, *British Journal of Industrial Relations*, **53**(3): 508–32.

Parker, B. and Caine, D. (1996) Holonic modelling: human resource planning and the two faces of Janus. *International Journal of Manpower*, **17**(8): 30–45.

Parker, G., MacKenzie, M. and Hall, B. (2016) Britain Breaks with Europe. *Financial Times Weekend*, June 25, p. 1.

Parker, J., Mars, L., Ransome, P. and Stanworth, H. (2003) *Social Theory: A Basic Tool Kit*. Basingstoke: Palgrave Macmillan.

Parker, J., Stanworth, H., Mars, L. and Ransome, P. (2015) *Explaining Social Life: A Guide To Using Social Theory*. Basingstoke: Palgrave Macmillan.

Parker, M. (2000) *Organizational Culture and Identity*. London: Sage.

Parker, O. and Wright, L. (2001) The missing link: Pay and employee commitment. *Ivey Business Journal*, **65**(3), 70–79.

Parker, P., Hall, D. T. and Kram, K. E. (2008) Peer coaching: a relational process for accelerating career learning. *Academy of Management Learning and Education*, 7(4): 487–503.

Parry, E. (2011) An examination of the e-HRM as a means to increase the value of the HR function. *International Journal of Human Resource Management*, **22**(5): 1146–62.

Parry, E. and Tyson, S. (2008) An analysis of the use and success of online recruitment methods in the UK. *Human Resource Management Journal*, **18**(3): 257–74.

Parry, E. and Wilson, H. (2009) Factors influencing the adoption of online recruitment. *Personnel Review*, **38**(6): 655–73.

Parsons, D. (2010) Medical-workforce planning: an art or science? *Human Resource Management International Digest*, **18**(5): 36–8.

Parsons, T. (1951) *The Social System*. Glencoe, IL: Free Press.

Parzefall, M.-R. and Salin, D. (2010) Perceptions of and reactions to workplace bullying: a social exchange perspective. *Human Relations*, **63**(6): 761–80.

Patel, R. (2009) *The Value of Nothing*. Toronto, Ontario: HarperCollins.

Paton, R., Peters, G., Storey, J. and Taylor, S. (2007) *Handbook of Corporate University Development: Managing Strategic Learning Initiatives in Public and Private Domains*. Aldershot: Gower.

Patterson, M. G., West, M. A., Lawthon, R. and Nickell, S. (1997) *Impact of People Management Practices on Business Performance*. London: Institute of Personnel and Development.

Patterson, M., Rick, J., Wood, S., Carroll, C., Balain, S. and Booth, A. (2007) Review of the validity and reliability of measures of human resource management. Sheffield: Institute of Work Psychology.

Pattisson, P. (2013) Revealed: Qatar's World Cup 'slaves'. September 25. www.theguardian.com/world/2013/sep/25/revealed-qatars-world-cup-slaves (accessed August 27, 2016).

Pattisson P. (2016) UK building firms accused of labour abuses in Qatar. The Guardian, April 14, p. 14.

Patton, K. R. and Daley, D. M. (1998) Gainsharing in Zebulon: what do workers want? *Public Personnel Management*, **27**, 117–311.

Payne, J., McDonald, S. and Hamm, L. (2013) Production teams and producing racial diversity in workplace relationships. *Sociological Forum*, **28**(2): 326–50.

Payne, S. C., Horner, M. T., Boswell, W. R., Schroeder, A. N. and Stine-Cheyne, K. J. (2009) Comparison of online and traditional performance appraisal systems. *Journal of Managerial Psychology*, **24**(6): 526–44.

Peck Kem, L. (2015) The HR leadership diet: trimming the fat and building up muscle for a sustainable future-ready workforce. In D. Ulrich, W. Schiemann and L., Sartain (eds) *The Rise of HR: Wisdom from 73 Thought Leaders*. Alexandria, VA: HR Certification Institute.

Pedler, M. (2008) *Action Learning for Managers*. Aldershot: Gower.

Pedler, M., Boydell, T. and Burgoyne, J. (1988) *The Learning Company Project Report*. Sheffield: Manpower Services Commission.

Pedler, M., Burgoyne, J. and Boydell, T. (1991) *The Learning Company: A Strategy for Sustainable Development*. Maidenhead: McGraw-Hill.

Pedler, M., Burgoyne, J. and Boydell, T. (2013) *A Manager's Guide To Self-Development* (6th edn). London: McGraw-Hill

Peiperl, M. A. (2001) Best practice: Getting 360-degree feedback right. *Harvard Business Review*, January: 142–7.

Pelletier, K. L. (2010) Leader toxicity: an empirical investigation of toxic behavior and rhetoric. *Leadership*, **6**(4): 373–89.

Peltonen, T. (2006) Critical theoretical perspectives on international human resource management. In G. K. Stahl and I. Bjorkman (eds) *Handbook of Research in International Human Resource Management*, (pp. 523–35). Cheltenham: Edward Elgar.

Peña, I. and Villasalero, M. (2010) Business strategy, human resource systems, and organizational performance in the Spanish banking industry. *International Journal of Human Resource Management*, **21**(15): 2864–88.

Pendleton, A. (1997) What impact has privatization had on pay and employment? *Relations Industrielles/ Industrial Relations*, **52**(3): 554–82.

Pennell, K. (2010) The role of flexible job descriptions in succession management. *Library Management*, **31**(4/5): 279–90.

Pennycook, M., Cory, G. and Alakeson, V. (2013) *A Matter of Time: The Rise of Zero-hours Contracts*. London: Resolution Foundation.

Penrose, E. T. (1959) *The Theory of the Growth of the Firm*. Oxford: Blackwell.

Peritz, I. and Friesen, J. (2010) Multiculturalism's magic number. *Globe and Mail*, October 2, pp. A14–15.

Perkins, S. and White, G. (2009) Modernising pay in the UK public services: trends and implications. *Human Resource Management Journal*, **20**(3): 244–57.

Perraudin, F. (2016) UN urges Tory rethink on trade union bill. The Guardian, February 15, p. 6.

Perren, L. and Burgoyne, J. (2002) *Management and Leadership Abilities: An Analysis of Texts, Testimony and Practice*. Report from the SME working group. London: Council for Excellence in Management and Leadership.

Perron, G. M., Raymond, P. C. and Duffy, J. F. (2006) Improving environmental awareness training in business. *Journal of Cleaner Production*, **14**: 551–62.

Peters, P., Poutsma, E., Van Der Heijden, I. J. M ., Bakker, A. B. and De Bruijn, T. (2014) Enjoying new ways to work: an HRM-process approach to study flow. *Human Resource Management*, **53**(2): 271–90.

Peters, T. and Waterman, R. (1982) *In Search of Excellence*. New York: Harper & Row.

Peterson, C. (2015) Ethics: the price of admission in high-performing organizations. In D. Ulrich, W. Schiemann and L. Sartain (eds) *The Rise of HR: Wisdom from 73 Thought Leaders*. Alexandria, VA: HR Certification Institute.

Pettijohn, L. S., Parker, S., Pettijohn, C. E. and Kent, J. L. (2001) Performance appraisals: usage, criteria and observations. *Journal of Management Development*, **20**(9): 754–71.

Pfeffer, J. (1994) *Competitive Advantage Through People: Understanding the Power of the Workforce*. Boston, MA: Houghton Mifflin.

Pfeffer, J. (1998) *The Human Equation*. Boston, MA: Harvard Business School Press.

Pfeffer, J. (2005) Changing mental models: HR's most important task. *Human Resource Management*, **44**(2): 123–8.

Philips, L. (2007) Go green now to combat climate change. *People Management*, August 23.

Phillips, J. J. (1996a) *Accountability in Human Resource Management*. Houston, TX: Gulf Publishing.

Phillips, J. (1996b) Measuring the ROI: the fifth level of evaluation. *Technical and Skills Training*, April: 10–13.

Phillips, J. (2005) Measuring up. *People Management*, April 7: 42–3.

Phillips, J. M. (1998) Effects of realistic job previews on multiple organizational outcomes: a meta-analysis. *Academy of Management Journal*, **41**(6): 673–90.

Phillips, J. M., Gully, S. M., McCarthy, J. E., Castellano, W. G. and Kim, M. S. (2014) Recruiting global travelers: the role of global travel recruitment messages and individual differences in perceived fit, attraction, and job pursuit intentions. *Personal Psychology*, **67**(1): 153–201.

Phillips, P. and Phillips, E. (1993) *Women and Work: Inequality in the Canadian Labour Market*. Toronto, Ontario: Lorimer.

Phillips, R. (1995) Coaching for higher performance. *Executive Development*, **8**(7): 5–7.

Pichler, S. (2012) The social context of performance appraisal and appraisal reactions: a meta-analysis. *Human Resource Management*, **51**(5): 709–32.

Pickard, J. (1997) Vocational qualifications. *People Management*, July 10: 26–31.

Pickard, J. (2001) When push comes to shove. *People Management*, **7**(23): 30–5.

Pierce, J. L., Jussila, I. and Cummings, A. (2009) Psychological ownership within the job design context: revision of the job characteristics model. *Journal of Organizational Behavior*, **30**(4): 477–96.

Piketty, T. (2014) *Capital in the Twenty-First Century*, Cambridge, MA: Belknap Press.

Pil, F. K. and Macduffie, J. P. (1996) The adoption of high-involvement work practices. *Industrial Relations: A Journal of Economy and Society*, **35**(3): 423–55.

Pilch, T. (2000) *Dynamic Reporting for a Dynamic Economy*. London: Academy of Enterprise.

Pilch, T. (2006) *Diversity and Economy*. London: Smith Institute.

Piore, M. and Sabel, C. (1984) *The Second Industrial Divide*. New York: Basic Books.

Piotrowski, C. and Armstrong, T. (2006) Current recruitment and selection practices: a national survey of Fortune 1000 firms. *North American Journal of Psychology*, December: 488–93.

Pitcher, G. (2008) Backlash against human resource management partner model as managers question results. *Personnel Today*, September 17.

Pitts, G. (2005) CEO's harmonious-society plan? Fire 14,000 staff. *Globe and Mail*, July 6, p. A1.

Plachy, R. J. (1987) Writing job descriptions that get results. *Personnel*, October: 56–63.

Platt, L. (1997) Employee work–life balance: the competitive advantage. In F. Hesselbein, M. Goldsmith and R. Beckhard (eds) *The Drucker Foundation, the Organization of the Future* (Chapter 32). San Francisco, CA: Jossey-Bass.

Plimmer, G. (2015a) Public outsourcing jumps under coalition. *Financial Times*, April 30.

Plimmer, G. (2015b) Workplaces divided by a common language. *Financial Times*, July 9, p. S1.

Poell, R. (2013) Workplace learning theories and practices. In C. Valentin and J. Walton (eds) *Human Resource Development: Practices and Orthodoxies* (pp. 19–32). Basingstoke: Palgrave Macmillan.

Poell, R. F. and Rocco, T. S. and Roth, G. L. (eds) (2015) *The Routledge Companion to Human Resource Development* (pp. 531–41). London: Routledge.

Pohler, D. and Luchak, A. (2015) Are unions good or bad for organizations? The moderating role of management's response. *British Journal of Industrial Relations*, **53**(3): 423–59.

Polanyi, M. (1967) *The Tacit Dimension*. Garden City, NY: Doubleday.

Pollard, E. and Hillage, J. (2001) *Exploring e-Learning*. Report No. 376. Brighton: Institute for Employment Studies.

Pollert, A. (1988) Dismantling flexibility. *Capital and Class*, (34): 42–75.

Pollert, A. (1991) *Farewell to Flexibility?* Oxford: Blackwell.

Pollitt, C. (2000) Is the emperor in his new underwear?: an analysis of the impacts of public management reform. *Public Management*, **2**(2): 181–99.

Pollitt, D. (2005) E-recruitment gets the Nike tick of approval. *Human Resource Management International Digest*, **13**(2): 33–5.

Pollitt, D. (2007) Software solves problem of global succession planning at Friesland Foods. *Human Resource Management International Digest*, **15**(6): 21–23.

Pollitt, D. (2008) Online recruitment connects 3 with top talent. *Human Resource Management International Digest*, **16**(4): 25–6.

Poon, J. (2004) Effects of performance appraisal politics on job satisfaction and turnover intention. *Personnel Review*, **33**(3): 322–34.

Porter, M. (1980) *Competitive Strategy*. New York: Free Press.

Porter, M. (1985) *Competitive Advantage: Creating and Sustaining Superior Performance*. New York: Free Press.

Porter, M. E. (1990) The competitive advantage of nations. *Harvard Business Review* **68**(2): 73–93.

Porter, M. E. (2004) *Competitive Strategy: Techniques for Analyzing Industries and Competitors*. New York: Free Press.

Porter, M. E. and Kramer, M. R. (2006) Strategy and society: the link between competitive advantage and corporate social responsibility. *Harvard Business Review*, December: 78–93.

Porter, M. E. and Kramer, M. R. (2011) The big idea: creating shared value. *Harvard Business Review*, **89**(1): 2.

Posthuma, R., Morgeson, F. and Campion, M. (2002) Beyond employment interview validity: a comprehensive narrative review of recent research and trends over time. *Personnel Psychology*, **55**: 1–82.

Potočnik, K. and Anderson, N. (2012) Assessing innovation: a 360-degree appraisal study. *International Journal of Selection and Assessment*, **20**(4): 497–509.

Potosky, D. and Bobko, P. (2004) Selection testing via the internet: practical considerations and exploratory empirical findings. *Personnel Psychology*, **57**: 1003–34.

Powell, J. H. and Wakeley, T. (2003) Evolutionary concepts and business economics: towards a normative approach. *Journal of Business Research*, **56**: 153–61.

Powell, M., Duberley, J., Exworthy, M., Macfarlane, F. and Moss, P. (2013) Has the British National Health Service (NHS) got talent? A process evaluation of the NHS talent management strategy? *Policy Studies*, **34**(3): 291–309.

Power, S., Brown, P., Allouch, A. and Tholen, G. (2013) Self, career and nationhood: the contrasting aspirations of British and French elite graduates. *British Journal of Sociology*, **64**(4): 578–59.

Prahalad, C. K. and Doz, Y. L. (1987) *The Multinational Mission: Balancing Local Demands and Global Vision*. New York: Free Press.

Premack, S. L. and Wanous, J. P. (1985) A meta-analysis of realistic job preview experiments. *Journal of Applied Psychology*, **70**(4): 706–19.

Preskill, H. (2008) Evaluation's second act: a spotlight on learning. *American Journal of Evaluation*, **29**(2): 127–38.

Press Association (2015) Strike closes entire London Underground, The Guardian, August 6, p. 9.

Proença, M. T. and de Oliveira, E. T. (2009) From normative to tacit knowledge: CVs analysis in personnel selection. *Employee Relations*, **31**(4): 427–47.

Prokopenko, J. (1994) The transition to a market economy and its implications for HRM in Eastern Europe. In P. S. Kirkbride (ed.) *Human Resource Management in Europe* (pp. 147–63). London: Routledge.

Prowse, P. and Prowse, J. (2010) Whatever happened to human resource management performance? *International Journal of Productivity and Performance Management*, **59**(2): 145–62.

Pulakos, E. D. and Schmitt, N. (1995) Experienced-based and situational questions: studies of validity. *Personnel Psychology*, **48**: 289–309.

Pulakos, E. D., Hanson, R. M., Arad, S. and Moye, N. (2015) Performance management can be fixed: an on-the-job experiential learning approach for complex behavior change. *Industrial and Organizational Psychology*, **8**(1): 51–76.

Pulignano, V. and Stewart, P. (2006) Bureaucracy transcended? New patterns of employment regulation and labour control in the international automotive industry. *New Technology, Work and Employment*, **21**(2): 90–106.

Pulignano, V., Meardi, G. and Doerflinger, N. (2015) Trade unions and labour market dualisation: a comparison of policies and attitudes towards agency and migrant workers in Germany and Belgium. *Work, Employment and Society*, **29**(5): 808–25.

Pun, K. F. and White, A. S. (2005) A performance measurement paradigm for integrating strategy formulation: a review of systems and frameworks. *International Journal of Management Reviews*, **7**(1): 49–71.

Punnett, B., Crocker, O. and Stevens, M. (1992) The challenge for women expatriates and spouses: some empirical evidence. *International Journal of Human Resource Management*, **3**(3): 585–92.

Purcell, J. (1989) The impact of corporate strategy on human resource management. In J. Storey (ed.) *New Perspectives on Human Resource Management* (pp. 67–91). London: Routledge.

Purcell, J. (1995) Corporate strategy and its link with human resource management strategy. In J. Storey (ed.) *Human Resource Management: A Critical Text* (pp. 63–86). London: Routledge.

Purcell, J. (1999) Best practice and best fit: chimera or cul-de-sac? *Human Resource Management Journal*, **9**(3): 26–41.

Purcell, J. (2001) The meaning of strategy in human resource management: a critical text. In J. Storey (ed.) *Human Resource Management* (pp. 59–77). London: Thomson Learning.

Purcell, J. and Ahlstrand, B. (1994) *Human Resource Management in the Multi-divisional Company*. Oxford: Oxford University Press.

Purcell, J. and Hutchinson, S. (2007) Front-line managers as agents in the HRM-performance causal chain: theory, analysis and evidence. *Human Resource Management Journal*, **17**(1): 3–20.

Purcell, J. and Kinnie, N. (2008) HRM and business performance. In P. Boxall, J. Purcell and P. Wright (eds) *The Oxford Handbook of Human Resource Management* (pp. 533–51). Oxford: Oxford University Press.

Purcell, J. and Sisson, K. (1983) Strategies and practices in the management of industrial relations. In G. Bain (ed.) *Industrial Relations in Britain* (pp. 95–120). Oxford: Blackwell.

Purcell, J., Kinnie, N., Hutchinson, S., Rayton, B. and Swart, J. (2003) *Understanding the People and Performance Link: Unlocking the Black Box*. London: Chartered Institute of Personnel and Development.

Purcell, J., Kinnie, N., Swart, J., Rayton, B. and Hutchinson, S. (2009) *People Management and Performance*. London: Routledge.

Pye, M., Cullinane, J. and Harcourt, M. (2001) The right to refuse unsafe work in New Zealand. *New Zealand Journal of Industrial Relations*, **26**(2): 199–216.

Pyman, A., Holland, P., Teicher, J. and Cooper, B. (2010) Industrial relations climate, employee voice and managerial attitudes to unions: an Australian study. *British Journal of Industrial Relations*, **48**(2): 460–80.

Qin, X., Ren, R., Zhang, Z. X. and Johnson, R. E. (2015) Fairness heuristics and substitutability effects: inferring the fairness of outcomes, procedures, and interpersonal treatment when employees lack clear information. *Journal of Applied Psychology*, **100**(3): 749.

Quinn, B. (2011) UK's largest greenhouse complex investigated for 'sweatshop labour.' April 29. https://www.theguardian.com/environment/2011/apr/29/greenhouse-thanet-earth-workers.

Raelin, J. (2011) Work-based learning: how it changes leadership. *Development and Learning in Organizations*, **25**(5): 17–20.

Raja, J. Z., Green, S. D., Leiringer, R., Dainty, A. and Johnstone, S. (2013) Managing multiple forms of employment in the construction sector: implications for HRM. *Human Resource Management Journal*, **23**(3): 313–28.

Rajouria, S. (2015) World Cup corruption: the bigger scandal. July 6. *American Prospect*. prospect.org/article/world-cup-corruption-bigger-scandal (accessed July 15, 2016).

Ram, M. (2013) Critical action learning: extending its reach. *Action Learning: Research and Practice*, **9**(3): 219–24.

Ram, M., Edwards, P., Gilman, M. and Arrowsmith, J. (2001) The dynamics of informality: employment relations in small firms and the effects of regulatory change. *Work, Employment & Society*, **15**(4), 845–61.

Ramsay, H., Scholarios, D. and Harley, B. (2000) Employees and high-performance work systems: testing inside the black box. *British Journal of Industrial Relations*, **38**(4): 501–31.

Ramsay, S., Troth, A. and Branch, S. (2011) Work-place bullying: a group processes framework. *Journal of Occupational and Organizational Psychology*, **84**: 799–816.

Ramus, C. A. (2001) Organizational support for employees: encouraging creative ideas for environmental sustainability. *California Management Review*, **44**: 85–105.

Ramus, C. A. (2002) Encouraging innovative environmental actions: what companies and managers must do. *Journal of World Business*, **37**: 151–64.

Ramus, C. A. and Steger, U. (2000) The role of supervisory support behaviours and environmental policy in employee 'eco-initiatives' at leading-edge European companies. *Academy of Management Journal*, **43**: 605–26.

Randell, G. (1994) Employee appraisal. In K. Sisson (ed.) *Personnel Management* (pp. 221–52). Oxford: Blackwell.

Rangel, B., Chung, W., Harris, T. B., Carpenter, N. C., Chiaburu, D.S and Moore, J. L. (2015) Rules of engagement: the joint influence of trainer expressiveness and trainee experiential learning style on engagement and training transfer. *International Journal of Training and Development*, **19**(1): 18–31.

Rankin, J. (2015) Fewer women leading FTSE firms than men called John. The Guardian, March 6. https://www.theguardian.com/business/2015/mar/06/johns-davids-and-ians-outnumber-female-chief-executives-in-ftse-100 (accessed August 14, 2016).

Rao, A. S. (2007) Effectiveness of performance management systems: an empirical study in Indian companies. *International Journal of Human Resource Management*, **18**(10): 1812–40.

Rarick, C. A. and Baxter, G. (1986) Behaviourally anchored rating scales (bars): an effective performance appraisal approach. *SAM Advanced Management Journal*, Winter: 36–9.

Rashidi, R. (2015) A review of performance management system. *International Journal of Academic Research*, **7**(1): 210–14.

Ravenscroft, A., Schmidt, A., Cook, J. and Bradley, C. (2012) Designing social media for informal learning and knowledge maturing in the digital workplace. *Journal of Computer Assisted Learning*, **28**(3): 235–49.

Rawls, J. (1971) *A Theory of Justice*. Cambridge, MA: Harvard University Press.

Ray, C. A. (1986) Corporate culture: the last frontier of control? *Journal of Management Studies*, **23**(3): 287–97.

Razzaque, J. and Richardson, B. (2006) Public participation in environmental decision making. In B. Richardson and S. Wood (eds) *Environmental Law for Sustainability* (pp. 165–94). Oxford: Hart.

Ready, D. and Conger, J. (2007) Make your company a talent factory. *Harvard Business Review*, **85**(6): 68–77.

Rebelo, T. M. and Gomes, A. (2011) Conditioning factors of an organizational learning culture. *Journal of Workplace Learning*, **23**(3): 173–94.

Redman, T. (2001) Performance appraisal. In T. Redman, and A. Wilkinson (eds) *Contemporary Human Resource Management* (pp. 57–95). Harlow: Pearson Education.

Redman, T., Snape, E., Thompson, D. and Ka-Ching Yan, F. (2000) Performance appraisal in an NHS hospital. *Human Resource Management Journal*, **10**(1): 48–62.

Redman, T., Hamilton, P., Mallock, H. and Kleymann, B. (2011) Working here makes me sick! The consequences of sick building syndrome. *Human Resource Management Journal*, **21**(1): 14–27.

Reed, J. (2007) *Appreciative Enquiry*. London: Sage.

Rees, T. (1998) *Mainstreaming Equality in the European Union: Education, Training and Labour Market Policies*. London: Routledge.

Rees, W. E. (1995) More jobs, less damage: a framework for sustainability, growth and employment. *Alternatives*, **21**(4): 24–30.

Reilly, B., Paci, P. and Holl, P. (1995) Unions, safety committees and workplace injuries. *British Journal of Industrial Relations*, **33**(2): 275–87.

Reilly, P. (2005) Get the best from knowledge workers. *People Management*, **29**(September): 52–3.

Remler, D. K. and Van Ryzin, G. G. (2011) *Research Methods in Practice: Strategies for Description and Causation*. Los Angeles, CA: Sage.

Renwick, D., Redman, T. and Maguire, S. (2008) *Green HRM: A Review, Process Model, and Research Agenda*. Discussion Paper Series No. 2008. Sheffield: University of Sheffield Management School.

Renwick, D., Redman, T. and Maguire, S. (2013) Green human resource management: a review and research agenda. *International Journal of Management Reviews*, **15**: 1–14.

Renwick, D. W. S., Jabbour, C., Muller-Camen, M, Redman, T. and Wilkinson, A. (2016) Contemporary developments in green (environmental) HRM scholarship. *International Journal of Human Resource Management*, **27**(2): 114–28.

Revans, R. (1982) *The Origins and Growth of Action Learning*. Bromley: Chartwell-Bratt.

Reynolds, M. (1997) Learning styles: a critique. *Management Learning*, **28**(2): 115–33.

Reynolds, M. (2009) Wild frontiers – reflections on experiential learning. *Management Learning*, **40**(4): 387–92.

Reynolds, M. and Vince, R. (2007) Introduction. In M. Reynolds and R. Vince (eds) *Handbook of Experiential Learning and Management Education* (pp.1–18). Oxford: Oxford University Press.

Riach, P. A. and Rich, J. (2002) Field experiments of discrimination in the market place. *Economic Journal*, **112**(483): 480–518.

Richardson, J., McBey, K. and McKenna, S. (2008) Integrating realistic job previews and realistic living conditions previews. *Personnel Review*, **37**(5): 490–508.

Rick, J. and Briner, R. (2000) Psychosocial risk assessment: problems and prospects. *Occupational Medicine*, **50**: 310–14.

Rigg, C., Stewart, J. and Trehan, K. (2007) *Critical Human Resource Development: Beyond Orthodoxy*. Harlow, FT/Prentice Hall.

Risher, H. (1978) Job evaluation: mystical or statistical. *Personnel*, **55**: 23–36.

Ritzer, G. (2000) *The McDonaldization of Society* (New Century edn). Thousand Oaks, CA: Pine Forge Press.

Ritzer, G. (2004) *The McDonaldization of Society* (Revised New Century edn). Thousand Oaks, CA: Pine Forge Press.

Robbins, P. (2004) *Political Ecology*. Oxford: Blackwell.

Roberts, G. (1997) *Recruitment and Selection*. London: Institute of Personnel and Development.

Roberts, J. (2006) Limits to communities of practice. *Journal of Management Studies*, **43**(3): 623–39.

Roberts, Z. (2001) HR can lower NHS death rates. *People Management*, **70**(20): 8.

Robertson, I. T., Baron, H., Gibbons, P., MacIver, R. and Nyfield, G. (2000) Conscientiousness and managerial performance. *Journal of Occupational and Organizational Psychology*, **73**(2): 171–81.

Robertson, J. L. and Barling, J. (2015a) The role of leadership in promoting workplace pro-environmental behaviors. In J. L. Robertson and J. Barling (eds) *The Psychology of Green Organizations* (pp. 164–86): New York: Oxford University Press.

Robertson J. L. and J. Barling (eds) (2015b) *The Psychology of Green Organizations* (pp. 164–86). New York: Oxford University Press.

Robinson, S. (2010) Leadership ethics. In J. Gold, R. Thorpe and A. Mumford (eds) *Handbook of Leadership and Management Development* (pp. 175–96). Aldershot: Gower.

Roche, W. K. (2009) Who gains from workplace partnership? *International Journal of Human Resource Management*, **20**(1): 1–33.

Rod, M. and Ashill, N. J. (2013) The impact of call centre stressors on inbound and outbound call-centre agent burnout. *Managing Service Quality*, **23**(3): 245–64.

Rodger, A. (1970) *The Seven Point Plan* (3rd edn). London: National Foundation for Educational Research.

Rodgers, H., Gold, J., Frearson, M., Holden, R. (2003a) The rush to leadership: explaining leadership development in the public sector. Paper presented at the Leadership Conference, Lancaster, UK.

Rodgers, H., Gold, J. Frearson, M., and Holden, R. (2003b) *International Comparator Contexts: The Leading Learning Project*. London: Learning and Skill Research Centre.

Rodrik, D. (2011) *The Globalization Paradox*. New York: Norton.

Rogaly, B. (2008) Intensification of workplace regimes in British horticulture: the role of migrant workers. *Population, Space and Place*, **14**: 497–510.

Rohrbach, D. (2007) The development of knowledge societies in 19 OECD countries between 1970 and 2002. *Social Science Information*, **46**(4): 655–89.

Rollinson, D., Hook, C., Foot, M. and Handley, J. (1996) Supervisor and manager styles in handling discipline and grievance, Part 2: Approaches to handling discipline and grievance. *Personnel Review*, **25**(4): 38–55.

Rose, M. (2000) Target practice. *People Management*, **6**(23): 44–5.

Ross, I. and MacDonald, G. (1997) Scars from stress cut deep in workplace. *Globe and Mail*, October 9, p. B16.

Ross, L., Rix, M. and Gold, J. (2005) Learning distributed leadership, Part 1. *Industrial and Commercial Training*, **37**(3): 130–7.

Rothwell, W. J. (2011) Replacement planning: a starting point for succession planning and talent management. *International Journal of Training and Development*, **15**(1): 87–99.

Rounce, K., Scarfe, A. and Garnett, J. (2007) A work-based learning approach to developing leadership for senior health and social care professionals. *Education and Training*, **49**(3): 218–26.

Rousseau, D. M. (1995) *Psychological Contracts in Organizations: Understanding Written and Unwritten Agreements*. Thousand Oaks, CA: Sage.

Rousseau, D. M. and Ho, V. T. (2000) Psychological contract issues in compensation. In S. L. Rynes and B. Gerhart (eds) *Compensation in Organizations: Current Research and Practice* (pp. 273–310). San Francisco, CA: Jossey-Bass.

Rowley, C. and Bae, J. (2002) Globalization and transformation of human resource management in South Korea. *International Journal of Human Resource Management*, **13**(3): 522–49.

Rubery, J. (2006) Labour markets and flexibility. In S. Ackroyd, R. Batt, P. Thompson and P. Tolbert (eds) *The Oxford Handbook of Work and Organization* (pp. 31–51). Oxford: Oxford University Press.

Ruddick, G. (2016) Rich pickings: Forbes reveal fall of £50bn in wealth of world's top 20. The Guardian, March 2, p. 3.

Rupp, D. E., Shao, R., Thornton, M. A. and Skarlicki, D. P. (2013) Applicants' and employees' reactions to corporate social responsibility: the moderating effects of first-party justice perceptions and moral identity. *Personnel Psychology*, **66**: 895–933.

Russ-Eft, D. and Preskill, H. (2005) In search of the holy grail: return on investment evaluation in human resource development. *Advances in Developing Human Resources*, **7**(1): 71–85.

Russell, B. (2008) Call centres: a decade of research. *International Journal of Management Reviews*, **10**(3): 195–219.

Russell, S. V. and McIntosh, M. (2011) Changing organizational culture for sustainability. In *The Handbook of Organizational Culture and Climate* (pp. 393–411). London: Sage.

Russo, M. V. and Fouts. P. A. (1997) A resource-based perspective on corporate environmental performance and profitability. *Academy of Management Journal*, **40**(3): 534–59.

Ryan, A. M and Ployhart, R. E. (2014) A century of selection. *Annual Review of Psychology*, **65**: 693–717.

Ryan, A. M. and Wessel, J. L. (2015) Implications of a changing workforce and workplace for justice perceptions and expectations. *Human Resource Management Review*, **25**(2): 162–75.

Ryan, J. C. and Tipu, S. A. (2009) An instrument for the self-appraisal of scientific research performance. *International Journal of Productivity and Performance Management*, **58**(7): 632–44.

Sadler-Smith, E. (2006) *Learning and Development for Managers*. Oxford: Blackwell.

Saffie-Robertson, M. C. and Brutus, S. (2014) The impact of interdependence on performance evaluations: the mediating role of discomfort with performance appraisal. *International Journal of Human Resource Management*, **25**(3): 459–73.

Said, E. (1993): *Culture and Imperialism*. New York: Alfred A. Knopf.

Saint-Onge, H. and Wallace, D. (2012) *Leveraging Communities of Practice for Strategic Advantage*. Burlington, MA: Elsevier.

Sako, K. and Tierney, A. (2005) *Sustainability of Business Service Outsourcing: The Case of Human Resource Outsourcing (HRO)*. AIM Working Paper. London: Advanced Institute of Management.

Saks, A. M. (2000) *Research, Measurement, and Evaluation of Human Sources*. Scarborough, Ontario: Nelson/Thompson Learning.

Salerno, S., Nunziante, A. and Santoro, G. (2015) Competences and knowledge: key-factors in the smart city of the future. *Knowledge Management and E-Learning*, **6**(4): 356–76.

Salgado, J. F. (1997) The five factor model of personality and job performance in the European Community. *Journal of Applied Psychology*, **82**(1): 30–43.

Salvatori, A. (2015) The effects of the EU equal-treatment directive for fixed-term workers: evidence from the UK. *British Journal of Industrial Relations*, **53**(2): 278–307.

Sambrook, S. and Stewart, J. (2005) A critical review of researching human resource development: the case of a pan-European project. In C. Elliott and S. Turnbull (eds) *Critical Thinking in Human Resource Development* (pp. 67–84). London: Routledge.

Sambunjak, D., Straus, S. and Marusić, A. (2006) Mentoring in academic medicine. *Journal of the American Medical Association*, **296**(9): 1103–15.

Sammalisto, K. and Brorson, T. (2008) Training and communication in the implementation of environmental management system (ISO 14001): a case study at the University of Gavle, Sweden. *Journal of Cleaner Production*, **16**: 299–309.

Samuel, P. and Bacon, N. (2010) The contents of partnership agreements in Britain 1990–2007. *Work, Employment and Society*, **24**(3): 430–48.

Sánchez, M. P., Elena, S. and Castrillo, R. (2009) Intellectual capital dynamics in universities: a reporting model. *Journal of Intellectual Capital*, **10**(2): 307–24.

Sanders, K. and Frenkel, S. (2011) HR-line management relations: characteristics and effects. *Journal of Human Resource Management*, **22**(8): 1611–17.

Sanyo Electric Co., Ltd., Annual Report 2006, http://panasonic.net/sanyo/corporate/ir_library/pdf/annualreports/ar-2006-e.pdf (accessed December 2016).

Sanyo Electric Co., Ltd., Sustainability Report 2006, https://www.panasonic.com/global/corporate/sustainability/pdf/kan2006_e.pdf (accessed December 2016).

Sass, R. (1982) Safety and self-respect. *Policy Options*, July–August: 17–21.

Saul, J. R. (2005) *The Collapse of Globalism*. Toronto, Ontario: Viking.

Saul, J. R. (2008) *A Fair Country*. Toronto, Ontario: Viking.

Saunders, D. (2010) Just watch us. *Globe and Mail*, December 18, p. F4.

Saunders, J. and Hunter, I. (2007) *Human Resource Outsourcing: Solutions, Suppliers, Key Processes and the Current Market*. London: Orion Partners.

Saunders, P., Huynh, A. and Goodman-Delahunty, J. (2007) Defining workplace bullying behaviour professional lay definitions of workplace bullying. *International Journal of Law and Psychiatry*, **30**(4–5): 340–54.

Savage, M. (2015) *Social Class in the 21st Century*. London: Pelican.

Sayer, A. (2000) *Realism and Social Science*. London: Sage.

Sayer, D. (1991) *Capitalism and Modernity: Excursus on Marx and Weber*. London: Routledge.

Sayim, K. Z. (2010) Pushed or pulled? Transfer of reward management policies in MNCs. *International Journal of Human Resource Management*, **21**(14): 2631–58.

Scarbrough, H. (2000) The HR implications of supply chain relationships. *Human Resource Management Journal*, **10**(1): 5–17.

Scarbrough, H. and Swan, J. (2001) Explaining the diffusion of knowledge management: the role of fashion. *British Journal of Management*, **12**(1): 3–12.

Schäffer, U., Mahlendorf, M. D. and Rehring, J. (2014) Does the interactive use of headquarter performance measurement systems in foreign subsidiaries endanger the potential to profit from local relationships? *Australian Accounting Review*, **24**(1): 21–38.

Schatsky, D. and Schwartz, J. (2015) *Global Human Capital Trends 2015*. Westlake, TX: Deloitte University Press.

Schein, E. H. (1990) *Organizational culture. American Psychologist*, **45**(2):109–19.

Schein, E. (2010) *Organizational Culture and Leadership* (4th edn). San Francisco, CA: Jossey-Bass.

Schleich, J. and Gruber, E. (2008) Beyond case studies: barriers to energy efficiency in commerce and the services sector. *Energy Economics*, **30**(2): 449–64.

Schlosberg, D. (1999) *Environmental Justice and the New Pluralism: The Challenge of Difference for Environmentalism*. Oxford: Oxford University Press.

Schmidt, F. L. (2002) The role of general cognitive ability and job performance: why there cannot be a debate. *Human Performance*, **15**: 187–210.

Schmitt, N. (2014) Personality and cognitive ability as predictors of effective performance at work. *Annual Review Organisational Psychology and Organisational Behavior*, **1**: 45–65.

Schmitt, N. and Kim, B. (2008) 'Selection decision making'. In P. Boxall, J. Purcell and P. Wright (eds) *The Oxford Handbook of Human Resource Management* (pp. 300–23). Oxford: Oxford University Press.

Schnabel, C. (2003) Determinants of trade union membership. In J. T. Addison and C. Schnabel (eds) *International Handbook of Trade Unions* (pp. 13–43). Cheltenham: Edward Elgar.

Schneider, B. (1987) The people make the place. *Personnel Psychology*, **40**: 437–53.

Schneider, B. (2000) The psychological life of organizations. In N. Ashkanasy, C. Wilderon and M. Peterson (eds) *Handbook of Organizational Culture and Climate* (pp. xvii–xxi). Thousand Oaks, CA: Sage.

Schneider, R. (2001) Variety performance. *People Management*, **7**(9): 26–31.

Scholarios, D. and Taylor, P.(2014) 'Decommissioned vessels'—performance management and older workers in technologically-intensive service work. *Technological Forecasting and Social Change*, **89**: 333–42.

Schön, D. A. (1983) *The Reflective Practitioner: How Professionals Think in Action*. London: Maurice Temple Smith.

Schuler, R. S. (1989) Strategic human resource management and industrial relations. *Human Relations*, **42**(2): 157–84.

Schuler, R. S. (1992) Strategic human resource management: linking people with the strategic needs of the business. *Organizational Dynamics*, **21**: 18–31.

Schuler, R. S. and Jackson, S. (1987) Linking competitive strategies and human resource management practices. *Academy of Management Executive*, **1**(3): 209–13.

Schuler, R., Dowling, P. and De Cieri, H. (1993) An integrative framework of strategic international human resource management. *Journal of Management*, **19**(2): 419–59.

Schuler, R. S., Jackson, S. and Storey, J. (2001) HRM and its links with strategic management. In J. Storey (ed.) *Human Resource Management: A Critical Text* (2nd edn) (pp. 114–30). London: Thompson Learning.

Schultz, T. W. (1981) *Investing in People: The Economics of Population Quality*. Berkeley, CA: University of California Press.

Schumacher, E. F. (1973) *Small is Beautiful: A Study of Economics as if People Really Mattered*. New York: Harper Collins.

Scott, B. and Revis, S. (2008) Talent management in hospitality: graduate career success and strategies. *International Journal of Contemporary Hospitality Management*, **20**(7): 781–91.

Scott, M. (1998) *Value Drivers*. Chichester: John Wiley & Sons.

Scott, E. (2005) The Ethics of Human Resource Management. In, J. Budd and J. Scoville (eds.) *The Ethics of Human Resources and Industrial Relations. Labour and Employment Relations* Series, pp. 173–202.

Scott, S. G. and Einstein, W. O. (2001) Strategic performance appraisal in team-based organizations: one size does not fit all. *Academy of Management Executive*, **15**(2): 107–16.

Scott-Dixon, K. (2004) *Doing IT: Women Working in Information Technology*. Toronto, Ontario: Sumach Press.

Scottish Government (2014) *Working Together Review*, Edinburgh: Scottish Government.

Scullion, H. (2001) International human resource management. In J. Storey (ed.) *Human Resource Management: A Critical Text* (2nd edn) (pp. 288–313). London: Thompson Learning.

Scullion, H. and Linehan, M. (eds) (2005) *International Human Resource Management: A Critical Text* (2nd edn). Basingstoke: Palgrave Macmillan.

Scullion, H. and Starkey, K. (2000) The changing role of the corporate human resource function in the international firm. *International Journal of Human Resource Management*, **11**(6): 1061–81.

Seal, W. and Ye, L. (2014) The balanced scorecard and the construction of a management control discourse. *Journal of Accounting and Organizational Change*, **10**(4): 466–485.

Sealy, R., Vinnicombe, S. and Singh, V. (2008) *The 2008 Female FTSE Report: A Decade of Delay*. Cranfield: Cranfield School of Management.

Séguin, R. (2010) Quebec labour, student groups unite to fight to right. *Globe and Mail*, November 6, p. A16.

Self, D. R., Armenakis, A. A. and Schraeder, M. (2007) Organizational change content, process, and context: a simultaneous analysis of employee reactions. *Journal of Change Management*, **7**: 211–29.

Selznick, P. (1957) *Leadership and Administration*. New York: Harper & Row.

Senge, P. (1990) *The Fifth Discipline*. New York: Doubleday.

Sengupta, S., Whitfield, K. and McNabb, B. (2007) Employee share ownership and performance: golden path or golden handcuffs? *International Journal of Human Resource Management*, **18**(8): 1507–38.

Sennett, R. (1998) *The Corrosion of Character*. New York: Norton.

Sennett, R. (2012) *Together: The Rituals, Pleasures and Politics of Cooperation*. New Haven, CT: Yale University Press.

Sewell, G. (1998) The discipline of teams: the control of team-based industrial work through electronic and peer surveillance. *Administrative Science Quarterly*, **43**: 397–428.

Shane, J. M. (2010) Performance management in police agencies: a conceptual framework. *Policing: An International Journal of Police Strategies and Management*, **33**(1): 6–29.

Shankleman, J. (2014). Mark Carney: most fossil fuel reserves can't be burned. The Guardian, October 13. https://www.theguardian.com/environment/2014/oct/13/mark-carney-fossil-fuel-reserves-burned-carbon-bubble (Accessed December 2016).

Sharma, R. (2014) The impact of e-HR: human resources in the digital age (an analysis of the issues and challenges in the Indian scenario). *Journal of Advanced Research in HR and Organizational Management*, **1**(1/2): 26–32.

Shaw, J. D., Duffy, M. K., Johnson, J. L. and Lockhart, D. E. (2005) Turnover, social capital losses and performance. *Academy of Management Journal*, **48**(4): 594–606.

Sheehan, C., DiCieri, H. and Holland, P. (2013) The changing role of human resources management in the employment relationship. In J. Teicher, P., Holland, and R. Gough (eds) *Australian Workplace Relations* (pp. 103–17). New York: Cambridge University Press.

Sheffield, J. and Coleshill, P. (2001) Developing best value in a Scottish local authority. *Measuring Business Excellence*, **5**(2): 31–8.

Sheldon, P. and Sanders, K. (2016) Contextualizing HRM in China: differences within the country. *International Journal of Human Resource Management*, **27**(18): 2017–33.

Shenkar, O. (1995) *Global Perspectives on Human Resource Management*. Englewood Cliffs, NJ: Prentice Hall.

Shibata, H. (2002) Wage and performance appraisal systems in flux: a Japan–United States comparison. *Industrial Relations*, **41**(4): 629–52.

Short, D., Keefer, J. and Stone, S. (2009) The link between research and practice: experiences of HRD and other professions. *Advances in Developing Human Resources*, **11**: 420–37.

Shrivastava, P. (1995) The role of corporations in achieving ecological sustainability. *Academy of Management Journal*, **20**(4): 936–60.

Siebert, W. S. and Zubanov, N. (2009) Searching for the optimal level of employee turnover: a study of a large U.K. retail organization. *Academy of Management Journal*, **52**(2): 294–313.

Siemens, G. (2014) *Connectivism: A Learning Theory for the Digital Age*. Arlington, TX: UT Arlington, LINK Research Lab.

Sikora, D. M. and Ferris, G. R. (2014) Strategic human resource practice implementation: the critical role of line management. *Human Resource Management Review*, **24**(3): 271–81.

Sillup, G. P. and Klimberg, R. (2010) Assessing the ethics of implementing performance appraisal systems. *Journal of Management Development*, **29**(1): 38–55.

Silvi, R., Bartolini, M., Raffoni, A. and Visani, F. (2015) The practice of strategic performance measurement systems: models, drivers and information effectiveness. *International Journal of Productivity and Performance Management*, **64**(2): 194–227.

Simms, M. and Holgate, J. (2010) Organising for what? Where is the debate on the politics of organizing? *Work, Employment and Society*, **24**(1): 157–68.

Simon, S. and Eby, L. (2003) A typology of negative mentoring experiences: a multidimensional scaling study, *Human Relations*, **56**(9): 1083–106.

Simosi, M. and Xenikou, A. (2010) The role of organizational culture in the relationship between leadership and organizational commitment: an empirical study in a Greek organization. *International Journal of Human Resource Management*, **21**(10): 1598–616.

Simula, H. and Ahola, T. (2014) A network perspective on idea and innovation crowdsourcing in industrial firms. *Industrial Marketing Management*, **43**(3): 400–8.

Singh, R. and Jain, N. (2014) To study the effectiveness of HRM practice in textile industries, in Madhya Pradesh, India. *Global Journal of Human Resource Management*, **2**(3): 59–72.

Singh, V. (2002) *Managing Diversity for Strategic Advantage*. London: Council for Excellence in Management and Leadership.

Sisodia, R., Wolfe, D. and Sheth, J. (2014) *Firms of Endearment: How World-class Companies Profit from Passion and Purpose* (2nd edn). Upper Saddle River, NJ: Pearson.

Sisson, K. and Storey, J. (2000) *The Realities of Human Resource Management: Managing the Employment Relationship*. Buckingham, Oxford University Press.

Skivenes, M. and Trygstad, S. (2010) When whistle-blowing works: the Norwegian case. *Human Relations*, **63**(7): 1071–97.

Sklair, L. (2002) *Globalization: Capitalism and its Alternatives* (3rd edn). New York: Oxford University Press.

Slocum, J., Lei, D. and Buller, P. (2014) Executing business strategies through human resource management practices. *Organizational Dynamics*, **43**: 73–87.

Sloman, M. (2005) *Training to Learning*. London: Chartered Institute of Personnel and Development.

Smethurst, S. (2004) The allure of online. *People Management*, 29 July: 38–40.

Smircich, L. (1983) Concepts of culture and organizational analysis. *Administrative Science Quarterly*, **28**(3): 339–58.

Smith, A. (1776/1982) *The Wealth of Nations*. Harmondsworth: Penguin.

Smith, A. R. (1980) *Corporate Manpower Planning*. London: Gower Press.

Smith, D. and Chamberlain, P. (2015) On the blacklist: how did the UK's top building firms get secret information on their workers? February 27. https://www.theguardian.com/uk-news/2015/feb/27/on-the-blacklist-building-firms-secret-information-on-workers (accessed September 14, 2016).

Smith, G. (2015) Can there be a moral economy on gas? *Scottish Left Review*, (89), September/October, p. 20.

Smith, K. J. (2015) Conducting thorough job analyses and drafting lawful job descriptions. *Employment Relations Today*, (Winter): 95–9.

Smith, L. (1993) Quoted in: Managing AIDS: how one boss struggled to cope. *Business Week*, February 1, p. 48.

Smith, P. and Morton, G. (1993) Union exclusion and the decollectivization of industrial relations in contemporary Britain. *British Journal of Industrial Relations*, **31**(1): 97–114.

Smith, P. and Morton, G. (2006) Nine years of New Labour: neoliberalism and workers' rights. *British Journal of Industrial Relations*, **44**(3): 401–20.

Smither, J., Reilly, R., Millsap, R., Pearlman, K. and Stoffey, R. (1993) Applicant reactions to selection procedures. *Personnel Psychology*, **46**: 49–76.

Smither, J., London, M., Flautt, R., Vargas, Y. and Kucine, I. (2003) Can working with an executive coach improve multi-source feedback ratings over time? A quasi-experimental field study. *Personnel Psychology*, **56**(1): 23–44.

Smither, J., London, M. and Reilly, R. (2005) Does performance improve following multisource feedback? A theoretical model, meta-analysis, and review of empirical findings. *Personnel Psychology*, **58**: 33–66.

Smither, J. W., Brett, J. F. and Atwater, L. E. (2008) What do leaders recall about their multisource feedback? *Journal of Leadership and Organizational Studies*, **14**(3): 202–18.

Smith Institute (2014) *Outsourcing the Cuts: Pay and Employment Effects of Contracting Out*. London: Smith Institute.

Sneade, A. (2001) Trade union membership 1999–2000: an analysis of data from the certification officer, and The Labour Force Survey. *Labour Market Trends*, September: 433–41.

Snell, S. A., Youndt, M. A. and Wright, P. M. (1996) Establishing a framework for research in strategic human resource management: merging source theory and organizational learning. *Research in Personnel and Human Resources Management*, **14**: 61–90.

Solberg, E. and Dysvik, A. (2016) Employees' perceptions of HR investment and their efforts to remain internally employable: testing the exchange-based mechanisms of the 'new psychological contract'. *International Journal of Human Resource Management*, **27**(9): 909–27.

Solnet. D., Kralj, A. and Kandampully, J. (2012) Generation Y employees: an examination of work attitude differences. *Journal of Applied Management and Entrepreneurship*, **17**(3): 36–55.

Soltani, E., ven der Meer, R. and Williams, T. (2005) A contrast of HRM and TQM approaches to performance management: some evidence. *British Journal of Management*, **16**(3): 211–30.

Song, J., Lim, D. H., Kang, I. G. and Kim, W. (2014) Team performance in learning organizations: mediating effect of employee engagement. *Learning Organization*, **21**(5): 290–309.

Soper, S. (2011) Inside Amazon's Warehouse. The Morning Call, September 18. http://articles.mcall.com/2011-09-18/news/mc-allentown-amazon-complaints-20110917_1_warehouse-workers-heat-stress-brutal-heat (Accessed December 2016).

Soylu, S. and Sheehy-Skeffington, J. (2015) Asymmetric intergroup bullying: the enactment and maintenance of societal inequality at work. *Human Relations*, **68**(7): 1099–129.

Sparrow, A., Elgot, J. and Davies, R. (2016) Theresa May to call for unity, equality and successful exit from EU. www.theguardian.com/politics/2016/jul/11/theresa-may-to-call-for-unity-equality-and-successful-exit-from-eu (accessed October 2016).

Sparrow, P. (2008) Performance management in the UK. In A. Varma, P. S. Budwar and A. Denisi (eds) *Performance Management Systems: A Global Perspective* (pp. 131–46). Abingdon: Routledge.

Sparrow, P., Brewster, C. and Harris, H. (2004) *Globalizing Human Resource Management*. London: Routledge.

Sparrow, P., Scullion, H. and Farndale, E. (2011) Global talent management: new roles for the corporate HR function? In H. Scullion and D. Collings (eds) *Global Talent Management*, New York: Routledge.

Spencer, B. and Kelly, J. (2015) Workers and union HRD. In R. F. Poell, T. S. Rocco and G. L. Roth (eds) *The Routledge Companion to Human Resource Development* (pp. 78–88). London: Routledge.

Spender, J.-C. (2008) Organizational learning and knowledge management: whence and whither? *Management Learning*, **39**(2): 159–76.

Spicer, A. (2015) The flaw in Amazon's management fad. The Guardian. August 17. https://www.theguardian.com/commentisfree/2015/aug/17/amazon-management-fad-rank-yank-jeff-bezos (accessed October 2016).

Spillane, J. (2006) *Distributed Leadership*. San Francisco, CA: Jossey-Bass.

Spillane, J. P., Camburn, E. M., Pustejovsky, J., Pareja, A. S. and Lewis, G. (2008) Taking a distributed perspective. *Journal of Educational Administration*, **46**(2): 189–213.

Spitzmüller, C., Neumann, E., Spitzmüller, M. et al. (2008) Assessing the influence of psychosocial and career mentoring on organizational attractiveness. *International Journal of Selection and Assessment*, **16**(4): 403–15.

Spychalski, A. C., Quiñones, M. A., Gaugler, B. B. and Pohley, K. (1997) A survey of assessment center practices in the United States. *Personnel Psychology*, **50**, 71–90.

Squires, G. (2001) Management as a professional discipline. *Journal of Management Studies*, **38**(4): 473–87.

Stahl, G. K. and Björkman, I. (eds) (2006) *Handbook of Research in International Human Resource Management*. Cheltenham: Edward Elgar.

Standing, G. (2011) *The Precariat: The New Dangerous Class*. London: Bloomsbury Academic.

Standing, G. (2014) Understanding the precariat through labour and work. *Development and Change*, **45**(5): 963–80.

Stanton, P. and Nankervis, A. (2011) Linking strategic HRM, performance management and organizational effectiveness: perceptions of managers in Singapore. *Asia Pacific Business Review*, **17**(1): 67–84.

Starik, M. and Rands, G. P. (1995) Weaving an integrated web: multilevel and multisystem perspectives of ecologically sustainable organizations. *Academy of Management Review*, **20**: 908–35.

Stavrou, E., Brewster, C. and Charalambous, C. (2010) Human resource management and firm performance in Europe through the lens of business systems: best fit, best practice or both? *International Journal of Human Resource Management*, **21**(7): 933–62.

Sternberg, R. J. and Horvath, J. A. (eds) (1999) *Tacit Knowledge in Professional Practice: Researcher and Practitioner Perspectives*. Mahwah, NJ: Lawrence Erlbaum.

Stevens, J. (2005) *High Performance Wales: Real Experiences, Real Success*. Cardiff: Wales Management Council.

Stewart, H. (2009) Economists tell Queen how they failed to see the recession coming. *The Observer*, July 27, p. 1.

Stewart, H. (2015) The great wages crash, The Guardian, 30 January, p. 1.

Stewart, J. (2007) The ethics of HRD. In C. Rigg, J. Stewart and K. Trehan (eds) *Critical Human Resource Development: Beyond Orthodoxy* (pp. 59–78): Harlow: Prentice Hall.

Stewart, J. (2010) E-learning for managers and leaders. In J. Gold, R. Thorpe and A. Mumford (eds) *The Gower Handbook of Leadership and Management Development* (pp. 441–56). Aldershot: Gower.

Stewart, J. (2015) Strategic HRD. In R. F. Poell, T. S. Rocco and G. L. Roth (eds) (2015) *The Routledge Companion to Human Resource Development* (pp. 203–11). London: Routledge.

Stewart, R. (1975) *Contrasts in Management*. Maidenhead: McGraw-Hill.

Stiglitz, J. E. (2010) Contagion, liberalization, and the optimal structure of globalization. *Journal of Globalization and Development*, **1**(2): Article 2.

Stiglitz, J. E. (2010a) *Freefall: Free Markets and the Sinking of the Global Economy*. London: Allen Lane.

Stiglitz, J. E. (2013) *The Price of Inequality*. London: Penguin.

Stiglitz, J. E. (2015) *The Great Divide*. London: Allen Lane.

Stober, D. and Grant A. M. (eds) (2008) *Evidence-Based Coaching Handbook*. New York: John Wiley & Sons.

Stohl, C. and Cheney, G. (2001) Participatory processes/ paradoxical practices. *Management Communications Quarterly*, **14**(3): 349–407.

Stone, D., Deadrick, D. L., Lukaszewski, K. M. and Johson, R. (2015) The influence of technology on the future of human resource management. *Human Resource Management Review*, **25**(2): 216–31.

Stoner, J. S. and Gallagher, V. C. (2010) Who cares? The role of job involvement in psychological contract violation. *Journal of Applied Social Psychology*, **40**(6): 1490–514.

Storey, J. (1983) *Managerial Prerogative and the Question of Control*. London: Routledge & Kegan Paul.

Storey, J. (ed.) (1989) *New Perspectives on Human Resource Management*. London: Routledge.

Storey, J. (1992) *Developments in the Management of Human Resources*. Oxford: Blackwell.

Storey, J. (1995a) Human resource management: still marching on or marching out? In J. Storey (ed.) *Human Resource Management: A Critical Text* (pp. 3–32). London: Routledge.

Storey, J. (ed.) (1995b) *Human Resource Management: A Critical Text*. London: Routledge.

Storey, J. (2001) Human resource management today: an assessment. In J. Storey (ed.) *Human Resource Management: A Critical Text* (2nd edn) (pp. 3–20). London: Thompson Learning.

Storey, J. (ed.) (2007) Human resource management today: an assessment. In J. Storey (ed.) *Human Resource Management: A Critical Text* (pp. 3–20). London: Thompson Learning.

Storey, J., Cressey, P., Morris, T. and Wilkinson, A. (1997) Changing employment practices in UK banking: case studies. *Personnel Review*, **26**(1): 24–42.

Strauss, G. (1998) An overview. In F. Heller, E. Pusic, G. Strauss and B. Wilpert (eds) *Organizational Participation: Myth and Reality* (pp. 8–39). Oxford: Oxford University Press.

Strauss, G. (2006) Worker participation: some under-considered issues. *Industrial Relations*, **45**(4): 778–803.

Strebler, M., Robinson, D. and Heron, P. (1997) *Getting the Best Out of Your Competencies*. Report No. 334. Brighton: Institute for Employment Studies.

Stredwick, J. and Ellis, S. (2005) *Flexible Working* (2nd edn). London: Chartered Institute of Personnel and Development.

Streeck, W. (1987) The uncertainties of management in the management of uncertainty. *Work, Employment and Society*, **1**: 281–308.

Streeck, W. and Visser, J. (1997) The rise of the conglomerate union. *European Journal of Industrial Relations*, **3**(3): 305–32.

Stuart M. (2015) Letter to editor: 'Trade union bill not backed by evidence', and signed by 110 others. The Guardian, August 18, p. 30.

Sturges, J., Conway, N. and Liefooghe, A. (2010) Organizational support, individual attributes, and the practice of career self-management behavior. *Group and Organization Management*, **35**(1):108–41.

Su, S., Baird, K. and Blair, B. (2009) Employee organizational commitment: the influence of cultural and organizational factors in the Australian manufacturing industry. *International Journal of Human Resource Management*, **20**(12): 2494–516.

Sullivan, R. (2010) Labour market or labour movement? The union density bias as barrier to labour renewal. *Work, Employment and Society*, **24**(1): 145–56.

Sullivan, S. and Arthur, M. (2006) The evolution of the boundaryless career concept: examining physical and psychological mobility. *Journal of Vocational Behavior*, **69**: 19–29.

Sullivan, S. E., Forret, M. L., Mainiero, L. A. and Terjesen, S. (2007) What motivates entrepreneurs? An exploratory study of the kaleidoscope career model and entrepreneurship. *Journal of Applied Management and Entrepreneurship*, **12**: 4–19.

Sullivan, S. E., Forret, M. L., Carraher, S. M. and Mainiero, L. A. (2009) Using the kaleidoscope career model to examine generational differences in work attitudes. *Career Development International*, **14**(3): 284–302.

Sullivan, T. (2014) Greedy institutions, overwork, and work-life balance. *Sociological Inquiry*, **84**(10): 1–15.

Sumelius, J., Björkman, I., Ehrnrooth, M., Mäkelä, K. and Smale, A. (2014) What determines employee perceptions of HRM process features? The case of performance appraisal in MNC subsidiaries. *Human Resource Management*, **53**(4): 569–92.

Sumithra, C. G. (2015) Competency based e learning systems an analytical study of select corporate enterprises in Bangalore. *DHARANA*, **8**(2): 84–96.

Sumner, J. (2005) *Sustainability and the Civil Commons: Rural Communities in the Age of Globalization*. Toronto, Ontario: University of Toronto Press.

Sundgren, M. and Styhre, A. (2006) Leadership as de-paradoxification: leading new drug development work at three pharmaceutical companies, *Leadership*, **2**(1): 31–52.

Sung, J. and Ashton, D. (2005) *High Performance Work Practices: Linking Strategy and Skills to Performance Outcomes*. London: Department of Trade and Industry/Chartered Institute of Personnel and Development.

Sung, S.Y. and Choi, J. N. (2014) Multiple dimensions of human resource development and organizational performance. *Journal of Organizational Behavior*, **35**(6): 851–87.

Suutari, V. and Viitala, R. (2008) Management development of senior executives: methods and their effectiveness. *Personnel Review*, **37**(4): 375–92.

Svensson, S. (2012) Flexible working conditions and decreasing levels of trust. *Employee Relations*, **34**(2): 126–37.

Swart, J., Price, A., Mann, C. and Brown, S. (2004) *Human Resource Development: Strategy and Tactics*. London: Butterworth-Heinemann.

Swedberg, R. (2005) *The Max Weber Dictionary: Keywords and Central Concepts*. Stanford: Stanford University Press.

Swinburne, P. (2001) How to use feedback to improve performance. *People Management*, **7**(11): 46–7.

Syal, R. (2015) Building firms make court apology for blacklisting workers. The Guardian, October 9.

Sylva, H. and Mol, S. (2009) E-Recruitment: a study into applicant perceptions of an online application system. *International Journal of Selection and Assessment*, **17**(3): 311–22.

Szamosi, L. T., Wilkinson, A., Wood, G. and Psychogios, A. (2010) Developments in HRM in south-eastern Europe. *International Journal of Human Resource Management*, **21**(14): 2521–8.

Szymanski, D. and Feltman, C. (2015a) Linking sexually objectifying work environments among waitresses to psychological and job-related outcomes. *Psychology of Women Quarterly*, **39**: 390–404.

Szymanski, D. and Feltman, C. (2015b) The psychological toll of being a Hooters waitress. News. com.au. September 1. http://www.news.com.au/lifestyle/health/mind/the-psychological-toll-of-being-a-hooters-waitress/news-story/819984b433e9b70985baa764e282bd8f (accessed October 2016).

Tahvanainen, M. and Suutari, V. (2005) Expatriate performance management in MNCs. In H. Scullion and M. Linehan (eds) *International Human Resource Management* (pp. 91–113). Basingstoke: Palgrave Macmillan.

Tamkin, P. (2014) High performance work practices. Brighton: Institute for Employment Studies.

Tamkin, P. and Denvir, A. (2006) *Strengthening the UK Evidence Base on Management and Leadership Capability*. Brighton: IES

Tamkin, P., Barber, L. and Dench, S. (1997) *From Admin to Strategy: The Changing Face of the HR Function*. Report No. 32. Brighton: Institute for Employment Studies.

Tamkin, P., Aston, J., Cummings, J. et al. (2002) *A Review of Training in Racism Awareness and Valuing Cultural Diversity*. Brighton: Institute of Employment Studies.

Tamkin, P., Giles, L., Campbell, M. and Hillage, J. (2004) *Skills Pay: The Contribution of Skills to Business Success*. Brighton: Institute for Employment Studies.

Tamkin, P., Albert, A., Reid, B. et al. (2010) *High Performance Working: Case Studies Analytical Report*. Evidence Report No. 21. Wath-upon-Dearne: UK Commission for Employment and Skills.

Tan, J.-S. (1998) Communication, cross-cultural. In M. Poole and M. Warner (eds) *Handbook of Human Resource Management* (pp. 492–97). London: Thomson Business.

Tansley, C., Turner, P. and Foster, C. (2007a) *Talent: Strategy, Management, Measurement. Research into Practice*. London: Chartered Institute of Personnel and Development.

Tansley, C., Turner, P., Foster, C., Harris, L., Stewert, J. and Sempik, A. (2007b) *Talent Strategy, Management and Measurement*. London: Chartered Institute of Personnel and Development.

Taras, D. and Kaufman, B. (2006) Non-union employee representation in North America: diversity, controversy and uncertain future. *Industrial Relations Journal*, **37**(5): 513–42.

Tatli, A. (2011) A multi-layered exploration of the diversity management field: diversity discourses, practices and practitioners in the UK. *British Journal of Management*, **22**: 238–53.

Tatli, A., Mulholland, G., Ozbilgin, M. and Worman, D. (2007) *Managing Diversity in Practice: Supporting Business Goals*. London: Chartered Institute of Personnel and Development.

Taylor, P. (2013). Performance management and the new workplace tyranny: A report for the Scottish Trades Union Congress. University of Strathclyde, Glasgow.

Taylor, F. W. (1911) *The Principles of Scientific Management*. New York: Harper.

Taylor, H. (1991) The systematic training model: corn circles in search of a spaceship? *Management Education and Development*, **22**(4): 258–78.

Taylor, M. and Taylor, A. (2014) Performance measurement in the Third Sector: the development of a stakeholder-focussed research agenda. *Production Planning and Control*, **25**(16): 1370–85.

Taylor, P. (2010) The globalization of service work: analysing the transnational call centre value chain. In P. Thompson and C. Smith (eds) *Working Life* (pp. 244–68). Basingstoke: Palgrave Macmillan.

Taylor, P. and Bain, P. (1998) An assembly line in the head: the call centre labour process. *Industrial Relations Journal*, **30**(2): 101–17.

Taylor, P. and Bain, P. (2005) Indian calling to the far away towns. *Work, Employment and Society*, **19**(2): 261–82.

Taylor, P. and Connelly, L. (2009) Before the disaster: health and safety and working conditions at a plastic factory. *Work, Employment and Society*, **23**(1): 160–8.

Taylor, P., Cunningham, I., Newsome, K. and Scholarios, D. (2010) 'Too scared to go sick' – reformulating the research agenda on sickness absence. *Industrial Relations Journal*, **41**(4): 270–88.

Taylor, S. (1998) *Employee Resourcing*. London: Institute of Personnel Development.

Taylor, S. and Bright, D. S. (2011) Open-mindedness and defensiveness in multisource feedback processes: a conceptual framework. *Journal of Applied Behavioral Science*, **47**: 432–60.

Taylor, S. and Napier, N. (1996) Working in Japan: lessons from women expatriates. *Sloan Management Review*, **37**: 125–44.

Taylor, S., Beechler, S. and Napier, N. (1996) Toward an integrative model of strategic international human resource management. *Academy of Management Review*, **21**(4): 959–85.

Teece, D. J. (2007) Explicating dynamic capabilities: the nature and microfoundations of (sustainable) enterprise performance. *Strategic Management Journal*, **28**(13): 1319–50.

Teece, D., Pisano, G. and Shuen, A. (1997) Dynamic capabilities and strategic management. *Strategic Management Journal*, **18**(7): 509–33.

Templer, A. J. and Cawsey, T. F. (1999) Rethinking career development in an era portfolio careers. *Career Development International*, **4**(2): 70–6.

Templer, K. J., Tay, C. and Chandrasekar, N. A. (2006) Motivational cultural intelligence, realistic job preview, realistic living conditions preview, and cross-cultural adjustment. *Group and Organization Management*, **31**(1): 154–73.

Temporal, P. (1978) The nature of non-contrived learning and its implications for management development. *Management Education and Development*, **9**: 20–3.

Teo, S. T. and Rodwell, J. J. (2007) To be strategic in the new public sector, HR must remember its operational activities. *Human Resource Management*, **44**: 265–84.

Terry, M. (2003) Can partnership reverse the decline in of British trade unions? *Work, Employment and Society*, **17**(3): 459–72.

Tharp, C. (2015) Context matters: building strategic HR from the outside in. In D. Ulrich, W. Schiemann and L. Sartain (eds) *The Rise of HR: Wisdom from 73 Thought Leaders* (pp. 75–80). Alexandria, VA: HR Certification Institute.

Thompson, M. and Ponak, A. (2005) The management of industrial relations. In M. Gunderson, A. Ponak and Taras, D. (eds) *Union–Management Relations in Canada* (5th edn) (pp. 112–33). Toronto, Ontario: Pearson.

Thompson, P. (1989) *The Nature of Work* (2nd edn). Basingstoke: Palgrave Macmillan.

Thompson, P. (2003) Disconnected capitalism: or why employers can't keep their side of the bargain. *Work Employment and Society*, **17**(2): 359–78.

Thompson, P. and Harley, B. (2008) HRM and the worker: labour process perspectives. In P. Boxall, J. Purcell and P. Wright (eds) *The Oxford Handbook of Human Resource Management* (pp. 147–65). Oxford: Oxford University Press.

Thompson P. and McHugh, D. (2009) *Work Organisations: A Critical Approach* (4th edn). Basingstoke: Palgrave Macmillan.

Thompson, P. and Smith, C. (eds) (2010) *Working Life*. Basingstoke: Palgrave Macmillan.

Thompson, P. and van den Broek, D. (2010) Managerial control and workplace regimes. *Work, Employment and Society*, **24**(3): 1–12.

Thornhill, A., Saunders, M. N. K. and Stead, J. (1997) Downsizing, delayering – but where's the commitment. *Personnel Review*, **26**(1): 81–98.

Thornton, G. and Gibbons, A. (2009) Validity of assessment centers for personnel selection. *Human Resource Management Review*, **19**(3): 69–187.

Thorpe, R., Gold, J., Anderson, L., Burgoyne, J., Wilkinson, D. and Malby, B. (2008) *Towards Leaderful Communities in the North of England* (2nd edn). Cork: Oak tree Press.

Thorpe, R., Gold, J. and Lawler, J. (2011) Locating distributed leadership. *International Journal of Management Reviews*, **13**: 239–50.

Thunnissen, M., Boselie, P. and Fruytier, B. (2013) Talent management and the relevance of context: towards a pluralistic approach. *Human Resource Management Review*, **23**(4): 326–36.

Tilly, C. (2008) *Democracy*. Cambridge: Cambridge University Press.

Today's Zaman (2015) Turkish women still struggling to access employment market. September 5. www.todayszaman.com/business_turkish-women-still-struggling-to-access-employment-market_398272.html (accessed August 15, 2016).

Tomlinson, K. (2003) *Effective Interagency Working: A Review of the Literature and Examples from Practice*. LGA Research Report No. 40. Slough: National Foundation for Educational Research.

Ton, Z. and Huckman, R. S. (2008) Managing the impact of employee turnover on performance: the role of process conformance. *Organization Science*, **19**(1): 56–68.

Topcic, M., Baum, M. and Kabst, R. (2016) Are high-performance work practices related to individually perceived stress? A job demands-resources perspective. *International Journal of Human Resource Management*, **27**(1): 45–66.

Topham, G. (2015) Walsh's pay rises up to £6.4m after airline group's €1bn profit. The Guardian, March 6, p. 33.

Topham, G. (2016) Eurostar workers to strike in dispute over work-life balance. The Guardian. August 10. https://www.theguardian.com/business/2016/aug/10/eurostar-workers-strike-august-row-work-life-balance (accessed August 12, 2016).

Toplis, J., Dulvicz, V. and Fletcher, C. (2005) *Psychological Testing* (4th edn). London: Chartered Institute of Personnel and Development.

Topping, A. (2015) Gender pay gap will not close for 70 years at current rate, says UN. The Guardian, March 5, p. 1.

Torbiörn, I. (2005) Staffing policies and practices in European MNCs: strategic sophistication, culture-bound policies or ad hoc reactivity? In H. Scullion and M. Linehan (eds) *International Human Resource Management* (pp. 47–68). Basingstoke: Palgrave Macmillan.

Torres, R. T., Preskill, H. and Piontek, M. E. (2005) *Evaluation Strategies for Communicating and Reporting: Enhancing Learning in Organizations*. Thousand Oaks, CA: Sage.

Torres, R., Fenwick, C., Tobin, S., Horne, R. and Rafferty, J. (2015) *OECD Report, World Employment and Social Outlook 2015: The Changing Nature of Jobs?* Geneva: International Labour Organization.

Torrington, D. (1998) Discipline and dismissals. In M. Poole and M. Warner (eds) *The Handbook of Human Resource Management* (pp. 498–506). London: International Thomson Business Press.

Tosey, P. (2010) Neuro-linguistic programming for leaders and managers. In J. Gold, R. Thorpe and A. Mumford (eds) *The Gower Handbook of Leadership and Management Development* (pp. 313–30). Aldershot: Gower.

Toulson, P. K. and Dewe, P. (2004) HR accounting as a measurement tool. *Human Resource Management Journal*, **14**(2): 75–90.

Townley, B. (1994) *Reframing Human Resource Management*. London: Sage.

Townley, B. (2014) Selection and appraisal. In Storey, J. (ed.) *New Perspectives on HRM* (pp. 92–109). London: Routledge.

Townsend, K., Wilkinson, A., Allan, C. and Bamber, G. (2012) Mixed signals in HRM: the HRM role of hospital line managers. *Human Resource Management Journal*, **22**: 267–82.

Trades Union Congress (1999) *Partners for Progress: New Unionism in the Workplace*. London: TUC.

Trades Union Congress (2007) *Bullying at Work: Guidance for Safety Representatives*. London: TUC.

Trades Union Congress (2009) Bullying boss blamed for breakdown. *Risks*, 396.

Trades Union Congress (2010) *One Million Climate Jobs*. London: TUC.

Trades Union Congress (2011) *Unions, Collective Bargaining and Employment Relations Project. Research Bulletin* Number 2. London: TUC.

Trades Union Congress (2015) In parts of Britain half of jobs pay less than living wage. February 24. ww.tuc.org.uk (accessed July 9, 2015).

Trades Union Congress (2016a) TUC backs Teresa May's call for workers on company boards. Press release. https://www.tuc.org.uk/economic-issues/industrial-issues/tuc-backs-theresa-may%E2%80%99s-call-workers-company-boards (accessed July 11, 2016).

Trades Union Congress (2016b) *Challenging racism after the EU referendum*. London: TUC.

Trades Union Congress and New Economics Foundation (2015) *Outsourcing Public Services*. London: TUC.

Trapp, R. (2005) The mirror has two faces. *People Management*, May 19: 40–2.

Travaglione, A. and Cross, B. (2006) Diminishing the social network in organizations: does there need to be such a phenomenon as "survivor syndrome" after downsizing? *Strategic Change*, **15**: 1–13.

Travis, A. (2011) Probation officers spend 75% of time on red tape, report finds. The Guardian, July 27, p. 7.

Travis, A. (2016) G4S suspended police control-room employees over 'bogus' 999 calls, The Guardian, May 24, p. 11.

Treanor, J. (2015a) Workers demotivated by high executive pay, survey reveals. The Guardian, December 18, p. 35.

Treanor, J. (2015b) Mark Carney calls on businesses to disclose carbon footprints. The Guardian, June 26. https://www.theguardian.com/business/2015/jun/26/mark-carney-calls-on-businesses-to-disclose-carbon-footprints (accessed December 12, 2016).

Tremblay, D.-G. (2003) Telework: a new mode of gendered segmentation? Results from a study in Canada. *Canadian Journal of Communication*, **28**(4): 461–78.

Trevino, L. and Nelson, K (2011) *Managing Business Ethics: Straight Talk About How To Do It Right* (5th edn). USA: John Wiley & Sons.

Trevor, J. (2009) Can pay be strategic? In S. Corby, S. Palmer and E. Lindop (eds) *Rethinking Reward* (pp. 21–40). Basingstoke: Palgrave Macmillan.

Truss, C. (2001) Complexities and controversies in linking HRM with organizational outcomes. *Journal of Management Studies*, **38**(8): 1121–49.

Tsoukas, H. (2000) Knowledge as action, organization as theory. *Emergence*, **2**(4): 104–12.

Tucker, R. C. (1978) *The Marx–Engels Reader*. New York: Norton.

Tulip, S. (2004) Hired education. *People Management*, September 30: 46–9.

Tung, R. (1988) *The New Expatriates*. Boston, MA: Ballinger.

Tung, R. (1998) A contingency framework for selection and training of expatriates revisited. *Human Resource Management Review*, **98**(8): 23–38.

Turner, C. and McCarthy, G. (2015) Coachable moments: identifying factors that influence managers to take advantage of coachable moments in day-to-day management. *International Journal of Evidence Based Coaching and Mentoring*, **13**(1): 1–14.

Turner, G. (1996) Human resource accounting – whim or wisdom? *Journal of Human Resource Costing and Accounting*, **1**(1): 63–73.

Tyson, S. (1995) *Human Resource Strategy*. London: Pitman.

Tziner, A., Joanis, C. and Murphy, K. R. (2000) A comparison of three methods of performance appraisal with regard to goal properties, goal perception and ratee satisfaction. *Group and Organization Management*, **25**(2): 175–90.

Uen, J. F., Ahistrom, D., Chen, S. and Liu, S. (2015) Employer brand management, organizational prestige and employees' word-of-mouth referrals in Taiwan. *Asia Pacific Journal of Human Resources*, **53**(1): 104–23.

UK Commission for Employment and Skills (2009) *Ambition 2020, World Class Skills and Jobs for the UK*. London: UKCES.

UK Commission for Employment and Skills (2010) *Developing Leadership and Management Skills through Employer Networks*. London: UKCES.

UK Commission for Employment and Skills (2011) *Skills for Jobs: Today and Tomorrow*: London: UKCES.

UK Commission for Employment and Skills (2012) *Understanding Training Levies*. London: UKCES.

UK Commission for Employment and Skills (2014) *Employer Skills Survey 2013: UK Results*. London: UKCES.

Ulhoi, J. P. and Madsen, H. (1996) The greening of European management education. In W. Wehrmeyer (ed.) *Greening People: Human Resource Management* (pp. 289–300). Sheffield Greenleaf.

Ulrich, D. (1997) *Human Resource Champions. The Next Agenda for Adding Value and Delivering Results*. Boston, MA: Harvard Business School Press.

Ulrich, D. (1998) A new mandate for human resources. *Harvard Business Review*, **76**: 124–34.

Ulrich, D. (2011) Integrated talent management. In K. Oakes, and P. Galagan (eds) *The Executive Guide to*

Integrated Talent Management (pp. 189–211). Alexandria, VA: ASTD Press.

Ulrich, D. and Beatty, R. W. (2001) From partner to players. *Human Resource Management*, **40**(4): 293–307.

Ulrich, D. and Brockbank, W. (2005*) The HR Value Proposition*. Boston, MA: Harvard Business School Press.

Ulrich, D., Brockbank, W., Johnson, D. and Younger, J. (2007) Human resource competencies: responding to increased expectations. *Employee Relations Today*, **34**(3): 1–12.

Ulrich, D., Alenn, J., Brockbank, W., Younger, J. and Nyman, M. (2009) *HR Transformation: Building Human Resources From the Outside In*. New York: McGraw-Hill.

Ulrich, D., Younger, J., Brockbank, W. and Ulrich, M. (2012) *HR from the Outside In: Six Competencies for the Future of Human Resources*. New York: McGraw-Hill.

Ulrich, L. and Trumbo, D. (1965) The selection interview since 1949. *Psychological Bulletin*, **63**: 100–16.

University and College Union (2015) Over half of universities and colleges use lecturers on zero-hour contracts. https://www.ucu.org.uk/6749 (accessed May 5, 2016).

Union of Concerned Scientists. What Are Tar Sands? (no date) Online, available at http://www.ucsusa.org/clean-vehicles/all-about-oil/what-are-tar-sands#.WEmautWLSUk (Accessed December 2016).

Urban, J. B., Hargreaves, M. and Trochim, W. (2014) Evolutionary evaluation: implications for evaluators, researchers, practitioners, funders and the evidence-based program mandate. *Evaluation and Program Planning*, **45**: 127–39.

Uy, M., Chan, K.-Y., Yoke, L., Sam, Y. L., Ringo, M. and Cherny, O. (2015) Proactivity, adaptability and boundaryless career attitudes: the mediating role of entrepreneurial alertness. *Journal of Vocational Behavior*, **86**: 115–23.

Vachon, T.E., Wallace, M. and Hyde, A. (2016) Union Decline in a Neoliberal Age: Globalization, Financialization, European Integration, and Union Density in 18 Affluent Democracies, *Socius: Sociological Research for a Dynamic World* Volume 2: 1–22. doi: 10.1177/2378023116656847.

Vaiman, V., Scullion, H. and Collings, D. (2012) Talent management decision making. *Management Decision*, **50**(5): 925–41.

Valentine, K. (2014) Tar sands oil development is more toxic than previously thought, study finds. February 4. https://thinkprogress.org/tar-sands-oil-development-is-more-toxic-than-previously-thought-study-finds-aef580e996cd#.mebuolccr/ (accessed March 9, 2016).

Van Der Heijden, B. I. Peters, P. and Kelliher, C. (2015) New ways of working and employability. In R. F. Poell, T. S. Rocco and G. L. Roth (eds) *The Routledge Companion to Human Resource Development* (pp. 542–51). London: Routledge.

Van der Locht, M., Van Dam, K. and Chiaburu, D. (2013) Getting the most of management training: the role of identical elements for training transfer. *Personnel Review*, **42**(4): 422–39.

VandeWalle, D., Ganesan, S., Challagalla, G. N. and Brown, S. P. (2000) An integrated model of feedback-seeking behavior: disposition, context and cognition. *Journal of Applied Psychology*, **85**(6): 96–103.

Van Dierendonck, D., Haynes, C., Borrill, C. and Stride, C. (2007) Effects of upward feedback on leadership behaviour toward subordinates. *Journal of Management Development*, **26**(3): 228–38.

Van Ewijk, A. R. (2011) Diversity and diversity policy: diving into fundamental differences. *Journal of Organizational Change Management*, **24**(5): 680–94.

Van Greuningen, M., Batenburg, R.S. and Van der Velden, L.F. J. (2012) Ten years of health workforce planning in the Netherlands: a tentative evaluation of GP planning as an example. *Human Resources for Health*, **10**(21) doi: 10.1186/1478–4491–10–21.

Van Hoye, G. (2013) Recruiting through employee referrals: an examination of employees' motives. *Human Performance*, **26**: 451–64.

Van Knippenberg, D. and Sitkin, S. B. (2013) A critical assessment of charismatic—transformational leadership research: back to the drawing board? *Academy of Management Annals*, 7(1): 1–60.

van Neikerk, S. (2015) South Africa. In Neale, J., Spence, T., and Ytterstad, A. (eds) *Global Climate Jobs* (pp. 30-33), http://www.climate-change-jobs.org/node/37 (accessed December 2016).

van Vijfeijken, H., Kleingeld, A., van Tuijl, H., Algera, J. and Thierry, H. (2002) Task complexity and task, goal, and reward interdependence in group performance management: a prescriptive model. *European Journal of Work and Organizational Psychology*, **11**(3): 363–83.

van Wanrooy, B., Bewley, H., Bryson, A. et al. (2013a) *Employment Relations in the Shadow of Recession: Findings from the 2011 Workplace Employment Relations Study*. Basingstoke: Palgrave Macmillan.

van Wanrooy, B., Bewley, H. and Bryson, A. (2013b) *The 2011 Workplace Employment Relations Study: first findings*. https://www.gov.uk/government/uploads/system/uploads/attachment_data/file/336651/bis-14-1008-WERS-first-findings-report-fourth-edition-july-2014.pdf (accessed October 2016).

Varma, A., Pichler, S. and Budhwar, P. (2011) The relationship between expatriate job level and host country national categorization: an investigation in the UK. *International Journal of Human Resource Management*, **22**(1): 103–20.

Verbeke A. (2013) *International Business Strategy* (2nd edn). Cambridge: Cambridge University Press.

Verma, A. (1995) Employee involvement in the workplace. In M. Gunderson and A. Ponak (eds) *Union–Management Relations in Canada* (3rd edn) (pp. 281–308). Don Mills, Ontario: Addison-Wesley.

Verma, A. (2005) What do unions do to the workplace? Union effects on management and HRM policies. *Journal of Labor Research*, **26**: 421–55.

Verma, A. and Taras, D. (2001) Employee involvement in the workplace. In M. Gunderson, A. Ponak and D. Taras (eds) *Union–Management Relations in Canada* (4th edn) (pp. 447–85). Don Mills, Ontario: Addison-Wesley.

Vesala, H. and Tuomivaara, S. (2015) Slowing work down by teleworking periodically in rural settings? *Personnel Review*, **44**(4): 511–28.

Victor, B. and Boynton, A. (1998) *Invented Here: Maximizing Your Organization's Internal Growth and Profitability*. Boston, MA: Harvard Business School Press.

Vidal, J. (2011) U.S. target EU members over stand on genetically modified crops. *Globe and Mail*, January 1, p. A11.

Vidal J. (2013) Toxic e-waste dumped in poor nations, says UN. https://www.theguardian.com/global-development/2013/dec/14/toxic-ewaste-illegal-dumping-developing-countries (accessed March 9, 2016).

Vilela, B. B., Gonzalez, J. A. V., Ferrin, P. F. and Araujo, M. L. (2007) Impression management tactics and affective context: influence on sales performance appraisal. *European Journal of Marketing*, **41**(5/6): 624–39.

Vince, R. and Reynolds, M. (2010) Leading reflection: developing the relationship between leadership and reflection. In J. Gold, R. Thorpe and A. Mumford (eds) *The Gower Handbook of Leadership and Management Development* (pp. 331–46). Aldershot: Gower Press.

Vining, A. R. (2011) Public agency external analysis using a modified "five forces" framework. *International Public Management Journal*, **14**(1): 63–105.

Visier (2014) 2014 Survey report – the state of workforce analytics and planning. www.visier.com/lp/2014-survey-report-the-state-of-workforce-analytics-and-planning/ (accessed July 26, 2015).

Visser, J. (2013) *Data Base on Institutional Characteristics of Trade Unions, Wage Setting, State Intervention and Social Pacts, 1960–2011 (ICTWSS Version 4.0)*. Amsterdam: Amsterdam Institute for Advances Labour Studies, University of Amsterdam.

Visser, J. and Waddington, J. (1996) Industrialization and politics: a century of union structural developments in three European countries. *European Journal of Industrial Relations*, **2**(1): 21–53.

Vroom, V. H. (1964) *Work and Motivation*. New York: John Wiley & Sons.

Vukotich, G. (2014) 360° feedback: ready, fire, aim—issues with improper implementation. *Performance Improvement*, **53**(1): 30–5.

Vygotsky, L. S. (1978) *Mind and Society: The Development of Higher Mental Process*. Cambridge, MA: Harvard University Press.

Wachman, R. and Wearden, G. (2010) Northern Rock to cut 650 jobs. June 8. https://www.theguardian.com/business/2010/jun/08/northern-rock-cuts-jobs (accessed August 21, 2016).

Wachsund, E. and Blind, K. (2016) More labour market flexibility for more innovation? Evidence from employer–employee linked micro data. *Research Policy*, **45**(5): 941–50.

Wackernagel, M., Schulz, N. B., Deumling, D. et al. (2002) Tracking the ecological overshoot of the human economy. *Proceedings of the National Academy of Sciences*, **99**(14): 9266–71.

Waddington, J. (1988) Business unionism and fragmentation within the TUC. *Capital and Class*, (36): 7–15.

Waddington, J. (1992) Trade union membership in Britain, 1980–1987: unemployment and restructuring. *British Journal of Industrial Relations*, **30**(2): 7–15.

Waddington, J. and Whitston, C. (1994) The politics of restructuring: trade unions on the defensive in Britain since 1979. *Relations Industrielles/Industrial Relations*, **49**(4): 794–817.

Waddington, J. and Whitston, C. (1997) Why do people join unions in a period of membership decline? *British Journal of Industrial Relations*, **35**(4): 515–46.

Wagner, R. F. (1949) The employment interview: a critical summary. *Personnel Psychology*, **2**: 17–46.

Wajcman, J. (1998) *Managing Like a Man*. University Park, PA: Pennsylvania State University Press.

Wajcman, J. (2000) Feminism facing industrial relations in Britain. *British Journal of Industrial Relations*, **38**(2): 183–201.

Wakeling, A. (2014) *Give and Take? Unravelling the True Nature of Zero-hours Contracts*. ACAS Policy

Discussion Papers. London: Advisory, Conciliation and Arbitration Service.

Walker, H., Sisto, L. and McBain, D. (2008) Drivers and barriers to environmental supply chain management practices: lessons from the public and private sectors. *Journal of Purchasing and Supply Management*, **14**(1): 69–85.

Walker, H. J., Bauer, T. N., Cole, M. S., Bernerth, J. B., Feild, H. S. and Short, J. C. (2013) Is this how I will be treated? Reducing uncertainty through recruitment interactions. *Academy of Management Journal*, **56**(5): 1325–47.

Wall, T. D. and Clegg, C. W. (1998) Job design. In C. L. Cooper and C. Argyris (eds) *The Concise Blackwell Encyclopedia of Management* (pp. 337–9). Oxford: Blackwell.

Wall, T. D. and Wood, S. J. (2005) The romance of human resource management and business performance, and the case for the big science. *Human Relations*, **58**(4): 429–61.

Wallace, H. M. L., Hoover, K. F. and Pepper, M. B. (2014) Multicultural ethics and diversity discourse. *Equality, Diversity and Inclusion*, **33**(4): 318–33.

Wal-Mart (2015) Global responsibility report. https://cdn.corporate.walmart.com/c0/24/2383f0674d27823dcf7083e6fbc6/2015-global-responsibility-report.pdf (accessed April 14, 2016).

Walton, J. (2005) Would the real corporate university please stand up. *Journal of European Industrial Training*, **29**(1): 7–20.

Walton, R. (1985) From control to commitment in the workplace. *Harvard Business Review*, March/April: 77–84.

Warhurst, C. and Findlay, P. (2012) *More Effective Skills Utilisation: Shifting the Terrain of Skills Policy in Scotland*. SKOPE Research Paper No. 107. Cardiff: Cardiff University.

Warhurst, C., Eikhof, D. R. and Haunschild, A. (2008) *Work Less, Live More? Critical Analysis of the Work–Life Boundary*. Basingstoke: Palgrave Macmillan.

Warhurst, R. P. (2013) Learning in an age of cuts: managers as enablers of workplace learning. *Journal of Workplace Learning*, **25**(1): 37–57.

Warr, P. (2008) Work values: some demographic and cultural correlates. *Journal of Occupational and Organizational Psychology*, **81**: 751–75.

Warren, T. (2015) Work-time underemployment and financial hardship: class inequalities and recession in the UK. *Work, Employment and Society*, **29**(2): 191–212.

Watkins, K. E. and Marsick, V. J. (1996) *Dimensions of the Learning Organization Questionnaire (DLOQ)*. Warwick, RI: Partners for the Learning Organization.

Watson, S. and Harmel-Law, A. (2010) Exploring the contribution of workplace learning to an HRD strategy in the Scottish legal profession. *Journal of European Industrial Training*, **34**(1): 7–22.

Watson, T. (1994) Recruitment and selection. In Sisson, K. (ed.) *Personnel Management* (pp. 185–252). Oxford: Blackwell.

Watson, T. (1999) Human resourcing strategies. In J. Leopold, L. Harris and T. Watson (eds) *Strategic Human Resourcing* (pp. 17–38). London: Pitman.

Watson, T. (2004) HRM and critical social sciences. *Journal of Management Studies*, **41**(3): 447–67.

Watson, T. and Harris, P. (1999) *The Emergent Manager*. London: Sage.

Watson, T. J. (2008) *Sociology, Work and Industry*. London: Routledge.

Watson, T. J. (2010) Critical social science, pragmatism and the realities of HRM. *International Journal of Human Resource Management Studies*, **21**(6): 915–31.

Watson, T. J. Leopold, J. and Watling, D. (2009) Strategic choice in patterns of employment relationships. In J. Leopold and L. Harris (eds) *The Strategic Management of Human Resources* (2nd edn) (pp. 442–72). Harlow: Prentice Hall.

Weale, S. (2000) Law: is it safe to speak out? It's a year since the new legislation was passed to protect whistleblowers at work. Sally asks if it's working. The Guardian, July 3, p. 8.

Weale, S. (2015) Four in 10 new teachers quit within a year. The Guardian, March 31, 2015.

Webb, S. and Webb, B. (1911) *Industrial Democracy*. London: Longmans.

Weber, B. (2011) Oil sands polluting Alberta watersheds, panel reports. *Globe and Mail*, March 10, p. A5.

Weber, M. (1903–1917/1949) *The Methodology of the Social Sciences* (eds E. Shils and H. Finch). New York: Free Press.

Weber, M. (1904–1905/2002) *The Protestant Ethic and the Spirit of Capitalism*. London: Penguin.

Weber, M. (1922/1968) *Economy and Society*. New York: Bedminster.

Wedderburn, Lord (1986) *The Worker and the Law* (3rd edn). Harmondsworth: Penguin.

Weer, C. H., DiRenzo, M. S. and Shipper, F. M. (2015) A holistic view of employee coaching: a longitudinal investigation of the impact of facilitative and pressure-based coaching on team effectiveness. *Journal of Applied Behavioral Science*, **52**(2): 187–214.

Wehrmeyer, W. (ed.) (1996) *Greening People: Human Resources and Environmental Management*. Sheffield: Greenleaf.

Wei, L.-Q. and Lau, C.-M. (2010) High performance work systems and performance: the role of adaptive capability. *Human Relations*, **63**(10): 1487–511.

Wei, L.-Q., Liu, J. and Herndon, N. C. (2011) SHRM and product innovation: testing the moderating effects of organizational culture and structure in Chinese firms. *International Journal of Human Resource Management*, **22**(1): 19–33.

Weichman, D. and Ryan, A. (2003) Reactions to computerized testing in selection contexts. *International Journal of Selection and Assessment*, **11**: 215–29.

Wiek, A., Farioli, F., Fukushi, K., and Yarime, M. (2012). Sustainability science: Bridging the gap between society. *Sustainability Science*, **7**(1), 1–4.

Welbourne, T. and Trevor, C. (2000) The roles of departmental and position power in job evaluation. *Academy of Management Journal*, **43**(4): 761–71.

Weldy, T. G. (2009) Learning organization and transfer: strategies for improving performance. *Learning Organization*, **16**(1): 58–68.

Weldy, T. G. and Gillis, W. E. (2010) The learning organization: variations at different organizational levels. *Learning Organization*, **17**(5): 455–70.

Wells, D. (1993) Are strong unions compatible with the new model of human resource management? *Relations Industrielles/Industrial Relations*, **48**(1): 56–84.

Wells, G. (1999) *Dialogic Inquiry: Towards a Sociocultural Practice and Theory of Education*. New York: Cambridge University Press.

Wenger, E. C. and Snyder, W. M. (2000) Communities of practice: the organizational frontier. *Harvard Business Review*, January–February: 139–45.

West, M. A., Borrill, C., Dawson, J., et al. (2002) The link between the management of employees and patient mortality in acute hospitals. *The International Journal of Human Resource Management*, 13(8): 1299–1310.

Western, S. (2008) *Leadership: A Critical Text*. London: Sage.

Westley, F. and Mintzberg, H. (2007) Visionary leadership and strategic management. *Strategic Management Journal*, **10**(1): 17–32.

Wheelen, T. L. and Hunger, J. D. (2014) *Strategic Management and Business Policy* (14th edn). New York: Pearson.

Whelan, E. and Carcary, M. (2011) Integrating talent and knowledge management: where are the benefits? *Journal of Knowledge Management*, **15**(4): 675–87.

Whitley, R. (1999) *Divergent Capitalism: The Social Structuring and Change of Business Systems*. Oxford: Oxford University Press.

Whitmore, J. (2002) *Coaching for Performance: Growing People, Performance and Purpose* (3rd edn). London: Nicholas Brealey.

Whittaker, D. H. (1990) *Managing Innovation: A Study of British and Japanese Factories*. Cambridge: Cambridge University Press.

Whittington, R. (1993) *What is Strategy and Does it Matter?* London: Routledge.

Whyman, P. B., Baimbridge, M. J., Buraimo, B. A. and Petrescu, A. I. (2015) Workplace flexibility practices and corporate performance: evidence from the British private sector. *British Journal of Management*, **26**: 347–64.

Wickens, P. (1987) *The Road to Nissan*. London: Palgrave Macmillan.

Wiek, A., Farioli, F., Fukushi, K. and Yarime, M. (2012) Sustainability science: bridging the gap between society. *Sustainability Science*, **7**(1): 1–4.

Wiggins, J. S. (ed.) (1996) *The Five-factor Model of Personality*. New York: Guildford Publications.

Wilk, S. and Cappelli, P. (2003) Understanding the determinants of employer use of selection methods. *Personnel Psychology*, **57**: 103–24.

Wilkinson, A. and Townsend, K. (2011) The changing face of work and industrial relations. In K. Townsend and A. Wilkinson (eds) *Research Handbook on Work and Employment Relations* (pp. 1–10). Cheltenham: Edward Elgar.

Wilkinson, R. and Pickett, K. (2010) *The Spirit Level: Why Equality is Better for Everyone*. London: Penguin.

Williams, C. (2003) Sky service: the demands of emotional labour in the airline industry. *Gender, Work and Organization*, **10**(5): 513–50.

Williams, R. (1976) *Keywords: A Vocabulary of Culture and Society*. New York: Oxford University Press.

Williams, R. (1983) *Keywords*. New York: Oxford University Press.

Williams, S., Abbott, B. and Heery, E. (2011) Non-union, worker representation through civil society organizations: evidence from the United Kingdom. *Industrial Relations Journal*, **42**(1): 69–85.

Willmott, H. (1984) Images and ideals of managerial work. *Journal of Management Studies*, **21**(3): 349–68.

Willmott, H. (1993) 'Strength is ignorance: freedom is slavery': managing culture in modern organizations. *Journal of Management Studies*, **30**(4): 515–52.

Willmott, H. (1995) The odd couple?: re-engineering business processes; managing human relations. *New Technology, Work and Employment*, **10**(2): 89–97.

Wilson, J. P. and Western, S. (2000) Performance appraisal: an obstacle to training and development. *Journal of European Industrial Training*, **24**(7): 384–90.

Wilson, K. and Jones, R. (2008) Reducing job-irrelevant bias in performance appraisals: compliance and beyond. *Journal of General Management*, **34**(2): 57–70.

Wilson, R. and Hogarth, T. (2003) *Tackling the Low Skills Equilibrium: A Review of Issues and Some New Evidence*. London: Department of Trade and Industry.

Winfield, N. (2011) EU, oil companies begin Libya evacuations. February 21. www.chron.com/disp/story.mpl (accessed March 3, 2011).

Winstanley, D. and Woodall, J. (eds) (2000) *Ethical Issues in Contemporary Human Resource Management*. Basingstoke: Palgrave Macmillan.

Wirz, A., Melchers, K. G., Lievens, F., De Corte, W. and Kleinmann, M. (2013) Trade-offs between assessor team size and assessor expertise in affecting rating accuracy in assessment centers. *Revista de Psicología del Trabajo y de las Organizaciones*, **29**(1): 13–20.

Witherspoon, P. D. (1997) *Communicating Leadership*. Boston: Allyn & Bacon.

Witz, A. (1986) Patriarchy and the labour market: occupational control strategies and the medical division of labour. In D. Knights and H. Willmott (eds) *Gender and the Labour Process* (pp. 14–35). Aldershot: Gower.

Wollstonecraft , M. (1792/2004) *A Vindication of the Rights of Woman* (ed. M. Brody). London: Penguin Classics.

Womack, J., Jones, D. and Roos, D. (1990) *The Machine that Changed the World*. New York: Rawson Associates.

Wood, I., Rodgers, H. and Gold, J. (2004) Picturing prejudice: learning to see diversity. Paper presented at the Fifth HRD Conference, Limerick University, May.

Wood, S. (1996) High commitment management and payment systems. *Journal of management Studies*, **33**(1): 53–77.

Wood, S. (2000) The BJIR and industrial relations in the new millennium. *British Journal of Industrial Relations*, **38**(1): 1–5.

Wood, S., Moore, S. and Willman, P. (2002) Third time lucky for statutory recognition in the UK. *Industrial Relations Journal*, **33**(3): 215–33.

Wood, S., Holman, D. and Stride, C. (2006) Human resource management and performance in UK call centres. *British Journal of Industrial Relations*, **44**(1): 99–124.

Woodall, J. (2001) Editorial. *Human Resource Development International*, **4**(3): 287–90.

Woodall, J., Scott-Jackson, W., Newham, T. and Gurney, M. (2009) Making the decision to outsource human resources. *Personnel Review*, **38**(3):236–52.

Woodruffe, C. (2000) *Development and Assessment Centres* (3rd edn). London: Chartered Institute of Personnel and Development.

Working Group Contribution to the IPCC Fifth Assessment Report Climate Change 2013. The physical science basis summary for policymakers. https://www.ipcc.ch/pdf/assessment-report/ar5/wg1/WGIAR5_SPM_brochure_en.pdf (accessed October 2016).

World Commission on Environment and Development (1987) *Our Common Future*. New York: Oxford University Press.

World Health Organization (2011) www.who.int/about/definition (accessed March 9, 2011).

World Health Organization (2016) WHO definition of health. www.who.int/about/definition/en/print.html (accessed September 14, 2016).

Wray-Bliss, E. (2005) Abstract ethics, embodied ethics: the strange marriage of Foucault and positivism in labour process theory. In C. Grey and H. Willmott (eds) *Critical Management Studies: A Reader* (pp. 383–417). Oxford: Oxford University Press.

Wright, M. (1996) The collapse of compulsory unionism? Collective organization in highly unionized British companies, 1979–1991. *British Journal of Industrial Relations*, **34**(4): 497–513.

Wright, P. and Gardner, T. (2003) The human resource–firm performance relationship. Methodological and theoretical challenges. In D. Holman, T. Hall, C. Clegg, P. Sparrow, and A. Howard (eds) *The New Workplace: A Guide to the Human Impact of Modern Work Practices* (pp. 311–29). London: John Wiley & Sons.

Wright, P. M. and Boswell, W. R. (2002) Desegregating HRM: a review and synthesis of micro and macro human resource management research. *Journal of Management*, **28**(3): 247–76.

Wright, P. M., Gardner, T. M. and Moynihan, L. M. (2003) The impact of HR practices on the performance of business units. *Human Resource Management Journal*, **13**(3): 21–36.

Wright, P., Gardner, T., Moynihan, L. and Allen, M. (2005) The relationship between HR practices and firm performance: examining causal order. *Personnel Psychology*, **58**(2): 409–46.

Yakabuski, K. (2008) The kindness of corporations. Report on business. *Globe and Mail*, July–August: 66–71.

Yammarino, F. J. and Atwater, L. E. (1997) Implications of self–other rating agreement for human resources management. *Organizational Dynamics*, **25**(4): 35–44.

Yang, C.-M., Shin, N.-Y., Weng, M.-W. and Hsu, C.-H. (2014) Using a two-dimensional mean value matrix (TDMVM) to improve users' satisfaction with government e-recruitment website. *Journal of Software*, **10**(1): 82–93.

Yanow, D. (2000) Seeing organizational learning: a 'cultural' view. *Organization*, **7**(2): 247–68.

Yanow, D. (2004) Translating local knowledge at organizational peripheries. *British Journal of Management*, **15**(1): 9–25.

Yap, M. H. T. and Ineson, E. M. (2012) Diversity management: the treatment of HIV-positive employees. *AIDS Care*, **24**(11): 1349–58.

Yen, Y.-S. (2014) The interaction effect on customer purchase intention in e-commerce. *Asia Pacific Journal of Marketing and Logistics*, **26**(3): 472–93.

Youndt, M. A., Snell, S. A., Dean, J. W. and Lepak, D. P. (1996) Human resource management, manufacturing strategy and firm performance. *Academy of Management Journal*, **39**: 836–66.

Yu, G. and Park, J. (2006) The effect of downsizing on the financial performance and employee productivity of Korean firms. *International Journal of Manpower*, **27**: 230–50.

Yuhas, A. (2014) Amazon banks on rise of the robots to speed online orders to customers. The Guardian, December 1. https://www.theguardian.com/technology/2014/dec/01/amazon-robots-online-orders-customers.

Yu, K. Y. T. (2014) Person-organization fit effects on organizational attraction: a text of an expectations-based model. *Organizational Behavior and Human Decision Processes*, **124**(1): 75–94.

Zainab, B., Bhatti, M. A., Pangil, F. B. and Battour, M. M. (2015) E-training adoption in the Nigerian civil service. *European Journal of Training and Development*, **39**(6): 538–64.

Zeytinoglu, I. U., Denton, M., Plenderleith, J. and Chowhan, J. (2015) Associations between workers' health, and non-standard hours and insecurity: the case of home care workers in Ontario, Canada. *International Journal of Human Resource Management*, **26**(19): 2503–22.

Zhang, Y. and Albrecht, C. (2010) The role of cultural values on a firm's strategic human resource management development: a comparative study of Spanish firms in China. *International Journal of Human Resource Management*, **21**(11): 1911–30.

Zhang, Y. and Begley, T. M. (2011) Perceived organizational climate, knowledge transfer and innovation in China-based research and development companies. *International Journal of Human Resource Management*, **22**(1): 34–56.

Zheng, C., Kashi, K., Fan, D., Molineux, J. and Shan Ee, M. (2016) Impact of individual coping strategies and organisational work–life balance programmes on Australian employee well-being. *International Journal of Human Resource Management*, **27**(5): 501–26.

Zhu, C. J., Cooper, B. K., Fan, D. and De Cieri, H. (2013) HR practices from the perspective of managers and employees in multinational enterprises in China: alignment issues and implications. *Journal of World Business* **48**: 241–50.

Zibarras, L. and Ballinger, C. (2011) *Promoting Environmental Behaviour in the Workplace: A Survey of UK Organisations. A report produced by the Department of Psychology, City University, London for British Psychological Society Division of Occupational Psychology Green Working Group*. Leicester: British Psychological Society.

Zide, J., Elman, B., Shahani-Denning, S. (2014) LinkedIn and recruitment: how profiles differ across occupations. *Employee Relations*, **36**(5): 583–604.

Ziegler, M. F., Paulus, T. and Woodside, M. (2014) Understanding informal group learning in online communities through discourse analysis. *Adult Education Quarterly*, **64**(1): 60–7.

Zilahy, G. (2003) Organizational factors determining the implementation of cleaner production in the corporate sector. *Journal of Cleaner Production*, **12**: 311–19.

Zutshi, A. and Sohal, A. (2004) Environmental management system adoption by Australian organizations, Part 1: Reasons, benefits and impediments. *Technovation*, **24**: 335–57.

name index

Page numbers marked with an asterisk (*) denote website addresses on those pages.

3M 515
3 (mobile phone company) 152

A

Aaltio-Marjosola, I. 488
Ababneh, K. I. 158
Abbott, Andrew 426
Abeysekera, L. 491
Abraham, S. E. 210
Accenture 130
Accounting for People Task
  Force 135
Ackers, P. 55, 335, 343
Ackroyd, S. 93, 215, 355, 484,
  494
Adair, J. 462
Adams, J. S. 266
Adamson, S. J. 175
Adams, R. J. 316, 317
Addison, J. 77, 354
Adidas 143*
Adler, L. 155
Adler, N. J. 17, 473, 539, 541
Advanced Institute of
  Management 448–9
Advisory, Conciliation and
  Arbitration Service
  (ACAS) 6–7, 107*, 155*,
  202*, 306*, 325, 337, 361*
Agrawal, V. 120
Aguinis, H. 191, 192, 198, 203
Agyeman, J. 521
Ahlstrand, B. 41, 54, 72
Ahmed, I. Z. 143, 148, 149, 171
Ahola, T. 207–8
Ahonen, P. 119
Akerjordet, K. 166
Alagaraja, M. 224, 232
Alban-Metcalfe, J. 447
Alberta Energy 372
Albizu, E. 431
Albrecht, C. 491, 539, 541
Alcázar, F. M. 119, 121

Alfes, K. 191, 201
Alghafri, A. A. 253
Alimo-Metcalfe, B. 447
Ali, N. N. K. 110
Alis, D. 122
Allen, D. 151
Allen, K. 369
Allen, M. R. 38
Allinson, C. W. 236
Almeida, S. 541
Alniaçik, E. 146
Altman, Ruth 292
Alvesson, M. 31, 472, 480,
  485, 492
Amati, Chiara 13–14, 402
Amazon 72, 87, 92, 385,
  474–5, 489–90
Ambasna-Jones, M. 472
Amicus (trade union) 316*
Amin, M. R. 109
Amiti, M. 129
Amnesty International 376, 377
Anand, R. 119
Andersen, S. C. 186–7, 190, 208
Andersen, T. J. 50
Anderson, B. A. 540–1
Anderson, C. 197
Anderson, D. 123, 399
Anderson, J. 236
Anderson, L. 463
Anderson, N. 212
Anderson, O. R. 237
Anderson, V. 247, 250, 466
Andolšek, D. M. 16
Andrews, R. 39
Anseel, F. 195, 197, 455
Anthony, P. 31
Antonacopoulou, E. P. 224, 459
Antonioni, D. 212, 455
Antoun, C. 145
Appelbaum, E. 55
Appelbaum, S. H. 133
Arber, S. 472
Ardichvili, A. 46, 369
Aries, E. 341
Aristotle 375–6
Armstrong, M. 191, 203

Armstrong, S. J. 236
Armstrong, T. 143
Arnett, D. 227
Arnett, G. 42
Arrowsmith, J. 261, 285, 287
Arshad, R. 14
Arthur, J. 91
Arthur, J. B. 79
Arthur, M. 177
Arthur, M. B. 177
Arthurs, A. J. 115
Arvey, R. D. 161
Asahi Glass 384
Asch, D. 92
Ashby, K. 394
Ashikali, T. 120
Ashill, N. J. 128
Ashkanasy, N. M. 90, 472, 478
Ashley, L. 117, 156–7
Ashley, Mike 72, 261, 333, 445
Ashman, I. 133, 370
Ashton, D. 234
Asmuß, B. 199
Astakhova, M. N. 73, 79
Atkinson, J. S. 121, 430
Atkinson, W. 234
ATL (trade union) 316*
Atwater, L. E. 212
Atzeni, M. 3
Audia, P. 196, 455–6
Au Optronix 384
Australian Human Resources
  Institute (AHRI) 380*
Australian Medical
  Association 380
Australian Wheat Board 377*
Autor, D. 234
Avdagic, S. 31
Avolio, B. J. 447, 453
Awan, A. G. 115
Axis Bank 185
Axtell, C. 153

B

Babbage, Charles 424
Babbie, E. 28
Bach, S. 126

subject index

Page numbers marked with an asterisk (*) denote website addresses on those pages. HRM stands for human resource management.